# GENDER AND
# WOMEN'S STUDIES

The naemes of our nations do not fit within the boarders of this map

They Spill into the lakes, rivers and ocens.

Vuntut  Inuvialuit
Deguth
Draanjik  Gwichyaa
Teetl'it  Sahtú  Kitlinermiut  Netsilingmiut  Iglulingmiut
Tr'ondëk Hwëch'in  Utkuhiksalingmiut
Tanana  Hanningajurmiut  Tununirmiut
Tutchone  Denesoline Nations  Ihalmiut
Kaska Dena  Akikinirmiut  Kangiqliniqmiut
Harvaqtuurmiut  Qaernermiut
Tahltan  Aivilingmiut  Tarramiut
Wetal  Paallirmiut
K'yak áannii  Nisga'a  Siquinirmiut
Dane-za  Sayisi Dene  Ahialmiut  Sikumiut
Gitxsan  Itivimiut
Gitxaala  Hoteladi  Iyuw Imuun
Nuxalk  Siksikawa  Thlingchadinne
Secwepemc  Tsuu T'ina  Nihithawiwin  Innu  Beothuk
Tsuu T'ina  Nakawē  Mushkegowuk
Niitsitapi  Iyiyiw Iyimiwin
Akisq'nuk  Nehiyawak  Omushkego  Iynu Ayamun  Gespegeoag
Sto:to  Aapatohsipikani  Nakoda  Sigenigteoag
Ktunaxa  Ilili mowin  Nehiramowin  Segepenegatig  Onamag
Syilx  Kainaa  Peskotomuhkati  Esgigeoag
Aamsskaapipikani  Wazhashk-Onigamininiwag  Odishkwaagamlig  Gespogoitnag
Goojijwininiwag
Misi-zaagiwininiwag  Wyandotte
Baawitigowininiwag
Tignontati
Attawandaron

This map represents Indigenous territories around the time of European contact in what is now Canada. As our book is rooted most firmly in the Canadian context, we wish to begin by acknowledging and honouring the Indigenous peoples who are the original inhabitants of this land.

# ARTIST'S STATEMENT

English is my first language, it is my only language, and it is not my language. My first word was "Mama." I learned to speak and to say, "I love you." It was when I started school, when language was taken out of my mouth and put onto the page, that I started to understand it as a system—a complex system that I could not control and was constantly failing at. As an Indigenous woman, I learned the ways that language was used to alienate and oppress my family, my ancestors, and the ways it continues to oppress me, both as a cultural experience and a disabled experience.

The first word I learned in Lenape was *Kawinganoowl'looma*, "I am glad to see you." I learned to say *Katawalill*, "I love you." I learned to say *Anushiik*, "Thank you."

In the classroom, we meticulously sort out our thoughts and ideas through language and writing. We share and exchange little pieces of our knowledge and ourselves—words in the air and words on the page. Language is not neutral. It lives in our bodies, our memories, and our imaginations, and holds immense power.

When making this map, I used Aaron Carapella's Tribal Nations Maps as a source (www.tribalnationsmaps.com). He did meticulous research to correctly record the names of the Nations pre-European contact. However, my brain tricks me and reverses letters, fills in gaps, and makes them up. Is your Nation's name spelled correctly? Is it on the map? Have you read these words before? Can you sound them out and wrap your mouth and tongue around the unfamiliar letters?

Vanessa Dion Fletcher
www.dionfletcher.com

# GENDER AND WOMEN'S STUDIES

## Critical Terrain

*Second Edition*

Edited by Margaret Hobbs and Carla Rice

WOMEN'S PRESS

Toronto | Vancouver

**Gender and Women's Studies: Critical Terrain, Second Edition**
Edited by Margaret Hobbs and Carla Rice

First published in 2018 by
**Women's Press, an imprint of CSP Books Inc.**
425 Adelaide Street West, Suite 200
Toronto, Ontario
M5V 3C1

**www.womenspress.ca**

**Library and Archives Canada Cataloguing in Publication**

Gender and women's studies in Canada
    Gender and women's studies : critical terrain / edited by Margaret Hobbs and Carla Rice. -- Second edition.

Previously published under title: Gender and women's studies in Canada.
Includes bibliographical references.
Issued in print and electronic formats.
ISBN 978-0-88961-591-5 (softcover).--ISBN 978-0-88961-592-2 (PDF).--
ISBN 978-0-88961-593-9 (EPUB)

    1. Feminism--Canada.  2. Women--Canada.  3. Women's studies--Canada.
I. Hobbs, Margaret (Margaret Helen), editor  II. Rice, Carla, editor  III. Title.
IV. Title: Gender and women's studies in Canada.
HQ1181.C3G46 2018              305.420971         C2018-901296-X
                                                  C2018-901297-8

Text design by Elisabeth Springate
Typesetting by Peggy and Co. Design Inc.
Cover design by Em Dash
Cover image: *She Who Stands Tall*, by Christi Belcourt, 2007

18   19   20   21   22         5  4  3  2  1

Printed and bound in Canada by Webcom

# DEDICATION

*To the prior generations of feminist thinkers and
activists who have made this project possible*

*To Carla's faux daughters, Claire Dion Fletcher and Vanessa
Dion Fletcher; Marg's nieces and stepdaughter—Laura Harris,
Emily Harris, and Genevieve Sweigard—and our students,
whose insight and energy continue to instruct and inspire us*

*To the succeeding generations who will carry the struggle, and the vision, forward*

# TABLE OF CONTENTS

# ACKNOWLEDGEMENTS

First and foremost, Carla would like to thank her tomboy "big sister" and co-conspirator, Marg Hobbs, who taught her how to teach in gender and women's studies and who mentored her in the challenges and pleasures of delivering the first-year course. Marg wants to thank her lipstick fem friend and co-editor, Carla Rice, for her inspiring pedagogy, but mostly for making this project a lot of fun. And thanks to our families and our partners, Gisele Lalonde and Susan Dion, for their love, support, and patience through the long hours and late nights of lively Skype (and now Zoom) meetings and writing sessions.

We would like to acknowledge the financial assistance of the Frost Centre for Canadian Studies and Indigenous Studies at Trent University and the Re•Vision Centre for Art and Social Justice at the University of Guelph. We are grateful to feminist scholar Katharine Bausch for her invaluable assistance with material for the Snapshots and Soundwaves, and feminist artist and photographer Michelle Peek, whose expertise was central in the selection of artwork for this edition. We also want to thank our past and present colleagues in Gender and Women's Studies at Trent, especially Marg McGraw, Colleen O'Manique, Joan Sangster, Katharine Bausch, Megan Gaucher, May Chazan, Nadine Changfoot, Julia Smith, Carol Williams, Paula Butler, Sedef Arat-Koç, Nan Peacock, and Karen Sutherland, as well as the many teaching assistants who have shared with us the joys and challenges of the first-year course. We are grateful to the guest speakers who contributed to the vibrancy of the introductory course. Special thanks to Shirley Williams and Marrie Mumford, whose annual visits to our classroom for so many years enriched our students', and our own, understanding of Indigenous women's resurgence in the areas of language, culture, and the arts.

Finally, we appreciate the support of the staff at Canadian Scholars/Women's Press who have skillfully guided us through two editions of this book. In particular, we thank those at the press with whom we worked most closely to produce this second edition: Lily Bergh (publisher), Natalie Garriga (editorial/production manager), Martha Hunter (former acquisitions editor), and Casey Gazzellone (copy editor and permissions coordinator extraordinaire). They have all worked tirelessly in helping to implement our vision for *Gender and Women's Studies: Critical Terrain*.

# INTRODUCTION

## Mapping the Terrain of Gender and Women's Studies

Another world is not only possible, she's on her way. Maybe many of us won't be here to greet her,
but on a quiet day, if I listen very carefully, I can hear her breathing.
—*Arundhati Roy, War Talk (2003, p. 75)*

The first problem for all of us, men and women, is not to learn, but to unlearn.
—*Gloria Steinem, "'Women's Liberation' Aims to Free Men, Too," Washington Post (1970, p. 192)*

As we thought about this introduction, we were reminded of these two quotations, the first by Arundhati Roy, who describes herself as an "Indian novelist, activist, and world citizen," and the second by American feminist activist and journalist Gloria Steinem. Roy opens us up to the transformative potential of social justice and solidarity by prompting us to hold fast to the belief that another world is possible, that there are alternatives to inequalities that are deepening the new global world order. We have to keep alive visions of gender and economic justice; they can move us, inspire us, sustain us, and galvanize us as thinkers and activists, as global citizens and as members of local communities, working for change. Steinem's words signal that the road ahead is not easy, that it involves a process of critical examination of many of our most taken-for-granted truths and belief systems about the world around us. It is through unlearning as much as learning that we begin to see how inequalities have been created and hence how they can be challenged and undone. Unlearning and learning are intertwined in a continual, connected process: the unpacking of prior knowledge and assumptions is important in making space for new versions and visions of social realities.

This volume engages with these practices: unlearning/learning and envisioning change. We aim to offer a broad selection of writings from a range of authors and perspectives to help introduce you to a field that is at the forefront of critical thinking about inequalities and social justice. This introduction provides students with an entry point to consider what gender and women's studies involves, how it has changed in recent years, and why it continues to be a meaningful and socially relevant area of inquiry. In what follows, we focus mainly on gender and women's studies in the North American context, which itself has been shaped by broader global shifts within both feminism and the political and economic landscape. We discuss some of the main goals and theoretical developments of gender and women's studies, and highlight key features of this book. We conclude with some thoughts about the process of critical thinking and how it might apply to your reading of the material in the text.

# WHAT IS GENDER AND WOMEN'S STUDIES?

As students coming into gender and women's studies introductory classes, you will have different ideas of what to expect. While some of you may have been introduced to gender and women's studies perspectives through a course, extracurricular involvement at high school, conversations with family and friends, or social media and popular culture, for many of you this is your first conscious engagement with this field. You likely have many questions: What is this field variously called "women's studies," "women's and gender studies," "gender and women's studies," or other similar names? (For a brief discussion of the shift from *women* to *gender* in the title of many programs see Hobbs and Rice, 2011a.) How does what I learn here differ from and add to what I am studying in my other courses? How relevant is gender and women's studies to my own life and to my future? Will these perspectives be useful to me in the workforce? Will the topics and approaches introduced in this class reflect or revise my understanding of local and global social relations and structures? How might my values and world view be enriched? What is feminism and do I have to be a feminist to take this course?

As you begin this journey, you should know that gender and women's studies is not one thing. It is not one perspective or one analysis but many, expressed differently by scholars and activists whose ideas and approaches differ from one another, shaped by their own backgrounds, interests, training, experience, and understandings of the world. Not surprisingly, then, introductory courses in this field are also diverse. Some professors might choose to introduce you to the field through a few specific themes, perhaps highlighting gendered analyses of popular culture or recent writings from the "third wave" of feminism. Some might engage more with international contexts and others with North America, and some focus mainly on the present while others explore women's historical experiences as well. Most introductory courses, however, aim for fairly broad fare, taking you through gender and women's studies across a range of themes, issues, and contexts.

Despite the differences in our approaches and perspectives, there is considerable overlap in what instructors in North American universities and colleges are trying to accomplish as they introduce you to what has been, and continues to be, a powerfully influential and transformative field. A number of years ago, we conducted an informal survey of course outlines and website descriptions of introductory gender and women's studies courses. The following list highlights some commonly shared goals guiding the teaching of entry-level courses in gender and women's studies:

- To introduce students to women's/gender studies as a broad, dynamic, interdisciplinary, and global field of inquiry, and to familiarize students with some of the major issues, debates, and approaches in gender and feminist scholarship and activism
- To complicate commonly presumed understandings of concepts like "women," "sex," "gender," "race," and "disability" by examining how these categories have been "constructed" (or created by society) and how they shape ideas and experiences of human difference
- To analyze and challenge hierarchical and intersecting relations of power influenced by gender, sexuality, class, race, ethnicity, ability, and other categories of difference
- To understand how power relations are embedded in institutions and in everyday, taken-for-granted social relations, practices, and values
- To highlight affinities and differences among self-identified women and gender non-conforming people, both within North America and worldwide, and to analyze intersecting social, cultural, political, and economic systems that shape their lives and agency
- To explore the multiple pathways and forms of individual and collective resistance to injustice and inequities in the past and the present, and to

analyze creative visions and strategies for change in local and global contexts

- To inspire and empower students to develop their knowledge of feminist scholarship and to engage critically in their communities at local, national, or global levels
- To develop students' skills in critical thinking and analysis, reading, and writing, and to create classroom environments that support learners' respectful debate and disagreement

These goals reflect a vision of gender and women's studies grounded in knowledge that is continuously shifting as the field develops and its insights deepen. Feminist scholars in the past and present have explored how ideas about gender work at interpersonal and institutional levels to shape social relations and the lived experiences of diverse people. Their explorations of gender, in relation to other social categories of identity and other axes of power, have been transforming the so-called traditional disciplines such as history, philosophy, politics, psychology, biology, and sociology, while also producing new syntheses of knowledge that we call *interdisciplinary* or even *transdisciplinary*.

When women's studies courses and programs emerged in North America in the 1960s and 1970s, a period of widespread protest against social and economic injustices, they joined other scholars—for example, in Canadian studies, Native studies, and labour studies—who were similarly interested in pressing beyond the limits of the older disciplines. Like these other interdisciplinary fields informed by critiques of social inequalities and visions of social justice, women's studies aimed to understand social relations in order to change them. You will notice from the goals summarized above that the field continues to offer tools, wisdom, and perspectives enabling a critical engagement with the world and its power structures. At the same time, gender and women's studies offers pathways through which we can better understand ourselves, our diverse experiences and identities, and our relationships with others in the wider world.

# CURRENT TRENDS IN GENDER AND WOMEN'S STUDIES

Gender and women's studies courses, and indeed this textbook, have been shaped in important ways by recent debates and new insights emerging from feminist scholarship. The ideas and the tools they suggest also come out of women's and social justice movements, from diversely positioned and marginalized people and grassroots communities, locally and globally, at the forefront of feminist thought and action.

Below we describe four of these major trends that together are making gender and women's studies perspectives more relevant than ever before in the critical task of understanding the world in which we live and the major challenges we face as a human community. This list is not exhaustive; there are many other trends shaping the field and the curriculum itself. Exciting feminist work is currently coming from disability studies, fat studies, and posthuman studies, and we anticipate that scholarship in these areas will significantly reshape gender and women's studies over the next decade. In the meantime, it is important for instructors and students alike to reflect upon and engage with the following four distinct, though overlapping, trends:

1. The concept and practice of intersectionality
2. Queering gender and women's studies
3. Indigenizing and decolonizing gender and women's studies
4. Globalizing, internationalizing, and transnationalizing gender and women's studies

## 1. The Concept and Practice of Intersectionality

"Intersectionality" is a concept and an approach to understanding the lives and experiences of individuals and groups of people in their diversity and complexity. Emerging as a theoretically important and challenging term in feminist scholarship, *intersectionality* is often used to describe the idea that women, men, and gender variant people live multiple layered identities and simultaneously experience oppression and privilege. The Canadian Research Institute for the Advancement of Women explains an intersectional approach as attempting "to understand how multiple forces work together and interact to reinforce conditions of inequality and social exclusion" (CRIAW, 2006, p. 5).

Intersectionality is not a new concept. The term itself was conceived in the early 1990s by African American feminists and critical race scholars Patricia Hill Collins (1990) and Kimberlé Crenshaw (1994), and the ideas associated with it have since been adapted, developed, and debated by feminist scholars, activists, and organizations in North America and elsewhere. Intersectionality critiques the limitations of perspectives that look narrowly at social relations through a gender lens alone, and encourages a wider view focused on the multiple components of identity and intersecting "axes" of power that constitute individuals' experiences in the world (Karpinski, 2007; Yuval-Davis, 2006). Intersectional theories and methods work, for example, to explore the specific ways in which factors such as gender, sexuality, Indigeneity, class, race, disability, geography, refugee and/or immigrant status, size, and age interact to shape people's social positioning. Such differences are also examined in the context of the larger social and political forces and institutions that create unequal access to power and privilege. Colonialism, capitalism, neo-liberalism, the World Trade Organization (WTO), and social welfare policies are all important examples. By examining the complexities and specificities of identities and social locations, intersectionality explores how women, men, and gender non-conforming people occupy many different and contradictory positions in social relations of power.

## 2. Queering Gender and Women's Studies

Recent developments in gender, queer, and trans theory and activism across North America have placed a spotlight on gender and sexuality as socially created constructs. In response, women's studies, which initially placed women squarely—some say narrowly—in the centre of analysis, is broadening its focus, and engaging more fully with issues and explorations of masculinities, queer and sexuality studies, and "transfeminism." At their heart, gender and queer theory involve critically analyzing the binary (either/or) categories of woman/man and femininity/masculinity by calling into question "the notion of two discrete tidily organized sexes and genders" (Scott-Dixon, 2006, p. 12). This rich theory base has arisen out of gay, lesbian, bisexual, and trans (GLBT) studies, itself a fairly new area of academic inquiry that seeks to understand and contextualize gendered and sexed bodies/identities and erotic desires and practices in different times and places (Meem et al., 2010; Stombler et al., 2010). GLBT studies, along with gender studies, has done much to explore sexual diversity, showing how dominant ideas and norms about sexuality, sexed bodies, and sexual practices and identities are not rooted naturally in the facts of biology, but are socially constructed in various ways by different societies. Queer theory goes further, aiming not only to interrogate sexuality norms, but also to turn upside down the very idea of "the normal"; namely, "everything in the culture that has occupied a position of privilege, power, and normalcy, starting with heterosexuality" (Bacon, 2006, p. 259). Adding another layer of nuance and complexity, transfeminism has emerged at the intersections of feminist and trans theory as a vibrant gender-inclusive field dedicated to ending the oppression of all gender crossing, gender diverse, gender non-conforming, and gender independent people (Scott-Dixon, 2006). At the same time, Indigenous thinkers who self-identify as "Two Spirit" and queer have worked to reclaim their bodies and erotic lives from colonial systems that attempted to impose sexist structures as well as sexual and gender norms onto Indigenous peoples as an integral part of colonization processes (Driskill et al., 2011).

## 3. Indigenizing and Decolonizing Gender and Women's Studies

The increased attention to decolonization and Indigenization in gender and women's studies comes from the proliferation of Indigenous scholarship and activism, and the critique of the historical marginalization of Indigenous perspectives in much of North American feminist thought and practice. "Indigenizing" involves the integration of Indigenous knowledge and perspectives into what counts as knowledge. As such, it goes well beyond the additive approach of writing Indigenous women in to existing Western theories, or squeezing their experiences into one or two classes in a gender and women's studies course. Instead the challenge for gender and women's studies teachers and students is to centre Indigeneity more fully by weaving it through and across studies of particular themes and issues; by valuing Indigenous knowledge forms; by analyzing colonialism and its continuing legacies for Indigenous women, men, and Two-Spirit and queer people; and by understanding the diversity of their lives and perspectives.

The closely related concept of "decolonizing" refers to the anti-colonial project of critiquing Western world views and challenging the oppressive power structures that they uphold. According to Maori scholar Linda Tuhiwai Smith (1999), decolonizing, "once viewed as the formal process of handing over the instruments of government, is now recognized as a long-term process involving bureaucratic, cultural, linguistic, and psychological divesting of colonial power," including in the academy (p. 98). For Davis (2010), decolonization of gender and women's studies means displacing white, Western subjectivities from the centre of course texts and topics, and disrupting Eurocentric, First World privilege through an examination of colonial relations from the perspectives of colonized others. Indigenous feminists, including Leanne Betasamosake Simpson (Michi Saagiig Nishnaabeg) (2011), Emma LaRocque (Métis) (2007), and Joyce Green (Ktunaxa/Cree-Scots Métis) (2007) see such anti-colonial feminist

approaches as critical to grasping urgent issues faced by Indigenous women today. For example, Sarah Hunt (Kwagiulth) (2016) argues that because sexual violence has been used as a weapon of colonialism to destroy and assimilate Indigenous peoples into a white, racist, sexist hierarchy, anti-violence and anti-colonial struggles cannot be separated if feminists hope to end violence against *all* women.

## 4. Globalizing, Internationalizing, and Transnationalizing Gender and Women's Studies

These terms themselves, as well as the practices they entail, are the subject of considerable debate. Sometimes they are used interchangeably. Increasingly, however, the language of global feminism, and hence calls for "globalizing" the curriculum, is giving way to the politics of "internationalizing" and/or "transnationalizing." For many, the term *global* in relation to feminism is too reminiscent of the condescension and denial of differences evident in past Western feminists' scholarly and activist approaches to women in the "Third World" (Grewal & Kaplan, 2006; Mohanty, 1991; Shohat, 2001). *Internationalization* is often employed as a broad umbrella term encompassing various practices and methods, extending feminism's focus beyond the Western world. Such endeavours, however, if not accompanied by a self-reflective critique of the limits of Western world views, can produce knowledge that reinforces, rather than challenges, dominant cultural stereotypes and misunderstandings.

Mohanty, for example, described three models for internationalizing gender and women's studies. She critiqued the "feminist as tourist" approach, which simply adds "Third World" and Indigenous women into existing analytic frameworks, stereotyping them as either hapless victims or romantic heroines. The "feminist as explorer" model can be problematic by focusing on women's lives in specific geographic contexts (through courses such as "Women in India," "Third World Women," etc.) without a sustained analysis of structural power relations. Mohanty (2003) instead encouraged a third alternative approach, "feminist solidarity," which recognizes differences and hierarchies of power within and across borders while building on affinities and common interests. Increasingly a transnational lens (as opposed to an international one) is promoted as a richer way to "teach students how to think about gender in a world whose boundaries have changed" (Kaplan & Grewal, 2002, p. 79). Transnational approaches emphasize the movement of money, labour, information, and culture across national borders; they draw out how histories of colonization and, more recently, globalization structure inequalities; and they explore the possibilities for solidarity among women and social movements organizing across geographic boundaries. In a transnationalized gender and women's studies curriculum, Canada and the United States can still be examined, but they are not centred (Mohanty in Dua & Trotz, 2002).

These theoretical and political shifts have challenged gender and women's studies to develop more nuanced theories and methods for understanding social relations and differences. Many instructors and students have taken up that challenge by becoming more inclusive of gender and queer theory (see Enke, 2012, in this volume); by better integrating Indigenous feminist thought, issues, and activism (St. Denis, 2007); by focusing on the gendered genesis and impacts of colonization and globalization in Canada and around the world (Mohanty, 2003); and by questioning their own positioning and implicatedness in current conditions (Blyth, 2008; Dion, 2009). Most feminist educators believe that a sustained focus on sexism is still necessary in gender and women's studies classrooms, especially in the face of deepening global gender inequities. At the same time, the theoretical insights offered by gender and queer theory, Indigenous feminism, and transnational feminist thought and activism have led many to radically rethink the subject and focus of gender and women's studies. In this book, we invite you to engage with

new knowledge and methods emerging from the field and contribute to conversations about the challenges we face in our local and global communities.

## FEATURES OF THIS BOOK

*Gender and Women's Studies: Critical Terrain* grew out of a familiar annual ritual for many introductory course instructors: the quest to find the perfect text that will engage and inspire students while guiding them skillfully through the dizzying array of concepts, theories, issues, approaches, histories, and contexts that constitute contemporary feminist and gender scholarship. We have a confession: we have never really liked textbooks. As undergraduate students, we had many occasions to throw our textbooks against the wall—once we awoke from the snooze induced by boredom. What, then, are we doing collaborating on our own introductory textbook in gender and women's studies?

Over time, we have come to appreciate how a textbook can help instructors and students navigate the dynamic and swiftly changing terrain of gender and women's studies. A text provides students with a concrete tangible work that they can hold in their hands as a guide. At its best, it can provide intellectual glue that makes more readily apparent the themes and flow of the course, as well as the interconnections between topics and the context within which particular pieces should be read. A textbook can include important learning and research aids such as guiding questions, relevant websites, and definitions of key terms. Textbooks that include a diversity of feminist authors introduce learners to multiple perspectives and current debates about topics related to women, gender, feminism, and social justice. We believe it is valuable for students, beginning in first year, to sharpen their analytic skills and develop their own positions in relation to a *multiplicity* of ideas and arguments.

Of course, the perfect text does not, and cannot, exist. Even with a more modest goal in mind, our own attempt at an introductory textbook has proved challenging, and certainly humbling. One of the most difficult parts of the process has been trimming to a reasonable size our initial wish list of wonderful feminist writings. By editing many pieces for length, we have been able to assemble a broadly representative sampling of works. *Critical Terrain* contributes to the growing list of innovative texts on the North American market by offering what we hope you will find to be an appealing collection with several unique characteristics and tools for students and instructors. We present below some of the main features of both the first and second editions of this book. These were inspired by a wide reading of existing textbooks, an appreciation for both classic insights and new theoretical developments shaping the field, and a recognition of the diversity of readership.

- *Multiplicity of disciplines and fields:* Because gender and women's studies is multidisciplinary and interdisciplinary, we provide writings that give you, as students, exposure to feminist scholarship from across disciplines as well as within the newer interdisciplinary and transdisciplinary gender and women's studies stream. Sociology, psychology, history, philosophy, Indigenous studies, literature, cultural studies, biology, science studies, Canadian studies, political economy, and anthropology are some of the areas represented in this text.
- *Historical and contemporary contexts:* Many gender and women's studies texts lean heavily on present-day concerns and circumstances. We chose selections that balance contemporary analyses with historical ones. To address broader society's historical amnesia, we aimed for readings that build a strong foundation in the history of women and other marginalized groups (such as Indigenous and racialized people, people with disabilities, and gender and sexual minorities).
- *Diversity of authors:* We think that it is important to feature work by a broad range of authors

from various social, economic, and geographic identities and locations. Different viewpoints from diversely located writers can generate critical debate about issues such as the relevance of gender and women's studies, men's relationship to feminism, gender and sexual minority and trans perspectives, gendered and racialized beauty ideals, impacts of globalization on women workers, and reproductive technologies. Thus, we highlight the richness of the literature and the diversity of gendered experiences, perspectives, and analyses. We include voices from the margins as well as the centre.
- *Current and classic selections:* While it can be tempting to showcase the newest writing that is stretching the boundaries of feminist ideas and actions, there is great value in revisiting some of the classic works. We have incorporated older and newer selections to honour the powerful contributions of multiple generations of feminist thinkers, to recognize the interconnectedness of the past and the present, and to acknowledge the indebtedness of contemporary insights to the work, knowledge, and struggle of those who came before.
- *Canadian, North American, and Indigenous content:* When we started thinking about this textbook, American collections dominated the market, but there are now an increasing number of Canadian-oriented contributions available. We believe that not just in Canadian, but also in North American classrooms, there should be some focus on Canada, partly to challenge commonly voiced assumptions that gender and other inequalities exist mainly beyond Canadian borders (over "there"). Consideration of the specificity of issues in Canada and North America provides you with critical perspectives on the immediate political, social, economic, and geographic context, where you can also begin to untangle the multiple and complex relations of power between "the West and the rest." We have tried to integrate a focus

on Indigenous women and colonial histories within Canada and North America, not merely in a few separate sections of the book, but as sustained themes throughout. There is an exciting and growing body of First Nations, Métis, and Inuit women's and Two-Spirit people's writing, including work by Indigenous feminists, and incorporating this work across the themes builds breadth and depth of understanding.

- *Global/transnational content:* Although it is useful to emphasize Canadian and North American specificity, we make links to broader global trends and to the diversity of gendered experiences within and between different parts of the world. We hope to encourage you to think about the local and the global as mutually constitutive. Analyses of global systems and institutions of power are introduced, and material by and about women in various locations is included. Throughout this volume, we try to avoid the "feminist as tourist model" so aptly critiqued by Mohanty (2003), where women from other countries are merely added in to existing Eurocentric frameworks. By foregrounding Canada and North America, we do not take up fully Mohanty's challenge to internationalize gender and women's studies curriculum in accordance with the "feminist solidarity" model that she promoted. Yet our approach still draws on her insights and those of other transnational feminist scholars.

- *Multiple genres and styles:* As instructors, we appreciate materials that vary genres and styles, exposing students to the numerous forms in which feminist ideas are created, sharpening learners' skills at reading across disciplines, and celebrating variety in ways of learning and knowing. In addition to standard scholarly articles, we include reports, news clips, fact sheets, website materials, short fiction, poetry, interviews, personal narratives, and, unique to this second edition, original artwork. Personal stories and creative works can teach different truths and move audiences in different ways, and often more intimately, than

straight scholarly pieces. Popular works by activists or activist organizations ground the material in practice and let students in on strategies and debates from inside the ranks of social justice movements. We hope these works also inspire you to see the relevance of gender and women's studies, and generate ideas for action-oriented praxis.

- *Tools and insights for education and action:* To enhance the learning process, we have included several teaching tools. Students and teachers will find useful learning aids in the form of textboxes, activist insights, illustrations and artwork, charts, lists, fact sheets, graphs, newspaper articles, maps, and activist campaign materials. We have chosen materials and teaching aids with attention to the wide variation in identities, ages, backgrounds, interests, literacy levels, and other academic skills among the student body. Instructors have access to a companion Teacher's Guide with critical questions, teaching tips, and suggested classroom activities and assignments designed to deepen students' reading and critical thinking skills.

- *Balance of bad news/good news:* Gender and women's studies instructors are well aware that students can be overwhelmed with the "bad news" about gendered and other socially created inequalities. This is particularly evident when we examine indicators such as growing disparities between the wealthy and the poor within and among nations in contemporary neo-liberal times. The optimism that fuelled second-wave feminists is not as accessible for a host of different reasons, yet we want to teach, learn about, and build on signs of hope. Throughout the reader, we highlight diverse examples and case studies of resistance in order to dispel lingering myths about the supposed powerlessness of marginalized groups; to challenge gendered, classed, racialized, and ablest stereotypes; and to convey a sense of the vibrancy of human agency. Because organized and collective activism, as well as individual actions, can create change, we have included selections that introduce and analyze the limits and possibilities of resistance in its various forms. Many students and instructors yearn to explore and share ideas about what we can do—as individuals and in groups of our own making and choosing—to participate in social justice projects.

## CRITICAL THINKING FOR CHANGE

As professors in gender and women's studies for a combined 30-plus years, we believe that a grounding in the theories, methods, and values of our field is critically important in an historical moment marked in many ways by pessimism, uncertainty, and austerity. Feminism has made significant strides toward gender equality, yet feminist and justice movements in Canada and around the world have faced enormous challenges in recent decades—the rise of economic globalization and the neo-liberal erosion of social welfare, equality rights, and economic security for women, racialized people, people with disabilities, and the poor are only a few egregious examples of troubling trends. In 2004, well-known Canadian feminist Judy Rebick commented on some of these setbacks in Canada:

> The triumph of neo-liberal/neo-conservative politics has dealt a mortal blow to a feminism that seeks economic and social equality. The gains we have made are threatened by the increasing impoverishment of women, even as a few climb the heights of corporate, professional and political success; by the shocking degradation of women in international sex slavery; the overwhelming burden of the double day; longer, rather than shorter, work times; the rise of racism, militarism and the security state; the monopoly of men on power; closer ties, especially military ties, with the United States; and the continuing scourge of war and violence against women and children. (Rebick, 2004, March 15)

Critical problems require critical thinking. The theories, tools, and world views found in gender and women's studies build our capacities for thinking our way through pressing social problems and for beginning to imagine more just alternatives. Beyond introducing students to vitally important content, the field offers vibrant learning opportunities that teach critical thinking for both personal and social transformation.

But what, then, is *critical thinking*? Feminist theorist and educator bell hooks writes that "thinking is an action" (2010, p. 7). Thinking is active because it involves asking questions and seeking answers in order to understand how the world works. hooks argues that students' passion for knowledge often gets undermined when educational institutions value the consumption of information over the teaching of skills needed to think critically. People commonly assume that being critical means responding negatively and often dismissively to others' ideas. Critical engagement, however, does not mean just fault-finding. Instead it involves learning to think carefully and skillfully to analyze and evaluate the truth, value, and meaning of an idea or position. It is active and participatory. It is also hard work. Critical thinking is a process of discerning what is significant about an issue or topic; analyzing and evaluating other people's thinking about it; questioning the merit and consequences of different positions, including our own; and working to create new knowledge (hooks, 2010). Critical thinking provides a way to expand our consciousness and strive for greater understanding across differences. Because of this, many progressive educators see it as a tool for fostering freedom, democracy, and equality (Freire, 2000, 2005; hooks, 2010).

*Conversation* is integral to critical thinking. hooks (2010) insists that dialogue enables students to find their voices, identify the issues that matter to them, discover new ways of seeing and knowing, and better remember the ideas exchanged in the classroom. As students taking gender and women's studies, you have opportunities to engage in many kinds of conversations: with instructors, other students, and, importantly, with the authors of the texts you read. At the same time, like many learners in introductory classes, you may have come to university or college perplexed about *how* to read assigned texts, listen to lectures, or enter into conversations about what you have read and heard. We must remind ourselves that people engaged in conversation are not passive; rather we are alive, open, reflective, and reaching for understanding to deepen, strengthen, and communicate knowledge.

In any learning situation, teachers and students enter a relationship. Lecturers have significant responsibilities, but so too do students. The first is *listening*—again an active, participatory process. Listening does not mean you stop thinking. Rather it means striving to make meaning of the speaker's message by working to digest and understand, and from there to analyze and reflect on what they are saying. At the same time, pausing to listen does not mean that you must agree with what is being said. Remember that teaching and learning are processes and that knowledge is always changing and evolving. As listeners, it is your responsibility to acknowledge what you are learning, but also what remains unclear, underdeveloped, or open to question. Careful listening can lead to well thought-out disagreement and dissent, which are vitally important to critical thinking.

A second set of responsibilities involves *self-reflection*, or examining your responses to others' ideas and questioning how your preconceptions and social positioning may be implicated in your hearing. We each bring our personal histories, identities, social relationships, commitments, values, and politics to our listening. Rather than the common knee-jerk reaction of rejecting new ideas outright, particularly those that challenge dominant thought and the status quo, how can you take seriously unfamiliar ways of thinking? What do your immediate responses to these ideas teach you about yourself and, possibly, your own positionality? Your job is to look for points of connection that can

aid in meaning-making while opening yourself to the possibility that the new ideas and vantage points might actually change you. They might take you someplace else, to transport you to new understanding.

A third challenge is *speaking up* and articulating your thoughts, ideas, and positions effectively and respectfully. While speaking in groups can be nerve-racking, finding your voice and figuring out how to use it is a valuable skill whether you continue in academe, pursue a professional degree, or directly enter the workforce. Both generosity and intellectual rigour are vital to creating an ethical space for sharing ideas and learning from each other. But how can you contribute to creating that space? Before and as you speak, keep reflecting: What is the point of my question or comment? You might also be thinking about your position in relation to the subject under discussion by asking yourself: Who am I in relationship to this topic? What do I bring that can give a unique perspective on this topic? How does my position influence my understanding?

This brings us to the fourth challenge: *critical reading*. The core elements of critical thinking discussed above are also foundational to critical reading. Engagement with written texts similarly demands listening, self-reflection, and even speaking, since you are entering into dialogue with the author. The Academic Skills Centre at our university encourages students to ask questions of the text, to respond to it and to evaluate it—in short, to "make it *mean* something to you" (Academic Skills Centre at Trent University, 2015; emphasis ours). Reading requires different approaches to understanding and meaning-making, depending on the type of text you are examining. As you look at each selection in this textbook, it is useful to consider first the genre of the work. Is it a scholarly article? A report by a government or community organization? A newspaper article? A work of art? A fictional short story? A poem? A personal narrative or an interview? A map, chart, or other kind of illustration? The specific questions you ask as an active reader might vary across genres. At the same time, there are some overarching questions that can guide you in your comprehension and interpretation. Here we outline eight points of entry involving probes intended to facilitate your reading as an active and interactive process.

## QUESTIONS FOR CRITICAL READING

1. How and where does this selection fit into the parts and sections of this text and of your course? How does it relate to the main themes examined in this part and section?
2. Is the subject matter new to you, or do you have some familiarity with it?
3. What are the main ideas? How are these ideas presented? How do they relate to what is being addressed in this part of the textbook and in your class?
4. If you are reading a scholarly article, what is the central argument or thesis? What information is used as evidence to support the argument? Is the argument persuasive?
5. How might this selection relate to key concepts emphasized in this part of the textbook and in your class?
6. Is the piece trying to challenge and change dominant thinking about something, deepen and transform your understanding, encourage personal reflection, and/or mobilize you to action?
7. Does the piece resonate with your own experiences and/or analyses of the issue or topic? Are there elements that you are questioning? What remains confusing, unclear, or underdeveloped?
8. Why is this piece significant? Why do you think it was included as one of your readings?

## THE CRITICAL TERRAIN OF THIS BOOK

We have organized this book into six thematic parts. Within each part, there are between two and six sections that develop the topics and address some key debates in feminist scholarship and activism.

Part 1:  Foundations: Why Gender and Women's Studies? Why Feminism?
Part 2:  Constructions of Sex and Gender
Part 3:  Gendered Identities
Part 4:  Cultural Representations and Body Politics
Part 5:  Gendering Globalization, Migration, and Activism
Part 6:  Organizing for Change

The second edition contains significant revisions to the table of contents. Of the 81 chapters, 43 are new to this edition. Of the 47 textboxes (called Snapshots and Soundwaves in this edition), 25 are newly added. Significantly the second edition features 10 works of activist art, along with a commissioned original artistic map by Indigenous disability-identified artist Vanessa Dion Fletcher (Lenape/Potawatomi). The overall structure of the book is generally the same, although we changed a few of the headings and added a new subsection on "Gender, Migration, and Citizenship." We increased the content on contemporary activist movements (including Black Lives Matter, Idle No More, disability justice, and hashtag activism); trans and gender-queer identities and politics; and feminist disability perspectives. We also added material on Islamophobia and the politics of veiling, Indigenous sovereignty and cultural resurgence, intersex, and sex work as labour.

The "critical terrain" signalled in our title has multiple meanings for this volume and for the future of gender and women's studies. Certainly the theoretical trends we have outlined, and that are taken up throughout the book, constitute critical shifts in a field that is continuously being re-mapped. Marginalized peoples around the world are facing critical problems requiring critical thought and action by all of us as members of local and global communities. We are at a critical juncture where systems of power and political ideologies are heightening divisions between people, pushing certain groups further to the margins. In this context, feminism offers critical insights and tools for transforming landscapes of inequalities.

As we pass this book over to you, we hope that you will be informed, engaged, challenged, and inspired by the content and the range of selections. Each piece offers its unique wisdom, and we hope that you will discover your own treasures in these pages. We also hope you will attend to the diversity of voices, issues, identities, and perspectives, taking care to reflect on their meanings and their contributions to feminist critical thought and action. Finally we hope that this textbook facilitates your social justice consciousness as it also fosters your intellectual and creative capacities to appraise and envision different avenues for change. We invite you into the conversation, and like to imagine you discussing, sharing, and debating the ideas with others in various forums and contexts.

*Note:* Portions of this introduction were adapted from two articles: "Rethinking Women's Studies: Curriculum, Pedagogy, and the Introductory Course," published in *Atlantis: A Women's Studies Journal* (2011a), and "Reading Women's and Gender Studies in Canada: A Review of Recent Introductory Textbooks," published in *Canadian Woman Studies* (2011b).

## REFERENCES

Academic Skills Centre at Trent University. (2015). "Reading Critically and Efficiently: Strategies for Successful Study." Retrieved from: https://www.trentu.ca/academicskills/documents/ReadingCritically.pdf.

Bacon, Jen. (2006). "Teaching Queer Studies at a *Normal* School." *Journal of Homosexuality, 52*(1/2), 257–83.

Blyth, Molly. (2008). "'So, What's a White Girl Like Me Doing in a Place Like This?' Re-Thinking Pedagogical Practices in an Indigenous Context." *Resources for Feminist Research, 33*(1/2), 63–80.

Canadian Research Institute for the Advancement of Women (CRIAW). (2006). *Intersectional Feminist Frameworks: An Emerging Vision*. Ottawa, ON: Canadian Research Institute for the Advancement of Women.

Collins, Patricia Hill. (1990). *Black Feminist Thought: Knowledge, Consciousness, and the Politics of Empowerment* (1st ed.). Boston, MA: Unwin Hyman.

Crenshaw, Kimberlé. (1994). "Mapping the Margins: Intersectionality, Identity Politics, and Violence against Women of Color." In Martha Fineman & Roxanne Mykitiuk (Eds.), *The Public Nature of Private Violence* (pp. 93–118). New York, NY: Routledge.

Davis, Dawn Rae. (2010). "Unmirroring Pedagogies: Teaching with Intersectional and Transnational Methods in the Women and Gender Studies Classroom." *Feminist Formations, 22*(1), 136–62.

Dion, Susan. (2009). *Braiding Histories: Learning from Aboriginal Peoples' Experiences and Perspectives*. Vancouver: University of British Columbia Press.

Driskill, Qwo-Li, Heath Justice, Daniel, Miranda, Deborah A., & Tatonetti, Lisa. (2011). *Sovereign Erotics: A Collection of Two-Spirit Literature*. Tuscon, AZ: University of Arizona Press.

Dua, Ena, & Trotz, Alissa (Eds.). (2002). "Transnational Pedagogy: Doing Political Work in Women's Studies. An Interview with Chandra Talpade Mohanty." *Atlantis: A Women's Studies Journal, 26*(2) (Spring/Summer), 66–77.

Freire, Paulo. (2000). *Pedagogy of the Oppressed: 30th Anniversary Edition*. New York, NY: Continuum.

Freire, Paulo. (2005). *Education for Critical Consciousness*. New York, NY: Continuum.

Green, Joyce. (2007). "Taking Account of Aboriginal Feminism." In Joyce Green (Ed.), *Making Space for Indigenous Feminism* (pp. 20–32). Black Point, NS: Fernwood.

Grewal, Inderpal, & Kaplan, Caren (Eds.). (2006). *An Introduction to Women's Studies: Gender in a Transnational World* (2nd ed.). Boston, MA: McGraw-Hill.

Hobbs, Margaret, & Rice, Carla. (2011a). "Rethinking Women's Studies: Curriculum, Pedagogy, and the Introductory Course." *A Women's Studies Journal, 35*(2), 139–49.

Hobbs, Margaret, & Rice, Carla. (2011b). "Reading Women's and Gender Studies in Canada: A Review of Recent Introductory Textbooks." *A Women's Studies Journal, 29*(1/2), 201–07.

hooks, bell. (2010). *Teaching Critical Thinking: Practical Wisdom.* New York, NY: Routledge.

Hunt, Sarah. (2016). "Representing Colonial Violence: Trafficking, Sex Work, and the Violence of Law." *Atlantis: Critical Studies in Gender, Culture & Social Justice, 37*(2), 25–39.

Kaplan, Caren, & Grewal, Inderpal. (2002). "Transnational Practices and Interdisciplinary Feminist Scholarship: Refiguring Women's and Gender Studies." In Robyn Wiegman (Ed.), *Women's Studies on Its Own: A Next Wave Reader in Institutional Change* (pp. 66–81). London, UK: Duke University Press.

Karpinski, Eva. (2007). "'Copy, Cut, Paste': A Reflection on Some Institutional Constraints of Teaching a Big Intro Course." *Resources for Feminist Research, 32*(3/4), 44–53.

LaRocque, Emma. (2007). "Metis and Feminist: Ethical Reflections on Feminism, Human Rights, and Decolonization." In Joyce Green (Ed.), *Making Space for Indigenous Feminism* (pp. 53–71). Black Point, NS: Fernwood.

Meem, Deborah, Gibson, Michelle, & Alexander, Jonathan (Eds.). (2010). *Finding Out: An Introduction to LGBT Studies.* Thousand Oaks, CA: Sage.

Mohanty, Chandra Talpade. (1991). "'Under Western Eyes': Feminist Scholarship and Colonial Discourses." In Chandra Talpade Mohanty, Ann Russo & Lourdes Torres (Eds.), *Third World Women and the Politics of Feminism* (pp. 51–80). Bloomington, IN: Indiana University Press.

Mohanty, Chandra Talpade. (2003). "'Under Western Eyes' Revisited: Feminist Solidarity through Anticapitalist Struggles." In Chandra Talpade Mohanty (Ed.), *Feminism without Borders: Decolonizing Theory, Practicing Solidarity* (pp. 221–51). Durham, NC: Duke University Press.

Rebick, Judy. (2004, March 15). "We've Come Part Way, Baby: A New Opportunity Has Opened for the Women's Movement." rabble.ca. Retrieved from: http://rabble.ca/news/weve-come-part-way-baby.

Roy, Arundhati. (2003). *War Talk.* Cambridge, MA: South End Press.

Scott-Dixon, Krista (Ed.). (2006). *Trans/forming Feminisms: Trans-Feminist Voices Speak Out.* Toronto, ON: Sumach.

Shohat, Ella. (2001). "Area Studies, Transnationalism, and the Feminist Production of Knowledge." *Signs: Journal of Women in Culture and Society, 26*(4), 1269–72.

Simpson, Leanne Betasamosake. (2011). *Dancing on Our Turtle's Back: Stories of Nishnaabeg Re-Creation, Resurgence and a New Emergence.* Winnipeg, MB: ARP Books.

Smith, Linda Tuhiwai. (1999). *Decolonizing Methodologies: Research and Indigenous Peoples.* London, UK: Zed Books.

St. Denis, Verna. (2007). "Feminism Is for Everybody: Aboriginal Women, Feminism, and Diversity." In Joyce Green (Ed.), *Making Space for Indigenous Feminism* (pp. 33–52). Black Point, NS: Fernwood.

Steinem, Gloria. (1970, June 7). "'Women's Liberation' Aims to Free Men, Too.'" *The Washington Post*, 192.

Stombler, Mindy, Baunach, Dawn M., Burgess, Elisabeth O., Donnelly, Denise, Simonds, Wendy, & Windsor, Elroi J. (Eds.). (2010). *Sex Matters: The Sexuality and Society Reader* (3rd ed.). Toronto, ON: Allyn & Bacon.

Yuval-Davis, Nira. (2006). "Intersectionality and Feminist Politics." *European Journal of Women's Studies, 13*(3), 193–209.

# PART 1

## Foundations: Why Gender and Women's Studies? Why Feminism?

> To be truly visionary we have to root our imagination in our concrete reality while simultaneously imagining possibilities beyond that reality.
>
> —*bell hooks, Feminism Is for Everybody: Passionate Politics (2000, p. 110)*

Part 1 addresses popular misconceptions and stereotypes about feminism, and discusses men's engagements with feminism in contemporary North America. We review some markers of progress and continuing inequalities in Canada and the United States. The concept of "intersectionality" is introduced as a tool to understand diverse gendered experiences and the relations of women, men, and gender non-conforming people to systems of power and inequality.

### Part 1A: This Is What a Feminist Looks Like

This section introduces you to different ways in which feminism has been understood and practised in the past and present. The articles offer multiple definitions of feminism, examine its history and relevance, and consider the many myths and stereotypes associated with the term.

### Part 1B: Diversity and Intersectionality

The second section examines social differences, in particular differences informed by gender, race, class, sexuality, disability, geography, histories of colonization and slavery, and embodiment. It also introduces the idea of intersectionality to understand/analyze how these social differences shape people's lives.

### Part 1C: Accounting for Inequalities

In this section, we provide an overview of key markers of progress and continuing inequalities in the North American and global contexts. Issues introduced include the gender gap in political representation, income inequality, gendered and racialized labour markets, social programs, childcare, and women's unpaid labour.

# CHAPTER 1

## Excerpts from *Feminism Is for Everybody*

*bell hooks*

bell hooks is a leading feminist theorist and cultural critic, whose work focuses on the interconnectedness of race, gender, culture, and class. The author of over 30 books, she has been recognized with numerous awards and has been named one of the most influential American thinkers by *Publisher's Weekly* and the *Atlantic Monthly*, and one of the world's top 100 visionaries by *Utne Reader*. *Ain't I a Woman: Black Women and Feminism* and *Feminism Is for Everybody* (excerpted here) are among her most well-known books.

## INTRODUCTION: COME CLOSER TO FEMINISM

Everywhere I go I proudly tell folks who want to know who I am and what I do that I am a writer, a feminist theorist, a cultural critic. I tell them I write about movies and popular culture, analyzing the message in the medium. Most people find this exciting and want to know more. Everyone goes to movies, watches television, glances through magazines, and everyone has thoughts about the messages they receive, about the images they look at. It is easy for the diverse public I encounter to understand what I do as a cultural critic, to understand my passion for writing (lots of folks want to write, and do). But feminist theory—that's the place where the questions stop. Instead I tend to hear all about the evil of feminism and the bad feminists: how "they" hate men; how "they" want to go against nature—and god; how "they" are all lesbians; how

"they" are taking all the jobs and making the world hard for white men, who do not stand a chance.

When I ask these same folks about the feminist books or magazines they read, when I ask them about the feminist talks they have heard, about the feminist activists they know, they respond by letting me know that everything they know about feminism has come into their lives third hand, that they really have not come close enough to feminist movement to know what really happens, what it's really about. Mostly they think feminism is a bunch of angry women who want to be like men. They do not even think about feminism as being about rights—about women gaining equal rights. When I talk about the feminism I know—up close and personal—they willingly listen, although when our conversations end, they are quick to tell me I am different, not like the "real" feminists who hate men, who are angry. I assure them I am as real and as radical a feminist as one can be, and if they dare to come closer to feminism they will see it is not how they have imagined it.

*****

I have wanted them to have an answer to the question "What is feminism?" that is rooted neither in fear or fantasy. I have wanted them to have this simple definition to read again and again so they know: "Feminism is a movement to end sexism, sexist exploitation, and oppression." I love this definition [...] because it so clearly states that the movement is not about being anti-male. It makes it clear that the problem is sexism. And that clarity helps us remember that all of us, female and male, have been socialized from birth on to accept sexist thought and action. As a consequence, females can be just as sexist as men. And while that does not excuse or justify male domination, it does mean that it would be naive and wrongminded for feminist thinkers to see the movement as simplistically being for women against men. To end patriarchy (another way of naming the institutionalized sexism) we need to be clear that we are all participants in perpetuating sexism until we change our minds and hearts, until we let go of sexist thought and action and replace it with feminist thought and action.

Males as a group have and do benefit the most from patriarchy, from the assumption that they are superior to females and should rule over us. But those benefits have come with a price. In return for all the goodies men receive from patriarchy, they are required to dominate women, to exploit and oppress us, using violence if they must to keep patriarchy intact. Most men find it difficult to be patriarchs. Most men are disturbed by hatred and fear of women, by male violence against women, even the men who perpetuate this violence. But they fear letting go of the benefits. They are not certain what will happen to the world they know most intimately if patriarchy changes. So they find it easier to passively support male domination even when they know in their minds and hearts that it is wrong. Again and again men tell me they

have no idea what it is feminists want. I believe them. I believe in their capacity to change and grow. And I believe that if they knew more about feminism they would no longer fear it, for they would find in feminist movement the hope of their own release from the bondage of patriarchy.

It is for these men, young and old, and for all of us, that I have written this short handbook, the book I have spent more than 20 years longing for. I had to write it because I kept waiting for it to appear, and it did not. And without it there was no way to address the hordes of people in this nation who are daily bombarded with anti-feminist backlash, who are being told to hate and resist a movement that they know very little about. There should be so many little feminist primers, easy to read pamphlets and books, telling us all about feminism, that this book would be just another passionate voice speaking out on behalf of feminist politics. There should be billboards; ads in magazines; ads on buses, subways, trains; television commercials spreading the word, letting the world know more about feminism. We are not there yet. But this is what we must do to share feminism, to let the movement into everyone's mind and heart. Feminist change has already touched all our lives in a positive way. And yet we lose sight of the positive when all we hear about feminism is negative.

When I began to resist male domination, to rebel against patriarchal thinking (and to oppose the strongest patriarchal voice in my life—my mother's voice), I was still a teenager, suicidal, depressed, uncertain about how I would find meaning in my life and a place for myself. I needed feminism to give me a foundation of equality and justice to stand on. Mama has come around to feminist thinking. She sees me and all her daughters (we are six) living better lives because of feminist politics. She sees the promise and hope in feminist movement. It is that promise and hope that I want to share with you in this book, with everybody.

Imagine living in a world where there is no domination, where females and males are not alike or even always equal, but where a vision of mutuality is the ethos shaping our interaction. Imagine living in a world where we can all be who we are, a world of peace and possibility. Feminist revolution alone will not create such a world; we need to end racism, class elitism, imperialism. But it will make it possible for us to be fully self-actualized females and males able to create beloved community, to live together, realizing our dreams of freedom and justice, living the truth that we are all "created equal." Come closer. See how feminism can touch and change your life and all our lives. Come closer and know firsthand what feminist movement is all about. Come closer and you will see: feminism is for everybody.

## FEMINIST POLITICS: WHERE WE STAND

Simply put, feminism is a movement to end sexism, sexist exploitation, and oppression. [...]

As all advocates of feminist politics know, most people do not understand sexism, or if they do, they think it is not a problem. Masses of people think that feminism is always and only about women seeking to be equal to men. And a huge majority of these folks think feminism is anti-male. Their misunderstanding of feminist politics reflects the reality that most folks learn about feminism from patriarchal mass media. The feminism they hear about the most is portrayed by women who are primarily committed to gender equality—equal pay for equal work, and sometimes women and men sharing household chores and parenting. They see that these women are usually white and materially privileged. They know from mass media that women's liberation focuses on the freedom to have abortions, to be lesbians, to challenge rape and domestic violence. Among these issues, masses of people agree with the idea of gender equity in the workplace—equal pay for equal work.

Since our society continues to be primarily a "Christian" culture, masses of people continue to believe that god has ordained that women be subordinate to men in the domestic household. Even though masses of women have entered the workforce, even though many families are headed by women who are the sole breadwinners, the vision of domestic life which continues to dominate the nation's imagination is one in which the logic of male domination is intact, whether men are present in the home or not. The wrongminded notion of feminist movement which implied it was anti-male carried with it the wrongminded assumption that all female space would necessarily be an environment where patriarchy and sexist thinking would be absent. Many women, even those involved in feminist politics, chose to believe this as well.

There was indeed a great deal of anti-male sentiment among early feminist activists who were responding to male domination with anger. It was that anger at injustice that was the impetus for creating a women's liberation movement. Early on most feminist activists (a majority of whom were white) had their consciousness raised about the nature of male domination when they were working in anti-classist and anti-racist settings with men who were telling the world about the importance of freedom while subordinating the women in their ranks. Whether it was white women working on behalf of socialism, black women working on behalf of civil rights and black liberation, or Native American women working for Indigenous rights, it was clear that men wanted to lead, and they wanted women to follow. Participating in these radical freedom struggles awakened the spirit of rebellion and resistance in progressive females and led them towards contemporary women's liberation.

As contemporary feminism progressed, as women realized that males were not the only group in our society who supported sexist thinking and behavior—that females could be sexist as well—anti-male sentiment no longer shaped the movement's consciousness. The focus shifted to an all-out effort to create gender justice. But women could not band together to further feminism without confronting our sexist thinking. Sisterhood could not be powerful as long as women were competitively at war with one another. Utopian visions of sisterhood based solely on the awareness of the reality that all women were in some way victimized by male domination were disrupted by discussions of class and race. Discussions of class differences occurred early on in contemporary feminism, preceding discussions of race. Diana Press published revolutionary insights about class divisions between women as early as the mid-'70s in their collection of essays *Class and Feminism*. These discussions did not trivialize the feminist insistence that "sisterhood is powerful," they simply emphasized that we could only become sisters in struggle by confronting the ways women—through sex, class, and race—dominated and exploited other women, and created a political platform that would address these differences.

Even though individual black women were active in contemporary feminist movement from its inception, they were not the individuals who became the "stars" of the movement, who attracted the attention of mass media. Often individual black women active in feminist movement were revolutionary feminists (like many white lesbians). They were already at odds with reformist feminists who resolutely wanted to project a vision of the movement as being solely about women gaining equality with men in the existing system. Even before race became a talked about issue in feminist circles it was clear to black women (and to their revolutionary allies in struggle) that they were never going to have equality within the existing white supremacist capitalist patriarchy.

From its earliest inception feminist movement was polarized. Reformist thinkers chose to emphasize gender equality. Revolutionary thinkers did not want simply to alter the existing system so that women would have more rights. We wanted to transform that system, to bring an end to patriarchy and sexism. Since patriarchal mass media was not interested in the more revolutionary vision, it never received attention in mainstream press. The vision of "women's liberation" which captured and still holds the public imagination was the one representing women as wanting what men had. And this was the vision that was easier to realize. Changes in our nation's economy, economic depression, the loss of jobs, etc., made the climate ripe for our nation's citizens to accept the notion of gender equality in the workforce. […]

Most women, especially privileged white women, ceased even to consider revolutionary feminist visions, once they began to gain economic power within the existing social structure. Ironically, revolutionary feminist thinking was most accepted and embraced in academic circles. In those circles the production of revolutionary feminist theory progressed, but more often than not that theory was not made available to the public. It became and remains a privileged discourse available to those among us who are highly literate, well-educated, and usually materially privileged. […]

Lifestyle feminism ushered in the notion that there could be as many versions of feminism as there were women. Suddenly the politics was being slowly removed from feminism. And the assumption prevailed that no matter what a woman's politics, be she conservative or liberal, she too could fit feminism into her existing lifestyle. Obviously this way of thinking has made feminism more acceptable because its underlying assumption is that women can be feminists without fundamentally challenging and changing themselves or the culture. […]

Feminist politics is losing momentum because feminist movement has lost clear definitions. We have those definitions. Let's reclaim them. Let's share them. Let's start over. Let's have T-shirts and bumper stickers and postcards and hip-hop music, television and radio commercials, ads everywhere and billboards, and all manner of printed material that tells the world about feminism. We can share the simple yet powerful message that feminism is a movement to end sexist oppression. Let's start there. Let the movement begin again.

---

*Source:* hooks, bell. (2000). Excerpted from "Introduction" and "Chapter 1: Feminist Politics." In *Feminism Is for Everybody: Passionate Politics* (pp. vii–x, 1–6). London, UK: Pluto Press.

# CHAPTER 2

## What's Feminism Done (For Me) Lately?

*Victoria L. Bromley*

Victoria L. Bromley is an award-winning teacher and former assistant professor at the Pauline Jewett Institute of Women's and Gender Studies at Carleton University. She is the author of *Feminisms Matter: Debates, Theories, Activism* and "Women's Studies: Are We 'Broad' Enough?" published in *Atlantis: Critical Studies in Gender, Culture & Social Justice.*

We made it! We are equal. Feminism is no longer necessary. And, of course, feminism is dead. The struggle is over and we can put our concerns to rest. These are some of the tenets that we often hear. It makes us feel good to think that things are not as bad for women and other marginalized groups as they were in the past. Social commentary of this brand is often paired with the familiar preface for gender equality assertions: "I'm not a feminist but …" What follows is a laundry list of values or aspirations that most people can agree on, such as equal pay, women's equal access to education, ending violence against women and children, women's right to enter the professions of medicine or engineering, and women's right to vote.

## I'M NOT A FEMINIST BUT...

Feminism offers a way to see ourselves and the world anew. Fortified with feminist analyses, we can challenge the negative images that bombard us every day and the bad things happening around us. It enables us to reject the bad stuff and move on to the good. The good is the stuff anyone can get behind, like equal rights, equal pay, environmental justice, and just plain old "I'm OK the way I am" and "I don't have to change who I am for anybody." These ideas are empowering.

I always ask my students during the first class, "How many of you are feminists?" About 10 per cent of students in my large first-year class usually claim this political identity. Yet I am always surprised by how many students look confused at my question. I commonly follow up with more acceptable questions such as how many of you believe in equal rights? Equal pay? Equal access to education? Reproductive freedom? Accessible and affordable child-care? Ending violence against women? Invariably most students raise their hands and I welcome them to the idea that these beliefs might mean they are feminists.

Our reluctance to link feminism to social justice issues is based on the negative stereotypes of feminists that dominate popular culture. Who wants to be seen as one of those card-carrying, angry, loud, man-hating "'Feminazis'"? Our reluctance to raise our hands and identify as feminists could also mean that we are not sure how others will interpret our version of feminism. Yes, there are many kinds of feminism, and we may not agree with everything other feminists say or do, so we keep quiet. But if feminism at its core includes both theory and practice to end sexism and other systems of oppression, is rooted in social justice, and demands social change, how can we not speak out?

Oh, but we *have* been speaking out! Feminists have been raising their voices for years. Social change doesn't happen easily. It is created through struggle, protest, and a commitment to a better world. It is rooted in concepts of social justice. Feminists have been very successful in making social change and achieving many of their goals. Unfortunately, many of the hard-fought struggles and important gains have become conventional common sense. I say *unfortunately* because such incredible successes make the significant changes in North American societies less visible. Many of the hard-won achievements by women's and other social movements now inform popular understandings of *normal* in North American culture. Most of us accept that with citizenship comes the right to vote regardless of one's gender, race, class, or sexuality, and that equal pay is a good idea, at least in principle. We also think that equality and freedom from discrimination are important goals for any society. However, these seemingly common-sense notions were not always part of our collective consciousness. Consequently, we may take them for granted.

It is important to recognize that in the mid-twentieth century, the women's movement emerged alongside many other social justice movements. All of these movements inspired each other, learned from each other, and created a wider context for social change and the questioning of many well-established customs, laws, and social practices that fostered inequalities and oppressions. As a way to understand the past and to support future feminist activism, we will examine the many links between women's movement and other social justice movements, including the peace movement, civil rights movement, Indian/Native rights movement, and gay/lesbian rights movement. The purpose here is to provide an understanding of where we were, how far we have come (at least in some ways), and what is at stake.

## SOCIAL CHANGE AND SOCIAL JUSTICE

In North America, the 1960s and 1970s were a period of social and political upheaval that made people both hopeful for and fearful of change. In the United States, the government was preoccupied with the Cold War and defeating the Soviet Union. This international focus affected domestic politics. Anti-war and peace movements were visible and vocal, with students and others protesting American involvement in the Vietnam War. The slogan "Make love not war" could be heard on the streets and in the news. Canada did not experience the same level of protest, and its international ambitions were not as intimately tied to victory in Vietnam as it was in the United States, but national debates still ensued, particularly as American draft resisters sought refuge across the border. The oil crisis also emerged in the 1970s. American reliance on oil laid the foundation for a new phase of U.S. imperialism and interventions in attempts to retain control over global oil reserves.

At the same time, the movement for civil rights in the United States was making race relations front-page news. African American students, with the support of local communities and the NAACP (National Association for the Advancement of Colored People), sparked a movement to end racial segregation in the American South when they peacefully sat down at lunch counters reserved for whites and requested service. The first lunch counter sit-in was launched in Wichita, Kansas, in July 1958, and by August of that year, integration was achieved. [...] Thousands of ordinary people protested everything from segregation on interstate buses to segregation in education and employment throughout the 1960s. Martin Luther King Jr. and Malcolm X, who articulated different ideas about how to bring white supremacy to an end, became the best-known spokesmen for that movement. White supremacy refers to the belief that white people are superior to all others, which has resulted in the systemic privileging of white people. Federal legislation, culminating in the Civil Rights Act of 1964, made racial segregation in schools, workplaces, and public facilities illegal and prohibited discrimination on the basis of race. It also made discrimination on the basis of sex, religion, or national origin illegal. The passing of the 1965 National Voting Rights Act, which banned voter prerequisites and qualifications such as literacy tests, ended the legal disenfranchisement experienced by African Americans, women, and the poor. Making discrimination illegal, however, does not mean that racism ceases to operate. But it was the bravery and creativity of ordinary women and men that inspired the nation and encouraged other oppressed people to create their own movements.

Canada's history of racial exclusion differs sharply from that of the United States. Canada's experience of race relations is much less openly confrontational, and the mass demonstrations, sit-ins, protests, and marches that marked the 1960s in the United States were less visible, although protests did occur. [...] But slavery, segregation, and racism did happen and racism continues in Canada to this day. Exclusionary practices in Canada relied extensively on unwritten conventions and social attitudes rather than the formal legal structures used in the southern United States.

## Viola Desmond—A Canadian Civil Rights Activist

It is perhaps fitting that the little-known hero of Canadian civil rights fought her battle in Nova Scotia, where segregation was socially, but not legally, sanctioned. Often compared to Rosa Parks, who refused to give up her seat on a Montgomery, Alabama, bus in 1955, Viola Desmond had refused to give up her seat in a New Glasgow, Nova Scotia, movie theatre in 1946 (McNeil 2005, 65; Smith 2008, 17).

Viola Desmond requested a ticket for a main floor house seat at the Roseland Theatre; however, the white teller sold her a ticket for the designated black seating area in the balcony. The teller apologized and explained that she was unable to sell Desmond a main floor ticket. Nonetheless, Viola Desmond took a main floor seat in protest of the unlawful segregation policy of the Roseland Theatre. The white theatre manager insisted that Desmond move to the balcony, and when she refused, the white police chief was called. Desmond was dragged from the theatre and arrested. Although the theatre imposed designated "white" and "black" seating, the practice of segregation was not based in law. Since Desmond could not be prosecuted for sitting in a white-designated area, the white police magistrate charged her with tax evasion. Since the Roseland Theatre charged forty cents for main floor seats, and thirty for balcony seats, and Desmond was sold a balcony seat, she was technically guilty of tax evasion on the difference between the two ticket prices, which amounted to one cent in tax. Shocked and troubled by her arrest and conviction, Viola Desmond launched an appeal with the assistance of the newly organized Nova Scotia Association for the Advancement of Coloured People (NSAACP), the black community, and the black press (Backhouse 1999).

Their collective effort to challenge Desmond's conviction and end racial segregation in theatre seating was defeated in 1947 when the Nova Scotia

*continued*

Supreme Court dismissed the application for judicial review. Viola Desmond continued to be an avid anti-racism activist until she died in 1965, without redress for her conviction.

In 2010, the Premier of Nova Scotia, Darrell Dexter, offered a long overdue apology when Viola Desmond was granted a posthumous pardon. At the announcement ceremony, the first black Lieutenant Governor of Nova Scotia, Mayann Francis, stated, "It is only on rare occasions ... that a society comes together to undo the wrongs of the past" (Parliament of Canada 2010). Efforts are underway to designate a provincial holiday to honour Viola Desmond.[1]

Canadians often take pride in the romanticized history of the Underground Railroad, which brought many black people to Canada from the United States. Following the second Fugitive Slave Act of 1850 in the United States, which allowed free blacks, former, and escaped slaves to be re-enslaved, many African Americans fled to Canada. In the years following the American Civil War (1861–65), the majority of blacks returned to their communities in the United States, disappointed not to have found the freedom from racial oppression promised in Canada. Many Canadians are unaware of the long history of black people's presence in Canada, which dates back to 1608 when the first named "negro" servant, Mathieu de Coste, was recorded in Nova Scotia. The first recorded black slave was Oliver le Jeune, who was brought from Madagascar to Quebec in 1632 (Winks 1997, 61). Black people came to Canada in various other ways as well. Following the American Revolution, Black Loyalists, many of whom were slaves who fought for the British, and were therefore seen as traitors to the newly established United States, were promised land and freedom by the British in Canada in 1783. The British also exiled some former slaves known as the Maroons, to Nova Scotia in 1796 (Winks 1997; Mensah 2010). This group of escapees had wreaked havoc on the British colony of Jamaica by raiding plantations and liberating slaves.

Native Americans were also actively protesting during the 1960s and 1970s in the United States. [...] The American Indian Movement (AIM) sought sovereignty over Native American lands and for Native peoples with a focus on treaty rights and the objective of preserving tradition and culture. AIM organized the Trail of Broken Treaties march on Washington in 1971, which offered a framework for negotiating tribal sovereignty within the federal system, and its members were key actors in the occupations of historic sites (Deloria and Lytle [1984] 1998; Ward and Vander Wall 1988). Many Aboriginal people living in Canada travelled to the United States to join AIM and support Native self-determination.

Like many Native American groups in the United States, Canadian First Nations, Métis, and Inuit are bound by land treaties and subject to the dictates of the Canadian government, rather than constituting self-determining nations. The descendants of those who lived in the area now known as Canada, prior to European contact, are referred to as First Nations peoples. The name signifies their status as one of Canada's founding nations, together with English and French. Métis are Native peoples of mixed North American Aboriginal and European heritage, who self-identify as Métis. Inuit are Native peoples of northern Labrador, northern Quebec, Nunavut, and the Northwest Territories. Together, these three groups are understood as Aboriginal peoples of Canada. But not all Aboriginal groups ceded their lands to the Canadian government, and there are many ongoing disputes with federal and provincial governments over title and land rights. The revision of the 1876 Indian Act in 1951 allowed some traditional ceremonies, such as potlatch and pow-wows, to be practiced once again. The 1951 Act instituted changes to Indian Status, which determined who was and who was not eligible to claim Indian Status. The 1951 revision ultimately excluded many women who were born with Indian Status and later lost their Status, as did their children and grandchildren, because they married a non-Indian.

Conversely, non-Status Indian women who married Status Indian men became Status Indians. Native people actively challenged this sexist legislation since it prohibited non-Status Indians from having property on Indian Reserves. A Status Indian woman who married a non-Indian man and then later got divorced could not return to her reserve to live, as housing would no longer be available to her (Green 2001; Lawrence 2003; Moss 1990).

Protests and legal challenges led to the passage of Bill C-31 in 1985, which reinstated some women and children's Indian Status. However, even with this bill's revised calculations, Aboriginal people continue to be denied Status as they "marry out." The federal government is therefore increasingly able to shrug off its responsibilities to Aboriginal people. The number of Status Indians will continue to decline as children of Status and non-Status relationships are eventually cut off.

All this history may seem unconnected to feminisms, and to some, perhaps a bit boring, but understanding the diversity of historical movements helps us to imagine this dynamic and socially and politically charged era. It was this environment that supported the development of new feminist thinking and the invigoration of women's movement.

Imagine change brewing all around you, because the 1960s also witnessed the emergence of the gay rights movement. Like the peace movement, this movement emerged in the era of Cold War politics. This context was particularly important as governments of the day increased the state regulation and repression of homosexuality, guided by assumptions about "subversives" and deviant identities as vulnerable to blackmail and communist influences. These views dictated practices that resulted in the expulsion of gays and lesbians from the military and government institutions, as well as heightened policing of gay bars and social spaces in both Canada and the United States (Andersen 2006; Kinsman 1995, 2010; Smith 2008). [...]

While gays and lesbians had been organizing in an ad hoc fashion around education, acceptance, and the de-pathologization of homosexuality since the 1950s, the time was now ripe for concerted social change. Moved by the fervour of social movements in 1960s and 1970s, particularly the women's and civil rights movements, in which gays and lesbians were already participating, gays and lesbians shifted their agenda to a more liberatory focus. [...]

Gay liberation has been celebrated since 1970 across the United States and elsewhere, commonly in June to commemorate the Stonewall riots. Gay Pride parades and events attempt to make homosexuality more visible, celebrate diverse gay identities, and ultimately make homosexuality socially acceptable. In 2003, the Supreme Court's landmark ruling in *Lawrence v. Texas* held that states cannot criminalize consenting adults who engage in sodomy in the privacy of their homes. In effect, *Lawrence* struck down all remaining state sodomy laws (Andersen 2006; Smith 2008). However, gays, lesbians, bisexuals, and trans and queer people remain subject to legal and social regulation in many areas, including same-sex marriage, adoption, child custody, health care, and employment, among others.

In Canada, an amendment to the Criminal Code in 1969 repealed the sodomy laws to decriminalize consensual sex for those twenty-one years of age and over. Interestingly, this amendment was part of a package of legal reforms proposed in 1967 by then Minister of Justice Pierre Trudeau, which also included greater access to abortion and the relaxation of divorce laws. Pierre Trudeau introduced the bill into Parliament and made headlines with his legendary statement, "The state has no place in the bedrooms of the nation" (Smith 2008).

Nonetheless, the unjust Toronto bathhouse raids of 1981 resulted in the arrest of close to 300 men on February 5. Targeting four of six popular gay bathhouses, Toronto police, together with the Ontario Attorney General's Office, engaged in massive raids, employing tactics to terrify and humiliate bathhouse patrons. Following the arrests, police contacted employers notifying them of their employees' arrests. As a result, many of the men arrested lost their jobs (Bérubé 2003). On February 6, the day after the first bathhouse raids, several thousand people marched on the Division 52 police station to protest the targeting of gays and lesbians by police. Weeks later, over 4,000 people gathered at Queen's Park demanding an investigation into the raids. On March 6, gay and lesbian activists, including MP Svend Robinson, author Margaret Atwood, and Reverend Brent Hawkes (who went on a hunger strike until an independent investigation of the raids was initiated), gathered for a Gay Freedom Rally (CBC 2012; Thomas 2011). In the official investigation that followed, police were condemned for their actions and the right to engage in consensual sex in private spaces was confirmed. It is reported that Operation Soap, as the raids were called, and the "policing" of the three subsequent protests, cost taxpayers an estimated $10 million. Pride Day was first celebrated in Toronto on June 28, 1981, with 1,500 participants, and is touted as North America's largest Gay Pride parade, with more than one million people now attending the celebrations.

This brief summary paints a complex picture of social justice movements in the 1960s and 1970s. Women were active in all of these social justice movements and in the struggle for what was then being called women's liberation. While each movement was distinct, it offered the possibility of crossover participation and synergy on multiple issues. Synergy, where one issue is connected to other issues to bolster change at many levels, is evident in the struggle for Native women's rights (see text box Synergy Among and Across Movements: The Case of Native Women's Rights in Canada).

Women's movement has never been homogeneous or linear. A homogeneous movement would assume that all the women who participated were the same—they would look the same, think the same, act the same, and want the same results. However, the women who participated in "Women's Liberation" have always been of all races, ethnicities, sexual orientations, abilities, and classes. Not surprisingly, this diversity has brought a plethora of issues to the table and has resulted in multiple paths and many twists and turns complicating women's movement. It has also resulted in conflicts, debates, and exclusions.

The process of trying to set priorities and frame a cohesive and unified agenda is where women's movement gets its bad reputation as a white, middle-class movement. And, to some extent, this seemed like the case as the mainstream media created celebrities out of prominent white women such as Betty Friedan, who published *The Feminine Mystique* (1963) documenting women's unhappiness as "the problem that has no name." Gloria Steinem also became famous during this era, which put her in the position of speaking for all women, as well as Jane Fonda, who became the face of women's involvement in the anti-war movement. […] While these women may have been the chosen darlings of the media, many more women of various backgrounds were working tirelessly, marching, advocating, and struggling for social change beyond the focus of the cameras.

## WOMEN'S MOVEMENT IS COMPLEX, MULTIPLE, AND DIVERSE

[In the United States,] Betty Friedan was the co-founder of the National Organization for Women (NOW) along with the Reverend Pauli Murray, who was the first African American woman to become an Episcopal priest. This pair showed the diversity of women's representation in the movement. As the co-founder of NOW, Friedan also participated in some of the ongoing conflicts, debates, and exclusions that plagued women's movement, particularly in her notorious 1969 reference to lesbians as the "lavender menace." Not until 1977 did NOW embrace lesbian rights as a fundamental feminist goal.

While lesbians were active in the gay rights movement, many also claimed a feminist consciousness. Evidence of this synergy across movements is presented in the radical feminist *Redstockings Manifesto* (1969), which defined lesbianism as a political identity and a choice, which women should embrace. The *Manifesto* called on all women to unite in the struggle for liberation and all men to give up their male privilege and support women's liberation as a goal of humanity. It promoted consciousness-raising to expose and eradicate patriarchy, which it argued was the root of women's oppression.

## Synergy Among and Across Movements: The Case of Native Women's Rights in Canada

Aboriginal peoples have historically had a variety of ways of organizing gendered relationships and expectations that varied over time and in different communities. With the creation of the Canadian nation, Aboriginal women's roles and status were defined by laws and customs that were particular to them but not created by them. In Canada, the Indian Act governed Aboriginal Status, and when Mary Two-Axe Early, Jeannette Lavell, Irene Bedard, and Sandra Lovelace lost their Status and were permanently banned from their ancestral lands, like so many Status Indian women who married non-Indians, they fought back. Loss of Status meant that these women were no longer able to live, own property, or be buried on their reserves. They were prohibited from participating in reserve politics through council meetings or elections, or having any say in band decision-making.

Unwilling to accept the exile of any Aboriginal women from their Native lands, in the 1950s Mary Two-Axe Early began her life of activism and protest, founding the organization Equal Rights for Indian Women in 1969 (the forerunner to the national Indian Rights for Indian Women, founded in 1973). Recognizing the dynamic synergy of the time

and understanding the importance of the Royal Commission on the Status of Women as a means for change, Two-Axe Early presented a petition before the Commission, challenging the government to rectify the loss of Native women's Status under the Indian Act. Spurred by the contradictions of living on the reserve but not being able to inherit property due to loss of Status, Two-Axe Early testified to the Commission (Green 2001; Two-Axe Early 1994). Hers was but one voice among the many Native women who had lost their Indian Status through marriage. Jeannette Lavell and Irene Bedard took their case all the way to the Supreme Court of Canada. They claimed that the Indian Act was discriminatory under the Canadian Bill of Rights (1960). Disappointingly, the Court ruled in 1973 that the Indian Act was exempt from the Canadian Bill of Rights (Bear 1991; Lawrence and Anderson 2003; Moss 1990).

On the heels of this decision, Mary Two-Axe Early, together with sixty other women from Kahnewake, took their struggle for Native women's rights global. Two-Axe Early and the others attended the United Nations' First International Conference on Women in Mexico City, which marked the International Year of the Woman in 1975. However, when they returned they found that the band council had evicted them from their homes, following government legislation and using the Indian Act. With heightened national and international publicity around the plight of Native women, the band was forced to withdraw their eviction notices, but the issue of Indian Status remained unresolved (Gehl 2000; Lawrence and Anderson 2003).

Again taking sexist discrimination against Native women global, Sandra Lovelace, a Maliseet from the Tobique Reserve in New Brunswick who lost her Status after marrying out, took her struggle to the United Nations. Lovelace and her children had been denied housing, health care, and access to education on the Tobique Reserve. Unwilling to be denied her birthright, Lovelace took her challenge to the United Nations Human Rights

*continued*

Committee in 1977. She argued that the Indian Act violated Article 27 of the International Covenant on Civil and Political Rights, which Canada had ratified the year before. It took four years for the United Nations to rule against the Canadian government. The 1981 ruling was a significant victory for Aboriginal women in Canada, even if it was only symbolic. While the United Nations ruled that the Indian Act breeched Aboriginal women's rights by denying them Status, international agreements and decisions by United Nations committees and courts do not supersede the laws of sovereign countries like Canada (Bear 1991; Gehl 2000; Lawrence and Anderson 2003; Moss 1990; Two-Axe Early 1994). [...]

[In 2010] the government introduced Bill C-3, the Gender Equality in Indian Registration Act, amending C-31; they claimed this would confer Status on thousands of previously ineligible descendants of Aboriginal women. The Native Women's Association of Canada (NWAC) argues that the bill fails to address the issue of the privileging of men in the second-generation cut-off for Indian Status. Consequently, those who trace their heredity through maternal ties will be denied Status if they were born prior to 1951, whereas those who trace it through paternal ties will be able to gain Status (NWAC 2012). [...]

Aboriginal groups in Canada, including the Native Women's Association of Canada, the Métis National Council, and the Chiefs of Ontario, are raising new questions about Native identity that move beyond the Status debates, arguing that as self-determining nations, Aboriginal peoples have the right to define who is and who is not an Indian, not the government of Canada. They contend that Indian identity cannot be measured by "blood quantity" as Indian Status currently attempts to do. Accordingly, Aboriginal people are still in jeopardy of extinction under the Indian Act. Instead, Native identity must be understood as the outcome of a complex configuration of social, cultural, and political forces (Chiefs of Ontario 2010; Hodgson-Smith 2010; Lavell 2010; NWAC 2012).

There are multiple problems that arise from viewing patriarchy as the common oppressor of women. First, this view supposes that men are the targets of feminism, giving credit to the backlash. Second, it fails to recognize the intersections of race and class as culpable in the oppression of all people. Black feminists have argued that, unlike the suburban middle-class white women trapped in their homes of whom Friedan writes about, black women often found their homes a place of refuge from racism and solidarity with men. Working-class women activists have also raised issues of workplace oppression and the role of capitalism as implicated with patriarchy.

In Canada, women were participating in many of the same debates. In 1970, the Royal Commission on the Status of Women Report documented women's inequality in Canada and offered recommendations for its eradication. Recommendations to all levels of government were made, such as the choice for women to work outside the home, the establishment of a universal childcare program, joint parental responsibility for children, implementation of affirmative action policies to overcome the discrimination against women, a commitment to publicly funded reproductive health care, and the establishment of a Committee on the Status of Women.

In response to the Report, the National Ad Hoc Committee on the Status of Women (NAC) formed in 1971 as a national advocacy group. Like the public face of women's movement suggests, NAC's early leadership was white and middle class. This failure to be representative of the diversity of Canadian women fostered friction and dissention among NAC members. It was not until the 1990s that racialized women claimed their place as leaders of NAC. Under the leadership of Sunera Thobani (1993–96) and Joan Grant-Cummings (1996–2000), NAC expanded its focus to address both national and international concerns including racism, refugee issues, global trade, and United Nations programs for women. Unfortunately, NAC has suffered from economic woes. Federal government funding cuts, an end to funding for advocacy organizations, and widespread backlash against feminisms and women's movement have stifled much of NAC's advocacy work, and questions as to whether it still even exists abound.[2] Other feminist organizations have jumped into the fray to support women's movement; however, these too have suffered from slashed budgets and backlash.

## ABORTION RIGHTS AND WOMEN'S MOVEMENT

Prior to 1969, abortion was illegal in Canada. Many women who sought to terminate a pregnancy had back-street abortions, which were performed in non-medical settings and rarely by accredited doctors. In desperation, women put themselves through dangerous and painful processes to induce miscarriages. Some women threw themselves down flights of stairs, ingested toxic substances, or inserted objects into their cervixes. Such options for terminating an unwanted pregnancy could have devastating outcomes. With no legal access to birth control, single mothers were particularly stigmatized as "bad girls," "loose women," and certainly not the kind of gals that you would take home to meet your mother. While not all feminists were (or are) pro-choice, the issue of abortion has been an important issue for women's movement.

Under such circumstances, we might assume that feminists and women activists would be thrilled when the Canadian government passed an abortion law in 1969. However, this legislation only partially legalized abortion. While the law served as the federal government's response to emergency rooms flooded by women seeking treatment from botched abortions, feminists and women's groups argued that the partial legalization of abortion was not enough. The law not only limited abortion procedures to accredited hospitals, prohibiting the establishment of women's clinics, but worse, a woman would only be granted an abortion if it were approved by a Therapeutic Abortion Committee. Such committees consisted of four doctors who would determine whether carrying the pregnancy to term would be detrimental to the woman's health. Needless to say, this process took time. And time was something that pregnant women seldom had.

To protest the inadequacies of the law, seventeen activists took to the road in March 1970, with the goal of arriving in Ottawa on Mother's Day, in what became known as the Abortion Caravan (Rebick 2005). What better day to reflect on the effects of pregnancy, both wanted and unwanted, than Mother's Day? The caravan began its journey in Vancouver and travelled east across Canada. It stopped in cities and towns along the way to rally support for the full legalization of abortion. Women waved clothes hangers and bottles of drain cleaner to represent the dangers of illegal abortion and the narrow-sightedness of the new law. The caravan got a lot of press, especially for leaving a coffin on Prime Minister Trudeau's doorstep to represent all the women who had died from illegal abortions. But this was nothing compared to the coverage that the thirty-five feminist abortion activists who chained themselves to chairs and demanded the legalization of abortion on demand received. These women activists so disrupted Parliament that it was forced to close (Sethna and Hewitt 2009).

These were just the first steps in the long and difficult struggle to the 1988 Morgentaler decision by the Supreme Court of Canada, which struck down the 1969 law as unconstitutional. The issue of abortion galvanized women in Canada and made "a woman's right to choose" a reality, with abortion clinics in almost every province.

Canada's struggle for reproductive choice was fortified by the 1973 United States Supreme Court decision in *Roe v. Wade*, which made first-trimester abortions legal. It did so by recognizing that the right of women to make choices about bearing children is central to their ability to participate fully and equally in society. This landmark decision derived its authority from the United States Supreme Court decisions, beginning in the 1920s, that interpreted constitutional guarantees of liberty as the individual's right to privacy in decisions about childrearing, procreation, the use of contraception, and marriage.

Prior to *Roe v. Wade*, it is estimated that anywhere from 200,000 to 1.2 million illegal abortions were performed each year in the United States (Cates et al. 2003). Although determining the effects of illegal abortions and their subsequent complications is difficult to calculate, it has been estimated that as many as 5,000 to 10,000 women died each year (NARAL). The historic verdict settling *Roe v. Wade* was the outcome of laborious work by women's movement, supported by medical, public health, legal, and religious organizations. As we can see, women's movement was as varied as the women and men who participated in it.

## LIFE WITHOUT WOMEN'S MOVEMENT

Can you imagine what your life would look like if women's movement had not been so successful? Without women's movement, marriage would still be the crowning achievement of any young woman's career. Convention would still demand that a woman take her husband's name. No-fault divorce would be unheard of. A "broken home" due to divorce would be blamed on the woman's inability to keep her marriage together, and it would still be a social stigma to be divorced or to come from a family where divorce occurred. Women, of course, would be wholly responsible for everything related to the home, except for any major decisions because those decisions would be the domain of men.

Sex, if you were having it, would only be permitted within marriage and then not necessarily a choice. Rape within marriage would not be a crime, but considered a man's right of access to his wife. Unmarried women would be divided into those who do and those who don't. And, if a baby resulted from doing it, the child would be stigmatized for life by its "illegitimacy." Sexual pleasure would be a uniquely male experience and women would still (secretly) be looking for the vaginal orgasm.

Fewer than half of women would work outside the home and they would earn, on average, just $0.52 for every dollar earned by a man. Women's paid employment would be seen as temporary until their real careers of marriage and motherhood began. Women's earnings would not be considered critical to family survival; rather, they would be thought of as "mad money" to be used by women haphazardly and according to their whims. As a result, women would be paid less, as their wages were not considered essential. "Help Wanted: Male" or "Help Wanted: Female" would divide classified ads in newspapers. Women would work predominantly as secretaries, nurses, teachers, domestics, and in other low-wage service jobs. Bosses could ask women if their husbands had given them permission to work, if they planned to have children, or if they intended to have more children. Women workers could be demoted or fired for getting pregnant; and sexual harassment on the job would be a regular occurrence with little recourse. The glass ceiling would be even more visible (Baumgardener and Richards 2010).

Since girls would be educated in "Home Economics" in high school, they'd be able to cook and sew, but changing the oil in their cars or fixing a faulty light switch would have to be left to the boys who took shop class. Of course, to ensure that boys could boil water and sew on a button when they left their mothers, they could take a class in "Bachelor Studies." But once they were married, they could expect to rely on their wives for such menial tasks. Girls would be rewarded academically for their talents of sitting quietly and listening passively. Math and science would be the privileged domain of boys, even if a girl showed some promise or skill. Curriculum and academic testing would reflect boys' experiences rather than girls', and, if girls happened to show up in a textbook, they were likely to be insignificant characters. The phrase "boys will be boys" would be bantered around as if it could explain anything and everything that wasn't quite right.

There would be no Little League sports for girls and no mandate to ensure their physical education. If a girl "got herself pregnant," she was the one who would get expelled from school. There would be no women's studies programs, and the fields of critical race studies, sexuality studies, and queer studies would be even more unimaginable.

Gender inequality in medical treatment and research remains a problem. One example of how gender is ignored in the field of medicine is in the area of oral contraceptives. Why isn't there an oral contraceptive for men? Well, apparently scientists are working on it. However, the male pill is still years away from approval (Goodman 2008). So, not only do men not have to take a pill but also women have to put up with the consequences of taking it. We can control our fertility with a little pill, but we have to deal with the side effects of weight gain, headaches, and the possible risks of cancer. Is this gender equality? I'm not advocating for male contraceptives that risk men's health and well-being; that certainly wouldn't be the equality that feminists are looking for. What feminists want are safe contraceptives, whether for men or women. They want more research and better testing before contraceptives are marketed to ensure that they are safe.

Another place where gender plays an important role is in the diagnosis and treatment of cardiovascular disease. Did you know that heart disease is still thought of as a health risk predominantly for men? When women go to the emergency room fearing a heart attack, they could be sent home without treatment, since they don't present with the same symptoms as men. Even when women have all the classic signs—chest pains, nausea, radiating pain in the left arm—cardiac tests can come back as "normal." Indigestion, gall bladder problems, anxiety, or stress are the most common misdiagnoses. Women are made to feel embarrassed about making a big deal of their health concerns and pain. If you're a woman under the age of fifty-five, you are seven times more likely to be misdiagnosed when the problem is really heart disease (Pope et al. 2000). In 2005, only 8 per cent of family and 17 per cent of cardiologists knew that more women die from heart disease than men each year (Mosca et al. 2005). More shockingly, women are five times more likely to die of heart disease than breast cancer and all other cancers combined (Lloyd-Jones et al. 2010).

Speaking of breast cancer, without pink ribbon campaigns spurred by women's movement, awareness about breast cancer and funding for research might not exist. Some caution needs to be raised here, however. As corporations jump on the philanthropy bandwagon, accusations of pinkwashing grow. For feminist critics, pinkwashing refers to the ways in which businesses brand their products as supporting the fight against breast cancer, as a means for boosting sales and ultimately revenues (King 2006; Landman 2008; Lubitow and Davis 2011; Pool 2011). In this competitive environment for donations, there is concern that a greater proportion of the money raised is allocated to fundraising than to research. And researchers are spending more time applying for funds, taking precious time away from their research, than ever before (Johnson 2011). While the management of breast cancer has improved considerably and success rates for remission are high, these results are not universal and women still die from this disease. Is this what success looks like?

Without the women's movement, campaigns to end violence against women would be virtually unknown. Take Back the Night marches, the White Ribbon Campaign, and the 16 Days of Activism to End Violence Against Women would not be on the radar. Women would still be encouraged to stay in abusive marriages. There would be no women's shelters for abused women and their children, and rape crisis lines and sexual assault centres would not exist. Even with women's movement, these critical resources are underfunded and often on the verge of closing because of budget shortfalls.

As for finances, without women's movement, married women would be unable to get a loan without their husbands co-signing, and their credit ratings would be tied to their husbands rather than to them. Single women would have difficulty renting an apartment, since landlords would want steady long-term renters and, after all, a single woman is bound to be married soon. If not married, what would women be doing living on their own? Landlords would need to worry about propriety, for the sake of the good tenants. The fear that single women are loose, that they could be having men over at all hours or even running a brothel would continue to be a widely held and dominant view.

The achievements of women's movement are seldom discussed outside of the classroom, but they are considerable: pay equity; the recognition of unpaid work as real work; affirmative action policies; freedom from sexual harassment on the job; legislation to criminalize rape in marriage; women's right to education in the professions (medicine, engineering, law, and business); and shared responsibility for parenting. Our failure to recognize and acknowledge the difficult struggles of the past, which made these accomplishments part of what we think of as *normal*, is the very reason that they may be in jeopardy in the future.

## BACKLASH AGAINST FEMINISM AND WOMEN'S MOVEMENT

Backlash is a concept that has been discussed in feminist circles since the 1990s, when Susan Faludi wrote *Backlash: The Undeclared War on Women* (1991). Feminism, she argued, was being blamed for anything and everything, from high divorce rates, children's failure in school, and job loss, to economic recession. Backlash is an aggressive and violent reaction to social changes that challenge the status quo. By status quo, I mean the power and privilege that dominate societies. Those who have it attempt to keep it at all costs, because they believe that they will be the losers if women's equality becomes a reality. Just imagine, women's movement is moving along, maybe under duress, but still moving forward and, suddenly, those with the most power who are benefiting from the way things are start to get scared. [...]

Affirmative action policies, such as equity hiring policies, ensure that historically marginalized groups like women, racialized people, and those with disabilities, have an opportunity to participate. This means that some white guy doesn't get the job that he previously could have counted on simply because he is some white guy. Cries of "This is reverse discrimination!" can be heard everywhere. But were we concerned when a woman or person of colour was the one who did not get the job, even when their qualifications were equal or better than the white guy's?

The highly publicized idea that women are already equal, and therefore that no one needs to be a feminist and there is no need for women's movement, can easily be challenged. Just think about women's earnings compared to men's, or the epidemic of violence against women, or inadequacies in health research when men's experience is the measure of treatment. Women are definitely not equal. And, if we have "been there and done that," why do funding cuts continue to plague women's advocacy organizations, shelters, and sexual assault centres? And why is the accessible and affordable childcare that was advocated for and recommended more than forty years ago by the Royal Commission on the Status of Women in Canada and by NOW in the United States still not a reality?

After more than 100 years of women's movement, much work remains to be done. In answer to our demands for equity and social changes, feminists have been basically told "If it ain't broke, don't fix it." These clichés are borrowed when a task is too hard or will take too long to complete. However, if everyone used this excuse, then things would never change, and we already know that things are not fine the way they are. Yet "I'm not a feminist" still resonates with many.

## CONCLUSION

We have seen in this chapter that the struggle for equality and social justice is a long and as yet unfinished battle. We explored the complex landscape of mid-twentieth century social justice movements—the peace movement, the civil rights movement, the Indian/Native rights movement, and the gay/lesbian rights movement—to show how these were interconnected with feminists and women's movement. It is clear from these struggles that social change does not simply happen. The tremendous accomplishments and social change achieved by feminists and social justice activists required hard work, tough decisions, massive organizing, and innovative theorizing.

## NOTES

1. On December 8, 2016, the federal government of Canada announced that Viola Desmond will be featured on the new $10 banknote to be released in 2018.

2. Editors' update: the National Ad Hoc Committee on the Status of Women (NAC) no longer formally exists.

## REFERENCES

Andersen, Ellen Ann. 2006. *Out of the Closets & into the Courts: Legal Opportunity Structure and Gay Rights Litigation.* Ann Arbor: University of Michigan Press.

Backhouse, Constance. 1999. *Colour-Coded: A Legal History of Racism in Canada, 1900–1950.* Toronto: University of Toronto Press.

Baumgardener, Jennifer, and Amy Richards. 2010. *Manifesta: Young Women, Feminism, and the Future.* New York: Farrar, Straus and Giroux.

Bear, Shirley. 1991. "You Can't Change the Indian Act?" In *Women and Social Change,* ed. Jerri Wine and Janice Ristock, 198–220. Toronto: James Lorimer and Company Publishers.

Bérubé, Allan. 2003. "The History of Gay Bathhouses." *Journal of Homosexuality* 44 (3): 33–53. http://dx.doi.org/10.1300/J082v44n03_03.

Canada. Parliament of Canada. 2010. *Debates of the Senate.* 3rd Session, 40th Parliament. 147 No. 8, October 21.

Cates Jr, Williard, et al. 2003. "The Public Health Impact of Legal Abortion: 30 Years Later." *Perspectives on Sexual and Reproductive Health* 35 (1): 25–8. doi: 10.1111/j.1931-2393.2003.tb00081.x.

CBC Digital Archives. "The Toronto Bathhouse Raids." Accessed April 20, 2012. http://www.cbc.ca/archives/categories/politics/rights-freedoms/gay-and-lesbian emergence-out-in-canada/the-toronto-bathhouse-raids.html.

Chiefs of Ontario. 2010. "Bill C-3 and the Indigenous Right to Identity." Prepared for the Standing Committee on Aboriginal Affairs and Northern Development. April 20. http://64.26.129.156/misc/CIO.pdf (link no longer active).

Deloria, Vine, and Clifford Lytle. (Original work published 1984) 1998. *The Nations Within: The Past and the Future of American Indian Sovereignty.* Austin: University of Texas Press.

Faludi, Susan. 1991. *Backlash: The Undeclared War on Women.* New York: Crown.

Friedan, Betty. 1963. *The Feminine Mystique.* New York: W.W. Norton.

Gehl, Lynn. 2000. "'The Queen and I': Discrimination against Women in the Indian Act Continues." *Canadian Woman Studies* 20 (2): 64–9.

Goodman, Adam. 2008. "The Long Wait for Male Birth Control." *Time.com.* August 3. Accessed January 14, 2011. http://content.time.com/time/health/article/0,8599,1829107,00.html.

Green, Joyce. 2001. "Canaries in the Mines of Citizenship: Indian Women in Canada." *Canadian Journal of Political Science* 34 (4): 715–38. https://doi.org/10.1017/S0008423901778067.

Hodgson-Smith, Kathy. 2010. Métis National, *Standing Committee on Aboriginal Affairs and Northern Development Council Standing Committee Hearing,* April 15. http://www.ourcommons.ca/DocumentViewer/en/40-3/AANO/meeting-9/evidence#T OC-TS-1700.

Johnson, Erica. 2011. "Cancer Society Spends More on Fundraising Than Research." *CBC News.* July 6. Accessed April 12, 2012. http://www.cbc.ca/news/canada/cancer-society-spends-more-on-fundraising-than-research-1.1080909.

King, Samantha. 2006. *Pink Ribbons, Inc.: Breast Cancer and the Politics of Philanthropy.* Minneapolis: University of Minnesota Press.

Kinsman, Gary. 1995. "'Character Weaknesses' and 'Fruit Machines': Towards an Analysis of the Anti-Homosexual Security Campaign in the Canadian Civil Service." *Labour/Le Travail* 35: 133–61. http://dx.doi.org/10.2307/25143914.

Kinsman, Gary. 2010. "Against National Security: From the Canadian War on Queers to the War on Terror." In *Locating Global Order: American Power and Canadian Security after 9/11,* ed. Wayne S. Cox and Bruno Charbonneau, 149–66. Vancouver: UBC Press.

Landman, Anne. 2008. "Pinkwashing: Can Shopping Cure Breast Cancer?" *Center for Media and Democracy.* http://www.prwatch.org/node/7436.

Lavell, Jeannette. 2010. *Standing Committee on Aboriginal Affairs and Northern Development Council Standing Committee Hearing,* April 13. http://www.ourcommons.ca/DocumentViewer/en/40-3/AANO/meeting-8/evidence.

Lawrence, Bonita. 2003. "Gender, Race, and the Regulation of Native Identity in Canada and the United States: An Overview." *Hypatia* 18 (2): 3–31. http://dx.doi.org/10.1111/j.1527-2001.2003.tb00799.x.

Lawrence, Bonita, and Kim Anderson. 2003. *Strong Women Stories: Native Vision and Community Survival.* Toronto: Sumach Press.

Lloyd-Jones, Donald, Robert J. Adams, Todd M. Brown, Mercedes Carnethon, Shifan Dai, Giovanni De Simone, Bruce Ferguson, Earl Ford, Karen Furie, Cathleen Gillespie, et al. 2010. "Heart Disease and Stroke Statistics—2010 Update: A Report from the American Heart Association." *Circulation* 121 (7): e46–215. https://doi.org/10.1161/CIRCULATIONAHA.109.192667.

Lubitow, Amy, and Mia Davis. 2011. "Pastel Injustice: The Corporate Use of Pinkwashing for Profit." *Environmental Justice* 4 (2): 139–44. http://dx.doi.org/10.1089/env.2010.0026.

McNeil, Daniel. 2005. "Afro(Americo)centricity in Black (American) Nova Scotia." *Canadian Review of American Studies* 35 (1): 57–85.

Mensah, Joseph. 2010. *Black Canadians: History, Experiences, Social Conditions.* Black Point, NS: Fernwood Publishing.

Mosca, Lori, et al. 2005. "National Study of Physician Awareness and Adherence to Cardiovascular Disease Prevention Guidelines." *Circulation* 111 (4): 499–510.

https://doi.org/10.1161/01.CIR.0000154568.43333.82. Medline: 15687140.

Moss, Wendy. 1990. "Indigenous Self-Government in Canada and Sexual Equality under the Indian Act: Resolving Conflicts between Collective and Individual Rights." *Queen's Law Journal* 15: 279–306.

NWAC (Native Women's Association of Canada). 2012. "Shadow Report." United Nations Committee on the Elimination of Racial Discrimination. 80th Session. February 13–March 9. Geneva. Accessed January 30, 2012. https://www.nwac.ca/wp-content/uploads/2015/05/2012-NWAC-CERD-Submission.pdf.

Pool, Léa. 2011. *Pink Ribbons Inc.* [film] Montreal: National Film Board of Canada.

Pope, J. Hector, Tom P. Aufderheide, Robin Ruthazer, Robert H. Woolard, James A. Feldman, Joni R. Beshansky, John L. Griffith, and Harry P. Selker. 2000. "Missed Diagnoses of Acute Cardiac Ischemia in the Emergency Department." *New England Journal of Medicine* 342 (16): 1163–70. https://doi.org/10.1056/NEJM200004203421603. Medline: 10770981.

Rebick, Judy. 2005. *Ten Thousand Roses: The Making of a Feminist Revolution.* Toronto: Penguin Canada.

Redstockings. 1969. "Redstockings Manifesto." In *Feminist Theory: A Reader,* ed. Wendy Kolmar and Frances Bartkowski, 220–21. Boston: McGraw-Hill Higher Education.

Sethna, Christabelle, and Steve Hewitt. 2009. "Clandestine Operations: The Vancouver Women's Caucus, the Abortion Caravan, and the RCMP." *Canadian Historical Review* 90 (3): 465–95. https://doi.org/10.3138/chr.90.3.463.

Smith, Malinda. 2008. "'How Long, Not Long': Local and Global Anti-Racism Struggles." *Ardent* 1 (1): 8–22.

Thomas, Nicki. 2011. "Thirty Years after the Bathhouse Raids." *Toronto Star.* February 4. Accessed April 20, 2012. https://www.thestar.com/news/gta/2011/02/04/thirty_years_after_the_bathhouse_raids.html.

Two-Axe Early, Mary. 1994. "Indian Rights for Indian Women." In *Women, Feminism, and Development,* ed. Huguette Dagenais and Denise Piché, 429–33. Montreal: McGill-Queen's University Press.

Ward, Churchill, and Jim Vander Wall. 1988. *Agents of Repression: The FBI's Secret Wars against the Black Panther Party.* Boston: South End Press.

Winks, Robin. 1997. *The Blacks in Canada*. Montreal: McGill-
    Queen's University Press.

*Source:* Bromley, Victoria L. (2012). Excerpted from
    "Chapter 2: What's Feminism Done (For Me) Lately?
    Feminist Contributions." In *Feminisms Matter:
    Debates, Theories, Activism* (pp. 13–26, 29–34).
    Toronto, ON: University of Toronto Press.

## BAD FEMINIST MANIFESTO

*Roxane Gay*

Roxane Gay's writing appears in *Best American Mystery Stories 2014, Best American Short Stories 2012, American Short Fiction,* and many others. She is a contributing opinion writer for *The New York Times* and author of the books *Ayiti, An Untamed State, Difficult Women,* and the *New York Times* bestselling books *Bad Feminist* and *Hunger.* She is also the author of *World of Wakanda* for Marvel.

I am failing as a woman. I am failing as a feminist. To freely accept the feminist label would not be fair to good feminists. If I am, indeed, a feminist, I am a rather bad one. I am a mess of contradictions.

There are many ways in which I am doing feminism wrong, at least according to the way my perceptions of feminism have been warped by being a woman.

I want to be independent, but I want to be taken care of and have someone to come home to. I have a job I'm pretty good at. I am in charge of things. I am on committees. People respect me and take my counsel. I want to be strong and professional, but I resent how hard I have to work to be taken seriously, to receive a fraction of the consideration I might otherwise receive. Sometimes I feel an overwhelming need to cry at work, so I close my office door and lose it.

I want to be in charge, respected, in control, but I want to surrender, completely, in certain aspects of my life. Who wants to grow up?

When I drive to work, I listen to thuggish rap at a very loud volume, even though the lyrics are degrading to women and offend me to my core. The classic Ying Yang Twins song "Salt Shaker"? It's amazing. "Bitch you

gotta shake it till your camel starts to hurt." Poetry. (I am mortified by my music choices.) I care what people think.

Pink is my favourite colour. I used to say my favourite colour was black to be cool, but it is pink—all shades of pink. If I have an accessory, it is probably pink. I read *Vogue,* and I'm not doing it ironically. I once live-tweeted the September issue.

I love dresses. For years I pretended I hated them, but I don't. Maxi dresses are one of the finest clothing items to become popular in recent memory. I have opinions on maxi dresses! I shave my legs! Again, this mortifies me. If I take issue with the unrealistic standards of beauty women are held to, I shouldn't have a secret fondness for fashion and smooth calves, right?

I know nothing about cars. When I take my car to the mechanic, they are speaking a foreign language. I still call my father with questions about cars, and am not terribly interested in changing any of my car-related ignorance.

Despite what people think based on my writing, I very much like men. They're interesting to me, and I mostly wish they'd be better about how they treat women so I wouldn't have to call them out so often. And still, I put up with nonsense from unsuitable men even though I know better and can do better. I love diamonds and the excess of weddings. I consider certain domestic tasks as gendered, mostly all in my favour because I don't care for chores—lawn care, bug killing and trash removal, for example, are men's work.

Sometimes—a lot of the time, honestly—I totally fake "it" because it's easier. I am a fan of orgasms, but they take time, and in many instances I don't want to spend that time. All too often I don't really like the guy enough to explain the calculus of my desire. Then I feel guilty because the sisterhood would not approve. I'm not even sure what the sisterhood is, but the idea of a sisterhood menaces me, quietly, reminding me of how bad a feminist I am.

I love babies, and I want to have one. I am willing to make certain compromises (not sacrifices) in order to do so—namely, maternity leave and slowing down at work to spend more time with my child, writing less so I can be more present in my life. I worry about dying alone, unmarried and childless, because I spent so much time pursuing my career and accumulating degrees. This kind of thinking keeps me up at night, but I pretend it doesn't because I am supposed to be evolved. My success, such as it is, is supposed to be enough if I'm a good feminist. It is not enough. It is not even close. Because I have so many deeply held opinions about gender equality, I feel a lot of pressure to live up to certain ideals. I am supposed to be a good feminist who is having it all, doing it all. Really, though, I'm a woman in her 30s, struggling to accept herself and her credit score. For so long I told myself I was not this woman—utterly human and flawed. I worked overtime to be anything but this woman, and it was exhausting and unsustainable and even harder than simply embracing who I am.

Maybe I'm a bad feminist, but I am deeply committed to the issues important to the feminist movement. I have strong opinions about misogyny, institutional sexism that consistently places women at a disadvantage, the inequity in pay, the cult of beauty and thinness, the repeated attacks on reproductive freedom, violence against women, and on and on. I am as committed to fighting fiercely for equality as I am committed to disrupting the notion that there is an essential feminism.

At some point, I got it into my head that a feminist was a certain kind of woman. I bought into grossly inaccurate myths about who feminists are—militant, perfect in their politics and person, man-hating, humourless. I bought into these myths even though, intellectually, I know better. I'm not proud of this. I don't want to buy into these myths any more.

Bad feminism seems the only way I can both embrace myself as a feminist and be myself, so I write. I chatter away on Twitter about everything that makes me angry and all the small things that bring me joy. I write blogposts about the meals I cook as I try to take better care of myself, and with each new entry I realize that I'm undestroying myself after years of allowing myself to stay damaged. The more I write, the more I put myself out into the world as a bad feminist but, I hope, a good woman—I am being open about who I am and who I was and where I have faltered and who I would like to become. No matter what issues I have with feminism, I am a feminist. I cannot and will not deny the importance and absolute necessity of feminism. Like most people, I'm full of contradictions, but I also don't want to be treated like shit for being a woman. I am a bad feminist. I would rather be a bad feminist than no feminist at all.

---

*Source:* Gay, Roxane. (2014). Excerpted from *Bad Feminist: Essays*. London, UK: Constable & Robinson. Retrieved from *The Guardian*, August 2, 2014: https://www.theguardian.com/world/2014/aug/02/bad-feminist-roxane-gay-extract.

# CHAPTER 3

## Anishinaabe-kwe and/or Indigenous Feminist?

*Wanda Nanibush*

Wanda Nanibush is Anishinaabe-kwe from Beausoleil First Nation. She is the curator of Indigenous art at the Art Gallery of Ontario (AGO). Nanibush has a Master's degree in visual studies from the University of Toronto, where she has also taught graduate courses. She currently teaches at OCAD University. Her curatorial credits include Rita Letendre: Fire & Light (AGO, 2017); Toronto: Tributes + Tributaries, 1971–1989 (AGO, 2016); The Fifth World (Mendel Art Gallery, 2015); and Sovereign Acts (currently touring). Her work has been included in publications such as *Time, Temporality and Violence in International Relations,* and *This Is an Honour Song: Twenty Years since the Blockades.* Nanibush has published articles in *Art in America, Canadian Art,* and *C Magazine,* as well as over 15 catalogue essays on artists. She is currently completing two films and her first book, entitled *Violence No More: The Rise of Indigenous Women.*

*I am a woman of my people*
*I am an image and word warrior*
*I am Anishinaabe*
*I am a worker*
*I am my language*
*I am a daughter, aunt, sister*
*I am water*
*I am land*
*I speak/act against violence against women, water,*
    *children, land*
*I speak/act with the ancestors and knowledge keepers*

I remember when I decided to add *kwe* to *Anishinaabe* a few years ago and how much of a struggle it was at first. This struggle marks out some of the pathways I have found to and from western feminisms and something we could call Indigenous feminisms. Sharing this journey opens up a space for thinking about the contradictions that structure my relationship to the word and the analysis called feminism and to the identity called feminist.

*Kwe* means woman in my language and placing it attached to my identity as an Anishinaabe meant making it essential to my understanding of my culture, as an entry point to myself. For some people, this is easy: they are comfortable having the world divided up between men and women, and thinking of women as essential in their capacity to bear children. I was always keenly aware of the oppressions that could be contained in defining women by their wombs. This analysis came from watching many women in the many foster homes where I grew up in chained to kitchens, kids and caretaking. I saw men sit at tables, eat quickly and leave before the "mother" ever sat down. I saw girls and mothers cleaning houses on a regular basis while boys were exempt. It seemed to be a very thankless life. I saw menopause hit women with a desire for their own passions, life goals and leisure. I swore as a young girl that I wouldn't enter a kitchen because it took up so much time and I wanted to read, write, dance and change the world.

I was in care with my brothers and nephews and nieces and eventually just one brother. I lived in homes with a lot of boys. I always say I was raised by my brothers. I was always more comfortable around boys and men. Some of that is my natural rejection of most femininity as a child and some of it comes from hearing how men speak about women. Respect as a woman seemed really hard to come by. I thought to myself, if I can't have their respect as a woman then I could get it by being more like a man—by being smarter, stronger and need-less.

I remember a group of girls in my elementary school berating me for being too physical, too strong. I decided I would hang with the boys then. Boys always told you the truth and were quick to get over things. There is also a cultural element to this because I felt like the manipulation and passive aggressive behaviour young white girls enact was learned from their mothers and I knew it was a white thing. It had to do with the limited powers women had to exert in their lives. Passive aggression in some ways is suppressed desire for freedom. When I moved back to the reservation when I was 12, I realized my way of being a strong woman was acceptable and cultivated there. I no longer felt like a boyish girl because all the girls seemed this way, partly because femininity does not define womanhood or girlhood on the rez. [...]

I had a baby when I was 20, on purpose, in order for my child's spirit to speak to my mother's spirit who had just died. When my mother died, I understood myself as a woman in a new way. I saw my own oppressions and labour as a woman joining hers and my sister's. I had to think about what kind of mother I wanted to be. Western thought taught me to challenge mother as my primary identity and Anishinaabe thought taught me to place children at the centre of our communities and worlds. I did both, raising my son to see me as a woman with desires and aspirations but also mothering him as the centre of the future of our people. I thought a lot about how he would be as a man.

When I added *kwe* to my identity, I began to see the diversity of constructions of women and started to seek alternatives within my own culture to western feminism. I have always been influenced by two westerners: Judith Butler and Emma Goldman. Butler because she challenges heterosexuality and understands how we perform and become women. Goldman because she had a keen sense of herself as a revolutionary individual and how to practice an anti-authoritarian ethic. As "Nish," we raise our kids in anti-authoritarian ways and this is one connection to *kwe*. We let their spirits develop freely and without violence. Of course feminism becomes important when we think about the current state of violence against women and children in our communities today. As an analysis that understands patriarchy, it is important because colonialism enforced patriarchy in our communities where women had previously enjoyed equality or had more power than men.

In 2012, I decided to look at the work of Rebecca Belmore, who I felt could help me think through the meaning of *kwe* from outside of where I had been learning it, which was in the teachings of elders. I knew that my responsibility was to protect the earth, the water and the children. I understood that ways of being as a mother could be learned from our first mother, the earth. I was beginning to understand the type of power women have because they bear children and how that did not have to be a limit to our freedom. But these teachings, coupled with queer theory and the activism I embedded in my everyday life, weren't great bedmates.

Belmore's solo exhibition was called *KWE* and examined the complicated and fertile relationship between Indigenous women, art and feminism. *KWE* asked, what does the cultural specificity of Anishinaabe add to or change when we consider the meanings of being and becoming a woman for an artist who does not do ceremony? Belmore's artistic practice has always engaged the question of what it is to be an Anishinaabe-kwe artist here and now. The very real aspects of patriarchy and its embeddedness in both Indigenous and Canadian communities through colonialism, especially in terms of the violence against women, is the subject of much of Belmore's work. As an Anishinaabe-kwe artist, she engages on multiple levels with her cultures, practices and stories on the role of women while keeping Indigenous self-determination central.

Belmore's insightful and aesthetically beautiful critiques play with the patriarchal present, underscoring the need for an understanding of colonialism within feminisms today. As a curator, I kept the meaning of *KWE* unspoken and let the work speak for itself. The underlying analysis of power in society whereby Indigenous women fall to the bottom of

any measures of health, wealth or protection is why many people see Belmore's work as feminist. Her body and her sister's body were present in almost every work. The presence of an Indigenous woman's body pushes through stories of victimhood to resilience and strength, it pushes through the overwhelming denigration of stereotypes, and it pushes through its absence in reform and revolution narratives. Women's work. As a child I hated that, but as a curator I understand it as fundamental to the meaning of *kwe*, and that the problem isn't how much we do but its value and place in society. Anishinaabe culture allowed me to consider possibilities as yet unthought in the west and unpracticed in our societies today: more genders than two; accounting for and valuing women's needs and labour based on their differences; the idea that a man can live as a woman; the idea that it doesn't matter who you sleep with but what responsibilities you take up; the idea that women can have power without becoming violent, aggressive, adversarial or colonial; the idea that differences mean an expansion of society and special powers in the individual; and that the spirit of the individual should never be crushed. I don't call myself a *feminist* (identity statement) because Indigenous people have spent generations being named by others and I want control over my own naming, but I also think of Indigenous women as the earliest feminists and I value the analysis of western feminisms. Adding *kwe* to my identity captures all of these paths for me and, since I am comfortable with contradictions, it is unfinished in terms of where it will take me next.

*Source:* Nanibush, Wanda. (2017). "Anishinaabe-kwe and/or Indigenous Feminist?" First published in *C Magazine, 132*(Winter), 53–56.

**Figure 3.1:** Rebecca Belmore, *KWE*, 2012, Installation view, photograph by Toni Hafkenscheid. Justina M. Barnicke Gallery.

*Source:* Justina M. Barnicke Gallery.

## 15 INDIGENOUS FEMINISTS TO KNOW, READ, AND LISTEN TO

*Abaki Beck*

Abaki Beck is a writer and activist whose writing has been published in *Bitch Magazine*, *Aperture*, and *The Establishment*, among other media. Beck has worked for the U.S. House of Representatives and conducted oral history research on Blackfeet food sovereignty, and is currently in the field of urban planning and community development. Beck is the founder and editor of POC Online Classroom, a website that curates social justice readings, resources, and syllabi, and is also the co-editor of the *Daughters of Violence* zine. She is a mixed-race Indigenous person enrolled in the Blackfeet Nation of Montana.

> I think it's in all of our best interests to take on gender violence as a core resurgence project, a core decolonization project, a core of any Indigenous mobilization … This begins for me by looking at how gender is conceptualized and actualized within Indigenous thought because it is colonialism that has imposed an artificial gender binary in my nation.
> —*Leanne Betasamosake Simpson*

Despite our profound contributions to our own communities and the nation as a whole, Native American stories and voices have been long ignored by mainstream social culture. Native Americans—and Native American women, trans, and nonbinary folks in particular—face a unique set of oppressions, including the ongoing impacts of settler colonialism. Settler colonialism works to erase Indigenous people, both literally and culturally: from physical war and violence, to removal from lands, to forced assimilation. These histories continue to render Native Americans and Native issues nearly invisible to the national eye. Even within intersectional feminist discussions and organizing, I find myself thinking, where are the radical Indigenous feminists? Why are our stories not valued and our voices not more amplified?

This erasure may lull us into believing that there simply aren't Indigenous feminists who are as prolific as Audre Lorde or Gloria Anzaldúa. But this is far from the truth. From Sydney Freeland, a Navajo filmmaker who focuses on stories about trans communities, to Sarah Deer, a Muscogee (Creek) lawyer fighting violence against Native women, these activists, writers, creators, and scholars fight for justice for Indigenous people and for the voices of their communities.

## 1. Leanne Betasamosake Simpson (Michi Saagiig Nishnaabeg)

Leanne Simpson is an activist, scholar, writer, and poet. She was heavily involved with the Idle No More movement that raised awareness of treaty betrayals and environmental injustices impacting First Nations people. Her book *Islands of Decolonial Love*, a mixture of poetry and short stories, includes a powerful spoken word collaboration with musicians that brings an interactive, multilayered perspective to her poems. She writes on critical topics such as decolonizing education by recognizing land as pedagogy, contemporary manifestations of colonial gender violence, and the connections between Black and Indigenous fights for justice. In addition to writing, she has worked as an independent scholar for over a decade and lectures at universities across Canada.

## 2. LaDonna Brave Bull Allard (Standing Rock Sioux)

LaDonna Brave Bull Allard is an activist and tribal historian who is a leader in the fight against the Dakota Access Pipeline. In April 2016, she founded the Sacred Stone Camp on her land, which was the first resistance camp of the #NoDAPL movement and some of the closest tribally owned land to the construction site. Since the founding of the Sacred Stone Camp, thousands of water protectors camped and organized to prevent the construction of the Dakota Access Pipeline. Because of activists like LaDonna, the #NoDAPL movement grew to be one of the most powerful and widely supported Indigenous rights movements in recent decades.

## 3. Audra Simpson (Mohawk)

Audra Simpson is a scholar and professor whose research focuses on the politics of recognition—particularly, the Kahnawà:ke Mohawk struggles in asserting their legal and cultural rights across settler-imposed borders. Her book, *Mohawk Interruptus: Political Life Across the Borders of Settler States,* explores how Kahnawà:ke

Mohawks maintain their sovereignty through traditional governance and a rejection of both U.S. and Canadian citizenship. Her book was celebrated by Indigenous studies scholars as a critical addition to scholarship on tribal community and national identity. As an anthropologist, a field that is notorious for exploiting and thinking of Natives only in the past tense, Simpson pushes against these notions by centering on Native epistemologies.

## 4. Haunani Kay-Trask (Hawaiian)

Writer, educator, and activist Haunani Kay-Trask is a strong Hawaiian nationalist. She is an advocate for Indigenous Hawaiian rights and is vocal against the U.S. military presence and the tourism industry in Hawaii. She is the author of several books of nonfiction and poetry. Her book, *From a Native Daughter: Colonialism and Sovereignty in Hawaii,* explores the ongoing discrimination and denial of rights to Native Hawaiians. In the book, she analyzes Hawaiian activism against U.S. imperialism—from the advocacy of Ka Lahui Hawai'i, a Native Hawaiian self-governing organization, to on-campus organizing by Indigenous students at the University of Hawaii.

## 5. Beatrice Medicine (Standing Rock Sioux)

Beatrice Medicine was one of the most prominent Native American female anthropologists, whose writing has focused particularly on Native women. Her book, *The Hidden Half: Studies of Plains Indian Women* (edited with Patricia Albers), was one of the first studies to center on the lives of Native American women specifically. In addition to working as a professor and scholar, she also served on the school board of her home reservation and taught classes at Native American Educational Services in Chicago, Illinois, a college dedicated to educating non-traditional students on community building. Because of her broad expertise and advocacy, she was often called as an expert witness in trials related to Native American issues, including the trial against activists who occupied Wounded Knee in 1973.

## 6. Chrystos (Menominee)

Chrystos is a Two-Spirit poet and activist. Their poetry explores issues of colonialism, genocide, violence against Native people, queerness, street life, and more. Their work has been featured in various anthologies, including the renowned *This Bridge Called My Back: Writings by Radical Women of Color*, edited by Cherrie Moraga and Gloria Anzaldúa. They are the author of five poetry anthologies. Chrystos's book *Not Vanishing*, published in 1998, was a best seller. Throughout their poetry, they often include clichés, plays on words, and rhymes as a refusal to separate spoken word and oral tradition from poetry.

## 7. Winona LaDuke (White Earth Ojibwe)

Environmental activist and author Winona LaDuke is perhaps the most well-known name on this list. Winona LaDuke has founded two prominent organizations: Honor the Earth and the White Earth Land Recovery Project. Honor the Earth, which she cofounded with the Indigo Girls, raises awareness of and provides financial support to environmental justice issues in Native communities. The White Earth Land Recovery Project buys land formerly owned by non-Natives on the White Earth Ojibwe Reservation and repurposes it to restore traditional land ownership and stewardship. Much of the work of this organization focuses on food sovereignty, including the preservation of wild rice fields. LaDuke also ran as Vice President on a Green Party ticket alongside Ralph Nader in 1996 and 2000.

## 8. Sarah Deer (Muscogee [Creek])

Sarah Deer is a lawyer, professor, and advocate who has worked for victims' rights and sexual violence prevention for decades. She was an instrumental activist in the 2013 reauthorization of the Violence Against Women Act, which expanded tribal jurisdiction to prosecute non-Native perpetrators of domestic and sexual violence.

Her book, *The Beginning and End of Rape: Confronting Sexual Violence in Native America,* is a collection of critical essays on violence against Native women. She provides a historical overview of the intersecting violences that contribute to the high rates of sexual violence against Native Americans today, from the history of rape and sex trafficking of Indigenous people to the destruction of tribal legal systems to protect their own citizens.

## 9. Beth Brant (Mohawk)

Beth Brant is one of the first prominent Native American lesbian writers. First published as part of *Sinister Wisdom* in 1984, the anthology *Gathering of Spirit: A Collection by North American Indian Women*, which she edited, was later published independently in 1988. This was the first anthology of Native American women's writing edited by a Native American woman. She went on to publish several poetry and essay collections on topics such as Mohawk identity, queerness, and feminism. She also edited an oral-history anthology of Mohawk elders titled *I'll Sing 'til the Day I Die: Conversations with Tyendinaga Elders.*

## 10. Mishuana Goeman (Tonawanda Band of Seneca)

Mishuana Goeman is a scholar and professor whose work focuses on settler colonialism, gender violence, and Native women's cultural production. Her work provides a feminist perspective to colonial spatial definitions of Native land (national or reservation borders) and bodies, analyzing how colonialism attempts to impose a new spatial reality on Indigenous people. In her book *Mark My Words: Native Women Mapping Our Nations*, she uses literature written by Native women to argue that women's writing centering on Indigenous knowledge is essential to help define our nations outside of settler standards and to support ongoing decolonization efforts.

## 11. Suzan Shown Harjo (Cheyenne and Hodulgee Muscogee)

Suzan Shown Harjo is a policy advocate and writer. She served as the congressional liaison on Indian Affairs for President Jimmy Carter and, in the late 1980s, as the president of the National Congress of American Indians, an advocacy organization that unites tribal representatives from across the nation. She was involved with the passage of several important laws pertaining to Native American rights, including the American Indian Religious Freedom Act (1978), the National Museum of the American Indian Act (1989), and the Native American Graves Protection and Repatriation Act (1990). She received the Presidential Medal of Honor from President Barack Obama in 2014.

## 12. Brenda Child (Red Lake Ojibwe)

Brenda Child is a scholar and professor who has studied histories of boarding schools, Ojibwe women's activism, Indigenous education, and Ojibwe labor, among other topics. Her debut book, *Boarding School Seasons: American Indian Families, 1900 to 1940,* used letters between parents and their children in boarding schools to explore the deep emotional impact of these assimilationist institutions. In her 2012 book, *Holding the World Together: Ojibwe Women and the Survival of Community*, she outlines the profound ways that Ojibwe women have contributed to strengthening their communities for centuries—from helping to mediate between tribes and European fur traders to organizing to ameliorate urban Indian poverty after World War II.

## 13. Sydney Freeland (Navajo)

Sydney Freeland is a transgender filmmaker who uses film to combat stereotypes about Native Americans and highlight the experiences of queer and trans people. Her debut feature length film, *Drunktown's Finest*, follows the lives of three young people living on the Navajo Reservation: a young father-to-be, a transgender woman who dreams of being a model, and a woman who was adopted by a white Christian family. The film's name is a riff off an offensive ABC news segment that labeled Gallup, New Mexico, as "Drunk Town, USA." Freeland also directed the web series *Her Story,* which revolves around queer and trans women, and was nominated for an Emmy.

## 14. Nicole Tanguay (Cree)

Nicole Tanguay is a Two-Spirit poet, playwright, musician, and advocate for Indigenous rights. Their poetry—which has been featured in anthologies such as *Miscegenation Blues: Voices of Mixed Race Women* and *The Colour of Resistance: A Contemporary Collection of Writing by Aboriginal Women*—explores topics like racism, environmental destruction, and violence against Indigenous peoples. Their poetry is raw and in your face, often tangling visceral descriptions of trauma, grief, and pain with the everyday survivance of Indigenous people. In "Blood," for example, they memorialize Indigenous women who died "lying in the streets/ and in gutters of hell/ waiting for the great God to remember them/ for who they are/ children of this land." They view poetry as a form of resistance and education on critical social justice issues.

## 15. Leslie Marmon Silko (Laguna Pueblo)

Leslie Marmon Silko is a prolific novelist, poet, and essayist and a key figure in the First Wave of the Native American Renaissance. Her novels are rooted in a Laguna Pueblo landscape and history, with her characters often striving to maintain their traditional or tribal lifestyles despite Western cultural imperialism. Her debut novel, *Ceremony*, follows the struggles of a Native American World War II veteran returning to his civilian life and finding strength in revitalizing his tribal spirituality. *Ceremony* challenges the Western canon by weaving Laguna stories throughout the novel in a poetic, viva voce style.

From initial colonial wars, to forced boarding schools, to the Dakota Access Pipeline, tribal communities have survived because of the relentless strength and knowledge of our grandmothers, aunties, and ancestors. These contemporary scholars, poets, activists, and filmmakers continue this long legacy of Indigenous feminist resistance. For Indigenous people and settlers/allies alike, it is crucial that we listen to these voices, honor their wisdom, and empower their work.

*Source:* Beck, Abaki. (2017, September 18). "15 Indigenous Feminists to Know, Read, and Listen To." *Bitch Magazine* (originally published April 19, 2017). Retrieved from: https://www.bitchmedia.org/article/15-indigenous-feminists-know-read-and-listen.

## ACTIVIST INSIGHT: ALICE WALKER (1944–)

Alice Walker is an African American author, poet, and activist. Born February 9, 1944, Walker grew up in the southern United States, near Eatonton, Georgia. She has published many works of fiction and non-fiction, as well as anthologies and poetry. Walker's 1982 novel *The Color Purple* was awarded the National Book Award and the 1983 Pulitzer Prize for Fiction, making her the first African American woman writer to receive this prestigious literary award. To date, Walker's books have sold more than 15 million copies, and her works have been translated into more than two dozen languages.

Throughout her literary career, Walker has remained a committed activist, devoting her time to many causes, including the civil rights movement, the women's movement, and, most recently, the movements to end the wars in the Middle East. The excerpt that appears below comes from Walker's first collection of essays, entitled *In Search of Our Mothers' Gardens* and published in 1983. In it, Walker uses the term "womanist" for the first time to refer to the experiences of women of colour. This piece remains an important contribution to feminist thought.

### Womanist

1. From *womanish*. (Opp. of "girlish," i.e., frivolous, irresponsible, not serious.) A black feminist or feminist of color. From the black folk expression of mothers to female children, "You acting womanish," i.e., like a woman. Usually referring to outrageous, audacious, courageous, or *willful* behavior. Wanting to know more and in greater depth than is considered "good" for one. Interested in grown-up doings. Acting grown up. Being grown up. Interchangeable with another black folk expression: "You trying to be grown." Responsible. In charge. *Serious*.

2. *Also:* A woman who loves other women, sexually and/or nonsexually. Appreciates and prefers women's culture, women's emotional flexibility (values tears as natural counterbalance of laughter), and women's strength. Sometimes loves individual men, sexually and/or nonsexually. Committed to survival and wholeness of entire people, male *and* female. Not a separatist, except periodically, for health. Traditionally universalist, as in: "Mama, why are we brown, pink, and yellow, and our cousins are white, beige, and black?" Ans.: "Well, you know the colored race is just like a flower garden, with every color flower represented." Traditionally capable, as in: "Mama, I'm walking to Canada and I'm taking you and a bunch of other slaves with me." Reply: "It wouldn't be the first time."

3. Loves music. Loves dance. Loves the moon. *Loves* the Spirit. Loves love and food and roundness. Loves struggle. *Loves* the folk. Loves herself. *Regardless*.

4. Womanist is to feminist as purple to lavender.

*Source:* Walker, Alice. (1983). *In Search of Our Mothers' Gardens: Womanist Prose* (pp. x–xii). San Diego, CA: Harcourt Brace Jovanovich.

# CHAPTER 4

## The Historical Case for Feminism

*Estelle Freedman*

Estelle Freedman is the Edgar E. Robinson Professor in U.S. History at Stanford University and a co-founder of the Program in Feminist, Gender, and Sexuality Studies. Her research areas include the history of women and social reform, including feminism and prison reform, and the history of sexuality. Her book *No Turning Back: The History of Feminism and the Future of Women*, from which the following piece is taken, has been praised as one of the most comprehensive and analytical studies of feminism to date. Freedman is the recipient of an impressive list of teaching and mentorship awards.

In the past two centuries, a revolution has transformed women's lives. Unlike national revolutions, this social upheaval crosses continents, decades, and ideologies. In place of armed struggle it gradually sows seeds of change, infiltrating our consciousness with the simple premise that women are as capable and valuable as men. To measure the breadth of this ongoing upheaval of old patterns, consider the way feminist movements have transformed law and politics, from divorce reforms in Egypt and sexual harassment cases in Japan and the United States to the nomination of equal numbers of male and female candidates by French political parties. Or note the change in leadership: During the 1990s, 90 percent of the world's nations elected women to national office, and women served as heads of state in more than twenty countries. Just as important, consider the thousands of grassroots organizations such as Women in Law and Development in Africa, the National Black Women's Health Project in the United States, and the Self-Employed Women's Association in India. Women's movements have never been so widespread.

In *No Turning Back* I explain why and how a feminist revolution has occurred. I argue that two related historical transitions have propelled feminist politics. First, the rise of capitalism disrupted older, reciprocal relations within families in ways that initially enhanced men's economic opportunities and defined women as their dependants. Second, new political theories of individual rights and representative government that developed alongside capitalism extended privileges to men only. In response, feminist movements named these disparities as unjust, insisting on the value of women's economic contributions and the justice of political rights for women. In short, the market economies and democratic systems that now dominate the world create both the need for feminism and the means to sustain it.

Feminist politics originated where capitalism, industrial growth, democratic theory, and socialist critiques converged, as they did in Europe and North America after 1800. Women and their male allies began to agitate for equal educational, economic, and political opportunities, a struggle that continues to the present. By 1900 an international women's movement advanced these goals in urban areas of Latin America, the Middle East, and Asia. Since 1970 feminism has spread globally, in both industrialized nations and in the developing regions where agriculture remains an economic mainstay.

Given their specific historical origins, the feminist politics initially forged in Europe and North America have not simply expanded throughout the world. Elsewhere, abundant forms of women's resistance to men's patriarchal authority predated Western democratic theories; they continue to influence feminist movements today. Socialist responses to capitalism invite quite different women's politics than where free markets prevail. Both the term *feminism* and the politics it represents have been continually transformed by the evolving responses of women and men from a variety of cultures. Indeed, women's politics have developed organically in settings so diverse that the plural *feminisms* more accurately describes them.

By the year 2000 these growing international movements to improve women's lives increasingly influenced each other, due in part to the forum provided by the United Nations Decade for Women from 1975 to 1985 and the follow-up conference in Beijing in 1995. While they share the conviction that women deserve full human rights, international feminisms often diverge in their emphases. Only some concentrate solely on women, while others recognize complex links to the politics of race, class, religion, and nationality. Despite these differences, most Western feminists have learned that global economic and political justice are prerequisites to securing women's rights. Women in the developing world have found that transnational feminist movements can help establish strategic international support for their efforts at home.

None of these feminist movements has proceeded without opposition, including formidable backlash in every era in which women have gained public authority. Nonetheless, at the beginning of the twenty-first century the historical conditions that promote feminism can be found in much of the world: Whether through the influence of Western economic and political systems, the refashioning of earlier practices, or both, an impressive array of movements now attempts to empower women. At present, economic globalization, along with international efforts to create stable democratic governments, suggests that new forms of feminism will continue to surface. Because of their flexibility and adaptability, women's political movements, whether explicitly labeled feminist or not, have set much of the world's agenda for the twenty-first century.

## THE HISTORY OF A TERM

Since I use *feminism* to describe movements whose participants do not necessarily apply that label themselves, I want to acknowledge at the outset the specific historical origins of this term. *Feminism* is a relatively recent word. First coined in France in the 1880s as *féminisme*, it spread through European countries in the 1890s and to North and South America by 1910. The term combined the French word for woman, *femme*, and *-isme*, which referred to a social movement or political ideology. At a time when many other "isms" originated, including socialism and communism, *féminisme* connoted that women's issues belonged to the vanguard of change. The term was always controversial, in part because of its association with radicalism and in part because proponents themselves disagreed about the label. Although self-defined *socialist feminists* appeared in Europe as early as 1900, many socialists who supported women's emancipation rejected the label *feminist*. They believed that middle-class demands for suffrage and property rights did not necessarily speak to working women's needs for a living wage and job security. Middle-class women also hesitated to call themselves feminists, especially when the term implied a claim to universal rights as citizens rather than particular rights as mothers.

*****

From its origins through the social upheavals of the 1960s, *feminist* remained a pejorative term among most progressive reformers, suffragists, and socialists around the world. Even as universal adult suffrage gradually extended to women—in England in 1928, in countries such as France, Japan, Mexico, and China by the late 1940s—few politically engaged women called themselves feminists. Within the international women's movement, participants debated whether the term *humanist* rather than *feminist* best applied to them. Nations ruled by communist parties, such as China and later Cuba, officially pronounced the emancipation of women as workers, but their state-sanctioned women's organizations rejected the feminist label and their suppression of oppositional political discourse precluded feminist politics.

A critical turning point in the history of feminisms occurred during the politically tumultuous 1960s. Women's politics revived in the West, at first under the banner of "women's liberation." Although the press quickly derided adherents by calling them "women's libbers," this second wave proved quite tenacious. By this time, both capitalist and socialist economies had drawn millions of women into the paid labor force, and civil rights and anticolonial movements had revived the politics of democratization. In Europe and the United States, millions of women expected to earn wages as well as raise children. The old feminist calls for economic and political equality, and a new emphasis on control over reproduction, resonated deeply across generations, classes, and races.

Western women's movements also significantly expanded their agendas after the 1960s. Along with demands for economic and political rights, women's liberation revived a politics of difference through its critique of interpersonal relations. Women's liberation championed both women's *equality* with men in work and politics and women's *difference* from men within the arenas of reproduction and sexuality. In this way the two competing strains of equality and difference began to converge. Within a decade, the older term *feminist* began to be used to refer to the politics of this new movement, deepening its radical connotation but potentially widening its appeal. At about the same time, the introduction of the term *gender*, rather than *sex*, signaled feminists' growing belief that social practices, and not only biology, have constructed our notions of male and female.

By 1980 an umbrella usage of the term *feminism* took hold in Western cultures. Anyone who challenged prevailing gender relations might now be called a feminist, whether or not they lived long before the coining of the term *feminism*, agreed with all the tenets of women's liberation, or claimed the label. A generation of Western women came of age influenced by feminism to expect equal opportunities. The majority of this generation often proclaimed, "I'm not a feminist, but …," even as they insisted on equal pay, sexual and reproductive choice, parental leave, and political representation. The children they raised, both male and female, grew up influenced by these feminist expectations but not necessarily comfortable with the term. Outside the West, the term *feminism* could still evoke a narrow focus on equal rights. Thus a 1991 essay in the influential Indian women's journal *Manushi*, titled "Why I Do Not Call Myself a Feminist," contrasted Western concerns about women's rights with broader human rights and social justice campaigns that address the needs of both men and women in developing countries.[1]

The term *feminism*, in short, has never been widely popular. Yet the political goals of feminism have survived—despite continuing discomfort with the term, a hostile political climate, and heated internal criticism—largely because feminism has continually redefined itself.

Over the past twenty-five years, for example, activists have amended the term to make it more compatible with their unique perspectives. Self-naming by black feminists, Asian American feminists, Third World feminists, lesbian feminists, male feminists, ecofeminists, Christian feminists, Jewish feminists, Islamic feminists, and others attests to the malleability of the label and to the seemingly contradictory politics it can embrace. To make the movement more racially inclusive, the African American writer Alice Walker once coined *womanist* to refer to a "Black feminist or feminist of color." In the 1990s young women in the United States, such as Walker's daughter, promised to go beyond the second wave of feminism by forging a more racially and sexually diverse movement that emphasized female empowerment rather than male oppression. "I'm not post-feminist," Rebecca Walker explained in 1992, "I'm the Third Wave."[2] Significantly, this generation reclaims rather than rejects the term *feminist*. Internationally as well, more women's organizations incorporate the word, such as the Feminist League in Central Asia, the Center for Feminist Legal Research in New Delhi, and the Working Group Toward a Feminist Europe.

By the 1990s the cumulative contributions of working-class women, lesbians, women of color, and activists from the developing world had transformed an initially white, European, middle-class politics into a more diverse and mature feminist movement. Taking into account the range of women's experiences, feminists have increasingly recognized the validity of arguments that once seemed contradictory. Instead of debating whether women are similar to or different from men, most feminists now recognize that both statements are true. Instead of asking which is more important, gender or race, most feminists now acknowledge the indivisibility and interaction of these social categories. Along with demanding the right to work, feminists have redefined work to include caring as well as earning. Along with calling for women's independence, feminists have recognized the interdependence of all people, as well as the

interconnection of gender equality with broader social justice movements.

## DEFINING FEMINISM TODAY

Given its changing historical meanings, is there any coherence to *feminism* as a term? Can we define it in a way that will embrace its variety of adherents and ideas? For my purposes, a four-part definition contains the critical elements of feminisms, including views that may be shared by those who claim the label as well as many who reject it.

> Feminism is a belief that women and men are inherently of equal worth. Because most societies privilege men as a group, social movements are necessary to achieve equality between women and men, with the understanding that gender always intersects with other social hierarchies.

Each of the four components of this working definition—equal worth, male privilege, social movements, and intersecting hierarchies—requires some clarification. I use *equal worth* rather than *equality* because the latter term often assumes that men's historical experience—whether economic, political, or sexual—is the standard to which women should aspire. The concept of equal worth values traditional female tasks, such as childbearing and child care, as highly as other kinds of work historically performed by men. It also allows us to recognize that women's different experiences can transform, and not simply integrate, political life.

The term *privilege* can refer to formal political rights such as suffrage and the right to hold office, but privilege can also include more personal entitlements, such as the greater social value placed on male children as expressed by strong parental preference for boys across cultures. Privilege also ensues when societies have a sexual double standard that allows male heterosexual autonomy, punishing women but not men who seek non-marital sexual expression.

To refer to feminism in terms of *social movements* may conjure images of people marching in the streets or rallying around political candidates, but it may also mean individual participation, such as enrolling in a women's studies class or engaging in artistic or literary creativity that fosters social change. While women may participate in a variety of social movements—civil rights, ecology, socialism, even fundamentalism—those movements cannot be feminist unless they explicitly address justice for women as a primary concern. Thus human rights or nationalist movements that insist on women's human rights and women's full citizenship may be feminist, while those that overlook or affirm patriarchal authority cannot be.

Similarly, feminism must recognize the integral relationship of gender to other forms of *social hierarchy*, especially those based on class, race, sexuality, and culture. Despite the prevalence of hierarchies that privilege men, in every culture some women (such as elites or citizens) enjoy greater opportunities than many other women (such as workers or immigrants). Some women always have higher status than many men. If we ignore these intersecting hierarchies and create a feminism that serves only the interests of women who have more privilege, we reinforce other social inequalities that disadvantage both women and men in the name of improving women's opportunities.

The overlapping identities of women as members of classes, races, and nations raise questions about the usefulness of the category *woman* itself. I use the term but with the recognition that there is no single, universal female identity, for gender has been constructed differently across place and time. Because of historical, social, national, and personal differences, women cannot assume a sisterhood, even though we can find common ground on particular issues. At the same time, feminism cannot deny the significance of gender in a world in which 70 percent of those living in poverty and two-thirds of those who are illiterate are female.

Feminists must continually criticize two kinds of false universals. We must always ask not only "What about women?" (What difference does gender make?) but also "Which women?" (What difference do ideas about race, class, or nationality make?). [...] I believe that we must question both the assumption that the term *man* includes woman as well and the assumption that the term *woman* represents the diversity of female experience.

## NOTES

1.  Madhu Kishwar, "Why I Do Not Call Myself a Feminist," *Manushi* 61 (1991), 2–8.
2.  Alice Walker, *In Search of Our Mothers' Gardens: Womanist Prose* (New York: Harcourt Brace Jovanovich, 1983), xi; Rebecca Walker, "Becoming the Third Wave," *Ms.* 2:4 (1992), 39–41.

*Source:* Freedman, Estelle. (2002). Excerpted from "Chapter 1: The Historical Case for Feminism." In *No Turning Back: The History of Feminism and the Future of Women* (pp. 1–11). New York, NY: Ballantine Books.

# CHAPTER 5

## This Is What a Feminist Looks Like

*Shira Tarrant*

Shira Tarrant is a professor in the Department of Women's, Gender & Sexuality Studies at California State University–Long Beach, as well as a recognized author, social critic, and expert on gender politics, pop culture, and masculinity. Her recent books cover a wide range of topics from pornography to men's role in feminism, including *New Views on Pornography*; *Gender, Sex, and Politics*; *The Pornography Industry: What Everyone Needs to Know*; and *Men and Feminism*.

Brandon Arber is a feminist. During college, he was the captain of his swim team and an all-around jock. For Brandon, feminism is a moral belief. It's about thinking girls and women shouldn't be raped, abused, discriminated against, or denied health services, especially if they get pregnant. When it comes down to it, he says, feminism is a viable approach to guiding decisions in our personal, political, and public lives. To Brandon, it's just common sense to believe in egalitarian values. It makes sense to care for all people and to bring about a better world.

\*\*\*\*\*

Derrais Carter graduated from the University of Kansas, where he majored in sociology and African American studies. When Derrais started college, he fell in love with hip-hop and feminism. In fact, hip-hop is what led Derrais to feminist politics when he started thinking about rap lyrics and what he calls "the battlefield of identity." Being a feminist gave Derrais a platform for changing his life and how he understands his relations with others. "I began to see women as more than a video prop, extra, and eye candy," Derrais writes in his essay "This Is What a Feminist Looks Like." Instead he realized that women are highly misrepresented figures in society whom he had been "conditioned to mistreat and ignore." When Derrais taught a group of high school students one summer, the conversation led to culture, capitalism, and globalization. "By understanding feminism," Derrais says, "we were able to talk about how our 'needs' can exploit women in various other countries. The discussion made all of us think more about how we are all connected."

Still, being a male feminist is a rough road, Derrais says. People are full of race- and gender-based assumptions. "As a black male in college, I was often assumed to be on an athletic scholarship," he explains. "And when I wear my 'This Is What a Feminist Looks Like' T-shirt, people have accused me of trying to get laid." Others have said the same about his job at the campus women's center. "I used to get angry about it. Now I see these comments as mere ignorance and a failure to accept that there are men who truly care about women's issues."

Current feminist perspectives are challenging concepts of gender in fresh, new ways. More men are getting involved in feminist movements led by women. And there are plenty of examples of gender activism initiated by men, such as One in Four and Men Can Stop Rape, programs that work to prevent sexual assault. Colleges and universities are increasingly shifting from women's studies to programs that study gender and sexuality more broadly. At the same time, more guys are becoming interested in feminism. As Julie Bindel reports in the *Guardian*, increasing numbers of men are enrolling in courses with feminist content and perspectives.

*****

## THERE'S ROOM FOR MEN

One question that often comes up is how feminism is relevant to men. If feminism is a women's movement, then where do men fit in?

The idea that only women can be feminists is based on essentialism—the assumption that men and women possess inherent behavioral traits based on biological sex. Sometimes people think the term "feminist men" is an oxymoron, says sociologist Michael Kimmel. In his essay "Who's Afraid of Men Doing Feminism?" Kimmel explains that essentialism leads us to think that a feminist man is either not a "real" man or he cannot be a real feminist.

But just as being a woman doesn't make someone a feminist, being a man doesn't automatically mean

he's not one. The "feminist-equals-woman" equation is a dangerous way of thinking, explains Judith Grant, author of *Fundamental Feminism*. That perspective blurs the point that feminism is about the interpretive lens we're using, not women's experience as women. Anyway, not all women are the same, just like all men aren't the same. Our gender position is always affected by our socioeconomic, racial, national, sexual, and religious identities.

"Feminism is a political way of thinking," explains Matthew Shepherd in *Feminism, Men, and the Study of Masculinity*. "And, like all political thought," Shepherd writes, the attractions of feminism "cut across sex." Being a feminist doesn't require certain plumbing. It requires a certain consciousness. Feminism is about using a particular lens that filters how we understand the world. This lens is analytical and always puts gender front and center. Feminists don't necessarily think that men and women are the same. Instead, they question the assumptions that biology is destiny and that might makes right. Feminists ask why difference comes at such a high price.

Essentialism also reinforces the binary idea that there are only two, opposite genders; in doing so, it limits our understanding of gender politics. Thinking of feminist-as-female excludes transgender, genderqueer, and intersex people, which is inconsistent with the principles of gender justice. According to activist and scholar Susan Stryker, the rise of queer and transgender studies has challenged essentialist-based politics. In her essay "(De)Subjugated Knowledge," Stryker writes that trans studies calls for "new analyses, new strategies and practices, for combating discrimination and injustice based on gender inequality." If we think of feminism as something that women do or believe in, then we conflate feminism with women. This essentializes a political perspective while paradoxically arguing against essentialist foundations.

Feminism benefits from men's participation. When men are involved in gender justice efforts, it maximizes the potential for deep, sustained social change. One practical advantage is that there is strength in numbers and feminism could use more allies. Plus, for the moment, as violence-prevention expert Jackson Katz suggests, men can be heard in ways that women still can't be heard. "Sexist?" Katz asks rhetorically. "Maybe. But effective? Yes."

Men's participation in feminism is not an invitation for male chivalry or for "protecting our women." A protectionist model actually perpetuates the gender stereotypes that are part of the problem, not part of the solution. Getting men involved with feminism means holding men personally and institutionally accountable for the sexist abuse of power, explains Katz. We need more men to challenge other men's sexism or misogyny as it manifests in all sorts of ways. Katz challenges men to move beyond defensive posturing and be willing to call it like it is.

*****

## JOINING THE STRUGGLE

When punk-rock feminist Chris Crass was hanging out with anarchist political groups in Southern California, his commitment to gender justice went hand in hand with opposing war, feeding homeless people through Food Not Bombs, and supporting students' rights. Chris recognized that ending sexism is key to radical change both within political movements and throughout broader society. For Chris, this continues to mean working with women and men as "allies to each other in the struggle to develop models of anti-racist, class-conscious, pro-queer, feminist manhood that challenges strict binary gender roles and categories." For Grantlin Schafer, being a "comrade in struggle" means working to prevent male violence through his job as an antiviolence educator for a sexual and domestic violence center in Loudoun County, Virginia. These men provide just two examples of the myriad ways men can get involved in feminism.

Nighat Gandhi explains that feminism is about transforming institutions such as the law, the family, the workplace, or marriage to weed out their injustices. Feminists don't necessarily want to destroy these institutions and practices. Many feminists simply want to see them changed into more equitable situations. Men are not excluded from these efforts. In fact, Gandhi says, men should very much feel a part of feminism.

Jackson Katz points out that Americans like to brag how we're "the freest country on earth," yet half of us don't even feel free enough to walk by ourselves at night. Many women aren't even safe in their own homes. By conservative estimates, 20 percent of adolescent girls have been physically or sexually assaulted by a dating partner. Two-thirds of American men responding to a major American public opinion poll in 2000 said that domestic violence is very or fairly common. And 92 percent of people who answered a 2005 national survey said that "family violence is a much bigger problem than people think." And these issues are not unique to the United States.

As Katz points out, it's a mistake to think of sexual assault or domestic violence as "women's issues." Men's violence against women is really more about men than it is about women, Katz explains in *The Macho Paradox: Why Some Men Hurt Women and How All Men Can Help.* What he means is that because men are the "ones committing the vast majority of the violence," it's time for men to face up and do something about it. We live our lives *in relation* to other people, Katz notes. Something that affects women no doubt affects men—and vice versa.

[…] When it comes to issues such as pay inequity or male violence toward women, there's a tremendous amount of work that men can do to stop the problem *before* it even happens! Prevention is the real solution. The most important thing is that we talk with each other as we continue coalition building between women and men and across the political spectrum.

## JUSTICE IS A RENEWABLE RESOURCE

Some men steer clear of feminism because they have been taught that it's a movement to take power, resources, authority, and perks from men. The real issue is *not* what men might lose: All of us—women and men alike—actually have a lot to gain from feminism. The problem is that power is often seen as a limited resource. This view of power assumes that if one group gains power, another loses it. Or that if one person achieves resources, it must necessarily happen at someone else's expense.

This scarcity model assumes that there are limited resources in the world and that if I get mine, you can't have yours. For those accustomed to this kind of thinking, the assumption is that if women gain power, men will necessarily lose it. But instead of thinking that equality and justice are finite resources (like fossil fuels), there are other ways to view it. If our power grid is fueled by wind or sun, one person's increase in power doesn't mean that there's less to go around. It is possible that *we* can work cooperatively toward achieving egalitarian conditions. It is possible to think of power as an infinite resource that won't run out when we challenge harmful or limiting gender expectations.

Feminism is about breaking down gender expectations that limit everyone. Feminism holds the potential for each of us to experience a fuller range of possibilities to exist freely in the world and to explore our full humanity while minimizing or eradicating oppression, subjugation, and patterns of domination.

Although equality and gender justice are unlimited resources, feminism does challenge men to change their behavior and to change systems from which they benefit. This requires hard work that some men resist—relinquishing some of the privileges that come with being a man, rethinking sexual pleasure that relies on a woman's denigration, and surrendering unearned authority.

Feminism is a movement for ending gender-based oppression and all forms of related patterns of domination and subjugation in our homes, our communities, and the world. There is a serious and growing movement of men who stand beside women in tackling issues of gender, race, class, sexuality—as well as enormous, complex problems such as war, imperialism, and globalization. These issues are all part of the same package and feminism can be used to address each of them, and more. Sociopolitical issues as seemingly diverse as sexual harassment and the war in Iraq are linked by similar patterns of domination, in which people or groups attempt to obtain power over others. Feminism can offer a new vision of shared power.

## WHO ME? A FEMINIST?

Sometimes guys don't get involved with feminist politics because they don't feel welcome. Even walking into a women's studies classroom for the first time can be a challenging experience. Men frequently don't engage with feminism because they think the issues don't involve them. They just can't relate. Or it never occurred to them to get involved in the first place. Not because they're bad men. Maybe it just never crossed their minds.

At the same time, feminist groups that are made up largely of women may intentionally or inadvertently exclude men. Cliques happen anywhere. Politics is no exception. Even social justice and gender politics. It happens. We won't pretend it doesn't.

Men might sometimes feel intimidated by feminism. Or they can believe (or presume) that they are unwelcome to join activist groups. It might feel uncomfortable or strange to stand in a bookstore looking at the feminist titles on the shelves. And sometimes stereotypes about feminists act as barriers that impede men's (and women's) participation.

*****

## DO I HAVE TO CALL MYSELF ONE?

What's in a name? Does it matter if you call yourself a feminist, a pro-feminist, a feminist ally, or even a member of the Men's Auxiliary? What if you practice your politics and don't want to label yourself?

Debates over terminology are nothing new—and they aren't limited to men. In the 1940s and '50s, for example, there were those who promoted women's rights and who objected to oppressions of all sorts, but who distanced themselves from the term *feminist*. Back then there were all sorts of reasons some people shied away from the label. To call oneself a feminist risked evoking images of being militant, racist, a sexual prude, bourgeois, strident, or just plain selfish. Similar assumptions are still made today. Both men *and* women who identify as feminists risk being called what historian Leila Rupp refers to as manhaters and crazies, kooks or queers.

Because there is concern that feminism focuses primarily on white women's issues and uncritically assumes white experience as the norm, some shy away from the term *feminist* because it doesn't go far enough. Thinkers and activists have developed terminology and frameworks to intentionally reflect the matrix of race, class, gender, and ethnicity. Womanism, for example, focuses on how black women experience power, oppression, and status within the social hierarchy. Womanism uses this concept as a base for advocating social change and improved gender politics by providing an option for social and political analysis that makes black women and other women of color central. […]

Some men who recognize these problems of gender repression, misogyny, sexism, and the politics of domination take a stand by identifying as feminists. Others call themselves pro-feminists, feminist allies, antisexist activists, or even "meninists"—a global group of men who, according to Feminist.com, "believe in and support the feminist principles of women's political, social, and economic equality." These are people who understand that men are not

born on Mars and women are not born on Venus but, rather, that *we* are all born on the same planet as equals. Like male feminists, men who are allies actively support gender justice. They "believe that women as a group suffer inequalities and injustices in society, while men as a group receive various forms of power and institutional privilege," writes Australian scholar Michael Flood in his pro-feminist FAQ. These antisexist men resist using the term *feminist* in describing themselves because, while they support gender equity and oppose sexism, they see their role as supporting women who have done feminist work for so long. Pro-feminists want neither to colonize feminism nor to act as if they've got all the answers.

There's no reason to shy away from claiming the term *feminist*, though our commitment to sociopolitical improvement may be more important than what we call ourselves. A person can be political without a label and sometimes we might not want to be tied down by a label at all. But particular labels can tell us about a person's politics. And when it comes to the long history of feminist efforts, there have been many men working alongside women in the struggle for gender equality.

## REFERENCES

Arber, Brandon. "It's Just Common Sense," in Shira Tarrant, ed., *Men Speak Out: Views on Gender, Sex, and Power*. New York: Routledge, 2008, pp. 163–164.

Bindel, Julie. "The New Feminists." *Guardian*, Tuesday, November 28, 2006, p. 12.

Carter, Derrais. "This Is What a Feminist Looks Like," in Shira Tarrant, ed., *Men Speak Out: Views on Gender, Sex, and Power*. New York: Routledge, 2008, p. 152.

Crass, Chris. "How Can I Be Sexist? I'm an Anarchist!" in Shira Tarrant, ed., *Men Speak Out: Views on Gender, Sex, and Power*. New York: Routledge, 2008, p. 284.

Flood, Michael. "Frequently Asked Questions about Pro-Feminist Men and Pro-Feminist Men's Politics." www.xyonline.net/misc/pffaq.html. Accessed June 23, 2008.

Gandhi, Nighat. "Can Men Be the Allies of Feminism?" www.xyonline.net/Canmenbeallies.shtml. Accessed June 23, 2008.

Grant, Judith. *Fundamental Feminism: Contesting the Core Concepts of Feminist Theory.* New York: Routledge, 1993, p. 109.

Katz, Jackson. *The Macho Paradox: Why Some Men Hurt Women and How All Men Can Help.* Naperville, IL: Sourcebooks, 2006, pp. 1–3, 15, and 16.

Kimmel, Michael S. "Who's Afraid of Men Doing Feminism?" in Tom Digby, ed., *Men Doing Feminism (Thinking Gender).* New York: Routledge, 1998.

Rupp, Leila J. "The Women's Community in the National Women's Party, 1945 to the 60s." *Signs,* vol. 10, no. 4 (1985), p. 722.

Schafer, Grantlin. "Breaking the Silence One Mile at a Time," in Shira Tarrant, ed., *Men Speak Out: Views on Gender, Sex, and Power.* New York: Routledge, 2008.

Shepherd, Matthew. "Feminism, Men, and the Study of Masculinity: Which Way Now?," in Steven P. Schacht and Doris W. Ewing, eds., *Feminisms and Men: Reconstructing Gender Relations.* New York: New York University, 1998, p. 174.

Stryker, Susan. "(De)Subjugated Knowledge: An Introduction to Transgender Studies," in Susan Stryker and Stephen Whittle, eds., *The Transgender Studies Reader.* New York: Routledge, 2006, p. 7.

*Source:* Tarrant, Shira. (2009). Excerpted from "Chapter 1: Overview and Introductions: This Is What a Feminist Looks Like." In *Men and Feminism* (pp. 1–2, 15–21, 23–25). New York, NY: Perseus Books.

# CHAPTER 6

## Why Intersectionality Can't Wait

*Kimberlé Crenshaw*

Kimberlé Crenshaw teaches courses in civil rights, critical race studies, and constitutional law at the University of California–Los Angeles and Columbia School of Law. She is a founder and leader in the intellectual movement called Critical Race Theory. She is also co-founder of the African American Policy Forum, a think tank that promotes efforts to dismantle structural inequality. Crenshaw's publications include *Critical Race Theory* and *Words That Wound: Critical Race Theory, Assaultive Speech and the First Amendment*.

Intersectionality was a lived reality before it became a term.

Today, nearly three decades after I first put a name to the concept, the term seems to be everywhere. But if women and girls of color continue to be left in the shadows, something vital to the understanding of intersectionality has been lost.

In 1976, Emma DeGraffenreid and several other black women sued General Motors for discrimination, arguing that the company segregated its workforce by race and gender: Blacks did one set of jobs and whites did another. According to the plaintiffs' experiences, women were welcome to apply for some jobs, while only men were suitable for others. This was of course a problem in and of itself, but for black women the consequences were compounded. You see, the black jobs were men's jobs, and the women's jobs were only for whites. Thus, while a black applicant might get hired to work on the floor of the factory if he were male, if she were a black female she would not be considered. Similarly, a woman might be hired as a secretary if she were white, but wouldn't have a chance at that job if she were black. Neither the black jobs nor the women's jobs were appropriate for black women, since they were neither male nor white. Wasn't this clearly discrimination, even if some blacks and some women were hired?

Unfortunately for DeGraffenreid and millions of other black women, the court dismissed their claims. Why? Because the court believed that black women should not be permitted to combine their race and gender claims into one. Because they could not prove that what happened to them was just like what happened to white women or black men, the discrimination that happened to these black women fell through the cracks.

It was thinking about why such a "big miss" could have happened within the complex structure of anti-discrimination law that the term *intersectionality* was born. As a young law professor, I wanted to define this profound invisibility in relation to the law. Racial and gender discrimination overlapped not only in the workplace but in other arenas of life; equally significant, these burdens were almost completely absent from feminist and anti-racist advocacy. Intersectionality, then, was my attempt to make feminism, anti-racist activism, and anti-discrimination law do what I thought they should—highlight the multiple avenues through which racial and gender oppression were experienced so that the problems would be easier to discuss and understand.

Intersectionality is an analytic sensibility, a way of thinking about identity and its relationship to power. Originally articulated on behalf of black women, the term brought to light the invisibility of many constituents within groups that claim them as members, but often fail to represent them. Intersectional erasures are not exclusive to black women. People of color within LGBTQ movements, girls of color in the fight against the school-to-prison pipeline, women within immigration movements, trans women within feminist movements, and people with disabilities fighting police abuse—all face vulnerabilities that reflect the intersections of racism, sexism, class oppression, transphobia, able-ism and more. Intersectionality has given many advocates a way to frame their circumstances and to fight for their visibility and inclusion.

Intersectionality has been the banner under which many demands for inclusion have been made, but a term can do no more than those who use it have the power to demand. And not surprisingly, intersectionality has generated its share of debate and controversy.

Conservatives have painted those who practice intersectionality as obsessed with "identity politics." Of course, as the DeGraffenreid case shows, intersectionality is not just about identities but about the institutions that use identity to exclude and privilege. The better we understand how identities and power

work together from one context to another, the less likely our movements for change are to fracture.

Others accuse intersectionality of being too theoretical, of being "all talk and no action." To that I say we've been "talking" about racial equality since the era of slavery and we're still not even close to realizing it. Instead of blaming the voices that highlight problems, we need to examine the structures of power that so successfully resist change.

Some have argued that intersectional understanding creates an atmosphere of bullying and "privilege checking." Acknowledging privilege is hard—particularly for those who also experience discrimination and exclusion. While white women and men of color also experience discrimination, all too often their experiences are taken as the only point of departure for all conversations about discrimination. Being front and center in conversations about racism or sexism is a complicated privilege that is often hard to see.

Although the president's [Barack Obama's] recent call to support black women was commendable, undertaking intersectional work requires concrete action to address the barriers to equality facing women and girls of color in U.S. society.

Intersectionality alone cannot bring invisible bodies into view. Mere words won't change the way that some people —the less-visible members of political constituencies—must continue to wait for leaders, decision-makers and others to see their struggles. In the context of addressing the racial disparities that still plague our nation, activists and stakeholders must raise awareness about the intersectional dimensions of racial injustice that must be addressed to enhance the lives of all youths of color.

This is why we continue the work of the #WhyWeCantWait campaign, calling for holistic and inclusive approaches to racial justice. It is why "Say Her Name" continues to draw attention to the fact that women too are vulnerable to losing their lives at the hands of police. And it is why thousands have agreed that the tragedy in Charleston, S.C., demonstrates our need to sustain a vision of social justice that recognizes the ways racism, sexism and other inequalities work together to undermine us all. We simply do not have the luxury of building social movements that are not intersectional, nor can we believe we are doing intersectional work just by saying words.

*Source:* Crenshaw, Kimberlé. (2015, September 24). "Why Intersectionality Can't Wait." *The Washington Post.* Retrieved from: https://www.washingtonpost.com/news/in-theory/wp/2015/09/24/why-intersectionality-cant-wait/?utm_term=.4aa8101c2cf9.

## THE DANGERS OF A SINGLE STORY

*Chimamanda Ngozi Adichie*

Chimamanda Ngozi Adichie was born in Nigeria. She is the author of the novels *Purple Hibisicus, Half of Yellow Sun,* and *Americanah,* which won the National Book Critics Circle Award for Fiction. She has also written several short stories and essays, including "We Should All Be Feminists," that have been featured in various publications including *The New Yorker* and *The Financial Times.* Her work has been translated into over 30 languages.

I come from a conventional, middle-class Nigerian family. My father was a professor. My mother was an administrator. And so we had, as was the norm, live-in domestic help, who would often come from nearby rural villages. So, the year I turned eight, we got a new house boy. His name was Fide. The only thing my mother told us about him was that his family was very poor. My mother sent yams and rice, and our old clothes, to his family. And when I didn't finish my dinner, my mother would say, "Finish your food! Don't you know? People like Fide's family have nothing." So I felt enormous pity for Fide's family.

Then one Saturday, we went to his village to visit, and his mother showed us a beautifully patterned basket made of dyed raffia that his brother had made. I was startled. It had not occurred to me that anybody in his family could actually make something. All I had heard about them was how poor they were, so that it had become impossible for me to see them as anything else but poor. Their poverty was my single story of them.

Years later, I thought about this when I left Nigeria to go to university in the United States. I was 19. My American roommate was shocked by me. She asked where I had learned to speak English so well, and was confused when I said that Nigeria happened to have English as its official language. She asked if she could listen to what she called my "tribal music," and was consequently very disappointed when I produced my tape of Mariah Carey.

She assumed that I did not know how to use a stove.

What struck me was this: She had felt sorry for me even before she saw me. Her default position toward me, as an African, was a kind of patronizing, well-meaning pity. My roommate had a single story of Africa: a single story of catastrophe. In this single story, there was no possibility of Africans being similar to her in any way, no possibility of feelings more complex than pity, no possibility of a connection as human equals. [...]

So, after I had spent some years in the U.S. as an African, I began to understand my roommate's response to me. If I had not grown up in Nigeria, and if all I knew about Africa was from popular images, I too would think that Africa was a place of beautiful landscapes, beautiful animals, and incomprehensible people, fighting senseless wars, dying of poverty and AIDS, unable to speak for themselves and waiting to be saved by a kind, white foreigner. I would see Africans in the same way that I, as a child, had seen Fide's family.

*Source:* Adichie, Chimamanda Ngozi. (2009, July). Excerpted from *The Dangers of a Single Story*. TED Talk. Retrieved from: https://www.ted.com/talks/chimamanda_adichie_the_danger_of_a_single_story/transcript?language=en.

# CHAPTER 7

## The Myth of Shared Womanhood and How It Perpetuates Inequality

*Mia McKenzie*

Mia McKenzie is a writer, activist, and the founder of the website *Black Girl Dangerous* (BGD). McKenzie identifies as a queer Black feminist and uses her writing and website to make space for LGBTQ people of color. Her debut novel, *The Summer We Got Free*, received a Lambda Literary Award in 2013. Her essays and short stories appear regularly on BGD as well as in various publications. McKenzie presents talks that centre on the intersections of race, class, queerness, and gender at universities and conferences across the United States.

I've been thinking a lot about shared female identity. A lot of people seem to think that being born with female parts bonds you in some significant way to other people who are born with female parts. In order to get the most out of all that bonded-female-parts-ness, there are events and outings that welcome female-born people only, places where we can listen to the music "we" like and talk about our periods or something. It goes like this: "women" have a different experience in the world than "men" and therefore understand each other on some deep level and in some universal way because of that experience. While I agree, of course, with that first part, I find the last part really tricky.

I don't feel any universal connection with all people who are born with female parts. I'm not sure I know anyone who actually does, not when you really break it down. Because, despite what mainstream (white) feminism and tampon commercials would have us believe, "shared" female experience isn't really all that "shared" at all.

Let's take for example a well-known issue that affects women—the issue of "equal pay." We've all heard the statistic: in the US, women make 77 cents for every dollar a man makes on average. That sucks. But it's not quite the shared experience it seems. A recent report by the National Partnership for Women & Families shows that black women only make 70 cents for every dollar a man makes on average, and only 64 cents compared to every dollar paid to a white, non-Hispanic man. And Latinas make only 55 cents for every dollar made by a white, non-Hispanic man. Well, damn. That 77 cents never looked so good.

Of course, it's not just economics. There are many ways in which factors such as race, sexuality, gender presentation, and (dis)ability make the "collective" experience of one group of women vastly different from that of another. According to RAINN (Rape, Abuse & Incest National Network), 91% of people who are raped in the US are women. So, rape is a universal issue for women, right? Of course. When you break it down, though, "universal" gets complicated. The rate of rape and attempted rape for white women is 17.7%. For American Indian/Alaskan women it's 34.1%. And women with disabilities are raped at a rate at least twice that of women overall. So while "women" have a collective experience of being more vulnerable to rape, some women are a whole lot more vulnerable to it than others. While that first statistic is always used to suggest a shared female experience of the world, the statistics that follow it show that women's experiences aren't really all that shared. Or at least not equally shared. Not anywhere *near* equally.

Despite these and a hundred other examples, the myth of shared female experience prevails. Why? Well, the easy answer is that because "women" are so vulnerable to so many different injustices, even if that vulnerability is vastly different from one group to another, lumping us all in together gives us a louder voice and more power to change things. Even if that's true, the downside of all this lumping together is significant. Because it allows the people with the loudest voices within the group to always be dominating the conversation. And because those voices rarely, if ever, even understand the experiences of the less-heard members of the group, not only can they not speak for them (which they shouldn't be doing anyway), *they can rarely even understand the importance of making space for them to speak for themselves.*

This is why today's mainstream feminist movements are still so white, even though women of color are 36.3% of the women in this country [United States]. It's why, even though "marriage equality" is all over the news all the time, you rarely see lesbians of color, and you never see disabled lesbians or trans lesbians, on TV. Because the voice of the privileged majority, even within a presumed non-privileged group, doesn't

end up raising the voices of the less-heard group; it usually just drowns them out. What you end up with is groups within groups that feel, and are, completely disconnected from one another. So is the case with women in this country. (This also describes queer community and people of color community as a whole, and QTPOC community specifically.)

Yet, the myth of shared female experience persists. It gets used by certain groups, including Michigan Womyn's Music Festival,[1] to exclude trans women because they presumably don't have all the parts necessary to participate in this "universal" female experience that doesn't actually exist anyway. The idea that cis women who attend this festival have a shared experience of womanhood—an experience that stretches like a rainbow bridge across race, sexuality, (dis)ability and economic class—that is so certain that no one without a vagina could possibly understand any of it is, frankly, absurd.

As a black, queer, cis woman who was raised working class, I feel almost completely disconnected from the experiences of white, straight, trans women who were raised wealthy. And much more so from the experiences of white, straight, cis women who were raised middle-class. Put me in a room full of either of these groups of women and I wouldn't be able to get away fast enough. I'd feel *incredibly* out of place.

In fact, put me in a room full of black lesbians and I won't likely do a whole lot of bonding. A room full of queer black women nerd-types? Ok, now we're getting closer.

Here's a quick list of rooms full of people where I will likely bond, in order of best to worst.

1.  Black queer women who are nerdy in bookish ways, regardless of economic class.
2.  Other queer women of color who are nerdy in bookish ways, who are working class.
3.  Other queer women of color who are nerdy in bookish ways, regardless of class.
4.  Black women, regardless of class and sexuality, who are nerdy in bookish ways.

5. Other women of color, regardless of class and sexuality, who are nerdy in bookish ways.

You see how complicated this is already??? A room full of white women is going to be somewhere around number 1006. Seriously, a "room full" of white women of any sort is a room I'm going to leave really quickly, and probably only have stumbled into by accident while looking for the bathroom.

My point is, possession of vaginas in and of themselves is neither what define women nor what bond women to each other. Shared experiences of the world, which include experiences of race, sexuality, (dis)ability, economic class, any number of nuanced vulnerabilities, love of french fries, etc. is what bonds women to each other. And continuing to talk about "women" as this vagina-having-but-otherwise-unspecific group,

rather than looking closer and breaking down the ways in which our specific experiences of the world are impacted by race, sexuality, etc., only perpetuates the inequalities we're supposed to be trying to eradicate.

## NOTE

1. After 40 years in existence, the festival shut down after 2015, following controversies surrounding its "womyn-born-womyn" policy.

*Source:* McKenzie, Mia. (2014). Excerpted from "The Myth of Shared Womanhood and How it Perpetuates Inequality." In *Black Girl Dangerous on Race, Queerness, Class and Gender* (pp. 106–111). Oakland, CA: BDG Press.

# CHAPTER 8

## Intersectional Feminist Frameworks: A Primer

*Canadian Research Institute for the Advancement of Women (CRIAW)*

The Canadian Research Institute for the Advancement of Women (CRIAW) provides tools and resources to support researchers and organizations in advancing social justice and equality for all women. Its focus is on generating and promoting urgently needed feminist research, and making it available for public advocacy and education. CRIAW's projects include *Intersectional Feminist Frameworks*, which aims to promote inclusiveness in research, and *FemNorthNet*, which seeks to engage women living in Northern communities in research on their experiences and needs due to economic restructuring.

## INTRODUCTION

While Canada has experienced substantial economic growth over the last decade, poverty continues to persist and grow in Canada. If you're a woman or child, you may be counted among those most affected. One in seven (2.4 million) women live in poverty in this country.[1]

What's worse—if you are an Aboriginal woman, a woman of colour, an immigrant woman, a woman with a disability, a lone mother, or a senior woman, you face an even greater chance of being counted among Canada's poor. In 2003, 38% of lone-parent families headed by mothers had incomes that were less than the after-tax Low Income Cut-Offs. In comparison, only 13% of lone-parent families headed by fathers, and 7% of two-parent families, faced this situation.[2]

These numbers tell us that despite the efforts of many different groups to end poverty and create a more just society, we've made little headway. In fact, poverty is intensifying for those living closest to society's margins.

After years of working towards greater equality for women, CRIAW believes that different approaches are needed to make real social and economic change—approaches that offer diverse contributions, and that work from Intersectional Feminist Frameworks (IFFs).

IFFs offer alternative frameworks to viewing economic and social change that value and bring together the visions, directions, and goals of women from very diverse experiences and different perspectives.

In this document CRIAW hopes to foster interest in IFFs and encourage their use by women's and social justice organizations.

## A Case for IFFs

Intersectional Feminist Frameworks (IFFs) aim to foster understanding of the many circumstances that combine with discriminatory social practices to produce and sustain inequality and exclusion. IFFs look at how systems of discrimination, such as colonialism and globalization, can impact the combination of a person's

- social or economic status,
- race,
- class,
- gender,
- sexuality,
- ability,
- geographic location,
- citizenship and nationalities, and/or
- refugee and immigrant status.

## Understanding IFFs

While IFFs are not new, many social activists face an ongoing challenge of developing, understanding, and applying these frameworks. However, CRIAW has identified emerging approaches and principles of IFFs that are based on countless conversations and represent many different views.

Some common underlying themes of IFFs include

- using tools for analysis that consider the complexities of women's lives;
- making sure policy analysis is centred on the lives of those most marginalized;
- attempting to think about women's lives in holistic ways when making policies;
- valuing self-reflection in our social justice beliefs so that we are aware of how we are all caught up in systems of power and privilege;
- integrating world views and knowledge that have historically been marginalized;

- understanding that women's varying histories have created many social identities, which place them in different positions of hierarchical power;
- making efforts to challenge binary thinking that sustains inequalities, such as able/disabled, gay/straight, white/black, man/woman, West/East, and North/South; and
- revealing that this binary thinking is a result of unequal power relations.

From these themes it's clear that Intersectional Feminist Frameworks (IFFs) are

- fluid, changing, and continuously negotiated;
- specific to the interaction of a person or group's history, politics, geography, ecology, and culture;
- based upon women's specific locations and situations rather than upon generalizations;
- diverse ways to confront social injustices, which focus on many types of discrimination rather than on just one; and
- locally and globally interconnected.

## THE WAY FORWARD: SHIFTING TO IFFS

Organizations and individuals who actively engage with IFFs' approaches and principles can be sure to uproot some tensions and challenges, as previously held beliefs and focal points are reexamined. But the adoption of IFFs by policy-makers and activists has the potential to generate equitable and broad-based social and economic change.

IFFs crack open oppressive structures and practices without ranking the fight against one oppression over the fight against another. Putting these types of frameworks in place is urgently needed if we hope to one day see a just society.

## Practising IFFs in Social Justice and Policy Work

Today's struggles for equality are being fought from many different levels and perspectives. The following two examples show concrete ways that IFFs could bring about new understandings and strategies for change. The first illustrates the use of IFFs in understanding immigration and refugee policies, while the second takes a look at using IFFs to fight for an end to poverty. [...]

## Immigrant and Migrant Women— Viewed through IFFs

Many activists and policy-makers have applied Gender-Based Analysis (GBA) to Canadian immigration policy and procedures to underscore the inequities faced by women applicants. But the reality of women crossing borders is much more complex than this analysis captures.

The following two situations highlight some of the strengths of using IFFs to address Canadian immigration policy and procedures.

### I. Broadening the Scope of Analysis

GBA use in immigration law captures most women's reliance on male spouses because of the way the Canadian immigration classification system is structured. In this gendered dilemma, immigrant and migrant women may face

- difficulty attending English/French language training programs;
- isolation without English language training;
- inadequate or unaffordable child care;
- unemployment; and
- lack of access to a social support network.

While gender plays a significant role, IFFs take note of many other factors in the immigration process to better understand the interlocking impact of racism, sexism, ageism, and discrimination based on language, sexuality, and/or disability upon migrant women. These factors include the

- demand for poorly paid and highly skilled workers in Canada and other Western countries;
- connections between policies on trade, labour, citizenship, education, training, social welfare, health, military, national security, and human rights; and
- historical links between colonialism, nation formation, global economies, and immigration policies.

### II. Strengthening Domestic Worker Advocacy

For years domestic worker advocacy groups have tried to challenge and change the government's Live-in Caregiver Program.[3] This program forces foreign domestic workers to live with their employer as a visa condition.

There is sizeable evidence that women are more vulnerable to abuse, exploitation, and isolation as live-in workers. Even with this knowledge, Canada refuses to listen to advocacy groups and end the live-in requirement, and Canadians remain unaware of these workers' mistreatment.

At face value the Live-in Caregiver Program appears

- economically supportive of migrant women,
- sympathetic to poor women migrating to Canada, and
- helpful for privileged women and families in Canada who require extensive child care.

Yet the live-in requirement results in workers being

- vulnerable to extended overtime hours without appropriate compensation, if any;
- unable to take skills training courses;
- unable to establish meaningful networks; and
- fearful of reporting any violation on the part of the employer.

IFFs can help build solid support and recognition for domestic workers by viewing gender alongside other forms of oppression that attempt to take away migrant women's power. A review of the Live-in Caregiver Program by advocacy groups and the Canadian government through IFFs would

- expose the role of colonialism and Canada's racist and sexist immigration policies in shaping this program;
- force this issue to become all of society's problem and not only the problem of the women facing the abuse;
- reveal how immigration, employment standards, citizenship, and restrictive labour policies combine to exclude and limit equal treatment of racialized women;
- show how Canada's lack of good-quality, affordable child care spaces mean that affluent Canadian women and their families can meet their child care needs through this program, leading to the exploitation of many migrant women from the South, while lower-income women in Canada, including many women with disabilities, Aboriginal women, racialized women, and women living in rural areas, have few or no child care alternatives; and
- explain the reluctance of governments to address unfair working conditions that are structured into the Live-in Caregiver Program.

## Ending Poverty through IFFs

Many anti-poverty campaigns focus their fight upon income gaps created through capitalism. IFFs, however, provide tremendous opportunities for radically re-envisioning such campaigns. For example, IFFs speak to the

- racialization of poverty through slavery, colonization, and labour migration;

- social exclusion of women already pushed to the margins through limited access to housing, child care, education, social services, citizenship, and a living wage; and
- enforcement of poverty through social and economical policies such as the Indian Act and the Immigration and Refugee Protection Act.

As IFFs are used to deal with poverty, social systems that crush the poor become exposed. IFFs make it clear that poverty is not simply about finding and keeping a job, although that is important. It may also be about

- having access to one's culture, religion, and language;
- being part of a supportive community;
- living in decent housing;
- being accepted for who you are no matter what you look like; and
- having access to health, education, and welfare services where your dignity as a human being equal to all others is respected.

Fighting poverty is about fighting social injustice across many fronts.

\*\*\*\*\*

## Choosing IFFs

IFFs are beginning to show signs of success for some organizations—particularly those with flexible structures open to change. Recently one community and campus radio station surveyed its ethnic programming to find out which shows provided information and discussion on gay, lesbian, bisexual, and transgendered topics. This survey helped identify the need for expression of issues found within already marginalized groups. Station coordinators demonstrated IFFs' principles by

- challenging programmers to think about who their audience includes;
- thinking about their listeners more holistically by offering more inclusive programming and messages; and
- opening up a self-reflection process for the station's staff and the programmers' social justice beliefs.

How and where social justice and feminist activists begin their analysis depends on the specific conditions of the lives of those with whom they are working. It's important to remember that IFFs

- are flexible and open to shifts and changes in the political, social, economic, and cultural order;
- have multiple points of entry, engagement, and discussion that cannot be determined in advance (i.e., gender may not be the most useful entry point to understand particular issues or situations);
- can inform government policy and organizing strategies for activists in many different areas (i.e., labour, anti-poverty, immigration, and environmental issues can be viewed from these frameworks);
- are challenging to adopt—growing pains and tensions are part of the process as previous beliefs are reflected upon; and
- aim to elicit broad-based social and economic change.

As women's movements are now globally connected, an expanded and diverse range of tools and resources for analysis and activism are available to challenge dominant powers. Shifting to IFFs is one way to access the range of marginalized knowledges that are available to social justice activists around the world.

## NOTES

1. CRIAW (2005). *Women and Poverty Fact Sheet* (3rd ed.) Ottawa: Canadian Research Institute for the Advancement of Women.

2. Statistics Canada (2005). *Women in Canada: A Gender-Based Statistical Report* (5th ed.).

3. *Editors' Note*: The Live-in Caregiver Program was suspended in 2014, leaving behind a large backlog of permanent resident applications, along with confusion and fear among migrant caregivers about pathways to permanent residence under the old and new caregiver programs. Caregivers are no longer required to live in their employer's home, but there are new barriers to qualify for permanent residence.

---

*Source:* Canadian Research Institute for the Advancement of Women (CRIAW). (2006). Excerpted from *Intersectional Feminist Frameworks: A Primer* (pp. 5–16, 21–22). Ottawa, ON: CRIAW. Retrieved from: http://www.criaw-icref.ca/en/product/intersectional-feminist-frameworks--a-primer.

## CONCEPTUALIZING INTERSECTIONALITY

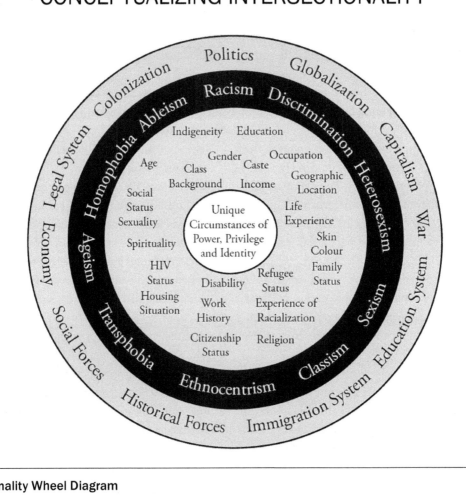

**Intersectionality Wheel Diagram**

- Innermost circle represents a person's unique circumstances.
- Second circle from inside represents aspects of identity.
- Third circle from inside represents different types of discrimination/isms/attitudes that impact identity.
- Outermost circle represents larger forces and structures that work together to reinforce exclusion.

Note: It is impossible to name every variety of discrimination, identity, or structure. These are just examples to help give you a sense of what intersectionality is.

*Source:* Simpson, Joanna. (2009). *Everyone Belongs: A Toolkit for Applying Intersectionality* (p. 5). Ottawa, ON: Canadian Research Institute for the Advancement of Women.

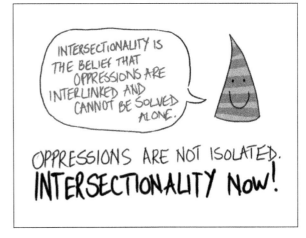

**Bob the Triangle**

*Source:* Dobson, Miriam. (2013). *Intersectionality: A Fun Guide*. Retrieved from: https://miriamdobson.com/2013/07/12/intersectionality-a-fun-guide-now-in-powerpoint-presentation-formation/.

## ACTIVIST INSIGHT: SOJOURNER TRUTH
## (1797–1883)

**Sojourner Truth, circa 1870, National Portrait Gallery, Smithsonian Institution.**

*Source:* Photograph courtesy of Wikimedia Commons.

One critical thematic of feminism that is perennially relevant is the important question of what it means to be a woman under different historical circumstances. Throughout the 1970s and the 1980s, this concern was the subject of major debate as the concept of "global sisterhood" was critiqued for its failure to fully take on board the power relations that divided us.

A century earlier, contestations among feminists involved in anti-slavery struggles and campaigns for women's suffrage also foregrounded similar conflicts. Their memory still resonates with us because the interrelationships between racism, gender, sexuality, and social class were at the heart of these contestations. [The] 19th century political locution "Ain't I a Woman?," by fundamentally challenging all ahistoric or essentialist notions of "woman," neatly captures all the main elements of the debate on "intersectionality." We regard the concept of "intersectionality" as signifying the complex, irreducible, varied, and variable effects which ensue when multiple axes of differentiation—economic, political, cultural, psychic, subjective, and experiential—intersect in historically specific contexts. The concept emphasizes that different dimensions of social life cannot be separated out into discrete and pure strands.

The phrase *Ain't I a Woman?* was first introduced into North American and British feminist lexicon by an enslaved woman, Sojourner Truth (the name she took, instead of her original name, Isabella, when she became a travelling preacher). We know from the biographies of black women such as Sojourner Truth that many of them spoke loud and clear. They would not be caged by the violence of slavery even as they were violently marked by it. Sojourner Truth's 1851 speech at the Women's Rights Convention in Akron, Ohio, very well demonstrates the historical power of a political subject who challenges imperatives of subordination and thereby creates new visions. Sojourner Truth was born into enslavement (to a wealthy Dutch slave-owner living in New York). She campaigned for both the abolition of slavery and for equal rights for women. Since she was illiterate throughout her life, no formal record of the speech exists and, indeed, two different versions of it are in existence.

This cutting-edge speech (in all senses of the term) deconstructs every single major truth-claim about gender in a patriarchal slave social formation. More generally, the discourse offers a devastating critique of the socio-political, economic, and cultural processes of "othering" whilst drawing attention to the simultaneous importance of subjectivity—of subjective pain and violence that the inflictors do not often wish to hear about or acknowledge. Simultaneously, the discourse foregrounds the importance of spirituality to this form of political activism when existential grief touches ground with its unconscious and finds affirmation through a belief in the figure of a Jesus who listens. Political identity here is never taken as a given but is performed through rhetoric and narration. Sojourner Truth's identity claims are thus relational, constructed in relation to white women and all men and clearly demonstrate that what we call "identities" are not objects but processes constituted in and through power relations.

It is in this sense of critique, practice, and inspiration that this discourse holds crucial lessons for us today. Part lament, but defiant, articulating razor-sharp politics but with the sensibility of a poet, the discourse performs the analytic moves of a "decolonised mind." It refuses all final closures. We are all in dire need of decolonized open minds today. Furthermore, Sojourner Truth powerfully challenges essentialist thinking that a particular category of woman is essentially this or essentially that (e.g., that women are necessarily weaker than men or that enslaved black women were not real women).

*Source:* Brah, Avtar, & Phoenix, Ann. (2004). Adapted from "Ain't I A Woman? Revisiting Intersectionality." *Journal of International Women's Studies, 5*(3), 76–77.

## Women's Rights Convention in Akron, Ohio, 1851 Speech

Well, children, where there is so much racket there must be something out of kilter. I think that 'twixt the negroes of the South and the women at the North, all talking about rights, the white men will be in a fix pretty soon. But what's all this here talking about?

That man over there says that women need to be helped into carriages, and lifted over ditches, and to have the best place everywhere. Nobody ever helps me into carriages, or over mud-puddles, or gives me any best place! And ain't I a woman? Look at me! Look at my arm! I have ploughed and planted, and gathered into barns, and no man could head me! And ain't I a woman? I could work as much and eat as much as a man—when I could get it—and bear the lash as well! And ain't I a woman? I have borne thirteen children, and seen most all sold off to slavery, and when I cried out with my mother's grief, none but Jesus heard me! And ain't I a woman?

Then they talk about this thing in the head; what's this they call it? [member of audience whispers, "intellect"]

That's it, honey. What's that got to do with women's rights or negroes' rights? If my cup won't hold but a pint, and yours holds a quart, wouldn't you be mean not to let me have my little half measure full?

Then that little man in black there, he says women can't have as much rights as men, 'cause Christ wasn't a woman! Where did your Christ come from? Where did your Christ come from? From God and a woman! Man had nothing to do with Him.

If the first woman God ever made was strong enough to turn the world upside down all alone, these women together ought to be able to turn it back, and get it right side up again! And now they is asking to do it, the men better let them.

Obliged to you for hearing me, and now old Sojourner ain't got nothing more to say.

---

*Source:* Truth, Sojourner, as recounted by Frances Gage. (1863). *Sojourner Truth Memorial Committee.* Retrieved from: http://sojournertruthmemorial.org/sojourner-truth/her-words/.

# CHAPTER 9

## Reformulating the Feminist Perspective: Giving Voice to Women with Disabilities

*Neita Kay Israelite and Karen Swartz*

Neita Kay Israelite is a professor emerita in the Faculty of Education and Graduate Program in Critical Disability Studies at York University. Her research and teaching focus on disability and inclusion, including university experiences of students with disabilities, identity construction of hard-of-hearing adolescents, and transition and adjustment issues.

Karen Swartz is director of York University's Physical, Sensory & Medical Disability Services, where she supports and advocates on behalf of university students, staff, and faculty living with disabilities. Her research focuses on postsecondary education and disability.

This essay focuses on women with disabilities, a significant and growing segment of Canadian society. According to Statistics Canada (2001), 3.6 million Canadians—12.4% of the population—have disabilities, and more than 50% of them are women. The rate of disability increases with age. Of children from birth to age 14, 3.3% have a disability; amongst working-age adults aged 15 to 64, 9.9% have a disability. This figure rises to 40.5% for Canadians over the age of 65, and more than 50% for those over the age of 75 (Government of Canada, 2002). With more people living longer, and the tendency of women to outlive men, we can expect the number of disabled women to continue to grow.

Persons with disabilities demonstrate relatively high rates of unemployment and low rates of work-related earnings in comparison to those without disabilities. Not surprisingly, women with disabilities have even higher rates of unemployment and lower earnings than their male counterparts (Bunch & Crawford, 1998; Fawcett, 1996). Women with disabilities in Ontario demonstrate exceptionally low rates of workforce participation, and nearly one-third live in poverty.

Despite the growing number of women with disabilities and the challenges they face, disabled women constitute a group that is typically marginalized by the mainstream feminist movement (as well as the masculinist disability movement). As Barbara Cassidy, Robina Lord, and Nancy Mandell point out (1998), feminist analyses of women's oppression tend to take white middle-class women as the norm. Those who differ from this norm with regard to their physical, sensory, or mental status—i.e., women with disabilities—as well as those who differ with regard to factors such as race, class, or ethnicity, are often "left out without anyone noticing they are absent" (Cassidy, Lord, & Mandell, 1998, p. 33).

Our essay begins with an overview of the two major models of disability: the medical model and the social model. Next, we review feminist debates on two critical concerns regarding the social model: (1) its exclusion of the subjective experience of people with disabilities, and (2) its exclusion of discourses on the body and the reality of impairment. Finally, we take up critiques of mainstream feminism by feminist disability theorists.

Throughout this essay, we use personal accounts of women with disabilities to illuminate critical aspects of our discussion. Most of the narratives were collected by second author Karen Swartz (2003) in her participatory qualitative research study of the life transitions of university women with disabilities. These accounts are augmented by narratives of women and girls with disabilities gathered by first author Neita Israelite and her colleagues in several qualitative research projects (Israelite, 2003; Israelite, Karambatsos, Pullan, & Symanzik, 2000; Israelite, Swartz, Huynh, & Tocco, 2004).

The disability field is currently split regarding the use of "disability-first" versus "person-first" terminology (Marks, 1999). Disability-first (i.e., disabled women) is preferred by some women as it acknowledges the community and culture of disabled people and the primacy of disability in their lives; person-first (i.e., women with disabilities) is preferred by other women as it acknowledges the primacy of their personhood. We use both terms in recognition of both points of view.

# MODELS OF DISABILITY

Two major theoretical positions inform attitudes and beliefs about disability: the traditional medical model, and the social model.

## The Medical Model

The medical model assumes that differences from the norm in terms of physical, sensory, or mental capabilities produce a defective member of society. This model holds that any difficulties people with disabilities experience are due to problems within the individual, and not because of environmental, societal, physical, or attitudinal barriers within the larger society. For instance, it is assumed that women with physical disabilities will have problems with public transit because they cannot climb stairs, that women who are deaf will have parenting problems because they cannot hear their children's voices, and that women with visual impairments will have problems with employment because they cannot read work manuals.

A critical dimension of the medical model is the notion of power. Considering disability as a defect within the individual allows those who are not disabled to take charge. This gives rise to a patriarchal-like set of dynamics in which power is held by, and transferred through, nondisabled people, who are often doctors, allied health professionals, clinicians, or educators. Their professional dominance has led to the medicalization of disability—the extension of the power and influence of medicine such that it "dominates the daily lives and experiences of many disabled people" (French & Swain, 2001, p. 738). One byproduct of this form of social control is labelling, a "medical discourse of diagnosis of impairment" (Swain & Cameron, 1999, p. 77), in which the impairment, nature of the remediation, or the individual's assistive devices become a description of her identity. In a study of attitudes toward university students with disabilities

(Israelite et al., 2000), a disabled woman complained about nondisabled peers who identify people with disabilities in terms of their assistive devices:

> One of the things that I consistently state when I speak in public is that I am not my machine.... And I'm sure it can be said ... whether that machine happens to be a computer or a wheelchair or a hearing aid. If you can't see the person, then you haven't seen me.

Some disabled people internalize medicalized identities to such an extent that they even refer to themselves in terms of a medical definition rather than "an affirming self-definition" (Marks, 1999, p. 69). In interviews with hard-of-hearing high school students (Israelite, 2003), one young woman with congenital (from birth) hearing loss called herself a "hearing aid" student; another with recently acquired loss said, "Now I am a 'hearing impaired.'"

## The Social Model

In contrast to the medical model, the social model views disability as a social identity. It holds that the "problem" of disability is inherent not in the individual, but rather in the social structure. In social model theory, the following distinction is made between impairment and disability:

> Impairment is the functional limitation within the individual caused by physical, mental, or sensory impairment. Disability is the loss or limitation of opportunities to take part in the normal life of a community on an equal level with others due to physical and social barriers. (Barnes, 1991, p. 2)

Therefore, the cause of disability is not impairment per se, but society's failure to provide appropriate services and to adequately ensure that the needs of people with disabilities are fully taken into account. Disability,

from this perspective, is constructed as all the things that impose restrictions on people with disabilities, such as individual prejudice, institutional discrimination, inequitable legislation, and restrictive school and work environments. Participants in a study of school-to-work transitions (Israelite et al., 2004) were disabled by a range of restrictions in the workplace. For instance, when a woman with a physical impairment approached a potential place of employment for a job application, she discovered that the human resources building was not wheelchair accessible:

> I went into the human resources building to pick up an application and I couldn't get in because I got stuck. I had to go all the way around to the back and come through, and I just knew that it didn't feel right. If you can't get into the human resources building to get an application, you know, it already discourages you by thinking, "Why would they want me when they wouldn't even let me in?"

Another woman in the study felt that prospective employers seriously underestimated the abilities of disabled people:

> They think, they assume, the job is too big for you. They underestimate you. And they have no faith in you or confidence. And you tell them you can do it successfully ... But generally they'll tell you, "Oh, you can't do it."

The attitudes this woman describes exemplify some of the taken-for-granted or commonly held beliefs that people without disabilities hold about those with disabilities. In our culture, physical, sensory, and mental impairments are often considered to have far-reaching effects on ability. Although such beliefs may be unconscious, they nevertheless strongly influence behaviour and expectations.

Taken-for-granted beliefs play a large part in widespread assumptions of dysfunction regarding the sexuality of disabled women, such as the myth that they are unfit as sexual partners. The women in Karen Swartz's (2003, pp. 21, 22) study, for example, said that, as they were growing up, they got the constant message from nondisabled peers that they were undesirable:

> What I found in high school, a lot of times, was when you try to pursue somebody you're interested in, they wouldn't even look at you twice. There was that perception of, "Oh, you have a disability, part of your body is broken, so therefore you're not a sexual being."

Taken-for-granted beliefs also contribute to marginalization, a process that relegates women who "fall out of the scope of what is currently defined as socially acceptable" (Rauscher & McClintock, 1997, p. 198) to the outer margins of economic and social power and the cultural life of a society, leading to their exclusion from a range of social, cultural, and economic experiences that are part of the everyday lives of non-disabled women. [...]

Since its original conception in Britain more than two decades ago, the social model has had a profound influence on the lives of people with disabilities. At the theoretical level, this model demonstrates "how the previously taken-for-granted, naturalistic category 'disability' is in reality an artificial and exclusionary social construction that penalizes those people who do not conform to mainstream expectations of appearance, behaviour, and/or economic performance" (Tregaskis, 2002, p. 457).

At the personal level, the social model has "liberated individual disabled people from the burden of personal tragedy, the oppression of individual inadequacies" (Morris, 1996, p. 12) by helping them understand that it is an impaired society, not their impaired bodies, that is responsible for the discrimination, marginalization, and exclusion they face.

# FEMINIST CRITIQUES OF THE SOCIAL MODEL

Although the social model has been beneficial to disabled people in both theory and praxis, it has been criticized for its failure to address the complexity of factors that shape the production of disability. Some prominent feminist debates deal with the exclusion of the subjective experience of people with disabilities from many social model accounts as well as the exclusion of discussions of the body and the reality of impairment.

## Subjective Experience and Social Model Theory

Feminists with disabilities such as Susan Wendell (1996), Jenny Morris (1996), and Carol Thomas (1999) have put forward accounts of disability in which personal narratives play an important role. Given the inequitable power differentials that characterize relations between women with and without disabilities, these women emphasize the necessity of foregrounding the individual experiences of disabled women as a vehicle for understanding their collective oppressions (Tregaskis, 2002). Other writers (e.g., Sheldon, 1999) argue that such analyses are too individualized and prioritize subjective experiences of disability over more theoretical explanations. Our position, however, is in line with Carol Thomas, who points out that "by taking the personal experiences of disabled women as their starting point and writing themselves into their own analyses, disabled feminist writers ... are thus building upon well-established practices among feminist writers more generally" (1999, p. 70). Giving voice to the personal narratives of women with disabilities is also an important way of increasing the general public's sense of social responsibility while informing and clarifying social model theory.

## The Body, Impairment, and Social Model Theory

Recent critiques of the social model focus on the exclusion of discussions of the body and impairment from many social model accounts. Many feminist disability theorists (e.g., Crow, 1996; French, 1994; Morris, 1991; Thomas, 1999; Wendell, 1996) and some masculinist disability theorists (e.g., Abberley, 1987; Hughes, 1999; Hughes & Paterson, 1997; Paterson & Hughes, 1999) take issue with the social model because it neither connects with the embodied experience nor the pain associated with impairment. Some theorists (e.g., French, 1994; Wendell, 1996) argue that the only way for the social model to move forward is to integrate the experience of impairment—the pain and the real limitations—with the experience of disability. Susan Wendell, who has an acquired physical disability, writes that disabled feminists should be discussing "how to live with the suffering body, with that which cannot be noticed without pain, and that which cannot be celebrated without ambivalence" (1996, p. 179). [...]

Sally French, who has a visual impairment, points out that it is her actual lack of visual acuity, and not some barrier created by a sighted society, that prevents her from recognizing people and reading nonverbal cues in social situations.

> While I agree with the basic tenets of [the social] model and consider it to be the most important way forward for disabled people, I believe that some of the most profound problems experienced by people with certain impairments are difficult, if not impossible, to solve by social manipulation. (1993, p. 17)

Social model proponents such as Michael Oliver (1996) point out that the original goal of the social model, when it was proposed more than 20 years ago, was to eradicate what they identify as the "true causes" of disability: societal discrimination and prejudice.

The fact that these causes still permeate the lives of women with disabilities is exemplified by their reaction to workplace prejudice and discrimination in our study of school-to-work transitions (Israelite et al., 2004, p. 20):

> It gets right to the core of your identity. You begin to question, "What is my role in this world."

> I thought, "Oh my God, this is what it's like out there. Oh my God, how am I going to find a job?"

Some disability scholars are calling for an updated version of the social model, one that acknowledges the relevance of bodily experience to the lives of disabled people. They argue that by not incorporating impairment, the social model concedes the body to medicine, thus giving tacit permission for it to be understood in terms of the medical model (Hughes & Paterson, 1997). Bill Hughes and Kevin Paterson (1997) assert that there is a need to wrest control of the impairment discourse from the medical profession and to establish the impaired body as an integral part of what it means to be disabled. This would entail, in part, "tackling the very real repulsion that society feels for the impaired body" (Tregaskis, 2002, p. 464). This repulsion was something that most of the participants in Karen Swartz's (2003, p. 27) study had not only experienced, but also internalized, to a significant extent. One woman explained:

> What you stare at in the mirror is not just something that is going to go away. You're not going to wake up from a dream. This is reality.

Impairment theory provides an explanation that, in keeping with the social model, places the responsibility for "the problem of repulsion" on nondisabled people. Claire Tregaskis (2002) explains that, "in reality, it is the non-disabled gaze which creates abnormality, and that actually it is the gaze that is disfigured, not the [disabled] 'other' who is being gazed at" (p. 463). This point is clearly illustrated in the comments of two women in Karen Swartz's (2003, p. 27) study:

> The only time I saw myself as disabled was when … someone said, "Oh what happened to you?" [I would reply] "Oh what do you mean what happened to me? Oh yeah. Oh God. Oh you're talking about that."

> [You have to] realize what you are feeling isn't you. It is the images that somebody else has transferred on to you.

*****

## DISABILITY THEORISTS CRITIQUE FEMINIST THEORY

Many women with disabilities write that they feel marginalized within the feminist movement. Their experience is that mainstream feminist theories tend to privilege "the functional capabilities and social roles characteristic of 'normal' women" (Kittay, Schriempf, Silvers, & Wendell, 2001, p. viii), often not taking women with disabilities into account. Feminist disability scholars share in the marginalization. Carol Thomas cites the cases of Jenny Morris (1991, 1996) and Susan Wendell (1996), both of whom have acquired disabilities. These scholars were accepted as feminist thinkers and writers until they became disabled; after that, they, too, found themselves marginalized from feminist scholarship.

According to feminist scholars Fine and Asch (1988):

> Women with disabilities traditionally have been ignored not only by those concerned about disability but also by those examining

women's experiences. Even the feminist scholars to whom we owe great intellectual and political debts have perpetuated this neglect. The popular view of women with disabilities has been one mixed with repugnance. Perceiving disabled women as childlike, helpless, and victimized, nondisabled women have severed them from the sisterhood in an effort to advance more powerful, competent, and appealing female icons. As one feminist academic said to the nondisabled co-author of this essay: "Why study women with disabilities? They reinforce traditional stereotypes of women being dependent, passive and needy." (pp. 3–4)

Several of Karen Swartz's (2003) participants said that during their childhood, doctors, teachers, counselors, and even some family members encouraged them, through both implicit and explicit messages, to be passive and dependent rather than strong and independent. They were dismayed when they got to university to find that such attitudes still predominated. One woman sought out courses in Women's Studies in the hopes of finding answers to her questions about the oppression of disabled women. She was dismayed to find that even a course on the history of women did not address this issue:

> I won't take a women's history course because it doesn't cover disabled women. You can't tell me that disabled women didn't exist.… I think we need to make professors more aware and almost demand that it get put on the curriculum. I mean if they can study women's issues, gay issues, African American issues. We are part of society and we deserve to be studied. (p. 37)

Feminist disability scholars agree with this student's assessment of university programs and have proposed ways of infusing disability issues into the postsecondary curriculum and making the experience of disabled women more central to teaching and research in Women's Studies (e.g., Garland-Thomson 2002; Linton, 1997). Rosemary Garland-Thomson (2002) argues for the positioning of feminist disability studies as a field of academic study and the inclusion of feminist disability theory as a major subgenre of feminist theory. Garland-Thomson is but one of many feminist scholars calling for the inclusion of the ability/disability binary as a category of analysis alongside gender, race, age, and social class in feminist analyses of oppression.

*\*\*\*\*\**

Disability is a fluid category. Some women are born with disabilities; others acquire them. Some are disabled for some portion of their lives, others for their whole lives. Virtually all women can expect to become disabled if they live long enough. Within the disability movement, masculinist disability scholars have been too slow to acknowledge the gendered nature of disability. Within the feminist movement, nondisabled feminist scholars have been too slow to acknowledge the importance of the disability to identity construction and feminist analyses of oppression. Sadly, what Marion Blackwell-Stratton, Mary Lou Breslin, Arlean Mayerson, and Susan Bailey stated in 1988 still holds true: "For the disabled feminist, neither the disability movement nor the women's movement fully addresses her concerns" (p. 307).

As Garland-Thomson so aptly states:

> Disability—like gender—is a concept that pervades all aspects of culture: its structuring institutions, social identities, cultural practices, political positions, historical communities, and the shared human experience of embodiment.... To understand how disability operates is to understand what it means to be fully human. (2002, p. 4)

## REFERENCES

Abberley, P. (1987). The concept of oppression and the development of a social theory of disability. *Disability, Handicap, and Society*, 2, 5–20.

Barnes, C. (1991). *Disabled People in Britain and Discrimination: A Case for Anti-Discrimination Legislation*. London: Hurst.

Blackwell-Stratton, M., Breslin, M., Mayerson, A., & Bailey, S. (1988). Smashing icons: Disabled women and the disability and women's movements. In M. Fine & A. Asch (Eds.), *Women with Disabilities: Essays in Psychology, Culture, and Politics* (pp. 306–332). Philadelphia: Temple University Press.

Bunch, M., & Crawford, C. (1998, June). *Persons with Disabilities: Literature Review of the Factors Affecting Employment and Labor Force Transitions*. Hull: Human Resources Development Canada. Retrieved June 19, 2003, from http://www.hrdc-drhc.gc.ca/sp-ps/arb-dgra/publications/research/disability.shtml.

Cassidy, B., Lord, R., & Mandell, N. (1998). Silenced and forgotten women: Race, poverty, and disability. In N. Mandell (Ed.), *Feminist Issues: Race, Class, and Sexuality* (2nd ed.) (pp. 27–54). Toronto: Prentice-Hall.

Crow, L. (1996). Including all of our lives: Renewing the social model of disability. In J. Morris (Ed.), *Encounters with Strangers: Feminism and Disability* (pp. 206–226). London: Women's Press.

Fawcett, G. (1996). *Living with Disability in Canada: An Economic Portrait*. Hull: Office for Disability Issues, Human Resources Development Canada.

Fine, M., & Asch, A. (Eds.). (1988). *Women with Disabilities: Essays in Psychology, Culture, and Politics*. Philadelphia: Temple University Press.

French, S. (1993). Disability, impairment, or something in between. In J. Swain, V. Finkelstein, S. French, & M. Oliver (Eds.), *Disabling Barriers, Enabling Environments*. Buckingham: Open University Press.

French, S. (1994). *On Equal Terms: Working with Disabled People*. Oxford: Butterworth-Heinemann.

French, S., & Swain, J. (2001). The relationship between disabled people and health and welfare professionals. In G. Albrecht, K. Seelman, & M. Bury (Eds.), *Handbook of Disability Studies* (pp. 734–753). Thousand Oaks: Sage.

Garland-Thomson, R. (2002). Integrating disability theory, transforming feminist theory. *Feminist Disability Studies* [Special issue] [Electronic version]. *NWSA Journal*, 14 (3), 1–32.

Government of Canada. (2002). *Advancing the Inclusion of Persons with Disabilities*. Hull: Human Resources Development Canada. Retrieved March 12, 2004, from www.hrdc-drhc.gc.ca/bcph-odi.

Hughes, B. (1999). The construction of impairment: Modernity and the aesthetic of oppression. *Disability & Society*, 14, 155–172.

Hughes, B., & Paterson, K. (1997). The social model of disability and the disappearing body: Towards a sociology of impairment. *Disability & Society*, 12, 325–340.

Israelite, N. (2003). *Identity construction of hard-of-hearing adolescents*. Unpublished raw data.

Israelite, N., Karambatsos, S., Pullan, J., & Symanzik, A. (2000, June). *Attitudes of university students toward students with disabilities*. Paper presented at the annual meeting of the Society for Disability Studies, Chicago, IL.

Israelite, N., Swartz, K., Huynh, J., & Tocco, A. (2004). *Postsecondary students and graduates with disabilities: The school-to-work transition*. Manuscript submitted for publication.

Kittay, E., Schriempf, A., Silvers, A., & Wendell, S. (2001). Introduction. *Feminism and Disability* [Special issue] [Electronic version]. *Hypatia*, 16 (4), vii–xii.

Linton, S. (1997). *Claiming Disability: Knowledge and Identity*. New York: New York University Press, p. 94.

Marks, D. (1999). *Disability: Controversial Debates and Conversations*. London: Routledge.

Morris, J. (1991). *Pride against Prejudice: Transforming Attitudes to Disability*. London: Women's Press.

Morris, J. (1996). Introduction. In J. Morris (Ed.), *Encounters with Strangers: Feminism and Disability* (pp. 1–16). London: Women's Press.

Oliver, M. (1996). *Understanding Disability: From Theory to Practice*. New York: St. Martin's Press.

Paterson, K., & Hughes, B. (1999). Disability studies and phenomenology: The carnal politics of everyday life. *Disability & Society*, 14, 597–610.

Rauscher, L., & McClintock, J. (1997). Ableism curriculum design. In M. Adams, L.A. Bell, & P. Griffen (Eds.), *Teaching for Diversity and Social Justice* (pp. 198–231). New York: Routledge.

Sheldon, A. (1999). Personal and perplexing: Feminist disability politics evaluated. *Disability & Society*, 14, 643–657.

Swain, J., & Cameron, C. (1999). Unless otherwise stated: Discourses of labeling and coming out. In M. Corker & S. French (Eds.), *Disability Discourse* (pp. 68–78). Buckingham: Open University Press.

Swartz, K. (2003). *Life transitions of student with disabilities revisited: A feminist approach*. Unpublished manuscript. York University, Toronto, Canada.

Thomas, C. (1999). *Female Forms: Experiencing and Understanding Disability*. Buckingham: Open University Press.

Tregaskis, C. (2002). Social model theory: The story so far. *Disability & Society*, 17, 457–470.

Wendell, S. (1996). *The Rejected Body: Feminist Philosophical Reflections on Disability*. New York: Routledge.

**Source:** Isrealite, Neita Kay, & Swartz, Karen. (2004). "Reformulating the Feminist Perspective: Giving Voice to Women with Disabilities." In Althea Prince & Susan Silva-Wayne (Eds.), *Feminisms and Womanisms: A Women's Studies Reader* (pp. 471–479). Toronto, ON: Women's Press.

# CHAPTER 10

## The Question of Gender

*Raewyn Connell and Rebecca Pearse*

Raewyn Connell is a professor emerita at the University of Sydney. She was one of the founders of the study of masculinity and published *Masculinities* in 1995. The concept of "hegemonic masculinity" was introduced in the book and has been particularly influential and controversial. Connell has been an advisor to United Nations initiatives on gender equality and peacemaking.

Rebecca Pearse is a professor in the Department of Political Economy at the University of Sydney. Previously, she was a post-doctoral fellow working at the Australian National University on a project entitled *Gendered Excellence in the Social Sciences.* Pearse has expertise in the political economy of climate and energy policy, social responses to environmental change, the sociology of knowledge, and feminism and gender relations.

## NOTICING GENDER

One night a year, the attention of the TV-watching world is focused on Hollywood's most spectacular event, the Oscar award ceremony. Famous people are driven up in limousines in front of an enthusiastic crowd, and in a blizzard of camera flashes they walk into the auditorium—the men in tuxedoes striding easily, the women going cautiously because they are wearing low-cut gowns and high-heeled shoes. As the evening wears on, awards are given out for film score, camera work, script writing, direction, best foreign film, and so on. But in the categories that concern the people you see on screen when you go to the movies, there are two awards given: best actor and best actress; best supporting actor and best supporting actress.

The internet is saturated with images of glamorous people, from models in advertisements to all kind of celebrities and public figures. When pop star Miley Cyrus performed at the MTV Music Video Awards (VMA) in 2013, the images of her sexually provocative dancing travelled at incredible speed across the world. After the event, Cyrus tweeted, "Smilers! My VMA performance had 306,000 tweets per minute. That's more than the blackout or Superbowl! [*sic*]." Major news and entertainment websites, social media, blogs, and Youtube channels sent waves of chatter through cyberspace. Much of it was about whether the public was prepared for the transformation of Cyrus from child star to sex symbol.

Whilst women's bodies are common elements of the visual images we consume on the web, women are much less likely to be producing web content. In a recent member survey, Wikipedia discovered that less than 15 per cent of people who write content for the online encyclopedia are women. Internet access is also uneven. In 2013 the multinational computer technology firm Intel found that nearly 25 per cent fewer women internationally have internet access than men. Whilst in a small number of affluent nations like France and the United States women actually have slightly higher rates of internet access, the gender gap reaches nearly 45 per cent in sub-Saharan Africa.

In politics women continue to be the minority. Every year a "family photo" is taken at G20 meetings, where heads of government and their senior finance and central bank representatives meet to discuss the international financial system. In 2013, four women stood among twenty national leaders in the photo, representing Germany, Brazil, South Korea, and Argentina. The imbalance is commonly more pronounced. There has never been a woman head of government in modern Russia, China, France, Japan, Egypt, Nigeria, South Africa, or Mexico. There has only been one each in the history of Brazil, Germany, Britain, Indonesia, and Australia. Statistics from the Inter-Parliamentary Union showed that in 2013, 79.1 per cent of members of the world's parliaments were men.

Among senior ministers the predominance of men is even higher. In 2012, only four countries in the world had women making up half of a national ministry (Norway, Sweden, Finland, and Iceland). More typical figures for women in ministerial roles were 21 per cent (Australia, Mexico), 11 per cent (China, Indonesia, Japan), 6 per cent (Malaysia), and 0 per cent (Lebanon, Papua New Guinea). The few women who do get to this level are usually given the job of running welfare or education ministries. Men keep control of taxation, investment, technology, international relations, police, and the military. Every

Secretary-General of the United Nations and every head of the World Bank has been a man.

Women's representation in politics has changed slowly over time, and with difficulty. French lawyer Christine Lagard was the first woman ever to head the International Monetary Fund in 2011. The world average number of women in parliaments increased from 10 per cent in 1995 to 20 per cent in 2012. Australia's first women Prime Minister, Julia Gillard, served for three years with a record eight women in ministry and five in cabinet. She was then thrown out of power in a party coup. The new conservative government elected in 2013 had only one woman in cabinet.

What is true of politics is also true of business. Of the top 200 businesses listed on the Australian stock exchange in 2012 (including those that publish the mass-circulation magazines), just seven had a woman as Chief Executive Officer (CEO). Of the 500 giant international corporations listed in Fortune magazine's 'Global 500' in 2013, just 22 had a woman CEO. Such figures are usually presented by saying that women now form 4.4 per cent of the top business leadership around the world. It's more informative to say that men compose 95.6 per cent of that leadership.

Women are a substantial part of the paid workforce, lower down the hierarchy. They are mostly concentrated in service jobs—clerical work, call centres, cleaning, serving food, and professions connected with caring for the young and the sick, i.e., teaching and nursing. In some parts of the world, women are also valued as industrial workers, for instance in microprocessor plants, because of their supposedly 'nimble fingers'. Though the detailed division between men's and women's work varies in different parts of the world, it is common for men to predominate in heavy industry, mining, transport, indeed in most jobs that involve any machinery except a sewing machine. World-wide, men are a large majority of the workforce in management, accountancy, law, and technical professions such as engineering and computing.

Behind the paid workforce is another form of work—unpaid domestic and care work. In all contemporary societies for which we have statistics, women do most of the cleaning, cooking and sewing, most of the work of looking after children, and almost all of the work of caring for babies. (If you don't think this is work, you haven't done it yet.) This work is often associated with a cultural definition of women as caring, gentle, self-sacrificing, and industrious, i.e., as good mothers. Being a good father is rarely associated with cutting school lunches and wiping babies' bottoms—though there are now interesting attempts to promote what in Mexico has been called '*paternidad afectiva*', i.e., emotionally engaged fatherhood. Normally, fathers are supposed to be decision-makers and breadwinners, to consume the services provided by women and represent the family in the outside world.

Women as a group are less likely to be out in the public world than men, and, when they are, have fewer resources. In almost all parts of the world, men are more likely to have a paid job. The world 'economic activity rate' for women has crept up, but is still just over two-thirds of the rate for men. The main exceptions are Scandinavia and parts of West Africa, where women's relative labour force participation rates are unusually high. But in some Arab states, women's participation rates are one-quarter the rate for men, and in much of South Asia and Latin America, they are about half the rate for men.

Once women are in the paid workforce, how do their wages compare? Over thirty years after the United Nations adopted the Convention on the Elimination of All Forms of Discrimination against Women (CEDAW) in 1979, nowhere in the world are women's earned incomes equal to men's. Women are often engaged in low-wage employment, and still receive 18 per cent less than men's average wages. In some countries, the gender pay gap is much bigger. Zambia has the largest gender pay gap at almost 46 per cent (2005), followed by South Korea with 43 per cent (2007) and Azerbaijan with 37 per cent (2008). Part of any gender gap in income can be explained by the pattern of women being more likely to work fewer hours and more likely to

be unemployed. Other reasons relate to discriminatory wage practices and to women's overrepresentation in low-paid jobs.

Therefore, most women in the world, especially women with children, are economically dependent on men. Some men believe that women who are dependent on them must be their property. This is a common scenario in domestic violence: when dependent women don't conform to demands from their husband or boyfriend, they are beaten. This creates a dilemma for the women, which is very familiar to domestic violence services. They can stay, and put themselves and their children at high risk of further violence; or go, and lose their home, economic support, and status in the community. If they go, certain husbands are so infuriated that they pursue and kill the wives and even the children.

Men are not beaten up by their spouses so often, but men are at risk of other forms of violence. Most assaults reported to the police, in countries with good statistics on the matter, are by men on other men. Some men are beaten, indeed some are murdered, simply because they are thought to be homosexual; and some of this violence comes from the police. Most of the prisoners in gaols are men. In the United States, which has the biggest prison system in the world, the prison population in 2011 was 1.59 million, and 93 per cent of them were men. Most deaths in combat are of men, because men make up the vast majority of the troops in armies and militias. Most industrial accidents involve men, because men are most of the workforce in dangerous industries such as construction and mining.

Men are involved disproportionately in violence partly because they have been prepared for it. Though patterns of child rearing differ between cultures, the situation in Australia is not unusual. Australian boys are steered towards competitive sports such as football, where physical dominance is celebrated, from an early age—by their fathers, by schools, and by the mass media. Boys also come under peer pressure to show bravery and toughness, and learn to fear being classified as *sissies* or *poofters* (a local term meaning effeminate or homosexual). Being capable of violence becomes a social resource. Working-class boys, who don't have the other resources that will lead to a professional career, become the main recruits into jobs that require the use of force: police, the military, private security, blue-collar crime, and professional sport. It is mainly young women who are recruited into the jobs that repair the consequences of violence: nursing, psychology, and social work.

So far, we have listed an assortment of facts, about mass media, about politics and business, about families, and about growing up. Are these random? Modern thought about gender starts with the recognition that they are not. These facts form a pattern; they make sense when seen as parts of the overall gender arrangement, which this chapter will call the 'gender order,' of contemporary societies.

To notice the existence of the gender order is easy; to understand it is not. Conflicting theories of gender now exist [...], and some problems about gender are genuinely difficult to resolve. Yet we now have a rich resource of knowledge about gender, derived from decades of research, and a fund of practical experience from gender reform. We now have a better basis for understanding gender issues than any previous generation had.

## UNDERSTANDING GENDER

In everyday life we take gender for granted. We instantly recognize a person as a man or woman, girl or boy. We arrange everyday business around the distinction. Conventional marriages require one of each. Mixed doubles tennis requires two of each, but most sports require one kind at a time.

Most years, next to Oscar night, the most popular television broadcast in the world is said to be the American Super Bowl, another strikingly gendered event: large armoured men crash into each other while chasing a pointed leather bladder, and thin women in short skirts dance and smile in the pauses. Most of us cannot crash or dance nearly so well, but we do our best in other ways. As women or men we slip our feet into differently shaped shoes, button our shirts on opposite sides, get our heads clipped by different hairdressers, buy our pants in separate shops, and take them off in separate toilets.

These arrangements are so familiar that they can seem part of the order of nature. Belief that gender distinction is 'natural' makes it scandalous when people don't follow the pattern—for instance, when people of the same gender fall in love with each other. So homosexuality is frequently declared 'unnatural' and bad.

But if having sex with a fellow-woman or a fellow-man is unnatural, why have a law against it? We don't provide penalties for violating the third law of thermodynamics. Anti-gay ordinances in US cities, police harassment of gay men in Senegal, the criminalization of women's adultery in Islamic Sharia law, the imprisonment of transsexual women for violating public order—such things only make sense because these matters are *not* fixed by nature.

These events are part of an enormous social effort to channel people's behaviour. Ideas about gender-appropriate behaviour are constantly being circulated, not only by legislators but also by priests, parents, teachers, advertisers, retail mall owners, talk-show hosts, and disc jockeys. Events like Oscar night and the Super Bowl are not just consequences of our ideas about gender difference. They also help to *create* gender difference, by displays of exemplary masculinities and femininities.

Being a man or a woman, then, is not a pre-determined state. It is a *becoming*, a condition actively under construction. The pioneering French feminist Simone de Beauvoir put this in a classic phrase: 'One is not born, but rather becomes, a woman.' Though the positions of women and men are not simply parallel, the principle is also true for men: one is not born masculine, but has to become a man.

This process is often discussed as the development of 'gender identity', [...] a name for the sense of belonging to a gender category. Identity includes our ideas of what that belonging means, what kind of person we are, in consequence of being a woman or a man. These ideas are not presented to the baby as a package at the beginning of life. They develop (there is some controversy about exactly when), and are filled out in detail over a long period of years, as we grow up.

As de Beauvoir further recognized, this business of becoming a gendered person follows many different paths, involves many tensions and ambiguities, and sometimes produces unstable results. Part of the mystery of gender is how a pattern that on the surface appears so stark and rigid, on close examination turns out so complex and uncertain.

So we cannot think of womanhood or manhood as fixed by nature. But neither should we think of them as simply imposed from outside, by social norms or pressure from authorities. People construct themselves as masculine or feminine. We claim a place in the gender order—or respond to the place we have been given—by the way we conduct ourselves in everyday life.

Most people do this willingly, and often enjoy the gender polarity. Yet gender ambiguities are not rare. There are masculine women and feminine men. There are women in love with other women, and men in love with other men. There are women who are heads of households, and men who bring up children. There are women who are soldiers, and men who are nurses. Sometimes the development of 'gender identity' results in intermediate, blended, or sharply contradictory patterns, for which we use terms like *effeminate*, *camp*, *queer*, and *transgender*.

Psychological research suggests that the great majority of us combine masculine and feminine characteristics, in varying blends, rather than being all one or all the other. Gender ambiguity can be an object of fascination and desire, as well as disgust. Gender impersonations are familiar in both popular and high culture, from the cross-dressed actors of Shakespeare's stage to movies starring transsexual women and drag queens like *Hedwig and the Angry Inch* (2001), *Priscilla, Queen of the Desert* (2004), and *Hairspray* (2007).

There is certainly enough gender blending to provoke heated opposition from movements dedicated to re-establishing 'the traditional family', 'true femininity,' or 'real masculinity'. By 1988 Pope John Paul II had become so concerned that he issued an Apostolic Letter, *On the Dignity and Vocation of Women*, reminding everyone that women were created for motherhood and their functions should not get mixed up with those of men. In a Christmas address in 2012, Pope Benedict XVI criticized gender theory directly. He argued: "People dispute the idea that they have a nature, given by their bodily identity that serves as a defining element of the human being. They deny their nature and decide that it is not something previously given to them, but that they make it for themselves." This is a good summary of a central insight from gender theory. Of course, the Pope was arguing against it, saying that an essential, biological nature should determine our personal and public lives. These efforts to maintain essentialist ideas about fixed womanhood and manhood are themselves strong evidence that the boundaries are none too stable.

But these are not just boundaries; they are also inequalities. Most churches and mosques are run exclusively by men, and this is part of a larger pattern. Most corporate wealth is in the hands of men, most big institutions are run by men, and most science and technology is controlled by men. In many countries, including some with very large populations, women are less likely than men to have been taught to read. For instance, recent adult literacy rates in India stood at 75 per cent for men and 51 per cent for women; in Nigeria, 72 per cent for men and 50 per cent for women. On a world scale, two-thirds of illiterate people are women. In countries like the United States, Australia, Italy, and Turkey, middle-class women have gained full access to higher education and have made inroads into middle management and professions. But even in those countries many informal barriers operate to keep the very top levels of power and wealth mostly a world of men.

There is also unequal respect. In many situations, including the cheerleaders at the football game, women are treated as marginal to the main action, or as the objects of men's desire. Whole genres of humour—bimbo jokes, woman-driver jokes, mother-in-law jokes—are based on contempt for women's triviality and stupidity. A whole industry, ranging from heavy pornography and prostitution to soft-core advertising, markets women's bodies as objects of consumption by men. Equal opportunity reforms in the workplace often run into a refusal by men to be under the authority of a woman. Not only do most religions prevent women from holding major religious office, they often treat women symbolically as a source of defilement for men.

Though men in general benefit from the inequalities of the gender order, they do not benefit equally. Indeed, many pay a considerable price. Boys and men who depart from dominant definitions of masculinity because they are gay, effeminate, or considered wimpish are often subject to verbal abuse and discrimination, and are sometimes the targets of violence. Men who conform to dominant definitions of masculinity may also pay a price. Research on men's health shows that men have a higher rate of industrial accidents than women, have a higher rate of death by violence, tend to eat a worse diet and drink more alcohol, and (not surprisingly) have more sporting injuries. In 2012, the life expectancy for men in the United States was calculated at 76 years, compared with 81 years for women. In Russia, after the restoration of capitalism, life expectancy for men was 63 years, compared with 75 years for women.

Gender arrangements are thus, at the same time, sources of pleasure, recognition, and identity, and sources of injustice and harm. This means that gender is inherently political—but it also means the politics can be complicated and difficult.

Inequality and oppression in the gender order have repeatedly led to demands for reform. Movements for change include campaigns for women's right to vote, and for women's presence in anti-colonial movements and representation in independent governments. There are campaigns for equal pay, for women's right to own property, for homosexual law reform, for women's trade unionism, for equal employment opportunity, for reproductive rights, for the human rights of transsexual men and women and transgender people; and campaigns against discrimination in education, against sexist media, against rape and domestic violence.

Political campaigns resisting some of these changes, or seeking counter-changes, have also arisen. The scene of gender politics currently includes anti-gay campaigns, anti-abortion ('pro-life') campaigns, a spectrum of men's movements, and a complex international debate about links between Western feminism and Western cultural dominance in the world. One of the most striking waves of change underway now is the legalization of gay marriage. Same-sex couples are now able to marry in 13 US states and Washington, DC.[1] This is a fast-growing reform movement mostly in the global North, but also in Latin America. Of the 16 countries that permit gay men and lesbians to marry, 9 have made this reform since 2010.

In this history, the feminist and gay movements of the 1960s–1970s were pivotal. They did not reach all their political goals, but they had a profound cultural impact. They called attention to a whole realm of human reality that was poorly understood, and thus created a demand for understanding as well as action. This was the historical take-off point of contemporary gender research. Political practice launched a deep change—which increasingly seems like a revolution—in human knowledge.

## NOTE ON SOURCES

Most of the statistics mentioned in this chapter, such as income, economic activity rates, and literacy, can be found in the United Nations Development Programme's *Human Development Report* (UNDP 2013), or online tables regularly published by the United Nations Statistics Division. Figures on parliamentary representation and numbers of ministers are from Inter-Parliamentary Union (2013), and on managers, from the Workplace Gender Equality Agency, *Fortune*, and CNN. Sources of information on men's health can be found in Schofield et al. (2000). Gender wage gap figures are taken from the International Trade Union Confederation report *Frozen in Time: Gender Pay Gap Unchanged for 10 Years* (ITUC 2012). The quotation on *woman* is from Simone de Beauvoir's *The Second Sex* (1949: 295).

## NOTE

1. In 2015, the US Supreme Court ruled that the constitution guarantees the right to same-sex marriage.

## REFERENCES

de Beauvoir, Simone. 1949. *The Second Sex*. Harmondsworth: Penguin (1972 edition).

Inter-Parliamentary Union. 2013. 'Women in national parliaments: Situation as of 1 July', http://ipu.org/wmn-e/world.htm (accessed 20 March 2014).

ITUC. 2012. *Frozen in Time: Gender Pay Gap Unchanged for 10 Years*. Brussels: International Trade Union Confederation.

Schofield, T., R.W. Connell, I. Walker, J. Wood, and D. Butland. 2000. 'Understanding men's health: A gender relations approach to masculinity, health and illness', *Journal of American College Health* 48 (6): 247–56.

UNDP. 2013. *Human Development Report 2013: The Rise of the South: Human Progress in a Diverse World*. New York: United Nations Development Programme.

*Source:* Connell, Raewyn, & Pearse, Rebecca. (2014). Excerpted from "Chapter 1: The Question of Gender." In *Gender: In World Perspective, 3rd Edition* (pp. 1–12). Cambridge, UK: Polity Press.

# SNAPSHOTS & SOUNDWAVES 7

## BECAUSE IT'S 2016!

*Canadian Feminist Alliance for International Action (FAFIA)*

Canadian Feminist Alliance for International Action (FAFIA) is an alliance of women's organizations at the national, provincial, territorial, and local levels. Its mandate is to advance women's equality in Canada by working for the full implementation of the international human rights treaties and agreements that Canada has ratified. FAFIA provides training and resources on women's human rights instruments and helps women to engage in using those instruments to address inequalities in their lives.

## Introduction

For Canadian women, the last decade has been shocking. The Harper Conservative government was hostile to women's non-governmental organizations, human rights advocates, and to women's equality claims, creating fear and silence.[1] It made new and deeper cuts to programs and benefits that are crucial to women.[2] Shrinking social programs and services, which are the building blocks of women's equality, moved women backwards. These actions hit Indigenous women, racialized women, women with disabilities, Muslim women, immigrant women, and single mothers especially hard. Twenty years ago, Canada was number one on UN gender equality indexes. In 2014, Canada ranked 25th.[3]

This CEDAW review happens at an important moment for Canadian women. Canada has a new federal Liberal government and a Prime Minister who says he is a feminist. The tone of government has changed and a national inquiry into missing and murdered Indigenous women and girls has been launched. These are welcome shifts.

Facts demonstrate, however, that there is a lot to do and to undo and many steps must be taken by federal, provincial and territorial governments in Canada to fulfill the rights set out in the *Convention on the Elimination of All Forms of Discrimination against Women* [CEDAW]. Canadian women need new, ambitious and transformative plans with adequate resource allocations in order to move forward. [...]

### Canada's Failure to Recognize Social and Economic Rights

At the February 2016 review of Canada by the Committee on Economic, Social and Cultural Rights (CESCR), CESCR criticized Canada for failing to recognize social and economic rights as justiciable rights and failing to provide domestic remedies for their violation.[4] This failure by Canada is a serious concern for women.

\* \* \* \* \*

## Women's Poverty and Income Inequality

About 13.5% of women in Canada live in poverty according to Statistics Canada's 2011 figures.[5] Particular groups of women have much higher rates of poverty:

- 37% of First Nations women (off reserve);[6]
- 23% of Métis and Inuit women;[7]
- 20% of immigrant women;[8]
- 28% of racialized women;[9]
- 27.5% of women with severe disabilities;[10]
- 28.3% of single women;[11]
- 23% of single mothers;[12] and
- 34% of single women over 65.[13]

Further, women's average incomes are about two-thirds of men's in Canada.[14] The gender income gap has narrowed a bit over twenty years, but Canada is ranked 11th among 17 comparable countries by the Conference Board of Canada.[15]

Women are poorer than men in Canada, are more likely to be poor, and more likely to live in deeper poverty.[16] As the data shows, particular groups of women are even more likely to be poor, and to have lower incomes, such as racialized, immigrant women or women with disabilities.

This income inequality has deep roots. Women are poorer than men because they have been assigned the role of unpaid caregiver and nurturer for children, men and old people; because in the paid labour force they perform caregiving and support work which is devalued and lower paid; because there is a lack of safe affordable childcare and this constrains women's participation in the paid labour force; because women, particularly racialized, immigrant women and women with disabilities, are devalued workers, and more likely to be in precarious work; and because women incur economic penalties when they are not attached to men and when they have children alone.[17]

For women, poverty and economic inequality have gendered, harmful consequences. Poor women are less able to protect themselves from being treated as sexual commodities and nothing more, and more likely to accept sexual commodification, prostitution and subordination in order to survive. They lose sexual autonomy in relationships. Their vulnerability to rape and assault is magnified. Their ability to care for their children is compromised, and they are more likely to have their children taken away in the name of "protection," often because they do not have adequate housing and cannot supply proper food or ensure safe conditions. Without adequate incomes, women cannot secure stable housing and become homeless, increasing their exposure to violence. They have no political voice or influence. They are over-policed and under-protected by police. Without access to adequate social programs, including adequate social assistance and social services, such as shelters and transitional housing, women are much less able to resist or escape subordination and violence.[18]

## Inadequate Social Programs

*Inadequate Social Assistance*
In Canada, welfare (social assistance) is a program of last resort. It is only available to persons who have no alternative income to rely on. Unfortunately, welfare rates in Canada are set so low that women who are reliant on social assistance are stuck in poverty rather than being helped out of it.

The Caledon Institute's report on welfare rates for 2013 shows that welfare incomes for all households in all jurisdictions fall well below the poverty line, as measured by Statistics Canada's after tax low-income cut-offs.[19] The effect of below poverty line welfare rates is that recipients cannot afford adequate food and shelter.

\* \* \* \* \*

*Lack of Affordable, Safe, Public Childcare*
77% of mothers with children between 3 and 5 years old are in the labour force.[20] Yet, Canada still does not have a national childcare program. Canadian women scramble to find safe childcare and struggle to pay for it. Eight years ago the CEDAW Committee expressed its

concerns with Canada's "lack of affordable quality child-care spaces," particularly for low-income women raising children,[21] and urged Canada "to step up its efforts to provide a sufficient number of affordable childcare spaces."[22] Forty-six years ago the Royal Commission on the Status of Women called for a national childcare program, describing it as the "ramp" to women's equality. But today regulated childcare is available for only 24% of Canadian children under five.[23]

Canada (outside of Quebec) is assessed poorly on childcare by Canadian[24] and international experts. At 0.25% of GDP, Canada's public investment in childcare is about one-half of the Organisation for Economic Co-operation and Development (OECD) average and one-third of the minimum recommended level.[25] As a result, Canada has among the lowest levels of access to childcare and the highest parent fees in the OECD. [...]

The new Government of Canada has promised to transfer funds to provinces, territories and Indigenous communities for some childcare programs under a National Early Learning and Childcare Framework.[26] The 2016 Budget set aside funds for these transfers to start in 2017.

This promised funding, while welcome, is not, by itself, a national childcare program. Canadian women need the Government of Canada to develop and immediately implement a comprehensive national approach to child-care, so that its leadership, and funding, can ensure affordable, quality, accessible childcare for all families and decent wages for childcare workers.

\* \* \* \* \*

### Women and Employment

*Wage Inequality*

Canadian women are paid less than their male counter-parts in nearly all sectors of the economy.[27] This occurs regardless of women's level of education.[28] Even those women with comparable levels of education, experience,

and responsibilities to men are usually paid less.[29] Women who work in female dominated occupations typically have lower rates of pay than those who work in male dominated occupations.[30] For racialized women,[31] women with disabilities[32] and Indigenous women,[33] the gender pay gap is even wider.[34]

- Comparing women and men who work full-time, full-year, women take home 20% less, on average, than men.[35]
- The pay gap between men and women in Canada is double that of the global average;[36] is the 8th larg-est gender wage gap among OECD countries;[37] and the World Economic Forum ranks Canada's wage equality in 27th place.[38] This gender wage gap has changed little since 1977.[39]
- Women are the majority of minimum wage workers (between $10–$13 across Canada);[40] are nearly twice as likely as men to work in minimum wage jobs;[41] and nowhere in Canada does working full-time for minimum wage earn a woman enough income to meet the poverty line, even for a single person.[42]
- Women are more likely than men to hold multiple, part time jobs.[43] In 2013, 26% of women worked part-time, while only 11% of men worked part-time.[44]
- The wage gap is worse for women with disabilities and for Indigenous and racialized women. Women with disabilities earn 32% less than women overall, and 57% less than men.[45] Racialized women earn 70.5% as much as racialized men.[46] Indigenous women who live off-reserve earn 68.5% as much as Indigenous men living off-reserve.[47] All of these groups earn less than non-racialized men.

## NOTES

1. The silencing of advocacy in Canada, including attacks on many women's and human rights organizations, is documented by Voices-Voix, online: <http://voices-voix.ca/>.

2. See FAFIA, *Women's Inequality in Canada*, Submission to the CEDAW Committee (September 2008) at 8, online:

<http://tbinternet.ohchr.org/Treaties/CEDAW/Shared%20
Documents/CAN/INT_CEDAW_NGO_CAN_42_8234_E.
pdf>. (For other commentary, see "For women, Harper's
government has been a Disaster," ipolitics (22 September
2015), online: <http://ipolitics.ca/2015/09/22/
for-women-harpers-government-has-been-a-disaster/>).

3.  UNDP, Human Development/Gender Equality Index, online:
<http://hdr.undp.org/en/composite/GII>.

4.  Committee on Economic, Social and Cultural Rights,
57th Sess, 7th Mtg, UN Doc E/C.12/2016/SR7 (2016)
at para 41, online: <https://documents-dds-ny.un.org/
doc/UNDOC/GEN/G16/037/75/PDF/G1603775.
pdf?OpenElement>; Committee on Economic, Social
and Cultural Rights, *Concluding Observations on the
Sixth Report of Canada*, UN Doc. E/C.12/CAN/CO/6 (4
March 2016) at paras 5–6, online: <http://tbinternet.
ohchr.org/_layouts/treatybodyexternal/Download.
aspx?symbolno=E%2fC.12%2fCAN%2fCO%2f6&Lang=en>.

5.  Statistics Canada, *Persons in Low Income after Tax (In
Percent, 2007 to 2011)*, Catalogue No 75-202-X (June
2013), online: <http://www.statcan.gc.ca/tables-tableaux/
sum-som/l01/cst01/famil19a-eng.htm> [Statistics Canada,
Persons in Low Income].

6.  Vivian O'Donnell & Susan Wallace, *Women in Canada: A
Gender-Based Statistical Report First Nations, Métis and
Inuit Women*, Statistics Canada, Catalogue No 89-503-X
(July 2011), online: <http://www.statcan.gc.ca/pub/89-
503-x/2010001/article/11442-eng.pdf>.

7.  *Ibid.*

8.  Tina Chui, *Women in Canada: A Gender-based Report
Immigrant Women*, Statistics Canada, Catalogue No 89-
503-X (July 2011), online: <http://www.statcan.gc.ca/
pub/89-503-x/2010001/article/11528-eng.pdf>.

9.  Tina Chu and Hélène Maheux, *Women in Canada: A Gender-
Based Statistical Report Visible Minority Women*, Statistics
Canada, Catalogue No 89-503-X (July 2011), online: <http://
www.statcan.gc.ca/pub/89-503-x/2010001/article/11527-
eng.pdf>.

10.  DAWN Canada, "Factsheet: Women with Disabilities and
Poverty" (2015), online: <http://www.dawncanada.net/
issues/issues/fact-sheets-2/poverty/>.

11.  Statistics Canada, Persons in Low Income, *supra* note 5.

12.  *Ibid.*

13.  *Ibid.*

14.  Statistics Canada, *Average Total Income of Women and
Men, 1976 to 2008*, Catalogue No 89-503-X, Table 202-
0407, Chart 1, (13 May 2013), online: <http://www.statcan.
gc.ca/pub/89-503-x/2010001/article/11388/c-g/c-g001-
eng.htm>.

15.  Conference Board of Canada, *Gender Income Gap* (January
2013), online: <http://www.conferenceboard.ca/hcp/
details/society/gender-income-gap.aspx>.

16.  Monica Townson, *Women's Poverty and the Recession*,
Canadian Centre for Policy Alternatives (2009), online:
<https://www.policyalternatives.ca/sites/default/files/
uploads/publications/National_Office_Pubs/2009/
Womens_Poverty_in_the_Recession.pdf>); Monica
Townson (commentary), *Canadian Women on Their Own
Are the Poorest of the Poor*, Canadian Centre for Policy
Alternatives (8 September 2009), online: <https://
www.policyalternatives.ca/publications/commentary/
canadian-women-their-own-are-poorest-poor>.

17.  Shelagh Day, "The Indivisibility of Women's Human Rights"
(2003) 20:3 *Canadian Woman Studies* 11 at 12.

18.  Canadian Women's Foundation, *The Facts about Women
and Poverty* (30 March 2013), online: <http://www.
canadianwomen.org/sites/canadianwomen.org/files//
FactSheet-EndPoverty-ACTIVE%20-%20May%2030.pdf>.

19.  Ann Tweddle, Ken Battle & Sherri Torjman, *Welfare in
Canada 2013*, Caledon Institute of Social Policy (2014)
at 48, online: <http://www.caledoninst.org/Publications/
PDF/1057ENG.pdf>.

20.  Martha Friendly, Bethany Grady, Lyndsay Macdonald & Barry
Forer, *Early Childhood Education and Care 2014*, Childcare
Canada (2015), online: <http://www.childcarecanada.
org/publications/ecec-canada/16/03/early-childhood-
education-and-care-canada-2014> [Friendly, *Early
Childhood Education and Care 2014*].

21.  Committee on the Elimination of Discrimination against
Women, *Concluding Observations of the Committee on
the Elimination of Discrimination against Women*, UN Doc
CEDAW/C/CAN/CO/7, (7 November 2008) note 4 at para 39.

22. *Ibid.* at para 40.

23. Friendly, *Early Childhood Education and Care 2014, supra* note 32.

24. Child Care Advocacy Association of Canada (CCAAC) & Coalition of Child Care Advocates of BC (CCCABC), *A Tale of Two Canadas: Implementing Rights in Early Childhood* (February 2011), online: <http://www.cccabc.bc.ca/res/rights/ccright_tale2can_brief.pdf>.

25. OECD, *Directorate for Education, Starting Strong II: Early Childhood Education and Care* (Paris: OECD, 2006), online: <http://www.oecd.org/edu/school/startingstrongiiearlychildhoodeducationandcare.htm>. (Note that this is the most current complete data on Canadian ECEC available from the OECD; based on available information in Canada, ECEC funding has undoubtedly increased since 2006, as several provinces have added full day kindergarten, while childcare funding has continued to grow slowly. No comparative data, however, are available as Canada's entries in the OECD Family Database (2009) and other international sources are incomplete.)

26. The Canadian Press, "'Ambitions' for Childcare Agenda for Federal-Provincial Talks," *CBC* (4 February 2016), online: <http://www.cbc.ca/news/politics/social-service-ministers-child-care-meeting-1.3433626>.

27. Canadian Centre for Policy Alternatives, *Progress on Women's Rights: Missing in Action* (2014) at 9, 11, online: <https://www.policyalternatives.ca/sites/default/files/uploads/publications/National%20office/2014/11/Progress_Women_Beijing20.pdf> [CCPA, Progress on Women's Rights]; Government of Canada, *Twentieth Anniversary of the Fourth World Conference on Women and the Adoption of the Beijing Declaration and Platform for Action Canada's National Review* (June 2014) at 11, online: <http://www.unece.org/fileadmin/DAM/Gender/publication/Canada_National_Review_Beijing_20.pdf>

28. Statistics Canada, *Study: Cumulative Earnings by Major Field of Study, 1991 to 2010* (28 October 2014), online: <http://www.statcan.gc.ca/pub/11-626-x/11-626-x2014040-eng.htm>.

29. *Ibid.*

30. Kate McInturff & Paul Tulloch, *Narrowing the Gap: The Difference That Public Sector Wages Make* (Ottawa: Canadian Centre for Policy Alternatives, 2014) at 7, online: <https://www.policyalternatives.ca/sites/default/files/uploads/publications/National%20Office/2014/10/Narrowing_the_Gap.pdf> [McInturff et al., Narrowing the Gap].

31. Statistics Canada, *Women in Canada Visible Minority Women: Lower Employment Income* (2015), online: <http://www.statcan.gc.ca/pub/89-503-x/2010001/article/11527-eng.htm#a19>.

32. National Union of Public and General Employees, *Facts about Women and Economic Wellbeing* (2011) at 2, online: <https://alltogethernow.nupge.ca/facts-about-womens-economic-well-being> [NUPGE, Facts].

33. McInturff et al., Narrowing the Gap, *supra* note 30 at 4.

34. NUPGE, Facts, *supra* note 32 at 2.

35. CCPA, Progress on Women's Rights, *supra* note 27 at 9.

36. "Gender Pay Gap in Canada More Than Twice Global Average, Study Shows," *The Globe and Mail* (5 May 2015), online: <http://www.theglobeandmail.com/news/british-columbia/gender-pay-gap-in-canada-more-than-twice-global-average-study-shows/article24274586/>.

37. Equal Pay Coalition, *Gender Wage Gap: Full Time Employees*, online: <http://equalpaycoalition.org/calculating-the-pay-gap/> (see also <https://www.oecd.org/gender/data/genderwagegap.htm>).

38. Ricardo Husmann et al., *The Global Gender Gap Report 2014*, World Economic Forum (2014) at 65, online: <http://www3.weforum.org/docs/GGGR14/GGGR_CompleteReport_2014.pdf>.

39. *Ibid.*

40. Government of Canada Labour Program, *Current and Forthcoming Minimum Hourly Wage Rates for Experienced Adult Workers in Canada* (August 2016), online: <http://srv116.services.gc.ca/dimt-wid/sm-mw/rpt1.aspx>.

41. Diane Galarneau and Eric Fecteau, *The Ups and Downs of Minimum Wage*, Statistics Canada (2006), online: <http://www.statcan.gc.ca/pub/75-006-x/2014001/article/14035-eng.htm#a6>.

42. Canada Labour Congress, *Minimum Wage in Canada* (April 2015) at 8, online: <http://canadianlabour.ca/sites/default/files/media/minwagecanada-2015-04-13%20%281%29.pdf>.

43. CCPA, Progress on Women's Rights, *supra* note 27 at 8.

44. *Ibid.*

45. NUPGE, Facts, *supra* 32 at 2; also see CCPA, Progress on Women's Rights, *supra* note 27 at 9, 19.

46. NUPGE, Facts, *ibid.* at 2.

47. *Ibid.*

*Source:* Canadian Feminist Alliance for International Action (FAFIA). (2016, October). Excerpted from *Report to the Committee on the Elimination of Discrimination against Women (CEDAW).* Ottawa, ON: FAFIA. Retrieved from: http://fafia-afai.org/wp-content/uploads/2016/10/FAFIA-Coalition-report.pdf.

# CHAPTER 11

## Conceptual Guide to the Unpaid Work Module

*Marion Werner, Leah F. Vosko, Angie Deveau, Giordana Pimentel,
and Deatra Walsh, with past contributions from Abetha Mahalingam,
Nancy Zukewich, Krista Scott-Dixon, Megan Ciurysek, and Vivian Ngai*

Marion Werner was a researcher at the Gender and Work Database (GWD) and is currently an associate professor in the Department of Geography, University at Buffalo, SUNY. She researches economic restructuring, the gendered and racialized politics of labour, and agro-food systems and policies. She is the author of *Global Displacements: The Making of Uneven Development in the Caribbean*.

Leah Vosko is project director of the GWD and professor of political science and Canada Research Chair in the Political Economy of Gender and Work at York University. She is recognized internationally for her scholarship on work, gender, citizenship, migration, and labour markets.

Angie Deveau is completing a PhD in gender, feminist, and women's studies at York University. Her research interests include a focus on women's unpaid work and gender, health, and social policy.

Giordana Pimentel completed her Master's degree at York University, where she researched women's constitutional rights under Section 15 of the Charter.

Deatra Walsh is director of the Poverty Reduction Division with the Government of Nunavut. She holds a PhD in sociology from Memorial University of Newfoundland, and her research interests include precarious employment and its gendered dimensions, and rural labour mobility.

# INTRODUCTION

This module explores how particular forms of unpaid work—like caregiving, domestic work, and volunteering—are defined, socially valued, organized, and gendered. Its purpose is twofold: to provide statistical data and library resources on the measurement of unpaid work in Canada, and to illustrate how unpaid work is shaped by gender relations as they intersect with "race," ethnicity, (dis)ability, age, and sexuality. […]

Unpaid work refers to the production of goods or services that are consumed by those within or outside a household, but not for sale in the market (OECD 2011). An activity is considered "work" (vs. "leisure") if a third person could be paid to do a certain activity (OECD 2011).

It is widely recognized that women—in Canada and beyond—perform the bulk of unpaid work in households and in the paid labour force (see, for example, Armstrong and Armstrong 2001; Beneria 1999; Luxton 1980; Marshall 2006; Mies 1986; Zukewich 2002). This work is often socially, politically, and economically devalued because "work" is often defined in conventional statistics as paid activities linked to the market (Beneria 1999). Despite the efforts of several generations of feminist scholars to make unpaid work visible, it remains marginalized in most methods of measuring economic activity.

In recent decades, many women's groups have struggled to have unpaid work taken more seriously in national statistical surveys. In the 1990s, as a result of sustained and multi-faceted attempts by Canadian women's groups to challenge statisticians on the notion that only paid labour contributes to production, Statistics Canada included an in-depth question about the amount of time individuals spent on unpaid work in the 1996 Census (Luxton and Vosko 1998). Over time, other national statistical agencies have devised guidelines and surveys for identifying and classifying various types of unpaid work (EUROSTAT 2004; Picchio 1998). […]

# KEY CONCEPTS

## Unpaid Informal Caregiving

Unpaid informal caregiving encompasses care and assistance provided by individuals to other individuals outside of civic or voluntary organizations (Zukewich 2002). This work is often similar in character to paid caregiving occupations such as those related to childcare provision, nursing, and home care. These are typically among the lowest paid occupations in the labour force.

The burden of unpaid informal caregiving falls disproportionately on women (Baxter et al. 2005; MacDonald et al. 2005). Unpaid informal caregivers are often family members, relatives, friends, and volunteers (Luxton 2006; Zukewich 2002). The recipients of care are usually children, elders, individuals who are ill, or people with disabilities, as well as individuals within the paid workforce like supervisors, co-workers, and friends (see Unpaid Work in Paid Workplaces). For example, in 2003, 62 percent of mothers were primary caregivers in homes where Canadian children with disabilities lived compared to three percent of fathers (Yantzi and Rosenberg 2008). As women age, their care work seldom diminishes and may even increase (Gattai and Musatti 1999). A large proportion of grandmothers are responsible for the care of their grandchildren (Bracke et al. 2008). Moreover, increasing numbers of elderly women are responsible for the care of their husbands (Paun 2003).

Caregiving accounts for a large proportion of unpaid work performed by individuals. Although unpaid informal caregiving benefits society, as well as caregivers and care recipients, it still lacks social recognition and is not counted as part of a country's productive output (Elson 1999; ILO 2007). Feminist economists estimate that, were it to be counted, this type of work would account for at least half of a given country's total Gross National Product (GNP) (Elson 1999; ILO 2007). Thus, for some scholars conducting research in the area of gender and work, a central concern involves measuring and assigning value to unpaid informal caregiving, and highlighting the sex/gender divisions that exist when it comes to who performs such types of work. Some analysts, such as Zukewich (2003), argue that only when adequate tools are created to measure and value unpaid informal caregiving will we have a better understanding of how the social and economic costs of sustaining ourselves and dependents relate to individuals' capacity to engage in the labour force.

Although men's participation in childcare duties within dual-income families has increased over the last three decades, women remain responsible for the largest share of unpaid caregiving within the home despite their growing participation in paid employment (Marshall 2006). Moreover, in single-earner households, 89 percent of mothers stay at home to fulfill caregiving responsibilities (Ibid.). Given the gendered character of unpaid informal caregiving, women's rights activists have advocated for state-supported universal childcare (see, for e.g., Mahon 2000; Prentice 2004). Efforts to institute a universal program at the federal level have largely failed. Provinces remain the main source of child-care subsidization and federal monies that could be put towards childcare are often used for other ends (e.g., tax credits, early learning initiatives, etc.) (Battle 2006; Campbell 2006; Friendly et al. 2007; Mahon 2006; Vosko 2006). Since 1997, Québec has offered extensive support for childcare and remains the only Canadian province to do so. Despite this advance, resources for childcare in Québec are not equitably distributed: children from working class and poor families access poorer quality facilities than their middle and upper class counterparts (Mahon 2006).

The growing participation of women in the paid workforce and the lack of state support for elder and child caregiving has created a "care deficit" in many countries of the global North. To fill this gap, governments promote the immigration of women, many of whom are women of colour, from poorer countries in the global South (Beneria 2008; Lawson 2007; Pratt 2003). This practice reproduces the care deficit in migrants' home countries since women migrants are often legally restricted or economically unable to bring their children with them when they migrate to work (Beneria 2008; Pratt 2005; Raghuram et al. 2009). It is also premised upon the growing number of temporary categories of migration and precarious forms of employment.

## Volunteering

Unpaid work that extends beyond one's own household into the households of others and social institutions more broadly is generally classified as "volunteer work." These activities are integral to maintaining the labour force, although they are rarely recognized as such. Beneria (1999) defines volunteer work as unpaid work performed for recipients who are not members of the immediate family and for which there is no direct payment (see also Gaskin 2003; Taylor 2004). Volunteer work includes both work done for formal organizations as well as help and care provided in an informal manner by individuals for other individuals.

Women's volunteer work predominates in institutions and sectors that are associated with the feminized work of care such as schools, hospitals, and voluntary services related to elder and childcare. In instances where these services are restructured, and fewer financial resources are dedicated to them, mostly female volunteers become essential sources of unpaid labour, tied to the overarching belief in a woman's "natural" capacity to carry out care work (Baines 2004; Denton et al. 2002). In contrast, men are more likely than women to take on leadership roles in their volunteer work, as well as more maintenance, coaching, or teaching positions (Rotolo and Wilson 2007).

## Unpaid Work in Paid Workplaces

Various types of unpaid work are performed by individuals in the workplace itself and often mis-recognized as volunteer work. As with other forms of unpaid work, the bulk of this work is undertaken by women. Forrest (1998) documents how women carry out unpaid work on-the-job outside their formal job requirements. These activities include cleaning, informal caregiving, serving other individuals, and maintaining interpersonal relations. The latter activity can involve empathy work: the often taxing efforts of employees to establish personal connections by means of listening and attending to the emotional needs of their clients, co-workers, or employers (Kosny and MacEachen 2009). Despite the benefits of the various unpaid work activities to workplaces, they still remain largely invisible. There is a tendency among policy makers, employers, and analysts to define paid work as time and effort spent directly in the production of goods and services for the market and thus to discount unpaid work in the workplace.

This form of unseen and unpaid work can be strongly associated with female-dominated and feminized occupations and sectors. For example, Baines (2004; 2009) documents the increasing reliance upon unpaid work performed by mostly female employees in the social service sector. These activities include unpaid policy- and service-building work, fundraising, and unpaid care for social service clients and their families. Restructuring of social services—linked to privatization—and declining state support for them have led to increased demands upon workers in this sector to perform these unpaid duties for their own or other service agencies.

Finally, unpaid work is being extended into paid workplaces through immigrant settlement processes. Many immigrants looking to access employment in their respective professional fields are required to gain "Canadian work experience" in the form of unpaid work. While this work is officially termed "volunteer work," it differs from standard definitions of volunteering (see above) in terms of motivation, experience, and sector (McLaren and Dyck 2004; Slade and Schugurensky 2010). Immigrants are compelled to undertake unpaid work due to their exclusion from the Canadian labour market. Their unpaid work is not

ancillary to workplaces, as helpers; rather, they perform similar functions as paid workers. Immigrants undertaking unpaid work to obtain "Canadian worker experience" not only perform unpaid work in non-profit or community agencies but also in for-profit companies (e.g., banks) and the public sector (Ibid.).

## Unpaid Domestic Work

An analysis of types of unpaid domestic work continues to reveal sex/gender divisions of labour in households. Although the gap between men's and women's performance of domestic work has narrowed slightly, a greater share of housework in Canada continues to be performed by women (Marshall 2006). Findings from the 2006 Census reveal little change in this pattern (e.g., see Statistics Canada 2006 Census Table). Although a majority of women engage in paid work, women remain disproportionately responsible for daily housework in dual-earner families. Thus, women carry the double burden of paid and unpaid work. Social context matters, however. The composition of families—especially the numbers and ages of children and multigenerational households—influence the number of hours spent on performing domestic duties, and the burden of this work on women (Marshall 2006; McMullin 2005). The timing of life transitions, specifically ages of marriage and child-bearing, also shapes the distribution of unpaid domestic work between women and men partners in households (McMullin 2005). As McMullin observes in her study of generational patterns of unpaid work in Canadian families, women who married and had children early in life are more likely to undertake more unpaid domestic work responsibilities than their older female counterparts.

The home has long been a site where unpaid domestic work is combined with paid employment, especially for women. Historically, paid work in the home (or homework) has been associated with women's work in systems of industrial production in, for example, the garment industry (Ng et al. 1999; Scott

1988). The reorganization of industry and changes in information technology have seen more workers in white collar occupations such as writers, editors, programmers, and software engineers shift to perform paid work in the home, with growing numbers of men working from home. Despite this shift, gendered divisions and uneven normative expectations regarding housework continue to persist in homes where paid work is also undertaken in either industrial or white collar sectors (Osnowitz 2005; see also Bernstein et al. 2001; Mirchandani 2000). Men working from home are more likely to segregate paid work from unpaid housework in comparison to their female counterparts, for whom this divide tends to be especially blurred, leading to longer hours of paid and unpaid work arranged in fragmented periods. The isolated and unregulated nature of homework tends to consolidate uneven gendered roles in these households (Ibid.). Furthermore, women who shoulder the dual burden of paid labour and unpaid work in the home are more likely to suffer from related stress and adverse effects on their physical and mental health (MacDonald et al. 2005; Marshall 2006).

The list of unpaid domestic activities in the Canadian Census illustrates the diversity and indispensability of these activities. Tasks include meal preparation and clean-up; clothing care; cleaning; plant and garden care; home maintenance/management; care for children and adults; unpaid help to other households; shopping or obtaining services; travel as part of care or obtaining services; and unpaid work in family businesses. Each category of unpaid work also includes a subset of tasks. For example, care to children includes attending to their health needs, supervising their education, transporting them to school and other activities, "babysitting," and so forth.

## Unpaid Subsistence Activities

Subsistence and/or survival-based activities form yet another type of unpaid work performed predominantly by women that is socially undervalued and made invisible in economic accounts of work. Subsistence activities can include the cultivation of vegetables, fetching wood and water, and the care of livestock animals, especially important for farming households' economies (Beneria 1999; Teitelbaum and Beckley 2006). While subsistence activities are often associated with so-called developing countries in the global South, they remain vital to livelihoods in industrial economies, especially in rural areas. In rural communities in Canada, for example, subsistence activities are important not solely due to economic need; these also form part of communities' cultural identity, heritage, and survival (Teitelbaum and Beckley 2006). Women's participation in subsistence production tends to be underestimated, especially where it is classified as unpaid family work (Philipps 2008a; 2008b). [...]

## Unpaid Family Work

Unpaid family work refers to the direct contributions of unpaid family members to production for the market, work that is officially counted under another member of the household. For example, one household member may be constructed legally as an owner or entrepreneur although the business may also rely upon the unpaid work of relatives who assist in the business' operations (Philipps 2008a; 2008b). Unpaid family work is generally performed by women from diverse geographical and social locations, such as immigrants, farm wives, and executive/political spouses.

In Canada, although initially associated with unpaid work on farms, unpaid family work is increasingly comprised of immigrant women and their family members who contribute to small businesses officially belonging to one member of the household (often, a male head of the household) (Philipps 2008a; 2008b). For example, the work of many Chinese immigrant women in Canada is categorized as unpaid in small businesses run by male heads of the household (Man 1997). Unpaid family work and its gendered dimensions also persist on farms. Women engage in long hours of on-farm unpaid work, activities also often combined with off-farm paid labour. Kubik and Moore (2005) document high rates of stress among Saskatchewan farm wives, linked to the triple burden of unpaid family work, unpaid domestic work, and paid off-farm labour.

***

# REFERENCES

Armstrong, P. and Armstrong, H. (2001). *The Double Ghetto: Canadian Women and Their Segregated Work*. Toronto: Oxford University Press.

Baines, D. (2004). "Caring for Nothing: Work Organization and Unwaged Labour in Social Services." *Work, Employment and Society*, 18(2), 267–295.

Baines, D. (2009). "Seven Kinds of Work—Only One Paid: Raced, Gendered and Restructured Work in Social Services." *Atlantis*, 28(2), 19–29.

Battle, K. (2006). *The Incredible Shrinking $1,200 Child Care Allowance: How to Fix It*. Ottawa: Caledon Institute of Social Policy.

Baxter, J., Hewitt, B., and Western, M. (2005). "Post-Familial Families and the Domestic Division of Labour." *Journal of Comparative Family Studies*, 36(4), 583–600.

Beneria, L. (1999). "The Enduring Debate over Unpaid Labour." *International Labour Review*, 138(3), 287–309.

Beneria, L. (2008). "The Crisis of Care, International Migration, and Public Policy." *Feminist Economics*, 14(3), 1–21.

Bernstein, S., Lippel, K., and Lamarche, L. (2001). *Women and Homework: The Canadian Legislative Framework*. Ottawa: Status of Women Canada.

Bracke, P., Christiaens, W., and Wauterickx, N. (2008). "The Pivotal Role of Women in Informal Care." *Journal of Family Issues*, 29(10), 1348–1378.

Campbell, A. (2006). "Proceeding with 'Care': Lessons to Be Learned from the Canadian Parental Leave and Quebec Daycare Initiatives in Developing a National Childcare Policy." *Canadian Journal of Family Law*, 22(2), 171–222.

Denton, M., Zeytinoglu, I. U., Davies, S., and Lian, J. (2002). "Job Stress and Job Dissatisfaction of Homecare Workers in the Context of Health Care Restructuring." *Work, Health and Quality of Life*, 32(2), 327–357.

Elson, D. (1999). *Gender-Neutral, Gender-Blind, or Gender-Sensitive Budgets? Changing the Conceptual Framework to Include Women's Empowerment and the Economy of Care*. London: Commonwealth Secretariat.

EUROSTAT. (2004). *Working Paper on Comparative Time Use Statistics Database European Union*.

Forrest, A. (1998). "The Industrial Relations Significance of Unpaid Work." *Labour/Le Travail*, 42, 199–225.

Friendly, M., Beach, J., Ferns, C., and Turiano, M. (2007). *Trends and Analysis 2007: Early Childhood Education and Care in Canada 2006*. Toronto: Childcare Resource and Research Unit.

Gaskin, K. (2003). *A Choice Blend: What Volunteers Want from Organisation and Management*. London: Institute for Volunteering Research.

Gattai, F. B. and Musatti, T. (1999). "Grandmothers' Involvement in Grandchildren's Care: Attitudes, Feelings, and Emotions." *Family Relations*, 48(1), 35–42.

International Labour Organization. (2007). *Overview of Gender-Responsive Budget Initiatives*. Geneva: International Labour Organization.

Kosny, A. and MacEachen, E. (2009). "Gendered, Invisible Work in Non-Profit Social Service Organizations: Implications for Worker Health and Safety." *Gender, Work, and Organization*, 17(4), 1–22.

Kubik, W. and Moore, R. J. (2005). "Health and Well-Being of Farm Women: Contradictory Roles in the Contemporary Economy." *Journal of Agricultural Safety and Health*, 11(2), 249–256.

Lawson, V. (2007). "Geographies of Care and Responsibilities." *Annals of the Association of American Geographers*, 97(1), 1–11.

Luxton, M. (1980). *More Than a Labour of Love: Three Generations of Women's Work in the Home*. Toronto: Women's Press.

Luxton, M. (2006). "Friends, Neighbours, and Community: A Case Study of the Role of Informal Caregiving in Social Reproduction." In Meg Luxton and Kate Bezanson (Eds.), *Social Reproduction: Feminist Political Economy Challenges Neo-Liberalism*. (pp. 263–292). Montreal and Kingston: McGill-Queen's University Press.

Luxton, M. and Vosko, L. F. (1998). "Where Women's Efforts Count: The 1996 Census Campaign and 'Family Politics' in Canada." *Studies in Political Economy*, 56, 49–89.

MacDonald, M., Phipps, S., and Lethbridge, L. (2005). "Taking Its Toll: The Influence of Paid and Unpaid Work on Women's Well-Being." *Feminist Economics*, 11(1), 63–94.

Mahon, R. (2000). "The Never-Ending Story: The Struggle for Universal Child Care Policy in the 1970s." *Canadian Historical Review*, 81(4), 582–615.

Mahon, R. (2006). "Of Scalar Hierarchies and Welfare Redesign: Child Care in Three Canadian Cities." *Transactions of the Institute of British Geographers*, 31(4), 452–466.

Man, G. (1997). "Women's Work Is Never Done: Social Organization of Work and the Experience of Women in Middle-Class Hong Kong Chinese Immigrant Families in Canada." In V. Demos and M. Texler Segal (Eds.), *Advances in Gender Research, vol. 2.* (pp. 183–226). Greenwich: JAI Press Inc.

Marshall, K. (2006). "Converging Gender Roles." *Perspectives on Labour and Income*, 18(3), 7–19.

McLaren, A. T. and Dyck, I. (2004). "Mothering, Human Capital and the 'Ideal Immigrant.'" *Women's Studies International Forum*, 27(1), 41–53.

McMullin, J. A. (2005). "Patterns of Paid and Unpaid Work: The Influence of Power, Social Context, and Family Background." *Canadian Journal on Aging/La Revue Canadienne Du Vieillissement*, 24(3), 225–236.

Mies, M. (1986). *Patriarchy and Accumulation on a World Scale: Women in the International Division of Labour.* London and Atlantic Highlands: Zed Books.

Mirchandani, K. (2000). "'The Best of Both Worlds' and 'Cutting My Own Throat': Contradictory Images of Home-Based Work." *Qualitative Sociology*, 23(2), 159–182.

Ng, R., Yuk-Lin Wong, R., and Choi, A. (1999). *Home Working: Home Office or Home Sweatshop? Report of Homeworkers in Toronto's Garment Industry.* Toronto: Centre for the Study of Education and Work.

OECD. (2011). *Society at a Glance 2011—OECD Social Indicators OECD Publishing.* http://www.oecd.org/els/social/indicators/SAG.

Osnowitz, D. (2005). "Managing Time in Domestic Space: Home-Based Contractors and Household Work." *Gender & Society*, 19(1), 83–103.

Paun, O. (2003). "Older Women Caring for Spouses with Alzheimer's Disease at Home: Making Sense of the Situation." *Health Care for Women International*, 24(4), 292–312.

Philipps, L. (2008a). "Helping Out in the Family Firm: The Legal Treatment of Unpaid Market Labor." *Wisconsin Journal of Law, Gender & Society*, 23, 65–112.

Philipps, L. (2008b). "Silent Partners: The Role of Unpaid Market Labor in Families." *Feminist Economics*, 14(2), 37–57.

Picchio, A. (1998). "Wages as a Reflection of Socially Embedded Production and Reproduction Processes." In Linda Clarke, Peter De Gijsel and Jorn Janssen (Eds.), *The Dynamics of Wage Relations in the New Europe.* (pp. 195–602). London: Kluwer.

Pratt, G. (2003). "Valuing Childcare: Troubles in Suburbia." *Antipode*, 35(3), 581–602.

Pratt, G. (2005). "From Migrant Women to Immigrant: Domestic Workers Settle in Vancouver, Canada." In Lise Nelson and Joni Seager (Eds.), *A Companion to Feminist Geography.* (pp. 123–137). Maldan: Blackwell Publishing.

Prentice, S. (2004). "Manitoba's Childcare Regime: Social Liberalism in Flux." *Canadian Journal of Sociology*, 29(2), 193–207.

Raghuram, P., Madge, C., and Noxolo, P. (2009). "Rethinking Responsibility and Care in a Postcolonial World." *Geoforum*, 40(1), 5–13.

Rotolo, T. and Wilson, J. (2007). "Sex Segregation in Volunteer Work." *The Sociological Quarterly*, 48(3), 559–585.

Scott, J. (1988). *Gender and the Politics of History.* New York: Columbia University Press.

Slade, B. and Schugurensky, D. (2010). "Starting from Another Side, the Bottom: Volunteer Work as a Transition into the Labour Market for Immigrant Professionals." In P. Sawchuk and A. Taylor (Eds.), *Challenging Transitions in Learning and Work: Perspectives on Policy and Practice.* (pp. 231–243). Rotterdam: Sense Publishers.

Statistics Canada. (2006). *Population 15 Years and Over by Hours Spent Doing Unpaid Housework, by Sex, by Census Metropolitan Areas.* http://www12.statcan.gc.ca/census-recensement/2006/

consultation/92-135/definitions-eng.cfm#d21.

Taylor, R. (2004). "Extending Conceptual Boundaries: Work, Voluntary Work and Employment." *Work, Employment & Society*, 18(1), 29–49.

Teitelbaum, S. and Beckley, T. (2006). "Hunted, Harvested and Homegrown: The Prevalence of Self-Provisioning in Rural Canada." *Journal of Rural and Community Development*, 1(2), 114–130.

Vosko, L. F. (2006). "Crisis Tendencies in Social Reproduction: The Case of Ontario's Early Years Plan." In Kate Bezanson and Meg Luxton (Eds.), *Social Reproduction: Feminist Political Economy Challenges Neo-Liberalism*. Montreal and Kingston: McGill-Queen's University Press.

Yantzi, N. M. and Rosenberg, M. W. (2008). "The Contested Meanings of Home for Women Caring for Children with Long-Term Care Needs in Ontario, Canada." *Gender, Place and Culture*, 15(3), 301–315.

Zukewich, N. (2002). *Using Time Use Data to Measure and Value Unpaid Caregiving Work*. (Master of Arts in Canadian Studies, Carleton University).

Zukewich, N. (2003). "Unpaid Informal Caregiving." *Canadian Social Trends* 70. Ottawa: Statistics Canada: 14–18.

---

*Source:* Werner, Marion, Vosko, Leah F., Deveau, Angie, Pimentel, Giordana, & Walsh, Deatra, with past contributions from Mahalingam, Abetha, Zukewich, Nancy, Scott-Dixon, Krista, Ciurysek, Megan, & Ngai, Vivian. (n.d.). Excerpted from *Conceptual Guide to the Unpaid Work Module.* Toronto, ON: Gender and Work Database. Retrieved from: http://www.genderwork.ca/gwd/modules/unpaid-work/.

# SNAPSHOTS & SOUNDWAVES 8

## UNPAID WORK: A GLOBAL VIEW

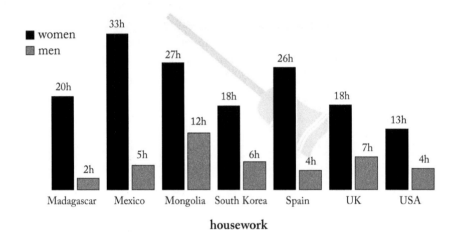

**housework**

**child care**

---

**Gender Division of Labor**

Hours spent each week on cooking, cleaning, and childcare, most recent since 2000, selected countries

*Source:* Seager, Joni. (2009). "Gender Division of Labour." Plate no. 25. In *The Penguin Atlas of Women in the World, 4th edition* (pp. 70–71). New York, NY: Penguin.

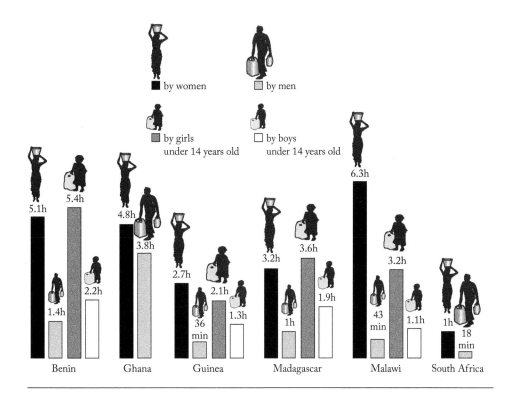

## Water Carriers

Average hours per week spent fetching water, 1998–2005

*Source:* Seager, Joni. (2009). "Water Carriers." Plate no. 25. In *The Penguin Atlas of Women in the World, 4th Edition* (pp. 70–71). New York, NY: Penguin.

# PART 2

## Constructions of Sex and Gender

One is not born, but rather becomes, a woman.
—*Simone de Beauvoir, The Second Sex (1974, p. 301)*

[Woman] is a term in process, a becoming, a constructing that cannot rightfully
be said to originate or to end.
—*Judith Butler, Gender Trouble (1990, p. 33)*

Part 2 explores the role of Western science and culture in making social differences and hierarchies based on categories such as sex, gender, race, ability, class, and sexuality. We highlight concepts like "essentialism" and "social constructionism," examine feminist critiques of and contributions to science, and trace scientific and social constructions of differences across time and place.

### Part 2A: The Construction of Sexed Bodies

In the first section, we introduce feminist and critical theory that challenges Western culture's taken-for-granted and deeply held ideas about sexed bodies. We call into question sexual binaries of male and female bodies, and invite students to consider alternative ways of conceptualizing sex differences.

### Part 2B: The Making of "Difference" and Inequalities

We are particularly interested in this section in examining feminist critiques of Western science and its role in constructing dualist thinking and hierarchical categories of difference based on ideas about sex, race, and disability. We see some of the ways in which inequalities among groups of people have been constructed, maintained, justified, and resisted. Students are also introduced to new ways of thinking about the relationship of biology and culture as interactive.

## Part 2C: Gender Construction and Performativity

Here we explore the social construction of our gendered identities through language and everyday practices. We introduce the concept of gender performativity, as well as important insights from contemporary analyses of masculinity and men's political involvement in feminism. We take up key perspectives in queer theory, which trouble gender binaries and challenge the narrow rigidity of dominant constructions of masculinity and femininity.

## Part 2D: The Construction of Sexuality

We examine in this section how social constructionist theory has been applied to historical and contemporary studies of sexuality within Canadian and global contexts. We invite students to assess critically the "naturalness" of heterosexuality, heterosexism, and homophobia, as well as the ethics of scientific research on sexual orientation. In addition, we begin to explore how ableism has, intentionally or not, shaped the politics and practices of social movements, focusing specifically on queer organizing.

# CHAPTER 12

## Introduction to *Beyond the Natural Body*

*Nelly Oudshoorn*

Nelly Oudshoorn is a professor of technology dynamics and health care at the University of Twente in the Netherlands, where she researches medical technology, and information and communication technology. Her scholarly works looking at the development of the "male pill" and the naming of "sex" hormones uncover some of the ways that science is implicated in creating and maintaining sex differences.

\*\*\*\*\*

What about sex and the body? [...] During the second wave of feminism that started in the 1970s, (fe)male bodies were of central concern in many debates, although in a rather peculiar way. Feminist biologists, like myself, were certain that biological determinism had to be rejected. We knew that nature does not determine what we mean when we use terms such as woman, body, femininity. We chose this position to contest those opponents of feminism who suggested that social inequality between women and men is primarily rooted in biological sex differences. According to this opinion, social changes demanded by feminists are wishful thinking because biology, rather than society, sets constraints on the behavior and abilities of women. Biology is destiny, and feminists simply have to accept this reality.

\*\*\*\*\*

Feminist biologists and historians of science did not hesitate to make [a] crucial move in exposing the myth of the natural body. Ruth Bleier, Ruth Hubbard, Evelyn Fox Keller and Helen Longino suggested that anatomical, endocrinological or immunological "facts" are anything but self-evident.[1] From these feminist scholars, I adopted the intellectually challenging and politically relevant notion that there does not exist an unmediated natural truth of the body. Our perceptions and interpretations of the body are mediated through language and, in our society, the biomedical sciences function as a major provider of this language. This view of the body is linked to a critical reappraisal of the status of biomedical knowledge. If understanding the body is mediated by language, scientists are bound by language as well. Consequently, the assumption that the biomedical sciences are the providers of objective knowledge about the "true nature" of the body could be rejected. This really changed my view of science and the world.

What is science all about if scientists are not discovering reality? In search of an answer to this question, I was inspired by the literature of the emerging field of social studies of science that introduced the powerful idea that scientific facts are not objectively given, but collectively created. This implies a totally different perspective on what scientists are doing: scientists are actively constructing reality, rather than discovering reality. For the debate about the body, this means that the naturalistic reality of the body as such does not exist; it is created by scientists as the object of scientific investigation (Duden 1991: 22). The social constructivist approach opened up a whole new line of research exposing the multiple ways in which the biomedical sciences as discursive technologies (re)construct and reflect our understanding of the body. The body, in all its complexities, thus achieved an important position on the feminist research agenda.

*****

## SEX AND THE BODY

In these biomedical discourses, the construction of the body as something with a sex has been a central theme all through the centuries. The myriad ways in which scientists have understood sex provide many illuminating counter-moves to the argument that sex is an unequivocal, ahistorical attribute of the body that once unveiled by science is valid everywhere and within every context. Early medical texts in particular challenge our present-day perceptions of male and female bodies. For our postmodern minds, it is hard to imagine that for two thousand years, male and female bodies were not conceptualized in terms of differences. Medical texts from the ancient Greeks until the late eighteenth century described male and female bodies as fundamentally similar. Women had even the same genitals as men, with one difference: "theirs are inside the body and not outside it." In this approach, characterized by Thomas Laqueur as the

"one-sex model," the female body was understood as a "male turned inside herself," not a different sex, but a lesser version of the male body (Laqueur 1990). Medical textbooks of this period show drawings of the female genitals that stress their resemblance to male genitalia so vividly that one could believe them to be representations of the male penis. For thousands of years, the "one-sex model" dominated biomedical discourse, even to such an extent that medical texts lacked a specific anatomical nomenclature for female reproductive organs. The ovary, for instance, did not have a name of its own but was described as the female testicle, thus referring again to the male organ. The language we are now familiar with, such as vagina and clitoris, simply did not exist (Laqueur 1990: 5, 96).

This emphasis on similarities rather than differences is also present in the texts of anatomists who studied parts of the body other than the reproductive organs. For Vesalius, the father of anatomy, "sex was only skin deep, limited to differences in the outline of the body and the organs of reproduction. In his view, all other organs were interchangeable between the sexes" (Schiebinger 1989: 189). In his beautiful drawings of the skeleton in *Epitome*, an anatomical atlas that appeared in 1543, Vesalius did not give sex to the bony structure of the body (Schiebinger 1989: 182). This (as we would now perceive it) "indifference" of medical scientists to bodily differences between the sexes does not seem to be a consequence of ignorance of the female body. Since the fourteenth century, the dissection of women's bodies was part of anatomical practice (Schiebinger 1989: 182). According to Laqueur, the stress on similarities, representing the female body as just a gradation of one basic male type, was inextricably intertwined with patriarchal thinking, reflecting the values of an overwhelmingly male public world in which "man is the measure of all things, and woman does not exist as an ontologically distinct category" (Laqueur 1990: 62).

It was only in the eighteenth century that biomedical discourse first included a concept of sex that is more familiar to our present-day interpretations of the male and the female body. The long-established tradition that emphasized bodily similarities over differences began to be heavily criticized. In the mid-eighteenth century, anatomists increasingly focused on bodily differences between the sexes, and argued that sex was not restricted to the reproductive organs, or as one physician put it: "the essence of sex is not confined to a single organ but extends, through more or less perceptible nuances, into every part" (Schiebinger 1989: 189). The first part of the body to become sexualized was the skeleton. If sex differences could be found in "the hardest part of the body," it would be likely that sex penetrated "every muscle, vein, and organ attached to and molded by the skeleton" (Schiebinger 1989: 191). In the 1750s, the first female skeletons appeared in medical textbooks. Londa Schiebinger has described how anatomists paid special attention to those parts of the skeleton that would become socially significant, amongst which was the skull. The depiction of the female skull was used to prove that women's intellectual capacities were inferior to those of men (Schiebinger 1986). The history of medicine in this period contains many illustrations of similar reflections of the social role of women in the representation of the human body. Anatomists of more recent centuries "mended nature to fit emerging ideals of masculinity and femininity" (Schiebinger 1989: 203). In nineteenth-century cellular physiology, the medical gaze shifted from the bones to the cells. Physiological "facts" were used to explain the passive nature of women. The biomedical sciences thus functioned as an arbiter in socio-political debates about women's rights and abilities (Laqueur 1990: 6, 215). By the late nineteenth century, medical scientists had extended this sexualization to every imaginable part of the body: bones, blood vessels, cells, hair and brains (Schiebinger 1989: 189). Only the eye seems to have no sex (Honegger 1991: 176). Biomedical discourse thus shows a clear shift in focus from similarities to differences. The female and the male body now became conceptualized in terms of opposite

bodies with "incommensurably different organs, functions, and feelings" (Laqueur 1990: viii).

Following this shift, the female body became the medical object *par excellence* (Foucault 1976), emphasizing woman's unique sexual character. Medical scientists now started to identify the "essential features that belong to her, that serve to distinguish her, that make her what she is" (Laqueur 1990: 5). The medical literature of this period shows a radical naturalization of femininity in which scientists reduced woman to one specific organ. In the eighteenth and nineteenth centuries, scientists set out to localize the "essence" of femininity in different places in the body. Until the mid-nineteenth century, scientists considered the uterus as the seat of femininity. This conceptualization is reflected in the statement of the German poet and naturalist Johann Wolfgang von Goethe (1749–1832): Der Hauptpunkt der ganzen weiblichen Existenz ist die Gebaermutter (The main point (or the essence) of the entire female existence is the womb) (Medvei 1983: 213).

In the middle of the nineteenth century, medical attention began to shift from the uterus to the ovaries, which came to be regarded as largely autonomous control centers of reproduction in the female animal, while in humans they were thought to be the "essence" of femininity itself (Gallagher and Laqueur 1987: 27). In 1848, Virchow (1817–1885), often portrayed as the founding father of physiology, characterized the function of the ovaries:

> It has been completely wrong to regard the uterus as the characteristic organ.... The womb, as part of the sexual canal, of the whole apparatus of reproduction, is merely an organ of secondary importance. Remove the ovary, and we shall have before us a masculine woman, an ugly half-form with the coarse harsh form, the heavy bone formation, the moustache, the rough voice, the flat chest, the sour and egoistic mentality and the distorted outlook ... in short, all that we

admire and respect in woman as womanly, is merely dependent on her ovaries. (Medvei 1983: 215)

The search for the female organ *par excellence* was not just a theoretical endeavor. The place in the body where the "essence" of femininity was located became the object of surgical interventions. The ovaries, perceived as the "organs of crises," became the paradigmatic object of the medical specialty of gynecology that was established in the late nineteenth century (Honegger 1991: 209, 211). The medical attention given to the ovaries resulted in the widespread practice of surgical operations for removal of the ovaries in many European countries, as well as in the United States. In the 1870s and 1880s, thousands of women were subjected to this drastic procedure for the treatment of menstrual irregularities and various neuroses (Corner 1965: 4).

Early in the twentieth century, the "essence" of femininity came to be located not in an organ but in chemical substances: sex hormones. The new field of sex endocrinology introduced the concept of "female" and "male" sex hormones as chemical messengers of femininity and masculinity. This hormonally constructed concept of the body has developed into one of the dominant modes of thinking about the biological roots of sex differences. Many types of behaviour, roles, functions and characteristics considered as typically male or female in western culture have been ascribed to hormones. In this process, the female body, but not the male body, has become increasingly portrayed as a body completely controlled by hormones. At this moment, the hormones estrogen and progesterone are the most widely used drugs in the history of medicine. These substances are a popular means of controlling fertility and are used for numerous other purposes: as menstruation regulators or abortifacients, in pregnancy tests and as specific medications for female menopause. Hormones are produced by pharmaceutical companies and delivered to women through a worldwide distribution network, including Third World countries (Wolffers et al. 1989: 27). This was not so a century ago. Our grandmothers did not know of any hormones: estrogen and progesterone as such did not exist in the nineteenth century. The concept of hormones was coined in 1905, and it took two decades before pharmaceutical companies began the mass production of hormones. Nowadays millions of women take hormonal pills and many of us have adopted the hormonal model to explain our bodies.

*****

Feminist studies have pointed out that cultural stereotypes about women and men play an important role in shaping scientific theories. The major question that emerges then is: To what extent do scientists use cultural notions as resources in their research practice?

## NOTE

1. Bleier (1984, 1986); Hubbard (1981); Hubbard et al. (1982); Keller (1982, 1984); Longino (1990); Longino and Doell (1983). In contrast to feminist sociologists, feminist biologists considered the body as relevant for the feminist research agenda. Actually, feminist biologists have adopted this position from the beginning of the debate about sex and gender. My account of the history of feminist studies should therefore not be read as a story of continuity and progress. There have been, and still are, many different positions in this debate about sex, gender and the body.

# REFERENCES

Bleier, R. (1984) *Science and Gender: A Critique of Biology and Its Theories on Women*. New York: Pergamon.

Bleier, R. (ed.) (1986) *Feminist Approaches to Science*. New York: Pergamon.

Corner, G.W. (1965) "The Early History of Oestrogenic Hormones," *Proceedings of the Society of Endocrinology* 33: 3–18.

Duden, B. (1991) *The Woman beneath the Skin: A Doctor's Patients in Eighteenth-Century Germany*. Cambridge, Mass., and London: Harvard University Press.

Foucault, M. (1976) *Histoire de la sexualité, 1: La volonté de savoir*. Paris: Gallimard.

Gallagher, C., Laqueur T., (eds) (1987) *The Making of the Modern Body: Sexuality and Society in the Nineteenth Century*. Berkeley, Los Angeles and London: University of California Press.

Honegger, C. (1991) *Die Ordnung der Geslechter Die Wissenschaften vom Menschen und das Weib*. Frankfurt and New York: Campus Verlag.

Hubbard, R. (1981) "The Emperor Doesn't Wear Any Clothes: The Impact of Feminism on Biology," in D. Spender (ed.), *Men's Studies Modified: The Impact of Feminism on the Academic Disciplines*. Oxford and New York: Pergamon.

Hubbard, R., Henifin, M.S., Fried, B. (eds) (1982) *Biological Woman: The Convenient Myth*. Cambridge, Mass.: Schenkman.

Keller, E. Fox (1982) "Feminism and Science," *Signs: Journal of Women in Culture and Society* 7 (1): 589–595.

Keller, E. Fox (1984) *Reflections on Gender and Science*. New Haven, Conn.: Yale University Press.

Laqueur, T. (1990) *Making Sex: Body and Gender from the Greeks to Freud*. Cambridge, Mass., and London: Harvard University Press.

Longino, H. (1990) *Science as Social Knowledge: Value and Objectivity in Scientific Inquiry*. Princeton, NJ, and Oxford: Princeton University Press.

Longino, H., Doell, R. (1983) "Body, Bias and Behavior: A Comparative Analysis of Reasoning in Two Areas of Biological Science," *Signs: Journal of Women in Culture and Society* 9 (2): 207–227.

Medvei, V.C. (1983) *A History of Endocrinology*. The Hague: MTP Press.

Schiebinger, L. (1986) "Skeletons in the Closet: The First Illustrations of the Female Skeleton in the Nineteenth-Century Anatomy," *Representations* 14: 42–83.

Schiebinger, L. (1989) *The Mind Has No Sex? Women in the Origins of Modern Science*. Cambridge, Mass., and London: Harvard University Press.

Wolffers, I., Hardon, A., Janssen, J. (1989) *Marketing Fertility: Women, Menstruation and the Pharmaceutical Industry*. Amsterdam: Wemos.

**Source:** Oudshoorn, Nelly. (1994). Excerpted from *Beyond the Natural Body: An Archaeology of Sex Hormones* (pp. 1–4, 6–10). Abingdon, UK: Routledge.

# ACTIVIST ART 1

## ASSIGNED MALE

*Sophie Labelle*

Sophie Labelle is a trans author, cartoonist, and public speaker from Montreal. She is especially known for her webcomic *Assigned Male*. Labelle grew up in rural Quebec, is a former elementary school teacher, and was the camp coordinator for Gender Creative Kids Canada. She is active in the trans rights movement and organizes conferences about trans history and transfeminism.

*Assigned Male* is a webcomic and series of zines tackling issues of gender norms and privilege. It tells the story of Stephie, a young trans girl discovering and embracing her gender.

*Source:* Labelle, Sophie. (2016, September 28). "#254." *Assigned Male*. Retrieved from: http://assignedmale.tumblr.com/post/151053988052/an-anecdote-a-participant-of-lgbt-youth-scotlands.

*Source:* Labelle, Sophie. (2015, August 28). "#121." *Assigned Male*. Retrieved from: http://assignedmale.tumblr.com/post/127783970357/fridays-update-this-is-a-discussion-that-i-often.

# CHAPTER 13

## How the Practice of Sex-Testing Targets Female Olympic Athletes

*Kate Allen*

Kate Allen writes about science and technology for the *Toronto Star*'s foreign desk. She is interested in all things great and geeky—from particle physics to paleontology and everything in between.

Sometime in 2011 or 2012, four elite female athletes travelled from their homes to a clinic in France.

They were all tall, flat-chested and muscular. Though they ranged in age from 18 to 21, none of the women had ever menstruated. Hormonal screening at the hands of anti-doping officers and team doctors had detected high levels of natural testosterone, so the athletes had come to be examined at a medical centre in Nice.

Doctors inspected the women's genitalia and found some atypical features. But genetic analysis and physical exams revealed something more unusual: all four had XY chromosomes rather than the usual female XX, and their internal reproductive glands were testes, not ovaries.

The athletes were diagnosed with 5-alpha reductase deficiency. Because of a genetic quirk, their bodies do not produce an enzyme that converts testosterone into a secondary hormone involved in the development of male characteristics. These women were chromosomally male, but had lived their lives, and competed athletically, as women.

The women, the doctors reported in a 2013 journal article, had "many questions" about the biological landmarks of female life: child-bearing, menstruation, sex. But from a competitive perspective, there was a different concern. Their testosterone levels were considered by the International Olympic Committee [IOC] and International Association of Athletics Federations [IAAF] to be in the male range, and therefore too high to compete fairly.

The doctors proposed a solution: gonadectomies, or surgical removal of their reproductive organs; clitoridectomies, or partial surgical removal of their clitorises; and, later, surgeries to feminize their vaginas and estrogen replacement therapy. These measures were not medically necessary, but after a year, the women would be cleared to compete. All four agreed.

Criticism from bioethicists, sports activists and intersex scholars was loud and furious.

Had these perfectly healthy women really just undergone clitoral mutilation for the purposes of sport? The athletes were competing with the hormones their bodies produced naturally, not doping—why is natural genetic variation policed in female athletes, but celebrated in men, like freakishly tall basketball players? What evidence is there, anyway, that testosterone is the sole predictor of superior athletic performance?

If the particulars were new, the fight itself was not. Ever since women began competing at elite levels, sports governing bodies like the Olympics have been searching for a way to cleanly divide men from women. Supporters say these boundaries are necessary to create a level playing field for female athletes.

Critics charge that these divisions are just metastasized social anxieties about gender. It is certainly true that crucial leaps in our understanding of sex differentiation were the result of studying animals and humans that warp our binary definitions. Even hard-nosed scientists admit that the field floats atop a fathomless public fascination: what makes a man, and what makes a woman?

But the more research we do, the less easy it is to answer that with a clear biological boundary. The public is by now used to the idea that sex is biological while gender is a social construct. But where in our biology does sex reside: in our genes, in our genitals, in our hormones? And is it even possible to separate biological sex from the environmental influence of gender?

"It is very difficult to come up with an absolute line," says Arthur Arnold, distinguished professor of integrative biology and physiology at the University of California Los Angeles. "The Olympic committees have struggled with this and have had different lines, all of which have broken down in various ways."

Last year, the IAAF was forced to lift its rules on female athletes and testosterone, and the IOC has begrudgingly followed suit. When the Games begin in Rio [2016 Summer Olympics in the city of Rio de Janeiro, Brazil] on Aug. 5, there will be no policy in place at all. It's not clear what tests or policies will eventually replace the revoked rules—or even if there should be a policy.

"It's kind of a mess," says Arnold.

\*\*\*\*\*

## THE SEX VERIFICATION TEST

At the 1936 Olympics, officials said they had conducted a "sex check" on an American gold-medal sprinter, Helen Stephens. Stephens had narrowly beaten a Polish runner, Stella Walsh, and Polish newspapers questioned the American's true gender.

Stephens "passed" the first known sex verification test. Officials, apparently, did not feel the need to examine Walsh.

In 1980, Walsh was murdered in a robbery in Cleveland. An autopsy revealed she had ambiguous genitalia, including a tiny, nonfunctioning penis. The revelation caused an uproar. In the *Star*, a headline declared "Olympic star Stella was a man." Along with media worldwide, the paper repeated that as fact over the decades.

But the coroner actually found that Walsh's cells were mismatched: some carried XY chromosomes, and some carried chromosomes with one X, not

**Figure 13.1: Helen Stephens, right, returns to the U.S. from the 1936 Berlin Olympics. Stephens "passed" the first known sex verification test.**

*Source:* Getty Images.

two. This type of "mosaicism" is caused by embryonic cell division errors, and is also called "mixed gonadal dysgenesis."

Walsh had mixed chromosomes, mixed internal sex organs and mixed external genitalia. As for her gender identity, the coroner, Samuel Gerber, offered his own assessment. "Socially, culturally and legally, Stella Walsh was accepted as a female for 69 years. She lived and died a female."

Western anthropologists have long fixated on "third" genders in other cultures: the Samoan Fa'afafine, the South Asian Hijra. But in international sports, authorities found increasingly laboured ways to split the two sexes, eventually mandating sex testing in the 1960s.

"Every generation of sex testing has been accompanied by a generation of activists and critics, and they've all pretty much had the same criticisms—which is that sex cannot be differentiated so easily," says Sandy Wells, a doctoral candidate at the University of British Columbia who studies the history of these policies.

At first, athletes were asked to appear naked before a panel of doctors. The "nude parades" were criticized as humiliating and abandoned.

Critics today would add they are diagnostically useless. Features like clitoromegaly—an atypically enlarged clitoris—are associated not only with intersex conditions but with premature birth and nerve tumours. "Guess what—everyone's body is different," says Wells. "More often than you'd think, the opinion of the panel would be contradictory."

Barr Body testing, more dignified and supposedly more scientific, used cells from a cheek swab, stained and examined under a microscope, to detect a bundled, silenced X chromosome, found in most cells of XX females and visible as a dark blot.

Maria José Martinez-Patiño, a Spanish hurdler, failed a Barr Body chromosome test in 1985. She was stripped of her national records and had her sports scholarship revoked. "I felt ashamed and embarrassed," Martinez-Patiño wrote decades later. "I lost friends, my fiancé, hope and energy. But I knew that I was a woman."

Martinez-Patiño has androgen insensitivity syndrome. Her chromosomal sex is XY and she has male internal sex organs, but a genetic mutation means her androgen receptors don't work. "When I was conceived, my tissues never heard the hormonal messages to become male," she wrote.

She developed as a typical female, and she and her family never doubted her gender. As an athlete, she could not make use of her body's testosterone. Armed with medical evidence, the hurdler fought the IAAF and won permission to race again. Absent from competition for three years, however, she failed to qualify for the next Olympics.

Through the decades, scientists joined in criticizing the tests as inaccurate and unethical. Nevertheless, athletes who had always known themselves to be women continued to be traumatically "outed." Between three and 15 athletes at every Games failed a sex test, a figure that does not count those who slunk away from sport to avoid humiliation.

The IAAF finally sponsored two medical-scientific symposia, which concluded what critics said all along: female athletes with sex-related genetic abnormalities, including mosaicism, androgen insensitivity syndrome and 5-alpha reductase deficiency do not enjoy any unfair physical advantage beyond the range of normal human variability. Blanket sex-testing is arbitrary and discriminatory.

The IAAF dropped the practice in 1991. But the IOC lumbered on. It replaced Barr Body testing with DNA tests to locate the newly discovered SRY gene on the Y chromosome. At the 1996 Games, eight female athletes were found positive for SRY. All had androgen insensitivity syndrome or 5-alpha reductase deficiency, and they were eventually cleared.

Dozens of scientific and medical societies had by this point called for the elimination of sex testing, including the American Medical Association and the Canadian and Australian genetics societies.

Whether it was the censure of scientists, disapproval from many athletes, or the cost of a program that had never caught a man masquerading as a woman—its stated purpose—the IOC finally dropped blanket sex testing in 1999.

It was a short-lived victory. Both the IAAF and IOC had retained an important condition: they could medically evaluate an athlete if necessary. A decade later, the case of Caster Semenya would convulse the sports world all over again.

## "JUST LOOK AT HER"

When Caster Semenya, the South African 800-metre runner, posted dominant wins in two championships in 2009, word leaked that officials had singled her out for a sex test. As her white competitors publicly questioned the muscular black woman's femininity—"just look at her," one said—Semenya underwent a battery of invasive physical and psychological exams.

Again, an athlete who had lived her life as a woman was barred from competition as her gender was publicly, humiliatingly scrutinized. Semenya was cleared to run again in 2010. [...]

In the wake of that furor, the IAAF adopted new regulations on "female hyperandrogenism." The IOC followed suit. Female athletes with testosterone levels "within the male range" would be unable to compete, unless they lowered their levels with drugs or surgery. (Those with androgen insensitivity syndrome were excused.)

The sports bodies said the new policies were not sex tests—they were tests for unfair advantage. Observers were dismayed, if not incredulous.

"I'm very proud of my association with the Olympic movement," says Bruce Kidd, who participated in numerous Games as an athlete, journalist and social scientist, and is now the principal of University of Toronto Scarborough. But, Kidd says, "for a movement that has long tried to link science and scholarship to its mission, it's an embarrassment."

Testosterone is a natural place to park suspicions about the source of athletic advantage. Men's testosterone levels are about 10 times higher than women's, and elite male athletes are demonstrably faster and stronger than elite female athletes.

IAAF researchers found that women with XY-chromosome disorders of sex development, who have significantly higher testosterone than is typical, are "dramatically" overrepresented among elite athletes compared to the general population.

What's more, anabolic steroids—the drug of choice for East Germany's state-sponsored doping program, Canadian sprinter Ben Johnson, and baseball's Barry Bonds—usually consist of synthetic testosterone.

But no study has ever shown that performance—say, finishing times in a race—correlates to athletes' levels of testosterone. Testosterone is a complicated, dynamic substance: finishing a marathon causes it to plummet in men, while positive feedback from a coach can cause it to shoot up.

Like every other biological marker, testosterone's ability to cleanly divide two binary sexes is muddled, especially in athletes.

In one study of nearly 700 Olympians participating in 15 sports, 13.7 per cent of women had natural testosterone levels above the typical female range, 4.7 per cent were within the male range, and 16.5 per cent of men had levels below the typical male range, with some falling into the female range. An IAAF study on 849 female athletes, excluding competitors with intersex traits and other genetic sex diversity, still found outliers.

If hyperandrogenic women are overrepresented in elite sports, they themselves are still vastly outranked by female athletes who are winning with typical hormones.

As for the cheaters, there is little evidence that synthetic or "exogenous" testosterone behaves the same way as natural or "endogenous" testosterone, which is produced by and responds to a dynamic system of hormones.

**Figure 13.2: Women at the Olympics: Female participants through the years**

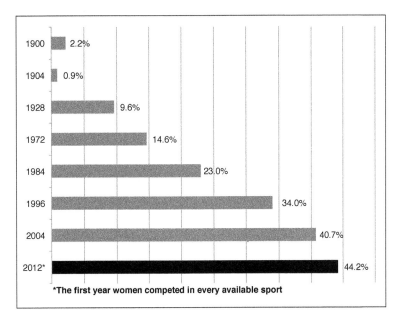

*The first year women competed in every available sport

*Source:* Data from International Olympic Committee. (2016, January). "Factsheet: Women in the Olympic Movement." Lausanne, Switzerland: Olympic Studies Centre.

"There is every reason to be really cautious about how we fill in those gaps, because we tend to fill them in a way that fits really pre-scientific ideas about masculinity and femininity," says Barnard College's Rebecca Jordan-Young.

Kidd was part of a team that took the hyperandrogenism rules to the Court of Arbitration for Sport after a young Indian sprinter with hyperandrogenism, Dutee Chand, was barred from competition.

"We have said all along that we support the anti-doping prohibitions against exogenous … pharmaceutically created testosterone. But we are bitterly opposed to the idea that a woman can't run on her own chemicals," Kidd said.

In July 2015, the court found that indirect evidence indicates testosterone probably confers an advantage. But it was not convinced that testosterone explained the entire performance gap between men and women, a difference in the range of 10 to 12 per cent. If testosterone confers an advantage in the realm of 1 to 3 per cent, it is no different from other variables that conspire to produce a superior athlete: height, muscle mass, oxygen uptake.

The ruling suspended the IAAF's regulations, citing lack of scientific evidence. But it raised questions that venture well beyond science: what is fairness, really, in the world of elite sport?

Those who decried the court's ruling cited a desire to maintain a level playing field for women. Female athletes themselves want that: the British world-record-holding marathoner, Paula Radcliffe, testified in support of the IAAF, and Maria José Martinez-Patiño, the banned hurdler, co-authored an article that concluded some rule must exist.

But why are women the only ones who need the playing field levelled? Is it fair to compete against LeBron James, Michael Phelps or Usain Bolt? Sports celebrates outliers on the spectrum of genetic diversity. No one is hunting for male athletes who produce vastly more testosterone than their peers, or enjoy any other freakish advantage.

We don't know the names of the four young female athletes who travelled to France, or anything about their athletic or personal lives, only that they were from developing countries. But because of the court's decision—affirmed by the IOC—their irreversible gonadectomies would no longer be necessary to compete. And of course their partial clitoridectomies, a cosmetic procedure, were never necessary.

Nobody knows what will happen next. The IAAF has two years from last July's ruling to produce evidence supporting the hyperandrogenism regulations. Even some supporters don't think they will: the science of sex and athletic advantage is just too elusive. Should declaring a gender identity be enough? Should we do away with divisions entirely?

Kidd points out we don't actually know how much of the 10- to 12-per-cent male advantage is the result of social context rather than biology.

"Will women run as fast as men in some events if genuine equality is achieved—if the genetic pool out of which female Olympians are drawn is the same, and there is the same motivational encouragement, the same financial encouragement?" he asks.

"We're living in an experiment."

*Source:* Allen, Kate. (2016, July 31). Excerpted from "How the Practice of Sex-Testing Targets Female Olympic Athletes." *Toronto Star.* Retrieved from: https://www.thestar.com/news/world/2016/07/31/why-the-olympics-cant-figure-out-who-is-a-man-and-who-is-a-woman.html.

# CHAPTER 14

## Contesting Intersex

*Georgiann Davis*

Georgiann Davis is an assistant professor in sociology at the University of Nevada–Las Vegas. She is current president of interACT: Advocates for Intersex Youth, and former president of the AIS-DSD (Androgen Insensitivity Syndrome – Disorder of Sex Development) Support Group. Davis has written numerous articles on intersex in various outlets ranging from *Ms. Magazine* to the *American Journal of Bioethics*. In her book, *Contesting Intersex: The Dubious Diagnosis*, Davis explores how intersex is defined, experienced, and contested in contemporary U.S. society.

## INTRODUCTION: "YOU'RE IN THE MONKEY CAGE WITH ME"

Summer in Chicago is a time for exploring the city, visiting Lake Michigan, enjoying great food, and debating the causes of the Cubs' inability to win. However, in the summer of 2008, a group of more than one hundred visitors chose to stay in their run-of-the-mill conference hotel rather than discover what Chicago has to offer. Mostly white middle class women, young and old, from around the country, they had come to the Windy City for the annual meeting of the Androgen Insensitivity Syndrome Support Group–USA (AISSG-USA).

Unlike most other national conferences, this one had no posters with its name decorating the hotel. Instead, the signs that led attendees to their registration site displayed a colorful orchid and the words "Women's Support Group" in bold letters, followed by "Please do not disturb." Curious hotel employees and guests found the meeting mysterious. One employee asked me, "Why are all of you needing support?" I shrugged my shoulders, not sure how to respond.

In fact, the ambiguity of the signs was appropriate to the purpose of the meeting, whose attendees were distinguished by the fact that the sex they were born with had been deemed biologically ambiguous by the medical profession. To put it another way, almost everyone at the meeting had been born with an intersex trait (or accompanied someone born with an intersex trait). In many instances, the result was physical bodies incongruent with sex chromosomes. In the past, these individuals might have been considered *hermaphrodites*, a term that some—but not all—in the intersex community now consider derogatory. Terms less contentious today include *intersex*, *intersex traits*, *intersexuality*, and *intersexual*.

This work is about how *intersex* is defined, experienced, and contested in contemporary U.S. society. I argue that medical professionals have replaced intersex language with disorder of sex development nomenclature, a linguistic move designed to reclaim their authority and jurisdiction over the intersex body. Ironically, this disorder of sex development (DSD) terminology was strategically introduced in 2005 by Cheryl Chase, a prominent intersex activist, and her allies, who had hoped the new nomenclature would improve medical care for those born with intersex traits. Instead, as I show here, DSD terminology has heightened tension within the intersex community. Some individuals born with intersex traits are embracing the new nomenclature; others resist it, citing the pathologization that underlies the term *disorder*; a few are indifferent to diagnostic labels and think individuals should use whatever term(s) they prefer. My hope is that *Contesting Intersex* will tease apart the tensions over terminology in the intersex community, while also showing how power resides in diagnostic labels.

Although *intersex* is itself a term whose meaning is contested, in general it is used to describe the state of being born with a combination of characteristics (e.g., genital, gonadal, and/or chromosomal) that are typically presumed to be exclusively male or female. People with androgen insensitivity syndrome (AIS), for example, have XY chromosomes and testes "but lack a key androgen receptor"[1] that consequently prevents their bodies from responding during gestational development and beyond to the normal amounts of *androgens* (an umbrella term for testosterone) their testes produce. Depending upon how much androgen the receptor blocks, some AIS individuals have ambiguous external genitalia (usually a larger clitoris that resembles a small penis) with either internal or external testes, while others have an outwardly "normal"-looking vagina with a shortened vaginal canal, no uterus, and undescended testes. [...]

There is no simple medical explanation for the cause(s) of intersex, no agreement on what defines intersex, and no formal record of those born with such "abnormalities." All of these lacks presumably contribute to the challenge of establishing the frequency of intersex. Still, estimates have been made, with the most-used figure suggesting 1 in 2,000 people is intersex, but because estimates drastically vary across publications,[2] I'm uncomfortable offering my own estimate. What I do know, however, is that intersex people exist all around the world.

Estimates of intersex in the population did not matter to the conference attendees, who shared a unique medical history and had a strong connection with one another. They were there to support one another in healing from what, for many, has been a life full of medical lies, deception, and unnecessary surgical intervention. Yet if you had happened to stumble into that Chicago hotel that summer weekend, you would have had no idea of what had brought the attendees together. Without the "Women's Support Group" signs, you might have imagined that you were interrupting a meeting of sorority sisters or a family reunion. A group official told me that one reason for the secrecy was to prevent any attendees from feeling uncomfortable or "freakish." This was also why the support group's public website did not name the conference location. I found AISSG-USA through that very website, as I searched the Internet for information about *my* intersex "abnormality." As a twenty-seven-year-old individual with complete androgen insensitivity syndrome (CAIS), I had met only one other intersex person, a friend from work who was as private about her diagnosis as I was about mine. I wanted to know more about intersex, and I started my search for information online. [...]

I was diagnosed with CAIS around the age of thirteen. I was experiencing abdominal pains, and my mother thought I would soon begin menstruating, a rite of passage for women in my family, as in many other families. However, my period never came. The abdominal pain went away, but my mother was concerned enough to seek medical advice. I soon found myself in an endocrinologist's office, wondering why so many doctors were literally looking over—and within—my body. At the time, the doctors told me I had underdeveloped ovaries that had a very high risk of being cancerous and would need to be surgically removed before my eighteenth birthday. But the doctors were lying: The purported ovaries were actually undescended testes. Encouraged by medical providers, my parents went along with the lie, and when I was seventeen, I had surgery to remove the supposedly dangerous organs.

I would not see a doctor again, or discover that I had an intersex trait, until, at nineteen, I relocated to a new area far from my childhood medical providers, where I sought new doctors. As is customary, they requested that I bring my medical records with me to my appointment for a routine physical. When I finally got my hands on my surgical records, I read them in utter disbelief. That was my first encounter with the truth about my body and the medically unnecessary surgery I had undergone. At that time, it made me deeply uncomfortable to learn that I had XY chromosomes and testicular feminization syndrome—the label for my trait when I was initially diagnosed. I was in tears as I read what one gynecologist had written in my medical file: "After extensive discussion I feel pt [patient] needs surgery to have gonads removed. She is not aware of any chromosomal studies and most literature agrees it best she not be aware of the chromosome studies. She has been told she is missing her uterus, she does have a vagina. She has no tubes. She has been told she may have streaked ovaries and they should be removed because of the possibility of developing gonadal cancer" (personal medical records, November 26, 1997).

I was shocked and confused. Why had my medical providers and parents lied to me for so many years? I thought I'd had surgery because of a health risk. Was having an intersex trait that horrible? I remember thinking I must be a real freak if even my parents hadn't been able to tell me the truth. I ran to the dumpster outside my building and threw my records away, not wanting to be reminded of the diagnosis or the surgery that couldn't be undone.

Almost a decade later, I was finally emotionally ready to confront my medical past, and I requested another set of my records. I was exploring feminist theories and gender and sexuality scholarship in my sociology doctoral program, an incredibly empowering experience that positioned me to revisit my personal experience with sex, gender, and sexuality binaries. Our assigned readings and thoughtful classroom discussions encouraged me to delve deeply into my medical history, first with close graduate school friends and faculty, eventually with anyone who cared to listen. Finally feeling liberated, I sought others like me, which is how I ended up at my first intersex support group conference, which happened to be in Chicago that year.

This project was born during that emotional weekend, which will forever mark my first involvement with the intersex community. Although I entered the weekend as an individual with an intersex trait looking for peers, by its end I was determined to pursue a sociological analysis of intersex in contemporary U.S. society. Despite my personal experience with intersex, I was initially concerned that I would have difficulty gaining access to a community that hasn't had the best experiences with researchers, notably psychologist John Money, whose work was discredited after the discovery of his falsified data and unethical research practices. I was wrong: AISSG-USA was incredibly supportive of my research, as was each of the other organizations I studied. It became clear during data collection that my personal experience with intersexuality provided an inroad into the field and community that would eventually become my second home. In the fall of 2013, I was elected president of the AIS-DSD Support Group, the new name of AISSG-USA, which had just started to allow men with intersex traits to attend their annual meeting.

As a result of the access, support, and assistance I received in connecting with intersex community members, I was able to collect a tremendous amount of data in a relatively short time. During this period, I formed friendships throughout the intersex community, to which I am now permanently connected. For I am not only studying the intersex community, I'm in it. As Peggy, a fifty-six-year-old with an intersex trait, said to me, "I feel that you're going to be on my side. You're not like someone at the zoo saying, 'Well I'm a human being and I'm taking notes on the monkeys.' You're in the monkey cage with me."

Like that of many of my research participants, my experience with intersexuality has left me with some horrific physical and emotional scars. However, it has also become the core of my intellectual passion and academic commitment. On January 7, 2010, in the midst of my data collection, I met fifty-three-year-old Cheryl Chase, who was instrumental in the rise of the intersex rights movement nearly two decades earlier. As we finished our emotionally intense interview, Chase wrote on a piece of paper, "Georgiann, Finish your PhD and change the world!" That note, along with a framed picture of the two of us, greets me every time I sit down at my desk. It is not just memorabilia from the field; it is symbolic of my commitment to *our* entire community, no matter how divided—over medical terminology and how best to advocate for change—we are today.

\*\*\*\*\*

## THE DUBIOUS DIAGNOSIS

I started *Contesting Intersex* with one broad question in mind: How did *intersex* become a *disorder of sex development*? I've argued that a good part of the answer to this question has to do with medical authority and jurisdiction over the intersex body. While Cheryl Chase and her allies came up with and advocated for the new DSD terminology, hoping it would improve intersex medical care, the phrase was formally introduced by the medical profession. DSD nomenclature initiated the transformation of intersex advocacy from collective confrontation to contested

collaboration. Today, DSD terminology has come to replace intersex language in almost all corners of the medical profession, a change that dismays at least some members of the intersex community.

The rapid and widespread acceptance of *DSD* by medical providers has been striking, but it can be explained by its context. When the terminological shift occurred in 2005, medical control over intersex was in jeopardy as a result of a confluence of factors, including feminist critiques of intersex medical care [...] and intersex activism. As public awareness rose about the prevalence of medically unnecessary surgeries on intersex people, it seemed impossible that medical providers could continue to treat intersex traits as they had been doing. But when intersex traits were reinvented as disorders of sex development—itself an act of powerful evidence for the social construction of medical diagnoses—medical providers had the perfect opportunity to reassert their authority over intersex and reclaim jurisdiction over the intersex body in treating this new disorder. The fact that many medical providers hold essentialist understandings of sex, gender, and sexuality—tending to see all three as biologically prescribed and, in many cases, neatly correlated—made them more open to and quick to accept the idea of *disorders* of sex development, not to mention the pathologization its language implies.

But at the same time as DSD nomenclature has taken off in the medical profession, it has been a major source of tension in the intersex community, especially since it was officially introduced by the medical profession in the "Consensus Statement on Management of Intersex Disorders" (Houk et al. 2006; Hughes et al. 2006; Lee et al. 2006). Some intersex people accept DSD language, which allows them access to biological citizenship and its benefits, including supportive relationships with medical providers and family members, though at the cost of feeling stigmatized for being labeled as having a disorder. Intersex people who reject DSD language tend to reject the idea that sex, gender, and sexuality are biologically prescribed bodily phenomena and instead embrace intersex itself as a powerful identity. In doing so, they challenge gender essentialist ideologies. However, I argue that by rejecting DSD terminology, they also limit their access to biological citizenship and its benefits.

Though DSD nomenclature has heightened divides in the intersex community, most intersex people agree that surgeries designed to "normalize" the intersex body shouldn't be performed until individuals are old enough to make their own decisions. This is an important goal our community shares, grounded in a desire to improve the lives of future generations of intersex people. But we need to remember that surgical interventions are not the exclusive cause of our struggles as intersex people, for even those who have escaped surgery struggle with intersex. This leads me to conclude that those struggles are not solely the result of dangerous interactions with the scalpel. Rather, they emerge out of the broader medicalization process, specifically the ongoing struggle to challenge the belief that we are abnormal, a belief held, alas, by too many of us, as well as much of the medical profession and society at large.

Given this challenge, our intersex community cannot afford in-group conflict over terminology. We need to be conscious of the origins and history of DSD terminology, but when we think about what needs to change to benefit future generations of intersex people, people should be able to choose whatever term—or terms—they find suitable: *intersex*; *intersex traits*; *intersex conditions*; *intersexed*; *intersexual*; *disorder of sex development*; *difference of sex development*; the abbreviation *DSD*; *diverse reproductive development* (*DRD*); *diverse sex development*, also known as *intersex* (*DSDI*); *intersex*, also known as *differences in reproductive development* (*IDSD*); *conditions affecting reproductive development* (*CARD*); *congenital atypical reproductive development* (*CARD*); *conditions related to reproductive development* (*CRD*); *variations of reproductive development* (*VRD*); *hermaphrodite*; a term we have not yet come up with; or no term at all. This flexibility will provide us with more open access to biological citizenship, which I have shown has

significant, though not exclusive, value. It will allow us to devote our time to other matters, such as ending the shame and secrecy tied to the intersex diagnosis.

Like some of my research participants, I find the word *disorder* pathologizing, but if strategically employing DSD nomenclature results in higher-quality medical care, why shouldn't we use it or some variation of it, including *differences* of sex development? While I find value in Audre Lorde's (1984) claim that the "master's tools will never dismantle the master's house" (112), meaning that using the tools of oppression can't end oppression, sometimes we need to access powerful institutions in order to create change. Because *intersex* has historically been situated in the medical institution, we need to access that institution, which means that sometimes we need to work with its terms, even *disorder of sex development*. But we can control how we approach that term by acknowledging—and pushing medical professionals to acknowledge—that sex, gender, and sexuality, as well as medical diagnoses, are socially constructed phenomena embedded within a system of stratification. There is power in a name, and the intersex community can and should use that power to its advantage.

Since the publication of the "Consensus Statement on Management of Intersex Disorders" (Houk et al. 2006; Hughes et al. 2006; Lee et al. 2006), the global intersex community has experienced several significant events that have raised public awareness about intersex in ways that have significant potential to shift the definition, status, and experience of intersex for years to come. The years 2012 and 2013, in particular, brought new political visibility to the intersex community. In 2012, the Swiss National Advisory Commission on Biomedical Ethics[3] and the German Ethics Council[4] independently offered opinions that critiqued the contemporary state of intersex medical care. In 2013, the United Nations Special Rapporteur on Torture condemned the medical profession's nonconsensual surgical treatment of intersex by associating it with torture.[5] The New Jersey Senate approved a bill that will allow intersex and trans people to change the gender listed on their birth certificates without surgery,[6] and a new German law came into effect that allows parents of intersex children to register their children as "X," rather than "M" or "F," on birth certificates.[7] Members of the intersex community often disagree on the implications of these events—for instance, the new German law has been criticized[8] for forcing intersex children into an arbitrary third option ("X"), unlike the law passed in Australia, also in 2013, that allows adults to choose a third gender designation on government-issued personal documents.[9]

*****

## Actions for Liberation

Despite recent attention on intersex, too much shame, secrecy, and stigma remain associated with intersex traits. My hope is that, regardless of our genitalia and our experiences with intersex, we can continue to fight for liberation from the shackles society rigidly ties to intersex bodies. We can begin to do this, I argue, by directly confronting the gender structure. When we make the gender structure visible—that is, when we understand how gender constrains us at the institutional, individual, and interactional levels of society—we diminish at least some of the powerful control it has over our lives. [...]

Given my personal, professional, and ethical commitment to the intersex community, I want to conclude *Contesting Intersex* by using the information and insights I have derived from my research to offer seven actions for liberation that intersex activists and our allies can take to decrease intersex stigma and the shame and secrecy that surrounds it. [...]

### Action #1: Stop the Surgeries
The first action in a liberatory transformation of the lives of intersex people must involve holding medical professionals responsible for violating medical protocols during the medical management of

intersexuality. Although both the 2000 committee statement "Evaluation of the Newborn with Developmental Anomalies of the External Genitalia" and the 2006 "Consensus Statement on Management of Intersex Disorders" are critical of the medically unnecessary surgical modification of intersex bodies (Committee 2000; Hughes et al. 2006; Lee et al. 2006; Houk et al. 2006), these surgeries continue under the guise of protecting children from health risks, especially cancer, even as these cancer claims are inconsistent at best and fallacious at worst.[10] There are no official estimates on the number of intersex people who have been subjected to medically unnecessary surgical interventions. However, my interviews with medical professionals indicate that such procedures are still quite common. Scholars who were studying the community years before I did noted the physical and emotional scarring caused by intersex "normalization" surgery (e.g., Holmes 2008; Karkazis 2008; Preves 2003), yet, as I've documented, these struggles continue to persist throughout the intersex community. [...]

### Action #2: Work with—Not for—Doctors
Liberatory transformation will also require that medical professionals engage in collective collaboration with intersex people and our families while simultaneously calling for us to be open to collaborating with doctors to promote change. Providers must be willing to learn from the intersex community and share at least some of their authority over intersex traits and the intersex body. There is no question that medical professionals who treat intersex traits are trying to help their patients, yet the majority of them are working exclusively from a medicalized body of knowledge and strategies acquired during their medical educations. However, for intersex people to achieve a true liberatory transformation, medical professionals need to extend their scope by engaging with, valuing the knowledge of, and even welcoming the tools of other stakeholders, including people in the intersex community and sociocultural scholars. [...]

The medical profession is a powerful institution. It is in our interest to work with that power to promote change. With supportive medical allies as our secret weapons, we can work together to change intersex medical care.

### Action #3: Expand and Diversify Peer Support

Liberatory transformation also depends upon expanding and diversifying peer support and the informational biocitizenship such support enables. When I asked research participants what advice they would give to someone recently diagnosed with an intersex trait, almost everyone said they would strongly encourage that person to meet other intersex people. Intersex people, me included, find solace in knowing we are not alone in our experience of being differently bodied. My interviews with parents confirmed the value of peer support. Parents with whom I spoke reported that meeting other parents of intersex children was emotionally empowering. [...]

Given the importance of peer support, I strongly recommend that all intersex groups strive toward being more inclusive of all intersex people, regardless of their gender expression. [...] There also needs to be more collaboration across intersex organizations toward a shared goal of increasingly racial and class diversity throughout the global intersex community. As it stands today, the intersex community consists largely of individuals privileged by race and class. We must actively work to diversify our community.

### Action #4: Replace Fear with Power

In order to achieve liberatory transformation, we must replace the fear of not fitting into the sex binary with the power we gain by educating others about sex variability. In my interviews with intersex people, I saw that the individuals who are most emotionally comfortable with their intersex diagnosis are those who do not feel constrained by the difference but rather embrace it as part of their identity. Many of these individuals speak publicly about their lived experiences. [...] This public exposure seems to be related to both a positive sense of self for these individuals and a destigmatization of intersexuality that benefits the entire intersex community. [...]

### Action #5: Embrace Feminist Ideas

If we believe, as my research suggests, that ideas can themselves be liberatory, and classrooms can be spaces where these liberatory ideas are shared (e.g., hooks 1994), then another step we must take on our road to liberatory transformation is to embrace the insights of feminist scholarship. Exposure to feminist scholarship created strikingly different outcomes for my research participants. Individuals who encountered feminist scholarship in formal educational settings or were introduced to it by friends or the media reported much more positive senses of self and were much more comfortable with their intersex trait than those who weren't.

\*\*\*\*\*

### Action #6: Recognize Social Constructions

This sixth action for a liberatory transformation builds on the previous action and calls for us to understand that phenomena throughout the world are constructed by various institutions in ways that maintain and perpetuate inequalities. The medical profession is just one example of such an institution. In the intersex community, the most debilitating phenomena include sex, gender, sexuality, and medical diagnoses, all of which tend to be viewed as indisputable characteristics of the body or, in the case of diagnoses, indisputable descriptions of those characteristics. It is not common to recognize sex, gender, sexuality, and even medical diagnoses as socially constructed through various social institutions, but doing so could be liberatory for the intersex community. [...]

### Action #7: Listen to Children

I see the seventh and final action as one of the most important. We must respect and include children's voices in the medical decision-making process. [...]

More often than not, medical providers ignore intersex children. That is, children's voices aren't usually heard in both specific decisions about their own bodies or in larger debates about intersex medical care, despite the fact that they are the ones most affected by the medical management of intersex traits. In most cases, medically unnecessary surgical interventions on intersex bodies happen to children—that is, to minors who cannot legally make their own decisions, or, if they are babies or toddlers, cannot even formulate their own opinions. Many medical providers who treat intersex children do not seriously consider children's wishes in the medical decision-making process. In order to value children's voices, medical providers would need to avoid all medically unnecessary interventions until children were mature enough to make their own decisions about their bodies. Given that these irreversible procedures are more often than not cosmetic, shouldn't intersex children have the right to delay or refuse them? I'm not suggesting that all medical recommendations pertaining to a child's intersex trait should be withheld until the child is mature enough to assess them. Rather, I'm suggesting that in the case of medically unnecessary and irreversible surgical interventions, we need to listen to intersex children and involve them in the decision-making process.

## NOTES

1. Cited from Sharon Preves's (2003) *Intersex and Identity*, p. 27.
2. For a further discussion of estimates of intersex in the population, see Melanie Blackless et al. (2000) and Anne Fausto-Sterling (2000, 53).
3. See Swiss National Advisory Commission on Biomedical Ethics (2012).
4. See German Ethics Council (2012).
5. See Feminist Newswire (2013).
6. See Kelly (2013).
7. See Nandi (2013).
8. Hida Viloria, a well-known intersex activist, offered a critique at Advocate.com. See Viloria (2013).

9. See Zara (2013).
10. See Rola Nakhal et al. (2013), Rebecca Deans et al. (2012), J. Pleskacova et al. (2010), Leendert H.J. Looijenga et al. (2007), Martine Cools et al. (2006), and Deborah Merke and Stefan Bornstein (2005).

## REFERENCES

Blackless, Melanie, Anthony Charuvastra, Amanda Derryck, Anne Fausto-Sterling, Karl Lauzanne, and Ellen Lee. 2000. "How Sexually Dimorphic Are We? Review and Synthesis." *American Journal of Human Biology* 12(2): 151–66.

Committee on Genetics: Section on Endocrinology and Section on Urology. 2000. "Evaluation of the Newborn with Developmental Anomalies of the External Genitalia." *Pediatrics* 106(1): 138–42.

Cools, Martine, Stenvert L.S. Drop, Katja P. Wolffenbuttel, J. Wolter Oosterhuis, and Leendert H.J. Looijenga. 2006. "Germ Cell Tumors in the Intersex Gonad: Old Paths, New Directions, Moving Frontiers." *Endocrine Reviews* 27(5): 468–84.

Deans, R., S. M. Creighton, L. M. Liao, and G. S. Conway. 2012. "Timing of Gonadectomy in Adult Women with Complete Androgen Insensitivity Syndrome (CAIS): Patient Preferences and Clinical Evidence." *Clinical Endocrinology* 76(6): 894–98.

Fausto-Sterling, Anne. 2000. *Sexing the Body: Gender Politics and the Construction of Sexuality*. New York, NY: Basic Books.

Feminist Newswire. 2013. "UN Condemns 'Normalization' Surgeries of Intersex Children." *Feminist Majority Foundation Blog*. Accessed January 31, 2015. http://feminist.org/blog/index.php/2013/02/08/un-condemns-normalization-surgeries-of-intersex-children/.

German Ethics Council. 2012. "Press Release: Intersex People Should Be Recognized, Supported and Protected from Discrimination." *Deutscher Ethikrat*. Accessed January 31, 2015. http://www.ethikrat.org/files/press-release-2012-01.pdf/.

Holmes, Morgan. 2008. *Intersex: A Perilous Difference*. Selinsgrove, Pa.: Susquehanna University Press.

hooks, bell. 1994. *Teaching to Transgress: Education as the Practice of Freedom*. New York, NY: Routledge.

Houk, Christopher P., Ieuan A. Hughes, S. Faisal Ahmed, Peter A. Lee, and Writing Committee for the International Intersex Consensus Conference Participants. 2006. "Summary of Consensus Statement on Intersex Disorders and Their Management." *Pediatrics* 118(2): 753–57.

Hughes, Ieuan A., Christopher Houk, S. Faisal Ahmed, Peter A. Lee, and LWPES1/ESPE2 Consensus Group. 2006. "Consensus Statement on Management of Intersex Disorders." *Archives of Disease in Childhood* 91(7): 554–63.

Karkazis, Katrina. 2008. *Fixing Sex: Intersex, Medical Authority, and Lived Experience*. Durham, N.C.: Duke University Press.

Kelly, Ashlee. 2013. "New Jersey Senate Panel Approves Trans and Intersex Birth Certificate Bill." *Gay Star News*. Accessed January 31, 2015. https://www.gaystarnews.com/article/new-jersey-senate-panel-approves-trans-and-intersex-birth-certificate-bill141213/.

Lee, Peter A., Christopher P. Houk, S. Faisal Ahmed, and Ieuan A. Hughes. 2006. "Consensus Statement on Management of Intersex Disorders." *Pediatrics* 118(2): 488–500.

Looijenga, Leendert H.J., Remko Hersmus, J. Wolter Oosterhuis, Martine Cools, Stenvert L.S. Drop, and Katja P. Wolffenbuttel. 2007. "Tumor Risk in Disorders of Sex Development (DSD)." *Best Practice & Research Clinical Endocrinology & Metabolism* 21(3): 480–95.

Lorde, Audre. 1984. *Sister Outsider: Essays & Speeches by Audre Lorde*. Berkeley, Calif.: Crossing Press.

Merke, Deborah P., and Stefan R. Bornstein. 2005. "Congenital Adrenal Hyperplasia." *The Lancet* 365(9477): 2125–36.

Nakhal, Rola S., Margaret Hall-Craggs, Alex Freeman, Alex Kirkham, Gerard S. Conway, Rupali Arora, Christopher R. J. Woodhouse, Dan N. Wood, and Sarah M. Creighton.

2013. "Evaluation of Retained Testes in Adolescent Girls and Women with Complete Androgen Insensitivity Syndrome." *Radiology* 268(1): 153–60.

Nandi, Jacinta. 2013. "Germany Got It Right by Offering a Third Gender Option on Birth Certificates" *The Guardian*. Accessed January 31, 2015. http://www.theguardian.com/commentisfree/2013/nov/10/germany-third-gender-birth-certificate.

Pleskacova, J., R. Hersmus, J. W. Oosterhuis, B. A. Setyawati, S. M. Faradz, M. Cools, K. P. Wolffenbuttel, J. Lebl, S. L. Drop, and L. H. Looijenga. 2010. "Tumor Risk in Disorders of Sex Development." *Sexual Development* 4(4/5): 259–69.

Preves, Sharon. 2003. *Intersex and Identity: The Contested Self*. New Brunswick, N.J.: Rutgers University Press.

Swiss National Advisory Commission on Biomedical Ethics. 2012. "On the Management of Differences of Sex Development: Ethical Issues Relating to 'Intersexuality.'" *Swiss National Advisory Commission on Biomedical Ethics*. Accessed January 31, 2015. http://www.nek-cne.ch/fileadmin/nek-cne-dateien/Themen/Stellungnahmen/en/NEK_Intersexualitaet_En.pdf.

Viloria, Hida. 2013. "Germany's Third-Gender Law Fails on Equality." *Advocate.com*. Accessed January 31, 2015. https://www.advocate.com/commentary/2013/11/06/op-ed-germany%E2%80%99s-third-gender-law-fails-equality.

Zara, Christopher. 2013. "Intersex Australia: Third Gender Allowed on Personal Documents in Addition to Male and Female." *International Business Times*. Accessed January 31, 2015. http://www.ibtimes.com/intersex-australia-third-gender-allowed-personal-documents-addition-male-female-1307843.

*Source:* Davis, Georgiann. (2015). Excerpted from *Contesting Intersex: The Dubious Diagnosis* (pp. 106, 145–148, 156–162, 164–166, 171, 179, 189–208). New York, NY: NYU Press.

## DEFINING GENITALS: WHO WILL MAKE ROOM FOR THE INTERSEXED?

Between 1.7 and 4% of the world population is born with intersex conditions, having primary and secondary sexual characteristics that are neither clearly male nor female.[1] The current recommended treatment for an infant born with an intersex condition is genital reconstruction surgery to render the child as clearly sexed either male or female.[2] Every day in the United States, five children are subjected to genital reconstruction surgery that may leave them with permanent physical and emotional scars.[3] Despite efforts by intersexed people to educate the medical community about their rejection of infant genital reconstruction surgery, the American medical community has not yet accepted the fact that differences in genital size and shape do not necessarily require surgical correction.[4]

## Size Does Matter

The size of an infant's genitals is important to physicians who "manage" the sex assignment of intersexed infants. In her book entitled *Lessons from the Intersexed*, Suzanne Kessler explores how physicians use size to determine the appropriateness of genitals.

### Ranges of Medically Acceptable Infant Clitoral and Penile Lengths

How big must a clitoris be before physicians decide it is too large? ... In spite of there being a table of standards, physicians are more likely to refer to the average clitoris in food terminology, such as a pea or a small bean. In general, medical standards do not allow clitorises larger than .9 centimeters (about ⅜ of an inch). [...]

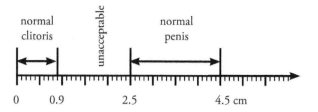

When is a penis too small? In general, medical standards permit infant penises as small as 2.5 centimeters (about one inch) to mark maleness, but usually not smaller. [Boys with penises smaller than 2.5 centimeters may be reassigned as girls based on the assumption that] a male infant needs a penis of a certain size in order to be accepted by family and peers. [The figure shown here] indicates standard clitoral and penile lengths for infants, revealing that intermediate area of phallic length that neither females nor males are permitted to have.

## NOTES

1. Anne Fausto-Sterling, *Sexing the Body: Gender Politics and the Construction of Sexuality* 51 (2000) (reporting that 1.7% of the population may be intersexed); Julie A. Greenberg, *Defining Male and Female Intersexuality and the Collision between Law and Biology*, 41 Ariz. L. Rev. 265, 267 (1999) (reporting that Johns Hopkins sex researcher John Money estimates the number of people born with ambiguous genitals at 4%). Historically, people with intersex conditions were referred to as "hermaphrodites" but this word has been rejected as embodying many of the misperceptions and mistreatment of intersexed people. Raven Kaldera, *American Boyz Intersexuality Flyer*, *at* http://www.amboyz.org/intersection/flyerprint.html (last visited Mar. 27, 2004).

2. Hazel Glenn Beh & Milton Diamond, *An Emerging Ethical and Medical Dilemma: Should Physicians Perform Sex Assignment Surgery on Infants with Ambiguous Genitalia?* 7 Mich. J. Gender & L. 1, 3 (2000); Fausto-Sterling, *supra* note 1, at 45; *see infra* note 4.

3. Emi Koyama, *Suggested Guidelines for Non-Intersex Individuals Writing about Intersexuality and Intersex People*, at http://isna.org/faq/writing-guidelines.html (last visited Mar. 27, 2004). *But see* Beh & Diamond, *supra* note 2, at 17 (estimating the number of sex reassignments in the United States at 100 to 200 annually).

4. Kishka-Kamari Ford, *"First Do No Harm"—The Fiction of Legal Parental Consent to Genital-Normalizing Surgery on Intersexed Infants*, 19 Yale L. & Pol'y Rev. 469, 471 (2001).

---

*Sources:* Haas, Kate. (2004). "Who Will Make Room for the Intersexed?" *American Journal of Law & Medicine, 30*(1), 41–68; Kessler, Suzanne J. (1998). *Lessons from the Intersexed.* New Brunswick, NJ: Rutgers University Press. Reprinted in Caron, Sandra L. (2007). *Sex Matters for College Students: FAQs in Human Sexuality, 2nd Edition* (p. 23). Upper Saddle River, NJ: Pearson Prentice Hall.

# CHAPTER 15

## Dueling Dualisms

*Anne Fausto-Sterling*

Anne Fausto-Sterling is a professor emerita at Brown University and fellow of the American Association for the Advancement of Science. She is one of the world's leading researchers on the development of sexual identity and the biology of gender, and her trail-breaking works on gender and sexuality include *Myths of Gender* and *Sexing the Body: Gender Politics and the Construction of Sexuality* (excerpted below).

## MALE OR FEMALE?

In the rush and excitement of leaving for the 1988 Olympics, Maria Patiño, Spain's top woman hurdler, forgot the requisite doctor's certificate stating, for the benefit of Olympic officials, what seemed patently obvious to anyone who looked at her: she was female. But the International Olympic Committee (IOC) had anticipated the possibility that some competitors would forget their certificates of femininity. Patiño had only to report to the "femininity control head office,"[1] scrape some cells off the side of her cheek, and all would be in order—or so she thought.

A few hours after the cheek scraping, she got a call. Something was wrong. She went for a second examination, but the doctors were mum. Then, as she rode to the Olympic stadium to start her first race, track officials broke the news: she had failed the sex test. She may have looked like a woman, had a woman's strength, and never had reason to suspect that she wasn't a woman, but the examinations revealed that

Patiño's cells sported a Y chromosome, and that her labia hid testes within. Furthermore, she had neither ovaries nor a uterus. According to the IOC's definition, Patiño was not a woman. She was barred from competing on Spain's Olympic team.

Spanish athletic officials told Patiño to fake an injury and withdraw without publicizing the embarrassing facts. When she refused, the European press heard about it and the secret was out. Within months after returning to Spain, Patiño's life fell apart. Spanish officials stripped her of past titles and barred her from further competition. Her boyfriend deserted her. She was evicted from the national athletic residence, her scholarship was revoked, and suddenly she had to struggle to make a living. The national press had a field day at her expense. As she later said, "I was erased from the map, as if I had never existed. I gave twelve years to sports."[2]

Down but not out, Patiño spent thousands of dollars consulting doctors about her situation. They explained that she had been born with a condition called *androgen insensitivity*. This meant that, although she had a Y chromosome and her testes made plenty of testosterone, her cells couldn't detect this masculinizing hormone. As a result, her body had never developed male characteristics. But at puberty her testes produced estrogen (as do the testes of all men), which, because of her body's inability to respond to its testosterone, caused her breasts to grow, her waist to narrow, and her hips to widen. Despite a Y chromosome and testes, she had grown up as a female and developed a female form.

Patiño resolved to fight the IOC ruling. "I knew I was a woman," she insisted to one reporter, "in the eyes of medicine, God and most of all, in my own eyes."[3] [...] After two and a half years, the International Amateur Athletic Federation (IAAF) [now called the International Association of Athletics Federations] reinstated her, and by 1992, Patiño had rejoined the Spanish Olympic squad, going down in history as the first woman ever to challenge sex testing for female athletes. Despite the IAAF's flexibility, however, the IOC has remained adamant: even if looking for a Y chromosome wasn't the most scientific approach to sex testing, testing *must* be done.

\*\*\*\*\*

## SEX OR GENDER?

Until 1968, female Olympic competitors were often asked to parade naked in front of a board of examiners. Breasts and a vagina were all one needed to certify one's femininity. But many women complained that this procedure was degrading. Partly because such complaints mounted, the IOC decided to make use of the modern "scientific" chromosome test. The problem, though, is that this test, and the more sophisticated polymerase chain reaction to detect small regions of DNA associated with testes development that the IOC uses today, cannot do the work the IOC wants it to do. A body's sex is simply too complex. There is no either/

or. Rather, there are shades of difference. [...] One of the major claims I make in this book is that labeling someone a man or a woman is a social decision. We may use scientific knowledge to help us make the decision, but only our beliefs about gender—not science—can define our sex. Furthermore, our beliefs about gender affect what kinds of knowledge scientists produce about sex in the first place.

Over the last few decades, the relation between *social expression* of masculinity and femininity and their *physical underpinnings* has been hotly debated in scientific and social arenas. In 1972, the sexologists John Money and Anke Ehrhardt popularized the idea that sex and gender are separate categories. *Sex*, they argued, refers to physical attributes and is anatomically and physiologically determined. *Gender* they saw as a psychological transformation of the self—the internal conviction that one is either male or female (gender identity) and the behavioral expressions of that conviction.[4]

Meanwhile, the second-wave feminists of the 1970s also argued that sex is distinct from gender—that social institutions, themselves designed to perpetuate gender inequality, produce most of the differences between men and women.[5] Feminists argued that although men's and women's bodies serve different reproductive functions, few other sex differences come with the territory, unchangeable by life's vicissitudes. If girls couldn't learn math as easily as boys, the problem wasn't built into their brains. The difficulty resulted from gender norms—different expectations and opportunities for boys and girls. Having a penis rather than a vagina is a sex difference. Boys performing better than girls on math exams is a gender difference. Presumably, the latter could be changed even if the former could not.

Money, Ehrhardt, and feminists set the terms so that *sex* represented the body's anatomy and physiological workings and *gender* represented social forces that molded behavior. Feminists did not question the realm of physical sex; it was the psychological and cultural meanings of these differences—gender—that was at issue. But feminist definitions of sex and gender left open the possibility that male/female differences in cognitive function and behavior could *result* from sex differences, and thus, in some circles, the matter of sex versus gender became a debate about how "hardwired" intelligence and a variety of behaviors are in the brain, while in others there seemed no choice but to ignore many of the findings of contemporary neurobiology.

In ceding the territory of physical sex, feminists left themselves open to renewed attack on the grounds of biological difference. Indeed, feminism has encountered massive resistance from the domains of biology, medicine, and significant components of social science. Despite many positive social changes, the 1970s optimism that women would achieve full economic and social equality once gender inequity was addressed in the social sphere has faded in the face of a seemingly recalcitrant inequality.[6] All of which has prompted feminist scholars, on the one hand, to question the notion of sex itself,[7] while on the other to deepen their inquiry into what we might mean by words such as *gender, culture,* and *experience.* The anthropologist Henrietta A. Moore, for example, argues against reducing accounts of gender, culture, and experience to their "linguistic and cognitive elements." [...] I argue, as does Moore, that "what is at issue is the embodied nature of identities and experience. Experience … is not individual and fixed, but irredeemably social and processual."[8]

Our bodies are too complex to provide clear cut answers about sexual difference. The more we look for a simple physical basis for "sex," the more it becomes clear that "sex" is not a pure physical category. What bodily signals and functions we define as male or female come already entangled in our ideas about gender. Consider the problem facing the International Olympic Committee. Committee members want to decide definitively who is male and female. But how? [...] Could the IOC use muscle strength as some measure of sex? In some cases. But the strength of men and women, especially highly

trained athletes, overlaps. [...] And although Maria Patiño fit a commonsense definition of femininity in terms of looks and strength, she also had testes and a Y chromosome. But why should these be the deciding factors?

The IOC may use chromosome or DNA tests or inspection of the breasts and genitals to ascertain the sex of a competitor, but doctors faced with uncertainty about a child's sex use different criteria. They focus primarily on reproductive abilities (in the case of a potential girl) or penis size (in the case of a prospective boy). If a child is born with two X chromosomes, oviducts, ovaries, and a uterus on the inside, but a penis and scrotum on the outside, for instance, is the child a boy or a girl? Most doctors declare the child a girl, despite the penis, because of her potential to give birth, and intervene using surgery and hormones to carry out the decision. Choosing which criteria to use in determining sex, and choosing to make the determination at all, are social decisions for which scientists can offer no absolute guidelines.

## REAL OR CONSTRUCTED?

I enter the debates about sex and gender as a biologist and a social activist. Daily, my life weaves in and out of a web of conflict over the politics of sexuality and the making and using of knowledge about the biology of human behavior. The central tenet of this book [*Sexing the Body: Gender Politics and the Construction of Sexuality*] is that truths about human sexuality created by scholars in general and by biologists in particular are one component of political, social, and moral struggles about our cultures and economies. At the same time, components of our political, social, and moral struggles become, quite literally, embodied, incorporated into our very physiological being. My intent is to show how these mutually dependent claims work, in part by addressing such issues as how—through their daily lives, experiments, and medical practices—scientists create truths about sexuality; how our bodies incorporate and confirm these truths; and how these truths, sculpted by the social milieu in which biologists practice their trade, in turn refashion our cultural environment.

My take on the problem is idiosyncratic, and for good reason. Intellectually, I inhabit three seemingly incompatible worlds. In my home department, I interact with molecular biologists, scientists who examine living beings from the perspective of the molecules from which they are built. They describe a microscopic world in which cause and effect remain mostly inside a single cell. Molecular biologists rarely think about interacting organs within an individual body, and even less about how a body bounded by skin interacts with the world on the other side of the skin. Their vision of what makes an organism tick is decidedly bottom up, small to large, inside to outside.

I also interact with a virtual community—a group of scholars drawn together by a common interest in sexuality—and connected by something called a listserv. On a listserv, one can pose questions, think out loud, comment on relevant news items, argue about theories of human sexuality, and report the latest research findings. The comments are read by a group of people hooked together via electronic mail. My listserv (which I call "Loveweb") consists of a diverse group of scholars—psychologists, animal behaviorists, hormone biologists, sociologists, anthropologists, and philosophers. Although many points of view coexist in this group, the vocal majority favor body-based, biological explanations of human sexual behavior. [...]

Unlike molecular biologists and Loveweb members, feminist theorists view the body not as essence, but as a bare scaffolding on which discourse and performance build a completely acculturated being. Feminist theorists write persuasively and often imaginatively about the processes by which culture molds and effectively creates the body. Furthermore, they have an eye on politics (writ large), which neither molecular biologists nor Loveweb participants have. Most feminist scholars concern themselves with real-world power relationships. They have often come to their theoretical

work because they want to understand (and change) social, political, and economic inequality. Unlike the inhabitants of my other two worlds, feminist theorists reject what Donna Haraway, a leading feminist theoretician, calls "the God-trick"—producing knowledge from above, from a place that denies the individual scholar's location in a real and troubled world. Instead, they understand that all scholarship adds threads to a web that positions racialized bodies, sexes, genders, and preferences in relationship to one another. New or differently spun threads change our relationships, change how we are in the world.

Traveling among these varied intellectual worlds produces more than a little discomfort. When I lurk on Loveweb, I put up with gratuitous feminist-bashing aimed at some mythic feminist who derides biology and seems to have a patently stupid view of how the world works. When I attend feminist conferences, people howl in disbelief at the ideas debated on Loveweb. And the molecular biologists don't think much of either of the other worlds. The questions asked by feminists and Loveweb participants seem too complicated; studying sex in bacteria or yeast is the only way to go.

To my molecular biology, Loveweb, and feminist colleagues, then, I say the following: as a biologist, I believe in the material world. As a scientist, I believe in building specific knowledge by conducting experiments. But as a feminist Witness (in the Quaker sense of the word) and in recent years as a historian, I also believe that what we call "facts" about the living world are not universal truths. Rather, as Haraway writes, they "are rooted in specific histories, practices, languages and peoples."[9] Ever since the field of biology emerged in the United States and Europe at the start of the nineteenth century, it has been bound up in debates over sexual, racial, and national politics. And as our social viewpoints have shifted, so has the science of the body.

Many historians mark the seventeenth and eighteenth centuries as periods of great change in our concepts of sex and sexuality.[10] During this period, a notion of legal equality replaced the feudal exercise of arbitrary and violent power given by divine right. As the historian Michel Foucault saw it, society still required some form of discipline. A growing capitalism needed new methods to control the "insertion of bodies into the machinery of production and the adjustment of the phenomena of population to economic processes."[11] Foucault divided this power over living bodies (*bio-power*) into two forms. The first centered on the individual body. The role of many science professionals (including the so-called human sciences—psychology, sociology, and economics) became to optimize and standardize the body's function.[12] In Europe and North America, Foucault's standardized body has, traditionally, been male and Caucasian. And although this [chapter] focuses on gender, I regularly discuss the ways in which the ideas of both race and gender emerge from underlying assumptions about the body's physical nature. Understanding how race and gender work—together and independently—helps us learn more about how the social becomes embodied.

Foucault's second form of bio-power—"*a biopolitics of the population*"[13]—emerged during the early nineteenth century as pioneer social scientists began to develop the survey and statistical methods needed to supervise and manage "births and mortality, the level of health, life expectancy and longevity."[14] For Foucault, "discipline" had a double meaning. On the one hand, it implied a form of control or punishment; on the other, it referred to an academic body of knowledge—the discipline of history or biology. The disciplinary knowledge developed in the fields of embryology, endocrinology, surgery, psychology, and biochemistry have encouraged physicians to attempt to control the very gender of the body—including "its capacities, gestures, movements, location and behaviors."[15]

By helping the normal take precedence over the natural, physicians have also contributed to populational biopolitics. We have become, Foucault writes, "a society of normalization."[16] One important mid-twentieth-century sexologist went so far as to name the male and female models in his anatomy text Norma and Normman [*sic*].[17] Today, we see the notion of pathology applied in many settings—from the sick, diseased, or different body, to the single-parent family in the urban ghetto. But imposing a gender norm is socially, not scientifically, driven. The lack of research into the normal distributions of genital anatomy, as well as many surgeons' lack of interest in using such data when they do exist [...], clearly illustrate this claim. From the viewpoint of medical practitioners, progress in the handling of intersexuality involves maintaining the normal. Accordingly, there *ought* to be only two boxes: male and female. The knowledge developed by the medical disciplines empowers doctors to maintain a mythology of the normal by changing the intersexual body to fit, as nearly as possible, into one or the other cubbyhole.

One person's medical progress, however, can be another's discipline and control. Intersexuals such as Maria Patiño have unruly—even heretical—bodies. They do not fall naturally into a binary classification; only a surgical shoehorn can put them there. But why should we care if a "woman" (defined as having breasts, a vagina, uterus, ovaries, and menstruation) has a "clitoris" large enough to penetrate the vagina of another woman? Why should we care if there are individuals whose "natural biological equipment" enables them to have sex "naturally" with both men and women? Why must we amputate or surgically hide that "offending shaft" found on an especially large clitoris? The answer: to maintain gender divisions, we must control those bodies that are so unruly as to blur the borders. Since intersexuals quite literally embody both sexes, they weaken claims about sexual difference.

*****

Euro-American ways of understanding how the world works depend heavily on the use of dualisms—pairs of opposing concepts, objects, or belief systems. [...]

Why worry about using dualisms to parse the world? I agree with the philosopher Val Plumwood, who argues that their use makes invisible the interdependencies of each pair. This relationship enables sets of pairs to map onto each other. Consider an extract of Plumwood's list:

**Table 15.1**

| Reason | Nature |
|---|---|
| Male | Female |
| Mind | Body |
| Master | Slave |
| Freedom | Necessity (nature) |
| Human | Nature (nonhuman) |
| Civilized | Primitive |
| Production | Reproduction |
| Self | Other |

In everyday use, the sets of associations on each side of the list often run together. "Culture," Plumwood writes, accumulates these dualisms as a store of weapons "which can be mined, refined and redeployed. Old oppressions stored as dualisms facilitate and break the path for new ones."[18] For this reason, even though my focus is on gender, I do not hesitate to point out occasions in which the constructs and ideology of race intersect with those of gender.

Ultimately, the sex/gender dualism limits feminist analysis. The term *gender*, placed in a dichotomy, necessarily excludes biology. As the feminist theorist Elizabeth Wilson writes: "Feminist critiques of the stomach or hormonal structure … have been rendered unthinkable."[19] […] Such critiques remain unthinkable because of the real/constructed divide (sometimes formulated as a division between nature and culture), in which many map the knowledge of the real onto the domain of science (equating the constructed with the cultural). Dichotomous formulations from feminists and nonfeminists alike conspire to make a sociocultural analysis of the body seem impossible.

Some feminist theorists, especially during the last decade, have tried—with varying degrees of success—to create a nondualistic account of the body. Judith Butler, for example, tries to reclaim the material body for feminist thought. Why, she wonders, has the idea of materiality come to signify that which is irreducible, that which can support construction but cannot itself be constructed?[20] We have, Butler says (and I agree), to talk about the material body. There *are* hormones, genes, prostates, uteri, and other body parts and physiologies that we use to differentiate male from female, that become part of the ground from which varieties of sexual experience and desire emerge. Furthermore, variations in each of these aspects of physiology profoundly affect an individual's experience of gender and sexuality. But every time we try to return to the body as something that exists prior to socialization, prior to discourse about male and female, Butler writes, "we discover that matter is fully sedimented with discourses on sex and sexuality that prefigure and constrain the uses to which that term can be put."[21]

Western notions of matter and bodily materiality, Butler argues, have been constructed through a "gendered matrix." That classical philosophers associated femininity with materiality can be seen in the origins of the word itself. "Matter" [is] derived from *mater* and *matrix*, referring to the womb and problems of reproduction. In both Greek and Latin, according to Butler, matter was not understood to be a blank slate awaiting the application of external meaning. "The matrix is a … formative principle which inaugurates and informs a development of some organism or object … for Aristotle, 'matter is potentiality, form actuality.' … In reproduction women are said to contribute the matter, men the form."[22] As Butler notes, the title of her book, *Bodies That Matter*, is a well-thought-out pun. To be material is to speak about the process of materialization. And if viewpoints about sex and sexuality are already embedded in our philosophical concepts of how matter forms into bodies, the matter of bodies cannot form a neutral, pre-existing ground from which to understand the origin of sexual difference.

Since matter already contains notions of gender and sexuality, it cannot be a neutral recourse on which to build "scientific" or "objective" theories of sexual development and differentiation. At the same time, we have to acknowledge and use aspects of materiality "that pertain to the body." "The domains of biology, anatomy, physiology, hormonal and chemical composition, illness, age, weight, metabolism, life and death" cannot "be denied."[23] The critical theorist Bernice Hausman concretizes this point in her discussion of surgical technologies available for creating male-to-female versus female-to-male transsexual bodies. "The differences," she writes, "between vagina and penis are not merely ideological. Any attempt to engage and decode the semiotics of sex … must acknowledge that these physiological signifiers have functions in the real that will escape … their function in the symbolic system."[24]

To talk about human sexuality requires a notion of the material. Yet the idea of the material comes to us already tainted, containing within it pre-existing ideas about sexual difference. Butler suggests that we look at the body as a system that simultaneously produces and is produced by social meanings, just as any biological organism always results from the combined and simultaneous actions of nature and nurture.

Unlike Butler, the feminist philosopher Elizabeth Grosz allows some biological processes a status that pre-exists their meaning. She believes that biological instincts or drives provide a kind of raw material for the development of sexuality. But raw materials are never enough. They must be provided with a set of meanings, "a network of desires"[25] that organize the meaning and consciousness of the child's bodily functions. This claim becomes clear if one follows the stories of so-called wild children raised without human constraints or the inculcation of meaning. Such children acquire neither language nor sexual drive. While their bodies provided the raw materials, without a human social setting the clay could not be molded into recognizable psychic form. Without human sociality, human sexuality cannot develop.

Grosz tries to understand how human sociality and meaning that clearly originate outside the body end up incorporated into its physiological demeanor and both unconscious and conscious behaviors.

Some concrete examples will help illustrate. A tiny gray-haired woman, well into her ninth decade, peers into the mirror at her wrinkled face. "Who is that woman?" she wonders. Her mind's image of her body does not synchronize with the mirror's reflection. Her daughter, now in her mid-fifties, tries to remember that unless she thinks about using her leg muscles instead of her knee joint, going up and down the stairs will be painful. (Eventually, she will acquire a new kinesic habit and dispense with conscious thought about the matter.) Both women are readjusting the visual and kinesic components of their body image, formed on the basis of past information, but always a bit out of date with the current physical body. How do such readjustments occur, and how do our earliest body images form in the first place? Here we need the concept of the psyche, a place where two-way translations between the mind and the body take place—a United Nations, as it were, of bodies and experiences.

In *Volatile Bodies*, Elizabeth Grosz considers how the body and the mind come into being together. To facilitate her project, she invokes the image of a Möbius strip as a metaphor for the psyche. The Möbius strip is a topological puzzle (Figure 15.1), a flat ribbon twisted once and then attached end to end to form a circular twisted surface. One can trace the surface, for example, by imagining an ant walking along it. At the beginning of the circular journey, the ant is clearly on the outside. But as it traverses the twisted ribbon, without ever lifting its legs from the plane, it ends up on the inside surface. Grosz proposes that we think of the body—the brain, muscles, sex organs, hormones, and more—as composing the inside of the Möbius strip. Culture and experience would constitute the outside surface. But, as the image suggests, the inside and outside are continuous and one can move from one to the other without ever lifting one's feet off the ground.

**Figure 15.1: Möbius Strip**

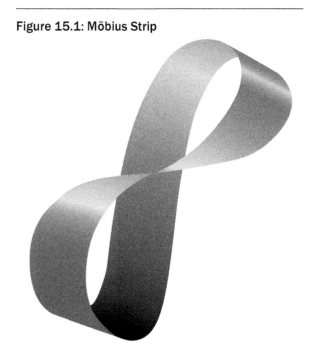

*Source:* Courtesy of John Harrison.

As Grosz recounts, psychoanalysts and phenome-nologists describe the body in terms of feelings.[26] The mind translates physiology into an interior sense of self. Oral sexuality, for example, is a physical feeling that a child and later an adult translates into psycho-sexual meaning. This translation takes place on the inside of the Möbius surface. But as one traces the surface toward the outside, one begins to speak in terms of connections to other bodies and objects— things that are clearly not-self. Grosz writes, "Instead of describing the oral drive in terms of what it feels like … orality can be understood in terms of what it does: creating linkages. The child's lips, for example, form connections … with the breast or bottle, pos-sibly accompanied by the hand in conjunction with an ear, each system in perpetual motion and in mutual interrelation."[27]

Continuing with the Möbius analogy, Grosz envisions that bodies create psyches by using the libido as a marker pen to trace a path from biological processes to an interior structure of desire. It falls to

a different arena of scholarship to study the "outside" of the strip, a more obviously social surface marked by "pedagogical, juridical, medical, and economic texts, laws, and practices" in order to "carve out a social subject … capable of labor, or production and manipu-lation, a subject capable of acting as a subject."[28] Thus, Grosz also rejects a nature versus nurture model of human development. While acknowledging that we do not understand the range and limits of the body's pliability, she insists that we cannot merely "subtract the environment, culture, history" and end up with "nature or biology."

## BEYOND DUALISMS

Grosz postulates innate drives that become organized by physical experience into somatic feelings, which translate into what we call emotions. Taking the innate at face value, however, still leaves us with an unexplained residue of nature. Humans are biological and thus in some sense natural beings *and* social and in some sense artificial—or, if you will, constructed entities. Can we devise a way of seeing ourselves, as we develop from fertilization to old age, as simultan-eously natural and unnatural? During the past decade, an exciting vision has emerged that I have loosely grouped under the rubric of developmental systems theory, or DST. What do we gain by choosing DST as an analytic framework?

Developmental systems theorists deny that there are fundamentally two kinds of processes: one guided by genes, hormones, and brain cells (that is, nature), the other by the environment, experience, learning, or inchoate social forces (that is, nurture). The pioneer systems theorist, philosopher Susan Oyama, promises that DST "gives more clarity, more coherence, more consistency and a different way to interpret data; in addition it offers the means for synthesizing the con-cepts and methods … of groups that have been working at cross-purposes, or at least talking past each other for decades." Nevertheless, developmental systems theory is no magic bullet. Many will resist its insights because, as Oyama explains, "it gives less … guidance on fundamental truth" and "fewer conclusions about what is inherently desirable, healthy, natural or inevitable."[29]

How, specifically, can DST help us break away from dualistic thought processes? Consider an example described by systems theorist Peter Taylor: a goat born with no front legs. During its lifetime, it managed to hop around on its hind limbs. An anatomist who studied the goat after it died found that it had an S-shaped spine (as do humans), "thickened bones, modified muscle insertions, and other correlates of moving on two legs."[30] This (and every goat's) skeletal system developed as part of its manner of walking. Neither its genes nor its environment determined its anatomy. Only the ensemble had such power. Many developmental physiologists recognize this principle. As one biologist writes, "enstructuring occurs during the enactment of individual life histories."[31]

A few years ago, when the neuroscientist Simon LeVay reported that the brain structures of gay and heterosexual men differed (and that this mirrored a more general sex difference between straight men and women), he became the center of a firestorm.[32] Although an instant hero among many gay males, he was at odds with a rather mixed group. On the one hand, feminists such as myself disliked his unquestioning use of gender dichotomies, which have in the past never worked to further equality for women. On the other, members of the Christian right hated his work because they believe that homosexuality is a sin that individuals can choose to reject. LeVay's, and later geneticist Dean Hamer's, work suggested to them that homosexuality was inborn or innate.[33] The language of the public debate soon became polarized. Each side contrasted words such as *generic, biological, inborn, innate,* and *unchanging* with *environmental, acquired, constructed,* and *choice.*

The ease with which such debates evoke the nature/nurture divide is a consequence of the poverty of a nonsystems approach. Politically, the nature/nurture framework holds enormous dangers. Although

some hope that a belief in the nature side of things will lead to greater tolerance, past history suggests that the opposite is also possible. Even the scientific architects of the nature argument recognize the dangers. In an extraordinary passage in the pages of *Science*, Dean Hamer and his collaborators indicated their concern: "It would be fundamentally unethical to use such information to try to assess or alter a person's current or future sexual orientation. Rather, scientists, educators, policy-makers and the public should work together to ensure that such research is used to benefit all members of society."[34]

The feminist psychologist and critical theorist Elisabeth Wilson uses the hubbub over LeVay's work to make some important points about systems theory. Many feminist, queer, and critical theorists work by deliberately displacing biology, hence opening the body to social and cultural shaping. This, however, is the wrong move to make. Wilson writes: "What may be politically and critically contentious in LeVay's hypothesis is not the conjunction neurology-sexuality per se, but the particular manner in which such a conjunction is enacted."[35] An effective political response, she continues, doesn't have to separate the study of sexuality from the neurosciences. Instead, Wilson, who wants us to develop a theory of mind and body—an account of psyche that joins libido to body—suggests that feminists incorporate into their worldview an account of how the brain works that is, broadly speaking, called connectionism.

The old-fashioned approach to understanding the brain was anatomical. Function could be located in particular parts of the brain. Ultimately, function and anatomy were one. […] Many scientists [still] believe that a structural difference represents the brain location for measured behavioral differences. In contrast, connectionist models argue that function emerges from the complexity and strength of many neural connections acting at once. The system has some important characteristics: the responses are often nonlinear, the networks can be "trained" to respond in particular ways, the nature of the response is not easily predictable, and information is not located anywhere—rather, it is the net result of the many different connections and their differing strengths.

The tenets of some connectionist theory provide interesting starting points for understanding human sexual development. Because connectionist networks, for example, are usually nonlinear, small changes can produce large effects. One implication for studying sexuality: we could easily be looking in the wrong places and on the wrong scale for aspects of the environment that shape human development. Furthermore, a single behavior may have many underlying causes, events that happen at different times in development. I suspect that our labels of *homosexual*, *heterosexual*, *bisexual*, and *transgender* are really not good categories at all, and are best understood only in terms of unique developmental events affecting particular individuals. Thus, I agree with those connectionists who argue that "the developmental process itself lies at the heart of knowledge acquisition. Development is a process of emergence."[36]

In most public and most scientific discussions, sex and nature are thought to be real, while gender and culture are seen as constructed. But these are false dichotomies.

## NOTES

We have cut extensively the notes and references, which were lengthy in the original.

1. Hanley 1983.
2. Quoted in Carlson 1991, p. 27.
3. Ibid. The technical name for Patiño's condition is Androgen Insensitivity Syndrome. It is one of a number of conditions that leads to bodies having mixtures of male and female parts. Today, we call such bodies *intersexes*.
4. [...] Money and Ehrhardt 1972, p. 4. [...]
5. See, for example, Rubin 1975. Rubin also questions the biological basis of homosexuality and heterosexuality. Note that feminist definitions of gender applied to institutions as well as personal or psychological differences.
6. For a discussion of this recalcitrance in terms of gender schema in adulthood, see Valian 1998a, 1998b.
7. [...] Burke 1996; Dreger 1998b; Feinberg 1996; Haraway 1989, 1997; Hausman 1995; Kessler and McKenna 1978; and Rothblatt 1995. [...]
8. Moore 1994, pp. 2–3.
9. Haraway 1997, p. 217. See also Foucault 1970; Gould 1981; Schiebinger 1993 a, b.
10. During this time, Foucault maintains, the change from Feudalism to Capitalism required a new concept of the body. Feudal lords applied their power directly. Peasants and serfs obeyed because God and their sovereign told them to (except, of course, when they revolted, as they did from time to time). The punishment for disobedience was, to the modern eye, violent and brutal: drawing and quartering. For a stunning description of this brutality, see the opening chapters of Foucault 1979.
11. Foucault 1978, p. 141.
12. These efforts created "an *anatomo-politics of the human body*" (Foucault 1978, p. 139; emphasis in the original).
13. Foucault 1978, p. 139; emphasis in the original.
14. Ibid. [...]
15. Sawicki 1991, p. 67 [....]
16. Foucault 1980, p. 107.
17. Quoted in Moore and Clarke 1995, p. 271.
18. Plumwood 1993, p. 43. Plumwood also argues that dualisms "result from a certain kind of denied dependency on a subordinated other." The denial, combined with a relationship of domination and subordination, shape the identity of each side of the dualism (ibid., p. 41). [...]
19. Wilson 1998, p. 55.
20. In her words, she "wants to ask how and why 'materiality' has become a sign of irreducibility, that is, how is it that the materiality of sex is understood as that which only bears cultural constructions and, therefore, cannot be a construction" (Butler 1993, p. 28).
21. Ibid., p. 29.
22. Ibid., p. 31.
23. Ibid., p. 66.
24. Hausman 1995, p. 69.
25. Grosz 1994, p. 55.
26. Phenomenology is a field that studies the body as an active participant in the creation of self. [...]

27. Grosz 1994, p. 116.

28. Ibid., p. 117. [...]

29. Oyama 1985, p. 9. The revised and expanded edition of Oyama's book is due out in the year 2000 (Duke University Press).

30. Taylor 1998, p. 24.

31. Ho 1989, p. 34. [...]

32. LeVay's results still await confirmation and in the meantime have been subject to intense scrutiny (LeVay 1991). See Byne 1995; Byne and Parsons 1993; and Fausto-Sterling 1992a and 1992b. [...]

33. [...] Hamer et al. 1993.

34. Extraordinary, because it is not customary to use a strictly scientific report to discuss the potential social implications of one's work. Hamer et al. 1993, p. 326.

35. Wilson 1998, p. 203.

36. Elman et al. 1996, p. 359. See also Fischer 1990.

# REFERENCES

Burke, P. 1996. *Gender shock: Exploding the myth of male and female.* New York: Doubleday.

Butler, J. 1993. *Bodies that matter: On the discursive limits of sex.* New York: Routledge.

Byne, W. 1995. Science and belief: Psychological research on sexual orientation. *Journal of Homosexuality* 28(3–4): 303–44.

Byne, W., and B. Parsons. 1993. Human sexual orientation: The biological theories reappraised. *Archives of General Psychiatry* 50(March): 228–39.

Carlson, A. 1991. When is a woman not a woman? *Women's Sports and Fitness* 13: 24–29.

Dreger, A.D. 1998. *Hermaphrodites and the medical invention of sex.* Cambridge: Harvard University Press.

Elman, J.L., E.A. Bates, et al. 1996. *Rethinking innateness: A connectionist perspective on development.* Cambridge: MIT Press.

Fausto-Sterling, A. 1992a. Why do we know so little about human sex? *Discover* 13: 6, 28–30.

Fausto-Sterling, A. 1992b. *Myths of gender: Biological theories about women and men.* New York: Basic Books.

Feinberg, L. 1996. *Transgender warriors.* Boston: Beacon Press.

Fischer, R. 1990. Why the mind is not in the head but in the society's connectionist network? *Diogenes* 151(Fall): 1–28.

Foucault, M. 1978. *The history of sexuality.* New York: Pantheon.

Foucault, M. 1980. Two lectures. In *Power/knowledge: Selected interviews and other writings 1972–1977 by Michel Foucault,* ed. C. Gordon. New York: Pantheon, 78–108.

Grosz, E. 1994. *Volatile bodies: Towards a corporeal feminism.* Bloomington: Indiana University Press.

Hamer, D., S. Hu, et al. 1993. Linkage between DNA markers on the X chromosome and male sexual orientation. *Science* 261: 321–25.

Hanley, D.F. 1983. Drug and sex testing: Regulations for the international competition. *Clinics in Sports Medicine* 2: 13–17.

Haraway, D. 1989. *Primate visions.* New York: Routledge.

Haraway, D. 1997. *Modest_Witness@Second_Millennium. FemaleMan©_Meets_OncoMouse™.* New York: Routledge.

Hausman, B.L. 1995. *Changing sex: Transsexualism, technology, and the idea of gender in the 20th century.* Durham: Duke University Press.

Ho, M.W. 1989. A structuralism of process: Towards a post-Darwinian rational morphology. In *Dynamic Structures in Biology,* ed. B. Goodwin, A. Sibatani, and G. Webster. Edinburgh: Edinburgh University Press, 31–48.

Kessler, S.J., and W. McKenna. 1978. *Gender: An ethnomethodological approach.* New York: Wiley.

LeVay, S. 1991. A difference in hypothalamic structure between heterosexual and homosexual men. *Science* 253: 1034–37.

Money, J., and A.A. Ehrhardt. 1972. *Man and women, boy and girl.* Baltimore: Johns Hopkins University Press.

Moore, H.L. 1994. *A passion for difference: Essays in anthropology and gender.* Bloomington: Indiana University Press.

Moore, L.J., and A.E. Clarke. 1995. Clitoral conventions and transgressions: Graphic representations in anatomy texts, c1900–1991. *Feminist Studies* 21(2): 255–301.

Oyama, S. 1985. *The ontogeny of information.* Cambridge: Cambridge University Press.

Plumwood, V. 1993. *Feminism and the mastery of nature.* New York: Routledge.

Rothblatt, M. 1995. *The apartheid of sex: A manifesto on the freedom of gender.* New York: Crown.

Rubin, G. 1975. The traffic in women: Notes on the "political economy" of sex. In *Toward an anthropology of women*, ed. R.R. Reiter. New York: Monthly Review Press, 157–210.

Sawicki, J. 1991. *Disciplining Foucault*. New York: Routledge.

Schiebinger, L. 1993a. Why mammals are called mammals: Gender politics in eighteenth-century natural history. *American Historical Review* 98(2): 382–411.

Schiebinger, L. 1993b. *Nature's body: Gender in the making of modern science*. Boston: Beacon Press.

Taylor, P.J. 1998. Natural selection: A heavy hand in biological and social thought. *Science as Culture* 7(1): 5–32.

Valian, V. 1998a. Running in place. *The Science* (January/February): 18–23.

Valian, V. 1998b. *Why so slow? The advancement of women*. Cambridge: MIT Press.

Wilson, E. 1998. *Neural geographies: Feminism and the microstructure of cognition*. New York: Routledge.

**Source:** Fausto-Sterling, Anne. (2000). Excerpted from "Chapter 1: Dueling Dualisms." In *Sexing the Body: Gender Politics and the Construction of Sexuality* (pp. 1–8, 21–27). New York, NY: Basic Books.

# CHAPTER 16

## Women's Brains

*Stephen Gould*

Stephen Gould was a highly influential paleontologist, evolutionary biologist, and award-winning popular science writer. Among the best-known scientists of his generation, he held the position of Alexander Agassiz professor of zoology at Harvard University and was curator of paleontology at Harvard's Museum of Comparative Zoology. Gould also wrote numerous widely read books, as well as regularly contributed essays to *Natural History Magazine* that uncovered and critiqued scientific sexism and racism in research.

In the prelude to *Middlemarch*, George Eliot lamented the unfulfilled lives of talented women:

> Some have felt that these blundering lives are due to the inconvenient indefiniteness with which the Supreme Power has fashioned the natures of women; if there were one level of feminine incompetence as strict as the ability to count three and no more, the social lot of women might be treated with scientific certitude.

Eliot goes on to discount the idea of innate limitation, but while she wrote in 1872, the leaders of European anthropometry were trying to measure "with scientific certitude" the inferiority of women. Anthropometry, or measurement of the human body, is not so fashionable a field these days, but it dominated the human sciences for much of the nineteenth century and remained popular until intelligence testing replaced skull measurement as a favored device for making invidious comparisons among races, classes, and sexes. Craniometry, or measurement of the skull, commanded the most attention and respect. Its unquestioned leader, Paul Broca (1824–80), professor of clinical surgery at the Faculty of Medicine in Paris, gathered a school of disciples and imitators around himself. Their work, so meticulous and apparently irrefutable, exerted great influence and won high esteem as a jewel of nineteenth-century science.

Broca's work seemed particularly invulnerable to refutation. Had he not measured with the most scrupulous care and accuracy? (Indeed, he had. I have the greatest respect for Broca's meticulous procedure. His numbers are sound. But science is an inferential exercise, not a catalog of facts. Numbers, by themselves, specify nothing. All depends upon what you do with them.) Broca depicted himself as an apostle of objectivity, a man who bowed before facts and cast aside superstition and sentimentality. He declared that "there is no faith, however respectable, no interest, however legitimate, which must not accommodate itself to the progress of human knowledge and bend before truth." Women, like it or not, had smaller brains than men and, therefore, could not equal them in intelligence. This fact, Broca argued, may reinforce a common prejudice in male society, but it is also a scientific truth. L. Manouvrier, a black sheep in Broca's fold, rejected the inferiority of women and wrote with feeling about the burden imposed upon them by Broca's numbers:

> Women displayed their talents and their diplomas. They also invoked philosophical authorities. But they were opposed by *numbers* unknown to Condorcet or to John Stuart Mill. These numbers fell upon poor women like a sledge hammer, and they were accompanied by commentaries and sarcasms more ferocious than the most misogynist imprecations of certain church fathers. The theologians had asked if women had a soul. Several centuries later, some scientists were ready to refuse them a human intelligence.

Broca's argument rested upon two sets of data: the larger brains of men in modern societies, and a supposed increase in male superiority through time. His most extensive data came from autopsies performed personally in four Parisian hospitals. For 292 male brains, he calculated an average weight of 1,325 grams; 140 female brains averaged 1,144 grams for a difference of 181 grams, or 14 percent of the male weight. Broca understood, of course, that part of this difference could be attributed to the greater height of males. Yet he made no attempt to measure the effect of size alone and actually stated that it cannot account for the entire difference because we know, a priori, that women are not as intelligent as men (a premise that the data were supposed to test, not rest upon):

> We might ask if the small size of the female brain depends exclusively upon the small size of her body. Tiedemann has proposed this explanation. But we must not forget that women are, on the average, a little less intelligent than men, a difference which we should not exaggerate but which is, nonetheless, real. We are therefore permitted to suppose that the relatively small size of the female brain depends in part upon her physical inferiority and in part upon her intellectual inferiority.

In 1873, the year after Eliot published *Middlemarch*, Broca measured the cranial capacities of prehistoric skulls from L'Homme Mort cave. Here he found a difference of only 99.5 cubic centimeters between males and females, while modern populations range from 129.5 to 220.7. Topinard, Broca's chief disciple, explained the increasing discrepancy through time as a result of differing evolutionary pressures upon dominant men and passive women:

> The man who fights for two or more in the struggle for existence, who has all the responsibility and the cares of tomorrow, who is constantly active in combating the environment and human rivals, needs more brain than the woman whom he must protect and nourish, the sedentary woman, lacking any interior occupations, whose role is to raise children, love, and be passive.

In 1879, Gustave Le Bon, chief misogynist of Broca's school, used these data to publish what must be the most vicious attack upon women in modern scientific literature (no one can top Aristotle). I do not claim his views were representative of Broca's school, but they were published in France's most respected anthropological journal. Le Bon concluded:

In the most intelligent races, as among the Parisians, there are a large number of women whose brains are closer in size to those of gorillas than to the most developed male brains. This inferiority is so obvious that no one can contest it for a moment; only its degree is worth discussion. All psychologists who have studied the intelligence of women, as well as poets and novelists, recognize today that they represent the most inferior forms of human evolution and that they are closer to children and savages than to an adult, civilized man. They excel in fickleness, inconstancy, absence of thought and logic, and incapacity to reason. Without doubt there exist some distinguished women, very superior to the average man, but they are as exceptional as the birth of any monstrosity, as, for example, of a gorilla with two heads; consequently, we may neglect them entirely.

Nor did Le Bon shrink from the social implications of his views. He was horrified by the proposal of some American reformers to grant women higher education on the same basis as men:

A desire to give them the same education, and, as a consequence, to propose the same goals for them, is a dangerous chimera.… The day when, misunderstanding the inferior occupations which nature has given her, women leave the home and take part in our battles; on this day a social revolution will begin, and everything that maintains the sacred ties of the family will disappear.

Sound familiar?[1]

I have reexamined Broca's data, the basis for all this derivative pronouncement, and I find his numbers sound but his interpretation ill-founded, to say the least. The data supporting his claim for increased difference through time can be easily dismissed.

Broca based his contention on the samples from L'Homme Mort alone—only seven male and six female skulls in all. Never have so little data yielded such far-ranging conclusions.

In 1888, Topinard published Broca's more extensive data on the Parisian hospitals. Since Broca recorded height and age as well as brain size, we may use modern statistics to remove their effect. Brain weight decreases with age, and Broca's women were, on average, considerably older than his men. Brain weight increases with height, and his average man was almost half a foot taller than his average woman. I used multiple regression, a technique that allowed me to assess simultaneously the influence of height and age upon brain size. In an analysis of the data for women, I found that, at average male height and age, a woman's brain would weigh 1,212 grams. Correction for height and age reduces Broca's measured difference of 181 grams by more than a third, to 113 grams.

I don't know what to make of this remaining difference because I cannot assess other factors known to influence brain size in a major way. Cause of death has an important effect: degenerative disease often entails a substantial diminution of brain size. (This effect is separate from the decrease attributed to age alone.) Eugene Schreider, also working with Broca's data, found that men killed in accidents had brains weighing, on average, 60 grams more than men dying of infectious diseases. The best modern data I can find (from American hospitals) records a full 100-gram difference between death by degenerative arteriosclerosis and by violence or accident. Since so many of Broca's subjects were very elderly women, we may assume that lengthy degenerative disease was more common among them than among the men.

More importantly, modern students of brain size still have not agreed on a proper measure for eliminating the powerful effect of body size. Height is partly adequate, but men and women of the same height do not share the same body build. Weight is even worse than height, because most of its variation reflects nutrition rather than intrinsic size—fat versus skinny exerts little influence upon the brain. Manouvrier took up this subject in the 1880s and argued that muscular mass and force should be used. He tried to measure this elusive property in various ways and found a marked difference in favor of men, even in men and women of the same height. When he corrected for what he called "sexual mass," women actually came out slightly ahead in brain size.

Thus, the corrected 113-gram difference is surely too large; the true figure is probably close to zero and may as well favor women as men. And 113 grams, by the way, is exactly the average difference between a 5-foot 4-inch and a 6-foot 4-inch male in Broca's data. We would not (especially us short folks) want to ascribe greater intelligence to tall men. In short, who knows what to do with Broca's data? They certainly don't permit any confident claim that men have bigger brains than women.

To appreciate the social role of Broca and his school, we must recognize that his statements about the brains of women do not reflect an isolated prejudice toward a single disadvantaged group. They must be weighed in the context of a general theory that supported contemporary social distinctions as biologically ordained. Women, blacks, and poor people suffered the same disparagement, but women bore the brunt of Broca's argument because he had easier access to data on women's brains. Women were singularly denigrated but they also stood as surrogates for other disenfranchised groups. As one of Broca's disciples wrote in 1881: "Men of the black races have a brain scarcely heavier than that of white women." This juxtaposition extended into many other realms of anthropological argument, particularly to claims that, anatomically and emotionally, both women and blacks were like white children—and that white children, by the theory of recapitulation, represented an ancestral (primitive) adult stage of human evolution. I do not regard as empty rhetoric the claim that women's battles are for all of us.

Maria Montessori did not confine her activities to educational reform for young children. She lectured on anthropology for several years at the University of Rome, and wrote an influential book entitled *Pedagogical Anthropology* (English edition, 1913). Montessori was no egalitarian. She supported most of Broca's work and the theory of innate criminality proposed by her compatriot Cesare Lombroso. She measured the circumference of children's heads in her schools and inferred that the best prospects had bigger brains. But she had no use for Broca's conclusions about women. She discussed Manouvrier's work at length and made much of his tentative claim that women, after proper correction of the data, had slightly larger brains than men. Women, she concluded, were intellectually superior, but men had prevailed heretofore by dint of physical force. Since technology has abolished force as an instrument of power, the era of women may soon be upon us: "In such an epoch there will really be superior human beings, there will really be men strong in morality and in sentiment. Perhaps in this way the reign of women is approaching, when the enigma of her anthropological superiority will be deciphered. Woman was always the custodian of human sentiment, morality and honor."

This represents one possible antidote to "scientific" claims for the constitutional inferiority of certain groups. One may affirm the validity of biological distinctions but argue that the data have been misinterpreted by prejudiced men with a stake in the outcome, and that disadvantaged groups are truly superior. In recent years, Elaine Morgan has followed this strategy in her *Descent of Woman*, a speculative reconstruction of human prehistory from the woman's point of view—and as farcical as more famous tall tales by and for men.

I prefer another strategy. Montessori and Morgan followed Broca's philosophy to reach a more congenial conclusion. I would rather label the whole enterprise of setting a biological value upon groups for what it is: irrelevant and highly injurious. George Eliot well appreciated the special tragedy that biological labeling imposed upon members of disadvantaged groups. She expressed it for people like herself—women of extraordinary talent. I would apply it more widely—not only to those whose dreams are flouted but also to those who never realize that they may dream—but I cannot match her prose. In conclusion, then, the rest of Eliot's prelude to *Middlemarch*:

> The limits of variation are really much wider than anyone would imagine from the sameness of women's coiffure and the favorite love stories in prose and verse. Here and there a cygnet is reared uneasily among the ducklings in the brown pond, and never finds the living stream in fellowship with its own oary-footed kind. Here and there is born a Saint Theresa, foundress of nothing, whose loving heartbeats and sobs after an unattained goodness tremble off and are dispersed among hindrances instead of centering in some long recognizable deed.

## NOTE

1.  When I wrote this essay, I assumed that Le Bon was a marginal, if colorful, figure. I have since learned that he was a leading scientist, one of the founders of social psychology, and best known for a seminal study on crowd behavior, still cited today (*La psychologie des foules,* 1895), and for his work on unconscious motivation.

*Source:* Gould, Stephen. (1980). "Women's Brains." In *The Panda's Thumb: More Reflections in Natural History* (pp. 152–159). New York, NY: Norton.

# CHAPTER 17

## Freaks and Queers

*Eli Clare*

Eli Clare is a writer, speaker, activist, teacher, and poet. His areas of expertise and activism are disability, queer, and trans rights and integrating ableism into feminist understandings of oppression. *Exile and Pride,* from which the following selection is taken, has established Clare as one of the leading writers on the intersections of queerness and disability. In his most recent book, *Brilliant Imperfection: Grappling with Cure,* Clare uses memoir, history, and critical analysis to explore cure—the deeply held belief that body-minds considered broken need to be fixed. He has also published a collection of poetry entitled *The Marrow's Telling: Words in Motion.*

## FREAK SHOW

The history of freakdom extends far back into western civilization. The court jester, the pet dwarf, the exhibition of humans in Renaissance England, the myths of giants, minotaurs, and monsters all point to this long history, which reached a pinnacle in the mid-1800s to mid-1900s. During that century, freaks were big entertainment and big business. Freak shows populated the United States, and people flocked to the circus, the carnival, the storefront dime museum. They came to gawk at "freaks," "savages," and "geeks." They came to be educated and entertained, titillated and repulsed. They came to have their ideas of normal and abnormal, superior and inferior, their sense of self, confirmed and strengthened. And gawk they did. But who were they gawking at? This is where I want to start.

Whatever these paying customers—*rubes* in circus lingo—believed, they were not staring at freaks of nature. Rather, the freak show tells the story of an elaborate and calculated social construction that utilized performance and fabrication as well as deeply held cultural beliefs. At the center of this construction is the showman, who, using costuming, staging, elaborate fictional histories, marketing, and choreography, turned people from four groups into freaks. First, disabled people, both white people and people of color, became Armless Wonders, Frog Men, Giants, Midgets, Pinheads, Camel Girls, Wild Men of Borneo, and the like. Second, nondisabled people of color—bought, persuaded, forced, and kidnapped to the United States from colonized countries all over the world—became Cannibals and Savages. Third, nondisabled people of color from the United States became Natives from the Exotic Wilds. And fourth, nondisabled people with visible differences—bearded women, fat women, very thin men, people covered with tattoos, intersex people—became wondrous and horrifying exhibits. Cultural critic and disability theorist Rosemarie Garland-Thomson argues that the differences among these sometimes overlapping groups of people melded together:

> Perhaps the freak show's most remarkable effect was to eradicate distinctions among a wide variety of bodies, conflating them under a single sign of the freak-as-other.... [A]ll the bodily characteristics that seemed different or threatening to the dominant order merged into a kind of motley chorus line of physical difference on the freak show stage.... [A] nondisabled person of color billed as the "Fiji Cannibal" was equivalent to a physically disabled Euro-American called the "Legless Wonder."[1]

In the eyes of many rubes, particularly white and/or nondisabled folks, the freak show probably was one big melting pot of difference and otherness. At the same time, the differences among the various groups of people who worked as freaks remain important to understanding the freak show in its entirety. But whatever the differences, all four groups held one thing in common: nature did not make them into freaks. The freak show did, carefully constructing an exaggerated divide between "normal" and Other, sustained in turn by rubes willing to pay good money to stare.

Hiram and Barney Davis performed wildly for their audiences, snapping, snarling, talking gibberish from stage. The handbill sold in conjunction with their display described in lengthy, imagined detail "What We Know About Waino and Plutano, the Wild Men of Borneo." In reality, Hiram and Barney were white, cognitively disabled brothers from an immigrant farm family who lived in Ohio. Their mother, after many offers which she refused, finally sold them to a persistent showman for a wash pan

full of gold and silver. Off-stage, Hiram and Barney were quiet, unassuming men. In one photo, they stand flanking their manager Hanford Lyman. Their hair falls past their shoulders; they sport neatly trimmed goatees; Hiram folds his hands in front of him; Barney cocks his hands on his hips; they look mildly and directly into the camera.

Ann Thompson, a white woman born without arms, posed as "The Armless Wonder." From stage, she signed and sold photographs as souvenirs, writing with her toes sayings like, "So you perceive it's really true, when hands are lacking, toes will do," or more piously, "Indolence and ease are the rust of the mind." In her autobiography, which she hawked along with her photos and trinkets, Ann presented herself as a respectable, religious lady. In one photo, she sits beside her husband and son, all of them wearing formal Victorian clothing.

William Johnson, a cognitively disabled African American man from New Jersey, became the "What Is It?," the "missing link," the "Monkey Man." He wore hairy ape-like costumes, shaved his head bald except for a little tuft at the very top, and posed in front of a jungle backdrop. The showmen at P. T. Barnum's American Museum in New York City described William as "a most singular animal, which though it has many of the features and characteristics of both the human and the brute, is not, apparently, either, but in appearance, a mixture of both—the connecting link between humanity and brute creation."[2] Although the way in which he came to the freak show is unknown—Barnum may have bought him at a young age and coerced him into performing at first—William died in his 80s at home, a rich and well-liked man, referred to, by his co-workers, as the "dean of freaks."

Charles Stratton, a working-class short person—*dwarf* in medical terminology—from Connecticut worked the freak show as General Tom Thumb. He played the role of a European aristocrat, complete with resplendent suits, a miniature carriage pulled by ponies, and meetings with rich and famous people around the world, becoming in the process a rich man himself. When Charles and Mercy Lavinia Warren Bump, a short woman who also worked the freak show, fell in love and decided to get married, P. T. Barnum set out, in an extravagant example of showmanship, to turn their wedding into a huge media spectacle. He was successful; 2,000 people attended the event, and the *New York Times* ran a full-page story, headlined "Loving Lilliputians." Charles and Mercy played their roles and used the publicity to springboard another European tour.

Two Congolese men and thirteen Congolese women, wearing large, heavy jewelry in their pierced lips, were bought by circus agent Ludwig Bergonnier and shipped from Africa to the United States. The poster advertising their display in the Ringling Brothers Circus freak show proclaimed them "Genuine Monster-Mouthed Ubangi Savages World's Most Weird Living Humans from Africa's Darkest Depths." The women were forced to wear only gunny sack skirts; the men, given only loincloths, carried spears. Ubangi was a name randomly pulled off a map of Africa and had no relationship to where these women and men had actually lived. Their real names and actual homeland are unknown.

The Davis brothers, Thompson, Johnson, Stratton, the now unknown African men and women did not slide into the world as infant freaks. They were made freaks, socially constructed for the purposes of entertainment and profit. This construction depended not only upon the showmanship of the "freaks" and their managers. It also capitalized on the eagerness of rubes to gawk at freaks and on the ableism and racism, which made the transitions from disabled white person, disabled person of color, nondisabled person of color, to freak even possible. Without this pair of oppressive ideologies, the attendant fear and hatred of all disabled people and all people of color, and the desire to create an Other against whom one could gauge her/his normality, who could ever believe for even one farcical moment that William Johnson was Darwin's missing link; Barney Davis, a wild man from Borneo; Ann Thompson, an armless wonder?

*Ann, in that photo of you with your husband and son, you sit on a rug decorated with crosses, a rug you crocheted. The showmen made a big deal of your dexterity. But did you learn to crochet as a freak show stunt? Or did you, like so many women of your time, sew and knit, embroider and crochet, simply as a necessity and a pastime?*

Within this context of ableism and racism, the people who worked the freak show did not live only as victims. Many of the "freaks" themselves—particularly those who were not cognitively disabled or brought to the United States from Africa, Asia, South and Central America, the Pacific islands, and the Caribbean—controlled their own acts and displays, working alongside their managers to shape profitable shows. Many of them made decent livings; some, like Charles Stratton, Mercy Lavinia Warren Bump, and William Johnson, even became wealthy. When P. T. Barnum lost all his money in a bad business deal, Stratton came out of semi-retirement and rescued him by agreeing to go on yet another lucrative European tour. Others, like the Hilton sisters, conjoined twins who worked in the mid-1900s, became their own managers, or, like Bump and her Lilliputian Opera Company, formed their own performing groups, which were employed by dime museums and traveling vaudeville companies. In other words, white, nondisabled freak show owners and managers didn't only exploit "their freaks." The two groups also colluded together to dupe the audience, to make a buck off the rube's gullibility. Within the subculture of the freak show, rubes were understood as exploited victims—explicitly lied to, charged outrageous sums for mere trinkets, pickpocketed, or merely given incorrect change at the ticket counter.

*Charles, there is a picture of you, taken during a visit with the Queen of England. You have a miniature sword drawn and are staging a fight with a poodle. Your wife, Mercy, writes of embarrassment and outrage. Of presidential candidate Stephen Douglas, she remembers: "He expressed great pleasure at again seeing me, and as I stood before him he took my hand and, drawing me toward him, stooped to kiss me. I instinctively* drew back, feeling my face suffused with blushes. It seemed impossible to make people at first understand that I was not a child."[3] *Did you share her embarrassment and outrage as you faced that poodle? Or did you and Barnum laugh long and hard as you concocted your stunts?*

The questions about exploitation are complicated; simple answers collapse easily. Robert Bogdan, in his history *Freak Show*, excerpts a letter he received from freak show manager Ward Hall: "I exhibited freaks and exploited them for years. Now you are going to exploit them. The difference between authors and the news media, and the freak show operators is that we paid them." Bogdan comments, "[Hall's] use of the word *exploit* was playful. He does not think he exploited them. He had a business relationship, complete with contract, with his troupe of human oddities. His livelihood depended on them, as theirs did on him. He had no pretensions of doing good…."[4] Although Bogdan chronicles the social construction of freaks in amazing detail and refuses to situate the people who worked the freak shows as passive victims, I believe he is reaching toward a simple answer to the question of exploitation.

Hall's exploitation of people who worked as freaks may not have revolved around ableism and racism. Maybe he wasn't acting out of fear and hatred of disabled people and people of color, out of his internal psychological sense and the external legislated reality of privilege. And then again, maybe he was. But most certainly, like all the people who profited from the freak show, he used ableism and racism to his benefit. This use of oppression by white, nondisabled businessmen is common, fraught, and ultimately unacceptable. In his letter, Hall explicitly casts himself as a boss exploiting his workers, placing the freak show within the context of capitalism. Bogdan defends Hall in a backhanded way when he writes: "[Hall] had no pretensions of doing good." But since when do bosses in most profit-making business have real pretensions of doing good by their workers? Doing good may be a byproduct of making profit, but only a byproduct.

Is Hall any less exploitative because he was acting as a boss rather than, or in addition to, a racist white person and an ableist nondisabled person?

Any estimation of exploitation in the freak show needs to also include Hall and "his troupe of human oddities" colluding together to exploit the rube. Sometimes, this exploitation carried with it a sense of absurdity, a sense that the rubes would believe anything, that they were simple, gullible fools. Other times, this exploitation was pure thievery, the sideshow creating situations in which it was easy to steal the rube's money. But to cast the audience only as victim neglects the very real ways in which the freak show bolstered white people's and nondisabled people's sense of superiority and well-being. The social construction of freaks always relied upon the perceived gap between a rube's normality and a freak's abnormality. Unsurprisingly, normality was defined exclusively in terms of whiteness and able-bodiedness.

The complexities of exploitation pile up, layer upon layer. White people and nondisabled people used racism and ableism to turn a profit. The freak show managers and owners were bosses and as such had power over their workers, the people who worked as freaks. Boss and worker together consciously manipulated their audience. That same audience willingly used lies to strengthen its own self-image. Given this maze of relationships, I have trouble accepting the assessment that exploitation in the freak show, if it existed at all, wasn't truly serious. Rather, I believe it exerted influence in many directions.

Working as a freak never meant working in a respectful, liberating environment, but then disabled people had no truly respectful and liberating options available to them in the mid-1800s. They could beg in the streets. They could survive in almshouses, where, as reformer Dorothea Dix put it, mentally ill people and developmentally disabled people lived "in cages, closets, cellars, stalls, pens! Chained naked, beaten with rods, and lashed into obedience."[5] They could live behind closed doors with their families. Consider William Johnson. As a Black, cognitively disabled man who apparently had no surviving family, he had few options. P. T. Barnum found William's counterpart, the woman displayed as the female "What Is It?," abandoned in an outhouse, covered with shit, left to die. In a world such as this, where the freak show existed alongside the street, the almshouse, the outhouse, William's position as the "dean of freaks," although dehumanizing in a number of ways, doesn't look so bad.

*William, late after the exhibits had closed, the rubes gone home, did you and your friends gather backstage to party, passing a bottle of whiskey round and round? Did you entertain some more, pull out your fiddle and play silly squeaky songs? Or did you sit back and listen to one joke after another until you were breathless with laughter?*

In many ways, working as a freak was similar to working as a prostitute. Cultural worker and working-class scholar Joe Kadi writes, "Left-wing working-class analysis … situates prostitution within the context of capitalism (one more *really* lousy job), celebrates the women who survive, thumbs its nose at the moralistic middle-class attitudes that condemn without understanding, and relays the women's stories and perspectives."[6] This same theoretical and political framework can be used to examine the job of freak. Clearly, working as a freak meant working a lousy job, many times the *only* job available, in a hostile ableist and racist world. Sometimes, the job was lousier than others. The African women and men who performed as "Ubangi savages" made a nickel on every photograph they sold, nothing else; whereas their manager, Ludwig Bergonnier, made $1,500 a week renting "his display" to the Ringling Brothers Circus. In contrast, Charles Stratton became rich, owning a horse farm and a yacht. Still others, like William Johnson, found community among the people who worked the freak show.

*You who ended up in the history books named only "Ubangi Savages," no names of your own: night after night, you paraded around the circus tent, air sticky against your bare skin, burlap prickly against your covered skin. Did you come to hate Bergonnier?*

What did the people who worked as freaks think of their jobs, their lives? I want to hear their stories,

but like the stories of other marginalized people, they were most often never told, but rather eaten up, thrown away, lost in the daily grind of survival. Some of these people didn't read or write, due to their particular disabilities or to the material/social circumstances of their lives. Or, as in the case of many of the people brought here from other countries, they didn't speak English and/or didn't come from cultures that passed stories through the written word. A few people who worked the freak show did write autobiographies, but these pamphlets or books were mostly part of the whole production, sold alongside the handbills and photos. These stories ended up being part of the showmen's hyperbole. So, in order to reconstruct, celebrate, and understand the lives of the people who worked the freak show, I rely on historians, like Robert Bogdan, who have sifted through thousands of handbills, posters, newspaper articles, and promotional garbage used to create The Armless Wonder, The Wild Men of Borneo. In large part, I will never truly know their lives but can only use my imagination, political sensibilities, and intuition to fill the holes between the outrageous headlines in the *New York Times* and other newspapers and the outrageous handbills sold at the carnival.

The historians who moralize about the freak show frustrate me. These academics will take a detail, like the fact that Hiram and Barney Davis's mother sold her sons to a showman, and use it to demonstrate just how despicable showmen could be and how oppressive the freak show was. The disturbing fact that many of the people who worked as freaks—disabled people from the United States[7] as well as people from colonized countries—were sold into the business needs to be examined. The question, why were they sold, has to be asked. Certainly, in many cases, the answer must revolve around fear and hatred, undiluted ableism and racism, imperialism, and capitalism. But consider Hiram and Barney. They were sold for a wash pan full of gold and silver. What did that wash pan mean to their mother, Catherine Davis? My sources suggest, although don't explicitly state, that the Davises were a *poor* immigrant farm family. Did that gold and silver mean economic survival to Catherine Davis? What happened to working-class and poor disabled people who needed care but whose families could not provide it? The options did not abound: the almshouse, the street, the freak show. Rather than moralize and condemn, I want freak show historians to examine the whole context, including racism, ableism, and classism, and begin to build a complex understanding of exploitation. Like the women Joe Kadi refers to in her analysis of prostitution, the people who worked as freaks—especially those who had some control over their own display—grasped an exploitative situation in an exploitative world and, as often as possible, turned it to their benefit.

At the same time, the people who had the least power in the freak show—people from colonized countries and cognitively disabled people—underscore just how exploitative this institution could be. Many of the people of color brought to the United States died bleak deaths of pneumonia, pleurisy, or tuberculosis. They died on the long ship rides. They died wanting desperately to return to their home countries. They did not want to be part of the freak show; they never came to like the freak show; they didn't become showmen and -women in their own right. Instead, the circus, the dime museum, the vaudeville act, the natural history museum were simply sites of imperialist atrocity. Likewise, cognitively disabled people most frequently had no control over their displays. Some lacked the abilities to say yes or no to their own exhibition; others were simply trapped by unscrupulous managers, who typically were also their legal guardians. Although some cognitively disabled people had what appear to be good and happy relationships with their managers, the dual role of showman and legal guardian is a setup for exploitation.

The display of both groups of people capitalized on the theory of the time that nondisabled people of color and cognitively disabled people embodied the missing link between primates and humans.

Eminent zoologist Baron Georges Cuvier wrote in the early 1800s:

> The negro race is confined to the south of Mount Atlas. Its characteristics are, black complexion, woolly hair, compressed cranium, and flattish nose. In the prominence of the lower part of the face, and the thickness of the lips, it manifestly approaches the monkey tribe.[8]

Much the same was believed about cognitively disabled people. Following the same train of thought as Cuvier, German scientist Carl Vogt wrote in 1867 even more explicitly about evolutionary theory:

> Microcephalics [people with a type of cognitive disability medically known as microcephalia] must necessarily represent an earlier developmental state of the human being … they reveal to us one of the milestones which the human passed by during the course of his historical evolution.[9]

The racism and ableism imbedded in these theories intersect intensely in the exhibition of cognitively disabled people of color. Consider the story of two cognitively disabled siblings kidnapped as children from San Salvador. Called "Maximo" and "Bartola," they were declared to be from "a long-lost race of Aztecs." Scientists and anthropologists studied them; showmen displayed them. Both groups helped create and defend the "long-lost race" fabrication, anthropologists to substantiate their theories, showmen to make money, each feeding off the other. They used a variety of observations as their proof. They emphasized physical attributes associated with being disabled by microcephalia, particularly short stature and a slightly sloping skull. They took note of "Maximo's" and "Bartola's" dark skin and thick black hair. They made much of their subjects' language use and food preferences, citing the cultural differences between "civilized" white people and "barbaric" people of color. They exaggerated the specific cognitive impairments of "Maximo" and "Bartola." In short, these white, nondisabled men totally intertwined race and disability; racism and ableism, to create "their freaks."

In one set of photos, "Maximo" and "Bartola" are stripped naked, posed against a blank wall. I imagine scientists measuring the diameter of their skulls, the length of their legs, taking notes about their skin color and speech patterns, then snapping these pictures to add to their documentation. A second set of photos has them sitting against a stone wall. "Maximo" wears striped pants and a shirt with a big sun on its front. "Bartola's" dress has a zig-zag design woven through it. Their hair is teased into big, wild afros. "Maximo" looks dazedly beyond the camera; "Bartola" looks down. I imagine showmen carefully arranging their props, calculating their profits. There are no complex or ambiguous answers here to the questions of power, control, and exploitation.

During the freak show's heyday, today's dominant model of disability—the medical model—did not yet exist. This model defines disability as a personal problem, curable and/or treatable by the medical establishment, which in turn has led to the wholesale medicalization of disabled people. As theorist Michael Oliver puts it:

> Doctors are centrally involved in the lives of disabled people from the determination of whether a foetus is handicapped or not through to the deaths of old people from a variety of disabling conditions. Some of these involvements are, of course, entirely appropriate, as in the diagnosis of impairment, the stabilisation of medical condition after trauma, the treatment of illness occurring independent of disability, and the provision of physical rehabilitation. But doctors are also involved in assessing driving ability, prescribing wheelchairs, determining the allocation

of financial benefits, selecting educational provision and measuring work capabilities and potential; in none of these cases is it immediately obvious that medical training and qualifications make doctors the most appropriate persons to be so involved.[10]

In the centuries before medicalization, before the 1930s and '40s when disability became a pathology and the exclusive domain of doctors and hospitals, the Christian western world had encoded disability with many different meanings. Disabled people had sinned. We lacked moral strength. We were the spawn of the devil or the product of god's will. Our bodies/minds reflected events that happened during our mothers' pregnancies.

At the time of the freak show, disabled people were, in the minds of nondisabled people, extraordinary creatures, not entirely human, about whom everyone—"professional" people and the general public alike—was curious. Doctors routinely robbed the graves of "giants" in order to measure their skeletons and place them in museums. Scientists described disabled people in terms like "female, belonging to the monocephalic, ileadelphic class of monsters by fusion,"[11] language that came from the "science" of teratology, the centuries-old study of monsters. Anthropologists studied disabled people with an eye toward evolutionary theory. Rubes paid good money to gawk.

*Hiram, did you ever stop mid-performance, stop up there on your dime museum platform and stare back, turning your mild and direct gaze back on the rubes, gawking at the gawkers, entertained by your own audience?*

At the same time, there were signs of the move toward medicalization. Many people who worked as freaks were examined by doctors. Often, handbills included the testimony of a doctor who verified the "authenticity" of the "freak" and sometimes explained the causes of his or her "freakishness." Tellingly, doctors performed this role, rather than anthropologists, priests, or philosophers. But for the century in which the freak show flourished, disability was not yet inextricably linked to pathology, and without pathology, pity and tragedy did not shadow disability to the same extent they do today.

Consequently, the freak show fed upon neither of these, relying instead on voyeurism. The "armless wonder" played the fiddle on stage; the "giant" lived as royalty; the "savage" roared and screamed. These performances didn't create freaks as pitiful or tragic but as curious, odd, surprising, horrifying, wondrous. Freaks were not supercrips. They did not *overcome* disability; they *flaunted* it. Nor were freaks poster children, the modern-day objects of pity, used to raise money on the telethon stage. Instead, the freaks performed, and the rubes gawked. In a culture that paired disability and curiosity, voyeurism was morally acceptable. Thus, people flocked without shame or compunction to see the "freaks," primed by cultural beliefs about disability to be duped by the lies and fabrications created at the freak show.

In the same way, cultural beliefs about race—notions about the "wild savage," the "noble savage," and an eagerness to see both—made the exhibition of nondisabled people of color at the freak show and other venues extraordinarily profitable. Take, for example, the display of Filipino people at the 1904 World's Fair in St. Louis. The exhibit was billed as the "Igorot Village," complete with mostly naked women and men dancing wildly and eating dog stew. One among many "anthropological" displays at the Fair, the Village, as a near perfect representation of the "wild savage," attracted by far the most Fair-goers and media attention. Christopher Vaughan, in his article "Ogling Igorots," writes:

> The "civilized" Visayans, despite offering hourly theatrical and orchestral performances—concluding with "The Star Spangled Banner," sung in English by the entire village—went relatively ignored in comparison with the Igorots.... Gate receipts at the Igorot concession nearly quadrupled

the total for the Visayans and tripled that of the colorful Moros.[12]

It was all too easy for white people to gawk at people of color, using the image of dog-eating savages from far-away "uncivilized" islands both to create and strengthen their sense of white identity and white superiority.

During this same period of time, imperialism had intensified to a fevered pitch, both abroad in places like the Philippines and at home as white people continued to subjugate and destroy Native peoples and cultures. By the time of the 1904 World's Fair, the United States had won the Spanish-American War and gained control over the Philippines. In explaining his decision to solidify the United States' colonial rule there, President McKinley referred to "our civilizing mission." What better way to justify that mission, than to display Filipino people as "uncivilized savages"?

This interplay between politics and the freak show also occurred on the national level. For instance, the missing-link evolutionary theory, used so profitably by showmen, supported slavery before Emancipation and the suppression of civil rights after. But the freak show didn't only *use* this ideology. The display of Black and white cognitively disabled people and nondisabled people of color as the "missing link" and the "What Is It?" actually bolstered the theory. The scientists and politicians could point to William Johnson and say, "See, here is living proof. Look at this creature." In doing so, they were reaffirming the less-than-human status of people of color and rationalizing much of their social and political policy. Simply put, the freak show both fed upon and gave fuel to imperialism, domestic racist politics, and the cultural beliefs about "wild savages" and white superiority.

The decline of the freak show in the early decades of the 20th century coincided with the medicalization of disability. As pity, tragedy, and medical diagnosis/treatment entered the picture, the novelty and mystery of disability dissipated. Explicit voyeurism stopped being socially acceptable except when controlled by the medical establishment. And later in the 20th century, as colonized people of color fought back successfully against their colonizers and as legal segregation in the United States ended and civil rights started to take hold, the exhibition of people of color also became, at least ostensibly, unacceptable. Along with these changes came a scorn for the freak show as an oppressive institution from the bad old days. But I'm not so sure the freak show is all that dead.

Consider Coco Fusco and Guillermo Gomez-Peña's performance piece "The Couple in the Cage," created in 1992 as part of the "500 Years of Resistance" celebration.[13] Fusco and Gomez-Peña costumed themselves in everything from false leopard skins to mirrored sunglasses and posed as native people from a newly discovered tribe. They toured natural history museums, art galleries, and street corners in a cage, performing the script of exotic and noble "savages." In the long tradition of showmen and -women, they even invented an island in the Gulf of Mexico from which they supposedly came and, as they toured, didn't let on to their ruse. Fusco and Gomez-Peña expected their audiences to immediately recognize the parody. Instead, as documented in a video shot at the scene of several performances[14] many people apparently took the ruse seriously. Some people expressed shock and disgust. Others, particularly white people, expounded on their theories about why Fusco paced back and forth, why Gomez-Peña grunted, staring out at the audience. Still others paid 50 cents for Polaroid pictures of the "savages" posed at their bars. Whether these people were serious, whether they all left the performance sites still duped, whether they truly believed their own theories is not clear. But at least to some extent, it appears that "The Couple in the Cage" easily replicated the relationship between rube and freak—even as there are significant differences between this performance art piece and the freak show—suggesting that the old images of race, rather than being dead, live painfully close to the surface.

The scorn for the freak show also assumes that the bad old days were really awful, but I'm not so sure that they were in actuality all that bad for some of the "freaks." Listen to the stories Robert Waldow and Violet and Daisy Hilton tell. All of them lived during the freak show's decline as medicalization took hold.

Robert Waldow, a tall man born in the 1920s, resisted becoming a giant, a freak. He wanted to be a lawyer, but unable to get the necessary education, he turned to shoe advertising. And later, after being pursued for years by showmen, he worked for the circus, earning a large salary and refusing to participate in the hype that would have made him appear taller than he really was. At the same time, doctors also pursued Robert, reporting him to be the tallest man in the world—this being medical hype, not circus hype. They refused to leave him alone. In 1936, a Dr. Charles Humberd showed up uninvited at the Waldows' home. Robert refused a physical exam and wouldn't cooperate with the interview. Humberd left disgruntled and the next year, unbeknownst to the Waldows, published an article in the *Journal of the American Medical Association* called, "Giantism: A Case Study," in which Robert became a case study of a "preacromegalic giant." Because of the article, which cast him as a surly brute, Robert and his family were deluged with unwelcome attention from the media, the general public, and the medical establishment. In the biography *The Gentleman Giant*, Waldow's father reveals that Robert was far more disturbed and angered by his dealings with doctors than with showmen.

Conjoined twins Daisy and Violet Hilton echo this reaction. These women worked the circus, carnival, and vaudeville circuits from the time they could talk. Early on, their abusive guardians controlled and managed the show. They would lock Daisy and Violet away for days at a time to ensure that no one but rubes paying good money could see them. Later, after a court order freed the sisters, they performed on their own. The cover of one publicity pamphlet has Daisy playing the saxophone, Violet, the piano, and both of them smiling cheerfully at the viewer. Much of their lives they spent fighting poverty as the freak show's popularity waned. And yet in their autobiography, they write about "loath[ing] the very tone of the medical man's voice" and fearing that their guardians would "stop showing us on stage and let the doctors have us to punch and pinch and take our picture always."[15] Try telling Robert Waldow and the Hilton sisters how enlightened today's medical model of disability is, how much more progressive it is than the freak show, how bad the bad old days were. Try telling Coco Fusco and Guillermo Gomez-Peña that the freak show is truly dead.

The end of the freak show meant the end of a particular kind of employment for the people who had worked as freaks. For nondisabled people of color from the United States, employment by the 1930s didn't hinge heavily on the freak show, and so its decline didn't have a huge impact. And for people from Africa, Asia, South and Central America, the Pacific islands, and the Caribbean, the decline meant only that white people had one less reason to come kidnap and buy people away from their homes. But for disabled people—both people of color and white people—the end of the freak show almost guaranteed unemployment, disability often being codified into law as the inability to work.

In the '30s when Franklin Roosevelt's work programs employed many people, the federal government explicitly deemed disabled people unable to work, stamping their work applications "P. H. Physically handicapped. Substandard. Unemployable," sending them home with small monthly checks. The League of the Physically Handicapped protested in Washington, DC, occupying the Work Progress Administration's offices, chanting, "We want jobs, not tin cups."[16] In this climate, as freak show jobs disappeared, many disabled people faced a world devoid of employment opportunities.

Listen, for instance, to Otis Jordan, a disabled African American man who works the Sutton Sideshow, one of the only remaining freak shows in the country, as "Otis the Frog Man." In 1984, his exhibit was banned from the New York State Fair when someone lodged a complaint about the indignities of displaying disabled people. Otis responded, "Hell, what does she [the woman who made the complaint] want from me—to be on welfare?"[17] Working as a freak may have been a lousy job, but nonetheless it was a job.

## PRIDE

Now with this history in hand, can I explain why the word *freak* unsettles me, why I have not embraced this piece of disability history, this story of disabled people who earned their livings by flaunting their disabilities, this heritage of resistance, an in-your-face resistance similar to "We're here, we're queer, get used to it"? Why doesn't the word *freak* connect me easily and directly to subversion? The answer I think lies in the transition from freak show to doctor's office, from curiosity to pity, from entertainment to pathology. The end of the freak show didn't mean the end of our display or the end of voyeurism. We simply traded one kind of freakdom for another.

Take, for instance, public stripping, the medical practice of stripping disabled children to their underwear and examining them in front of large groups of doctors, medical students, physical therapists, and rehabilitation specialists. They have the child walk back and forth. They squeeze her muscles. They watch his gait, muscle tension, footfall, back curvature. They take notes and talk among themselves about what surgeries and therapies they might recommend. Since the invention of video cameras, they tape the sessions. They justify public stripping by saying it's a training tool for students, a way for a team of professionals to pool knowledge.[18] This isn't a medical practice of decades gone by. As recently as 1996, disability activist Lisa Blumberg reported in *The Disability Rag* that "specialty" clinics (cerebral palsy clinics, spina bifida clinics, muscular dystrophy clinics, etc.) at a variety of teaching hospitals regularly schedule group—rather than private—examinations and conduct surgery screenings in hospital amphitheaters.[19] Excuse me, but isn't public stripping exactly what scientists and anthropologists did to "Maximo" and "Bartola" a century ago? Tell me, what is the difference between the freak show and public stripping? Which is more degrading? Which takes more control away from disabled people? Which lets a large group of nondisabled people gawk unabashedly for free?

Today's freakdom happens in hospitals and doctors' offices. It happens during telethons as people fork over money out of pity, the tragic stories milked until they're dry. It happens in nursing homes where severely disabled people are often forced to live against their wills. It happens on street corners and at bus stops, on playgrounds and in restaurants. It happens when nondisabled people stare, trying to be covert, smacking their children to teach them how to pretend not to stare. A character in the play *P.H.reaks: The Hidden History of People with Disabilities* juxtaposes the voyeurism of the freak show with the voyeurism of everyday life, saying:

> We're always on display. You think if I walked down the street of your stinking little nowhere town people wouldn't stare at me? Damn right they would, and tell their neighbors and friends and talk about me over dinners and picnics and PTA meetings. Well, if they want to do that, they're going to have to pay me for that privilege. You want to stare at me, fine, it's 25 cents, cash on the barrel. You want a picture, that's another quarter. My life story. Pay me. You think I'm being exploited? You pay to go to a baseball game, don't you?[20]

Today's freakdom happens all the time, and we're not even paid for it. In fact, disabled people have, as a group, an astounding unemployment rate of 71 percent.[21] When we do work, we make 64 cents to a nondisabled worker's dollar.[22]

We don't control today's freakdom, unlike the earlier freak show freakdom, which sometimes we did. The presentation of disability today has been shaped entirely by the medical establishment and the charity industry. That is, until the disability rights movement came along. This civil rights and liberation movement established Centers for Independent Living all over the country, working to redefine the concept of independence. These centers offer support and advocacy, helping folks find accessible housing and personal attendants, funding for adaptive equipment and job training. Independent living advocates measure independence not by how many tasks one can do without assistance, but by how much control a disabled person has over his/her life and by the quality of that life.

The movement founded direct-action, rabble-rousing groups, like ADAPT[23] and Not Dead Yet,[24] that disrupt nursing home industry conventions, blockade non-accessible public transportation, occupy the offices of politicians committed to the status quo, and protest outside courtrooms. Disabled people have a history of direct-action protest, beginning with the League of the Physically Handicapped's WPA protest. In 1977, disabled people occupied the HEW (Department of Health, Education, and Welfare) offices in San Francisco for 25 days, successfully pressuring politicians into signing Section 504 of the Rehabilitation Act, the first civil rights legislation in the United States for disabled people.[25] And today, ADAPT is rabble-rousing hard, both on the streets and in Congress, to pass legislation that would make it more possible for people with significant disabilities to live in homes of their own choosing, rather than nursing homes.

The movement is creating a strong, politicized disability culture with a growing body of literature, performances, humor, theory, and political savvy. We have theater, dance, poetry, anthologies, fiction, magazines, art exhibits, film festivals, analysis, and criticism written by disabled folks, conferences, and a fledgling academic discipline called disability studies. At the same time, there are disabled people working to crossover into mainstream culture, working to become models photographed for the big-name fashion magazines, actors in soap operas, sitcoms, and Hollywood movies, recognized artists, writers, and journalists.

The movement lobbied hard for laws to end separate and unequal education, for comprehensive civil rights legislation. The 1990 Americans with Disabilities Act (ADA) did not spring from George H. W. Bush's head, fully formed and shaped by his goodwill and understanding of disability issues. Rather, lawyers schooled in disability rights and disabled White House appointees with a stake in disability politics crafted the bill, disability lobbyists educated and lobbied hard, and grassroots disability activists mobilized to get the ADA passed. In short, the disability rights movement founded in the same storm of social change as women's liberation and gay/lesbian liberation, riding on the energy and framework created by the Black civil rights movement, came along and is undoing internalized oppression, making community, creating a culture and sense of identity, and organizing to change the status quo.

These forces are taking freakdom back, declaring that disabled people will be at the center of defining disability, defining our lives, defining who we are and who we want to be. We are declaring that doctors and their pathology, rubes and their money, anthropologists and their theories, gawkers and their so-called innocuous intentions, bullies and their violence, showmen and their hype, Jerry Lewis and his telethon, government bureaucrats and their rules will no longer define us. To arrive as a self-defined people, disabled people, like other marginalized people, need a strong sense of identity. We need to know our history, come to understand which pieces of that history we want to make our own, and develop a self-image full of pride. The women and men who worked the freak show, the freaks who knew how to flaunt their disabilities—the

tall man who wore a top hat to add a few inches to his height, the fat woman who refused to diet, the bearded woman who not only refused to shave, but grew her beard longer and longer, the cognitively disabled person who said, "I know you think I look like an ape. Here let me accentuate that look"—can certainly teach us a thing or two about identity and pride.

Pride is not an inessential thing. Without pride, disabled people are much more likely to accept unquestioningly the daily material conditions of ableism: unemployment, poverty, segregated and substandard education, years spent locked up in nursing homes, violence perpetrated by caregivers, lack of access. Without pride, individual and collective resistance to oppression becomes nearly impossible. But disability pride is no easy thing to come by. Disability has been soaked in shame, dressed in silence, rooted in isolation.

In 1969 in the backwoods of Oregon, I entered the "regular" first grade after a long struggle with the school officials who wanted me in "special education," a battle won only because I had scored well on an IQ test, my father knew the principal, and the first grade teacher, who lived upriver from us, liked my family and advocated for me. I became the first disabled kid to be mainstreamed in the district. Eight years later, the first laws requiring public education for disabled kids, Individuals with Disabilities Education Act (IDEA) and Section 504, were signed. By the mid-1980s, mainstreaming wasn't a rare occurrence, even in small, rural schools, but in 1969 I was a first.

No one—neither my family nor my teachers—knew how to acknowledge and meet my particular disability-related needs while letting me live a rather ordinary, rough-and-tumble childhood. They simply had no experience with a smart, gimpy six-year-old who learned to read quickly but had a hard time with the physical act of writing, who knew all the answers but whose speech was hard to understand. In an effort to resolve this tension, everyone ignored my disability and disability-related needs as much as possible. When I had trouble handling a glass of water, tying my shoes, picking up coins, screws, paper clips, writing my name on the blackboard, no one asked if I needed help. When I couldn't finish an assignment in the allotted time, teachers insisted I turn it in unfinished. When my classmates taunted me with *retard*, *monkey*, *defect*, no one comforted me. I rapidly became the class outcast, and the adults left me to fend for myself. I took as much distance as I could from the kids in "special ed." I was determined not to be one of them. I wanted to be "normal," to pass as nondisabled, even though my shaky hands and slurred speech were impossible to ignore.

Certainly, I wasn't the only disabled person I knew. In Port Orford, many of the men had work-related disabilities: missing fingers, arms, and legs, broken backs, serious nerve damage. A good friend of my parents had diabetes. A neighbor girl, seven or eight years younger than me, had CP much like mine. My best friend's brother had a significant cognitive disability. And yet I knew no one with a disability, none of us willing to talk, each of us hiding as best we could.

No single person underlines this ironic isolation better than Mary Walls, who joined my class in the fourth grade. She wore hearing aids in both ears and split her days between the "regular" and the "special ed" classrooms. We shared a speech therapist. I wish we had grown to be friends, but rather we became enemies, Mary calling me names and me chasing her down. I understand now that Mary lived by trying to read lips, and my lips, because of the way CP affects my speech, are nearly impossible to read. She probably taunted me out of frustration, and I chased her down, as I did none of my other bullies, because I could. I understand now about horizontal hostility: gay men and lesbians disliking bisexual people, transsexual women looking down on drag queens, working-class people fighting with poor people. Marginalized people from many communities create their own internal tensions and hostilities, and disabled people are no exception. I didn't have a disabled friend until I was in my mid-20s, and still today most of my close friends, the people I call "chosen family," are nondisabled. Often, I feel like an impostor as I write about disability, feel that

I'm not disabled enough, not grounded deeply enough in disability community, to put these words on paper. *This* is the legacy for me of shame, silence, and isolation.

Pride works in direct opposition to internalized oppression. The latter provides fertile ground for shame, denial, self-hatred, and fear. The former encourages anger, strength, and joy. To transform self-hatred into pride is a fundamental act of resistance. In many communities, language becomes one of the arenas for this transformation. Sometimes, the words of hatred and violence can be neutralized or even turned into the words of pride. To stare down the bully calling *cripple*, the basher swinging the word *queer* like a baseball bat, to say "Yeah, you're right. I'm queer, I'm a crip. So what?" undercuts the power of those who want us dead.

*****

Whatever we name ourselves, however we end up shattering our self-hatred, shame, silence, and isolation, the goal is the same: to end our daily material oppression.

## NOTES

1. Rosemarie Garland-Thomson, *Extraordinary Bodies: Figuring Physical Disability in American Culture and Literature* (New York: Columbia University Press, 1997), 62–63.
2. Robert Bogdan, *Freak Show: Presenting Human Oddities for Amusement and Profit* (Chicago: University of Chicago Press, 1988), 136.
3. Quoted in Lori Merish, "Cuteness and Commodity Aesthetics: Tom Thumb and Shirley Temple" in *Freakery: Cultural Spectacles of the Extraordinary Body*, ed. Rosemarie Garland-Thompson (New York: New York University Press, 1996), 190.
4. Bogdan, *Freak Show*, 268.
5. Quoted in Joseph Shapiro, *No Pity: How the Disability Rights Movement Is Changing America* (New York: Times Books, 1993), 59.

6.  Joanna Kadi, *Thinking Class: Sketches from a Cultural Worker* (Boston: South End Press, 1996), 103.

7.  For instance, before the end of slavery, enslaved children born disabled were often sold to showmen, sometimes for large sums of money. Conjoined twins Millie and Christina McCoy, born into slavery in 1852, brought their enslaver $30,000.

8.  Quoted in Beruth Lindfors, "Circus Africans," *Journal of American Culture* 6.2 (1983): 9.

9.  Quoted in Nigel Rothfels, "Aztecs, Aborigines, and Ape-People: Science and Freaks in Germany, 1850–1900" in *Freakery*, 158.

10. Michael Oliver, *The Politics of Disablement* (New York: St. Martin's Press, 1990), 48.

11. Bogdan, *Freak Show*, 230.

12. Christopher Vaughan, "Ogling Igorots" in *Freakery*, 222.

13. This year-long celebration, marking the 500th-year anniversary of Christopher Columbus's arrival in the Americas, focused on people of color's ongoing resistance to racism, imperialism, and genocide.

14. *The Couple in the Cage: A Guatinaui Odyssey*, prod. and dir. Coco Fusco and Paula Heredia, 31 min., sd., col. with b&w sequences, 4 3/4 cm (Chicago: Authentic Documentary Productions/Video Data Bank, 1993), videodisc/DVD.

15. Quoted in Bogdan, *Freak Show*, 173.

16. Shapiro, *No Pity*, 63–64.

17. Bogdan, *Freak Show*, 280.

18. Lisa Blumberg, "Public Stripping" in *The Ragged Edge: The Disability Experience from the Pages of the First Fifteen Years of The Disability Rag*, ed. Barrett Shaw (Louisville: Avocado Press, 1994), 73–77.

19. Lisa Blumberg, "Public Stripping Revisited," *The Disability Rag* 17.3 (1996): 18–21.

20. Doris Baizley and Victoria Ann Lewis, *P.H.*reaks: The Hidden History of People with Disabilities* in *Beyond Victims and Villains*, ed. Victoria Ann Lewis (New York: Theatre Communications Group, 2006), 78–79.

21. Disability Rights Nation, "'Nearly Half of Us Don't Know About the ADA,' Says New Harris Poll," *Ragged Edge* 19.5 (1998): 5.

22. Shapiro, *No Pity*, 28.

23. ADAPT (American Disabled for Attendant Programs Today) can be reached at 1640 E. Second St., Suite 100, Austin, TX 78702. Telephone: (512) 442-0252. www.adapt.org | adapt@adapt.org.

24. Not Dead Yet can be reached at 497 State St., Rochester, NY 14608-1642. Contact: Diane Coleman, telephone: (585) 697-1640. www.notdeadyet.org | ndycoleman@aol.com.

25. Shapiro, *No Pity*, 66–70.

*Source:* Clare, Eli. (1999). Excerpted from "Freaks and Queers." In *Exile and Pride: Disability, Queerness, and Liberation* (pp. 85–109). Durham, NC: Duke University Press.

## IMAGINING DISABILITY FUTURES

*Alison Kafer*

Alison Kafer is associate professor and chair of the Department of Feminist Studies at Southwestern University. Her research interests are in disability studies; feminist, crip, and queer theory; and activism. Kafer has written several articles that have appeared in the *Journal of Women's History* and *Feminist Disability Studies*, among other journals and collections. The excerpt that appears below comes from her book *Feminist, Queer, Crip*, published in 2013. Since then, it has fast become a classic in feminist, disability, and queer studies.

> I dream of more inclusive spaces.
> —*Kavitha Koshy, "Feels Like Carving Bone"*

I have never consulted a seer or psychic; I have never asked a fortune-teller for her crystal ball. No one has searched my tea leaves for answers or my stars for omens, and my palms remain unread. But people have been telling my future for years. Of fortune cookies and tarot cards they have no need: my wheelchair, burn scars, and gnarled hands apparently tell them all they need to know. My future is written on my body.

In 1995, six months after the fire, my doctor suggested that my thoughts of graduate school were premature, if not misguided. He felt that I would need to spend the next three or four years living at home, under my parents' care, and only then would it be appropriate to think about starting school. His tone made it clear, however, that he thought graduate school would remain out of reach; it was simply not in my future. What my future did hold, according to my rehabilitation psychologist and my recreation therapist, was long-term psychological therapy.

My friends were likely to abandon me, alcoholism and drug addiction loomed on my horizon, and I needed to prepare myself for the futures of pain and isolation brought on by disability. Fellow rehab patients, most of whom were elderly people recovering from strokes or broken hips, saw equally bleak horizons before me. One stopped me in the hallway to recommend suicide, explaining that life in a wheelchair was not a life worth living (his son, he noted offhandedly, knew to "let him go" if he was eventually unable to walk).

My future prospects did not improve much after leaving the rehabilitation facility, at least not according to strangers I encountered, and continue to encounter, out in the world. A common response is for people to assume they know my needs better than I do, going so far as to question my judgement when I refuse their offers of help. They can apparently see into my immediate future, forecasting an inability to perform specific tasks and predicting the accidents and additional injuries that will result. Or, taking a longer view, they imagine a future that is both banal and pathetic: rather than involving dramatic falls from my wheelchair, their visions assume a future of relentless pain, isolation, and bitterness, a representation that leads them to bless me, pity me, or refuse to see me altogether. Although I may believe I am leading an engaging and satisfying life, they can see clearly the grim future that awaits me: with no hope of a cure in sight, my future cannot be anything but bleak. Not even the ivory tower of academia protected me from these dismal projections of my future: once I made it to graduate school, I had a professor reject a paper proposal about cultural approaches to disability; she cast the topic as inappropriate because [it was] insufficiently academic. As I prepared to leave her office, she patted me on the arm and urged me to "heal," suggesting that my desire to study disability resulted not from intellectual curiosity but from a displaced need for therapy and recovery. My future, she felt, should be spent not researching disability but overcoming it.

These grim imagined futures, these suggestions that a better life would of necessity require the absence of impairment, have not gone unchallenged. My friends, family, and colleagues have consistently conjured other futures for me, refusing to accept ableist suggestions that disability is a fate worse than death or that disability prohibits a full life. Those who have been most vocal in imagining my future as ripe with opportunities have been other disabled people, who are themselves resisting negative interpretations of their futures. They tell stories of lives lived fully, and my future, according to them, involves not isolation and pathos but community and possibility: I could write books, teach, travel, love, and be loved; I might raise children or become a community organizer or make art; I could engage in activist struggles for the rights of disabled people or get involved in other movements for social justice.

At first glance, these contradictory imagined futures have nothing in common: the first casts disability as pitiable misfortune, a tragedy that effectively prevents one from leading a good life, while the second refuses

such inevitability, positioning ableism—not disability—as the obstacle to a good life. What these two representations of the future share, however, is a strong link to the present. How one understands disability in the present determines how one imagines disability in the future; one's assumptions about the experience of disability create one's conception of a better future.

If disability is conceptualized as a terrible unending tragedy, then any future that includes disability can only be a future to avoid. A better future, in other words, is one that excludes disability and disabled bodies; indeed, it is the very *absence* of disability that signals this better future. The *presence* of disability, then, signals something else: a future that bears too many traces of the ills of the present to be desirable. In this framework, a future with disability is a future no one wants, and the figure of the disabled person, especially the disabled fetus or child, becomes the symbol of this undesired future. As James Watson—a geneticist involved in the discovery of DNA and the development of the Human Genome Project—puts it, "We already accept that most couples don't want a Down child. You would have to be crazy to say you wanted one, because that child has no future."[1] Although Watson is infamous for making claims about who should and shouldn't inhabit the world, he's not alone in expressing this kind of sentiment.[2] Watson's version simply makes clear some of the assumptions underlying this discourse, and they are assumptions that cut to the heart of this project. The first is that disability is seen as the sign of no future, or at least of no good future. The second, and related, assumption is that we all agree; not only do we accept that couples don't want a child with Down syndrome, we know that anyone who feels otherwise is "crazy." To want a disabled child, to desire or even to accept disability in this way, is to be disordered, unbalanced, sick. "We" all know this, and there is no room for "you" to think differently.

It is this presumption of agreement, this belief that we all desire the same futures, that I take up in this work. I am particularly interested in uncovering the ways the disabled body is put to use in these future visions, attending to both metaphorical and "corporeal presence and absence."[3] I argue that disability is disavowed in these futures in two ways: first, the value of a future that includes disabled people goes unrecognized, while the value of a disability-free future is seen as self-evident; and second, the political nature of disability, namely its position as a category to be contested and debated, goes unacknowledged. The second failure of recognition makes possible the first; casting disability as [a] monolithic fact of the body, as beyond the realm of the political and therefore beyond the realm of debate or dissent, makes it impossible to imagine disability and disability futures differently. Challenging the rhetoric of naturalness and inevitability that underlies these discussions, I argue that decisions about the future of disability and disabled people are political decisions and should be recognized and treated as such. Rather than assume that a "good" future naturally and obviously depends upon the eradication of disability, we must recognize this perspective as colored by histories of ableism and disability oppression. Thus, in tracing these two failures of recognition—the disavowal of disability from "our" futures—I imagine futures otherwise, arguing for a cripped politics of access and engagement based on the work of disability activists and theorists.

What *Feminist, Queer, Crip* offers is a politics of crip futurity, an insistence on thinking these imagined futures—and hence, these lived presents—differently. [...] I hold on to an idea of politics as a framework for thinking through how to get "elsewhere," to other ways of being that might be more just and sustainable. In imagining more accessible futures, I am yearning for an elsewhere—and, perhaps, an "elsewhen"—in which disability is understood otherwise: as political, as valuable, as integral.

Before going any further, I admit to treading tricky ground here. "A future with disability is a future no one wants": while I find it absolutely essential to dismantle the purported self-evidence of that claim, I can't deny that there is truth to it. Not only is there abstract truth

to it, there's personal, embodied truth: it is a sentiment I myself hold. As much joy as I find in communities of disabled people, and as much as I value my experiences as a disabled person, I am not interested in becoming more disabled than I already am. I realize that position is itself marked by an ableist failure of imagination, but I can't deny holding it. Nor am I opposed to prenatal care and public health initiatives aimed at preventing illness and impairment, and futures in which the majority of people continue to lack access to such basic needs are not futures I want. But there is a difference between denying necessary health care, condoning dangerous working conditions, or ignoring public health concerns (thereby causing illness and impairment) and recognizing illness and disability as part of what makes us human.[4]

*＊＊＊＊＊*

I became disabled before I began reading feminist theory, yet it was feminist theory that led me to disability studies. It was through reading feminist theoretical approaches to the body that I came intellectually to understand disability as a political category rather than an individual pathology or personal tragedy. Feminist theory gave me the tools to think through disability and the ways in which assumptions about disability and disabled bodies lead to resource inequalities and social discrimination. Just as feminist theorists had questioned the naturalness of femininity, challenging essentialist assumptions about "the" female body, I could question the naturalness of disability, challenging essentialist assumptions about "the" disabled body. My understanding of the political/relational model of disability has been made possible by my engagement with the work of feminist theorists [...]. Simply put, feminism has given me the theoretical tools to think critically about disability, the stigmatization of bodily variation, and various modes and strategies of resistance, dissent, and collective action.

## NOTES

1. Michael Gerson, "The Eugenics Temptation," *Washington Post,* October 24, 2007. A19.

2. I have borrowed my phrasing here from Ruth Hubbard. See her "Abortion and Disability: Who Should and Who Should Not Inhabit the World?" in *The Disability Studies Reader*, ed. Lennard J. Davis (New York: Routledge, 2006). 93–103.

3. Monica J. Casper and Lisa Jean Moore, *Missing Bodies: The Politics of Visibility* (New York: New York University Press, 2009), 4.

4. For an account of disability as human biodiversity, see Rosemarie Garland-Thomson, "Welcoming the Unbidden: The Case for Preserving Human Biodiversity," in *What Democracy Looks Like: A New Critical Realism for a Post-Seattle World,* ed. Amy Schrager Lang and Cecelia Tichi (New Brunswick: Rutgers University Press, 2006), 77–87. See also Kenny Fries, *The History of My Shoes and the Evolution of Darwin's Theory* (New York: Carroll & Graf, 2007).

*Source:* Kafer, Alison. (2013). Excerpted from "Introduction: Imagined Futures." In *Feminist, Queer, Crip* (pp. 1–4, 14). Bloomington, IN: Indiana University Press.

# ACTIVIST ART 2

## ALISON LAPPER PREGNANT

*Marc Quinn*

Marc Quinn (born 1964) is a leading contemporary British artist. Quinn makes art about what it is to be a person living in the world—whether his work concerns our relationship with nature and how that relationship is mediated by our desires; what identity and beauty mean and why we feel compelled to transform our identities and bodies; or representations of pressing issues in contemporary social history. He has exhibited internationally in many museums and galleries.

**Source:** Quinn, Marc. (2005). "Alison Lapper Pregnant." *The Complete Marbles*. Retrieved from: http://marcquinn.com/artworks/single/alison-lapper-pregnant1.

Marc Quinn's iconic sculpture *Alison Lapper Pregnant* is a portrait of disabled artist Alison Lapper when she was eight months pregnant. He notes that when he was making marble sculptures for *The Complete Marble* series (1999–2005),

> they seemed to me like public sculptures from the future. But now that Alison Lapper is in Trafalgar Square, the present has caught up to the future. Marble is the material used to commemorate heroes, and these people seem to me to be a new kind of hero—people who instead of conquering the outside world have conquered their own inner world and gone on to live fulfilled lives. To me, they celebrate the diversity of humanity. Most monuments are commemorating past events; because Alison is pregnant it's a sculpture about the future possibilities of humanity.

In *The Complete Marbles* series, Quinn explores the contradictions between our outside appearance and inner being. The figures celebrate imperfection and the beauty of different kinds of bodies as well as the strength and vitality of the human spirit.

Of the original sculpture (first exhibited in Trafalgar Square in 2005–2007), Alison Lapper has said: "I regard it as a modern tribute to femininity, disability and motherhood. It is so rare to see disability in everyday life—let alone naked, pregnant and proud."

---

*Source:* Quinn, Marc. (2005). "Alison Lapper Pregnant" (Artist Statement). Retrieved from: http://marcquinn.com/artworks/single/alison-lapper-pregnant1.

# ON RACE AND RACISM

## Ten Things Everyone Should Know About Race

Our eyes tell us that people look different. No one has trouble distinguishing a Czech from a Chinese, but what do those differences mean? Are they biological? Has race always been with us? How does race affect people today?

There's less—and more—to race than meets the eye:

1. *Race is a modern idea.* Ancient societies, like the Greeks, did not divide people according to physical distinctions, but according to religion, status, class, even language. The English language didn't even have the word "race" until it turns up in a 1508 poem by William Dunbar referring to a line of kings.

2. *Race has no genetic basis.* Not one characteristic, trait, or even gene distinguishes all the members of one so-called race from all the members of another so-called race.

3. *Human subspecies don't exist.* Unlike many animals, modern humans simply haven't been around long enough or isolated enough to evolve into separate subspecies or races. Despite surface appearances, we are one of the most genetically similar of all species.

4. *Skin color really is only skin deep.* Most traits are inherited independently from one another. The genes influencing skin color have nothing to do with the genes influencing hair form, eye shape, blood type, musical talent, athletic ability, or forms of intelligence. Knowing someone's skin color doesn't necessarily tell you anything else about him or her.

5. *Most variation is within, not between, "races."* Of the small amount of total human variation, 85% exists within any local population, be they Italians, Kurds, Koreans, or Cherokees. About 94% can be found within any continent. That means two random Koreans may be as genetically different as a Korean and an Italian.

6. *Slavery predates race.* Throughout much of human history, societies have enslaved others, often as a result of conquest or war, even debt, but not because of physical characteristics or a belief in natural inferiority. Due to a unique set of historical circumstances, ours [European and North American] was the first slave system where all the slaves shared similar physical characteristics.

7. *Race and freedom evolved together.* The U.S. was founded on the radical new principle that "All men are created equal." But our early economy was based largely on slavery. How could this anomaly be rationalized? The new idea of race helped explain why some people could be denied the rights and freedoms that others took for granted.

8. *Race justified social inequalities as natural.* As the race idea evolved, white superiority became "common sense" in America. It justified not only slavery but also the extermination of Indians, exclusion of Asian immigrants, and the taking of Mexican lands by a nation that professed a belief in democracy. Racial practices were institutionalized within American government, laws, and society.

9. *Race isn't biological, but racism is still real.* Race is a powerful social idea that gives people

different access to opportunities and resources. Our government and social institutions have created advantages that disproportionately channel wealth, power, and resources to white people. This affects everyone, whether we are aware of it or not.

10. *Colorblindness will not end racism.* Pretending race doesn't exist is not the same as creating equality. Race is more than stereotypes and individual prejudice. To combat racism, we need to identify and remedy social policies and institutional practices that advantage some groups at the expense of others.

*Source:* California Newsreel. (2003). "RACE—The Power of an Illusion: Ten Things Everyone Should Know about Race." San Francisco, CA: California Newsreel. Retrieved from: http://newsreel.org/guides/race/10things.htm.

## Racism in Canada: A Timeline

1608   The French introduce Black slavery into Canada.

1613   French and English practise genocide and attempt to exterminate the Beothuck people from Newfoundland.

1709   Proclamation makes slavery legal in French Canada.

1763   European settlers exploit, kill, and infect Indigenous peoples with tuberculosis and smallpox in order to obtain Indigenous land. For instance, Lord Jeffrey Amherst practises germ warfare by giving out smallpox-infected blankets.

1763   Through the Treaty of Paris, France cedes Canada to Britain. One effect of this transfer in power is the legal strengthening of slavery in Canada.

1784   Race riot in Shelburne and Birchtown, Nova Scotia. A mob destroys Black people's property and drives Blacks out of the townships.

1875   Chinese Canadians are disenfranchised.

1876   Canada passes the Indian Act as one tool to eradicate Indigenous culture and expropriate land and resources for profit and settlement.

1880s–1996   Government/church-run residential schools are established. Indigenous children are taken from parents to be "civilized and educated" and "to kill the Indian in the child."

1885   In response to white Canada's racist fears of Chinese immigration, the federal government passes the Chinese Immigration Act, which introduced the Head Tax.

1900s   Federal government officials engage in a campaign to discourage Black American applicants from settlement and rejected them on the basis of medical or other grounds. The Ontario legislature establishes segregated schools for Black people (in place until 1964). Black people are refused service and segregated in restaurants, theatres, and recreational facilities.

1907   The Asiatic Exclusion League forms with the goal of restricting Asian admission to Canada. The League carries out a major demonstration, which culminates in the worst race riot in the history of British Columbia.

1910   The Canadian Immigration Act creates a list of preferred and non-preferred countries, with British and white European immigrants on the "preferred" list and the rest of the world, made up largely of people of colour, on the "non-preferred" list.

1923   The Chinese Exclusion Act bans Chinese immigration until 1947.

1942   Canada closes its doors to Jewish refugees fleeing Hitler's Final Solution. Of all the Western countries, Canada admits the fewest Jewish refugees.

1942–1947   The federal government forced Japanese Canadians into internment camps and confiscated their property.

1955   Canadian Domestic Workers Program is established to deal with the chronic shortage of Canadian workers prepared to accept low wages and undesirable working conditions as domestic servants. The program initially targets Black women from the Caribbean, and later women from the Philippines.

1960s/1970s     Africville, a Black settlement near Halifax, Nova Scotia, is demolished and its residents are forced to relocate. Vancouver City Council destroys Hogan's Alley, Vancouver's Black community, with the construction of the Georgia Street Viaduct.

1995     As part of the federal budget, the government imposes the Right of Landing Fee, widely known as the Head Tax. The fee of $975 applies to all adults, including refugees, becoming permanent residents. In 2000, the government rescinds the fee for refugees, but maintains it for immigrants.

2002     The Immigration and Refugee Protection Act comes into force in 2002 and as a "security" measure in the wake of the September 11, 2001, attacks. The Act erodes basic rights in Canada, with some of the worst impacts being experienced by refugees and immigrants.

*Source:* Vancouver Status of Women. (2008). Adapted from *History in Our Faces on Occupied Land: A Race Relations Timeline*. Vancouver, BC: Vancouver Status of Women. Retrieved from: http://www.anti-racism.ca/content/history-our-faces-occupied-land-race-relations-timeline.

# CHAPTER 18

## Do Muslim Women Really Need Saving?

*Lila Abu-Lughod*

Lila Abu-Lughod is the Joseph L. Buttenwieser Professor of Social Science in the Department of Anthropology at Columbia University. Abu-Lughod's work focuses on the relationship between cultural forms and power, the politics of knowledge and representation, and the dynamics of gender and the question of women's rights in the Middle East. Many of her works have become classics in the fields of women's studies and anthropology.

What are the ethics of the current "War on Terrorism," a war that justifies itself by purporting to liberate, or save, Afghan women? Does anthropology have anything to offer in our search for a viable position to take regarding this rationale for war?

I was led to pose the question of my title in part because of the way I personally experienced the response to the U.S. war in Afghanistan. Like many colleagues whose work has focused on women and gender in the Middle East, I was deluged with invitations to speak—not just on news programs but also to various departments at colleges and universities, especially women's studies programs. Why did this not please me, a scholar who has devoted more than 20 years of her life to this subject and who has some complicated personal connection to this identity? Here was an opportunity to spread the word, disseminate my knowledge, and correct misunderstandings. The urgent search for knowledge about our sister "women of cover" (as President George Bush so marvelously called them) is laudable and when it comes from women's studies programs where "transnational feminism" is now being taken seriously, it has a certain integrity (see Safire 2001).

My discomfort led me to reflect on why, as feminists in or from the West, or simply as people who have concerns about women's lives, we need to be wary of this response to the events and aftermath of September 11, 2001. I want to point out the minefields—a metaphor that is sadly too apt for a country like Afghanistan, with the world's highest number of mines per capita—of this obsession with the plight of Muslim women. I hope to show some way through them using insights from anthropology, the discipline whose charge has been to understand and manage cultural difference. At the same time, I want to remain critical of anthropology's complicity in the reification of cultural difference.

## CULTURAL EXPLANATIONS AND THE MOBILIZATION OF WOMEN

It is easier to see why one should be skeptical about the focus on the "Muslim woman" if one begins with the U.S. public response. I will analyze two manifestations of this response: some conversations I had with a reporter from the PBS *NewsHour with Jim Lehrer* and First Lady Laura Bush's radio address to the nation on November 17, 2001. The presenter from the *NewsHour* show first contacted me in October to see if I was willing to give some background for a segment on Women and Islam. I mischievously asked whether she had done segments on the women of Guatemala, Ireland, Palestine, or Bosnia when the show covered wars in these regions; but I finally agreed to look at the questions she was going to pose to panelists. The questions were hopelessly general. Do Muslim women believe "x"? Are Muslim women "y"? Does Islam allow "'z" for women? I asked her: If you were to substitute Christian or Jewish wherever you have Muslim, would these questions make sense? I did not imagine she would call me back. But she did, twice, once with an idea for a segment on the meaning of Ramadan and another time on Muslim women in politics. One was in response to the bombing and the other to the speeches by Laura Bush and Cherie Blair, wife of the British Prime Minister.

What is striking about these three ideas for news programs is that there was a consistent resort to the cultural, as if knowing something about women and Islam or the meaning of a religious ritual would help one understand the tragic attack on New York's World Trade Center and the U.S. Pentagon, or how Afghanistan had come to be ruled by the Taliban, or what interests might have fueled U.S. and other interventions in the region over the past 25 years, or what the history of American support for conservative groups funded to undermine the Soviets might have been, or why the caves and bunkers out of which Bin Laden was to be smoked "dead or alive," as President Bush announced on television, were paid for and built by the CIA.

In other words, the question is why knowing about the "culture" of the region, and particularly its religious beliefs and treatment of women, was more urgent than exploring the history of the development of repressive regimes in the region and the U.S. role in this history. Such cultural framing, it seemed to me, prevented the serious exploration of the roots and nature of human suffering in this part of the world. Instead of political and historical explanations, experts were being asked to give religio-cultural ones. Instead of questions that might lead to the exploration of global interconnections, we were offered ones that worked to artificially divide the world into separate spheres—recreating an imaginative geography of West versus East, us versus Muslims, cultures in which First Ladies give speeches versus others where women shuffle around silently in burqas.

Most pressing for me was why the Muslim woman in general, and the Afghan woman in particular, were so crucial to this cultural mode of explanation, which ignored the complex entanglements in which we are all implicated, in sometimes surprising alignments. Why were these female symbols being mobilized in this "War against Terrorism" in a way they were not in other conflicts? Laura Bush's radio address on November 17 [2001] reveals the political work such mobilization accomplishes. On the one hand, her address collapsed important distinctions that should have been maintained. There was a constant slippage between the Taliban and the terrorists, so that they became almost one word—a kind of hyphenated monster identity: the Taliban-and-the-terrorists. Then there was the blurring of the very separate causes in Afghanistan of women's continuing malnutrition, poverty, and ill health, and their more recent exclusion under the Taliban from employment, schooling, and the joys of wearing nail polish. On the other hand, her speech reinforced chasmic divides, primarily between the "civilized people throughout the world" whose hearts break for the women and children of

Afghanistan and the Taliban-and-the-terrorists, the cultural monsters who want to, as she put it, "impose their world on the rest of us."

Most revealingly, the speech enlisted women to justify American bombing and intervention in Afghanistan and to make a case for the "War on Terrorism" of which it was allegedly a part. As Laura Bush said, "Because of our recent military gains in much of Afghanistan, women are no longer imprisoned in their homes. They can listen to music and teach their daughters without fear of punishment. [...] The fight against terrorism is also a fight for the rights and dignity of women" (U.S. Government 2002).

These words have haunting resonances for anyone who has studied colonial history. Many who have worked on British colonialism in South Asia have noted the use of the woman question in colonial policies where intervention into sati (the practice of widows immolating themselves on their husbands' funeral pyres), child marriage, and other practices was used to justify rule. As Gayatri Chakravorty Spivak (1988) has cynically put it: white men saving brown women from brown men. The historical record is full of similar cases, including in the Middle East. In turn of the century Egypt, what Leila Ahmed (1992) has called "colonial feminism" was hard at work. This was a selective concern about the plight of Egyptian women that focused on the veil as a sign of oppression but gave no support to women's education and was professed loudly by the same Englishman, Lord Cromer, who opposed women's suffrage back home.

Sociologist Marnia Lazreg (1994) has offered some vivid examples of how French colonialism enlisted women to its cause in Algeria. [...] Lazreg (1994) also gives memorable examples of the way in which the French had earlier sought to transform Arab women and girls. She describes skits at awards ceremonies at the Muslim Girls' School in Algiers in 1851 and 1852. In the first skit, written by "a French lady from Algiers," two Algerian Arab girls reminisced about their trip to France with words including the following:

> Oh! Protective France: Oh! Hospitable
>     France! ...
> Noble land, where I felt free
> Under Christian skies to pray to our God: ...
> God bless you for the happiness you bring us!
> And you, adoptive mother, who taught us
> That we have a share of this world,
> We will cherish you forever!
>     [Lazreg 1994:68–69]

These girls are made to invoke the gift of a share of this world, a world where freedom reigns under Christian skies. This is not the world the Taliban-and-the-terrorists would "like to impose on the rest of us."

Just as I argued above that we need to be suspicious when neat cultural icons are plastered over messier historical and political narratives, so we need to be wary when Lord Cromer in British-ruled Egypt, French ladies in Algeria, and Laura Bush, all with military troops behind them, claim to be saving or liberating Muslim women.

## POLITICS OF THE VEIL

I want now to look more closely at those Afghan women Laura Bush claimed were "rejoicing" at their liberation by the Americans. This necessitates a discussion of the veil, or the burqa, because it is so central to contemporary concerns about Muslim women. This will set the stage for a discussion of how anthropologists, feminist anthropologists in particular, contend with the problem of difference in a global world. In the conclusion, I will return to the rhetoric of saving Muslim women and offer an alternative.

It is common popular knowledge that the ultimate sign of the oppression of Afghan women under the Taliban-and-the-terrorists is that they were forced to wear the burqa. Liberals sometimes confess their surprise that even though Afghanistan has been liberated from the Taliban, women do not seem to be throwing off their burqas. Someone who has worked in Muslim regions must ask why this is so surprising. Did we expect that once "free" from the Taliban they would go "back" to belly shirts and blue jeans, or dust off their Chanel suits? We need to be more sensible about the clothing of "women of cover," and so there is perhaps a need to make some basic points about veiling.

First, it should be recalled that the Taliban did not invent the burqa. It was the local form of covering that Pashtun women in one region wore when they went out. The Pashtun are one of several ethnic groups in Afghanistan, and the burqa was one of many forms of covering in the subcontinent and Southwest Asia that has developed as a convention for symbolizing women's modesty or respectability. The burqa, like some other forms of "cover," has, in many settings, marked the symbolic separation of men's and women's spheres, as part of the general association of women with family and home, not with public space where strangers mingled.

Twenty years ago, the anthropologist Hanna Papanek (1982), who worked in Pakistan, described the burqa as "portable seclusion." She noted that many saw it as a liberating invention because it enabled women to move out of segregated living spaces while still observing the basic moral requirements of separating and protecting women from unrelated men. Ever since I came across her phrase "portable seclusion," I have thought of these enveloping robes as "mobile homes." Everywhere, such veiling signifies belonging to a particular community and participating in a moral way of life in which families are paramount in the organization of communities and the home is associated with the sanctity of women.

The obvious question that follows is this: If this were the case, why would women suddenly become immodest? Why would they suddenly throw off the markers of their respectability, markers, whether burqas or other forms of cover, which were supposed to assure their protection in the public sphere from the harassment of strange men by symbolically signaling

to all that they were still in the inviolable space of their homes, even though moving in the public realm? Especially when these are forms of dress that had become so conventional that most women gave little thought to their meaning.

To draw some analogies, none of them perfect, why are we surprised that Afghan women do not throw off their burqas when we know perfectly well that it would not be appropriate to wear shorts to the opera? At the time these discussions of Afghan women's burqas were raging, a friend of mine was chided by her husband for suggesting she wanted to wear a pantsuit to a fancy wedding: "You know you don't wear pants to a WASP wedding," he reminded her. New Yorkers know that the beautifully coiffed Hasidic women, who look so fashionable next to their dour husbands in black coats and hats, are wearing wigs. This is because religious belief and community standards of propriety require the covering of the hair. They also alter boutique fashions to include high necks and long sleeves. As anthropologists know perfectly well, people wear the appropriate form of dress for their social communities and are guided by socially shared standards, religious beliefs, and moral ideals, unless they deliberately transgress to make a point or are unable to afford proper cover. If we think that U.S. women live in a world of choice regarding clothing, all we need to do is remind ourselves of the expression, "the tyranny of fashion."

What had happened in Afghanistan under the Taliban is that one regional style of covering or veiling, associated with a certain respectable but not elite class, was imposed on everyone as "religiously" appropriate, even though previously there had been many different styles, popular or traditional with different groups and classes—different ways to mark women's propriety, or, in more recent times, religious piety. Although I am not an expert on Afghanistan, I imagine that the majority of women left in Afghanistan by the time the Taliban took control were the rural or less educated, from nonelite families, since they were the only ones who would not emigrate to escape the hardship and violence that has marked Afghanistan's recent history. If liberated from the enforced wearing of burqas, most of these women would choose some other form of modest headcovering, like all those living nearby who were not under the Taliban—their rural Hindu counterparts in the North of India (who cover their heads and veil their faces from affines) or their Muslim sisters in Pakistan.

Even *The New York Times* carried an article about Afghan women refugees in Pakistan that attempted to educate readers about this local variety (Fremson 2001). The article describes and pictures everything from the now iconic burqa with the embroidered eyeholes, which a Pashtun woman explains is the proper dress for her community, to large scarves they call chadors, to the new Islamic modest dress that wearers refer to as *hijab*. Those in the new Islamic dress are characteristically students heading for professional careers, especially in medicine, just like their counterparts from Egypt to Malaysia. One wearing the large scarf was a school principal; the other was a poor street vendor. The telling quote from the young street vendor is, "If I did [wear the burqa] the refugee would tease me because the burqa is for 'good women' who stay inside the home" (Fremson 2001:14). Here you can see the local status associated with the burqa—it is for good respectable women from strong families who are not forced to make a living selling on the street.

The British newspaper *The Guardian* published an interview in January 2002 with Dr. Suheila Siddiqi, a respected surgeon in Afghanistan who holds the rank of lieutenant general in the Afghan medical corps (Goldenberg 2002). A woman in her sixties, she comes from an elite family and, like her sisters, was educated. Unlike most women of her class, she chose not to go into exile. She is presented in the article as "the woman who stood up to the Taliban" because she refused to wear the burqa. She had made it a condition of returning to her post as head of a major hospital when the Taliban came begging in 1996, just eight months after firing her along with other women. Siddiqi is described as thin, glamorous,

and confident. But further into the article, it is noted that "her graying bouffant hair is covered in a gauzy veil" (Goldenberg 2002:38). This is a reminder that though she refused the burqa, she had no question about wearing the chador or scarf.

Finally, I need to make a crucial point about veiling. Not only are there many forms of covering, which themselves have different meanings in the communities in which they are used, but also veiling itself must not be confused with, or made to stand for, lack of agency. As I have argued in my ethnography of a Bedouin community in Egypt in the late 1970s and 1980s (1986), pulling the black head cloth over the face in front of older, respected men is considered a voluntary act by women who are deeply committed to being moral and have a sense of honor tied to family. One of the ways they show their standing is by covering their faces in certain contexts. They decide for whom they feel it is appropriate to veil.

To take a very different case, the modern Islamic modest dress that many educated women across the Muslim world have taken on since the mid-1970s now both publicly marks piety and can be read as a sign of educated urban sophistication, a sort of modernity (e.g., Abu-Lughod 1995, 1998; Brenner 1996; El Guindi 1999; MacLeod 1991; Ong 1990). As Saba Mahmood (2001) has so brilliantly shown in her ethnography of women in the mosque movement in Egypt, this new form of dress is also perceived by many of the women who adopt it as part of a bodily means to cultivate virtue, the outcome of their professed desire to be close to God.

Two points emerge from this fairly basic discussion of the meanings of veiling in the contemporary Muslim world. First, we need to work against the reductive interpretation of veiling as the quintessential sign of women's unfreedom, even if we object to state imposition of this form, as in Iran or with the Taliban. (It must be recalled that the modernizing states of Turkey and Iran had earlier in the century banned veiling and required men, except religious clerics, to adopt Western dress.) What does freedom mean if we accept the fundamental premise that humans are social beings, always raised in certain social and historical contexts and belonging to particular communities that shape their desires and understandings of the world? Is it not a gross violation of women's own understandings of what they are doing to simply denounce the burqa as a medieval imposition? Second, we must take care not to reduce the diverse situations and attitudes of millions of Muslim women to a single item of clothing. Perhaps it is time to give up the Western obsession with the veil and focus on some serious issues with which feminists and others should indeed be concerned.

Ultimately, the significant political-ethical problem the burqa raises is how to deal with cultural "others." How are we to deal with difference without accepting the passivity implied by the cultural relativism for which anthropologists are justly famous—a relativism that says it's their culture and it's not my business to judge or interfere, only to try to understand. Cultural relativism is certainly an improvement on ethnocentrism and the racism, cultural imperialism, and imperiousness that underlie it; the problem is that it is too late not to interfere. The forms of lives we find around the world are already products of long histories of interactions.

I want to explore the issues of women, cultural relativism, and the problems of "difference" from three angles. First, I want to consider what feminist anthropologists […] are to do with strange political bedfellows. I used to feel torn when I received the e-mail petitions circulating for the last few years in defense of Afghan women under the Taliban. I was not sympathetic to the dogmatism of the Taliban; I do not support the oppression of women. But the provenance of the campaign worried me. I do not usually find myself in political company with the likes of Hollywood celebrities (see Hirschkind and Mahmood 2002). I had never received a petition from such women defending the right of Palestinian women to safety from Israeli bombing or daily harassment at checkpoints, asking the United States to reconsider

its support for a government that had disposed them, closed them out from work and citizenship rights, refused them the most basic freedoms. Maybe some of these same people might be signing petitions to save African women from genital cutting, or Indian women from dowry deaths. However, I do not think that it would be as easy to mobilize so many of these American and European women if it were not a case of Muslim men oppressing Muslim women—women of cover for whom they can feel sorry and in relation to whom they can feel smugly superior. Would television diva Oprah Winfrey host the Women in Black, the women's peace group from Israel, as she did RAWA, the Revolutionary Association of Women of Afghanistan, who were also granted the *Glamour Magazine* Women of the Year Award? […]

To be critical of this celebration of women's rights in Afghanistan is not to pass judgment on any local women's organizations, such as RAWA, whose members have courageously worked since 1977 for a democratic secular Afghanistan in which women's human rights are respected, against Soviet-backed regimes or US-, Saudi-, and Pakistani-supported conservatives. Their documentation of abuse and their work through clinics and schools have been enormously important.

It is also not to fault the campaigns that exposed the dreadful conditions under which the Taliban placed women. […] It is, however, to suggest that we need to look closely at what we are supporting (and what we are not) and to think carefully about why. How should we manage the complicated politics and ethics of finding ourselves in agreement with those with whom we normally disagree? I do not know how many feminists who felt good about saving Afghan women from the Taliban are also asking for a global redistribution of wealth or contemplating sacrificing their own consumption radically so that African or Afghan women could have some chance of having what I do believe should be a universal human right— the right to freedom from the structural violence of global inequality and from the ravages of war, the everyday rights of having enough to eat, having homes for their families in which to live and thrive, having ways to make decent livings so their children can grow, and having the strength and security to work out, within their communities and with whatever alliances they want, how to live a good life, which might very well include changing the ways those communities are organized.

Suspicion about bedfellows is only a first step; it will not give us a way to think more positively about what to do or where to stand. For that, we need to confront two more big issues. First is the acceptance of the possibility of difference. Can we only free Afghan women to be like us or might we have to recognize that even after "liberation" from the Taliban, they might want different things than we would want for them? What do we do about that? Second, we need to be vigilant about the rhetoric of saving people because of what it implies about our attitudes.

Again, when I talk about accepting difference, I am not implying that we should resign ourselves to being cultural relativists who respect whatever goes on elsewhere as "just their culture." I have already discussed the dangers of "cultural" explanations; "their" cultures are just as much part of history and an interconnected world as ours are. What I am advocating is the hard work involved in recognizing and respecting differences—precisely as products of different histories, as expressions of different circumstances, and as manifestations of differently structured desires. We may want justice for women, but can we accept that there might be different ideas about justice and that different women might want, or choose, different futures from what we envision as best (see Ong 1988)? We must consider that they might be called to personhood, so to speak, in a different language.

Reports from the Bonn peace conference held in late November to discuss the rebuilding of Afghanistan revealed significant differences among the few Afghan women feminists and activists present. RAWA's position was to reject any conciliatory

approach to Islamic governance. According to one report I read, most women activists, especially those based in Afghanistan who are aware of the realities on the ground, agreed that Islam had to be the starting point for reform. Fatima Gailani, a U.S.-based advisor to one of the delegations, is quoted as saying, "If I go to Afghanistan today and ask women for votes on the promise to bring them secularism, they are going to tell me to go to hell." Instead, according to one report, most of these women looked for inspiration on how to fight for equality to a place that might seem surprising. They looked to Iran as a country in which they saw women making significant gains within an Islamic framework—in part through an Islamically oriented feminist movement that is challenging injustices and reinterpreting the religious tradition.

The situation in Iran is itself the subject of heated debate within feminist circles, especially among Iranian feminists in the West (e.g., Mir-Hosseini 1999; Moghissi 1999; Najmabadi 1998, 2000). It is not clear whether and in what ways women have made gains and whether the great increases in literacy, decreases in birthrates, presence of women in the professions and government, and a feminist flourishing in cultural fields like writing and filmmaking are because of or despite the establishment of a so-called Islamic Republic. The concept of an Islamic feminism itself is also controversial. Is it an oxymoron or does it refer to a viable movement forged by brave women who want a third way?

One of the things we have to be most careful about in thinking about Third World feminisms, and feminism in different parts of the Muslim world, is how not to fall into polarizations that place feminism on the side of the West. I have written about the dilemmas faced by Arab feminists when Western feminists initiate campaigns that make them vulnerable to local denunciations by conservatives of various sorts, whether Islamist or nationalist, of being traitors (Abu-Lughod 2001). As some like Afsaneh Najmabadi are now arguing, not only is it wrong to see history simplistically in terms of a putative opposition between Islam and the West (as is happening in the United States now and has happened in parallel in the Muslim world), but it is also strategically dangerous to accept this cultural opposition between Islam and the West, between fundamentalism and feminism, because those many people within Muslim countries who are trying to find alternatives to present injustices, those who might want to refuse the divide and take from different histories and cultures, who do not accept that being feminist means being Western, will be under pressure to choose, just as we are: Are you with us or against us?

My point is to remind us to be aware of differences, respectful of other paths toward social change that might give women better lives. Can there be a liberation that is Islamic? And, beyond this, is liberation even a goal for which all women or people strive? Are emancipation, equality, and rights part of a universal language we must use? [...] In other words, might other desires be more meaningful for different groups of people? Living in close families? Living in a godly way? Living without war? I have done fieldwork in Egypt over more than 20 years and I cannot think of a single woman I know, from the poorest rural to the most educated cosmopolitan, who has ever expressed envy of U.S. women, women they tend to perceive as bereft of community, vulnerable to sexual violence and social anomie, driven by individual success rather than morality, or strangely disrespectful of God.

Mahmood (2001) has pointed out a disturbing thing that happens when one argues for a respect for other traditions. She notes that there seems to be a difference in the political demands made on those who work on or are trying to understand Muslims and Islamists and those who work on secular-humanist projects. She, who studies the piety movement in Egypt, is consistently pressed to denounce all the harm done by Islamic movements around the world—otherwise, she is accused of being an apologist. But there never seems to be a parallel demand for those

who study secular humanism and its projects, despite the terrible violences that have been associated with it over the last couple of centuries, from world wars to colonialism, from genocides to slavery. We need to have as little dogmatic faith in secular humanism as in Islamism, and as open a mind to the complex possibilities of human projects undertaken in one tradition as the other.

## BEYOND THE RHETORIC OF SALVATION

Let us return, finally, to my title, "Do Muslim Women Need Saving?" The discussion of culture, veiling, and how one can navigate the shoals of cultural difference should put Laura Bush's self-congratulation about the rejoicing of Afghan women liberated by American troops in a different light. It is deeply problematic to construct the Afghan woman as someone in need of saving. When you save someone, you imply that you are saving her from something. You are also saving her *to* something. What violences are entailed in this transformation, and what presumptions are being made about the superiority of that to which you are saving her? Projects of saving other women depend on and reinforce a sense of superiority by Westerners, a form of arrogance that deserves to be challenged. All one needs to do to appreciate the patronizing qualities of the rhetoric of saving women is to imagine using it today in the United States about disadvantaged groups such as African American women or working-class women. We now understand them as suffering from structural violence. We have become politicized about race and class, but not culture.

As anthropologists, feminists, or concerned citizens, we should be wary of taking on the mantles of those 19th-century Christian missionary women who devoted their lives to saving their Muslim sisters. One of my favorite documents from that period is a collection called *Our Moslem Sisters*, the proceedings of a conference of women missionaries held in Cairo in 1906 (Van Sommer and Zwemer 1907). The subtitle of the book is *A Cry of Need from the Lands of Darkness Interpreted by Those Who Heard It*. Speaking of the ignorance, seclusion, polygamy, and veiling that blighted women's lives across the Muslim world, the missionary women spoke of their responsibility to make these women's voices heard. As the introduction states, "They will never cry for themselves, for they are down under the yoke of centuries of oppression" (Van Sommer and Zwemer 1907:15). "This book," it begins, "with its sad, reiterated story of wrong and oppression is an indictment and an appeal.... It is an appeal to Christian womanhood to right these wrongs and enlighten this darkness by sacrifice and service" (Van Sommer and Zwemer 1907:15).

One can hear uncanny echoes of their virtuous goals today, even though the language is secular, the appeals not to Jesus but to human rights or the Liberal West. [...]

Could we not leave veils and vocations of saving others behind and instead train our sights on ways to make the world a more just place? The reason respect for difference should not be confused with cultural relativism is that it does not preclude asking how we, living in this privileged and powerful part of the world, might examine our own responsibilities for the situations in which others in distant places have found themselves. We do not stand outside the world, looking out over this sea of poor benighted people, living under the shadow—or veil—of oppressive cultures; we are part of that world. Islamic movements themselves have arisen in a world shaped by the intense engagements of Western powers in Middle Eastern lives.

A more productive approach, it seems to me, is to ask how we might contribute to making the world a more just place. A world not organized around strategic military and economic demands; a place where certain kinds of forces and values that we may still consider important could have an appeal and where there is the peace necessary for discussions, debates, and transformations to occur within communities. We need to ask ourselves what kinds of world conditions we could contribute to making such that popular desires will not be overdetermined by an overwhelming sense of helplessness in the face of forms of global injustice. Where we seek to be active in the affairs of distant places, can we do so in the spirit of support for those within those communities whose goals are to make women's (and men's) lives better? Can we use a more egalitarian language of alliances, coalitions, and solidarity, instead of salvation?

Even RAWA, the now celebrated Revolutionary Association of the Women of Afghanistan, which was so instrumental in bringing to U.S. women's attention the excesses of the Taliban, has opposed the U.S. bombing from the beginning. They do not see in it Afghan women's salvation but increased hardship and loss. They have long called for disarmament and for peacekeeping forces. Spokespersons point out the dangers of confusing governments with people, the Taliban with innocent Afghans who will be most harmed. They consistently remind audiences to take a close look at the ways policies are being organized around oil interests, the arms industry, and the international drug trade. They are not obsessed with the veil, even though they are the most radical feminists working for a secular democratic Afghanistan. Unfortunately, only their messages about the excesses of the Taliban have been heard, even though their criticisms of those in power in Afghanistan have included previous regimes. A first step in hearing their wider message is to break with the language of alien cultures, whether to understand or eliminate them. Missionary work and colonial feminism belong in the past. Our task is to critically explore what we might do to help create a world in which those poor Afghan women, for whom "the hearts of those in the civilized world break," can have safety and decent lives.

# REFERENCES

Abu-Lughod, Lila. (1986). *Veiled Sentiments: Honor and Poetry in a Bedouin Society.* Berkeley: University of California Press.

———. (1995). Movie Stars and Islamic Moralism in Egypt. *Social Text* (42), 53–67.

———. (1998). *Remaking Women: Feminism and Modernity in the Middle East.* Princeton: Princeton University Press.

———. (2001). Orientalism and Middle East Feminist Studies. *Feminist Studies* 27(1), 101–113.

Ahmed, Leila. (1992). *Women and Gender in Islam.* New Haven: Yale University Press.

Brenner, Susanne. (1996). Reconstructing Self and Society: Javanese Muslim Women and "the Veil." *American Ethnologist* 23(4), 673–697.

El Guindi, Fadwa. (1999). *Veil: Modesty, Privacy and Resistance.* Oxford: Berg.

Fremson, Ruth. (2001). Allure Must Be Covered. Individuality Peeks Through. *New York Times*, November 4: 14.

Goldenberg, Suzanne. (2002). The Woman Who Stood Up to the Taliban. *The Guardian*, January 24. Electronic document, https://www.theguardian.com/world/2002/jan/24/gender.uk1.

Hirschkind, Charles, and Saba Mahmood. (2002). Feminism, the Taliban, and the Politics of Counter-Insurgency. *Anthropological Quarterly* 75(2), 107–122.

Lazreg, Marnia. (1994). *The Eloquence of Silence: Algerian Women in Question.* New York: Routledge.

MacLeod, Arlene. (1991). *Accommodating Protest.* New York: Columbia University Press.

Mahmood, Saba. (2001). Feminist Theory, Embodiment, and the Docile Agent: Some Reflections on the Egyptian Islamic Revival. *Cultural Anthropology* 16(2), 202–235.

Mir-Hosseini, Ziba. (1999). *Islam and Gender: The Religious Debate in Contemporary Iran.* Princeton: Princeton University Press.

Moghissi, Haideh. (1999). *Feminism and Islamic Fundamentalism.* London: Zed Books.

Najmabadi, Afsaneh. (1998). Feminism in an Islamic Republic. In *Islam, Gender and Social Change.* Yvonne Haddad and John Esposito, eds. 59–84. New York: Oxford University Press.

———. (2000). (Un)Veiling Feminism. *Social Text* (64), 29–45.

Ong, Aihwa (1988). Colonialism and Modernity: Feminist Re-Presentations of Women in Non-Western Societies. *Inscriptions* 3–4, 79–93.

———. (1990). State versus Islam: Malay Families, Women's Bodies, and the Body Politic in Malaysia. *American Ethnologist* 17(2), 258–276.

Papanek, Hanna. (1982). Purdah in Pakistan: Seclusion and Modern Occupations for Women. In *Separate Worlds.* Hanna Papanek and Gail Minault, eds. 190–216. Columbus: South Asia Books.

Safire, William. (2001). "On Language." *New York Times Magazine*, October 28: 22.

Spivak, Gayatri Chakravorty. (1988). Can the Subaltern Speak? In *Marxism and the Interpretation of Culture.* Cary Nelson and Lawrence Grossberg, eds. 271–313. Urbana: University of Illinois Press.

U.S. Government. (2002). Electronic document, http://www.whitehouse.gov/news/releases/2001/11/20011117 (link no longer active). Accessed January 10.

Van Sommer, Annie, and Samuel M. Zwemer, eds. (1907). *Our Moslem Sisters: A Cry of Need from Lands of Darkness Interpreted by Those Who Heard It.* New York: Fleming H. Revell Co.

---

***Source:*** Abu-Lughod, Lila. (2002). Excerpted from "Do Muslim Women Really Need Saving? Anthropological Reflections on Cultural Relativism and Its Others." *American Anthropologist, 104*(3), 783–790.

# ACTIVIST ART 3

## TECHNICOLOR MUSLIMAH

*Saba Taj*

"I am Saba Taj, a queer Muslim femme mixed-media visual artist and activist whose work centers around identity and challenging Islamophobia and sexism. I have struggled with my Muslim identity and its seeming contradictions with the other parts of myself, but have come to wholly embrace it as an essential part of who I am by rejecting monolithic interpretations of what it means to be Muslim. Over the years, my explorations of identity have grown increasingly intersectional, confronting Islamophobia's connections to systemic oppression rooted in anti-black racism and imperialism."

*—From Carol Kuruvilla, "Queer Muslim Artist Saba Taj Sees Her Art as an Act of Resistance," HuffPost News (2016, June 24)*

[Top row] Amna, Student; Sarah, Mother;
[Bottom row] Taiyyaba, Attorney; Mona, Doctor.

**Source:** Taj, Saba. (2011). "Technicolor Muslimah." *Portraits of American Muslim Women*. Retrieved from: http://www. artbysaba.com/technicolor-muslimah-2011---2014.

Modern treatment of Muslim subject matter in art and media is closely tied to the political and religious controversy that seems to be pervasive in these "exotic" countries of the East. While much of the conflict is real, oftentimes, visual media and "Muslim art" do nothing to lessen the perception of all Muslims as exotic, "other," and entirely homogenous. Truly, much art and writing relies on the juxtaposition of the traditional and the taboo within Islam—emphasizing that the East is in exact opposition to the West. This portrayal is a farce. There is a massive community of Muslims who live in Western countries who are not antithetical to "the West." This community is made up of individuals, each with their own unique mosaic of culture and experiences. Islam is not a tiny box. It is not one-dimensional, and neither are the people who identify as Muslim. That such a simplistic perception of these peoples has persisted into our world today is unacceptable. There is a place for everyone in this country [United States], yet these people have continued to be not only homogenized, but vilified.

I have created a series of fifteen portraits of Muslim women in acrylic paint. The women are rendered in bright colors, which, in itself, is a departure from how Muslim women are often portrayed. I chose women because I believe that they are often the clearest representatives of the Muslim world, and the most misunderstood. This series focuses on aspects of these women that need to be explored—their humor, their joy, and their kindness. Each woman is identified as Muslim by her headscarf. This visual symbol is truly the only suggestion of her religion, because my perspective here is humanist. In addition, eleven of the paintings are presented with props to further support the theme of humor, or to identify the subjects as American, as well as Muslim. [...] The fifteenth portrait is a bit of a departure from the rest of the group. The subject faces the viewer directly, with an assertive gaze. We know nothing of her but her name. This portrait is especially important, because it indicates that the story is not over. This joyful portrayal of Muslim women is only one aspect amongst the kaleidoscope of qualities that these women possess. She is the blank slate. She is asking the viewer, "So what do you think of me, now?" She anchors the series, and asks the viewers to look back upon themselves. What do we know of her, if she does not tell us? Even in this age of instant information, we have a tendency to see a woman wearing a hijab, and imagine a patriarch forcing that veil upon her. We have an obsession with that piece of cloth and all that we think it represents. The assumption is that these women are being oppressed, that they are imprisoned within layers of cloth. This closed-minded perspective imprisons far too many. Those who fall prey to this misconception are preventing themselves from seeing how dynamic these women truly are, from seeing that they are American women who make their own choices. The hijab truly recedes into the background in these paintings, and the vibrant women within them shine through—in technicolor.

*Source:* Taj, Saba. (2013). "Technicolor Muslimah: A Lighter & Brighter Side." *Muslimah: Muslim Women's Art & Voices.* New York: Global Fund for Women. Retrieved from: http://muslima.globalfundforwomen. org/content/technicolor-muslimah.

# CHAPTER 19

## X: A Fabulous Child's Story

*Lois Gould*

Lois Gould was an acclaimed American writer, known for her novels, memoirs, and other works about women's lives. Her only children's story, *X: A Fabulous Child's Story*, was first published in *Ms.* magazine in 1972 and has become a feminist classic. She wrote a column for *The New York Times*, and served as editor of the *Ladies Home Journal* and other national magazines.

Once upon a time, a baby named X was born. This baby was named X so that nobody could tell whether it was a boy or a girl. Its parents could tell, of course, but they couldn't tell anybody else. They couldn't even tell Baby X, at first.

You see, it was all part of a very important Secret Scientific Xperiment, known officially as Project Baby X. The smartest scientists had set up this Xperiment at a cost of Xactly 23 billion dollars and 72 cents, which might seem like a lot for just one baby, even a very important Xperimental baby. But when you remember the prices of things like strained carrots and stuffed bunnies, and popcorn for the movies and booster shots for camp, let alone twenty-eight shiny quarters from the tooth fairy, you begin to see how it adds up.

Also, long before Baby X was born, all those scientists had to be paid to work out the details of the Xperiment, and to write the *Official Instruction Manual* for Baby X's parents and, most important of all, to find the right set of parents to bring up Baby X. These parents had to be selected very carefully. Thousands of volunteers had to take thousands of tests and answer thousands of tricky questions. Almost everybody failed because, it turned out, almost everybody really wanted either a baby boy or a baby girl, and not Baby X at all. Also, almost everybody was afraid that a Baby X would be a lot more trouble than a boy or a girl. (They were probably right, the scientists admitted, but Baby X needed parents who wouldn't mind the Xtra trouble.)

There were families with grandparents named Milton and Agatha, who didn't see why the baby couldn't be named Milton or Agatha instead of X, even if it *was* an X. There were families with aunts who insisted on knitting tiny dresses and uncles who insisted on sending tiny baseball mitts. Worst of all, there were families that already had other children who couldn't be trusted to keep the secret. Certainly not if they knew the secret was worth 23 billion dollars and 72 cents—and all you had to do was take one little peek at Baby X in the bathtub to know if it was a boy or a girl.

But, finally, the scientists found the Joneses, who really wanted to raise an X more than any other kind of baby—no matter how much trouble it would be. Ms. and Mr. Jones had to promise they would take equal turns caring for X, and feeding it, and singing it lullabies. And they had to promise never to hire any baby-sitters. The government scientists knew perfectly well that a babysitter would probably peek at X in the bathtub, too.

The day the Joneses brought their baby home, lots of friends and relatives came over to see it. None of them knew about the secret Xperiment, though. So the first thing they asked was what kind of a baby X was. When the Joneses smiled and said, "It's an X!," nobody knew what to say. They couldn't say, "Look at her cute little dimples!" And they couldn't say, "Look at his husky little biceps!" And they couldn't even say just plain "kitchycoo." In fact, they all thought the Joneses were playing some kind of rude joke.

But, of course, the Joneses were not joking. "It's an X" was absolutely all they would say. And that made the friends and relatives very angry. The relatives all felt embarrassed about having an X in the family. "People will think there's something wrong with it!" some of them whispered. "There *is* something wrong with it!" others whispered back.

"Nonsense!" the Joneses told them all cheerfully. "What could possibly be wrong with this perfectly adorable X?" Nobody could answer that, except Baby X, who had just finished its bottle. Baby X's answer was a loud, satisfied burp.

Clearly, nothing at all was wrong. Nevertheless, none of the relatives felt comfortable about buying a present for a Baby X. The cousins who sent the baby a tiny football helmet would not come and visit any more. And the neighbors who sent a pink-flowered romper suit pulled their shades down when the Joneses passed their house.

The *Official Instruction Manual* had warned the new parents that this would happen, so they didn't fret about it. Besides, they were too busy with Baby X and the hundreds of different Xercises for treating it properly. Ms. and Mr. Jones had to be Xtra careful about how they played with little X. They knew that if they kept bouncing it up in the air and saying how *strong* and *active* it was, they'd be treating it more like a boy than an X. But if all they did was cuddle it and kiss it and tell it how *sweet* and *dainty* it was, they'd be treating it more like a girl than an X.

On page 1,654 of the *Official Instruction Manual*, the scientists prescribed: "plenty of bouncing and plenty of cuddling, *both*. X ought to be strong and sweet and active. Forget about *dainty* altogether."

Meanwhile, the Joneses were worrying about other problems. Toys, for instance. And clothes. On his first shopping trip, Mr. Jones told the store clerk, "I need some clothes and toys for my new baby." The clerk smiled and said, "Well, now, is it a boy or a girl?" "It's an X," Mr. Jones said, smiling back. But the clerk got all red in the face and said huffily, "In that case, I'm afraid I can't help you, sir." So Mr. Jones wandered helplessly up and down the aisles trying to find what X needed. But everything in the store was piled up in sections marked "Boys" or "Girls." There were "Boys' Pajamas" and "Girls' Underwear" and "Boys' Fire Engines" and "Girls' Housekeeping Sets." Mr. Jones went home without buying anything for X. That night, he and Ms. Jones consulted page 2,326 of the *Official Instruction Manual*. "Buy plenty of everything!" it said firmly.

So they bought plenty of sturdy blue pajamas in the Boys' Department and cheerful flowered underwear in the Girls' Department. And they bought all kinds of toys. A boy doll that made pee-pee and cried, "Pa-pa." And a girl doll that talked in three languages and said, "I am the Pres-i-dent of Gen-er-al Mo-tors." They also bought a storybook about a brave princess who rescued a handsome prince from his ivory tower, and another one about a sister and brother who grew up to be a baseball star and a ballet star, and you had to guess which was which.

The head scientists of Project Baby X checked all their purchases and told them to keep up the good work. They also reminded the Joneses to see page 4,629 of the *Manual*, where it said, "Never make Baby X feel *embarrassed* or *ashamed* about what it wants to play with. And if X gets dirty climbing rocks, never say 'Nice little Xes don't get dirty climbing rocks.'"

Likewise, it said, "If X falls down and cries, never say 'Brave little Xes don't cry.' Because, of course, nice little Xes *do* get dirty, and brave little Xes *do* cry. No matter how dirty X gets, or how hard it cries, don't worry. It's all part of the Xperiment."

Whenever the Joneses pushed Baby X's stroller in the park, smiling strangers would come over and coo: "Is that a boy or a girl?" The Joneses would smile back and say, "It's an X." The strangers would stop smiling then, and often snarl something nasty—as if the Joneses had snarled at *them*.

By the time X grew big enough to play with other children, the Joneses' troubles had grown bigger, too. Once a little girl grabbed X's shovel in the sandbox, and zonked X on the head with it. "Now, now, Tracy," the little girl's mother began to scold, "little girls mustn't hit" and she turned to ask X, "Are you a little boy or little girl, dear?"

Mr. Jones, who was sitting near the sandbox, held his breath and crossed his fingers.

X smiled politely at the lady, even though X's head had never been zonked so hard in its life. "I'm a little X," X replied.

"You're a *what*?" the lady exclaimed angrily. "You're a little b-r-a-t, you mean!"

"But little girls mustn't hit little Xes, either!" said X, retrieving the shovel with another polite smile. "What good does hitting do, anyway?"

X's father, who was still holding his breath, finally let it out, uncrossed his fingers, and grinned back at X.

And at their next secret Project Baby X meeting, the scientists grinned, too. Baby X was doing fine.

But then it was time for X to start school. The Joneses were really worried about this, because school was even more full of rules for boys and girls, and there were no rules for Xes. The teacher would tell boys to form one line, and girls to form another line. There would be boys' games and girls' games, and boys' secrets and girls' secrets. The school library would have a list of recommended books for girls,

and a different list of recommended books for boys. There would even be a bathroom marked BOYS and another one marked GIRLS. Pretty soon, boys and girls would hardly talk to each other. What would happen to poor little X?

The Joneses spent weeks consulting their *Instruction Manual* (there were 249½ pages of advice under "First Day of School"), and attending urgent special conferences with the smart scientists of Project Baby X.

The scientists had to make sure that X's mother had taught X how to throw and catch a ball properly, and that X's father had been sure to teach X what to serve at a doll's tea party. X had to know how to shoot marbles and how to jump rope and, most of all, what to say when the Other Children asked whether X was a Boy or a Girl.

Finally, X was ready. The Joneses helped X button on a nice new pair of red-and-white checked overalls, and sharpened six pencils for X's new pencilbox, and marked X's name clearly on all the books in its nice new bookbag. X brushed its teeth and combed its hair, which just about covered its ears, and remembered to put a napkin in its lunchbox.

The Joneses had asked X's teacher if the class could line up alphabetically, instead of forming separate lines for boys and girls. And they had asked if X could use the principal's bathroom, because it wasn't marked anything except BATHROOM. X's teacher promised to take care of all those problems. But nobody could help X with the biggest problem of all—Other Children.

Nobody in X's class had ever known an X before. What would they think? How would X make friends?

You couldn't tell what X was by studying its clothes—overalls don't even button right-to-left, like girls' clothes, or left-to-right, like boys' clothes. And you couldn't guess whether X had a girl's short haircut or a boy's long haircut. And it was very hard to tell by the games X liked to play. Either X played ball very well for a girl, or else X played house very well for a boy.

Some of the children tried to find out by asking X tricky questions, like "Who's your favorite sports star?" That was easy. X had two favorite sports stars: a girl jockey named Robyn Smith and a boy archery champion named Robin Hood. Then they asked, "What's your favorite TV program?" And that was even easier. X's favorite TV program was "Lassie," which stars a girl dog played by a boy dog.

When X said that its favorite toy was a doll, everyone decided that X must be a girl. But then X said that the doll was really a robot, and that X had computerized it, and that it was programmed to bake fudge brownies and then clean up the kitchen. After X told them that, the Other Children gave up guessing what X was. All they knew was they'd sure like to see X's doll.

After school, X wanted to play with the Other Children. "How about shooting some baskets in the gym?" X asked the girls. But all they did was make faces and giggle behind X's back.

"How about weaving some baskets in the arts and crafts room?" X asked the boys. But they all made faces and giggled behind X's back, too.

That night, Ms. and Mr. Jones asked X how things had gone at school. X told them sadly that the lessons were okay, but otherwise school was a terrible place for an X. It seemed as if Other Children would never want an X for a friend.

Once more, the Joneses reached for their *Instruction Manual.* Under "Other Children," they found the following message: "What did you Xpect? *Other Children* have to obey all the silly boy-girl rules, because their parents taught them to. Lucky X—you don't have to stick to the rules at all! All you have to do is be yourself. P.S. We're not saying it'll be easy."

X liked being itself. But X cried a lot that night, partly because it felt afraid. So X's father held X tight, and cuddled it, and couldn't help crying a little, too. And X's mother cheered them both up by reading an Xciting story about an enchanted prince called Sleeping Handsome, who woke up when Princess Charming kissed him.

The next morning, they all felt much better, and little X went back to school with a brave smile and a clean pair of red-and-white checked overalls.

There was a seven-letter-word spelling bee in class that day. And a seven-lap boys' relay race in the gym. And a seven-layer-cake baking contest in the girls' kitchen corner. X won the spelling bee. X also won the relay race. And X almost won the baking contest, except it forgot to light the oven. Which only proves that nobody's perfect.

One of the Other Children noticed something else, too. He said: "Winning or losing doesn't seem to count to X. X seems to have fun being good at boys' skills *and* girls' skills."

"Come to think of it," said another one of the Other Children, "maybe X is having twice as much fun as we are!"

So after school that day, the girl who beat X at the baking contest gave X a big slice of her prizewinning cake. And the boy X beat in the relay race asked X to race him home.

From then on, some really funny things began to happen. Susie, who sat next to X in class, suddenly refused to wear pink dresses to school any more. She insisted on wearing red-and-white checked overalls—just like X's. Overalls, she told her parents, were much better for climbing monkey bars.

Then Jim, the class football nut, started wheeling his little sister's doll carriage around the football field. He'd put on his entire football uniform, except for the helmet. Then he'd put the helmet in the carriage, lovingly tucked under an old set of shoulder pads. Then he'd start jogging around the field, pushing the carriage and singing "Rockabye Baby" to his football helmet. He told his family that X did the same thing, so it must be okay. After all, X was now the team's star quarterback.

Susie's parents were horrified by her behavior, and Jim's parents were worried sick about his. But the worst came when the twins, Joe and Peggy, decided to share everything with each other. Peggy used Joe's hockey skates, and his microscope, and took half his newspaper route. Joe used Peggy's needlepoint kit, and her cookbooks, and took two of her three baby-sitting jobs. Peggy started running the lawn mower, and Joe started running the vacuum cleaner.

Their parents weren't one bit pleased with Peggy's wonderful biology experiments, or with Joe's terrific needlepoint pillows. They didn't care that Peggy mowed the lawn better, and that Joe vacuumed the carpet better. In fact, they were furious. It's all that little X's fault, they agreed. Just because X doesn't know what it is, or what it's supposed to be, it wants to get everybody *else* mixed up, too!

Peggy and Joe were forbidden to play with X anymore. So was Susie, and then Jim, and then *all* the Other Children. But it was too late; the Other Children stayed mixed up and happy and free, and refused to go back to the way they'd been before X.

Finally, Joe and Peggy's parents decided to call an emergency meeting of the school's Parents' Association, to discuss "The X Problem." They sent a report to the principal stating that X was a "disruptive influence." They demanded immediate action. The Joneses, they said, should be *forced* to tell whether X was a boy or a girl. And then X should be *forced* to behave like whichever it was. If the Joneses refused to tell, the Parents' Association said, then X must take an Xamination. The school psychiatrist must Xamine it physically and mentally, and issue a full report. If X's test showed it was a boy, it would have to obey all the boys' rules. If it proved to be a girl, X would have to obey all the girls' rules.

And if X turned out to be some kind of mixed-up misfit, then X should be Xpelled from the school. Immediately!

The principal was very upset. Disruptive influence? Mixed-up misfit? But X was an Xcellent student. All the teachers said it was a delight to have X in their classes. X was president of the student council. X had won first prize in the talent show, and second prize in the art show, and honorable mention in the science fair, and six athletic events on field day, including the potato race.

*Nevertheless,* insisted the Parents' Association, X is a Problem Child. X is the Biggest Problem Child we have ever seen!

So the principal reluctantly notified X's parents that numerous complaints about X's behavior had come to the school's attention. And that after the psychiatrist's Xamination, the school would decide what to do about X.

The Joneses reported this at once to the scientists, who referred them to page 85,759 of the *Instruction Manual.* "Sooner or later," it said, "X will have to be Xamined by a psychiatrist. This may be the only way any of us will know for sure whether X is mixed up—or whether everyone else is."

The night before X was to be Xamined, the Joneses tried not to let X see how worried they were. "What if—?" Mr. Jones would say. And Ms. Jones would reply, "No use worrying." Then a few minutes later, Ms. Jones would say, "What if—?" and Mr. Jones would reply, "No use worrying."

X just smiled at them both, and hugged them hard and didn't say much of anything. X was thinking, What if—? And then X thought: No use worrying.

At Xactly nine o'clock the next day, X reported to the school psychiatrist's office. The principal, along with a committee from the Parents' Association, X's teacher, X's classmates, and Ms. and Mr. Jones, waited in the hall outside. Nobody knew the details of the tests X was to be given, but everybody knew they'd be *very* hard, and that they'd reveal Xactly what everyone wanted to know about X, but were afraid to ask.

It was terribly quiet in the hall. Almost spooky. Once in a while, they would hear a strange noise inside the room. There were buzzes. And a beep or two. And several bells. An occasional light would flash under the door. The Joneses thought it was a white light, but the principal thought it was blue. Two or three children swore it was either yellow or green. And the Parents' Committee missed it completely.

Through it all, you could hear the psychiatrist's low voice, asking hundreds of questions, and X's higher voice, answering hundreds of answers.

The whole thing took so long that everyone knew it must be the most complete Xamination anyone had ever had to take. Poor X, the Joneses thought. Serves X right, the Parents' Committee thought. I wouldn't like to be in X's overalls right now, the children thought.

At last, the door opened. Everyone crowded around to hear the results. X didn't look any different; in fact, X was smiling. But the psychiatrist looked terrible. He looked as if he was crying! "What happened?" everyone began shouting. Had X done something disgraceful? "I wouldn't be a bit surprised!" muttered Peggy and Joe's parents. "Did X flunk the *whole* test?" cried Susie's parents. "Or just the most important part?" yelled Jim's parents.

"Oh, dear," sighed Mr. Jones.

"Oh, dear," sighed Ms. Jones.

"*Sssh,*" ssshed the principal. "The psychiatrist is trying to speak."

Wiping his eyes and clearing his throat, the psychiatrist began, in a hoarse whisper. "In my opinion," he whispered—you could tell he must be very upset—"in my opinion, young X here—"

"Yes? Yes?" shouted a parent impatiently.

"*Sssh!*" ssshed the principal.

"Young *Sssh* here, I mean young X," said the doctor, frowning, "is just about—"

"Just about *what*? Let's have it!" shouted another parent.

"… just about the *least* mixed-up child I've ever Xamined!" said the psychiatrist.

"Yay for X!" yelled one of the children. And then the others began yelling, too. Clapping and cheering and jumping up and down.

"*SSSH!*" ssshed the principal, but nobody did.

The Parents' Committee was angry and bewildered. How *could* X have passed the whole Xamination? Didn't X have an *identity* problem? Wasn't X mixed up at *all*? Wasn't X *any* kind of a misfit? How could it *not* be, when it didn't even *know* what it was? And why was the psychiatrist crying?

Actually, he had stopped crying and was smiling politely through his tears. "Don't you see?" he said. "I'm crying because it's wonderful! X has absolutely no identity problem! X isn't one bit mixed up! As for being a misfit—ridiculous! X knows perfectly well what it is! Don't you, X?" The doctor winked. X winked back.

"But what *is* X?" shrieked Peggy and Joe's parents. "*We* still want to know what it is!"

"Ah, yes," said the doctor, winking again. "Well, don't worry. You'll all know one of these days. And you won't need me to tell you."

"What? What does he mean?" some of the parents grumbled suspiciously.

Susie and Peggy and Joe all answered at once. "He means that by the time X's sex matters, it won't be a secret anymore!"

With that, the doctor began to push through the crowd toward X's parents. "How do you do," he said, somewhat stiffly. And then he reached out to hug them both. "If I ever have an X of my own," he whispered, "I sure hope you'll lend me your instruction manual."

Needless to say, the Joneses were very happy. The Project Baby X scientists were rather pleased, too. So were Susie, Jim, Peggy, Joe, and all the Other Children. The Parents' Association wasn't, but they had promised to accept the psychiatrist's report, and not make any more trouble. They even invited Ms. and Mr. Jones to become honorary members, which they did.

Later that day, all X's friends put on their red-and-white checked overalls and went over to see X. They found X in the back yard, playing with a very tiny baby that none of them had ever seen before. The baby was wearing very tiny red-and-white checked overalls.

"How do you like our new baby?" X asked the Other Children proudly.

"It's got cute dimples," said Jim.

"It's got husky biceps, too," said Susie.

"What kind of baby is it?" asked Joe and Peggy.

X frowned at them. "Can't you tell?" Then X broke into a big, mischievous grin. "It's a Y!"

*Source:* Gould, Lois. (1998). "X: A Fabulous Child's Story." In Blyth McVicker Clinchy & Julie K. Norem (Eds.), *The Gender and Psychology Reader* (pp. 523–530). New York, NY: NYU Press.

## UNDERSTANDING MASCULINITIES: THE WORK OF RAEWYN CONNELL

Raewyn Connell is a professor emerita at the University of Sydney. She was one of the founders of the study of masculinity and published *Masculinities* in 1995. The concept of "hegemonic masculinity" was introduced in the book and has been particularly influential and controversial. Connell has been an advisor to United Nations initiatives on gender equality and peacemaking and is considered one of the pre-eminent scholars of global masculinities. A sociologist by training, Connell has won numerous awards for her contributions to the study of sex and gender. Below are some of her key insights about the workings of masculinity.

- *Multiple Masculinities.* Historians and anthropologists have shown that there is no one pattern of masculinity that is found everywhere. Different cultures and different periods of history construct masculinity differently. Equally important, more than one kind of masculinity can be found within a given cultural setting. Within any workplace, neighbourhood or peer group, there are likely to be different understandings of masculinity and different ways of "doing" masculinity.

- *Hierarchy of Masculinities.* Different masculinities do not sit side-by-side like dishes in a smorgasbord; there are definite relations between them. Typically, some masculinities are more honoured than others. Some may be actively dishonoured, for example, homosexual masculinities in modern western culture. Some are socially marginalized, for example, the masculinities of disempowered ethnic minorities. Some are exemplary, taken as symbolizing admired traits, for example, the masculinities of sporting heroes.

- *Hegemonic Masculinity.* The form of masculinity that is culturally dominant in a given setting is called "hegemonic masculinity." "Hegemonic" signifies a position of cultural authority and leadership, not total dominance; other forms of masculinity persist alongside. The hegemonic form need not be the most common form of masculinity. Hegemonic masculinity is, however, highly visible. It is likely to be what casual commentators have noticed when they speak of "the male role." Hegemonic masculinity is hegemonic not just in relation to other masculinities, but in relation to the gender order as a whole. It is an expression of the privilege men collectively have over women. The hierarchy of masculinities is an expression of the unequal shares in that privilege held by different groups of men.

- *Active Construction of Masculinities.* Masculinities do not exist prior to social behaviour, either as bodily states or fixed personalities. Rather, masculinities come into existence as people act. They are accomplished in everyday conduct or organizational life, as patterns of social practice. In other words, we "do gender" in everyday life. However, masculinities are far from settled. From bodybuilders in the gym, to managers in the boardroom, to boys in the elementary school playground, a great deal of effort goes into the making of conventional, as well as non-conventional, masculinities. Recent research on homosexual men shows that for men too, identity and relationships involve a complex and sustained effort of construction.

- *Dynamics of Masculinities.* Since different masculinities exist in different cultures and historical epochs, we can deduce that masculinities are able to change. Masculine identities are not fixed but are dynamic; particular masculinities are composed, de-composed, contested and replaced. Sometimes, this process of contestation and change finds spectacular public expression, in large-scale rallies or demonstrations. More often, it is local and limited. Sometimes, it becomes conscious and deliberate; at other times, it is non-conscious.

---

*Source:* Connell, Raewyn. (2002). Slightly modified from "Understanding Men: Gender Sociology and the New International Research on Masculinities." *Social Thought and Research, 24*(1–2), 13–31.

# IT'S THE MASCULINITY, STUPID!

*Jackson Katz and Jeremy Earp*

Jackson Katz is internationally renowned for his groundbreaking scholarship and activism on issues of gender, race, and violence. He has long been a major figure and thought leader in the growing global movement of men working to promote gender equality and prevent gender violence.

Jeremy Earp is the production director of the Media Education Foundation and the director of several films on media culture and politics, including *Tough Guise 2: Violence, Manhood & American Culture*, featuring and based on the work of Jackson Katz. Below is an excerpt from their interview on the throwback allure of Donald Trump.

Donald Trump's advantage over Hillary Clinton with white voters has been one of the most talked-about story lines of the 2016 presidential campaign. What's received far less attention is the fact that men make up the overwhelming majority of Trump's white base of support. [...]

**JE: In your new book, *Man Enough?* you look at how cultural ideals of manhood have shaped the way we see the presidency and the qualifications of presidential candidates. How do differences in men's and women's voting patterns, the so-called gender gap, factor into your analysis?**

JK: One of the main things I look at in the book is why so many men—white men in particular—have been abandoning the Democratic Party over the past 40-plus years and identifying as Republicans and conservatives. For decades it has flummoxed both Democrats and many on the left that millions of working and downwardly mobile middle-class white guys vote for the party that delivers tax cuts to the wealthy and seeks to eliminate programs that are designed to help working families. Why do they vote against what many of us see as their self-interest? I've tried to demonstrate that millions of white guys have an emotional and identity investment in a certain ideology and style of manhood. We hear a lot about men voting based on things like national security and free enterprise and taxes and the economy, but I think this misses how their identities as men are also at work here. In the simplest terms, I'm saying it's the masculinity, stupid!

**JE: How does your analysis apply to the current campaign? Polls show Trump with a massive advantage over Hillary with men, specifically *white* men—a much greater margin than Hillary's advantage with women overall.[1]**

JK: I think the gigantic and historic gender gap we're seeing is the natural outgrowth of Trump doubling down on Republican strategy that goes back decades—a strategy designed, at its core, to target white voters, especially white male voters, and run up huge margins with them. The problem with this strategy, of course, is that the percentage of white men as a share of the total electorate has been shrinking. That's why so many Republicans have been arguing for years that the party needs to modify its approach and grow its voting base, and it's why so many of them have been recoiling in horror at Trump's approach. Trump and his people clearly aren't buying any of this. They've obviously made a calculation that they can win without growing the base so long as they can capture something like 70% of the white male vote, which would be a historic record. They've been very up front about this. Trump's former campaign manager, Corey Lewandowski, who's now working for CNN, said after Trump's immigration speech on August 31 that the chief goal of the speech was to "lock in the white guys" who are Trump's core voters. This was an incredibly revealing statement, but most commentators ignored it, focusing instead on how Trump's aggressive and uncompromising tone might be turning off swing voters and women.

JE: **Why do you think that is? When gender comes up in discussions of politics, why does the conversation always seem to turn to women and women's voting patterns, leaving men off the hook?**

JK: I think it's partly an analytic blind spot, rooted in the fact that we're not used to seeing dominant groups as "groups" at all. It's the same with discussions about race. When most people hear the word "race," they tend to think about people of color, not whites, because white people are the unexamined norm we measure other racial groups against. In the same way, when gender comes up, the conversation typically turns to "women's issues" and the kind of things that motivate women voters. What's mostly missing is any kind of sustained look at the *male* side of the gender gap, the material and symbolic factors that have driven *men's* voting patterns over the years.

JE: **A lot's been made of Trump's genius as a media impresario, especially his mastery of television. In your view, what is it about Trump's media performance *as a man* that seems to be resonating so powerfully with white guys of very different class backgrounds?**

JK: When you listen to Trump's supporters, they say over and over again that what Trump says isn't as important as *how* he says it. They love the confident, aggressive, forceful, and unfiltered way he expresses himself, the fact that he doesn't back down, doesn't apologize even when he's obviously wrong. That he refuses to be "politically correct." It's the whole straight-shooter cowboy thing, the sense that he tells it like it is. This is exactly what people used to say about Ronald Reagan—that they may not have always agreed with him, but at least they knew where he stood. A lot of people were drawn to his persona, especially men, and white working-class men in particular. And I think Trump is tapping into a lot of these same longings for a throwback to the days when men were men.

JE: **In a lot of the mainstream commentary on the gender gap, it seems to be assumed that men are somehow hardwired to be more conservative than women. What's your take on this?**

JK: The right-wing echo chamber of talk radio, Fox News, and alt-right media, especially, make it seem like American men emerge from the womb as natural Republicans and conservatives. But what this forgets is that working-class and blue collar white men in the United States were rock-solid Democrats for decades, beginning with the 1930s New Deal and all the way through the 1960s. During those years, most blue-collar white guys wouldn't have dreamed of voting Republican, who were seen as the party of effete country club elites, out-of-touch aristocrats, and snobs who were hostile to the interests of the average working man.

**JE: When, and why, did that start to change?**

JK: For me, the watershed year is 1972, when Richard Nixon won a crushing 49-state landslide victory over South Dakota Senator George McGovern. Nixon won huge numbers of blue collar white men who had been rock-solid Democrats since FDR and the New Deal, setting in motion the political realignment that shapes presidential politics to this day. Since 1972, Republicans have not only succeeded in positioning themselves as the party of white people in the post-Civil Rights era, but as the party of *real men.* They've also managed, on a parallel track, to cast the Democrats not only as the party of African-Americans and people of color, but also as the party of soft and weak men, an ineffectual collection of weak-kneed, emasculated intellectuals who align themselves with women and gays and turn their backs on the real-world issues that real men care about in a dangerous world full of real threats. There's no question race was also absolutely central to these shifts, but race isn't enough to explain why so many white men fled the Democratic Party while so many white women stayed put. I don't think we can separate the race politics from the gender politics.

**JE: Are there other factors involved here?**

JK: I think some of the Democratic Party's diminished strength with white working men can also be traced to the decline of the labor movement as a traditional source of masculine strength. As blue collar manufacturing jobs have been shipped overseas, a lot of dislocated, alienated, and screwed-over white working-class guys have gravitated toward the tough-guy

rhetoric and symbolism of the Republicans to hold on to their manhood. The Republican Party may offer working-class white men very little in terms of actual policies that benefit them, but at least they offer them a kind of cultural recognition and validation.

**JE: Beyond the optics and rhetoric, are there actual issues Republicans have seized on to speak to these men?**

JK: There are a number of key issues that have allowed Republican candidates to reach out to male voters, especially working-class white guys, and establish their masculine chops. The gun issue, for example, is clearly about much more than legalistic debates about the proper interpretation of constitutional rights. For many gun-owning men, the issue is intensely personal and goes to core aspects of their identity. [...] And there's a whole range of issues like this—military spending, law and order, etc.—that speak to white men, emotionally, as men.

**JE: How does the right-wing narrative about liberal elitism come into play here?**

JK: When conservatives go on and on about Democrats being cultural elitists who look down on average folks, it's really just another way of feminizing them. If Democrats are unassertive, effete, and urbane intellectuals who use genteel, condescending language, then how can they be trusted to provide tough leadership and act in the interests of the hardscrabble working men of the American heartland? Trump has gotten a lot of mileage out of this mentality. Even though he grew up the pampered child of complete and utter privilege, his brash personal style and bravado have signaled to a lot of working-class white guys that he's one of them, a "real man" and a "blue collar billionaire" who understands them—the kind of guy, in Clint Eastwood's words, who can fight back against the liberal "wussification" of America. It's totally emotional, it's all about white men's identities, and it has nothing to do with how Republican policies will affect working-class men and women in the real world.

**JE: And yet conservatives have somehow been able to frame "identity politics" as this emotionally sensitive stuff that only liberals and left-wingers engage in.**

JK: Exactly. If you're not straight, white, and male, and you assert your rights based on your gender or racial or ethnic identities, you get accused of playing identity politics; you're criticized for playing the "woman card" or the "race card." At the same time, if you're a woman who supports a woman candidate, or a person of color who supports a person of color, you're dismissed for allowing your own personal identity to cloud your judgment. It's as though only subordinate groups have identities, only people of color and women and LGBTQ people are prone to thinking about politics and the world through the lens of their experience as gendered and racial beings. And it's as though straight white guys are somehow immune to all of this, which is obviously ridiculous. Trump and his handlers have very clearly, and by their own admission, been playing the "man card"—the *white* man card—again and again during this campaign.

---

## Note

1. *Editors' note*: This interview was conducted prior to the 2016 U.S. presidential election held on November 8, 2016. Trump lost the popular vote but won the election.

---

*Source:* Katz, Jackson, & Earp, Jeremy. (2016, September 26). Excerpted from "It's the Masculinity, Stupid! An Interview with Jackson Katz on the Throwback Allure of Donald Trump." *Media Education Foundation*. Reprinted from *Huffington Post*, October 2, 2016: http://www.huffingtonpost.com/entry/its-the-masculinity-stupid-an-interview-withjackson_us_57f197b9e4b07f20daa10e6f. Full interview can be found at: http://www.mediaed.org/itsthe-masculinity-stupidan-interview-with-jackson-katz-on-the-throwback-allure-of-donald-trump/.

# CHAPTER 20

## Gender in Personal Life

*Raewyn Connell and Rebecca Pearse*

Raewyn Connell is a professor emerita at the University of Sydney. She was one of the founders of the study of masculinity and published *Masculinities* in 1995. The concept of "hegemonic masculinity" was introduced in the book and has been particularly influential and controversial. Connell has been an advisor to United Nations initiatives on gender equality and peacemaking.

Rebecca Pearse is a professor in the Department of Political Economy at the University of Sydney. Previously, she was a postdoctoral fellow working at the Australian National University on a project entitled *Gendered Excellence in the Social Sciences.* Pearse has expertise in the political economy of climate and energy policy, social responses to environmental change, the sociology of knowledge, and feminism and gender relations.

To most people, being a man or a woman is above all a matter of personal experience. It is part of the way we grow up, the way we conduct family life and sexual relationships, the way we present ourselves in everyday situations, and the way we see ourselves. This chapter examines some issues that arise in this realm of intimacy, and reflects on how to understand what happens here.

\*\*\*\*\*

## GROWING UP GENDERED: SEX ROLE SOCIALIZATION

When sex role theory provided the main framework of gender studies, there was a straightforward account of how people acquired gender. Babies were identified as either female or male and put in pink and blue clothes respectively. The blue babies were expected to behave rougher and tougher, to be more demanding and vigorous. In time, they were given toy guns, footballs, and computer games. The pink babies were expected to be more passive and compliant, also prettier. As they grew older, they were dressed in frilly clothes, given dolls and makeup kits, told to take care of their appearance and be polite and agreeable.

Put more formally, the idea was that 'sex roles' were acquired by socialization. Various 'agencies of socialization', notably the family, the school, the peer group, and the mass media, took the growing child in hand. Through an immense number of small interactions, these agencies conveyed to the girl or the boy the social 'norms' or expectations for behaviour. This could be done by imitating admired 'role models', such as a father might be for a boy; or it could be done piecemeal. Compliance with the norms would lead to rewards, or 'positive sanctions': smiles from mother, approval from friends, good marks at school, success in the dating game, appointment to a good job. Nonconformity or deviance would lead to negative sanctions, all the way from frowns to getting beaten up or sent to gaol.

With this mixture of positive and negative reinforcement, most children would learn the gender-appropriate behaviour, develop the traits the society thought appropriate for women or for men, and thus 'internalize' the norms. As fully socialized members of society, they would in turn apply negative sanctions to deviants, and convey the norms to the next generation. Of course, the process could go wrong, for instance if fathers disappeared from families and boys lacked role models, which would probably lead to juvenile delinquency.

There is something to be said for this story of how gender is acquired, but there are also severe problems with it; so severe, in fact, that the socialization model should be abandoned.

First, it is too monolithic. The world does not consist of neatly homogeneous cultures. Cultures were smashed, fragmented, and re-composed by conquest, colonization, migration, and contemporary globalization. The ethnic pluralism of modern societies mixes traditions. The model of sex role socialization mistakes what is dominant for what is normative. Further, multiple patterns arise within gender relations. [...] There are always multiple patterns of masculinity and femininity to complicate the picture of learning.

Second, the socialization model supposes that learning gender is a matter of acquiring traits, that is, regularities of character that will produce regularities of behaviour. Sex role theory, basically, is a version of the difference model of gender. But, major differences in traits between women and men (or between girls and boys) are hard to detect.

Third, the socialization model pictures the learner as passive, the agencies of socialization as active. In real life, gender learning does not look like this. Consider the American elementary schools studied by Barrie Thorne (1993). The boys and girls here are not lying back and letting the gender norms wash over them. They are constantly active. They sometimes accept gender divisions supplied by adults and sometimes don't. They set up their own gender divisions in the playground, and then disrupt them. They try out gendered self-presentations (e.g., the older girls putting on lip gloss); they complain, joke, fantasize, and question about gender. Similar energy appears in other studies of schools. [...]

The socialization model seems to miss the pleasure that is obvious in much gender learning; the resistance which many young people put up to hegemonic definitions of gender; and the difficulty involved in constructing identities and working out patterns of conduct in a gender order marked by power, violence, and alienated sexualities. [...]

Fourth, the socialization model recognizes just one direction of learning—towards or away from the sex role norms. This makes it hard to understand the shifts of direction that often appear in a young person's life, coming apparently from nowhere. There can be a shift of attachment from mother to father, a new level of aggression, a sudden burst of sexual activity, a turning away from girls or boys. Rather than just failing to 'internalize' the gender patterns of her/his parents, a young person may vehemently reject them, criticize their political or human inadequacy, and launch out on a search for something different.

*****

# A BETTER ACCOUNT: EMBODIED LEARNING

A good account of how we acquire gender must recognize both the contradictions of development, and the fact that learners are active, not passive. It must recognize the agency of bodies in the social world, since the active learner is embodied. It must recognize the power and the complexity of the institutions that occupy the learner's world. It must give an account of the gender competencies that are learned, and the different life projects in which they are used. And it must recognize historical change in all these respects.

The pleasure involved in learning gender is to some extent a bodily pleasure, pleasure in the body's appearance and in the body's performance. Bodily changes such as menarche, first ejaculation, the 'breaking' of a boy's voice, and the development of a girl's breasts are important, but their meanings remain ambiguous until they are given definition by the society's gender symbolism.

Because gender practice involves bodies but is not biologically determined, the learned behaviour may be hostile to bodies' physical well-being. Young men in rich countries such as the United States and Australia, enacting their fresh-minted masculinities on the roads, die in appalling numbers in traffic accidents, at a rate four times higher than young women. A large number of adolescent girls and young women go in for dieting, in an attempt to maintain their heterosexual attractiveness. For a smaller number, this escalates into life-threatening anorexia. In poorer countries, the circumstances are different but the stakes are also very high. In the Palestinian confrontation with Israeli occupation, the intifada, most of the direct resistance has been carried out by very young men and boys. As Julie Peteet (1994) showed in a terrifying ethnography, being beaten or arrested by the Israeli army and police became a kind of rite of passage into masculinity for Palestinian youth; and some of them were killed.

Embodied learners encounter the gender regimes of the institutions they come in contact with. The socialization model was right about the importance of the family, the school, and the media in children's lives, but failed to recognize the internal complexity of the gender regimes of these institutions. In a school, teachers and peer groups present a range of different patterns of masculinity and femininity to the children. [...]

The diversity of gender patterns among children and youth shows up with particular clarity in research that looks across different social groups. Stephen Frosh, Ann Phoenix, and Rob Pattman, in a very perceptive study called *Young Masculinities* (2002), report on 11- to 14-year-old boys in 12 secondary schools across London. They show that ethnic position is prominent in London boys' views about masculinity—Afro-Caribbean boys being thought high in masculinity and Asian boys low. Relationships with schools are ambivalent, academic success being both desired and thought feminine. Above all, the study shows that diversity in the boys' lives exists in tension with 'canonical narratives' of masculinity, i.e., a hegemonic pattern (an admired physical toughness, sports skills, heterosexuality). All boys acknowledge the hegemonic masculinity but most do not fully inhabit it. Rather, their adolescence is marked by a complex negotiation with definitions of gender, in which they may criticize some versions of masculinity as too tough, while rejecting others as effeminate.

Much of young people's learning about gender is learning what we might call gender competence. Young people learn how to navigate the local gender order and the gender regimes of the institutions they deal with. They learn how to adopt a certain gender identity and produce a certain gender performance—how to 'do gender', as West and Zimmerman (1987) famously put it. Young people also learn how to distance themselves from a given gender identity, how to joke about their own performance. Most boys and girls fail to match gender ideals of handsomeness, beauty, skill, achievement, or recognition. But most of them cope. [...]

Gender configurations, being patterns of activity, are not static. Masculinity and femininity are 'projects', to use a term suggested by the philosopher

Jean-Paul Sartre (1968). They are patterns of a life-course projected from the present into the future, bringing new conditions or events into existence. Simone de Beauvoir's *The Second Sex* (1949) includes a long section that discusses alternative life projects for women as they existed in European society and history. There is likely to be overlap in the gender projects, a degree of social standardization of individual lives. These common trajectories of gender formation are what researchers pick up as patterns of masculinity or femininity in life-history and ethnographic research.

Gender projects are not one-dimensional or smooth, and may involve heavy costs. Any trajectory involves a number of distinct moments in which different gender commitments are made, different strategies are adopted, or different resolutions of gender issues are achieved. This can be seen in the lives of a group of men from the Australian 'green' movement (Connell 1995: ch. 5). Most of them grew up in homes with a conventional gender division of labour, and in childhood and adolescence began to make a commitment to hegemonic masculinity. But this moment of engagement was followed by a moment of negation, as they started to distance themselves from hegemonic masculinity, for a variety of reasons, including family conflict. Most then, in the counter-culture or in the green movement, encountered feminism and were obliged to confront gender issues head-on: this was a moment of separation from hegemonic masculinity. Some were still at this point when we interviewed them. Some, however, had moved on to a moment of contestation, starting a political project of reforming masculinity and committing themselves to gender equality.

The diversity of masculinities and femininities shown by a great deal of gender research implies different trajectories of gender formation. Class inequalities, ethnic diversity, regional difference, national origin, and migration create different experiences of childhood. Major social changes may alter relations between parents and children. [...]

The diversity of trajectories is shown in a British study, Gillian Dunne's *Lesbian Lifestyles* (1997). Some of the women she interviewed served an 'apprenticeship' to conventional femininity, some were tomboys; some grew up in families with a conventional division of labour, some in egalitarian homes. Dunne emphasizes the agency of the girls in responding to these experiences. But she also notes the intractability of the gender order. As they moved into adolescence, where the 'romance' and 'dating' culture ruled, many of the girls found the middle ground in gender relations, which they had previously occupied, disappearing beneath their feet. As one woman, Connie, recalls:

> The whole thing changed, suddenly they became totally different people. I thought what is this thing that happens to everyone else and doesn't happen to me? ... I didn't know how to behave, quite honestly. They all seemed to have this secret code that they all learned, and I didn't. They all knew how to behave at discos, and I would sit pinned to the wall terrified. Where did they learn this? I didn't have it. It was some sort of pattern of social behaviour that everyone fell into, and I didn't have it—God! ... The big 'goo goo' eyes came out, the painted faces, and the frocks, and all that stuff, and the act, the peacock act, basically attracting.

As the gender order changes, new trajectories become possible. In parts of the world influenced by the Women's Liberation movement, young women growing up in the following decades had their own dilemmas about jobs, marriage, and children, as can be seen in the stories told in Chilla Bulbeck's three-generation study, *Living Feminism* (1997). But they did not face the same impasse as women of earlier generations. Belief in gender equality has also spread among younger men, in some places. Witness the national study of men in Germany by Paul Zulehner and Rainer Volz (1998), where men below 50 endorse a gender-equal model of family life, and reject 'traditional' norms, much more often than men above 50.

# DISCOURSE AND IDENTITY

Perhaps the commonest way of understanding the presence of gender in personal life is through the concept of 'gender identity'. The term 'identity' shifted meaning during its long history. [...] Erik Erikson's famous *Childhood and Society* (1950) interpreted a range of modern personal, social, and political problems as difficulties in achieving identity. [...]

To Erikson, the term *identity* meant the coherence of the psychological mechanisms by which the ego handles the pressures that impinge on it—from the unconscious mind, on the one side, and the outside world, on the other. The question 'who am I?' is, in principle, answered by the ego's success in mastering the trials and tribulations of psychological development. This was, Erikson thought, a particularly important issue in adolescence.

The key application of this concept to gender was made by the American psychiatrist Robert Stoller (1968), who altered it in two ways. First, the 'core gender identity' that Stoller saw as the basis of adult personality was supposed to be formed very early in life, not in adolescence. Second, the concept of identity acquired a different frame of reference. Erikson referred to the integration of the ego as a whole. Stoller's conception was much more specific. To talk of 'gender identity' is to talk only of one aspect of the person—her or his involvement in gender relations or sexual practice.

To Stoller, this narrower focus did not matter because he assumed that the integration of the personality as a whole was largely focused on the sense of being a male or a female. But on any other view of personality and social process, an exclusive focus on gender is a problem. We can speak just as meaningfully of 'racial identity', 'generational identity', or 'class identity'. If we acknowledge the 'constant interweaving' (Bottomley 1992) of these social relations, which is now common in discussions of intersectionality, we must attend to these other forms of identity in order to understand gender identity. The concept of 'gender identity' formulated by Stoller thus leads towards a conception of identity as inherently plural rather than unitary.

A model of identity built on gender dichotomy was easily accepted by the 1970s because American feminist research emphasized gender difference in the rearing of children. [...]

Though it has been well established that men can 'mother' (Risman 1986), it is still the case that, in contemporary Western society, few of them do. But the reasons for this may be economic rather than psychological. Introducing paid leave for fathers of young children, in Scandinavia, has been a successful reform (Holter 2003). There has also been more recognition [...] that we do not find dichotomous gender patterns in adult personalities. [...]

The trend has therefore been to speak of multiple gender and sexual identities. [...] The concept of 'identity' has increasingly been used for claims made by individuals about who they are in terms of difference from other people.

This is closely related to the growth, especially in the United States, of identity politics. One becomes a member of a social movement by claiming the identity (as Black, as a woman, as lesbian, etc.) that the movement represents. Queer politics takes the process a step further. Queer activists have challenged taken-for-granted communities by emphasizing their diversity: highlighting the presence of Black lesbians in white-dominated lesbian communities, for instance. Yet the queer movement has, ironically, generated a spectacular new identity, LGBT (lesbian, gay, bisexual, transgender), sometimes expanded by adding TQI (transsexual, queer, intersex) and even others who can be assembled under the umbrella as 'sexual minorities'. LGBT persons, and the LGBT community, are now familiar entities in human rights talk and sexual politics.

Even the identities on which social movements have been based prove, on close examination, to be less solid than we might think. Arne Nilsson's (1998) beautifully crafted study of homosexual history in the Swedish city of Gothenburg identifies three ways of being homosexual: 'so', commonly a bit effeminate; 'real men', often working-class youth; and '*fjollor*', flamboyant queens. Three identities, perhaps? But Nilsson also shows how the patterns of homosexual life grew out of the structure of the industrial and maritime city. Among the conditions shaping sexuality were crowded housing, a sharp gender division of labour, high density of men in public spaces, a non-respectable working-class street life, connections to other cities via the shipping trade, certain patterns of policing, and the poverty of many young men, who might enter homosexual relationships for a period and then move on.

The distinctive forms of homosexual practice changed as these conditions changed. The 1950s saw rising affluence in Sweden, suburban working-class housing, the growth of the welfare state, and moral panics about the seduction of youth. A sharper cultural distinction between heterosexual and homosexual people followed the increasing privacy of sexual conduct itself. Thus, the configurations of sexual and social practice which might easily be read as 'identities' were dependent on historically transitory social conditions, and for many participants were only a limited part of their whole sexual life-history. [...]

Is a unified identity really so desirable? To weld one's personality into a united whole is to refuse internal diversity and openness, perhaps to refuse change. Major reform in gender relations may well require a loss of self, an experience of gender vertigo, as part of the process. This seemed common among the group of men in the Australian 'green' movement who were trying to change traditional masculinity. [...] But how far can changing gender configurations go? We now turn to [other] cases recognized in gender studies.

## TRANSITION, TRANSGENDER, AND TRANSSEXUAL

One of the most dramatic proofs of the importance of social processes in gender, and a familiar disproof of biological essentialism, is the fact that different

societies have recognized different gender categories. There are not only women and men; there might also be third genders, or variations on two that seem to multiply the gender categories in which people can live.

This question has intrigued gender researchers, and there is a large ethnographic literature addressed to categories such as the *berdache*, the 'two-souled' people of Indigenous cultures in the south-western region of North America (Williams 1986), who have male bodies, a social position closer to that of women than of men, and great spiritual power. Javanese society traditionally provided a space for *banci*, people with male bodies and women's dress who typically have sex with straight men. In Brazil, there are *travesti*, often in poverty and making their living as sex workers, who are physically male but feel themselves feminine, and have sex with men within a sexual culture that makes a strong distinction between the insertive and the receptive partner.

These groups are all different from each other, and it is debated whether the idea of a 'third gender' makes sense for any of them. Certainly, all such patterns can change, as shown in Thailand. In research by Peter Jackson (1997), the traditional Thai sex/gender categories for males were *phuchai* (man, mainly heterosexual) and *kathoey* (effeminate or cross-gender, receptive homosexual). Under the impact of international gay culture, these categories have not disappeared. Rather, they have been elaborated with a series of additions: *bai* (bisexual), *gay-king* (homosexual, preferring to be insertor), *gay-queen* (usually effeminate, preferring to be receptive), and *gay-quing* (masculine or effeminate, and sexually versatile).

Even within the gender order of the global North, which emphasizes a dichotomy of man and women, there are opportunities for violating the boundaries, whether in a carnival mood or with great seriousness. A well-known study by Marjorie Garber, *Vested Interests* (1992), finds an astonishing range of cross-dressing practices, in theatre, film, the sex industry, religion, music, detective stories, television ... ranging from Marlene Dietrich's top hat to Boy George's dresses.

People who somehow live across gender boundaries, who don't just dip in and out, have intrigued gender analysts within Western culture as much as 'third gender' categories have intrigued ethnographers. [...]

[After] the social science of gender was well developed, 'transsexuals', as such people came to be called in the 1950s, still appeared to psychiatrists and sociologists as a kind of natural experiment exposing the mechanism of the gender system. The story of the creation of 'transsexualism' as a medical syndrome, the ambiguous role of doctors, and the controversy within the medical profession has been well told (Meyerowitz 2002; Stryker 2008), and interested readers can find many of the key documents in Susan Stryker and Stephen Whittle's admirable *Transgender Studies Reader* (2006).

With the rise of performative theories of gender, there has been great interest in variations in gender and violations of norms. If normative gender is brought into being performatively, then by changing the performative actions, we should be able to create non-normative gender. This line of thought gave rise in the 1990s to a transgender movement influenced by queer theory, mainly in the United States, which has since had considerable impact across the world. This movement emphasized the instability of gender boundaries, rejected the 'binary' of male and female, and tried in various ways to live outside, or beyond, or across, gender categories. Kate Bornstein's *Gender Outlaw: On Men, Women, and the Rest of Us* (1994) is perhaps the best-known statement from this movement.

The analysis of gender in the present chapter suggests an important difference between this transgender movement, focused on the symbolic dimension of gender and trying to break down or blur the symbolic categories of gender, and the projects of transition between locations in the gender order that since about 1950 have been called transsexual. Viviane Namaste in *Invisible Lives* (2000) challenges transgender discourse, urging attention to the real-life experiences, subjectivities, and struggles of transsexual men and

women that are 'erased' by queer theory as well as by government agencies. Simply accessing health care and social services, as Namaste's research in Canada shows, can be very difficult for people making transitions. Yet the state, and the world of institutions more generally, is critically important for transsexual women. Namaste's studies in her important book *Sex Change, Social Change* (2011) show the struggles for recognition and safety that have to be carried on—in prisons, in the media, in universities, in social services, in human rights forums.

The following account is based on the analysis in Raewyn Connell's paper 'Transsexual Women and Feminist Thought' (2012), where more detail will be found. Whereas transgender stories mostly emphasize the fluidity of gender, transsexual autobiographies mostly emphasize gender's stability, indeed its intransigence. This is abundantly clear in the best social-scientific study of gender transition, Henry Rubin's *Self-Made Men* (2003). The gender project, to use the term introduced earlier in this chapter, is consistent over time—however 'wrong' in terms of conventional social embodiment it may be.

Experiences of contradictory embodiment are central in transsexual women's lives. This is well shown in the survey undertaken by Claudine Griggs (1998) as well as autobiographies such as Katherine Cummings' *Katherine's Diary* (1992). Transsexual women describe these experiences in different ways: having a man's body and a woman's body at the same time, or one emerging from the other, or—the traditional one—being trapped in the wrong body. These figures of speech have aroused scorn, but they do highlight the importance of social embodiment. Transsexuality is best understood not as a syndrome nor as a discursive position, but as a bundle of life trajectories that arise from contradictions in social embodiment. Transsexual women's narratives speak of recognition: sometimes a dramatic moment, sometimes a gradually growing awareness, but centrally a matter of recognizing a fact about oneself, that one is a woman despite having a male body.

But this recognizing is a fearful thing, because the central contradiction in transsexuality is so powerful. This fact is totally at odds with what everyone around knows, and with what the transsexual woman knows too, being also recognizable as a man (or boy, since this often happens in youth). And there is no walking away from this terror: gender is intransigent, both as a structure of the society and as a structure of personal life. Some transsexual women try to keep the contradiction inside their skins, and ride out the terror. Some kill themselves; it's not clear how many, but there are high rates of attempted suicide. Moving towards transition is an attempt to end this precarious practice and achieve a settlement.

Because the contradiction is one of embodiment, transition now usually involves modifications to the body with medical aid. This involves a number of procedures: psychiatric screening, hormonal treatment (mainly oestrogen for transsexual women, testosterone for transsexual men), surgery ('top' and 'bottom' in different packages), electrolysis, vocal training, and sometimes others. The process is unavoidably traumatic, as shown in Griggs' (1996) superb narrative of reassignment surgery.

There is nothing pretty about gender reassignment; these are rough measures and have rough results. Though media and scholarly attention have focused obsessively on the surgery, that is only part of the medical treatment, and medical treatment is only part of transition. A huge amount of other work is to be done. This includes raising funds; getting personal support, post-operative care, legal documentation; finding housing; dealing with relationship crises; dealing with a workplace or finding work; dealing with bodily changes; gaining social recognition; and dealing with hostility. Any of these may be uppermost in turn.

This work, as the sociology of gender would lead us to expect, engages all the dimensions of the gender order; it is not only about sexuality or identity. It is structured by the inequalities of the gender order; the process is not the same for transsexual women

and transsexual men. Transsexual women are shedding the patriarchal dividend that accrues to men as a group, in labor markets, finance markets (e.g., housing), family status, professional authority, and so on. A small but path-breaking econometric study by Kristen Schilt and Matthew Wiswall (2008) in the United States finds there is an economic penalty in transition for both men and women, but transsexual men eventually are better paid after transition than before, while transsexual women lose, on average, nearly one-third of their income.

A great deal rests on the responses of others. Transition puts partnerships, especially marriages, at acute risk: a wife's position in the gender order is seriously challenged, and may be traumatically undermined, by a husband's moves towards transition. With transsexual women's children, too, relationships may end at transition. Even when they continue, both child and parent have to handle the significant loss that occurs in transition. Gender relations are embodied; here it is embodied fatherhood being lost, and it is not only the transitioning woman who pays the price. These issues have become more prominent in autobiographies, such as the very readable account of transition by Jennifer Boylan (2003). As Boylan's story shows, families can be resilient, and partnerships and parent/child relationships can be re-woven. Indeed, family members may be vital supports during transition.

Gatekeepers for jobs and housing have to be negotiated with. According to recent research by Schilt and Wiswall (2008) in the United States, transsexual women have different workplace strategies. Some respond by concealing their stories—the 'stealth' strategy—while others are not only open about their transition, but contest rather than conform to sexist conventions. These studies, however, had mainly middle-class samples. A lot of working-class transsexual women have always survived by sex work. There is a certain clientele of straight men who are excited by transsexual women. But this does not mean they respect them. [...] For that kind of reason, sex work is likely to be a precarious milieu, exposing transsexual women to high levels of HIV infection and violence (Garofalo et al. 2006; Namaste 2009).

In the past, feminists have often held negative views of transsexual women. This is less common now, and some transsexual women are well-recognized feminists. Most transsexual women are not banner-bearers for any cause. Gender transition only happens through severe contradictions in personal life, which can be unbearable, and commonly absorb a great deal of energy simply to hold together. Transsexual lives can be made harder, as Namaste says, by denial of recognition from institutions or movements. Yet in some sense these lives do show the potentials for change that lie in the historical process of social embodiment, and they enrich the project of gender justice that feminism has launched.

## REFERENCES

Bottomley, Gillian. 1992. *From Another Place: Migration and the Politics of Culture*. Cambridge: Cambridge University Press.

Bornstein, Kate. 1994. *Gender Outlaw: On Men, Women, and the Rest of Us*. New York: Routledge.

Boylan, Jennifer Finley. 2003. *She's Not There: A Life in Two Genders*. New York: Broadway Books.

Bulbeck, Chilla. 1997. *Living Feminism: The Impact of the Women's Movement on Three Generations of Australian Women*. Cambridge: Cambridge University Press.

Connell, Raewyn. 1995. *Masculinities*. Cambridge: Polity.

Connell, Raewyn. 2012. 'Transsexual women and feminist thought: Toward a new understanding and new politics', *Signs* 37 (4): 857–81.

Cummings, Katherine. 1992. *Katherine's Diary: The Story of a Transsexual*. Melbourne: Heinemann.

de Beauvoir, Simone. 1949. *The Second Sex*. Harmondsworth: Penguin (1972 edition).

Dunne, Gillian A. 1997. *Lesbian Lifestyles: Women's Work and the Politics of Sexuality*. Basingstoke: Macmillan.

Erikson, Erik H. 1950. *Childhood and Society*. London: Imago.

Frosh, Stephen, Ann Phoenix and Rob Pattman. 2002. *Young Masculinities: Understanding Boys in Contemporary Society*. Basingstoke: Palgrave.

Garafalo, Robert, Joanne Deleon, Elizabeth Osmer, Mary Doll and Gary W. Harper. 2006. 'Overlooked, misunderstood and at-risk: Exploring the lives and HIV risk of ethnic minority male-to-female transgender youth', *Journal of Adolescent Health* 38 (3): 230–6.

Garber, Marjorie. 1992. *Vested Interests: Cross-Dressing and Cultural Anxiety*. New York: Routledge.

Griggs, Claudine. 1996. *Passage through Trinidad: Journal of a Surgical Sex Change*. Jefferson: McFarland & Co.

Griggs, Claudine. 1998. *S/he: Changing Sex and Changing Clothes*. New York: Bloomsbury.

Holter, Øystein Gullvåg. 2003. *Can Men Do It? Men and Gender Equality—the Nordic Experience*. Copenhagen: Nordic Council of Ministers.

Jackson, Peter A. 1997. '*Kathoey*><Gay><Man: The historical emergency of gay male identity in Thailand', in *Sites of Desire, Economies of Pleasure*, edited by Lenore Manderson and Margaret Jolly. Chicago: University of Chicago Press.

Meyerowitz, Joanne. 2002. *How Sex Changed: A History of Transsexuality in the United States*. Cambridge: Harvard University Press.

Namaste, Viviane K. 2000. *Invisible Lives: The Erasure of Transsexual and Transgendered People*. Chicago: University of Chicago Press.

Namaste, Viviane K. 2009. 'Undoing theory: The "transgender question" and the epistemic violence of Anglo-American feminist theory', *Hypatia* 24 (3): 11–32.

Namaste, Viviane K. 2011. *Sex Change, Social Change: Reflections on Identity, Institutions, and Imperialism*. Toronto: Canadian Scholars' Press.

Nilsson, Arne. 1998. 'Creating their own private and public: The male homosexual life space in a Nordic city during high modernity', *Journal of Homosexuality* 35: 81–116.

Peteet, Julie. 1994. 'Male gender and rituals of resistance in the Palestinian Intifada: A cultural politics of violence', *American Ethnologist* 21: 31–49.

Risman, Barbara J. 1986. 'Can men "mother"? Life as a single father', *Family Relations* 35: 95–102.

Rubin, Henry. 2003. *Self-Made Men: Identity and Embodiment among Transsexual Men*. Nashville: Vanderbilt University Press.

Sartre, Jean-Paul. 1968. *Search for a Method*. New York: Vintage.

Schilt, Kristen, and Matthew Wiswall. 2008. 'Before and after: Gender transitions, human capital, and workplace experiences,' *The B.E. Journal of Economic Analysis & Policy* 8(1): article 39.

Stoller, Robert J. 1968. *Sex and Gender, vol. 1: On the Development of Masculinity and Femininity*. London: Hogarth Press.

Stryker, Susan. 2008. *Transgender History*. Berkeley: Seal Press.

Stryker, Susan, and Stephen Whittle, eds. 2006. *The Transgender Studies Reader*. New York: Routledge.

Thorne, Barrie. 1993. *Gender Play: Girls and Boys in School*. New Brunswick: Rutgers University Press.

West, Candace, and Don H. Zimmerman. 1987. 'Doing gender', *Gender and Society* 1: 125–51.

Williams, Walter L. 1986. *The Spirit and the Flesh: Sexual Diversity in American Indian Culture*. Boston: Beacon Press.

Zulehner, Paul M., and Rainer Volz. 1998. *Männer im Aufbruch: wie Deutschlands Männer sich selbst und wie Frauen sie sehen*. Ostfildern: Schwabenverlag.

---

*Source:* Connell, Raewyn, & Pearse, Rebecca. (2014). Excerpted from "Chapter 6: Gender in Personal Life." In *Gender: In World Perspective, 3rd Edition* (pp. 93, 96–111). Cambridge, UK: Polity Press.

# SNAPSHOTS & SOUNDWAVES 14

## TRANSFEMINIST TERMS AND CONCEPTS

*A. Finn Enke*

A. Finn Enke is a professor of history and of gender and women's studies, and the director of the LGBT Studies Certificate Program at the University of Wisconsin–Madison. Enke's work focuses on the history of sexuality and gender, primarily in 20th century United States, and on feminist, queer, and transgender social movements and theory.

This is not a glossary of all terms relevant to transgender studies, trans histories, and trans lives. It would be impossible to be exhaustive here, as the list of terms related to cultural and community-based gender practices is literally infinite. Neither is it definitive: meanings and uses change across time and place.

Language itself is a social activity; words, phrases, and uses effectively communicate only within a community that grants rough consensus to that particular expression. At the same time, language adapts around cultural changes and may be open to new words and new grammars; in the same measure, communities and individuals do learn new languages all the time. Since the 1960s, the concept of "gender inclusive" language has gone from referring to the once radical practice of saying "people" instead of "men," "person" instead of "man," and "he and she" instead of just "he" to today, when "gender-inclusive" might refer to language that does not impose binary gender and honors the actual gender diversity of human lives.

The English language imposes binary gender, and, in many cases, it requires work to circumvent this imposition. In contrast to many languages, English does not gender all nouns or attach gender to the first person singular ("I"). However, most singular pronouns ("he," "she") are gendered, as are some familial terms (e.g., "aunt," "uncle"). In many cases, English provides a neutral choice (one can say "child" rather than "son" or "daughter"), but speech customs may make certain options feel awkward. Workers in many service-sector jobs are taught to greet customers as "ma'am," "sir," or "ladies"; this is an entirely gratuitous gender imposition that may feel polite and even friendly to some people, but to others it may feel irritating if not violent.

Transliteracy suggests the following:

- Become more aware of when the language, culture, or simply one's own habits of speech are imposing gender.
- Consider one's own attachments or intentions with such speech.
- Learn to use alternatives.

These are ways to begin to change cultural consensus in language. This does not mean doing away with gender-specific language; it means developing additional fluencies to respect the complexity of gender.

**Gender-Inclusive Pronouns (often called gender-neutral):** ze/hir/hir, they/them/theirs (subject/object/possessive, respectively). Gender-inclusive pronouns are not associated with a specific gender and thereby do not ascribe gender. In English, the plural "they" is an example. The singular "they" dates back to the fifteenth century and is common in some parts of the English-speaking world, but in most places in North America, the singular "they" is less familiar. For the singular, our most common options ("he" and "she") are specifically gendered. Trans-aware communities developed the use of ze/hir/hir as gender-inclusive alternatives. In more recent years, they/them/their is becoming even more popular as a singular pronoun.

*Usage considerations:* For many trans people who identify as men or women, use of inclusive pronouns can feel like an offensive refusal to recognize their gender identity. At the same time, the fact that many people identify with one of the binary pronouns does not preclude using inclusive pronouns as a *general* practice for all people, conveying that we do not know how other people identify their own gender and also that some people do not identify with either of the binary options. In some communities and classrooms, "ze" and/or "they" are used universally and with complete fluency. However, these options have yet to circulate through mainstream culture, and thus their use must be considered political and pedagogical.

**Sex:** From the perspective of evolutionary biology, human sex is conventionally classified in two categories (female and male) according to whether a body produces eggs or sperm. Associated with this characteristic are others, such as genital morphology, chromosomal makeup, and genetic factors that affect secondary sex characteristics (body hair, breasts, and so forth). The variety of factors involved and the natural variation in all of them have led to greater acknowledgment of the fact that humans exceed sexual dimorphism (that is to say, male and female are not neatly distinct) and also that it would be theoretically possible to group humans into more than two sex categories.

**Legally Recognized Sex Status:** People's legal existence in the United States is accompanied by the requirement to have a legally recognized sex status, but in practice, sex status is indicated by multiple and at times competing factors. Legal sex is designated on such documents as birth certificates, passports, Social Security cards, and state IDs. Because such documents are purportedly used for identification, institutions place great weight on whether a person "looks like" the sex indicated on the document. In the absence of federal law, the ease with which identity documents may be changed varies according to laws established at the state and/or local level and according to bureaucratic idiosyncrasies. For these reasons, a person's identity documents may not all have the same sex designation, and the concept of "legal sex" itself is a bit of an oxymoron.

**Intersex Conditions:** More than thirty variations in sexual development fall under the category of intersex conditions. Some of these lead to ambiguity in genital morphology, others to secondary sex characteristics less commonly associated with genetic sex, and so forth.

*Usage considerations:* In recent years, medical institutions have come to favor the term "Disorders of Sexual Development" (DSD). Some people with intersex conditions prefer this term over "intersex"; others identify as intersex, or as persons with intersex conditions, and many feel that DSD is pathologizing and depoliticizing.

**Gender:** Gender results from cultural practices of ordering or organizing different types of people according to bodies and behaviors. Social gender has mainly to do with a combination of the expectations assigned to one's sex and the role one plays in one's society. Because each culture establishes its own categorizations of norms for genders, gender conformity and gender crossing are necessarily culturally specific. In many societies, production, reproduction, consumption, and distribution are infused with and constitute gender.

**Gender Identity:** One's sense of one's self as a gendered person (e.g., as man, woman, both, neither, or some other configuration of gender). A person's gender identity may or may not match the sex assigned at birth or current legal sex as indicated on any of the several documents indicating sex, and it may or may not conform to conventional expectations of maleness or femaleness, including expectations of what a man's or woman's body looks like.

**Gender Expression:** How people express, wear, enact, and perform gender through behavior, mannerism, clothing, speech, physicality, and selective body modification.

**Transgender:** The term "transgender" incorporates distinct but overlapping arenas of social organization. "Transgender" may be used as:

- The *name of a social movement* that insists on the right of all people to determine for themselves their own personal and legal gender statuses (gender self-determination), freedom of gender identity and gender expression for all people, and civil and social rights for all people regardless of gender identity, gender expression, and body type.
- An *ever-expanding social category* that incorporates the broadest possible range of gender nonconformity for the purposes of movement building, organizing, and social-service recognition. In the United States and Canada, this may include transsexuals, transvestites, cross-dressers, female and male impersonators, persons with intersex conditions, butches, studs, femmes, fem queens, drag queens, drag kings, feminine-identified men, masculine-identified women, MTF, FTM, trannies, gender variants, gender queers, boi dykes, trans men, trans guys, trans women, bigender, two spirit, intergender, neutrois, pan gender, third gender, gender fluid, and so forth. People who place themselves in any of the above categories may or may not identify with the collective term "transgender." [...]

**Transsexual:** Medical and popular term describing persons with significant cross-gender identity. Due to varying life circumstances, transsexuals may or may not live in their gender identity some of or all the time; depending on medical access, legal options or restrictions, financial means, physical appropriateness, and desire, transsexuals may or may not change bodily characteristics and/or achieve legal sex reassignment through hormonal and surgical means.

**MTF (Male to Female, also MtF, M2F):** A trans spectrum indicating movement from male (assignment at birth based on perceived physical sex) to female (gender identity); it includes personal and sometimes social recognition of feminine and/or female identity; MTF may or may not include hormonal and/or surgical modifications and/or sex reassignment.

**FTM (Female to Male, also FtM, F2M):** A trans spectrum indicating movement from female (assignment at birth based on perceived physical sex) to male (gender identity); it includes personal and sometimes also social recognition of masculine and/or male identity; FTM may or may not include hormonal and/or surgical modifications and/or sex reassignment.

*Usage consideration:* MTF and FTM are often preferred as adjectives modifying a noun, such as "person" or "spectrum," rather than as a noun substitute. For example, just as one is a "transgender person" rather than "a transgender," one might prefer to be considered an "MtF person" or "person on an MtF spectrum" rather than "an MtF."

**Trans (trans-, trans*) and Trans People:** At this time, "trans" is an inclusive and respectful term available for use by people outside trans communities as well as by those who identify with or as trans; as a general term, it avoids the subcultural specificities and alliances that require specialized knowledge for appropriate use.

*Usage considerations:* "Transgender," "transsexual," and "trans" are words that have institutional recognition in many English-speaking countries, but many people who would be included under the "transgender umbrella" do not identify with them. For example, some people with trans histories reject being considered trans-(anything) but instead are men or women, period. Furthermore, identities are generally community-specific and thus may also be specific to class, race, nationality, location, age, and so forth. [...]

**Cisgender, Cissexual:** From the Latin prefix "cis," meaning on the same side or staying with the same orientation, "cisgender" and "cissexual" name the characteristic of staying with or being perceived to stay with the gender and/or sex one was assigned at birth.

**Cis-privilege:** The privilege and power accorded to people who are perceived to follow the norms associated with the sex they are perceived to be and assumed to have been assigned at birth. People who trans gender as well as people who do not may receive cis-privileges, and people who do not intentionally trans gender as well as people who do are denied cis-privileges if they fail to pass (or pass enough) in the sex/gender they are expected to be.

**Sexual Preference (or Identity or Orientation):** Sexual identity and gender identity are two different things.

Sexual identity (or preference) has to do with sexual, erotic, and/or emotional attractions, interests, and orientations. For each person, sexual identity may have nothing or everything to do with gender identity and body type. Like all people, trans people may be gay, bi, lesbian, straight, asexual, pansexual, queer, and so forth; similarly, people across all sexual identities may or may not be trans.

**A Note on Transgender and Intersex:** These two categories are distinct but may overlap and form an alliance. As with the general population, some people who have intersex conditions are trans-identified; in addition, some trans people may consider their trans-ness itself to be one form of intersex condition. [...] Trans and intersex movements achieve alliance based on the overlap (some people occupy both categories), especially on the shared goal of sex/gender self-determination and the right to respectful medical care.

---

*Source:* Enke, A. Finn. (2012). Excerpted from "Note on Terms and Concepts." In *Transfeminist Perspectives in and beyond Transgender and Gender Studies* (pp. 16–20). Philadelphia, PA: Temple University Press.

# CHAPTER 21

## Between the Village and the Village People: Negotiating Community, Ethnicity, and Safety in Gender Fluid Parenting

*May Friedman*

May Friedman is an associate professor at Ryerson University in the School of Social Work and in the Ryerson/York University Joint Graduate Program in Communication and Culture. Her recent publications include "Reproducing Fat-Phobia: Reproductive Technologies and Fat Women's Right to Mother" and "Here Comes a Lot of Judgement: Honey Boo Boo as a Site of Reclamation and Resistance."

"Why don't you just buy him a gun? It would be just as dangerous!" This is my mother's impassioned response to my decision to allow my four-year-old son to wear a skirt.

Although I am explicit about my feminist values and have attempted to raise my children in a gender fluid context, this is the moment where all of the vague allusions I have made come to a head, where all the dolls and trucks for my sons and daughter unambiguously solidify into a message my mother finally can't ignore: I am going to honour my small son's sartorial decision-making and allow him to wear "girls'" clothing. All the groundwork I had thought I'd laid over the years has obviously not made the impression I expected because my mother is exactly as shocked as she would have been had I given my boy a loaded gun.

I attempt to weakly deflect her anger, to shield my children from her outrage, to explain my commitment to this value system, but leave her house with a sick feeling in the pit of my stomach. My mother, notorious for calling me multiple times a day, does not communicate with me for more than a week and takes weeks longer to drop her frosty tone.

There are a number of ways to read this interaction. On the one hand, it is easy to give a simple reading: my mother, an older, immigrant woman, is unfamiliar with contemporary outlooks on gender and is thus amusingly outraged by this most gentle of forays into gender fluidity. A more nuanced response would look at the oppression and danger experienced in her countries of origin and would respond to her passion as a natural extension of her complicated life history. Alternatively, we may examine my mother's strongly normative gender identity as a safety blanket as her other identities (age, citizenship, ethnicity) have been shifting and unstable.

All of these readings of our conversation are true, and yet none are adequate, none address how bereft I feel at her scorn and fury, or how complicated are the intricacies of our relationship, and of her relationship to her grandson and subsequent grandchildren. These readings are also not the story I want to tell, of the simple uneducated Orientalized immigrant woman who doesn't "get" "our" enlightened values (Arat-Koç). That reading is both disrespectful to my mother (and my roots) and doesn't acknowledge the force of our familial ties.

If there is a village raising my children, my mother is on the town council. She is a central part of our lives, and the tension between the need for her support and her inability—for whatever reason—to share my parenting values cannot be read as her "simpleness." The truth is far from simple.

## SHARING THE CARING

How do we take care? How can we ensure that our children live safe and authentic lives? I increasingly find myself with two competing and contradictory responses to this question. Answer one says that we cannot provide safety alone, that mythic nuclear families are simply insufficient to provide for the complex needs of children, and indeed, their parents (Kinser). The second answer, however, is the answer that comes when I am frightened. When I am made aware of my race, I want to protect my children from racism. When I fear the repercussions of living in a female body, I want to surround them with enlightened feminists. And when they explore their gender diversity, using the tools I have been trying to give them for years, I am shocked by my own hesitation, my own fear and desire to limit their environment to safe allies. Yet to do so is to court disaster in other realms.

I've written about our need to assume responsibility for one another, as individuals, families, and communities (Friedman). As a social work academic, I am strongly committed to the notion of shared responsibility culminating in the formal response of a robust welfare state. I believe that we all experience contingencies in our lives and that having a strong societal support system (not merely the informal networks of family and friends) is essential to our continued well-being (Baines). This is especially so in the wearying realm of parenthood where liberal individualism would have us, mothers in particular, assume sole responsibility for the avalanche of minutiae associated with maintaining life and socializing small humans (O'Reilly). On a political level, I advocate for national childcare, state support for single mothers and other impoverished parents. On both instrumental and psychological levels, I do not believe we were meant to go it alone. This can be seen in my parenting practice, in my attempt to ensure that my children experience multiple secure attachments to their caregivers. Aiming to disrupt the perceived normativity of our immediate family, we discuss our kids' "grown-ups"—Mama, Daddy, Safta, Saba, Sabrina, Doda Judy, Bubie, Zadie, their teachers, our neighbours, friends, etc. And indeed, especially in their infancies, it felt like we were able to participate in a nuanced patchwork of caregiving, assisted by those around us in negotiating the work of sustaining young life.

It may seem that my commitment to this shared and communal parenting practice is born from ideology, yet, like all praxis, it begins with very tangible realities: in my case, the reality of blending complicated and intense employment with a desire for multiple children. I can no longer say whether my commitment to communality grew with my family or allowed my family to grow, yet here we are with many, many allies in our parenting (though of course, the final burdens of total responsibility, and the legal assignment of liability remain my partner's and mine alone). What I could not foresee as my children's needs grew beyond immediate physical care and increasingly into the realm of political and emotional choices, was the impact of diversifying their care team beyond our intimate bubble. If we share their care, we have a different responsibility to allow others to weigh in on parenting choices, a notion that is anathema in a neo-liberal environment that controls parental choice through dominant discourse, but purports to leave the transmission of values to parents alone. When my children were tiny, I would have blithely agreed that monolithic parental control was both unrealistic and not in children's best interest. Then I bought my son a skirt.

## FEMINISM AS A SECOND LANGUAGE

I did not grow up with feminism. Unlike many of my friends and colleagues who became politicized in childhood or adolescence, who attended protests and discussed the intersections of personal and political with their families of origin, my consciousness was raised at a much later stage. It was not until graduate school (shortly after my enormous spectacle of a wedding, complete with name change) that my "click" moment occurred. Suddenly, I found language to describe the nagging discomfort I had felt for years, the vague recognition that things were not as they should be. My indistinct commitment to a moral life was abruptly reconfigured as a strong dedication to social justice.

The contemporary feminism that I espouse engages with critical race theory and a reckoning of both heterosexism and homophobia, considers the social model of disability and (less than I'd like) the impact of class (Hernández and Rehman; Wilson, Sengupta, and Evans); it functions as "a polysemic site of contradictory positionalities" (Shohat 2). This post-structuralist, post-colonial moment has allowed me to make sense of my own life and identity as well as the complex world I inhabit. My engagement with

feminism thus affected my parenting before I even began to grow my family. I knew the impact of gender, race, and class on my own life; I could see more clearly my areas of privilege. Most of all, I wanted to live an empowered life despite motherhood, and wanted to ensure that my children had complete access to all opportunities and experiences, regardless of their sex or gender. My commitment to these ideals grew quickly alongside my parenting. I was frustrated at the extent to which becoming parents allowed my relationship with my partner to regress to problematic gender roles (though years of provocative conversation have had a remarkable impact on these concerns). I was, and am, incredibly dismayed at the limitations placed on my older son and daughter in particular, the extent to which my son has been dubbed smart and strong, lauded for his physical ability, while my daughter was praised for her beautiful penmanship (pengirlship?) and capacity for independent play. One of the many joys of welcoming our third child was the extent to which this little person was allowed a distinct personality without every trait, every difference from his siblings, being immediately put down to sex.

Co-parenting with my partner has itself required an intense negotiation, and an awareness of the ways that parenting in a heterosexual union presents its own version of gender entrenchment. His martial arts training, my baking, my preference for laundry while he takes out the garbage—these hobbies and chores are not benign choices. Likewise, when we play to our strengths as parents, my children may view their female parent doing detail oriented work and keeping track of things like appointments and deadlines, while their male parent may sometimes seem like more fun. On the other hand, there are ways we subvert these binaries, make choices that work against expectations. Certainly, we stand together in our attempts to maintain an awareness of the ways that gender works on us and with us as parents, and as people.

Gender fluid parenting isn't about letting them wear each the "other" gender's clothes, though of course, we encourage them to do so. It isn't about buying them dolls and trucks. It's about aiming for ongoing complicated conversations that encourage them to understand how their ideas and identities are formed. It's about helping them keep doors open, to allow them to become their most authentic selves. This involves an exploration of race, of ability, a consideration of the reading of my fat, brown body and their white skin and the ways other identities intersect with gender. It's about asserting both the centrality of gender on their lives, and, simultaneously, its fundamental irrelevance.

These are radical values, ideas that are fundamentally contrary to the dominant discourses about how boys and girls, and mothers and fathers, *should* act. It's an uphill battle to uphold these values in the face of school, media, peers, and virtually all other influences blaring the need for specific and delineated gender that matches genitalia, to encourage critical thought instead of mindless conformity. As Dan Kois asserts, "… any parent raising kids in 2012 knows that it's still not simple navigating a culture that seems intent on selling princess dresses to girls (even if the princesses who wear them are spunky, smart, and Brave) and superhero outfits to boys (even if the superheroes are—well, they're pretty much still all muscly dudes)." It is tempting to believe that I am best served by protecting my kids as much as possible from the influence of the outside world, by aiming to limit their loving relationships to only myself and my co-parent, or perhaps a tiny circle of allies. Yet to do so works in direct conflict with my aim to remain empowered as a mother. In my particular context, empowered motherhood is achieved by allowing my children to be bombarded with love, by inviting the people in my family and community to join me in caring for these young people. Asking for help, asking for community, however, makes the "values" message less coherent, and, especially in the case of intimate caregivers like my mother, requires that I cede control, that I grant buy-in. I cannot share my children solely on my terms without severely restricting my access to both instrumental and emotional support.

## HAVING IT ALL

Suggesting that my children benefit from a wealth of caregivers only to give me a break diminishes the full potential of these contradictory and complicated relationships. By spending time with many people who love them, my children have learned to embrace ambiguity, to understand (respectful) conflict, and have had their certainty about adult omnipotence severely challenged. Arguably, their capacity for critical thought has been extended by their access to so many different points of view. They have learned about things that I cannot teach them. When they talk to their grandfather about how he left his whole family behind to avoid remaining a soldier, they learn about gender. When they learn about their grandmother's experiences in law school while parenting their father as a young child, they learn about heteronormativity. When they witness, or talk to their aunt about her decision to parent her children in a hyper-gendered way, they are exercising their critical capacity to understand how gender marks our beliefs and intersects with systems such as religion and class. Both positive and negative influences thus allow my children to learn much more than they would if I restricted them, by some wizardry, to a perfect progressive enclave. Yet such an analysis does not take into account their safety, the ways that I flinch when a family member says something homophobic, or how I recoil when the conversation turns to a patronizing analysis of racialized nannies, and the trouble with finding "good help." I am looking for "good help," and I am frightened of the implications of sharing my children with people who love them, but who do not express that love in terms of acceptance or respect for difference. I am especially fearful of the implications of normative gender models, given the high rate of suicide among gender diverse young people: Kim Pearson of the Trans Youth Family Allies suggests that "Trans kids are the highest suicide risk on the planet, bar none" (quoted in Green). I cannot say whether my children will push beyond the limits of the sexes listed on their birth certificates, but I will be damned if I will lose them because they are afraid to.

Given the impossibility of "safe space," I nonetheless want to help my children avoid hateful influences, to feel free to explore their potential, especially with people who purport to love them. It is sometimes tempting to limit access in the name of safety. As I navigate this terrain, I realize the extent to which I remain closeted about my beliefs and desires in the heart of my family of origin. I take note of the ways that my decision to partner with a man has allowed me to "pass" for so long that I have forgotten the depth of the normativity with which I was raised. Yet to portray my origins as normative is also a distortion, also doesn't tell the whole story.

## OUTSIDE/IN

Some days, it feels like I live my life in two modes. I am the confident feminist academic, examining representations of motherhood in the public sphere and teaching my students about the perils of hegemonic identity markers. Other times, however, I'm just "Baby May."

"Baby May" is the way I'm known in my family of origin. Nine years younger than my only sibling, I will never not be the baby, no matter how many degrees I get or children I bear. And because sometimes I am weary of arguing, it is sometimes comforting to retreat to this place, a place where critical thought is given much less value than high fashion.

Coming from extreme poverty, racism, and marginalization, the class privilege that my family of origin has achieved is tempered by insecurity, by experiences as both refugees and immigrants. Our shifting geographical base has prioritized our familial connections, which may be why being "Baby May" is so seductive, so safe. In their own ways, my family and community of origin are quite politicized but are often very conservative as a means of erasing their past vulnerabilities and maintaining their own need

for untouchable safety in the present day. Their biases and hostilities toward my progressive beliefs are not borne of ignorance, but of a complex amalgam of fear, history, and love—of a feeling that their conservatism will save my children and me the pain of being an outsider, of being reviled for my identity. Bizarrely, in my particular experience, my family and I are attempting to solve the same problem—responding to difference—by enacting two opposing solutions. I attempt to embrace difference and fluidity in gender, sexuality, and in all other realms. They smile grimly at my naïveté and advise me, in their words and their actions, to avoid standing out, to annihilate difference whenever possible and to "pass" for as long as I can.

The conservatism of my places of origin makes me deeply uncomfortable, but it is its own sort of home. By contrast, emigrating to my progressive neighbourhood downtown has surrounded me with parenting allies, with hip gender-bending kids on the monkey bars at our local park. Yet this shift has not always been perfectly comfortable. In some respects, I feel unstably situated in this domain, surrounded by relatively class-privileged and educated (and overwhelming white) neighbours. As Paula Austin beautifully articulates, "I have felt left out of feminism mostly because it leaves out women who looked like my mother" (167). Like others who inhabit liminal identities (Walker; Weiner-Mahfuz), sometimes I feel like an outlier wherever I dwell.

I fear that by analyzing my own experiences, I lend fuel to the stereotypical construction of raised consciousness as solely the domain of privileged bodies, and of gender fluidity as exclusively a white enterprise (Tokawa). I cringe a bit when I am admired for my parenting practice, when I hear "they are so lucky to have you!" The cringing is because I am merely muddling my way through, making endless, future-therapy-inducing errors, scolding when I should listen, pushing away when I should gather my children close, wrestling with the challenge of being myself and being accountable. I can't hear that I'm doing this well when I know how many ways

I may be parenting poorly. At the same time, however, there is a deeper discomfort behind my resistance to acknowledging the praise of my parenting practice: especially when issued in response to my concerns about difficult moments with other loved ones and caregivers, these accolades feel fraught. Sometimes, it feels like the subtext of the compliment is an acknowledgement that we are so much more enlightened than our forebears; that we are more educated than the people around us.

As someone who did not grow up steeped in feminism, this analysis makes me squirm. It feels like so recently that I was the person making ham-handed comments, that I could so easily have stayed in my well-intentioned, charity model, uncritical compassion. I am aware of the ways that the rhetoric, in my case, may be true—that I have had my consciousness raised through education, and that that is an unearned and complicated privilege. I am also aware of the politicization of many of the people around me through sites of extreme oppression, of my immigrant and Aboriginal colleagues who understand "revolution" in visceral ways that I will never access, of my marginalized friends who know the meaning of activism in their bodies, in tangible and critical moments. I don't want to write the story of the educated English speaking daughter who raises her kids "right," protecting them from the biased and unenlightened views of her immigrant parents. That story is limited and limiting and does everyone, my parents, my children, and myself, a great disservice.

My resistance to the notion of gender fluid parenting as exclusively the domain of educated Western parents does not merely take issue with this supposition as a misrepresentation of the many forms of complicated gender expression that occur in non-Western contexts (Comeau). Rather, on a personal level, I fear my children becoming entitled to activism. Suddenly, I am raising the people who will blithely discuss the protests they attended with their mama, who will take for granted the need for social transformation. In this context, it can be easy to raise children who

will become unthinkingly critical, who will develop a critical lens that may not be informed by the hard work of consciousness raising, but will instead merely allow them to see critical thought as a new dogma, a "right way" in opposition to the thoughtless people around them. As one respondent in a study done by Tey Meadow suggests, however, this is not the goal of gender fluid parenting: "I don't think parenting is having our kids grow up and making little us's. It's how do we create the safe, comfortable, competent environment where they get to grow up and be themselves, whoever that is? And are there limits to that? Yes, but within a certain broad bandwidth they get to discover who they are" (737).

## CONCLUSIONS

I want my children to play with gender. I want my children to be critical and authentic and to have the relative safety to name and choose their identity markers. Fostering a thoughtful response to difference, however, means understanding my mother's rage. It means understanding both why I believe my mother is wrong, that my son should get his skirt, and also her complex and convoluted reasons for being so very angry. It means teaching my children to challenge, rather than to dismiss. As Amber Kinser writes, "Every moment of mother-relating for me also is a moment of relating-in-multiplicity, of trying to reduce the friction of opposing demands of multiple selves and relationships. Survival in feminist mothering necessitates coming to see this rubbing against, this friction, this tension, not as purely oppositional and therefore needing to be resolved, but as inherent and necessary, and not in need of fixing" (124).

Teaching critical thought, teaching my children to challenge is not best done alone. I cannot model a successful critique of a neo-liberal paradigm of individualism and efficiency by keeping them to myself in order to ensure a coherent message. Instead, I have to hope that being surrounded by love and contradiction will hone their critical skills, that being forced to confront differences of opinion (some of them very painful) will give them a greater capacity for understanding. I appreciate that this response invites controversy, that in inviting dialogue rather than certainty I may expose my children to hatred, that I am privileging imperfect love over perfect safety. Yet this is all I know how to do, not following any manual, not following any sage advice, but just trusting my instincts, navigating this knife edge between where I am and where I come from and hoping that I will not fail too badly, that my best will be good enough.

## REFERENCES

Arat-Koç, Sedef. "Whose Social Reproduction? Transnational Motherhood and Challenges to Feminist Political Economy." *Social Reproduction: Feminist Political Economy Challenges Neo-Liberalism.* Eds. Kate Bezanson and Meg Luxton. Montreal: McGill-Queen's University Press, 2006. 75–92. Print.

Austin, Paula. "Femme-Inism: Lessons of My Mother." *Colonize This: Young Women of Color on Today's Feminism.* Eds. Daisy Hernández and Bushra Rehman. Emeryville: Seal Press, 2002. 157–169. Print.

Baines, Donna, ed. *Doing Anti-Oppressive Practice: Social Justice Social Work.* Halifax: Fernwood Publishing, 2011. Print.

Comeau, Lisa M. "Towards White, Anti-Racist Mothering Practices: Confronting Essentialist Discourses of Race and Culture." *Journal of the Association for Research on Mothering* 9.2 (2007): 20–30. Print.

Friedman, May. *Mommyblogs and the Changing Face of Motherhood.* Toronto: University of Toronto Press, 2013. Print.

Green, Jesse. "S/He: Why Parents of Transgender Children Are Faced with a Difficult Decision." *New York Magazine.* Web. 27 May, 2012.

Hernández, Daisy, and Bushra Rehman, eds. *Colonize This! Young Women of Color on Today's Feminism.* Emeryville: Seal Press, 2002. Print.

Kinser, Amber E. "Mothering as Relational Consciousness." *Feminist Mothering.* Ed. Andrea O'Reilly. Albany: SUNY Press, 2008. 123–142. Print.

Kois, Dan. "Free to Be." *Slate.* Web. 22 October, 2012.

Meadow, Tey. "'Deep Down Where the Music Plays': How Parents Account for Childhood Gender Variance." *Sexualities* 14.6 (2011): 725–747. Print.

O'Reilly, Andrea, ed. *Mother Outlaws: Theories and Practices of Empowered Mothering.* Toronto: Women's Press, 2004. Print.

Shohat, Ella. *Taboo Memories, Diasporic Voices.* Durham: Duke University Press, 2006.

Tokawa, Kenji. "Why You Don't Have to Choose a White Boy Name to be a Man in this World." *Gender Outlaws: The Next Generation.* Eds. Kate Bornstein and S. Bear Bergman. Berkeley: Seal Press, 2010. Print.

Walker, Rebecca. *Black, White and Jewish: Autobiography of a Shifting Self.* New York: Riverhead Books, 2001. Print.

Weiner-Mahfuz, Lisa. "Organizing 101: A Mixed-Race Feminist in Movements for Social Justice." *Colonize This: Young Women of Color on Today's Feminism.* Eds. Daisy Hernández and Bushra Rehman. Emeryville: Seal Press, 2002. 29–39. Print.

Wilson, Shamillah, Anasuya Sengupta, and Kristy Evans, eds. *Defending Our Dreams: Global Feminist Voices for a New Generation.* London: Zed Books, 2005. Print.

**Source:** Friedman, May. (2013). "Between the Village and The Village People: Negotiating Community, Ethnicity, and Safety in Gender Fluid Parenting." In Joy Green & May Friedman (Eds.), *Chasing Rainbows: Exploring Gender Fluid Parenting Practices* (pp. 99–110). Bradford, ON: Demeter Press.

## MEN AND FEMINISM

*The White Ribbon Campaign*

## Who We Are

White Ribbon is the world's largest movement of men and boys working to end violence against women and girls, promote gender equity, healthy relationships and a new vision of masculinity.

Starting in 1991, we asked men to wear white ribbons as a pledge to never commit, condone or remain silent about violence against women and girls. Since then the White Ribbon has spread to over 60 countries around the world.

We work to examine the root causes of gender-based violence and create a cultural shift that helps bring us to a future without violence.

Our vision is for a masculinity that embodies the best qualities of being human. We believe that men are part of the solution and part of a future that is safe and equitable for all people.

Through education, awareness-raising, outreach, technical assistance, capacity building, partnerships and creative campaigns, White Ribbon is helping create tools, strategies and models that challenge negative, outdated concepts of manhood and inspire men to understand and embrace the incredible potential they have to be a part of positive change.

## What We Do

White Ribbon positively engages men, young men and boys through relevant educational programming that challenges language and behaviours, as well as harmful ideas of manhood that lead to violence against women.

Our programming includes:

**Workshops, Talks, and Presentations**

- Engaging workshops, presentations and talks with elementary, middle, high school and post-secondary students.
- Trainings and presentations for educators and teacher candidates around promoting gender equality in classrooms and schools.
- Sessions explore realities for women and girls as well as pressures on men and boys and ways they can become allies for change that affects everyone.
- Topics include "Building Allyship Together With Women and Girls to End Gender-Based Violence," "Building Allyship and Unpacking 'Bro-Culture,'" "Building Allyship and Exploring My Own Role and Commitment to Ending Gender-Based Violence," and "Building Allyship Through Story-Telling and Action Planning."

### It Starts With You, It Stays With Him

- Encouraging and inspiring fathers, father figures, educators, community leaders, coaches and family members to embrace being positive, strong role models for the young men and boys around them by valuing women as equal and teaching how to have healthy, equal relationships.
- Tips, Tools, e-Modules and Videos to view and share.

### Draw The Line

- Interactive campaign that aims to engage Ontarians in a dialogue about sexual violence.
- Challenging common myths about sexual violence, equipping bystanders with information on how to intervene safely and effectively.
- Series of scenario postcards and posters, PSAs and podcasts.
- Resources include: Drawling the Line on Sexual Violence: A Guide for Ontario Educators (Grades 1-8); Drawing the Line on Sexual Violence: A Guide for Ontario Educators (9-12).

### Boys Conferences

- Annual conferences in partnership with Elementary Teachers' Federation of Ontario bringing boys together to discuss gender equality, respect and healthy relationships and steps they can take to make a difference. Uses interactive workshops, drama, art, video, peer educators and other engaging facilitation styles, guest speakers.

### Huddle Up & Make The Call

- Utilizes the power of student-led initiatives and athlete testimonials to address gender-based violence in secondary schools in the Greater Toronto Area.
- Promoting and supporting equitable, healthy relationships and safe environments for all students, Make The Call empowers and inspires students to engage their peers and communities in ending all forms of violence against women and girls.
- This initiative is proudly brought to you by the Toronto Argonauts and White Ribbon, with support from Status of Women Canada and Tim Hortons.

### National Community of Practice [NCoP] Project

- Funded by Status of Women Canada, White Ribbon worked in collaboration with nine women's, youth, and community-based organizations across Canada to create a community of practice. Together we shared lessons learned, key challenges, and developed a national evaluation framework for gender-based violence prevention programming. The national evaluation framework is a comprehensive tool which assesses changes across individual, social, organizational and community capacity. To learn more about CoP national partners and examples of the ways in which men and boys are interrogating their power and privilege to promote gender equality, visit the National community of practice toolkit (http://www.canpreventgbv.ca/toolkit/about-the-toolkit/).

### What Makes A Man Conference

- What Makes A Man is a discussion-focused event exploring how ideas of masculinity and gender affect everyone in all walks of life. The unique trademark of WMAM is how we reduce the line between expert and listener, as we are all experts in our lived experiences! Diverse speakers share short informal talks designed to spark a following discussion with the audience.

### The Education and Action Kit

- White Ribbon's Education and Action Kit is used by hundreds of thousands of teachers and students in 3000 schools across North America. Teachers and students have used the Kit and related White Ribbon resources with enormous success. The Kit combines in-class lessons with school-wide projects to raise awareness about violence against women, and to promote ideals about gender equality and healthy relationships. It is designed as a positive resource for both females and males.

**Campaign in a Box**

- The Campaign in a Box is a set of fully interactive exercises designed to help teach and promote healthy equal relationships among boys and girls in grades 5-8.

*Source:* Excerpted from the White Ribbon Campaign. (n.d.) Retrieved from: www.whiteribbon.ca.

*Source:* Men Can Stop Rape. (2008). Retrieved from: http://www. mystrength.org/8.0.html (site no longer active). Current campaigns can be found here: http://www.mencanstoprape.org.

# CHAPTER 22

## Troubling Genders, Subverting Identities:
## An Interview with Judith Butler

*Vasu Reddy and Judith Butler*

Judith Butler is Maxine Elliot Professor in the Department of Comparative Literature and the Program of Critical Theory at the University of California–Berkeley. Her many honours include the Brudner Prize from Yale University, the Adorno Prize from the City of Frankfurt, the Andrew Mellon Award for Distinguished Academic Achievement in the Humanities, and the Albertus Magnus Professorship from the City of Cologne, Germany. She is considered a leading intellectual in gender, feminist, and queer studies, and her books have been translated into more than twenty languages. Butler's theory of performativity, introduced in her book *Gender Trouble*, has significantly shaped our understanding of gender and has had a major influence on feminist and queer scholarship.

Vasu Reddy is the executive director of the Human and Social Development research programme at the Human Sciences Research Council (HSRC). He is an honorary associate professor and research fellow at the University of KwaZulu-Natal.

In this interview we engage Judith Butler, one of the most challenging, influential and refreshing thinkers of our time. [...]

It is difficult to summarize the work of Butler. [...] In one sense her ongoing tenacious interrogation of the ontology of language and discourse is critical to her thinking [...]. Whereas some critics have venomously indicated that her work represents a verbal politics as opposed to a concern with the material conditions of women's lives, Butler's work (indeed her ideas), however, demonstrate otherwise. Since the publication of *Gender Trouble*, her work continues to shape, impact and influence different fields of inquiry, including and especially gender and sexuality studies, feminist and queer theory, cultural studies and, to some extent the humanities academy as a whole. In the preface to the second edition of *Gender Trouble: Feminism and the Subversion of Identity* (1999: xvi), a foundational text in critical gender studies, Butler writes:

> Despite the dislocation of the subject that the text performs, there is a person here: I went to many meetings, bars, and marches and saw many kinds of genders, understood

myself to be at the crossroads of some of them, and encountered sexuality at several of its cultural edges.

Her work disturbs, provokes and challenges the relationship between politics and the critique of identity, thereby implying that her experiential ground continues to remain intact in relation to her verbal politics (1999: xxii):

> What continues to concern me most is the following kinds of questions: what will and will not constitute an intelligible life, and how do presumptions about normative gender and sexuality determine in advance what will qualify as the 'human' and the 'livable'.

It is especially in this context that we invite (and encourage) our diverse readership to consider Butler's thinking in relation to how men and women may continue to engage theory and analysis from an activist perspective.

**Vasu: You have been critical about the essentialism in some feminist work, including the reluctance of some feminists to return to biology. You are also critical of the essentialism evident in some aspects of the gay and queer movements. Added to this is your view that categories such as 'man', 'woman', 'male' and 'female' are too displaced. Why?**

Judith: The debate between essentialism and social constructionism was strong about ten years ago. I find that the terms have become complicated recently. It is no longer possible to take a strict view on either side. I was part of a group of feminists (there were many I would include in this group) who were very concerned about how the categories of 'woman' or 'women' were used and understood in feminist discourse. [...] If I want to be able to refer to the gender that I am, the sex that I am, the way I see the world, and I need

these references in order to define myself, I better know what these terms imply before I commit myself to them as part of any self-description. It is for this reason, if not for others, that it is crucial to find out the meaning of the category of 'women' as it has been historically wrought and politically mobilized.

**Vasu: You turn to performativity as a possible improvement on social construction. You emphasise that identity or, for that matter, gender identity is a performative construct? What is the logic in conceiving identity in this way? [...]**

Judith: The first point to understand about performativity is what it is not: identities are *not* made in a single moment in time. They are made again and again. This does not mean identities are made radically new every time they are made, but only that it takes some time for identities to be brought out; they are dynamic and historical. In fact if we ask what is distinctive about 'being' human, it will probably turn out that human being is always about becoming. There is always a question of what I will become, even if I am living in such a way that seeks to refuse that question. There is always a question of whether what I was yesterday will be precisely the same as what I become in time. Tomorrow is there a possibility for me to become otherwise than what I am? This is not just a question of a private struggle with the self, but of the social terms by which identities are supported and articulated. In this sense it is always in the context of a certain constellation of social power that I am able to pose the question of my own becoming differently. Through what constellations of social discourse and power was I brought into the world? And how is it that I might inhabit or revise the world such that my own way of being might also change? We are interpreted by social means; the language we have for what is most intimately our own is already given to us from elsewhere. This means that in the most intimate encounters with ourselves, the most intimate moments of disclosure, we call upon a language that we never made in order to say who we are. In this sense we are exposed to the social, impinged upon by the social, in ways that precede my doing, but any doing that might come to be called my own is dependent upon this very unchosen domain. My view is that there are norms into which we are born—gendered, racial, national—that decide what kind of subject we can be, but in being those subjects, in occupying and inhabiting those deciding norms, in incorporating and performing them, we make use of local options to rearticulate them in order to revise their power. Norms cannot be embodied without an action of a specific kind, and they cannot continue to enforce themselves without a continual action. It is in the thinking through of this action that change can happen, since we are acting all the time in the ways that we enact, repeat, appropriate and refuse the norms that decide our social ontology. You will see that I subscribe neither to free will nor to determinism in these debates. Social terms decide our beings, but they do not decide them once and for all. They also establish the conditions by which a certain constrained agency, even a decision, is possible on our parts.

**Vasu: Your theory of materialisation renders the material category of sex into a site of permanent contestation? If this is a correct assessment, why do you hold this view, and what spin-offs does it hold for understanding agency and the subject?**

Judith: I began the theory of materialisation in response to the question of the physical matter that is said to constitute lived bodies. [...] I think if we want to accord dignity to bodies, to their suffering, to their desires, then we cannot reduce the body in advance to the status of pure matter.

The body is a site of vulnerability, of longing, of suffering, disease, reproduction (sometimes), dying and death. To understand any of these profoundly human dimensions of bodily experience, we have to consider the body as something that not only occupied specific sites and places, but something that is also in time, temporalised. It is impinged upon, for instance, by social norms, but it also enters into extended ways of living, modes of appropriating and re-enacting social norms, ways of giving material substance to norms that can only be described as processes in time. So whatever concept of 'materiality' we come up with to describe the living and dying of bodies will have to be one that takes time into account, not as a contingent feature of bodily experience, but as a necessary one. It would be wrong to think about bodies as inert matter; except in those cases where they have ended up in that state by virtue of death [...] Cultural imprints on the body become a part of the very physiology of the body, so that it becomes impossible to separate the biological from the cultural in ways that some people used to do. Our responses to social environments over time are part of what produces the so-called 'facts' of the biological body. And all such a formulation implies is that it will not work to separate the body from cultural discourse. That said, causal models that reduce culture to biology or biology to culture misrepresent the dynamic and historical process of their interplay. [...] As a consequence, we should not treat the body as a kind of slate or surface on which cultural meanings are imposed. The body is that which embodies and enacts certain kinds of social meanings. [...]

**Vasu: In the past decade, the world has witnessed an increase in the homophobia displayed by several African leaders. Like Zimbabwean president Mugabe, his counterparts from Namibia, Swaziland, Zambia, Uganda and Kenya have virulently opposed homosexuality, labelling it**

a 'scourge' that goes against Christian teachings and African traditions. In *Excitable Speech* (1997) you address some of these issues in relation to hate speech. Are these expressions of 'excitable speech' in any way unique to Africa, and what observations do you have about this beyond the description that these utterances are examples of hate speech and homophobic discourse?

**Judith:** You know, I think that there are questions that arise when Mugabe makes his claims comparing homosexuals to animals or saying that lesbian and gay people sacrifice their very status as human beings by virtue of their homosexuality. In such extreme statements, it is not only a matter of Mugabe having the right to express his private view. His speech is public discourse, and it affects employment, it affects where people can move, it affects who can make a housing claim, who may secure adoption rights, who has access to health care, who lives and who dies. I fear that these are murderous words.

**Vasu:** In *Bodies That Matter* you raise the question of 'freedom of choice' and that our gender choices are limited rather than 'free'. In what ways are our gender choices limited, and what concerns does this raise for questions about agency?

**Judith:** Many people tend to think within the terms of a classical political liberalism, assuming that either we are free or we are restrained. For me, though, restraint is a condition of freedom. By the fact that we are socially constructed, we were born into a world we never made. We do not have a lot of choice about who our parents are, who raises us. There are many things that come to us from the outside that we do not choose. And yet there is always the question of how to live these various conditions. You'll note that 'live' becomes a transitive verb. And I do not believe that these various conditions determine

us absolutely, although sometimes social power can take away our lives or the lives of others, and agency is vitiated. Social conditions that determine us absolutely, restrict us absolutely, and actually produce victims of all of us. Sometimes this describes the situation well, especially when we are, quite against our will, subject to an annihilating violence. But it would be wrong to devise a theory about social construction that takes that model as the norm. If we were to do so, then, we are always already victims. And no political agency can be derived from this view. On the other hand, the classical liberal position tends to counsel that it does not matter what your social conditions are. If freedom is an inherent attribute of every human, then every human can and ought to 'rise above' social conditions and act. I accept neither the social determinism view nor the classical liberal one.

We cannot become anything we want. You know, there is one reading of *Gender Trouble*, which suggests that a person can become one thing one day and then something radically different the next. I don't think that's true. There is another reading of *Gender Trouble* that concludes that we are fully constituted, we are fully constructed and that means that there is no freedom. I do not think that is true either. I think they are both misunderstandings of what I'm trying to do—understandable misunderstandings, since they subscribe to the two oppositional moments within the framework that I am trying to displace. What is the dilemma of what it is to be constructed, to live that construction, to be part of an ongoing process of constructing? What is done to me, and what is it I do with what is done to me?

**Vasu:** Like *Gender Trouble*, *Bodies That Matter*, and *Excitable Speech*, *The Psychic Life of Power* extends your argument about identity, focusing on how gender 'accomplishments' such as masculinity and femininity, and 'achievements' such as heterosexuality come about. Here too you situate homosexuality at the heart of a 'homosexually panicked' culture. Could you expand on your thinking here?

**Judith:** It comes down to the question of whose lives are regarded as worthy lives, and whose illness is worthy of treatment, and whose dying and death is worthy of acknowledgment and grief. These are issues raised by gay politics during the AIDS crisis, but they are compounded now as the AIDS crisis continues in Africa, and racialisation within the contemporary geopolitical sphere compounds each and every one of these questions. In the North American context, grieving became a political issue with the onset of the AIDS crisis in the '80s and early '90s, and indeed continuing into present time. One of the reasons that lives lost through AIDS were difficult to grieve in the US, and why there was such an important activism centring on public mourning, such as the Names Project, the Quilt, is that it seemed that homosexuality was in this culture, not a real love, and gay lives were not as visible and real as others, and so their deaths, especially their deaths from a stigmatised disease remained, at first, unspeakable, and unmournable. Members of the dominant culture looked over at gay people and silently and openly concluded, 'well their lives are not real lives anyway' and 'their loves are not real loves anyway', and 'their losses are not real losses anyway'; they are just 'playing' or they are just 'copying', or they are just living in a 'shadow world', or an 'unreal world', they haven't 'grown up', or their relations are not legitimate in the way that heterosexual marriages are, then it follows that these lives are devalued, lost before they are lost, unworthy of public grief. [...] If the part of the population that has died is the one 'we never loved', then they are also those we never lost. And yet, there is an elusive death that haunts dominant culture in ways that cannot be readily explained. [...]

**Vasu:** In *What's Left of Theory?* you engage at length with the political uses of theory and literature. Some related questions: Is it still appropriate to talk about the political uses of theory and literature? Is literary theory dead? Where is theory today?

**Judith:** When some critics claim that 'theory is dead' it seems to me that the statement 'theory is dead' is an effort to drive a nail into the coffin and that, in fact, proves that theory is alive. So rather the statement is an effort to accomplish something and make theory into past history. In fact I think it has evolved into a new kind of scholarly work that is much more engaged in cultural practices and popular culture. Most significant is the way that new theory 'moves' between social theory and literary criticism, economic analysis or political theory; it has become disseminated into various disciplinary frames. Certain theoretical questions have hardly gone away. For example, how do we think about the subject? How do we think about explanation? How do we think about interpretation? What is the nation? What is the political? We have to be able to speak not only about this or that political institution or structure, this or that national formation, but the political as a way that groups live together in power. Surely it is theoretical to ask, how might we live with the notion of the future? Literature engages in the charting of possible worlds, theory engages in the charting of possible worlds, it schematises possibility, it does not always tell us what possibilities to realise, or where to go with them, but it opens up a way of seeing the world that can be very disorienting, that can produce another sense of reality, that can destabilise the status quo, that can question deeply what we take for granted as naturalised or realistic versions of the status quo, and that helps open up possibility. [...] If theory does this, then it can be absolutely exhilarating in so far as it opens up this world we thought was so closed to us. [...]

# REFERENCES

Butler J (1990; 1999) *Gender Trouble: Feminism and the Subversion of Identity*, New York & London: Routledge.

Butler J (1993) *Bodies That Matter: On the Discursive Limits of "Sex"*, New York & London: Routledge.

Butler J (1997) *The Psychic Life of Power: Theories in Subjection*, Stanford: Stanford University Press.

Butler J (1997) *Excitable Speech: A Politics of the Performative*, New York & London: Routledge.

Butler J, Guillory J and Thomas K (eds) (2000) *What's Left of Theory? New Works on the Politics of Literary Theory*, London: Routledge.

**Source:** Reddy, Vasu, & Butler, Judith. (2004). Excerpted from "Troubling Genders, Subverting Identities: Interview with Judith Butler." *Agenda, 18*(62), 115–123.

# CHAPTER 23

## Becoming 100 Percent Straight

*Michael A. Messner*

Michael A. Messner is a professor of sociology and gender studies at the University of Southern California. His research areas include men and masculinity, gender relations, and the gendered division of labour in organized sports and athletics. He is the author of over a dozen books, including a history of men's involvement in the anti-violence movement called *Some Men: Feminist Allies and the Movement to End Violence against Women*. He also continues a now 25-year longitudinal study of coverage of women's and men's sports on TV news and highlights shows.

In 1995, as part of my job as the president of the North American Society for the Sociology of Sport, I needed to prepare an hour-long presidential address for the annual meeting of some 200 people. This presented a challenge to me: how might I say something to my colleagues that was interesting, at least somewhat original, and above all, not boring. Students may think that their professors are especially dull in the classroom but, believe me, we are usually much worse at professional meetings. For some reason, many of us who are able to speak to our classroom students in a relaxed manner, using relatively jargon-free language, seem to become robots, dryly reading our papers—packed with impressively unclear jargon—to our yawning colleagues.

Since I desperately wanted to avoid putting 200 sport studies scholars to sleep, I decided to deliver a talk which I entitled "Studying up on Sex." The title, which certainly did get my colleagues' attention, was intended as a play on words, a double entendre. "Studying up" has one generally recognizable colloquial meaning, but in sociology it has another. It refers to studying "up" in the power structure. Sociologists have perhaps most often studied "down"—studying the poor, the blue- or pink-collar workers, the "nuts, sluts, and perverts," the incarcerated. The idea of "studying up" rarely occurs to sociologists unless and until we live in a time when those who are "down" have organized movements that challenge the institutional privileges of elites. For example, in the wake of labor movements, some sociologists like C. Wright Mills studied up on corporate elites. Recently, in the wake of racial and ethnic civil rights movements, some scholars like Ruth Frankenberg have begun to study the social meanings of "whiteness." Much of my research, inspired by feminism, has involved a studying up on the social construction of masculinity in sport. Studying up, in these cases, has raised some fascinating new and important questions about the workings of power in society.

However, I realized that when it comes to understanding the social and interpersonal dynamics of sexual orientation in sport, we have barely begun to scratch the surface of a very complex issue. Although sport studies have benefited from the work of scholars such as Helen Lenskyj (1986, 1997), Brian Pronger (1990), and others who have delineated the experiences of lesbians and gay men in sports, there has been very little extension of their insights into a consideration of the social construction of heterosexuality in sport. In sport, just as in the larger society, we seem obsessed with asking "How do people become gay?" Imbedded in the question is the assumption that people who identify as heterosexual or "straight" require no explanation, since they are simply acting out the "natural" or "normal" sexual orientation. We seem to be saying that the "sexual deviants" require explanation, while the experience of heterosexuals, because we are considered normal, seems to require no critical examination or discussion. But I knew that a closer look at the development of sexual orientation or sexual identity reveals an extremely complex process. I decided to challenge myself and my colleagues by arguing that although we have begun to "study up" on corporate elites in sport, on whiteness, on masculinity, it is now time to extend that by studying up on heterosexuality.

But in the absence of systematic research on this topic, where could I start? How could I explore, raise questions about, and begin to illuminate the social construction of heterosexuality for my colleagues? Fortunately, for the previous two years I have been working with a group of five men (three of whom identified as heterosexual, two as gay) mutually to explore our own biographies in terms of the earlier bodily experiences that helped to shape our gender and sexual identities. We modeled our project after that of a German group of feminist women, led by Frigga Haug, who created a research method which they call "memory work." In short, the women would mutually choose a body part, such as "hair," and each

would then write a short story based on a particularly salient childhood memory that related to their hair (for example, being forced by parents to cut one's hair, deciding to straighten one's curly hair in order to look more like other girls, etc.). Then the group would read all of the stories and discuss them one by one in the hope of gaining more general understanding of, and raising new questions about, the social construction of "femininity." What resulted from this project was a fascinating book called *Female Sexualization* (Haug 1987), which my men's group used as the inspiration for our project.

As a research method, memory work is anything but conventional. Many sociologists would argue that this is not really a "research method" at all. The information that emerges from the project cannot be used very confidently as a generalizable "truth," and in this sort of project the researcher is simultaneously part of what is being studied. How, my more scientifically oriented colleagues might ask, is the researcher to maintain his or her objectivity? My answer is that in this kind of project objectivity is not the point. In fact, the strength of this sort of research is the depth of understanding that might be gained through a systematic group analysis of one's experience, one's subjective orientation to social processes. A clear understanding of the subjective aspect of social life—one's bodily feelings, emotions, and reaction to others—is an invaluable window that allows us to see and ask new sociological questions about group interaction and social structure. In short, group memory work can provide an important, productive, and fascinating insight on social reality, though not a complete (or completely reliable) picture.

As I pondered the lack of existing research on the social construction of heterosexuality in sport, I decided to draw on one of my own stories from my memory work in the men's group. Some of my most salient memories of embodiment are sports memories. I grew up as the son of a high school coach, and I eventually played point guard on my dad's team. In what follows, I juxtapose my story with that of a gay former Olympic athlete, Tom Waddell, whom I had interviewed several years earlier for a book on the lives of male athletes (Messner 1994).

Many years ago, I read some psychological studies that argued that even for self-identified heterosexuals it is a natural part of their development to have gone through "bisexual" or even "homosexual" stages of life. When I read this, it seemed theoretically reasonable, but did not ring true in my experience. I have always been, I told myself, 100 percent heterosexual! The group process of analyzing my own autobiographical stories challenged the concept I had developed of myself, and also shed light on the way in which the institutional context of sport provided a context for the development of my definition of myself as "100 percent straight." Here is one of the stories.

> When I was in the 9th grade, I played on a "D" basketball team, set up especially for the smallest of high school boys. Indeed, though I was pudgy with baby fat, I was a short 5'2", still pre-pubescent with no facial hair and a high voice that I artificially tried to lower. The first day of practice, I was immediately attracted to a boy I'll call Timmy, because he looked like the boy who played in the *Lassie* TV show. Timmy was short, with a high voice, like me. And like me, he had no facial hair yet. Unlike me, he was very skinny. I liked Timmy right away, and soon we were together a lot. I noticed things about him that I didn't notice about other boys: he said some words a certain way, and it gave me pleasure to try to talk like him. I remember liking the way the light hit his boyish, nearly hairless body. I thought about him when we weren't together. He was in the school band, and at the football games, I'd squint to see where he was in the mass of uniforms. In short, though I wasn't conscious of it at the time, I was infatuated with Timmy—I had

a crush on him. Later that basketball season, I decided—for no reason that I could really articulate then—that I hated Timmy. I aggressively rejected him, began to make fun of him around other boys. He was, we all agreed, a geek. He was a faggot.

Three years later, Timmy and I were both on the varsity basketball team, but had hardly spoken a word to each other since we were freshmen. Both of us now had lower voices, had grown to around 6 feet tall, and we both shaved, at least a bit. But Timmy was a skinny, somewhat stigmatized reserve on the team, while I was the team captain and starting point guard. But I wasn't so happy or secure about this. I'd always dreamed of dominating games, of being the hero. Halfway through my senior season, however, it became clear that I was not a star, and I figured I knew why. I was not aggressive enough.

I had always liked the beauty of the fast break, the perfectly executed pick and roll play between two players, and especially the long twenty-foot shot that touched nothing but the bottom of the net. But I hated and feared the sometimes brutal contact under the basket. In fact, I stayed away from the rough fights for rebounds and was mostly a perimeter player, relying on my long shots or my passes to more aggressive teammates under the basket. But now it became apparent to me that time was running out in my quest for greatness: I needed to change my game, and fast. I decided one day before practice that I was gonna get aggressive. While practicing one of our standard plays, I passed the ball to a teammate, and then ran to the spot at which I was to set a pick on a defender. I knew that one could sometimes get away with setting a face-up screen on a player, and then as he makes contact with you, roll your back to him and plant your elbow hard in his stomach. The beauty of this move is that your own body "roll" makes the elbow look like an accident. So I decided to try this move. I approached the defensive player, Timmy, rolled, and planted my elbow deeply into his solar plexus. Air exploded audibly from Timmy's mouth, and he crumbled to the floor momentarily.

Play went on as though nothing had happened, but I felt bad about it. Rather than making me feel better, it made me feel guilty and weak. I had to admit to myself why I'd chosen Timmy as the target against whom to test out my new aggression. He was the skinniest and weakest player on the team.

At the time, I hardly thought about these incidents, other than to try to brush them off as incidents that made me feel extremely uncomfortable. Years later, I can now interrogate this as a sexual story, and as a gender story unfolding within the context of the heterosexualized and masculinized institution of sport. Examining my story in light of research conducted by Alfred Kinsey a half-century ago, I can recognize in myself what Kinsey saw as a very common fluidity and changeability of sexual desire over the life-course. Put simply, Kinsey found that large numbers of adult, "heterosexual" men had previously, as adolescents and young adults, experienced sexual desire for males. A surprisingly large number of these men had experienced sexual contact to the point of orgasm with other males during adolescence or early adulthood. Similarly, my story invited me to consider what is commonly called the "Freudian theory of bisexuality." Sigmund Freud shocked the post-Victorian world by suggesting that all people go through a stage, early in life, when they are attracted to people of the same sex.[1] Adult experiences, Freud argued, eventually led most people to shift their sexual desire to what he

called an appropriate "love object"—a person of the opposite sex. I also considered my experience in light of what lesbian feminist author Adrienne Rich called the institution of compulsory heterosexuality. Perhaps the extremely high levels of homophobia that are often endemic in boys' and men's organized sports led me to deny and repress my own homoerotic desire through a direct and overt rejection of Timmy, through homophobic banter with male peers, and the resultant stigmatization of the feminized Timmy. Eventually, I considered my experience in the light of what radical theorist Herbert Marcuse called the sublimation of homoerotic desire into an aggressive, violent act as serving to construct a clear line of demarcation between self and other. Sublimation, according to Marcuse, involves the driving underground, into the unconscious, of sexual desires that might appear dangerous due to their socially stigmatized status. But sublimation involves more than simple repression into the unconscious. It involves a transformation of sexual desire into something else—often into aggressive and violent acting out toward others. These acts clarify the boundaries between oneself and others and therefore lessen any anxieties that might be attached to the repressed homoerotic desire.

Importantly, in our analysis of my story, the memory group went beyond simply discussing the events in psychological terms. The story did perhaps suggest some deep psychological processes at work, but it also revealed the importance of social context—in this case, the context of the athletic team. In short, my rejection of Timmy and the joining with teammates to stigmatize him in 9th grade stands as an example of what sociologist R. W. Connell calls a moment of engagement with hegemonic masculinity, where I actively took up the male group's task of constructing heterosexual/masculine identities in the context of sport. The elbow in Timmy's gut three years later can be seen as a punctuation mark that occurred precisely because of my fears that I might be failing in this goal.

It is helpful, I think, to compare my story with gay and lesbian "coming out" stories in sport. Though we have a few lesbian and bisexual coming out stories among women athletes, there are very few from gay males. Tom Waddell, who as a closeted gay man, finished sixth in the decathlon in the 1968 Olympics, later came out and started the Gay Games, an athletic and cultural festival that draws tens of thousands of people every four years. When I interviewed Tom Waddell over a decade ago about his sexual identity and athletic career, he made it quite clear that for many years sports was his closet:

> When I was a kid, I was tall for my age, and was very thin and very strong. And I was usually faster than most other people. But I discovered rather early that I liked gymnastics and I liked dance. I was very interested in being a ballet dancer … [but] something became obvious to me right away—that male ballet dancers were effeminate, that they were what most people would call faggots. And I thought I just couldn't handle that … I was totally closeted and very concerned about being male. This was the fifties, a terrible time to live, and everything was stacked against me. Anyway, I realized that I had to do something to protect my image of myself as a male—because at that time homosexuals were thought of primarily as men who wanted to be women. And so I threw myself into athletics—I played football, gymnastics, track and field … I was a jock—that's how I was viewed, and I was comfortable with that.

Tom Waddell was fully conscious of entering sports and constructing a masculine/heterosexual athletic identity precisely because he feared being revealed as gay. It was clear to him, in the context of the 1950s, that being known as gay would undercut his claims to the status of manhood. Thus, though he described the athletic closet as "hot and stifling," he remained there until several years after his athletic retirement. He even knowingly played along with

locker room discussions about sex and women as part of his "cover."

> I wanted to be viewed as male, otherwise I would be a dancer today. I wanted the male, macho image of an athlete. So I was protected by a very hard shell. I was clearly aware of what I was doing … I often felt compelled to go along with a lot of locker room garbage because I wanted that image—and I know a lot of others who did too.

Like my story, Waddell's points to the importance of the athletic institution as a context in which peers mutually construct and reconstruct narrow definitions of masculinity. Heterosexuality is considered to be a rock-solid foundation of this concept of masculinity. But unlike my story, Waddell's may invoke a dramaturgical analysis.[2] He seemed to be consciously "acting" to control and regulate others' perceptions of him by constructing a public "front stage" persona that differed radically from what he believed to be his "true" inner self. My story, in contrast, suggests a deeper, less consciously strategic repression of my homoerotic attraction. Most likely, I was aware on some level of the dangers of such feelings, and was escaping the risks, disgrace, and rejection that would likely result from being different. For Waddell, the decision to construct his identity largely within sport was to step into a fiercely heterosexual/masculine closet that would hide what he saw as his "true" identity. In contrast, I was not so much stepping into a "closet" that would hide my identity; rather, I was stepping out into an entire world of heterosexual privilege. My story also suggests how a threat to the promised privileges of hegemonic masculinity—my failure as an athlete—might trigger a momentary sexual panic that can lay bare the constructedness, indeed, the instability of the heterosexual masculine identity.

In either case, Waddell's or mine, we can see how, as young male athletes, heterosexuality and masculinity was not something we "were," but something we were doing. It is significant, I think, that although each of us was "doing heterosexuality," neither of us was actually "having sex" with women (though one of us desperately wanted to). This underscores a point made by some recent theorists that heterosexuality should not be thought of simply as sexual acts between women and men. Rather, heterosexuality is a constructed identity, a performance, and an institution that is not necessarily linked to sexual acts. Though for one of us it was more conscious than for the other, we were both "doing heterosexuality" as an ongoing practice through which we sought to do two things:

- avoid stigma, embarrassment, ostracism, or perhaps worse if we were even suspected of being gay;
- link ourselves into systems of power, status, and privilege that appear to be the birthright of "real men" (i.e., males who are able to compete successfully with other males in sport, work, and sexual relations with women).

In other words, each of us actively scripted our own sexual and gender performances, but these scripts were constructed within the constraints of a socially organized (institutionalized) system of power and pleasure.

## QUESTIONS FOR FUTURE RESEARCH

As I prepared to tell this sexual story publicly to my colleagues at the sport studies conference, I felt extremely nervous. Part of the nervousness was due to the fact that I knew some of them would object to my claim that telling personal stories can be a source of sociological insights. But a larger part of the reason for my nervousness was due to the fact that I was revealing something very personal about my sexuality in such a public way. Most of us are not accustomed to doing this, especially in the context of

a professional conference. But I had learned long ago, especially from feminist women scholars, and from gay and lesbian scholars, that biography is linked to history. Part of "normal" academic discourse has been to hide "the personal" (including the fact that the researchers are themselves people with values, feelings, and, yes, biases) behind a carefully constructed facade of "objectivity." Rather than trying to hide or be ashamed of one's subjective experience of the world, I was challenging myself to draw on my experience of the world as a resource. Not that I should trust my experience as the final word on "reality." White, heterosexual males like me have made the mistake for centuries of calling their own experience "objectivity," and then punishing anyone who does not share their world view by casting them as "deviant." Instead, I hope to use my experience as an example of how those of us who are in dominant sexual/racial/gender/class categories can get a new perspective on the "constructedness" of our identities by juxtaposing our subjective experiences against the recently emerging world views of gay men and lesbians, women, and people of color.

Finally, I want to stress that in juxtaposition neither my own nor Tom Waddell's story sheds much light on the question of why some individuals "become gay" while others "become" heterosexual or bisexual. Instead, I should like to suggest that this is a dead-end question, and that there are far more important and interesting questions to be asked:

- How has heterosexuality, as an institution and as an enforced group practice, constrained and limited all of us—gay, straight, and bi?
- How has the institution of sport been an especially salient institution for the social construction of heterosexual masculinity?
- Why is it that when men play sports they are almost always automatically granted masculine status, and thus assumed to be heterosexual, while when women play sports, questions are raised about their "femininity" and sexual orientation?

These kinds of questions aim us toward an analysis of the workings of power within institutions—including the ways that these workings of power shape and constrain our identities and relationships—and point us toward imagining alternative social arrangements that are less constraining for everyone.

## NOTES

1. The fluidity and changeability of sexual desire over the life course is now more obvious in evidence from prison and military populations, and single-sex boarding schools. The theory of bisexuality is evident, for example, in childhood crushes on same-sex primary schoolteachers.
2. Dramaturgical analysis, associated with Erving Goffman, uses the theater and performance to develop an analogy with everyday life.

## REFERENCES

Haug, Frigga (1987) *Female Sexualization: A Collective Work of Memory.* London: Verso.

Lenskyj, Helen (1986) *Out of Bounds: Women, Sport and Sexuality.* Toronto: Women's Press.

Lenskyj, Helen (1997) "No fear? Lesbians in sport and physical education." *Women in Sport and Physical Activity Journal* 6(2): 7–22.

Messner, Michael A. (1994) "Gay athletes and the Gay Games: In interview with Tom Waddell," in M.A. Messner and D.F. Sabo (eds) *Sex, Violence and Power in Sports: Rethinking Masculinity.* Freedom: The Crossing Press, pp. 113–19.

Pronger, Brian (1990) *The Arena of Masculinity: Sports, Homosexuality and the Meaning of Sex.* New York: St. Martin's Press.

*Source:* Messner, Michael A. (1999). "Becoming 100 Percent Straight." In Jay Coakley & Peter Donnelly (Eds.), *Inside Sports* (pp. 104–110). London, UK: Routledge.

## THE HETEROSEXUAL QUESTIONNAIRE

*Martin Rochlin*

Martin Rochlin was a scholar, activist, and pioneer in the field of gay-affirmative psychotherapy. Through his clinical practice, mentorship of students, professional presentations, and public appearances, he promoted the rights of sexual minorities. Rochlin was a leader in the campaign that resulted in the removal of homosexuality from the list of mental disorders in the *Diagnostic and Statistical Manual of Mental Disorders*. His heterosexual questionnaire, originally published in 1972, is still widely reprinted in textbooks and anthologies in gender and women's studies and sociology.

1. What do you think caused your heterosexuality?
2. When and how did you decide that you were a heterosexual?
3. Is it possible that your heterosexuality is just a phase you may grow out of?
4. Is it possible that your heterosexuality stems from a neurotic fear of others of the same sex?
5. If you have never slept with a person of the same sex, is it possible that all you need is a good gay lover?
6. Do your parents know that you are straight? Do your friends and/or roommate(s) know? How did they react?
7. Why do you insist on flaunting your heterosexuality? Can't you just be who you are and keep it quiet?
8. Why do heterosexuals place so much emphasis on sex?
9. Why do heterosexuals feel compelled to seduce others into their lifestyles?
10. A disproportionate majority of child molesters are heterosexual. Do you consider it safe to expose children to heterosexual teachers?
11. Just what do men and women *do* in bed together? How can they truly know how to please each other, being so anatomically different?
12. With all the societal support marriage receives, the divorce rate is spiraling. Why are there so few stable relationships among heterosexuals?
13. Statistics show that lesbians have the lowest incidence of sexually transmitted diseases. Is it really safe for a woman to maintain a heterosexual lifestyle and run the risk of disease and pregnancy?
14. How can you become a whole person if you limit yourself to compulsive, exclusive heterosexuality?
15. Considering the menace of overpopulation, how could the human race survive if everyone were heterosexual?
16. Could you trust a heterosexual therapist to be objective? Don't you feel s/he might be inclined to influence you in the direction of her/his own leanings?

17. There seem to be very few happy heterosexuals. Techniques have been developed that might enable you to change if you really want to. Have you considered trying aversion therapy?
18. Would you want your child to be heterosexual, knowing the problems that s/he would face?

*Source:* Rochlin, Martin. (1995). "The Language of Sex: The Heterosexual Questionnaire." In Adie Nelson & Barrie William Robinson (Eds.), *Gender in the 1990s: Images, Realities, and Issues* (pp. 38–39). Toronto, ON: Nelson Canada.

# CHAPTER 24

## The Ethics of Genetic Research
## on Sexual Orientation

*Udo Schüklenk, Edward Stein, Jacinta Kerin, and William Byne*

Udo Schüklenk is a professor and Ontario Research Chair in Bioethics in the Department of Philosophy at Queen's University. A leading expert in the field of bioethics (the study of ethics in health care), he has authored or co-authored a number of books and over 100 academic papers. His research interests are in the area of public health issues and infectious disease control. He is the joint editor-in-chief of *Bioethics* and *Developing World Bioethics*.

Edward Stein is a professor of law and the founding director of the Family Law, Policy, and Bioethics Program at the Cardozo School of Law in New York City. He is the author of *The Mismeasure of Desire: The Science, Theory, and Ethics of Sexual Orientation* and editor of *Forms of Desire: Sexual Orientation and the Social Constructionist Controversy*.

Jacinta Kerin completed her PhD in bioethics at Monash University in 2004. Her research concerns focus on the philosophy of science, ethics, and feminism.

William Byne is an associate professor and director of the Laboratory of Neuroanatomy and Morphometrics at Mount Sinai School of Medicine in New York City. He is co-editor of the book *Treatment of Transgender Children and Adolescents* and editor-in-chief of the academic journal *LGBT Health*.

Research on the origins of sexual orientation has received much public attention in recent years, especially findings consistent with the notion of relatively simple links between genes and sexual orientation.

*****

## ETHICAL CONCERNS

We have several ethical concerns about genetic research on sexual orientation. Underlying these concerns is the fact that even in our contemporary societies, lesbians, gay men, and bisexuals are subject to widespread discrimination and social disapprobation. Against this background, we are concerned about the particularly gruesome history of the use of such research. Many homosexual people have been forced to undergo "treatments" to change their sexual orientation, while others have "chosen" to undergo them in order to escape societal homophobia. All too often, scientifically questionable "therapeutic" approaches destroyed the lives of perfectly healthy people. "Conversion therapies" have included electroshock treatment, hormonal therapies, genital mutilation, and brain surgery.[1] We are concerned about the negative ramifications of biological research on sexual orientation, especially in homophobic societies. In Germany, some scholars have warned of the potential for abuse of such genetic research, while others have called for a moratorium on such research to prevent the possible abuse of its results in homophobic societies. These warnings should be taken seriously.

We are concerned that people [are] conducting research on sexual orientation work within homophobic frameworks, despite their occasional claims to the contrary. A prime example is the German obstetrician Günter Dörner, whose descriptions of homosexuality ill-conceal his heterosexism. Dörner writes about homosexuality as a "dysfunction" or "disease" based on "abnormal brain development." He postulates that it can be prevented by "*optimizing*" natural conditions or by "*correcting* abnormal hormonal concentrations prenatally" (emphasis added).[2] Another example is provided by psychoanalyst Richard Friedman, who engages in speculation about nongay outcome given proper therapeutic intervention.[3] Research influenced by homophobia is likely to result in significantly biased accounts of human sexuality; further, such work is more likely to strengthen and perpetuate the homophobic attitudes on which it is based.

## SEXUAL ORIENTATION RESEARCH IS NOT VALUE NEUTRAL

Furthermore, we question whether those who research sexual orientation can ever conduct their work in a value-neutral manner. One might think that the majority of American sex researchers treat homosexuality not as a disease, but rather as a variation analogous to a neutral polymorphism. To consider whether or not this is the case, one must look at the context in which interest in sexual orientation arises. Homophobia still exists to some degree in all societies within which sexual orientation research is conducted. The cultures in which scientists live and work influence both the questions they ask and the hypotheses they imagine and explore. Given this, we believe it is unlikely that the sexual orientation research of any scientist (even one who is homosexual) will escape some taint of homophobia.

*****

We are not claiming that all researchers are homophobic to some degree whether or not they are aware of it. Nor are we talking about the implicit or explicit intentions of individual sexual orientation researchers. Rather, we are seeking to highlight that the very motivation for seeking the "origin" of homosexuality has its source within social frameworks that are pervasively homophobic. Recognition that scientific projects are constituted by, and to some degree complicit in, social structures does not necessarily entail that all such science should cease. At the very least, however, it follows that sexual orientation research and its use should be subject to critique. Such a critique will call into question the claim that, by treating homosexuality as a mere variation of human behavior, researchers are conducting neutral investigations into sexual orientation.

*****

*Normativity of Naturalness and Normality.* Why is there a dispute as to whether homosexuality is natural or normal? We suggest it is because many people seem to think that nature has a prescriptive normative force such that what is deemed natural or normal is necessarily good and therefore *ought* to be. Everything that falls outside these terms is constructed as unnatural and abnormal, and it has been argued that this constitutes sufficient reason to consider homosexuality worth avoiding.[4] Arguments that appeal to "normality" to provide us with moral guidelines also risk committing the naturalistic fallacy. The naturalistic fallacy is committed when one mistakenly deduces from the way things are to the way they ought to be. For instance, Dean Hamer and colleagues commit this error in their *Science* article when they state that "it would be fundamentally unethical to use such information to try to assess or alter a person's current or future sexual orientation, either heterosexual or homosexual, or other normal attributes of human behavior."[5] Hamer and colleagues believe that there is a major genetic factor contributing to sexual orientation. From this, they think it follows that homosexuality is normal, and thus worthy of preservation. Thus, they believe that genetics can tell us what is normal, and that the content of what is normal tells us what ought to be. This is a typical example of a naturalistic fallacy.

Normality can be defined in a number of ways, but none of them direct us in the making of moral

judgments. First, normality can be reasonably defined in a *descriptive* sense as a statistical average. Appeals to what is usual, regular, and/or conforming to existing standards ultimately collapse into statistical statements. For an ethical evaluation of homosexuality, it is irrelevant whether homosexuality is normal or abnormal in this sense. All sorts of human traits and behaviors are abnormal in a statistical sense, but this is not a sufficient justification for a negative ethical judgment about them.

Second, "normality" might be defined in a functional sense, where what is normal is something that has served an adaptive function from an evolutionary perspective. This definition of normality can be found in sociobiology, which seeks biological explanations for social behavior. There are a number of serious problems with the sociobiological project.[6] For the purposes of this argument, however, suffice it to say that even if sociobiology could establish that certain behavioral traits were the direct result of biological evolution, no moral assessment of these traits would follow. To illustrate our point, suppose any trait that can be reasonably believed to have served an adaptive function at some evolutionary stage is normal. Some questions arise that exemplify the problems with deriving normative conclusions from descriptive science. Are traits that are perpetuated simply through linkage to selectively advantageous loci less "normal" than those for which selection was direct? Given that social contexts now exert "selective pressure" in a way that nature once did, how are we to decide which traits are to be intentionally fostered?

*****

*U.S.-Specific Arguments.* In the United States, several scholars and lesbian and gay activists have argued that establishing a genetic basis for sexual orientation will help make the case for lesbian and gay rights. The idea is that scientific research will show that people do not choose their sexual orientations and therefore they should not be punished or discriminated against in virtue of them. This general argument is flawed in several ways.[7] First, we do not need to show that a trait is genetically determined to argue that it is not amenable to change at will. This is clearly shown by the failure rates of conversion "therapies."[8] These failures establish that sexual orientation is resistant to change, but they do not say anything about its ontogeny or etiology. Sexual orientation can be unchangeable without being genetically determined. There is strong observational evidence to support the claim that sexual orientation is difficult to change, but this evidence is perfectly compatible with nongenetic accounts of the origins of sexual orientations. More importantly, we should not embrace arguments that seek to legitimate homosexuality by denying that there is any choice in sexual preference because the implicit premise of such arguments is that if there *was* a choice, then homosexuals would be blameworthy.

Relatedly, arguments for lesbian and gay rights based on scientific evidence run the risk of leading to impoverished forms of lesbian and gay rights. Regardless of what causes homosexuality, a person has to decide to publicly identify as a lesbian, to engage in sexual acts with another woman, to raise children with her same-sex lover, or to be active in the lesbian and gay community. It is when people make such decisions that they are likely to face discrimination, arrest, or physical violence. It is decisions like these that need legal protection. An argument for lesbian and gay rights based on genetic evidence is impotent with respect to protecting such decisions because it focuses exclusively on the very aspects of sexuality that might not involve choices.

Another version of this argument focuses on the specifics of U.S. law. According to this version, scientific evidence will establish the immutability of sexual orientation, which, according to one current interpretation of the Equal Protection Clause of the Fourteenth Amendment of the U.S. Constitution, is one of three criteria required of a classification if it is to evoke heightened judicial scrutiny. While this line of argument has serious internal problems,[9] such an argument, like a good deal of American bioethical reasoning, has limited or no relevance to the global context. Since the results of the scientific research are not confined within American borders, justifications that go beyond U.S. legislation are required.

The same sort of problem occurs in other defenses of sexual orientation research that discuss possible ramifications in U.S.-specific legislative terms. For instance, Timothy Murphy claims that, even if a genetic probe predictive of sexual orientation were available, mandatory testing would be unlikely.[10] He bases this claim on the fact that in some states employment and housing discrimination against homosexual people is illegal. In many countries, however, the political climate is vastly different, and legal anti-gay discrimination is widespread. And there is evidence that scientific research would be used in a manner that discriminates against homosexuals.[11] [For example,] in Singapore, homosexual sex acts are a criminal offense. The Singapore Penal Code sections 377 and 377A threaten sentences ranging from two years to life imprisonment for homosexual people engaging in same-sex acts. Not coincidentally, in light of our concerns, a National University of Singapore psychiatrist recently implied that "pre-symptomatic testing for homosexuality should be offered in the absence of treatment,"[12] thereby accepting the idea that homosexuality is something in need of a cure.

*Genetic Screening.* Several attempts to defend sexual orientation research against ethical concerns related to the selective abortion of "pre-homosexual" fetuses have been made. It has been claimed that this sort of genetic screening will not become commonplace because "diagnostic genetic testing is at present the exception rather than the rule."[13] While this may indeed be true in the U.S., it has far more to do with the types of tests currently offered than with a reluctance on the part of either the medical profession or the reproducing public to partake of such technology. For example, the types of tests available are diagnostic for diseases and are offered on the basis of family history or specific risk factors. The possibility of tests that are supposed to be (however vaguely) predictive of behavioral traits opens genetic technology to a far greater population, especially when the traits in question are undesired by a largely prejudiced society.

Furthermore, it has been claimed that the medical profession would not advocate such a test that does not serve "important state interests" (p. 341). This argument not only ignores the existence of homophobia among individuals within medicine,[14] it assumes also that public demand for genetic testing varies predominantly according to medical advice. However, should such a test become available, the media hype surrounding its market arrival would render its existence common knowledge, which, coupled with homophobic bias, would create a demand for the test irrespective of its accuracy and of any kind of state interest. Furthermore, this argument ignores the fact that genetic screening for a socially undesirable characteristic has already been greeted with great public demand in countries such as India, where abortion on the basis of female sex is commonplace, irrespective of its legality.[15] Techniques to select the sexual orientation of children, if made available, might well be widely utilized.[16]

*****

*The Value of Knowing the Truth.* Finally, various scholars appeal to the value of the truth to defend research on sexual orientation in the face of ethical concerns. Scientific research does, however, have its costs and not every research program is of equal importance. Even granting that, in general, knowledge is better than ignorance, not all risks for the sake of knowledge are worth taking. With respect to sexual orientation, historically, almost every hypothesis about the causes of homosexuality led to attempts to "cure" healthy people. History indicates that current genetic research is likely to have negative effects on lesbians and gay men, particularly those living in homophobic societies.[17]

## A GLOBAL PERSPECTIVE

Homosexual people have in the past suffered greatly from societal discrimination. Historically, the results of biological research on sexual orientation have been used against them. We have analyzed the arguments offered by well-intentioned defenders of such work and concluded that none survive philosophical scrutiny. It is true that in some countries in Scandinavia, North America, and most parts of Western Europe, the legal situation of homosexual people has improved, but an adequate ethical analysis of the implications of genetic inquiry into the causes of sexual orientation must operate from a global perspective. Sexual orientation researchers should be aware that their work may harm homosexuals in countries other than their own. It is difficult to imagine any good that could come of genetic research on sexual orientation in homophobic societies. Such work faces serious ethical concerns so long as homophobic societies continue to exist. Insofar as socially responsible genetic research on sexual orientation is possible, it must begin with the awareness that it will not be a cure for homophobia and that the ethical status of lesbians and gay men does not in any way hinge on its results.

## NOTES

1.  Jonathan Ned Katz, *Gay American History* (New York: Thomas Crowell, 1976), pp. 197–422.

2.  Günter Dörner, "Hormone-Dependent Brain Development and Neuroendocrine Prophylaxis," *Experimental and Clinical Endocrinology* 94 (1989): 4–22.

3.  Richard C. Friedman, *Male Homosexuality: A Contemporary Psychoanalytic Perspective* (New Haven: Yale University Press, 1988), p. 20.

4.  Michael Levin, "Why Homosexuality Is Abnormal," *Monist* 67 (1984): 251–83.

5.  Dean Hamer et al., "A Linkage between DNA Markers on the X Chromosome and Male Sexual Orientation," *Science* 261 (1993): 326.

6.  Philip Kitcher, *Vaulting Ambition: Sociobiology and the Quest for Human Nature* (Cambridge: MIT Press, 1985).

7.  Edward Stein, "The Relevance of Scientific Research Concerning Sexual Orientation to Lesbian and Gay Rights," *Journal of Homosexuality* 27 (1994): 269–308.

8.  Charles Silverstein, "Psychological and Medical Treatments of Homosexuality," in *Homosexuality: Research Implications for Public Policy*, ed. J.C. Gonsiorek and J.D. Weinrich (Newbury Park: Sage, 1991), pp. 101–14.

9.  Janet Halley, "Sexual Orientation and the Politics of Biology: A Critique of the New Argument from Immutability," *Stanford Law Review* 46 (1994): 503–68.

10.  Timothy Murphy, "Abortion and the Ethics of Genetic Sexual Orientation Research," *Cambridge Quarterly of Healthcare Ethics* 4 (1995): 341.

11.  Paul Billings, "Genetic Discrimination and Behavioural Genetics: The Analysis of Sexual Orientation," in *Intractable Neurological Disorders, Human Genome, Research, and Society*, ed. Norio Fujiki and Darryl Macer (Christchurch and Tsukuba: Eubios Ethics Institute, 1993), p. 37; Paul Billings, "International Aspects of Genetic Discrimination," in *Human Genome Research and Society*, ed. Norio Fujiki and Darryl Macer (Christchurch and Tsukuba: Eubios Ethics Institute, 1992), pp. 114–17.

12.  L.C.C. Lim, "Present Controversies in the Genetics of Male Homosexuality," *Annals of the Academy of Medicine Singapore* 24 (1995): 759-62.

13.  Murphy, "Abortion and the Ethics of Genetic Sexual Orientation Research," p. 341.

14.  Kevin Speight, "Homophobia Is a Health Issue," *Health Care Analysis* 3 (1995): 143–48.

15.  Kusum, "The Use of Prenatal Diagnostic Techniques for Sex Selection: The Indian Scene," *Bioethics* 7 (1993): 149–65.

16.  Richard Posner, *Sex and Reason* (Cambridge, Mass.: Harvard University Press, 1992), p. 308.

17.  For further elaborations on this argument, see Edward Stein, Udo Schüklenk, and Jacinta Kerin, "Scientific Research on Sexual Orientation," in *Encyclopedia of Applied Ethics*, ed. Ruth Chadwick (San Diego: Academic Press, 1997).

*Source:* Schüklenk, Udo, Stein, Edward, Kerin, Jacinta, & Byne, William. (1998). Excerpted from "The Ethics of Genetic Research on Sexual Orientation." *Hastings Centre Report, 7*(4), 6, 8–13.

## HOMOPHOBIA, HETEROSEXISM, AND HETERONORMATIVITY

Below are two definitions by noted American feminists Suzanne Pharr and Audre Lorde. Pharr is a long-time activist and organizer for social and economic justice movements, and author of *Homophobia: A Weapon of Sexism*. Lorde was a writer, poet, and activist, and a key figure in the Black feminist and lesbian movements of the 1970s and 1980s.

Pharr and Lorde each define homophobia and heterosexism in a different way. What does each writer contribute to your understanding of these concepts?

### *Homophobia: A Weapon of Sexism*, Suzanne Pharr

Homophobia works effectively as a weapon of sexism because it is joined with a powerful arm, heterosexism. Heterosexism creates the climate for homophobia with its assumption that the world is and must be heterosexual and its display of power and privilege as the norm. Heterosexism is the systemic display of homophobia in the institutions of society. Heterosexism and homophobia work together to enforce compulsory heterosexuality and that bastion of patriarchal power, the nuclear family. The central focus of the rightwing attack against women's liberation is that women's equality, women's self-determination, women's control of our own bodies and lives will damage what they see as the crucial societal institution, the nuclear family.

### *Scratching the Surface*, Audre Lorde

*Heterosexism:* The belief in the inherent superiority of one pattern of loving and thereby its right to dominance. *Homophobia:* The fear of feelings of love for members of one's own sex and therefore the hatred of those feelings in others.

---

### How Do You Recognize Homophobia in Yourself and Others?

### *The Campaign to End Homophobia*, Cooper Thompson and Barbara Zoloth

There are four distinct but interrelated types of homophobia: personal, interpersonal, institutional, and cultural.

*Personal homophobia* is prejudice based on a personal belief that lesbian, gay, and bisexual people are sinful, immoral, sick, inferior to heterosexuals, or incomplete women and men.

Personal homophobia is experienced as a feeling of fear, discomfort, dislike, hatred, or disgust with same-sex sexuality. Anyone, regardless of their sexual orientation or preference, can experience personal homophobia; when this happens with lesbian, gay, and bisexual people, it is called *internalized homophobia*.

*Interpersonal homophobia* is individual behavior based on personal homophobia. This hatred or dislike may be expressed by name-calling, telling "jokes," verbal and physical harassment, and other individual acts of discrimination.

Interpersonal homophobia, in its extreme, results in lesbians, gays, and bisexuals being physically assaulted for no other reason than their assailants' homophobia. Most people act out their fears of lesbian, gay, and bisexual people in non-violent, more commonplace ways. Relatives often shun their lesbian, gay, and bisexual family members; co-workers are distant and cold to lesbian, gay, and bisexual colleagues; heterosexual friends aren't interested in hearing about their lesbian, gay, and bisexual friends' relationships.

*Institutional homophobia* refers to the many ways in which government, businesses, churches, and other institutions and organizations discriminate against people on the basis of sexual orientation. Institutional homophobia is also called *heterosexism*.

Institutional homophobia is reflected in religious organizations which have stated or implicit policies against lesbians, gays, and bisexuals leading services; agencies which refuse to allocate resources to services to lesbian, gay, and bisexual people; and governments which fail to insure the rights of all citizens, regardless of their sexual orientation.

*Cultural homophobia* refers to social standards and norms which dictate that being heterosexual is better or more moral than being lesbian, gay, or bisexual, and that everyone is or should be heterosexual. Cultural homophobia is also called *heterosexism*.

Cultural homophobia is spelled out each day in television shows and print advertisements where virtually every character is heterosexual, every erotic relationship involves a female and a male, and every "normal" child is presumed to be attracted to and will eventually marry someone of the other sex. In the few cases where lesbians, gays, or bisexual people are portrayed, they are usually unhappy, stereotyped, engaged in self-destructive behaviors, or ambivalent about their sexual orientation.

## Heteronormativity

### *Identity and Opportunity,* Miriam Smith

Heteronormativity means that social organization is structured around the assumption that heterosexual sexual preference and heterosexual coupling is the dominant mode of sexual, intimate, and family organization and that homosexuality is deviant. Even when dominant norms are not openly homophobic or hostile towards homosexuality, lesbian and gay people are outside of the "norm." So, for example, people are usually assumed to be heterosexual unless they state or are shown to be otherwise, an assumption that is an example of "heteronormativity." Some lesbian and gay people label themselves "queer"—traditionally a hostile epithet aimed at them—in part to call attention to the power of "naming" as a means of enforcing social expectations and defining "normalcy." Heteronormativity is not confined to social attitudes, norms, and values but is also enshrined in public policies. Until very recently, same-sex couples [in Canada] were not entitled to benefits provided to heterosexual couples, such as pensions or medical benefits provided by private or public sector employers. Such policies are "heteronormative" because they assume that heterosexual couples are the only form of couple or the only form of couple that is worthy of the social and economic support they provide.

***Sources:*** Pharr, Suzanne. (1988). *Homophobia: A Weapon of Sexism* (p. 16). Inverness, CA: Chardon Press; Lorde, Audre. (1984). "Scratching the Surface: Some Notes on Barriers to Women and Loving." In Audre Lorde (Ed.), *Sister Outsider: Essays and Speeches* (p. 45). Freedom, CA: The Crossing Press. Originally published in *The Black Scholar, 9*(7) (1978), 31–35; Thompson, Cooper, & Zoloth, Barbara. (1990). Excerpted from "The Campaign to End Homophobia: Homophobia Pamphlet." *Campaign to End Homophobia* (pp. 1–2). Retrieved from: http://www.cooper-thompson.com/essays/PDF/Homophobia.pdf; Smith, Miriam. (2012). "Identity and Opportunity: The Lesbian and Gay Rights Movement." In Maureen Fitzgerald & Scott Rayter (Eds.), *Queerly Canadian: An Introductory Reader in Sexuality Studies* (p. 122). Toronto, ON: Canadian Scholars' Press.

# THE "FRUIT MACHINE"

*Sherry Aske and Trevor Pritchard*

Sherry Aske is a news editor, presenter, and producer at *CBC Ottawa*. Trevor Pritchard is a writer, editor, radio producer, and photographer. Most recently, he has worked as a radio producer with *CBC* in Ottawa and Saskatoon.

It's not fiction—although it sounds like something straight out of a dystopian novel.

The so-called "fruit machine" was a homosexuality detection system commissioned by the Canadian government during the Cold War—and developed largely by a psychologist at Carleton University in Ottawa—to keep LGBT people out of the public service or military.[1]

While the machine is long gone, its legacy is back in the news after the federal government was hit with a class-action lawsuit this week from former public servants who lost their jobs because of their sexual orientation.

Gay and lesbian civil servants were driven out of the Canadian military and public service beginning in the 1950s, but the practice continued after homosexuality was removed from the Criminal Code in the 1960s.

At the time, homosexuals were perceived by the government as weak, unreliable and potentially disloyal. The government feared they might be easy targets for Soviet spies who could blackmail them into giving up important secrets—and thus commissioned the machine to determine a person's sexual identity through involuntary biological responses.

The project "was a series of psychological tests," said Patrizia Gentile, an associate professor at Carleton University and the [co-]author of *The Canadian War on Queers*.

In one test, for example, subjects were shown pictures that would "arouse desire," said Gentile, while cameras took pictures of their pupils, to see if they dilated.

## "Product of His Time"

The machine was used by the federal government throughout the 1960s, until the Defence Research Board—which was later folded into the Department of National Defence—pulled funding in 1967.

The device was never able to establish a "discernable difference," between the biological responses of heterosexuals and LGBT individuals, Gentile wrote in her book.

The machine was based on research by Frank Robert Wake, a Carleton University psychologist who died in 1993.

"I think he was a product of his time, definitely. But that doesn't of course excuse the fact that he came up with research that was discriminatory and harmful to a lot of people's lives," Gentile told CBC Radio's *Ottawa Morning* on Thursday.

"He is part of the Cold War culture and this culture of fear, where homosexuals and communists were conflated."

According to Doug Elliott, a longtime gay rights activist and the Toronto lawyer leading the class-action lawsuit, as many as 9,000 people could be eligible to join it.

The Liberal government is planning an apology to the country's LGBT community for the past discrimination, but it's unclear when it will act.[2]

*Source:* Aske, Sherry, & Pritchard, Trevor. (2016, November 3). "How the Cold War 'Fruit Machine' Tried to Determine Gay from Straight." *CBC News.* Retrieved from: http://www.cbc.ca/news/canada/ottawa/archives-homosexuality-dector-fruit-machine-1.3833724.

## NOTES

1. For more information, please follow the link to the CBC Digital Archives video on the "fruit machine": http://www.cbc.ca/archives/entry/rcmp-uses-fruit-machine-to-detect-gays.

2. Prime Minister Justin Trudeau delivered this historic apology to LGBTQ2 Canadians on November 28, 2017.

# CHAPTER 25

## Loving Women in the Modern World

*Leila J. Rupp*

Leila J. Rupp is the interim dean of social sciences and distinguished professor in the Department of Feminist Studies at the University of California–Santa Barbara. An historian by training, she was editor of the *Journal of Women's History* for many years. She researches and publishes widely in the areas of women's movements, sexualities, and comparative and transnational women's history. Among her many books, Rupp co-edited the ninth edition of *Feminist Frontiers*, a widely used anthology of feminist writings. Her most recent co-edited volume, *Understanding and Teaching U.S. Lesbian, Gay, Bisexual, and Transgender History*, received a Lambda Literary Award for Best Anthology.

What does it mean to be a "lesbian" in the modern world? In the 21st century it means loving women, desiring women, forming relationships with women, engaging in sexual behaviour with women, claiming an identity as a lesbian, and perhaps forming communities with other lesbians, although not all of these are necessary to the definition. But what do we make of women who loved, desired, formed relationships with and had sex with women before the concept and identity of "lesbian" were available? What do we make of such women in cultures that have different categories of gender and sexual behaviour? We might call them "lesbian-like" or talk of same-sex love, desire or sexual acts.[1] What is crucial is that we contemplate, as best we can, the ways in which women in the past and in different parts of the world negotiated and understood their desire, love and self-conceptions.

I explore here different patterns of loving women in various parts of the world, from around the beginning of the 19th century up to the present. It is impossible, of course, to be comprehensive, since research on many societies remains sketchy or is entirely lacking. Nor is there space to do justice to more than a few places. But my aim is to give a sense of women's lives with other women before, during and after the "discovery," naming and claiming of lesbian identity. Although lesbianism is often dismissed in societies subject to Western imperialism as an imported perversion (and in Western societies traditionally attributed to those of "other" races, classes or nations), women all around the world have found many ways of loving other women.

The story of loving women in the modern world is a tale of women who dressed and passed as men and who married women, of female-husbands and manly women, of romantic friends who made lives together, of trysts in domestic spaces, of secretive and not-so-secretive communities, of sapphists and female inverts and marriage-resisters and bulldaggers and butches and fems and lesbians. Yet it is not simply a tale of women with same-sex desires freeing and naming themselves as the modern world came into being. What history teaches us is how differently sexuality has been conceived and practised in the past and in various societies, and how mistaken we are to think solely in terms of progress. As a way of disrupting a narrative of progress, I have approached the history of loving women thematically, looking first at marrying women, then desiring women, and finally at women claiming diverse identities.

## MARRYING WOMEN

One of the most persistent patterns of what may or may not accurately be called female same-sex sexuality is the case of women crossing the gender line to live as men and to marry women. What we do not know in such cases is whether women became men solely for the economic and social freedom that male dress and employment provided, whether a sexual motivation figured in their decisions, or whether they conceived of themselves as something akin to transgendered, even if no such concept existed. We are particularly in the dark about the motives of their wives. What we do know is that such gender-crossing and marriage to women existed in a number of contexts.

Consider the story of Edward De Lacy Evans, born a woman, who lived as a man for twenty-three years in Victoria, Australia.[2] The case came to light in 1879 when he was forcibly stripped for a bath, having just arrived at Kew Asylum in Melbourne. Evans had emigrated to Australia from Ireland in 1856 as Ellen Tremaye, but after working for a short time as a domestic servant began dressing as a man and married one of his shipmates. He went to work as

a miner and, when his first wife left him for another man, explaining that Evans was actually a woman, he married a young Irishwoman. When she died, he married a third young woman, who bore a child after being impregnated by her sister's husband. Although Evans claimed the child as his own, it was the birth, it seems, that sent Evans to the asylum.

What grabbed public interest was not the masquerade itself but the three marriages. Newspaper stories reported Evans's interest in women on board ship, and one journalist concluded that "the woman must have been mad on the subject of sex from the time she left Ireland."[3] The fact that Evans had been committed may have explained his sexual deviance, but how was one to account for his wives? It was difficult to ignore the fact that his third wife had borne a child, so therefore must have engaged in sexual intercourse with a man. Although she claimed not to know either that Evans was a woman or how she became pregnant, her speculation that Evans had one night substituted a real man for himself suggested that she and Evans did indeed regularly have sex. One newspaper story reported that his wives did not expose him because they were "nymphomaniacs," suggesting knowledge of the emerging medical literature that linked excessive heterosexual desire and prostitution with female same-sex sexuality. When Evans's wife eventually named her brother-in-law as the father of the child in a bid for support, Evans testified in court that he had witnessed the two in bed together, but that it was so painful he could barely speak of it.

Evans's story, like so many tales of women who became men and married women, leaves us uncertain what to think.[4] Clearly there was more here at stake than occupational mobility. That Evans loved and desired women seems evident, but did he think of himself as male? Did his wives? What was crucial to the public commentary was the insistence that gender transgression was a sign of mental illness, and in fact the doctors proclaimed Evans cured only when he donned female clothing.

In other cultures in other parts of the world, "manly women" might marry women without the need for deception. The crucial difference was societal acceptance of gender-crossing or the existence of a third (or more) category of gender. In some Native American cultures, what are called "two-spirit" manly females are conceptualized as a mixture of the masculine and feminine, a gender apart from either women, men or womanly men. The two-spirit role has to do with spirituality, occupation, personality and gender more than sexuality, so when sex does take place between a manly woman and another woman, it may technically be "same-sex sex"—because the bodies involved are physiologically alike—but in fact the sex is more accurately conceptualized as cross-gender.[5] Among the Mohaves, *hwames* are women who take on male roles and who are able to marry women and serve as fathers of children borne by their wives.

*****

Native American societies were not the only ones that conceptualized multiple genders and allowed same-sex but cross-gender relationships, nor were they the only social group in which two biological women might marry one another. In more than thirty African groups woman–woman marriage has been, and in some cases still is, a possibility. As among the Mohaves, a female husband could be the father of children born to her wife from a union with a biological male. In that sense, she is a "social male." In at least some cases, such a role involved male dress and occupations, as for third-gender Native Americans. In Nigeria in the 1990s, an elderly Ohagia Igbo *dike-nwami* ("brave-woman") by the name of Nne Uko told an ethnographer that she "was interested in manly activities" and felt that she was "meant to be a man."[6] Although she was divorced from a husband, she farmed and hunted, joined men's societies and married two women who gave birth to children biologically fathered by her brother. The fundamental reason for the existence of such marriages is economic

and familial: if a woman cannot conceive, she can continue her family line by taking a wife who will bear children. Women might choose a female husband for a number of reasons, including the possibility of greater sexual freedom, more companionship, less quarrelling and physical violence, distaste for men, more input in household decisions or more bridewealth.[7] We know little or nothing about the emotional and sexual aspects of having a female husband, although scholars tend to insist that sex is not a part of such marriages. One ethnographer who spent two years studying the Bangwa of Cameroon in the 1970s suggested the presence of at least an emotional component when he described his best woman informant's relationship with one of her wives, commenting on "their obvious satisfaction in each other's company."[8]

A quite different kind of marriage from one in which a partner passed as a man or became a social male developed in the Euro-American world in the late 18th and early 19th centuries. As an ideology of sexual difference between women and men took hold among the urban middle classes, the phenomenon known as "romantic friendship" flourished. Women, assigned the domestic sphere of the home and assumed to be emotional and asexual, developed strong and passionate ties to other women that thrived in addition to or alongside marriage to men. When romantic friends in certain privileged circumstances chose not to marry as expected, they sometimes formed marriage-like relationships that became known in the United States, because of their prevalence in the north-east, as "Boston marriages."

No doubt the most famous marriage between romantic friends was that of Eleanor Butler and Sarah Ponsonby, who ran away together from their aristocratic Irish homes in 1778 when they were thirty-nine and twenty-three respectively. Although Butler, the elder of the pair, dressed and behaved in a masculine manner, they lived respectably, if eccentrically and not without occasional criticism, in a rural retreat in Wales for fifty-one years. As the "Ladies of Llangollen" they came to embody romantic friendship and the possibility of marriage, in practice if not in name, between two women. They called each other "my Better Half," "my Sweet Love" and "my Beloved."[9] Visitors flocked to their home, newspaper accounts described their house and garden, and other women who loved women viewed them as icons of female love. Anne Lister, a member of the Yorkshire gentry who was quite forthright about her love and lust for women, visited the Ladies in 1822 and felt a connection. She concluded that the long marriage between the two women must have been held together by "something more tender still than friendship."[10] When Butler died, leaving Ponsonby almost penniless, friends managed to arrange for Butler's pension to be paid to her—in effect a recognition that they had been married.

*****

The Ladies of Llangollen […] lived in [a society] that did not have a category for women who married women. Their relationship [was] nonetheless accepted, or at least tolerated, because of class privilege and because of ignorance, wilful or otherwise, that sexual relationships formed part of the arrangement. In 19th-century England and Wales, as throughout Europe and the United States, romantic friendships crossed the boundaries of respectability if there was too much gender transgression or suspicion of sexual activity beyond kissing and cuddling, as we shall see. But by the end of the 19th century, as the science of sexology began to describe and categorize masculine women and women with same-sex desires as "inverts" or "perverts," everything began to change.

Consider the case of Alice Mitchell and Freda Ward in late 19th-century Memphis, Tennessee. Mitchell, a middle-class white nineteen-year-old, fell in love with her seventeen-year-old friend Freda Ward (known as 'Fred') and hatched a plot to dress as a man, run away with her and marry her. To this point their attachment seemed, to their families, to fit the familiar pattern of romantic friendship. Then

Ward's family uncovered the plot and sent back Mitchell's engagement ring and other tokens of their love, forbidding them to see each other. Even worse from Mitchell's perspective, Ward began to be courted by a man. Early on in their plans to run away, Mitchell had said that she would kill Ward if she backed out of her promise to marry her, and she acted on this threat by slashing Ward's throat on the streets of Memphis in 1892. The case attracted attention from doctors and the popular press not only because of its drama, but also because it seemed to fit so perfectly the newly emerging theory of gender inversion and sexual deviance as inextricably linked. That is, Alice Mitchell became the embodiment of the "invert" or "lesbian" in American medical and popular discourse.[11] Her family's strategy for the defence was to have her declared insane, and she died in an asylum.

Across the Atlantic, at about the same time, the Hungarian count Sandor Vay was accused by his father-in-law not only of forgery, but also of fraud, since he "was only a woman, walking around in masculine clothes."[12] Unlike Mitchell, Vay was a "passing woman" who was raised as a boy, had affairs with women and worked as a journalist and writer. His father-in-law testified that one could see the shape of (rather large) male equipment between Vay's legs, and Vay's wife reported that she had given herself to him and had had no idea prior to his arrest that he was not biologically a man. Yet other witnesses testified that they knew the count to be a woman. The doctor who reported on the case to the court was himself confused, finding it difficult to deal with the masculine countess as a lady and much "easier, natural, and more correct" to think of Sandor as "a jovial, somewhat boyish student."[13] At this point the medical authorities proceeded from the story of a passing woman to a diagnosis of inversion and mental illness. As in the case of Alice Mitchell, the emerging ideas of the sexologists concerning gender inversion and same-sex sexual desire came to the fore. Sandor Vay was to Hungary, and to Europe more generally, what Alice Mitchell was to the United States: the embodiment of a sexual invert.

Once women who passed as men became defined in Euro-American cultures as sexual inverts and subsequently as mannish lesbians, marriages between women—whether passing women, manly women, social males, female husbands or romantic friends—had the potential to take on an air of sexual deviance. Nevertheless, some women continued to cross the gender line secretly, to live their lives as men and to marry women. Billy Tipton, a US jazz musician, originally invented himself as a man in order to earn a living during the Depression, but in 1989, when he died, his secret was revealed. He had been married several times and had adopted sons, and none of his immediate family—including his wives—knew that he had been born a woman.[14]

In the contemporary world, women in a few places can actually marry. In Belgium, Canada, Denmark, The Netherlands, Sweden and, in the United States, Massachusetts, lesbian marriages are taking place. Even in India, a society that does not condone same-sex relations, the fact that the Hindu Marriage Act allows diverse communities to define marriage means that some same-sex couples are able get married.[15] In the 1990s in a very poor rural region of India, Geeta, a woman from a *dalit* or "untouchable" family who was married to an abusive husband, met Manju, an older woman whose masculinity had won her a great deal of respect and power in her village. They came to know each other at a residential school run by a women's organization devoted to equality and empowerment, and they fell in love. As Geeta put it, "I do not know what happened to me when I met Manju but I forgot my man. I forgot that I had been married. We were so attracted to each other that we immediately felt like husband and wife."[16] Geeta accepted Manju as her husband at a Shiva temple, Manju's family accepted Geeta as a daughter-in-law, and Manju became both a second mother and a father to Geeta's daughter.

Marriage between women, then, has a long and complicated history. Many of the stories of women who married other women involve gender transgression, whether secret or open. Some take place in societies that recognize more than two genders or, for a variety of reasons, accept the idea of women as social males. There are many reasons why women might choose to cross the gender line or identify with a third or fourth gender, sexual desire for other women being only one. We know even less about why women might choose to marry female husbands. But what is clear is that women in various places in modern history have chosen to live their lives with other women.

## DESIRING WOMEN

What do we know of women's sexual activities with one another, much less of their desires? This is a question not only of evidence, but also of interpretation. What counts as "sex"? Kissing, hugging, cuddling? And what about acts that seem clearly sexual from a contemporary Western perspective but might have little to do with erotic desire in other contexts? These are tricky questions. What we do know is that, despite all the obstacles, some record of women's same-sex desires has survived.

Let us begin with romantic friendship in the 18th- and 19th-century Western world, since one of the central debates in the history of sexuality hinges on the question of whether or not these passionate, intense, loving and physically affectionate relationships included sex, by which we presumably mean the involvement of genitals and/or sexual desire and/or sexual gratification. Certainly some of what romantic friends wrote to each other sounds like declarations of desire. There is Alice Baldy, a white woman from the US state of Georgia, writing in 1870 to her beloved, Josie Varner: "Do you know that if you only touch me, or speak to me there is not a nerve or fibre in my body that does not respond with a thrill of delight?"[17] Or 19th-century Czech writer Božena Němcové writing to Sofie Rottová, a fellow author: "Believe me, sometimes I dream that your eyes are right in front of me, I am drowning in them, and they have the same sweet expression as they did when they used to ask: 'Božena, what's wrong? Božena, I love you.'"[18] Or African-American poet Angelina Weld Grimké writing in 1896 to her school friend Mamie Burrell: "Oh Mamie if you only knew how my heart beats when I think of you and it yearns and pants to gaze, if only for one second upon your lovely face."[19] Are these expressions of physical desire? Formulaic expressions of friendship? Or sometimes the former, sometimes the latter and sometimes both?

One of the cases that most troubles our understanding of the relationship between romantic friendship and sexual desire is that of Scottish schoolteachers Jane Pirie and Marianne Woods. In the early 19th century, Pirie and Woods fulfilled a dream by establishing a school together in Edinburgh. Then their plans all came crashing down one day when one of their students, Jane Cumming, born of a liaison between an Indian woman and an aristocratic Scottish man serving the empire in the East, reported shocking behaviour to her grandmother. According to Jane Cumming, the two teachers visited each other in bed, lay one on top of the other, kissed and shook the bed. Furthermore, Cumming reported that Jane Pirie said one night, "You are in the wrong place," and Marianne Woods replied "I know," and asserted that she was doing it "for fun." Another night, said Cumming, Pirie had whispered, "Oh, do it, darling." And she described a noise she heard as similar to "putting one's finger into the neck of a wet bottle."[20]

One can only imagine the reactions of the judges in the case, forced to make an impossible choice between believing that respectable Scottish schoolteachers might engage in sexual behaviour or believing that decent schoolgirls could make up such tales. As one judge put it, making clear the acceptability of normal romantic friendship, "Are we to say that every woman who has formed an intimate friendship and has slept in the same bed with another is guilty? Where is the innocent woman in Scotland?"[21] Ultimately, they had to decide whether Pirie and Woods kissed, caressed and fondled "more than could have resulted from ordinary female

friendship," suggesting a line between affectionate behaviour and sexuality that could be crossed.[22] The only way out of the dilemma was provided by Jane Cumming's heritage and childhood in India, where surely, many of the judges decided, she must have learned not only about sex, but also about sexual relations between women—something no respectable Scottish schoolgirl would be able to imagine.

*****

In describing and defining lesbianism, sexologists have left us some of the first detailed and reliable records of female same-sex sexual behaviour. Despite the filter of the doctors' own intentions and interpretations, women's voices do sometimes break through. In one famous US study of "sex variants" in New York in the 1930s, women described their sex lives and bragged about their ability to satisfy their lovers. Perhaps playing with both traditional notions about lesbians and the experts' belief in the hypersexuality of black women, a number of African-American subjects boasted of their sexual technique: "I insert my clitoris in the vagina just like the penis of a man…. Women enjoy it so much they leave their husbands."[23] Far more reliable are oral histories collected by historians sympathetic to their narrators. In the working-class lesbian bar culture of 1940s and 1950s Buffalo, New York, white, black and Native American butches saw their role as pleasuring their fems, primarily through tribadism or what they called "friction."[24] Oral sex became more acceptable in the 1950s at the same time that the idea of the "untouchable" or "stone butch"—the "doer" who did not let her lover make love to her—became more firmly entrenched. As one stone butch from the 1950s put it, "I wanted to satisfy them, and I wanted to make love—I love to make love. I still say that's the greatest thing in the world."[25]

These varied sources from different places provide evidence of kissing, the caressing of breasts, tribadism, manual stimulation, the use of dildoes, and oral sex. Sex practices change over time and vary in different cultures. But what all this evidence makes clear is that there is a long history of women desiring other women and acting on that desire. How women thought about what they did with each other, both before and after "lesbian" became a possible identity, we know less about. Yet women who loved women did, in different contexts, come to define identities that were based on their love and desire.

## CLAIMING AN IDENTITY

The story of the emergence of lesbian identity has both geographical and chronological limitations, but the notion of love, sexual desire or sexual activity making one a kind of person has more fluid boundaries. That is, the term *lesbian* has a relatively recent origin in Western culture, but there were other words or concepts that women applied to themselves to describe their desires and actions. Before the invention of the term *homosexuality* in 1869, Anne Lister saw her love and desire for women as a defining characteristic. She knew the term *Saffic*, considered her attraction to women natural, and proclaimed proudly that "I love, & only love, the fairer sex & thus beloved by them in turn, my heart revolts from any other love than theirs."[26]

At the same time we need to remember that there have always been, and still are, women who love and desire other women but do not see that as defining their identities in any way. In Lesotho, for example, a small, poor country entirely enclosed by South Africa, women love other women and engage in activities that seem to a modern Western sensibility to be sexual; yet they neither identify as a particular category of "sexual being" nor even define what they do as "sex," which in Lesotho requires a penis.[27] As in much of the rest of the world, women must expect to marry and bear children. But boarding-school girls pair up as "Mummy" and "Baby" and kiss, rub each other's bodies, sometimes have genital contact, and jealously guard their relationships. Older women greet each other with long "French" kisses, fondle one another and engage in tribadism and cunnilingus, all of which they describe as "loving each other," "staying together nicely," "holding each other" or "having a nice time together," but not as sex.[28] And they are not lesbians.

In other cultures, women may engage in actions that provide an identity, but not one that corresponds to the concept "lesbian." At the end of the 19th century in Canton, a Chinese silk-producing area, women organized "sworn sisterhoods" (*zishu*) and identified as "marriage-resisters" (*dushen zhyyi nüzi*, literally "women believing in remaining single").[29] Although there were economic and cultural reasons behind their decision, commentators at the time attributed the phenomenon in part to the fact that women "acquired intimate friends with whom they practiced homosexual love."[30]

Once the sexologists had undertaken the process of naming and defining the kind of people who loved others of the same sex, what did such definitions mean to women who loved other women? For some, the medicalization of same-sex love brought unwanted attention and shame; for others, self-understanding and an identity. Jeannette Marks, a professor of English at Mount Holyoke College, Massachusetts, who lived in an intimate relationship with Mary Woolley, the college's president from 1901 to 1937, was one who worried that others might see her as a lesbian. [...]

On the other hand, the concept of lesbianism as a defining characteristic allowed some women to embrace their own sexuality more fully. British feminist Frances Wilder expressed her gratitude to homosexual sexologist Edward Carpenter, whose work made her realize that she "was more closely related to the intermediate sex than I had hitherto imagined."[31] In *The Well of Loneliness*, Radclyffe Hall has her famous character Stephen discover her true nature when she finds a copy of Richard von Krafft-Ebing's monumental work *Psychopathia Sexualis*. Hall hoped that her novel would help young women like herself come to terms with their desires, as well as elicit sympathy from heterosexual readers.[32]

But it would be a mistake to assume that the experts defined lesbian identity independently, leaving women-loving women either to reject or embrace what was offered them. For the sexologists fashioned their analyses from what they saw around them, including the cases of women such as Alice Mitchell and Sandor Vay. And in the early 20th century a self-fashioning of the modern lesbian was taking place in communities where women with same-sex desires found others like themselves.

In Paris, the salon of the American Natalie Clifford Barney was the heart of one such lesbian community from the 1890s to the 1930s. A wealthy heiress, Barney wasted no time agonizing over the conclusions of the sexologists. Secure in her sexual desire for women, feminine in her self-presentation and protected by class privilege, Barney flourished in an environment in which homosexuality was celebrated among the elite. In her salon, she gathered around her a coterie of writers, artists and lovers whose works celebrated lesbianism. And she eschewed shame: "Albinos aren't reproached for having pink eyes and whitish hair, why should they [society] hold it against me for being a lesbian? It's a question of nature: my queerness isn't a vice, isn't 'deliberate,' and harms no one."[33] Flamboyant and self-confident, Barney had no qualms about flaunting her non-monogamous lesbianism.

Berlin, too, was home in the 1920s to a vibrant lesbian world. Until the Nazi rise to power, an astonishing number of lesbian clubs, bars, balls, groups, circles and publications catered to women who loved women, and cabaret acts openly represented lesbian love.[34] The periodical *Die Freundin* ("The Girlfriend"), published in Berlin from 1924 to 1933, directed its stories and articles to women described as "same-sex loving" (*gleichgeschlechtlichliebend*), "homosexual" (*homosexuell*), "homoerotic" (*homoerotisch*) or "lesbian" (*lesbisch*).[35] The transnational aspects of lesbian culture among elites is evident in the title of another periodical published in Berlin in the 1930s. *Garçonne* (the French for "boy" with an added feminine ending, meaning

also an "emancipated woman") catered to a lesbian and male transvestite audience.[36] Both periodicals featured photographs and illustrations of a variety of lesbians: some cross-dressed, some in butch–fem couples, some entirely feminine.

New York was also home to commercial and private venues that catered to a crowd with same-sex desires, and not just to elite women. By the 1920s, two neighbourhoods—Greenwich Village and Harlem—had established reputations as welcoming places for lesbians as well as gay men. Like Paris and Berlin, both districts were also artistic and bohemian centres. The Harlem Renaissance in particular spread word of lesbian love through literature, art and the blues. Lucille Bogan, in "B.D. Women Blues," sang of "bulldagger" women, and in fact many of the great women blues singers were themselves lesbian or bisexual. Mabel Hampton, a black performer who in her teens lived in Harlem, described private parties where women who desired women might meet: "The bulldykers used to come and bring their women with them, you know."[37]

Such vibrant lesbian communities were the exception rather than the rule, however, for in much of the world the idea that women should live independently of men remained unthinkable. But even where the conditions for such lesbian communities were lacking, the language of same-sex love began to enter the vernacular. In Republican China, indigenous developments—such as the emergence of marriage resistance, the widespread existence of same-sex love relations in sex-segregated schools, and changes in gender roles accompanying urbanization—combined with the translation of the work of Western sexologists and drew attention to the new concept of "same-sex love" (*tongxing ai*) that had migrated from Japan.[38] A number of women writers from the progressive May Fourth movement wrote about love between women, often telling of relationships between women in school. One such author, Lu Yin, in *Lishi's Diary* (1923) tells the story of a woman who does not wish to marry and whose feelings for her school friend Yuanqing change from "ordinary friendship" to "same-sex romantic love." They make plans to live together, and Lishi that night dreams that they are rowing a boat in the moonlight. Then Yuanqing's mother forces her to move away and plans to marry her off to her cousin. Yuanqing writes to Lishi, "Ah, Lishi! Why didn't you plan ahead! Why didn't you dress up in men's clothes, put on a man's hat, act like a roan, and visit my parents to ask for my hand?"[39] In the end, Yuanqing repudiates their dream and Lishi dies of melancholia. Lu Yin herself married twice, but her writings suggest that she struggled with lesbian desire. She described her urge to dress as a man and visit a brothel, although she feared that if anyone found out, they would have "dreadful suspicions" about her.[40]

*****

In the 1960s and 1970s, in conjunction with movements for social justice that were appearing around the world, women who identified as lesbians began to speak out and organize public protests, even in places where that put them in a great deal of danger. When the United Nations-sponsored first International Women's Year Conference came to Mexico City in 1975, the press attacked the lesbian presence as imported and alien to Mexican culture, but four years later a group of lesbians promoted their cause publicly at the first World Sexology Congress.[41] In South Africa, groups such as Sunday's Women in Durban, the GLOW (Gay and Lesbian Organization of the Witwatersrand), Lesbian Forum in Soweto-Johannesburg, and Lesbians in Love and Compromising Situations (LILACS) in Cape Town emerged during the 1980s.[42] Lesbians with sufficient class or organizational privilege connect at international feminist and gay/lesbian conferences such as those sponsored by the International Lesbian and Gay Association. The Asian Lesbian Network brings together lesbians from ten Asian countries and Asian lesbians living outside Asia, and the Encuentros de Lesbianas Feministas are conferences for lesbians in Latin America and the Caribbean.[43]

Claiming an identity—as Saffic or lesbian; as a marriage-resister, a *garçonne* or a bulldagger; as *bombero* (literally "firefighter," for butch) or *mucama* ("housemaid," for fem) in Argentina or as *chapatbaz* (women who engage in tribadism) in Urdu—requires one to have a concept of a particular kind of person with which one can relate, a notion that there are others like oneself with whom one might build a community. Although identity is important to the construction of the modern lesbian, we must remember that there are still women all around the globe who are crossing the gender line, loving women and engaging in sexual relations without thinking of themselves as lesbians.

## LOVING WOMEN

What does it mean to love women in the modern world? As all of these manifestations of relationships between women make clear, there are many and various ways in which women love other women. Some cross the gender line to marry their lovers. [...] And others, in different ways, celebrated their love, claimed an identity and joined together to make the world a more hospitable place for loving women.

## NOTES

1. Judith M. Bennett, "'Lesbian-Like' and the Social History of Lesbianisms," *Journal of the History of Sexuality*, vol. 9, no. 1–2 (2000), pp. 1–24; Leila J. Rupp, "Toward a Global History of Same-Sex Sexuality," *Journal of the History of Sexuality*, vol. 10, no. 2 (2001), pp. 287–302.

2. Lucy Chesser, "'A Woman Who Married Three Wives': Management of Disruptive Knowledge in the 1879 Australian Case of Edward De Lacy Evans," *Journal of Women's History*, vol. 9, no. 4 (1998), pp. 53–77.

3. Ibid., p. 60.

4. See Rudolf Dekker and Lott van de Pol, *The Tradition of Female Transvestism in Early Modern Europe* (London

1989); and Julie Wheelwright, *Amazons and Military Maids: Women Who Dressed As Men in Pursuit of Life, Liberty and Happiness* (London 1989).

5.  See Sabine Lang, "Various Kinds of Two-Spirit People: Gender Variance and Homosexuality in Native American Communities," in Sue-Ellen Jacobs, Wesley Thomas and Sabine Lang (eds.), *Two-Spirit People* (Urbana 1997), pp. 100–118; and Walter L. Williams, *The Spirit and the Flesh: Sexual Diversity in American Indian Culture* (Boston 1986).

6.  Quoted in Joseph M. Carrier and Stephen O. Murray, "Woman–Woman Marriage in Africa," in Stephen O. Murray and Will Roscoe (eds.), *Boy-Wives and Female Husbands: Studies in African Homosexualities* (New York 1998), p. 259.

7.  See Carrier and Murray, *Boy-Wives*.

8.  Quoted in Carrier and Murray, *Boy-Wives*, p. 263.

9.  Quoted in Martha Vicinus, *Intimate Friends: Women Who Loved Women, 1778–1928* (Chicago 2004), p. 9.

10. Ibid., p. 45.

11. See Lisa Duggan, *Sapphic Slashers: Sex, Violence and American Modernity* (Durham 2000).

12. Quoted in Geertje Mak, "Sandor/Sarolta Vay: From Passing Woman to Invert," *Journal of Women's History*, vol. 16, no. 1 (2004), p. 54.

13. Ibid., p. 61.

14. See Diane Wood Middlebrook, *Suits Me: The Double Life of Billy Tipton* (New York 1998).

15. Ruth Vanita, "CLAGS Reports," *Centre for Lesbian and Gay Studies News*, vol. 14, no. 2 (2004), p. 14.

16. Quoted in Amanda Lock Swarr and Richa Nagar, "Dismantling Assumptions: Interrogating 'Lesbian' Struggles for Identity and Survival in India and South Africa," *Signs: Journal of Women in Culture and Society*, vol. 29 (2004), p. 500.

17. Quoted in Elizabeth W. Knowlton, "'Only a Woman Like Yourself': Rebecca Alice Baldy, Dutiful Daughter, Stalwart Sister and Lesbian Lover of Nineteenth-Century Georgia," in John Howard (ed.), *Carryin' On in the Lesbian and Gay South* (New York 1997), p. 48.

18. Quoted in Dasa Francikova, "Female Friends in Nineteenth-Century Bohemia: Troubles with Affectionate Writing and 'Patriotic Relationships,'" *Journal of Women's History*, vol. 12, no. 3 (2000), pp. 23–28, quotation on p. 24.

19. Quoted in Gloria T. Hull, *Color, Sex and Poetry: Three Women Writers of the Harlem Renaissance* (Bloomington 1987), p. 139.

20. Quoted in Lillian Faderman, *Scotch Verdict* (New York 1983), p. 147.

21. Ibid., p. 281.

22. Ibid., p. 82.

23. Quoted in Jennifer Terry, *An American Obsession: Science, Medicine and Homosexuality in Modern Society* (Chicago 1999), p. 242.

24. See Elizabeth Lapovsky Kennedy and Madeline D. Davis, *Boots of Leather, Slippers of Gold: The History of a Lesbian Community* (New York 1993).

25. Ibid., p. 204.

26. Anne Lister, *I Know My Own Heart: The Diaries of Anne Lister (1797–1810)*, ed. Helena Whitbread (London 1988), p. 145.

27. Kendall, "'When a Woman Loves a Woman' in Lesotho: Love, Sex, and the (Western) Construction of Homophobia," in Stephen O. Murray and Will Roscoe (eds.), *Boy-Wives and Female Husbands: Studies in African Homosexualities* (New York 1998), pp. 223–41.

28. Ibid., p. 233. On boarding-school relationships, Kendall cites Judith Gay, "Mummies and Babies and Friends and Lovers in Lesotho," *Journal of Homosexuality*, vol. 11, no. 3–4 (1985), pp. 97–116.

29. See Tze-lan D. Sang, *The Emerging Lesbian: Female Same-Sex Desire in Modern China* (Chicago 2003), pp. 52, 377.

30. Ibid., p. 52.

31. Quoted in Carroll Smith-Rosenberg, "Discourses of Sexuality and Subjectivity: The New Woman, 1870–1936," in Martin Bauml Duberman, Martha Vicinus and George Chauncey (eds.), *Hidden from History: Reclaiming the Gay and Lesbian Past* (New York 1989), p. 275.

32. See Vicinus, *Intimate Friends*, p. 217.

33. Ibid., pp. 189–90.

34. See the articles in *Eldorado: Homosexualle Frauen und Männer in Berlin 1850–1950*, exh. cat., Berlin, Schwules Museum (Berlin 1984).

35. Katharine Vogel, "Zum Selbstverständnis lesbischer Frauen in der Weimarer Republik," in *Eldorado*, pp. 162–68.

36. Quoted in Petra Shlierkamp, "Die Garçonne," in *Eldorado*, p. 173.

37. Joan Nestle, "Excerpts from the Oral History of Mabel Hampton," *Signs: Journal of Women in Culture and Society*, vol. 18 (1993), p. 933.

38. See Sang, *The Emerging Lesbian*.

39. Ibid., p. 139.

40. Ibid., p. 144.

41. Claudia Hinojosa, "Mexico," in Bonnie Zimmerman (ed.), *Lesbian Histories and Cultures* (New York 2000), pp. 494–96.

42. Ian Barnard, "South Africa," in Zimmerman, *Lesbian Histories and Cultures*, pp. 721–22.

43. Julie Dorf, "International Organizations," in Zimmerman, *Lesbian Histories and Cultures*, pp. 398–400.

*Source:* Rupp, Leila J. (2006). Excerpted from "Loving Women in the Modern World." In Robert Aldrick (Ed.), *Gay Life and Culture: A World History* (pp. 223–247). New York, NY: Universe.

# CHAPTER 26

## "Stand Up" for Exclusion? Queer Pride, Ableism, and Inequality

*Danielle Peers and Lindsay Eales*

Danielle Peers is an assistant professor in the Faculty of Physical Education and Recreation at the University of Alberta. Peers's work focuses on adapted physical activity, socio-cultural sport and movement studies, and critical disability studies. A former Paralympic medallist, Peers works with art-based and autoethnographic research methods involving video, creative movement, and creative writing.

Lindsay Eales is a Vanier scholar and PhD student in the Faculty of Physical Education and Recreation at the University of Alberta. Eales studies, choreographs, and performs integrated dance, as well as disability and Mad performance art. As co-artistic director of CRIPSiE (Collaborative Radically Integrated Performers Society in Edmonton), she has spent the last ten years creating vibrant movement communities that appreciate diversity and reimagine disability.

It was Queer Pride Week 2011 in Edmonton, as we began to write this piece. Our city's billboards are wrapped with rainbow-colored posters of young scantily-clad men with bulging... muscles. Unfortunately, we have come to expect a significant dose of ableism, ageism, racism and fatphobia at Pride festivals across North America. In 2011, however, the Edmonton Pride Festival Society[1] made ableism official!

Edmonton Pride's official slogan in 2011 was "STAND UP."[2] Although dismayed by the ableist[3] language, we were hoping, at the very least, that this slogan signaled a move towards a more political Pride: A move away from the festival that had renamed itself after a bank two years ago and that had begun banning some political queer groups from marching (most notably in Toronto). But what Edmonton Pride is standing up for this year is *not* greater equity. The event listings tell the disappointing story: "Stand up... and boogie"; and "Stand up... and barbeque"—as if there was nothing of political value left for queers to "stand up" for.

The Pride slogan, poster and website, however, demonstrate that there is still much work to be done. On the poster, "STAND UP"[4] is written in white monolithic letters below the *diversity*-rainbow-colored silhouettes of six immaculately non-diverse bodies in progressive stages of getting up to stand. On one side of the poster are three square, thin, muscular silhouettes: one in "thinker" pose; one crouching as though about to begin a sprint; and one standing with arms and legs wide apart, taking up space. On the other side are three smaller, super-thin-yet-curvy multi-colored figures: one on knees and bum sitting in a "schoolgirl" pose (like the pornography pose, minus the braids and the kilt); one on knees with head thrown back to show off large, perky breasts; one standing with arms and legs pulled together to make space for the more masculine standing counterpart. The Edmonton Pride website bears the slogan and poster below a banner photograph which features scantily-clad, athletic-looking white-skinned men wearing afro-like wigs. There is still so much work to be done.

Among the many race, gender and ability issues with these images of supposed queer diversity is the noticeable lack of fat, gender-queer, wheeling, scootering, ageing, small-statured, cane-wielding, pre-pubescent and dog-guided members of our queer communities. The *lack* of any significantly diverse bodies in the *diversity* poster and website might not have struck many Pride-goers as strange, however, since many of these bodies are structurally excluded from Queer[5] events, in general.

Every summer, for example, the Edmonton Pride Festival Society rents one of the most accessible[6] venues in Edmonton, and, through great expense and logistical prowess, manages to transform it into an almost entirely inaccessible space (despite years of being offered free or cheap alternatives for rendering the space more accessible). Year round, gay parties and events are held almost exclusively in bars or galleries that are up or down at least a flight of stairs. Most of these events don't allow minors, won't accommodate wheelchairs, have gender-segregated washrooms and are not set up for those who see or hear in non-normative ways. With few "standing up" against (or perhaps even taking note of) these exclusions, many community members end up having to *sit* out most "queer" events.

Of course, mainstream gay movements are perhaps too easy targets. [...] We ask: Are our academic, artistic and activist movements that claim to be equity-based any less ableist and any more accessible than the Edmonton Pride example herein?

In Robert McRuer's groundbreaking work, *Crip Theory: Cultural Signs of Queerness and Disability*,[7] he argues that the exclusion, marginalization or complete erasure of disability is common to contemporary queer politics and to activist politics more generally. One of his most poignant examples is the 2004 World Social Forum[8] (WSF) in Mumbai, India, a global activist network that protested the World Economic Forum by collectively imagining alternatives to globalized capitalism. The WSF earned protests of its own, however, due to its lack of accessibility and the organizers' refusal to include a speaker on disability issues. The WSF's slogan was "Another World Is Possible," yet it remained somewhat impossible for WSF activists to imagine disability as having a place in this new world, let alone in the movement that might create it.

There is an eerie familiarity to this seeming impossibility of imagining accessibility and disability issues as vital components of social movements. Think about it. Have you recently attended any of the following:

- Equity-based academic conferences or lectures organized without any physical, visual or audio accessibility forethought?
- Take back the night or G8 marches planned on inaccessible routes?
- Film festivals in which wheelchair users are deemed fire hazards and are not allowed in the theatre, and where captions are turned off because normate[9] audience members find them "distracting"?
- Expensive queer parties or fundraisers held in spaces with gender-segregated washrooms, inaccessible entrances and no minors allowed?

More importantly, did you notice these structural exclusions at the time? People often don't notice these barriers because excluded bodies usually cannot enter these spaces to demonstrate their inaccessibility. It is a self-fulfilling prophecy and one that has very real consequences for the bodies and communities that are excluded, as well as for those of us who fail to address these systemic exclusions.

Odds are, however, that some of you *have* noticed some of these barriers at least some of the time. There are, after all, vibrant activist communities that work hard at identifying and creatively responding to the ways that they participate in the inequitable treatment and exclusion of others. [...]

As inundated as we are with the inequitable politics of Pride, Edmontonians are finally getting a taste of equity-oriented queer celebrations. The Exposure Queer Arts and Culture Festival[10] is making radical moves towards removing barriers to their festival and to Edmonton's queer scene in general. It started with their "All Bodies Pool Party": an outdoor, wheelchair accessible, pay-what-you-can, all-ages, all-gender affair. Finally, queer Edmontonians—like queers elsewhere—have a choice: "Stand Up!" for the ableism of Pride, or sit in on an accessible queer/crip celebration of swimming, mobilizing and imagining more inclusive images, activities, events and communities.

## NOTES

1.  Edmonton Pride Festival. (2012). Home. Retrieved from http://www.edmontonpride.ca/

2.  Edmonton Pride Festival. (2012). Home. Retrieved from http://www.edmontonpride.ca/

3.  Fedcan Blog. (2011). Home. Retrieved from http://blog.fedcan.ca/tag/ableism-and-disability/ (link no longer active).

4.  Edmonton Pride Festival. (2012). Home. Retrieved from http://www.edmontonpride.ca/

5.  Queer Studies. (2011, December 17). Retrieved December 29, 2011 from Wikipedia: http://en.wikipedia.org/wiki/Queer_studies

6.  Accessibility. (2012, January 2). Retrieved January 2, 2012 from Wikipedia http://en.wikipedia.org/wiki/Accessibility

7.  McRuer, R. (2006). *Crip Theory: Cultural Signs of Queerness and Disability.* New York: New York University Press.

8.  World Social Forum. (2011, December 30). Retrieved on January 1, 2012, from Wikipedia: http://en.wikipedia.org/wiki/World_Social_Forum#2004_World_Social_Forum

9.  Editors' Note: Feminist disability studies scholar Rosemarie Garland-Thomson coined the term *normate* as a way of describing all those who derive privilege for mentally and physically fitting the characteristics that western cultures deem as typical or normative.

10.  Exposure. (n.d.). The 5th Annual Exposure. Retrieved from http://www.exposurefestival.ca/

*Source:* Peers, Danielle, & Eales, Lindsay. (2012). Excerpted from "'Stand Up' for Exclusion? Queer Pride, Ableism and Inequality." In Malinda S. Smith & Fatima Jaffer (Eds.), *Beyond the Queer Alphabet: Conversations on Gender, Sexuality & Intersectionality* (pp. 39–41). Ottawa, ON: Canadian Federation for the Humanities and Social Sciences.

# PART 3

## Gendered Identities

Movements begin when people refuse to live divided lives.
—*Parker J. Palmer, quoted in The Cultural Creatives:*
*How 50 Million People Are Changing the World (2000, p. 20)*

This part of the book examines gendered identities, systemic inequalities, and the power of stereotypes. We emphasize some of the main institutions in societies that shape gendered social relations through, for example, the family, the community, the educational system, and the state. The main focus is on practices and legacies of colonization and imperialism.

## Part 3A: Thinking about Difference and Identity

We introduce here some basic concepts for understanding constructions of difference and identity in the contemporary social world. These include critical writings on identity, difference, stereotyping, racism, white privilege, microaggression, and culture. We use South Asian girls' struggles for belonging as a North American case study that illustrates the significance of race to women's lives.

## Part 3B: Histories and Legacies of Colonialism and Imperialism

In this section, we take up histories and legacies of slavery, colonization, and imperialism, nationally and transnationally. We introduce readers to "difficult knowledge" about the histories of slavery and colonization in Canada and North America as well as the implicatedness of whiteness in colonialism and imperialism. We examine legacies of racism and colonialism today by exploring how race and gender interact in diverse women's lives. This section and the next also work together to ground and elaborate our analysis of colonization by examining its specific operations and consequences for one group in particular: Indigenous women within what is now called Canada.

## Part 3C: Indigenous Women: Resistance and Resurgence

We turn in this section to examining Indigenous women's individual and collective strategies for survival and resistance in North America in the past and present. We highlight women's involvements in political activism; community leadership; artistic expression, including performance and poetry; and various strategies employed to negotiate and challenge colonial imagery and institutions.

# CHAPTER 27

## Stereotyping As a Signifying Practice

*Stuart Hall*

Stuart Hall was a leading cultural theorist and sociologist, and one of the founding figures of British cultural studies. Hall was director of the Centre for Contemporary Cultural Studies at Birmingham University in England, where he played an instrumental role in expanding the scope of cultural studies to include an analysis of race and gender. He later became a professor of sociology at the Open University. The British newspaper *The Observer* has called him "one of the country's leading cultural theorists."

We need to reflect on how a racialized regime of representation actually works. Essentially, this involves examining more deeply the set of representational practices known as *stereotyping*. [...] Stereotyping reduces people to a few, simple, essential characteristics, which are represented as fixed by Nature.

Stereotyping as a signifying practice is central to the representation of racial difference. But what is a stereotype? How does it actually work? In his essay on "Stereotyping," Richard Dyer (1977) makes an important distinction between *typing* and *stereotyping*. He argues that, without the use of *types*, it would be difficult, if not impossible, to make sense of the world. We understand the world by referring individual objects, people, or events in our heads to the general classificatory schemes into which—according to our culture—they fit. Thus, we "decode" a flat object on legs on which we place things as a "table." We may never have seen that kind of "table" before, but we have a general concept or category of "table" in our heads, into which we "fit" the particular objects we perceive or encounter. In other words, we understand "the particular" in terms of its "type." We deploy what Alfred Schutz called *typifications*. In this sense, "typing" is essential to the production of meaning.

Richard Dyer argues that we are always "making sense" of things in terms of some wider categories. Thus, for example, we come to "know" something about a person by thinking of the *roles* which he or she performs: is he/she a parent, a child, a worker, a lover, boss, or an old age pensioner? We assign him/her to the *membership* of different groups, according to class, gender, age group, nationality, "race," linguistic group, sexual preference, and so on. We order him/her in terms of *personality type*—is he/she a happy, serious, depressed, scatter-brained, over-active kind of person? Our picture of who the person "is" is built up out of the information we accumulate from positioning him/her within these different orders of typification. In broad terms, then, "a *type* is any simple, vivid, memorable, easily grasped and widely recognized characterization in which a few traits are foregrounded and change or 'development' is kept to a minimum" (Dyer, 1977, p. 28).

What, then, is the difference between a *type* and a *stereotype*? *Stereotypes* get hold of the few "simple, vivid, memorable, easily grasped and widely recognized" characteristics about a person, *reduce* everything about the person to those traits, *exaggerate* and *simplify* them, and *fix* them without change or development to eternity. So the first point is—*stereotyping reduces, essentializes, naturalizes, and fixes "difference."*

Secondly, *stereotyping deploys a strategy of "splitting."* It divides the normal and the acceptable from the abnormal and the unacceptable. It then *excludes* or *expels* everything which does not fit, which is different. Dyer argues that "a system of social- and stereo-types refers to what is, as it were, within and beyond the pale of normalcy [i.e., behaviour which is accepted as "normal" in any culture]. Types are instances which indicate those who live by the rules of society (social types) and those who the rules are designed to exclude (stereotypes). For this reason, stereotypes are also more rigid than social types … [B]oundaries … must be clearly delineated and so stereotypes, one of the mechanisms of boundary maintenance, are characteristically fixed, clear-cut, unalterable" (ibid., p. 29). So, *another feature of stereotyping is its practice of "closure" and exclusion. It symbolically fixes boundaries, and excludes everything which does not belong.*

Stereotyping, in other words, is part of the maintenance of social and symbolic order. It sets up a symbolic frontier between the "normal" and the "deviant," the "normal" and the "pathological," the "acceptable" and the "unacceptable," what "belongs" and what does not or is "Other," between "insiders" and "outsiders," Us and Them. It facilitates the "binding" or bonding together of all of Us who are "normal" into one "imagined community"; and it sends into symbolic exile all of Them—"the Others"—who are in some way different—"beyond the pale." Mary Douglas (1966), for example, argued that whatever is "out of place" is considered as polluted, dangerous, taboo. Negative feelings cluster around it. It must be symbolically excluded if the "purity" of the culture is to be restored. The feminist theorist Julia Kristeva calls such expelled or excluded groups "abjected" (from the Latin meaning, literally, "thrown out") (Kristeva, 1982).

The third point is that *stereotyping tends to occur where there are gross inequalities of power.* Power is usually directed against the subordinate or excluded group. One aspect of this power, according to Dyer, is *ethnocentrism*—"the application of the norms of one's own culture to that of others" (Brown, 1965, p. 183). [Derrida argued] that, between binary oppositions like Us/Them, "we are not dealing with … peaceful coexistence … but rather with a violent hierarchy. One of the two terms governs … the other or has the upper hand" (1972, p. 41).

In short, stereotyping is what Foucault called a "power/knowledge" sort of game. It classifies people according to a norm and constructs the excluded "other." Interestingly, it is also what Gramsci would have called an aspect of the struggle for hegemony. As Dyer observes, "The establishment of normalcy (i.e., what is accepted as 'normal') through social- and stereo-types is one aspect of the habit of ruling groups … to attempt to fashion the whole of society according to their own world view, value system, sensibility and ideology. So right is this world view for the ruling groups that they make it appear (as it *does* appear to them) as 'natural' and 'inevitable'—and for everyone—and, in so far as they succeed, they establish their hegemony" (Dyer, 1977, p. 30). Hegemony is a form of power based on leadership by a group in many fields of activity at once, so that its ascendancy commands widespread consent and appears natural and inevitable.

# REFERENCES

Brown, R. (1965) *Social Psychology*. London/New York, Macmillan.

Derrida, J. (1972) *Positions*. Chicago, University of Chicago Press.

Douglas, M. (1966) *Purity and Danger*. London, Routledge & Kegan Paul.

Dyer, R. (ed.) (1977) *Gays and Film*. London, British Film Institute.

Kristeva, J. (1982) *Powers of Horror*. New York, Columbia University Press.

---

*Source:* Hall, Stuart. (2002). Excerpted from "The Spectacle of the 'Other.'" In *Representation: Cultural Representations and Signifying Practices* (pp. 257–259). London, UK: Open University.

# CHAPTER 28

## Undoing the "Package Picture" of Cultures

*Uma Narayan*

Uma Narayan is a professor of philosophy and Andrew W. Mellon Chair of the Humanities at Vassar College in the United States. Her research and teaching areas include
contemporary moral issues, feminist theory, and global feminism. She is co-editor of
a number of anthologies and the author of *Dislocating Cultures: Identities, Traditions
and Third World Feminism*. Narayan's work is especially influential for challenging the
common misconception that feminism is solely a Western notion.

Many feminists of color have demonstrated the
need to take into account differences among
women to avoid hegemonic gender-essentialist
analyses that represent the problems and interests
of privileged women as paradigmatic. As feminist
agendas become global, there is growing feminist
concern to consider national and cultural differences
among women. However, in attempting to take seriously these cultural differences, many feminists risk
replacing gender-essentialist analyses with culturally essentialist analyses that replicate problematic
colonialist notions about the cultural differences
between "Western culture" and "non-Western cultures" and the women who inhabit them (Narayan
1998). Seemingly universal essentialist generalizations
about "all women" are replaced by culture-specific
essentialist generalizations that depend on totalizing
categories such as "Western culture," "non-Western
cultures," "Indian women," and "Muslim women."
The picture of the "cultures" attributed to these groups

of women remains fundamentally essentialist, depicting as homogeneous groups of heterogeneous peoples
whose values, ways of life, and political commitments
are internally divergent.

I believe that many contemporary feminists are
attuned to the problem of imposing Sameness on
Other women but fail to register that certain scripts
of Difference can be no less problematic. Cultural
imperialism in colonial times denied rather than
affirmed that one's Others were "just like oneself,"
insisting on the colonized Others' difference from
and inferiority to the Western subject. Insistence
on sharp contrasts between "Western culture" and
"Other cultures" and on the superiority of Western
culture functioned as justifications for colonialism.
However, this self-portrait of Western culture had
only a faint resemblance to the political and cultural
values that actually pervaded life in Western societies. Thus, liberty and equality could be represented
as paradigmatic Western values at the very moment

when Western nations were engaged in slavery, colonization, and the denial of liberty and equality to large segments of Western subjects, including women.

Anticolonial nationalist movements added to the perpetuation of essentialist notions of national culture by embracing, and trying to revalue, the imputed facets of their own culture embedded in the colonialists' stereotypes. Thus, while the British imputed "spiritualism" to Indian culture to suggest lack of readiness for the worldly project of self-rule, many Indian nationalists embraced this definition to make the anticolonialist and nationalist argument that their culture was distinctive from and superior to that of the West. Thus, sharply contrasting pictures of Western culture and of various colonized national cultures came to be reiterated by both colonizers and colonized.

Prevalent essentialist modes of thinking about cultures depend on a problematic picture of what various cultures are like, or on what I call the "Package Picture of Cultures." This view understands cultures on the model of neatly wrapped packages, sealed off from each other, possessing sharply defined edges or contours, and having distinctive contents that differ from those of other "cultural packages." I believe that these packages are more badly wrapped and their contents more jumbled than is often assumed and that there is a variety of political agendas that determine who and what are assigned places inside and outside a particular cultural package.

The essentialist Package Picture of Cultures represents cultures as if they were entities that exist neatly distinct and separate in the world, independent of our projects of distinguishing among them, obscuring the reality that boundaries between them are human constructs, underdetermined by existing variations in worldviews and ways of life. It eclipses the reality that the labels currently used to demarcate particular cultures themselves have a historical provenance and that what they individuate as one culture often changes over time. For example, while a prevailing picture of Western culture has it beginning in ancient Greece and perhaps culminating in the contemporary

United States, a historical perspective would register that the ancient Greeks did not define themselves as part of "Western culture" and that "American culture" was initially distinguished from "European culture" rather than assimilated to it under the rubric "Western culture." The *Shorter Oxford English Dictionary* indicates that the use of the term *Western* to refer to Europe in distinction to *Eastern* or *Oriental* began around 1600, testimony to its colonial origins. Similarly, *Indian culture* is a label connected to the historical unification of an assortment of political territories into *British India*, a term that enabled the nationalist challenge to colonialism to emerge as *Indian*. Labels that pick out particular cultures are not simple descriptions that single out already distinct entities; rather, they are arbitrary and shifting designations connected to political projects that, for different reasons, insist on the distinctness of one culture from another.

The Package Picture of Cultures also assumes that the assignment of individuals to specific cultures is an obvious and uncontroversial matter. Under the influence of this picture, many of us assume that we know as a simple matter of fact to what "culture" we and others belong. I invite readers who think that they are members of Western culture or American culture to ask themselves what they have in common with the millions of people who would be assigned to the same cultural package. Do I share a common culture with every other Indian woman, and, if so, what are the constituent elements that make us members of the same culture? What is *my* relationship to Western culture? Critical reflection on such questions suggests that the assignment of individuals to particular cultures is more complicated than assumed and that it is affected by numerous, often incompatible, political projects of cultural classification.

The Package Picture of Cultures mistakenly sees the centrality of particular values, traditions, or practices to any particular culture as a given and thus eclipses the historical and political processes by which particular values or practices have come to be deemed central components of a particular culture.

It also obscures how projects of cultural preservation themselves change over time. Dominant members of a culture often willingly discard what were previously regarded as important cultural practices but resist and protest other cultural changes, often those pertaining to the welfare of women. For instance, Olayinka Koso-Thomas's work reveals that in Sierra Leone virtually all the elaborate initiation rites and training that were traditional preliminaries to female circumcision have been given up because people no longer have the time, money, or social infrastructure for them. However, the rite of excision, abstracted from the whole context of practices in which it used to be embedded, is still seen as a crucial component of "preserving tradition" (Koso-Thomas 1987, 23). Feminists need to be alert to such synecdochic moves, whereby parts of a practice come to stand in for the whole, because such substitutions conceal important dimensions of social change.

Feminist engagement with cultural practices should be attentive to a process that I call "selective labeling," whereby those with social power conveniently designate certain changes in values and practices as consonant with cultural preservation and others as cultural loss or betrayal. Selective labeling allows changes approved by socially dominant groups to appear consonant with the preservation of essential values or core practices of a culture, while depicting changes that challenge the status quo as threats to that culture. The Package Picture of Cultures poses serious problems for feminist agendas in third-world contexts, since it often depicts culturally dominant norms of femininity, along with practices that adversely affect women, as central components of cultural identity and casts feminist challenges to norms and practices affecting women as cultural betrayals (Narayan 1997).

Giving up the Package Picture's view of cultural contexts as homogeneous helps us see that sharp differences in values often exist among those described as members of the same culture while among those described as "members of different cultures" there are often strong affinities in values, opening up liberating possibilities with respect to cross-cultural feminist judgments. For instance, the values and judgments of a Western feminist may diverge greatly from those of politically conservative members of her "package," while they might converge quite strongly with those of an Indian feminist counterpart. A Western feminist accused of imposing Western values in her negative judgment of an Indian cultural practice could, for instance, point out that her judgments correspond closely to those of some Indian feminists. Making this assertion does require her to be informed about Indian feminists' analyses of the practice and to use her critical judgment when such analyses disagree, as sometimes happens. Feminists can avoid the Package Picture of Cultures by attending to the historical variations and ongoing changes in cultural practices, to the wide range of attitudes toward those practices manifested by different members of a culture, and to the political negotiations that help to change the meanings and significances of these practices. Such attention would facilitate informed and astute feminist engagement with women's issues in national contexts different from their own.

## REFERENCES

Koso-Thomas, Olayinka. 1987. *The Circumcision of Women*. New York: Zed.

Narayan, Uma. 1997. *Dislocating Cultures: Identities, Traditions, and Third World Feminism*. New York: Routledge.

Narayan, Uma. 1998. "Essence of Culture and a Sense of History." *Hypatia* 13(2): 86–106.

**Source:** Narayan, Uma. (2000). Excerpted from "Undoing the 'Package Picture' of Cultures." *Signs: Journal of Women in Culture and Society, 25*(4), 1083–1086.

# ACTIVIST ART 4

## MISS CANADIANA

*Camille Turner*

Camille Turner is an artist, educator, and cultural producer whose work explores themes of race, space, home, and belonging. Miss Canadiana, one of her earliest projects, challenges perceptions of Canadianness and troubles the unspoken binary of "real Canadian" and "diverse other." Turner is the founder of Outterregion, an Afro-futurist performance group. She is a graduate of OCAD University and York University's Masters in Environmental Studies Program, where she is currently a PhD candidate.

*Hometown Queen.*

**Source:** Turner, Camille. (2011). "Hometown Queen." *Miss Canadiana.* Retrieved from: http://camilleturner.com/project/miss-canadiana/.

My image as Miss Canadiana points to the contradiction of the Canadian mythology. My body, as a representative of Canadian heritage, is surprising only because Blackness is perceived as foreign in Canada. (Camille Turner)

Miss Canadiana is a persona created and performed by Camille Turner since 2002. She has made appearances across Canada and has represented Canada in the UK, Germany, Senegal, Australia, Cuba, Jamaica and Mexico. Documentation of the performances has been included in numerous exhibitions and festivals.

*Hometown Queen* is a series of staged photographs of Miss Canadiana returning to Camille's hometown of Hamilton, Ontario.

I created the Hometown Queen series to re-write my personal history and to pay homage to my complicated relationship with Hamilton [Ontario], my hometown. The Hamilton I grew up in was a proud, hard-working steel town with a no-nonsense attitude. On the one hand, I admire this city's fierce resistance to the influence of nearby sprawling full-of-itself Toronto. On the other hand, growing up there I witnessed and experienced many incidents of blatant bigotry. I couldn't wait to get away from Hamilton when I was young but now I realize that this complex city made me the person I am today—always looking beneath the surface and recognizing the irony in everything around me. (Camille Turner)

---

*Source:* Turner, Camille. (n.d.). *Miss Canadiana* (Artist Statement). Retrieved from: http://camilleturner.com/project/miss-canadiana/.

# HOW TO KNOW IF YOU ARE WHITE

*Mia McKenzie*

Mia McKenzie is a writer, activist, and the founder of the website *Black Girl Dangerous* (BGD). McKenzie identifies as a queer Black feminist and uses her writing and website to make space for LGBTQ people of color. Her debut novel, *The Summer We Got Free*, received a Lambda Literary Award in 2013. Her essays and short stories appear regularly on BGD as well as in various publications. McKenzie presents talks that centre around the intersections of race, class, queerness, and gender at universities and conferences across the United States.

When I talk about "white people" I am talking about people who exist in bodies that give them access to white privilege. Some people exist in these bodies and get these privileges but don't ID as white. The thing about whiteness, though, is that you don't have to claim it to have it. You may not want to be white, for whatever reasons, but you don't choose whiteness. Whiteness chooses you. And when it does, it gives you—whether you want or acknowledge them or not—a whole slew of privileges that non-white folks don't get. Even if you are poor. Even if you are a woman. Even if you are queer and/or trans. Even if you are elderly. Even if you are a person with a disability. All of these things will, of course, affect your life in enormous ways and affect your access to any number of things. But they don't erase whiteness.

So if you're confused about whether or not whiteness has chosen you, here's a few questions to help you sort it out.

1. Do you look white? If this seems in any way like a complicated question, it can be easily discerned by walking into a fancy store (in clean, neat clothing) and seeing how the people who work there treat you. Do you get dirty looks upon entering? Do the shopkeepers glance at each other with worry? Do you notice people following you around to make sure you're not stealing anything? If not, you may be white.

2. When you are walking down the street and a cop car rolls by, do you feel safer because the police are around? Because they are there to protect you should something go wrong? If so, you may be white.

3. Do people ask you where you're from, and when you answer, "I'm from here," do they ask, "No, like, where are you *from* from?" If not, you may be white.

4. Are people visibly surprised when you are smart and articulate? If not, you may be white.

5. Have you ever been mistaken for a valet while wearing a suit? If not, you may be white.

6. Does the idea of driving through Mississippi fill you with apprehension? If not, you may be white.

7.  Do people reach out and touch your hair/body without your permission and then accuse you of being too sensitive or of overreacting when you don't like it? If not, you may be white.

8.  Do you regularly experience racism (note: racism is a system in which people are given less access to employment, education, safe and adequate housing, legal representation, etc. based on their race; racism is not people "not liking you" because of your race)? If not, you may be white.

9.  Do you see a lot of people who are the same color as you in movies, on TV, in magazines, etc. who are not portraying stereotypes or caricatures? If so, you may be white.

10. When you stand up for yourself, do people accuse you of being too angry? If not, you may be white.

11. Do people assume, without knowing you or ever speaking to you, that you are unintelligent, a criminal, good with computers, a terrorist, lazy, that you don't speak English, or that you are poor? If not, you may be white.

Hope this helps!

---

*Source:* McKenzie, Mia. (2014). "How to Know If You Are White." In *Black Girl Dangerous: On Race, Queerness, Class and Gender* (pp. 70–72). Oakland, CA: BGD Press.

# CHAPTER 29

## Women's Experience of Racism:
## How Race and Gender Interact

*Marika Morris, Canadian Research Institute
for the Advancement of Women (CRIAW)*

Marika Morris is an adjunct research professor in the School of Indigenous and Canadian Studies at Carleton University in Ottawa, Ontario. Prior to earning her PhD, she was the research coordinator for the Canadian Research Institute for the Advancement of Women. Morris is the author of *Participatory Research and Action: A Guide to Becoming a Researcher for Social Change.* In her research, she recognizes the interconnectedness between policy, economy, and society at federal, provincial, and municipal levels.

*The purpose of this fact sheet is to provide easy-to-understand statistical information and research on how women experience racism, and to provide suggestions for resources and action. We hope it will serve as a basic introduction for people with no knowledge of how race and gender affect women's lives. [...]*

Anti-racism does not mean pretending that race doesn't exist. It means recognizing racism; effectively and constructively challenging racism in yourself and others; and eliminating racism embedded in public policy, workplaces, and every other area of life.

## JOBS/INCOME

Racism and sexism combine to produce more economic inequalities for racialized women than for either white women or racialized men. Average annual income for 1995/96[1]:

$31,117: All Canadian men
$23,600: Visible minority men
$19,208: All Canadian women
$18,200: Aboriginal men
$16,600: Visible minority women
$13,300: Aboriginal women

Over half or nearly half of some racialized groups of women in Canada are living in poverty: 52% of women of Arab/West Asian (Middle Eastern) ancestry, 51% of women of Latin American ancestry, 47% of Black women, and 43% of Aboriginal women live in poverty. In the case of the first two groups, recent immigration may be a factor. Racialized immigrant women face more roadblocks to employment in Canada. More often than not, foreign university degrees and qualifications and foreign work experience are not recognized because Canada has inadequate systems to judge academic equivalencies.[2] Although governments invest in English or French as a second language programs, existing programs are inadequate to meet the need. Many women in particular are not receiving enough language training to integrate themselves as full participants in Canadian society. Racism is a major barrier to employment: Many employers and managers make assumptions about work habits, suitability of certain types of work, and ability to "fit in" on the basis of skin colour, or assume that someone who speaks English or French with a different accent is stupid.[3] In the case of Black women and Aboriginal women, long-standing policies and practices of racism and marginalization keep almost half (over 40%) of these groups of women living in poverty, compared with 19% of women who are not visible minorities.[4] In 1996, 17% of visible minority women in Canada had a university degree compared to 12% of Canadian women who did not belong to a visible minority group. Nevertheless, 15% of visible minority women were unemployed, compared with 9% of non-visible-minority women.[5]

## What the Words Mean

*Aboriginal or Indigenous peoples:* "Native" peoples, including First Nations, Inuit, Métis, and status and non-status Indians.

*Immigrant:* An immigrant is someone who moves to Canada with the intention of staying permanently. Immigrants come from all over the world: Asia, Africa, Europe, North or South America, or Oceania. Immigrants can be white or people of colour, and speak English, French, or another language as a mother tongue.

*Racialized:* This word has been used in different ways by different people. In this fact sheet, *racialized* will refer to anyone who experiences racism because of his or her race, skin colour, ethnic background, accent, culture, or religion. In this fact sheet, *racialized* includes people of colour, Aboriginal peoples, and ethnic, linguistic, religious, or cultural minorities who are targets of racism. When terms such as *women of colour* are used, they refer only to that group, as Canadian statistics are often collected separately for *visible minority*, *Aboriginal*, and *immigrant* groups. Racialized women have different cultures, histories, religions, family norms, life experiences, and are subject to different stereotypes. What they have in common is they are *racialized*—that is, they are subject to racism and made to feel different because of their racial/ethnic background.

*Refugee:* Refugees move to Canada under a special category ("refugee") because they are fleeing persecution or war in their own countries.

*Visible minority, racial minority, women/people of colour: Visible minority* tends to be used by the Canadian government, and will be used in this fact sheet when reporting statistics collected by the federal government. These terms do not include Aboriginal peoples.

Some people are now using the term *racialized* to refer to this group, to show that "race is socially constructed." For example, in Canada "Irish" and "French Canadians" used to be considered races. There were signs saying "No Irish allowed" and Irish people were discriminated against in employment. Racist hatred has nothing to do with the target groups and everything to do with how dominant groups in a society identify non-dominant groups for discrimination.

## HOUSING

Racial discrimination in housing is well documented. Jamaican and Somali immigrants had particular difficulties in finding rental housing because of some landlords' perceptions of these groups.[6] Race is also a barrier to home ownership. Two studies of Black and white people in Toronto (matched for income and family characteristics) found a lower rate of home ownership among Black people.[7] There is also a racist perception that Chinese immigrants in British Columbia's Lower Mainland, for example, are "taking over," particularly certain suburbs like Richmond.[8] No one seems to feel that white people have "taken over" certain communities, even though all white people in Canada are immigrants or the descendants of immigrants. Research has shown that racialized immigrant women can experience extreme forms of discrimination when finding housing, especially if they are single parents. They are very vulnerable to abuse by landlords.[9]

---

### What Racism Affects

Racism affects

- housing
- jobs
- self-esteem
- health
- and every aspect of your life

If you are subject to racism, it may cost you money, a place to live, a job, your self-respect, your health, or your life. Women who experience racism may live through it in a different way from men, and from each other.

---

## ACCESS TO JUSTICE

For racialized women, gender-based violence is not the only type of violence they experience: race and gender combine to increase their likelihood of being assaulted. For example, [in 1971 the young Cree woman] Helen Betty Osbourne was brutally gang-raped, tortured, and killed by a group of white men, and the white townsfolk kept a conspiracy of silence about her rapists and murderers. Because of the documented racism of Canada's police forces, criminal justice system, and jails,[10] racialized women may be reluctant to call police in cases of domestic assault out of loyalty to their family and community, or because they do not wish to fuel racist stereotypes about their community or to subject themselves or family members to a racist system. Refugees from places in which police forces, the military, and the government were involved in violence against civilians, including organized or systemic rape of women, may have no trust in systems of authority.[11] Aboriginal women are subject to racism in the courts, and are overrepresented in Canadian jails, which is a soul-destroying experience. Aboriginal women make up over 20% of Canada's female prison population, but only 2% of the female population of Canada.[12] In Canada, you are more likely to be sent to jail if you are poor or racialized.[13] Programs in jail are often not appropriate for racialized women.[14]

---

### More Words and Ideas

*Overt racism:* Racism can be overt, such as calling people names, beating them up, excluding them on the basis of race or ethnicity. Some companies ask employment agencies for white candidates only.

*Covert, subtle, or "polite" racism:* Lets you know you are different, that the most salient characteristic about you is your race, rather than your personality, your achievements as an individual, or anything else.

*Structural racism:* Not all racism is as obvious as beating someone up or even secretly excluding someone while being polite to his or her face. Racism can be structural (it's a part of every aspect of society). Sometimes, structural racism in hiring is not conscious or deliberate: People tend to hire those they know, people like themselves, or they advertise the job among their own networks. When the majority of people in decision-making positions are white men,

*continued*

they tend to hire other white men. Employment equity programs are supposed to get companies and government departments to expand their networks, to ensure that racialized communities hear about job opportunities, to give them a fair chance, and to introduce anti-discrimination policies and workshops in the workplace.

### "But All That Is in the Past. Why Can't We Forget about It?"

It's obviously not in the past. Take a look at the statistics about how racism affects access to housing, jobs, health, justice, and citizenship. The past also shapes people's experiences in the present. For example, for over 100 years, a Canadian government policy to assimilate Aboriginal peoples by taking children away from their families to residential schools—where they were punished for speaking their language, practising their own cultural and religious traditions, and where they were often the victims of physical and sexual abuse—left generations of Aboriginal peoples without parenting skills, without self-esteem, and feeling ashamed of who they were and hopeless about the future. Survivors of residential schools are still trying to heal from the damage.

## HEALTH

Racism itself can cause illness. When people are overtly racist, it translates into poorer health for the targets of racism.[15] Structural racism can also cause illness and death. Language and cultural barriers mean less access to life-saving medical procedures.[16] Structural racism leading to less income and social status has a direct impact on health.[17] Another example of structural racism is using standards developed in research using white men to measure health and health risks when these standards may

not be the same for women, racialized people, and particularly racialized women.

Some women refugees in Canada have experienced rape during wartime and have seen their children and other family members tortured and killed. This has particular physical and mental health consequences. Some women have been subject to female genital mutilation, which may also pose health problems and isolate them from health care providers and from women outside their communities.[18]

Women tend to be the health guardians of their families, and sacrifice paid work and personal happiness to care for sick relatives. Greater vulnerability to illness and less access to health care and home care services for racialized communities[19] mean more unpaid health care work for racialized women, which can have an impact on their own health.

## RACIALIZED SEXUALITY

Racialized women are often sexualized in racist ways. This is one of the ways racism and sexism can combine. For women of colour, sexual harassment can be racialized. A man might sexually harass a woman of colour by making racist comments or assumptions about her sexuality. Women of Asian origin are often stereotyped as exotic and obedient. Black women are stereotyped as highly sexual and available.[20] It is possible that women of colour face more sexual harassment and may be more vulnerable to sexual assault because of racist stereotypes. In addition, if they are harassed or assaulted, racist stereotypes on the part of the police and the courts mean they may have less access to justice. Racialized women who are lesbian, bisexual, or transgendered face homophobia and racism from mainstream society; marginalization from their own communities; and racism, exclusion, and stereotyping from movements seeking gay, lesbian, bisexual, and transgendered rights.

### "Why Can't Women Just Join Together As a Sisterhood Instead of Bringing Up Things That Divide Us?"

Kalwant Bhopal says that the idea of sisterhood implies that all women experience the same oppression, but solidarity implies an understanding that the struggles of all women are different, but interconnected. Métis anti-racist, feminist activist educator Jean Fyre Graveline discusses the myths that "skin colour doesn't matter," "we are all equal," "we all have equal opportunity to succeed." She draws on Aboriginal healing methods to show that we are all interconnected, but we must recognize that people have different privileges that affect how people work together. To build a strong women's movement and a strong society, we must face head-on the challenges of racism and how it interacts with many other factors to produce our different life experiences.

## SCHOOLS

School curricula tend to erase the contributions of racialized women in building Canada. For example, many Canadians still believe that Canada is made of "two founding peoples" (English and French), and do not learn about the 10,000-year history of Aboriginal women and men on this land, Canada's own history of slavery prior to 1833 and the particular suffering of Black women slaves, the interaction of racism and sexism in Canada's old law banning men of Asian origin from employing white women, the trafficking of Aboriginal women as prostitutes by white male Indian agents, a law (which lasted until 1946) that banned women of Chinese origin from becoming citizens, or the fact that Aboriginal women and men did not receive the federal vote until 1960, 42 years after the full federal vote was granted to white women. When they learn about the contributions of racialized people to Canada, it tends to be about those of racialized men. In addition, teachers may treat racialized

students differently, sometimes without realizing they are doing so. Some racialized students do not do well at school because of their teachers' racist low expectations of them.[21] Both sexist and racist expectations of teachers and guidance counsellors can have a profound effect on the lives of racialized girls. A study found that young Canadian-born Black francophone and anglophone women and men living in Montreal also experienced racial confrontations and harassment by fellow students in English and French elementary and high schools.[22]

## MEDIA

The media portrayal of white women still leaves a lot to be desired, but the media portrayal of racialized women is worse. Apart from a small minority of racialized women who appear to be confident, whole people, racialized people in general and racialized women in particular are underrepresented in Canadian television drama and news media relative to their proportion in the Canadian population, and where racialized women do appear, they are often relegated to stereotypical positions.[23]

## SELF-ESTEEM

Racism can create feelings of powerlessness and low self-esteem,[24] which have an impact on health, happiness, and life chances.

### "What about Reverse Racism?"

*Reverse racism* is a term mainly used by people to justify their own racism. Some people defend white privilege by saying, "Well, such-and-such a group is racist too." The big difference is because white people, particularly white men, are overrepresented in positions of power relative to their proportion in the population, white racism against other groups often

*continued*

means lost job opportunities, particularly for racialized women. There are so few racialized women in positions of power that if some of them dislike white men, it has no real effect on white men. Quite frankly, after experiencing the horrible effects of racism, the onus is not on racialized women to embrace and trust white people, but on white people to stop being racist.

*Reverse racism* is also used to describe employment equity programs by people who believe such programs are "race-based, gender-based hiring systems." What these people do not want to acknowledge is that in the absence of employment equity systems, there is often an unwritten race-based, gender-based hiring system that favours white men, which is why white men are overrepresented in decision-making positions. [...] Employment equity is not an attack on white men. It is a mechanism to ensure that everyone has a fair chance.

can be abused and threatened with deportation if they complain. Many women do not know their rights.

### Racism Hurts the Country and the World

White people unknowingly experience immediate benefits of racism, such as access to housing and jobs because racialized candidates have been turned down. However, in the end, racism destroys community and individual well-being. Hatred, suspicion, lack of trust, putting up barriers between oneself and others, [...] or seeing someone [negatively because of his or her race create] conflicts and problems in the country and [elsewhere] in the world. Racial discrimination is also a terrible waste of human resources, which hurts our economy as a whole.

## CITIZENSHIP AND IMMIGRATION

Canada claims to have a non-racist, non-sexist immigration system. Why, then, is there an overrepresentation of Canadian overseas immigration offices in the United States and Europe, when most of Canada's immigrants now come from Asia?[25] Canada's immigration system divides people into classes: If you have enough money, you can buy your way in under the investor class. Canada judges independent-class immigrants according to a point system, which gives points for education and for speaking one of Canada's official languages, for example. This discriminates against women because "women have been denied access to education, training and employment opportunities. As a result, most women entering Canada are unable to qualify as independent immigrants."[26] Most women enter Canada as sponsored immigrants, which means that they are financially dependent on their sponsors, usually their husbands, for a period of 10 years. It means they do not qualify for many social services or programs. It gives husbands and other sponsors a huge amount of power over women, who

## DOMESTIC WORKERS

Some advocates refer to the federal government's immigration Live-in Caregiver Program[27] as "a form of slavery." Women from other countries and regions, particularly the Philippines and the Caribbean, come to Canada because of a lack of economic alternatives in their own countries, in order to send money back to support their children and other relatives. This obligation and lack of choices makes them very vulnerable to abuse of all kinds. Women who come to Canada under the Live-in Caregiver Program must live in their employer's home (which increases their vulnerability to sexual assault, eliminates privacy, and means they are on call 24 hours a day and are usually not paid for overtime). They can work only for the employer who is listed on the Employment Authorization (EA) form and cannot take other work. They can stay in Canada only until the date specified on the EA. They are frequently unaware of their rights, and employers have threatened them with deportation and other measures to ensure their silence about abusive working conditions.[28]

> ### "What about So-and-So Who's in a Position of Power? Doesn't That Mean All Racialized Women Can Make It If They Work Hard Enough?"
>
> A few token racialized women in positions of power does not mean that things are fine for all racialized women, or that racism and sexism do not exist. Many racialized women have worked very hard to get where they are, and many have worked very hard and not reached their goals because of racist attitudes and structures.

## HATE CRIMES

In Toronto, there are about 300 overt acts of racism every year, involving mainly vandalism and assault, particularly against Jewish and Black people. However, these statistics are from before September 11 [2001], after which there was a huge increase in vandalism and assault of Muslims and people who looked like they might be of Arab origin, as well as bombings and vandalism of Muslim, Jewish, and Hindu places of worship.[29] Hate crimes, in terms of being beaten because of your race, ethnicity, or religion, can lead to injury, permanent disability, or death. Hate crimes involving vandalism of places of worship or other buildings or objects identified with a group can leave the community fearful and feeling excluded from society. Women may have particular safety concerns as the targets of sexual as well as physical assault.

## ASSUMPTIONS THAT REFLECT GENDERED RACISM

### Assumptions That All People of Colour Are Immigrants

White women who emigrate from the United States or other primarily English- or French-speaking countries are often not viewed as immigrants, but as Canadians who were born elsewhere. Women of colour who were born in Canada are often viewed as immigrants, even though they are not. They are asked, "Where are you from?" If they answer, "Edmonton," they are then asked, "No, where are you really from?" They are made to feel like foreigners in their own country.

### Assumptions That Racialized Women Are Not Feminists

Some people assume that women may have certain beliefs and outlooks depending on their racial, ethnic, or religious background. Women of South Asian ancestry (including India and Pakistan) are often assumed to want to have only sons. Muslim women who wear the *hijab* (head scarf) are often assumed not to be feminists, or to be subservient to men. The only way to know what a woman believes is by asking her.

### Resistance to Acknowledging Racism

Most Canadians know that to be racist is a bad thing, so they deny being racist. However, many Canadians continue to hold stereotypes that benefit white people and hurt everyone else in very real ways. Some people think racism is about only a few isolated incidents perpetrated by a few ignorant individuals. However, there have recently been a number of disturbing comments by people with decision-making power over others, such as these examples from early 2002 alone:

- Ontario Finance Minister Jim Flaherty suggested in January 2002 that Aboriginal peoples were not "real people."[30] Flaherty held the purse strings for every initiative in Ontario, and came in second in the leadership race to become premier of Ontario.
- Saskatchewan Member of Parliament Roy Bailey publicly stated in January 2002 that Dr. Rey Pagtakhan, the new minister for veterans' affairs, was unsuited for the job because he is "Asiatic."[31]

- PEI Member of the Legislative Assembly Wilbur MacDonald said in an April 2002 speech that "the white human race is on a fast track which will destroy us … we're not at the present time keeping up with the numbers of people who are in our society…. England, for example, is being taken over by British West Indies people, France is being taken over by another group of people. It won't be long in the United States … [that] Spanish people will be taking over…. We're going to deteriorate in our population too…."[32]

Racism is *systemic*. It's not about a few individuals. Racism pervades the structures of our society, such as our government, our schools, the labour market, the immigration system, the justice system, police forces, and so on.

## INTERNALIZED RACISM

Racialized people can also be racist, both in terms of accepting mainstream views about other racial, ethnic, and cultural groups, and in terms of believing the repeated racist messages they have heard all their lives. Everyone has a voice in their head that repeats messages about good and bad, right and wrong, from when we were growing up. When someone has grown up with racism, that voice can be internalized, that is, the voice repeats the racist messages throughout life, about not being good enough. It can also harm that person's relationships with people within their community. One example of this is in Beatrice Culleton's book, *In Search of April Raintree*, in which two Métis sisters grow up in separate foster homes. One can "pass for white" and the other has darker skin. The lighter-skinned sister, despite her lighter skin, grew up being called "half-breed," "dirty Indian," etc., and was mistreated by her white foster family, while the darker-skinned sister grew up in a Métis-positive home. The lighter-skinned sister is ashamed to be seen with her darker-skinned sister, and renounces

her heritage and wants to "live like a white person." This is internalized racism, and it has an effect on the relationship between the sisters. It is when even some small part of you believes the racist garbage you have heard. It can affect how you live your life. Developing high self-esteem and modelling this for others is a powerful act of resistance.

## RACE INTERACTS WITH MANY OTHER FACTORS

[Race can interact with] class, income, occupation, social status, language, physical appearance, culture, religion, ability, sexual orientation, age, immigration status, Indian status, personal background, and experience.

## NOTES

1.  The averages for all men and all women in Canada are 1995 data from the 1996 Census, reported in Statistics Canada, 1996 Census: Sources of Income, Earnings, and Total Income, and Family Income, *The Daily*, May 12, 1998. The other data are from Statistics Canada, *Women in Canada 2000: A Gender-Based Statistical Report* (Ottawa: Minister of Industry, 2000).
2.  National Organization of Immigrant and Visible Minority Women of Canada (NOIVMC), *A Survey of Immigrant and Visible Minority Women on the Issue of Recognition of Foreign Credentials* (Ottawa: NOIVMC, 1996).
3.  West Coast Domestic Workers Association website: www. vcn.bc.ca/wcdwa/eng_1.htm.
4.  Statistics Canada, *Women in Canada 2000: A Gender-Based Statistical Report* (Ottawa: Minister of Industry, 2000), p. 246.
5.  Statistics Canada, *Women in Canada 2000*, pp. 224, 226.
6.  Kenneth Dion, Immigrants' Perceptions of Housing Discrimination in Toronto: The Housing New Canadians Project, *The Journal of Social Issues*, volume 57, number 3 (Fall 2001): 523–39.

7. Joe T. Darden and Sameh M. Kamel, Black and White Differences in Homeownership Rates in the Toronto Census Metropolitan Area: Does Race Matter?, *The Review of Black Political Economy*, volume 28, number 2 (Fall 2000): 53–76; Andrejs Skaburskis, Race and Tenure in Toronto, *Urban Studies*, volume 33 (March 1996): 223–52.

8. Brian K. Ray, Greg Halseth, and Benjamin Johnson, The Changing "Face" of the Suburbs: Issues of Ethnicity and Residential Change in Suburban Vancouver, *International Journal of Urban and Regional Research*, volume 21 (March 1997): 75–99.

9. Sylvia Novac, Immigrant Enclaves and Residential Segregation: Voices of Racialized Refugee and Immigrant Women, *Canadian Woman Studies*, volume 19, number 3 (Fall 1999): 88–93.

10. Commission on Systemic Racism in the Ontario Criminal Justice System, *Report of the Commission on Systemic Racism in the Ontario Criminal Justice System* (Toronto: Queen's Printer for Ontario, 1995); Jean Charles Coutu, *La Justice pour et par les autochtones* (Québec: Ministre de la Justice du Québec, 1995); A. Currie and George Kiefl, *Ethnocultural Groups and the Justice System in Canada: A Review of the Issues* (Ottawa: Department of Justice Canada, 1994); Commission on Systemic Racism in the Ontario Criminal Justice System, *Racism behind Bars: The Treatment of Black and Other Racial Minority Prisoners in Ontario Prisons* (Toronto: Queen's Printer for Ontario, 1994); Urban Alliance on Race Relations, *Race and the Canadian Justice System: An Annotated Bibliography* (Toronto: Urban Alliance on Race Relations, 1995); the Hon. Louise Arbour, *Commission of Inquiry into Certain Events at the Prison for Women in Kingston* (Ottawa: Public Works and Government Services, 1996).

11. Amnesty International, *Women's Rights Are Human Rights: Resources for Information and Action* (Ottawa: Amnesty International Canada, 2002): www.amnesty.ca/women/index.html.

12. Statistics Canada, *Women in Canada 2000*, p. 177.

13. Canadian Association of Elizabeth Fry Societies, *Factsheet: Justice and the Poor* (Ottawa: CAEFS, no date): www.elizabethfry.ca/eweek02/factsht.htm#justice; Elizabeth Comack, Vanessa Chopyk, and Linda Wood, *Mean Streets? The Social Locations, Gender Dynamics, and Patterns of Violent Crime in Winnipeg* (Ottawa: Centre for Policy Alternatives, December 2000).

14. Kelly Blanchette, *Risk and Need among Federally Sentenced Female Offenders: A Comparison of Minimum, Medium, and Maximum Security Inmates* (Ottawa: Research Division, Correctional Service of Canada, 1997); Barbara Bloom, Gender-Responsive Programming for Women Offenders: Guiding Principles and Practices, *Forum on Corrections Research*, volume 11, number 3 (2000): 22–27; Canadian Association of Elizabeth Fry Societies (CAEFS), *Position of the Canadian Association of Elizabeth Fry Societies (CAEFS) regarding the Classification and Carceral Placement of Women Classified as Maximum Security Prisoners* (Ottawa: CAEFS, 1997); Kim Pate, *Complaint regarding the Discriminatory Treatment of Federally Sentenced Women by the Government of Canada* (Ottawa: Canadian Association of Elizabeth Fry Societies, 2001): www.elizabethfry.ca/complain.htm.

15. See Nancy Krieger and Stephen Sidney, Racial Discrimination and Blood Pressure: The CARDIA Study of Young Black and White Adults, *American Journal of Public Health*, volume 86, number 19 (October 1996): 1370–78; Wornie L. Reed, Suffer the Children: Some Effects of Racism on the Health of Black Infants, in Peter Conrad and Rochelle Kern (Eds.), *The Sociology of Health and Illness: Critical Perspectives* (New York: St. Martin's Press, 1994), pp. 314–27, quoted in Boston Women's Health Book Collective, *Our Bodies, Ourselves for the New Century* (New York: Touchstone, 1998), p. 683.

16. T. Gregory Hislop, Chong The, Agnes Lai, Tove Lobo, and Victoria M. Taylor, Cervical Cancer Screening in BC Chinese Women, *BC Medical Journal*, volume 42, number 10 (December 2000): 456–60.

17. Income is the primary determinant of health, beyond smoking, "lifestyle choices," and genetic endowment: see Andrew Haines and Richard Smith, Working Together to Reduce Poverty's Damage, *British Medical Journal*, volume 317 (February 22, 1997): 529; Dennis Raphael, Health Inequalities in Canada: Current Discourses and Implications for Public Health Action, *Critical Public Health*, volume 10, number 2 (2000): 193–216; Pat Armstrong, Hugh Armstrong, and David Coburn, *Unhealthy Times: Political*

*Economy Perspectives on Health and Care* (Oxford: Oxford University Press, 2001). […]

18. Canadian Women's Health Network, *Female Genital Mutilation and Health Care: Current Situation and Legal Status Recommendations to Improve the Health Care of Affected Women* (Ottawa: Health Canada Women's Health Bureau, 2000): www.cwhn.ca/resources/fgm.

19. Mary Ann Mulvihill, Louise Mailloux, and Wendy Atkin, *Advancing Policy and Research Responses to Immigrant and Refugee Women's Health in Canada* (Ottawa: Centres of Excellence for Women's Health, Health Canada, 2001): www.cewh-cesf.ca/resources/im-ref_health/im_ref_health.pdf.

20. Philomena Essed, *Towards a Methodology to Identify Converging Forms of Everyday Discrimination* (New York: United Nations, no date), quoted in Canadian Feminist Alliance for International Action (FAFIA), *Report on Canada's Compliance with the International Convention on the Elimination of All Forms of Racial Discrimination in Response to Canada's 13th and 14th Reports to the Committee in the Elimination of All Forms of Racial Discrimination*, FAFIA Think Tank Paper no. 3 (Ottawa: FAFIA, August 2001).

21. See Canadian Race Relations Foundation (CRRF), *Racism in Our Schools: What to Know about It; How to Fight It* (Toronto, CRRF, 2000): www.crr.ca/en/MediaCentre/FactSheets/FACTJune2000.pdf.

22. Micheline Labelle, Daniel Salée, and Yolande Frenette, *Civic Incorporation or Exclusion? Representation of Citizenship among Second-Generation Youth of Jamaican and Haitian Origin in Montreal* (Montréal: Centre de recherche sur l'immigration, l'ethnicité et la citoyenneté (CRIEC): www.unites.uqam.ca/criec.

23. MediaWatch, *Front and Centre: Minority Representation on Television* (Toronto: MediaWatch, no date), data collected in 1993: www.mediawatch.ca/research/front.

24. Josephine Enang, Mothering at the Margins: An African-Canadian Immigrant Woman's Experience, *Canadian Women's Health Network* (Spring 2001): 7–8: www.cwhn.ca.

25. Applicants who immigrate to Canada must submit their applications to the Canadian embassy, consulate, or commission nearest them. There are six such offices in the United States alone, whereas many Asian countries do not have even one, and India, one of the largest countries in the world, has only one for the whole country. See Citizenship and Immigration Canada, *Immigration Processing Missions Abroad*: www.cic.gc.ca/english/info/emission.html.

26. Judy Vashti Persad and Véronica Moreno, *Community Development with Immigrant Women: A Resource Kit for Community Educating and Organizing* (Toronto: Cross Cultural Communication Centre, 1990), p. 21.

27. West Coast Domestic Workers Association website: http://www.wcdwa.ca/.

28. Canadian Human Rights Commission (CHRC), *Annual Report 2001* (Ottawa: CHRC, 2002).

29. Canadian Race Relations Foundation (CRRF), "Flaherty: Enough Is Enough: Says the Executive Director of the CRRF," News release (Toronto: CRRF, January 22, 2002).

30. Canadian Race Relations Foundation, ""Asiatic' Remark Inappropriate: A Statement from the Executive Director," News release (Toronto: CRRF, January 2002).

31. Wilbur MacDonald speaking in the PEI legislature, *Hansard*, Prince Edward Island Legislative Assembly, Third session of the 61st General Assembly, April 19, 2002: www.gov.pe.ca/leg/hansard/2002spring.

---

*Source:* Morris, Marika. (2002). Excerpted from "Women's Experience of Racism: How Race and Gender Interact" (pp. 1–12). Ottawa, ON: CRIAW. Retrieved from: http://www.criaw-icref.ca/en/product/womens-experience-of-racism-how-race-and-gender-interact.

# CHAPTER 30

## The Hall of Shame: Lies, Masks, and Respectful Femininity

*Amita Handa*

Amita Handa is a scholar, author, and DJ. She currently works as a student equity adviser for the Toronto District School Board. She has an MA in women's studies and a PhD in sociology, and has produced cutting-edge Canadian research focusing on issues of cultural conflict among second-generation South Asian youth. Her book, *Of Silk Saris and Mini Skirts: South Asian Girls Walk the Tightrope of Culture,* from which we have drawn the following selection, has been described as "an articulate and richly textured account of South Asian girls' attempts to 'fit in' without abandoning their diasporic roots."

In my interviews with young South Asian women it became apparent that parental and community regulation of women's sexuality was tied into protecting young women from the ills of Western society. All the women in my study knew how they had to behave in order to be accepted as "good" daughters and community members. They were all concerned about their sexual reputations in one way or another and were very aware that their behaviour has an impact on how their family is viewed by the rest of the community. In their experience, their reputation, and the resulting family reputation, was closely monitored by community members: relatives, family friends, and acquaintances. What struck me as familiar and noteworthy were the lengths to which we would go to protect our reputations, and the extent to which our lives were experienced as fragmented. This fragmentation meant that the codes of femininity we observed outside the home were completely different to those observed within the family and community. Our good reputations were always ultimately based on our sexual reputations, although much of the discourse around reputation was embedded in taken-for-granted notions of feminine codes of behaviour; hence its sexual subtext was often implicit.

## MIS-USES OF THE BODY

The debates involving women in colonial India are not only a historical example of how women come to represent and maintain cultural boundaries but the illustration of a process of contestation over cultural difference. There are continuities between this earlier period of colonialism and nationalism and the present diasporic context. [...] Specifically, there are parallels between colonial racism and Canadian racism, and the South Asian diaspora mirrors, in significant ways, the Indian nation-state. In the diasporic context young women continue to mark boundaries of cultural difference. These boundaries are maintained through notions of femininity that regulate the body in how it is adorned, what it consumes, and where it goes (meaning women can go [to] only certain places at certain times).

Leslie Roman has argued that the body is a primary site on which notions of femininity are constructed.[1] She shows how bodily consumption and adornment are tied into sexual reputation, and how control of the body is an expression of social control. As a mechanism of social control, "dirtiness" is linked not only to health but also to prevailing cultural norms around order and propriety. Individuals who transgress these are seen as vulgar and bad.[2] Roman applies this theoretical framework to her study of girls in a Catholic high school. She points out that for women, smoking is associated with "low" behaviour, such as alcoholism, and "provocative" dress. It suggests a "looser construction of the body; a body freed to its desires, so to speak, as well as a rejection of the 'little girl,' the niceness, the willingness to get along, the softness," that often characterizes dominant notions of femininity.[3] Roman found that the "'price' of freedom of the body—freedom to be at ease in public arenas, to wear comfortable and casual clothes, to smoke cigarettes—was the loss of a good reputation."

For the young women I interviewed, maintaining a notion of difference from white Canadians is also contingent on notions of appropriate femininity. Like most girls, South Asian teenagers face community sanctions if their conduct does not conform to expected feminine behaviour. Regulations and sanctions are strategies of identification and a means by which community is imagined and produced. It is through the sanctioning of those who transgress the boundaries that communities are constituted as bounded entities. By observing specific norms of conduct, "we" come to feel identity with each other and see ourselves as different from "others."

Most of the women I spoke with defined normative feminine behaviour by things they were not supposed to do: drinking, smoking, doing drugs, and dating boys. What they were expected to do included studying hard, going to family and community gatherings, and helping with domestic duties. For South Asian women, negotiating their femininities doesn't just affect their sexual reputations—it also indicates their degree of allegiance to an ethnic collectivity. The danger of engaging in immoral activities is associated with the outside world. Nina explained that much of her life outside the home was hidden from her parents and that they did not understand or accept many of the things that she wanted to do: "Indian girls are not supposed to drink or smoke or go out, you know. My parents think, well you know, if you go out so much, if you're going to clubs and stuff, it looks so bad on you. Like I know friends whose parents think, well you know, if you go to a club nobody's going to marry you, because you're always going out all the time and you're doing this and that."

Nina shows how the East/West dualism is embedded in codes of feminine behaviour that regulate drinking, smoking, and social (potentially sexual) affiliations. A woman's failure to comply with these codes brands her with an unscrupulous sexual reputation and will eventually inhibit her marriageability. Nina explains how restrictions on freedom of movement and bodily expression are synonymous with being South Asian. Her ethnic identity depends on complying with these restrictions around femininity. Notions of South Asian-ness and femininity are integral to each other, so that transgressing the norms of one category simultaneously destabilizes the other. Later, Nina said about her friends: "They're aware that I am Indian 'cause they, I mean, I feel like I constantly have to explain to them why I am

Indian, because of the way my parents are. I have to explain that I can't do this with you, I can't do this with you. Why? Because my parents are Indian and that's why I can't." Here, the restriction of social activities by parents becomes part of what actually defines being South Asian.

\*\*\*\*\*

## GEOGRAPHY OF GENDER

As mentioned previously, the boundary of ethnicity is often dependent on gender. Characteristics that have become associated with gender serve to carve out ethnic identity and what most often distinguishes one ethnic collective from another are "rules relating to sexuality, marriage and family … and a *true* member will perform these roles properly" (my emphasis).[4] Gender and ethnicity work together in establishing definitions of identity, and notions of cultural authenticity help to maintain regulations around "appropriate" femininity. This became apparent during the course of these conversations.

My interviews often began with an exploration of school environments, and I used these discussions to explore the young women's sense of ethnic identity vis-à-vis their sense of belonging in relation to other cultural groups. In all of the interviews it was often implicit that they had to be different from "Canadian women," by which they meant white women. I observed the contest between East and West in the various discourses that construct white and South Asian women's sexualities in contrast with one another. I spoke with Salimah, for example, about the various cultural groups in her school, and we began to tease out some of the ways in which South Asian women were located differently from white women in relation to sexuality. In a discussion of stereotypical representations Salimah said: "Okay, when I see white girls, I can generalize here, most white girls are more giving, like fast sexually, you know. Even

though Indian girls aren't [fast], well not all, but I'm just saying they're taught not to be. But I don't think that's enforced in, in you know, white families. I know of this one girl whose mother bought her the pill. That would never happen in an Indian family."

The East-West dualism operates as an organizing category in her talk and she points to the oppositional relationship between brown and white women. Here, brown/white stands in for East/West. Part of what differentiates South Asian and white girls are codes around sexual behaviour and family acceptance of (heterosexual) sexuality: Salimah shows that in order to be seen as good girls, young South Asian women must conform to sexual norms that are not associated with what white girls do.

Within modernity, unresolved fears about modern social progress, anxieties about social change, and the possibility that unregulated freedom could cause moral and social disintegration have been projected onto both youth and women. We have also seen how the West has become synonymous with modernity, while the East is associated with tradition or pre-modernity. The young women in my study suggest that fears about modern change are manifested in fears about westernization. Within South Asian communities, in the sexualized discourse of East as pure and West as temptress, women are often positioned as sexual by the mere fact of living in the modern West. Salimah talked about how diasporic sexuality is viewed by those "back home."

[…] [There's] definitely a double standard. 'Cause I want to meet a really nice sweet guy kind of thing, but once you get them, *they don't want the modern girl, they don't want that girl who could be smart or anything.* They want that girl who's going to do everything for them, who's going to be that typical Indian girl. You know, and that's not what Canada's producing at the moment, I'm not lying. That's another thing, the Pakistani cricket team was here and one of the guys met this girl and phoned her and said, "Oh I want to get with you" and this and that. And she's like, "What do you think I am? *Just 'cause I'm from Canada I'm a slut? Just 'cause I'm from Canada, I'm not your typical one*, so you can turn around and do anything with me?" That's what a lot of Indian girls are getting slack for, just 'cause they're from Canada, they're modernized, and they're not what people want them to be. [my emphasis]

Salimah begins by commenting on how men are threatened by women's independence and popularity. For her the typical Pakistani girl fits modern colonial notions of South Asian womanhood: servitude, docility, and chastity. A typical Canadian woman, on the other hand, is seen as sexually active and associated with modernity. Modern is defined as both intelligent and sexually promiscuous. There is also a subtext of cultural authenticity; living in Canada makes one less Pakistani than living "back home."

[...] Salimah's comments indicate that the discourse around sexuality is not just about the relationship between white and brown. Even within the category of "brown" some forms of sexual behaviour are seen as more authentic than others. Let us refer back to Yuval-Davis's claim about the boundaries of ethnic identity being dependent on gender. From Salimah's account we can see that the definition of South Asian is contingent on the degree to which it is associated with the non-West. The non-West is not defined just geographically, however; it is also contingent upon certain sexual codes, whereby women become the territory upon which East is constructed as pure and West as degenerate. This moral discourse views the modern/West as a sexual threat to notions of South Asian femininity and thereby constructs women on a modern terrain as sexually available to men. Salimah's passage maps out Canada as a modern terrain. This terrain is gendered and thus a South Asian girl's mere residency in the modern positions her as a sexual object.

Most of the young women I interviewed commented on how their parents often referenced "back home" as a standard of measure. [...] Alka shows how the myth of "back home" works in regulating young women's sexualities. She addresses this myth in relation to upper-class youth culture in India:

I went to boarding school in India for six months.... And I go back there every year and I know. I mean, [...] girls go out left, right, and centre. Where they go out? To clubs and you name it. The only happening thing right now is big clubs and nice hotels and whatever. They go out for coffee, they come home late nights, even. I'm talking about even in the most decent homes they go out, they go out guys and girls. I mean you should see New Year's, it's a blast there.... But the really funny thing is that when I go back it's like freedom like you wouldn't believe. I get freedom like you wouldn't believe and I enjoy it. That's why I like India a lot, 'cause I get freedom like you wouldn't....

Alka explodes the "back home" myth by revealing that the worst fears about women and the West are actually occurring in the East. The strictness and sexual propriety associated with the homeland are displaced by her account of experiencing more freedom in India itself than she does here in the Toronto diasporic community. Why, then, maintain the fantasy? Because this myth serves as a means to hold on to a notion of protection, purity, and propriety associated with the East. This protection from modernity may be all the way back home, but it serves as a distant standard to aspire to. This myth also justifies the regulation and protection of women on diasporic terrain by giving permission for the reproduction of "Indian" (from India) in Canada.

# WHITE LIES, BROWN PARENTS

All of the girls I interviewed admitted that they lied to their parents. While most teenagers do not share everything with their parents, I was struck by how instrumental lying is in maintaining the next-to-impossible status of the good South Asian girl. Salimah told me she "had to lie," although she had mixed feelings about it. She explained that her parents viewed her as an innocent, good daughter and that it was very important for her to maintain this image: "I lie to my parents a lot, and if I started thinking that I feel bad about lying then there wouldn't be much to my life. It's kind of like living, doing what you have to do. I do feel bad about lying, but I want to keep my parents happy. If I didn't lie I wouldn't get anywhere. And I do feel bad about lying that much but I'd feel more bad if … I want to keep my parents happy. I really do. I really look for their approval."

I recall learning about concealment as central to ideas of respect in my own family, when I found a pack of Du Maurier cigarettes in my older brother's room. He was smoking but hiding it from my parents. Later that evening, my father lit up a cigar with some friends, a habit he indulged in occasionally. My grandparents were not at home. He was smoking but hiding it from his parents. The next day, I saw my grandfather come inside from an afternoon walk, and I detected the smell of bidis (Indian cigarettes) on his breath. He realized that his secret had been found out. "Shhh, please don't tell anyone," he said. He was smoking but hiding it from everyone! Over time I realized: it was not that nobody knew about each other's smoking, but that not openly engaging in a behaviour that was deemed negative was enmeshed in notions of respect.

For the women I interviewed, lying is used not only to negotiate freedom, but also to uphold the good girl image in the eyes of their parents and the larger South Asian community. Even when family members are aware that their daughters are engaged in activities deemed inappropriate by family and community members, they participate in

maintaining the lie. To speak about these activities honestly is considered to be disrespectful. In addition to upholding the image of goodness for family and community, however, with their peers the girls had to negotiate another set of expectations. With friends, they often lied about lying, because they found those who were able to participate more freely in the social world often did not understand the necessity for masking. Lying, it seemed, conformed only too well to the stereotype of the South Asian girl. For example, Nina explained that she could not be open with her white friends about the extent to which she lied to her parents:

> It is easier to turn to them [South Asian friends] than to my other friends sometimes, when they don't understand and I, I feel like I'm being put down, like my own character is being put down.… They go, "Why can't you argue with your parents?" And I tell them that I try to. But I feel like they're putting me down.… They go, "But why don't you be stronger?" and they don't realize that I'm trying to be really, really strong and they don't understand that and I get really defensive.… They go, "Oh but if I was your parents' daughter, they would die, they wouldn't last," and I go, "If you were my parents' daughter then you wouldn't be like the way you are now."

In relation to her friends, lying represents not being rebellious enough. Acquiescing to authority is equivalent to docility and does not measure up to the carefree, heroic rebellious image of the westernized teenager. And yet for Nina in relation to her parents, telling the truth risks the loss of a good reputation.

Although most girls crossed over the boundaries of proper femininity, many of them did not feel that they were "bad" girls. Yet they knew that in the eyes of their parents they would be seen as disobedient or immoral and therefore un-Indian. Defining South Asian femininity as synonymous with the restrictions around self-determination that I have spoken about leaves very little room for a self-definition that describes the reality of the young women's lived experiences. I found that young women were able to negotiate their freedom and sexual reputations through the use of clothing. Lying, in this case, takes the form of masking and manipulating femininity. Salimah described her relationship to clothing:

> They [parents] don't mind me wearing normal clothes and everything. The only thing they don't like is ripped jeans, anything that is tight. I'm not allowed to wear shorts, all that kind of stuff. One story, it was in the summer, I was in shorts and all of a sudden I see my dad at the end of the driveway and I started waving to my dad [instinctively] and he started driving by and then I realized. So I jumped into a bush and I changed and my friend's just watching me and watching my dad driving by, and I changed in the bush, in the mud and everything, and I got up and she said, "Ahh, he's gone," and I'm like, "Oh shit, oh well" [laughter].[5]

In her study of working-class girls in England, Susan Lees showed that young women walk a tightrope in order to negotiate their reputations.[6] She argues that both "good" girls and "bad" girls stake out their femininity through clothing. Good girls must negotiate the next-to-impossible line between adhering to the ideals of beauty and attractiveness and appearing too sexual. In my conversation with Tina and Pam […] they pointed to how dress conveys certain meanings around traditional and modern, good girls and bad girls:

> *Tina:* Well okay, you have your modern Indian girl and the traditional.… Okay, if you see like the traditional Indian girl, they're more like, okay, study well, do what your parents say, and there's lots of them. I'm talking the traditional Indian girl.

> *Pam:* Okay there's this girl.… We went to Square One one day, I saw her walking into the mall with her father, plain face okay? When we saw her in the mall later on, she left her father and she was wearing bright red lipstick and makeup and everything, and I bet she like washes her face by the time she goes and sees her dad again, and goes home like nothing happened. And I see this girl go to dances and …
> *Tina:* Ahh, she's pretty, ahh, promiscuous.

The sisters indicate how girls manipulate their femininity through fashion in order to suit the dictates of a particular context. For the girl they discuss, the mall represents a public space where she negotiates contradictory codes of femininity. Her dilemma is similar to Salimah's description of changing clothes in the bushes. The fear of getting caught by her father translates into getting caught for wearing clothes that transgress the boundaries of appropriate femininity. The trouble is, of course, that appropriate femininity is defined differently in other social spaces, to which these young women also wish to belong.

*****

While lying helps young women gain more freedom, it also helps them negotiate their reputations. Lying gives them some control over their reputations at home and school. While the emotional cost of "living lies" is extremely high for these young women, for many South Asian women honesty is too high a price to pay. It carries the risk of exclusion from the definition of "South Asian." Walking this tightrope of upholding community identity in a white dominant context brings with it a tremendous amount of emotional stress. Constantly masking or hiding parts of the self which are not accepted either by the world of peers or parents has a serious negative effect on self-esteem and self-worth. It is seldom that all the parts of the self can be celebrated, approved of, and accepted.

Defiance of adulthood is manifested for youth in terms of challenging and defying authority. For young women this takes place on the sexual terrain; manipulating their femininities and transgressing expected codes of behaviour. In its narrative of womanhood, the South Asian community draws on nationalist constructions of femininity that are in direct opposition to discourses around teens in the West. While white girls may defy social norms around growing up through dress and "sexual deviance" (i.e., sexual expression), for South Asian girls, rebellion against the responsible adult citizen narrative is also seen as a defiance of cultural identity and a disloyalty to ethnic membership. South Asian girls in Canada have to negotiate contradictory messages about their sexuality. On the one hand, they "get slack" because they are modernized; not being "typical" makes them open to assumptions about their sexual availability. On the other hand, being South Asian in Canada automatically sets them up as sexually unavailable in relation to dominant white culture. According to the latter, the typical South Asian girl is a patriarchal construction of docility and passivity. Her subjectivity is depersonalized and disregarded by a discursive construction that locates her as a victim within a cultural problematic only. While these narratives regulate and limit the lives of young South Asian women, I would like to place them within the wider context of Canadian racism. An allegiance to certain authentic notions of tradition and culture is also a means by which to articulate a standpoint against a racist and assimilationist white Canadian society. In this sense diaspora is a complex and overlapping space: it disrupts some normative categories while simultaneously reproducing others. In the context of negative or absent representations, notions of South Asian cultural authenticity also serve as a powerful site of resistance.

## NOTES

1. Leslie Roman, "Intimacy, Labour, and Class."
2. M. Douglas, *Purity and Danger.*
3. Roman, "Intimacy, Labour, and Class," pp. 134, 136.
4. Floya Anthias and Nira Yuval-Davis, Introduction to *Woman-Nation-State*, p. 102.
5. The regulation of women's bodies through social sanctions and controls, such as the bodily controls that Leslie Roman speaks about (in "Intimacy, Labour, and Class"), has been documented in both sociological as well as anthropological research. See S. Ardener, "Introduction: The Nature of Women in Society"; S. Ortner and H. Whitehead, "Introduction: Accounting for Sexual Meanings," pp. 1–28; E.M. Schur, *Labelling Women Deviant*; C. Smart and B. Smart, *Women, Sexuality and Social Control.* Feminist scholars have also illustrated that women who challenge the norms of appropriate feminine behaviour are often open to social disapproval through the "sexualization" of their behaviour. For example, L.S. Smith has argued that girls who transcend the norms of femininity through delinquent behaviour are portrayed by adults in the legal system as sexually promiscuous (1978, pp. 74–86).
6. Susan Lees, *Losing Out: Sexuality and Adolescent Girls.*

## REFERENCES

Anthias, F. and N. Yuval-Davis. Introduction to *Woman-Nation-State*. Ed. F. Anthias and N. Yuval-Davis. London: Macmillan, 1989.

Ardener, S. "Introduction: The Nature of Women in Society." *Defining Females*. Ed. S. Ardener. New York: Wiley, 1978.

Douglas, M. *Purity and Danger*. London: Routledge, 1984.

Lees, S. *Losing Out: Sexuality and Adolescent Girls*. London: Hutchinson, 1986.

Ortner, S. and H. Whitehead. "Introduction: Accounting for Sexual Meanings." *Sexual Meanings*. Ed. S. Ortner and H. Whitehead. Cambridge: Cambridge University Press, 1981, pp. 1–28.

Roman, L.G. "Intimacy, Labour, and Class: Ideologies of Feminine Sexuality in the Punk Slam Dance." *Becoming Feminine: The Politics of Popular Culture*. Ed. L.G. Roman, L.K. Christian-Smith, with E. Ellsworth. London: The Falmer Press, 1988.

Schur, E.M. *Labelling Women Deviant*. Philadelphia: Temple University Press, 1984.

Smart, C. and B. Smart. *Women, Sexuality and Social Control*. London: Routledge, 1978.

Smith, L.S. "Sexist Assumptions and Female Delinquency: An Empirical Investigation." *Women, Sexuality and Social Control*. Ed. C. Smart and B. Smart. London: Routledge, 1978, 74–86.

---

*Source:* Handa, Amita. (2003). Excerpted from "The Hall of Shame: Lies, Masks, and Respectful Femininity." In *Of Silk Saris and Mini Skirts: South Asian Girls Walk the Tightrope of Culture* (pp. 107–128). Toronto, ON: Women's Press.

## ACTIVIST INSIGHT: FRANCHESCA RAMSEY ON MICROAGGRESSIONS AND BEING AN ALLY

American actress, comedian, and blogger Franchesca Ramsey, known online as Chescaleigh, went viral in January 2012 when she posted a video called "Sh*t White Girls Say...to Black Girls." The video uses humour to expose *microaggressions*—the everyday insults, dismissals, and indignities that white people inflict upon people of colour. The term is now being used by other marginalized groups (e.g., sexual and gender minorities, people with disabilities) to describe the slights, stereotypes, and insults that they confront. The video currently has over 12 million views and has been featured on many news and popular culture programs. Check it out on her YouTube channel here: www.youtube.com/watch?v=ylPUzxpIBe0.

Ramsey also posted a video entitled "5 Tips for Being an Ally," which you can view here: www.youtube.com/watch?v=_dg86g-QIMO.

# CHAPTER 31

## The Secret of Slavery in Canada

*Afua Cooper*

Afua Cooper is a scholar, author, and poet. She is an associate professor and holds the James Robinson Johnston Chair in Black Canadian Studies at Dalhousie University in Halifax, Nova Scotia. She is a leading authority on Black Canadian history and slavery. Cooper has published multiple books of poetry and historical fiction and non-fiction, and has curated exhibits on African Canadian history and the transatlantic slave trade. The following selection is from her national bestseller, *The Hanging of Angelique: The Untold Story of Canadian Slavery and the Burning of Old Montréal*, which was a finalist for the Governor General's Literary Awards.

Slavery is Canada's best-kept secret, locked within the national closet. And because it is a secret it is written out of official history. But slavery was an institutionalized practice for over two hundred years. Canada also engaged in the nefarious business of slaving. Stephen Behrendt, a historian and demographer of slavery, reveals that the shipyards of several of the older Canadian colonies constructed ships for use in the British slave trade.[1] Canada might not have been a slave society—that is, a society whose economy was based on slavery—but it was a society with slaves. It shared this feature with virtually all other New World societies. Contrary to popular belief, slavery was common in Canada.

The reluctance to discuss and accept Canada as a place where slavery was institutionalized for 206 years is understandable. In North America, we associate the word *slavery* with the United States, not Canada, because the American economy, especially the southern portion, was fuelled by the labour of millions of African slave captives. In the story of North American slavery, we associate Canada with "freedom" or "refuge," because during the nineteenth century, especially between 1830 and 1860, the period known as the Underground Railroad era, thousands of American runaway slaves escaped to and found refuge in the British territories to the north. Therefore, the image of Canada as "freedom's land" has lodged itself in the national psyche and become part of our national identity. One result is the assumption that Canada is different from and morally superior to that "slave-holding republic," the United States.

When most people think of slavery, they see a huge cotton or sugar cane plantation worked by hundreds of slaves, with blood dripping down their backs as they endure constant whipping from the slave-drivers.

The slaveholder (usually a male) sits on the verandah of his mansion, fanned by docile young slaves. This lurid image is drawn from a southern United States or Caribbean version of slavery, and most people cannot associate it with Canada's early history. Yet the White settlers who colonized Canada during both the French and English periods were indeed slaveholders.

Scholars have painted a pristine picture of Canada's past. It is difficult to find a scholarly or popular publication on the country's past in which images, stories, and analyses of slave life are depicted. We read numerous accounts of pioneer life without learning that some of these pioneers were enslaved people who, like the free White pioneers, built roads and highways, constructed homesteads, fought off bears, caught beavers, established farms from forests, and helped in the defence of the young country.[2] People of African descent, free and enslaved, have vanished from national narratives. It is possible to complete a graduate degree in Canadian studies and not know that slavery existed in Canada.

A useful definition of slavery is the robbery of one's freedom and labour by another, usually more powerful person. Violence and coercion are used to carry out the theft and to keep the slave captive in the condition of bondage and servitude. This definition applies to slavery in Canada. Laws were enacted and institutions created to rob persons of their freedom and labour and keep them in perpetual servitude. In the earliest era of colonial rule in Canada, both Aboriginal peoples and Africans and their descendants were enslaved (Aboriginal slaves were colloquially termed *Panis*). From 1628 to 1833, slavery was a legal and acceptable institution in both French and British Canada and was vigorously practised.

The colonists in New France wanted slaves, especially Black slaves. In all European New World settlements, large percentages of the Native populations were exterminated through genocide, the harsh conditions of slavery, and the arrival of new diseases in their midst. In enslavement, the Native populations declined rapidly, which gave Europeans the notion that

Natives could not withstand slavery. In the belief that Blacks were sturdier people, Europeans began to bring African captives into the colonies to work as slaves. On the whole, Blacks appeared somewhat better able to withstand the physical demands of slavery: they lived a little longer than the Native people. Canada's political and administrative leaders—suave, urbane, and educated men, some of whom spent time in the tropical colonies—knew this. They therefore used their power and influence to bring Black slaves into the country.

\*\*\*\*\*

As French colonists settled in Canada and expanded their colonizing ventures, it became clear that the available labour force could not meet the demands created by a burgeoning economy. Thus, New France began its colonial life with a chronic labour shortage. Even though a system of indentureship had been set in place, with contract labourers coming from France to serve out an indenture, it did not solve the problem. Seeing the prosperity of their New England neighbours, a prosperity based on slave labour, *les Canadiens* hit on the idea that slavery was exactly what their colony needed.

\*\*\*\*\*

By 1690, New France had a population of 12,000. But it was not enough. The labour shortage continued. In 1688, bowing to pressure from the settlers, the governor, Marquis de Denonville, and the intendant, Jean Bochart de Champigny, wrote to Louis XIV, requesting permission to introduce Black slaves into the colony. [...]

The following year, the king gave his consent, though he expressed doubts about the effects of the severe Canadian climate on slaves from the tropics. Despite his concerns, enslaved Africans were brought into the colony. Further royal consent was given in 1701, and slavery began to take root.

\*\*\*\*\*

With or without help from the Crown, New France's colonists were able, with varying degrees of success, to obtain enslaved Africans. One method available to the French was the use of Native allies. The Abenaki and sometimes the Iroquois captured Black slaves from the English to the south and sold them to the French settlers in Canada. However, there were also legal transactions between the French and the English: French colonists bought Black slaves from New York, New England, the Carolinas, and other American colonies. Enslaved Africans also came to New France from the West Indies, from Africa, and from Europe.

In Montréal, which eventually would have the largest slave population in the colony, the first Black person recorded as a slave in the register of the church of Notre-Dame is simply named "Louis." It is noted that he was a native of Madagascar and was twenty-six at the time of his baptism on May 24, 1692. Louis Lecomte-Dupre owned Louis, the slave. On the same day, another slave, Pierre Célestin, age twenty-four, was baptized as well. Also a native of Madagascar, his owner was Pierre Leber. It would seem that both of these slaves received the first names of their owners.[3]

\*\*\*\*\*

The French empire in the West Indies was built on sugar production and the labour of enslaved Africans. The Code Noir, a French legal code, regulated slavery in the West Indies. Though it was never made law in Canada, New France's slaveholders applied the Code Noir when they thought it necessary. […] Under the Code Noir, slaves were declared "movable," that is, personal property, in the same category as livestock, furniture, and trade goods. The Code Noir regulated other aspects of slave life, such as relations between master and slave, the status of slave children, slave marriages, and so forth.[4]

\*\*\*\*\*

Imperial edicts and local laws also consolidated, regularized, and protected slavery in New France and enshrined the rights of colonists to own slaves. In 1701, Louis XIV gave his full consent to Black slavery in Canada, authorizing "its colonists to own slaves … in full proprietorship."[5] This consent was merely academic, because Canadians had already been doing so.

\*\*\*\*\*

Black slavery in Canada was patriarchal, meaning that the male slaveholder was the head of an extended family that included people he was related to by marriage and blood (his wife and children) and enslaved persons. Slaves often lived in the same houses as their owners, ate the same food, were baptized by their owners, and had owners or their close relatives as godparents, and sometimes they received the name of the owner's family.

The paternalistic nature of slavery in New France had much to do with the scarcity of labour in a growing colony: slaves were a valuable resource. Yet the economy, largely based on the fur trade, did not demand large gangs of labourers in the way that an agriculturally based economy would have. True, in Canada, agriculture was an important secondary economic activity, and many of the White colonists were farmers who did use slaves as farm labourers. Canada's economic model made for a form of slavery that was, to some degree, different from the slavery seen across the southern United States. It was more in line with the type of slavery found in colonial New England and New York.

Slaves in Canada engaged in a variety of occupations—from rat catcher to hangman—but most worked as house servants, as farm labourers, or in skilled occupations. In New France, and later in British Canada, slaves were owned by a variety of individuals and corporations. The Church, the nobility, merchants, lawyers, government officials, gentry, soldiers, seigneurs, tavern-keepers, farmers, business people, and artisans all held slaves. The merchant elite, as a group, held the largest number of enslaved people.

[…] The majority of this population lived in the three main centres of the colony: Montréal, Trois-Rivières, and the capital, Québec. This made slavery in New France a more or less urban phenomenon. By the end of the French period, in 1760, seventy-seven percent of all enslaved people lived in urban areas, with fifty-two percent of this group residing in Montréal alone.[6] Living in cities, the enslaved had some mobility and so became acquainted with the geography of their locale. This knowledge, in many instances, accounted for their frequent escapes.

Generally speaking, the kind of work enslaved people did ensured close proximity to their owners. Even if relationships between owners and slaves were hostile, the two parties nonetheless maintained physical domestic closeness. Enslaved people could legally marry, with the permission of their owners, and upon death were usually given a Christian burial. New France's slaves also had certain rights typically reserved for free persons in the rest of the New World. For example, they could serve as witnesses at religious functions and could petition against free persons.[7]

*****

Enslaved Africans were hired out, […] and they were also sold and bought. On September 25, 1743, Charles Réaume drew up a contract in the office of a Québec notary to sell five enslaved Africans to Louis Cureux. […]

The entire slave party was sold for 3,000 livres.

The French colonists and rulers also gave away slave children as gifts:

> In July, 1748, Jean-Pierre Roma, Commandant for the King at the Island of St. Jean [Prince Edward Island] … on his passage to Québec, made a singular Gift to his friend, Fleury de la Gorgendière…. He gave him a mulatto Girl, five months old and named Marie.

> The child was born at Québec, February 20, 1848; she was baptized the following day, and her godfather and godmother were M. Perrault, a merchant, and Marie-Anne Roma, daughter of Commandant Roma.

> The gift made to M. Fleury de la Gorgendière is explained by the fact that the mother of the child, the slave of Roma, died in giving it birth. Roma, not being able to charge himself with raising the orphan, preferred to give it to M. Fleury de la Gorgendière.

> The deed is drawn up by the Notary, Jean-Claude Panet, July 15, 1748; and it is the stipulation that in case of the death of Fleury and his wife, the mulatto will return to Mlle [Mademoiselle] Roma (her godmother). If she cannot take her, it is stipulated that she will receive her freedom.[8]

This sad story hides as much as it reveals. The slave mother died giving birth to her child, and her owner gave the baby away because he felt he could not raise her himself. The child, described as a mulatto, was called an "orphan." But for a child to be created, a father had to be involved. Who was the child's father? Was it Roma himself? Was that why he felt so obliged to find a home for the child, and why he gave her away to his trusted friend instead of selling her? A veil of semi-protectiveness was drawn around the slave baby. Not only was she given to someone whom Roma believed would care for her, but Roma's daughter was the baby's godmother and a stand-in parent if that became necessary. The baby's mother remained nameless, but we know a few things about her: she was a Black woman; she was Roma's slave; and she died in childbirth.

Enslaved Africans in Canada reacted to slavery in much the same way that slaves did in other New World societies and took steps to wreak revenge on their owners. They ran away, talked back, broke tools, were disobedient, threatened their owners, organized slave uprisings, and in two cases allegedly set major fires that devastated colonial towns.

Slaves also died young. The average age of death for Panis was 17.7 years, and for Blacks, 25.2. Only a few Blacks lived to be 80.[9]

During the French period, enslaved Panis were more numerous than enslaved Africans because Panis were easier to obtain. This situation would be reversed with the Conquest of Canada.

In 1760, at the end of the Seven Years War between Britain and France, Britain conquered Canada. Three years later, by the Treaty of Paris, France ceded Canada to Britain. New France ceased to be, and the Canadian territory seized by the British was renamed and transformed into the colony of Québec. By the time of the conquest, over 1,500 Black slaves had landed in Canada.

With the 47th article of the treaty of capitulation, signed between the victorious British and the defeated French, the British confirmed the rights of the French colonists to own and retain their slaves.

*****

With its successes in the Seven Years War, Britain became the strongest power in the world. By this time, it was also the most powerful slave trading nation. [...] By the time of the Conquest of Canada, Britain had transported hundreds of thousands of captive Africans to the New World in numerous slave ships. Britain also had a large slave empire centred in the West Indies and the United States, with slave colonies in southern India and south Africa.

If the enslaved Canadian Blacks and Panis thought the Conquest would deliver a chance for freedom, they were wrong. The British conquest led to the intensification of slavery in Canada. Britain had

the resources to pump slaves into Canada; however, no large-scale shipments of slaves were required to provide the Canadian colonists with slave labour. With Canada now a British possession, land-hungry British-American colonists to the south began migrating in large numbers to the new territory. The post-Conquest immigrants brought their Black slave labourers with them, thus increasing the slave population in Canada.

The British preferred Black slaves to enslaved Panis, and, having the resources, ensured that more Black bondspeople would enter the colony. As a result, under the British regime, Black enslaved labourers became more numerous than Panis. Consequently, enslavement gradually became identified solely with Africans.

*****

The British conquerors introduced the printing press and the newspaper to the newly acquired territory. From these papers, we learn that slaves in the new dispensation, as in the old regime, continued to run away. Throughout the colonial period, English-language newspapers regularly announced slave flight. These advertisements give us insight into the enslaved people, their condition, and their responses to slavery.

*****

[One] runaway was the slave woman Cash.

*Quebec Gazette*, October 19, 1769

On Sunday morning … a Negro wench named Cash, twenty-six years old … speaks English and French very fluently, carried with her a considerable quantity of linen and other valuable effects not her own; and as she has also taken with her a large bundle of wearing apparel belonging to herself, consisting of a black satin cloak, caps, bonnets, ruffles, ribbons, six or seven petticoats, a pair of old stays, and many other articles of value which cannot be ascertained, it is likely that she may change her dress.

Cash absconded with a large portion of her owner's wardrobe and must have thought of using these clothes as a means of disguise. Or, quite likely, she felt that her owner owed her all that she took.

From these ads, we learn that many slaves were bilingual, sometimes multi-lingual. We often learn of a slave's knowledge of skills and trades. For example, one Pompey was noted to be a sailor. And we get a description of the kind of clothes the runaways wore.

Where would slaves run? Slave runaways could take refuge with sympathetic Natives in the Upper Country or disappear into some frontier communities. Escaping to land held by a foreign power was another possibility, as was escaping via ship to the West Indies or Florida. But it is likely that slaves like Cash and others who came with their owners from places such as New England and New York were running *back* to these places—places they knew and where they may have had relatives. When going back to the thirteen colonies, escapees traversed a reverse Underground Railroad.

*****

*Marronage*, the act of running away, could be either temporary or permanent. With temporary (or *petit*) *marronage*, enslaved persons ran away for a few days or weeks because they were upset and angry with their owners. However, they intended to go back. Temporary *marronage* was a weapon enslaved Africans used to show their owners that they did not have to "put up with it." It also showed that slaveholders did not have complete ownership over the bodies of their slave property. Permanent *marronage* meant that the captives escaped and lived in freedom in hard-to-reach places such as forests, wildernesses, swamps, and mountain strongholds.[10]

Newspapers in the colony of Québec were not the only ones that broadcasted the flight of slaves. In the forty years after the Conquest, and in the early years of the nineteenth century, ads for runaway and missing slaves also graced the pages of colonial newspapers in New Brunswick, Nova Scotia, and Upper Canada.

The sale of slaves was another feature of life in Canada. The value of slave property depended on physical health (acquired immunity from smallpox was an asset), special aptitudes, age, and sex, among other factors. Olivier Le Jeune was sold for 50 livres in 1628. Marie-Joseph Angélique was sold for a barrel of gunpowder. In 1738, in Montréal, Catherine Raimbault sold two of her Black male slaves, Laramee, aged thirty, and Charles, aged ten, for 200 and 570 livres respectively. That a ten-year-old child fetched more than a thirty-year-old man is not strange, given that slaves died so young in the colony. The seller and purchaser probably knew that Laramee did not have long to live, while the boy could potentially render fifteen more years of service.

In the post-Conquest period, a woman skilled in housework could fetch between £30 and £50. The woman described in this ad would likely have commanded a good price:

*Quebec Gazette*, February 23, 1769

Mr. Prenties has to sell a negro woman, aged 25 years, with a mulatto male child, 9 months old. She was formerly the property of General Murray; she can be well recommended for a good house servant; handles milk well and makes butter to perfection.

*****

[Such ads] reveal, certainly, that slaves were seen as chattel, like horses or harnesses. They also tell us that women's primary occupation was that of domestic. Black women laboured in the homes of their owners doing all manner of housework, including child care.

The image of the Black woman who "understands thoroughly every kind of housework," the tireless domestic, has persisted throughout the centuries. […]

Sale of slaves was usually a transaction between two parties, but sometimes slaves were sold publicly. The same Mr. Prenties who advertised in February 1769 was not successful in selling his slaves. Six months later, he chose to do so at a public market. "To be sold at public vendue … a negro woman aged 25, with a mulatto child, male.…"[11]

Slave ads pertaining to women and children often indicate that children were sold with their mothers. Some of these children are described as mulattoes, the fathers of whom are "unknown." The relatively large mulatto population at the time of the Conquest reveals that White men often sired the children of Black women, most of whom were enslaved women. This fact must be placed in the context of the power relationships in slave societies. White men owned Black women's bodies and what came out of those bodies. Black women were regularly subjected to sexual assaults by their owners and other White men. If the women were impregnated and had children, these children inherited the status of their mothers and were enslaved. It mattered little that the children's fathers were White men, sometimes very prominent White men; what mattered was that their mothers were enslaved and Black. One of the most dehumanizing aspects of slavery was the loss of control that Black people, especially women, experienced over their bodies.[12]

One commentator on Canadian slavery makes light of the sexual abuse that Black women faced when he casts them as seducers whose charms (hapless) White men cannot resist.[13] Slaveholders who sexually abused Black women, kept them as concubines, and impregnated them may have subscribed to this sentiment. It is a common attitude of those in power. Refusing to take responsibility for their offence, they blame the victim.

The American Revolutionary War (1776–1783) produced a further expansion of slavery in Canada.

Many Americans who remained loyal to the Crown fled to Canada, with their enslaved chattel, on the heel of British defeat by the American forces. At least 35,000 of these Loyalists fled to Nova Scotia. Five thousand were Black, both slave and free; however, the majority were free. The expansion of Nova Scotia's population led, in 1784, to the province being divided to create New Brunswick. This new province got its share of free and enslaved Black Loyalists. Likewise, some Black Loyalists made it into Prince Edward Island.

About 10,000 Loyalists—White, Black, and Native—came to the province of Québec. However, unlike in the Maritime provinces, most of the Québec Black Loyalists were enslaved. They came with their White owners from New York, New England, Virginia, the Carolinas, and other parts of the thirteen colonies. Some of the enslaved Blacks were also in the parties of members of the Iroquois Confederacy.

\*\*\*\*\*

In Upper Canada and Québec (renamed Lower Canada after 1791), though many Blacks were free people, the majority were enslaved. The enslaved population, brought to Canada mainly by White Loyalists (members of the Mohawk elite also held Black slaves), came with a variety of skills, which they used in the founding and development of the colonies. Slaves worked as millwrights, blacksmiths, coopers, printers, and tinsmiths. They felled trees, made roads, opened highways, and worked as domestics, nannies, and farm labourers. James Walker insists that "we cannot understand early pioneer history unless we acknowledge that slavery existed.…"[14] By 1793, it is estimated that there were five hundred slaves in Upper Canada.

Like many of the families of the old French regime, most of Upper Canada's leading families, including many of the province's founding fathers and mothers, were slaveholders.

\*\*\*\*\*

Peter Russell, a member of the Executive Council and future provincial administrator, held at least five slaves, four of whom comprised one family: a woman named Peggy and her three children. Peggy and her family lived with Russell and big sister Elizabeth in their town home in York (now part of Toronto).[15]

*****

Peggy, the mother of three children, Milly, Amy, and Jupiter, and the wife of a free Black man named Pompadour, was a disobedient and recalcitrant slave who bucked the Russells' authority by talking back to them and running away whenever she felt like it. On more than one occasion, her master had her confined to the town's jail. Jupiter, her son, was also a runaway and "disobedient"; he too was lodged in jail for his rudeness and "saucy ways." Peter Russell determined to get Peggy off his hands by selling her to another member of the colonial elite, slaveholder Matthew Elliott, then living in Sandwich.

*****

Peter Russell, an Anglo-Irish man, accepted the institution of slavery in Upper Canada even though in Britain itself slavery was on the decline. He behaved like a typical American slaveholder: he separated families if he saw fit, he punished and imprisoned his slaves, and when they would not "obey" he sold them. He was not going to put Peggy on the auction block; rather, he was selling her through a more "genteel" method. Nevertheless, the result would be the same: Peggy would be separated from her husband and children.

Yet, contrary to a once-popular belief that slave masters had "absolute authority" over their slaves, Russell was not in total control. If conditions were not to their liking, slaves often tried in subtle and not so subtle ways to live within the bounds of the institution on their own terms, to change the frame of reference. Peggy was doing just that when she left the Russell household to live "at large."

Peggy's way of dealing with her enslavement paralleled that of enslaved people throughout the Americas and Canada. […] Peggy may not have tried to make a permanent bid for her freedom because she had young children and wanted to remain with her family. What Peggy engaged in was *petit marronage*, running away temporarily to protest one's enslavement, or taking a vacation of sorts to escape the vagaries of slave life.

*****

Even though York was a small town, others would employ and harbour Peggy while knowing she belonged to someone else. Because there was a labour shortage, Peggy could find sympathizers who would take her in. Who knows what was going on in the Russell household that led Peggy to run from it. Was she sexually abused by either owner? It seems that her relationship with Elizabeth Russell, in particular, was strained. Peter Russell, in his letter to Elliott, said that Peggy showed a "disposition at times to be very troublesome," revealing that Peggy was an incorrigible slave. She would not behave.

*****

By 1806, Peter Russell, who by this time was no longer the provincial administrator, was at the point of desperation. He wanted to rid himself of Peggy and her son, Jupiter. He advertised in the *York Gazette*:

February 19, 1806, To Be Sold:

A Black woman named Peggy, aged forty years, and a Black boy, her son, named Jupiter, aged about fifteen years, both of them the property of the subscriber. The woman is a tolerable cook and washerwoman, and perfectly understands making soap and candles. The boy is tall and strong for his age, and has been employed in the country business, but brought up principally as a house servant. They are each of them servants for life. The price of the woman is one hundred and fifty dollars. For the boy two hundred dollars, payable in three years, with interest from the day of sale, and to be secured by bond, &c. But one-fourth less will be taken for ready money.

If the Russells seem to have been "reluctant" masters, Peggy and her family were "irresolute" slaves. What is quite clear is that Peggy and her family pushed and pulled at slavery and sought to effect their freedom or gain concessions. […]

Common people also bought, held, and sold slaves. In the *Niagara Herald*, on January 2, 1802, we find "for sale, a negro slave, 18 years of age, stout and healthy, has had the smallpox and is capable of service either in the house or out of doors." In the same paper, on January 18: "For sale, negro man and woman, the property of Mrs. Widow Clement. They have been bred to the work of the farm; will be sold on highly advantageous terms for cash or lands. Apply to Mrs. Clement."

Colonists could also place ads when they wished to buy slaves. The *Niagara Gazette* and *Oracle* of January 11, 1797, ran the following: "Wanted to purchase, a negro girl from seven to twelve years of age of good disposition. For full particulars, apply to … W.J. Cooke, West Niagara."

How were enslaved people treated? Some masters baptized their slaves, married them, and remembered them in their wills. One salient example of a "good and paternalistic master" is Robert I.D. Gray. He apparently treated his slave family well, and provided generously for them in his will, manumitting them and setting up a trust fund for them. Yet not even he could free the slaves while he lived. They had to wait until he died, and therefore had no further use of their time and labour, to get their freedom. Another slaveholder, Isaac Bennett, made provision in his will for the education and freedom of his two slave boys.

But, for every humane master, there was a brutal one to match.

*****

Black people, then, throughout the length and breadth of British North America, were owned, bought, and sold by White colonists. The lives of the Black enslaved people and their offspring were regulated and circumscribed by those who owned them and the legal resources they could access. Slavery was as Canadian as it was American or West Indian. It is important to note, though, that in this period of the mid- to late eighteenth century, there were also free Black communities in British North America. In Nova Scotia and New Brunswick, Black people of Loyalist origin built free villages and towns in such places as Preston, Shelburne, Birchtown, and Saint John. In fact, these and others became the first free Black communities in North America. However, the residents of these communities faced extreme hostility from Whites. […]

Slavery did not remain unchallenged. And the enslaved were always the first to challenge the conditions of their servitude. We have seen that they ran away and performed other hostile acts against their owners. However, the first official challenge to slavery came from the top down and occurred in the colony of Upper Canada. Colonel John Graves Simcoe, veteran of the Revolutionary War, arrived in Canada in 1792 to take up the post of lieutenant governor of the new province of Upper Canada. Simcoe had been a member of the British Parliament and supported antislavery measures in its House. On arriving in Canada (he came by way of Montréal), Simcoe realized the extent of slaveholding among the White population and is reputed to have said that, under his governorship, he would not discriminate "between the natives of Africa, America, or Europe."[16] On reaching Upper Canada, Simcoe was determined to abolish slavery.

He had his chance in March 1793, when he heard of the case of Chloe Cooley, a slave woman who was manhandled, tied up with ropes, and thrown in a boat by her owner, William Vrooman of Queenston in the Niagara district. Vrooman then rowed the boat to the New York side of the Niagara River and sold his slave to someone on the American side. Eyewitnesses related that Cooley "screamed violently and made resistance."[17] Simcoe decided to prosecute Vrooman, but his chief justice told him he did not have a leg to stand on, since slavery was legal in the British empire and Vrooman was well within his rights to dispose of his slave in any manner he wished. Simcoe then decided to prosecute Vrooman for disturbing the peace.

Later, Simcoe gathered enough support in the legislative and executive councils and the assembly to push for a bill on the immediate abolition of slavery in the province. But it was not to be. The slaveholders inside his parliament and those outside were outraged at his audacity and fought him. They claimed that slave labour was essential for the economic life of the colony and that Simcoe would ruin them if he abolished slavery. [...] So Simcoe backed off, and he and his advisers worked out a compromise. In July 1793, "An act to prevent the further introduction of slaves and to limit the term of contracts for servitude within this province" was pushed through the legislature.[18] The title of the act tells us that it was a compromise indeed. Nothing was said about abolition, because that was not the act's intent. The act did not free a single slave.

It did accomplish other things. First, it confirmed that current slaves would remain slaves. Slaveholders had pushed for this, and they got it. Now they could breathe a sigh of relief. Second, the act banned the introduction of new slaves. Third, the children of current slaves would gain their freedom upon reaching twenty-five, and if they had children before they reached that magic number, their children would be automatically free.

Interestingly, the act did not prevent the sale of slaves across international borders. Many slaveholders saw this loophole and, like Vrooman, sold their slaves into New York.

Upper Canadian slaves who were hoping to be freed by Simcoe's bill had to look for their freedom elsewhere. In 1787, the Northwest Territory (Michigan, Indiana, Ohio, Illinois, Wisconsin, and part of Minnesota) issued an ordinance prohibiting slavery. Vermont and other parts of New England had also abolished slavery by this date. And, in 1799, New York made provisions for the gradual abolition of slavery. As a result, many Upper Canadian enslaved Blacks escaped into these free territories.[19] So numerous were some of these former Canadians in American cities that, in Detroit, for example, a group of former Upper Canadian slaves formed a militia in 1806 for the defence of the city against the Canadians. They also fought against Canada in the War of 1812.

If Simcoe's bill had a redeeming feature, it was the article that prohibited the importation of new slaves into the province. This meant, in effect, that slavery would decline, as it could not be expanded through importation. Perhaps, more important, it also meant that any foreign slaves would be immediately freed upon reaching the soil of Upper Canada. That was what began the Underground Railroad for enslaved Americans. By the War of 1812, they had heard of this novel situation and many began making the trek northward. The paradox is inescapable: at the same time, many Upper Canadian slaves were making the trek southward to freedom in Michigan and New England.

\*\*\*\*\*

In the other provinces, there was some movement against slavery. A few legislators in Lower Canada tried to copy Simcoe's bill, but they were roundly defeated by the slaveholding interests in the House. One such pro-slavery legislator, a slaveholder himself, was none other than Québec nationalist Joseph Papineau. It would be the courts in Lower Canada, not the government, that would move against slavery. Some Québec slaves took their masters to court, claiming that their masters were holding them illegally. In 1797, the courts began to rule in favour of the enslaved. In some instances in Nova Scotia and New Brunswick, local courts also freed some slaves who petitioned for their freedom. The slaveholders of Prince Edward Island, on the other hand, held fast to their right to own enslaved property. Slaves there did not even bother to present their case in court. Gradually, over time, slavery declined in the five colonies that made up British North America. It would eventually come to an end in 1834, when the British Parliament outlawed and abolished it in all its territories.

Though the story of slavery in Canada has been silenced, those who owned slaves and those whose actions impinged directly on the lives of the enslaved did not adopt a secretive pose in their dealings with their slave property. Government officials deliberated slavery as a public issue. Various statutes and acts concerning Black enslavement came from the imperial and provincial parliaments. The courts also documented the presence of slaves and their concerns. Further, census takers counted enslaved Blacks among the general population. In fact, in the years following the Revolutionary War, there were at least two censuses done to count the number of slaves in the populations of Upper and Lower Canada.[20] As important, enslaved people bore witness to their own presence through flight and other subversive actions.

## NOTES

1. Stephen D. Behrendt, *The Atlantic Slave Trade* [CD ROM] (Cambridge: Cambridge University Press, 1999). This database has information on over 30,000 slave ships used in the British trade.

2. James Walker, a historian at the University of Waterloo, discusses how Black history is missing from pioneer history. See James Walker, *A History of Blacks in Canada* (Hull: Ministry of State for Multiculturalism, 1980), 1–7.

3. O.M.H. Lapalice, "Les Esclaves noir à Montréal sous l'ancien régime," *Canadian and Numismatic Journal* 12 (1915): 139.

4. William Riddell, "The Code Noir," *Journal of Negro History* 10, no. 3 (1925): 321–28.

5. Robin W. Winks, *The Blacks in Canada: A History* (Montréal: McGill-Queen's University Press, 1997), 1.

6. Ibid., 9. See also Marcel Trudel, *L'esclavage au Canada Français: Histoire et conditions de l'esclavage* (Québec: Les Presses Universitaire Laval, 1960), 130. On demography, see Kenneth Donovan, "Slaves and Their Owners in Ile Royale," *Acadiensis* xxv, no. 1 (Autumn 1995, pp. 3–32), 3.

7. See Winks, *The Blacks in Canada*, 11.

8. William Riddell, "An Early Canadian Slavery Transaction," *Journal of Negro History* 13, no. 2 (1928): 207. The translation is Riddell's. The original is in French and is taken from Pierre Georges Roy, *Le bulletin des recherches historiques* 33, no. 8: 584.

9. Winks, *The Blacks in Canada*, 10.

10. See Bernard Moitt, "Women and Resistance," in *Women and Slavery in the French Antilles, 1635–1848* (Bloomington: Indiana University Press, 2001), 125–50.

11. Hurbert Neilson, "Slavery in Old Canada, before and after the Conquest," *Transactions of the Literary and Historical Society of Quebec* 2, no. 26 (1906): 35.

12. See Dorothy Roberts, *Killing the Black Body: Race, Reproduction, and the Meaning of Liberty* (New York: Vintage Books, 1999), 23–25; Maureen Elgersman, *Unyielding Spirits: Black Women and Slavery in Early Canada and Jamaica* (New York: Garland Publishing, 1999), 21–38.

13. Trudel, *L'eslavage au Canada Français*, 258.

14. Walker, *A History of Blacks in Canada*, 6.

15. The Russells wrote about their slave woman Peggy and her family. Much of Peggy's story is contained in the Russell Papers, a portion of which is Elizabeth Russell's diary, housed at the Baldwin Room, Toronto Public Library. Sections of Elizabeth's diary are reprinted in Edith Firth, *Town of York, 1791–1815* (Toronto: Champlain Society, 1962).

16. Winks, *The Blacks in Canada*, 96.

17. Peter Martin, a free Black man, and William Grisley, a White man, witnessed Vrooman binding and disposing of Chloe Cooley. Martin and Grisley related the matter to Simcoe and some members of his Executive Council. See E.A. Cruikshank, ed., *The Correspondence of Lieut. Governor John Graves Simcoe* [hereafter cited as Simcoe

Papers], vol. 1 (Toronto: Ontario Historical Society, 1923–31), 304.

18. For the complete "Act to Prevent Further Introduction of Slaves ...," see Nancy Power and Michael Butler, *Slavery and Freedom in Niagara* (Niagara-on-the-Lake: Niagara Historical Society, 1993), Appendix A. The act can also be viewed in *Statutes of Ontario, 1791–1840*, or on the Archives of Ontario Black history website.

19. William Riddell, "The Slave in Canada," *The Journal of Negro History* 3 (July 1920): 324. Henry Lewis, a former slave of William Jarvis, escaped to Schenectady, New York, and wrote to his ex-owner, offering to buy himself. See Henry Lewis to William Jarvis, 3 May 1798, Jarvis Papers, Toronto Public Library.

20. Two censuses of slaves in the Niagara district of Upper Canada were carried out in 1783. The Lower Canadian census was done in 1784. See Winks, *The Blacks in Canada*, 35; Power and Butler, *Slavery and Freedom*, 13–15.

*Source:* Cooper, Afua. (2006). Excerpted from *The Hanging of Angelique: The Untold Story of Canadian Slavery and the Burning of Old Montréal* (pp. 68–81, 83–98, 100–105). Toronto, ON: Harper Collins.

# ACTIVIST ART 5

## YOU ARE MY SUNSHINE

*Wangechi Mutu*

Mutu was born in Nairobi, Kenya, and lives and works in Brooklyn, NY. She is best known for her large-scale collages depicting female figures in lush, otherworldly land-scapes. Her work explores issues of gender, race, war, globalization, colonialism, and the eroticization of the Black female body. She creates mysterious cyborgian figures pieced together with human, animal, machine, and monster parts. She often combines found materials and magazine cutouts with sculpture and painted imagery, sampling from sources as diverse as African traditions, international politics, the fashion indus-try, and science fiction. Wangechi Mutu is considered one of the most important con-temporary African artists working today. Her art has been exhibited around the world and has achieved widespread acclaim.

*Source:* Mutu, Wangechi. (2015). "You are My Sunshine." Collage painting on paper, 24 x 36 in. Retrieved from: http://wangechimutu.com/.

The piece, "You Are My Sunshine," was exhibited at the Africa's Out! inaugural event at the Barbara Gladstone Gallery in Manhattan on June 5, 2015. Mutu founded Africa's Out! as an artistic and political response to the recent criminalization of homosexuality in African countries like Nigeria and Uganda. Africa's Out!, explains Mutu, "is our sincere effort to counter this with joy, support and celebration." "I thought I'm going to call it Africa's Out! because it will be about ... you know, what is out," she said. "We're here and we're all over. We're out of the bag. We're confident, we're capable, we're evolved, we're full and we're ready. So, Africa's Out!"

*Source:* Sommerfeldt, Chris. (2015, June 14). Adapted from "Africa's Out!: Wangechi Mutu's Initiative to Celebrate African Diversity." *Kenyan Vibe*. Retrieved from: https://www.kenyanvibe.com/africas-out-wangechi-mutus-initiative-to-celebrate-african-diversity/.

# CHAPTER 32

## Black Women Rage

*Wendy Brathwaite*

Wendy (Motion) Brathwaite is a poet, performer, and award-winning spoken word and hip hop artist. Her work addresses some of the difficult realities of African Canadian life in Greater Toronto, including racism, marginalization, gender inequalities, and Black motherhood. She is the author of two published works of poetry, *Motion in Poetry* and *40 Dayz,* and the play *Aneemah's Spot.*

Black Woman rage makes us take to the stages
Up front at rallies
Leading black families
Black woman rage is a thing of beauty
Doing our duty,
making our roles
Suffering in silence, giving the bad eye
Calling on God,
dealing with spirits
Jah-Jah takes over as riddims move hips
Cusses come from full brown female lips
Black woman rage is a sight to behold
Working the fields
suns beat on bent backs
Black songs rise with density of deep sound
Deep pasts seep to all who have the ear—
Can you understand the meaning
of Rage … Black … Woman … Song?
Sad, true, throaty, tired
Awakened

As we stretch to the heights of creation
Leggo our hand in the offending face
Stay in our place? What place?
When we just be all over …
Never removed as we feed the masses
with milk, poems and minds
Full breasts and asses
Queen Nzinga looks on
as we swing our small axes
through the forests of fearsome shadows
that mean us no good
We learn to run from home-grown licks
Give 2 snaps up
and stand akimbo
as only Raging Black Women could.
We beat the drums to call on the sisters
to pass on the secrets that only mothers know.
two hundred and forty days of
two heart-beats, two sighs,
two souls, two-fold life-form multiply

with the powers of Yin and Yang
One moment kisses to heal the sting of her strong
    hand
Raging, Woman Black—
back to the basics of the Motherland …
Speak your story, speak
sister songs
and weep if you will
at the rage that kept us frozen, still
under humping weights
that pinned us in darkened places
Rage that kept us from killing our rapists
In order to maintain we paralyzed ourselves instead
They left us for dead
They *thought* we were
dead
But we don't die,
we …
grow, laugh, spread, cry
Daughters of the cotton and cane
cannot wither and die.

*Source:* Brathwaite, Wendy. (2002). "Black Women Rage." In *Motion in Poetry* (pp. 27–29). Toronto, ON: Three O'Clock Press.

# CHAPTER 33

## The Construction of a Negative Identity

*Kim Anderson*

Kim Anderson (Cree Métis) is an associate professor of family relations and applied nutrition at the University of Guelph. She is well known for her book *A Recognition of Being: Reconstructing Native Womanhood,* which was followed by *Life Stages and Native Women: Memory, Teachings and Story Medicine.* Anderson has conducted several research projects in collaboration with the Ontario Federation of Indigenous Friendship Centres (OFIFC), most recently on projects about Indigenous knowledge transfer in urban communities, and gender and life stage factors in urban Indigenous governance.

*Princess, Princess, calendar girl,*
*Redskin temptress, Indian pearl.*
*Waiting by the water*
*For a white man to save.*
*She's a savage now remember—*
*Can't behave!*[1]

These lines, taken from Monique Mojica's play *Princess Pocahontas and the Blue Spots,* capture the essence of how Indigenous women in the Americas are stereotyped: as sexual temptresses, aligned with nature, savagely promiscuous, and in need of salvation from the white man. Every North American is familiar with the imagery and connotations of the Indian princess and the "squaw," and as Indigenous women of the twenty-first century we continue to endure the Halloween Pocahottie costumes, the "dirty squaw"

catcalls, and the landscapes with names like "Squaw Valley." Where do the Indian princess and squaw images come from? How did they become so widespread, and how do they affect the day-to-day lives of contemporary Native women?

As I explored these questions, I discovered that both the Indian princess and the dirty, easy squaw were invented and then reinforced because they proved useful to the colonizer. The Indian princess upholds settler entitlement to the land as she is the one who invited the white man in. The "uncivilized" squaw justifies the violence involved in this process. To me, these images are like a disease that has spread through both the Native and the non-Native mindset. In tracing this development, I hope to highlight a renewed understanding of Native womanhood that will help us to recover our strength, self-esteem, and dignity.

# ROOTS OF A NEGATIVE FEMALE IMAGE

In both Western and Indigenous frameworks, Native women have historically been equated with the land. The Euro-constructed image of Native women, therefore, mirrors Western attitudes toward the earth. Sadly, this relationship has typically developed within the context of control, conquest, possession, and exploitation. The Euro-Canadian image of Native women has been constructed within this context and has evolved along with the evolving relationship of European people to this continent.

When they first arrived on Turtle Island in the sixteenth century, Europeans produced images of Native womanhood to symbolize the magnificent richness and beauty they encountered. This was the phase of the great mother, the Indian Queen. Cherokee scholar Rayna Green described the personification of "America" typical to this period (1575–1765):

> Draped in leaves, feathers, and animal skins, as well as in heavy jewelry, she appeared aggressive, militant, and armed with spears and arrows. Often she rode on an armadillo, and stood with her foot on the slain body of an animal or human enemy. She was the familiar mother-goddess figure—full bodied, powerful, nurturing but dangerous—embodying the wealth and danger of the New World.[2]

"Exotic, powerful, dangerous and beautiful," this Native female symbol represented both "American liberty and European virtue,"[3] but as the European settler became more familiar with the land, the queen was demoted. Colonial claims to the land would work only if the queen became more accessible, less powerful, and within the grasp of the white man. Out of this need, the "Indian princess" was born. The queen was transformed from a mother-goddess figure to a girlish-sexual figure, for who can own a mother or dominate the gods?

"Indian princess" imagery constructed Indigenous women as the virgin frontier, the pure border waiting to be crossed.[4] The enormous popularity of the princess lay within her erotic appeal to the covetous European male wishing to lay claim to the "new" territory. This equation of the Indigenous woman with virgin land, open for consumption, created a Native female archetype that, as Elizabeth Cook-Lynn has pointed out, could then be "used for the colonizer's pleasure and profit."[5]

Richard Slotkin's work offers valuable insights into how such fantasies of border crossing underpin settler/invader identity building and nationalism in the United States. He writes about the myth of the American frontier, where the white hero must cross the border into the lands of the "primitive" where he is regenerated through acts of violence.[6] These notions of border crossing, possession, and achieving a sense of renewal and belonging are dependent on the conquest and consumption of Native women and are ubiquitous in North American his-story and storytelling. They have been promoted through other popular his-storical characters like Sacajewea, the Shoshone woman who purportedly led explorers Lewis and Clark into the interior of the North American continent.[7] In Canada, we have Tekakwitha, the seventeenth-century "Mohawk Saint" who is eroticized by the white males who have written about her because she represents another version of transformative borderlands.[8] Further abroad, the story is the same. In her essay connecting Pocahontas in North America, Malintzin in Mexico, and Krotoa in South Africa, Pamela Scully writes: "The overly sexualized native woman surfaces in the sources of European exploration in places as diverse as North America, the South Pacific, East Indies and West Africa."[9]

The erotic image of Native female as "new" territory to be conquered persists to this day. You need only glance at posters of Walt Disney's *Pocahontas* to be confronted with a contemporary example of this archetype. We see a voluptuous yet innocent-looking Native (but not too Native) "girl," who will soon be conquered and consumed by the adventurous young white male. In her book *Killing the Indian Maiden: Images of Native American Women in Film*, M. Elise Marubbio points out that images of the princess and sexualized maiden persist into films she reviewed into the 1990s, and that the end of the story typically involves the death of the Native woman.[10] Chris Finley has written about the problematic representation of Sacajawea in the 2006 film *Night at the Museum*, where Sacajawea is "a Celluloid Maiden character that loves white men and aids in conquest."[11] While it may be possible to interpret characters like Pocahontas or Sacajewea as strong Indigenous leaders,[12] the mainstream interpretation of these mythic characters is quite the opposite: Native women (and, by association, the land) are "easy, available, and willing" for the white man, and conquest, consumption, and disappearance are the end result.[13]

Whereas the Indian princess has been popular and has a long history, her "darker twin," the "squaw," is also ubiquitous.[14] As with other colonial his-stories, once Indigenous peoples began to resist colonization, new archetypes emerged. Indigenous women world-wide became symbols of the troublesome colonies, and in the Americas the squaw emerged. Carol Douglas Sparks has traced the princess-to-squaw devolution in colonizer accounts of the Navajo.[15] The virgin-princess, so commonly found in white male adventurer records of the nineteenth century, is soon transformed. While the princess held erotic appeal for the covetous imperial male wishing to claim the "new" territory, the squaw drudge justified the conquest of an uncivilized terrain: "Americans found squaw drudges far more comfortable than these outspoken and powerful women, whose presence defied colonial rationalizations. Not only could the squaw be pitied, but her very existence justified American intrusion into her land and society."[16]

In her book, *Capturing Women: The Manipulation of Cultural Imagery in Canada's Prairie West*, Sarah Carter demonstrates how both the Canadian state and the national press deliberately promoted "dirty squaw"

imagery in the late 1800s.[17] At the time of settler invasion in western Canada, "dirty squaw" fiction was useful for a number of reasons. The uncivilized squaw provided a backdrop for the repressive measures against the Native population of the time. Like the men who were depicted as savage warriors, the women were reported to be "violent instigators of atrocities" (against whites),[18] thereby justifying colonial violence against Indigenous peoples. The image of the Native woman as the beast of burden in her society was drawn up to demonstrate the superiority of European wom-anhood and femininity (after all, white women did not "labour"), and the necessity for replacing Native wom-anhood with European womanhood. David Smits has written about how "the squaw" was thus constructed in contrast to the civilized, white "Victorian lady."[19]

As Native peoples were increasingly forced off their homelands, and women lost their status and role as producers within the economic structure of their societies, they were further cast as lazy and slovenly. Women were no longer able to provide for their families because they had lost the means to produce primary goods, such as clothing and food. They became dependent upon purchased goods and an economy in which they held no power. The dirty squaw conveniently took the blame for the increasing poverty in Indigenous communities and deflected attention from government and public complicity in the devastation of Indigenous peoples. If Native women were constructed as "squaws," dirty, lazy, and slovenly, it was faster to cover up the reality of Native women who were merely struggling with the increasingly inhuman conditions on reserve:

> In the unofficial and unpublished reports of reserve life … it was widely recognized that problems with reserve housing and health had little to do with the preferences, temper-ament, or poor housekeeping abilities of the women. Because of their poverty, the people were confined in one-room shacks, which were poorly ventilated and were impossible

to keep clean because they had dirt floors and were plastered with mud and hay. One inspector of the agencies noted in 1891 that the women did not have soap, towels, wash basins, or wash pails, nor did they have any means of acquiring them. Similarly, it was frequently noted that the women were short of basic clothing and had no textiles or yarn to work with. Yet in official public statements, the tendency was to ascribe blame to the women rather than drawing attention to conditions that would injure the reputation of government administration.[20]

Similarly, if Native women were portrayed as poor parents, it was then excusable for the state to remove Native children and place them in residential schools and foster homes.

Native female sexuality was also transformed into the "squaw" who was "lewd and licentious" and morally reprehensible. This representation was projected onto Native women to excuse the mistreatment they endured from white settler males. Within the context of late nineteenth-century morality, it was easier to blame Native women than to challenge the behaviour of the heroes on the frontier. The narrative espousing how "easy" Native women were was developed to cover up the fact that white males were involved in unmarried sexual activity and that state officials were perpetrators of sexual assault. This tactic is common in rape cases and is well entrenched in the Western consciousness: blame women for the sexual deviance of certain men. As part of the Native woman-blaming campaign, the *Toronto Daily Mail* of February 2, 1886, railed: "The character of the men of this country has been assailed."[21]

The squalor of the media-driven uncivilized easy squaw was further intended to guard against interracial marriages, thus protecting racial "purity" in the new country: "There were fears that the Anglo-Celts might be overrun by more fertile, darker and lower people, who were believed to be unable to control

their sexual desires."[22] The moral reform movement of the late 1880s in the West embraced images of the dirty squaw in an effort to keep the races segregated and to keep the white race pure. The dirty, dark squaw not only justified the deplorable treatment of Indigenous peoples, she also created a gauge against which white femininity could be measured and defined. Where Native women were powerful physical workers, white women were encouraged to be weak and frail. The Native woman thus was reinvented as a drudge. Where Native women had sexual liberty, white women were restricted from pleasure. The Native woman was then perceived as easy. Where Native women resisted the increasing restrictions and poverty of reserves, white women were expected to be models of domesticity, industriousness, and obedience. The Native woman had to be reconstructed as deficient in order to prop up the image of the white woman.

Since contact with the Europeans, Native women have been trapped within a dichotomous world view, where everything is either good or bad, dark or light, pure or corrupt. The Euro-constructed Indigenous woman with her dark ways, her squalor and corruption makes the construction of whiteness all the more attractive in the North American subconscious. In terms of female identity, the Native woman must endure the Western framework of virgin-whore, which was translated to princess-squaw and slapped on top of the complex understanding of Native womanhood that had existed for tens of thousands of years. This his-story continues to interfere with the lives of contemporary Native women.

## GHOSTS OF THE SQUAW AND THE PRINCESS

The majority of Native women will tell you that they have been called a "squaw"; this label has been applied to Native women right across North America. There are accounts from women of nations as widespread as the Mi'kmaq (Rita Joe) and the Pawnee/Otoe (Anna Lee Walters).[23] Native girls begin to hear racial/sexual slurs from an early age, often before they even understand the terms themselves. Anishinaabe professor Shirley Williams says she remembers hearing white boys singing, "Squaws along the Yukon aren't good enough for me." The boys would follow up with, "Would two dollars be enough?," playing on the myth that Native women are "easy." [...]

The "squaw" remains alive and well in the North American imaginary. The February 2, 2015, cover of "Canada's National Magazine," *Maclean's*, featured a photo of Cree writer and broadcaster Rosanna Deerchild, with the caption "They call me a stupid squaw, or tell me to go back to the rez."[24] Deerchild notes that she is harassed every few weeks on the streets of Winnipeg, stating "someone honks at me, or yells out 'How much' from a car window."[25] This squaw image is not only stamped on the North American subconscious when it comes to Native women, but also on land, place, and products such as "squaw brand sifted peas" and "Siwash squaw apples."[26] In her article "The S-Word: Discourse, Stereotypes, and the American Indian Woman," Debra Merskin writes that she found 4.8 million hits in a Google search of the term *squaw*, and that "most are linked to resorts, casinos or about landforms."[27] Efforts on the part of Indigenous peoples and allies to change such labelling are often resisted. Merskin points out that Native Americans have not had the same success at changing stereotypes as other marginalized groups and that the racist and sexist messages in this labelling reify "the hierarchical position of dominant Euro-American culture by controlling access to resources and power."[28] [...]

When negative images of Native women are so ingrained in the North American consciousness that even children participate in using them, it is easy to see how Native women might begin to think of themselves as "easy squaws." Janice Acoose describes how these negative images affected her consciousness.

I learned so passively to accept and internalize the easy squaw, Indian-whore, dirty Indian, and drunken Indian stereotypes that subsequently imprisoned me, and all Indigenous peoples, regardless of our historic, economic, cultural, spiritual, and geographical differences.... I shamefully turned away from my history and cultural roots, becoming, to a certain extent, what was encouraged by the ideological collusiveness of text books, and the ignorant comments and peer pressure from non-Indigenous students.[29]

Many Native female writers—including Joanne Arnott, Beth Brant, Maria Campbell, Janet Campbell Hale, Beatrice Culleton, Paula Gunn Allen, Lee Maracle, and Anna Lee Walters[30]—have provided accounts of how they or other Native women have fostered destructive and hateful attitudes toward themselves. This self-hatred is rooted in internalized racism, which comes from the negative self-concepts of racist stereotypes like the squaw. Internalized racism spreads like a disease through Native communities.[31] It makes us doubt the validity of the existence of our people, and thus ourselves.

Whereas the squaw is overtly negative, the Indian princess can be trickier to unpack. This is because the Indian princess today is often disguised as the honouring of an Indigenous female icon. In 2000, the United States released the "Sacagawea dollar," a commemorative coin, demonstrating the Shoshone woman's "eagerness to lead the way."[32] In other instances, commemoration of the archetypical "Indian maiden" involves adopting her identity. Rebecca Blevins Faery has written about her experience of going to Pocahontas, Iowa, to witness the opening of Disney's *Pocahontas*.[33] At this event, the white settlers of the town dressed up in beaded headbands, sang pioneer anthems, and sold white-looking dolls of Pocahontas. Where does such an inclination come from? Indigenous scholars such as Phillip Deloria and Shari Huhndorf have documented how North American traditions of "playing Indian" allow settlers to claim a sense of entitlement to the territory and assuage negative feelings about the violence that has facilitated their occupation.[34] Too often we find ourselves confronting these situations. I remember being taken off guard by a Pocahontas number at one of my daughter's dance shows—an honour that made me want to crawl under the seat. But at least I had the advantage of having read Indigenous and other critical race theorists to know why it feels so wrong to be faced with such images.[35]

Although the Indian princess can appear in such manifestations as children's Halloween or dance costumes, she is more often than not sexualized. As with the squaw, this imagery validates racist attitudes about the promiscuity and sexual availability of Indigenous women. This understanding finds its way into our lives and our communities. Sometimes, it means constantly having to fend off the advances of people with an appetite for the "Other."[36] It may involve a continual struggle to resist crass, sexualized interpretations of one's being. It often involves violence, or the threat of rape. In her autobiography, Métis performing artist and writer Morningstar Mercredi tells a story that demonstrates the connection between sexualization of Native women, settler conquest and consumption, and nationalized identity. She writes about living in western Canada, where "walking down most city streets guarantees a proposition"[37] and recalls being solicited by a white worker in an oil camp, who tells her "They say you're not a real Canadian till you've had an Indian woman...."[38]

Plains Cree/Métis professor Emma LaRocque asserts that "the dehumanizing portrayal of the squaw and the over-sexualization of Native females such as Disney's Pocahontas surely render all Native female persons vulnerable."[39] After telling me, "Since childhood, I have had to walk through a maze of racist and sexist assaults on me," she told me a story that offered a striking image of the perceived worthlessness of Native female existence as it has too often been understood by the dominant society:

My first experience of when I was conscious of this kind of assault happened when I was about ten years old. I was sitting in a café in my hometown, reading a comic book, as I [was] wont to do. Minding my own business. I don't know where my parents were, but I just remember a big, fat, red-faced white guy coming in. Leering at me. I don't even think I could identify what that look was because I had been so safe at home and in my community. I had never been attacked, and I didn't know what on earth that was. This guy, he throws a quarter. I still remember, and I still see that quarter rolling right past my Coke bottle. He threw a quarter and he said, "Want to go for a ride, little squaw?"

LaRocque acknowledges the danger she was in at that moment, and how racist stereotypes endanger Native girls and women: "To this day, I am profoundly grateful he did nothing else. He could have just picked me up and taken me away. Nobody would have known the difference." She asks, "Where do these men get off on attacking little children, teenagers, regular-aged women and grandmothers? It has to come from some conditioning, some horrendous sociological, racist, and sexist conditioning, to be so inhumane to your co-human beings. It is really stunning."

Negative images of Native women, whether in historical accounts, anecdotes, jokes, movies, or Canadian literature,[40] are at the root of stories like that of Helen Betty Osbourne, a sixteen-year-old Native woman who was picked up by four white men and brutally raped and murdered in The Pas, Manitoba, in 1971. This story remains fixed in the consciousness of many Native women as it demonstrates how mainstream society interprets violence against Native women, especially when it is committed by whites. In my conversation with Gertie Beaucage (Anishinaabe), she pointed out that Osbourne was killed because she was expected to be "easy," and yet she resisted the sexual assault of the white men who attacked her.

As Emma LaRocque has further pointed out, "In the minds of 'good boys who did bad things,' it is not the place of 'squaws' to resist white power, especially power snakily connected to the male ego."[41]

The Osbourne case eventually received a moderate amount of publicity because of the injustices it represented. There are, however, many more Native women's tales that would reveal the minimal worth placed on Native female lives. In our conversations, Lee Maracle (Sto:lo) and Catherine Martin (Mi'kmaq) have demonstrated to me that the notion that Native women are there for the sexual taking has been acted out from one side of the continent to the other. Maracle recalls her childhood on the West Coast:

> In my village, every single weekend … men came into the village, picked up little children, took them to the gravel pit, raped them—sometimes killed them—and were never prosecuted. I personally was chased in automobiles by white men. And when I went to swear out a complaint, they said it was in my imagination. I had charged a white man with assault, and I was called not a credible witness. Those things happen in our personal lives.

Maracle attributes this to the "permission that white society gave to white men to enter our communities, murder, pillage, rape, and plunder us at will." [...]

Hereditary Wet'suwet'en Chief Theresa Tait lives in central British Columbia. When I spoke with her about this issue, she told me that in the previous decade there had been at least five Indigenous women who had been killed in her local area, with little investigation and next to no media coverage about these incidents. In the years since I first spoke with Tait, Indigenous women and their allies have worked diligently to raise awareness and demand action to address the travesty of the more than 1,000 cases of missing and murdered Indigenous women in Canada,

and the lack of attention to the issue. In spite of reports by Amnesty International (2004), the Native Women's Association of Canada (2009), and the Royal Canadian Mounted Police (2014) and countless efforts of grassroots activism, the Canadian state has only recently begun to address missing and murdered Indigenous women as an issue warranting immediate investigation in the form of a national inquiry.[42]

Native women seeking justice against the violence in their lives are overshadowed by the image of the squaw. In her study of how race figures into sexual abuse trials, Sherene Razack notes that Indigenous women are treated as "inherently rapeable" because of assumptions made about Native female promiscuity and the insistence that a rape victim who has passed out because of alcohol is considered to have suffered less of a violation.[43] A Native woman who is drunk is deemed particularly unworthy of humane treatment, and Native women who are involved in abusive relationships may not feel comfortable calling the police in the case of domestic violence because they may be seen as "at fault," or deserving of the abuse.[44] As recent evidence has proven, calling the police might put an Indigenous woman's safety further at risk. In 2011, for example, a northern Manitoba Royal Canadian Mounted Police (RCMP) officer arrested an intoxicated Indigenous woman, but then took her out of her cell and brought her home "to pursue a personal relationship."[45] According to the RCMP adjudication documents obtained by the Canadian Broadcasting Corporation (CBC), "Fellow officers teased and goaded him by text message to see 'how far he would go,'" and his senior officer told him "You arrested her, you can do whatever the f--k you want to do."[46] For this, the offending officer was given a "reprimand" and docked seven days' pay.[47]

As Indigenous women's testimony here and elsewhere indicates, these violent, racist, and sexist practices are not isolated incidents, nor are they historical. In 2013, the international organization Human Rights Watch released an 89-page report entitled *Those Who Take Us Away: Abusive Policing*

**Figure 34.1: The Triangle of Oppression**

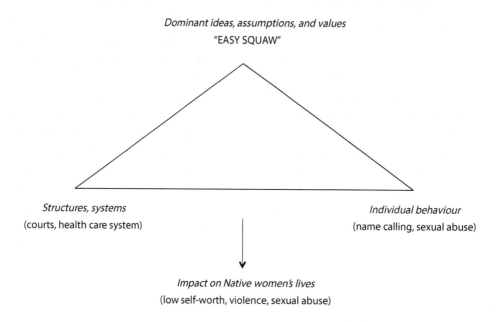

*Dominant ideas, assumptions, and values*
"EASY SQUAW"

*Structures, systems*
(courts, health care system)

*Individual behaviour*
(name calling, sexual abuse)

*Impact on Native women's lives*
(low self-worth, violence, sexual abuse)

*and Failures in the Protection of Indigenous Women and Girls in Northern BC*, detailing, among other abuses, physical and sexual assault on Indigenous women by the police.[48] The connection to stereotypes is evident when considering their findings that "At times the physical abuse was accompanied by verbal racist or sexist abuse."[49] The impact on Native women's daily lives is profound: "Concerns about police harassment led some women—including respected community leaders—to limit their time in public places where they might come into contact with officers."[50] The construction of a negative identity can rule a Native woman's experience, as these stories demonstrate. The triangle of oppression (see Figure 34.1), developed by the Doris Marshall Institute,[51] is a useful tool for analyzing how the oppression functions.

Each point of the triangle supports the others to maintain the oppression of Native women. If Native women are constructed as "easy squaws" and are locked into this imagery through the behaviour of individuals, they will continue to be rendered worthless in public institutions such as courtrooms or hospitals, or in relations with police. If we treat Native women as easy or drunken squaws on the street, or in environments or institutions that are supposed to serve or protect women, we perpetuate negative stereotypes that will further enable individuals to abuse Native females, and so on. Negative Native female images are part of a vicious cycle that deeply influences the lives of contemporary Native women. We need to get rid of the images, the systems that support them, and the abusive practices carried out by individuals.

## NOTES

1.  Monique Mojica, *Princess Pocahontas and the Blue Spots* (Toronto: Women's Press, 1991), 21.

2.  Rayna Green, "The Pocahontas Perplex: The Image of the Indian Woman in American Culture," in *Native Women's*

*History in Eastern North America before 1900: A Guide to Research and Writing*, edited by Rebecca Kugel and Lucy Eldersveld Murphy (Lincoln: University of Nebraska Press, 2007), 7–26.

3.  Ibid.

4.  This was a typical application of Indigenous women in other colonial contexts, as explained in Ann McClintock, *Imperial Leather: Race, Gender, and Sexuality in the Colonial Context* (New York: Routledge, 1995).

5.  Elizabeth Cook-Lynn, *Why I Can't Read Wallace Stegner and Other Essays* (Madison: University of Wisconsin Press, 1996), 145.

6.  Richard Slotkin, *Gunfighter Nation: The Myth of the Frontier in Twentieth-Century America* (New York: Atheneum, 1992), 14.

7.  Kim Anderson, "Native Women, the Body, Land, and Narratives of Contact and Arrival," in *Storied Communities: Narratives of Contact and Arrival in Constituting Political Community*, ed. Hester Lessard, Rebecca Johnson, and Jeremy Webber (Vancouver: UBC Press, 2010), 167–88. See also Gail Guthrie Valaskakis, "Sacajawea and Her Sisters: Images and Native Women," *Indian Country: Essays on Contemporary Native Culture* (Waterloo: Wilfrid Laurier University Press, 2005), 125–150.

8.  Valaskakis, "Indian Country"; Allan Greer, *Mohawk Saint: Catherine Tekakwitha and the Jesuits* (New York: Oxford University Press, 2005).

9.  Pamela Scully, "Malintzin, Pocahontas, and Krotoa: Indigenous Women and Myth Models of the Atlantic World," *Journal of Colonialism and Colonial History* 6, no. 3 (2005): 151.

10. Elise M. Marubbio, *Killing the Indian Maiden: Images of Native American Women in Film* (Lexington: University Press of Kentucky, 2006).

11. Chris Finley, "Violence, Genocide, and Captivity: Exploring Cultural Representations of Sacajawea as a Universal Mother of Conquest," *American Indian Culture and Research Journal* 35, no. 4 (2011): 198.

12. Beth Brant, *Writing as Witness: Essay and Talk* (Toronto: Women's Press, 1994), 83–103; Clara Sue Kidwell, "Indian Women as Cultural Mediators," *Ethnohistory* 39, no. 2 (Spring 1992): 97–107.

13. Cook-Lynn, *Why I Can't Read Wallace Stegner and Other Essays*, 106. See also Anderson, "Native Women, the Body,

Land," and Marubbio, *Killing the Indian Maiden*.

14. Green, "The Pocahontas Perplex," 20.

15. Carol Douglas Sparks, "The Land Incarnate: Navajo Women and the Dialogue of Colonialism," in *Negotiators of Change: Historical Perspectives on Native American Women*, ed. Nancy Shoemaker (New York: Routledge, 1995), 135–56.

16. Ibid., 147.

17. Sarah Carter, *Capturing Women: The Manipulation of Cultural Imagery in Canada's Prairie West* (Montreal: McGill-Queen's University Press, 1997), 158–93.

18. Ibid., 160.

19. David Smits, "The 'Squaw Drudge': A Prime Index of Savagism," in *Native Women's History in Eastern North America before 1900: A Guide to Research and Writing*, ed. Rebecca Kugel and Lucy Eldersveld Murphy (Lincoln: University of Nebraska Press, 2007), 27–49.

20. Ibid., 162.

21. Ibid., 183.

22. Ibid., 191.

23. Rita Joe, *Song of Rita Joe: Autobiography of a Mi'kmaq Poet* (Charlottetown: Ragweed Press, 1996), 62; Anna Lee Walters, *Talking Indian: Reflections on Survival and Writing* (Ithaca: Firebrand Books, 1992), 211.

24. Nancy Macdonald, "Welcome to Winnipeg, Where Canada's Racism Problem Is at Its Worst," *Maclean's: Canada's National Magazine*, February 2, 2015, 22.

25. Ibid.

26. Debra Merskin, "The S-Word: Discourse, Stereotypes, and the American Indian Woman," *The Howard Journal of Communications* 21, no. 4 (2010): 354.

27. Ibid., 348.

28. Ibid., 360.

29. Janice Acoose, *Iskwewak-Kah'Ki Yan Ni Nahkomakanak: Neither Indian Princesses nor Easy Squaws, Second Edition* (Toronto: Women's Press, 2016).

30. Joanne Arnott, *Breasting the Waves: On Writing and Healing* (Vancouver: Press Gang, 1995), 76; Brant, *Writing as Witness*, 13, 119–20; Maria Campbell, *Halfbreed* (Toronto: McClelland & Stewart Limited, 1973), 47, 90; Janet Campbell Hale, *Bloodlines: Odyssey of a Native Daughter* (New York: HarperPerennial, 1993), 139–40; Beatrice Culleton, *In Search of April Raintree* (Winnipeg: Pemmican

Publications, 1983); Paula Gunn Allen, *The Sacred Hoop: Recovering the Feminine in American Indian Tradition* (Boston: Beacon Press, 1986), 48–49; Lee Maracle, *I Am Woman* (Vancouver: Press Gang Publishers, 1996), 14–19; Anna Lee Walters, *Talking Indian*, 52.

31. Barbara-Helen Hill, *Shaking the Rattle: Healing the Trauma of Colonization* (Penticton: Theytus Books, 1995).

32. It is easy to find online information describing the "Sacagawea dollar." See, for example, http://www.pcgs.com/News/Dollar-Coins-Sacagawea-Design-Unveiled-At-White-House.

33. Rebecca Blevins Faery, *Cartographies of Desire: Captivity, Race, and Sex in the Shaping of an American Nation* (Norman: University of Oklahoma Press, 1999), 145–52.

34. Phillip Deloria, *Playing Indian* (New Haven: Yale University Press, 1998); Shari M. Huhndorf, *Going Native: Indians in the American Cultural Imagination* (Ithaca: Cornell University Press, 2001).

35. I found it very helpful when I first read about "eating the other" in bell hooks. See bell hooks, *Black Looks: Race and Representation* (Toronto: Between the Lines Press, 1992), 21–39.

36. Ibid., 25.

37. Morningstar Mercredi, *Morningstar: A Warrior's Spirit* (Regina: Coteau Books, 2006), 129.

38. Ibid., 127.

39. Emma LaRocque, "The Colonization of a Native Woman Scholar," in *Women of the First Nations: Power, Wisdom, and Strength*, ed. Christine Miller and Patricia Chuchryk (Winnipeg: University of Manitoba Press, 1996), 12.

40. See Acoose, *Iskwewak*.

41. Emma LaRocque, "Tides, Towns, and Trains," in *Living the Changes*, ed. Joan Turner (Winnipeg: University of Manitoba Press, 1990), 87.

42. Amnesty International, *Stolen Sisters: A Human Rights Response to Discrimination and Violence against Indigenous Women in Canada* (London: Amnesty International, 2004); Native Women's Association of Canada, *Voices of Our Sisters in Spirit: A Research and Policy Report to Families and Communities*, 2nd ed. (Pointe-Claire: Ohsweken Gibson Library Connections, 2009); Royal Canadian Mounted Police, *Missing and Murdered Aboriginal Women: A National Operational Overview* (Ottawa: Government of Canada, 2014).

43. Sherene Razack, *Looking White People in the Eye: Gender, Race, and Culture in Courtrooms and Classrooms* (Toronto: University of Toronto Press, 1998), 68–72. See also Sherene Razack, "Gendered Racial Violence and Spatialized Justice: The Murder of Pamela George," *Canadian Journal of Law and Society* 15, no. 2 (2000): 91–130.

44. Anne McGillivary and Brenda Comaskey, *Black Eyes All of the Time: Intimate Violence, Aboriginal Women, and the Justice System* (Toronto: University of Toronto Press, 1999), 100.

45. Holly Moore, "Mountie Takes Aboriginal Home from Jail Cell to Pursue Relationship," *CBC News Online*, January 8, 2015.

46. Ibid.

47. Ibid.

48. Human Rights Watch, *Those Who Take Us Away: Abusive Policing and Failures in the Protection of Indigenous Women and Girls in Northern British Columbia, Canada* (Toronto: Human Rights Watch, 2013), http://www.hrw.org/reports/2013/02/13/those-who-take-us-away.

49. Ibid., 8.

50. Ibid.

51. Rick Arnold, Bev Burke, Carl James, D'Arcy Martin, and Barb Thomas, *Educating for a Change* (Toronto: Between the Lines and the Doris Marshall Institute for Education and Action, 1991), 91–92.

# REFERENCES

Acoose, Janice. *Iskwewak Kah'Ki Yan Ni Nahkomakanak: Neither Indian Princesses Nor Easy Squaws*. 2nd ed. Toronto: Women's Press, 2016.

Allen, Paula Gunn. *The Sacred Hoop: Recovering the Feminine in American Indian Tradition*. Boston: Beacon Press, 1986.

Amnesty International. *Stolen Sisters: A Human Rights Response to Discrimination and Violence against Indigenous Women in Canada*. London: Amnesty International, 2004.

Anderson, Kim. "Native Women, the Body, Land, and Narratives of Contact and Arrival." In *Storied Communities: Narratives of Contact and Arrival in Constituting Political*

*Community*, edited by Hester Lessard, Rebecca Johnson, and Jeremy Webber, 167–88. Vancouver: UBC Press, 2010.

Arnold, Rick, Bev Burke, Carl James, D'Arcy Martin, and Barb Thomas. *Educating for a Change*. Toronto: Between the Lines and the Doris Marshall Institute for Education and Action, 1991.

Arnott, Joanne. *Breasting the Waves: On Writing and Healing*. Vancouver: Press Gang Publishers, 1995.

Blevins Faery, Rebecca. *Cartographies of Desire: Captivity, Race, and Sex in the Shaping of an American Nation*. Norman: University of Oklahoma Press, 1999.

Brant, Beth. *Writing as Witness: Essay and Talk*. Toronto: Women's Press, 1994.

Campbell, Maria. *Halfbreed*. Toronto: McClelland & Stewart, 1973.

Campbell Hale, Janet. *Bloodlines: Odyssey of a Native Daughter*. New York: Harper Perennial, 1993.

Carter, Sarah. *Capturing Women: The Manipulation of Cultural Imagery in Canada's Prairie West*. Montreal: McGill-Queen's University Press, 1997.

Cook-Lynn, Elizabeth. *Why I Can't Read Wallace Stegner and Other Essays*. Madison: University of Wisconsin Press, 1996.

Culleton, Beatrice. *In Search of April Raintree*. Winnipeg: Pemmican Publications, 1983.

Deloria, Phillip. *Playing Indian*. New Haven: Yale University Press, 1998.

Finley, Chris. "Violence, Genocide, and Captivity: Exploring Cultural Representations of Sacajawea as a Universal Mother of Conquest." *American Indian Culture and Research Journal* 35, no. 4 (2011): 191–208.

Green, Rayna. "The Pocahontas Perplex: The Image of the Indian Woman in American Culture." In *Native Women's History in Eastern North America before 1900: A Guide to Research and Writing*, edited by Rebecca Kugel and Lucy Eldersveld Murphy, 7–26. Lincoln: University of Nebraska Press, 2007.

Greer, Allan. *Mohawk Saint: Catherine Tekakwitha and the Jesuits*. New York: Oxford University Press, 2005.

Hill, Barbara-Helen. *Shaking the Rattle: Healing the Trauma of Colonization*. Penticton: Theytus Books, 1995.

hooks, bell. *Black Looks: Race and Representation*. Toronto: Between the Lines Press, 1992.

Huhndorf, Shari M. *Going Native: Indians in the American Cultural Imagination*. Ithaca: Cornell University Press, 2001.

Human Rights Watch. *Those Who Take Us Away: Abusive Policing and Failures in the Protection of Indigenous Women and Girls in Northern British Columbia, Canada*. Human Rights Watch, 2013. http://www.hrw.org/reports/2013/02/13/those-who-take-us-away.

Joe, Rita. *Song of Rita Joe: Autobiography of a Mi'kmaq Poet*. Charlottetown: Ragweed Press, 1996.

Kidwell, Clara Sue. "Indian Women as Cultural Mediators," *Ethnohistory* 39, no. 2 (Spring 1992): 97–107.

LaRocque, Emma. "Tides, Towns, and Trains." In *Living the Changes*, edited by Joan Turner, 76–90. Winnipeg: University of Manitoba Press, 1990.

———. "The Colonization of a Native Woman Scholar." In *Women of the First Nations: Power, Wisdom, Strength*, edited by Christine Miller and Patricia Chuchryk, 11–18. Winnipeg: University of Manitoba Press, 1996.

Macdonald, Nancy. "Welcome to Winnipeg, Where Canada's Racism Problem Is at Its Worst." *Maclean's* (February 2, 2015), 16–24.

Maracle, Lee. *I Am Woman*. Vancouver: Press Gang Publishers, 1996, 14–19.

Marrubio, M. Elise. *Killing the Indian Maiden: Images of Native American Women in Film*. Lexington: University Press of Kentucky, 2006.

McClintock, Ann. *Imperial Leather: Race, Gender, and Sexuality in the Colonial Context*. New York: Routledge, 1995.

McGillivary, Anne, and Brenda Comaskey. *Black Eyes All of the Time: Intimate Violence, Aboriginal Women, and the Justice System*. Toronto: University of Toronto Press, 1999.

Mercredi, Morningstar. *Morningstar: A Warrior's Spirit*. Regina: Coteau Books, 2006.

Merskin, Debra. "The S-Word: Discourse, Stereotypes, and the American Indian Woman." *The Howard Journal of Communications* 21, no. 4 (2010): 345–66.

Mojica, Monique. *Princess Pocahontas and the Blue Spots*. Toronto: Women's Press, 1991.

Moore, Holly. "Mountie Takes Aboriginal Home from Jail Cell to Pursue Relationship." *CBC News Online*, January 8, 2015.

Native Women's Association of Canada. *Voices of Our Sisters in Spirit: A Research and Policy Report to Families and*

*Communities*, 2nd ed. Pointe-Claire: Ohsweken Gibson Library Connections, 2009.

Razack, Sherene. *Looking White People in the Eye: Gender, Race, and Culture in Courtrooms and Classrooms*. Toronto: University of Toronto Press, 1998.

———. "Gendered Racial Violence and Spatialized Justice: The Murder of Pamela George." *Canadian Journal of Law and Society* 15, no. 2 (2000): 91–130.

Royal Canadian Mounted Police. *Missing and Murdered Aboriginal Women: A National Operational Overview*. Ottawa: Government of Canada, 2014.

Scully, Pamela. "Malintzin, Pocahontas, and Krotoa: Indigenous Women and Myth Models of the Atlantic World." *Journal of Colonialism and Colonial History* 6, no. 3 (2005).

Slotkin, Richard. *Gunfighter Nation: The Myth of the Frontier in 20th Century America*. New York: Atheneum, 1992.

Smits, David. "The 'Squaw Drudge': A Prime Index of Savagism." In *Native Women's History in Eastern North America before 1900: A Guide to Research and Writing*, edited by Rebecca Kugel and Lucy Eldersveld Murphy, 27–49. Lincoln: University of Nebraska Press, 2007.

Sparks, Carol Douglas. "The Land Incarnate: Navajo Women and the Dialogue of Colonialism. In *Negotiators of Change: Historical Perspectives on Native American Women*, edited by Nancy Shoemaker, 135–56. New York: Routledge, 1995.

Valaskakis, Gail Guthrie. *Indian Country: Essays on Contemporary Native Culture*. Waterloo: Wilfrid Laurier University Press, 2005.

Walters, Anna Lee. *Talking Indian: Reflections on Survival and Writing*. Ithaca: Firebrand Books, 1992.

---

*Source:* Anderson, Kim. (2016). Excerpted from "The Construction of a Negative Identity." In *A Recognition of Being: Reconstructing Native Womanhood,* 2nd edition (pp. 79–92). Toronto, ON: Women's Press.

## COLONIZATION AND THE INDIAN ACT

The Indian Act is a Canadian federal law that governs in matters pertaining to Indian status, bands, and Indian reserves. Throughout history, it has been highly invasive and paternalistic, as it authorizes the Canadian federal government to regulate and administer in the affairs and day-to-day lives of registered Indians and reserve communities. This authority has ranged from overarching political control, such as imposing governing structures on Aboriginal communities in the form of band councils, to control over the rights of Indians to practice their culture and traditions. The Indian Act has also enabled the government to determine the land base of these groups in the form of reserves, and even to define who qualifies for Indian status. While the Indian Act has undergone numerous amendments since it was first passed in 1876, today it largely retains its original form. The Indian Act is a part of a long history of assimilation policies that were intended to terminate the cultural, social, economic, and political distinctiveness of Aboriginal peoples by absorbing them into mainstream Canadian life and values.

\* \* \* \* \*

The Indian Act has been highly criticized for its gender bias as another means of terminating one's Indian status, thus excluding women from their Aboriginal rights. Legislation stated that a status Indian woman who married a non-Indian man would cease to be an Indian. She would lose her status, and with it, she would lose treaty benefits, health benefits, the right to live on her reserve, the right to inherit her family property, and even the right to be buried on the reserve with her ancestors. However, if an Indian man married a non-status woman, he would keep all his rights. Even if an Indian woman married another Indian man, she would cease to be a member of her own band and become a member of his. If a woman was widowed, or abandoned by her husband, she would become enfranchised and lose status altogether. Alternatively, if a non-Native woman married an Indian man, she would acquire status. In all these situations, a woman's status was entirely dependent on her husband.

***Source:*** Indigenous Foundations. (2009). Excerpted from "The Indian Act" by Eric Hanson. *University of British Columbia*. Vancouver, BC: University of British Columbia. Retrieved from: http://indigenousfoundations.arts.ubc.ca/ the_indian_act/#introduction.

# Excerpts from the Indian Act of Canada

## 1. The Indian Act, 1876

*Terms*
3. The following terms contained in this Act shall be held to have the meaning hereinafter assigned to them ...

1) The term "band" means any tribe, band or body of Indians who own or are interested in a reserve or in Indian lands in common, of which the legal title is vested in the Crown ...
3) The term "Indian" means
   *First.* Any person of Indian blood reputed to belong to a particular band;
   *Second.* Any legitimate child of such person;
   *Thirdly.* Any woman who is or was lawfully married to such person.

   (a) Provided that any illegitimate child, unless having shared with the consent of the band in the distribution of moneys of such band for a period exceeding two years, may, at any time, be excluded from the membership thereof by the band, if ... sanctioned by the Superintendent-General: ...
   (c) Provided that any Indian woman marrying any other than an Indian or non-treaty Indian shall cease to be an Indian in any respect within the meaning of this Act....
   (d) Provided that any Indian woman marrying an Indian of any other band shall cease to be a member of the band to which she formerly belonged, and become a member of the band ... of which her husband is a member:
   (e) Provided also that no half-breed in Manitoba who has shared in the distribution of half-breed lands shall be accounted an Indian; and that no half-breed head of family (Except the widow of an Indian, or a half-breed who has already been admitted into a treaty), shall ... be accounted an Indian, or entitled to be admitted into any Indian treaty....

5) The term "reserve" means any tract or tracts of land set apart by treaty or otherwise for the use of, benefit of or granted to a particular band of Indians, of which the legal title is the Crown's, but which is unsurrendered, and includes all the trees, wood, timber, soil, stone, minerals, metals or other valuables thereon or therein....

*Protection of Reserves*
11. No person ... other than an Indian of the band, shall settle, reside or hunt upon, occupy or use any land or marsh, or shall settle, reside upon or occupy any road, or allowance for roads running through any reserve belonging to ... such a band; ...

*Privileges of Indians*
64. No Indian or non-treaty Indian shall be liable to be taxed for any real or personal property, unless he holds real estate under lease or in fee simple, or personal property, outside of the reserve or special reserve, in which case he shall be liable to be taxed for such real or personal property at the same rate as other persons in the locality in which it is situated....

*Disabilities and Penalties*
72. The Superintendent-General shall have the power to stop the payment of the annuity and interest money of any Indian who may be proved, to the satisfaction of the Superintendent-General, to have been guilty of deserting his family, and the said Superintendent-General may apply the same towards the support of any family, woman or child so deserted; also to stop the payment of the annuity and interest money of any woman having no children, who deserts her husband and lives immorally with another man....

*Enfranchisement*
86. Whenever any Indian man, or unmarried woman, of the full age of twenty-one years, obtains the consent of the band of which he or she is a member to become enfranchised ... the local agent shall report ... the name of the applicant to the Superintendent-General; whereupon the Superintendent-General ... shall authorize some

competent person to report whether the applicant is an Indian who, from the degree of civilization to which he attained, and the character for integrity, morality, and sobriety which he bears, appears to be qualified to be [enfranchised]:

(I) Any Indian who may be admitted to the degree of Doctor of Medicine, or to any other degree by any University of Learning, or who may be admitted in any Province of the Dominion to practice law ... or who may enter Holy Orders or who may be licensed by any denomination of Christians as a Minister of the Gospel, shall *ipso facto* become and be enfranchised under this Act.

Assented to 12 April 1876

**2. The Indian Act, 1970**

*Administration*
3. (I) This Act shall be administered by the Minister of Indian Affairs and Northern Development, who shall be the superintendent-general of Indian affairs....

*Definition and Registration of Indians*
5. An Indian Register shall be maintained in the Department [of Indian Affairs], which shall consist of Band Lists and General Lists and in which shall be recorded the name of every person who is entitled to be registered as an Indian....

11. Subject to section 12, a person is entitled to be registered if that person
(a) [is] entitled to hold, use or enjoy the lands and other immovable property belonging to the various tribes, bands or bodies of Indians in Canada;
(b) is a member of a band ...
(c) is a male person who is a direct descendant in the male line of a male person described in paragraph (a) or (b);
(d) is the legitimate child of
  (i) a male person described in paragraph (a) or (b), or
  (ii) a person described in paragraph (c);

(e) is the illegitimate child of a female person described in paragraph (a), (b) or (d); or
(f) is the wife or widow of a person who is entitled to be registered by virtue of paragraph (a), (b), (c), (d), or (e)....

12. (I) The following persons are not entitled to be registered ...
(a) a person who
  (i) has received or has been allotted half-breed lands or money scrip,
  (ii) is a descendant of a person described in sub-paragraph (i),
  (iii) is enfranchised....
(b) a woman who married a person who is not an Indian, unless that woman is subsequently the wife or widow of a person described in section 11....

14. A woman who is a member of a band ceases to be a member of that band if she marries a person who is not a member of that band, but if she marries a member of another band, she thereupon becomes a member of the band which her husband is a member....

*Enfranchisement*
[Previous sections pertaining to enfranchisement are replaced by sections 109–112.]
109. (I) On the report of the Minister that an Indian has applied for enfranchisement and that in his opinion the Indian
(a) is of the full age of twenty-one years,
(b) is capable of assuming duties and responsibilities of citizenship, and
(c) when enfranchised, will be capable of supporting himself and his dependents, the Governor in Council may by order declare that the Indian and his wife and minor unmarried children are enfranchised....

(2) On the report of the Minister that an Indian woman married a person who is not an Indian, the Governor in Council may by order declare that the woman is enfranchised as of the date of her marriage and, on the recommendation of the Minister may by order declare

that all or any of her children are enfranchised as of the date of the marriage or such other date as the order may specify....

### 3. Bill C-31: An Act to Amend the Indian Act, 1985

Clause 4. This amendment would substitute for the existing scheme of band membership....

It would also eliminate provisions relating to entitlement to registration that discriminate on the basis of sex and would replace them with non-discriminatory rules for determining entitlement. As well, it would eliminate the distinction between "legitimate" and "illegitimate" children and provide for the reinstatement of persons who have lost their entitlement to registration under discriminatory provisions or, in certain cases, through enfranchisement.

The proposed sections 5 to 7 would deal with registration in the Indian Register, sections 6 and 7 replacing the present sections 11 and 12....

6. (I) Subject to section 7, a person is entitled to be registered if ...
(c)    the name of that person was omitted or deleted from the Indian Register, or from a band list ... under subparagraph ... 12(1)(b), subsection 12(2) or subsection 109(2) ... or under any former provision of this Act relating to the same subject matter as any of those provisions....

*Clause 12:* The amendment to subsection 68(1) and the repeal of subsection 68(2) [based on section 72 in the 1876 Indian Act] would establish the same rule for male and female Indians with respect to support payments in circumstances such as desertion. The repeal of subsection 68(3) would remove a special rule for "illegitimate" children....

*Clause 14:* The repeal of sections 109 to 113 would remove the concept of enfranchisement from the Indian Act.

---

*Source:* Downe, Pamela J. (2005). Excerpted from "Excerpts from the Indian Act of Canada." In Lesley Biggs & Pamela J. Downe (Eds.), *Gendered Intersections: An Introduction to Women's and Gender Studies* (pp. 103–106). Black Point, NS: Fernwood.

# ACTIVIST ART 6

## INDIAN ACT

*Nadia Myre*

Nadia Myre (Anishinaabe) is an Indigenous Artist from Québec. She crafts exquisite works that weave together the complex histories of Aboriginal identity, nationhood, memory, and handicraft. Myre is a recipient of numerous awards, including the prestigious Sobey Art Award (2014). Her works may be found on permanent exhibition in many institutions, such as the Montreal Museum of Fine Arts and the National Gallery of Canada.

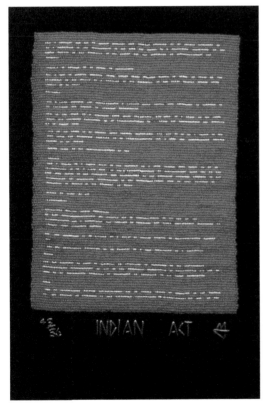

*Source:* Myre, Nadia. (2002). "Indian Act." Images from Cont[r]act, Solo Exhibition. Retrieved from: http://www.nadiamyre.net/work/#/contract/.

Indian Act speaks of the realities of colonization—the effects of contact, and its often-broken and untranslated contracts. The piece consists of all 56 pages of the Federal Government's Indian Act mounted on stroud cloth and sewn over with red and white glass beads. Each word is replaced with white beads sewn into the document; the red beads replace the negative space.

As an artist, I have been sourcing the material and intellectual culture of my ancestors. My mother was orphaned and through the experience of reclaiming our Native Status in 1997 as Algonquins and members of the Kitigan Zibi reserve in Maniwaki, Quebec, the exploration of my identity has become a major theme in my work. I am interested in the specificities and practices of the Anishinabeg as well as general pan-Indian experiences of stereotype and the struggle of reclamation. As such, my work has manifested in various ways, from deconstructing language to demonstrate shifts of meaning and power within the notions of 'desire' and the 'other', to working with raw materials in the traditions of my people. (Nadia Myre)

*Source:* Myre, Nadia. (n.d.). "Nadia Myre: Indian Act" (Artist Statement). *The Medicine Project*. Retrieved from: http://themedicineproject.com/nadia-myre.html.

# CHAPTER 34

## Regulating Native Identity by Gender

*Bonita Lawrence*

Bonita Lawrence (Mi'kmaw) is an associate professor in the Department of Equity Studies at York University. She is a founding member of the undergraduate program in Multicultural and Indigenous Studies, and of the upcoming graduate program in Indigenous Thought. Her research focuses primarily on urban, non-status, and Métis identities, federally unrecognized Aboriginal communities, Aboriginal peoples and the criminal justice system, and Indigenous nationhood and justice. Her well-known book *"Real" Indians and Others: Mixed-Blood Urban Native Peoples and Indigenous Nationhood* from which the following chapter is taken, explores many of these themes.

In Canada, a history of gender discrimination in the Indian Act has created an ongoing conflict within Native organizations and reserve communities around notions of individual and collective rights, organized along lines of gender. It is crucially important, then, to understand the central role that the subordination of Native women has played in the colonization process, in order to begin to see the violation of Native women's rights through loss of Indian status, not as the problems faced by individuals, but as a *collective* sovereignty issue.

## GENDERING INDIANNESS IN THE COLONIAL ENCOUNTER

The nation-building process in Canada began to accelerate between 1781 and 1830, in what is now Southern Ontario, when the British began to realize the necessity of bringing in settlers on the lands where previously they had engaged in the fur trade, to secure the territory they claimed against the threat of American expansion. Settlement of the area was only made possible as individual Anishinaabe (Ojibway) bands were gradually induced to cede, in small packages, the land immediately north of Lake Ontario and Lake Erie to the British. Many of these land surrenders were framed as peace treaties, to ensure that the British would be allies to the Ojibway against the possible northern encroachment of American settler violence; on this basis, only male leaders or representatives were asked to participate in treaty negotiation and the signing away of land (Schmalz 1991, 120–22).

In negotiating only with men, the British deliberately cut out the stabilizing presence of older women and the general authority that was given to their voices in major decisions concerning the land. As Kim Anderson has written, traditional Native societies were often matrilineal in very balanced ways (2000, 66–68). Even in societies where men made the decisions about which lands to hunt on each year, clans organized along the female line frequently controlled land inheritance. To bypass older women in traditional societies effectively removed from the treaty process the people centrally responsible for regulating land access.

Moreover, the British were confident in their knowledge that, as Major Gladwin articulated, "The free sale of rum will destroy them more effectively than fire and sword" (Schmalz 1991, 82). The "chemical warfare" of alcohol, deliberately introduced north of the Great Lakes after the Pontiac uprising of 1763, had an immediate and devastating effect on Ojibway communities in the Toronto and southwestern Ontario region, whose social disintegration and their resulting dependency on the British were devastating (Schmalz 1991, 87). In such circumstances, as the abilities of the men to make good choices for the future were increasingly destabilized by alcohol, it was frequently the women whose decision-making capabilities became crucial for the survival of the society as a whole. The fact that the women invariably spoke with the future of the children always in mind meant that "choices" being forced on the men, such as surrendering the lands they could no longer hunt or trap on in exchange for the promise of assistance in the transition to farming (or later, of jobs in resource development), were most strenuously resisted by the women, who saw holding on to the land base as the only way in which the social fabric of the society to nurture the next generation would survive at all.

Finally, as Kathleen Jamieson has noted, most of the early land treaties and Indian legislation were premised on the Indigenous peoples the English were most familiar with—the Anishinaabe (Ojibway) and Haudenosaunee (Iroquois) peoples. Especially in Haudenosaunee society, female-led clans held the collective land base for all of the nations of the confederacy. Removing women, then, was the key to privatizing the land base. For all of these reasons, a central aspect of the colonization process in Canada would be to break the power of Indigenous women within their nations (Jamieson 1978, 13).

It is also important to take into account not only the concerns of British colonial administrators, for whom Indian administration was but another post of the empire, but the fears of the growing body of white settlers, where colonial anxieties about white identity and who would control settler societies were rampant. As Ann Stoler has noted, the European settlements that developed on other people's lands have generally been obsessed with ways of maintaining colonial control and of rigidly asserting differences between Europeans and Native peoples to maintain white social solidarity and cohesion (Stoler 1991, 53). Colonial societies have had to invent themselves as new groupings of individuals with no organic link to one another, in settings that are often radically different from their places of origin. They have had to invent the social institutions that will then define them as a society—and they have to be capable of rationalizing or justifying their existence on other people's lands and the brutality through which their presence is maintained. The very existence of white settler societies is therefore predicated on maintaining racial apartheid, on emphasizing racial difference, both white superiority and Native inferiority.

This flies in the face of the actual origins of many white settlements in Canada—which frequently began with displaced and often marginal white men, whose success with the fur trade or settlement, and often their very survival, depended on their ability to insinuate themselves into Indigenous societies through intermarriage. The early days of European–Native contact frequently involved negotiated alliances with local Indigenous communities, often cemented through marriage. [...]

Meanwhile, the entire structure of the fur trade, in both eastern and western Canada, involved "country marriages" between European men and the Native women that the traders depended on so heavily for their survival—and a growing reliance on the mixed-blood children of these marriages to fill specific niches in the fur trade—which meant that, as time went on, the boundaries between who should be considered European and who should be considered Native (and by what means) have not always been clear. By the mid-nineteenth century, the presence of numerous mixed-blood communities in the Great Lakes area made it difficult for Anglo settlers to maintain clear boundaries between colonizers and colonized.[1] Social control was predicated on legally identifying who was white, who was Indian, and which children were legitimate progeny—citizens rather than subjugated Natives (Stoler 1991, 53). [...]

Moreover, fur trade society in western Canada, in the years before the 1885 Rebellion, was in many respects highly bicultural. Many settlements consisted primarily of white men married to Cree women, raising Cree families. While the language spoken in public was English, the language spoken in many of the homes was Cree. Clearly, if a white settler society modeled on British values was to be established, white women had to take the place of Native women, and Native women had to be driven out of the place they had occupied in fur trade society, a process that would continue through successive waves of white settlement, from the Great Lakes westward across the continent. The displacement of Native women from white society, and the replacement of the bicultural white society that their marriages to white men created to an openly white supremacist society populated by all-white families, was accomplished largely through the introduction of punitive laws in the Indian Act concerning prostitution and intoxication off-reserve.

These laws targeted Aboriginal women as responsible for the spread of venereal disease among the police and officials in western Canada and therefore increasingly classified urban Aboriginal women as prostitutes within the criminal code after 1892 (Carter 1997, 187).

*****

## GENDER DISCRIMINATION IN THE INDIAN ACT

Many of the legal disabilities for women in the Indian Act have existed as much by omission as by explicit statement through the use of the constant masculine term in the legislation, even though a separate legal regime has existed for Indian women with respect to marriage, childbirth, regulation of sexual conduct, exclusion from the right to vote or otherwise partake in band business, and rights to inherit and for a widow to administer her husband's estate. Because of the constant use of the masculine pronoun, confusion has existed at times in various communities as to whether Native women actually have any of the rights pertaining to men in much of the Indian Act legislation (Jamieson 1978, 56). Finally, definitions of Indianness have been asserted in such a patriarchal manner as to be fraught with discriminatory consequences for Indian women.

[...] Legislation in 1850 first defined Indianness in gendered terms, so that Indian status depended either on Indian descent or marriage to a male Indian. With the Gradual Enfranchisement Act of 1869, not only were wives removed from inheritance rights and automatically enfranchised with their husbands, but Section 6 began a process of escalating gender discrimination that would not be definitively changed until 1985. With this section, for the first time, Indian women were declared "no longer Indian" if they married anybody who lacked Indian status. On marrying an Indian from another "tribe, band, or body," she and her children now belonged to her husband's tribe only (Jamieson 1978, 29–30).

Prior to 1951, some recognition on a local basis was given to the needs of Indian women who were deserted or widowed. Indian women who lost their status were no longer legally Indian and no longer formal band members, but they were not considered to have the full rights that enfranchised women had. These women were often issued informal identity cards, known as "red tickets," which identified them as entitled to shares in treaty monies and recognized on an informal basis their band membership, to the extent that some of them were even able to live on the reserve. It was not until 1951 that women who lost their Indian status were also compulsorily enfranchised. This meant that they not only lost band membership, reserve residency, or any property they might have held on the reserve, but also access to any treaty monies or band assets (RCAP 1996, 19:301–02).

Section 6, governing loss of status, was only one of the many aspects of the 1869 legislation that limited the power of Native women in their societies. Particularly in the context of matrilineal practices, this act ripped huge holes in the fabric of Native life. The clan system of the Iroquois was disrupted in particularly cruel ways. Not only was the matrilineal basis of the society (and therefore its framework of land tenure) threatened by legislation that forced Native women to become members of their husbands' communities, but the manner in which white women received the Indian status of their husbands resulted in the births of generations of clanless individuals within reserve communities, since clan inheritance passed through the mother. Finally, in addition to these processes, which subverted and bypassed the power of Native women in matrilineal societies and opened up their lands for privatization, Native women were formally denied any political role in the governance of their societies. For example, when the 1869 legislation divided reserves into individual lots, married women could not inherit any portion of their husband's lots, and they lost their own allocations if they married non-Natives. After 1884, widows were allowed to inherit one-third of their husband's lot—if a widow was living with her husband at his time of death and was determined by the Indian agent to be "of good moral character" (RCAP 1996, 4:28–29). Meanwhile, in 1876, the Indian Act prevented Native women from voting in any decisions about surrender of reserve lands. The many ways in which Native women were rendered marginal in their communities by patriarchal colonial laws not only made it more difficult for them to challenge the tremendous disempowerment that loss of status represented—it made land theft much easier.

From the perspective of the colonial administration, the 1869 legislation had two primary goals—to remove as many individuals as possible from Indianness and, as part of this process, to enforce Indianness as being solely a state of "racial purity" by removing those children designated as "half-breed" from Indian communities. At the same time, however, if reserve residents were to grow increasingly mixed-blooded, it would facilitate their enfranchisement, as individuals who were "too civilized" to be Indians. In this respect, it is, of course, important to note that when white women married Native men, they also produced "half-breed" children, who nevertheless were allowed to stay in Native communities as Indians. Because of patriarchal notions that children were solely the products of their fathers, these children were not recognized by colonial administrators as half-breed. However, communities where there was a great deal of such intermarriage were often reported on approvingly, as when glowing comments were made about Caughnawaga (Kahnawake) in the 1830s that "there is scarcely a pure blooded Indian in the settlement" (Jamieson 1978, 23).

It is clear from the government debates at the time that this legislation was also aimed at undermining the collective nature of Native societies, where lands, monies, and other resources were shared in common. By restricting reserves only to those who were granted location tickets, by externalizing the Indian women who married white men and their children, and by forcing exogamy on Native women (where the custom in many communities was that Native men would join their wives' extended family, who controlled the land along clan lines), most of the collective aspects of Native society were to be subverted or suppressed.

In 1874, legislation altered and elaborated upon the definition of the term *Indian*, making Indian descent solely flowing from the male line. With this act, the status of the illegitimate children of Native women was also continuously subject to changing standards at the whim of the superintendent of Indian Affairs, depending on whether the father was known to be Native or not. The superintendent was also given the power to stop the payment of annuities and interest to any woman having no children, who deserted her husband, and "lived immorally with another man" (Jamieson 1978, 45). Other legislation criminalized Indian women further, targeting them as prostitutes and providing them with penalties of one hundred dollars and up to six months in jail. […]

The 1920s legislation that evicted or jailed Native "squatters" on band lands had severe implications for women who lost their status and were increasingly rendered homeless, especially if their husbands were not white but were, rather, nonstatus Indians or Métis, or if their marriages to white men failed, or they were widowed (Jamieson 1978, 51). […]

While the 1951 Indian Act represents a lessening of colonial control for Indian men, it actually heightened colonial regulation for Indian women in general and especially for those women who married non-Natives. The membership section became even more elaborate, couched in almost unreadable bureaucratic language, which spelled out not only who was entitled to be registered as an Indian but who was not. The male line of descent was further emphasized as the major criterion for inclusion—in fact mention of "Indian blood" was altogether removed. The areas of the act that dictated who was not an Indian included Section 12(1)(b), which removed the status of any woman who married a non-Indian (which included American Indians and nonstatus Native men from

Canada), and Section 12(1)(a)(iv), also known as the "double-mother" clause, which removed the status of any individual whose mother *and* paternal grandmother lacked Indian status prior to their marriages to Indian men. […]

The major change for Native women who "married out" was that from the date of their marriages they were not only automatically deprived of their Indian status and band rights, but by order of the governor-in-council they were declared enfranchised. Enfranchisement for these Indian women, however, did not involve the same conditions as those that had been experienced by Indian men and their families either through voluntary or involuntary enfranchisement. Individuals who enfranchised, voluntarily or involuntarily, had to have sufficient resources to survive off-reserve. No such condition was considered necessary for Indian women compulsorily enfranchised, since they were assumed to be, effectively, "wards" of their husband. […]

The financial losses experienced by Native women due to loss of status have been considerable. When enfranchised, the women were entitled to receive a per capita share of band capital and revenue, as well as the equivalent of twenty years' treaty money. Since the treaty money is either four or five dollars a year, depending on the treaty, the women were therefore entitled to receive either eighty or one hundred dollars. However, during the interval when large numbers of women were being enfranchised and "paid off," most Native communities had relatively few assets and revenue available to provide meaningful shares to the women. Many of those bands subsequently received significant monies from resource development, to which the enfranchised women and their children never had access.

Another series of financial losses that Native women experienced when they lost their Indian status included the lack of access to postsecondary-education funding, free day-care provisions in some communities, funding for school supplies and social schooling programs, housing policies that enabled on-reserve Indians to buy houses with assistance from the Central Mortgage and Housing Corporation and Indian Affairs, loans and grants from the Indian Economic Development Fund, health benefits, exemption from taxation and from provincial sales tax, hunting, fishing, animal grazing, and trapping rights, cash distributions from sales of band assets, and the ability to be employed in the United States without a visa and to cross the border without restrictions (Jamieson 1978, 70–71). Finally, Indian women were generally denied access to personal property willed to them, evicted from their homes, often with small children and no money (especially when widowed or separated), and generally faced hostile band councils and indifferent Indian Affairs bureaucrats (Jamieson 1978, 72).

However, it is the personal and cultural losses of losing status that Indian women have most frequently spoken about. Some of the costs have included being unable to participate with family and relatives in the life of their former communities, being rejected by their communities, being culturally different and often socially rejected within white society, being unable to access cultural programs for their children, and finally not even being able to be buried with other family members on the reserve. The extent of penalties and lack of compensation for losses suffered has made the forcible enfranchisement of Indian women "retribution, not restitution," what Justice Bora Laskin, in his dissenting opinion in *Lavell and Bedard*, termed "statutory banishment" (Jamieson 1978, 72).

Finally, in terms of Native empowerment generally, it is important to note that this "bleeding off" of Native women and their children from their communities was in place for 116 years, from 1869 until 1985. The phenomenal cultural implication hidden in this legislation is the sheer numbers of Native people lost to their communities. Some sources have estimated that by far the majority of the twenty-five thousand Indians who lost status and were externalized from their communities between

1876 and 1985 (Holmes 1987, 8) did so because of ongoing gender discrimination in the Indian Act.[2] But it is not simply a matter of twenty-five thousand individuals. If one takes into account the fact that for every individual who lost status and had to leave her community, all of her descendants (many of them the products of nonstatus Indian fathers and Indian mothers) also lost status and for the most part were permanently alienated from Native culture, the numbers of individuals who ultimately were removed from Indian status and lost to their nations may, at the most conservative estimates, number between one and two million.

By comparison, in 1985, when Bill C-31 was passed, there were only 350,000 status Indians still listed on the Department of Indian Affairs' Indian register (Holmes 1987, 54). In comparing the potential numbers of people lost to their Native communities because of loss of status with the numbers of individuals still considered Indian in 1985, the scale of cultural genocide caused by gender discrimination becomes visible. Because Bill C-31 allowed the most recent generation of individuals who had lost status to regain it, along with their children, approximately one hundred thousand individuals had regained their status by 1995 (Switzer 1997, 2). But the damage caused, demographically and culturally, by the loss of status of so many Native women for a century prior to 1985, whose grandchildren and great-grandchildren are no longer recognized—and in many cases no longer identify—as Indian, remain incalculable.

## THE STRUGGLE TO CHANGE THE INDIAN ACT

Given the accelerating gender discrimination in the Indian Act created by the modifications of 1951, Mohawk women in the 1960s created an organization known as Indian Rights for Indian Women, which attempted to address the disempowerment of Indian women, particularly with respect to loss of status. In

1971, Jeannette Corbiere Lavell and Yvonne Bedard, two Indian women who had lost status through their marriages, challenged the discriminatory sections of the Indian Act in the Canadian courts. [...]

Lavell challenged the deletion of her name from her band list, while Bedard, in a separate case, challenged the fact that her reserve was evicting her and her children from the house which her mother had willed to her, even though she was no longer married to her husband. Both women lost at the federal court level, but were successful at winning appeals, and their cases were heard together in the Supreme Court. Their argument was based on the fact that the Indian Act discriminated against them on the basis of race and sex, and that the Bill of Rights should therefore override the discriminatory sections of the Indian Act with respect to membership. [...]

In 1973, the Supreme Court, by a five-to-four decision, ruled against Lavell and Bedard. Among other reasons, the decision noted that since not all Indians were discriminated against, only Indian women who married non-Indians, then racial discrimination could not be said to exist; and since enfranchised Indian women gained the citizenship rights that made them equal (in law) to white women, then gender discrimination could not be said to exist. While this judgment clarified none of the issues, it did assert that the Bill of Rights could not take precedence over the Indian Act. Because of this decision, the Indian Act was exempt from the application of the Canadian Human Rights Act in 1977 (Holmes 1987, 5).

The Maliseet community of Tobique was the next focus of resistance. The women at Tobique began their struggle over the issue of homelessness—the manner in which their band council interpreted Indian Act legislation to suggest that Indian women had no right to own property on the reserve. As the women addressed the problems they faced, their struggle slowly broadened until their primary goal became changing the Indian Act (Silman 1987, 119–72). Since the decision in *Lavell and Bedard* had foreclosed any possibility of

justice within Canada, the Tobique women decided to support Sandra Lovelace in an appeal to the United Nations Human Rights Committee. Lovelace argued that Section 12(1)(b) of the Indian Act was in violation of Article 27 of the International Covenant on Civil and Political Rights, which provides for the rights of individuals who belong to minorities to enjoy their culture, practice their religion, and use their language in community with others from the group (Beyefsky 1982, 244–66). In 1981, the United Nations determined that Sandra Lovelace had been denied her cultural rights under Article 27 because she was barred from living in her community. Canada, embarrassed at the international level, at this point stated its intention to amend the discriminatory sections of the Indian Act. After some degree of consultation and proposed changes, Bill C-31, An Act to Amend the Indian Act, was passed in 1985.[3]

The violence and resistance that Native women struggling for their rights faced from male-dominated band councils and political organizations during this interval cannot be ignored.[4] For example, when Mary Two-Axe Early and sixty other Native women from Kahnawake (then known as the Caughnawaga band) chose to focus international attention on their plight by bringing their organization, Indian Rights for Indian Women, to the International Women's Year conference in Mexico City in 1975, they were all served with eviction notices in their absence by their band council (Jamieson 1979, 170). Meanwhile, when the Tobique women, protesting homelessness in their communities, occupied the band office in order to have a roof over their heads and draw attention to their plight, they were threatened with arrest by the band administration, physically beaten up in the streets, and had to endure numerous threats against their families from other community members.[5]

It has been the children of Native mothers and white, nonstatus Indian, or Métis fathers who have been forced to become urban Indians and who, in their Native communities of origin, are currently being regarded as outsiders because they *have* been labeled as "not Indian." Gender has thus been crucial in determining not only who has been able to stay in Native communities but who has been called mixed-blood and externalized as such. In this respect, gender discrimination in the Indian Act has shaped what we think about who is Native, who is mixed-blood, and who is entitled access to Indian land. These beliefs are only rendered more powerful by the strongly protectionist attitudes toward preserving Native culture as it is lived on reserves at present, where outsiders may be seen as profoundly threatening to community identity.

This history has even deeper repercussions, however, for Native communities today. Because the subordination of Indigenous women has been a central nexus through which colonizers have sought to destroy Indigenous societies, contemporary gender divisions created by the colonizer continue to subvert sovereignty struggles in crucial ways. And yet, almost inevitably, when issues of particular concern to Native women arise, they are framed as "individual rights," while in many cases, those who oppose Native women's rights are held to represent "the collective." In a context where a return to traditional collective ways is viewed as essential to surviving the ravages of colonization, Native women are routinely asked to separate their womanness from their Nativeness, as if violations of Native women's rights are not violations of Native rights.

## NOTES

1. Recent research has documented the presence of mixed-blood communities at no fewer than fifty-three locations in the Great Lakes region between 1763 and 1830 (RCAP 1996, I:150).

2. These figures include both those individuals who were enfranchised and those who lost their status because of gender discrimination in the Indian Act. However, the numbers of individuals who lost status due to enfranchisement only reached significant levels for a few years during the 1920s and 1930s, and the policy was ended

for everybody but women marrying non-Natives in 1951. By comparison, for over a century, the majority of individuals who lost status were Indian women who married out.

3. In April 1985, the Charter of Rights and Freedoms came into effect. The identity legislation within the 1951 Indian Act was in violation of Section 15(1), which prohibited discrimination on the basis of race and gender, as well as other particularities. Because of this, when Bill C-31 came into effect on 28 June 1985, its amendments to the 1951 act came into legal effect retroactively back to 17 April 1985, the date that the charter came into effect (Gilbert 1996, 129).

4. At the time of *Lavell and Bedard*, there were no women on the National Indian Brotherhood executive council, and the Association of Iroquois and Allied Indians, which first enlisted the help of the solicitor general and turned the tide against Lavell, represented twenty thousand Indian men (Jamieson 1978, 91).

5. The American Indian Movement, with long experience in defending traditional and grassroots Native people against "puppet" Indian governments, offered their assistance to the Tobique women. The women declined, however, for fear that the situation would escalate still further if AIM entered the reserve to support them (Silman 1987, 129–30).

## REFERENCES

Anderson, Kim. 2000. *A Recognition of Being: Reconstructing Native Womanhood*. Toronto: Second Story Press.

Beyefsky, Anne F. 1982. The Human Rights Committee and the Case of Sandra Lovelace. In *The Canadian Yearbook of International Law*, Vol. 20.

Carter, Sarah. 1997. *Capturing Women: The Manipulation of Cultural Imagery in Canada's Prairie West*. Kingston and Montreal: McGill-Queen's University Press.

Gilbert, Larry. 1996. *Entitlement to Indian Status and Membership Codes in Canada*. Toronto: Thompson Canada Ltd.

Holmes, Joan. 1987. *Bill C-31—Equality or Disparity? The Effects of the New Indian Act on Native Women*. Background Paper. Canadian Advisory Council on the Status of Women.

Jamieson, Kathleen. 1978. *Indian Women and the Law in Canada: Citizens Minus.* Canadian Advisory Council on the Status of Women and Indian Rights for Indian Women.

Jamieson, Kathleen. 1979. Multiple Jeopardy: The Evolution of a Native Women's Movement. *Atlantis* 4, no. 2:157–76.

Royal Commission on Aboriginal Peoples (RCAP). 1996. *For Seven Generations: Report of the Royal Commission on Aboriginal Peoples*, Vols. 1–5. Ottawa: Government of Canada.

Schmalz, Peter S. 1991. *The Ojibwa of Southern Ontario.* Toronto: University of Toronto Press.

Silman, Janet. 1987. *Enough Is Enough: Aboriginal Women Speak Out*, as told to Janet Silman. Toronto: Women's Press.

Stoler, Ann. 1991. Carnal Knowledge and Imperial Power: Gender, Race, and Morality in Colonial Asia. In *Gender at the Crossroads: Feminist Anthropology in the Post-Modern Era*, edited by Micaela di Leonardo. Berkeley: University of California Press.

Switzer, Maurice. 1997. Time to Stand Up and Be Counted. *The First Perspective* (December):2.

---

*Source:* Lawrence, Bonita. (2004). Excerpted from "Chapter 2: Regulating Native Identity by Gender." In *"Real" Indians and Others: Mixed Blood Urban Native Peoples and Indigenous Nationhood* (pp. 45–63). Vancouver, BC: UBC Press.

# SNAPSHOTS & SOUNDWAVES 22

## COLONIZATION AND RESIDENTIAL SCHOOLS

### Condensed Timeline of Events

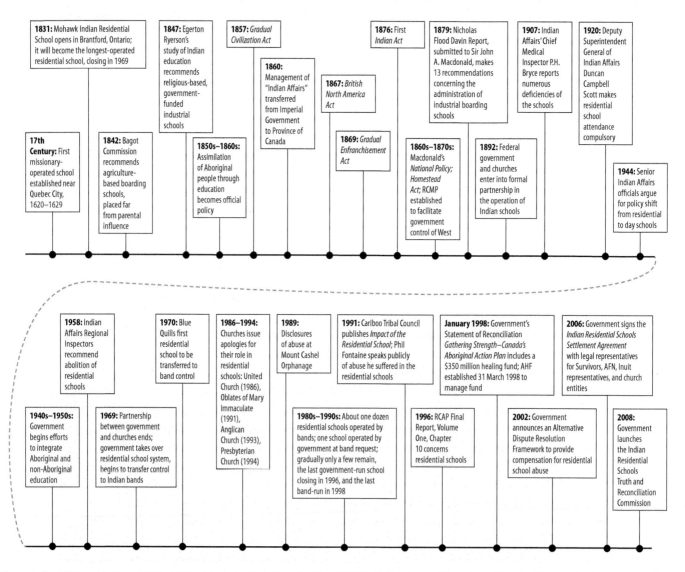

**1831:** Mohawk Indian Residential School opens in Brantford, Ontario; it will become the longest-operated residential school, closing in 1969

**1847:** Egerton Ryerson's study of Indian education recommends religious-based, government-funded industrial schools

**1857:** *Gradual Civilization Act*

**1876:** First *Indian Act*

**1879:** Nicholas Flood Davin Report, submitted to Sir John A. Macdonald, makes 13 recommendations concerning the administration of industrial boarding schools

**1907:** Indian Affairs' Chief Medical Inspector P.H. Bryce reports numerous deficiencies of the schools

**1920:** Deputy Superintendent General of Indian Affairs Duncan Campbell Scott makes residential school attendance compulsory

**17th Century:** First missionary-operated school established near Quebec City, 1620–1629

**1842:** Bagot Commission recommends agriculture-based boarding schools, placed far from parental influence

**1850s–1860s:** Assimilation of Aboriginal people through education becomes official policy

**1860:** Management of "Indian Affairs" transferred from Imperial Government to Province of Canada

**1867:** *British North America Act*

**1869:** *Gradual Enfranchisement Act*

**1860s–1870s:** Macdonald's *National Policy*; *Homestead Act*; RCMP established to facilitate government control of West

**1892:** Federal government and churches enter into formal partnership in the operation of Indian schools

**1944:** Senior Indian Affairs officials argue for policy shift from residential to day schools

**1958:** Indian Affairs Regional Inspectors recommend abolition of residential schools

**1970:** Blue Quills first residential school to be transferred to band control

**1986–1994:** Churches issue apologies for their role in residential schools: United Church (1986), Oblates of Mary Immaculate (1991), Anglican Church (1993), Presbyterian Church (1994)

**1989:** Disclosures of abuse at Mount Cashel Orphanage

**1991:** Cariboo Tribal Council publishes *Impact of the Residential School*; Phil Fontaine speaks publicly of abuse he suffered in the residential schools

**January 1998:** Government's Statement of Reconciliation *Gathering Strength—Canada's Aboriginal Action Plan* includes a $350 million healing fund; AHF established 31 March 1998 to manage fund

**2006:** Government signs the *Indian Residential Schools Settlement Agreement* with legal representatives for Survivors, AFN, Inuit representatives, and church entities

**1940s–1950s:** Government begins efforts to integrate Aboriginal and non-Aboriginal education

**1969:** Partnership between government and churches ends; government takes over residential school system, begins to transfer control to Indian bands

**1980s–1990s:** About one dozen residential schools operated by bands; one school operated by government at band request; gradually only a few remain, the last government-run school closing in 1996, and the last band-run in 1998

**1996:** RCAP Final Report, Volume One, Chapter 10 concerns residential schools

**2002:** Government announces an Alternative Dispute Resolution Framework to provide compensation for residential school abuse

**2008:** Government launches the Indian Residential Schools Truth and Reconciliation Commission

*Source:* Castellano, Marlene Brant, Archibald, Linda, & DeGagné, Mike. (2008). "A Condensed Timeline of Events (Residential Schools)." In *From Truth to Reconciliation: Transforming the Legacy of Residential Schools* (pp. 64–65). Ottawa, ON: Aboriginal Healing Foundation (now housed with the Legacy of Hope Foundation). Retrieved from: http://www.ahf.ca/downloads/from-truth-to-reconciliation-transforming-the-legacy-of-residential-schools.pdf.

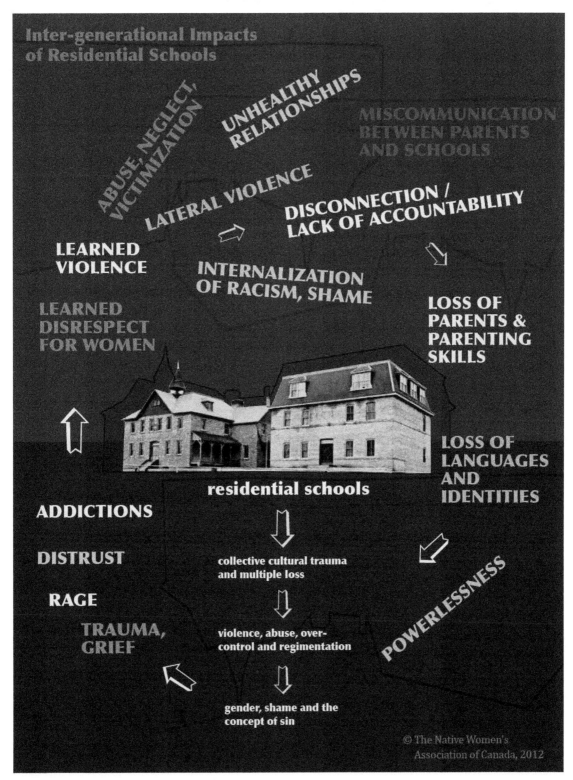

*Source:* The Native Women's Association of Canada (NWAC). (2012). "Inter-Generational Impacts of Residential Schools." Ottawa, ON: NWAC. Retrieved from: https://www.nwac.ca/wp-content/uploads/2015/05/Inter-generational-Impacts-of-Residential-Schools-Poster.pdf.

# ACTIVIST ART 7

## ANISHINAABE-KWE'S RESILIENCE

*Shirley Ida Williams née Pheasant*

Shirley Ida Williams is an Elder and member of the Bird Clan of the Ojibway and Odawa First Nations of Canada. She was born and raised at Wikwemikong First Nations Unceded Reserve on Manitoulin Island, and attended St. Joseph's Residential School in Spanish, Ontario. Williams is a professor emerita in the Chanie Wenjack School for Indigenous Studies at Trent University, where she developed and taught Nishnaabe language curriculum for many years. She continues to promote Nishnaabe language and culture through her work as a speaker, consultant, teacher, translator, and author.

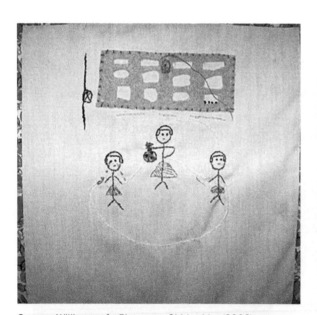

*Source:* Williams née Pheasant, Shirley Ida. (2009). "Anishinaabe-kwe's Resilience." From "Quilt 3 – Child Prisoners." *Living Healing Quilt Project*. Retrieved from: http://quiltinggallery.com/2009/01/22/anishinaabe-kwes-resilience.

*Source:* The Living Healing Quilt Project. (2008). "Quilt 3 – Child Prisoners." *Living Healing Quilt Project*. Retrieved from: http://quiltinggallery.com/2008/11/26/the-quilts-and-stories-from-the-living-healing-quilt-project/#child.

## Living Healing Quilt Project: Promoting Healing—One Stitch at a Time

*This post is part of the Living Healing Quilt Project that honours the strength, courage, and commitment of Indian Residential School survivors. This quilt block is from Quilt 3 – Child Prisoners.*

This is my story of how I maintained my resilience while I was at St. Joseph's Residential School in Spanish, Ontario.

My father used to give me $2.00 at the beginning of September and that $2.00 used to keep me in money until April, then I would say that I was broke. At the school, we had store hours once a month if we all behaved. The store had candies, chocolate bars, and jelly beans. Jelly beans were the cheapest to buy because one could buy 5 jelly beans for a penny! So I would get jelly beans for my comfort food.

Whenever my true friends or I got sick or lonely or if we got a scolding or strapping for speaking our language, one of the things that I did was get my bag of jelly beans. I would get my true friends together and we would gather outside somewhere and then we would circle around each other and share one jelly bean. This jelly bean had to be eaten and bitten equally by us! None would bite more than the other, but shared equally to wipe away our hurts.

After sharing our jelly bean, then we could wipe our hurts or loneliness and we would become strong again and able to laugh and to go on functioning in the school. We would tell ourselves that this is just for a time till we would be 16 years old and we would be free to leave here!

I used embroidery work to sew my piece. There are three girls that I remember that I was close with, Mary Ann, Mary Elizabeth and Louise from Gchi-minising. One of the girls has tears dripping from her face. The dresses we wore were grey or sometimes blue. The bag that I am holding is full of jelly beans and like I said if one of my friends got hurt or lonely we would get together to share this candy. The lines represent the sharing of hurt, the strength we had, and how we helped to nurture one another. From the sharing, we were able to survive and give caring to each other.

The fence represents how we were locked up and the broken green line represents the lack of kindness, love, and emotional support that we needed in order to grow mentally well. The yellow lines also represent the spiritual growth we got from each other in order to go on within the institution.

The school was gutted by fire in the 70s but the shell is still standing including the statue of St. Joseph.

*Source:* Williams née Pheasant, Shirley Ida. (2009, January 22). "Anishinaabe-kwe's Resilience" (Artist Statement). *Living Healing Quilt Project*. Retrieved from: http://quiltinggallery.com/2009/01/22/anishinaabe-kwes-resilience/.

# CHAPTER 35

## Nishnaabeg[1] Resurgence: Stories from Within

*Leanne Betasamosake Simpson*

Leanne Betasamosake Simpson is a renowned Michi Saagiig Nishnaabeg scholar, writer, and artist. Her work reveals the intersections between politics, story, and song, and brings audiences into a rich and layered world of sound, light, and sovereign creativity. Simpson was integral in the work of the 2012 Idle No More protests, and has been widely recognized as one of the most compelling Indigenous voices of her generation.

On June 21, 2009, a community procession of Michi Saagiig Nishnaabeg[2] dancers, artists, singers, drummers, community leaders, Elders, families and children walked down the main street of Nogojiwanong.[3] With our traditional and contemporary performers gently dancing on the back of our Mikinaag,[4] we wove our way through the city streets, streets where we had all indirectly, or directly, experienced the violence of colonialism, dispossession and desperation at one time or another. Our drummers provided the heartbeat; our singers provided the prayers. Settler-Canadians poked their heads out of office buildings and stared at us from the sidelines. "Indians. What did they want now? What did they want this time?" But that day, we didn't have any want. We were not seeking recognition or asking for rights. We were not trying to fit into Canada. We were celebrating our nation on our lands in the spirit of joy, exuberance and individual expression.

Our allies lined the streets offering smiles and encouraging shouts of approval. Flanked by huge, colourful puppets and a flock of sparkling bineshiinyag[5] made by local children, the procession was both strikingly disarming and deeply political at the same time. This was not a protest. This was not a demonstration. This was a quiet, collective act of resurgence. It was a mobilization and it was political because it was a reminder. It was a reminder that although we are collectively unseen in the city of Peterborough, when we come together with one mind and one heart we can transform our land and our city into a decolonized space and a place of resurgence, even if it is only for a brief amount of time. It was a reminder of everything good about our traditions, our culture, our songs, dances and performances. It was a celebration of our resistance, a celebration that after everything, we are still here. It was an insertion of Nishnaabeg presence.

As I walked down the main street of the place where I live with my family, I felt a mixture of strong emotions. As I saw my Haudenosaunee and Cree colleagues from the university walking with us, I felt a deepened sense of solidarity. This was a time in my life

I felt most connected to my community. But I was also afraid. I was afraid of the response of the non-Natives in my community. I was afraid they would throw things at us, that there would be confrontations, that there would be violence. I was afraid that my kids, having only known joy and beautiful things from their culture, would suddenly have their bubble burst and they would see the violent assault my generation of Indigenous assumes as normal.

The idea of a celebratory community procession is incredible to my eighty-something Nokomis.[6] Growing up on the reserve, and then living in Peterborough, the idea of "Indians" marching down the main street in a celebratory fashion seems fantastical to her at best. She can't believe that her great grandchildren feel proud, that in her words, "It is OK for them to be Indian." And in many ways, that was the point of the procession. The Nishnaabeg have been collectively dispossessed of our national territory; we are an occupied nation. Individually, we have been physically beaten, arrested, apprehended, interned in jails, sanitariums, residential or day schools and foster care. We have endured racist remarks when shopping or seeking healthcare and education within the city. We have stories of being driven to the outskirts of our city by police and bar owners and dropped off to walk back to our reserves. But that day, we turned inward to celebrate our presence and to build our resurgence as a community. For me, it was a beautiful day. I've never walked in solidarity with all of our Nishnaabeg families before, regardless of our individual political orientation. I've never had the opportunity to celebrate our survival, our continuance, our resurgence: all of the best parts of us. For an hour that day, we collectively transformed the streets of Peterborough back into Nogojiwanong, and forward into Nogojiwanong. For an hour that day, we created a space and a place where the impacts of colonialism were lessened, where we could feel what it feels like to be part of a united, healthy community, where our children could glimpse our beautiful visions for their future.

The procession made its way to the shores of Zaagigaans,[7] where we held a Powwow and artistic festival. The cycle of our Grand Entry into the streets of Peterborough was repeated as our Elders and dancers danced their way around the cedar arbor, and we started over once again. Together, we transformed National Aboriginal Day into something about resurgence for our community, instead of a shallow multicultural education day for Canadians to feel less guilty about their continued occupation of our lands. For me, our procession was a political act. We built a day where we put the health of our nation first. We strengthened our culture. We strengthened our relationships with each other and with Nogojiwanong. Nishnaabe Elder Edna Manitowabi says that one of the reasons our cultures and ways of life are important is that our culture brings our hearts great joy. Our culture is beautiful and loving, and it nurtures our hearts and minds in a way that enables us to not just cope, but to live. We always feel good after being out in the bush, or after ceremony. I thought of this that day as I walked. I thought of the word *eyaa'oyaanh*, which means who I am, the way I am living or becoming, my identity.[8] In order to have a positive identity, we have to be living in ways that illuminate that identity, and that propel us towards mino bimaadiziwin, the good life.[9]

## GAAWIIN NDA-GAJSII, WE ARE NOT SHAMEFUL

For most of the day, I thought about my Ancestors. I thought of the seeds they had planted so long ago to ensure that we were all there on that day in June, walking down our street together. And if I am honest, I also thought of the shame that I carry inside of me from the legacy of colonial abuse, the unspoken shame we carry collectively as Michi Saagiig Nishnaabeg. It is shame that is rooted in the humiliation that colonialism has heaped on our peoples for hundreds of years and is now carried within our bodies, minds and our hearts. It is shame that our ancestors—our families—did not rally hard enough against the colonial regime. It is shame that we were tricked into surrendering our life, land and sustenance during the Williams Treaty process. It is shame that makes us think that our leaders and Elders did not do the best they could. To me, this colonial shame felt like not only a tremendous burden to carry, but it also felt displaced. We are not shameful people. We have done nothing wrong. I began to realize that shame can only take hold when we are disconnected from the stories of resistance within our own families and communities. I placed that shame as an insidious and infectious part of the cognitive imperialism that was aimed at convincing us that we were a weak and defeated people, and that there was no point in resisting or resurging. I became interested in finding those stories of resistance and telling them so that our next generation would know. [...]

Michi Saagiig Nishnaabeg territory is located along the north shore of Lake Ontario, or Chi'Nbiish,[10] from Niagara Falls to Gananoque. Our old people referred to our nation as Kina Gchi Nishnaabegogaming: *Kina* meaning all; *Gchi* for big; and *ogamig* meaning the place of, where we live, where we make our living, the place that was given to us.[11] Our oral tradition tells of a beautiful territory covered with mature stands of white pine with trunks spanning seven feet and towering 200 feet overhead. The land was easy to travel through, with pine needles and a sparse understory as a result of a white pine canopy. There was a tall grass prairie where Peterborough stands today—a prairie that the Michi Saagiig Nishnaabeg maintained with controlled burns.[12] It's hard for me to imagine a land like that today, with southeastern Ontario farmland spanning out in all directions.

For my ancestors, the Michi Saagiig Nishnaabeg, our self-determination and sovereignty as part of the Nishnaabeg nation was relatively intact between 1700–1783.[13] Over the next forty years, we were forced to survive an intense, violent assault on our

lands and our peoples. By 1763, the British Crown no longer needed us as allies; soon loyalists streamed into our territory and began occupying Michi Saagiig Nishnaabeg lands. Over the next fifty years, our people survived pandemics, violence and assault, unjust treaty negotiations, occupation of our lands and a forced relocation—which, for some of us, resulted in a small and insufficient reserve at Alderville, a Methodist mission. Eventually, our system of governance was replaced by a colonial administration, as the planned assimilation strategy moved into full swing. By 1822—when many Nishnaabeg in the north and the west were still living as they always had—we were facing the complete political, cultural and social collapse of everything we had ever known.

My ancestors resisted and survived what must have seemed like an apocalyptic reality of occupation and subjugation in a context where they had few choices. They resisted by simply surviving and being alive. They resisted by holding onto their stories. They resisted by taking the seeds of our culture and political systems and packing them away, so that one day another generation of Michi Saagiig Nishnaabeg might be able to plant them. I am sure of their resistance, because I am here today, living as a contemporary Michi Saagiig Nishnaabeg woman. I am the evidence. Michi Saagiig Nishnaabeg people are the evidence. Now, nearly two hundred years after surviving an attempted political and cultural genocide, it is the responsibility of my generation to plant and nurture those seeds and to make our Ancestors proud.

Shame traps us individually and collectively into the victimry of the colonial assault, and travels through the generations, accumulating and manifesting itself in new and more insidious ways in each re-generation. The cycle of shame we are cognitively locked into is in part perpetuated and maintained by western theoretical constructions of "resistance," "mobilization" and "social movements," by defining what is and is not considered. Through the lens of colonial thought and cognitive imperialism, we are often unable to *see* our Ancestors. We are unable to *see* their philosophies and their strategies of mobilization and the complexities of their plan for resurgence. When resistance is defined solely as large-scale political mobilization, we miss much of what has kept our languages, cultures and systems of governance alive. We have those things today because our Ancestors often acted within the family unit to physically survive, to pass on what they could to their children, to occupy and use our lands as we always had. This, in and of itself, tells me a lot about how to build Indigenous renaissance and resurgence.

## A FLOURISHMENT OF THE INDIGENOUS INSIDE

[…] We have been resisting colonial imposition for four centuries. I think our communities know something about organizing, mobilizing and strategizing. I think our communities know quite a lot about living through the most grievous of circumstances.

Although I have been thinking about resistance for my entire adult life, it was not until I read Taiaiake Alfred's *Peace, Power and Righteousness: An Indigenous Manifesto* and then *Wasáse: Indigenous Pathways of Action and Freedom*, that I began to think about resurgence. Alfred's seminal works immediately spoke to my *(o)debwewin*, literally the sound my heart makes,[14] or "truth," because at the core of his work, he challenges us to reclaim the Indigenous contexts (knowledge, interpretations, values, ethics, processes) for our political cultures. In doing so, he refocuses our work from trying to transform the colonial outside into a flourishment of the *Indigenous* inside. We need to rebuild our culturally inherent philosophical contexts for governance, education, healthcare and economy. We need to be able to articulate in a clear manner our visions for the future, for living as Indigenous Peoples in contemporary times. To do so, we need to engage in *Indigenous* processes, since according to our traditions, the processes of engagement highly influences the outcome of the engagement itself. We need to do this on our own terms, without the

sanction, permission or engagement of the state, western theory or the opinions of Canadians. In essence, we need to not just figure out who we are; we need to re-establish the processes by which we live who we are within the current context we find ourselves. We do not need funding to do this. We do not need a friendly colonial political climate to do this. We do not need opportunity to do this. We need our Elders, our languages and our lands, along with vision, intent, commitment, community and ultimately, action. We must move ourselves beyond resistance and survival, to flourishment and mino bimaadiziwin.[15] If this approach does nothing else to shift the current state of affairs—and I believe it will—it will ground our peoples in their own cultures and teachings that provide the ultimate antidote to colonialism, which I believe is what Indigenous intellectuals and theorists[16] have been encouraging us to do all along. In this book [*Dancing on Our Turtle's Back*], I am interested in exploring these transformative contexts from within my own Nishnaabeg culture. Transforming ourselves, our communities and our nations is ultimately the first step in transforming our relationship with the state.

Building diverse, nation-culture-based resurgences means significantly re-investing in our own ways of being: regenerating our political and intellectual traditions; articulating and living our legal systems; language learning; ceremonial and spiritual pursuits; creating and using our artistic and performance-based traditions. All of these require us—as individuals and collectives—to diagnose, interrogate and eviscerate the insidious nature of conquest, empire and imperial thought in every aspect of our lives. It requires us to reclaim the very best practices of our traditional cultures, knowledge systems and lifeways in the dynamic, fluid, compassionate, respectful context within which they were originally generated. A critical level of anti-colonial interrogation is required in order for us to be able to see the extraordinarily political nature of Nishnaabeg thought.

Ethically, it is my emphatic belief that the land, reflected in Nishnaabeg thought and philosophy, compels us towards resurgence in virtually every aspect. Walking through the bush last spring with my children, the visual landscape reminded me of this. We saw Lady Slippers, and I was reminded of our name for the flower and the story that goes with it,[17] and then moss, and then butterflies.[18] Then we saw a woodpecker[19] and I thought of a similar story. Finally, we walked through a birch stand and I thought of Nanabush, Niimkiig and birch bark.[20] Our Nishnaabeg landscape flourishes with our stories of resistance and resurgence, yet through colonial eyes, the stories are interpreted as quaint anecdotes with "rules" of engagement and consequence. Interpreted within our cultural web of non-authoritarian leadership, non-hierarchical ways of being, non-interference and nonessentialism,[21] the stories explain the resistance of my Ancestors and the seeds of resurgence they so carefully saved and planted. So I could then assume my responsibility as a Michi Saagiig Nishnaabeg to care take of their garden, eventually passing those responsibilities on to my grandchildren. [...]

While it is my firm belief that there is much work to be done within our nations in terms of building resurgence—both political and cultural—within a nation-based framework, I don't believe this is *all* we need to do. According to our Seven Fires Prophecy, much work needs to be done to decolonize the state, Indigenous-state relations and Canada in order for the Eighth Fire to be lit.[22] At this point, to me, it seems rather futile to be engaged in scholarly and political processes, trying to shift these relationships when there is no evidence there exists the political will to do so on the part of the Canadian state. There is no opportunity; and putting our energies into demanding that the state recognize us seems depressing, futile and a waste of energy, given the condition of our communities. I also believe Nishnaabeg philosophy propels us to focus on ourselves in terms of transformation. However, I do not wish to criticize the work of Indigenous academics who chose to engage, interrogate and struggle with the dominant white paper liberalism that plagues Indigenous-state relations in Canada. The seminal works of many of my colleagues are at their core aimed at decolonizing the Canadian state, political systems and legal system in order to demand political relationships based on recognized Indigenous nations and alternatives to rights-based approaches. While this body of work searches for solutions within federalism that do not subsume Indigenous self-determination, agency and sovereignty, there is also important work to be done within our nations. This is the work that is my focus, because these are the things that I am constantly thinking about, talking about and asking Elders about. My approach to this work is not rooted solely in the intellectual; it is rooted in my spiritual and emotional life, as well as my body; and it is explored through my Nishnaabeg name, my clan, my Michi Saagiig Nishnaabeg roots and my own individual being. It is not better or worse than any other Michi Saagiig Nishnaabeg's contribution. It is simply a reflection of my own current ideas and thinking and is not meant to reflect the views of my broader nation, or to be comprehensive in any manner.

In my own life, I have been taught by a handful of Elders that embody Nishnaabeg thought in a way that I worry we are losing. These Elders are fluent language speakers. They embody gentleness and kindness. And what struck me immediately—and continues to do so twenty years later—is that they rejected rigidity and fundamentalism as colonial thinking. Their ways of being in the world and their interpretations of our teachings were reflective of a philosophical state, a set of values and ethics and a way of being in the world where they didn't feel the need to employ exclusionary practices, authoritarian power and hierarchy. They "protected" their interpretations by embodying them and by living them. They "resisted" colonialism by living within Nishnaabeg contexts. When I moved back into the southeastern regions of my territory, I was immediately struck by moralistic judgment, rules to constrict and control social behaviours within my community, and a more formalized hierarchy to restrict access to knowledge, which to me is reminiscent of colonial thought and religious fundamentalism.[23] This was not my understanding or interpretation of my own cultural teachings. I was taught that individual Nishnaabe had the responsibility of interpreting the teachings for themselves within a broader shared collective set of values that placed great importance on self-actualization, the suspension of judgment, fluidity, emergence, careful deliberation and an embodied respect for diversity.

There exists very little in the academic literature conceptualizing and exploring resistance and resurgence from within Indigenous thought.[24] My perspective is that the process of resurgence must be Indigenous at its core in order to reclaim and re-politicize the context and the nature of Nishnaabeg thought. Nishnaabeg thought was designed and conceptualized to perpetuate the holistic well being of Nishnaabeg people through a series of cultural and political manifestations, including government, education and restorative justice that promoted mino bimaadiziwin. Our ways of being promoted the good life or continuous rebirth at every turn: in the face of political unrest, "natural disasters" and even genocide. Nishnaabeg thought provides us with the impetus, the ethical responsibility, the strategies and the plan of action for resurgence. We have a responsibility to the coming generations to maintain that resurgence in the midst of an all-out colonial attack and in the more insidious decentralized post-colonial-colonialism.[25] Nishnaabeg thought was not meant to promote assimilation or normalization within a colonial context. It was not meant to be reduced and relegated to a decorative window dressing in western scholarship.

## AANJI MAAJITAAWIN,[26] THE ART OF STARTING OVER

I am writing this at a time when Canada is busy talking about "reconciliation" at every turn, while at the same time using the *Indian Act* to enforce a band council "government" against the will of the

Algonquins of Barriere Lake. "Reconciliation" is being promoted by the federal government as a "new" way for Canada to relate to Indigenous Peoples, and it isn't just government officials that are promoting the idea. I have heard heads of universities talk about reconciliation; I have read journalist's op-ed pieces; I have heard mayors talk about reconciliation as they open local Aboriginal events. But the idea of reconciliation is not new. Indigenous Peoples attempted to reconcile our differences in countless treaty negotiations, which categorically have not produced the kinds of relationships Indigenous Peoples intended. I wonder how we can reconcile when the majority of Canadians do not understand the historic or contemporary injustice of dispossession and occupation, particularly when the state has expressed its unwillingness to make any adjustments to the unjust relationship. Haudenosaunee scholar and orator Dan Longboat recently reminded me of this, when he said that treaties are not just for governments, they are for the citizens as well.[27] The people also have to act in a manner that is consistent with the relationships set out in the treaty negotiation process. If Canadians do not fully understand and embody the idea of reconciliation, is this a step forward? It reminds me of an abusive relationship where one person is being abused physically, emotionally, spiritually and mentally. She wants out of the relationship, but instead of supporting her, we are all gathered around the abuser, because he wants to "reconcile." But he doesn't want to take responsibility. He doesn't want to change. In fact, all through the process he continues to physically, emotionally, spiritually and mentally abuse his partner. He just wants to say sorry so he can feel less guilty about his behaviour. He just wants to adjust the ways he is abusing; he doesn't want to stop the abuse. Collectively, what are the implications of participating in reconciliation processes when there is an overwhelming body of evidence that in action, the Canadian state does not want to take responsibility and stop the abuse? What are the consequences for Indigenous Peoples of participating in a process that attempts to absolve Canada of past wrong doings, while they continue to engage with our nations in a less than honourable way?

Those that chose to participate in reconciliation processes do so believing that participation could potentially bring more positive change than non-participation. They may be right. But our eyes need to be wide open if we are entering this process. As reconciliation has become institutionalized,[28] I worry our participation will benefit the state in an asymmetrical fashion, by attempting to neutralize the legitimacy of Indigenous resistance. If reconciliation is focused only on residential schools rather than the broader set of relationships that generated policies, legislation and practices aimed at assimilation and political genocide, then there is a risk that reconciliation will "level the playing field" in the eyes of Canadians. In the eyes of liberalism, the historical "wrong" has now been "righted" and further transformation is not needed, since the historic situation has been remedied. I worry the historical context for contemporary Indigenous-state contention becomes co-opted in this model, because the perception of most Canadians is that post-reconciliation, Indigenous Peoples no longer have a legitimate source of contention.[29] I also worry that institutionalization of a narrowly defined "reconciliation" subjugates treaty and nation-based participation by locking our Elders—the ones that suffered the most directly at the hands of the residential school system—in a position of victimhood. Of course, they are anything but victims. They are our strongest visionaries and they inspire us to vision alternative futures. Are we participating in a process that allows the state to co-opt the individual and collective pain and suffering of our people, while also criminalizing the inter-generational impacts of residential schools and ignoring the larger neo-assimilation project to which our children are now subjected?

For reconciliation to be meaningful to Indigenous Peoples and for it to be a decolonizing force, it must be interpreted broadly. To me, reconciliation must be grounded in cultural generation and political resurgence. It must support Indigenous nations in regenerating our languages, our oral cultures, our traditions of governance and everything else residential schools attacked and attempted to obliterate.[30] Reconciliation must move beyond individual abuse to come to mean a collective re-balancing of the playing field. This idea is captured in the Nishnaabeg concept *Aanji Maajitaawin*: to start over, the art of starting over, to regenerate. Reconciliation is a process of regeneration that will take many years to accomplish. We have to regenerate our languages so we have communities of fluent speakers. We have to regenerate the conditions that produce leaders and political systems based on our collective Nishnaabeg values, political processes and philosophies. Canada must engage in a decolonization project and a re-education project that would enable its government and its citizens to engage with Indigenous Peoples in a just and honourable way in the future.

From a Nishnaabeg theoretical and legal perspective, regeneration or restoration is at the core of re-balancing relationships. Nishnaabeg legal systems are, at their core, restorative. Restorative processes rely upon the abuser taking full responsibility for his/her actions in a collective setting, amongst the person s/he violated, and amongst the people both the perpetrator and the survivor hold responsibilities to—be that their extended family, clan or community. In the case of state-perpetuated residential schools, the tables would be turned in a Nishnaabeg legal system. The survivors would have agency, decision-making power, and the power to decide restorative measures. In the case of the Community Holistic Circles of Healing in Hollow Water First Nation,[31] the abuser must take responsibility for his or her actions and is required to sit in a circle of community Elders, the extended family of the survivor and his or her extended family (who are there to support him or her through this process). Everyone participating in the circle has a chance to speak or to share their thoughts, feelings and perspectives. The survivor has the choice to share whatever he or she feels most appropriate. Imagine government officials, church officials, nuns, priests and teachers from a particular residential school in a circle with the people that had survived their sexual, physical, emotional and spiritual abuse. This is a fundamentally different power relationship between perpetrators of violence and survivors of that violence, where the abusers must face the full impact of their actions. Reconciliation then becomes a process embodied by both the survivor and the perpetrator. And part of restoration means that the community maintains the authority to make that individual accountable for future wrongs. The interrogation is focused on the perpetrator of the violence, not on the survivors. The responsibility and the authority for restoration are in the agency of the survivors, not the perpetrators themselves. The authority to hold the state accountable then rests with Indigenous nations, not the liberal state.[32]

Restorative models work in Nishnaabeg communities because ethically taking responsibility for one's actions is paramount in the healing or restoration process; as well, the purpose of these models in the long term is the rehabilitation and restoration of all of those individuals back into mino bimaadiziwin. These models put the hens in charge of the hen house and the fox under interrogation. If it is truly time to talk "reconciliation," then how we reconcile is critically important. I can see no evidence whatsoever that there exists a political will on the part of the state to do anything other than neutralize Indigenous resistance, so as to not impinge upon the convenience of the settler-Canadians. The only way to not be co-opted is to use our own legal and political processes to bring about justice.

In the words of Dene scholar Glen Coulthard, our culturally inherent political theory provides Indigenous Peoples with mechanisms for "critically revaluating, reconstructing and redeploying culture and tradition in ways that seek to prefigure, alongside those with similar ethical commitments, a radical alternative to the structural and psycho-affective facets of colonial domination."[33] Our liberatory and inherent theories of resurgence also do not tell

us to persistently search through the web of colonial traps for settler political recognition and to gleefully accept white paper liberalism designed to redistribute resources and rights, placating the guilt of settler Canadians and neutralizing Indigenous resistance. Our inherent theories of resurgence are transformative and revolutionary. They are meant to propel and maintain social, cultural and political transformative movement through the worst forms of political genocide; and I think it is important to understand them as such.

While there are Indigenous scholars, leaders and activists engaged in broadening the state's conceptualization of reconciliation in order to re-align it with the political goals of Indigenous Peoples, again, I worry about emphasis. This cannot become the bulk of our work or take up the bulk of our resources. Perhaps good things will come out of this process, particularly for residential school survivors. Perhaps our communities will be able to use something from this "reconciliation process" to meet some of their goals, but we need to enter into this carefully and with critical eyes that are guided by the whole picture.

[...] I have been careful throughout this chapter to not define "resurgence." It is my hope that readers will take the concepts and ideas presented in this book, return to their own communities, teachings, languages and Elders or Knowledge Holders, and engage in a process where they figure out what "resurgence" means to them, and to their collective communities. This chapter is what resurgence means to me, at this point in my life. And while this is a personal process, I believe it is also important to collectivize these discussions and processes. In sharing my thoughts on this, my hope is that readers will take what is useful to them and illuminate it in their lives and their work, while leaving the parts that they disagree with to die within these pages. I know my thinking on this will change, because the process I am engaged with is transformative. As my language skills increase, so will my thinking. As I move through different stages in my life, so will my thinking.

In our ceremonies, we have a beautiful and sacred Nishnaabeg song, commonly referred to as our Prophecy Song. My understanding is that the Prophecy Song is very, very ancient.[34] The grammatical structure is such that it is the voices and words of our Ancestors as the beginning of the Seven Fires Prophecy, singing encouragement to the coming generations who are responsible for building a Nishnaabeg resurgence in the Seventh Fire. The song is an incredible gift from my Ancestors. It is a song of resistance and resurgence; and when we sing it, its haunting melody fills our hearts with hope, with love, with beauty and thanksgiving. It is a single song that has the power to liberate us from shame. Aambe Maajaadaa![35]

## NOTES

1. *Nishnaabeg* is translated as "the people" and refers to Ojibwe, Odawa (Ottawa), Potawatomi, Michi Saagiig (Mississauga), Saulteaux, Chippewa and Omámíwinini (Algonquin) people. Nishnaabeg people are also known as Nishinaabeg, Anishinaabeg, Anishinaabek and Anishinabek, reflecting different spelling systems and differing dialects. I have used many Nishnaabemowin (Ojibwe language) words throughout this chapter, and I have used the dialects of the people who taught me the words. The words I learned from Doug Williams are in the Michi Saagiig Nishnaabeg or eastern Ontario dialect. Shirley Williams and Isadore Toulouse speak Odawa or the central/Manitoulin dialect. There are also a few words in the northwestern dialect. I am a language learner, not a fluent speaker, and any mistakes are my own. I have, however, tried to check each word that is unfamiliar to me with an Elder who is a fluent language speaker to ensure that I am using the word correctly, even if the word is coming from a reputable dictionary. In Michi Saagiig Nishnaabeg contexts, I have tried to use our spelling—Nishnaabe or Nishnaabeg (plural), when referring to the work of other writers from the northwest parts of our territory. I have used the spelling they use in their work. Because there are too many examples of academics who

are not fluent speakers using Nishnaabemowin words incorrectly, I have referenced all but the most common Nishnaabemowin words in the text.

2. *Michi Saagiig Nishnaabeg* means the Nishnaabeg people who live or dwell at the mouth of a large river. Michi Saagiig Nishnaabeg Elder Doug Williams explained to me that this is the way his Elders referred to themselves. Peterborough, ON, October 26, 2010. This is similar to Basil Johnston's Mizhi-zaugeek, *Anishinaubae Thesaurus*, Michigan State University Press, East Lansing, MI, 2006, 14. Michi Saagiig or "Mizhi-zaugeek" people live at the eastern doorway of the Nishnaabeg nation, located in what is now known as eastern Ontario. According to Doug Williams, the word *Mississauga* is an anglicized version of Michi Saagiig or Mizhi-zaugeek.

3. *Nogojiwanong* is the Michi Saagiig name for Peterborough, Ontario, and means "the place at the end of the rapids." It is commonly used amongst Nishnaabeg people in Peterborough.

4. Turtle.

5. Birds.

6. Grandmother.

7. This is the name for Little Lake and it means "little lake." I learned this word from Doug Williams. Waawshkigaamagki (Curve Lake First Nation), July 15, 2010. Shirley Williams showed me how to spell it. Peterborough, ON, September 20, 2010.

8. To me, this word means that in order to have a Nishnaabeg identity, one must live that identity in all of its many and beautiful diverse forms. The spelling and full meaning of this word was taught to me by Shirley Williams. Peterborough, ON, September 19, 2010.

9. The art of living the good life. Winona LaDuke also translates *mino bimaadiziwin* to mean "continuous rebirth." Scott Lyons writes that we should use the bimadizi form of the word to keep with the verb-based traditions of the language. Language expert Shirley Williams translates *bimadizi* to mean he/she is living, and *bimaadiziwin* as an abstract noun meaning "the art of living life." Peterborough, ON, September 12, 2010. As a concept, mino bimaadiziwin is commonly used in Nishnaabeg teachings. I worry though that it is becoming almost an overused and over simplified concept in Nishnaabeg scholarship particularly amongst

non-speakers and cultural beginners (Christine Sy also brought up this point in previous drafts). While I still find mino bimaadiziwin to be an important concept, I use it while keeping these observations in mind.

10. *Chi'Nbiish*, literally "big water," is the Michi Saagiig Nishnaabeg name for Lake Ontario, according to Doug Williams. Peterborough, ON, November 30, 2010.

11. Doug Williams. Peterborough, ON, November 30, 2010. I specifically asked Doug if there was a term our ancestors used to refer to their "nation," and this was his response. My interest in this came out of a conversation with Niigaanwewidam James Sinclair that took place in November 2010.

12. Doug Williams, Keynote Speaker. Peterborough Race Relations Committee, Dreams of Beans Coffee House, Peterborough, ON, November 18, 2010.

13. Brian Osborne and Michael Ripmeester, "The Mississaugas between Two Worlds: Strategic Adjustments to Changing Landscapes of Power," *Canadian Journal of Native Studies*, 1997, XVII(2): 259–291.

14. Jim Dumont, Nishnaabeg Elder. Explained in a workshop as part of his presentation at the Elders' Conference, Trent University, Peterborough, ON, February 20, 2010.

15. Mino bimaadiziwin is a phrase that is used to denote "living the good life" or "the art of living the good life." Winona LaDuke translates the term as "continuous rebirth," (Winona LaDuke, *Our Relations: Struggles for Land and Life*, South End Press, Cambridge, MA, 1994, 4, 132), so it means living life in a way that promotes rebirth, renewal, reciprocity and respect. It is my understanding that although there are many ways to live the good life and that within Nishnaabeg contexts, there is no dichotomy between the "good life" and the "bad life," rather living in a good way is an ongoing process.

16. By here, I mean Elders, Faith-Keepers, Clan-Mothers, traditional leaders, Grandmothers, Grandfathers, language-keepers and Knowledge-Holders, not western-trained academics, and I specifically mean those Elders, Faith-Keepers, Clan-Mothers, traditional leaders, Grandmothers, Grandfathers, language-keepers and Knowledge Holders that are able to interpret our teachings through the language in a way that embodies their Nishnaabeg essence,

rather than in a way that locks us into a fundamentalist preservation framework.

17. For a written version of this story, see Lise Lunge-Larsen and Margi Preus, *The Legend of the Lady Slipper*, Houghton Mifflin, Boston, MA, 1999.

18. One version of this story exists in "The First Butterflies" in *Tales the Elders Told: Ojibway Legends* by Basil Johnston, Royal Ontario Museum, Toronto, ON, 1983, 12–17; another exists in John Borrows' *Drawing Out Law: A Spirit's Guide*, University of Toronto Press, Toronto, ON, 2010, 14–16.

19. Basil Johnston, "The Woodpecker" in *The Bear-Walker and Other Stories*, Royal Ontario Museum, Toronto, ON, 1983, 49–55.

20. *Niimkiig* means thunderbirds. For a version of this story, see Wendy Makoons Geniusz's "Nenabozho and the Animkikiig" in *Our Knowledge Is Not Primitive: Decolonizing Botanical Anishinaabe Teachings*, Syracuse University Press, Syracuse, NY, 2009, 136–140.

21. Kiera Ladner, "Women and Blackfoot Nationalism," *Journal of Canadian Studies*, 2000, 35(2): 35–61; Rupert Ross, *Dancing with a Ghost: Exploring Indian Reality*, Reed Books Canada, Markham, ON, 1992, 11–38, 116–125; and Emma LaRoque, "Métis and Feminist" in Joyce Green, ed., *Making Space for Indigenous Feminism*, Fernwood Publishing, Halifax, NS, 2007, 63.

22. For a broader discussion, see Leanne Simpson, "Oshkimaadiziig, the New People," in Leanne Simpson, ed., *Lighting the Eighth Fire: The Liberation, Resurgence, and Protection of Indigenous Nations*, Arbeiter Ring Publishing, Winnipeg, MB, 2008, 13–21.

23. This exists in all parts of the territory; this is just how I came to understand it. Compare this section with Taiaiake Alfred, *Wasáse: Indigenous Pathways of Action and Freedom*, Broadview Press, Peterborough, ON, 2005, 197–198. I have also discussed my observations with Doug Williams, which he felt were consistent with Michi Saagiig Nishnaabeg interpretations. Waawshkigaamagki (Curve Lake First Nation), July 15, 2010.

24. Leanne Simpson, "Oshkimaadiziig, the New People," in Leanne Simpson, ed., *Lighting the Eighth Fire: The Liberation, Resurgence, and Protection of Indigenous Nations*, Arbeiter Ring Publishing, Winnipeg, MB,

2008, 13–21. Alfred explores these concepts within Haudenosaunee thought in Taiaiake Alfred, *Wasáse: Indigenous Pathways of Action and Freedom*, Broadview Press, Peterborough, ON, 2005.

25. Taiaiake Alfred, *Wasáse: Indigenous Pathways of Action and Freedom*, Broadview Press, Peterborough, ON, 2005, 58.

26. *Aanji maajitaawin* means to start over, the art of starting over, or regeneration. Shirley Williams, Peterborough, ON, September 19, 2010.

27. Haudenosaunee scholar Roronhiakewen Dan Longboat, Peterborough, ON, September 9, 2010.

28. I recognize that this discussion is delicate in that I do not want to offend or disregard the experiences, thoughts and perspectives of residential school survivors, nor is it my intent to criticize my colleagues who are working with the Truth and Reconciliation Commission. My intent here is to examine the wider political forces shaping this process of reconciliation.

29. I wrote this while listening to (and was influenced by) Fiona MacDonald's oral presentation, *Democratic Multinationalism: A Political Approach to Indigenous State Relations in Canada*, Canadian Political Science Association Annual Meeting, June 3, Concordia University, Montreal, QC.

30. This idea came out of a discussion with Kiera Ladner on August 15, 2010.

31. A description of Hollow Water First Nation's Community Holistic Circle Healing is available at <www.iirp.org/article_detail.php?article_id=MDco>. I have worked with the community of Hollow Water since 1997 and have witnessed several CHCH circles.

32. I recognize here that survivors may not want to face their abusers in this fashion. My point here is to bring attention to the shift in power and emphasis in Indigenous restorative processes.

33. Glen S. Coulthard, "Subjects of Empire," *Contemporary Political Theory,* 2007, 6: 437–460.

34. My understanding is my own interpretation of the teachings of Edna Manitowabi, who initially shared the song with me, and explained its meaning. Stoney Lake, ON, December 14, 2010.

35. The first line of the song is "Aambe Maajaadaa!," literally "Come On! Let's get going!"

*Source:* Simpson, Leanne Betasamosake. Excerpted from "Nishnaabeg Resurgence: Stories from Within." In *Dancing on Our Turtle's Back: Stories of Nishnaabeg Re-Creation, Resurgence, and a New Emergence* (pp. 11–29). Winnipeg, MB: ARP Books, 2011.

# CHAPTER 36

## The Braiding Histories Stories

*Susan D. Dion and Michael R. Dion*

Susan Dion is an Indigenous scholar (Potawatami/Lenape) and associate professor in the Faculty of Education at York University in Toronto. Dion works in collaboration with the Toronto District School Board Aboriginal Education Centre on research and program development. She is widely consulted by diverse community groups, workplaces, and government ministries. Her most well-known book is *Braiding Histories: Learning from Aboriginal Peoples' Experiences and Perspectives*.

Michael Dion is an independent Potawatomi/Lenape researcher and creative writer, as well as a chef and caregiver. He is a co-author of "The Braiding Histories Stories," which is excerpted below.

## INTRODUCTION

*Braiding Histories: Learning from the Life Stories of First Nations People* is the title of a writing project that we have been working on for the past eight years. Michael and I are brother and sister. We are (re)telling the stories of our ancestors in response to the need for 'tellings' that will disrupt the taken for granted way of knowing about First Nations people that we see produced and reproduced in educational sites. Michael and I are of mixed Aboriginal (Leni Lenape/ Potawatami) and non-Aboriginal (Irish/French) ancestry. We are (re)telling the stories of our ancestors while conscious of our pedagogical and political responsibilities. Through our (re)tellings, we hope to contribute to an alternative way of knowing about

First Nations people and the relationship between First Nations people and Canadians, a way of knowing that will engage our readers in a rethinking of their current understanding.

One of the Braiding Histories stories is included in this paper, as well as our reflections on the stories. [...]

## (RE)TELLING AUDREY'S STORY

What we've learned about the theory of enunciation is that there's no enunciation without positionality. You have to position yourself somewhere in order to say anything at all ... the past is not only a position from which to speak, but it is also an absolutely necessary resource in what one has to say. (Hall, 1989, p. 18)

## Reflections on Loss and Respect

In part, our (re)telling project emerged from the desire to understand and explore our position as people of Aboriginal ancestry. Thinking about our project, Michael and I recognize that our need to speak has everything to do with our position, yet there was an uncertainty about that position. In thinking about our ancestry, we found ourselves confronted with the following questions. Can you be Aboriginal if you didn't grow up within an Aboriginal community? If you had no access to Aboriginal languages, to cultural practices, are you still Aboriginal? What does it mean to be Aboriginal and, more specifically, what does it mean to us? Many Aboriginal people in Canada have been denied their community, and so much Aboriginal culture has been destroyed. To a certain extent, being Aboriginal in Canada means living with that loss. How did we live with that loss? What did it mean for our mother and for us? With these questions, we turned to our mother and began our project with her story.

We recognized our mother's story as one of strength, pride, and respect. We learned about loyalty, hard work, and caring from our mother and saw these as elements of the story of Aboriginal people that we wanted to pass on to our readers. In our mother's story, we also saw the opportunity to explore the policy of forced assimilation and its impact on Aboriginal individuals and communities.

This story is about the impact of systemic discrimination on the day-to-day lived experiences of First Nations people. Being poor is not something restricted to Aboriginal people, but the segregation on reserves and the extent of discrimination Aboriginal people have had to endure is something we want our readers to be aware of. In some ways, what we want to express in this story is very subtle and therefore especially difficult to put into words. In the description of home, school, work, relationship, and family, we hope to create a scene of recognition wherein our readers will come to recognize what the loss of Aboriginal language and culture has meant to individuals. This story is not just about loss; it is about a woman being disconnected from her culture and the constant struggle to demonstrate to herself and others the pride that she carries. It is about the desire on the part of her and her children to reconnect with Aboriginal culture and the strength that comes with that.

In its affirmation of beauty, strength, and pride, our mother's story reflects the humanity of Aboriginal people. It also presents her experience of the violence of discrimination and the shame she was made to feel. Engaging with her story and the contradictions of her life, Michael and I and Mom found an understanding of complex family relationships that nurtured old wounds. The story fulfilled a healing role personally and has the potential to contribute to healing on a community level.

The story we tell is of our mother's strength and the discrimination she experienced in Canadian society. We ask readers to consider:

- What does that mean to me?
- What does that mean to my understanding of what it means to be Canadian?
- What does that mean to my understanding of Aboriginal people today?
- How is my experience of being Canadian different from Aboriginal peoples' experience of Canada?
- What is the past that all Canadians are called to reckon with?

In the (re)telling of our mother's story, we recognize a significant risk. The hearing of the story is easily limited to the story of one woman's strength in the face of adversity. Is it possible that our readers will refuse to attend to the source of the adversity and refuse to ask: Why the adversity?

Our (re)telling calls the reader's attention to the context of telling. The motivating question from which the story emerges is: Why didn't Audrey tell? The potential for engaging the question is presented to the readers and readers are called upon to consider: What did she not want to tell? Why did she not want to tell? And (drawing on Aboriginal conceptions of story): Why am I being asked to hear this story? What am I meant to learn from the story? Will our readers recognize that the story is not a request to change what happened in the past but to alter what they know and how they know the past?

*****

## Audrey's Story

At the end of my day, I like listening to Aboriginal flute music. I turn out the electric lights, light a few candles, and sink into my favorite blue chair. It is an old but sturdy chair, re-covered more than once. I can feel the new, soft, velvety material as my hands stroke the arms. I remember, when you children were young, walking into the living room and one of you would immediately jump out of the chair shouting, "Mom's chair, Mom's chair." I give the arm another soft caress and listen to the relaxing, even soothing sounds of the flutes. The music evokes feelings of connection, and I remember.

I was born on March 28, 1930 to Effie and Victor Tobias on the Moravian Town Indian reserve and was named Audrey Angela. I never could figure out why my mother couldn't have put it the other way around. I always hated my odd sounding name. I thought Angela would have been a much better choice. It sounded pretty.

Our house was set back from the dirt road, past a dried out, scruffy lawn. It was a very small, two story, wood frame house. The ground floor was one big open room. There was a table and a wood stove on one side and a bed for my parents and baby sister Elizabeth on the other side. I slept upstairs with my four brothers and sister. There was a curtain dividing the girls' side from the boys' side. In the summer, it was stuffy and hot, but the winters were cold. Lying in bed with my sister, I would try to ignore the cold, but the flimsy shingles rattling in the wind made it hard to sleep. The closest we came to insulation was the newspaper my brothers and I stuffed into the space between the walls and the roof. In the morning, we would struggle, pushing the rickety old beds from one side of the room to the other. Stretching with all our might with fists full of newspaper, we tried to remember where the gusts of wind from the night before had blown in. The floor was just as bad. In the fall, the whole family would work at collecting dirt to pack around the bottom of the house. This banking was supposed to stop the wind from gusting below the floorboards on cold winter days. But no matter how much newspaper and mud we packed in, it was impossible to keep the cold out of that house.

We grew most of our own food in a large vegetable lot out behind the house. In the spring, the ground had to be prepared and the seeds planted. One of my happy childhood memories is playing "Peter Cotton Tail" in the garden during the late summer. When the garden was in full growth, my sister Joan, who always played the part of Mr. McGregor, would try to catch me and my brother Ken sneaking food out of the garden. If she caught us, she would scare us and we would run away. In the fall, the garden was a lot of hard work. We had to pick the vegetables and store them in the 'dug out.' We would be eating the potatoes, carrots, onions, squash, and turnips until just after Christmas when the vegetables would run out, and there was not much to eat. January and February were hungry months. For supper, Mom would cook a pot of macaroni and mix it with a can of tomatoes. At breakfast, we would sit around the table watching her mix flour and water in a big bowl. She would take a wad of the gooey mixture in her hands, roll it into little strings and drop them into a pot of boiling water. I called this stuff "slippery mush." With canned milk and sugar, it was good, but most of the time we had to eat it plain.

There were no jobs on the reserve. My father worked a few months of the year at a sawmill in town, and during the spring, he fished, but there were many months when there was no work. During the winter, I remember Mom was always busy weaving baskets. Dad would go into the bush and cut down a certain kind of tree. Then came the work of preparing the wood for weaving. I remember them cutting and pounding the strips of wood. The strips had to be soaked in the wash tub for a couple of days, and then there was more cutting and splitting. When the strips were the right thickness, Mom and Dad would smooth the edges with sandpaper. Sometimes they would dye the slats to make fancy patterns in the baskets. Grandma taught Mom how to weave when she was little, and Mom taught us. We made laundry baskets, waste paper baskets, and baby cradles. When we had a stack of baskets ready, Mom and Dad would go into town and sell them.

I knew that my family belonged to the Delaware Nation. What I did not know then is that Delaware is the English name given to my father's people. The original name of my father's nation is Leni Lenape. My mother's family belongs to the Potawatami Nation, and she was from the nearby reserve on Walpole Island. I can picture my father and his friends sitting by the wood stove singing in the Lenape language, but I never learned to speak Lenape. My father went to residential school, and when he became a parent, he believed that it was best for his children not to know their own language and culture. He said that we needed to know the ways of the white community. My two older brothers went to the residential school at Muncey Town. Thankfully, by the time I was ready for school, the residential school had been closed down. We went to a small school on the reserve where the Anglican minister was the teacher. He was very strict and did not hesitate to use the strap. He taught us about the Europeans who discovered and conquered the Americas. We read stories about the white settlers who came and built a country out of nothing. The teacher and the lessons made us feel like nothing, as

though we were nothing until the settlers arrived. It wasn't true. We had our own good way of living before the Europeans arrived. We knew how to take care of ourselves.

I was nine years old when I first moved off the reserve. Just after WWII began, my father and brother joined the army and were stationed in Petawawa. My mother took the rest of us kids and moved to a small town near Hamilton so that we would be closer to Dad and my brother Albert. There was work for Aboriginal people doing manual labour on the farms in the area. Mom went to work on one of the farms, and we kids went to a school in the town of Aldershot. The teachers at this school were not quite as bad as the minister on the reserve, but still we were made to feel that because we were Indians we were not as good as the white children. The white families owned the farms our parents worked on, and the tone of the teachers' voices let us know where we belonged on the social ladder.

When my father and brother joined the army, our whole family became enfranchised. This meant that legally we became Canadian citizens. Mom and Dad were eligible to vote, but we lost our Indian status and all treaty rights. At one point, before the war had ended, we moved back to the reserve but stayed less than a year. As non-status Indians, we were not entitled to a house. We lived with Grandma for a while, but we really needed a house of our own. We moved back to Aldershot, and when I was nineteen years old, I left home and moved to Hamilton where I looked for work as a waitress.

After my family was enfranchised, I believed that I was no longer Indian. But being Indian was not something I could put on and off like a pair of shoes. Even if the government of Canada no longer considered me Indian, the people I met in my day-to-day life were not willing to let me forget that I was. In those days, there were places I could look for a job and other places I could not even consider applying. There were stores and restaurants I could go into, but there were many where I would not even think of going. Signs in store front windows read, "No Indians Allowed," and in other places, a look of disgust from the clerks was enough to send me back out onto the street. I finally found a job as a waitress at a restaurant owned by a Chinese family, and I worked very hard. I was determined to make something of my life. I wanted to be a part of Canadian society; I wanted to fit in. I needed to prove that I was just as good or better than the other people I worked with.

I met your father at the restaurant where I was working. Lindy was a regular customer. He was kind, attractive, and he was white. The waitresses were scheming, trying to match Lindy up with one of their pretty friends. But Lindy often sat in my section, and we would talk and laugh together while I served his food. I thought he was just being friendly. He was not Indian, and I never really believed that he would be interested in me. One night as I approached his table, Lindy stood up and said, "I have something to give you." When I asked, "What?" he kissed me. I think that our fate was sealed with that kiss. We started seeing each other regularly, and before too long, we were married. I remember the Catholic priest who rather reluctantly agreed to marry us. When the brief ceremony was over, he mumbled just loud enough for us to hear, "It'll never last."

But the priest was wrong. It did last. Life was not easy, but Lindy and I loved and supported each other for over fifty years. We lived in Hamilton until 1965 when your dad was offered a better job in a smaller city. We thought the move to a smaller town would be good for us, so in 1965, we moved to Sarnia. In some ways, life in Sarnia was better, but in some ways it was harder. We were the only family of mixed race living in an all white middle-class neighborhood. Some people were very friendly. Remember the couple who lived across the street? You kids always thought they were grouchy, but they always waved and said hello to us. Not like the family who lived up the street. They had two little girls about the same age as you, but those girls were never allowed to play with you.

Looking for a job in Sarnia was horrible. When I went to apply, lots of people just told me to get out. But I needed a job, and I kept on looking. Finally, I got a job driving a coffee truck. It was hard. I felt like I was always working and always tired, but we had a home and a good life. I worked at that job for twelve years and drove a taxi for eight years before I retired.

I grew up at a time when Indians were considered savages who had no culture and nothing of value to offer me or anyone else. I was made to feel that to be successful I had to become a non-Indian. At home, at school, or at church I had no opportunity to learn about Aboriginal culture. I knew nothing about Lenape language, history, and ceremonies. When you and your brothers and sister asked, "What was it like when you were little?" I did not know what to tell you. But you wouldn't be discouraged. You and your brother kept asking questions. On Sunday afternoons while I was in the kitchen baking with you kids at my elbows wanting to stir, pour, and lick the spoon, you two would start again with the questions. My hands were busy stirring, measuring, and pouring but my mind was free to think. Maybe it was the warmth and security in that kitchen, maybe it was the civil rights movement of the sixties and the rise of the National Indian Brotherhood. Whatever it was, while I prepared the cakes, cookies, and pies that you kids would devour, I began to realize that maybe there was something I could tell, that maybe it was important for you to know a little bit about what it was like for me when I was growing up.

It was hard for me, but that was when I began to tell you a few of the stories. When I look at you today, I see a commitment to family, a joy in the telling and hearing of stories, and a deep sense of responsibility to our ancestors. This is a part of our Aboriginal culture that was not lost.

Today, I am a widow and live in Toronto, close to some of my family. Each night, I listen to the music of the flutes, and I know who I am.

\*\*\*\*\*

## CONCLUSION

Writing the *Braiding Histories* stories, Michael and I created a project that provided us with the opportunity to investigate and "learn from" the lived experiences of Aboriginal people. (Re)membering and (re)telling the stories of our ancestors, the project became for us a labour of self-understanding. Through our research and writing, we came to recognize ourselves in relationship with Aboriginal people, and shared our stories in the hope of contributing to a new and just relationship between Aboriginal people and Canadians.

While the stories are for us a source of affirmation and connection, they call attention to a history many Canadians would rather forget. Our (re)tellings were purposefully written with the intention of offering readers an alternative listening position. Turning to Aboriginal conceptions of history and story, reconceptions of cultural representation in the field of anthropology, and conceptions of testimony and witnessing, we began to think about and understand how relationship, attention to detail, and concerns with representing the suffering of others were critical to our project of retelling. Building on the strength of our relationship, Michael and I composed stories that would offer readers the opportunity to recognize themselves as something other than "perfect strangers" in their relationship with Aboriginal people. Sharing detailed stories of the lived experiences of Aboriginal people and their response to colonization, we hoped to initiate a recognition that, as individuals and as Canadians, our readers share a history intertwined with the stories of Aboriginal people. It was our intention to offer stories that would initiate attachment to, and implication in, the stories of colonization, calling for a responsible response.

The work of writing the *Braiding Histories* stories was an important first step that provided the space for exploring loss, celebrating reconnection, and recognizing the possibilities for continued learning from Aboriginal world views and value systems. [...]

In our research and writing process, we often found ourselves confronted with the task of (re)telling from texts written by non-Aboriginal writers. We searched their stories and "found in translation" the strength and humanity that had been subverted by colonization. As Linda Tuhiwai Smith (1999) writes, "colonized peoples have been compelled to define what it means to be human because there is a deep understanding of what it has meant to be considered not fully human, to be *savage*" (p. 26). [...]

Knowing the past helps us to understand the present and create a more just future. The project of (re)telling contributes to our understanding of the need to continue listening and learning from and with Aboriginal people.

## REFERENCES

Hall, Stuart. (1989). Ethnicity: Identity and difference. *Radical America, 23* (4), 9–21.

Smith, L. T. (1999). *Decolonizing Methodologies: Research and Indigenous Peoples.* New York: St. Martin's Press.

*Source:* Dion, Susan D., & Dion, Michael R. (2004). Excerpted from "The Braiding Histories Stories." *Journal of the Canadian Association of Curriculum Studies, 2*(1), 77–100.

# CHAPTER 37

## The Cattle Thief (1894)

*E. Pauline Johnson*

E. Pauline Johnson (Tekahionwake) (1861–1913) was a popular late 19th-century/early 20th-century Canadian writer, poet, and performer. Born at Six Nations of the Grand River First Nation, Ontario, she was the daughter of a Mohawk father and an English mother. Her poems and performances before largely Euro-Canadian audiences highlighted the intersection of her two heritages. Feminist and Indigenous scholars have recently reconsidered Johnson's writings and performance career, re-evaluating her as a complex and contradictory figure who engaged with and resisted dominant ideas about race, gender, Indigenous rights, and Canada.

They were coming across the prairie, they were
  galloping hard and fast;
For the eyes of those desperate riders had sighted
  their man at last—
Sighted him off to Eastward, where the Cree
  encampment lay,
Where the cotton woods fringed the river, miles
  and miles away.
Mistake him? Never! Mistake him? the famous
  Eagle Chief!
That terror to all the settlers, that desperate Cattle
  Thief—
That monstrous, fearless Indian, who lorded it over
  the plain,
Who thieved and raided, and scouted, who rode
  like a hurricane!
But they've tracked him across the prairie; they've
  followed him hard and fast;

For those desperate English settlers have sighted
  their man at last.

Up they wheeled to the tepees, all their British
  blood aflame,
Bent on bullets and bloodshed, bent on bringing
  down their game;
But they searched in vain for the Cattle Thief: that
  lion had left his lair,
And they cursed like a troop of demons—for the
  women alone were there.
"The sneaking Indian coward," they hissed; "he
  hides while yet he can;
He'll come in the night for cattle, but he's scared to
  face a *man*."
"Never!" and up from the cotton woods rang the
  voice of Eagle Chief;
And right out into the open stepped, unarmed, the
  Cattle Thief.

Was that the game they had coveted? Scarce fifty
    years had rolled
Over that fleshless, hungry frame, starved to the
    bone and old;
Over that wrinkled, tawny skin, unfed by the
    warmth of blood.
Over those hungry, hollow eyes that glared for the
    sight of food.

He turned, like a hunted lion: "I know not fear,"
    said he;
And the words outleapt from his shrunken lips in
    the language of the Cree.
"I'll fight you, white-skins, one by one, till I kill
    you *all*," he said;
But the threat was scarcely uttered, ere a dozen
    balls of lead
Whizzed through the air about him like a shower
    of metal rain,
And the gaunt old Indian Cattle Thief dropped
    dead on the open plain.
And that band of cursing settlers gave one
    triumphant yell,
And rushed like a pack of demons on the body that
    writhed and fell.
"Cut the fiend up into inches, throw his carcass on
    the plain;
Let the wolves eat the cursed Indian, he'd have
    treated us the same."
A dozen hands responded, a dozen knives gleamed
    high,
But the first stroke was arrested by a woman's
    strange, wild cry.
And out into the open, with a courage past belief,
She dashed, and spread her blanket o'er the corpse
    of the Cattle Thief;
And the words outleapt from her shrunken lips in
    the language of the Cree,
"If you mean to touch that body, you must cut your
    way through *me*."
And that band of cursing settlers dropped
    backward one by one,

For they knew that an Indian woman roused, was a
    woman to let alone.
And then she raved in a frenzy that they scarcely
    understood,
Raved of the wrongs she had suffered since her
    earliest babyhood:
"Stand back, stand back, you white-skins, touch
    that dead man to your shame;
You have stolen my father's spirit, but his body I
    only claim.
You have killed him, but you shall not dare to touch
    him now he's dead.
You have cursed, and called him a Cattle Thief,
    though you robbed him first of bread—
Robbed him and robbed my people—look there, at
    that shrunken face,
Starved with a hollow hunger, we owe to you and
    your race.
What have you left to us of land, what have you left
    of game,
What have you brought but evil, and curses since
    you came?
How have you paid us for our game? how paid us
    for our land?
By a *book*, to save our souls from the sins you
    brought in your other hand.
Go back with your new religion, we never have
    understood
Your robbing an Indian's *body*, and mocking his *soul*
    with food.
Go back with your new religion, and find—if find
    you can—
The *honest* man you have ever made from out a
    *starving* man.
You say your cattle are not ours, your meat is not
    our meat;
When *you* pay for the land you live in, *we'll* pay for
    the meat we eat.
Give back our land and our country, give back our
    herds of game;
Give back the furs and the forests that were ours
    before you came;

Give back the peace and the plenty. Then come
with your new belief,
And blame, if you dare, the hunger that *drove* him
to be a thief."

*Source:* Johnson, E. Pauline. (1894). "The Cattle Thief."
Reprinted from: http://www.canadianpoetry.ca/
confederation/johnson/white_wampum/the_cattle_
thief.htm.

# CHAPTER 38

## I Am Not Your Princess (1988)

*Chrystos*

Chrystos is a Menominee poet, artist, and activist. She writes on a range of themes, from extremely personal poems that deal with difficult family relations, love, and lust, to political pieces that speak out against the forced invisibility of Indigenous peoples. Her work has been published in numerous anthologies such as *This Bridge Called My Back: Writings by Radical Women of Color* and *Living the Spirit: A Gay American Indian Anthology*.

## PREFACE

Because there are so many myths & misconceptions about Native people, it is important to clarify myself to the reader who does not know me. I was not born on the reservation, but in San Francisco, part of a group called "Urban Indians" by the government. I grew up around Black, Latin, Asian & white people & am shaped by that experience, as well as by what my father taught me. He had been taught to be ashamed & has never spoken our language to me. Much of the fury which erupts from my work is a result of seeing the pain that white culture has caused my father. It continues to give pain to all of us. I am not the "Voice" of Native women, nor representative of Native women in general. I am not a "Spiritual Leader," although many white women have tried to push me into that role. While I am deeply spiritual, to share this with strangers would be a violation. Our rituals, stories & religious practices have been stolen & abused, as has our land. I don't publish work which would encourage this—so you will find no creation myths here. My purpose is to make it as clear & as inescapable as possible, what the actual, material conditions of our lives are. Hunger, infant mortality, forced sterilization, treaty violations, the plague of alcohol & drugs, ridiculous jail terms, denial of civil rights, radiation poisoning, land theft, endless contrived legal battles which drain our wills, corrupt "tribal" governments, harassment & death at the hands of the BIA & FBI are the realities we face. Don't admire what you perceive as our stoicism or spirituality—work for our lives to continue in our own Ways. Despite the books which still appear, even in radical bookstores, we are not Vanishing Americans.

# I AM NOT YOUR PRINCESS

Sandpaper between two cultures which tear
one another apart I'm not
a means by which you can reach spiritual understanding or even
learn to do beadwork
I'm only willing to tell you how to make fry bread
1 cup flour, spoon of salt, spoon of baking powder
Stir   Add milk or water or beer until it holds together
Slap each piece into rounds          Let rest
Fry in hot grease until golden
This is Indian food
only if you know that Indian is a government word
which has nothing to do with our names for ourselves
I won't chant for you
I admit no spirituality to you
I will not sweat with you or ease your guilt with fine turtle tales
I will not wear dancing clothes to read poetry or
explain hardly anything at all
I don't think your attempts to understand us are going to work so
I'd rather you left us in whatever peace we can still
scramble up        after all you continue to do
If you send me one more damn flyer about how to heal myself
for $300 with special feminist counseling
I'll probably set fire to something
If you tell me one more time that I'm wise I'll throw up on you
Look at me
See my confusion         loneliness         fear         worrying about all our
struggles to keep        what little is left for us
Look at my heart         not your fantasies        Please don't ever
again tell me about your Cherokee great-great grandmother
Don't assume I know every other Native Activist
in the world personally        That I even know names of all the tribes
or can pronounce names I've never heard
or that I'm expert at the peyote stitch
If        you ever
again tell me
how strong I am
I'll lay down on the ground & moan so you'll see
at last         my human weakness        like your own
I'm not strong        I'm scraped
I'm blessed with life while so many I've known are dead

I have work to do       dishes to wash       a house to clean
There is no magic
See my simple cracked hands which have washed the same things
you wash       See my eyes dark with fear in a house by myself
late at night       See that to pity me or to adore me
are the same
1 cup flour, spoon of salt, spoon of baking powder, liquid to hold
Remember this is only my recipe       There are many others
Let me rest
here
at least

---

*Source:* Chrystos. Excerpted from "Preface" and "I Am Not Your Princess." (1988). In *Not Vanishing* (pp. 66–67). Vancouver, BC: Press Gang, 1988.

# CHAPTER 39

## "You Can't Change the Indian Act?"

*Shirley Bear with the Tobique Women's Group*

Shirley Bear (Maliseet) is a multimedia artist, writer, activist, and First Nation herbalist and Elder. Born on the Tobique First Nation in New Brunswick, Bear has been a long-time advocate for the rights of Indigenous women, and has played a crucial role in promoting Indigenous arts and artists in Canada. She has served as cultural adviser at the British Columbia Institute of Technology, education adviser at the Emily Carr Institute of Art and Design, and as resident Elder for the First Nations House of Learning at the University of British Columbia.

In Canada, the Indian Act is federal legislation that governs the day-to-day lives of more than 350,000 Aboriginal peoples of whom there are approximately 200,000 residing on "Indian reserves." The Indian Act, legislated in 1869, explicitly defines Canada's original inhabitants, not by blood or familial association, but by marriage. Until 1985, "Indian status" was determined by a patrilineal system: that is, by a person's relationship to "a male person who is a direct descendant in the male line of a male person…." When a woman born of "Indian status" married a non-status man, even a non-status Native or Métis man, she lost her original status and was never able to regain it even if she was divorced or widowed. Along with losing her status, a woman lost her band membership, her property, inheritance, burial, medical, educational, and voting rights on the reserve. However, when a non-status female married a status male, "Indian status" was conferred upon her.

A section of the offending pre-1985 Indian Act reads:

Persons not entitled to be registered

12 (1) The following persons are not entitled to be registered, namely:

(b) a woman who married a person who is not an Indian, unless that woman is subsequently the wife or widow of a person described in section 11.

In June 1985, the Canadian Parliament passed C-31, ending more than 100 years of legislated sexual discrimination against Native Indian women. The passage of legislation to amend the Indian Act marked the culmination of a long campaign by Native women to regain their full Indian status, rights, and identity. This chapter is the story of an extraordinary group of women from Tobique Reserve in New Brunswick who have been in the forefront of that struggle.

These women are uniquely diverse ideologically, psychologically, and functionally. This is a fairly small group of individuals who came together through their awareness of the injustices toward women (in particular, Aboriginal women) in Canada. *Enough Is Enough: Aboriginal Women Speak Out* (1987), compiled and introduced by Janet Silman of Winnipeg, chronicles via a series of personal interviews the events that led up to the now controversial Bill C-31.

My involvement with the Tobique Women's Group started with my activities on the Big Cove Reserve involving the unjust treatment of single mothers and housing. In late 1980, members of the Tobique Women's Group invited me to participate in a meeting of Aboriginal women interested in establishing a political body that would represent the Aboriginal women of New Brunswick. A provincial conference at Fredericton created a reorganized Native Women's Council, which remained a daughter organization of the National Native Indian Women's Association of Canada. The women, whose stories are told in *Enough Is Enough*, grew up on the Tobique Reserve, a community located between the St. John and Tobique rivers in New Brunswick. The community is better known to its residents as Negoot Gook.

In this chapter, I wish to share with the reader my perceptions of who we are and how we developed into "political activists" as we were later known. This will be done in conjunction with excerpts from *Enough Is Enough: Aboriginal Women Speak Out*.

Activism, social or political, starts when one understands that her deprivation of power stems from an injustice toward her. This growing awareness may take many years to develop, as it did for a small group of women from the Tobique Indian Reserve (Negoot Gook).

## EARLY RECOLLECTIONS

Ida Paul is the eldest of the women featured in *Enough Is Enough*. Her earliest memories recount:

> My father was working in the woods where the men would be gone for two or three months in the winter trapping for furs. When my mother died, they couldn't reach him, and when he got back she was already buried. I was four and my sister Lilly was two. Later, my father came back and gave me away to an Indian man and his French wife in Edmundston and Lilly went to a family in Old Town, Maine. We couldn't go to school in the winter time—no shoes. When I was fourteen, my grandmother said to me, "Now that you are fourteen, you have to go out and earn your own living." I'd go from one place to another, staying with different people— for a while here, for a while there. I stayed with Madeline for a time, but her husband would say, "I've got kids of my own to feed. I can't afford to keep you." He went down to McPhail's store (McPhail was the Indian agent and owned the store) and asked him for some money for my keep, but McPhail refused, saying, "No, she's got a father. He has to look after her." I met Frank about that time and married him when I was seventeen.

Lilly Harris, Ida Paul's sister, also remembers the hard times as a child without a home. Lilly, unlike her sister, became actively political with the women of the Tobique. Lilly recalls:

> My mother died when I was two so I stayed with my grandmother and shifted around, sometimes with my older sisters. I went to school till about the fourth grade, but couldn't go to school in winter time—no

shoes. One day, my girl friend's father left the mother and the children. The mother got some help from the Indian agent, so that my little friend got a pair of rubber boots. She told me to go down and ask the Indian agent. She said, "He gave me a pair so I can go to school. You go down and ask him." I went down early in the morning and sat there. I sat there all day while he was seeing everybody else. I asked him, "I can't go to school. I need a pair of rubbers," and he said, "You've got a father. Let him buy you shoes." So after all that, the Indian agent wouldn't give me no shoes. When I was fourteen, I left. It was especially hard for orphaned children and for women who didn't have husbands.

Eva (Gookum) Saulis—Gookum, meaning aunt, is the name she's known by in the whole community—grew up in what she calls good old times. Gookum's mother and father had a small farm on the Tobique Reserve. Gookum recalls:

I had nine brothers in all; I was the only girl. The old times were good for my mother, good for us too. By the time I was born, everybody was Roman Catholic. There must have been Indian celebration days and stories, of course, but the priests were so against anything traditional, I think they tried to break all those traditions. When people say, "The missionaries christianized the Indians," that means that they tried to take their language, their traditions, their legends, everything. When the missionaries came, they told us to bow our heads and pray. When we looked up, our land was gone.

Mavis Goeres grew up on the Tobique Reserve in the 1930s and 1940s and she remembers:

At a very early age, my brother quit school and went out working in the woods with my father. They'd be gone all winter long. I don't remember our family ever having a hard time. We had a lot of fun growing up here. We made our own fun and there wasn't any drinking or drugs involved. When I was fifteen years old, I went away to pick potatoes. I was in the eleventh grade and I met a man and got married.

Juanita Perley was the first woman to actively challenge the Reserve administration by taking over a public building. Juanita recalls some early memories and impressions:

The reserve was a really beautiful place to live, for children growing up especially. When people went shopping, they never got money to buy the groceries; the Indian agent would write up a purchase order at his own store—McPhail's store. They'd be making fun of the Indian people that came in—they called us "gimmes"—like "gimme this," "gimme that." I always resented the way the white people treated us and even today resent it—I don't like them one bit, and I don't care if that is printed in the book either!

Glenna Perley is considered by the Tobique Women's Group to be their strength and sustaining courage and is also very respected within the larger community. Her mother died when she was quite young and she recalls living with her grandmother:

When I was living with my grandmother, she would talk to me a lot about religion—but, even though she was a good Catholic, it was her Indian religion she would talk about. Without the ways my grandmother taught me, maybe I would have turned to drinking, but I know I'm strong and that's why, I guess.

Caroline Ennis has devoted a large portion of her time since 1977 to right the unjust attitudes and practices toward women, in particular toward Aboriginal women in Canada. When Glenna asked her to arrange media coverage of the first housing protest on the Tobique Reserve, Caroline's first recollections are about injustices toward her mother:

I don't remember much about my father but I know my mother left him because he used to drink and beat her up. Tobique was a nice place for kids to grow up in. You made your own fun. I didn't feel poor because everybody else around here was poor too.

In 1977, Sandra Lovelace-Sappier, as a woman who had lost her Indian status through the discriminatory clause, 12 (1)(b), of the Indian Act, agreed to take her case to the United Nations Human Rights Committee. Of her early life, Sandra remembers:

We were really poor because my mom brought us four girls up by herself. At first, we went to school on the reserve. The nuns taught us and we couldn't talk Indian. They used to tell us we were dirty. They made us ashamed we were Indians. After grade six, we went to school down town and there was a lot of "Go back where you came from." The white kids would make fun of us, put us down because we were Indians, so I quit school about grade eight. I figured if this is what the world is like, I don't want to be around white people. I left home at about seventeen, went with a bunch of girls to work at a potato factory in Maine.

Karen Perley, Sandra's sister, is a committed person in community activities. Karen recalls:

I grew up without my father being around. In this little school on the reserve, the nuns used to show preference to the light-skinned kids. I was really religious and I used to pray every morning, every night and sometimes in the afternoon. I would pray that I would wake up the next morning and have blue eyes. In 1966, when Carl and I left for California, I was fifteen.

A child of the sixties, during the "hippie" movement, Bet-te Paul is a single mother of two, by choice. Her commitment to the Aboriginal peoples is definitely radical by any standards. She doesn't recall much about her early life on the reserve.

Joyce (YC) Sappier, Bet-te's mother, grew up with her grandmother and was one of the original occupiers of the public buildings at the Tobique Reserve in 1977.

Cheryl Bear is the youngest member of the Tobique Women's Group, but a seasoned woman activist. Cheryl has a strong sense of her rights as a person. She has lived through very difficult relationships. She says of her early life:

I enjoyed growing up on the reserve—I had a good childhood. I was raised by my grandparents. I was spoiled, I guess, to put it bluntly. I quit school in grade eight. I regret quitting school almost every day now—got married when I was fifteen.

My early memories on the Tobique Reserve include the freedom of movement we had. Children spent much time in creative play without the worries of physical harm. Being a typically dark-skinned person, I also recall the different treatment I received from our grade school teachers, the nuns. Growing up, we all knew that we were different from the time we started school. Some of us were painfully aware that the difference was also something to be ashamed of. We didn't realize that this was in violation of our rights, or that it was wrong for the religious who were our teachers to exercise these types of practices and attitudes. We didn't know what it was called; we just knew that it didn't feel good.

The women grew up experiencing different levels of consciousness, but each one was starting to internalize and intellectualize the various forms of injustices that they were either experiencing or living. From as early as 1950, some women were returning to their original home communities only to realize for the first time that they did not belong. We may have been told previously that we were no longer Indian, but that had no impact on us until our return. I returned in 1960 after a marriage breakup and my father said that they could not afford to feed me and my two children because we were not Indian or even belonged in Tobique. Because there was no employment on the reserve, we were forced to move out.

## THE LAW IS THE LAW

The attitudes at the time that the Tobique Women's Group came together in the early 1970s reflected the subordination of the Aboriginal peoples. The law was the law, i.e., the Indian Act was considered to be the final arbiter of all matters among Aboriginal peoples, and between Aboriginal peoples and government bureaucracy. One exception to this attitude has always been the Six Nations Confederacy, consisting of the Oneida, Tuscarora, Mohawk, Seneca, Cayuga, and Onondaga. They always knew they were sovereign and this has been reflected in their treatment of Six Nations women.

The activism of the Tobique Women's Group was preceded by the actions of other Aboriginal women. Mary Two-Axe Early was the first Aboriginal woman to speak out publicly against the section of the Indian Act that stripped women of their rights if they married non-status men. In the 1950s, after marrying a non-status man, she moved back to the Mohawk Reserve in Quebec that had been her birthplace. She was not refused the right to reside in the community of her birth, since, in accordance with Mohawk culture, the community has always been matrilineal. However, Section 12 (1)(b) did prevent her from having access to financial support; it would also have prevented her from being buried in the community of her birth. In the seventies, other Native women began to organize across Canada, with the offending section of the Indian Act being one of the major issues they raised. In 1973, the Supreme Court of Canada heard the cases of Jeanette Lavell and Yvonne Bedard against Section 12 (1)(b). In a five-to-four decision, the court ruled that the Indian Act was *exempt* from the Canadian Bill of Rights.

Organizations such as the National Indian Brotherhood (formed in the 1950s to represent status Indians, socially and politically) mounted a lobbying campaign against Lavall and Bedard. Their argument was that it was necessary for the Indian Act to be kept intact for use as a bargaining lever with the federal government and that any tampering—such as amending Section 12 (1)(b)—would play into the government's 1969 White Paper plan of doing away with special Indian status and assimilating Indians into the mainstream of Canada. It was against this historical background that the women of Tobique began their activism.

## AN ISSUE OF HOUSING

In 1976, Juanita Perley's husband threw her and their 10 children out of their home and won the legal argument that she had no right to their house. The house was in his name only and only he had any legal right to it. But Juanita, a woman of petite stature, was not going to put up with any nonsense and, more importantly, was not going to see her family be broken up like this and forced to live in the streets. So she occupied a public building. Juanita recounts:

> It was Labour Day weekend when we first got thrown out. When I moved all of the kids

up to the band office, the RCMP showed up. It was the first time here that anyone had occupied a public building. The police said that I was going to be arrested for breaking and entering. He said, "I'm going to charge you with B and E." I replied, "What's that, bacon and eggs?"

When Cheryl Bear's marriage broke down, she was in need of housing so she moved into the next available house and found that it had been destined for someone else—but she remained strong and stayed. Cheryl's grandfather was encouraging and gave her the spiritual strength needed to maintain her decision.

In 1977, Glenna Perley and Gookum Saulis would no longer put up with housing conditions and the unjust treatment toward women and children in Negoot Gook. They organized women to protest against inadequate housing by occupying the Tobique (Negoot Gook) band office. What started out to be an issue of poor housing for women was soon usurped by the media to be an issue of status. One headline in the *Telegraph-Journal* in 1977 read, "Women Occupy Band Office—Want Indian Act Changes."

The women in the book identify in their stories where the change began to take place from the Tobique women's original concerns about housing to the media emphasis on the status issue.

*Caroline Ennis:* "It was status women who were having trouble with housing. When I got involved in the demonstrations and lobbying, it wasn't for the non-status thing; it was purely a women's thing."

*Juanita Perley:* "This business about women getting kicked out of their homes, it goes way back."

*Cheryl Bear:* "See, the woman was supposed to move out with the kids, and it was the man's house."

*Karen recalls her mother's situation:* "My mother had tried to get some help with the house. She said, 'The men are getting helped more than the women are.'"

The women who had lost their status were moving back to the Tobique Reserve after marriage break-ups or becoming widowed, and were experiencing difficulties finding housing for themselves and their children. Four of the women tell about their feelings and sudden awareness of their non-status positions:

*Lilly Harris:* "When we were growing up, nobody talked about status and non-status. When I married I lost my status, but I didn't know it at the time. I didn't find out until I moved back in the mid-1970s."

*Mavis Goeres:* "I find out that white women are Indians now, but I'm not! Here, when I came back, men could kick their wife and children out because the Indian Act made the man sole owner of the house."

*Joyce Sappier:* "No, I never knew I'd lost it because I didn't sell my rights."

*Sandra Lovelace-Sappier:* "I had gone to the band office before and asked for a house for myself and my child. I'd had to pitch a tent because I couldn't find a place to stay. They'd told me I had no rights, that I was non-status. That was when Dan and Caroline Ennis approached me about taking my case to the United Nations."

## The Occupation of the Band Office

In late August, women from the Tobique Reserve demonstrated in front of the band office over housing. A demonstration was also staged in front of the Indian Affairs office in Fredericton, NB. At the end of August, women of the Tobique began to occupy the band office.

There were frightening instances of verbal and physical harassment toward the women who were protesting, and their children. Some members of the Tobique Reserve took the women's action as a personal affront against them and their chief and his supporters; this resulted in a counterattack. In early September, the women were served with an injunction from the chief and council ordering them out of the band office, but they disregarded it. In mid-September, the band administration moved all of their equipment and files out of the band office, but the women remained. An election was called on October 3, 1977, and a new chief was declared who supported the women's issue. (Unfortunately, he was pressured to resign within a year.) On October 4, 1977, fire was set to the band office. Fortunately, no one was hurt and the women started to move out gradually, although there had been no adequate resolution to the question of adequate housing. The women recall experiences related to the occupation:

*Bet-te:* "We didn't really move in; we were just going to sit there until we got a meeting with the chief and council. That's actually how the occupation got started."

*Glenna:* "Really, we went in mainly to try and talk to the chief."

*Karen:* "The chief treated us like we were invisible, like he couldn't see us. A lot of reserve residents cooked meals and sent them over."

*Glenna:* "Then they wanted to put us in jail."

*Caroline:* "The situation got more volatile as the occupation continued."

*Bet-te:* "We were, 'the shit disturbers, radicals, white-washed, women's lib' ... we were just women who needed decent homes."

*Joyce:* "I got evicted because I believed so strongly in what the women were fighting for."

*Bet-te:* "That's around the time the violence really started. The occupation wasn't only hard on us; it was hard on the other reserve residents, too. When it really got bad, we had guns in the band office."

*Glenna:* "In interviews (during the occupation), that's when I realized non-status was the main problem I was talking about."

The women discussed the actual violence that they and their children experienced during the three-month occupation. All the while, they sought help from other political organizations and received very little response from the Native Indian groups or from the Department of Indian Affairs. The main help came from some reserve residents, namely the elders, and non-Indian women's groups.

On December 29, 1977, Sandra Lovelace (Sappier) filed a complaint against Canada with the United Nations Human Rights Committee in Geneva, Switzerland. For the next four years, the main focus was on the discriminatory clause, Section 12 (1)(b), of the Indian Act, which dictates a Native woman's loss of Indian status should she marry a non-status man. And, in 1981, the United Nations Human Rights Committee found Canada in breach of the International Covenant on Civil and Political Rights over sexual discrimination.

## THE 100-MILE WALK

In the meantime, the women never let up on the lobbying momentum. The housing problem did not lessen because the band administration had gone through more changes, only to find itself with the same leadership that had precipitated the original band office occupations. But by now the women were aware of the power of the political lobby outside of their own community.

In July 1979, the women who had occupied the Tobique band office saw that the situation was not getting any better, so they decided to organize a 100-mile walk from Oka, Quebec (outskirts of Montreal), to Ottawa. This walk by women and children attracted national attention. Native peoples from British Columbia, the Yukon, Northwest Territories, Ontario, and Quebec joined the 100-mile march. During the walk, the participants became more vocal about the non-status issue. Sandra Lovelace, who participated in the walk, gave a number of interviews to the press, and the issue of the discriminatory Indian Act Clause 12 (1)(b) received cross-country coverage to the exclusion of the many other concerns of the walkers. The issues that had inspired the walk were not restricted to the sexual discrimination of 12 (1)(b), but included living conditions on the reserves, housing, and distribution of resources. The walk received so much attention that government officials had to take notice and start addressing the issues that the women were talking about. The number of walkers grew from 50 to more than 200 by the time they reached Parliament Hill in Ottawa. Publicity from the walk precipitated a meeting with Prime Minister Joe Clark, his wife Maureen McTeer, and a number of Cabinet ministers. The women were assured that the government would be making moves to change the Indian Act. Some of the women described their feelings as they made the historic 100-mile walk to Ottawa:

*Caroline:* "We wanted to raise public consciousness about Native women's problems, and mainly the walk was over housing. I know the RCMP kept an eye on us during the walk, too, … but really, what threat could we be to the country anyway?"

*Sandra:* "When we started out on the walk, getting on the bus here on the reserve, you should have seen the men. They were standing outside laughing at us, saying, 'You fools, what are you going to accomplish?'"

*Lilly:* "Oh, it was hot, but most people walked all of the way. I was 62 when we made the walk. I think I was the oldest walker."

*Caroline:* "I'll never forget that hectic first morning at breakfast. We filled the whole restaurant. We had thought we could stay overnight at the Catholic school or some kind of retreat house where they had all kinds of room, but the priest wouldn't let us. We got denied help from the Catholic priests along the route."

*Glenna:* "When we passed this one reserve, people had sandwiches for us. They knew we would be walking by there around noon hour, so all these women got together and had lunches out along the road. I'll never forget that."

*Karen:* "We had meetings and meetings. Walking during the day and meetings at night. We'd have meetings to decide whether we should have a meeting."

*Caroline:* "We got more and more media coverage as we went along."

*Karen:* "We told people a lot about housing, of course. Then reporters started asking Sandra about 12 (1)(b) and sexual discrimination in the Indian Act."

*Sandra:* "It all happened on the walk."

*Karen:* "The last day of the walk before arriving in Ottawa, the women from the NIB (National Indian Brotherhood) offices came and joined us. They were all in their high heels, fancy clothes, the kind of fancy tee-shirts the NIB used to give out, nail polish on their fingers. And here we were, grubby and sweaty."

*Sandra:* "We really didn't think anybody would listen to us, or that we would accomplish anything. Just getting there was emotional."

*Lilly:* "There was a big rally when we got to Parliament Hill, speeches, television cameras. People had hot dogs and hamburgers, cold drinks for us."

*Gookum:* "I looked back to see all them women come walking up. They looked so determined."

*Bet-te:* "I got chills seeing that."

*Gookum:* "I felt like crying."

*Karen:* "Oh jeez, it was so emotional—tears coming down our eyes, crying. I hadn't realized that we had made such an impact, but we did. I'd thought, here we are walking all this way and nobody cares, but they did!"

The positive outcomes of the walk were that $300,000 extra housing money was allotted to Tobique Reserve, and the Native Women's Association of Canada received a major increase in funding. But the women had to continue their lobbying after the walk. Unfortunately, Joe Clark's Conservative government was defeated shortly after the walk by the Liberal government of Pierre Trudeau, and no action was taken to change the Indian Act. The Tobique women believe that at no point during Trudeau's term of office did he show any interest in the plight of Native women or a willingness to consider changes in the Indian Act.

The women had continuing problems when they returned to the reserve. Only a fraction of the $300,000 allotted for housing as a result of the Walk was used for housing for single women and their children. Women in desperate need of housing were not getting it and women were still having difficulty getting the other material resources they needed to survive. In spite of efforts to directly pressure the band administration, and another brief occupation of the band office, only token gestures were made by the band council to meet women's needs.

## LOBBYING TO CHANGE THE INDIAN ACT

Taking the case of non-status women to the United Nations had initially been a strategy to put pressure on the Canadian government in order to make officials address the concerns Native women were raising. The Tobique women's strategy of going to the United Nations did exert tremendous pressure on the federal government to change the Indian Act.

On December 29, 1977, the complaint of Sandra Lovelace against the Canadian government was communicated to the Human Rights Committee in Geneva, Switzerland. Because of delays by the Canadian government in responding to the Human Rights Committee's request for information, the final verdict was not made until July 30, 1981. The UN Human Rights Committee ruled in Sandra Lovelace's favour, finding Canada in breach of the International Covenant because the Indian Act denied Sandra the legal right to live in the community of her birth.

The final ruling put additional pressure on the federal government to amend the Indian Act by "embarrassing" Canada—tarnishing the country's image—in the international community. Although the lobbying campaign to amend 12 (1)(b) of the

Indian Act seemed on the verge of victory, four more years of concentrated lobbying actually were necessary. During those subsequent years, Tobique women became seasoned lobbyists with an issue that had become a "political football."

The women became involved in a variety of activities that allowed them to exert influence. For example, Sandra Lovelace attended the 1981 UN Convention as a Canadian delegate, where she spoke about the condition of Indian women in Canada. Caroline Ennis became a member of NAC, where her activities strengthened the support of NAC and its member women's groups for the Native women's cause.

My appointment to the New Brunswick Advisory Council on the Status of Women gave us the influence we needed on the provincial level. It also enabled us to take active participation at the five annual First Ministers' conferences on constitutional Aboriginal matters because the Province of New Brunswick was willing to assert support on sexual equality.

The Tobique Women's Group has always supported that we, as Aboriginal peoples, should hold a special status in Canada, but we did not wish to see it entrenched in the Canadian Constitution, which was repatriated in 1982 without any guarantee that it would apply equally to men and women. It is necessary for this to happen as there is already evidence of continuing discriminatory treatment toward women. It is necessary to have some judicial recourse because Indians negotiating for self-government for Indian communities are making their own membership laws. The same sexual discrimination will happen as in the case of Sandra Lovelace, where women will be denied residence in their mother's and grandmother's birthplaces.

The lobbying continued with the development of a pamphlet identifying the offending law and explaining in detail how it affected women in Indian communities for more than 100 years. This is when I became totally committed and involved. It took several political lobbying trips to Ottawa and several more conferences to inform the people of Canada that this offending law had to be eliminated.

## REINSTATEMENT

By 1985, when Canada passed legislation to eliminate sexual discrimination from the Indian Act, the women of Tobique had seen how their power was being evidenced within the community. In 1982, it was largely their efforts that finally changed the band administration, by electing a chief who understood the issue of sexual discrimination, and who had given his assurance to change similar practices within his administration. The women started seeing a better situation for themselves. When the Indian Act changes came about through Bill C-31, the Tobique Reserve was ready and they hired women who had been in the lobby to change the Indian Act to develop policies to implement the new law.

The first thing was to reinstate to band membership of the Tobique Band all the women who had lost their status through 12 (1)(b) and subsequently all the first-generation children.

There was never any fear that we could not accommodate at the Tobique Reserve the number of people being reinstated, or what it would mean in terms of the services we would have to provide. Public statements accompanying the information on Bill C-31 were explicit in their assurances that the Indian reserves would not suffer any hardships from the possible influx of reinstated band members. The impact of Bill C-31 on the Tobique Reserve does not follow the same pattern as most other Indian reserves.

By the time the government was trying to determine how much money would be allocated for services to the total population increases, the Tobique Reserve already had a large number of non-status residents who were receiving health and welfare benefits. There were also a small number of people receiving education benefits. Concerning the Tobique Reserve, the Indian Affairs department of the federal government assessed the number of people reinstated against the total required increase of funds, but the actual funding that finally came through was inadequate.

Furthermore, the increase in residency was higher than we anticipated because Tobique had an open-door policy for reinstatement. The Tobique Women's Group would never regress in their political demands and activities. We addressed the injustices and demanded retribution. The issues that we lobbied for were rectified and we celebrated.

The comic but sad situation that has developed and is causing such confusion within our communities arises from the fact that the policy developers of the Canadian government, along with the intervention of Aboriginal political representatives, produced a compromising Bill C-31. The Tobique Women's Group specifically addressed the reinstatement of the offended women and their first-generation children. We did not lobby for the war veterans who had lost their status, nor for people who, for other reasons, wanted to enter the Canadian mainstream system. Confusion developed when other lobbying groups saw the momentum we created and insisted on being heard. The resulting Bill C-31 is a weak attempt by the government to appease all factions.

The underlying currents of dissatisfaction toward Indian community leaders because they cannot meet the demand for proper and satisfying services to every band member are causing an unhealthy social and psychological backlash in the communities.

Some of the following problems are causing hardships:

- The federal government has not lived up to its promised financial support.
- There is an existing housing shortage.
- Indian Act policies do not allow for an economic foundation to flourish and encourage a comfortable economic growth.
- The higher standards of education demanded by residents of the reserve are not being realized as a result of cutbacks and, in some instances, denials.
- Population has increased by 33 percent resulting from reinstatements.

It's a constant day-to-day negotiation between the reserve administration officers and the Department of Indian Affairs bureaucracy just to make sure that band members on the Tobique Reserve are not hungry, cold, or uneducated. Misinterpretations of the bill are delaying real progress. Too much energy is being wasted on this process. To the Tobique Women's Group, Bill C-31 meant only the beginning of a real growth of our community.

Many of the women whom we grew up with have returned, either alone, widowed, divorced, or with their retired husbands. In some cases, their children have decided to return and make their lives at their mother's birthplace. In any case, each person who has returned has brought a new viewpoint, a new energy, and a new confidence and pride in who he or she is. The grandmothers of this community express the joy that they feel for the return of their daughters who, through no fault of their own, were treated with such disrespect under and over the Canadian law. The book *Enough Is Enough: Aboriginal Women Speak Out* is about struggles; it's about lives and the political progression of this small group of very brave women who cared—and still care—as they continue to be involved in the community.

As of this writing, two of the women—Ida Paul and Lilly Harris—have since passed away. They encouraged us with their humour, common sense, and total support through the arduous journeys to Ottawa, fundraising, and the battles with band administrations. They are fondly remembered by the group and will continue to remain in our memories through these personal accounts.

The impact of Bill C-31 is being felt throughout Canada in different ways. In 1987, the federal government issued a report on the impact of Bill C-31 that did not involve input by the First Nations. After extensive lobbying from the three national political groups—the Assembly of First Nations, the Native Indian Women's Association of Canada, and the Native Council of Canada—an inquiry was developed that established consultation between these three groups and the federal government. The first phase has been realized, and some of the points that have been identified in presentations to the inquiry are the following:

- Bill C-31 has not improved the lives of Indian people, but has simply created more problems, tensions, and splits in communities.
- DIAND registration process has caused hardship for registrants.
- Many off-reserve registrants believe that all Indians should enjoy the same rights despite their place of residence.
- Insufficient information has been provided regarding the registration process and there is a lack of consistency in processing applications.
- Many registrants indicated that, once registered, they are given no further information as to eligibility for services, etc.... Regional organizations felt that they should receive funding to address this informational need of reinstated people.
- Presenters from bands and tribal councils felt that the federal government has not lived up to its promise to implement Bill C-31 with adequate lands and resources.
- Band and tribal council presenters indicated an increased pressure on program and service delivery coupled with inadequate resources to meet higher demands for these programs and services.
- Band and tribal councils noted that band staff and councils are not receiving adequate resources to deal with the range of issues brought forward by Bill C-31.
- Some presenters argued that the social, political, and cultural fabric of First Nations communities have been weakened by Bill C-31, while others felt that Bill C-31 has strengthened the community fabric.
- Organizations stated that, despite Bill C-31, discrimination continues to exist.

This, of course, is only a summary of the positions put forward to date. [...]

The realities of reserve life still reflect colonial influences. The Indian Act perpetuates those attitudes. This is a document that requires massive revision. It does not protect or enhance our original cultures.

Our land base is painfully small and meagrely supports its residents. Some of our reserves have to accommodate 180 families, a school, a church, and possibly a small administration office on a piece of land that is equivalent to the size of a farm in Quebec or Ontario, and definitely smaller than any farm in Saskatchewan.

As it stands, the Indian Act restricts individuals from using their land deeds for collateral for funding purposes, so this restricts individual initiatives in business.

The schooling that our people receive contradicts the philosophies that we are taught at home. When we attempt to form meaningful co-operatives, our Canadian-American-European learned standards get in the way and confuse our innate ideologies.

Self-government is a phrase that sounds like a fairy tale when you face the reality of the Indian Act. It can be changed, however. The Tobique Women's Group influenced changes. We hope that the First Nations of Canada will also take a real look at the situation the Original People are in as we enter our 600th year under colonialism.

We can do something about this situation.

We can change the world.

---

*Source:* Shirley Bear with the Tobique Women's Group. (1991). Excerpted from "You Can't Change the Indian Act?" In Jeri Dawn White & Janice L. Ristock (Eds.), *Women and Social Change: Feminist Activism in Canada* (pp. 198–220). Toronto, ON: James Lorimer.

# CHAPTER 40

## The Eagle Has Landed: Native Women, Leadership, and Community Development

*Sylvia Maracle*

Sylvia Maracle is a Mohawk Elder from the Tyendinaga Mohawk Territory who has worked extensively as a community organizer at the provincial and national levels. Recognized as a primary shaper of culture-based management principles, she has served as the executive director of the Ontario Federation of Indian Friendship Centres (OFIFC), vice president of the National Association of Friendship Centres (NAFC), president of the Native Women's Resource Centre (NWRC), and as a founding member of the Indigenous Studies PhD Council at Trent University. She lectures and writes about a range of topics, including urban development, women's issues, education, health, and wellness, the role of women in Indigenous self-government, and the cultural revitalization of Indigenous peoples. Recently, Maracle was named an Officer of the Order of Canada.

When I was a student in the early 1970s, a special teacher came to the Native Canadian Centre of Toronto. I will never forget what he said. Hopi Elder Thomas Banyaca shared a prophecy with us that day that I have since seen come alive. He came to tell us about the future of the Indigenous peoples of the Americas. In one powerful statement he made, he said that when the eagle landed on the Moon, the people would recover. Elder Banyaca's statement came directly from the Hopi prophecies. We were all astonished—the Apollo program had just landed its lunar module the *Eagle* on the Moon in 1969. The statement, "The *Eagle* has landed," thus foreshadowed major change in our communities.

In my lifetime, we have moved from people with crippling problems to communities that are slowly healing and reshaping our future. I have witnessed tremendous community development over the last thirty-five years, and much of it has been led by women. In this essay, I want to explore some of the ways in which urban Aboriginal women have developed the institutions that have helped to bring our people together to heal.

# BIRTH OF THE ABORIGINAL HEALING MOVEMENT

Thirty-five years ago, Aboriginal communities were struggling with rampant addictions, low education levels, poor housing, few employment opportunities and numerous family stresses. We had people whose lives had been profoundly scarred by the violence of residential school, training schools, adoption and other child and family service interventions, people who were apologetic for who they were. We had internalized the many forms of violence we experienced with colonization and had learned to express it laterally, against one another. Internalized colonization also meant we were not able to appreciate the value of our cultures or to see their application as vibrant and vital forms of community development. As communities, we lacked cohesiveness. We needed a vision.

Since that time, I have seen Native peoples make remarkable changes as they began the powerful movement towards cultural revitalization. Native peoples have taken up the consuming desire to ask the questions "Who am I? Where have I come from? Where am I going? What are my responsibilities?" I believe that Aboriginal women were the first ones to wake up to this process, and the first to take up their responsibilities.

I recall attending a conference entitled "Rève-Toi!" (Wake up!) that was hosted by the Quebec Native Women's Association in the early 1970s. I remember watching women wake up to the call and begin to see what it was they wanted. Whether their vision was a Friendship Centre, a Native women's centre, a shelter or a dance troupe, they were willing to work for it. In doing so, they encouraged the painters and craftspeople, the dreamers and the teachers and the clans to recover their vision and culture. This took place in urban and rural settings, but many Native women had moved into urban centres by the 1970s.

It's important to consider why so many Aboriginal women found themselves in urban settings. First Nations women may have come because they weren't

part of families that were popular. A number of Aboriginal women were victimized by the violence in their communities and were therefore forced to leave. Some had to leave when they married out and found themselves disenfranchised of their Indian status and band membership. Others left because they were not able to live with the very aggressive application of band policies that marginalized them as women in their communities, for example, in housing. There were also women who came to urban centres so their children could be educated. Many Métis and other non-status Aboriginal women came from communities that were never provided with a land base and were dispersed into the cities. For all of these reasons and more, Aboriginal women were forced to leave their communities, but they took their identities with them, as women, as clans, as Nations. And so, even though so many had no choice but to become urban, and some endured terrible experiences in the process, the creativity of these women turned hardship into opportunity. They knew that their families needed places to belong in urban settings as Native people, and so they created the very organizations that could help address their survival.

The beginnings of most of these organizations were very humble. No sooner were Native women established in urban settings than they would offer their homes for hospitality and even shelter for newcomers. From there, small gathering places were set up informally in somebody's garage or in a church basement. These places, funded by bake sales and the proceeds from selling beadwork or raffling quilts, and surviving on the volunteer work of community women, gradually grew into the first Friendship Centres. Sometimes Native women did it alone, and sometimes these centres were created through networks with other non-profit community groups or government agencies.

Their services started with tea and talk, and ultimately grew into sophisticated counselling and referral agencies. They gradually grew into the role of community development centres, attracting other

Native women who were able to envision, and ultimately create, community-based agencies to look at specific needs in the areas of housing, employment and addictions treatment, to name a few. Many women provided important economic support to themselves and their families as they began to earn salaries in Aboriginal community organizations. These emerging organizations were symbols of pride in our communities. Out of nothing but a dream, an idea, hard work and the creativity of community women, they became our social safety nets, cultural education centres and agents of change.

There is no evidence that the women who were involved in creating the early Friendship Centres ever thought that they would become social planning bodies, or social justice centres or house discussions about self-determination and self-governance. The women did not set out specifically to do these things, yet all of the actions we undertake today are the results of that early organizing and volunteering. Furthermore, women usually developed these community groups and organizations to support the well-being of the community before they undertook to develop community resources for themselves. It was not until the mid-1970s that organizations specifically for the support of women were developed.

## WOMEN'S CREATIVITY AND LEADERSHIP

In our communities, there are people who have titles and there are people who are leaders. These are not necessarily the same people. Our leaders are not necessarily the ones who have taken on a title. Natural leaders are the ones who seem to get things done. They have a healthy vision, possess knowledge, are passionately committed and have a personal leadership style that promotes action. Early on in our development, it was these natural leaders who worked to change our communities, and these leaders were, in overwhelming numbers, women.

While all this community development was happening, I saw the men rushing to keep up. They were our leaders in the formal sense, but they were running to catch up to their people. Many were not necessarily as healthy as their people yet. We know that a large percentage of our people have been affected by addictions, residential school trauma, criminal justice contact, violence and racism. All of these contributed to our generally unhealthy communities. Many who had been appointed our leaders at the time came from these roots as well, and many tried to lay claim to the work that the women had done.

Why was it primarily men who were occupying formal positions of leadership? When the treaty parties came to us, the Europeans didn't bring their women. In turn, they didn't want to deal with the women who were the leaders of our families, clans, communities and Nations. Colonial government policies and laws, including the *Indian Act*, reinforced political practices that excluded women. This interference ensured that only men carried titles like chief, band councillor and band administrator until very recently. In following these *Indian Act* practices over the past century, we have internalized the belief that those who carry these titles are the natural leaders of our communities. Many of us know that this is not always true, but public policy and negotiations with government continue to support this system of leadership, and often to the exclusion of women. For these reasons, it has been women who have led the challenge to change discriminatory practices and to look at more responsible leadership processes. I've seen governments prop up systems that governments have always propped up and watched women respond. That kind of advocacy had to occur at the community level where women could build organizations with mandates to challenge the way things were and to create change.

Some of our current notions of leadership were formed during the time that women were totally excluded from politics. Our development as peoples has been characterized by this tension between formal male leadership and informal female leadership, and there have been too few opportunities to recognize and celebrate what our women have done or to explore the distinct qualities of our women's leadership.

How do women approach leadership? Our traditions tell us that we are not the same as men, nor should we try to use the same approaches they use. I learned this lesson from my grandmother on a visit home from university in 1973. My grandmother had never been to school and was curious to know what I was learning. She had some seventy grandchildren and another thirty-two great-grandchildren, and at that point I was the only one who had gone to university. As she was one of the most magnificent people I knew, I wanted to prove that I was worthy of her question. I responded by saying that I was learning about women's liberation. It was the heyday of second-wave feminism and feminism was a hot topic, but my grandmother had no idea what I was talking about. When she asked me to explain what I meant by women's liberation, I replied that women wanted to be equal with their men. It was about equality, I thought. But when my grandfather translated these notions into Mohawk, my grandmother started laughing. She said something in Mohawk, and when I asked my grandfather to translate, he told me that her exact words were "Why would women want to lower themselves to be equal to men?"

I had intended to impress my grandmother with all my worldly knowledge, yet she humbled me with a few words, reminding me of how powerful we are as women and of the great responsibilities we carry for our people. To my grandmother, women were lowered to Mother Earth first, with the responsibility to create and nurture, and she believed it was our responsibility to complete creation. It is inevitable, therefore, that our recovery as peoples would be led by the women. This interaction with my grandmother helped me to understand the role of women in community development.

Real community development involves working hard, for long hours, without real compensation. Our women worked in community development because they were waking up to their responsibilities, and they had the vision. They did the work for the children, their family and the generations to come. They did it because they saw people living in ways that were not acceptable. They did it because many of the cultural teachings encouraged them to do it. Early community development allowed women to express who they were. They may have been driven out of their home community, but they were able to create a sense of community elsewhere, and especially in urban areas, which provided an anonymity and safety that allowed our women to freely express their creativity and vision.

In addition to vision, the early community development also created relationships, working partnerships and opportunities for sharing. I think that in real community development, there is a tendency to share the dream as opposed to the power. This is perhaps one of the fundamental differences between women's and men's approaches to community development. I have come to believe that it is not the power that is the ultimate end, it is the dream, and that this is the way that Aboriginal women have worked. For example, once these women got these organizations going, they did a remarkable thing as leaders: they let someone else take over. I think that this is a tremendous approach. To hand over one's vision to the next leader, natural or titled, is a very empowering thing. That is not to say that organizations that were the reflection of their leader did not suffer in some way when the founder left. But the fact that most of these founders had the vision to let other women take over attests to the unique leadership styles of Aboriginal women.

As a result of women's participation, I have seen an urban leadership that has become increasingly accountable. It's really hard to not tell your sister, daughter, aunt, mother or best friend what you are up to. I think it's a lot easier than being elected to formal leadership, where perhaps 30 percent of the community votes by ballot and puts you in power. Whether it was a conscious, long-range thought or a realization of a prophecy, I saw changes in leadership take place and people become more credible. I saw women engaging in more inclusive community-development processes.

Women are now 52 percent of the Aboriginal population, yet we are not 52 percent of the elected leadership of formal Aboriginal political organizations. When I look at urban organizations, I see a better representation of women than what I see among the chiefs, band councillors and leadership in the political organizations. Urban areas have long received more women who have been forced to migrate, and so they have participated in greater numbers in the labour force and in decision-making positions in our urban organizations.

Women's creativity continues to challenge and periodically threaten the processes in some of our organizations today. In the 1970s, Native women referred to the various First Nations organizations as male dominated. Métis and other non-status women have also encountered male domination in their organizations. We now see the establishment of women's secretariats and councils within First Nations and Métis politics as a response to the desire for women's involvement. But whether these will become real expressions of community development and empowerment remains to be seen.

## MOVING ON TO THE FUTURE

In the future, I think we are going to see more women creating partnerships and opportunities for sharing. It will be good to see all those women with all their energies pooled together. And although our initial urban leaders are ageing, many of those women who created the Friendship Centres and the network of other urban Aboriginal organizations are still around. They have provided the leadership today with the seeds to continue community development, and they continue to watch what we do to nurture those seeds and help them grow.

As more Aboriginal women become formal leaders, will we lose sight of those behaviours that encouraged our resiliency, brightness and creativity? Will we become part and parcel of the process that will limit young women's thinking? There wasn't an old guard when we came along, so there was no one to tell us what could or could not be done. At the present moment, I try very hard as part of my responsibility to encourage the next generation.

I worry that, as women leaders, we may have been negligent as mentors. When we were starting out, we benefited from the presence of those natural leaders who took the time to involve us and engage us, while building all of the organizations that they built. Now that we are involved in maintaining, improving, strengthening and expanding these groups, we have found ourselves too busy to mentor. We have to make time to talk with young people, especially young women, and to help them reflect on and analyze the issues that shape our leadership role. The other side of mentoring, however, is that those who want to be mentored have to be patient, ask questions, believe and commit their time and energies.

I think that many young women are again champing at the bit in terms of community development and leadership. Our women continue to be the cutting edge of our development and the voice that challenges our inequity. One way we see them doing this is in challenging some of our cultural practices. For example, there are increasing numbers of young women taking up singing and drumming, even though they are often met with resistance. These are seen historically as activities for our young men, but young women are challenging that cultural norm. The more they are told that it is not appropriate, the more they embrace it.

I think in the future, we will see young women leading our development into a number of new areas. They may already be leading the way in terms of health care, seniors' programming, culture-based education and holistic programming, as well as in entertainment and information technology. And of course it is our younger people, both women and men, who are already showing natural leadership in the arts, literature, and music and dance, through dreaming and creating new visions of being Aboriginal in the twenty-first century.

To foster community development, we need to actively engage our young men in undoing some of the gender stereotypes that they have learned. It is not acceptable in a healing community to encourage young men to drum and learn the teachings and have young women stand back. It is not acceptable in a healing community to organize athletic activities for boys and young men and have the young women stand around and watch. These conditions and experiences will bring forth the next generation of natural leaders, who will challenge the traditions they are given. Our job as adults will be to create safe spaces for both genders to develop, places where they can have conversations about each other in order to understand what they're feeling and thinking.

We continue to be affected and to feel the repercussion of formal political developments. It was, in large part, Indian Affairs policy and legislation that encouraged women to organize as Native women in the 1970s. For a period, there were some common areas of concern for all Aboriginal women. However, as our leadership evolved, so did the issues that they had to confront. While all of us face racism, poverty and loss of land, government legislation controls our realities in such different ways that many of us have questioned whether or not First Nations, Métis and Inuit women share enough similar circumstances that can be dealt with through common approaches. This has led to the same kind of fractionalization within the Aboriginal women's community that we see in the Aboriginal political organizations. We find ourselves having to organize separately according to how Canada has classified us, as First Nations, Métis or Inuit. And yet while we may have to organize in ways that differ from one another, ultimately we continue to face many common experiences as Aboriginal women.

I wonder how much the development of women's committees within the First Nations, Métis and Inuit political organizations will further fractionalize us. It is certainly envisioned as a strength in redirecting and redesigning the organizations as they were developed in the late 1960s and early 1970s. And yet it will take strong leaders to sit and talk about how they feel and to look to a future beyond their grandchildren's grandchildren in a time when all of our organizations are threatened by competition for federal government resources.

Urban women face specific circumstances. First Nations like to say that they represent the interests of their urban members, but they never talk to us or consult with us. The *Corbiere* decision[1] says that we have the right to be involved in the selection of leadership in our home First Nations. In reality, we are tolerated there, but not welcome. Furthermore, chiefs have claimed that they represent their people regardless of residency and without having to consult them. The *Corbiere* decision said yes to more representation and it also said that it was the right of the individual member of a First Nation to access services and professions where and how that individual chose to do so. To invoke our token involvement in the politics of our home communities, or to have our affairs governed exclusively from our home communities, may limit the creativity and the nurturing that has brought us this far. As urban women, we have to consider the impact of this representation on our development.

## FULL CIRCLE

As the numbers of Aboriginal peoples on the healing path increase, there will be questions and challenges about what to do after the healing is completed. We are not used to living life to its fullest, but rather to healing and helping others. We will need to learn how to balance the numerous aspects of life that we juggle: academic and lived experience, traditional culture and new forms of cultural expression, professional and personal life, and nurturing others versus nurturing ourselves.

As I understand it, leaders were traditionally understood to be servants of the people. The next generation will have to integrate this cultural practice into daily organizational behaviour. At the same time, there will be a need for more political savvy. This will mean that leaders will have to be more aware of politics that are both internal and external in order to facilitate community growth and development.

The process of colonization reinforces the divisions that undermine the power of the circle and cause women to distance themselves from one another. This has especially been done through the imposition of the labels *First Nations*, *Métis* and *Inuit*. Our early natural leaders used their collective power and efforts to create community-controlled organizations. Since then, divisiveness has been heightened and has become more pronounced. Increasingly, the fight for the future has become the fight for money. We focus on majority and minority power and use processes learned from the colonizers, not those roles and responsibilities we have learned to carry in our healing journey. These were not the values and practices of those women who created our early community organizations.

Our leaders will need to sit again with the eagle and all of our other teachers to reflect on what is important in our future, define what role they will play, identify shared dreams and then determine how this will be reflected in our organizations and communities. If we recognize and accept this visioning task, we will be much stronger in the next phase of community development.

There is no doubt that Aboriginal women are leading the way in recovering our health as peoples, implementing the prophecies, recreating communities and birthing new dreams. We are now living these responsibilities as formal and natural leaders. And when those original women who are still watching us ask, "What are these women doing with what we started?" we will have to acknowledge that there is still much to be done. There are entirely new challenges still to be met and many young voices still to be developed. With 50 percent of our population under the age of twenty-four and 40 percent under the age of sixteen, there is a huge population of young women coming forward.

I have no doubt that our power will continue. We will answer those original women by recognizing that we borrow from our children. We must commit ourselves to realizing those yet unmet prophecies and to being responsible leaders regardless of the structure of our organizations. We must promise that we will continue to dream. We must show those original women that the eagle has landed and that we have picked up our eagle feathers.

## NOTE

1. The Assembly of First Nations has produced a document on the *Corbiere* decision, which reads: "In *Corbiere*, the Supreme Court of Canada ruled that denying the vote to members because they live off reserve is a form of discrimination. *Corbiere* determined that voting rights could not be discriminatory. By creating this new category of discrimination, many questions were raised about other rights for non-resident members." See "The Corbiere Decision: What It Means for First Nations." *Assembly of First Nations*. Retrieved from: www.afn.ca.

*Source:* Maracle, Sylvia. (2003). "The Eagle Has Landed: Native Women, Leadership, and Community Development." In Kim Anderson & Bonita Lawrence (Eds.), *Strong Women Stories: Native Vision and Community Survival* (pp. 70–80). Toronto, ON: Sumach Press.

# PART 4

## Cultural Representations and Body Politics

Men act and women appear. Men look at women. Women watch themselves
being looked at. This determines not only most relations between men and
women but also the relation of women to themselves.... Thus she turns herself
into an object—and most particularly an object of vision: a sight.
—*John Berger, Ways of Seeing (1972, p. 47)*

Part 4 explores diverse representations of women, men, and gender non-conforming people
in contemporary popular culture, and examines some key issues concerning gendered and
sexed bodies, such as health care and women's health movements, menstruation, sexuality,
reproductive rights and justice, transphobia, violence, and beauty.

### Part 4A: Cultural Representations and the Creation of Desire
In this first section, we examine contemporary consumer culture, focusing on advertising,
music, television, children's animated films, magazines, and social media. We consider how
popular culture contributes to a "postfeminist sensibility." We explore image consumption as
an active, not merely passive, process and encourage students to question how particular
values and assumptions are "naturalized" through popular culture, and how these can
be challenged.

### Part 4B: Regulating Bodies and Desires
We look closely in this section at the social regulation of sexed bodies and sexualities in
contemporary image culture as well as in the all-important contexts of home, school, and
public spaces.

### Part 4C: Beauty Projects: Conformity and Resistance
In this section, we examine historical and contemporary beauty ideals and their gendered and
racialized implications. We look specifically at how feminists have analyzed body modification

projects (including weight loss, eating problems, skin lightening or tanning, and cosmetic surgery) as ways that women seek to conform to cultural ideals as well as resist bodily abjection and social exclusion. We invite students to reflect on "looking relations" and challenge myths surrounding fatness, disability, and aging.

## Part 4D: Politics of Health: From Medicalization to Health Care Reform

Here students are introduced to feminist and Indigenous critiques of the biomedical model of health and Western health care systems; feminist-inspired models of health and women's health movements; and social determinants of health. We consider particular health issues affecting diverse people, and we explore some of the challenges posed for health equity movements and activism in contemporary neo-liberal contexts in North America and around the world.

## Part 4E: Reproductive Rights and Justice

This section encourages a broad understanding of reproductive rights and justice, focusing on specific issues like birth control, abortion, and compulsory sterilization. We introduce students to multiple ways in which women's reproductive rights have been denied or limited historically and in contemporary contexts in North America and other parts of the world. Students also learn about women's active involvement in various reproductive rights and justice movements.

## Part 4F: Gender Violence

This section examines the nature, extent, and forms of gendered violence. We analyze in particular gendered and racialized violence targeting specific groups, including Indigenous women, Black women, and gender and sexual minorities. We expose and challenge common myths and misconceptions, present diverse narratives and analyses of experiences of violence, and examine actions and movements involved in violence prevention.

# Part 4A: Cultural Representations and the Creation of Desire

## SNAPSHOTS & SOUNDWAVES 23

### GENDER PLAY: MARKETING TO GIRLS

*Sharon Lamb, Lyn Mikel Brown, and Peggy Orenstein*

Sharon Lamb is a professor of counseling and school psychology in the College of Education and Human Development, and director of the Mental Health Counseling Program at the University of Massachusetts–Boston. She is a renowned expert on girls, sexuality, and popular culture.

Lyn Mikel Brown is a professor of education at Colby College in Waterville, Maine. She is highly acclaimed for her work on girls' social and psychological development.

Peggy Orenstein is an internationally renowned author, editor, and speaker about issues affecting girls and women. Her book *Cinderella Ate My Daughter: Dispatches from the Front Line of the New Girlie-Girl Culture* (excerpted below) examines the persistent ultra-feminine and hypersexual messaging directed at young girls.

### Sparkle, Sweetie!

- In 2007, we spent a whopping $11.5 billion on clothing for seven- to fourteen-year-olds, up from $10.5 billion in 2004.
- Close to half of six- to nine-year-old girls regularly use lipstick or gloss, presumably with parental approval; the percentage of eight- to twelve-year-olds who regularly use mascara and eyeliner doubled between 2008 and 2010, to 18 and 15 percent, respectively.
- "Tween" girls now spend more than $40 million a month on beauty products. No wonder Nair, the depilatory maker, in 2007 released Nair Pretty, a fruit-scented line designed to make ten-year-olds conscious of their "unwanted" body hair.

*Source:* Orenstein, Peggy. (2011). Excerpted from *Cinderella Ate My Daughter: Dispatches from the Front Lines of the New Girlie-Girl Culture* (p. 82). New York, NY: HarperCollins.

## Written on a Bikini Underwear Set for Sizes 4 and Up

P–perfect

O–off the hook

P–princess

S–stylin'

T–too cool for you

A–angel

R–rockin'

---

*Source:* Lamb, Sharon, & Brown, Lyn Mikel. (2007). Excerpted from *Packaging Girlhood: Rescuing Our Daughters from Marketers' Schemes* (p. 15). New York, NY: St. Martin's Press.

## Toys "R" Us as Alien Culture

A saunter through Toys "R" Us or Wal-Mart will teach you most of what you need to know about kids' toys. Three things will be apparent: (1) boys' toys and girls' toys are in separate aisles; (2) boys' toys are action toys, and girls' are homemaking, nurturing, or fashion toys; (3) boys' toys are red, blue, black, and green, and girls' are pink and purple. The way toys are advertised and sold, you'd think boys and girls came from different planets. The truth of the matter is that if men are from Mars and women are from Venus, it's because they've been educated in the language, customs, and behaviors of these stereotyped pseudo-planets from birth—and a lot of this education has been through toys. [...]

Since we're talking about planets, let's imagine we're aliens sent to Earth to gather information about human beings. We land in the girls' toys section of Toys "R" Us, Wal-Mart, or Target, thinking that what we see represents the people of this planet. Here is what we learn about these supposedly imaginative, industrious, and somewhat volatile earthlings:

- Humans are obsessed with pink.
- Humans nurture everything but especially babies, and they practice with baby dolls.
- Humans must look pretty and fashionable. They must also make everyone else look pretty and fashionable.
- Humans love jewelry and accessories, either to wear or to decorate with.
- Humans love to decorate houses.
- Humans clean, cook, and entertain.
- Wearing the right accessories is critically important.
- Humans shop.
- All humans are queens, brides, princesses, fairies, ballerinas, and mermaids, or they are sexy shopping divas, pop stars, and cheerleaders.
- Humans are really happy about all this.

## Educational Toys

Toys "R" Us isn't for everyone. Although it is a multinational, multiconglomerate corporation with about sixteen hundred stores in twenty-eight countries, there are alternatives. But before you decide to avoid Wal-Mart, Target, and the like, remember that choosing "educational" doesn't always mean choosing gender equity. Our kids love the Discovery Store and other stores like it. It has all sorts of cool science stuff about space, the earth, biology, and technology. But check out the catalog. Below is a list by gender of what kids featured in the catalog are doing. Guess which is the boys' list and which is the girls' list.

**List A**

Helping mother cut flowers with "home florist system"

Eating a snack

Playing indoor golf

Playing with an interactive educational globe

Hanging with Mom

Flying a kite

Watching someone launch a rocket

Getting money from a play ATM machine

Making a pot on a pottery wheel

Watching a kid use a radio-controlled hovercraft

**List B**

Looking through a telescope with Dad

Chasing a radio-controlled jet

Holding the controls of a radio-controlled jet

Playing a football game

Playing basketball

Flying a kite

Launching a rocket

Launching a UFO

Launching an air-powered glider

Using a spy tool off a spy utility belt

Using a metal detector

Wearing a Night Vision Communicator

Using a voice convertor system

Playing with a chemistry set or forensic lab

Looking through a telescope alone

Performing a magic trick

Working a radio-controlled hovercraft

Flying a radio-controlled helicopter

Particularly offensive is the thought that girls' play will involve shopping and could make use of a toy ATM machine. Where's the science and discovery in that? Also offensive is that she is used as a prop to observe and admire the boy working the controls for the radio-controlled hovercraft and launching a rocket. The only gender-neutral toy that the Discovery catalog features is the kite. Don't we want girls to discover the world, too?

*Source:* Lamb, Sharon, & Brown, Lyn Mikel. (2007). Adapted from *Packaging Girlhood: Rescuing Our Daughters from Marketers' Schemes* (pp. 212–214, 220–221). New York, NY: St. Martin's Press.

## WAYS OF SEEING

*John Berger*

John Berger (1926–2017) was a British cultural critic, novelist, poet, screenwriter, and painter. In 1972, during his stint as a BBC correspondent, Berger published *Ways of Seeing* as an accompaniment to a BBC documentary of the same name. Revolutionary for its time, the book engaged with the media theory concept of "the gaze." The theory of the gaze attempts to understand how people see gendered representations in visual culture. Important for feminist media studies, Berger argued that the gaze applies differently to men and women, meaning that men and women appear and are looked at differently. The man is looked at for his power and potency, while the woman is seen as an object to be manipulated, rather than an agent of her own destiny. His actions demonstrate self-mastery and ownership of what he surveys. Her actions show her susceptibility to being looked upon and appraised. This means, Berger argued, that ultimately men and women carry themselves differently in the world. Berger's theory of gendered gaze is elaborated on in the following excerpt from *Ways of Seeing*.

A woman must continually watch herself. She is almost continually accompanied by her own image of herself. Whilst she is walking across a room or whilst she is weeping at the death of her father, she can scarcely avoid envisaging herself walking or weeping. From earliest childhood she has been taught and persuaded to survey herself continually. And so she comes to consider the *surveyor* and the *surveyed* within her as the two constituent yet always distinct elements of her identity as a woman. She has to survey everything she is and everything she does because how she appears to men is of crucial importance for what is normally thought of as the success of her life. Her own sense of being in herself is supplanted by a sense of being appreciated as herself by another. [...]

Every woman's presence regulates what is and is not 'permissible' within her presence. Every one of her actions—whatever its direct purpose or motivation—is also read as an indication of how she would like to be treated. If a woman throws a glass on the floor, this is an example of how she treats her own emotion of anger and so of how she would wish it to be treated by others. If a man does the same, his action is only read as an expression of his anger. If a woman makes a good joke, this is an example of how she treats the joker in herself and accordingly of how she as a joker-woman would like to be treated by others. Only a man can make a good joke for its own sake.

One might simplify this by saying: *men act* and *women appear*. Men look at women. Women watch themselves being looked at. This determines not only most relations between men and women but also the relation of women to themselves. The surveyor of woman in herself is male: the surveyed female. Thus she turns herself into an object—and most particularly an object of vision: a sight.

*Source:* Berger, John. (2008, first published 1972). Excerpted from *Ways of Seeing* (pp. 46–47). London, UK: Penguin. For more information on John Berger and *Ways of Seeing*, check out the original BBC documentary here: www.youtube.com/watch?v=utEoRdSL1jo.

## "EATING THE OTHER": DESIRE AND RESISTANCE

*bell hooks*

bell hooks is a leading feminist theorist and cultural critic, whose work focuses on the interconnectedness of race, gender, culture, and class. The author of over 30 books, she has been recognized by numerous awards, such as The American Book Awards/Before Columbus Foundation Award, the Writer's Award from the Lila Wallace-Reader's Digest Fund, and The Bank Street College Children's Book of the Year. hooks has been named one of the most influential American thinkers by *Publisher's Weekly* and the *Atlantic Monthly*, and one of the world's top 100 visionaries by *Utne Reader*.

The excerpt below comes from a larger chapter in hooks's iconic work *Black Looks: Race and Representation*. In it, hooks discusses why white people are attracted to the culture of the "Other." She refers to the yearning to consume this culture as "eating the Other" and believes that this yearning comes from a sense that white people feel that their own culture lacks excitement and vitality.

Within current debates about race and difference, mass culture is the contemporary location that both publicly declares and perpetuates the idea that there is pleasure to be found in the acknowledgment and enjoyment of racial difference. The commodification of Otherness has been so successful because it is offered as a new delight, more intense, more satisfying than normal ways of doing and feeling. Within commodity culture, ethnicity becomes spice, seasoning that can liven up the dull dish that is mainstream white culture. Cultural taboos around sexuality and desire are transgressed and made explicit as the media bombards folks with a message of difference no longer based on the white supremacist assumption that "blondes have more fun." The "real fun" is to be had by bringing to the surface all those "nasty" unconscious fantasies and longings about contact with the Other embedded in the secret (not so secret) deep structure of white supremacy. [...]

When I began thinking and doing research for this piece, I talked to folks from various locations about whether they thought the focus on race, Otherness, and difference in mass culture was challenging racism. There was overall agreement that the message that acknowledgment and exploration of racial difference can be pleasurable represents a breakthrough, a challenge to white supremacy, to various systems of domination. The over-riding fear is that cultural, ethnic, and racial differences will be continually commodified and offered up as new dishes to enhance the white palate—that the Other will be eaten, consumed, and forgotten. After weeks of debating with one another about the distinction between cultural appropriation and cultural appreciation, students in my introductory course on black literature were convinced that something radical was happening, that these issues were "coming out in the open." Within a context where desire for contact with those who are different or deemed Other is not considered bad, politically incorrect, or wrong-minded, we can begin to conceptualize and identify ways that desire informs our political choices and affiliations. Acknowledging ways the desire for pleasure, and that includes erotic longings, informs our politics, our understanding of difference, we may know better how desire disrupts, subverts, and makes resistance possible. We cannot, however, accept these new images uncritically.

*Source:* hooks, bell. (1992). Excerpted from "Eating the Other: Desire and Resistance." In *Black Looks: Race and Representation* (pp. 21–22, 39). Boston, MA: South End Press.

# CHAPTER 41

## Postfeminist Media Culture: Elements of a Sensibility

*Rosalind Gill*

Rosalind Gill is a professor of cultural and social analysis in the Department of Sociology at City, University of London, in England. Among her many works, she is co-editor of *Aesthetic Labour: Beauty Politics in Neoliberalism*, author of *Gender and the Media*, and has produced two BBC documentaries. Her research focuses on gender and media, cultural and creative work, and mediated intimacy. For the last decade, she has made a significant contribution to debates about the "sexualization of culture."

## INTRODUCTION

The notion of *postfeminism* has become one of the most important and contested terms in feminist cultural analysis. In recent years, debates about everything from the history and exclusions of feminism to the gender consciousness (or otherwise) of young women and the ideological nature of contemporary media have crystallized in disagreements about postfeminism. As with *postmodernism* before it, the term has become overloaded with different meanings. [...]

However, after nearly two decades of argument about postfeminism, there is still no agreement as to what it is and the term is used variously and contradictorily to signal a theoretical position, a type of feminism after the Second Wave or a regressive political stance. Such disagreement would not necessarily be cause for alarm (but might merely be a sign of vibrant debate) were it not for two additional problems: first, the difficulty of specifying with any rigour the features of postfeminism; second, the problem with applying current notions to any particular cultural or media analysis. What makes a text postfeminist? What features need to be present in order for any media scholar to label something as postfeminist? In order to use the term *postfeminism* for analytical purposes, at minimum we need to be able to specify the criteria used to identify something as postfeminist.

To this end, this chapter aims to propose a new understanding of postfeminism which can be used to analyse contemporary cultural products. It seeks to argue that postfeminism is best thought of as a sensibility that characterizes increasing numbers of films, television shows, advertisements and other media products. [...] This piece begins the process of exploring and tentatively explicating the themes or features that characterize this sensibility. To do so, [...] it will engage with examples from a range of different media—from talk shows to lad magazines, and from 'chick lit' to advertising. It hopes to demonstrate the utility of the notion of postfeminism as a sensibility, and to contribute to the task of unpacking postfeminist media culture.

## UNPACKING POSTFEMINIST MEDIA CULTURE

This chapter will argue that postfeminism is understood best [...] as a sensibility. [...] This new notion emphasizes the contradictory nature of postfeminist discourses and the entanglement of both feminist and anti-feminist themes within them. It also points to a number of other relatively stable features that comprise or constitute a postfeminist discourse. These include the notion that femininity is a bodily property; the shift from objectification to subjectification; the emphasis upon self-surveillance, monitoring and discipline; a focus upon individualism, choice and empowerment; the dominance of a makeover paradigm; a resurgence in ideas of natural sexual difference; a marked sexualization of culture; and an emphasis upon consumerism and the commodification of difference. These themes coexist with, and are structured by, stark and continuing inequalities and exclusions that relate to 'race' and ethnicity, class, age, sexuality and disability as well as gender.

## FEMININITY AS A BODILY PROPERTY

One of the most striking aspects of postfeminist media culture is its obsessive preoccupation with the body. In a shift from earlier representational practices, it appears that femininity is defined as a bodily property

rather than a social, structural or psychological one. Instead of regarding caring, nurturing or motherhood as central to femininity (all of course highly problematic and exclusionary), in today's media, possession of a 'sexy body' is presented as women's key (if not sole) source of identity. The body is presented simultaneously as women's source of power and as always unruly, requiring constant monitoring, surveillance, discipline and remodelling (and consumer spending) in order to conform to ever-narrower judgements of female attractiveness.

Indeed, surveillance of women's bodies constitutes perhaps the largest type of media content across all genres and media forms. Women's bodies are evaluated, scrutinized and dissected by women as well as men, and are always at risk of 'failing'. This is most clear in the cultural obsession with celebrity, which plays out almost exclusively over women's bodies. Magazines such as *Heat* offer page after page of big colour photographs of female celebrities' bodies, with scathing comments about anything from armpit hair to visible panty lines, but focusing in particular upon 'fat' and, more recently, censuring women deemed to be too thin. So excessive and punitive is the regulation of women's bodies through this medium that conventionally attractive women can be indicted for having 'fat ankles' or 'laughter lines'. No transgression is seemingly too small to be picked over and picked apart by paparazzi photographers and writers. [...]

Ordinary (non-celebrity) women are not exempt. TV programmes such as *What Not to Wear* and *10 Years Younger* subject women to hostile scrutiny for their bodies, postures and wardrobes, and evaluations including the like of 'very saggy boobs' and 'what a minger'. [...]

Importantly, the female body in postfeminist media culture is constructed as a window to the individual's interior life. For example, in *Bridget Jones's Diary* (Fielding, 1997) when Bridget Jones smokes 40 cigarettes a day or consumes 'excessive' calories, we are invited to read this in psychological terms as indicative of her emotional breakdown. Today, a sleek, toned, controlled figure is normatively essential for portraying success. Yet there is also—contradictorily—an acknowledgement that the body is a canvas affording an image which may have little to do with how one feels inside. For example, after their break-ups with Brad Pitt and Tom Cruise respectively, Jennifer Aniston and Nicole Kidman were heralded across the media as 'triumphant' when they each first appeared in public—meaning that they successfully performed gleaming, commodified beauty and dazzling self-confidence, however hurt or vulnerable they may actually have felt. There was no comparable focus on the men.

## THE SEXUALIZATION OF CULTURE

The intense focus on women's bodies as the site of femininity is closely related to the pervasive sexualization of contemporary culture. Sexualization here refers both to the extraordinary proliferation of discourses about sex and sexuality across all media forms, referred to by Brian McNair (2002) as part of the 'striptease culture', as well as to the increasingly frequent erotic presentation of girls', women's and (to a lesser extent) men's bodies in public spaces. Newspapers' use of rape stories as part of a package of titillating material is well documented, and in the news media all women's bodies are available to be coded sexually, whether they are politicians, foreign correspondents or serious news anchors.

Different forms of sexualization are evident also in popular magazines. In the 'lad mags', sex is discussed through a vocabulary of youthful, unselfconscious pleasure-seeking, while in magazines targeted at teenage girls and young women it is constructed as something requiring constant attention, discipline, self-surveillance and emotional labour. Girls and women are […] responsible for producing themselves as desirable heterosexual subjects as well as pleasing men sexually, protecting against pregnancy and sexually-transmitted infections, defending their own sexual reputations and taking care of men's

self-esteem. Men, by contrast, are hailed as hedonists just wanting 'a shag'. The uneven distribution of these discourses of sex, even in a resolutely heterosexual context, is crucial to understanding sexualization (Gill, 2006; Tincknell et al., 2003). Put simply, in magazines aimed at straight women, men are presented as complex, vulnerable human beings. But in magazines targeted at those same men, women only ever discuss their underwear, sexual fantasies, 'filthiest moments' or body parts (Turner, 2005).

The lad magazines are emblematic of the blurring of the boundaries between pornography and other genres which has occurred in the last decade. 'Porno chic' has become a dominant representational practice in advertising, magazines, internet sites and cable television. Even children's television has adopted a sexualized address to its audience and between its presenters. The commercially-driven nature of this sexualization can be seen in the way that clothing companies target girls as young as five with thongs (G-strings), belly tops and T-shirts bearing sexually provocative slogans, such as 'When I'm bad I'm very, very bad, but when I'm in bed I'm better'. The use of the Playboy bunny icon on clothing, stationery and pencils aimed at the pre-teen market is but one example of the deliberate sexualization of children (girls). The 'girlification' of adult women such as Kylie Minogue and Kate Moss is the flipside of a media culture that promotes female children as its most desirable sexual icons.

## FROM SEX OBJECT TO DESIRING SEXUAL SUBJECT

Where once sexualized representations of women in the media presented them as passive, mute objects of an assumed male gaze, today sexualization works somewhat differently in many domains. Women are not straightforwardly objectified but are presented as active, desiring sexual subjects who choose to present themselves in a seemingly objectified manner because it suits their liberated interests to do so (Goldman, 1992). Nowhere is this clearer than in advertising which has responded to feminist critiques by constructing a new figure to sell to young women: the sexually autonomous heterosexual young woman who plays with her sexual power and is forever 'up for it'.

This shift is crucial to understanding the postfeminist sensibility. It represents a modernization of femininity to include what Hilary Radner has called a new 'technology of sexiness' (Radner, 1999) in which sexual knowledge and practice are central. Furthermore, it represents a shift in the way that power operates: from an external, male judging gaze to a self-policing, narcissistic gaze. It can be argued that this represents a higher or deeper form of exploitation than objectification—one in which the objectifying male gaze is internalized to form a new disciplinary regime. In this regime, power is not imposed from above or the outside, but constructs our very subjectivity. Girls and women are invited to become a particular kind of self, and are endowed with agency on condition that it is used to construct oneself as a subject closely resembling the heterosexual male fantasy found in pornography. [...]

The humorous tone that characterized early examples of this shift—the amusing bra adverts in which billboard models confidently and playfully highlighted their sexual power or traffic-stopping sexiness—should not imply that this shift is not, in fact, profoundly serious and problematic. In the last decade it has gone from being a new and deliberate representational strategy used on women (i.e. for depicting young women) to being widely and popularly taken up by women as a way of constructing the self. [...]

To be critical of the shift is not to be somehow 'anti-sex'—although in postfeminist media culture this position (the prude) is the only alternative discursively allowed (itself part of the problem, eradicating a space for critique). Rather it is to point to the dangers of such representations of women in a culture in which sexual violence is endemic, and to highlight the exclusions of this representational

practice—only *some* women are constructed as active, desiring sexual subjects: women who desire sex with men (except when lesbian women 'perform' for men) and only young, slim and beautiful women. As Myra Macdonald (1995) has pointed out, older women, bigger women, women with wrinkles, etc. are never accorded sexual subjecthood and are still subject to offensive and sometimes vicious representations. Indeed, the figure of the unattractive woman who wants a sexual partner remains one of the most vilified in a range of popular cultural forms. [...]

## INDIVIDUALISM, CHOICE AND EMPOWERMENT

Notions of choice, of 'being oneself' and 'pleasing oneself', are central to the postfeminist sensibility that suffuses contemporary western media culture. They resonate powerfully with the emphasis upon empowerment and taking control that can be seen in talk shows, advertising and makeover shows. A grammar of individualism underpins all these notions—such that even experiences of racism, homophobia or domestic violence are framed in exclusively personal terms in a way that turns the idea of the personal-as-political on its head. Lois McNay (1992) has called this the deliberate 'reprivatization' of issues which have become politicized only relatively recently.

One aspect of this postfeminist sensibility in media culture is the almost total evacuation of notions of politics or cultural influence. This is seen not only in the relentless personalizing tendencies of news, talk shows and reality TV, but also in the ways in which every aspect of life is refracted through the idea of personal choice and self-determination. For example, phenomena such as the dramatic increase in the number of women having Brazilian waxes (to remove pubic hair entirely and reinstate a prepubescent version of their genitalia) or the uptake of breast augmentation surgery by teenage girls are depicted widely as indicators of women 'pleasing themselves' and 'using beauty' to make themselves feel good. Scant attention is paid to the pressures that might lead a teenager to decide that major surgery will solve her problems, and even less to the commercial interests that are underpinning this staggering trend, such as targeted advertising by cosmetic surgery clinics and promotional packages which include mother and daughter special deals and discounts for two friends to have their 'boobs' done at the same time. The notion that all our practices are freely chosen is central to postfeminist discourses, which present women as autonomous agents no longer constrained by any inequalities or power imbalances whatsoever. [...] The shift to the notion that women just 'please themselves' presents women as entirely free agents and cannot explain why—if women are just pleasing themselves and following their own autonomously generated desires—the resulting valued 'look' is so similar—hairless body, slim waist, firm buttocks, etc. Moreover, it simply avoids all the interesting and important questions about the relationship between representations and subjectivity, the difficult but crucial questions about how socially-constructed, mass-mediated ideals of beauty are internalized and made our own.

What is striking is the degree of fit between the autonomous postfeminist subject and the psychological subject demanded by neoliberalism. At the heart of both is the notion of the 'choice biography' and the contemporary injunction to render one's life knowable and meaningful through a narrative of free choice and autonomy, however constrained one actually might be (Rose, 1996; Walkerdine et al., 2001). [...]

In *Bridget Jones's Diary* and in 'chick lit' more generally, achieving desirability in a heterosexual context is explicitly (re-)presented as something done for yourself, not in order to please a man. In this modernized, neoliberal version of femininity, it is absolutely imperative that one's sexual and dating practices be presented as freely chosen (however traditional, old-fashioned or inegalitarian they may be—involving strict adherence to rules, rationing oneself and not displaying any needs). [...]

## SELF-SURVEILLANCE AND DISCIPLINE

Intimately related to the stress upon personal choice is the new emphasis on self-surveillance, self-monitoring and self-discipline in postfeminist media culture. Arguably, monitoring and surveilling the self have long been requirements of the performance of successful femininity—with instruction in grooming, attire, posture, elocution and 'manners' being 'offered' to women to allow them to emulate more closely the upper-class white ideal. In women's magazines, femininity has always been portrayed as contingent—requiring constant anxious attention, work and vigilance, from touching up your make-up to packing the perfect capsule wardrobe, from hiding 'unsightly' pimples, wrinkles, age spots or stains to hosting a successful dinner party. However, what marks out the present moment as distinctive are three features. First, the dramatically increased intensity of self-surveillance, indicating the intensity of the regulation of women (alongside the disavowal of such regulation). Second, the extensiveness of surveillance over entirely new spheres of life and intimate conduct. Third, the focus upon the psychological—the requirement to transform oneself and remodel one's interior life.

Something of the intensity and extensiveness of the self-surveillance and discipline now normatively required of women can be seen in women's magazines in which bodily shape, size, muscle tone, attire, sexual practice, career, home, finances, etc. are rendered into 'problems' that necessitate ongoing and constant monitoring and labour. Yet, in an extraordinary ideological sleight of hand, this labour must be understood nevertheless as 'fun', 'pampering' or 'self-indulgence' and must *never* be disclosed. Magazines offer tips to girls and young women to enable them to continue the work of femininity but still appear as entirely confident, carefree and unconcerned about their self-presentation (as this is now an important aspect of femininity in its own right); for example, the solution to continuing a diet while at an important business lunch where everyone else is drinking is to order a spritzer (and surreptitiously to ask the waiter to make it largely mineral water). [...]

No area of a woman's life is immune from the requirement to self-survey and work on the self. More and more aspects of the body come under surveillance: you thought you were comfortable with your body? Well think again! When was the last time you checked your 'upper arm definition'? Have you been neglecting your armpits or the soles of your feet? Do you sometimes have (ahem) unpleasant odours?

But it is not only the surface of the body that needs ongoing vigilance—there is also the self: what kind of friend/lover/daughter/colleague are you? Do you laugh enough? How well do you communicate? Have you got emotional intelligence? In a culture saturated by individualistic self-help discourses, the self has become a project to be evaluated, advised, disciplined and improved or brought 'into recovery'. However, what is so striking is how unevenly distributed these quasi-therapeutic discourses are. In magazines, contemporary fiction and television talk shows, it is women, not men, who are addressed and required to work on and transform the self. Significantly, it appears that the ideal disciplinary subject of neoliberalism is feminine.

## THE MAKEOVER PARADIGM

More broadly, it might be argued that a makeover paradigm constitutes postfeminist media culture. This requires people (predominantly women) to believe, first, that they or their life is lacking or flawed in some way; second, that it is amenable to reinvention or transformation by following the advice of relationship, design or lifestyle experts and practising appropriately modified consumption habits. Not only is this the implicit message of many magazines, talk shows and other media content, but it is the explicit focus of the 'makeover takeover' (Hollows, 2000) that dominates

contemporary television. It began with food, homes and gardens, but has now extended to clothing, cleanliness, work, dating, sex, cosmetic surgery and raising children. [...]

As Helen Wood and Beverly Skeggs (2004) have argued, the ubiquity of such shows produce 'new ethical selves' in which particular forms of modernized and upgraded selfhood are presented as solutions to the dilemmas of contemporary life. The scenarios are profoundly classed and gendered and, as Angela McRobbie (2004a) points out, racialized too (if largely through exclusion), since the kind of hostile judgments routinely made of white working-class women would risk being heard as racist if made by white experts about black bodies, practices and lives. [...]

McRobbie points to the appalling nastiness and viciousness of the gendered and class animosities enacted, as the audience is encouraged to laugh at those less fortunate. However, in a programme such as *Wife Swap*, in which two married women (usually from dramatically different class backgrounds) swap lives, the orchestrated morality is sometimes more complicated, with middle-class 'career women' the target of attack for devoting too little time or attention to their children (alongside the attacks on working class women's poor food preparation or incompetence at helping with homework, which McRobbie describes). What is clear from even a cursory viewing of such shows is that women simply cannot win; inevitably, they will always 'fail'. But rather than interrogating femininity or social relations, or what we as a society expect of women, the shows offer no way of understanding this other than through the dramatized spectacle of conflict between two women. [...]

## THE REASSERTION OF SEXUAL DIFFERENCE

For a short time in the 1970s and 1980s, notions of male and female equality and the basic similarity of men and women took hold in popular culture, before this was resolutely dispensed with in the 1990s. A key feature of the postfeminist sensibility has been the resurgence of ideas of natural sexual difference across all media from newspapers to advertising, talk shows and popular fiction. One arena in which this played out was the media debate about masculinity, in which the figure of the 'New Man' was attacked by both women and men as asexual and not manly enough. New man was condemned as inauthentic and fake, and understood by many as an act or a pose that had arisen through what was presented as the hegemonic dominance of feminism, but had little to do with what men were actually like. Against this, the rise of the 'New Lad' in the 1990s was widely reported as an assertion of freedom against the stranglehold of feminism and—crucially—as an unashamed celebration of true or authentic masculinity, liberated from the shackles of 'political correctness'. New lad championed and reasserted a version of masculinity as libidinous, powerful and, crucially, different from femininity.

Importantly, these discourses of sexual difference were nourished both by the growing interest in evolutionary psychology, and developments in genetic science which held out the promise of locating a genetic basis for all human characteristics. Such developments, from concern about the existence of a 'gay gene' to attempts to identify the parts of the brain responsible for risk-taking (and to demonstrate that they were larger in men than in women), were accorded a huge amount of coverage in the press and on television, and it is significant that this interest coincided with a moment in which the lifestyle sections of newspapers were expanding and proliferating, filled in large part by articles focusing on the nature of gender and gender relations (see Gill, 2006).

In addition, notions of sexual difference were fed by the explosion of self-help literature which addressed—at least as its subtext—the question of why the 'battle of the sexes' continued despite (or, in some iterations, because of) feminism. One answer rang out loud and clearly from many texts: because men and women are fundamentally different.

Feminism was deemed to have lost its way when it tried to impose its ideological prescriptions on a nature that did not fit; what was needed, such literature argued, was a frank acknowledgement of difference rather than its denial. Spearheading the movement (or at least the publishing phenomenon) was John Gray, whose 'Mars and Venus' text (2002) soon became a whole industry. Gray's genius was in locating sexual difference as a psychological rather than essentially biological matter, and transposing old and cliched notions through the new and fresh metaphor of interplanetary difference, while (superficially at least) avoiding blame and criticism (a closer reading tells a different story). [...]

## IRONY AND KNOWINGNESS

No discussion of the postfeminist sensibility in the media would be complete without considering irony and knowingness. Irony can serve many functions. It is used in advertising to address what Goldman (1992) calls 'sign fatigue', by hailing audiences as knowing and sophisticated consumers, flattering them with their awareness of intertextual references and the notion that they can 'see through' attempts to manipulate them. Irony is used also as a way of establishing a safe distance between oneself and particular sentiments or beliefs, at a time when being passionate about anything or appearing to care too much seems to be 'uncool'. [...]

Most significantly, however, in postfeminist media culture irony has become a way of 'having it both ways', of expressing sexist, homophobic or otherwise unpalatable sentiments in an ironized form, while claiming this was not actually 'meant'. It works in various ways. As Whelehan (2000) and Williamson (2003) have argued, the use of retro imagery and nostalgia is a key device in the construction of contemporary sexism. Referencing a previous era becomes an important way of suggesting that the sexism is safely sealed in the past while constructing scenarios that would garner criticism if they were represented as contemporary. In the recent *'Happy Days'* advert for Citroën C3 cars, for example, the first frame shows a young woman having her dress entirely ripped off her body to reveal her bright red underwear (which matches the car). She screams, but the action soon moves on as the interest is in her body, not her distress. The 1950s iconography and soundtrack from the *Happy Days* show protects the advert from potential criticism: it is as if the whole thing is in ironic and humourous quotation marks. [...]

Irony also functions through the very extremeness of the sexism expressed: as though the mere fact that women are compared to 'rusty old bangers' or posed against each other in the 'dumbest girlfriend' competition is (perversely) evidence that there is no sexism (the extremeness of the sexism is evidence that there is no sexism). Magazine editors routinely trot out the line that it is all 'harmless fun' (when did 'harmless' and 'fun' become yoked together so powerfully?). [...]

Yet if we suspend our disbelief in the notion that it is 'just a laugh', we are left with a fast-growing area of media content (which profoundly influences other media) that is chillingly misogynist, inviting men to evaluate women only as sexual objects. A recent issue of *FHM* asks men: 'How much are you paying for sex?' Readers are invited to calculate their 'outgoings' on items such as drinks, cinema tickets and bunches of flowers, and then to divide the total by the number of 'shags' they've had that month in order to calculate their 'pay per lay'. Under a fiver per shag is 'too cheap—she is about the same price as the Cambodian whore'; around £11 to £20 is 'about the going rate for a Cypriot tart', and each shag should now be compared with the value and pleasure to be obtained from purchasing a new CD. Any more expensive than this and the lad should expect a performance worthy of a highly-trained, sexy showgirl (Turner, 2005).

It is hard to imagine any other group in society being so systematically objectified, attacked and vilified with so little opposition—which tells us something about the power of irony. Any attempt to offer a critique of such articles is dismissed by references to the critic's presumed ugliness, stupidity or membership of the 'feminist thought police'. Frequently, criticisms are pre-empted by comments which suggest that the article's writer is expecting 'blundering rants' from the 'council of women'. In this context, critique becomes much more difficult—and this, it would seem, is precisely what is intended.

## FEMINISM AND ANTI-FEMINISM

Finally, this chapter will turn to constructions of feminism, which are an integral feature of the postfeminist sensibility considered here. One of the things that makes the media today very different from the television, magazines, radio or press of the 1960s, 1970s and early 1980s is that feminism is now part of the cultural field. That is, feminist discourses are expressed within the media rather than simply being external, independent, critical voices. Feminist-inspired ideas burst forth from our radios, television screens and print media in TV discussions about date rape and sexualized imagery, in newspaper articles about women's experiences of war or the increasing beauty pressures on young girls, in talk shows about domestic violence or anorexia. Indeed, it might be argued that much of what counts as feminist debate in western countries today takes place in the media rather than outside it.

However, it would be entirely false to suggest that the media has somehow become feminist and has unproblematically adopted a feminist perspective. Instead it seems more accurate to argue that the media offers contradictory, but nevertheless patterned, constructions. In this postfeminist moment, as Judith Stacey (1987) has put it, feminist ideas are simultaneously 'incorporated, revised and depoliticised', and—let us add here—attacked. Angela McRobbie (2004b) has referred to this as the contemporary 'double entanglement' of neoliberal values in relation to gender, sexuality and family life, and a feminism that is part of common sense yet also feared, hated and fiercely repudiated.

What makes contemporary media culture distinctively postfeminist, rather than pre-feminist or anti-feminist, is precisely this entanglement of feminist and anti-feminist ideas. This can be seen clearly in the multimillion dollar publishing phenomenon of 'chick lit' in the wake of the success of *Bridget Jones's Diary*. In contemporary screen and paperback romances, feminism is not ignored or even attacked (as some backlash theorists might have it), but is simultaneously taken for granted and repudiated. A certain kind of liberal feminist perspective is treated as common sense, while at the same time feminism and feminists are constructed as harsh, punitive and inauthentic, not articulating women's true desires (Tasker and Negra, 2005). In some instances feminism is set up as policeman, disallowing women the pleasures of traditional femininity. [...]

In such romances, postfeminist heroines are often much more active protagonists than their counterparts in popular culture from the 1970s and 1980s. They value autonomy, bodily integrity and the freedom to make individual choices. However, what is interesting is the way in which they seem compelled to use their empowered postfeminist position to make choices that would be regarded by many feminists as problematic, located as they are in normative notions of femininity. They choose, for example, white weddings, downsizing, giving up work or taking their husband's name on marriage (McRobbie, 2004b). One reading of this may highlight the exclusions of Second Wave feminism, suggesting that it represents the 'return of the repressed'; the pleasures of domesticity or traditional femininity (Hollows, 2003). Another (not necessarily contradictory) reading might want to stress the ways in which pre-feminist ideals are being (seductively) repackaged as postfeminist freedoms (Probyn, 1997) in ways that do nothing to question normative heterosexual femininity. Two things are clear, however: postfeminism constructs an articulation or suture between feminist and anti-feminist ideas, and this is effected entirely through a grammar of individualism that fits perfectly with neoliberalism.

## CONCLUSION

This chapter has attempted to outline the elements of a postfeminist sensibility, [...] highlighting two key points about the sensibility sketched here: its intimate relation to feminism and to neoliberalism.

What makes a postfeminist sensibility quite different from both pre-feminist constructions of gender and feminist ones is that it is clearly a response to feminism. In this sense, postfeminism articulates a distinctively new sensibility. [...] Feminist ideas are at the same time articulated and repudiated, expressed and disavowed. Its constructions of contemporary gender relations are profoundly contradictory. On the one hand, young women are hailed through a discourse of 'can-do girl power', yet on the other hand, their bodies are powerfully reinscribed as sexual objects; women are presented as active, desiring social subjects, but they are subject to a level of scrutiny and hostile surveillance which has no historical precedent.

[...] It is precisely in the apparent contradictions of the postfeminist sensibility that the entanglement of feminist and anti-feminist discourses can be seen. The patterned nature of the contradictions is what constitutes the sensibility, one in which notions of autonomy, choice and self-improvement sit side-by-side with surveillance, discipline and the vilification of those who make the 'wrong' 'choices' (become too fat, too thin or have the audacity or bad judgement to grow older).

These notions are also central to neoliberalism and suggest a profound relation between neoliberal ideologies and postfeminism. In recent years a number of writers have explored neoliberalism in order to highlight the ways in which it has shifted from being a political or economic rationality to a mode of governmentality that operates across a range of social spheres (Brown, 2003; Rose, 1996). Neoliberalism is understood increasingly as constructing individuals as entrepreneurial actors who are rational, calculating and self-regulating. The individual must bear full responsibility for their life biography, no matter how severe the constraints upon their action.

However, what has not yet been examined is the relationship of neoliberalism to gender relations. But it appears from this attempt to map the elements of a postfeminist sensibility that there is a powerful resonance between postfeminism and neoliberalism. This operates on at least three levels. First, and most broadly, both appear to be structured by a current of individualism that has replaced almost entirely notions of the social or political, or any idea of the individual as subject to pressures, constraints or influence from outside themselves. Second, it is clear that the autonomous, calculating, self-regulating subject of neoliberalism bears a strong resemblance to the active, freely choosing, self-reinventing subject of postfeminism. These two parallels suggest, then, that postfeminism is not simply a response to feminism but also a sensibility at least partly constituted through the pervasiveness of neoliberal ideas. Third, however, is a connection which might imply that the synergy is even more significant: in the popular cultural discourses examined here, *women* are called on to self-manage and self-discipline. To a much greater extent than men, women are required to work on and transform the self, regulate every aspect of their conduct, and to present all their actions as freely chosen.

## REFERENCES

Brown, W. (2003) 'Neo-Liberalism and the End of Liberal Democracy', *Theory and Event* 7(1). Accessed 4 December 2006: http://muse.jhu.edu/journals/tae/.

Fielding, H. (1997) *Bridget Jones's Diary*. London: Picador.

Gill, R. (2006) *Gender and the Media*. Cambridge: Polity Press.

Goldman, R. (1992) *Reading Ads Socially*. London: Routledge.

Gray, J. (2002) *Men Are from Mars, Women are from Venus*. London: HarperCollins.

Hollows, J. (2000) *Feminism, Femininity, and Popular Culture*. Manchester: Manchester University Press.

Hollows, J. (2003) 'Feeling Like a Domestic Goddess: Postfeminism and Cooking', *European Journal of Cultural Studies* 6(2): 179–202.

Macdonald, M. (1995) *Representing Women: Myths of Femininity in the Popular Media*. London: Hodder.

McNair, B. (2002) *Striptease Culture: Sex, Media and the Democratisation of Desire*. London: Routledge.

McNay, L. (1992) *Foucault and Feminism: Power, Gender and the Self*. Cambridge: Polity Press.

McRobbie, A. (2004a) '"Notes on "*What Not to Wear*" and Post-Feminist Symbolic Violence', in L. Adkins and B. Skeggs (eds) *Feminism after Bourdieu*, pp. 99–109. Oxford: Blackwell.

McRobbie, A. (2004b) 'Post Feminism and Popular Culture', *Feminist Media Studies* 4(3): 255–64.

Probyn, E. (1997) 'New Traditionalism and Post-Feminism: TV Does the Home', in C. Brunsdon, J. D'Acci and L. Spigel (eds) *Feminist Television Criticism: A Reader*, pp. 126–37. Oxford: Blackwell.

Radner, H. (1999) 'Queering the Girl', in H. Radner and M. Luckett (eds) *Swinging Single*, pp. 1–38. Minneapolis: University of Minnesota Press.

Rose, N. (1996) *Inventing Ourselves: Psychology, Power and Personhood*. New York: Cambridge University Press.

Stacey, J. (1987) 'Sexism by a Subtler Name? Postindustrial Conditions and Post-Feminist Consciousness in the Silicon Valley', *Socialist Review* 17(6): 7–28.

Tasker, Y. and D. Negra (2005) '"In Focus" Postfeminism and Contemporary Media Studies', *The Cinema Journal* 44(2): 107–10.

Tincknell, E., C. Chambers, J. Van Loon and N. Hudson (2003) 'Begging for It: "New Femininities", Social Agency and Moral Discourse in Contemporary Teenage and Men's Magazines', *Feminist Media Studies* 3(1): 47–63.

Turner, J. (2005) 'Dirty Young Men', *Guardian Weekend* (22 Oct.). Retrieved from https://www.theguardian.com/theguardian/2005/oct/22/weekend7.weekend3.

Walkerdine, V., H. Lucey and J. Melody (2001) *Growing up Girl: Psychosocial Explorations of Gender and Class*. Basingstoke: Palgrave.

Whelehan, I. (2000) *Overloaded: Popular Culture and the Future of Feminism*. London: Women's Press.

Williamson, J. (2003) 'Sexism with and Alibi', *Guardian* (31 May). Retrieved from https://www.theguardian.com/media/2003/may/31/advertising.comment.

Wood, H. and B. Skeggs (2004) 'Notes on Ethical Scenarios of Self on British Reality TV', *Feminist Media Studies* 4(2): 205–8.

*Source:* Gill, Rosalind. (2007). Excerpted from "Postfeminist Media Culture: Elements of a Sensibility." *European Journal of Cultural Studies, 10*(2), 147–166.

## DISNEY'S VERSION OF GIRLHOOD

*Sharon Lamb and Lyn Mikel Brown*

Sharon Lamb is a professor of counseling and school psychology in the College of Education and Human Development, and director of the Mental Health Counseling Program at the University of Massachusetts–Boston. She is a renowned expert on girls, sexuality, and popular culture.

Lyn Mikel Brown is a professor of education at Colby College in Waterville, Maine. She is highly acclaimed for her work on girls' social and psychological development.

*Disney girls are women with Barbie doll bodies.* And, like Barbie, one small size fits all. The form-fitting clothing of these heroines proves it. They have the exotic made-up faces of women and the gowns and midriff-baring (Jasmine in *Aladdin*) bikini tops (Ariel in *The Little Mermaid*) of women. Not real women, of course—they're too perfect—but the male fantasy version. They arch their backs (did they use the same template for the Victoria Secret bra ad as they did for *The Little Mermaid* and *Pocahontas* bursting out of the water scenes?), toss their hair, smile sweetly, and speak softly. They're pretty when they're angry. Let's face it, changing skin and hair color and adding some exotic clothing does not a woman of color make. The one exception to this is Lilo and her older sister in *Lilo and Stitch*. What a relief to see real girls' bodies, faces, and personalities. No surprise—they don't make the princess doll set.

*Disney girls and women are gossips and chatter-boxes.* "Girls talk too much," Peter Pan complains after Wendy accosts him. Women in *The Little Mermaid* gossip around the washtub. Ursula the Sea Witch warns Ariel, "The men up there don't like a lot of chatter." In *Dumbo*, a mean-spirited female elephant announces to her friends, "Have I got a trunk full of dirt."

*Disney girls mother and do the housework.* And not only Snow White and Cinderella. Wendy mothers the Lost Boys, while the native woman in *Peter Pan* admonishes her, "No dance! Go gettum firewood" (adding a little racism to the mix). The little girl who catches Mowgli's eye in *The Jungle Book* sings, "I will have a handsome husband, and a daughter of my own. And I'll send her to fetch the water. I'll be cooking in the home." The soldiers in *Mulan* sing about a girl worth fighting for who cooks and waits at home.

*Disney girls have lovely voices.* From Snow White to Pocahontas, those girls can really warble. It's part of what makes them beautiful. They sing their desire and woes to animals and other nonhuman creatures because, and this is important:

*Disney girls have no support systems.* Except for Lilo who has her big sister, Disney girls don't have girlfriends and very little family. If they do, they leave them for princes or beasts or bandits (*Robin Hood*). Even after proving themselves, they find real honor with a husband (*Mulan*). They typically don't have mothers, and their fathers tend to be buffoons (*Beauty and the Beast*, *Aladdin*) or authoritarian jerks (*The Little Mermaid*).

*Disney girls can't resist a mirror.* Check out Tinker Bell measuring her hips in a hand mirror. She is clearly shocked at what she sees. Are they that wide? Dated, you say? Elastigirl, the mother in the Disney/Pixar movie *The Incredibles*, checks out her hips in a mirror in the same fashion. It seems that saving her family and the world just has to wait. Disney girls can make mirrors out of anything. Cinderella checks her hair in a wash bubble and later in a pond. Lady of *Lady and the Tramp* catches her image in a water bowl.

*Disney girls are incomplete without a man.* It is not only romance, it is romance in a reality that affirms male power. Male power is what Disney does best, and not just in the old Disney movies. Every Pixar movie to date is a male journey story. Yes, girls exist as primary characters in *A Bug's Life*, *The Incredibles*, *Finding Nemo*, and *Cars*, but the main character is male. Men provide the energy, the rules, and the hope for safety (*Mulan*, *Pocahontas*), while we're reminded with one-liners that girls are crybabies (*Chicken Little*) or need to be rescued (almost every movie). Disney girls will do anything to meet or be chosen by the man of their dreams. Ariel gives up her voice; Tinker Bell betrays Wendy; Cinderella's stepsisters fight over the prince and betray her. Disney is brilliant at retelling history and creating romance where none existed: between Pocahontas and John Smith or between Mulan and her officer. A girl can't have her own story or live a life

of bravery unless, in the end, she assumes her rightful place. She is not a Disney girl unless she marries.

*Powerful Disney women are evil and ugly.* Except for the grandmother spirit in *Pocahontas*, who shows up again in *Brother Bear*, when adult women exist they are typically vengeful and jealous of the Disney girl. They are also powerful and ugly: wicked stepmothers and queens (*Snow White*, *Cinderella*), ugly monsters and witches (*The Little Mermaid*, *The Sword and the Stone*, *Monsters, Inc.*). They are cruel and vengeful (Cruella DeVille in *101 Dalmatians* and the Queen of Hearts in *Alice in Wonderland*). Female power is itself evil: "It's time Ursula took matters into her own tentacles!" It is pretty clear to any little kid watching that dark skin is associated with evil. Check out Ursula or the evil queen in *Snow White* at their villainous peak. And while women with power will meet their demise in the most horrible ways—a stake through the heart, a car accident—Disney girls who recognize male power are rewarded with a place in his world: "Here she stands, the girl of his dreams" (*Cinderella*).

*Disney girls are innocent.* Tarty female characters in Disney movies pop up in funny places, usually in groups to underscore the Disney girl's singular innocence or to affirm a character's manliness: the busty barmaids in *Beauty and the Beast*, the sexy harem dancers in *Aladdin*, the vampish muses in *Hercules*. They are the girls that male characters like to flirt with but won't marry.

Let's be fair. We have welcomed the feisty, clever, and brave Disney girl of recent years. Look how Ariel defies her father and follows her heart! Isn't it great that Beauty is also a bit of a nerd and defiantly rejects the big handsome lout who pursues her? Isn't Pocahontas fearless, and isn't her relationship with her grandmother wonderful? Mulan really proves girls can do everything a guy can and, in this case, better than any other guy. Who wouldn't want their daughter to have such presence of mind and such impact on the world around her? The problem is that so much of the courage and feistiness is either in pursuit of romance or later put aside for it. Beauty endures horrific abuse to change her man; Ariel gives up her voice for her man; Pocahontas's goal is saving her man as much as preserving her homeland; Mulan's amazing feats dissolve in the presence of romance. This feels like a bait and switch. Draw a girl in with promises of something different and then bring in the same old thing through the back door.

* * * * *

## Questions for Critical Viewing

Whether you're watching old favourites or new movies, ask yourself the following questions about representations of girls, women, and gender relations.

1. Who does most of the rescuing, and who is being rescued?
2. Who is full of personality? Why can't a lead girl be the one with all the personality?
3. Is the best friend of the girl in the movie a real friend, or is she dropped as a character early on?
4. Who gets to drive the cool vehicles? The motorcycles and the ATVs?
5. Does there have to be a girl-meets-boy romantic ending? Can you think of another happily-ever-after scenario?
6. What does she wear at the end of the movie? A white gown? Why?
7. Are there girls that reflect your daughter's race, class, or sexual orientation? And why are so many people in this movie white and rich?
8. Are the partyers in the film stereotypically people of color?
9. Is there a gratuitous scene where the girl tries on clothes, goes shopping, or appears on a catwalk?
10. Do the parents have cool jobs (football coach, author, artist, rock-and-roll singer) or real ones?
11. Are feminist moms or businesswomen the enemy rather than a resource?
12. Who holds the powerful jobs? (Children Now reports that 71 percent of lawyers, 80 percent of CEOs, 92 percent of officials, and 80 percent of doctors on TV are men.)
13. What are the lead girl's interests, talents, skills, and hobbies?
14. Why do they make the mean girl so one-dimensionally mean?
15. Why are there so few women producers, writers, and directors? (When a program has at least one woman writer, a female director, or a female producer, the TV show or movie has 5 to 10 percent more female characters.)

*Source:* Lamb, Sharon, & Brown, Lyn Mikel. (2007). Excerpted from *Packaging Girlhood: Rescuing Our Daughters from Marketers' Schemes* (pp. 67–69, 91–93). New York, NY: St. Martin's Press.

# CHAPTER 42

## The Trouble with White Feminism: Whiteness, Digital Feminism, and the Intersectional Internet

*Jessie Daniels*

Jessie Daniels is a professor of sociology at Hunter College and at The Graduate Centre at The Graduate Centre at the City University of New York. In the early 2000s, she directed a large research project involving young men leaving Rikers Island, New York City's largest jail. A paper based on that project won the Sarah Mazelis Paper of the Year Award for 2011. Daniels's current research considers race and digital media technologies, and she is widely acclaimed for her work on Internet manifestations of racism. Her books include *Cyber Racism* and *White Lies*.

## INTRODUCTION

In the summer of 2013, writer and pop-culture analyst Mikki Kendall grew increasingly frustrated watching her friends being viciously attacked online, particularly by a White male academic who identified as a "male feminist." Kendall's friends, like her, are women of color engaged in digital activism through social media, particularly Twitter, and through writing in longer form on their own blogs and for online news outlets. Kendall's friends were being called names, bullied, and threatened by the self-professed male feminist. During a rather public meltdown, the man admitted that he had intentionally "trashed" women of color, posting on Twitter: "I was awful to you because you were in the way" (Kendall, 2013).

The behavior of this one man was hurtful and disappointing, but it was the inaction of prominent White feminist bloggers who failed to acknowledge the racist, sexist behavior of one of their frequent contributors that prompted Kendall to create #SolidarityIsForWhiteWomen. Kendall's hashtag quickly began trending on Twitter and ignited a wide range of discussions about hashtag campaigns as a form of cyberfeminist activism and, more broadly, about social media, feminism, and call-out culture. One journalist, Michelle Goldberg, excoriated Kendall specifically, and women of color more generally, for starting a "toxic Twitter war" that is destructive for feminism (Goldberg, 2014). [...]

Although a number of scholars have critiqued the first and second waves of feminist movements as rooted in Whiteness (Hull, Scott, & Smith, 1982; Truth,

2009; Ware, 1992), there is little existing literature that does lay out a systematic critique of Whiteness in contemporary digital feminist activism. To address this gap in our understanding of White feminism, I examine three case studies of White feminist activism: (1) Sheryl Sandberg's "Lean In" and "Ban Bossy" campaigns; (2) "One Billion Rising" campaign; and (3) "The Future of Online Feminism," a report authored by Vanessa Valenti and Courtney Martin for the #FemFuture project. Through these three case studies I will demonstrate some of the trouble with White feminism.

During the early days of the Internet, some scholars theorized that the emergence of virtual environments and an attendant culture of fantasy would mean an escape from the boundaries of race and the experience of racism. A few imagined that people would go online to escape their embodied racial and gender identities (Nakamura, 2002; Turkle, 1995) and some saw the Internet as a "utopia" where, as the 1990s telecom commercial rendered it, there is "no race, no gender." The reality that has emerged is quite different. Race and racism persist online in ways that are both new and unique to the Internet, alongside vestiges of centuries-old forms that reverberate significantly both offline and on (Brock, 2006, 2009; Daniels, 2009, 2013). The reality of the Internet we have today has important implications for understanding Whiteness and feminism.

The examination of Whiteness in the scholarly literature is well-established (Fine et al., 2004; Frankenberg, 1993; Hughey, 2010; Twine and Gallagher, 2008). Whiteness, like other racial categories, is socially constructed and actively maintained through social boundaries. A key strategy in maintaining these boundaries is through efforts to define who is, and is not, White. Ample historical evidence demonstrates that the boundaries of Whiteness are malleable across time, place, and social context (Allen, 1994; Daniels, 1997; Roediger, 2007; Wray, 2006). Another central mechanism of Whiteness is a seeming invisibility, or "unmarked" quality, that allows those

within the category "White" to think of themselves as simply human, individual, and without race, while Others are racialized (Dyer, 1988). At the same time, some scholars have noted that Whiteness can also be characterized by a paradoxical "hypervisibility" (Reddy, 1998). We know that Whiteness shapes housing (Low, 2009), education (Leonardo, 2009), politics (Feagin, 2012; Painter, 2010), law (Lopez, 2006; Painter, 2010), social science research methods (Arnesen, 2001; Zuberi & Bonilla-Silva, 2008), and indeed, frames much of our (mis)understanding of U.S. society (Feagin, 2010; Lipsitz, 2006; Mills, 1997; Painter, 2010).

*****

In the current multimedia landscape, Whiteness remains an infrequently examined part of feminist digital activism. While there is a growing literature about race and racism in Internet studies (Daniels, 2013), there has not been peer-reviewed academic scholarship to date that critically examines White feminism online. In the section that follows, I take up three case studies of White feminism.

## CASE STUDIES OF WHITE FEMINISM

I selected the following case studies for their prominence in American popular culture during 2012–2014. These three cases were also widely discussed among feminists online on blogs and through Twitter. All three of the case studies have strong components of online engagement and digital activism, both by design of their creators and through the comments of feminists and others who are critical of these projects.

### The "Lean In" and "Ban Bossy" Campaigns

Sheryl Sandberg is the Chief Operating Officer of Facebook and has recently emerged as a leading spokesperson for a particular kind of feminism.

Sandberg has explained that she was encouraged to write *Lean In: Women, Work and the Will to Lead* (2013) based on her 2010 talk at the Technology, Entertainment, Design (TED) conference, an online video which has received more than five million views. Sandberg's basic message is that there are so few women leaders in politics, government, and corporations because women are limiting themselves. If women can just get out of their own way and "lean in"—by which she means assert themselves in male-dominated offices and boardrooms—then the entire "power structure of the world" will be changed and this will "expand opportunities for all" (Sandberg, 2013). More than a mere self-help book, *Lean In* is also an online campaign and what Sandberg likes to refer to as "a movement." Sandberg hopes to inspire women to create their own "Lean In Circles," or peer support groups, to facilitate "leaning in."

Sandberg has conceded that she has only recently begun to identify as a feminist. Her book is her first public declaration of her feminism, but what she articulates is a form of liberal feminism long interwoven with Whiteness, class privilege, colonialism, and heteronormativity (Ahmed, 2006; Collins, 2002; Spelman, 1988; Srivastava, 2005). Sandberg's answer to her central question—"why there aren't more women leaders"—is not that there are structural barriers or systematic inequality, but that women need to change. The intended audience for Sandberg's message is specific and limited: she writes for women in corporate work environments who are heterosexual, married (or planning to marry), cisgender, middle to upper-middle class, predominantly (though not exclusively) White. Drawing on her experience as an executive at Facebook, and before that at Google, Sandberg instructs her audience on "choosing the right husband" (i.e., one who helps with domestic labor and child care). Searches for the words *lesbian*, *gay*, and *transgender* in the text of *Lean In* yield no results. Similarly, there are virtually no mentions of African American, Asian American, Native American, or Latina women in the book, nor any discussion of how "leaning in" might be different

for women who are not White. Such a narrow conceptualization of who is included in the category of "woman" fits neatly with liberal feminism.

The basic tenets of liberal feminism emphasize equal access to opportunity for women and men. The goal of liberal feminism is for women to attain the same levels of representation, compensation, and power in the public sphere as men. For change to happen, liberal feminists primarily rely on women's ability to achieve equality through their own individual actions and choices. [...] For Sandberg, the root cause of gender inequality rests with the individual choices women make, and to a lesser extent, society's beliefs about women, which women then internalize. For there to be "more women leaders," women need to shake off their temerity, sharpen their elbows, and claim their space at the corporate table. The praxis—the actual work involved that follows from such a perspective—becomes the "motivational work" women must do to and for themselves to fit into the male-dominated corporate structure, not the efforts to change that structure or the economic system upon which it rests.

Given the huge effort of this motivational work, Sandberg says, it is best to start early. Sandberg believes that young girls are being given the wrong messages in childhood, an idea that is also a familiar tenet of liberal feminism. According to Sandberg, girls with leadership potential are called "bossy," which is a pejorative in American culture, and they internalize this message. To create change, she envisions a world in which all little girls who were called "bossy" come to see themselves instead as "leaders." To facilitate this change, Sandberg has now launched a spin-off campaign, in partnership with the Girl Scouts, called "Ban Bossy." In the illustration for the campaign, a figure of a little girl sits with her head down, playing alone. The large, bold text reads: "Bossy holds girls back" (Girl Scouts of America, 2014). Below that, in a smaller font, the text reads: "Girls are twice as likely as boys to worry that leadership roles will make them seem 'bossy.'" At the bottom, the viewer is directed to visit BanBossy.com. The "twice as likely" claim about the greater concern among girls about seeming "bossy" is a cornerstone for the campaign. This fact is taken from a small subsample ($N = 360$) of a 2008 study conducted by the Girl Scout Research Institute; the subsample included those who said they were "not interested" in leadership positions (Girl Scout Research Institute, 2008).

While it is true that 29 percent of girls and 13 percent of boys in the subsample said "I do not want to seem bossy," this is somewhat misleading in light of the data from the larger sample. When looking at the larger sample ($N = 2,475$ girls, $N = 1,514$ boys), the data reveal that the lack of interest in leadership is disproportionately a problem among White youth. In fact, the data show that the proportion of youth who think of themselves as leaders is highest among African American girls (75 percent), African American boys (74 percent), and Hispanic girls (72 percent). It is lowest among boys who are White (32 percent) or Asian American (33 percent), and then among White girls (34 percent). Given this breakdown of the sample as a whole, the campaign to "ban bossy" seems to be an effort that would benefit young White girls most, as that is the cohort of girls least likely to see themselves as leaders.

Sandberg has enlisted the support of high-profile women of color to promote the "Ban Bossy" campaign. Some of the promotional posters feature a photo of Sheryl Sandberg, flanked by former U.S. Secretary of State Condoleezza Rice and Anna Maria Chávez, the CEO of the Girl Scouts of the USA. But the fact that Sandberg has enlisted some prominent women of color to sign on to her campaign does not change the fact that liberal feminism is consistent with White supremacy. [...]

In Sandberg's corporate-themed liberal feminism, there is no apparatus—either in theory or in practice—for dealing with race or racism. As long as these are, as bell hooks suggests, a "taboo subject" for liberal feminists, then liberal feminism will continue to be aligned with White supremacy. The focus in *Lean In* and "Ban Bossy" is on a feminism for women who are White, cisgender, heterosexual, married or about

to be, middle or upper-middle class, and working in corporations. Though this is a narrow and exclusive conceptualization of who is a "woman," this makes no difference for the ideologies and expressions of White feminism.

## One Billion Rising (OBR)

Eve Ensler is an American playwright most well known for her play *The Vagina Monologues* (1998) about rape and sexual violence. Ensler is also a feminist activist who has launched a number of campaigns intended to raise awareness about violence against women, among them the V-Day campaign to stop violence against women. Ensler's most recent endeavor, One Billion Rising (OBR), is an expansion of the V-Day franchise and intended to reach a broader global audience. As Ensler explains: "We founded V-Day, a global movement, to stop such violence 16 years ago, and we have had many victories. But still we have not ended the violence. On February 14, 2013, millions of people rose up and danced in 207 countries with our campaign One Billion Rising" (Ensler, 2013). Ensler has received numerous awards, including several honorary doctorate degrees, and admirers of her work point to the millions of dollars raised through V-Day events. A supporter of the One Billion Rising project of worldwide dancing praises it as a "good first step" toward how "highlighting a shared problem can encourage the sharing of solutions" (Filopovic, 2013). There is plenty of criticism of Ensler's work, as well; taken together, these illustrate some of the trouble with White feminism.

There is no [satisfactory] account available of why Ensler chose February 14 as the focus for her charitable efforts. [...] February 14 was already a signifier for the struggle of Indigenous women. Since 1990, Indigenous and First Nations women in Canada have led marches on February 14 to call attention to the violence against native women. These events, known as the "Memorial March for Missing and Murdered Indigenous Women" (shared using the hashtag #MMIW), began as a way to commemorate the murder of an Indigenous woman on Powell Street in Vancouver, Coast Salish Territories. If Ensler's V-Day had remained a New York City-based event, or even a U.S.-focused event, this confluence of dates might not have been an issue, but V-Day expanded to Canada. In an "Open Letter to Eve Ensler," Lauren Chief Elk (2013), a Native American activist, critiqued the organization's marketing campaign in Canada, writing:

> Your organization took a photo of Ashley Callingbull, and used it to promote V-Day Canada and One Billion Rising, without her consent. You then wrote the word "vanishing" on the photo, and implied that Indigenous women are disappearing, and inherently suggested that we are in some type of dire need of your saving. You then said that Indigenous women were V-Day Canada's "spotlight". V-Day completely ignored the fact that February 14th is an iconic day for Indigenous women in Canada, and marches, vigils, and rallies had already been happening for decades to honor the missing and murdered Indigenous women.

In response, Ensler and a spokesperson for OBR said they did not know that there was a conflict with the date, and then the spokesperson added, "every date in the calendar has importance." The move into Canada by Ensler's OBR on a day already commemorated by Indigenous women, using the photo of Ashleigh Callingbull without permission, and writing "vanishing" on it are forms of theft, appropriation, and erasure of Indigenous women and their activism. Theft, appropriation, and erasure are painful to those whose work is being stolen and whose very existence is being erased. Yet, through the lens of White feminism, it is difficult, if not impossible, to stay focused on Indigenous women's pain of erasure. As Lauren Chief Elk (2013) goes on to explain in her letter, "When I told you that your White, colonial, feminism is hurting us, you started crying. Eve, you are not the victim here." Theft, appropriation, and erasure are

key strategies of settler colonialism, a disturbingly consistent feature of OBR.

A central activity of OBR events is dancing. As Ensler explains, "It turns out that dancing, as the women of Congo taught me, is a most formidable, liberating and transformative energy" (Ensler, 2013). However, some Congolese women do not share Ensler's enthusiasm for dancing as a response to systematic sexual violence. In a meeting of "radical grassroots feminists" that she attended in London, Gyte (2013) described listening to a Congolese woman express anger toward One Billion Rising, using words like "insulting" and "neo-colonial" to describe the campaign. The woman pointed out that it would be difficult to imagine a White, middle-class, educated, American woman (like Ensler) turning up on the scene of some other kind of atrocity to tell survivors to "rise" above the violence they have seen and experienced by dancing—"imagine someone doing that to holocaust survivors" (Gyte, 2013). Ensler has made several trips to the Democratic Republic of Congo and reported for Western audiences on the use of rape as a weapon of war, which may be useful for raising awareness about systematic sexual violence, but the move to take a Congolese tradition of dance and use it as a campaign strategy for OBR suggests a form of appropriation. [...]

The White feminism of the OBR campaign is rooted in what Toni Morrison (1992) refers to as "sycophancy of White identity" in which White writers use Africa as a means to contemplate their own terror and desire (p. 19). When such critiques are levied at Ensler's work, often by women of color, many White feminists come to her defense to argue that she is "doing good work" and thus should be released from any obligation to respond to such criticism, as happened recently (Romano, 2015). When such a controversy erupts, it is then dismissed as the result of disgruntled, envious, or "angry" women of color who are "using" social media to "attack" well-meaning White feminists (Goldberg, 2014). [...]

The kinds of change brought about through Ensler's activism further highlight the trouble with

White feminism. In describing what change looks like as a result of OBR, Ensler (2013) writes:

> In Guatemala, Marsha Lopez, part of the V-Day movement since 2001, says the most important result of OBR was the creation of a law for the criminalisation of perpetrators who impregnate girls under 14 years old. The law also includes penalties for forced marriage of girls under 18.

Through speaking for and through Marsha Lopez of Guatemala, Ensler identifies "criminalization of perpetrators" as the greatest achievement of OBR. Such an approach to systematic sexual violence, which relies primarily on an engagement by the State, does not acknowledge—and indeed cannot conceptualize—the ways in which the State is an agent of sexual violence, nor does it acknowledge the ways in which the State enacts violence against some men. This is what Bernstein refers to as carceral feminism, with incarceration as the underlying paradigm for justice (Bernstein, 2014, p. 70). The focus on incarceration as a solution to gender inequalities is both insufficient to address the problems of systematic sexual violence (across differences of race, national context, and gender identity) and shifts the focus to another system of oppression that in the United States consumes the bodies of Black and Brown men. To be sure, the carceral paradigm of justice is part of the trouble with the White feminism of Ensler's One Billion Rising.

## The Future of Online Feminism

Digital activism is the most important advance in feminism in 50 years, but it is in crisis and unsustainable. This is the central message of a report released in April 2013 by the Barnard Center for Research on Women (BCRW). The report, called *The Future of Online Feminism* (using the hashtag #FemFuture), was written by Courtney Martin and Vanessa Valenti, both involved at different times with the prominent feminist blog Feministing.com. While less widely known than the work of Sandberg or Ensler, the report by Martin and Valenti seems to encapsulate a set of debates about digital activism; as with Sandberg and Ensler, the report illustrates some of the trouble with White feminism.

Martin and Valenti [...] approached BCRW about doing a report on the "online revolution" in feminism. A key observation of the report is that "many have called feminist blogs the 21st century version of consciousness raising" (Martin & Valenti 2013, p. 3). The 34-page report sets out an overview of what the authors call "online feminism," by which they mean blogs and online petitions in support of feminist issues. [...] While they recognize that the emergence of digital technologies has been a boon to feminist causes, Martin and Valenti contend that online feminism is at "a crisis point" because feminist bloggers are not getting paid for their activism, thus making such activism "unsustainable." But, as the BCRW's introduction to the report explains, "Martin and Valenti had a compelling vision to make the landscape of feminist writers and activists online stronger" and they proposed doing this through a variety of tactics (Martin & Valenti, 2013, p. 2).

When it was released, there was an immediate negative reaction to the report, which was voiced largely, but not exclusively, by women of color (Johnson, 2013; Loza, 2014). [...] Many of the criticisms of the report saw the invitation-only convening of "a core group of trailblazing feminists working online" as cliquish, if not elitist. Martin and Valenti write that "what transpired was no less than historic," but it is not clear what was historic about the gathering. Although the convening included a racially diverse group of feminists engaged online—a fact mentioned often to defend the report as inclusive—the document ultimately contains the vision of Martin and Valenti. The authors suggest the possibility of intersectionality when they write that theirs is "boundary-crossing work—cross-generational, cross-class, cross-race, cross just about every line that still divides us both within and outside of the feminist movement" (Martin & Valenti, 2013, p. 4). This is the only mention of race, generation, or class in the text. However, the report does mention a number of women of color who were included, without their permission and without invitations to the convening, as exemplars of online feminism. For many observers, the process of developing, writing, and releasing the report was one that centered elite White women's experiences while using the presence of women of color—at the convening and in textual examples—to avoid that insinuation. As Susana Loza (2014) observes, "The production of the #FemFuture report is emblematic of the White liberal feminist approach to its perceived exclusivity: symbolic multiculturalism."

The trouble with the White feminism of the report is rooted in the ideas, if not quite theories, that inform it. Martin and Valenti write that they were inspired to create a "feminist version" of something called "collective impact," a model for social change developed by nonprofit consultants John Kania and Mark Kramer. The central concept that Martin and Valenti take from this model is that the key to large-scale social change is convening power and agenda setting. What make these effective, according to Kania and Kramer (2011), is a "shared vision for change, one that includes a common understanding of the problem and a joint approach to solving it through agreed upon actions." The formidable challenge in trying to create a feminist version of the Kania and Kramer model is finding a "shared vision" among feminists that includes a "common understanding of the problem." It may be that Martin and Valenti believed that they had arrived at this based on the convening of 21 "trailblazing" feminists, but they did not—and, with such a small group, indeed could not, however diverse the group or well-intentioned the organizers. Instead, Martin and Valenti proceeded with the "convening power" and "agenda setting" without the shared vision and this, in many ways, illustrates some of the trouble with White feminism.

The crisis that the report identifies among feminist online activists is primarily an economic one, with affective peril a close second. It is not surprising, then, that the solutions Martin and Valenti offer include a wide range of tactics and strategies to make feminist

blogging economically lucrative and more emotionally satisfying. Some of the proposed solutions include sponsoring a "Feminist Business Boot Camp" (a weeklong opportunity to learn about business and financial structures and examine social business case studies), "Corporate Partnerships" (not every corporation's mission and operations would fit within the ethical and political framework that many online feminists demand of our partners), and "Self-Care & Solidarity Retreats" (in order to reconnect with renewed purpose and clarity). The proposed solutions in the report are a combination of economic empowerment and emotional uplift, with an ambitious overall goal: "We must create a new culture of work, a vibrant and valued feminist economy that could resolve an issue that's existed for waves before us" (Martin & Valenti, 2013, p. 23).

In many ways, what Martin and Valenti are proposing is a well-trod path in the world of women's blogging conferences, most notably the BlogHer franchise. At these blogging conferences, which began in 2005 to highlight the work of women bloggers, thousands of women, predominately White, come together looking for emotional support and for ways to "monetize"—make money from—their blogs. Although not explicitly a form of feminist organizing, there is a kind of women's empowerment ethos to these conferences. Reporters from *The New York Times* and the *Wall Street Journal* have covered the BlogHer conferences, but the Whiteness of women's blogging conferences is rarely remarked upon by the mainstream media. However, the racial composition of these conferences is set in relief when contrasted with the Blogalicious conference, developed and attended by African American women; there is also stark difference in sponsorship between the two conferences. Research on sponsorship at these conferences from 2007–2009 found that there were consistently more than 40 sponsors at BlogHer, many of them corporations such as GM, which provided cars for attendees, and some of the top tech firms, while there were fewer than 10 sponsors at Blogalicious, and many of these were small or single proprietor businesses (Daniels, 2011). The top women bloggers who are touted as financial success stories at BlogHer are almost always White (e.g., Heather Armstrong, a well-known "mommy blogger," is a millionaire), while women of color bloggers talk about the struggle to attract sponsorship for their blogs. This stark difference speaks to the racialized political economy in which White women earn more than African American, Native American, and Latina women; this includes income earned from doing work online, such as blogging for feminist causes. What Martin and Valenti miss […] is the way that race still matters in the economy. In contrast to some in the "waves that came before," who might have been critical of the idea of feminism joined seamlessly with capitalism, the Martin and Valenti report, like the women's blogging conferences, embraces the idea of a corporate-sponsored feminism. And this fits very neatly with White feminism.

## DISCUSSION

There are a number of challenges with discussing White feminism. For women of color, the initial challenge is simply being heard, as they are frequently ignored. Once their voices have registered, they risk being bullied and verbally abused (or worse). Most likely they will be called "angry," or in some cases, accused of starting a "war" (Goldberg, 2014). These misreadings of critique as attack cause some White women to further retreat from engaging about race and may lead to their excluding women of color from feminist organizing to avoid even the possibility of criticism. For White women like myself, speaking out about White feminism is to risk hurt feelings and the loss of connection with other White women—and the opportunities that come with that. […]

When Mikki Kendall's hashtag #SolidarityisforWhiteWomen was trending, many White feminists reported feeling hurt, attacked, wounded, or simply left out of the conversation (Van Deven, 2013). In many ways, the reaction to challenges to White feminism causes "unhappiness," which, as Sara Ahmed (2010) explains, can be a good thing:

To be willing to go against a social order, which is protected as a moral order, a happiness order is to be willing to cause unhappiness, even if unhappiness is not your cause. To be willing to cause unhappiness might be about how we live an individual life (not to choose "the right path" is readable as giving up the happiness that is presumed to follow that path).… To be willing to cause unhappiness can also be how we immerse ourselves in collective struggle, as we work with and through others who share our points of alienation. Those who are unseated by the tables of happiness can find each other.

[…] The era of digital activism presents new opportunities for digital feminism; at the same time, the intersectional Internet makes challenging hegemonic White feminism easier and more effective. Twitter, in particular, is changing the landscape of feminism. Loza (2014) notes the proliferation of hashtags created by feminists of color with intersectional themes and observes "these hashtags are a direct indictment of the parochial vision of online feminism articulated in the #FemFuture report."

Mikki Kendall agrees: "I do know that Twitter is changing everything. Now, people are forced to hear us and women of color no longer need the platform of White feminism because they have their own microphones" (qtd. in Vasquez, 2013). If the goal is a sustained critique of White feminism, then we have to see Twitter as a key tool in that effort.

To sustain a challenge to White feminism, we have to become more adept at critically examining Whiteness. As it is elsewhere in the sociopolitical landscape, when race is addressed in and by feminist blogs, the subject is nearly always raised by a person of color (de la Peña, 2010, p. 926). Challenging White feminism means, at the very least, bringing up race and recognizing that White people have race. To go further, we must understand the ways that constructing and protecting Whiteness has been a core feature in the rise of the popular Internet (de la Peña, 2010, p. 936), and we must join this with a dissection of how White feminism has benefitted from this technological development.

## CONCLUSION

[...] Challenging White feminism in favor of an intersectional feminism that centers the experiences of Black, Latina, Asian, Indigenous, queer, disabled, and trans women is to speak against a social order. To challenge White feminism is also to risk causing unhappiness, but this is a risk we must take so that we can find each other in our resistance to it.

## REFERENCES

Ahmed, S. N. (2006). *Queer phenomenology: Orientations, objects, others*. Durham: Duke University Press.

Ahmed, S. N. (2010). Feminist killjoys (and other willful subjects). *The Scholar and Feminist Online, 8*(3). Retrieved from http://sfonline.barnard.edu/polyphonic/print_ahmed.htm.

Allen, T. W. (1994). *The invention of the White race*. London: Verso.

Arnesen, E. (2001). Whiteness and the historians' imagination. *International Labor and Working-Class History, 60*, 3–32.

Bernstein, E. (2014). Militarized humanitarianism meets carceral feminism: The politics of sex, rights, and freedom in contemporary antitrafficking campaigns. *Signs, 36*(1), 45–72.

Brock, A. (2006). "A belief in humanity is a belief in colored men": Using culture to span the digital divide. *Journal of Computer-Mediated Communication, 11*(1), 357–374.

Brock, A. (2009). Life on the wire: Deconstructing race on the Internet. *Information, Communication & Society, 12*(3), 344–363.

Chief Elk, L. (2013). An open letter to Eve Ensler. Retrieved from http://chiefelk.tumblr.com/post/49527456060/an-open-letter-to-eve-ensler.

Collins, P. H. (2002). *Black feminist thought: Knowledge, consciousness, and the politics of empowerment*. New York: Routledge.

Daniels, J. (1997). *White lies*. New York: Routledge.

Daniels, J. (2009). *Cyber Racism: White supremacy online and the new attack on civil rights*. Lanham: Rowman & Littlefield.

Daniels, J. (2011). BlogHer and Blogalicious: Gender, race, and the political economy of women's blogging conferences. In R. Gajjala & Y. J. Oh (Eds.), *Cyberfeminism 2.0* (pp. 29–60). New York: Peter Lang.

Daniels, J. (2013). Race and racism in Internet studies: A review and critique. *New Media & Society, 15*(5), 695–719.

de la Peña, C. (2010). The history of technology, the resistance of archives, and the whiteness of race. *Technology and Culture, 51*(4), 919–937.

Dyer, R. (1988). White. *Screen, 29*(4), 44–65.

Ensler, E. (1998). *The vagina monologues*. New York: Random House.

Ensler, E. (2013, December 9). One Billion Rising: The 2014 campaign to end violence against women. *The Guardian*. Retrieved from https://www.theguardian.com/society/womens-blog/2013/dec/09/one-billion-rising-2014-campaign-end-violence-against-women-justice.

Feagin, J. R. (2010). *The White racial frame: Centuries of framing and counter-framing*. New York: Routledge.

Feagin, J. R. (2012). *White party, White government: Race, class, and U.S. politics*. New York: Routledge.

Filipovic, J. (2013, February 13). What makes One Billion Rising's invitation to dance a radical move. *The Guardian*. Retrieved from https://www.theguardian.com/commentisfree/2013/feb/14/one-billion-rising-invitation-dance-radical.

Fine, M., Weis, L., Pruitt, L. P., & Burns, A. (2004). *Off White: Readings on power, privilege, and resistance* (2nd ed.). New York: Routledge.

Frankenberg, R. (1993). *White women, race matters: The social construction of Whiteness*. Minneapolis: University of Minnesota Press.

Girl Scout Research Institute. (2008). *Change it up! What girls say about redefining leadership*. New York: Girl Scouts of the USA. Retrieved from http://www.girlscouts.org/research/pdf/change_it_up_executive_summary_english.pdf.

Goldberg, M. (2014, February 17). Feminism's toxic Twitter wars. *The Nation, 135*(7), 12–17.

Gyte, N. (2013, February 2). Why I won't support One Billion Rising. *Huffington Post*. Retrieved from http://www.

huffingtonpost.co.uk/natalie-gyte/one-billion-rising-why-i-wont-support_b_2684595.html.

Hughey, M. (2010). The (dis)similarities of White racial identities: The conceptual framework of "hegemonic Whiteness." *Ethnic and Racial Studies, 33*(8), 1289–1309.

Hull, G. T., Scott, P. B., & Smith, B. (Eds.). (1982). *But some of us are brave: Black women's studies.* New York: Feminist Press at CUNY.

Johnson, J. M. (2013, April 12). #FemFuture, history & loving each other harder. *Diaspora hypertext.* Retrieved from http://dh.jmjafrx.com/2013/04/12/femfuture-history-loving-each-other-harder/.

Kania, J., & Kramer, M. (2011). Collective impact. *Stanford Social Innovation Review*, Winter. Stanford: Stanford University.

Kendall, Mikki. (2013, August 14). #SolidarityisforWhiteWomen: Women of color's issue with digital feminism. *The Guardian.* Retrieved from http://www.theguardian.com/commentisfree/2013/aug/14/solidarityisforwhitewomen-hashtag-feminism.

Leonardo, Z. (2009). *Race, whiteness and education.* New York: Routledge.

Lipsitz, G. (2006). *The possessive investment in Whiteness* (2nd ed.). Philadelphia: Temple University Press.

Lopez, I. H. (2006). *White by law: The legal construction of race.* New York: New York University Press.

Low, S. M. (2009). Maintaining Whiteness: The fear of others and niceness. *Transforming Anthropology, 17*(2), 79–92.

Loza, S. (2014). Hashtag feminism, #SolidarityisforWhitewomen, and the other #FemFuture. *Ada: A Journal of Gender, New Media, and Technology, 5.* doi:10.7264/N337770V.

Martin, C., & Valenti, V. (2013). *The future of online feminism.* Retrieved from http://bcrw.barnard.edu/wp-content/nfs/reports/NFS8-FemFuture-Online-Revolution-Report.pdf.

Mills, C. W. (1997). *The racial contract.* Ithaca: Cornell University Press.

Morrison, T. (1992). *Playing in the dark: Whiteness in the literary imagination.* New York: Vintage.

Nakamura, L. (2002). *Cybertypes: Race, ethnicity, and identity on the Internet.* New York: Routledge.

Painter, N. (2010). *The history of White people.* New York: Norton.

Reddy, M. (1998). Invisibility/hypervisibility: The paradox of normative Whiteness. *Transformations, 9*(2), 55–64.

Roediger, D. R. (2007). *The wages of Whiteness: Race and the making of the American working class* (2nd ed.). London: Verso.

Romano, A. (2015). Rosie O'Donnell lashes out at feminists over "The Vagina Monologues." *The Daily Dot.* Retrieved from http://www.dailydot.com/politics/rosie-odonnell-eve-ensler-twitter/.

Sandberg, S. (2013). *Lean in: Women, work and the will to lead.* New York: Knopf.

Spelman, E. V. (1988). *Inessential woman: Problems of exclusion in feminist thought.* Boston: Beacon Press.

Srivastava, S. (2005). "You're calling me a racist?" The moral and emotional regulation of antiracism and feminism. *Signs, 40*(1), 29–62.

Truth, S. (2009). Ain't I a woman? In Paul Halsall (Ed.), *Internet modern history sourcebook.* New York: Fordham University. (December 1851).

Turkle, S. (1995). *Life on the screen: Identity in the age of the Internet.* New York: Simon & Schuster.

Twine, F. W., & Gallagher, C. (2008). Introduction: The future of Whiteness: A map of the Third Wave. *Ethnic and Racial Studies, 31*(1), 4–24.

Van Deven, M. (2013). The discomfort of #solidarityisfor Whitewomen. *In the Fray.* Retrieved from http://inthefray.org/2013/08/the-discomfort-of-solidarity/.

Vazquez, T. (2013, August 14). "Why "solidarity" is bullshit. *Bitch Magazine.* Retrieved from http://bitchmagazine.org/post/why-solidarity-is-bullshit.

Ware, V. (1992*). Beyond the pale: White women, racism, and history.* New York: Verso.

Wray, M. (2006). *Not quite White: White trash and the boundaries of Whiteness.* Durham: Duke University Press.

Zuberi, T., & Bonilla-Silva, E. (Eds). (2008). *White logic, White methods: Racism and methodology.* New York: Rowman & Littlefield.

*Source:* Daniels, Jessie. (2016). Excerpted from "The Trouble with White Feminism: Whiteness, Digital Feminism, and the Intersectional Internet." In Safiya Umoja Noble & Brendesha M. Tynes (Eds.), *The Intersectional Internet: Race, Sex, Class, and Culture Online* (pp. 41–43, 45–60). New York, NY: Peter Lang.

## ACTIVIST INSIGHT: SUEY PARK
## #NOTYOURASIANSIDEKICK

On December 14, 2013, graduate student Suey Park tweeted, "Be warned. Tomorrow morning we will be having a convo about Asian American Feminism with hashtag #NotYourAsianSidekick. Spread the word!!!!!!!" Within days, it trended globally, with over 50,000 tweets across 60 countries in 72 hours, sparking a worldwide conversation about feminism, race, and lived experiences. Park deliberately chose Twitter to begin a movement because it was a space "where people already gathered" and there were "conversations, consciousness raising, and resistance happening." There are many critics of using Twitter as a platform for social change. Park dismisses those critics, believing that "Twitter is a space where many people can have voices and generate change." What do you think? Below are Suey Park's reflections on social justice hashtags.

When I started graduate school and left behind a campus full of support and safety, I had a hard time adjusting and making friends. I never thought I would find friends through Twitter, but as I became physically ill, had knee surgery, and struggled as the only Asian American in my cohort, I quickly found that Twitter was my refuge and it became my community. Much like the stigma of online dating, I never thought I would meet people through Twitter because I never had a problem making friends before. However, with my passion for racial justice, I found it hard to meet people in graduate school with similar interests, and so connected by way of shared values and interests through Twitter.

It was surprising at first. Though relatively new to Twitter, it was an interface that was natural to me. All I did was to share my heartbreaks, my wins, and my frustration in a real and open way, and I found that my vulnerability drew in more followers, or friends as I call them. The only pro-tip I can give about using Twitter is to never forget that the people on the other side of the screen are as real as you are. If you forget this, then you are forgetting that communication technologies are not cold and mechanical, but are simply a platform to allow for human interaction.

In the last month, I've had everyone from huge corporations to education specialists reach out to me for tips on how to make a hashtag trend; most end up discouraged when they realize that although there are algorithms and metrics, as seen in the "Anatomy of a Hashtag" by *Al Jazeera*, it actually takes a community to create a trending hashtag.

But when I tell corporations this, they are frustrated by my explanation. The truth being that I have a physical illness, a disability, and a severe anxiety disorder. That means that from an early age I knew the importance of community and relying on others because I was too frail, too quiet, too sensitive to stand up for myself. And the beauty of learning such a lesson at an early age is that individualism was never an option for me.

Meanwhile, corporations are all about individualism rather than collective action for the benefit of an entire community. People participate in social justice hashtags because of their invested interest in them and not because I simply tell people to join. The viral success of #NotYourAsianSidekick after I first tweeted the tag on December 15, 2013, wasn't about me, but all of us.

My personal friends as well as my Twitter community really carried the conversation. My friend Juliet Shen encouraged me to take breaks for my health. She and my friends Cayden Mak and Justin Valas stayed up all night to monitor the tag and make sure that trolls and arguments did not destroy the generative conversation. Much to my delight, I woke up 8 hours later to see that #NotYourAsianSidekick was still trending, which I know was not my doing, but that of my friends and my community.

In the words of Jeff Yang (2013), who said it better than I ever could, "These threads won't weave themselves, nor will these chains break of their own accord, and unless we join hands and swim together, unless we become each others' sidekicks, the river of memory will sweep us away." And in the aftermath of #NotYourAsianSidekick, I still see the importance of continually unlearning scarcity myths. Until we first challenge American individualism in our own minds, we can never dismantle it at large.

And then I watched in horror as the media selectively left behind my comments on community and collective action, and instead focused on just me as an individual. As my friend Muna Mire (2014) recently wrote in her piece about Martin Luther King Jr.: "Movements don't happen because of charismatic individuals, movements happen because people organize, raise consciousness and treat each other and the oppressor humanely."

Similarly, the media made #NotYourAsianSidekick primarily about me and my colorblocked outfit—the now iconic green shirt and yellow skirt. Of course this makes sense as the media gets more clicks out of selling and commodifying me as a young Asian American woman, offering me 15 minutes of fame in return for my sidekick appearances.

So if not me as an individual, then what is the significance of #NotYourAsianSidekick?

Well, in her piece "The Revolution WILL be tweeted," Professor Imani Perry (2011) wrote: "Communication technologies are necessary tools for sharing the kind of news that gets people out of their seats. Mainstream media blackouts are impotent in the face of digital age couriers, carrying words like modern day David Walkers, Ida B. Wells or Paul Reveres. For today's freedom fighters, Twitter is one extremely useful technology. So if it's going to happen, the revolution indeed will be tweeted." She highlights how corporate-owned media will never broadcast a true movement whereas Twitter allows us to change the narrative and broadcast our own news.

When I first read Professor Perry's piece it felt like a call to action. From my experience organizing I saw that some old methods worked and that some felt stale and reproduced. I have long criticized protests for being manufactured in nature rather than organic. I yearned for a space where I could build and move in a way that was kind to my body and also creative in its intervention. After reading her piece and observing how many groups utilized Twitter to make change, I decided to give it a whirl.

In graduate school my favorite course was "Race and US Social Movements," and I found a repeated theme in which leaders would base where people already gathered to build movements with greater capacity and numbers. For me, that opportunity space was Twitter and my intention behind #NotYourAsianSidekick was the base build. Leading up to the global conversation, I already saw conversations, consciousness raising, and resistance happening. All I did was create a space where we could streamline our energies.

Although I organize outside of Twitter, I also see it as an extension of my work. It allows for a synergistic effect by allowing many individual voices to make a loud collective impact. Again to quote Jeff Yang (2013): "It's also more evidence of what I've referred to as our 'special mutant power' as Asian Americans—our ability to gather a thunderous hammerstrike of digital traffic and drop it from space on an unsuspecting target. We are, essentially, a kind of organically organized distributed denial of service attack, sending traffic soaring when we direct our attention at things we like, or don't like, as the case may be."

Many belittle the Twitter community and Twitter feminism (see Murphy, 2013) and I saw many patronizing opinions from leading white feminists following the release of "Can Feminist Hashtags 'Dismantle the State'?" (O'Connor, 2013). When my mentions were getting flooded with white feminists explaining to me that Twitter was useless, Mikki Kendall (@Karnythia), writer and founder of #SolidarityIsForWhiteWomen, tweeted at me "You're about to explain community to people that have none."

It's ironic, isn't it? That "thousands of feminists similarly gave an online middle finger to those that reject them, namely patriarchal Asian-American spaces and white feminists" as Kai Ma (2013) wrote. She also wrote "what pierced through the tweets was a broad slam around the silence from non-Asian feminists around our causes," and yet we saw the most vocal opposition after we dared to speak up.

Before all this started, a professor told me that Ella Baker used to ask "Who are your people?" A question I realized I first had to answer for myself before I could envision any next steps. As Professor and author Barbara Ransby (2011) wrote: "Ella Baker taught us how we ought to do our movement work: take time to be inclusive, be active listeners, walk the thorny and sometimes circuitous path of participatory democracy, mutual respect and genuine solidarity; and build campaigns from the bottom up not the top down. Today's progressives should take these lessons to heart, if they want to succeed in creating the social change our world desperately needs." For me, Twitter is a space where many people can have voices and generate change.

So what does it take to trend a hashtag? A community.

*Editors' Note*: Suey Park is now off Twitter after being "doxxed" following controversy stirred around another Twitter campaign she started, #CancelColbert. She launched the campaign to protest a race-based joke about Asian Americans made on the popular news satire show *The Colbert Report*.

## References

Ma, Kai. (2013, December 18). "#NotYourAsianSidekick Is Great. Now Can We Get Some Real Social Change?" *Time*. Retrieved from: http://ideas.time.com/2013/12/18/notyourasiansidekick-is-great-now-can-we-get-some-real-social-change/.

Mire, Muna. (2014, January 20). "Use Martin Luther King, Jr. Day to Rewrite Anti-Racist Mythology." *rabble.ca*. Retrieved from: http://rabble.ca/news/2014/01/use-martin-luther-king-jr-day-to-rewrite-anti-racist-mythology.

Murphy, Meghan. (2013, December 18). "The Trouble with Twitter Feminism." *Feminist Current*. Retrieved from: http://www.feministcurrent.com/2013/12/18/the-trouble-with-twitter-feminism/.

O'Connor, Maureen. (2013, December 23). "Can Feminist Hashtags 'Dismantle the State'?" *The Cut*. Retrieved from: https://www.thecut.com/2013/12/can-feminist-hashtags-dismantle-the-state.html.

Perry, Imani. (2011, October 15). "The Revolution WILL Be Tweeted." Retrieved from: http://imaniperry.typepad.com/imani_perry/2011/10/the-revolution-will-be-tweeted.html.

Ransby, Barbara. (2011, April 4). "Quilting a Movement." *In These Times*. Retrieved from: http://inthesetimes.com/article/7074/quilting_a_movement.

The Stream Team. (2013, December 18). "Anatomy of a hashtag: #NotYourAsianSidekick." *Al Jazeera America*. Retrieved from: http://america.aljazeera.com/watch/shows/the-stream/multimedia/multimedia/2013/12/anatomy-of-a-hashtagnotyourasiansidekick.html.

Yang, Jeff. (2013, December 19). "Why #NotYourAsianSidekick Started a Social Media Brushfire." *The Wall Street Journal*. Retrieved from: https://blogs.wsj.com/speakeasy/2013/12/19/why-notyourasiansidekick-started-a-social-media-brushfire/.

*Source:* Park, Suey. (2014, January 21). "The Viral Success of #NotYourAsianSidekick Wasn't about Me, but All of Us." *xoJane*. Retrieved from: http://www.xojane.com/issues/suey-park-notyourasiansidekick.

# SNAPSHOTS & SOUNDWAVES 28

## IF MEN COULD MENSTRUATE: A POLITICAL FANTASY

*Gloria Steinem*

Gloria Steinem is a celebrated American feminist writer, lecturer, and activist who has been actively involved in social justice movements for over 40 years. She co-founded *Ms.* magazine, helped to found *New York* magazine, and has published articles in *Esquire*, *The New York Times*, and numerous women's magazines and international publications. Her books include the bestsellers *Revolution from Within: A Book of Self-Esteem* and *Outrageous Acts and Everyday Rebellions*. Steinem has been honoured with many awards for her activism and journalism career.

A white minority of the world has spent centuries conning us into thinking that a white skin makes people superior—even though the only thing it really does is make them more subject to ultraviolet rays and to wrinkles. Male human beings have built whole cultures around the idea that penis envy is "natural" to women—though having such an unprotected organ might be said to make men vulnerable, and the power to give birth makes womb envy at least as logical.

In short, the characteristics of the powerful, whatever they may be, are thought to be better than the characteristics of the powerless—and logic has nothing to do with it.

What would happen, for instance, if suddenly, magically, men could menstruate and women could not?

The answer is clear—menstruation would become an enviable, boast-worthy, masculine event:

Men would brag about how long and how much.

Boys would mark the onset of menses, that longed-for proof of manhood, with religious ritual and stag parties.

Congress would fund a National Institute of Dysmenorrhea to help stamp out monthly discomforts.

Sanitary supplies would be federally funded and free. (Of course, some men would still pay for the prestige of commercial brands such as John Wayne Tampons, Muhammad Ali's Rope-a-Dope Pads, Joe Namath Jock

Shields—"For Those Light Bachelor Days," and Robert "Baretta" Blake Maxi-Pads.)

Military men, right-wing politicians, and religious fundamentalists would cite menstruation ("men-struation") as proof that only men could serve in the Army ("you have to give blood to take blood"), occupy political office ("Can women be aggressive without that steadfast cycle governed by the planet Mars?"), be priests and ministers ("How could a woman give her blood for our sins?") or rabbis ("without the monthly loss of impurities, women remain unclean").

Male radicals, left-wing politicians, mystics, however, would insist that women are equal, just different, and that any woman could enter their ranks if she were willing to self-inflict a major wound every month ("you MUST give blood for the revolution"), recognize the preeminence of menstrual issues, or subordinate her selfness to all men in their Cycle of Enlightenment. Street guys would brag ("I'm a three-pad man") or answer praise from a buddy ("Man, you lookin' good!") by giving fives and saying, "Yeah, man, I'm on the rag!" TV shows would treat the subject at length. ("Happy Days": Richie and Potsie try to convince Fonzie that he is still "The Fonz," though he has missed two periods in a row.) So would newspapers. (SHARK SCARE THREATENS MENSTRUATING MEN. JUDGE CITES MONTHLY STRESS IN PARDONING RAPIST.) And movies. (Newman and Redford in "Blood Brothers"!)

Men would convince women that intercourse was more pleasurable at "that time of the month." Lesbians would be said to fear blood and therefore life itself—though probably only because they needed a good menstruating man.

Of course, male intellectuals would offer the most moral and logical arguments. How could a woman master any discipline that demanded a sense of time, space, mathematics, or measurement, for instance, without that in-built gift for measuring the cycles of the moon and planets—and thus for measuring anything at all? In the rarefied fields of philosophy and religion, could women compensate for missing the rhythm of the universe? Or for their lack of symbolic death-and-resurrection every month?

Liberal males in every field would try to be kind: the fact that "these people" have no gift for measuring life or connecting to the universe, the liberals would explain, should be punishment enough.

And how would women be trained to react? One can imagine traditional women agreeing to all arguments with a staunch and smiling masochism. ("The ERA would force housewives to wound themselves every month": Phyllis Schlafly. "Your husband's blood is as sacred as that of Jesus—and so sexy, too!": Marabel Morgan.) Reformers and Queen Bees would try to imitate men, and pretend to have a monthly cycle. All feminists would explain endlessly that men, too, needed to be liberated from the false idea of Martian aggressiveness, just as women needed to escape the bonds of menses envy. Radical feminists would add that the oppression of the nonmenstrual was the pattern for all other oppressions. ("Vampires were our first freedom fighters!") Cultural feminists would develop a bloodless imagery in art and literature. Socialist feminists would insist that only under capitalism would men be able to monopolize menstrual blood....

In fact, if men could menstruate, the power justifications could probably go on forever.

If we let them.

---

*Source:* Steinem, Gloria. (1978, October). "If Men Could Menstruate: A Political Fantasy." *Ms.,* 110.

# CHAPTER 43

## Why Is America So Obsessed with Virginity?

*Anastasia Kousakis and Jessica Valenti*

Anastasia Kousakis is a freelance writer, editor, and director. She was the associate editor at the Progressive Book Club when this interview was conducted.

Jessica Valenti is a well-known American feminist writer, lecturer, and activist. She is the author of six books, including *The Purity Myth: How America's Obsession with Virginity Is Hurting Young Women*, which has been made into a documentary. She is also a co-editor of the anthology *Yes Means Yes: Visions of Female Sexual Power and a World without Rape*, which was named one of *Publishers Weekly*'s Top 100 Books of 2009. Her most recent book, *Sex Object: A Memoir* (2016), was a *New York Times* bestseller. Valenti is the founder of the award-winning blog Feministing.com, an online community run by and for young feminists.

Think you know the meaning of virginity? You'll be surprised to find out what Jessica Valenti discovered. In her book *The Purity Myth: How America's Obsession with Virginity Is Hurting Young Women*, the founder and [former] executive editor of Feministing. com takes on the virginity movement, and argues that it's high time we disassociate female morality and sexuality. I sat down with Valenti to discuss the book, the myths, and what's going on at those Purity Balls.

**AK: So, what is the purity myth?**

**JV:** The purity myth is the lie that virginity or sexual abstinence has some bearing on who we are as people, as good people, women in particular. More specifically, what the book talks about is how that lie and how that myth is really a driving force in a lot of the conservative moves to regress women's rights and to reinforce traditional gender roles. So, how they're using this myth of sexual purity, this fear of young women's sexuality, to promote their agenda for women.

**AK: You argue in the book that America is obsessed with virginity, female virginity specifically, and that there is, in fact, an entire movement fuelling this obsession. How exactly do you define the "virginity movement"?**

JV: The virginity movement, specifically, is a group of—and they certainly don't call themselves the virginity movement—conservatives, anti-feminist organizations, legislators, all with this really specific agenda in mind for women that's definitely regressive, definitely old school, definitely traditional. But instead of using the normal ways of pushing their agenda, they're really focusing on young women's sexuality as not only a scare tactic but as a salacious way to get their point across.

AK: **One of the more fascinating things that's revealed in your book is that there is actually no official medical definition of "virginity."**

JV: Right. Isn't that crazy!

AK: **How, then, is virginity defined by those who are working so hard to defend the so-called purity of girls and women?**

JV: The virginity movement uses the definition of virginity that's the most culturally accepted one—heterosexual intercourse. And I think that limited definition of virginity is probably why so many virginity pledgers have oral and anal sex, because they don't necessarily see it as infringing on their virginity.

AK: **So young people are engaging in sexual activity, and considering themselves still virgins because they say "If I have oral sex I can still be a virgin ..."**

JV: Right. And that's what I found really interesting when I interviewed Hanne Blank who wrote *Virgin: The Untouched History*, which is this amazing history of virginity. The reason she started to look into the definition of virginity was because she was answering young people's questions on this website she ran, and a lot of the questions were, "Am I still a virgin? I did such and such."

And she was like, "I don't know? Do you want to be?" She told all these really interesting stories of how young people will—I think she calls them Process Oriented Virgins—make excuses, like "Oh, yeah, I had sexual intercourse, but that's not really when I lost my virginity. I really lost my virginity when I did this." Or "I really lost my virginity when I had an orgasm." Everyone has different definitions for it.

AK: **In some ways, virginity, as it's defined by the virginity movement—**

JV: It's completely irrelevant.

AK: **And, if purity equals virginity then virginity is a myth, as well.**

JV: Right. Oh, I definitely think that virginity is a myth. I think that virginity is a huge lie. Having your first sexual encounter certainly is important, and I don't mean to demean anyone's understanding of their sexuality or how they want to think of themselves in that way. And I think that can be a really powerful experience and a wonderful first thing. But, as a concept it's more dangerous than not, because it puts us into these virgin or not virgin categories, which doesn't really give us a very nuanced perspective or understanding of sexuality.

AK: **Speaking of danger, what are the things that abstinence-only educators are actually teaching young children, particularly girls, and how are they dangerous?**

JV: Oh, there are so many! I don't think it's any secret that most abstinence-only education is medically inaccurate. They lie about contraception in terms of its failure rate; one class was taught that condoms cause cancer. What ends up happening for a lot of these kids is that they've been taught that birth control is ineffective or birth control is dangerous so they don't use it.

Outside of the medical and health dangers, there's also a social message being taught in abstinence-only education, which is that boys want sex and they'll do anything to get it, and girls own sex and have to keep it. It's up to young women to be the gatekeepers of sexuality. There's a lot of talk about dressing a certain way, you control what men think of you. It's this very disturbing message that somehow young women have control over male sexuality, and that you shouldn't get a guy too excited. Which, of course, lends itself to all sorts of victim blaming and sexual assault situations and things like that. So, that's also very dangerous.

AK: **Recently, teen mother Bristol Palin was asked about using contraception and she said, "Everyone should be abstinent … but it's not realistic at all." Do abstinence-only supporters and educators actually think what they're doing works? Or is there something more to it?**

JV: I think there are a lot of folks who believe that it truly works, because they have these kids and they're pledging their virginity. You know, not understanding that, of course, if you get a 14-year-old in front of their community members and church members and parents they're going to pledge their virginity. It's not like they're going to say no. So, yeah, I think [they think] they're being effective. But, they aren't honest about their larger agenda—that this isn't about keeping kids healthy, this isn't about teaching young people to make good choices sexually and morally. It's about reinforcing traditional gender roles in a really, really specific, rigid way. It's about relaying specific messages about sexuality and what's appropriate. And, of course, that's being straight and married and having kids.

AK: **The people behind the virginity movement go to great lengths to connect purity with abstinence, one of the more shocking examples are Purity Balls—which, you note, are federally funded [in the United States]. What are Purity Balls and why are we paying for them?**

JV: [Laughs] Purity Balls. I could talk about Purity Balls all day. Purity Balls are essentially daddy-daughter dances where young girls at some point in the evening will pledge their virginity to their fathers, and their fathers, in turn, will pledge to be the caretakers of said virginity. If you can watch a video, it's very, very disturbing. The language they use is mired in ownership and these really old school, antiquated norms about daddies owning their daughters. There's one video where the fathers give the daughters a necklace—it's a lock and a key. She keeps the lock and he keeps the key until the day she gets married and he gives the key/penis to her future husband. Very, very disturbing.

[Purity Balls are] put on by crisis pregnancy centers, which are federally funded through abstinence-only education money. What's really interesting about them is when people started to complain, "Where are the mother-son Purity Balls?" and people started to call them out on their patriarchal bullshit, if you will, they create something called Integrity Balls. Integrity Balls are mother-son dances, but instead of the son pledging his virginity to his mother and his mother pledging to protect his virginity until he gets married, the language is, "I vow to be abstinent because I don't want to do that to someone's future wife or someone's current daughter." It's still framed in this language of women-as-property.

AK: **Is this rooted in religion?**

JV: Purity Balls are definitely rooted in Christianity and Evangelical stuff, absolutely. But, I don't think it's necessarily relegated to one religion. A lot of folks are having the Purity Balls. More broadly, the idea of virginity and women's morality being tied up with virginity, young women being good when they're virgins, that's certainly not just a religious thing. It's a pretty culture-wide thing, I believe.

AK: **How does feminism factor into the virginity movement?**

JV: The most interesting thing to me about the virginity movement and what reveals their true agenda—that it's not just about helping women—is the fact that they're so antifeminist, and the fact that a lot of the books that are written about this, a lot of the speakers, either have ties to antifeminist organizations, like Independent Women's Forum or Concerned Women for America, or straight up blame feminism for the woes of young women today. They're very direct in saying that they think feminism is the problem, which I think is really telling—what does it say about their movement that they think that women's equality is a problem for women?

AK: **Admittedly, I never identified as a "feminist" in my teens and early 20s, and as recently as last weekend I heard a close female friend, who's 30, insist that she's not a feminist. What would you say to young women and girls who are reluctant to identify as feminist, especially those who are strong, independent, self-determined individuals? What is it about feminism, or the notion of feminism, that turns them off?**

JV: There are a couple of things. There are a lot of folks out there that don't identify as feminists because of more political reasons. A lot of women of color don't identify as feminists because of the racist history of the movement. I get that. But overwhelmingly what you see are a lot of women, especially young women, who have feminist ideals, who believe in feminist issues, who don't call themselves feminist because they're afraid of being called a man-hater or they're afraid of being called ugly—whatever bizarre antifeminist stereotype they believe. Or, they're afraid of being questioned. This is [true] for much younger women I've spoken to who are like, "I don't really know all that much about feminism and I don't want someone to be like, what is it about?" Young women already feel apprehensive in terms of talking about politics, and stuff like that, so [there's a] fear of being called out.

What I find really interesting about it is, once I do talk to younger women about feminism, and once you debunk those antifeminist myths and make clear that not only are these myths untrue but they exist for a reason, that they're really strategic, then they're like, "Oh. Yeah. That's true." So I think that it doesn't take much.

AK: **To get more young women, or women in general, on board …**

JV: Exactly. And the truth is there are a ton of young women out there who are doing feminist work who don't identify as feminists. And that's okay with me, too. You don't need to call yourself a feminist in order to be doing great feminist work. People often ask me that: Well don't you think it's important that they call themselves feminists? Not for me it's not. For them, though, there's a real benefit in calling yourself a feminist because you have access to this community and this support system that you may not know is there. So that's why I really try to encourage young women to not only keep believing in those feminist values, keep fighting for them, but also to identify as feminist for their own sake, and for their own well-being.

AK: **You write a lot about pornography in the book—how does pornography relate to the myth of purity?**

JV: Oh, God. So much. Mainstream pornography is very much tied up in the virgin-whore thing. They have virgin porn, they have barely-legal porn. This idea that the sexiest women are not women, they're girls. Then, of course, there's the whore porn where you have to do the most dirty, disgusting horrible things to someone. Porn plays into this dichotomous, binary vision of sexuality, that girls are either innocent and need to be taken advantage of, or they're whores who just want … I was going to say something disgusting but I won't. But, of course, as I say in the book, there's a lot of great feminist porn out there.

AK: **Yeah, you argue that there is a progressive approach to pornography.**

JV: I do think that. It's difficult because feminist porn is really dwarfed by the mainstream pornography industry. It's difficult to be like, "Oh it's fine because there's feminist porn," when there are a couple of feminist porn makers and this huge, multi-billion dollar porn industry. But, the answer of the virginity movement and the conservative movement has been trying to put it away and hide it which has not been effective, and just makes things worse. Instead of doing that, why don't we talk to the women, few as they may be, who are making progressive pornography, who are looking at sexuality in a complex way? Why don't we look to them for answers, not just about sexuality, but about pornography. When we talk about pornography, why aren't we talking to the people who are actually doing it right?

AK: **The purity movement has such a specific idea of what purity means—it's only white, female, heterosexual purity. Where do homosexuals and women of color fit into the picture?**

JV: Well, they are the impure ones. If some of us are pure and innocent, then the rest of us are dirty and bad. Certainly with women of color I'm not the first person to say this. It's not a new idea that they're so hypersexualized, that they're never considered the virgin, that they're never considered innocent. But I would argue that the same is true for queer women. They're queer—they're the "other" in that way. Any deviation from straight, vanilla, procreative sex is impure, dirty, wrong. That's why I even think masturbation is seen as impure—because it's not procreative, because it's purely for pleasure, it's bad. So lesbian sex, or gay male sex for that matter, is wrong, impure, dirty, bad. Which not only says terrible things about their homophobia and heteronormativity, but also says terrible things about what they think about sexual pleasure and its place in the world.

*Source:* Kousakis, Anastasia, & Valenti, Jessica. (2009, May 8). "Why Is America So Obsessed with Virginity?" *HuffPost Blog.* Retrieved from: https://www.huffingtonpost.com/anastasia-kousakis/why-is-america-so-obsesse_b_183798.html.

# CLITERACY, 100 NATURAL LAWS AND Άδάμας (UNCONQUERABLE)

*Sophia Wallace*

Sophia Wallace is an award-winning American conceptual artist who uses mixed media to explore how otherness is constructed visually on the gendered, sexualized, racialized body. Wallace has presented her work in major exhibitions across the United States and abroad. She has received international critical acclaim and viral exposure for "CLITERACY," a project addressing citizenship and body sovereignty using the medium of text-based objects, unauthorized street installation, performance, and sculptural forms.

**Source:** Wallace, Sophia. (2012). *CLITERACY, 100 Natural Laws.* Retrieved from: http://www.sophiawallace.com/cliteracy-100-natural-laws.

*CLITERACY, 100 Natural Laws,* is a mixed media project that explores a paradox; the global obsession with sexualizing female bodies in a world that is illiterate when it comes to female sexuality. *CLITERACY* is a new way of talking about citizenship, sexuality, human rights, and bodies. The project reveals the—phallic as neutral—bias in science, law, philosophy, politics, mainstream and even feminist discussion, and the art world—which is so saturated with the female body as subject. Using text as form, *CLITERACY* explores the construction of female sexual bodies as passive vehicles of reception defined by lack. It confronts a false body of knowledge by scientists who have resisted the idea of a unique, autonomous female body and rather studied what confirmed their assumption that women's anatomy was the inverse of male anatomy, and that reproduction was worthy of study, while female sexuality was most certainly not. In the last ten years there have been tremendous scientific breakthroughs in the understanding of the clitoris. The clitoris is exponentially larger and more complex than commonly thought. What we think of as the clitoris, is only the tip of the iceberg. While this discovery is shocking in its late arrival, the problem of global ILLCLITERACY is a salient allegory into the bigger problem of a female body, both cis and trans female, constructed with false information and a greater goal of control within culture that defines femaleness as inferior and female sexual organs as taboo. *CLITERACY* builds upon my photographic practice and ongoing exploration of how power shapes knowledge, often through use of the visual, for the purpose of reifying hierarchy.

# CHAPTER 44

## The Facilities

*Ivan Coyote*

Ivan Coyote is a Canadian spoken word performer, writer, and LGBTQI advocate. Coyote is the award-winning author of eleven books and creator of four short films, and has released three albums that combine storytelling with music. Coyote often grapples with complex and personal issues of gender identity in their work, as well as topics such as family, class, social justice, and queer liberation. In their book *Gender Failure* (co-authored with Rae Spoon and excerpted below), Coyote explores and exposes their failed attempts at fitting into the gender binary, and the harmful impacts of enforcing traditional gender roles.

I can hold my pee for hours. Nearly all day. It's a skill I developed out of necessity, after years of navigating public washrooms. I hold it for as long as I can, until I can get myself to the theatre or the green room or my hotel room, or home. Using a public washroom is a very last resort for me. I try to use the wheelchair-accessible, gender-neutral facilities whenever possible, always after a thorough search of the area to make sure no one in an actual wheelchair or with mobility issues is en route. I always hold my breath a little on the way out though, hoping there isn't an angry person leaning on crutches waiting there when I exit. This has never happened yet, but I still worry. Sometimes I rehearse a little speech as I pee quickly and wash my hands, just to be prepared. I would say something like, I apologize for inconveniencing you by using the washroom that is accessible to disabled people, but we live in a world that is not able to make room enough for trans people

to pee in safety, and after many years of tribulation in women's washrooms, I have taken to using the only place provided for people of all genders.

But I have never had to say any of this. Yet. Once at an airport, I was stopped by a janitor on my way out who reprimanded me for using a bathroom that wasn't meant for me, and I calmly explained to him that I was a transgender person, and that this was the only place I felt safe in, and then I noted that there were no disabled people lined up outside the washroom door, or parents with small children waiting to use the change table.

He narrowed his eyes at me. Then he said, "Okay, but next time you should …"

I waited for him to finish. Instead, he shook his head and motioned down the empty hallway with his mop handle that I should be off, that this conversation was now over.

I wondered later in the departure lounge exactly what it was he felt I should do next time? Hold it longer? Not have bodily functions at all? Use the men's room? The ladies'? Be someone else? Look different? Wear a dress? Not wear a tie? Cease and desist with air travel altogether? Do my part to dismantle the gender binary to make more room for people like myself?

I could write an entire book about bathroom incidents I have experienced. It would be a long and boring book where nearly every chapter ends the same, so I won't. But I could. Forty-four years of bathroom troubles. I try to remind myself of that every time a nice lady in her new pantsuit for travelling screams or stares at me, I try to remember that this is maybe her first encounter with someone who doesn't appear to be much of a lady in the ladies' room. That she has no way of knowing this is already the sixth time this week that this has happened to me, and that I have four decades of it already weighing heavy on my back. She doesn't know I have been verbally harassed in women's washrooms for years. She doesn't know I have been hauled out with my pants still undone by security guards and smashed over the head with a giant handbag once. She can't know that I have five cities and seven more airport bathrooms and eleven shows left to get through before I can safely pee in my own toilet. She can't know that my tampon gave up the ghost somewhere between the security line and the food court. I try to remember all that she cannot know about my day, and try to find compassion and patience and smile kind when I explain that I have just as much right to be there as she does, and then make a beeline, eyes down, shoulders relaxed in a non-confrontational slant, into the first stall on the left, closest to the door.

Every time I bring up or write about the hassles trans and genderqueer people receive in public washrooms or change rooms, the first thing out of many women's mouths is that they have a right to feel safe in a public washroom, and that, no offense, but if they saw someone who "looks like me" in there, well, they would feel afraid, too. I hear this from other queer women. Other feminists. This should sting less than it does, but I can't help it. What is always implied here

is that I am other, somehow, that I don't also need to feel safe. That somehow their safety trumps mine.

If there is anything I really do understand, it is being afraid in a public washroom. I am afraid in them all the time, with a lifetime of good reason. I wish that I had some evidence that harassing people in public washrooms really did originate from being afraid. I wish I could believe them that it starts with their own fear. What I suspect is more true is that their behavior begins with and is fed by a phobia. They are afraid of men in a women's washroom, because of what might happen. I am afraid of women in a women's washroom, because of what happens to me all the time.

I don't see cisgendered women who want to feel safe in a public washroom as my adversaries, though; what I see is the potential for many built-in comrades in the fight for gender-neutral, single-stall locking washrooms in all public places. Because the space they seek and the safety I dream of can be accomplished with the very same hammer and nails. Because what I do know for sure is that every single trans person I have ever spoken to, every single tomboy or woman who wears coveralls for her job or woman with short hair or recovering from chemo, or effeminate boy, or man who likes wearing dresses, or man with long hair that I have ever met is hassled or confronted or challenged nearly every other time they use a public washroom, anywhere. Always. Often. Every day. All the time. Incessantly. Repeatedly. Without mercy or respite. Everything from staring to pointing to screaming to physical violence.

This violence and harassment is justified by people claiming that they were afraid. But very rarely does it feel to me like the person harassing me is actually afraid. Startled, maybe, for a second or two. But when I explain that I was assigned female at birth, just like they were, they usually don't back down. Their fear doesn't disappear, or dissipate. This is right about the time their friend will shake their head at me as if to say, what do you expect? They will pat their friend on the back to comfort them. They both feel entitled to be in a public washroom, entitled enough that they

428 Part 4 Cultural Representations and Body Politics

get to decide whether or not I am welcome there. This feels to me like I am being policed, and punished for what I look like. This doesn't smell like fear to me. It reeks of transphobia.

It starts very early. I know a little girl, the daughter of a friend, who is a self-identified tomboy. Cowboy boots and caterpillar yellow toy trucks. One time I asked her what her favourite colour was and she told me camouflage. She came home last October in tears from her half-day at preschool with soggy pants because the other kids were harassing her when she used the girls' room at school and the teacher had instructed her to stay out of the boys' room. She had drunk two glasses of juice at the Halloween party and couldn't hold her pee any longer. She and her peers were four years old, they knew she was a girl, yet already they felt empowered enough in their own bigotries to police her use of the so-called public washrooms. I find it extremely hard to believe that these children were motivated by fear of another little girl. She was four years old and had already learned the brutal lesson that there was no bathroom door with a sign on it that welcomed people who looked like her. She had already been taught that bathrooms were a problem, and that problem started with her, and was hers alone.

My friend asked me to talk to her, and I did. I wanted to tell her that her mom and I were going to talk to the school and that it would all stop, but I knew this wasn't true. I wanted to say that it would be better when she got older, but I couldn't. I asked her to tell me the story of what happened. Asked her how it made her feel. Mad and sad, she told me. I told her she wasn't alone. She asked me if I had ever peed in my own pants. I told her yes, I had, but not for a long time. When you get bigger, your bladder grows bigger too, I told her. When you get old like me, you will be able to hold your pee for a lot longer, I promised her. Until you get home? she asked me. I said yes, until you can get home. She seemed to take some comfort in that.

So I get a little tired of having to swallow my lived experience to be force-fed someone else's what-ifs. I get tired of my safety coming second. I get tired of the realities of trans and gender non-conforming people's lives being overshadowed and ignored in favour of a boogey-man that might be lurking in the ladies room. I get really tired of being mistaken for a monster. I get tired of swallowing all these bathroom stories and smiling politely. But the last thing I can do is allow myself to get angry. Because if I get angry, then I am seen as even more of a threat. Then it's all my fault, isn't it?

Because then there is a man in the ladies' room, and for some reason, he's angry.

_Source:_ Coyote, Ivan. (2014). "The Facilities." In Ivan Coyote & Rae Spoon, _Gender Failure_ (pp. 205–210). Vancouver, BC: Arsenal Pulp Press.

## THE NEW SEX ED

*Forward Together*

Forward Together, formerly Asian Communities for Reproductive Justice (ACRJ), has been at the forefront of building a reproductive justice movement that understands the reproductive health and rights of marginalized women and girls within a social justice framework. Forward Together identifies itself as a multi-racial organization that works with community leaders and organizations to transform culture and policy to catalyze social change. Its mission is to ensure that women, youth, and families have the power and resources they need to reach their full potential.

## Introducing the New Sex Ed: Empowered Youth Strengthening Communities!

The New Sex Ed is a collaborative creation of the SexEd! Strategic Cohort, a movement-building vehicle of EMERJ (Expanding the Movement for Empowerment and Reproductive Justice). The five groups in SexEd! are all doing cutting-edge work on sexuality education in diverse communities across the country [United States]: Forward Together, California Latinas for Reproductive Justice, Colorado Organization for Latina Opportunity and Reproductive Rights, Illinois Caucus for Adolescent Health, and SPARK Reproductive Justice Now.

**Why Do We Need It?**

The growing awareness that abstinence-only education is a failed strategy creates an opportunity for us to demand the kind of sexuality education that will provide young people in all communities [with] the information, skills, and support they need to thrive. Comprehensive sexuality education (CSE) is useful, but we can do more to include the experiences and needs of communities of color, immigrant communities, LGBTQ communities, and others who have traditionally been left out of CSE programs and policies.

**What Does It Provide?**

The New Sex Ed has lots of tools and strategies that are holistic, grounded in our communities, and engages those whose experiences and realities are often overlooked. It is a resource for building a new movement for sexuality education in this country [United States] that is relevant to all people in all communities. Imagine that!

**What Can You Do with It?**

Use it, share it with your allies, and please let us know what worked and didn't work for you and your communities. Together we can work toward making sure that all of our communities have the support and resources they need to thrive!

# Sexuality Education Justice (SEJ) Framework

## What We Want: Our Vision

- We want sexuality education that has a *holistic* view of sexuality and sexual health, including positive body image, self-esteem, gender identity, sexual orientation, and communication and decision-making in relationships, and for sexuality to be seen as a part of life.
- We want sexuality education that goes *beyond a deficit-based disease and pregnancy prevention framework* to recognize and celebrate sexuality as a natural part of human development.
- We want *attention, commitment, and resources* that focus on promoting overall sexual health of all people, including marginalized communities—people of color, LGBTQ folks, people with disabilities, immigrants.
- Sexuality education is about *equity*, and we want quality sexuality education for all students and all people.
- Sexuality education is a *core part of people's lives*, not an extra issue that we work on.
- What we want is sexuality education JUSTICE.

## The Problem

- Abstinence-only education doesn't work, and even "comprehensive" sexuality education can be a *narrow, one-size-fits-all approach* that doesn't build on the strengths, histories, and experiences of young people, families, and communities.
- Some students get better sexuality education than others. In many cases, this is because some schools have more money and resources: *It's an issue of equity.*
- Educators, parents, and others who provide information about sexuality do not have tools to teach sexuality education that is *holistic, non-deficit based, and is relevant to our families, communities, and cultures.*

## The Solution: SEJ

Sexuality Education Justice is holistic.

- It addresses the *needs and realities of all people*—including people of color, Indigenous people, immigrants and English language learners, people with disabilities, LGBTQ people, people of faith, and people of all ages and genders—and is based on the lived experiences and cultural norms of these diverse groups of people.
- It incorporates *social, cultural, and economic support* for pregnant and parenting youth, including directly addressing stigma and demonization of young people of color.
- It addresses *cultural and societal myths, stereotypes, and barriers* (e.g., shame and guilt) around sexuality and positive sexuality.
- It's having the *power and resources* to make informed decisions about our gender, body, sexuality, relationships, and well-being.

## Why Do We Need SEJ?

- Sexuality education *impacts everyone*, not just the majority. So our approaches must resonate with all communities.
- Sexuality education must *support, not demonize*, communities that are "left out," e.g., those whose power to make decisions about their bodies is compromised by existing approaches to sexuality education, like communities of color, LGBT communities, teen parents, etc.
- Sexuality education must *build on the wisdom and experience of our communities*, and speak to the needs of our communities, in order to benefit our communities.

## How Do We Achieve SEJ?

By building on community strengths:

- *Youth* can engage in peer education, leadership development, and organizing to ensure that they and their peers are gaining the knowledge and power they need to make informed decisions about sex and sexuality.
- *Parents* can break the silence and fear around talking about sexuality with their children if they have the tools they need to do so. Parents care about what their children are learning, they want to develop trust with their children, and they are willing to stand up for what is best for their families.
- *Organizations* can ensure that the communities they serve have the culturally relevant support and resources that allow all people to make the best decisions for themselves regarding their gender, bodies, sexuality, and relationships through providing direct services, developing tools, advocating for policies, and organizing for change.

---

*Source:* Forward Together. (2010, July 13). "Introducing the New Sex Ed: Empowered Youth Strengthening Communities!" Retrieved from: http://www.reproductivejusticeblog.org/2010/07/introducing-new-sex-ed-empowered-youth.html; Forward Together. (2010). "Sexuality Education Justice Framework." Retrieved from: http://strongfamiliesmovement.org/sej-framework.

# CHAPTER 45

## Through the Mirror of Beauty Culture

*Carla Rice*

Carla Rice is a professor and Canada Research Chair in Care, Gender, and Relationships in the College of Social and Applied Human Sciences at the University of Guelph. She is a leader in the field of embodiment studies in Canada, and her research explores cultural representations of stories of body and identity. She is the founder of Re•Vision: The Centre for Art and Social Justice, a social research centre with a mandate to use arts-informed and community-engaged methods to foster inclusive communities, well-being, equity, and justice within Canada and beyond. Rice's notable books include *Gender and Women's Studies in Canada: Critical Terrain* and *Becoming Women: The Embodied Self in Image Culture*.

## INTRODUCTION

The body is an important identity project for girls coming of age in Westernized cultures. As a key self-making medium, many girls and women also experience their bodies as significant obstacles and sources of distress. On the positive side, bodies are sites of agency and empowerment, primary vehicles through which individuals explore, interact with, and understand the world. On the negative, bodies are objects of social scrutiny and sanction, fueling girls' dissatisfaction and deprecation. In this chapter, I explore the contradictory meanings young women hold regarding their bodies. Using the concept of the "material culture of beauty" and my own research on adult women's body histories, I reveal the ways in which cultural imaginings and gazes have shaped their body self-images. Narratives of embodiment from 100 ordinary Canadian women of varying body sizes and racial backgrounds and with and without disabilities and physical differences illustrate the fact that, although women of all ages have greater freedom to play with their appearance, cultural codes of beauty have become more narrowly defined over the past few decades. The result is a curious situation in which women are told to be and look however they wish all the while experiencing social sanction and derision if they step outside narrow boundaries of acceptable bodily self-presentations.

There is an upsurge of feminist writing about beauty, both critical and celebratory. Although feminist commentary on beauty has mushroomed since the 1970s, writers continue to wrestle with the same old debate: Are beauty practices manifestations of sexist, racist, and market oppression of women? Or, do they afford women opportunities for self-expression, empowerment, and pleasure? Some critics contend that patriarchal and commercial interests push women into painful beauty work to satisfy our culturally created desires and assuage fears of difference (Gill, 2009). Others argue that women are not cultural dupes but active agents who strategically alter their appearance in their best interests (Holliday & Sanchez Taylor, 2006). Body stories reveal the ways in which women of all shapes, sizes, and hues take up body ideals and identify multiple motivations for their beautifying practices, ranging from pleasure and convenience to self-esteem and economic advantage. The stories further disclose that although all women grapple with the contradictions of body practices that may oppress even as they empower, not all confront the same cultural looks and gazes. For example, young, thin, white women are more likely to be seen as the epitome of beauty; visibly disabled women as undesirable and sexless; Black women as sexually wild and aggressive; and Asian and South Asian women as meek or mysterious and exotic. The interplay of these stereotypes with body ideals calls for more intersectional understandings of the role that cultural imagery plays in women's lives. To help develop these sorts of interpretations, I explore the differing cultural gazes that diverse women confront, then move to examine the body projects they take up.

## THE UNEASY PRIMACY OF IMAGES

In Western culture, women are identified socially with their bodies. How the culture values or devalues physical features, sizes, and capacities has a significant impact on women's sense of body and self. In explaining why the body is so important to women's identity, French feminist Simone de Beauvoir famously wrote that, "one is not born, but becomes a woman" (1974, p. 249). She argues that women's bodies are central to this process; through media, medical systems, and

beauty culture, we learn how to fashion our bodies to "create" our gender. Since de Beauvoir, feminist critics looking at images of female bodies have noted that women tend to be positioned as "objects" of a male gaze (Mulvey, 1975). As critic John Berger (1980) said of the ways that women and men have been depicted in Western art and advertising: "… men act and women appear. Men look at women. Women watch themselves being looked at. This determines not only most relations between men and women but also the relation of women to themselves" (p. 47). Many in my study experienced being looked at as an everyday occurrence in their lives: "No one verbalizes it. It becomes the norm. 'He was looking at my tits.' 'He was looking at my ass'" (Sheila, 22, South Asian Canadian). In sexist visual society, where men as a group are handed greater power to determine women's desirability and value, girls grow up with varying degrees of insecurity about the beholder's assessment: "I see girls who are competent yet they fall apart because a guy walks in the door" (Andrea, 37, white Canadian). These "gendered looking relations" not only affected how the women I interviewed surveyed their bodies, but by teaching them certain ideals and norms of femininity and femaleness, also taught them to police the boundaries of their gendered and sexed embodiment.

How did gendered looking relations emerge? For most of us, mirrors are the oldest and most ubiquitous image-making technologies in our day-to-day lives. As cultural historians have shown, prior to the Victorian period, only the wealthy could afford mirrors. In the 16th century, for example, a small glass mirror framed in precious metals and jewels cost the equivalent of a luxury car in today's currency (Melchior-Bonnet, 2001). Technological advancements in the 19th century saw massive increases in mirror production and their installation in public and private spaces. The new department stores, such as Eaton's in Canada and Macy's in the United States, used reflecting surfaces to illuminate interiors with light as a way to encourage spending (O'Brien &

Szeman, 2004). At the same time, mirrors became permanent fixtures of middle-class homes as well as portable accessories for many girls and women. Thus, a majority of Western women began to subject their bodies to greater scrutiny only with the introduction of affordable image technologies—first mirrors, then photography and film (Rice, 2014).

In the 19th century, beauty was believed to derive from inner qualities such as character, morality, and spirituality. To orient female buyers toward consumption of cosmetics, marketers heightened women's image consciousness by reminding them of the critical gaze of others. For example, one ad from the 1920s warns women "Strangers' eyes, keen and critical—can you meet them proudly, confidently, without fear?" Another claims, "Your husband's eyes … more searching than your mirror."[1]

Surprisingly, while today large corporations control the cosmetics market, ordinary women were industry innovators. Canadian working-class farm girl Elizabeth Arden, poor Jewish immigrant Helena Rubinstein, and African American domestic servant and daughter of slaves Madame C. J. Walker became successful entrepreneurs. Feminist social historian Kathy Peiss (1998) suggests that these socially marginalized women built their businesses by attracting other women to act as sales agents and by using stories of their own struggles to attract customers. Early entrepreneurs brought to advertising the idea that women could improve their social situation through personal transformation.

By the 1920s, the beauty business had mushroomed into a mass market overtaken by male manufacturers (Peiss, 1998). Drawing on the social permissiveness of the period, advertisers connected women's cosmetic use with greater individuality, mobility, and modernity. While marketers sold makeup as a means for women to assert autonomy and resist outmoded gender expectations, by the end of the 1930s, messages increasingly equated beauty with a woman's "true femininity." For example, in one ad entitled "Beauty Lost—Beauty Regained," readers

are told how a "lovely lady who goes to pieces" recovers her mental health by "regaining her lost youth." Ads of the time encouraged women's investment in their appearance in the name of their emotional well-being and psychological health. When image became intertwined with a woman's identity, personality, and psychology in this way, modifying the body became, for many girls and women, a principal method of caring for the self. In this way, a woman's appearance came to be read as a prime measure of her self-esteem, feminine essence, and mental health.

During the Second World War, beauty became a means for women to support the war effort, with ad copy announcing that "beauty is a duty," that "fit" bodies increased women's productivity, while "lovely" faces enhanced troop morale. It was not until the 1950s that cosmetics companies began directly targeting teenage girls—who had started to hold part-time jobs and had their own disposable income—with ads designed to appeal to their sense of generational distinctiveness and romantic desires. With copy encouraging readers to get "The 'natural' look men look for," ads for *Seventeen Cosmetics* reinforced girls' desires to attract an admiring male gaze.

Arguably, these gazes have become even more complex in today's commercial culture, as women are encouraged to find pleasure in gazing at each other's images. For example, think about the typical cover of a *Cosmo*, *Vogue*, or other fashion magazine. As you consider the cover photo, ask yourself the following questions: "Who is the woman on the cover looking at?" "Who does she think is looking at her?" Your reflections might suggest that the cover image operates not only as an object of vision for *male* but also for *female* audiences. As viewers, we might imagine ourselves to be a male or female spectator looking at the model with envy or desire. Alternately, we might imagine ourselves to be the beautiful, sexy model looking back with confidence, desire, or conviction in our own desirability at the male and female spectators who are looking at us. In either case, through this relay of looks, the model becomes an object of desire for imagined spectators *who want her* and for those *who want to be like her*. While the idea that women find pleasure in looking at each other's bodies may appear less sexist than that of men evaluating female bodies, media critic Rosalind Gill argues that the shift from an "external, male judging gaze" to an internal "self policing" gaze may represent deeper manipulation, since it invites female audiences to become more adept at scrutinizing their own and other women's images (Gill, 2007, p. 151).

Image culture sends powerful messages about the rejected or "abject" body, which it subjects to invasive stares, gapes, and glares. In Western culture, the fat, aged, ambiguously gendered, racially marked, disabled or diseased, and physically different body is an object of fear and fascination. Julia Kristeva (1982) calls the abject the twisted braid of fear and fascination that people feel when they encounter bodily fluids, physical differences, disabilities, grave illness, and dying bodies. According to Kristeva, the abject is feared and rejected because it resists our drive to master and control our bodies. Physical features and processes treated as abject are those that remind us of the uncontainability of our bodies, our vulnerability to disease, the certainty of our death.

Rather than being an object of the gaze, abject bodies, according to disability theorist Rosemary Garland-Thomson, are subjected to "the stare" (2009). Staring is our compulsion to look at disaster called "the car wreck" phenomenon (p. 3); the visual gape we engage in when we can't pull our eyes away from the unfamiliar, unexpected, the strange. Women with disabilities, visible differences in particular, described the fearful and fascinated gape of non-disabled others: "There's a fascination with difference. People want the gory details of disability because they want to feel that they are better off" (Harriet, 34, WASP, chronic illness). Racialized women also reported that cultural stereotypes often informed and validated hyper-sexualizing looks onto their bodies: "From a lot of white men, I get sexual fascination: I'm the wild Black woman, with pronounced buttocks and thighs" (Marcia, 37, African Canadian, First Nations).

## BODY PROJECTS TODAY

As a result of the cultural meanings given to notions of desirability and difference, many girls and women come to relate to their bodies as self-making projects. The women who participated in this study, born in the 1960s onwards, from all walks of life in Canada are among the first generation to come of age in a world replete with image technologies of mirrors, cameras, and computers. Nearly every woman I spoke with recognized the controlling influence of different cultural and gendered gazes. While the experiences of this cohort varied depending on race, size, and ability, most women I spoke to also told of how their degree of dissatisfaction increased in adolescence, a time when they encountered mounting pressure to appear as desirable. Many came to see different body sites—including skin, weight, hair, and breasts—as projects and as problems. This included the 90% who saw themselves as over- or underweight; 80% who believed their breasts were too big or small; 60% who believed their skin was too dark and/or disliked their hair colour/texture; and 100% who began to remove unwanted body hair. Coming of age in a consumerist, image-oriented society, they dealt with the disparity between differences and ideals by imagining, as one participant put it, their best possible bodily self: "I never had an image of me that wasn't in the [wheel]chair. But I would create images of me looking different in the sense that I would be prettier, slimmer, more popular. The most attractive I could imagine becoming: my best possible image of myself" (Frances, 45, WASP, born with spina bifida). All navigated puberty and adolescence by envisioning or adopting diverse practices—from hair relaxing and eating disorders to dieting and cosmetic surgery—to remake their differences desirable.

The messages in today's magazines echo the efforts of the women in my study to close the gap between their body differences and desirable ideals. Fashion magazines are vehicles for delivering messages of the beauty business to female consumers; a primary purpose is to enlist readers into image enhancement through continuous consumption. Rather than advocating one ideal, magazines try to democratize beauty by convincing readers that they can achieve their "best bodies." This message enables girls' and women's expression of individuality and celebration of difference. Yet it also portrays body modification as critical to self-expression. In addition, it pulls diverse audiences into preoccupation with perpetual body improvement and purchase of products.

In what follows, I describe the various body projects that women in my study took up and consider how their motivations for engaging in bodywork varied depending on their race, ability, and size.

## Weight

In contemporary Western culture, people learn to value a certain size as part of the body beautiful. For example, the thin female body is associated with health, wealth, sexiness, and success. Despite a growing dialogue about body acceptance, fat is seen as unattractive, not physically or emotionally healthy, and lacking in self-control. Today's magazines criticize women's bodies, whatever their weight. Headlines such as "Battle of the Bones" and "Stars' Worst and Best Beach Bodies" regularly invite readers' criticism of famous bodies and encourage comparison based on looks and size. Coming of age in our size-obsessed culture, 66% of the women in this study came to feel their "too-big" bodies violated size standards and 24% that their "too-thin" ones failed to fit weight norms. The voices in their heads echoed messages from mainstream media: no size is acceptable or safe.

Historically and cross-culturally, fatness has been interpreted as both a sign of wealth and fertility and a signifier of disease and death. While the celebration and stigmatization of fat have fluctuated in different times among various cultures, concerns about the medical and moral risks of being overweight have intensified over the last century. In North America today, two competing frames shape the debate on overweight and obesity: Is it an "epidemic" or is it a "myth" (Lupton, 2012; Rice, 2007)? The first frame—the epidemic of obesity—dominates public debate. Global and national public health institutions have fuelled fear of fat by interpreting obesity as an escalating epidemic that threatens the health and fitness of populations and nations (World Health Organization, 2003). Beyond health problems, an increasing number of social problems are being blamed on fat, from global warming (Jacobson & McLay, 2006) to America's vulnerability to terrorist attacks (Associated Press, 2006). Despite the ubiquity of such moralistic medical messages, there is considerable uncertainty and controversy within obesity research itself about the causes, health consequences, measures, and treatment of obesity. More recently, social scientists, while not dismissing health concerns raised by doctors or governments, have questioned obesity researchers' assumptions and interests and begun to explore why our society has become so alarmed about fat (Gard & Wright, 2005).

Epidemiologists now suggest that rising weights in our society may be related to people's biology combined with obesity-causing environments (Brownell & Horgen, 2004). In addition, we simply do not know the health consequences of obesity. We know that the relationship between health and weight is a U-shaped curve, meaning that health risks increase at extreme under- and overweight (Gard & Wright, 2005). While high weight is associated with hypertension and heart disease, this association does not mean there is a causal relationship—in other words, there is no evidence that being fat in itself causes these health problems (Cogan & Ernsberger, 1999). To date, there are no safe, proven treatments for "excess" weight (Ernsberger & Koletsky, 1999). The most common treatments such as dieting, pills, and surgery all have health risks and consequences (Bennett & Gurin, 1983). Finally, weight measures such as the Body Mass Index (BMI) have also been called into question. BMI was originally meant as a screening tool (to tell if someone is at risk for developing a health problem) but it is now widely misused as a diagnostic tool (to tell if someone needs to lose weight) (Ikeda, Crawford, & Woodward-Lopez, 2006; Jutel, 2006). Kate Harding (2008) developed the *BMI Slide Show* to get people to think critically about BMI. Watch the slide show to assess whether you think the categories are skewed (https://kateharding.net/bmi-illustrated/).

Some critical scholars have written about "the obesity epidemic" as a moral panic, arguing that misplaced morality and ideological assumptions underlie our "war on fat" (Gard & Wright, 2005). They argue that in obesity science the causes of and solutions for obesity invariably come back to people's health practices. This view both ignores scientific uncertainty about the causes of weight gain and blames individuals by ignoring contexts such as poverty or weight prejudice that constrain their options for eating or activity.

Recent history shows that obesity epidemic discourses dominate cultural narratives partly because they dovetail with ongoing state-sponsored efforts designed to improve the health, fitness, and competitiveness of nations. From the late 1960s onwards, many Western governments, including Canada, initiated public education campaigns that advocated greater physical activity to prevent fatness and promote fitness in citizens (MacNeill, 1999). In response to growing concerns about excessive consumption and the sedentary lifestyles of Canadians, Prime Minister Pierre Elliott Trudeau launched the ParticipACTION Campaign in the early 1970s. It famously compared the fitness levels of a 30-year-old Canadian with a 60-year-old Swede. (See this ad at the ParticipACTION Archive Project http://scaa.sk.ca/gallery/participaction/english/home.html.) Many ParticipACTION ads imagined the ideal Canadian citizen as a thin, fit, white, able-bodied male. They further raised the spectre of the feminized, unfit, underdeveloped, and Third-World "Other," who threatened Canada's competitiveness on the global economic stage. However, the effectiveness of interventions that link fatness prevention to fitness promotion has never been established. Studies show

that fat children and adults are less likely to be physically active and more likely to have eating problems. Yet research has not revealed whether overeating and under-exercising increases weight, whether being fat increases one's susceptibility to problem eating and inactivity (Boutelle, Neumark-Sztainer, Story, & Resnick, 2002), or whether the association between behaviour and weight is mediated by other factors (such as genetics, food additives, and so on).

Some women in my research suggest that ParticipACTION ads disseminated throughout the 1970s and 1980s heightened their fear of fat and instilled the belief that their big bodies were "bad." By linking thinness with fitness and positioning fat as opposite to fit, ParticipACTION's popular "FitFat" ad conveyed the idea that fatness and fitness could *not* coexist in the same body. Those perceived as fat in childhood describe how demanding physical education programs introduced into schools often dissuaded them from participating in physical activity altogether. Adult enforcement of restrictive diets resulted in long-term struggles with food, including compulsive, binge, and secretive eating (Rice, 2007; 2009b). In other words, fatness prevention efforts contributed to producing the very behaviours and bodies that proponents were attempting to prevent!

> I remember this feeling of dread when the ["FitFat"] ad came on TV. Once my father and I were watching, I remember a man's voice saying, "This year fat's not where it's at." This made me so self-conscious.… (Maude, 27, white Canadian, blind from adolescence)

Although ParticipACTION ended in 2001, the Canadian federal government recently re-launched the campaign to stem rising levels of obesity, once again focusing on "over"weight children and adults as a high-risk group (Canadian Press, 2007). With a renewed focus on fatness prevention through fitness promotion, efforts to stem today's obesity epidemic may be leading a new cohort of large children to adopt problem eating and inactivity, possibly contributing to future problems with weight. This raises some critical questions for developing feminist-informed health and physical education policies and programs: What do you think a fat-friendly, girl-friendly, and disability-friendly physical education curriculum would look like? If you had the task of designing a feminist health promotion campaign, what messages would you want to convey to promote girls' health?

## Eating Distress

Although only about 3% of young women in North America have eating disorders according to medical criteria, 50% admit to extreme weight control, including fasting and vomiting (Neumark-Sztainer et al., 2002). The high prevalence of problem eating notwithstanding, eating disorders are interpreted as *mental illness* (American Psychiatric Association, 2013). However, feminist critics have long noted that an eating disorder, like all diagnoses, is a social construct (Rabinor, 2004). The term *disorder* incorrectly establishes a clear dichotomy between mental illness and wellness. Yet given the pressure for women to control their appetites and weights, it is often difficult to distinguish normal from pathological eating (Cohen, 2004; Rice & Langdon, 1991).

Unfortunately, few experts consider the concept of a *continuum* of eating problems. Beyond debates about eating disorder diagnoses, there are many problems with psychiatric labelling more generally—not only do labels stigmatize people, they also tend to be applied to the least powerful groups in society (Caplan & Cosgrove, 2004). Young women's emotional struggles tend to be pathologized more than young men's, so that there are fewer diagnoses to capture the downsides of masculinity (like excessive risk taking and inability to express emotion) than of femininity (depression and eating problems). Examples of psychiatric labels that have been proposed—such as dressing disorder and compulsive shopping disorder—expose

how power relations often arbitrate what is considered stereotypical behaviour and what is labelled a psychiatric condition.

Further, many feminists have been critical of psychiatric treatment for eating disorders that positions women as pathological for adopting socially induced behaviors (Rice, 1996). In her ethnographic research, Helene Gremillion (2003) has found that treatment programs tend to substitute one set of disciplinary practices that regulate women's bodies for another—disempowering female patients by replacing culturally condoned food and weight control with medically condoned surveillance of their eating and weight (LaMarre & Rice, 2015). Hospitalization can save lives, yet statistics belie the effectiveness of interventions: re-hospitalization of women with eating problems is common (Health Canada, 2002), creating a revolving-door experience that suggests that treatment often does not work.

Many of the women I interviewed described how they began demanding dieting and disordered eating as a way of amending what they saw as their abject body fat. Some talked of starting to eat secretively in childhood as a direct response to mothers' and doctors' enforced dieting routines while others took up disordered eating during adolescence to escape their "deviant" labels and answer pressure to appear as desirable. Whether they started secretive eating in childhood to resist adult imposition of restrictive diets or later adopted disordered eating to amend size differences, it is noteworthy that *all* participants perceived as fat eventually took up problem eating.

> At least I felt normal enough and desirable enough [when bulimic] that I could actually contemplate a sexual relationship. I could actually let go of protecting myself and enter into a relationship. (Gayle, 29, English-Métis Canadian)

Many people mistakenly believe that only privileged white girls have eating problems. Weight restriction became a way of life for a majority of women of *all* sizes and shapes I interviewed, whether Black, Asian, South Asian, or white. Some racialized participants told how ultra-thinness was viewed more critically in their communities, where images of attractive bodies spanned a broader range of sizes. However, most had grown up during a time when communities of colour constituted a small portion of the Canadian population, and thus many had little access to an alternative beauty aesthetic that called into question white weight standards. With stereotypic portrayals of starving African bodies circulating in Western media throughout the 1970s (such as in children's charity commercials), slenderness also became abject for Black women interviewed.

Growing up in a racially charged image environment, some Black women describe how they got caught between racist stereotypes of starving African bodies in mainstream media and sexist pressures to conform to conflicting feminine size ideals from both the dominant culture (thinness) and their communities (roundness). In my research, the meaning given to a woman's size depended on her race, which suggests that the emaciated brown body operates as an implicit Other against which the thin, white beauty ideal gets defined.

> A girl at school said I looked like starving kids in the World Vision commercial. That was the most hurtful thing anybody ever said to me. I thought, "I should be bigger and more normal because I look like those poster kids." (Rhonda, 32, West Indian Canadian)

## Skin

Historically, skin became women's first body project as they learned the power of complexion to advance or undermine their social inclusion. From ancient times, pallour was associated with high social status; women at work outdoors were tanned and aged faster, whereas women of high social status were not obliged to work in the fields but stayed indoors and were pale-skinned. From the 17th century onward, this superiority of white over dark was scientifically proclaimed, as white Europeans needed a convincing justification for systems of slavery and colonization that contradicted emerging political theories of human rights (Schiebinger, 1993). To rationalize the disenfranchisement of racialized peoples, scientists constructed a hierarchy of races based on physical traits such as skin colour and bone structure.

As a result of the legacies of Western colonization, racialization, and widespread sexism, many cultures still associate light skin with female beauty, and this fuels and is fuelled by a profitable business in skin-whitening products. While some feminists have suggested that skin whitening is a practice relegated to our racist past (Peiss, 1998), they are missing the rapidly growing global trade in skin-lightening products. Feminist critical race scholar Amina Mire (2005) has called this phenomenon "the globalization of white western beauty ideals." (If you doubt Mire's claim, do an internet search for "skin lightening." It will yield over a million links!) In the West, many cosmetics companies market skin lightening to aging white women by associating light skin with youth and beauty. In ads, the aging process frequently is framed as a pathological condition that can be mitigated through measures such as bleaching out "age spots." Globally, cosmetics companies also sell skin-whitening products to women of colour, often covertly via the internet in order to avoid public scrutiny or state regulation of their commodities and campaigns (Mire, 2005). This is partially because many products contain unsafe chemicals such as hydroquinone and mercury that inhibit the skin's melanin formation and are toxic. The dangers of mercury poisoning due to skin lighteners—neurological, kidney, and psychiatric damage—are well known. However, the hazards of hydroquinone, which has been shown to be scarring in high doses and to cause cancer in laboratory studies, are less well documented.

In Africa and other regions of the global South, skin whitening is traditionally associated with white colonial oppression. Because women who practise skin lightening were and are harshly judged as suffering from an "inferiority complex" due to colonization, many engage in the practice covertly (Mire, 2005). Companies thus rely on covert advertising to mitigate women's secret shame about their perceived physical deficiencies, as well as their need to conceal such practices in order to avoid condemnation. Companies selling covertly also avoid public scrutiny of product campaigns. In some campaigns, explicitly racist advertisements associate dark skin with "diseases" and "deformities" such as "hyperpigmentation" and "pigmentation pathologies." In contrast, they typically associate light skin with youth, beauty, health, and empowerment. In its online ads, L'Oréal, a leading manufacturer and marketer of skin-whiteners such as Bi-White and White Perfect, references the inferiority of dark skin and the superiority of light complexions. Bi-White features an Asian woman unzipping her darker skin. (See the ad at www.youtube.com/watch?v=l0zsVIA3x6Y.) Directed mainly to female Asian consumers, the ad uses medical language to suggest that Asian bodies produce too much melanin that Bi-White will block. As Mire (2005) writes, darkness is associated with falseness, dirtiness, ugliness, and disease. Lightness is seen as true, clean, healthy, and beautiful.

There is a growing trend for many Western-owned cosmetics corporations to rely less on covert internet marketing and more on splashy TV and print campaigns to reach customers in Asia. Since 1978, Hindustan Lever Limited, a subsidiary of the Western corporation Unilever, has sold its skin-whitening products to millions of women around the world (Melwani, 2007). Fair & Lovely, one of Hindustan Lever's best-known beauty brands, is marketed in over 38 countries and monopolizes a majority share of the skin-lightening market in India (Leistikow, 2003). One industry spokesperson stated that fairness creams are half of the skin-care market in India, and that 60 to 65% of Indian women use these products daily (Timmons, 2007). Ads for Fair & Lovely frequently feature depressed young women with few prospects who gain brighter futures by attaining their dream job or desired boyfriend after becoming fairer. Other commercials show shy young women who take charge of their lives and transform themselves into "modern" independent beauties. Appealing to women's dual aspirations for desirability and economic equality, ads feature taglines such as "Fair & Lovely: The Power of Beauty" and "Fair & Lovely: For Total Fairness" (Timmons, 2007). (See ads at www.youtube.com/watch?v=KIUQ5hbRHXk&NR=1.)

The accounts of racialized women in this study echo these ads' sensibilities in that all learned, often from both the dominant culture and their own communities, that lighter skin was associated with beauty, virtue, and economic opportunity.

> Being in the West Indian community, I was more attractive, and with people who weren't West Indian I was more acceptable because I wasn't as dark. So I had an easier time from all groups because I am supposedly that ideal. (Salima, 30, West Indian, South Asian Canadian)

Ironically, Western psychologists and psychiatrists have framed skin whitening as signs of mental illness, unconnected to colonial or other oppressive histories. In contrast, the experiences of informants suggest that skin-lightening practices are technologies of both oppression and opportunity, especially for racialized women who get caught between the colonizing effects of white supremacist ideals and competing desires for femininity and social acceptance (Rice, 2009a; 2009b). In their narratives, participants aspired to lighter (rather than white) ideals to straddle conflicting demands: to affirm their ethnic looks and escape being seen as Other. Many spoke of avoiding sunlight, wearing light concealer, and using skin lightening in an effort to create a desirable image that enabled them to evade demeaning racist and sexist comments while not completely erasing their embodied difference.

> We have a family friend who is a lot darker than we are. She bought Fair & Lovely and when everyone found out, they used to say, "Oh, she uses Fair & Lovely." The fact that we talked about it is mean. The fact that she feels she has to use it is terrible. (Preeta, 29, South Asian Canadian)

Many white women are well aware of the cultural associations of dark skin with devalued status. Yet in a cultural context where race is read off multiple body sites (skin colour, facial features, and so on), tanned skin may be viewed as a temporary, detachable adornment rather than an essential feature that signifies someone's racial status (Ahmed, 1998). It is in this context that white women often see skin darkening as a beauty project. After the First World War, tanning became a statement about high social status; a tan proclaimed the leisure to lie out in the sun and the money to go to tropical beaches in midwinter. White women who tan can thus connect their bronzed skin to health, wealth, and attractiveness, secure in the knowledge that they still are seen as white, regardless of the health implications (such as the increased risk of skin cancers and premature skin aging). These experiences, too, generate many questions: Why is there emphasis on white women's attainment of a sun-kissed glow while racialized women feel pressured to aspire to the glow of fairness? Is the obsession with fairness a bad case of a "colonial hangover," or is it an example of a Western cultural imperialism that uses global media to spread white beauty ideals?

## Hair

Within a racial hierarchy of beauty, Black women encounter complex messages about hair due to associations of long, flowing hair with social mobility and femininity. Beauty entrepreneur Madame C. J. Walker, who is credited with popularizing the "hot" comb for straightening hair, sold such products as Black women's "passport to prosperity" (Rooks, 1996, p. 65). She saw Black women's beauty in a political light—as a "vindication of black womanhood" demeaned by slavery and as a pathway to prosperity and respectability denied by white society.

Today, an estimated 80% of African American women straighten their hair (Swee, Klontz, & Lambert, 2000). In 1993, the World Rio Corporation marketed a hair-straightening product on its late-night infomercials that targeted these women. In the Rio ads, good hair was equated with straightened hair and bad hair with untamed curls. Ads used the now familiar format of abject *before* and ideal *after* shots featuring women who had been given a complete makeover. As critical race scholar Noliwe Rooks notes (1996), models in the *before* shots were without make-up, jewellery, or accessories (p. 123). They looked unhappy and their hair was unstyled and unkempt, almost made to look "primitive." The *after* shots featured women who had complete beauty makeovers. Although the manufacturers claimed Rio had low levels of acid, it actually contained harsh chemicals. Many who used it experienced hair loss, burns, blisters, and sores on their scalps. Of 340 000 people who purchased the product, over 3000 filed complaints, the largest number ever received in the United States for a cosmetic product (Swee, Klontz, & Lambert, 2000). Many Black women in my study explained how they used hair relaxers, not because they desired whiteness, but because they wanted to avoid racial Othering, as well as aspire to desirability, acceptability, and an enhanced self.

> In high school, people would say, "What are you?" I realized if I blow-dry my hair to get it straight I might not identify as anything separate.… The less I try to visually look like some stereotypes from the media or their beliefs, the less I am singled out. (Ada, 27, Trinidadian Canadian, African, and Chinese)

Not only do these attitudes have an impact on Black women's beauty perceptions but they also are linked to blocked educational and economic opportunities. Many African Canadian girls report witnessing or experiencing harassment in school arising from perceptions of their hue and hair. Some school boards in the United States have suspended African American students for wearing cornrows, dreadlocks, and other hairstyles seen as making an overly strong political statement (Rooks, 2001). Black women have even been fired from corporate jobs for styling their hair in dreadlocks and braids. Virtually all Black women I interviewed worried that if they wore their hair naturally, they would not succeed in their career or romantic aspirations. Seen in this light, it would be a mistake to interpret hair straightening as just another example of women's internalization of sexism and racism. Instead, their stories suggest that managed hair could carry social benefits, including boosting status and success.

> There's a lot of anger because if I go on interviews, people have a pre-made assumption about Black women and therefore about me. When I put in a bid for a job, it is all paper. So it isn't until the interview that they meet me. So you go into a room of ten people and they're all white. Then in walks little Blackie in her braids. You can see the shock on their faces. (Sharon, 31, West Indian, English Canadian)

Along with the presence of long-flowing hair on a woman's head, the absence of body hair is a critical characteristic of the acceptable female body. Few North American women removed their underarm or leg hair before the 20th century; with the rise of beauty culture and body-baring fashions, hair removal became commonplace by the end of the Second World War (Hope, 1982). To convince female consumers to buy depilatory products, early marketers framed any hair not on a woman's head as unsightly and ugly. At the same time, physicians began to label as pathological "excess" hair on parts of the female body typically associated with hair growth in men (Herzig, 2000).

From the pages of fashion magazines to illustrations in biology textbooks, the image of the hairless woman has emerged as a pervasive norm (Schick, Rima, & Calabrese, 2011). Although unshaven men are considered acceptable and their body hair removal optional, studies show that in Anglo-Western countries between 80 and 100% of women spend an average of 30 minutes per week removing unwanted face or body hair (PR Web, 2011). A strong cultural connection exists between hair and sex—the absence of body hair is interpreted as a sign of femaleness, whereas its presence signifies maleness (Toerien & Wilkinson, 2003).

A majority of women in this study committed at puberty to a lifetime of hair removal, which became a routine part of the hidden work of having an acceptable female body. The hairless norm is so ubiquitous that although pubic hair is an important marker of puberty, its discovery was horrifying and embarrassing for 25%, who had no prior knowledge that growing hair "down there" was typical. Many began removing leg and underarm hair to feel more attractive and a majority also told how they conformed as a way of shielding themselves from people's disapproval and their own discomfort. For some, facial hair was particularly frightening because it was read as a sign of maleness, visually undermining her sex and eliciting the scary feeling that she was not really a woman. Even though 40% of all women naturally grow facial hair (Bindel, 2010), being hirsute was emotionally and socially damaging for those in this study, fueling their depression, body consciousness, and fear of relationships.

Studies of racial differences in body hair are contradictory with some researchers claiming that Black, South Asian, and "Mediterranean" women are hairier than northern European women and others, that whites are the hairiest and Asian women the least hairy of all (Toerien & Wilkinson, 2003).

A majority of South Asian women identified body hair as a problem trait, far more than any other group I interviewed. Most assumed they were naturally hairier. But their accounts point to sexual dualism and racist stereotyping as the more likely roots of their hair worries. Historically, certain groups of racialized women, including darker-skinned African and Southern Asian as well as Indigenous South American women from the colonized world (and to a lesser extent, those from southern Europe), have been imagined as more hairy than white northern European women. In the wake of Darwin's theories of evolution, scientists began to see body hair as a measure of racial difference and to classify amounts and thicknesses of hair according to a racial hierarchy. By the Victorian era, scientists and the lay public exhibited great interest in racialized bearded women because they were seen to represent the missing link between animals and humans. In this context Julia Pastrana, a Mexican-American Indigenous woman, became a freak show performer in Europe due to her excess facial hair (caused by a rare condition called hypertrichosis). Associations between race and hair haunt the stories of South Asian Canadian women today who tell how their body hair conjured up ideas about racialized women as hairier, more masculine, and hyper-sexual within white-dominated culture.

Over the last several years, the Brazilian wax, which leaves behind a strip of hair above the pubic bone or takes all hair away, has gone from being a risqué novelty to a basic grooming practice. To give an indication of how popular pubic hair waxing has become, one researcher searching for the term "Brazilian wax" on the internet in 2001 yielded 133 hits (Labre, 2002); when I searched for the same phrase in 2011, I got close to 5 million. Surveys have found that 85 to 95% of Western women polled have tried removing hair from their groin area (Tiggemann & Hodgson, 2008); 50% regularly practise pubic-hair removal (Riddell, Varto, & Hodgson, 2010). Many shave or wax because they see their pubic hair as ugly and unclean. The association of female body hair with

the abject is highly evident in women's descriptions of their pre-shorn bodies as disgusting and gross.

## Breasts

Despite headlines to the contrary, cosmetic surgery rates in North America remain greatly skewed by gender: in 2010, over 91% of cosmetic procedures were performed on women by mostly male doctors who made up 91% of surgeons (American Society of Plastic Surgeons, 2011). According to the American Society for Aesthetic Plastic Surgery (2011), demand for plastic surgery increased by 9% in 2010 and by a whopping 155% since statistical collection began in 1997. Breast augmentation topped the list (318,123) beating out breast reduction (138,152), which placed fifth in popularity. It is difficult to get an accurate read on how many Canadian women seek breast surgery because the government does not keep track of procedures (Canadian Broadcasting Corporation, 2008). However, it is estimated that between 100,000 and 200,000 Canadian women have implants. Little reliable data are available on the race of those undergoing reductions and augmentations, but statistics indicate that 30% of all North American procedures in 2010 were performed on non-whites, who make up a growing percentage of recipients (American Society of Plastic Surgeons, 2011). The American Society of Plastic Surgeons (2011) reports that reductions are popular among African American women, while Asian American women most commonly request augmentations. These statistics do not reflect actual numbers, however, since the rise of medical tourism means more people seek out cheap surgeries in places like India, Costa Rica, and Thailand (Morgan, 1991; Morgan, 2009). As surgery goes global, augmentation has become the second most sought-after procedure, with reductions coming in sixth worldwide (International Society of Aesthetic Plastic Surgery, 2010).

Breast augmentations involving silicone gel or sacs were introduced in the 1960s but it was not until 1991 that controversy about the possible effects of these implants led to a moratorium on their general use (Heyes & Jones, 2009). Almost two decades after fears that leaks could cause connective tissue diseases (such as rheumatoid arthritis), North American governments approved a new generation of "safer" implants (for more information, go to http://www.hc-sc.gc.ca/hl-vs/iyh-vsv/med/implants-eng.php).

In the wake of this reversal, promotional pitches have escalated. Although direct-to-consumer advertising of medical drugs and devices is illegal in Canada, implant-promoting messages still trickle across our image-permeable border. Ads for the Natrelle Breast Enhancement Collection liken implants to jeans, shoes, and jewellery, framing augmentation as a fashion accessory rather than major surgery with risks. (View some examples at http://www.coloribus.com/adsarchive/prints/natrelle-breast-implants-shoes-10538005/.) On Facebook, Natrelle now gives away free "Breast Augmentation Kits" so that women considering implants can try different sizes at home. Earlier ads that used images of flowers, the word "blossom," and a just-out-of-puberty model suggest that the campaign is designed to appeal to an adolescent audience.

In makeover culture, cosmetic surgery is no longer reserved for celebrities or the superrich. Popular media and surgeons alike now promote procedures as viable solutions to ordinary image problems. Physicians have long framed surgical breast reduction as a necessary treatment for macromastia (big breasts), an apparent disorder causing physical pain and emotional problems (Mello, Domingos, & Miyazaki, 2010). More recently, the American Society of Plastic Surgeons has also classified small breasts as a disease: micromastia (Ehrenreich, 2001). Despite efforts to establish clear lines between elective and restorative surgery, labelling small breasts as a disease indicates that the boundaries between profit-driven medicine and the beauty industry have blurred as medicine transitions into big business (Sullivan, 2001).

Immersed as we are in a media sea of successful transformations, it is troubling that we don't have easy access to information about surgery's downside: the health consequences of reductions and augmentations. In my role as a researcher, I have spoken with women who were satisfied with their surgeries and had no regrets. However, in my former career as a clinician, I worked with those who bitterly regretted their decision. Some felt lied to, misled, kept in the dark about the procedure's negative consequences, and angry about the long-term costs to their bodies and lives. Beyond the pain, infection, and scarring associated with any surgery, complications from reductions and implants include partial or full loss of sexual sensation in the nipple, inability or restricted ability to breast-feed, and necrosis or death of nipple tissue (Reardon & Grogan, 2011). Of women receiving implants, most will have complications requiring additional surgery or implant removal (Tweed, 2003) because of rupture, deflation, and leakage that occurs in three-quarters of recipients (Brown et al., 2000). There is no medical consensus on how long implants last, although reputable surgeons acknowledge that *all* women with implants will require replacement at some future date (Singer, 2008). Anywhere from 25 to 100% of those with implants deal with capsular contracture, where scar tissue forms around the implant, causing implanted breasts to become hard, painful, or lopsided (Tweed, 2003). There may also be a link between silicone-gel implants and autoimmune diseases such as fibromyalgia (Brown et al., 2001).

The eight women in my own study who sought breast augmentations and reductions did so to avert harassing looks and hurtful comments, and to free themselves from stressful efforts to conceal their breast size and shape. As Debra Gimlin (2006) found in her research on women considering cosmetic surgery, those I interviewed described getting reductions and implants as a way to escape abjection more than to embody an ideal—as a means of alleviating negative feelings and alienation associated with being seen as an Other. Many experienced physical and psychological problems associated with too large or too small breasts that they connected to discomfort caused by looks, stares, and criticisms more than to the size of their breasts alone. At the same time, all were aware that to get Canada's publicly funded health insurance to cover the procedures they had to make the case that size constituted a serious medical, and not merely social, problem. Their accounts offer reasons for why women pursue surgical solutions without relying on the "beauty myth" as the main argument. Instead, as Holliday and Sanchez Taylor (2006) show, surgery seekers in this study exercised choice within a given set of constraints and engaged in a project of self-making using the options available.

> [Before my implants] I felt so uncomfortable hiding my breasts. I used to take off my bra, get under the covers, make sure it was dark so you couldn't see. I wouldn't let him touch the smaller one. If he did touch it, then he'd be "How come one's smaller?" (Maya, 22, Jamaican Canadian, disability from late childhood)

The surgical solution, though entirely understandable, is not without consequences that extend beyond each individual's health or wellness. In a context where the body is tied to a woman's morality and body modification is seen as a self-improvement strategy, there is a danger that what was once a difficult choice for some might become compulsory for many. Since a sizable minority of women now pursue surgery to enhance self-image or to ease emotional turmoil and, at times, physical pain, surgery's spread may create a conundrum for a majority since it contributes to a hierarchy of bodies and a narrowing of norms.

## CONCLUSION: RECOVERING BEAUTY?

In my research, women report two responses to beauty standards: changing their bodies, which can lead to harmful image problems and risky body alteration practices, or changing their situations, which can lead to improved bodily self-images. Many redirected their energy into creating life circumstances where self-worth was based on things other than appearance. Significantly, the capacity of each to alter her environment emerged in each narrative as key to a woman's control and ownership of image. Beyond individuals' improvisational efforts to affirm their embodied identities, other critical ways that activists change their situations is by changing their institutional and image environments. For instance, a "body equity" approach implemented in schools, health care settings, and other institutional sites advocates accepting diverse bodies and stopping stereotyping based on size, disability, and other differences (Rice & Russell, 2002). Similarly, altering image environments entails creating representations that celebrate bodily differences and that dare to depict the abject. For example, live performances by "fat drag" troupes such as *Pretty, Porky and Pissed Off* and the *Fat Femme Mafia* poke fun at cultural stereotypes about fat while the play *'Da Kink in My Hair* explores Black women's diverse embodiments and relationships to beauty. Photographer Holly Norris and model Jes Sachse have created *American Able* as a spoof of American Apparel ads to reveal how disabled women are made invisible in mass media. With creativity and courage, these artists and activists imagine new possibilities for representations.

For some feminist writers, the challenge is to rethink our concept of beauty itself (Felski, 2006) so that women can reclaim notions of beauty and "ugly" in their lives. While feminists during the second wave advocated for doing away with harmful beauty standards, contemporary scholars now contend that we cannot eliminate concepts of beauty entirely

(Rice, 2014). This is because judgments about what is beautiful may be universally present in societies (Holliday & Sanchez Taylor, 2006) and because there is no such thing as a "natural" body to which we can escape from imposed standards (Scott, 2005) (the natural and cultural are always shaping and transforming each other). For instance, Phoebe Farris (2013) explains that beauty has always been emphasized in Native American cultures, manifest through works of art and craft produced as well as in regalia worn and dances performed by contemporary Indigenous peoples.

Beyond recognising the futility of appealing to the "natural," some writers wonder what we would lose without beauty—without the visual and tactile, the gesture, smell, and sound, or any sensory pleasure in our lives (Colebrook, 2006). To change our image-driven, dominant conception of beauty, they argue instead for creating a feminist aesthetic—an inclusive theory of feminist beauty and sensory pleasure that incorporates the ugly. In order to reframe beauty in a way that avoids body shame, refuses to be reduced to the visual, affirms the ugly and includes anyone who seeks it, art historian Joanna Frueh develops the concept of "monster/beauty," a condition emerging "from intimacy with one's aesthetic/erotic capacity" (2001, p. 11). Rebecca Coleman and Mónica Figueroa (2010) recast beauty in a temporal sense, saying that its past and future orientation (longing for the body we once had or hope to have in the future) needs to give way to a present orientation to make it less cruel and harmful to women. Here beauty might function in women's lives not as a visual ideal to aspire to but as an embodied feeling of aliveness or vitality recognized as it is happening in the moment.

These are only a few examples that exist for altering our image landscapes and expanding possibilities for beauty and more meaningful representation of bodies. Much work remains to be done. It is up to each of us as individuals and in our communities to give careful thought to the images and narratives we produce and consume as well as the radical ways we might transform these as we chart our pathways forward.

## NOTE

1. Unless otherwise noted in a citation, all historical advertisements discussed in this chapter were retrieved from Ad Access On-Line Project, Duke University, at https://repository.duke.edu/dc/adaccess.

## REFERENCES

Ahmed, S. (1998). Animated borders: Skin, colour and tanning. In M. Shildrick & J. Price (Eds.), *Vital signs: Feminist reconfigurations of the bio/logical body* (pp. 45–65). Edinburgh, Scotland: Edinburgh University Press.

American Psychiatric Association. (2013). *Diagnostic and statistical manual of mental disorders: DSM-5*. Washington, DC: American Psychiatric Association.

American Society for Aesthetic Plastic Surgery. (2011). Demand for plastic surgery rebounds by almost 9%. *Statistics, surveys & trends*. Retrieved from www.surgery.org/media/news-releases/demand-for-plastic-surgery-rebounds-by-almost-9% (link no longer active).

American Society of Plastic Surgeons. (2011). *Report of the 2010 plastic surgery statistics: 2010 cosmetic demographics*. Retrieved from www.plasticsurgery.org/documents/News/Statistics/2010/plastic-surgery-statistics-full-report-2010.pdf.

Associated Press. (2006, March 2). Surgeon General: Obesity epidemic will dwarf terrorism threat. *CBSNews.com*. Retrieved from www.cbsnews.com/news/obesity-bigger-threat-than-terrorism/.

Bennett, W., & Gurin, J. (1983). *The dieter's dilemma: Eating less and weighing more*. New York, NY: Basic Books.

Berger, J. (1980). *Ways of seeing*. Harmondsworth, England: Penguin Books.

Bindel, J. (2010, August 20). Women: Embrace your facial hair! *The Guardian Online*. Retrieved from www.theguardian.com/lifeandstyle/2010/aug/20/women-facial-hair.

Boutelle, K., Neumark-Sztainer, D., Story, M., & Resnick, M. (2002). Weight control behaviors among obese, overweight, and non-overweight adolescents. *Journal of Pediatric Psychology, 27*(6), 531–540.

Brown, L., Middleton, M. S., Berg, W. A., Soo, M. S., &

Pennello, G. (2000). Prevalence of rupture of silicone gel breast implants in a population of women in Birmingham, Alabama. *American Journal of Roentgenology, 175*, 1–8.

Brown, L., Pennello, G., Berg, W. A., Soo, M. S., & Middleton, M. S. (2001). Silicone gel breast implant rupture, extracapsular silicone and health status in a population of women. *Journal of Rheumatology, 28*, 996–1103.

Brownell, K., & Horgen, K. (2004). *Food fight*. New York, NY: Contemporary Books.

Canadian Broadcasting Corporation. (2008, April 10). Cosmetic surgery: Balancing risk. *CBC News In Depth: Health*. Retrieved from www.cbc.ca/news2/background/health/cosmetic-surgery.html.

Canadian Press. (2007, February 19). $5M to bring back ParticipACTION exercise program. *CBCnews.ca*. Retrieved from www.cbc.ca/news/technology/5m-to-bring-back-participaction-exercise-program-1.640711.

Caplan, P., & Cosgrove, L. (Eds.). (2004). *Bias in psychiatric diagnosis*. Lanham, MD: Jason Aronson.

Cogan, J., & Ernsberger, P. (1999). Dieting, weight, and health: Reconceptualizing research and policy. *Journal of Social Issues, 55*(2), 187–205.

Cohen, E. (2004). The fine line between clinical and subclinical anorexia. In P. Caplan & L. Cosgrove, *Bias in psychiatric diagnosis* (pp. 193–200). Lanham, MD: Jason Aronson.

Colebrook, C. (2006). Introduction. *Feminist Theory, 7*(2), 131–142.

Coleman, R., & Figueroa, M. (2010). Past and future perfect? Beauty, affect and hope. *Journal for Cultural Research, 14*(4), 357–373.

de Beauvoir, S. (1974). *The second sex* (2nd ed.). (H. M. Parshley, trans.). New York, NY: Vintage Books.

Ehrenreich, B. (2001, June 24). Stamping out a dread scourge. *Time Magazine*. Retrieved from www.time.com/time/magazine/article/0,9171,159040,00.html.

Ernsberger, P., & Koletsky, P. (1999). Biomedical rationale for a wellness approach to obesity: An alternative to a focus on weight loss. *Journal of Social Issues, 55*(2), 221–259.

Farris, P. M. (2013). Indigenous beauty. In P. Z. Brand (Ed.), *Beauty unlimited* (pp. 162–174). Bloomington, IN: Indiana University Press.

Felski, R. (2006). "Because it is beautiful": New feminist perspectives on beauty. *Feminist Theory, 7*, 273–282.

Frueh, J. (2001). *Monster/beauty: Building the body of love*. Berkeley, CA: University of California Press.

Gard, M., & Wright, J. (2005). *Obesity epidemic: Science, morality and ideology*. New York, NY: Taylor and Francis.

Garland-Thomson, R. (2009). *Staring: How we look*. Toronto, ON: Oxford University Press.

Gill, R. (2007). Postfeminist media culture: Elements of a sensibility. *European Journal of Cultural Studies, 10*, 147–166.

Gill, R. (2009). Beyond the "sexualization of culture" thesis: An intersectional analysis of "sixpacks," "midriffs" and "hot lesbians" in advertising. *Sexualities, 12*, 137–160.

Gimlin, D. (2006). The absent body project: Cosmetic surgery as a response to bodily dys-appearance. *Sociology, 40*(4), 699–716.

Gremillion, H. (2003). *Feeding anorexia: Gender and power at a treatment center*. Durham, NC: Duke University Press.

Harding, K. (2008). BMI illustrated categories project. Retrieved from http://kateharding.net/bmi-illustrated/.

Health Canada. (2002). *A report on mental illnesses in Canada*. Ottawa, ON: Author.

Herzig, R. M. (2000). The woman beneath the hair: Treating hypertrichosis, 1870–1930. *NWSA Journal, 12*(3), 50–66.

Heyes, C. J., & Jones, M. (2009). Cosmetic surgery in the age of gender. In C. J. Heyes and M. Jones (Eds.), *Cosmetic surgery: A feminist primer* (pp. 1–17). Burlington, VT: Ashgate.

Holliday, R., & Sanchez Taylor, J. (2006). Aesthetic surgery as false beauty. *Feminist Theory, 7*, 179–195.

Hope, C. (1982). Caucasian female body hair and American culture. *Journal of American Culture, 5*(1), 93–99.

Ikeda, J., Crawford, P., & Woodward-Lopez, G. (2006). BMI screening in schools: Helpful or harmful. *Health Education Research, 21*(6), 761–769.

International Society of Aesthetic Plastic Surgery. (2010). Biennial global survey. ISAPS international survey on aesthetic/cosmetic procedures performed in 2009. Retrieved from www.yourplasticsurgeryguide.com/trends/2010-isaps-biennial-study.htm (link no longer active).

Jacobson, S., & McLay, L. (2006). The economic impact of obesity on automobile fuel consumption, *The Engineering Economist, 51*(4), 307–323.

Jutel, A. (2006). The emergence of overweight as a disease entity: Measuring up normality. *Social Science and Medicine, 63,* 2268–2276.

Kristeva, J. (1982). *Powers of horror: An essay on abjection.* (L. Roudiez, trans.). New York, NY: Columbia University Press.

Labre, M. P. (2002). The Brazilian wax: New hairlessness norm for women? *Journal of Communication Inquiry, 26*(2), 113–132.

LaMarre, A., & Rice, C. (2015). Normal eating as counter-cultural: Prescriptions and possibilities for eating disorder recovery. *Journal of Community & Applied Social Psychology, 25*(5), doi: 10.1002/casp.2240.

Leistikow, N. (2003, April 28). Indian women criticize "Fair and Lovely" ideal. *Women's E-News.* Retrieved from www.womensenews.org/story/the-world/030428/indian-women-criticize-fair-and-lovely-ideal.

Lupton, D. (2012). *Fat.* New York, NY: Taylor and Francis.

MacNeill, M. (1999). Social marketing, gender, and the science of fitness: A case study of ParticipACTION campaigns. In P. White & K. Young (Eds.), *Sport and gender in Canada* (pp. 215–231). Toronto, ON: Oxford University Press.

Melchior-Bonnet, S. (2001). *The mirror: A history.* (K. Jewett, trans.). New York, NY: Routledge.

Mello, A. A., Domingos, N. A., & Miyazaki, M. C. (2010). Improvement in quality of life and self-esteem after breast reduction surgery. *Aesthetic Plastic Surgery, 34*(1), 59–64.

Melwani, L. (2007, August 18). The white complex: What's behind the Indian prejudice for fair skin? *Little India.* Retrieved from www.littleindia.com/the-white-complex/.

Mire, A. (2005, July 28). Pigmentation and empire: The emerging skin-whitening industry. *Counterpunch Magazine Online.* Retrieved from www.counterpunch.org/2005/07/28/the-emerging-skin-whitening-industry/.

Morgan, K. (2009). Women and the knife: Cosmetic surgery and the colonization of women's bodies. In C. J. Heyes & M. Jones (Eds.), *Cosmetic surgery: A feminist primer* (pp. 49–77). Burlington, VT: Ashgate.

Morgan, M. (1991). Women and the knife: Cosmetic surgery and the colonization of women's bodies. *Hypatia, 6,* 25–53.

Mulvey, L. (1975). Visual pleasure and narrative cinema. *Screen, 16,* 6–18.

Neumark-Sztainer, D., Story, M., Hannan, P. J., Perry, C. L., & Irving, L. M. (2002). Weight-related concerns and behaviors among overweight and nonoverweight adolescents: Implications for preventing weight-related disorders. *Archives of Pediatrics & Adolescent Medicine, 156,* 171–178.

O'Brien, S., & Szeman, I. (2004). *Popular culture: A user's guide.* Toronto, ON: Nelson Education.

ParticipACTION Archive Project. Retrieved from www.digital.scaa.sk.ca/gallery/participaction/english/home.html.

Peiss, K. (1998). *Hope in a jar: The making of America's beauty culture.* New York, NY: Henry Holt.

PR Web. (2011, May 11). Veet® survey reveals groomed bikini lines more important to women than toned bodies. Retrieved from www.prweb.com/releases/2011/5/prweb8415224.htm.

Rabinor, J. R. (2004). The "eating disordered" patient. In P. Caplan & L. Cosgrove (Eds.), *Bias in psychiatric diagnosis* (pp. 189–192). Lanham, MD: Jason Aronson.

Reardon, R., & Grogan, S. (2011). Women's reasons for seeking breast reduction: A qualitative investigation. *Journal of Health Psychology, 16*(1), 31–41.

Rice, C. (1996). Trauma and eating problems: Expanding the debate. *Eating Disorders, 4,* 197–237.

Rice, C. (2007). Becoming "the fat girl": Acquisition of an unfit identity. *Women's Studies International Forum, 30*(2), 158–174.

Rice, C. (2009a). Imagining the other? Ethical challenges of researching and writing women's embodied lives. *Feminism & Psychology, 19,* 245–266.

Rice, C. (2009b). How big girls become fat girls: The cultural production of problem eating and physical inactivity. In H. Malson & M. Burns (Eds.), *Critical feminist perspectives on eating disorders: An international reader* (pp. 92–109). London, England: Psychology Press.

Rice, C. (2014). *Becoming women: The embodied self in image culture.* Toronto, ON: University of Toronto Press.

Rice, C., & Langdon, L. (1991). The use and misuse of diagnostic labels. *National Eating Disorder Information Centre Bulletin 6,* 1–4.

Rice, C., & Russell, V. (2002). *Embodying equity: Body image as an equity issue.* Toronto, ON: Green Dragon Press.

Riddell, L., Varto, H., & Hodgson, Z. G. (2010). Smooth talking: The phenomenon of pubic hair removal in women. *Canadian Journal of Human Sexuality, 19*, 121–130.

Rooks, N. (1996). *Hair raising: Beauty, culture, and African-American women.* New Brunswick, NJ: Rutgers University Press.

Rooks, N. (2001). Wearing your race wrong: Hair, drama and the politics of representation for African American women at play on a battlefield. In M. Bennett & V. Dickerson (Eds.), *Recovering the black female body: Self representations by African American women* (pp. 279–295). New Brunswick, NJ: Rutgers University Press.

Schick, V. R., Rima, B. N., & Calabrese, S. K. (2011). Evulvalution: The portrayal of women's external genitalia and physique across time and the current barbie doll ideals. *Journal of Sex Research, 48*(1), 74–81.

Schiebinger, L. (1993). *Nature's body: Gender and the making of modern science.* Boston, MA: Beacon Press.

Scott, L. (2005). *Fresh lipstick: Redressing fashion and feminism.* New York, NY: Palgrave.

Singer, N. (2008, January 17). Do my breast implants have a warranty? *New York Times.* Retrieved from www.nytimes.com/2008/01/17/fashion/17SKIN.html?r=1&oref=slogin.

Sullivan, D. A. (2001). *Cosmetic surgery: The cutting edge of commercial medicine in America.* New Brunswick, NJ: Rutgers University Press.

Swee, W., Klontz, K., & Lambert, L. (2000). A nationwide outbreak of alopecia associated with the use of hair-relaxing formulation. *Archives of Dermatology, 136*, 1104–1108.

Tiggemann, M., & Hodgson, S. (2008). The hairlessness norm extended: Reasons for and predictors of women's body hair removal at different body sites. *Sex Roles, 59*(11–12), 889–897.

Timmons, H. (2007, May 30). Telling India's modern women they have power. *New York Times Online.* Retrieved from www.nytimes.com/2007/05/30/business/media/30adco.html?ex=1181620800&en=201bcdec 2fbde98d&ei=5070&emc=eta1.

Toerien, M., & Wilkinson, S. (2003). Gender and body hair: Constructing the feminine woman. *Women's Studies International Forum, 26*(4), 333–344.

Tweed, A. (2003). *Health care utilization among women who have undergone breast implant surgery.* Vancouver, BC: British Columbia Centre of Excellence for Women's Health.

World Health Organization. (2003). *Controlling the global obesity epidemic.* Geneva, Switzerland. Retrieved from www.who.int/nutrition/topics/obesity/en/index.html.

---

**Source:** Rice, Carla. (2016). Excerpted from "Through the Mirror of Beauty Culture." In Nancy Mandell & Jennifer Johnson (Eds.), *Feminist Issues: Race, Class, and Sexuality, 6th Edition* (pp. 147–174). Toronto, ON: Pearson. Originally published as "Chapter 7: In the Mirror of Beauty Culture" in *Becoming Women* (2014) by Carla Rice. Toronto: UTP Press.

## ACTIVIST INSIGHT:
## INTERSECTIONAL BODY ACTIVISM

Body activism challenges us to think critically about the way our culture judges, oppresses, privileges, and silences people based on body size, shape, age, skin colour,
and perceived ability. Intersectional body activism asks us to also consider how society celebrates or marginalizes certain bodies based on identity markers such as
gender, race, class, and sexuality. The movement takes many forms, including the use
of social media as a place for discussion and consciousness raising. For instance, the
Tumblr feed "It Gets Fatter," was started by fat people of colour to discuss body posi-
tivity and to provide counter-narratives to normative beauty ideals. The site is a space
for people to post questions, poetry, video diaries, and other forms of media that consider questions of body image, race, class, sexuality, gender, ability, and social justice.
Check it out here: itgetsfatter.tumblr.com/.

Other activists are working to challenge media representations of idealized bodies
through popular culture forms. Check out this clip about the Pretty Big Movement, a
dance company that aims to change the narrative around which bodies are included in
the performing arts: thescene.com/watch/presents/pretty-big-movement-is-destroy-
ing-dancer-stereotypes?mbid=marketing_organic_cne_social_scene_status.

# CHAPTER 46

## Body Beautiful/Body Perfect: Where Do Women with Disabilities Fit In?

*Francine Odette*

Francine Odette is an educator, writer, community organizer, and activist. She is a faculty member at George Brown College in Toronto, where she co-designed a course entitled "Disability Discourse: The Experienced Life." Odette has spent over 25 years advocating for the rights of girls and women with disabilities. She has worked as a consultant, adviser, and researcher on numerous projects involving women in the education, arts, health, and work sectors. In 2008, she was awarded the YWCA Women of Distinction Award.

When I decided to write about the issue of body image and its impact on women with disabilities, the challenge brought with it a chance to explore the link between fat oppression and the experiences of women with disabilities. Unfortunately, little research has been conducted on this issue as it affects the lives of women with disabilities. This may reflect the belief that the lived experiences of many women with disabilities are not important or perceived as valid by mainstream researchers.

I do not represent the experiences of all women with disabilities regarding the issues of body image and self-perceptions; however, over the years I have listened to the stories of many women who have a range of disabilities. These women's disabilities include being non-verbal, [having] mobility [impairments], deafness, hard of hearing, and/or visual impairments. Many of these women spoke of their lives and how they have begun to deal with some of their concerns. While recognizing that the issues for women with disabilities may vary from those of non-disabled women, our lives, experiences, and fears are very similar.

Women are identified socially with our bodies. For women living in Western culture, thinness is often equated with health and success. We are taught early to be conscious of our body shape, size, weight, and physical attributes. The current cultural "norm" or ideal is unattainable for most women. Fat women, women with disabilities, women from particular racial or ethnic groups or with non-heterosexual orientation, and other women who do not conform to the prescribed norm of social desirability are often viewed as having experiences and attributes somewhat different from that of other women in this culture and as a result are often isolated.

Women with disabilities living in this society are not exempt from the influence of messages that attempt to dictate what is desirable and what is not in a woman. These messages are often internalized, and have an impact on how we see ourselves. The further we see ourselves from the popular standard of beauty, the more likely our self-image will suffer. We may experience a greater need to gain control over our bodies, either by our own efforts of restrictive eating and exercising, or the intrusive procedures performed by those deemed to be the "experts"—the medical profession.

We form images of ourselves early in infancy and these are confirmed or altered by the responses, or evaluations, made by others in our lives. Based on physical judgments, women with disabilities hear various messages from family, friends, and society at large about our perceived inability to participate in the roles that are usually expected of women. Society believes that lack of physical attractiveness, as defined by the dominant culture, hampers our ability to be intimate. These misperceptions hamper our ability to get beyond our physical differences, perpetuate body-image dissatisfaction, and contribute to eating problems.

Within this culture, having a disability is viewed negatively. This notion is supported by the fact that the lives of women with different disabilities are not reflected in the media. We are invisible. However, when our lives are spoken of, they are distorted through romantic or bizarre portrayals of child-like dependency, monster-like anger, or super-human feats. This increases the discomfort of others when in contact with women with disabilities, which in turn perpetuates the sense of "otherness" that women with disabilities may feel.

As women and individuals with disabilities, the messages that we receive often indicate the lack of role expectations for us. For young girls with disabilities, the invisibility of our lives becomes reinforced by the fact that popular advertising suggests the "normal" body is that which is desirable. Once these messages become internalized and reinforced, young girls and women with disabilities may try to compensate for their disabilities by striving to look as close to the nondisabled "norm" as possible. Similar to many non-disabled women's experiences, some girls and women with different disabilities may try to hide their bodies or change how their bodies look. Comfort and health may be sacrificed as we attempt to move closer to the realm of what the "normal" body appears to be by manipulating our bodies through continuous dieting, plucking, shaving, cutting, and constricting.

## MEDICALIZING OUR BODIES

Much feminist theory has been focused on identifying the reality that within Western culture, women's bodies are objectified for the purposes of male pleasure and domination. As a result, women's perceptions of themselves and their bodies become distorted. We are taught to mistrust our own experience and judgment about the notion of desirability and acceptance. These qualities are defined by the dominant culture. They are socially and economically defined by those in power—white, able-bodied, heterosexual men. Within this context, the body becomes a commodity with which one may bargain in order to obtain more desirable opportunities, for example, work or security (Szekely).

Feminist analysis identifies women's alienation from themselves and their bodies as a result of the objectification of the female body. However, a great deal of feminist analysis may not be reflective of all women's experience. The way in which women's bodies are portrayed as commodities in the media may not be a reality for many women labelled "disabled." In reflecting societal beliefs regarding disability, our bodies become objectified for the purposes of domination, but within a different context.

Traditionally, disability, whether it is visible or invisible, has tended to be viewed as something that is undesirable. Whether we are born with our disability or acquire it later, our bodies become objectified as part of the medical process. Medical examinations are often undertaken by groups of male doctors who, despite their aura of "professionalism," are still perceived by the patient as a group of anonymous men. Regular routines such as dressing ourselves or other activities are observed by doctors while on their "rounds," as this is seen as an excellent training for new doctors.

Many of us recount our experiences of having to display our bodies to groups of male doctors in the guise of "medical treatment" without prior knowledge or consent. We may have been asked to strip, walk back and forth in front of complete strangers so that they can get a better view of what the physical "problem" is, or to manually manipulate our limbs to determine flexibility and dexterity. Today, pictures or videos are taken of us and used as educational tools for future doctors, with little thought given to our needs to have control over what happens to our bodies or who sees us. While the medical profession attempts to maintain control over our bodies, some women with disabilities may attempt to regain control through dieting, binge-ing, or other methods of body mutilation.

Some disabled women speak of having numerous surgeries conducted with the hope of a "cure," when, in reality, the surgeries result in increased pain, discomfort, and [an] altered physical state of one's body. The concept of body image as it impacts young girls and women with disabilities is crucial, especially when one looks at instances where the functioning of certain body parts must change and be altered, resulting in scars, diminished sensation, or radically changing the physical state, for example, amputation, mastectomies. A common theme emerges between intrusive medical intervention and popular methods of cosmetic surgery; the perceived need to change or alter the "imperfect" body. For many women with disabilities, the message is clear—the way our bodies are now is neither acceptable nor desirable. To be non-disabled is the "ideal" and along with that comes the additional expectations for the quest of the "perfect body."

Body image, self-image, and esteem are often linked with the perceptions held by society, family, and friends. Disability is often seen as a "deficit" and women with disabilities must address the reality that the "ideal" imposed by the dominant culture regarding women's bodies is neither part of our experience nor within our reach. As women with disabilities, some of us experience difficulty in having others identify us as "female."

Disability and "differentness" results in many of us living our lives from the margins of society. As women with disabilities, we must begin to challenge the perceptions of "body beautiful" along with the perceptions held by some non-disabled feminists who resist the "body beautiful" but ignore or affirm the notion of the "body perfect." Disability challenges all notions of perfection and beauty as defined by popular, dominant culture. We must reclaim what has been traditionally viewed as "negative" and accentuate the reality that "differentness" carries with it exciting and creative opportunities for change. A lot can be learned by the experiences of women with different disabilities, as we begin the process of reclaiming and embracing our "differences." This includes both a celebration of our range of sizes and shapes and abilities.

## REFERENCE

Szekely, Eva. *Never Too Thin*. Toronto: Women's Press, 1988.

*Source:* Odette, Francine. (1994). "Body Beautiful/Body Perfect: Challenging the Status Quo. Where Do Women with Disabilities Fit In?" *Canadian Women's Studies/ les cahiers de la femme, 14*(3), 41–43.

# CHAPTER 47

## The Women's Health Movement in Canada: Looking Back and Moving Forward

*Madeline Boscoe, Gwynne Basen, Ghislaine Alleyne, Barbara Bourrier-Lacroix, and Susan White of the Canadian Women's Health Network*

The Canadian Women's Health Network (CWHN) was created in 1993 as a national organization to improve the health and lives of girls and women in Canada and the world by collecting, producing, and sharing knowledge, information, resources, and strategies dedicated to women's health and equality. Due to a lack of stable funding, the CWHN closed permanently in 2017.

You would be hard-pressed to find anyone who works in, or thinks about health in Canada today who did not agree, at least publicly, on the importance of social and economic conditions such as education, housing, environment, and gender on a person's health status. This broadened approach to health reflects a profound change in thinking and can be credited, in part, to the work of the women's health movement. This social movement was the first to bring together women's own experiences with health services, and their own opinions about their health concerns, with new visions, new information, and new methods of research and outcome evaluations. [...]

## IN THE BEGINNING

The 1960s, 1970s, and 1980s saw the rebirth of the women's movement and, in direct association with it, the women's health movement in Canada and around the world. Women came together to share experiences and knowledge. We looked at our cervixes, fit diaphragms, helped get each other off mood-altering drugs, and "caught" babies. We shared stories about our interactions with the medical system. We started asking questions. We understood that knowledge was power and sought information. Through debate and sharing, we developed new approaches. We realized that we could understand medical information if it was presented in an accessible form. We came to recognize the impact of issues such as violence and racism on our health. We realized that those who formulated the research questions controlled the answers. We understood that women's health is a political, social, and economic matter. We were, as Sharon Batt (1994) wrote, "Patient No More" and would be, to quote Sue Sherwin, "No Longer Patient."

Women gathered in discussion groups, educational forums, and consciousness-raising sessions. We created new avenues to develop our concerns and our ideas that broke down isolation and allowed for individual and group action. No one was just a "patient" or a doctor, or a nurse, or a therapist, or an academic. Health was something that mattered to all women.

The women's health movement made links and formed partnerships with other groups who shared our issues:

- consumer groups and self-help movements dealing with issues such as cancer, mental health, and addictions;
- anti-racism groups and those working on equity and access issues including First Nations and rural communities;
- those providing alternative and traditional healing;
- environmental and anti-nuclear groups;
- disability rights activists;
- medical reform groups, including those interested in health promotion and community development;
- the legal community, who helped us push companies and providers to be more responsive and responsible.

In part, the strength and endurance of the women's health movement has been a result of this network.

## SHAPING OUR ISSUES

Over the years, the women's health movement has focused on three main issues: the health care delivery system, the development and analysis of the social determinants of health, and a commitment to increase the participation of women in all aspects of health care.

> Improving the health status of women meant paying attention to education, economic and social policies, housing, and the environment.

The movement's critique of a health care system dominated by white, male health professionals began with exposing how lack of information prevented women from making informed decisions; how the power dynamics between health professionals (doctors [usually male] and nurses [female]) and between physicians and patients made it hard to question professional expertise or refuse treatment; how sexism, racism, paternalism, and other oppressions within the system led to our priorities not being addressed; how the growing pervasiveness of drugs and other technologies distorted the treatment and prevention programs women really needed (Batt 2002; Beck; Cohen and Sinding; Status of Women Canada).

Women also learned that some institutions had interests in conflict with ours. For example, the commercial push to market a drug and increase profits could supersede the obligation to make safe and effective medicines available and to do follow-up on a drug's safety.

The emphasis was on a woman-centred vision of health and wellness. We knew that improving the health status of women meant paying attention to education, economic and social policies, housing, and the environment. Gender was put up front and centre as a critical determinant of health. The analyses recognized and respected the diverse needs and realities of women's lives and the impact of these on their health status.

Women worked for the increased presence of women throughout the health care system. We looked at the research used to rationalize the existing approaches to our health concerns. We saw that women's issues and voices were absent in both asking the questions and seeking the answers and that none of it was "neutral." We saw that women were often excluded from clinical trials for new drugs and couldn't know if the medicine we were given was safe for us.

We fought for greater participation of women in all levels of the health care system including policy making. We pressed for and finally got Women's Health Bureaus or Departments in provincial governments, women's health committees in research and professional groups such as the Medical Research Council, a Women's Health Bureau inside Health Canada, women's health research centres in Ontario, and the establishment of the Centres of Excellence in Women's Health.

## CREATING WOMAN-CENTRED PROGRAMS AND SERVICES

Not satisfied with just offering critiques, women's health advocates also developed programs that reflected our vision of woman-centred care (Barnett, White and Horne). When we found existing services unresponsive or unyielding to our issues, we founded new, creative ones where all women would have opportunities to learn and freely discuss their concerns. We developed more equitable, non-hierarchical ways for health service providers to work with each other—and to work with women.

These activities fuelled a new approach to women's health and health services, one that required much more than pink walls or even "nicer" female doctors. We called for providers to listen to women's voices, putting women, not care providers, centre stage in the healthcare system. This approach, which we called a *woman-centred model*, had several themes or principles. These included:

- user control of health care delivery systems;
- establishing innovative services;
- creating resource centres;
- emphasizing self-help and peer support;

- obtaining appropriate and effective health promotion and education;
- deprofessionalizing medical knowledge and health service jobs;
- developing programs examining health issues in their social context;
- demanding equity in hiring practices;
- understanding that women are experts in their own needs and issues;
- providing continuity of care and care providers;
- having access to female practitioners.

From these principles came activities, programs, and services. One of the earliest was *Side-effects*, a play and popular education campaign about women and pharmaceuticals that made a remarkable cross-country tour in the early 1980s (Tudiver and Hall). Other examples included the formation of home birth and midwifery coalitions, the launching of the still-published *A Friend Indeed* newsletter on women and menopause, women-centred tobacco programs, the Montreal Health Press, environmental action groups, women and AIDS activities, endometriosis and breast cancer action groups, the disability rights organization DAWN, feminist counselling programs, women's shelters, traditional healing study groups, *HealthSharing* magazine, sexual assault support and action groups, anti-racism work, and community-based women's services such as Le Regroupement des centres de santé des femmes du Québec, Winnipeg's Women's Health Clinic, and the Immigrant Women's Health Centre in Toronto to name a few.

These organizations, programs, and services were characterized by innovation and social action. Their work recognized that women's health and well-being are deeply affected by poverty and class and by experiences of abuse and racism. Women who sought services in woman-centred programs experienced group-learning methods, peer support, or new types of care providers, such as nurse practitioners. Women experienced alternative delivery models, which increased their knowledge and sense of autonomy and competence. The programs provided examples of outreach to those women whom conventional medical service providers considered "hard to reach."

The development and evolution of these programs and services is the "happy" part of the story. Sadder, if not tragic, is that, despite women's best efforts, most of these programs and services, no matter their effectiveness, remained marginalized within the mainstream health delivery sector and/or have had their funding severely if not completely cut. Those that survive are the exception to the rule and even these have never received the funding that would make them universally accessible.

*****

## MOVING FORWARD

Women's health concerns have become very popular and "acknowledged" in the mainstream. This has proved to be both a blessing and a curse. Women's health advocates have achieved a certain level of recognition, but are always in danger of being co-opted or used by those who control the health system. The language of the women's movement has been taken on by governments and media, but too often without a deep commitment to giving women a real voice in health care policy and planning. We [...] know that there is still much to be accomplished. Today we can identify five broad challenges ahead for women's health in Canada.

### 1. Health Reform and Health Service Restructuring

The erosion of our publicly-funded, not-for-profit health insurance system and the accelerating growth of a two-tiered health system is a significant women's health issue. Though women and men are both affected by government cutbacks and rising health care expenditures, they do not have the same financial resources to cope with them and the impacts are different. Women, on average, earn less than men, are less likely to have supplementary health insurance coverage through their paid employment, and are more likely to live in poverty (Donner, Busch and Fontaine). As a result, women face a greater burden when health care costs are privatized.

And it is women who bear the burden when health care services are off-loaded from the institution to the home. Women provide 80 per cent of both paid and unpaid health care (Armstrong *et al.;* National Coordinating Group on Health Care Reform and Women). This inequitable situation results in increased stress, poverty, and social exclusion for these female caregivers.

Despite a 2002 Royal Commission on Health Care that clearly demonstrated the support for and superiority of the Canadian Medicare system (Romanow), action is missing. The Commission report itself was also lacking in almost any mention of women's health issues and concerns (National Coordinating Group on Health Care Reform and Women, 2003). The movements toward national home care and pharmacare programs seem to be fading. Primary care discussions make little if any mention of community health centres. Midwifery and feminist counselling services remain small and underfunded. Through the establishment of the Canadian Institutes for Health Research (CIHR) there has been an increase in support for academic research in gender health. But there is little funding for innovation or demonstration projects such as support for women's second stage housing, women-centred smoking cessation or addiction treatment, or mothering support.

The federal government, as well some provinces, have a commitment to undertake gender sensitive policy and program development, with, at the very least, uneven results. Provincial governments may have identified women as a priority population, produced a women's health plan, or set up Women's Health departments but without much effect on care. The hopes and requests for women-centred models of care remain.

There have been and continue to be huge cuts to the groups and ad hoc organizations that have provided much of the infrastructure for the women's health movement. Women's centres, community health centres, national and regional organizations [...] have all had their funding dramatically reduced or disappear altogether. Burn-out is common as staff members grow exhausted from unrealistic workloads to which are added the need to write seemingly endless funding proposals and reports (Scott 2003). The loss of these groups and programs is a "double-whammy": women lose services and programs providing practical examples of women-centred approaches, and also lose their work in promoting a health determinants approach in all service and policy areas.

## 2. The Continuing Medicalization of Women's Health

The biomedical-corporate model continues to dominate our health care system. Institutions, professional groups, and corporations in the medical field have significant built-in inertia, if not conflicts of interest, with the reforms envisioned by the women's health movement and the Beijing *Platform for Action* (United Nations), and indeed, Canadian government policy statements such as "Health For All" (Epp). For most, it is business as usual.

Despite years of mobilization and analysis, women's bodies and women's health issues continue to be over-medicalized, with women seen as incompetent and *all* our health issues in need of medical intervention. Among the latest examples are the widespread prescribing of hormone replacement for all menopausal women and the increasing use of epidural anesthesia for birthing women (Giving Birth in Canada; O'Grady).

This biomedical focus on the treatment of acute medical problems continues to colour the approach of health care providers as well as the media and politicians. In this reactive role, the health system continually allocates resources that result in questionable policy "choices" such as:

- Paying for breast cancer screening by mammography, but not for breast cancer support groups or smoking awareness and cessation programs, or for research into possible environmental causes (O'Leary Cobb).
- Directing some $100 million in federal/provincial "economic development" funds to drug companies to produce hormonal drugs for older women, with little or no support allocated to health education, menopause research, or ensuring streets are safe enough to encourage women to prevent osteoporosis through exercise (Batt 2002).
- Investing large amounts of public and private funds into "new" reproductive technologies while midwifery continues to struggle for recognition, and resources to support mothering and to address environmental contaminants that may lead to infertility are basically non-existent (Hawkins and Knox).
- Over-prescribing of Benzodiazepines. Women are not only more likely to be prescribed benzodiazepines compared to men, but are also more likely to be prescribed benzodiazepines for longer periods of time (Currie 2003).
- Over-prescribing selective serotonin uptake inhibitors (SSRIs) to treat depression and other mental health conditions while other effective interventions such as counselling or exercise remain unfunded and underutilized—and systemic changes in workplaces and elsewhere that lead to stress and depression are ignored (Currie 2005).

It took two decades of lobbying by women's health advocates before legislation to regulate the new reproductive technologies was introduced and passed into law *(An Act Respecting Assisted Human Reproduction and Related Research)*. The *Act* is just one step towards an overall strategy to improve the reproductive and sexual health of Canadians, a commitment made by the government several years ago in yet one more "green" paper. This strategy must include increasing access to emergency contraception and ensuring reliable, accessible information on sex education for women and girls across their life spans.

## 3. Quality Health Information for Women

For women to make informed choices, we must have access to accurate, timely, women-sensitive health information. But programs that used to fund groups creating information tools no longer exist. And while the explosive growth of the Internet seems to have created access to an enormous amount of information, it is not necessarily the knowledge women need or can access. In addition, most health research continues to lack an analysis of the differences between men and women or between women (Health Canada).

Community-based health providers have responded to the demand for health information by creating material, but have been constrained by limited funding and time. By contrast, advertising by the pharmaceutical industry has continued to permeate our media, not only to promote new products to professionals with expensive sophisticated techniques, but to produce health "information" brochures and other material that really should come from impartial, trusted, non-commercial sources. These same companies push their products to women—often flouting laws that prohibit direct-to-consumer advertising (Mintzes and Baraldi).

> Despite years of mobilization and analysis, women's bodies and women's health issues continue to be over-medicalized, with women seen as incompetent and *all* our health issues in need of medical interventions.

## 4. Public Policy—Is It Going to Be Healthy or Not?

While the federal government [in Canada] takes pride in its progressive health policy statements, we need actions not words.

Those government policy frameworks that emphasize a broad range of health determinants and have goals to achieve population health (Federal/Provincial/Territorial Advisory Committee on Population Health) overlap with a woman-centred holistic approach. However, many of the government's actions appear to ignore these commitments. No action has ever been taken to build in health impact assessments that would evaluate new policies or programs as possible causes of inequities in women's health.

The growing gap between the rich and the poor, both within Canada and internationally, points to a societal failure to protect citizens and increases ill health, not just for the impoverished, but for everyone. Poverty is increasingly becoming feminized. The dismantling of social programs such as housing and income support are felt everywhere in Canada, but this has a particular impact on the lives and health of women and children. Poverty is hazardous to women's health.

## 5. Changes in the Women's Health Movement

Women's health activists continue to struggle with whether or not to put our energies into modifying institutions or building new ones. Funding restraints make it more difficult for *all* the services envisioned by grassroots groups to be developed. When they are (under) funded they immediately develop long waiting lists and meeting needs becomes difficult if not impossible.

We are [...] made up of women who live at different levels of power and privilege. Our members have many different issues, priorities, and perspectives.

How to prioritize issues and resource allocation is far from clear.

Midwifery is an example of this potential stress—in effect, a competition for services between rich and poor women. Midwifery, fought for by a broad coalition of consumers, midwives, and public health staff, has finally been implemented in most provinces and territories. How can equal access for all women be ensured? Will midwifery services, in short supply at the present, be "overused" by women who have resources, while women who would most profit from midwifery services (adolescents, women with multiple problems, rural and northern women who have to leave their communities to birth) have the least chance of getting access to them? It is clear that many women would seek to improve their birth experience if they had the opportunity. What happens to the women most in need, whose voices are often absent?

## PROTECTING OUR VISION

The women's health movement has broadened and matured. Some of the coalitions created long ago remain, but even those that have come apart have continuing ties that have created an underlying network of individuals and groups who remain active and connected. And women need this network: the issues we have fought for remain as current and as real today as they were three decades ago. New problems have an all too familiar ring. The task is clearly not an easy one.

The changes that have been won have been the result of persistence and, at times, anger and pain. Not only has the health care system resisted us, but frequently women's wishes and concerns have been disregarded, no matter how clearly they were articulated, while at other times they have been co-opted. Gender parity in medical schools and the recognition of nurse practitioners are wonderful, but this is only a small step toward our vision. Having women in positions of power as physicians, health administrators, and politicians will continue to have some positive

effect. But this is not the only mechanism that we can rely on. As we all know, women frequently experience "glass ceilings" and "sticky floors." We also know that one's values cannot be automatically assumed because of gender.

We need to move from the *personal is the political* to *the communal good is in everyone's interest.* Individual health cannot exist without social justice. As individuals, we need to work on issues that are best for the community of women, even when these are not necessarily our personal priorities. Those of us working in the health service sector will need to join other groups to advocate for the systemic changes that will remove inequities such as poverty and racism that so strongly affect health. We need to ensure that whatever changes are made are not merely superficial or cosmetic changes laid over a biomedical service model, with no attention paid to the broader social determinants of health.

Women's health activists need not only to continue to lobby to reform and adapt existing institutions and professions, but we need to be sure this work doesn't lead to losing what has been achieved with the creation of alternative and new women-centred services and service providers. We must stay on guard to protect woman-centred research. We also need to consider creating a long-term demonstration fund for community-based, consumer-controlled services, particularly for women. We are, after all, retooling an industry.

We need mechanisms throughout the system to ensure that this dynamic process continues. Grassroots groups and a diverse range of citizen voices must maintain a strong leadership role as we move forward. We know that in times of confusion and constraint, dissent and critiques can be hard to hear. We will need to continue to build new alliances and new coalitions.

The women's health movement has provided a dynamic environment for some of the most creative debates and positive visions for a better, healthier future. Given the opportunity, there is no reason why we can't take on the challenges ahead.

# REFERENCES

*An Act Respecting Assisted Human Reproduction and Related Research*. Ottawa: Ministry of Supply and Services Canada, 2004.

Armstrong, Pat, Carol Amaratunga, Jocelyne Bernier, Karen Grant, Ann Pederson and Kay Willson. *Exposing Privatization: Women and Health Care Reform in Canada*. Aurora: Garamond, 2001.

Barnett, Robin, Susan White and Tammy Horne. *Voices from the Front Lines: Models of Women-Centred Care in Manitoba and Saskatchewan*. Winnipeg: Prairie Women's Health Centre of Excellence, 2002.

Batt, Sharon. *Patient No More: The Politics of Breast Cancer*. Charlottetown: Gynergy, 1994.

Batt, Sharon. *Preventing Disease: Are Pills the Answer?* Toronto: Women and Health Protection, 2002.

Beck, Christina S. *Partnership for Health: Building Relationships between Women and Health Caregivers*. Mahwah: Lawrence Erlbaum Associates, Inc., 1997.

Cohen, May and Chris Sinding. "Changing Concepts of Women's Health: Advocating for Change." *Women's Health Forum: Canadian and American Commissioned Papers*. Ottawa: Minister of Supply and Services Canada, 1996.

Currie, Janet. *Manufacturing Addiction: The Over-Prescription of Benzodiazepines and Sleeping Pills to Women in Canada*. Vancouver: British Columbia Centre of Excellence for Women's Health, 2003.

Currie, Janet. *The Marketization of Depression: Prescribing of SSRI Antidepressants to Women*. Toronto: Women and Health Protection, 2005.

Donner, Lissa, Angela Busch and Nahanni Fontaine. *Women, Income and Health in Manitoba: An Overview and Ideas for Action*. Winnipeg: Women's Health Clinic, 2002.

Epp, Jake. *Achieving Health for All: A Framework for Health Promotion*. Ottawa: Minister of Supply and Services Canada, 1986.

Federal/Provincial/Territorial Advisory Committee on Population Health. *Strategies for Population Health: Investing in the Health of Canadians*. Ottawa: Ministry of Supply and Services Canada, 1994.

*Giving Birth in Canada: A Regional Profile*. Ottawa: Canadian Institute for Health Information, 2004.

Hawkins, Miranda and Sarah Knox. *The Midwifery Option: A Canadian Guide to the Birth Experience*. Toronto: HarperCollins Canada Ltd., 2003.

Health Canada. Women's Health Bureau. *Exploring Concepts of Gender and Health*. Ottawa: Minister of Supply and Services Canada, 2003.

Mintzes, Barbara and Rosanna Baraldi. *Direct-to-Consumer Prescription Drug Advertising: When Public Health Is no Longer a Priority*. Toronto: Women and Health Protection, 2001.

National Coordinating Group on Health Care Reform and Women. *Women and Health Care Reform*. Winnipeg: National Coordinating Group on Health Care Reform and Women, 2002.

National Coordinating Group on Health Care Reform. *Reading Romanow: The Implications of the Final Report of The Commission on the Future of Health Care in Canada for Women*. Winnipeg: National Coordinating Group on Health Care Reform, 2003.

O'Grady, Kathleen. "Reclaiming Menopause: Another Look at HRT and the Medicalization of Women's Bodies." *Network* 5/6 (4/1) (2002): 3–4.

O'Leary Cobb, Janine. "Behind the Screens: Mammograms." *A Friend Indeed* 10(4) (2003).

Romanow, Roy J. *Building on Values: The Future of Health Care in Canada*. Final Report of the Commission on the Future of Health Care in Canada. Saskatoon: Commission on the Future of Health Care in Canada, 2002.

Scott, Katherine. *Funding Matters: The Impact of Canada's New Funding Regime on Nonprofit and Voluntary Organizations*. Ottawa: Canadian Council on Social Development, 2003.

Sherwin, Susan. *No Longer Patient: Feminist Ethics and Health Care*. Philadelphia: Temple University Press, 1992.

Status of Women Canada. *What Women Prescribe: Report and Recommendations from the National Symposium "Women in Partnership: Working towards Inclusive, Gender-Sensitive Health Policies."* Ottawa: Minister of Supply and Services Canada, 1995.

Tudiver, Sari and Madelyn Hall. "Women and Health Services Delivery in Canada: A Canadian Perspective." *Women's Health Forum: Canadian and American Commissioned Papers.* Ottawa: Minister of Supply and Services Canada, 1996.

United Nations. Department of Public Information. *Platform for Action and the Beijing Declaration: Fourth World Conference on Women, Beijing, China, 4-15 September, 1995.* New York, 1996.

*Source:* Boscoe, Madeline, Basen, Gwynne, Alleyne, Ghislaine, Bourrier-Lacroix, Barbara, & White, Susan, of the Canadian Women's Health Network. (2005). "The Women's Health Movement in Canada: Looking Back and Moving Forward." *Canadian Woman Studies/les cahiers de la femme,* 24(1), 7–13.

## ACTIVIST INSIGHT: *OUR BODIES OURSELVES*

*Source:* Boston Women's Health Book Collective.
(1973). *Our Bodies, Ourselves.* New York, NY:
Simon and Schuster.

*Source:* Boston Women's Health Book Collective, &
Norsigian, Judy. (2011). *Our Bodies, Ourselves.*
New York, NY: Simon and Schuster.

In 1969, as the women's movement was gaining momentum and influence in the Boston area and elsewhere around the United States, twelve women met during a women's liberation conference. In a workshop on "women and their bodies," they talked about their own experiences with doctors and shared their knowledge about their bodies. Eventually, they decided to form the Doctor's Group, the forerunner to the Boston Women's Health Book Collective (which was later called Our Bodies Ourselves), to research and discuss what they were learning about themselves, their bodies, health, and women.

The fruit of their discussions and research was a course booklet entitled *Women and Their Bodies*, a stapled newsprint edition published in 1970. The booklet, which put women's health in a radically new political and social context, became an underground success. In 1973, Simon & Schuster published an expanded edition, renamed *Our Bodies, Ourselves*.

Our Bodies Ourselves (OBOS) introduced these key ideas into the public discourse on women's health:

- That women, as informed health consumers, are catalysts for social change
- That women can become their own health experts, particularly through discussing issues of health and sexuality with each other
- That health consumers have a right to know about controversies surrounding medical practices and about where consensus among medical experts may be forming
- That women comprise the largest segment of health workers, health consumers, and health decision-makers for their families and communities, but are underrepresented in positions of influence and policy making
- That a pathology/disease approach to normal life events (birthing, menopause, aging, death) is not an effective way in which to consider health or structure a health system

## Mission

OBOS's current mission as a global feminist organization is to distill and disseminate health information from the best scientific research available as well as women's life experiences, so that individuals and communities can make informed decisions about health, reproduction, and sexuality. OBOS provides trustworthy educational resources worldwide, advocates for equitable public policies, and facilitates dialogue to inspire action on the social injustices affecting health and human rights.

*Source:* Our Bodies Ourselves. (2012). Adapted from "About Us" and "History." Retrieved from: www.ourbodiesourselves.org.

# CHAPTER 48

## Women, Disability, and the Right to Health

*Paula C. Pinto*

Paula C. Pinto is an activist and assistant professor at the School for Social and Political Sciences, University of Lisbon, Portugal, where she also coordinates the Observatory on Disability and Human Rights. In her roles as a researcher at the Centre for Public Administration and Public Policy in Lisbon, and as an invited faculty at the Technical University of Lisbon and the New University of Lisbon, she has contributed greatly to the field of disability rights in Portugal and abroad. Pinto is the author of a number of articles on disability, inclusion, and citizenship and human rights.

## INTRODUCTION

Few studies have examined intersections of gender and disability, especially in their implications for women. In fact, both the disability and feminist movements have been criticized for ignoring the issues facing disabled women (Begum, 1992; Gerschick, 2000; Lloyd, 2001; Morris, 1995; Nixon, 2009; Traustadottir, 1990). Disability analyses [typically ignore gender], portraying disabled people as a homogeneous group. Therefore, the distinct ways in which gender affects the lives of women and men with disabilities are rarely investigated or discussed; in practice, however, disability studies have mostly echoed male-centric perspectives while the specific realities and concerns of disabled women have remained obscured. Disability has also been largely disregarded in feminist thought, even after relationships between gender and other forms of oppression such as race and class were acknowledged and investigated. In short, the particular needs and perspectives of women with disabilities are hardly reflected in either the disability or the feminist literatures.

This chapter sets out to overcome this double marginalization by examining how gender and disability intersect to shape disabled women's health experiences. Naturally, with Nasa Begum (1992), I recognize that women with disabilities are themselves a diverse group and in this sense, multiple identities related to race, age, sexuality, and class are likely to compound or alleviate the forms of oppression they are subjected to. While addressing the complexity of all these interactions is beyond the scope of this chapter, it remains important not to overlook their significance.

In gendering disability and health, I want to avoid the pitfall of talking about disabled women experiencing a "double disadvantage." As pointed out by Jenny Morris (1995), this is neither truthful nor useful and leads to social constructs of these women as "passive victims of oppression" (p. 63). Feminist research on disabled women, on the contrary, must be empowering. By placing "women's subjective reality at its core" (p. 63), research must expose the prejudice that permeates social relations involving disabled women. At the same time it must recognize "the source of strength, celebration, or liberation" (p. 63) that disabled women find in their struggle to transform demeaning images of their lives. In an attempt to apply these principles here, the arguments throughout this chapter will be illustrated with stories of disabled women, including quotations from a pilot project in which I have been involved conducted with women with disabilities in Ontario, Canada. The decision to frame arguments in the language of human rights, with particular reference to the right to health, is also a deliberate intent to emphasize the humanness that fundamentally underlies disabled women's health experiences and needs—in other words, it highlights that what women with disabilities demand is nothing less than what all human beings are entitled to just by nature of their membership in the human family. Moreover, it is what the Canadian government (and many others all over the world) has subscribed and legally committed to under international human rights law, notably the recent Convention on the Rights of Persons with Disabilities.

## The Right to the Highest Attainable Standard of Health

The international human rights system comprises a number of legally binding instruments enacted under the patronage of the United Nations and other international organizations. The right to the highest attainable standard of health, commonly known as the right to health, is codified in several of them, including:

- the Covenant on Economic, Social, and Cultural Rights (CESCR)

- the Convention on the Rights of the Child (CRC)
- the Convention on the Elimination of Discrimination against Women (CEDAW)
- the Convention on the Rights of Persons with Disabilities (CRPD)

Canada is signatory to all of these treaties, thus subscribing to a broad conception of the right to health that encompasses access to timely and appropriate health care and also involves the underlying preconditions for a healthy life, such as access to safe drinking water and adequate sanitation, proper nutrition and housing, to mention just a few. Under current human rights law the international community recognizes that everyone has a right to health, which involves the right to access without discrimination the resources and conditions that enable each individual to enjoy "the highest attainable standard of health conducive to living a life with dignity." In the specific context of disability, the CRPD further highlights the importance of taking into account gender specificities in access to health care.

**Source:** United Nations. (2000). Convention on Economic, Social, and Cultural Rights.

According to official statistics (Statistics Canada, 2011), 1.7 million Canadian women aged 15 and over have a disability[1] compared to just under 1.5 million men. The experience of disability is thus more common among women than among men. The gap is particularly wide among seniors, as females tend to live longer than males and are therefore more likely to develop age-related chronic conditions that prevent them from participating in social activities. Disabled women are thus likely to face distinct and unique challenges. It therefore becomes crucial to understand how the simultaneous experience of disability and gender (Lloyd, 2001) affects women's lives.

This chapter will explore this theme by addressing four main topics: (1) access to health care and wellness; (2) sexual and reproductive rights; (3) gender-based violence; and (4) poverty. Not surprisingly, these are important topics for any discussion about women's health in general. In fact, as Carol Gill (1997) pointed out, "the needs and concerns of women with disability are less exotic than many non-disabled people might think" (p. 1). Certainly, some health issues for disabled women are amplified or given a particular emphasis because of the unique features that surround the experience of disability in our culture; nevertheless, in essence, they remain basic women's health issues.

## DEFINING DISABILITY AND GENDER

Before we can address the intersections of disability and gender we need to define what we mean by those concepts. Two broad models have shaped understandings of disability in Western societies. Traditional conceptions define disability as "a personal tragedy," the consequence of individual impairments and functional incapacities. Giving rise to actions aimed at repairing or eliminating individual impairments through therapeutic interventions, this approach became known as the "medical model" of disability. Over the last two decades, however, a vast number of disability scholars, many of whom are people with disability (Barnes, 1990; Finkelstein, 1980; Oliver, 1983, 1996; Rioux & Valentine, 2006), have been calling attention to the ways in which social, economic, and political structures, processes, and institutions disadvantage, oppress, and *disable* some members of the human family. By placing the problem outside the person and in society, this approach became known as the "social model" of disability. It is also the paradigm that informs this chapter. In this sense, the terms *disabled women* and *women with a disability* will be used interchangeably throughout this chapter, both to reflect an understanding of disability as socially created and to emphasize the human nature, rather

than the impairment, of those disabled by society. [...]

Much like disability, gender is socially construed through social and economic processes, practices, and relations. These relations are fundamentally unequal, marked by unequal access for women and men to material and non-material resources (Sen, George, & Östlin, 2002). Gender norms, values, and expectations become entrenched in particular roles, attributes, and responsibilities that are distinctly assigned to women and men in the family and in society. Given the fundamental inequalities that signal the roles and relations between women and men, gender is, above all, a powerful form of stratification that both influences and is influenced by all other physical and social markers such as class, race, sexual orientation, and disability.

In short, both disability and gender are *socio-political realities*, and as such they need to be understood in the context of social relations of power and control. In Western societies, disability status and female gender are usually associated with greater vulnerability and powerlessness, and therefore women with disabilities are potentially at greater risk than disabled men of facing discrimination and having their human rights violated (World Health Organization, 2011).

## ACCESS TO HEALTH CARE AND WELL-BEING

Gender inequities are widespread within health care systems globally. They may involve differential access to health care resources by women and men as well as discrepancies in the way the system responds to their health needs. These disparities tend to reflect broader and more profound socio-economic inequalities that distinguish the lives of women and men in most societies. Drawing on data from the Canadian Community Health Survey—CCHS 2009—a Statistics Canada report, "Women in Canada," shows that working-age women with disabilities visit health professionals more often than other women, yet they report poorer general health and lower mental health.

Disabled women's discrimination in the health care system is pervasive. Despite women's numerical supremacy, rehabilitation medicine has traditionally focused on the needs of men—the soldiers, the male workers, or the athletes who had acquired disabilities (Gill, 1997; Morrow, 2000; Tuck & Wallace, 2000). Therefore, conditions that affect mostly women, such as, for instance, chronic fatigue syndrome, continue to be less investigated and are less understood than those that typically affect men (i.e., spinal cord injury). Because disabled women's lives have been rendered invisible, the examination of how different disabilities impact general female health conditions and needs has also been neglected (Frazee, Gilmour, & Mikytiuk, 2006; Gill, 1997; Morrow, 2000). Not surprisingly, then, in several studies (Frazee et al., 2006; Masuda, 1999; Morrow, 2000; Odette et al., 2003) women with disabilities have identified a lack of information on issues so diverse, such as routine health care, nutrition, and safe sex as a barrier to health and wellness.

While many disabled women go without needed care, women's experiences in clinical encounters have also been problematic. In health settings, as Gill (1997) explains, disabled women are not just rendered invisible, they are often de-gendered and dehumanized too, viewed only from the prism of their disability or impairment. [...]

For many disabled women, medical practices are often oppressive rather than supportive. Women find themselves stigmatized and deprived of any privacy and dignity, as when, for instance, they are required to appear undressed in front of a group of health providers who examine them as if they were "a scientific experiment" (Frazee et al., 2006).

The professional gaze that may assume forms of "public stripping" (Gill, 1997) is certainly not an exclusive experience of women with disabilities, but "gender exacerbates the power difference between doctor and patient, making resistance or refusal to participate more difficult" (Frazee et al., 2006, p. 244). Moreover, due to prevailing normative standards

and representations of the female body, even beyond medical settings disabled women are caught between the intense "visibility" of their different bodies and the "invisibility" of their selves, desires, and needs as women and human beings. As Hilde Zitzelsberger (2005) has found in her qualitative study of women with physical disabilities and differences, this paradoxical experience constantly challenges disabled women's ability to build healthy lives and identities. For instance, Hope, a woman Zitzelsberger (2005) interviewed, noted:

> So the focus was on being physically visible. Not emotionally being visible because a person could stare at me and see my crutches, but they would not go any further than that. They would not go and think that I could be visible in many different ways. I could be visible as a woman that could have a relationship, as a woman that could be a friend to someone, as a woman that could be seen in a workplace, as a woman that could be a mother one day. (p. 394)

In addition to experiencing heightened in/visibility (Zitzelsberger, 2005), disabled women's access to health and wellness is further compromised by physical barriers and obstacles inscribed in the way health care is organized and delivered, which often does not take into account their varying needs and characteristics (Gill, 1997). Stairs and narrow doors, inaccessible medical equipment (making routine exams difficult or impossible), lack of staff to assist with transfers and communication, and tight scheduling (limiting time available to understand needs, explain procedures, and build reciprocal trust) are some of the most common obstacles disabled women have to put up with in their encounters with the health care system (Gill, 1997; Odette et al., 2003; Rajan, 2012). But it is the increasingly unpredictable access to medical services that women most fear. As Shirley Masuda (1999) found in her study, in contexts of fiscal restraint, disabled women are likely to experience the deterioration in health care and are concerned that financial policies will continue to affect the provision of care for them. One woman summarized: "Threatened cutbacks are very distressing. We live in fear of pain. Do they replace joints or do we have to pay?" (p. 9). In sum, disabled women are facing stigmatization and discrimination in the health care system, and their medical needs are not being adequately met. This represents a clear violation of their right to the highest attainable standard of health and a serious threat to their dignity and well-being.

## SEXUAL AND REPRODUCTIVE RIGHTS

Sexual and reproductive rights are of critical importance to all women, yet among those with disabilities, the term acquires a new and broader meaning. Non-disabled feminists fight sexist ideologies that reduce the lives of women to the role of mothers and nurturers; their arguments tend to focus on women's right to be free from unwanted pregnancy. But for disabled women, who have been sterilized without consent and denied the opportunity to mothering, the right to become pregnant and have a child—including a disabled child—and the right to refuse forced sterilization are equally or even more important (Kallianes & Rubenfeld, 1997; Pinto, 2008).

Social representations of the sexuality of disabled women are filled with contradictions. Construed as dependent, "eternal children," women with disabilities are often presumed to be asexual beings, with no desires, no sexual needs nor capacities. As such, they are not seen as in need of information about birth control, sexuality, and child-bearing (Traustadottir, 1990). But at the same time, efforts have always been made to block disabled women from participation in the sexual sphere. Historically, the reproductive abilities of disabled women, particularly those with learning disabilities, have been tightly controlled through institutionalization, forced sterilization, and social control. Many have lost custody of their children in divorce and others have had their children removed from their care by welfare agencies (Gill, 1997; Kallianes & Rubenfeld, 1997; O'Toole, 2002; Traustadottir, 1990). Therefore, for disabled women the choice of child-bearing is a political act that defies the social oppression they have been subjected to (Morris, 1995). They claim the right to be recognized as sexual, whether in lesbian or heterosexual relationships, and the power to control their fertility and to bear children if they so decide. They also demand access to necessary resources in support of their parenting role (DAWN Ontario, n.d.b). Yet they struggle to find sensitive and informed health providers to help them fully achieve these rights (Gill, 1997; Kallianes & Rubenfeld, 1997).

Little research has been conducted on the sexual health of disabled women (Rajan, 2012; Basson, 1998; Gill, 1997). Health providers receive insufficient training about disability and many fail to assess and adequately respond to women's concerns and needs. Providers' attitudes are often shaped by popular beliefs that portray women with disabilities as not sexually active, and in consequence disabled women may not receive appropriate medical care (Rajan, 2012; Barile, 2003; Riddel et al., 2003). This may have devastating consequences for their health.

Lack of knowledge about disability and its interacting effects with women's sexual and reproductive health may also reinforce health providers' disablist attitudes as Irene, a woman interviewed by Lipson and Rogers (2000), has experienced. She recounted:

> Well, they told me I couldn't get pregnant first off, because of hemorrhaging. He didn't think that the hips, my pelvic area, and my lower back would support the weight of a child. And they didn't feel confident that with all the pelvic and hip fractures that I would be able to accommodate birth. And then after I got pregnant, they tried to tell

me that I shouldn't keep him because he'd be brain damaged from all the Prozac and the drugs they were giving me. And I said I didn't care; he was a gift. (p. 18)

Despite the anxieties of health providers, Irene's baby was born healthy and without any known disabilities. Yet her story powerfully speaks of the many barriers facing disabled mothers—in particular, society's fears that they can only produce defective babies, and the increasing acceptance (inclusive within the women's movement) of selective abortion (the abortion of fetuses identified as disabled), which is seen by disabled people as an indication of how their lives are devalued in our society. […]

As with other areas of health, barriers to appropriate sexual and reproductive care for women with disabilities further include the physical inaccessibility of many medical facilities and equipment (Rajan, 2012; Barile, 2003), which prevent them from being assessed and receiving care. Different disabilities require different things: for those with physical impairments, it is important that physicians' offices, examination tables, and other screening technologies are accessible; for those who are blind, deaf, or deal with learning disabilities, the lack of alternative formats to convey information may become an excluding barrier. But for all, finding responsive, sensitive providers is critical (Rajan, 2012; Kallianes & Rubenfeld, 1997; Riddel et al., 2003). Reports of disabled women being abused during clinical assessments have been collected (Thomas, 2001). Access to gynecological care may be particularly constrained for women who have experienced sexual trauma. For these women, the consequences of not finding practitioners sensitive to their needs may even lead to avoidance of treatment (Rajan, 2012; Riddel et al., 2003).

Women with disabilities are not a homogeneous group, but they are all sexual beings with the potential to build relationships that include sexual aspects (Basson, 1998). As any other women, all are entitled to basic sexual and reproductive rights, including the right to enjoy their sexuality, the right to bear children, and the right to access appropriate care and resources to give birth to and raise their children.

## GENDER-BASED VIOLENCE

Violence against women is a persistent and pervasive phenomenon in contemporary societies (World Health Organization, 2005). Women with disabilities face the same risks as all other women, but they are also exposed to specific vulnerabilities related to their disability (Rajan, 2011; Nosek, Howland, & Rintala, 2001; Tilley, 1998). The issue of violence and abuse is therefore central for discussions of disabled women's health and well-being.

It has been reported (e.g., Barrett et al., 2009) that women with disabilities experience interpersonal violence almost twice as often as women without disabilities. Violence against disabled women encompasses a wide range of injurious acts, including deliberate physical, psychological, or sexual maltreatment or abuse, as well as more passive forms of neglect such as denial of food or medical care (DAWN Ontario, n.d.a). Verbal abuse, intimidation, social isolation and confinement, economic deprivation or exploitation, and abuse by the system, including refusal or unwillingness to provide needed care have also been described as typical forms of abuse of disabled women (Rajan, 2011; Mays, 2006). As in the non-disabled community, most of the abusive acts are perpetrated by men who tend to be close and well known to their victims (Mays, 2006; World Health Organization, 2005) and yet, because investigators rarely assume that disabled women have intimate partners, intimate partner violence often goes undetected (Barnett, Miller-Perrin, & Perrin, 2005).

A number of factors have been identified as contributing to disabled women's increased vulnerability to violence and abuse. First, it has been suggested that an increased dependency on a variety of people to provide assistance with daily activities greatly increases opportunities for abuse (Rajan, 2011; DAWN Ontario, n.d.a; Nosek, Howland, & Rintala, 2001; Nosek, Foley, Hughes, & Howland, 2001; Tilley, 1998). Receiving care often involves intimate and emotional contact, and many women have experienced violence at the hands of their caregivers, including spouses and boyfriends, personal assistants, physicians, and therapists. Abuse from caregivers has been reported to involve inappropriate touch, physically rough treatment, refusal to respect women's choices, or even theft of their money and property (Nosek, Foley, et al., 2001). In one study, a woman shared: "The orthotist told me he had to put his finger in my vagina to be sure the (artificial) leg fit right" (Nosek, Foley, et al., 2001). Dependency on perpetrators for daily survival activities accentuates the vulnerability of women with disabilities, who may feel compelled to tolerate acts of abuse, as this other woman in the same study confided: "The father of a girlfriend kissed and fondled me. This was in exchange for helping me up and down steps and the like …" (p. 184). Low self-esteem and systematic denial of their human rights are said to produce feelings of powerlessness and over-compliance among many disabled women (Rajan, 2011; Nosek, Howland, et al., 2001; Nosek, Foley, et al., 2001), diminishing their ability to escape abusive relationships. Lack of money, not knowing where to go for support, and lack of help from service providers can also result in women staying in abusive relationships for longer periods (Rajan, 2011).

A feminist approach, however, must go beyond acknowledging disabled women's vulnerabilities, or it will do little to challenge their stigmatization and marginalization (Mays, 2006). Rather, it must be able to place analyses of violence in the broader context of the oppressive relations of disablism and sexism that encircle the lives of many of these women. It must stress that abuse of disabled women is strongly linked to gendered inequalities in power, and the historical, social, and material conditions that perpetuate and reinforce the subordinate position of people with disabilities in our society. For disabled women, these translate into limited economic opportunities and lack of independence, persisting demeaning images, stereotypes, and gender norms […] (Mays, 2006) with potentially devastating consequences for women's health and well-being.

## Women with Disabilities Speak Out

The following are excerpts taken from interviews conducted by the author with women with disabilities, in Ontario, Canada:

**On Gender and Disability:**
"We are a male-dominant society, there are … a lot of issues that are women's issues that are magnified if you're a woman with disabilities." (Susan)

**On Women and Poverty:**
"I think that women are more likely to live in poverty than men, simply because men are expected to be bread-winners and … if a man and a woman apply for the same job … well [we'll] give it to him 'cause after all he's got a family to support. I've lost jobs where that thing was said to me … 'Well, … you know, … your application looks really good, but this fellow has to support a family….' Whereas … you know, women are expected to stay at home and look after the kids. 'You'll be alright, dear, you have a husband to look after you.'" (Laura)

**On Current Practices of Social Services:**
"They keep you afraid of fraud charges, you're afraid of losing your benefits, you're afraid if your mother comes and gives you $50 for your birthday because it's gonna get taken off your cheque, you're afraid that any minute the phone's gonna ring and you're gonna be audited…. If you have an anxiety disorder, that makes you ill." (Laura)

**On the Role of Policy:**
"For those of us with disabilities there are a lot of barriers that are there, just by the nature of our

*continued*

disabilities. And I think that the policy should be there to ensure that these barriers are removed ... whether [it] be for participation at society, everything from I can go to a coffee shop and have a coffee to I can compete and hopefully successfully obtain a high-paying job!" (Emma)

Consequences may be even harsher because a woman with disability may find it particularly difficult to leave a situation of abuse and find adequate support—neither disability-related programs nor existing services for victims of abuse are adequately prepared to respond to disabled women's needs in this area. While disability workers have traditionally disregarded issues of violence and abuse among their clients, many women's shelters do not accommodate women who are in wheelchairs or who need assistance with daily care and medication (Nosek, Howland, et al., 2001; Nosek, Foley, et al., 2001). Disabled women may also fear they will not be heard or believed when they speak out. Research conducted in Canada (Rajan, 2011) and in Sydney, Australia (Keilty & Connelly, 2001), has shown that disabled women, particularly those with learning disabilities, face numerous barriers when reporting to the police, including prevailing stereotypes that portray them as sexually promiscuous and unable to provide credible accounts, and police officers' lack of time to engage and effectively communicate with victims. Similar barriers are likely to be faced in other contexts by women experiencing different disabilities, further contributing to their social isolation and reinforcing abusers' assumptions that disabled women are "easy prey" (Nosek, Howland, et al., 2001). Not surprisingly then, research has also found that disabled women experience abuse and violence for significantly longer periods of time than women without disabilities (Nosek, Howland, et al., 2001). For some, suicide might be the only possible escape (DAWN Ontario, n.d.a).

# POVERTY

All of the barriers to health and well-being highlighted so far are further compounded by disabled women's lack of adequate income. Research in the general population has shown that, on average, people with better income enjoy better health. Among the population with a disability, a strong relationship between income and health has also been found. Disabled women in Canada are more likely than men to experience economic deprivation (Statistics Canada, 2008a, 2008b) and thus are at higher risk for ill health, too.

The problematic income situation of women with disabilities is linked to all the other issues they face, particularly the discrimination they experience in education and the labour market (Statistics Canada, 2008a). Official statistics in Canada show that the unemployment rate of people with disabilities is higher than that of adults without disabilities, disabled women being the least likely group to be employed (Statistics Canada, 2008a).

Women who are able to access work earned in 2006 an average income of $22,213, lower than that of non-disabled women ($28,942) and disabled men ($30,748) (Statistics Canada, 2008b). Many may end up with after-tax household incomes below Statistics Canada's low-income cut-off, defined as comprising people living in "straitened conditions."

The rate of low income is often related to the source of one's income. In the current disability income system, disabled women are particularly disadvantaged (Jongbloed, 1998). Programs linked to labour force attachment, such as employment insurance or workers' compensation, usually offer better benefits than social assistance, but women with disabilities are more likely to have government transfers as their primary source of income. It has been recognized that the great majority (70 percent) of those on social assistance live in low-income households (Office for Disability Issues, 2004); thus, disabled women face an increased risk of poverty. Even if they do receive benefits based on employment earnings, women experience discrimination because they tend to have been paid less than men and are more likely to have taken time off or worked part-time because of their traditional domestic roles. Yet, restrictions imposed on welfare programs over the last decade discourage many of them from exploring the possibility of a job to supplement their income for fear of losing their meagre, but secure, disability benefits (Jongbloed, 1998; Masuda, 1998).

In fact, over the last 20 years women have experienced increased difficulties in accessing the benefits and services they need, which makes their lives ever more difficult (Masuda, 1998). Cuts in home care and homemaking services, for instance, are leaving many disabled women with basic daily needs unmet. Reduced availability and repair of required technical devices, and less help for child care impact disabled women's ability to live independent lives and perform family roles. Cuts to staff in hospital and institutions jeopardize the quality of care to them, especially those who need extra help. All of these have negative consequences for women's health and well-being (Masuda, 1998).

Without an adequate income, disabled women become socially isolated (Schur, 2004). Many cannot access a secure place to live or buy healthy food. Adults with disabilities are twice as likely as those without disabilities to have experienced food insecurity, a risk particularly high among lone mothers. In fact, more than one in every three lone mothers with disabilities runs out of money for food at least once a year (Office of Disability Issues, 2004). Their health, and that of their children, is certainly impacted and their human rights and dignity are further eroded.

## CONCLUSION

Women with disabilities are an under-studied and underserved group. Like other women, their lives are constricted by social and economic disadvantages that undermine their dignity as human beings and their capacity for self-determination. Because of prevailing sexist and disablist ideologies, they experience high poverty rates, severe ratios of violence and abuse, and systematic denial of their sexual, reproductive, and health rights. All these affect their physical and mental health and well-being.

More research is needed to fully understand the interconnections of gender and disability and their health impacts on disabled women. Integrated approaches that combine insights from feminist and critical disability theories can be very useful to uncover structures and social relations of power and control that constrain disabled women's lives. Bringing together women with disabilities, researchers, and social activists, such efforts are elemental not only to an understanding of the inequalities facing disabled women, but also to political processes aiming at ending their discrimination and advancing their human rights.

## NOTE

1. Disability is equated with activity limitation caused by a long-term health condition or problem.

## REFERENCES

Barile, M. (2003). *Access to Breast Cancer Screening Programs for Women with Disabilities*. Montreal: Action des femmes handicappées de Montréal.

Barnes, C. (1990). *Cabbage Syndrome: The Social Construction of Dependence*. Lewes: Falmer Press.

Barnett, O., C. L. Miller-Perrin, & R. D. Perrin. (2005). *Family Violence across the Life Span: An Introduction* (2nd ed.). Thousand Oaks: Sage.

Barrett, K., B. O'Day, A. Roche, & B. L. Carlson. (2009). Intimate Partner Violence, Health Status and Health Care Access among Women with Disabilities. *Women's Health Issues* 19: 94–100.

Basson, R. (1998). Sexual Health of Women with Disabilities. *Canadian Medical Association Journal* 159(4): 359–362.

Begum, N. (1992). Disabled Women and the Feminist Agenda. *Feminist Agenda* 40: 70–84.

DAWN Ontario. (n.d.) (a). *Family Violence against Women with Disabilities.* Retrieved from dawn.thot.net/violence_wwd.html.

DAWN Ontario. (n.d.) (b). *Women with Disabilities and Reproductive Rights: Plain Language Fact Sheet.* Retrieved from dawn.thot.net/wwd_reproductive_rights.html.

Finkelstein, V. (1980). *Attitudes and Disabled People.* New York: World Rehabilitation Fund.

Frazee, C., J. Gilmour, & R. Mikytiuk. (2006). Now You See Her, Now You Don't: How Law Shapes Disabled Women's Experience of Exposure, Surveillance, and Assessment in the Clinical Encounter. In D. Pothier & R. Devlin (Eds.), *Critical Disability Theory: Essays in Philosophy, Politics, Policy, and Law* (pp. 223–247). Vancouver: UBC Press.

Gerschick, T. (2000). Toward a Theory of Disability and Gender. *Signs: Journal of Women in Culture and Society* 25(4): 1263–1268.

Gill, C. (1997). *Last Sisters: Health Issues of Women with Disabilities.* Retrieved from dawn.thot.net/cgill-pub.htm#top.

Jongbloed, L. (1998). Disability Income: The Experiences of Women with Multiple Sclerosis. *Canadian Journal of Occupational Therapy* 65(4): 193–201.

Kallianes, V., & P. Rubenfeld. (1997). Disabled Women and Reproductive Rights. *Disability & Society* 12(2): 203–221.

Keilty, J., & G. Connelly. (2001). Making a Statement: An Exploratory Study of Barriers Facing Women with an Intellectual Disability When Making a Statement about Sexual Assault to the Police. *Disability & Society* 16(2): 273–291.

Lipson, J. G., & J. G. Rogers. (2000). Pregnancy, Birth, and Disability: Women's Health Care Experiences. *Health Care for Women International* 21(1): 11–26.

Lloyd, M. (2001). The Politics of Disability and Feminism: Discord or Synthesis? *Sociology* 35(3): 715–728.

Masuda, S. (1998). *The Impact of Block Funding on Women with Disabilities.* Ottawa: DisAbled Women's Network (DAWN) Canada.

Masuda, S. (1999). *Women with Disabilities: We Know What We Need to Be Healthy!* Vancouver: British Columbia Centre of Excellence for Women's Health and DAWN Canada.

Mays, J. M. (2006). Feminist Disability Theory: Domestic Violence against Women with a Disability. *Disability & Society* 21(2): 147–158.

Morris, J. (1995). Creating a Space for Absent Voices: Disabled Women's Experience of Receiving Assistance with Daily Living Activities. *Feminist Review* 51(Autumn): 68–93.

Morrow, M. (2000). *The Challenges of Change: The Midlife Health Needs of Women with Disabilities.* Vancouver: British Columbia Centre of Excellence for Women's Health.

Nixon, J. (2009). Domestic Violence and Women with Disabilities: Locating the Issue on the Periphery of Social Movements. *Disability & Society* 24(1): 77–89.

Nosek, M. A., C. C. Foley, R. B. Hughes, & C. A. Howland. (2001). Vulnerabilities for Abuse among Women with Disabilities. *Sexuality and Disability* 19(3): 177–189.

Nosek, M. A., C. Howland, & I. Rintala. (2001). National Study of Women with Physical Disabilities: Final Report. *Sexuality and Disability* 19(1): 5–39.

Odette, F., K. K. Yoshida, P. Israel, A. Li, D. Ullman, A. Colontonio, H. Maclean, & D. Locker. (2003). Barriers to Wellness Activities for Canadian Women with Physical Disabilities. *Health Care for Women International* 24(2): 125–134.

Office for Disability Issues. (2004). *Advancing the Inclusion of Persons with Disabilities: A Government of Canada Report.* Ottawa: Social Development Canada.

Oliver, M. (1983). *Social Work with Disabled People.* Basingstoke: Macmillan.

Oliver, M. (1996). *Understanding Disability: From Theory to Practice.* London: Macmillan.

O'Toole, C. J. (2002). Sex, Disability, and Motherhood: Access to Sexuality for Disabled Mothers. *Disability Studies Quarterly* 22(4): 81–101.

Pinto, P. (2008). Re-Constituting Care: A Rights-Based Approach to Disability, Motherhood, and the Dilemmas of Care. *Journal of the Association for Research on Mothering* 10(Spring/Summer): 119–130.

Rajan, D. (2011). *Women with Disabilities and Abuse: Access to Services.* Ottawa: DAWN.

Rajan, D. (2012). Women with Disabilities and Breast Cancer Screening: An Environmental Scan. Identified Problems, Strategies, and Recommended Next Steps. Ottawa: DAWN and Canadian Breast Cancer Network.

Riddel, L., K. Greenberg, J. Meister, & J. Kornelsen. (2003). *We're Women Too: Identifying Barriers to Gynecologic and Breast Health Care for Women with Disabilities*. Vancouver: British Columbia Centre of Excellence for Women's Health.

Rioux, M. H., & F. Valentine. (2006). Does Theory Matter? Exploring the Nexus between Disability, Human Rights, and Public Policy. In D. Pothier & R. Devlin (Eds.), *Critical Disability Theory: Essays in Philosophy, Politics, Policy, and Law* (pp. 47–69). Vancouver: UBC Press.

Schur, L. (2004). Is There Still a "Double Handicap"? Economic, Social, and Political Disparities Experienced by Women with Disabilities. In B. G. Smith & B. Hutchison (Eds.), *Gendering Disability* (pp. 253–271). New Brunswick: Rutgers University Press.

Sen, G., A. George, & P. Östlin. (2002). Engendering Health Equity: A Review of Research and Policy. In G. Sen, A. George, & P. Östlin (Eds.), *Engendering International Health: The Challenge of Equity* (pp. 1–33). Cambridge: MIT Press.

Statistics Canada. (2008a). *Participation and Activity Limitation Survey 2006: Labour Force Experiences of People with Disabilities in Canada*. Retrieved from http://www5.statcan.gc.ca/olc-cel/olc.action?objId=89-628-X&objType=2&lang=en&limit=1.

Statistics Canada. (2008b). *Participation and Activity Limitation Survey 2006: Tables (Part V)*. Retrieved from http://www5.statcan.gc.ca/olc-cel/olc.action?objId=89-628- X&objType=2&lang=en&limit=1.

Statistics Canada. (2011). *Women in Canada: A Gender-Based Statistical Report*. Retrieved from http://www.statcan.gc.ca/pub/89-503-x/89-503-x2010001-eng.htm.

Thomas, C. (2001). Medicine, Gender, and Disability: Disabled Women's Health Care Encounters. *Health Care for Women International* 22(3): 245–262.

Tilley, C. M. (1998). Health Care for Women with Physical Disabilities: Literature Review. *Sexuality and Disability* 16(2): 87–102.

Traustadottir, R. (1990). *Obstacles to Equality: The Double Discrimination of Women with Disabilities*. Retrieved from dawn.thot.net/disability.htm.

Tuck, I., & D. Wallace. (2000). Chronic Fatigue Syndrome: A Women's Dilemma. *Health Care for Women International* 21(5): 457–466.

World Health Organization. (2005). *Multi-Country Study on Women's Health and Domestic Violence against Women: Summary Report of Initial Results on Prevalence, Health Outcomes, and Women's Responses*. Geneva: Author.

World Health Organization. (2011). *World Report on Disability*. Geneva: Author.

Zitzelsberger, H. (2005). (In)visibility: Accounts of Embodiment of Women with Physical Disabilities and Differences. *Disability & Society* 20(4): 389–403.

*Source:* Pinto, Paula C. (2015). Excerpted from "Women, Disability, and the Right to Health." In Pat Armstrong & Ann Pederson (Eds.), *Women's Health: Intersections of Policy, Research, and Practice, Second Edition* (pp. 137–152). Toronto, ON: Women's Press.

# SNAPSHOTS & SOUNDWAVES 32

## UNDERSTANDING THE SOCIAL DETERMINANTS OF HEALTH

*There are many definitions of the social determinants of health. Here are two influential ones:*

Social determinants of health are the economic and social conditions that influence the health of individuals, communities, and jurisdictions as a whole. Social determinants of health determine whether individuals stay healthy or become ill (a narrow definition of health). They also determine the extent to which a person possesses the physical, social, and personal resources to identify and achieve personal aspirations, satisfy needs, and cope with the environment (a broader definition of health). Social determinants of health are about the quantity and quality of a variety of resources that a society makes available to its members.

*Source:* Raphael, Dennis. (2004). *Social Determinants of Health: Canadian Perspectives.* Toronto, ON: Canadian Scholars' Press.

The social determinants of health are the conditions in which people are born, grow, live, work, and age, including the health system. These circumstances are shaped by the distribution of money, power, and resources at global, national, and local levels, which are themselves influenced by policy choices. The social determinants of health are mostly responsible for health inequities—the unfair and avoidable differences in health status seen within and between countries.

*Source:* World Health Organization. (2017). "Social Determinants of Health." Retrieved from: http://www.who.int/social_determinants/en/.

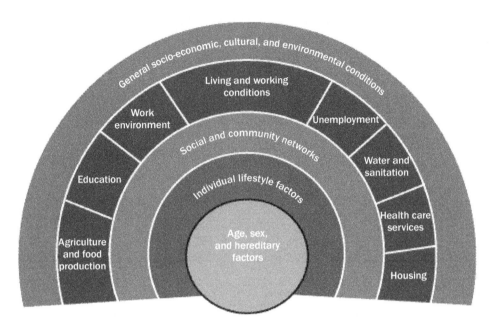

*Source:* Dahlgren, Göran, & Whitehead, Margaret. (1991). "The Main Determinants of Health." In *Policies and Strategies to Promote Social Equity in Health* (p. 11). Stockholm, Sweden: Institute for Futures Studies. Retrieved from: http://www.iffs. se/media/1326/20080109110739filmZ8UVQv2wQFShMRF6cuT.pdf.

## Fast Facts on the Social Determinants of Health

- Poverty, social exclusion, poor housing, and poor health systems are among the main social causes of ill health.

- Differences in the quality of life within and between countries affect how long people live. A child born in Japan has a chance of living 43 years longer than a child born in Sierra Leone.

- The probability of a man dying between the ages of 15 and 60 is 8.2 percent in Sweden, 48.5 percent in the Russian Federation, and 84.5 percent in Lesotho.

- In Australia, there is a 20-year gap in life expectancy between Australian Aboriginal and Torres Strait Islander peoples, and the Australian average.

- Low- and middle-income countries account for 85 percent of the world's road deaths.

- In 2002, nearly 11 million children died before reaching their fifth birthday—98 percent of these deaths were in developing countries.

- Inequality in income is increasing in countries that account for more than 80 percent of the world's population.

- Few governments have explicit policies for tackling socially determined health inequalities.

*Source:* World Health Organization. (2006). "Fact File: Social Determinants of Health." Retrieved from: http://www.who.int/features/factfiles/sdh/01_en.html.

# SNAPSHOTS & SOUNDWAVES 33

## HOW SEXISM AND RACISM DETERMINE HEALTH

### Sexism as a Determinant of Health

- Worldwide, women live an average four years longer than men.
- In 2011, women's life expectancy at birth was more than 80 years in 46 countries, but only 58 years in the WHO African region.
- Girls are far more likely than boys to suffer sexual abuse.
- Road traffic injuries are the leading cause of death among adolescent girls in high- and upper-middle-income countries.
- Complications from pregnancy and childbirth are an important cause of death among girls aged 15–19 in low- and middle-income countries.
- An estimated three million unsafe abortions occur globally every year among girls aged 15–19 years. Unsafe abortions contribute substantially to lasting health problems and maternal deaths.
- Every year, approximately 287,000 women die due to complications in pregnancy and childbirth; 99 percent of maternal deaths every year occur in developing countries.
- For women in their reproductive years (15–44), HIV/AIDS is the leading cause of death and disease worldwide. Unsafe sex is the main risk factor in developing countries.
- Women are more susceptible to depression and anxiety than men. Depression is the leading cause of disease burden for women in high-income and low- and middle-income countries.

- Breast cancer is the leading cancer killer among women aged 20–59 years worldwide.
- Globally, cardiovascular disease, often thought to be a "male" problem, is the leading killer of women.

*Source:* World Health Organization. (2013). Adapted from "Factsheet no. 334: Women's Health." Retrieved from: http://www.who.int/mediacentre/factsheets/fs334/en/index.html.

### Racism as a Determinant of Health

- Black women are significantly less likely than white women to receive minimum expected therapy for breast cancer.
- First Nations adults in Canada have a 20.8 percent higher rate of cancer than the general Canadian population.
- African Americans are significantly less likely to receive major colorectal treatment for their cancer, follow-up treatment, or chemotherapy.
- Black people are less likely to receive surgical treatment than white people, and they also have a shorter life expectancy than white people.
- Members of visible minorities were less likely to have been admitted to hospital, tested for prostate-specific antigen, administered a mammogram, or given a Pap test; members of visible minorities were less likely than white people to have had a mammogram or Pap test.

- In the United States, non-white people are treated by lower-quality surgeons, quality being measured by risk-adjusted mortality rates.
- Minoritized people were less likely than white people to have pain recorded even after adjustment for language differences.
- In health care settings with predominantly racial and ethnic minority people, 62 percent of those people were undertreated by WHO standards, and they were three times more likely to be under-medicated than those seen in non-minority settings.
- Many Indigenous peoples face racism and discrimination on a day-to-day basis. Cultural discontinuity, including loss of Indigenous languages, has been associated with higher rates of depression, alcoholism, suicide, and violence, and as having a greater impact on youth.
- A history of racial discrimination, social exclusion, and poverty can combine with mistrust and fear to deter members of racialized groups and Indigenous communities from accessing services and getting culturally appropriate care.

*Source:* McGibbon, Elizabeth A., & Etowa, Josephine B. (2009). Adapted from "Chapter 2: Racism as a Determinant of Health: Evidence for Change." In *Anti-Racist Health Care Practice* (pp. 54–58). Toronto, ON: Canadian Scholars' Press.

## A New Global Agenda for Health Equity

Our children have dramatically different life chances depending on where they were born. In Japan or Sweden, they can expect to live more than 80 years; in Brazil, 72 years; India, 63 years; and in one of several African countries, fewer than 50 years. And within countries, the differences in life chances are dramatic and are seen worldwide. The poorest of the poor have high levels of illness and premature mortality. But poor health is not confined to those worst off. In countries at all levels of income, health and illness follow a social gradient: the lower the socioeconomic position, the worse the health.

It does not have to be this way and it is not right that it should be like this. Where systematic differences in health are judged to be avoidable by reasonable action they are, quite simply, unfair. It is this that we label health inequity. Putting right these inequities—the huge and remediable differences in health between and within countries—is a matter of social justice. Reducing health inequities is, for the Commission on Social Determinants of Health, an ethical imperative. Social injustice is killing people on a grand scale.

*Source:* World Health Organization. (2008). "A New Global Agenda for Health Equity." In *Closing the Gap in a Generation: Health Equity through Action on the Social Determinants of Health*. Commission on Social Determinants of Health—Final Report. Geneva, Switzerland: WHO. Retrieved from: http://apps.who.int/iris/bitstream/10665/69832/1/WHO_IER_CSDH_08.1_eng.pdf.

# CHAPTER 49

## First Peoples, Second Class Treatment

*Billie Allan and Janet Smylie*

Billie Allan is an assistant professor in the School of Social Work at the University of Victoria in British Columbia. She is a former postdoctoral fellow and researcher at the Well Living House, an action research centre for Indigenous infants, children, and their families' health and well-being, located at the Centre for Research on Inner City Health, St. Michael's Hospital, in Toronto.

Janet Smylie is a professor in the Dalla Lana School of Public Health at the University of Toronto. One of Canada's first Métis physicians, Smylie is a respected international leader in the field of Indigenous health. She has practised and taught family medicine in diverse Indigenous communities. Her career has been focused on addressing inequities in the health of Indigenous peoples in Canada by bridging gaps in health knowledge and practice. Smylie currently holds a Canadian Institutes of Health Research Applied Public Health Chair in Indigenous Health Knowledge and Information at St. Michael's Hospital, where she directs the Well Living House and is an active staff physician.

*First Peoples, Second Class Treatment* explores the role of racism in the health and well-being of Indigenous peoples in Canada. We begin with an overview of the historical and contemporary contexts of racism, and the ways in which racism is fundamentally responsible for the alarming disparities in health between Indigenous and non-Indigenous peoples. [...]

## THE IMPORTANCE OF LOOKING AT RACISM AND INDIGENOUS HEALTH

Indigenous peoples' experiences are too often omitted in discussions of racism and anti-racism (Lawrence & Dua, 2005). The reasons for these omissions typically include a rationale that argues for recognition of the unique histories, policies and contemporary circumstances shaping the lives of Indigenous peoples (Nestel, 2012; Levy et al., 2013). While this recognition is important, these omissions may contribute to a continual "writing out" or "writing over" of

Indigenous experiences of racism, marginalization and violence, along with the strategies used to address and resist these same realities.

## THE IMPORTANCE OF CONTEXT

Stories about Indigenous health in Canada are frequently presented without the context needed to make sense of the information provided. For example, epidemiological data is often gathered, analyzed and shared without the inclusion of adequate context related to the historical and present-day impacts of colonial policies on the social determinants of health for Indigenous peoples. In addition, this data can be shared in the absence of the voices and perspectives of Indigenous people themselves (Smylie, 2014). [...]

While stories about Indigenous health are frequently marked by an absence of context, they can also be characterized by the presence of racist stereotypes and inaccuracies pervasive in mainstream Canadian narratives. These include the idea that genetic predeterminations—as opposed to factors like access to the social determinants of health—are responsible for the health inequities experienced by Indigenous peoples and other racialized groups. The importance of taking care to contextualize Indigenous peoples' health cannot be overstated since, as noted by Greenwood and de Leeuw (2012), a failure to do so may result in a presumption that the extremely poor health status and socioeconomic challenges faced by many Indigenous peoples is a matter only of physiological or biomedical failure (n.p.).

As a result, this chapter begins with a focus on providing some of the context necessary to understand stories about Indigenous health.

\*\*\*\*\*

## RACISM AND COLONIZATION

Racism and colonization are inextricably intertwined; Reading (2013) notes that the use of race as a category of identity began with European colonization of other continents. Despite the fact that race is a socially constructed category with no biological basis, it has been used for hundreds of years to argue for and promote hierarchies of supposed superiority and civility among "races" of people (Reading, 2013). Racism not only justified historic colonization but compounds its contemporary effects (Cunningham, 2009), contributing to, for example, the obstruction of Indigenous self-determination and failure to recognize treaty and land rights, the lack of access to services and resources, and the over-surveillance by criminal justice and child welfare systems. The continued marginalization and criminalization experienced by Indigenous peoples and people of colour occurs in direct relationship to the continued societal and systematic privileging of white people in Canadian society.

## IMPACTS OF COLONIZATION ON THE SOCIAL DETERMINATIONS OF HEALTH

Colonization has been recognized internationally as a key determinant of health for Indigenous peoples (Cunningham, 2009; Mowbray, 2007). In April 2007, an international delegation of Indigenous representatives met as part of ongoing consultations linked to the World Health Organization's Commission on Social Determinants of Health. The proceedings from this meeting included the statement: "Everyone agrees that there is one critical social determinant of health, the effect of colonization" (Mowbray, 2007).

In Canada, Indigenous conceptualizations of the social determinants of health have emphasized the fundamental role of colonization, racism, social exclusion and a lack of self-determination in the alarming disparities in Indigenous and non-Indigenous peoples' health. For example, Loppie Reading & Wien (2009) specifically identify the relationships between the factors listed above and determinants of health including health care, education, housing, employment, income, food security, community infrastructure, cultural continuity and environmental stewardship.

## The Indian Act

The institutionalization of colonial policies impacting the social determinants of health is illustrated by the Indian Act of 1876 which provided the federal government of Canada with the right to determine who can and cannot be an "Indian." In addition to entrenching government control of Indigenous identity, the Indian Act enabled the movement of First Nations peoples from their homelands onto "reserve lands" which were also controlled by the federal government on behalf of those they identified to be "Indian" (Smylie, 2009). The reserve system invested tremendous power into the hands of Indian agents who could govern the movement of Indians on and off reserve through a pass system (Coates, 2008). Removal to reserve lands had a devastating impact on Indigenous ways of knowing and being in relation to land, including the restriction of traditional hunting and gathering practices which were replaced by a constructed reliance on government rations of European foods. The Indian Act also included stipulations that barred legal representation, gathering to discuss Indigenous affairs, the use of mechanized farm equipment, the slaughter of livestock on-reserve for sustenance, and the sale of agricultural goods off-reserve (Coates, 2008; Harry, 2009). In addition, the Indian Act undermined the roles and responsibilities of women in previously matriarchal and/or matrilineal societies, preventing women's involvement in governance and rooting "Indian" identity in male lineage (Blair, 2005; Stevenson, 2011).

## Colonial Policies and the Métis

The Métis peoples originated in the 17th century with the intermarriage of the early waves of European (mainly French and Scottish) men and First Nations women in the western provinces (Smylie, 2009). In the following two centuries, the Métis nation birthed a distinct language (Michif) and culture, and occupied a key economic role in the fur trade (Smylie, 2009). The lasting effects of land dispossession, exclusion, racism and race-based persecution are reflected in the gross disparities in health status and social determinants of health that the Métis peoples suffer alongside First Nations and Inuit peoples. At the same time, the use of state-imposed definitions of Indigenous identity, particularly via the Indian Act, means that Métis peoples and non-Status First Nations people are excluded from many Aboriginal-specific health entitlements and services, including the Non-Insured Health Benefits (NIHB) program, further exacerbating health disparities (Bent, Havelock & Haworth-Brockman, 2007; Bourassa & Peach, 2009; Ghosh & Spitzer, 2014; Haworth-Brockman, Bent & Havelock, 2009; Wilson et al., 2013).

## Colonial Policy and Its Impact on Inuit Health and Well-Being

Inuit peoples traditionally resided in the territories above the treeline on the lands presently known as Canada, and compose part of the broader circumpolar Inuit population with traditional lands spanning Alaska, Greenland and Russia (Smylie, 2001; Smylie, 2009). Canada now recognizes four Inuit regions settled through extensive land claims, including Inuvialuit, Nunavut, Nunatsiavut and Nunavik (Inuit Tapiriit Kanatami, n.d.). The history of federal interference in Inuit life includes forced relocation to remote permanent villages (Smylie, 2009), as well as the mass slaughter of Inuit sled dogs,[1] both of which significantly impacted the previously nomadic ways of life. The rupture of traditional Inuit life, including hunting and gathering practices and social and family structures, through the introduction of European and Christian norms and values, residential schools and forced economic dependency on the federal government, has had a lasting impact on the health and well-being of Inuit peoples who experience some of the most extreme health disparities in Canada (Møller, 2005; Smylie, 2009).

## Residential Schools, the Sixties Scoop and Contemporary Child Welfare

Indigenous children were historically removed from the care of their families and communities to residential schools, a system of institutionalized education and care that lasted well over 100 years. The residential school system was intended to "kill the Indian in the child" and many, including former Prime Minister of Canada Paul Martin, have since recognized the implementation of the schools as an act of cultural genocide (Miller, 1996; Neu, 2000) which has had rippling multigenerational effects on survivors, their children, grandchildren and great-grandchildren. The sexual, emotional, physical, mental, spiritual and cultural abuse experienced by generations of Indigenous children who survived residential schools has resulted in deeply painful impacts on the physical, emotional, spiritual and mental health of survivors, their families and communities. This does not acknowledge the effects of the tremendous loss experienced by those families and communities whose children never returned, whose precious lives did not survive the horrors of these schools.

As concerns about poor conditions and widespread abuses surfaced, support for residential schools began to wane in the late 1940s and into the 1950s. This gave way to a new wave of assimilationist practices—beginning in the 1950s and peaking in the 1960s, there was an enormous influx of Indigenous children taken into the care of child welfare agencies which is now known as the Sixties Scoop (Sinclair, 2004). This era of mass apprehension meant that in

the matter of a decade approximately one in three Indigenous children was apprehended from the care of their families and communities (Fournier & Crey, 1997; Sinclair, 2007).

Overrepresentation of Indigenous children in child welfare remains an urgent and ongoing challenge facing Indigenous communities across Canada. While the most recent estimates suggest that Aboriginal peoples account for slightly more than 4 percent of the general Canadian population, Aboriginal children represent 48 percent of children in care (Statistics Canada, 2013a). [...]

The rupture of identity, family and community perpetrated through the practices identified above has had lasting and intergenerational impacts, substantially interfering with or completely impeding the transmission of values, beliefs and practices, including parenting practices. The ways in which the resulting intergenerational trauma and damage to Indigenous identity have impacted the health and well-being of Indigenous peoples has been extensively documented (Allan, 2013; Brave Heart, 1998; Desmarais, 2013; Menzies, 2008; Smith, Varcoe & Edwards, 2005; Wesley-Esquimaux & Smolewski, 2004). For example, a study of self-identified First Nations adults in Hamilton, Ontario found a population prevalence of post-traumatic stress disorder of 34 percent using the primary care PTSD screen (Smylie et al., 2011).

## Gendered Impact of Colonial Racism

Addressing the alarming health disparities and barriers to health care experienced by Indigenous women requires a foundational understanding of the historical and contemporary racist policies and practices that have shaped their lives, health and well-being, and access to health care. For example, it is critical to examine links between contemporary rates of infant mortality, maternal morbidity and mortality, and overall poorer health in the context of the history of forced sterilization of Indigenous women (Grekul, Krahn & Odynak, 2004), the undermining of traditional midwifery, mandatory medical evacuation for pregnant Indigenous women in remote communities, and the historic and ongoing racism evident in the disproportionate rates of child welfare intervention experienced by Indigenous women and their families.

Ongoing racism is also evident in the epidemic of violence against Aboriginal women, and the failure of the Canadian state to adequately investigate and address this violence. Aboriginal women in Canada experience higher rates than non-Aboriginal women of both spousal and non-spousal violence, and report more severe forms of violence (Mathyssen, 2011; Statistics Canada, 2013b). Indigenous women in Canada are more likely to be victims of homicide and, unlike their non-Indigenous counterparts (Statistics Canada, 2013b), are as likely to be murdered by a stranger or acquaintance as they are by an intimate partner (NWAC, 2010). Violence against Indigenous women is most painfully reflected in the mass numbers of missing and murdered Indigenous girls and women in Canada […].

# WHAT WE KNOW ABOUT THE MAGNITUDE OF RACISM EXPERIENCED BY INDIGENOUS PEOPLES IN CANADA AND ITS IMPACT ON HEALTH, WELL-BEING AND ACCESS TO HEALTH SERVICES

## What We Know: Experiences of Racism and Impacts on Health

In Canada, there is a range of survey data documenting the experiences of racial discrimination of Indigenous people (e.g. Regional Health Survey, Aboriginal Peoples Survey, Urban Aboriginal Peoples Study, Toronto Aboriginal Research Project and the Our Health Counts study) and a small but growing body of research focused on documenting and delineating the

relationship between racism and Indigenous health and health care access. These studies have found that many if not most Indigenous people in Canada experience racism on a recurring basis. It should also be noted that research from both Canada and the US indicates that experiences of racism are commonly underreported, such that presently available data can be best understood as an underestimate of the true prevalence of racism in Canada (Smylie, 2009; Wilson et al., 2013).

Current research also indicates that racism has direct impacts on health. A 2012 study by Currie et al. examining experiences of racism among Aboriginal university students in Edmonton, Alberta found that student reactions to racism were indicative of racial battle fatigue (Smith, Allen & Danley, 2007), described as the depletion of mental and physical resources due to the constant engagement of stress response systems to cope with ongoing discrimination (Currie et al., 2012; Smith et al., 2007). A study using data from the 2003 Canadian Community Health Survey (CCHS) demonstrates that there are health disparities experienced by racialized groups in Canada that cannot be explained by socioeconomic status, suggesting that these disparities are evidence of the "wear and tear of experiences of racism and discrimination in regular encounters with societal institutions and in everyday life" (Veenstra, 2009). These studies are supported by a growing body of research in the US and Australia identifying racism as a chronic stressor implicated in the health of African Americans and Indigenous Australians.

## Racism and the Health Care System

In the context of contemporary Indigenous health, Canada's race-based legislation has normalized the uneven distribution of health funding, resources and services according to state-constructed Indigenous identities such that only those classified by the Canadian government as status First Nations and Inuit peoples are entitled to the Non-Insured Health

Benefits (NIHB) program and to the Indigenous health services and support provided through the federal government via the First Nations and Inuit Health Branch. Métis and non-status First Nations lack access to these services and resources while facing the same determinants of health that have created egregious disparities in health in comparison to non-Indigenous people (Greenwood & de Leeuw, 2012; Loppie Reading & Wien, 2009; Smylie, 2009; Smylie & Adomako, 2009; Statistics Canada, 2008). At the same time, simply being eligible for NIHB does not necessarily ensure access since some services require on-reserve residency in order to receive funding for or access to a service or program, and the roster of approved services and medications is constantly changing (Haworth-Brockman et al., 2009; Mother of Red Nations, 2006). Moreover, the delivery of NIHB poses challenges to equitable access to health services in comparison to non-Indigenous people, particularly in northern and remote communities.

In addition to the uneven access to health services and resources created through the NIHB and other race-based policies, experiences and anticipation of racist treatment by health care providers also act as barriers to accessing needed health services for Indigenous peoples (Kurtz et al., 2008; Tang & Browne, 2008; Browne et al, 2011). For example, in examining the experiences of Indigenous and non-Indigenous persons accessing an inner-city emergency department, Browne et al. (2011) found that Indigenous participants described anticipating that being identified as Aboriginal and poor might result in a lack of credibility and/or negatively influence their chances of receiving help. This was such a common experience that participants actively strategized around how to manage negative responses from health care providers in advance of accessing care. In some cases, these experiences keep people from accessing health care at all.

Racism in the Canadian health care system can be fatal, a fact devastatingly illustrated by the death of Brian Sinclair, a 45-year-old Indigenous man who visited the emergency room of the Winnipeg Health Sciences Centre in 2008. Mr. Sinclair was referred to the ER by a community physician for a bladder infection. While he waited, Mr. Sinclair vomited on himself several times, and other ER visitors pled with nurses and security guards to attend to him (Puxley, 2013a, 2013b). Following a 34-hour wait, Mr. Sinclair died of the bladder infection in the waiting room without ever receiving treatment. The Sinclair family, their legal counsel and local Indigenous leaders asked a provincial inquest into the matter to strongly consider the ways in which Mr. Sinclair's race, disability (Mr. Sinclair was a double amputee and had suffered some cognitive impairment) and class resulted in his lack of treatment and subsequent death (Puxley, 2014). In February 2014, the Sinclair family withdrew from the provincial inquest due to frustration with its failure to examine and address the role of systemic racism in his death, and in the treatment of Indigenous peoples in health care settings more broadly (Sinclair, 2014).

*****

---

## CRITICAL NEXT STEPS

### Transforming the Conversation about Race and Health in Canada

In order to address the health disparities experienced by Indigenous peoples and racialized groups in Canada, we must accurately apprehend and engage the realities of our shared physical and societal landscape. This requires a fundamental acknowledgement of the historical and ongoing colonization of Indigenous peoples (Lawrence & Dua, 2005). This work also demands a foundational shift in how matters of racism and racialization are taken up by Canadian social institutions beyond the health care system, including education, child protection and justice, as well as how these issues are accounted for and addressed by public policies, formal legislation and mainstream stories. It requires a departure from the cherished image of Canada as a well-meaning, international peacekeeper and the imagined harmony of the multicultural mosaic, and a long walk towards truth and reconciliation in a country that our former Prime Minister [Stephen Harper] claims has "no history of colonialism" (Henderson & Wakeham, 2009). There is also much that can be learned from our international Indigenous colleagues regarding approaches to policymaking, programming, service provision and anti-racism interventions.

## Improving Indigenous Health Data Collection in Order to Address Racism as a Driver of Indigenous Health Disparities

[…] The available population health data for Indigenous peoples in Canada is a patchwork, drawing largely on sources with significant limitations (Anderson et al., 2006; Smylie & Anderson, 2006). Meaningful data is critical to understanding and addressing the role of racism in the health disparities experienced by Indigenous people living in Canada. This echoes the work of scholars from Australia and New Zealand who are at the forefront of advancing knowledge addressing the impact of racism on Indigenous health (Paradies et al., 2008) and their call for research in four key areas: 1) the prevalence and experience of racism experienced by Indigenous peoples across the life course; 2) the impact of racism on Indigenous health across the life course; 3) the development of measures to assess systemic racism against Indigenous peoples; and 4) identifying best practices in addressing systemic racism against Indigenous peoples.

We especially argue for concerted effort to develop or adapt effective interventions addressing attitudinal/interpersonal and systemic racism towards Indigenous peoples, and to undertake bold and brave evaluation of existing anti-racism strategies and interventions.

## NOTE

1. While the slaughter of Inuit sled dogs has long been denied by the federal government and the RCMP, the province of Quebec acknowledged and offered compensation of $3 million for the slaughter of sled dogs to the people of Nunavik in 2011 (Brennan, 2012; "Premier Charest's apology for dog killings," 2011–2012).

## REFERENCES

Allan, B. (2013). *Rupture, defragmentation and reconciliation: Re-visioning the health of urban Indigenous women in Toronto.* (Unpublished doctoral dissertation). University of Toronto, Toronto, Ontario.

Anderson, M., Smylie, J., Anderson, I., Sinclair, R. & Crengle, S. (2006). *First Nations, Métis, and Inuit health indicators in Canada. A background paper for the project Action Oriented Indicators of Health and Health Systems Development for Indigenous People in Australia, Canada and New Zealand.* Regina, SK: Indigenous Peoples' Health Research Centre.

Bent, K., Havelock, J. & Haworth-Brockman, M. (2007). *Entitlements and health services for First Nations and Métis women in Manitoba and Saskatchewan.* (Project #150). Winnipeg, MB: Prairie Women's Health Centre of Excellence.

Blair, P.J. (2005). *Rights of Aboriginal women on- and off-reserve.* Vancouver, BC: Scow Institute. Retrieved from: http://www.scowinstitute.ca/library/documents/RPRightsofWomen.pdf

Bourassa, C. & Peach, I. (2009). *Reconceiving notions of Aboriginal identity.* Ottawa, ON: Institute on Governance.

Brave Heart, M.Y. (1998). The return to the sacred path: Healing the historical unresolved grief response among the Lakota through a psychoeducational group intervention. *Smith College Studies in Social Work*, 68, 287–305.

Brennan, R.J. (2012). "Inuit communities finally get compensation for dog slaughter." *The Toronto Star.* Retrieved from: https://www.thestar.com/news/canada/2012/06/29/inuit_communities_finally_get_compensation_for_dog_slaughter.html

Browne, A.J., Smye, V., Rodney, P., Tang, S., Mussell, B. & O'Neil, J. (2011). Access to primary care from the perspective of Aboriginal patients at an urban emergency department. *Qualitative Health Research*, 21(3), 333–348.

Coates, K. (2008). *The Indian Act and the future of Aboriginal governance in Canada: Research paper for the National Centre for First Nations Governance*. Ottawa, ON: National Centre for First Nations Governance.

Cunningham, M. (2009). *Chapter V: Health. In United Nations, Permanent Forum on Indigenous Issues, State of the world's Indigenous peoples* (pp. 156–187). New York, NY: United Nations.

Currie, C.L., Wild, T.C., Schopflocher, D.P., Laing, L. & Veugelers, P. (2012). Racial discrimination experienced by Aboriginal university students in Canada. *Canadian Journal of Psychiatry*, 57(10), 617–625.

Desmarais, D.A. (2013). Colonialism's impact upon the health of Métis elderly: History, oppression, identity and consequences. (Doctoral dissertation). University of Regina, Regina, Saskatchewan.

Fournier, S. & Crey, E. (1997). *Stolen from our embrace: The abduction of First Nations children and the restoration of Aboriginal communities*. Vancouver, BC: Douglas & McIntyre.

Ghosh, H. & Spitzer, D. (2014). Inequities in diabetes outcomes among urban First Nation and Métis communities: Can addressing diversities in preventive services make a difference? *The International Indigenous Policy Journal*, 5(1). Retrieved from: http://ir.lib.uwo.ca/iipj/vol5/iss1/2

Greenwood, M. & de Leeuw, S. (2012). Social determinants of health and the future well-being of Aboriginal children in Canada. *Paediatrics and Child Health*, 17(7), 381–384.

Grekul, J., Krahn, A. & Odynak, D. (2004). Sterilizing the "feeble-minded": Eugenics in Alberta, Canada, 1929–1972. *Journal of Historical Sociology*, 17(4), 358–384.

Harry, K. (2009). *The Indian Act and Aboriginal women's empowerment: What front line workers need to know*. Vancouver, BC: Battered Women's Support Services.

Haworth-Brockman, M., Bent, K. & Havelock, J. (2009). Health research, entitlements and health services for First Nations and Métis women in Manitoba and Saskatchewan. *Journal of Aboriginal Health*, 4(2), 17–23.

Henderson, J. & Wakeham, P. (2009). Colonial reckoning, national reconciliation? First Peoples and the culture of redress in Canada. *English Studies in Canada*, 35(1), 1–26.

Inuit Tapiriit Kanatami. (n.d.). About ITK. Retrieved from: https://www.itk.ca/about-canadian-inuit/

Kurtz, D.L.M., Nyberg, J.C., Van Den Tillaart, S., Mills, B. & Okanagan Urban Aboriginal Health Research Collective (OUAHRC). (2008). Silencing of voice: An act of structural violence: Urban Aboriginal women speak out about their experiences with health care. *Journal of Aboriginal Health*, 4(1), 53–63.

Lawrence, B. & Dua, E. (2005). Decolonizing anti-racism. *Social Justice: A Journal of Crime, Conflict and World Order*, 32(4), 120–143.

Levy, J., Ansara, D. & Stover, A. (2013). *Racialization and health inequities in Toronto*. Toronto, ON: Toronto Public Health.

Loppie Reading, C. & Wien, F. (2009). *Health Inequalities and Social Determinants of Aboriginal Peoples' Health*. National Collaborating Centre for Aboriginal Health. Prince George, BC: National Collaborating Centre for Aboriginal Health.

Mathyssen, I. (2011). *Ending violence against Aboriginal women and girls: Empowerment—a new beginning: Report of the Standing Committee on the Status of Women*. Ottawa: Standing Committee on the Status of Women.

Menzies, P. (2008). Developing an Aboriginal healing model for intergenerational trauma. *International Journal of Health Promotion and Education*, 46(2), 41–48.

Miller, J. (1996). *Shingwauk's Vision: A history of Native residential schools*. Toronto, ON: University of Toronto Press.

Møller, H. (2005). *A problem of the government? Colonization and the socio-cultural experience of tuberculosis in Nunavut*. (Unpublished master's thesis). Copenhagen University, Copenhagen, Denmark.

Mother of Red Nations: Women's Council of Manitoba. (2006). *Twenty years and ticking: Aboriginal women, human rights and Bill C-31*. Winnipeg, MB: Author. Retrieved from: http://morn.cimnet.ca/cim/dbf/morn_billc31_complete.pdf?im_id=5088&si_id=92 (link no longer active)

Mowbray, M. (Ed.) (2007). *Social determinants and Indigenous health: The International experience and its policy implications*. Geneva, Switzerland: World Health Organization Commission on Social Determinants of Health.

Native Women's Association of Canada (NWAC). (2010). *What their stories tell us: Research findings from the Sisters in Spirit initiative.* Ottawa, ON: Author.

Nestel, S. (2012). *Colour coded health care: The impact of race and racism on Canadians' health.* Toronto, ON: Wellesley Institute.

Neu, D. (2000). Accounting and accountability relations: colonization, genocide and Canada's first nations. *Accounting, Auditing & Accountability Journal, 13*(3), 268–288.

Paradies, Y., Harris, R. & Anderson, I. (2008). *The impact of racism on Indigenous health in Australia and Aotearoa: Towards a research agenda (Discussion Paper No. 4).* Darwin, Australia: Cooperative Research Centre for Aboriginal Health.

Puxley, C. (2013a, October 24). "Woman tells inquest she tried to get nurses to check on man in Winnipeg ER." *MacLean's.* Retrieved from: http://www.macleans.ca/general/woman-tells-inquest-she-tried-to-get-nurses-to-check-on-man-in-winnipeg-er/

Puxley, C. (2013b, October 30). "Woman in ER where man died after lengthy wait says it was obvious he needed help." *MacLean's.* Retrieved from: http://www.macleans.ca/general/woman-in-er-where-man-died-after-lengthy-wait-says-it-was-obvious-he-needed-help/

Puxley, C. (2014, January 5). "Brian Sinclair inquest to look at hospital backlogs; man died after 34-hour ER wait." *CTV News.* Retrieved from: http://www.ctvnews.ca/canada/brian-sinclair-inquest-to-look-at-hospital-backlogs-man-died-after-34-hour-er-wait-1.1618464

Reading, C. (2013). *Understanding racism.* Prince George, BC: National Collaborating Centre for Aboriginal Health.

Sinclair, R. (2004). Aboriginal social work education in Canada: Decolonizing pedagogy for the seventh generation. *First Peoples Child & Family Review, 1*(1), 49–61.

Sinclair, R. (2007). Identity lost and found: Lessons from the sixties scoop. *First Peoples Child & Family Review, 3*(1), 65–82.

Sinclair, Robert. (2014, February 18). *Statement of Robert Sinclair re: withdrawal of Sinclair family from Phase 2 of the Brian Sinclair inquest.* Retrieved from: https://dl.dropboxusercontent.com/u/8827767/Withdrawal/2014-02-18%20Statement%20of%20Robert%20Sinclair%20FINAL.pdf (link no longer active)

Smith, D., Varcoe, C. & Edwards, N. (2005). Turning around the intergenerational impact of residential schools on Aboriginal people: Implications for health policy and practice. *Canadian Journal of Nursing Research, 37*(4), 38–60.

Smith, W.A., Allen, W.R. & Danley, L.L. (2007). "Assume the position … you fit the description": Campus racial climate and the psychoeducational experiences and racial battle fatigue among African American male college students. *American Behavioral Scientist, 51*(4), 551–578.

Smylie, J. (2001). SOGC policy statement: A guide for health professionals working with Aboriginal peoples: Cross cultural understanding. *Journal of the Society of Obstetricians and Gynaecologists of Canada, 100,* 157–200.

Smylie, J. (2009). Chapter 19: The health of Aboriginal peoples. In D. Raphael (Ed.), *Social determinants of health: Canadian perspectives, second edition* (pp. 280–304). Toronto, ON: Canadian Scholars' Press Inc.

Smylie, J. (2014). Indigenous Child Wellbeing in Canada. In A. C. Michalos (Ed.), *Encyclopedia of Quality of Life and Wellbeing Research* (pp. i–j). Dordrecht, Netherlands: Springer.

Smylie, J. & Adomako, P. (2009). *Indigenous children's health report: Health assessment in action.* Toronto, ON: St. Michael's Hospital.

Smylie, J. & Anderson, M. (2006). Understanding the health of Indigenous peoples in Canada: Key methodological and conceptual challenges. *Canadian Medical Association Journal, 175*(6), 602–602.

Smylie, J., Firestone, M., Cochran, L., Prince, C., Maracle, S., Morley, M., Mayo, S., Spiller, T. & McPherson, B. (2011). *Our Health Counts Urban Aboriginal Health Database Research Project – Community report First Nations adults and children, City of Hamilton.* Hamilton, ON: De Dwa Da Dehs Ney>s Aboriginal Health Centre.

Statistics Canada (2008). Aboriginal Peoples in Canada in 2006: Inuit, Métis, and First Nations, 2006 Census. Catalogue number 7-558-XIE. Ottawa, ON: Minister of Industry. Retrieved from: http://www12.statcan.ca/census-recensement/2006/as-sa/97-558/pdf/97-558-XIE2006001.pdf

Statistics Canada. (2013a). *Aboriginal Peoples in Canada: First Nations People, Métis and Inuit.* National Household

Survey, 2011. Catalogue no. 99-011-X2011001. Ottawa, ON: Minister of Industry. Retrieved from: http://www12.statcan.gc.ca/nhs-enm/2011/as-sa/99-011-x/99-011-x2011001-eng.cfm

Statistics Canada. (2013b). *Measuring violence against women.* Ottawa, ON: Author. Retrieved from: http://www.statcan.gc.ca/pub/85-002-x/2013001/article/11766-eng.pdf

Stevenson, W. (2011). Colonialism and First Nations women in Canada. In M. Cannon & L. Sunseri (Eds.), *Racism, colonialism, and indigeneity in Canada: A reader* (pp. 44–56). Don Mills, ON: Oxford University Press.

Tang, S. & Browne, A.J. (2008). 'Race' matter: Racialization and egalitarian discourses involving Aboriginal people in the Canadian health care context. *Ethnicity & Health*, 13(2), 109–127.

Veenstra, G. (2009). Racialized identity and health in Canada: Results from a nationally representative survey. *Social Science and Medicine*, 69, 538–542.

Wesley-Esquimaux, C.C. & Smolewski, M. (2004). *Historic trauma and Aboriginal healing.* Ottawa, ON: Aboriginal Healing Foundation.

Wilson, D., de la Ronde, S., Brascoupe, S., Apale, A.N., Barney, L., Guthrie, B., Horn, O., Johnson, R., Rattray, D. & Robinson, N. (2013). Health professionals working with First Nations, Inuit, and Métis consensus guideline. *Journal of Obstetrics & Gynaecology Canada*, 35(6) Suppl 2, S1–S52.

---

**Source:** Allan, Billie, & Smylie, Janet. (2015). Excerpted from *First Peoples, Second Class Treatment: The Role of Racism in the Health and Well-Being of Indigenous Peoples in Canada* (pp. 4–10, 12–17). Toronto, ON: The Wellesley Institute.

# CHAPTER 50

## HIV/AIDS, Globalization, and the International Women's Movement

*Sisonke Msimang*

Sisonke Msimang is a writer and activist whose work focuses on race, gender, and democracy. She is programme director for the Centre for Stories in Perth, Australia, an initiative that collects, preserves, and shares stories about migrants, refugees, and diverse people and places linked to the Indian Ocean Rim. Msimang is a Yale World Fellow, an Aspen New Voices Fellow, and was a Ruth First Fellow at the University of the Witwatersrand. She regularly contributes to *The Guardian* and *The New York Times*, among other publications, and has given a popular TED Talk called "If a Story Moves You, Act on It." Msimang has recently published her memoir, entitled *Always Another Country: A Memoir of Exile and Home.*

## HIV/AIDS AND GLOBALIZATION

Globalization has been described as "the drive towards an economic system dominated by supranational trade and banking institutions that are not accountable to democratic processes or national governments" (Globalization Guide, www.Globalizationguide. org/01.html). It is characterised by an increase in cross-border economic, social, and technological exchange under conditions of (extreme) capitalism. As human bodies move across borders in search of new economic and educational opportunities, or in search of lives free from political conflict and violence, they bring with them dreams and aspirations. Sometimes, they carry the virus that causes AIDS, and often, they meet the virus at their destinations.

As corporations increasingly patrol the planet, looking for new markets, and natural and human resources to exploit, they set up and abandon economic infrastructure—opening and closing factories, establishing hostels. In so doing, they create peripheral communities, hoping to benefit from employment and the presence of new populations where previously there were none. And when they move on, once they have found a cheaper place to go, they leave in their wake communities that are extremely susceptible to HIV/AIDS.

This is because the virus follows vulnerability, crosses borders with ease, and finds itself at home where there is conflict, hunger, and poverty. The virus is particularly comfortable where wealth and poverty co-exist—it thrives on inequality. It is not surprising, then, that Southern Africa provides an excellent case study of the collusion between globalizing processes and HIV/AIDS.

The economy of the region has been defined in the last two centuries by mining: gold and diamonds. In an era of plummeting gold prices, and an increasing shift towards the service industry, Southern Africa is shedding thousands of jobs. Yet the last century of globalization has provided a solid platform for the current AIDS crisis.

If there was a recipe for creating an AIDS epidemic in Southern Africa, it would read as follows: "Steal some land and subjugate its people. Take some men from rural areas and put them in hostels far away from home, in different countries if need be. Build excellent roads. Ensure that the communities surrounding the men are impoverished so that a ring of sex workers develops around each mining town. Add HIV. Now take some miners and send them home for holidays to their rural, uninfected wives. Add a few girlfriends in communities along the road home.

Add liberal amounts of patriarchy, both home-grown and of the colonial variety. Ensure that women have no right to determine the conditions under which sex will take place. Make sure that they have no access to credit, education, or any of the measures that would give them options to leave unhappy unions, or dream of lives in which men are not the centre of their activities. Shake well and watch an epidemic explode."

There's an optional part of the recipe, which adds an extra spice to the pot: African countries on average spend four times more on debt servicing than they do on health. Throw in a bit of World Bank propaganda, some loans from the IMF, and beat well. Voilà. We have icing on the cake.

As the gap between the rich countries of the North and the poor countries of the South grows, we are beginning to see serious differences in the ways that states can afford to take care of their citizens. Access to technology, drugs, and strong social safety nets in the North mean that HIV/AIDS is a manageable chronic illness in most developed countries. Yet there are pockets of poor, immigrant, gay, and otherwise marginalised communities within these countries, where HIV prevalence is on the rise. An analysis of the complex intersections between inequalities tells us that it is not enough to belong to a rich country—that alone does not protect you from vulnerability to HIV infection, nor does it guarantee treatment. Where you sit in relation to the state is equally important—whether you are a woman, a poor woman, a black woman, an educated woman, a lesbian, a woman with a disability who is assumed not to be having sex, an immigrant who is not entitled to many of the social security benefits of citizens. All these factors determine your vulnerability to HIV/AIDS.

Now what does this mean for a 25-year-old woman living in Soweto? Jabu works as a security guard at a shopping centre in Johannesburg. Every day she spends two hours travelling to work because of the distances the architects of apartheid set up between city centres and the townships that serviced them. Jabu is grateful to have a job. Her two little ones are in KwaZulu Natal with their grandmother until Jabu can get a stable job. She is on a month-to-month contract with the security company. She watches expensive cars all day, protecting their owners' investments while they work. The company doesn't want to take her on as staff so each month she faces the uncertainty of not having a job the next month. Joining a union is not an option—she's not technically a staff member and she can't afford to make trouble. Jabu's boyfriend Thabo drives a taxi. Their relationship saves her cash because he drives her to and from work every day—a saving of almost one third of her salary each month. She has another boyfriend at work, who often buys her lunch. She has to be careful that Thabo doesn't find out.

In addition to race, class, and gender, Jabu's life is fundamentally shaped by the forces of globalization—where she works and how secure that work is, where her children live, even how she arrives at work. These factors all influence her vulnerability to HIV infection.

## HIV/AIDS AND FEMINISM

During the last eight years of my work on sexual and reproductive rights, my focus has been primarily on HIV and AIDS. For me, the pandemic brings into stark relief the fact that states have failed to provide their citizens with the basic rights enshrined in the declaration of human rights.

Twenty years ago, AIDS was known as Gay-Related Immune Disease—so associated was it with gay men. Today, the face of AIDS has changed. It looks like mine. It is now black, female, and extremely young. In some parts of sub-Saharan Africa, girls aged 15–19 are six times more likely than their male counterparts to be HIV-positive. Something is very wrong.

In the next 10 years, the epidemic will explode in Asia and in Central and Eastern Europe as well as in Latin America. The pandemic will have profound effects on the burden of reproductive work that women do, and this in turn will have far-reaching consequences for the participation of women in politics, the economic sector, and other sectors of society. The very maintenance of the household, the work that feminist economists like Marilyn Waring, Diane Elson, and others tell us keeps the world running, may no longer be possible.

As older women are increasingly called upon to care for children, and as life expectancy shrinks to the forties and fifties, in Africa we face the prospect of a generation without grandparents, and an imminent orphan and vulnerable children crisis that will effectively leave kids to take care of kids. As the orphan crisis deepens, child abuse is on the rise. Girls without families to protect them are engaging in survival sex to feed themselves and their siblings, and we are told that communities will "cope." There is a myth of coping that pervades the development discourse on AIDS. What it really means is that women will do it. What it translates into is that families split up, girls hook for money and food, and a vicious cycle is born.

While there is some feminist analysis of the AIDS epidemic, we have not yet heard a rallying cry from the women's movement. A recent article by Noeleen Heyzer, UNIFEM's executive director, begins to formulate some arguments about why, in the context of AIDS, women can no longer wait for equality with men (www.csmonitor.com/2002/0718/p13s02-coop.html). Dr. Heyzer points out that it takes 24 buckets of water a day to care for a person living with AIDS—to clean sheets fouled by diarrhoea and vomit, to prepare water for bathing (sometimes several times a day), to wash dishes and prepare food. For women who must walk miles, and still do all the other chores that always need doing, the burden becomes unbearable.

This past spring in New York, I was asked to speak to a group at a high school in Brooklyn about HIV/AIDS and violence against women in the South African context. They were an intelligent group, well versed in feminism. I was not the only presenter. A young American woman who had worked with *Ms. Magazine* talked about pop culture, and the politics of wearing jeans and letting your G-string show. I left the meeting feeling disconcerted. I had made my presentation and received a few awkward questions about men in Africa. I cringed on behalf of my brothers because I certainly was not trying to demonise them, but the students were feeding into a larger narrative of the familiar discourse of black male laziness, deviancy, and sexual aggression that I was careful to point out to them. Aside from that, they found little else to talk about.

On the other hand, the woman from the US struck a chord with them. They talked about eating disorders and the media, about Britney Spears and Janet Jackson. It was fascinating. Having lived in the US, I was able to follow and engage, but my interests as an African feminist do not lie in this subject matter. It was a clear example of how far apart we, as feminists, sometimes are from one another.

Contexts vary, and of course the issues that are central in the global North will be different from those of Southern feminists. And amongst us there will be differences. I understood where the high school students were coming from. Indigenous feminism must be rooted in what matters most to women at a local level. At a global level within feminism, however, I fear that we may be in danger of replicating the G-strings versus AIDS conversation. I am worried by the relative silence from our Northern sisters about a pandemic that is claiming so many lives.

## A WAY FORWARD

In the context of HIV/AIDS, it is no longer enough to frame our conversations solely in terms of race, class, and gender. These are primary markers of identity, but increasingly, we need more. We need to look at where women are located spatially in relation to centres of political, social, and economic power. We need also to examine how where we live—rural, urban, North, or South—intersects with poverty and gender. We also need to think about how the experience of poverty interacts with, and not just intersects with, gender. Culture is another factor that deserves attention.

We are beginning to see dangerous patriarchal responses to the epidemic from virginity tests to decrees about female chastity from leaders. In part this is simply an extension of deeply rooted myths about female sexuality. However, with HIV/AIDS, it can also be attributed to the fact that in many cases women are the first to receive news of their sero-positive status. This is often during pre-natal screening, or when babies are born sick. Bringing home the "news" that there is HIV in the family often means being identified as the person who caused the infection in the first place. We know that, in the vast majority of cases, this is simply not true.

The Treatment Action Campaign (TAC), a movement begun by and for people living with HIV/AIDS in South Africa, has managed to mobilise national and international support for the idea of universal access to drugs for people with AIDS. The group began their campaign by using pregnant women as their rallying cry. The right to nevirapine for pregnant women opened the door for TAC's broader claims about the rights of all people with HIV/AIDS to HIV medication. The campaign has been hugely successful. TAC encouraged the South African government to take the pharmaceutical industry to court and the government won, paving the way for a win at the World Trade Organization. Companies' patent rights can no longer supersede the rights of human beings to access life-saving medicines.

TAC's strategy needs to be vigorously debated and analysed by feminists. TAC did not use arguments about reproductive and sexual rights. They simply said, "It is unfair for the government not to give drugs to pregnant women so they can save their babies' lives." It was a classic "woman as the vessel" argument. TAC's interest was not in women's rights—but in the rights of people living with HIV/AIDS, some of whom happen to be women. The campaign's success was largely based on the notion that the average South African found it difficult to accept that "innocent" babies would die because of government policy. This requires some serious feminist interrogation. TAC has since been pushed by gender activists within the movement to ensure that the drugs do not stop when the baby is born.

Gender activists to date have struggled to get their voices heard in the doctor-dominated AIDS world. The mainstream women's movement needs to get on board and face up to the challenge of HIV/AIDS. AWID's [Association for Women's Rights in Development] "Globalise This" campaign provides an opportunity to highlight the HIV/AIDS epidemic and the threat it poses to women.

At precisely the moment when we need international solidarity to focus on the impact of AIDS on poor women's lives, and their need to be able to control their lives and their bodies, we have to oppose the US administration's cutbacks on funding for essential reproductive health services. We are also still waiting for the G8 to enact their long-standing commitment to spend 0.7 per cent of GDP on overseas development assistance each year. How likely is it that they will ever reach this target if they focus instead on supporting the war against Iraq?

Our sisters in the North need to develop a consciousness about the fight against AIDS as a feminist fight. We need civil society and feminist voices in developing countries to challenge their governments to tackle HIV/AIDS as a health issue, as a human rights issue, and as a sexual and reproductive rights issue. If we lose this fight, it will have profound effects on the lives of girls and women into the next century.

*Source:* Msimang, Sisonke. (2003). "HIV/AIDS, Globalisation, and the International Women's Movement." *Gender and Development, 11*(1), 109–113.

# CHAPTER 51

## The Women Are Coming: The Abortion Caravan

*Judy Rebick*

Judy Rebick is one of Canada's best-known feminists and political commentators. She is the former Sam Gindin Chair in Social Justice and Democracy at Ryerson University in Toronto, and former president of the National Action Committee on the Status of Women. She is the founding publisher of rabble.ca, a progressive, independent news and discussion site. Rebick makes regular appearances on television and radio, contributes frequently to newspapers and magazines, and has authored several books, including *Transforming Power: From the Personal to the Political* and *Occupy This!* The following chapter is drawn from her book *Ten Thousand Roses: The Making of a Feminist Revolution*.

> If men could get pregnant, abortion would be a sacrament.
> —*Florynce R. Kennedy*[1]

The first national action of the women's movement in Canada was the 1970 abortion caravan. Seventeen members of the Vancouver Women's Caucus, one of the earliest women's liberation groups, decided to travel to Ottawa to protest the abortion law that had been passed by Parliament in 1969.

Up until 1969, abortion was illegal. Many women risked going to backstreet abortionists, who were rarely doctors, or tried to terminate a pregnancy themselves. Many pharmacists stocked slippery elm, which a woman would insert into her cervix, hoping for a miscarriage. Some desperate women douched with Lysol, threw themselves down stairs, or, in the mythology of the pro-choice movement, inserted a coat hanger into their vaginas. One of the strongest arguments for legal abortion was the number of women resorting to these drastic measures. According to one estimate, 33,000 illegal abortions were performed in Canada in 1959 alone. A botched abortion was the number one reason for hospital emergency admissions of young women in those years. But instead of making abortion completely legal, the 1969 law limited abortions to accredited hospitals and allowed them to be performed only when approved by a therapeutic abortion committee of four doctors, for reasons associated with the woman's health. That meant a woman often needed a letter from a psychiatrist to get a legal abortion.

The abortion caravan women set off from Vancouver with the goal of arriving in Ottawa in time for Mother's Day. They stopped in cities and towns along the way for meetings and protest rallies, getting extraordinary press coverage everywhere they went. In 1970 women's liberation was news.

As the first unified action of the women's movement, the abortion caravan revealed some of the differences emerging among feminists. Most of the travelling Vancouver women were active in the New Left and the anti-war movement. They had some political disagreements among themselves, but they managed to work together well until they hit Toronto, where socialist feminists and radical feminists had just experienced a split.

The caravan arrived in Ottawa to much excitement on Friday, May 8. More women arrived from Toronto and Montreal the next morning. On Saturday afternoon, 300 women and men marched on Parliament Hill and then held a meeting inside the Parliament Buildings. Angry that no representative of the government would meet with them, about 150 of the demonstrators headed to Prime Minister Pierre Elliott Trudeau's residence on Sussex Drive. Trudeau was not in town that weekend, but demonstrators managed to leave a coffin representing all the women who had died from illegal abortions at his doorstep. On the Monday, about 30 women chained themselves to their chairs in the galleries in the House of Commons, in tribute to the British suffragists who had chained themselves at Parliament to get the vote a century before.

Feminists saw Trudeaumania as sexist enthusiasm over the bachelor prime minister. For his part, Trudeau had little patience for the challenges coming from radical young women. Some of the abortion caravan women managed to meet with him months later in a Vancouver hotel. They made an impression. Maude Barlow, then Trudeau's adviser on women's issues, remembers that when she asked the prime minister to meet with representatives of the National Action Committee on the Status of Women, he responded, "Are those the same wild, wild women that I met with last year? If so, it may be counterproductive."

## IN CONVERSATION: BETSY MEADLEY WOOD, ELLEN WOODSWORTH, BONNIE BECKMAN, MARGO DUNN, MARCY COHEN, AND JACKIE LARKIN

*Betsy Wood:* The Vancouver Women's Caucus didn't last long, but it was the best group ever. It came out of Simon Fraser University. Ellen Woodsworth came from the University of British Columbia, but we were mostly from SFU. Driving to and from work is how I got into the women's caucus. I heard someone talking about it on the radio, and I thought, Wow! I lived in West Vancouver at the time, and all the women there were getting their tranquilizers and sleeping pills and wake-me-up pills. The NDP didn't even have a women's committee at the time. And here was this fantastic group that had everything together and was moving.

On Thanksgiving weekend of '69, we held the first western conference on women's liberation. There were about 100 women there. The Vancouver Women's Caucus put forward the idea of a women's cavalcade to Ottawa.

*Ellen Woodsworth:* We'd been having incredible discussions about what issue we could take up to mobilize all kinds of women, and abortion seemed like the right one.

*Margo Dunn:* We decided on a caravan because it was linked a bit to the On to Ottawa Trek of unemployed people in 1935.

*Marcy Cohen:* At that point the law was interpreted in such a way that you had to say you were not together emotionally to get an abortion. You had to go to a psychiatrist. A law doesn't mean much unless you change the climate.

*Jackie Larkin:* It didn't take long to arrive at the slogan "Free Abortion on Demand." If you are going to take on an issue, you are going to go all the way.

*Betsy:* Doctors wouldn't talk to you about abortion in those days. You would ask them, and they would look the other way.

*Marcy:* My first commitment was more abstract. I was a student radical and I wanted to make a difference and take the world on. It didn't really matter what issue. I remember coming to Vancouver from Calgary and not fitting in, and then the women's movement happened and it was an explosion. I could think and I could express myself and I was a person.

*Bonnie Beckman:* I was so new to it. I had been involved in some political stuff, but men controlled it. Women's liberation, what was that? I found this group and came away with a clear concept of what was being said. My impression was that the first thing we were going to do was repeal the abortion law. When we finished that, we were going to get 24-hour daycare. And when we finished that, we were going to get equal wages for work of equal value.

I had dropped out of high school and travelled around the world, and when I got back to Vancouver, I found all of this brewing. It was really exciting.

*Ellen:* We wanted liberation. We were just women strategizing with each other. Talking about patriarchy, talking about capitalism, talking about how we could mobilize women. I was secretly and in a positive way reading lesbian literature, which I couldn't share with anyone. But I knew this was going to open up. Abortion wasn't my issue personally, but there was momentum on it.

*Bonnie:* I had been trying to get a tubal ligation, and the doctors wouldn't let me have it. So my issue wasn't abortion, either. It was trying to come together in something that gave us a common language. The abortion issue lent itself very easily to a focused mobilization. As we radicalized, we were thinking what had big control over our lives—men, the media, advertising, and the state. Abortion was a great example of something you could go after the state on. All we had to do was change the law.

*Margo:* Abortion is the issue that has mobilized more women than any other. I feel as strongly now about it at the age of 60 as I did in my twenties.

*Betsy:* When the Women's Caucus started out, there were four things we stood for: equal pay, child care, abortion clinics, and birth control. When I went to the Women's Caucus, I didn't go because of abortion. I went for equal pay. But no matter what our primary issue was, everyone worked on preparing for the abortion caravan. Seventeen women from Vancouver made the trip.

*Bonnie:* We travelled in two cars and a van. Before we left, someone painted "Smash capitalism" on the van. We got to Kamloops and met in a church basement. There was a big debate. Some people wanted the slogan off the truck and other people were defending it, and the discussion went on and on. I hadn't participated in all the ideological discussions of the women's movement. I put my sleeping bag off in a corner and went to sleep.

*Betsy:* The slogan had never been talked about in the group, but there it was. I just about died. "Smash capitalism" is fine, but that wasn't the time or place for it. I felt we could gain a lot of support, and "smash capitalism" could cause us to lose people. The debate continued as we travelled.

We got fantastic publicity. We had sent out our poster, which was fabulous, to every paper across the country along with our schedule. Everywhere we went there was publicity waiting for us. In Calgary, I opened up the paper and I couldn't believe it. It seemed to me that the paper was all about reproduction, and before the caravan you wouldn't have seen that. That's how fast it changed.

*Ellen:* I don't think any social movement since the thirties had planned something on such a national scale. We were consciously using the media and trying to figure out how to get other women to join the campaign and build on it.

*Marcy:* We had guerrilla theatre portraying a backstreet abortion all the way across, too.

It was a better time economically. I was a student assistant, but I stopped working and did the caravan full time, without pay, of course. It was much easier to survive in those days.

*Jackie:* I was a national organizer for the Waffle in Ottawa at the time. They released me and let me work on the caravan. There was a strong cross-country connection of socialists, students, women, and anti-war activists. They were the framework for what happened.

*Margo:* We sent letters to women's groups across the country, telling them we were coming. Could they find us a place to stay and give us a little dinner, something simple like chili? So everywhere we went we'd stay in United Church basements and there'd be chili. It was chili all the way.

*Bonnie:* As we entered a town, we'd sit on the back of the van with our banners and really make an entrance.

*Margo:* The van had a coffin on top, which we had our luggage stowed in. The plan was ultimately to deliver the coffin to Sussex Drive.

Every day we had this routine: drive 300 miles, do guerrilla theatre, eat, and have a public meeting. We collectively decided who would deal with the media. Some women were experienced with the media and some hadn't done it before, and we rotated. It was very feminist, the entire internal organization. The public meeting would inevitably wind up with wrenching horror stories and tears. I still remember some of the stories. The meetings would go later than we'd planned. And then we'd go back to where we were staying and argue about taking "Smash capitalism" off the van and about whether or not we should be smoking dope on the caravan. Before we left Vancouver, we'd had a meeting with a radical lawyer who told us all the things we could get arrested for. We were ready to be arrested once we got to Ottawa. We had bail ready.

*Ellen:* It wasn't until we reached Ottawa that we really confirmed what we were going to do.

*Marcy:* I know we'd already had an idea of going into the House of Commons because I brought a mini-skirt to wear. We had tensions among ourselves about what we were going to do in the Ottawa action, and we also discussed this with women along the way. In Toronto, feminists were definitely positioned on different sides. People weren't talking to each other, and it galvanized the differences we had internally. I remember feeling that there was a lot of difficulty in Toronto, and later when we got to Ottawa.

The Ottawa women's group almost all came out of the left of the NDP and the student movement, so they were less ideological. We used to think of the Toronto women as too heavy, too ideologically intense. They were the heavy women's liberationists.

*Ellen:* We had one meeting organized at the University of Toronto, and people were not friendly to us. It was a whole different feeling than going through small towns and cities, where we had a real sense of exhilaration. In Toronto, women were icy cold, fighting each other, unclear if they were going to come to Ottawa and take this risk with us.

*Marcy:* We had to pander to the socialist feminists, exaggerating our internal differences so that the socialist feminists in Toronto would go with us.

*Margo:* When we arrived in Ottawa, we went to a meeting at a school with 200 women. That was Friday night.

*Jackie:* The demonstration happened Saturday. Women from Montreal and Toronto arrived on Saturday morning. The decision to go to Trudeau's house happened spontaneously.

*Marcy:* We had had a lot of demonstrations in Vancouver where we had taken over the streets, so at first the Ottawa demonstration seemed fairly tame. We were on the sidewalks, and we pushed people to take over the streets.

*Betsy:* And then the speeches were over and wham, people were saying, "On to Trudeau's house!"

*Margo:* Before the demonstration, there was a big meeting in the Railway Room in the Parliament Buildings. I remember I had the tools of an illegal abortion in my bag: a garden hose, a hanger, and a can of Drano. A security guard opened my purse, looked in, and waved me through. Grace MacInnis spoke at the meeting.[2] Henry Morgentaler spoke and was hissed for not being radical enough. Doris Powers, a woman from Toronto who was involved in an anti-poverty group, spoke too. I think it was her speech that kicked things over the edge. We were furious when we got out onto the streets.

*Betsy:* We had agreed that if John Munro, the minister of health; Trudeau; and John Turner, the minister of justice, wouldn't meet with us, we would issue a declaration of war against the Canadian government for May 11, 1970, at 3 P.M., the day after Mother's Day. I think Trudeau was off at some meeting and Munro had gone to Europe.

*Jackie:* None of the ministers showed up. When we got to Trudeau's house, there were only two RCMP guys there. They didn't know what to do with us, so we just sat down on the grass.

*Marcy:* We had linked arms because we expected to be stopped, but they didn't stop us, so we just kept going.

*Betsy:* The RCMP came and asked each of us if we were the spokesperson for the group, and we answered, "There are no leaders here."

*Margo:* There were all the angry poor women from the Just Society Movement, a Toronto anti-poverty group. I remember women saying, "We are going to stay here till Trudeau comes back." Gwen Hauser read a poem, and I gave the implements of illegal abortion to Gordon Gibson, Trudeau's staff assistant at the time, who had shown up. I remember people didn't know who he was.

*Margo:* We could have gotten into Trudeau's house if we had been prepared to break a window.

*Marcy:* But then we would have gotten arrested. So we went back to the school where we were meeting to plan Monday's action at the Parliament Buildings. There had started to be some scuffling on the lawn at Trudeau's, and we didn't want that. About 200 women came back to the school with us.

*Jackie:* The idea was to have a quick meeting and then have a party.

*Betsy:* We were going to have a debate about Monday's action, but the debate didn't happen. This is where Marcy and I parted company for a couple of years. Even teenagers who came with the women from Toronto could go into the Parliament Buildings, but only three of us from Vancouver could go in, and I wasn't going to be one of them. Finally Mary Trew stood up and said, "Is this a plan to keep Betsy out?" and a woman said, "Yes." The reason given was to protect me. If we were charged by the police, there would be trips back and forth to Ottawa, and since I had four kids, I couldn't afford it, or so they said.

*Marcy:* We were all part of the decision. It was torturous, and there was a lot of discussion as to who could hold the position of the group. There was a feeling that some people had a different philosophy from the rest of the group about how we should be arguing our position on abortion and how to deal with the police or a trial.

*Ellen:* Our differences were not only over the "Smash capitalism" slogan and dope smoking. We were debating whether we were for the right to abortion only, or whether we were fighting to smash a system.

*Margo:* I was one of the people who also wanted to go inside, and I didn't have any of the jeopardies that we had defined—women who were not citizens or had criminal records, anything that would make their case more difficult than others if they were nabbed. It narrowed down in my mind to who had been in the leadership. And to me that meant Marcy, Ellen, and Betsy. But there were these differences. There were lifestyle issues, issues around clothes, etcetera, and it was so important that the three women who might go to court be united. So I remember voting for someone other than Betsy.

*Marcy:* I had a lot of guilt about it. I knew that my feelings came from the experience of being in

Toronto and seeing the divisions between the socialist feminists and the radical feminists. Seeing Betsy gravitate to the radical feminists made me decide that if we were going to be at risk, we had to make sure we could carry the struggle. There was a continual struggle in terms of our differences, and if we were going to carry through what we had started, then we had to be solid and not risk breaking apart.

*Ellen:* We assumed that we were going to be arrested and that we would be in a political battle with the courts and with the media, and we wanted people to not be fighting each other too. We wanted to be able to continue mobilizing for women's liberation in Canada.

*Betsy:* The only division I saw was that this was not the place for "Smash capitalism" if you wanted to smash capitalism. Abortion was such a great thing for bringing people together, and that was what we should stick to. I felt we were safe. I wasn't afraid of going into the building because there was no way they were ever going to arrest us. But as sisters, everyone else was making up my mind for me.

*Jackie:* I think a lot of what went on was the political immaturity of the movement. If we go out on an abortion demonstration today, we don't worry about the politics of who is speaking; we get a broad cross-section of people. In those days the big issue was, did you have the right politics behind what you said? Here's an example. About a month after the abortion caravan, I was in Toronto, and Peggy Morton, a Toronto socialist feminist, sat on the steps of a co-op with me and said, "You know, we made a really big mistake when we went into the House of Commons," and I said "Oh, yeah?" and she said, "We should have been saying, 'Victory to the NLF.'"[3] It's exactly the same issue. If you are supporting abortion rights, then really you are in favour of smashing capitalism: that's what you guys argued then. Or if you are really going to support abortion, you

have to be a socialist feminist. It's bullshit, but that's what we were arguing.

*Marcy:* I don't agree that we were arguing that.

*Bonnie:* I think there was a generation gap happening, because Betsy was almost 20 years older than the rest of us. For me, this was very much about the way I wanted to change the world. Betsy, you came at it from a single-issue point of view, but you should have been participating. We wouldn't have been there if it hadn't been for you. But those were the times we lived in.

*Margo:* In the big meeting, there was a three-hour discussion about whether we should chain ourselves to the chairs in the parliamentary gallery. I remember someone saying we should chain ourselves like the suffragists did.

*Marcy:* I remember all this talking and talking and talking, and then suddenly it was Monday morning. We had borrowed a lot of things to get us ready to set off.

*Jackie:* I remember digging through people's cupboards in co-ops, trying to find nylons. We had to go out and buy gloves and purses.

*Ellen:* We strategized about who would go into which gallery and who would start the chant. If one person was taken out, what would we do? Go limp?

*Jackie:* I remember going up the elevator in the Parliament Buildings, and no one looking at one another.

*Marcy:* Standing in the line with all these people you knew, but everyone looked different because we were dressed up … our other selves.

*Margo:* There were three or four men from Ottawa who were beards for some of the women.[4] I think there were 35 or 36 who went inside. There was also a demonstration outside that was supposed to act as a camouflage.

*Jackie:* My chain didn't work in the end. My memory is that for half of the women who went in, the chains didn't hold.

*Ellen:* We also had to figure out how to get those goddamn chains out of our purses quietly. We tried not to be noisy or obvious, but we were listening to the MPs trashing some men in Vancouver who were marching across the border in Blaine to protest the war in Cambodia. Many of these men were our friends and lovers, so things started to move really fast back and forth across the gallery, and then it was pandemonium, people looking up and saying, "What's going on here?" They couldn't figure out where the shouting was coming from. Some people started to be dragged away. We went limp and they would try to drag us and we would go limp again. It took them quite a while.

*Margo:* There was a text, written collectively, we were going to read. One person was supposed to start, and then the next person would continue in the next gallery. That was the plan, but it didn't work out that way.

*Jackie:* The police took our chains. They didn't arrest us, but 10 women were taken down to the police station and then released.

*Margo:* Meanwhile outside, about 200 women wearing black headscarves walked two by two around the eternal flame. Our heads were bowed in mourning for the women who continued to die because of lack of access to safe abortion. At 3 P.M., we threw off the black scarves to reveal red ones and charged up the steps to begin the first action of the "war." We set fire to a placard containing the text of the law. Soon the women who had been in the House ran out to join us. We were surprised, but thrilled, that no one was arrested. The caravan shut down the House of Commons for 45 minutes, and we got tons of media coverage.

A few weeks later, back in Vancouver, the Vancouver Women's Caucus had a meeting with Trudeau. We met him at the Bayshore Inn. He had phoned from his plane to say he wanted to talk to us, and we only had three hours' notice to get women down there. We activated our phone trees. We got to the room in the Bayshore before Trudeau did. We discussed making him sit on the floor, but thought we wouldn't get away with it. We didn't want him sitting in the middle of the room, though, so we moved his chair off-centre. When he got there, we were relentless—it was great. And there was a lot of press.

*Bonnie:* I remember saying, "Look, we want this abortion law repealed," and he said, "Well, go and get the people to vote for it. You have the right to have it, but go and do the job." He wasn't against it. He said, "Go and convince people."

*Marcy:* The thing I remember about him was his arrogance. I remember him saying that if you needed an abortion and you had money, you could go to the States.

*Ellen:* And we were shouting, "Just society, just for the rich."

## NOTES

1.  Florynce Kennedy was the first African American woman to graduate from Columbia Law School. She was a flamboyant civil rights and feminist activist in the United States, well known for her quotable quotes. This one comes from a 1973 speech.

2.  Grace MacInnis was the only female member of Parliament at this time. She represented the NDP from Vancouver Kingsway.

3.  National Liberation Front in North Vietnam. The radical slogan in the anti-Vietnam War movement was "Victory to the NLF," whereas the unifying slogan was "Stop the War."

4.  Men who escorted the women to cover their true purpose.

*Source:* Rebick, Judy. (2005). Excerpted from "Chapter 3: The Women Are Coming: The Abortion Caravan." In *Ten Thousand Roses: The Making of a Feminist Revolution* (pp. 35–46). Toronto, ON: Penguin.

# CHAPTER 52

## The Coercive Sterilization of Aboriginal Women in Canada

*Karen Stote*

Karen Stote is an assistant professor in the Women and Gender Studies Program at Wilfrid Laurier University in Kitchener, Waterloo. She was awarded the competitive Joseph-Armand Bombardier Canada Graduate Scholarship from the Social Sciences and Humanities Research Council of Canada at both the Master's and Doctoral levels. Her research interests include Indigenous-settler relations, feminism, reproductive rights and justice, genocide studies, and eugenics in Canada. For many years, Stote has collaborated on various projects seeking to educate the public on Indigenous-settler issues. She is the author of the book *An Act of Genocide: Colonialism and the Sterilization of Aboriginal Women*.

This chapter considers the coercive sterilization of Aboriginal women [...]. In Canada, there exists but one concise history of eugenics, and other works dealing with sterilization have rarely progressed beyond an examination of the legislation itself.[1] Nonetheless, studies have confirmed that Aboriginal women were disproportionately targeted by enacted legislation in the province of Alberta.[2] Sterilization measures were also implemented in the absence of formal legislation. Evidence indicates this practice was carried out by eugenically minded doctors in Ontario and Northern Canada, where Aboriginal women were the prime targets.[3] No scholarship, however, has yet specifically referred to or conducted in-depth study of this practice as it was applied to Aboriginal women.

And although coercive sterilization policies have been recognized as racist, sexist, and imperialist, how this practice was carried out on Aboriginal women has yet to be fully understood within this larger context.

\*\*\*\*\*

## STERILIZATION AS A PUBLIC HEALTH MEASURE

Sexual sterilization gained prominence as a result of its support by the eugenics movement in the early 1900s.[4] As with any ideology, behind it were the historical and material relations that gave rise to its use as an explanation of, or justification for, the given social order. In this case, an industrializing capitalist state brought with it increasingly high rates of poverty, illness, and social problems for those being marginalized by the current system and facing increasing pressures to congregate in urban centers in search of a wage.[5] Eugenicists and others concerned with the costs of implementing public health measures (such as better sanitation and nutrition, living wages, or safer working and housing conditions in these centers) often explained the problems experienced by the masses as stemming from the innate traits of the poor, rather than as consequences of the way society was organized.[6] By locating the causes of the undesirable effects of the capitalist system within its victims, eugenic ideology, and the interventions proposed by many of its proponents—such as sterilization— worked to maintain the status quo and ensure business could continue as usual for those benefiting from relations of exploitation.

Just as the capitalist mode of production has been recognized as necessarily patriarchal, eugenicists were particularly concerned with women and their ability to reproduce. Due to this ability, women were considered by eugenicists as central to national progress and have been subject to interventions aimed at shaping their reproduction in the interests of the state.[7] […] At the same time as some women were encouraged to reproduce, namely upper- and middle-class women, the sexuality and reproductive potential of other women was considered threatening to the social order.

Impoverished and marginalized women and their children, who were often forced to rely on state aid or private charity, came to be viewed as a costly burden. They were also blamed for perpetuating social problems in society. The sterilization of these women, who often failed to conform to socially defined roles, was supported by many medical, philanthropic, and women's organizations as a solution to these problems.[8] These groups successfully lobbied government to adopt both positive and negative eugenic measures in the interest of economy.

Within the larger context of capitalist expansion, eugenic ideology was also employed by government officials as one means of justifying colonialist policies being imposed on Aboriginal peoples in Canada. The poor health, poverty, and other conditions experienced by Aboriginal peoples as a direct result of colonial policy then became indicative of their lower racial evolution.[9] A cursory glance at the annual reports of the Department of Indian Affairs from the late nineteenth and early twentieth centuries reveals many references that explain the epidemic proportions of tuberculosis and other sicknesses in Aboriginal communities as the result of the lower evolutionary state or inherent weakness of Aboriginal peoples, rather than as the result of contact with Europeans, the theft of Indian lands and resources, or the starvation policies imposed by the federal government.[10]

For the colonizing process to be successful, it has been central to impose western institutions and to subjugate Aboriginal women through their separation from the land, the control of their bodies, and those of their children.[11] Many organizations worked to reinforce notions of femininity and helped carry out a "civilizing mission" on Aboriginal women. Mariana Valverde demonstrates that the Women's Christian Temperance Union, the Salvation Army, and the National Council of Women often advanced eugenic arguments and helped create a climate in which some were considered undesirable: namely impoverished, "undomesticated," immigrant, and Aboriginal women.[12] Some of the most celebrated feminists in Canada created a space for themselves as colonial agents by reinforcing sexist and racist notions of womanhood and participating in the colonization of Aboriginal women.[13] Aboriginal women were often described as "savages," "depraved," or of "loose moral character," and their sexuality was intensely policed.[14] For those who proved unwilling to assimilate or whose sexuality was deemed difficult to control, sterilization was sometimes the result.

## STERILIZATION IN CANADA

Two provinces in Canada enacted formal sterilization legislation. Alberta had a Sexual Sterilization Act in effect from 1928 to 1972, and British Columbia, from 1933 to 1973.[15] Jana Grekul and Timothy Christian have both examined records dealing with Alberta's sterilization act and have found that in this province, Aboriginal women were disproportionately targeted and the number of those sterilized increased as the years passed.[16] Grekul and her colleagues Harvey Krahn and Dave Odynak found that Aboriginal peoples were overrepresented to the provincial Eugenics Board, and once approved for sterilization, were more likely to be subject to the procedure. They conclude that "Aboriginals were the most prominent victims of the Board's attention. They were overrepresented among presented cases and among those diagnosed as 'mentally defective.' Thus they seldom had a chance to say 'no' to being sterilized."[17]

In 1937, in order to protect government from liability and to avoid the impression that there was "a conspiracy for the elimination of the race by this means" the Department of Indian Affairs suggested efforts be made to obtain consent, if at all possible, prior to sterilization.[18] It is important to note that the failure of the Department of Indian Affairs to condemn the practice at this point was in effect to condone it. [...]

One must wonder what role this stance played in future actions. In that same year, the Act was amended under the pretense that it was too restrictive.[19] This 1937 amendment made a distinction between psychotic persons and those considered mentally defective, and excised the consent requirement for the latter.[20] The proportion of Aboriginal peoples sterilized by the Act rose steadily from 1939 onward, tripling from 1949 to 1959.[21] Even when opposition to the Act gained momentum and its repeal became more likely, the rate at which Aboriginal peoples were sterilized underwent a terrific increase, representing more than 25 percent of those sterilized. This led

Christian to write, "It is incredible that between 1969 and 1972, more Indian and Métis persons were sterilized than British, especially when it is considered that Indians or Métis were the least significant racial group, statistically, and British were the most significant."[22] However, consent for sterilization was only sought in 17 percent of Aboriginal cases. More than 77 percent were defined as mentally defective, and hence their consent was not needed.[23]

The federal government also undertook other measures to legitimize the provincial sterilization act: in 1951, an amendment to the Indian Act increased the application of provincial laws to Indians.[24] This amendment newly stipulates that a "mentally incompetent Indian" is to be defined according to the laws of the province in which "he" resides.[25] In other words, a mentally incompetent Indian was whatever a province deemed him or her to be.[26] Therefore, any provincial laws dealing with those defined as mentally incompetent could be applied to Aboriginal peoples, including the Sexual Sterilization Act.

This amendment also stipulated that the property of a mentally incompetent Indian could be denied to that person.[27] In the case of so-defined Indians living on reserve, their property would pass to the minister of Indian Affairs, to be sold, leased, or disposed of in any way deemed fit by the minister. For Indians living off reserve, property would pass to the province in which that Indian resided. The increased application of services to Aboriginal peoples by the provinces would also, by default, reduce services the federal government would need to provide.

Allowing for the transfer of property from Aboriginal peoples to the federal government and/or the provinces through a designation of mental incompetence was consistent with policy that had been established through the Indian Act, that of transferring land rights out of the hands of Aboriginal women and their peoples and into the hands of men: to Indian men if they met the definition of an Indian under the Act, or, if deemed "unfit" by the state, to white men, or the Canadian state.[28] As Kathleen

Jamieson has pointed out, "private rights in land inherited through the male were an indispensable component of this system, which had as its corollary control and repression of the sexuality of the female."[29]

In British Columbia, files documenting sterilizations have been thought to be lost or destroyed. However, Gail van Heeswijk has provided the first study of the Sexual Sterilization Act in this province by reviewing the Essondale Report, a document outlining the case histories of sixty-four patients sterilized under this legislation.[30] Over the course of the eight years discussed in the report, from 1935–1943, fifty-seven of the sixty-four individuals sterilized were women.[31] Van Heeswijk states the reason given for sterilization in thirty-five of these cases was promiscuous behavior. Furthermore, forty-six of the fifty-seven women sterilized were single, twenty-two had illegitimate pregnancies, and another five had their pregnancies terminated prior to or during the procedure.[32]

Though neither the Essondale Report nor van Heeswijk makes any mention of patients' ethnicity, some of the women sterilized at Essondale were Aboriginal. [...]

It is also known that the federal government provided financial support for its wards at Essondale. Though van Heeswijk states that fees for sterilizations were paid to the performing physician by the institution from which the inmate was referred, the arrangement was such that whenever possible, for Aboriginal charges, a per diem rate was paid to the institution by the federal government.[33] This was indeed in keeping with federal policy at the time.[34]

More recent information indicates that sterilizations were also performed on some of those institutionalized at the Woodlands School, a provincially-run institution housing children abandoned at birth, the disabled, and wards of the court. It is unclear whether sterilizations took place at Woodlands by way of transfer to the Essondale Hospital or whether they were arranged by family physicians in the community.[35] However, children were often admitted to this institution with the purpose of sanctioning their sterilization and the Department of National Health and Welfare did pay the per diem rate for Aboriginal wards in its care.[36]

Evidence indicates sterilizations were also performed in the absence of legislation. For example, Kathleen McConnachie has shown that sterilizations were carried out by eugenically minded doctors in the province of Ontario.[37] Due to the widespread opposition, primarily from the Catholic Church, doctors lobbied instead for an amendment to the Medical Act protecting those who performed such an operation from subsequent legal action. McConnachie concludes, "What lobbyists for sterilization legislation were striving for in the 1930s was legislative legitimization for the practice already widespread in the province."[38]

Largely due to the efforts of A.R. Kaufman, the rubber magnate who founded the Parent's Information Bureau (PIB), more than 1000 sterilizations were performed in Ontario. In many cases, these were done on a "goodwill" basis by physicians believing in the cause of eugenics and that sterilization was a viable means of preventing or alleviating poverty.[39] Kaufman stated that from 1930 to 1935, his PIB funded a number of "sympathetic surgeons" to operate on about 400 women in hospitals.[40] [...]

In addition, Kaufman claimed that between 1930 and 1969, 1000 male sterilizations were performed in the "sick room" at his rubber plant in Kitchener, Ontario. Following a PIB advertisement appearing in the *Kitchener Daily Record* in 1969 offering free sterilization to parents on welfare, nearly 700 of these procedures were performed.[41] [...]

The full extent to which sterilization was applied to Aboriginal peoples in Ontario is unclear. It is known that by 1928 Aboriginal peoples were being classified as mentally unfit and this was most often a precursor to sterilization. [...]

Though no sterilization legislation ever materialized in the North, on two occasions the Northwest Territories Council considered it, in consultation with the Department of Mines and Resources and the Department of Pensions and National Health.[42] [...]

On April 1, 1973, the Canadian Broadcasting Corporation's public affairs program *Weekend* aired a news story suggesting there was a calculated attempt to reduce the birth rate among Aboriginal peoples in Northern Canada.[43] The program discussed the linguistic barriers and the climate of paternalism that led to cases of Inuit women being sterilized without their knowledge. It also featured charges that some Inuit children were separated from their families, sometimes never to be seen again after being sent to hospitals in the South for medical treatment, and claimed that Inuit women were indeed sterilized without their consent both in the North and at the Charles Camsell Hospital in Alberta. [...]

In 1976, a series of articles by Robert Lechat alleged that the federal government was in fact intensifying a program of sterilizing Aboriginal peoples in the North. He claimed that women were sterilized without full knowledge or consent in six communities in the Keewatin District: in Repulse Bay, he alleged that out of twenty-two women between thirty and fifty years of age, ten were sterilized (45 percent); in Chesterfield Inlet, out of twenty-three women between thirty and fifty years of age, six were sterilized (26 percent); in Pelly Bay, out of eighteen women between the ages of thirty and fifty, five were sterilized (27 percent); and, in Gjoa Haven, out of forty-one women between thirty and fifty years of age, thirteen were sterilized (31 percent).[44] [...]

The numbers released as a result of a parliamentary inquiry [...] only dealt with the six settlements named by Lechat.[45] They indicate that a total of seventy sterilizations were performed on women from these northern areas over the course of the ten years under consideration. [...] With only one exception, the reason given for all of these sterilizations was multiparity, or having given birth to "two or more children." Despite governmental insistence that there was no policy of sterilization in the north, these figures do confirm the numbers reported by Lechat in his articles.[46]

Additional information drawn from this same collection of Medical Services files reveals that the sterilizations reported were only a fraction of those performed on Aboriginals. In a number set reporting sterilizations of Aboriginal women in the North from 1970 to 1973 [...], there were 180 sterilizations performed in the North in four years alone, with the greatest proportion of these performed in areas that were not targeted by the parliamentary inquiry. [...]

Additional information troubles these rates further, and indicates that the number of sterilizations performed on Aboriginal women could be much higher. At the request of Dr. Whiteside, a non-physician associated with the National Indian Brotherhood, the federal government made available the number of sterilizations performed on Aboriginal women, from 1971–1972, at hospitals run by the Department of National Health and Welfare.[47] Subsequent information released by Medical Services also provides the number of sterilizations for 1973 and 1974 at these same hospitals.

Over the course of the four years in question, at least 580 sterilizations were performed by doctors working at federally operated hospitals. Of these, at least 551 were on Aboriginal women. Based on additional information, forty-six more sterilizations were performed at the Charles Camsell hospital in 1970, and four sterilizations and one vasectomy were performed at the Inuvik General Hospital in that same year.[48]

*****

## THE LARGER IMPLICATIONS OF COERCIVE STERILIZATION

The evidence confirms what some have been claiming for many years, that Aboriginal women have been subject to sterilizations in Canada under questionable circumstances. It could be argued that while one can refer to eugenic sterilization as shameful and unjust, nonetheless one cannot paint all sterilizations performed on Aboriginal women as coercive: to do so would be to deny the agency of Aboriginal women to make choices about their own reproduction and continue the paternalism so rampant in past Indian policy. However, as the Committee to End Sterilization Abuse, formed in the mid-1970s in response to the overt reproductive abuses of marginalized women in the United States, stated:

> Forced infertility is in no way a substitute for a good job, enough to eat, decent education, daycare, medical services, maternal infant care, housing, clothing, or cultural integrity…. when society does not provide the basic necessities of life for everyone, there can be no such freedom of choice.[49]

Similarly, I argue that, until such conditions are met, until conditions of colonialism are ended and the longstanding policies and practices imposed on Aboriginal peoples by a foreign government are brought to a halt, and until Aboriginal peoples are returned lands, resources, and the freedom to provide for their own subsistence in ways they so choose, without stipulations, one cannot speak of freedom of choice.

Rather than address issues on this level, there is a tendency to speak of reproductive decisions as resulting simply from an individual woman's choice […]. However, this focus on individual choice serves to obfuscate the existence of any systematic abuse directed toward certain populations such as Aboriginal women. As Rickie Solinger writes:

> That is the problem with choice. In theory, choice refers to individual preference and wants to protect all women from reproductive coercion. In practice, though, choice has two faces. The contemporary language of choice promises dignity and reproductive autonomy to women with resources. For women without, the language of choice is a taunt

and a threat. When the language of choice is applied to the question of poor women and motherhood, it begins to sound a lot like the language of eugenics: women who cannot afford to make choices are not fit to be mothers. This mutable quality of choice reminds us that sex and reproduction—motherhood—provide a rich site for controlling women, based on their race and class "value."[50]

[…] Unequal relations did exist, and continue to exist, between Canada and Aboriginal peoples and, more specifically, between western medical practitioners and Aboriginal women, so that the context in which reproductive options arise and Aboriginal women must make choices continues to be one of colonialism and assimilation.

Coercive sterilization has indeed worked as one of many policies to undermine Aboriginal women and their ability to make decisions about their own lives. This practice can be linked to other explicit policies stemming from the Indian Act that have undermined Aboriginal women and denied them the ability to participate fully in life within their communities and is consistent with the provision of medical services in ways that promote assimilation and state control over Aboriginal bodies.[51] All these policies have worked to destroy the connections between Aboriginal women, their peoples, and their lands.

Sterilization also breaks the link between one generation and the next by breaking the connection between Aboriginal women and their future.[52] Other policies worked to do this as well, such as residential schooling or the "sixties scoop," which forcefully transferred Aboriginal children out of their communities and into non-Aboriginal families.[53] One must also consider that today there are more children in the child welfare system than there were at the height of residential school policy.[54] Interventions of this sort further perpetuate assimilation as these children are the least likely to ever return home and are most often disconnected from their communities and ways of life.

However, there is finality to the practice of sterilization. The break that comes from robbing Aboriginal women of the ability to reproduce cannot be undone, and effectively terminates the legal line of descendants able to claim Aboriginal status, thereby reducing the numbers of those to whom the federal government has longstanding obligations, whether these are founded in treaties, or are obligations stemming from the occupation of Aboriginal peoples' lands.

One could also argue that the sterilization of Aboriginal women allows the Canadian state to deny responsibility for and avoid doing something about the deplorable conditions in most Aboriginal communities, conditions recognized as the direct result of dispossession and colonialism. [...] It is certainly more cost-effective to curb Aboriginal women's reproductive capacities than to address the fundamental issues required to improve the living conditions into which Aboriginal children are born.

Indeed, one could argue that the coercive sterilization of Aboriginal women represented a cost-effective method that allowed the Canadian government to avoid accountability for the theft of Aboriginal lands and resources. The effects of the sterilization of Aboriginal women, whether intentional or not, are in line with past Indian policy and serve the political and economic interests of Canada. The point needs to be emphasized, then, that whether imposed coercively on one woman or many, this entire historical and material context gives sterilization larger implications when applied to Aboriginal women. It is this context that leads some to argue that this practice amounts to genocide under international law.[55]

## CONCLUSION

[...] The evidence reviewed confirms that Aboriginal women were indeed subject to sterilizations both under enacted legislation and in areas where no formal legislation was in existence. Though the federal government fell short of enacting legislation directly sanctioning the sterilization of Aboriginal peoples,

through its refusal to condemn the practice, by its enactment of policies and legislation affecting other aspects of Aboriginal life making sterilization more likely, and through its financial support to provinces, it did allow for these sterilizations to be carried out more effectively, both in its own institutions and in those under provincial control.

By grounding coercive sterilization within its larger historical and material context, I allow for it to be understood, not as an isolated instance of abuse, but as one of many policies employed to separate Aboriginal peoples from their lands and resources while reducing the numbers of those to whom the federal government has obligations. Policies like coercive sterilization have undermined Aboriginal women's ability to reproduce and have allowed the federal government to avoid effective and far-reaching solutions to public health problems in Aboriginal communities. In this sense, the results of the sterilization of Aboriginal women, whether intended or not, are in line with past Indian policy and serve the political and economic interests of Canada.

## NOTES

[Note that the endnotes were heavily edited down from the original due to space considerations]

1. Angus McLaren, *Our Own Master Race: Eugenics in Canada, 1885-1945* (Toronto: McClelland & Stewart, 1990); Richard Cairney, "Democracy Was Never Intended for Degenerates: Alberta's Flirtation with Eugenics Comes Back to Haunt It," *Canadian Medical Association Journal* 155, no. 6 (1996): 1-4; Timothy Caufield and G. Robertson, "Eugenic Policies in Alberta: From the Systematic to the Systemic?" *Alberta Law Review* 35, no. 1 (1996): 59-79; Terry Chapman, "Early Eugenics Movement in Western Canada," 9-17; Jana Grekul, "The Social Construction of the Feebleminded Threat: Implementation of the Sexual Sterilization Act in Alberta, 1929-1972" (PhD diss., University of Alberta, 2002); Gail van Heeswijk, "'An Act Respecting Sexual Sterilization': Reasons for Enacting and Repealing the Act" (MA diss., University of British Columbia, 1994).

2. Timothy J. Christian, *The Mentally Ill and Human Rights in Alberta: A Study of the Alberta Sexual Sterilization Act* (Edmonton: University of Alberta, Faculty of Law, 1974), 90; Jana Grekul, Harvey Krahn, and Dave Odynak, "Sterilizing the 'Feeble-Minded': Eugenics in Alberta, Canada, 1929–1972," *Journal of Historical Sociology* 17, no. 4 (2004): 358–84.

3. Cora B.S. Hodson, *Human Sterilization Today: A Survey of the Present Position* (London: Watts & Co., 1934), 39; Kathleen McConnachie, "Science and Ideology: The Mental Hygiene and Eugenics Movements in the Inter-War Years, 1919–1939" (PhD diss., University of Toronto, 1987), 213–44; Angus McLaren and Arlene Tigar McLaren, *The Bedroom and the State* (Toronto: McClelland and Stewart, 1986), 92–123; Robert Lechat, "Killing Our Future: Sterilization and Experiments," *Akwesasne Notes* (Early Spring, 1977): 5; "Many Inuit Sterilized, RC Says," *Globe and Mail*, October 9, 1976, 16; Robert Lechat, "Intensive Sterilization for the Inuit," *Eskimo* (Fall/Winter 1976): 5; Robert Lechat, "Sterilization of Inuit Is Exposed as National Scandal," *Sunday Express*, RG 29, Volume 2870, File 851-1-5, pt. 3C, Library and Archives Canada (LAC); Jamie Cohen and T. F. Baskett, "Sterilization Patterns in a Northern Canadian Population," *Canadian Journal of Public Health* 69 (1978): 222–24.

4. McLaren, *Our Own Master Race*, 89–107.

5. For an overview of the social conditions that gave rise to eugenics as an ideology, see Allan Chase, *The Legacy of Malthus: The Social Costs of the New Scientific Racism* (New York: Alfred A. Knopf, Inc, 1977), 2–175.

6. Francis Galton is credited with coining the term *eugenics* yet his ideas were influenced by the works of others who came before him, namely Thomas Malthus and Herbert Spencer. Chase, *The Legacy of Malthus*, 68–110; Thomas Malthus, *Essay on the Principle of Population* (London: Reeves and Turner, 1878).

7. Linda Gordon, *The Moral Property of Women: A History of Birth Control Politics in America* (Chicago: University of Illinois Press, 2002), 55–125; Carolyn Burdett, "The Hidden Romance of Sexual Science: Eugenics, the Nation and the Making of Modern Feminism," in *Sexology in Culture: Labeling Bodies and Desires*, ed. Lucy Bland and Laura Doan (Chicago: University of Chicago Press, 1998), 44–59.

8. McLaren, *Our Own Master Race*, 31, 128–144; Valverde, *The Age of Light, Soap and Water*, 48–49, 58–67.

9. Maureen K. Lux, *Medicine That Walks: Disease, Medicine, and Canadian Plains Native People, 1880–1940* (Toronto: University of Toronto Press, 2001), 138–224.

10. Edgar Dewdney, Indian Commissioner in 1886, referred to deaths on Indian reserves as directly due to hereditary disease which originated at a time prior to the beginning of federal responsibility. Canada, *Commons Debates*, April 15, 1886, 718–30, cited in Lux, *Medicine That Walks*, 141. In 1896, Dr. S.E. MacAdam blamed the high death rates in residential schools on the transition from savagery to civilization. Dr. Macadam to commissioner, June 5, 1896, quoted in Lux, *Medicine That Walks*, 110. In 1904, Frank Pedley, deputy superintendent of Indian Affairs, in attempting to answer why poor health was so prominent and mortality so high on Indian reserves, blamed the situation on the moral failings of Aboriginal peoples and some inherent defect on their part. Canada, *Sessional Papers*, vol. 11, no. 27, 1904, 238.

11. Sarah Carter, "First Nation Women of Prairie Canada in the Early Reserve Years, the 1870's to the 1920's: A Preliminary Inquiry," in *Women of the First Nations: Power, Wisdom and Strength*, ed. Christine Miller and Patricia Churchryk (Manitoba: University of Manitoba Press, 1996), 51–75; Mona Etienne and Eleanor Leacock, eds., *Women and Colonization* (New York: Praeger Publishers, 1980), 25–42; Winona Stevenson, "Colonialism and First Nations Women in Canada," in *Scratching the Surface: Canadian Anti-Racist Feminist Thought*, ed. Enakshi Dua and Angela Robertson (Toronto: Women's Press, 1999), 49–75.

12. Valverde, *The Age of Light, Soap and Water*, 32. For a specific example relating to Aboriginal women, see Pamela M. White, "Restructuring the Domestic Sphere—Prairie Indian Women on Reserves: Image, Ideology and State Policy, 1880–1930" (PhD diss., McGill University, 1987).

13. Emily Murphy, one of the "Famous Five" who succeeded in gaining the status of personhood for women under the British North America Act, argued that many of the women passing before her as magistrate court judge should be sterilized rather than incarcerated for their crimes. Jennifer Henderson, *Settler Feminism and Race Making in Canada*

(Toronto: University of Toronto Press, 2003), 159–208. Nellie McClung also advocated sterilization, and through her involvement with the Women's Christian Temperance Union, established home missions designed to "conquer racial poisons" by training "uncivilized" immigrant, impoverished, and Aboriginal women in the arts of "mothercraft," or on issues such as breastfeeding, bottle-feeding, domestic hygiene, and food preparation. Cecily Devereux, *Growing a Race: Nellie L. McClung and the Fiction of Eugenic Feminism* (Montreal & Kingston: McGill-Queen's University Press, 2005), 113–36. There are statues of the "Famous Five," which also includes Irene Parlby, Louise McKinney, and Henrietta Muir Edwards, erected in both Ottawa and Calgary.

14. Carter, "First Nation Women," 51–75; Robin Jarvis Brownlie, "Intimate Surveillance: Indian Affairs, Colonization, and the Regulation of Aboriginal Women's Sexuality," in *Contact Zones: Aboriginal and Settler Women in Canada's Colonial Past*, ed. Katie Pickles and Myra Rutherdale (Vancouver: UBC Press, 2005), 160–78; Joan Sangster, *Regulating Girls and Women: Sexuality, Family, and the Law in Ontario, 1920–1960* (Ontario: Oxford University Press, 2001), 168–93.

15. For Alberta, see Timothy J. Christian, *The Mentally Ill and Human Rights in Alberta: A Study of the Alberta Sexual Sterilization Act* (Edmonton: University of Alberta, Faculty of Law, 1974); A. Naomi Nind, "Solving an 'Appalling' Problem: Social Reformers and the Campaign for the Alberta Sexual Sterilization Act, 1928," *Alberta Law Review* 38, no. 2 (2003): 536–62. For British Columbia, see Angus McLaren, "The Creation of a Haven for 'Human Thoroughbreds': The Sterilization of the Feebleminded and the Mentally Ill in British Columbia," *Canadian Historical Review* 67 (1986): 127–50; Gail van Heeswijk, "'An Act Respecting Sexual Sterilization': Reasons for Enacting and Repealing the Act" (MA diss., University of British Columbia, 1994).

16. The Eugenics Board was presented with and passed 4,739 cases for sterilization, out of which 2,834 sterilization operations were performed. Aboriginal peoples comprised, on average, only 2.5 percent of the population but over 8 percent of those sterilized. Because these are averages, the actual proportion of the population that was Aboriginal fluctuated during the period in which sterilization was carried out, as did the number of those sterilized. Grekul, Krahn, and Odynak, "Sterilizing the 'Feeble-minded,'" 358–84.

17. Grekul, Krahn, and Odynak, "Sterilizing the 'Feeble-minded,'" 375.

18. Correspondence between the Department of Indian Affairs and the Eugenics Board (Eugenics Board meeting no. 83, May 31, 1937) cited in Grekul, "The Social Construction of the Feebleminded Threat," 156.

19. Grekul, "The Social Construction of the Feebleminded Threat," 4.

20. Mental defectiveness was defined as "a condition of arrested or incomplete development of mind existing before the age of eighteen years, whether arising from inherent causes or induced by disease or injury." The diagnosis was determined by a psychiatric evaluation, often coupled with one or a series of IQ tests. Statutes of Alberta, *Sexual Sterilization Act Amendment Act*, 1937, s. 2 (c).

21. Christian, *The Mentally Ill and Human Rights in Alberta*, 80–90.

22. Ibid., 90.

23. Grekul, Krahn, and Odynak, "Sterilizing the 'Feeble-minded,'" 375.

24. Statutes of Canada, *An Act to Amend the Indian Act*, 1951, c. 29, s. 88.

25. Ibid., s. 1.

26. Statutes of Alberta, *Sexual Sterilization Act Amendment Act*, 1937, s. 2 (c).

27. Statutes of Canada, *An Act to Amend the Indian Act*, 1951, c. 29, s. 51.

28. Kathleen Jamieson, "Sex Discrimination and the Indian Act," in *An Arduous Journey: Canadian Indians and Decolonization*, ed. Rick Ponting (Toronto: McClelland & Stewart, 1986), 112–36.

29. Jamieson, "Sex Discrimination and the Indian Act," 113.

30. The Essondale Hospital was one institution in which sterilizations took place. It has been renamed the Riverview Psychiatric Hospital. Correspondence, M. Stewart, August 17, 1945, GR 496, "Some Aspects of Eugenical Sterilization in British Columbia with Special Reference to Patients Sterilized from Essondale Provincial Mental Hospital since 1935," Box 38, file 3, Provincial Secretary, British Columbia Archives and Record Services.

31. Though the BC Act was enacted in 1933, the author states it only came into operation in 1935. The reason for the delay was the failure to appoint members to the Board of Eugenics. Van Heeswijk, "An Act Respecting Sexual Sterilization," 46.

32. Van Heeswijk, "An Act Respecting Sexual Sterilization," 51.

33. Van Heeswijk, "An Act Respecting Sexual Sterilization," 43.

34. Correspondence from the Department of Indian Affairs to P.E. Moore, Director, Indian and Northern Health Services, Department of National Health and Welfare, January 10, 1957, RG 29, "Mental Diseases," Volume 2971, File 851-4-300, pt. 1A, LAC.

35. Dulcie McCallum, *The Need to Know: Woodlands School Report, an Administrative Review* (British Columbia: Ministry of Children and Family Development, 2001), 23, 34; Public Guardian and Trustee of British Columbia, *The Woodlands Project July 2002–June 2004: A Report of the Public Guardian and Trustee of British Columbia* (August 2004), 20.

36. McCallum, *The Need to Know*, 23, 34; Robert Menzies and Ted Palys, "Turbulent Spirits: Aboriginal Patients in the British Columbia Psychiatric System, 1879–1950," in *Mental Health and Canadian Society: Historical Perspectives*, ed. James E. Moran and David Wright (Montreal & Kingston: McGill-Queen's University Press, 2006), 154 n11.

37. McConnachie, "Science and Ideology," 236–37.

38. Ibid., 237.

39. A.R. Kaufman, often referred to as the father of birth control in Canada, actively promoted sterilization as a means of addressing economic problems. Kaufman distributed birth control and provided sterilizations free of charge to his employees and those living in poor urban slums. He eventually expanded his services through the work of the Parents' Information Bureau and traveling nurses to Western parts of Canada. For more information on Kaufman and his activities, see McLaren and Tigar McLaren, *The Bedroom and the State*, 92–123; Fiona Alice Miller, "Population Control and the Perseverance of Eugenics: A Case Study of the Politics of Fertility Control, Alvin Ratz Kaufman, 1930–1979" (MA diss., University of Victoria, 1993); Linda Revie, "More Than Just Boots! The Eugenic and Commercial Concerns behind A. R. Kaufman's Birth Controlling Activities," *Canadian Bulletin of Mental Health* 23, no. 1 (2006): 119–43.

40. A.R. Kaufman, three-page typewritten speech for a 1975 public meeting of the Ontario Cabinet, Queen's Park, AO, Planned Parenthood Ontario Records, Series B, General Files, 1972–1979, "A. R. Kauffman" [sic] File 2, cited in Revie, "More Than Just Boots!," 127.

41. University of Waterloo, PIB, GA58, Box 2, "Correspondence," 1930–76, unpublished interview between Gerald Stortz and A.R. Kaufman, February 25, 1977; AO, Planned Parenthood Ontario Records, MU 4468, Series B, General Files, 1972–79, "A. R. Kauffman" [sic], A.R. Kaufman to Marilyn E. Schima, May 7, 1974, 2, cited in Revie, "More Than Just Boots!," 128.

42. A proposal for sterilization legislation was tabled on January 17, 1939 and November 21, 1941. Memorandum from Deputy Commissioner Gibson to Major McKeand, member of the Northwest Territories Council, January 17, 1939, RG 85, "Sterilization of Imbeciles," Volume 901, File 10109, LAC; Correspondence from J.J. Heagerty, M.D. to R.A. Gibson, November 25, 1941, RG 85, "Sterilization of Imbeciles," Volume 901, File 10109, LAC; Extract from the Minutes of the One Hundred and Thirty-Fourth Session of the Northwest Territories Council, November 21, 1941, RG 85, "Sterilization of Imbeciles," Volume 901, File 10109, LAC.

43. Jim Eayrs, "Sterilization of Eskimos," *Weekend*, April 1, 1973 (Canadian Broadcasting Corporation, NWT), Transcript, RG 29, "Birth Control," Volume 2870, File 851-1-5, pt. 3A, LAC.

44. "Killing Our Future: Sterilization and Experiments," *Akwesasne Notes* (Early Spring, 1977): 5; "Many Inuit Sterilized, RC Says," *Globe and Mail*, October 9, 1976, 16; Robert Lechat, "Intensive Sterilization for the Inuit," *Eskimo* (Fall/Winter 1976): 5; Robert Lechat, "Sterilization of Inuit Is Exposed as National Scandal," *Sunday Express*, RG 29, Volume 2870, File 851-1-5, pt. 3C, LAC.

45. Information compiled from the response received from Harkness, and subsequently submitted by Acting Assistant Deputy Minister, Medical Services Branch, Lyall M. Black to Christine Brydon, parliamentary returns officer, on December 1, 1976. Information Release, Parliamentary Returns Officer, December 1, 1976, RG 29, "Birth Control," Volume 2870, File 851-1-5, pt. 4, LAC.

46. These numbers were subsequently reported to Parliament by the Minister of National Health and Welfare Marc Lalonde on February 25, 1977, Canada, *House of Commons Debates*, February 25, 1977, 3430.

47. Correspondence from M.L. Webb, Assistant Deputy Minister, Medical Services, to Dr. Maurice Leclair, Deputy Minister of National Health, April 13, 1973, RG 29, "Birth Control," Volume 2870, File 851-1-5, pt. 3A, LAC.

48. Appendix P "Charles Camsell Hospital, Sterilization by Means of Tubal Ligation and Cauterization," RG, "Birth Control" Volume 2870, File 851-1-5, pt. 3A, LAC.

49. CESA Papers, quoted in Thomas M. Shapiro, *Population Control Politics: Women, Sterilization and Reproductive Rights* (Philadelphia: Temple University Press, 1985), 144.

50. Rickie Solinger, *Beggars and Choosers: How the Politics of Choice Shapes Adoption, Abortion, and Welfare in the United States* (New York: Hill and Wang, 2001), 223.

51. Sarah Carter argues that legislation embodied within the Indian Act left women who were defined as "Indian" with fewer fundamental rights than any other women or men in Canada. This is evident in the very definition of an Indian under the Act as "any Indian man and his wife." Carter, "First Nation Women," 51–75.

52. Randi Cull, "Aboriginal Mothering under the State's Gaze," in *"Until Our Hearts Are on the Ground": Aboriginal Mothering, Oppression, Resistance and Rebirth*, ed. D. Memee Lavell-Harvard and Jeannette Corbiere Lavell (Toronto: Demeter Press, 2006), 141–56.

53. On residential schools in Canada, see Roland Chrisjohn and Sherri Young, *The Circle Game: Shadows and Substance in the Indian Residential School Experience in Canada* (Vancouver: Theytus Press, 2006); on the child welfare system, Cindy Blackstock, Nico Trocme, and Marilyn Bennett, "Child Maltreatment Investigations among Aboriginal and Non-Aboriginal Families in Canada," *Violence against Women* 10, no. 8 (2004): 901–16; Pete Hudson and Brad McKenzie, "Child Welfare and Native People: The Extension of Colonialism," *The Social Worker* 49, no. 2 (1981): 63–66, 87–88.

54. Blackstock et al., "Child Maltreatment Investigations," 901–16.

55. Under Article II (d) of the Convention on the Prevention and Punishment of the Crime of Genocide, imposing measures to prevent births within a group constitutes an act of genocide under international law. How Canada has managed to avoid liability for this charge is the subject of forthcoming work. For a discussion of the sterilization of Native American women and the charge of genocide, see Ralstein Lewis, "The Continuing Struggle against Genocide: Indigenous Women's Reproductive Rights." *Wicazo SA Review* 20, no. 1 (2005): 71–95.

*Source:* Stote, Karen. (2012). Excerpted from "The Coercive Sterilization of Aboriginal Women in Canada." *American Indian Culture and Research Journal, 36*(3), 117–150.

# CHAPTER 53

## Debating Feminist Futures: Slippery Slopes, Cultural Anxiety, and the Case of the Deaf Lesbians

*Alison Kafer*

Alison Kafer is an associate professor and chair of the Department of Feminist Studies at Southwestern University in Georgetown, Texas. Her research interests are in disability studies, feminist, crip, and queer theory, and activism. Kafer has written several articles that have appeared in the *Journal of Women's History* and *Feminist Disability Studies*, among other journals and collections. The excerpt that appears below comes from her book *Feminist, Queer, Crip*, published in 2013. It has since become a classic in feminist, disability, and queer studies.

The pervasiveness of prenatal testing, and especially its acceptance as part of the standard of care for pregnant women, casts women as responsible for their future children's able-bodiedness/able-mindedness; prospective parents are urged to take advantage of these services so as to avoid burdening their future children with any disabilities. This notion of "burdening" children finds an echo in the debate over same-sex marriage, with LGBT couples cast as selfish parents, placing their own desires over the physical and mental health of their children (and, by extension, of all children). Moreover, according to Timothy Dailey of the Family Research Council, homosexual parents often "'recruit' children into the homosexual lifestyle" by modeling "abnormal sexuality."[1] The possibility that same-sex parents might produce queer children is one of the most common reasons given for opposing such families, a reasoning that takes for granted the homophobic worldview that queerness must be avoided at all costs.

It is in the literature of reproductive technologies and their "proper" use that heterocentrism and homophobia intersect powerfully with ableism and stereotypes about disability. These stories reveal profound anxieties about reproducing the family as a normative unit, with all of its members able-bodied/able-minded and heterosexual. At sites where disability, queerness, and reproductive technologies converge, parents and prospective parents are often criticized and condemned for their alleged misuse of technology. Assistive reproductive technologies are to be used only to deselect or prevent disability; doing otherwise—such as selecting for disability—means failing to properly reproduce the family.

In this chapter, I explore one such story in which ableism and heterocentrism combine, a situation in which parents were widely condemned for failing to protect their children from both disability and queerness. Sharon Duchesneau and Candace McCullough, a deaf lesbian couple in Maryland, attracted publicity and controversy for their 2001 decision to use a deaf sperm donor in conceiving their son. What most interests me about their story, and what I focus on here, is the consistency with which cultural critics and commentators took for granted the idea that a better future is one without disability and deafness. [Their story], in other words, centers around the proper use of assistive reproductive technology and the future of children.

*****

The story of Sharon Duchesneau and Candace McCullough [...] has been presented to the public almost exclusively in terms of what the future can, should, and will include. Whether warning of a slippery slope, of other disabled people "manufacturing" disabled children, or of "unnatural" lifestyles, commentators see the couple's selection of a deaf sperm donor as a sign of a dangerous future. I am less interested in arguing for or against these women's decision than in detailing how critics of the couple utilize dystopic rhetoric in their condemnations, presenting deafness and disability as traits that obviously should be avoided. [A] world free of impairment is portrayed as a goal shared by all, a goal that is beyond question or analysis, a goal that is natural rather than political.

# DEAF/DISABLED: A TERMINOLOGICAL INTERLUDE

For most hearing people, to describe deafness as a disability is to state the obvious: deaf people lack the ability to hear, and therefore they are disabled. For

some people, however, deaf and hearing alike, it is neither obvious nor accurate to characterize deafness as a disability and deaf people as disabled. Rather, Deaf people are more appropriately described as members of a distinct linguistic and cultural minority, more akin to Spanish speakers in a predominantly English-language country than to people in wheelchairs or people who are blind.[2] Spanish speakers are not considered disabled simply because they cannot communicate in English without the aid of an interpreter, and, according to this model, neither should Deaf people, who rely on interpreters in order to communicate with those who cannot sign, be considered disabled. Drawing parallels between Deaf people and members of other cultural groups, supporters of the linguistic-cultural model of deafness note the existence of a vibrant Deaf culture, one that includes its own language (in the United States, American Sign Language [ASL]), cultural productions (e.g., ASL poetry and performance), residential schools, and social networks, as well as high rates of intermarriage.[3] As Deaf studies scholar Harlan Lane explains, "[T]he preconditions for Deaf participation [in society] are more like those of other language minorities: culturally Deaf people campaign for acceptance of their language and its broader use in the schools, the workplace, and in public events."[4] This linguistic-cultural model of deafness shares a key assumption of the social model of disability—namely, that it is society's interpretations of and responses to bodily and sensory variations that are the problem, not the variations themselves.

*Everyone Here Spoke Sign Language*, Nora Groce's study of hereditary deafness on Martha's Vineyard from the early eighteenth century to the mid-twentieth century, provides an example of this perspective. Groce argues that genetic deafness and deaf people were so interwoven into the population that almost every person on the island had a deaf relative or neighbor.[5] As a result, "everyone [there] spoke sign language," a situation that proves it is possible for hearing people to share the responsibility of communication rather than simply expecting deaf people to lip-read and speak orally or alleviate their hearing loss with surgeries and hearing aids.[6] Groce's study challenges the idea that deafness precludes full participation in society, suggesting that the barriers deaf people face are due more to societal attitudes and practices than to one's audiological conditions. For those who subscribe to this worldview, deafness is best understood as a distinct culture in which one should feel pride, rather than as a disability.

Although some Deaf people are averse to the label "disabled," either because of their immersion in Deaf culture or because of an internalized ableist impulse to distance themselves from disabled people, others are more willing to explore the label politically. This kind of exploration is based on making a distinction between being labeled as "disabled" by others, especially medical or audiological professionals and the hearing world in general, and choosing to self-identify as disabled. Many Deaf people who choose to take up the label of disability do so for strategic reasons. For some, the decision stems from a desire to ally themselves with other disabled people. They recognize that people with disabilities and Deaf people share a history of oppression, discrimination, and stigmatization because of their differences from a perceived "normal" body. As a group, Deaf and disabled people can work together to fight discrimination, and they have done so since the birth of the modern disability rights movement in the late 1960s. Thus, while some Deaf people may be opposed to (or at the very least ambivalent about) seeing deafness as a disability, they may simultaneously be willing to identify themselves as disabled or to ally themselves with disabled people in order to work toward social changes and legal protections that would benefit both populations.[7]

Recognizing this affinity between disability and deafness is particularly important in an analysis of cure narratives and utopian discourse, because it is precisely the image of deafness as disability that animates these narratives. What makes the actions of parents who express a preference for a deaf baby—the

case under consideration here—so abhorrent to the larger culture is the refusal to eradicate disability from the lives of their children.

---

## REPRODUCING CULTURAL ANXIETY: THE CASE OF THE DEAF LESBIANS

In November 2001, [...] Sharon Duchesneau and Candace (Candy) McCullough, a white lesbian couple living in Maryland, had a baby boy named Gauvin, who was conceived by assisted insemination. Both Duchesneau, the birth mother, and McCullough, the adoptive mother, are deaf, as is their first child, Jehanne. Jehanne and her new brother Gauvin were conceived with sperm donated by a family friend, a friend who also is deaf. Duchesneau and McCullough had originally intended to use a sperm bank for the pregnancies, but their desire for a deaf donor eliminated that option: men with congenital deafness are precluded from becoming sperm donors; reminiscent of the eugenic concern with the "fitness" of potential parents, deafness is one of the conditions that sperm banks and fertility clinics routinely screen out of the donor pool. Several months after he was born, Gauvin underwent an extensive audiology test to determine if he shared his parents' deafness. To the delight of Duchesneau and McCullough, the diagnosis was clear: Gauvin had "a profound hearing loss" in one ear, and "at least a severe hearing loss" in the other.[8] Duchesneau noted that they would have accepted and loved a hearing child, but a deaf child was clearly their preference. "A hearing baby would be a blessing," Duchesneau explained, "a Deaf baby would be a special blessing."[9]

Liza Mundy covered Duchesneau and McCullough's story for the *Washington Post Magazine* in March of 2002, and her essay provided a detailed explanation of these women's reproductive choices. Although the piece acknowledged the criticisms lodged against Duchesneau and McCullough, it was largely sympathetic; Mundy took care to explain the women's understanding of Deaf identity and to situate them within a larger understanding of Deaf culture and community. She also, of necessity, mentioned the women's lesbian relationship, but it was not a central component of the piece. For Mundy, it was the women's deafness, and their decision to have deaf children within a larger Deaf community, that made their story newsworthy.

The piece made quite a splash, and the story of the Deaf lesbian couple was picked up by other newspapers and wire services. Papers across the United States and England ran versions of and responses to the story, and cultural critics from across the ideological spectrum began to weigh in. The Family Research Council, a Washington-based organization that "champions marriage and family as the foundation of civilization," issued a press release with comments from Ken Connor, the group's president at the time. Describing Duchesneau and McCullough as "incredibly selfish," Connor berated the pair for imposing on their children not only the "disadvantages that come as a result of being raised in a homosexual household" but also the "burden" of disability. Connor linked disability and homosexuality, casting both as hardships that these two women "intentionally" handed their children. The Family Research Council's press release closed with a quote from Connor that not only continued to link homosexuality with disability but also depicted both as leading toward a dystopic future: "One can only hope that this practice of intentionally manufacturing disabled children in order to fit the lifestyles of the parents will not progress any further. The places this slippery slope could lead to are frightening."[10] The use of the term *lifestyles*—a word frequently used to refer derisively to queers and our sexual/relational practices—effectively blurs deafness and queerness, suggesting that both characteristics are allegedly leading "us" down the road to ruin.

Indeed, the queerness of this future had everything to do with its portrayal as negative and

imperfect. Although Ken Connor and the Family Research Council probably would not celebrate the use of a Deaf sperm donor by a heterosexual couple, it is highly unlikely that they would have condemned it as aggressively or as publicly as they did here, casting such a move as the first step on a slippery slope into the unknown. (They have not gone on record, for example, condemning Deaf heterosexuals who have children.) The case of the Deaf lesbians acquired the mileage that it did because of its evocation of a queer disabled future; heterosexism and ableism intertwine, each feeding off and supporting the other.

The Family Research Council was not alone in discussing these women's desire for a Deaf baby in the context of their sexuality. Indeed, even some queer commentators found something troubling, and ultimately dystopic, about the idea. Queer novelist Jeanette Winterson seemed to suggest that it was precisely these women's queerness that made their decision so anathema:

> If either of the Deaf Lesbians in the United States had been in a relationship with a man, Deaf or hearing, and if they had decided to have a baby, there is absolutely no certainty that the baby would have been Deaf. You take a chance with love; you take a chance with nature, but it is those chances and the unexpected possibilities they bring, that give life its beauty.[11]

It is worth noting that Winterson appears concerned only about the loss of some possibilities, namely the possibility of having a hearing child. Screening out deaf donors from sperm banks also removes the chance of "unexpected possibilities," at least in terms of genetic deafness, but apparently the denial of that chance does not trouble her.

Winterson condemned Duchesneau and McCullough for removing the element of "chance" from their pregnancy and guaranteeing themselves a deaf baby, a guarantee that could not happen "with nature."[12] However, her remarks obscure the fact that the women's use of a deaf donor provided no such guarantee, a fact made clear in Mundy's article. Duchesneau, McCullough, and their deaf donor; Winterson's hypothetical deaf heterosexual couple: both groups would have exactly the same odds of having a deaf child, yet Winterson found no fault with the imagined heterosexual conception. She appears to believe that it is acceptable, if perhaps regrettable, for heterosexual deaf couples to have deaf children because such an act is "natural"; bearing deaf children becomes "unnatural" and thereby dangerous when it is done outside the bounds of a "normal, natural" relationship—an odd position for a queer writer to take and one that has certainly been influenced by dominant ableist culture.

Winterson clearly took for granted that "everyone" views these women's behavior as reprehensible; for her, it was a "simple fact" that life as a deaf person is inferior to life as a hearing person. Duchesneau and McCullough's refusal to accept this "simple fact," and their insistence that deafness is desirable, has made them the targets of criticism from across the political spectrum. Winterson echoed Connor's "slippery slope" rhetoric when she suggested that these women's actions will lead to other, allegedly even more troubling futures. "How would any of us feel," she asked, "if the women had both been blind and claimed the right to a blind baby?" The tone and content of Winterson's essay answers this question for her readers, making clear that "we" would feel justifiably outraged.[13] It is perhaps no accident that Winterson referred to "blind women" rather than "blind people," again implying that it might be "natural" for a heterosexual blind couple to reproduce, but not a lesbian one. She even drew on this image for the title of her essay, "How Would We Feel If Blind Women Claimed the Right to a Blind Baby?"

This rhetorical move—shifting from an actual case involving deafness to a hypothetical situation involving a different disability—is a popular strategy to convince a disabled person that her decision to choose for disability, either by having a disabled child or by refusing technological fixes, is misguided, illogical, and extreme. By decontextualizing the situation, removing it from a Deaf person's own sphere of reference, it is assumed that the Deaf person will be able to recognize her error in judgment. This practice suggests that some disabilities are worse than others, that eventually one can substitute a particular disability that is so "obviously" undesirable that the disabled person will change her mind. Cross-disability alliances are presumed to be nonexistent; it is assumed that all Deaf people believe it would be best to eliminate the birth of "blind babies" or people with X disability.

This story is complicated by the fact that Winterson's stance is not without basis. In the *Washington Post* story, McCullough does express a preference for a sighted child. According to Mundy,

> If they themselves—valuing sight—were to have a blind child, well then, Candy acknowledges, they would probably try to have it fixed, if they could, like hearing parents who attempt to restore their child's hearing with cochlear implants. "I want to be the same as my child," says Candy. "I want the baby to enjoy what we enjoy."[14]

McCullough and Duchesneau's position that Deaf babies are "special blessings" does not mean that they are not also simultaneously implicated in the ableism of the larger culture; their desire for deafness does not necessarily extend to a desire for any and all disabilities. Deaf and disabled people are not immune to the ableist—or homophobic—ideologies of the larger culture. (It is worth noting in this context, however, that McCullough does not express a desire for genetic testing and selective abortion).

Indeed, even some disabled queers mirrored the blend of heterocentrism and ableism circulating through mainstream responses to Duchesneau and McCullough's reproductive choices. A participant on the QueerDisability listserv, for example, found the couple's decision to choose a Deaf donor troubling, partly because of the hardships and social barriers their children would face, partly because of the alleged financial burden their children would place on the state. Echoing Winterson, the listserv member drew a distinction between the "naturally" Deaf children who result from heterosexual relationships and the "unnaturally," and therefore inappropriately, Deaf children who result from queer relationships. We are left to wonder how this community member would view the choice by an infertile heterosexual Deaf couple to use a Deaf sperm donor, whether that choice would be deemed more natural and therefore acceptable.[15] Her comments lead me to believe that she would, like Winterson, find less fault with the imagined heterosexual couple than with the real homosexual one: either deafness or homosexuality in isolation would be permissible, but the combination is too abnormal, too disruptive, too queer, even for some gays and lesbians and people with disabilities.

These kinds of responses to the use of assisted insemination by Deaf queers support Sarah Franklin's argument that, while reproductive technology "might have been (or is to a limited extent) a disruption of the so-called 'natural' basis for the nuclear family and heterosexual marriage, [it] *has instead provided the occasion for reconsolidating them.*"[16] With few exceptions, Franklin explains, the state has taken little action to guarantee queers and/or single parents equal access to assisted reproductive technologies, and prominent people in the field of reproductive medicine have been outspoken in their belief that these technologies should not be available to same-sex couples or single parents.[17] As sociologist Laura Mamo points out, "[A]ccess to reproductive technologies in the United States is from the outset a class-based and sexuality-based phenomenon, and the institutional organization of these services enacts the reproduction of class and sexuality hierarchies by assuring the survival and ongoing proportionality of middle-class (usually white) heterosexual families."[18]

Mamo details the ways in which lesbians and (single heterosexual women) are disadvantaged within the medical system. Insurance policies, for example, require a diagnosis of infertility before they agree to cover assistive technologies, yet such a diagnosis is difficult to make in the absence of heterosexual sex. Many lesbians want to use sperm donated by a friend or family member, yet some clinics forbid the use of sperm from a known donor unless the woman is married to the donor.[19] Dorothy Roberts and Elizabeth Weil note that many fertility clinics require proof of a "stable" marriage before initiating treatment, an open-ended requirement that has been used to block the treatment of queers, women of color, and poor people. California prohibits discriminating against queers in fertility treatments, but, as Elizabeth Weil argues, such discrimination can hide under other names. Guadalupe Benitez lost her case against the North Coast Women's Care Medical Group when they argued that they had refused to treat her not because she was a lesbian but because she was unmarried; in an earlier case, which the clinic lost, Benitez was able to prove that treatment had stopped because of her status as a lesbian.[20] Assisted insemination may make it easier for queers to bear children, thereby "unsettling the conflation of reproduction with heterosexuality," but heterocentric/homophobic attitudes may prevent, or at least hinder, their use of this technology.[21]

Dorothy Roberts notes that racism also plays a role in access to assisted reproductive technologies, as doctors are far less likely to recommend fertility treatments for black women than for whites.[22] Although clinics cannot legally discriminate against potential patients on the basis of race, they can neglect to inform people of color about all possible treatments. Ableist attitudes pose similar barriers to disabled people's use of assisted reproductive technologies. Many disabled women report being discouraged by their doctors and families from having children, a fact that suggests that they might not receive all the fertility assistance they need.[23] The policing of these technologies serves to reinforce the dominant vision of a world without impairment and to perpetuate the stigmatization of the queer, disabled, nonwhite body.

\*\*\*\*\*

None of the articles tracing the reproductive choices of Sharon Duchesneau and Candace McCullough questioned the assumption that a future without disability and deafness is superior to one with them. [...] The vast majority of public reactions to these women's choices tell a story about the appropriate place of disability/deafness in the future; it is assumed that everyone, both hearing and Deaf, disabled and nondisabled, will and should prefer a nondisabled, hearing child. Thus, the future allegedly invoked by the couple's actions is dangerous because it advocates an improper use of technology; technology can and should be used only to *eliminate* disability, not to *proliferate* it. Such a goal is *natural*, not *political*, and therefore neither requires nor deserves public debate.

## OPEN TO DEBATE? DISABILITY AND DIFFERENCE IN A FEMINIST FUTURE

[...] As manifested in the furor surrounding McCullough and Duchesneau's reproductive choices, disability is often seen as a difference that has no place in the future. Disability is a problem that must be eliminated, a hindrance to one's future opportunities, a drag on one's quality of life. Speaking directly about the Duchesneau and McCullough case, bioethicist Alta Charo argues, "The question is whether the parents have violated the sacred duty of parenthood, which is to maximize to some reasonable degree the advantages available to their children. I'm loath to say it, but I think it's a shame to set limits on a child's potential."[24] Similar claims are made in opposition to same-sex parenting; critics argue that children raised in queer households will have a lower quality of life

than children raised in heterosexual ones.[25] However, in both of these situations, it is assumed not only that disability and queerness inherently and irreversibly lower one's quality of life but also that there is only one possible understanding of "quality of life" and that everyone knows what "it" is without discussion or elaboration. [...]

Susan Wendell suggests that living with disability or illness "creates valuable *ways of being* that give valuable perspectives on life and the world," ways of being that would be lost through the elimination of illness and disability.[26] She notes, for example, that adults who require assistance in the activities of daily life, such as eating, bathing, toileting, and dressing, have opportunities to think through cultural ideals of independence and self-sufficiency; these experiences can potentially lead to productive insights about intimacy, relationship, and interdependence. "If one looks at disabilities as forms of difference and takes seriously the possibility that they may be valuable," argues Wendell,

> it becomes obvious that people with disabilities have experiences, by virtue of their disabilities, which non-disabled people do not have, and which are [or can be] sources of knowledge that is not directly accessible to non-disabled people. Some of this knowledge, for example, how to live with a suffering body, would be of enormous practical help to most people.... Much of it would enrich and expand our culture, and some of it has the potential to change our thinking and our ways of life profoundly.[27]

To eliminate disability is to eliminate the possibility of discovering alternative ways of being in the world, to foreclose the possibility of recognizing and valuing our interdependence.

To be clear, no policy decisions have been made as to which "defects" should be eliminated or about what constitutes a "defective" gene; with few exceptions, assisted reproductive technology remains largely unregulated in the United States. But the proliferation of prenatal testing and the increasing availability of pre-implantation genetic diagnosis certainly send a message about the proper and expected approach to disability. Public discussions of these technologies have lagged far behind their use and development, and they rarely include the perspectives of disabled people. As H-Dirksen L. Bauman argues, "Presumptions about the horrors of deafness are usually made by those not living Deaf lives."[28] [...] Moreover, as the debate surrounding Duchesneau and McCullough's reproductive choices makes clear, selecting for disability remains a highly controversial position, and hypothetical disabled children continue to be used to justify genetic research and selective abortion. "Curing" and eliminating disability—whether through stem cell research or selective abortion—is almost always presented as a universally valued goal about which there can, and should, be no disagreement.

I want to suggest that stories of Deaf lesbians intentionally striving for Deaf babies be read as counternarratives to mainstream stories about the necessity of a cure for deafness and disability, about the dangers of nonnormative queer parents having children. Their stories challenge the feasibility of technological promises of an "amazing future" in which impairment is cured through genetic and medical intervention, thereby resisting a compulsory able-bodied/able-minded heterosexuality that insists upon normal minds/bodies. It is precisely this challenge that has animated the hostile responses these families have received. Their choice to choose deafness suggests that reproductive technology can be used as more than a means to screen out alleged defects, that disability cannot ever fully disappear, that not everyone craves an able-bodied/able-minded future, that there might be a place for bodies with limited, odd, or queer movements and orientations, and that disability and queerness can indeed be desirable both in the future as well as now.

The story of the Deaf lesbians, Candace McCullough and Sharon Duchesneau, is only one among many. An ever-increasing number of memoirs, essays, and poems about life with a disability, as well as theoretical analyses of disability and able-bodiedness, tell other stories about disability [...]. There are stories of people embracing their bodies, proudly proclaiming disability as sexy, powerful, and worthy; tales of disabled parents and parents with disabled children refusing to accept that a bright future for our children precludes disability and asserting the right to bear and keep children with disabilities; and narratives of families refusing to accept the normalization of their bodies through surgical interventions and the normalization of their desires through heterocentric laws and homophobic condemnations. These stories deserve telling, and the issues they raise demand debate and dissent.

It is not that these tales are any less partial or contested than the others in public circulation; they, too, can be used to serve multiple and contradictory positions. Indeed, Lennard Davis argues that we need to question whether these kinds of reproductive decisions—choosing deafness and disability—are "radical ways of fighting against oppression" or "technological fixes in the service of a conservative, essentialist agenda."[29] I would only add that the two are not mutually exclusive; the same choice can serve both agendas. Just as selecting for girls can be as problematic as selecting for boys, with both choices potentially reliant on narrow gender norms and expectations, selecting for disability has the potential to reify categories of able-bodiedness as much as deselecting disability does. What is needed then are examinations of how particular choices function in particular contexts; what does it mean for lesbian parents to choose deafness in this context, or a single mother to refuse to terminate a pregnancy after receiving a Down diagnosis in that context? Such explorations are impossible as long as selecting for disability remains largely inconceivable, as long as we all assume—or are assumed to assume—that disability cannot belong in feminist visions of the future and that its absence merits no debate.

# NOTES

1. Timothy J. Dailey, "Homosexual Parenting: Placing Children at Risk," *Insight* no. 238, accessed November 8, 2006, www.frc.org. See also Caryle Murphy, "Gay Parents Find More Acceptance," *Washington Post*, June 14, 1999, A1.

2. The use of "Deaf," with a capital "D," emerged in the late twentieth century as a way to signal pride in one's identity and in the cultural practices and historical traditions of deaf people. Deaf with a capital letter is thus a way to draw attention to a cultural deaf identity, whereas Deaf with a small "d" simply connotes being unable to hear or hard-of-hearing. This use is not universally accepted, however, with some deaf people and deaf studies scholars moving away from the "big D/little d" convention. For a recent reflection on this question, and on larger questions of deaf identity, see Brenda Jo Brueggemann, *Deaf Subjects: Between Identities and Places* (New York: New York University Press, 2009); for discussion about the limitations of American discourses of deaf identity, see Susan Burch and Alison Kafer, eds., *Deaf and Disability Studies: Interdisciplinary Perspectives* (Washington, DC: Gallaudet University Press, 2010).

3. Carol Padden and Tom Humphries, *Deaf in America: Voices from a Culture* (Cambridge, MA: Harvard University Press, 1988); John Vickrey Van Cleve and Barry Crouch, *A Place of Their Own: Creating the Deaf Community in America* (Washington, DC: Gallaudet University Press, 1989).

4. Harlan Lane, "Constructions of Deafness," in *The Disability Studies Reader*, ed. Lennard J. Davis (New York: Routledge, 1997), 161. Lane acknowledges that there are differences between Deaf people and other linguistic minorities. He notes, "Deaf people cannot learn English as a second language as easily as other minorities. Second and third generation Deaf children find learning English no easier than their forbears, but second and third generation immigrants to the United States frequently learn English before entering school…. Normally, Deaf people are not proficient in this native language [sign language] until they reach school age. Deaf people are more scattered geographically than many linguistic minorities. The availability of interpreters is even more vital for Deaf people than for many other linguistic minorities because there are so few Deaf lawyers, doctors, and accountants, etc." Lane, "Constructions of Deafness," 163–64.

5. Nora Ellen Groce, *Everyone Here Spoke Sign Language: Hereditary Deafness on Martha's Vineyard* (Cambridge, MA: Harvard University Press, 1985). For a more recent discussion of deafness on Martha's Vineyard, see Annelies Kusters, "Deaf Utopias? Reviewing the Sociocultural Literature on the World's 'Martha's Vineyard Situations,'" *Journal of Deaf Studies and Deaf Education* 15, no. 1 (2010): 3–16.

6. Unfortunately, there is an extensive history of requiring Deaf people to do precisely that: to learn to lip-read, speak orally, and abandon signing, and to undergo painful surgeries and medical treatments in order to "correct" their hearing loss. Scholars of Deaf studies have documented histories of Deaf people being punished, often brutally, for engaging in sign language, and of the campaigns waged against residential schools and Deaf communities. In spite of such treatment, the Deaf community continued to use and fight for sign language. Robert M. Buchanan, *Illusions of Equality: Deaf Americans in School and Factory, 1850–1950* (Washington, DC: Gallaudet University Press, 1999); Susan Burch, *Signs of Resistance: American Deaf Cultural History, 1900 to World War II* (New York: New York University Press, 2002).

7. For one example of these kinds of coalitions, see Corbett Joan O'Toole, "Dale Dahl and Judy Heumann: Deaf Man, Disabled Woman—Allies in 1970s Berkeley," in *Deaf and Disability Studies: Interdisciplinary Perspectives*, ed. Susan Burch and Alison Kafer (Washington, DC: Gallaudet University Press, 2010), 162–87.

8. Liza Mundy, "A World of Their Own," *Washington Post Magazine*, March 31, 2002, www.washingtonpost.com. Sadly, Gauvin died suddenly and unexpectedly from an inherited condition (unrelated to his deafness). In sharp contrast to his birth, his passing was met with very little news coverage or public reaction.

9. Mundy, "A World of Their Own."

10. Family Research Council, "*Washington Post* Profiles Lesbian Couple Seeking to Manufacture a Deaf Child," *PR Newswire Association*, April 1, 2002. There are strong parallels here between Connor's warning and the eugenic tracts in

wide circulation in the late nineteenth and early twentieth centuries. Alexander Graham Bell, for example, worried about the development of deaf culture and any related rise in deaf populations. See his "Memoir Upon the Formation of a Deaf Variety of the Human Race" for one iteration of these fears. I thank Susan Burch for pointing me in the direction of this text.

11. Jeanette Winterson, "How Would We Feel If Blind Women Claimed the Right to a Blind Baby?" *Guardian* (UK), April 9, 2002.

12. For feminist and queer deconstructions of nature rhetoric, particularly uses of "nature" to proscribe gender and sexuality identities and practices, see, for example, Catriona Mortimer-Sandilands and Bruce Erickson, eds. *Queer Ecologies: Sex, Nature, Politics, Desire* (Bloomington: Indiana University Press, 2010); and Noël Sturgeon, *Environmentalism in Popular Culture: Gender, Race, Sexuality, and the Politics of the Natural* (Tucson: University of Arizona Press, 2009).

13. Winterson refers to McCullough and Duchesneau's decision as "a bad joke," a sign of "psychosis," "paranoid," and a form of "genetic imperialism."

14. Mundy, "A World of Their Own."

15. These comments were not left unaddressed by other members on the listserv, however. Participants questioned the assumptions about the "burdens" caused by disability and about the inappropriateness of Deaf women choosing a donor that reflected their own lives, a choice nondisabled couples make regularly. They also challenged the contention that Deaf children pose a financial strain on the state, arguing that economic arguments about the "strain" caused by people with disabilities have often been used to justify coerced and forced sterilization, institutionalization, and coerced abortion.

16. Sarah Franklin, "Essentialism, Which Essentialism? Some Implications of Reproductive and Genetic Technoscience," in *If You Seduce a Straight Person, Can You Make Them Gay? Issues in Biological Essentialism versus Social Constructionism in Gay and Lesbian Identities*, ed. John P. DeCecco and John P. Elia (Binghamton, NY: Harrington Park, 1993), 30; italics in original.

17. Patrick Steptoe, known as the "father of in vitro fertilization," remarked that "it would be unthinkable to willingly create a child to be born into an unnatural situation such as a gay or lesbian relationship." Quoted in Franklin, "Essentialism, Which Essentialism?" 31.

18. Mamo, *Queering Reproduction*, 72.

19. Ibid., 134.

20. Dorothy Roberts, *Killing the Black Body: Race, Reproduction, and the Meaning of Liberty* (New York: Vintage, 1998); Elizabeth Weil, "Breeder Reaction," *Mother Jones* 31, no. 4 (2006): 33–37.

21. Franklin, "Essentialism, Which Essentialism?" 29.

22. Roberts, *Killing the Black Body*, 254.

23. Jo Litwinowicz, "In My Mind's Eye: I," in *Bigger than the Sky: Disabled Women on Parenting*, ed. Michele Wates and Rowen Jade (London, UK: Women's Press, 1999).

24. Quoted in David Teather, "Lesbian Couple Have Deaf Baby by Choice," *Guardian* (UK), April 8, 2002, http://www.guardian.co.uk/world/2002/apr/08/davidteather.

25. Glenn Stanton from Focus on the Family scolds, "[A] wise and compassionate society always comes to the aid of children in motherless or fatherless families, but a wise and compassionate society never intentionally subjects children to such families. But every single same-sex home would do exactly that, for no other reason than that a small handful of adults desire such kinds of families." Same-sex households are to be discouraged, in other words, because they "subject" children to situations in which they will need "aid" and rescue. Quoted in McCreery, "Save Our Children/ Let Us Marry," 196.

26. Susan Wendell, "Unhealthy Disabled: Treating Chronic Illnesses as Disabilities," *Hypatia: A Journal of Feminist Philosophy* 16, no. 4 (2001): 31, emphasis in original.

27. Wendell, *Rejected Body*, 69.

28. H Dirksen L. Bauman, "Designing Deaf Babies and the Question of Disability," *Journal of Deaf Studies and Deaf Education* 10, no. 3 (2005): 313.

29. Lennard J. Davis, "Postdeafness," in *Open Your Eyes: Deaf Studies Talking*, ed. H-Dirksen Bauman (Minneapolis: University of Minnesota Press, 2008), 319.

# REFERENCES

Bauman, H-Dirksen L. "Designing Deaf Babies and the Question of Disability." *Journal of Deaf Studies and Deaf Education* 10, no. 3 (2005): 311–15.

Bell, Alexander Graham. *Memoir Upon the Formation of a Deaf Variety of the Human Race.* Washington, DC: National Academy of Sciences, 1884.

Brueggemann, Brenda. *Deaf Subjects: Between Identities and Places.* New York: New York University Press, 2009.

Buchanan, Robert M. *Illusions of Equality: Deaf Americans in School and Factory, 1850–1950.* Washington, DC: Gallaudet University Press, 1999.

Burch, Susan. *Signs of Resistance: American Deaf Cultural History, 1900 to World War II.* New York: New York University Press, 2002.

Burch, Susan, and Alison Kafer, eds. *Deaf and Disability Studies: Interdisciplinary Perspectives.* Washington, DC: Gallaudet University Press, 2010.

Dailey, Timothy J. "Homosexual Parenting: Placing Children at Risk." *Insight* 238, www.frc.org.

Davis, Lennard J. "Postdeafness." In *Open Your Eyes: Deaf Studies Talking,* ed. H-Dirksen Bauman, 314–25. Minneapolis: University of Minnesota Press, 2008.

Family Research Council. "*Washington Post* Profiles Lesbian Couple Seeking to Manufacture a Deaf Child." *PR Newswire Association, Inc.* April 1, 2002.

Franklin, Sarah. "Essentialism, Which Essentialism? Some Implications of Reproductive and Genetic Technoscience." In *If You Seduce a Straight Person, Can You Make Them Gay? Issues in Biological Essentialism versus Social Constructionism in Gay and Lesbian Identities,* ed. John P. DeCecco and John P. Elia, 27–40. Binghamton, NY: Harrington Park, 1993.

Groce, Nora Ellen. *Everyone Here Spoke Sign Language: Hereditary Deafness on Martha's Vineyard.* Cambridge, MA: Harvard University Press, 1985.

Kusters, Annelies. "Deaf Utopias? Reviewing the Sociocultural Literature on the World's 'Martha's Vineyard Situations.'" *Journal of Deaf Studies and Deaf Education* 15, no. 1 (2010): 3–16.

Lane, Harlan. "Constructions of Deafness." In *The Disability Studies Reader,* ed. Lennard J. Davis, 154–71. New York: Routledge, 1997.

Litwinowicz, Jo. "In My Mind's Eye: I." In *Bigger than the Sky: Disabled Women on Parenting,* ed. Michele Wates and Rowen Jade, 29–33. London, UK: Women's Press, 1999.

Mamo, Laura. *Queering Reproduction: Achieving Pregnancy in the Age of Technoscience.* Durham, NC: Duke University Press, 2007.

McCreery, Patrick. "Save Our Children/Let Us Marry: Gay Activists Appropriate the Rhetoric of Child Protectionism." *Radical History Review* 2008, no. 100 (2008): 186–207.

Mortimer-Sandilands, Catriona, and Bruce Erickson, eds. *Queer Ecologies: Sex, Nature, Politics, Desire.* Bloomington: Indiana University Press, 2010.

Mundy, Liza. "A World of Their Own." *Washington Post Magazine.* March 31, 2002.

Murphy, Caryle. "Gay Parents Find More Acceptance." *Washington Post.* June 14, 1999. http://www.washingtonpost.com/wp-srv/local/daily/june99/gays14.htm.

O'Toole, Corbett Joan. "Dale Dahl and Judy Heumann: Deaf Man, Disabled Woman—Allies in 1970s Berkeley." In *Deaf and Disability Studies: Interdisciplinary Perspectives,* ed. Susan Burch and Alison Kafer, 162–87. Washington, DC: Gallaudet University Press, 2010.

Padden, Carol, and Tom Humphries. *Deaf in America: Voices from a Culture.* Cambridge, MA: Harvard University Press, 1988.

Roberts, Dorothy. *Killing the Black Body: Race, Reproduction, and the Meaning of Liberty.* New York: Vintage, 1998.

Sturgeon, Noël. *Environmentalism in Popular Culture: Gender, Race, Sexuality, and the Politics of the Natural.* Tucson: University of Arizona Press, 2009.

Teather, David. "Lesbian Couple Have Deaf Baby by Choice." *Guardian* (UK). April 8, 2002. http://www.guardian.co.uk/world/2002/apr/08/davidteather.

Van Cleve, John Vickrey, and Barry Crouch. *A Place of Their Own: Creating the Deaf Community in America.* Washington, DC: Gallaudet University Press, 1989.

Weil, Elizabeth. "Breeder Reaction." *Mother Jones* 31, no. 4 (2006): 33–37.

Wendell, Susan. *The Rejected Body: Feminist Philosophical Reflections on Disability.* New York: Routledge, 1996.

———. "Unhealthy Disabled: Treating Chronic Illnesses as Disabilities." *Hypatia: A Journal of Feminist Philosophy* 16, no. 4 (2001): 17–33.

Winterson, Jeanette. "How Would We Feel If Blind Women Claimed the Right to a Blind Baby?" *Guardian* (UK). April 9, 2002. Features section, 9.

*Source:* Kafer, Alison. (2013). Excerpted from "Chapter 3: Debating Feminist Futures: Slippery Slopes, Cultural Anxiety, and the Case of the Deaf Lesbians." In *Feminist, Queer, Crip* (pp. 69–85, 197–203). Bloomington, IN: Indiana University Press.

# CHAPTER 54

## A Primer on Reproductive Justice and Social Change

## What Is Reproductive Justice?

*Loretta Ross*

Loretta Ross is a visiting associate professor in Women's Studies at Hampshire College in Amherst, Massachusetts. She is a co-founder and former national coordinator of the SisterSong Women of Color Reproductive Justice Collective. Her areas of expertise are women's issues, hate groups, racism and intolerance, human rights, and violence against women.

Reproductive Justice is the complete physical, mental, spiritual, political, social, and economic well-being of women and girls, based on the full achievement and protection of women's human rights. This definition, as outlined by Asian Communities for Reproductive Justice (ACRJ) [now called Forward Together], offers a new perspective on reproductive issues advocacy, pointing out that for Indigenous women and women of color, it is important to fight equally for (1) the right to have a child; (2) the right not to have a child; and (3) the right to parent the children we have, as well as to control our birthing options, such as midwifery. We also fight for the necessary enabling conditions to realize these rights. [...]

The Reproductive Justice framework analyzes how the ability of any woman to determine her own reproductive destiny is linked directly to the conditions in her community—and these conditions are not just a matter of individual choice and access. Reproductive Justice addresses the social reality of inequality, specifically, the inequality of opportunities that we have to control our reproductive destiny. Moving beyond a demand for privacy and respect for individual decision making to include the social supports necessary for our individual decisions to be optimally realized, this framework also includes obligations from our government for protecting women's human rights. Our options for making choices have to be safe, affordable, and accessible, three minimal cornerstones of government support for all individual life decisions.

One of the key problems addressed by Reproductive Justice is the isolation of abortion from other social justice issues that concern communities of color: issues of economic justice, the environment, immigrants' rights, disability rights, discrimination based on race and sexual orientation, and a host of other community-centered concerns. These issues directly affect an individual woman's decision-making process. By shifting the focus to reproductive oppression—the control and exploitation of women, girls, and individuals through our bodies, sexuality, labor, and reproduction—rather than a narrow focus on protecting the legal right to abortion, SisterSong Women of Color Reproductive Health Collective is developing a more inclusive vision of how to build a new movement.

Because reproductive oppression affects women's lives in multiple ways, a multi-pronged approach is needed to fight this exploitation and advance the well-being of women and girls. There are three main frameworks for fighting reproductive oppression defined by ACRJ:

1. Reproductive Health, which deals with service delivery,
2. Reproductive Rights, which addresses legal issues, and
3. Reproductive Justice, which focuses on movement building.

Although these frameworks are distinct in their approaches, they work together to provide a comprehensive solution. Ultimately, as in any movement, all three components—service, advocacy, and organizing—are crucial.

\*\*\*\*\*

Reproductive Justice focuses on organizing women, girls, and their communities to challenge structural power inequalities in a comprehensive and transformative process of empowerment. [...]

[...] We have to address directly the inequitable distribution of power and resources within the movement, holding our allies and ourselves responsible for constructing principled, collaborative relationships that end the exploitation and competition within our movement. We also have to build the social, political, and economic power of low-income women, Indigenous women, women of color, and their communities so that they are full participating partners in building this new movement. This requires integrating grassroots issues and constituencies that are multi-racial, multi-generational, and multi-class into the national policy arena, as well as into the organizations that represent the movement.

SisterSong is building a network of allied social justice and human rights organizations that integrate the reproductive justice analysis into their work. We are using strategies of self-help and empowerment so that women who receive our services understand they are vital emerging leaders in determining the scope and direction of the Reproductive Justice and social justice movements.

---

*Source:* Ross, Loretta. (2006). Excerpted from "What Is Reproductive Justice?" In *Reproductive Justice Briefing Book* (pp. 4–5). Atlanta, GA: SisterSong Women of Color Reproductive Justice Collective.

# Conditions of Reproductive Justice

*Rickie Solinger*

Rickie Solinger is an independent historian, curator, and lecturer. She is the author of numerous books and articles about reproductive, welfare, and prison politics, including the award-winning books *Wake Up Little Susie: Single Pregnancy and Race before Roe v. Wade* and *Beggars and Choosers: How the Politics of Choice Shapes Abortion, Adoption, and Welfare in the United States*. In addition to her scholarship, Solinger curates travelling art exhibitions across the United States, seeking to engage viewers and enrich opportunities for public education.

## REPRODUCTIVE JUSTICE RECOGNIZES WOMEN'S RIGHT TO REPRODUCE AS A FOUNDATIONAL HUMAN RIGHT

The right to be recognized as a legitimate reproducer regardless of race, religion, sexual orientation, economic status, age, immigrant status, citizenship status, ability/disability status, and status as an incarcerated woman encompasses the following:

### Women's Right to Manage Their Reproductive Capacity

1. The right to decide whether or not to become a mother and when
2. The right to primary culturally competent preventive health care
3. The right to accurate information about sexuality and reproduction
4. The right to accurate contraceptive information
5. The right and access to safe, respectful, and affordable contraceptive materials and services

6. The right to abortion and access to full information about safe, respectful, affordable abortion services
7. The right to and equal access to the benefits of and information about the potential risks of reproductive technology

### Women's Right to Adequate Information, Resources, Services, and Personal Safety While Pregnant

1. The right and access to safe, respectful, and affordable medical care during and after pregnancy, including treatment for HIV/AIDS, drug and alcohol addiction, and other chronic conditions, including the right to seek medical care during pregnancy without fear of criminal prosecution or medical interventions against the pregnant woman's will
2. The right of incarcerated women to safe and respectful care during and after pregnancy, including the right to give birth in a safe, respectful, medically appropriate environment

3. The right and access to economic security, including the right to earn a living wage
4. The right to physical safety, including the right to adequate housing and structural protections against rape and sexual violence
5. The right to practise religion or not, freely and safely, so that authorities cannot coerce women to undergo medical interventions that conflict with their religious convictions
6. The right to be pregnant in an environmentally safe context
7. The right to decide among birthing options and access to those services

## A Woman's Right to Be the Parent of Her Child

1. The right to economic resources sufficient to be a parent, including the right to earn a living wage
2. The right to education and training in preparation for earning a living wage
3. The right to decide whether or not to be the parent of the child one gives birth to
4. The right to parent in a physically and environmentally safe context
5. The right to leave from work to care for newborns or others in need of care
6. The right to affordable, high-quality child care

*Source:* Solinger, Rickie. "Conditions of Reproductive Justice." In *Reproductive Justice Briefing Book* (p. 42). Atlanta, GA: SisterSong Women of Color Reproductive Justice Collective.

# 10 Reasons to Rethink Overpopulation

*The Population and Development Program at Hampshire College*

The Population and Development Program (PopDev) is a center for critical thinking, learning, and advocacy on population and the environment based at Hampshire College in Amherst, Massachusetts. PopDev critiques the idea of "overpopulation," tracing its consequences in policy for reproductive health and family planning, environment and climate change, immigration, and international security. PopDev offers alternative frameworks for understanding population dynamics and creates activist tools, publications, and educational resources for organizers, students, policy-makers, and journalists.

A central requirement for reproductive justice is not only for women to have the right not to have children, but to also exercise the right to have children. Women have been denied this right through population control programs that care more about reducing birth rates than empowering women to have control over their reproductive health and rights. The ideology that informed the programs has not gone away, and below are 10 reasons why rethinking overpopulation is vital to creating the global understanding and solidarity needed to advance women's reproductive and sexual rights.

1. The population "explosion" is over. Although world population is still growing and is expected to reach 9 billion by the year 2050, the era of rapid growth is over. With increasing education, urbanization, and women's work outside the home, birth rates have fallen in almost every part of the world and now average 2.7 births per woman.
2. The focus on population masks the complex causes of poverty and inequality. A narrow focus on human numbers obscures the way different economic and political systems operate to perpetuate poverty and inequality. It places the blame on the people with the least amount of resources and power rather than on corrupt governments and rich elites.
3. Hunger is not the result of "too many mouths" to feed. Global food production has consistently outpaced population growth. People go hungry because they do not have the land on which to grow food or the money with which to buy it.
4. Population growth is not the driving force behind environmental degradation. Blaming environmental degradation on overpopulation lets the real culprits off the hook. The richest fifth of the world's people consume 66 times as many resources as the poorest fifth. The U.S., with a low fertility rate, is the largest emitter of greenhouse gases responsible for global warming.
5. Population pressure is not a root cause of political insecurity and conflict. Especially since 9/11, conflict in the Middle East has been linked to a "youth bulge" of too many young men whose numbers supposedly make them prone to violence.

Blaming population pressure for instability takes the onus off powerful actors and political choices.

6. Population control targets women's fertility and restricts reproductive rights. All women should have access to high-quality, voluntary reproductive health services, including safe birth control and abortion. In contrast, population control programs try to drive down birth rates through coercive social policies and the aggressive promotion of sterilization or long-acting contraceptives that can threaten women's health.

7. Population control programs have a negative effect on basic health care. Under pressure from international population agencies, many poor countries made population control a higher priority than primary health care from the 1970s on. Reducing fertility was considered more important than preventing and treating debilitating diseases like malaria, improving maternal and child health, and addressing malnutrition.

8. Population alarmism encourages apocalyptic thinking that legitimizes human rights abuses. Dire predictions of population-induced mass famine and environmental collapse have long been popular in the U.S. Population funding appeals still play on such fears even though they have not been borne out in reality. This sense of emergency leads to an elitist moral relativism, in which "we" know best and "our" rights are more worthy than "theirs."

9. Threatening images of overpopulation reinforce racial and ethnic stereotypes and scapegoat immigrants and other vulnerable communities. Negative media images of starving African babies, poor, pregnant women of color, and hordes of dangerous Third World men drive home the message that "those people" outnumber "us." Fear of overpopulation in the Third World often translates into fear of increasing immigration to the West, and thereby people of color becoming the majority.

10. Conventional views of overpopulation stand in the way of greater global understanding and solidarity. Fears of overpopulation are deeply divisive and harmful. In order to protect and advance reproductive rights in a hostile climate, we urgently need to work together across borders of gender, race, class, and nationality. Rethinking population helps open the way.

---

*Source:* Population and Development Program at Hampshire College. "10 Reasons to Rethink Overpopulation." In *Reproductive Justice Briefing Book* (pp. 31–32). Atlanta, GA: SisterSong Women of Color Reproductive Justice Collective.

# REPRODUCTIVE RIGHTS AROUND THE WORLD

Contraception

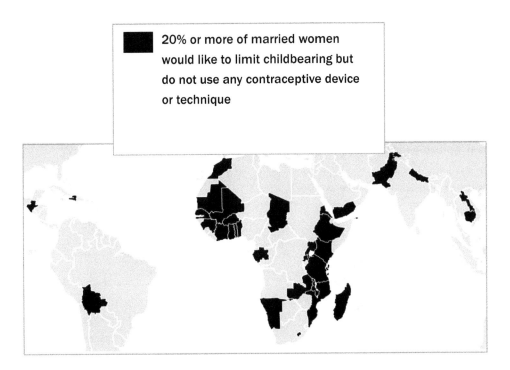

20% or more of married women would like to limit childbearing but do not use any contraceptive device or technique

**Unmet need, 2007**

*Source:* Seager, Joni. (2009). "Unmet Need, 2007." Plate no. 10 (Contraception). In *The Penguin Atlas of Women in the World, 4th Edition* (p. 36). New York, NY: Penguin.

**Types of contraception: Proportion of married or "in union" women worldwide using each method, late 1990s or latest available data**

*Source:* Seager, Joni. (2009). "Types of Contraception." Plate no. 10 (Contraception). In *The Penguin Atlas of Women in the World, 4th Edition* (p. 36). New York, NY: Penguin.

## Preventing Unsafe Abortion

Magnitude of the problem:

- 21.6 million women experience an unsafe abortion worldwide each year; almost all unsafe abortions occur in developing countries.
- 47,000 women die from complications of unsafe abortion each year.
- Deaths due to unsafe abortion remain close to 13 percent of all maternal deaths.

*Source:* World Health Organization. (2011). Adapted from "Executive Summary." In *Unsafe Abortion: Global and Regional Estimates of the Incidence of Unsafe Abortion and Associated Mortality in 2008, 6th Edition* (p. 1). Geneva, Switzerland: WHO. Retrieved from: http://apps.who.int/iris/bitstream/10665/44529/1/9789241501118_eng.pdf.

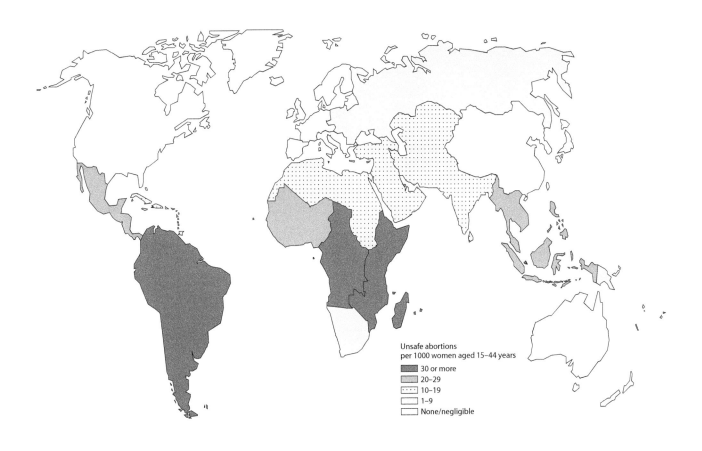

**Estimated annual number of unsafe abortions per 1000 women aged 15–44 years, by subregions, 2008**

*Source:* World Health Organization. (2011). "Figure 5: Estimated Annual Number of Unsafe Abortion per 1000 Women Aged 15–44 years, by Subregions, 2008." In *Unsafe Abortion: Global and Regional Estimates of the Incidence of Unsafe Abortion and Associated Mortality in 2008, 6th Edition* (p. 20). Geneva, Switzerland: WHO. Retrieved from: http://apps.who.int/iris/bitstream/10665/44529/1/9789241501118_eng.pdf.

## Maternal Mortality

**Race and mother-death in the U.S.**

Maternal deaths per 100,000 births, 2003

- African/American: 31
- Hispanic: 10
- white: 8

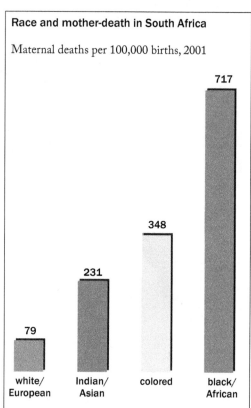

**Race and mother-death in South Africa**

Maternal deaths per 100,000 births, 2001

- white/European: 79
- Indian/Asian: 231
- colored: 348
- black/African: 717

### Maternal Mortality

*Source:* Seager, Joni. (2009). "Race and Mother-Death in the U.S./Race and Mother-Death in South Africa." Plate no. 12 (Maternal Mortality). In *The Penguin Atlas of Women in the World, 4th Edition* (p. 41). New York, NY: Penguin.

# CHAPTER 55

## Toronto and the Runaway Wives

*Margo Goodhand*

Margo Goodhand is the former editor-in-chief of the *Edmonton Journal* and the *Winnipeg Free Press*. She has been published in newspapers and magazines across Canada, including the *Globe and Mail* and *The Walrus*, as a syndicated columnist, news reporter, travel writer, editorial writer, and arts and book reviewer.

Marilyn Tinsley, her friends suspected, was a victim of abuse during her short marriage. She never talked about why she left her husband, a well-known musician in Toronto, a move that had propelled her and her two little girls into a marginal existence on welfare in the big city. But the 30-something Tinsley had a thing about domestic violence. She saw it; she noticed. She would sit on a stoop in her low-rent neighbourhood on Gothic Avenue near High Park and point out the women she claimed were being abused. And she railed against a system that was [indifferent] to their suffering.

"One day, we were sitting on the front porch discussing a woman who had just walked by with two black eyes and she said to me, 'Well, what are we going to do about it?'" recalls her one-time friend and neighbour Maggie (O'Brien) Longdon Reid. "And I said, 'Well I don't know about you, Marilyn, but I'm not going to do anything—why? What should I do?' And she read me the riot act. If you knew Marilyn, you'd know that I had to do something … I was terrified of Marilyn."

A woman with an Irish lilt still left from her birthplace, Reid doesn't look as though she has been terrified of anyone, anywhere. But she swears Marilyn goaded her into action. And that Marilyn—even way back in 1971, before anyone was doing anything about it—had a plan. "She laid it all out. She had a very clear vision. She wanted to provide this service, a wonderful service" for women and children fleeing an abusive home, Reid said.

Marilyn told Reid how hard it was for women in this situation to break free, to find work, to support their families. She talked about opening a house where they could stay, where they could help each other, where they could receive help from others finding training or a job and economic independence. And where they would be safe from harm. "I listened to her and I thought at the time…. Nobody's ever hit me or hurt me," Reid said.

Ideas like that cost money, and Marilyn had none. But she knew Maggie was good at getting things, and Maggie knew that was true. "I was a (city) project officer and I knew how to get money." So the conversation continued, and it was fierce. "Marilyn was not, she wasn't endearing, you know what I mean? A bit like a pitbull," Reid said. "Once she got on to you, you were done. She said 'so are you going to do anything or not?' and I said 'yeah, OK.'"

And then in 1972, in one of those serendipitous moments that change the world, Marilyn saw a sign. It read: "Want to do something for women in distress? If you're interested in forming a women's shelter, please come to this meeting."

Joice Guspie saw that poster, too. Guspie was a self-described "dope-smoking hippie" in her 20s, walking by the Women's Place at 31 Dupont Street—another federally funded feminist centre that opened in the early 1970s—when she saw it. She knew she had to sign up. And she knew why. She was haunted by an encounter with a battered woman that had happened a year or two prior, just outside her rooming house.

"She was freaked out, scared, and running from her husband. I knew I wanted to help her and I didn't know how. Finally, I called the police—I thought, they're the good guys, right? And the look on her face. I will never forget the look on her face when they took her away. She looked so betrayed. She knew the police would probably just call her husband. They probably ended up taking her home. I kept on telling her it would be OK. And my heart just sank because I knew it wasn't going to be OK. I betrayed her—but I really didn't know what else to do. When I saw that message on the board, I thought: This is what I need to do."

Darlene Lawson saw the sign at the Women's Place, where she had just begun hanging out. With its strong core of feminist founders, the centre was a singularly safe place for Toronto's gay women. Lawson was a 21-year-old sociology student and fledgling feminist [...]. "I was also at the very beginning of coming out as a lesbian," she said. "And the Women's Place was the only place that I knew of in the city to meet other women who were lesbian … so I roamed around there a little bit, didn't know anyone, extremely nervous and didn't know what I was doing with my life at this point. But it was all very exciting

at the same time. There was so much happening. It was such a vibrant time. When I saw the little sign on the bulletin board, it was like, OK, this is political and this is about women so it sounds good."

Darlene roped in four of her friends, all U of T students who shared a house with her at the time: Kate Hanson, Suzanne Alexanderson, Martha Ireland and Christine Poulter. The house was on Amelia Street, and Darlene's group of young, single, smart feminists were soon dubbed the "Amelia Street Mafia" by the rest of the fledgling group.

And then there was Barbara (Billie) Stone. Billie was recruited by her friend and colleague Maggie one day while on a break at 12 Madison, an addiction research foundation. Married with three children, and a decade older than these 20-something activists, Billie became somewhat of an Earth mother to the Amelia Street gang.

Billie thinks Maggie was the major impetus behind the group that straggled into the Dupont Street women's organizing centre that night in 1972, because she was so well-connected and charismatic. And Maggie credits Marilyn with the vision and the passion to start something new.

But in the end, the signs for the first battered women's shelter in Canada all point to a young feminist named Lynn Zimmer. "I put up the sign(s), and all these women showed up," Lynn said simply. She was 24, a Loyola College Communications Arts grad who had spent two years in newsroom purgatory working—and determinedly trying to revamp—the "women's section" of the *Peterborough Examiner* before trying out Osgoode Hall Law School in Toronto in 1971. She lasted a year. "It was the first year they had a significant number of women enrolled; 50 of us out of 300," she said, adding with a laugh, "There was definitely no feminist content. I remember one course that was so vile—it was Evidence, and the professor used to entertain us by having one 'really funny' sexual assault case every class. And of course I'd have to get up and say things and everybody would say—oh there she goes again!" [...]

[Zimmer] stopped attending the classes she hated and flunked. And she started volunteering at the Women's Place. But even there, she was restless. "It was a hotbed of women being mad about everything," she quipped. "[...] I kind of reached the point where I was sick of being mad about everything. I think I just needed something practical to do." The eldest in a Catholic family of eight, Zimmer started to look around for something that needed to be done.

"We had all these women calling (the Women's Place) and saying, could they come and stay? The story always seemed to be similar—I've got to get out of here. I went to welfare, but I can't get welfare if I don't have an address. And I can't get a place because I don't have any money." The only spots the centre could send them to were an overnight shelter for street women and a multipurpose place on Dundas Street that had "World War One veterans on the ground floor, and families on the other," Zimmer shudders. "It was just a horrible, classic shelter. The part that scandalized us the most was you had to line up for a bar of soap. That just totally put us over the edge."

She resolved to build something better. And made a little sign to recruit other women to the cause. And along came the Amelia Street gang led by Darlene, Joice, and the older, savvier women of the west-end—Maggie, Marilyn and Billie. [...]

As the group started to meet faithfully every week through the summer and fall of 1972, their vision became quite clear: to offer a temporary home for women and children in crisis, where they could be safe, and be given the time to regroup, get the help and support they needed, and get back on their feet.

"We didn't know that violence was going to be the big issue," Zimmer said, although some suspected it might. "We definitely were very clear that this is because there were women who were married to jerks and they were trapped and they needed a place to stay." Outside the group, the language was often different. It had to be. "We were very careful," Kate Hanson remembers. "Because at the time, the whole issue of wife abuse was not at all discussed or recognized in

any way. You couldn't even raise the question, actually, because men were terrified that women were getting uppity and their rights were going to be trampled. It was very strange." If the men weren't afraid of losing their status or wives, Hanson said, they were in denial—men don't abuse their wives, who could say such a thing? "So we just talked about women and children who were in crisis and needed housing."

The vision was also, always, to run this house as a collective, with everyone sharing in decision-making, everyone sharing in the work—a true collaborative democracy. [...]

"It was for women who needed a time span to sort of think about what's next—so it was not like an overnight shelter, not just about housing, not a one-night thing," said Martha Ireland, explaining why the word *shelter* didn't suit this new concept. "That's why it was called Interval House—because it was that interval between what you left and what you were going on to." [...]

At the time, Maggie was living with a city official who steered her to about six potential contacts there (she describes Toronto's city hall in the 1970s as a fairly "incestuous" little bureaucracy, where everybody knew everyone else). They all remember the group's presentation the fall of 1972 at city hall, armed with statistics from the various social service agencies they had visited. "A bunch of us went and watched," said Hanson. "The council was extremely dubious about the whole thing—'Is there an issue? Like, why are you even doing this?'"

All have fond memories of Toronto's mayor at the time, David Crombie. "He was intelligent, outgoing, approachable," said Hanson. "He was very enthusiastic about the project, particularly after Maggie presented the statistics. [...]"

Billie Stone remembers paying Crombie a separate visit later with Suzanne Alexanderson, to ask for a city grant—armed with nothing but passion for the project they had been meeting over for almost a year, and the knowledge that the mayor's wife, Shirley, was "into" women's issues. [...] Others went cap in hand to

United Way board member Helen Marchison. "She was wonderful. She thought we were gutsy and a little bit crazy," said Zimmer. "And she persuaded them to give us a $1,200 grant to cover first and last month's rent on a house."

There was no template for this kind of venture. There were no job descriptions, no protocols, no regulations. "We'd go to ask for money, and they'd ask us things like, 'Have any of you got any experience?'" Zimmer said. "And we'd say, 'We're a group of women and we know how to look after children, we know how to operate a kitchen, we know how to run a household—and, well, that's what this is. We're just running a household for a group of women who need to be somewhere for a short period until they get their lives all lined up.'" They may have been unprepared for the role they were about to take in so many families' shattered lives—but so were the women who would soon seek refuge with them. "We were all learning together," Zimmer said. [...]

"We could have stopped, we could have not shown up for the next meeting," Guspie pointed out. "We could have said, 'We'll never get the money.'" "But it was easier," Lawson countered. "The truth is it was easier in those days to do things." It is true. Incredibly, to them, federal government money was available seemingly to any community group with a good idea through the OFY and LIP programs,[1] now in their second year and gaining national attention.

The United Way's Marchison was supportive and encouraging, and—though they didn't supply any money or resources—so were places like the Toronto YWCA, the Family Service Association and the Distress Centre. The city proved to be a relatively easy sell, with the mayor (and his wife, Shirley, Interval House founders all point out) on board. It took a few trips to convince the bureaucrats. To this day, Maggie Reid jokes that they got the house because "Marilyn was so obnoxious. We went to see this guy. Marilyn was quiet. I did my charming thing. And then she thought he wasn't moving fast enough so she just went at him. She said to him—'so don't you

care? Are you the sort of man who beats your wife?' I think he was afraid of her," she laughed, "she was just this little thing but she was so fierce. People hated her or they loved her, one or the other. He said: 'Don't worry about it. We'll make sure you have a place.'"

The city finally found them a rental house at 173 Spadina Road that needed a lot of work inside, plus some major structural and plumbing renovations just to bring it to code—most of which were done either under the table or by friends of friends. Kate Hanson assembled the LIP grant application, putting it together at night at her father's office on his electric typewriter. Lo and behold, "the whole thing worked very well because within two or three months," Hanson said, "we got the grant to fund 12 positions—and we didn't even have 12 people! It was really excellent. We got paid $100 a week ($83.50 a week, once deductions were taken out), and it lasted about six months."

That funding arrived just as this pivotal year for Canadian women dawned—January 1973. And it kicked the women of Interval House into high gear. There was so much to be done: painting, renovating, furnishing and supplying the house; raising a capital fund from anyone who might give them money; reaching out to every social agency that would listen; figuring out who would do what and when. Among their first hires were Gale Carsenat and Louise Robinson (known as Lou). Later that year they were joined by Trudy Don, who would go on to become the face of Interval House for decades.

"I remember realizing the scope was so much bigger and so much more unbelievable because nothing like this had been done before. I was like, 'I can't believe I landed here, this is amazing,'" Lawson recalled.

The furniture arrived like magic, Zimmer said. Kind of. "We used to go out on garbage night at Forest Hill to get furniture," she laughed. The rest was donated. Billie Stone can't forget the night Darlene was driving her uncle's truck with a donated stove inside, and it stalled at Church Street. "I had to jump out of the truck and stop the traffic, and we pushed it across the road, with the stove inside. But we got it there," Stone said. "I had never driven a stick shift in my life," Lawson explained calmly. "I thought I'd figure it out on the way."

"It was a real group effort, getting the money in and at the same time setting up a whole stable of experts in different areas who could help women when they came into the house," said Hanson. "We had to know who they all were, who to contact and what they could do for any given woman's crisis. Right down to medical. We had to have it all. Between all of us, we put together a fairly substantial package of contacts in the social services that could help. It was a big deal." […]

They opened their doors April 1, 1973. Media coverage was limited, at first, but the founders will never forget the first big splash in the *Toronto Star*, on July 21, 1973. Reporter Sidney Katz spent a long time with them, Zimmer remembers—"schmoozing us," according to Gale Carsenat. They were shocked and angry when his section-front article appeared under the headline "The rising wave of runaway wives." The story begins with a hapless husband discovering a "so long" note pinned to his pillow from his wife, and goes on to brand it a new social trend: "Add one more man to the brotherhood of deserted husbands, a fast-growing group."[2]

"In the past it was nearly always the man who walked away from a distasteful domestic situation," Katz wrote. "Today the runaway wife is a familiar figure to welfare, police and government officials. Sometimes the women even leave their children behind." Then he interviews a number of deserted men on how tough their lives have become. "He basically lamented the fate of the poor misunderstood husbands!" said Zimmer. "We were so mad at him," Carsenat recalled. "It was like he had stabbed us."

It takes Katz eight paragraphs before he finally explains why the wife in his lead paragraph has decided to leave her distressed husband: his emotional abuse, escalating drinking problem and finally a physical assault ("The night before she left he had slapped her across the face while the couple next door were visiting"). He also mentions another "runaway" who left after she was thrown downstairs for forgetting to send her husband's suit to the cleaners. But he ends the article focusing on the plight of "the deserted fathers" who are struggling to find efficient housekeepers to replace their runaway wives. "I've been living this way for eight months," he quotes one newly abandoned dad, "and it's hell."

Forty years later, a few of the Interval House founders get together for drinks and dinner and every one of them remembers that article. They laugh about it now. At this same event, they hear that they were Canada's first battered women's shelter. "We thought we were first," Zimmer said with quiet satisfaction. "I always knew there was something out west that was really close, so I always figured like, let's not contest it, let's just say it was a spontaneous combustion thing and it just spread like wildfire. Because in our way, we each were the first, we didn't copy each other, we just did it. We had no idea how revolutionary it was," she added. "We thought it was exciting. But we really had no idea."

The names on their document of incorporation are Lynn Zimmer, Suzanne Alexanderson, Martha Ireland, Joice Guspie, Katherine Hanson, Maggie May (O'Brien) Longdon, Elizabeth Johnson, Marilyn Tinsley, Christine Poulter, Darlene Lawson and Barbara (Billie) Stone.

And Zimmer is right. Though many women's groups were struggling at the time to create places like Interval House, there really was some kind of social spontaneous combustion going on. An awakening, of sorts, combined with the right political climate. Canada's second state-funded shelter, by a nose, was a little house that got its grant approved in May 1973 and opened weeks later in a farming community smack dab in British Columbia's Bible Belt. The neighbourhood would never be the same again.

## NOTES

1.  OFY (Opportunities for Youth) and LIP (Local Initiatives Project) were federally funded jobs creation programs in the 1970s that funded many community organizations and initiatives.

2.  Katz, Sidney. "The Rising Wave of Runaway Wives: 'Women Are Liberating Themselves—They Say to Heck with It and Leave.'" *Toronto Star*, July 21, 1973.

*Source:* Goodhand, Margo. (2017). Excerpted from "Chapter 6: Toronto and the Runaway Wives." In *Runaway Wives and Rogue Feminists: The Origins of the Women's Shelter Movement in Canada* (pp. 49–59). Black Point, NS: Fernwood.

# CHAPTER 56

## The Ultimate Rape Victim

*Jane Doe*

The woman known as Jane Doe is an internationally recognized anti-rape writer, lecturer, and arts and culture worker. She successfully sued the Toronto Police for negligence and gender discrimination in the investigation of her rape, and subsequently changed Canadian law. In her acclaimed book, *Story of Jane Doe: A Book about Rape*, she positions sexual assault within the context of equity issues and integrates issues of race, immigration, colonialism, queerphobia, and sex work into her analysis. The Jane Doe case is widely cited in Canadian law textbooks and is studied in law schools internationally.

*I don't really know how to be a raped woman.* I didn't in 1986 and I don't today. I just have never completely figured it out. Being a raped woman has come to define me in some ways, but I struggle still to understand and define it personally, as opposed to the stereotypes. But I own those too. Trauma and despair have been mine. Depression and pain have marked me. Yet there is more. And less.

A raped woman is framed socially and within the law as something broken. Neither Madonna nor whore, but somewhere in between. The carrier of bad luck. There is a general but grudging acceptance that it isn't really her fault, but if she had done something else, gone in another direction, not had that drink or worn that dress or smiled that way, it might never have happened. And thank God it wasn't me or anyone I love. If it had to happen to someone, thank-you-God it was her.

Raped women make other people uncomfortable. Try talking about your rape with friends, at a dinner party or with family. The subject jump-starts every socialized and biological instinct to protect, to seek revenge, to contain, to minimize or to deny that the human psyche stores. The nature of these responses requires the woman to carefully select, when, to whom and how she will recount her experience. Or to decide if she should or can recount it at all. Ever.

Raped women are fallen women. Pushed really, but the shame is on them. A stain like original sin, not of their making but never to be removed or forgotten. Raped women cannot display their rage or joy or sexuality. They cannot be glamorous or successful or funny. They certainly cannot be agents of social and political change.

There are many reasons for this present and historical construction of the woman who has been raped. They are as intricate as political systems, as revered as sacraments.

\*\*\*\*\*

I have never allowed anyone to refer to me as a *rape victim*. Certainly for the time that buddy held a knife to my throat I was his victim and I cannot deny that. But every time that term is used to define me, I feel I am returned to that moment, that night of terror and helplessness. Nor am I fond of the label *survivor*. Like everyone else, I was already surviving the normal pain and hardships of life before I was raped, thank you very much. "Okay. So what do we call you?" you ask. Call me a woman. Call me a woman who has been raped. Call me a woman who has been raped by a man.

Rape victims are supposed to be helpless. We require assistance and must play a passive role while the good men, the police, lawyers and judges, punish the one, isolated bad man who committed the crime. Mass media reflect on and report their version of the raped or beaten woman as victim. Rape victims are othered, viewed as less than normal, unraped people. The term, its use and purpose, is not particular to the legal system and its players or the media. It is commonly used by members of the medical and helping professions as well, and by feminists.

A more appropriate language to describe these crimes of violence was developed by feminists during the seventies and eighties but has been all but forgotten. Look at terms like *wife assault*, *partner assault*, *domestic violence* and *family abuse*. Statistics overwhelmingly support the fact that these crimes are committed by men against women and children. And yet the language we use is gender-neutral. Listening to it, one could logically assume that the wife or partner had assaulted herself, that the children of the family were fighting with or abusing each other and that the violence referred to was homegrown as opposed to imported.

Not so long ago, women working in rape crisis centres and shelters developed language that identified the nature and perpetrator of the crime. Meaning men. Rape is about men. *Male violence* and *violence against women* were the terms we used. After a few years of this, and as we began to work with legal, social and

government systems in the hope of effecting change, after we accepted their money to pay our wages and signed on the dotted line of institutional bureaucracy, we were requested to alter our language, to cut back on the perceived "rhetoric" so as not to alienate or hurt the feelings of the men who were sensitive to our issues (and signed our cheques). The long-term effect has been the un-gendering of sexual assault. But what is its cause? What are its other components? How does it end? Who benefits? Why do men rape?

If rape hadn't existed by now, we would have invented it. The rape of women has immense economic, social and legal advantages that are seldom articulated. Put plainly, rape works. It is a tool of sexism, and like racism, it exists because it "works." Stay with me, don't go away, this gets interesting. As a white woman who is anti-racist, I work hard to understand the causes and effects of racism. I understand that I benefit socially and economically from racism, especially the systemic, institutionalized, polite form that Canada has perfected.

As a white woman, I am more employable, better paid and less fetishized than Native women or women of colour. My menfolk are not incarcerated or stopped by police at the same rate. My children are not taunted, bullied or subjected to discriminatory treatment based solely on their skin colour. I can move a little more freely, hold my head a little higher, because I am not a visible container for racial intolerance. In these ways I enjoy privilege based on my racial origin. This acknowledgement does not by itself make me a racist. It helps me to understand racism and how it works.

Similarly, men benefit in systemic and obvious ways from a society that is inherently sexist. Men earn more than women, hold more positions of power, are not responsible for the unpaid work of mothering, walk freely and are free to walk alone. They need not worry about unwanted pregnancies, body image, aging and financial security with anywhere near the same intensity as women. They do not consciously fear the stranger rapist or feel compelled to monitor the actions of strange women around them. They are not taught at a very early age that there is a damned good chance they will experience a form of male violence staved off only by their lifelong vigilance and the curtailing of certain actions, pleasures and freedoms they might otherwise enjoy.[1]

In Canada, the government statistics are that one in four men would rape if given the opportunity. This is unacceptable, frightening, outrageously high. But let's flip that stat for a moment and look at the inverse proposition: three out of four men would not rape. Indeed there are many more good men than bad. Where are they? What are they doing to address the rapes of their mothers, daughters, sisters and wives? How do I differentiate them from the bad guys? Sure, they're against rape, but do they understand the ways in which it maintains their privileged status as males? If rape is an extreme tool of sexism used to maintain the male status quo, doesn't it work for all men?

In lectures I have given, this is where good men redden, their brows furrow and they start to disengage. They don't understand and they ask what they can do, what they should do, but mostly they want to go home. At another time—and appropriately so—I might have said, "Read a book. Don't expect me to take responsibility for your consciousness-raising." But this is what I say here: It's hard to be a man. I shouldn't like to try it.

Men are still socialized from a very young age that to be emotional, delicate or tender is to be a girl, and that that is the worst they can be. They must not cry or play with nurture-based toys or wear pastels. They are overwhelmed with male images that drive cars, leave the house for the majority of the day, and return only to mete out discipline and to enjoy the labour of the more home-based female parent. Traditional family values do not require that men prepare food, clean, organize, schedule or provide health care at the same level as women or at all. Their leisure pursuits are sports or technology-based, their literacy level is lower than girls', their demonstrative signs of affection limited.

Our baby boys, whom we love and cherish and who are born to us free from malice or ill will, are conditioned to understand human sexuality as singular to their individual wants and needs, to translate "bitch" and "ho" as labels of both affection and contempt, to mistrust anything that "bleeds for five days every month and doesn't die," and to appreciate "gay," "faggot" and "queer" as variations of the greatest, most final insult of all.

A good friend of mine, a man who is sweet, smart and pro-feminist, has pointed out in more than one conversation about the meaning of life that his instinct, his motivation, is to follow his dick. To be true to it. I have challenged him on this, suggested that perhaps these are not quite the words he is reaching for when he discusses his life. But he stands firm, and I retreat, fearful that he really means what I think he means. Fearful that I really do—or don't—understand men and the cultural divide that distances them from me.

Every few decades and recently so, the tired sociological saw that men are biologically predetermined to rape is dressed up and trotted out to explain the eternal and rising incidence of the crime.[2] Women are cautioned to govern themselves accordingly given that the boys simply can't help it. The books, articles, columns that tooth the saw are well received and become the subject of circular logic and debate. What I cannot understand, am fascinated by, is that men themselves do not rebel against such a limited definition of their ethos and are not insulted by their group equation to molluscs and amphibian life.

*Good men don't do it. Our men don't do it.* What to make of the fact that 75 to 80 per cent of reported rapes are committed by men known to the women involved. The woman has no problem making an identification. The lighting is fine. She can provide you with her rapist's address and any other identifying information you could imagine. Some you could not. There is no need for a profile, criminal, geographic or artistic. Computer experts, criminologists, DNA and forensic scientists are not called in. They will not be part of the investigation into a crime that escalates yearly and has the lowest reporting rate of all violent crimes. That job goes to the uniformed officer who catches the 911 call or takes the report at the station. That officer has received a maximum of five days' training in a workshop called Family Violence, which blends the rape and sexual assault of adult women with similar crimes of violence committed against youth and children. The training is delivered by other police officers. A rape victim may talk about how well her assault was investigated, she might chide (never challenge) or horrify the cadets to attention with her story. The necessity for adequate diversity training to assist these young men in sexual-assault investigation—which cops themselves will tell you is the most murky and difficult crime to investigate—is ignored. Directives to increase the numbers of women and non-white police force applicants have failed or fallen far short of their projected marks.

Instead, increasingly significant portions of police budgets are designated for the purchase, maintenance and upgrading of computer technology to investigate and solve crime. VICAP and VICLAS, the systems used in Canada and the United States, are compatible with European and other international policing instruments. They are effective in dealing with international espionage, corporate and white-collar crimes, and auto, credit card or jewellery theft rings. And that's a good thing. Their efficacy in infiltrating prostitution, sex trade, pornography and child abuse networks is heralded by law enforcement officers. I'm sure they have been helpful in other violent crimes. But if you have not been raped by a stranger or an "anger retaliatory rapist" (who constitute only 25 per cent of the rapist population), your crime will not be compatible with computer technology. These tools and the information they store are based on faulty conclusions about empirical evidence. Which means they can be as racist and as sexist as the agents who design and interpret them. Only now they get to call profiling "science," so it acquires a whole new, if undeserved, credibility.

In the majority of rape cases, consent is the issue. The accused has agreed that there was sexual intercourse but it was, he swears, consensual. If the woman involved has prior activity that registers on the VICLAS system, it is used against her in a court of law. For instance, if the woman involved was raped before or if she did time for a crime she did or did not commit. If in the past she was apprehended by police under the Mental Health Act,[3] if she was hospitalized for postpartum depression or protested against government policies resulting in police apprehension, or if she whored to pay for college or drugs, fled her country of origin because of police abuse or was part of a Native roadblock, it will show up in a VICLAS search. (If you don't believe that this kind of information is collected and stored and available for some to access, take the time to file an Access to Information Act application on yourself. There is probably a file with your name on it.) Next, an "expert" witness will be hired to testify that you are a slut, addict, terrorist, deviant or other form of miscreant, and your rapist is free to rape you again or otherwise complicate your life. Actually, it probably won't even get as far as the expert-witness scenario because the rapist's lawyer can ask questions to elicit the information himself, or he can get it through his own computer search and not even have to pay for expert medical testimony.

One of the things we need if we are to encourage women to report is increased and ongoing training and education on rape and other crimes of violence committed against women by men, delivered by women who are professionals in the area, meaning women who work in shelters and rape crisis centres. This will only happen through police policy and operational changes in law enforcement practices. Changes that will also benefit policing. Changes that women have been suggesting globally. For decades.

Women who work in anti-violence, who write about it and educate others and have first hand experience of it, are the experts in the field of rape—not some Eliot Ness clone or computer nerd with a PhD. Hire us. And by the way, we will expect to be paid for our work.[4] The escalating focus on "stranger danger" by police through the media and with the assistance of so-called victim's rights groups has worked to maintain a climate of fear that ensures a large degree of control over how and where women live. Current warnings issued by police to alert communities of a serial rapist are fear-based and hysterical in language and nature. Instead of factual warnings that give us information about the dangerous men in our midst, they issue "don'ts" directed toward women, the people most at risk. The don'ts include:

Don't go out alone. Don't go out alone at night. Don't go out alone or at night unless accompanied by someone (male). Don't open the windows. Don't open the doors. Lock the windows and doors. Don't talk to strangers (men). Don't assist strangers (men). Don't take shortcuts. Alternate your daily routine and routes to work or school. Don't take elevators by yourself (or with strange men). Monitor the motions of the men around you. Don't ride the bus alone. Don't get off the bus alone. Leave your lights on. Don't use underground parking. Don't park on the street. Walk in pairs. Walk on the road. Walk down the middle of the road. Carry a cellphone. Don't struggle. Don't resist. Don't fight back. Don't arm yourself. Eat grass.

*Hey! We already don't do those things!* Tell us something we don't know. Give us adequate information that does not interfere with your investigation. Give us dates, times, locations, any description you might have, and let us work in community to craft solutions and to support you and each other.

And stop using the fear of strange men to deflect the bigger problems of sexual assault, beatings and other inhumane atrocities committed against us by men we know.

A lot of women have told me that they think it would be "worse" to be raped by a stranger than by a man you know. Personally, I think that in the larger sexual-assault lottery, I lucked out by being raped by a stranger.

For one thing, I was not assaulted by someone I loved or trusted or otherwise chose to let into my life. I did not have to deal with that level of emotional betrayal. For another, there was never any question of consent or introducing my past sexual history during the rapist's trial. Oh, his lawyer would have done it—in fact, there is even a pamphlet called "Whack the Sexual Assault Complainant at Preliminary Hearing," which advises defence lawyers on how to get women's past sexual history introduced at trial. Defence lawyer Michael Edelson wrote (originally in an article published in a professional journal called *Lawyers Weekly* in May 1988):

You have to go in there as defence counsel and whack the complainant hard … get all the medical evidence; get the Children's Aid Society records … and you've got to attack with all you've got so that he or she will say, "I'm not coming back."

The fact that I was raped by a stranger who was a serial offender with a history of identical crimes actually worked in my favour in court. It predisposed the police and the courts to believe that I was telling the truth and not making a false allegation. As a result, there was no legal basis to introduce my sexual history. (I did not dream that it or my medical and family histories would become issues in my civil trial twelve years later. In fact, if I had known it would come to that, I probably would not have proceeded.)

It is easier (but not a foregone conclusion) for the courts to establish lack of consent if the rapist is a stranger. The justice system is less likely to think or believe that you agreed to sex and then changed your mind or just made the whole thing up to get attention. It should be relatively safe to assume that if a strange guy has a knife at your throat, the issue of consent is not to be debated.[5]

Mind you, if you change the picture just a bit and make the man with the knife at your throat your husband, boyfriend or date, well maybe he thought you liked it that way because he'd done it before and you didn't call the police that time, or it was just a little fantasy so he's not guilty. Not really. If he doesn't have a weapon but hurts you with his hands or threatens to, drops something in your drink or withholds money or food or shelter unless you succumb, then your consent does become the issue. The only issue that matters. The fact that you had prior sexual relations with him (or others), had been sexually assaulted before, consumed drinks or drugs that night (or ever), the very fact that you knew him can be used against you in a court of law to raise doubt about your consent and to determine that he is not guilty.

And they wonder why more women don't report….

## NOTES

1. Again, the incidence of male-on-male violence is high and rising. Young men today, especially youth of colour, think twice about walking alone at night. Their mothers certainly worry about it. The subject I am addressing, however, is the rape and sexual assault of adult women by adult men, and how that works as a tool of sexism.
2. *A Natural History of Rape: Biological Basis of Sexual Coercion,* by Randy Thornhill and Craig T. Palmer (2000), is the most recent manifesto of this sort.
3. The Mental Health Act gives police the authority to arrest and incarcerate individuals they deem to be mentally ill who are held (but not charged) until the diagnosis is confirmed. The record of the arrest is permanent.
4. The point of payment for work done by professional women who consult with police departments on rape or wife assault is one of the hottest hot-button issues I have encountered in my work as Jane Doe. Even other women working in the area take issue with it, claiming it will further alienate police. Since 1975 anti-violence workers in Toronto have left their paid work to sit on panels and committees or go to meetings with police without financial reimbursement for wages and time lost. And to no effect. Would consultants on helicopter use and purchase or stun-gun efficacy in crime fighting work for free? Should they? The practice of not paying people for their work results in that work being undervalued or ignored. Not to mention poverty.
5. The film *The Accused*, starring Jodie Foster and based on a true story, is an example of the courts believing that a woman consented to a gang rape by strangers, even though she was sure she did not. We need not go as far as Hollywood to find examples. In Canada see *Regina v. Wald, Hockett and Girt*, Alberta Court of Appeal and *Regina v. Sansregret*, Supreme Court of Canada.

*Source:* Doe, Jane. (2003). Excerpted from *The Story of Jane Doe: A Book about Rape* (pp. 118–128). Toronto, ON: Random House Canada.

## ACTIVIST INSIGHT: 10 THINGS MEN CAN DO TO PREVENT GENDER VIOLENCE

*Jackson Katz*

Jackson Katz is internationally renowned for his groundbreaking scholarship and activism on issues of gender, race, and violence. He has long been a major figure and thought leader in the growing global movement of men working to promote gender equality and prevent gender violence. Katz is the creator, lead writer, and narrator of the award-winning *Tough Guise* documentary series about American manhood, media, and violence. He is the author of two books: *The Macho Paradox: Why Some Men Hurt Women and How All Men Can Help* and *Man Enough? Donald Trump, Hillary Clinton and the Politics of Presidential Masculinity.*

1. Approach gender violence as a *men's* issue involving men of all ages and socioeconomic, racial, and ethnic backgrounds. View men not only as perpetrators or possible offenders, but as empowered bystanders who can confront abusive peers.

2. If a brother, friend, classmate, or teammate is abusing his female partner—or is disrespectful or abusive to girls and women in general—don't look the other way. If you feel comfortable doing so, try to talk to him about it. Urge him to seek help. Or if you don't know what to do, consult a friend, a parent, a professor, or a counselor. *Don't remain silent.*

3. Have the courage to look inward. Question your own attitudes. Don't be defensive when something you do or say ends up hurting someone else. Try hard to understand how your own attitudes and actions might inadvertently perpetuate sexism and violence, and work toward changing them.

4. If you suspect that a woman close to you is being abused or has been sexually assaulted, gently ask if you can help.

5. If you are emotionally, psychologically, physically, or sexually abusive to women, or have been in the past, seek professional help *now*.

6. Be an ally to women who are working to end all forms of gender violence. Support the work of campus-based women's centers. Attend "Take Back the Night" rallies and other public events. Raise money for community-based rape crisis centers and battered women's shelters. If you belong to a team or fraternity, or another student group, organize a fundraiser.

7. Recognize and speak out against homophobia and gay-bashing. Discrimination and violence against LGBTQ people are wrong in and of themselves. This abuse also has direct links to sexism—e.g., the

sexual orientation of men who speak out against sexism is often questioned, a conscious or unconscious strategy intended to silence them. This is a key reason few men do speak out.

8. Attend programs, take courses, watch films, and read articles and books about multicultural masculinities, gender inequality, and the root causes of gender violence. Educate yourself and others about how larger social forces affect the conflicts between individual men and women.

9. Don't fund sexism. Refuse to purchase any magazine, rent any video, subscribe to any website, or buy any music that portrays girls or women in a sexually degrading or abusive manner. Speak out about cyber-sexism and misogynist attacks against women on social media sites such as Facebook, Twitter, and Tumblr. Protest sexism in new and old media.

10. Mentor and teach young boys about how to be men in ways that don't involve degrading or abusing girls and women (or men). Volunteer to work with gender violence-prevention programs, including anti-sexist men's programs. Lead by example.

---

*Source:* Katz, Jackson. (2013). Adapted from "10 Things Men Can Do to Prevent Gender Violence." *MVP Strategies*. Retrieved from: http://www.mvpstrat.com/resources/downloadable-tools/.

# CHAPTER 57

## Digital Defense: Black Feminists Resist Violence with Hashtag Activism

*Sherri Williams*

Sherri Williams is an assistant professor in the School of Communication at American University in Washington, DC. Her research interests are located at the intersection of social media, social justice, reality television, and mass media, and how people of colour use and are represented by these mediums. Williams has been interviewed by many prominent media outlets including *CNN*, *USA Today*, *Smithsonian Magazine*, and *Vice*.

Jada's sixteen-year-old half-clothed body was sprawled across the carpeted floor: eyes closed, mouth open, genitals exposed with one leg extended and the other slightly bent. Photos of the black high school student's body spread through social media after her alleged rape. People mocked her by photographing themselves lying on the floor with their legs bent and they posted those pictures with the hashtag #JadaPose. Quickly after those demeaning photos spread, Jada's alleged rape went viral in July 2014 after feminists responded with a bevy of supportive hashtags: #StandWithJada, #JusticeForJada, #JadaCounterPose, #SupportJada. A photo of Jada holding a sign with the hashtag #IAmJada in one hand and a raised clenched fist with the other circulated through social media. The violence committed against Jada became a spectacle on social media but it was also a catalyst for black feminists to move to use Twitter to combat the sexual brutalization that black women and girls have experienced throughout history.

Hashtags, especially on Twitter, have emerged as an effective way to share information and spur action about a demographic that seems to get little support from its nation—black women. Social media hashtags bring attention to black women's issues when traditional mainstream media newspaper articles and television stories ignore black women's concerns as they have for decades. Twitter is an important tool to inform the public of violence against black women because it enables anti-violence advocates to connect with the public and one another in real time without relying on the traditional news cycle or the mainstream media's problematic framing of sexual violence and black women. After Jada's alleged sexual assault became public, her case did not gain the same national media attention as the female teenage rape survivor in Steubenville, Ohio, who appeared to be white in online photos and whose rape was also mocked and displayed on social media. For Jada, there were no extensive stories broadcast on national news or segments with pundits and white feminists speaking on her behalf. When white feminists miss opportunities to stand with their black sisters and mainstream media overlooks the plight of nonwhite women, women of color use social media as a tool to unite and inform. Before national mainstream and online news media outlets reported on Jada, black feminists on social media were front and center spreading information about her.

In 1968 the final report of the National Advisory Commission on Civil Disorders, or Kerner Commission as it was informally known (named after the Commission's Chair, Governor Otto Kerner Jr.), identified the media as contributing to protests that erupted in the United States during the 1960s. Specifically, the report suggested that the mainstream media failed to show the nation the complexities and realities of black life. Now, almost fifty years after the Commission's report, media scholars continue to find that portrayals of people of color have not changed a great deal. Images of black criminality still dominate news coverage and white men maintain leadership positions in newsrooms (Carolyn Byerly and Clint C. Wilson 2009). Also, the progress gained for black reporters in mainstream newsrooms has been crushed in recent years. Between 1997 and 2013 almost 1,200 black journalists in daily newspaper newsrooms lost their jobs (Monica Anderson 2014).

Research consistently shows that black women sexual assault survivors have to fight not only their assailants when attacked, but also persistently racist stereotypes about their womanhood while seeking justice; they are judged by gendered and racialized stereotypes and not their individual actions (Kimberlé W. Crenshaw 1991). The negative images that circulate about black women render them as "not newsworthy" by many mainstream news organizations.

The way that black women sexual assault survivors are treated in the courtroom and the newsroom is another form of violence. The symbolic annihilation, the complete absence or trivialization in the media, of assaults against black women and girls mutes their

abuse, makes it invisible and erases their humanity thereby further violating black women and girls and inflicting more pain on them.

Black feminists' use of social media fills the gap in national media coverage of black women's issues, from the ways that race and gender affect the wage gap to the disproportionate amount of violence committed against black transgender women. Black Twitter often engages in critical discussions about gender and its impact on equity and liberation (Jamilah Lemieux 2014). During President Barack Obama's 2014 State of the Union address, black feminists on Twitter noted the absence of legislation that could help black women economically and politically using #BlackFeministFuture. After President Obama announced his "My Brother's Keeper" initiative to help young men of color advance, black feminists noted the need to help black girls now and not later with #WhyWeCantWait. Once the story of Renisha McBride, a nineteen-year-old black woman who was fatally shot in the face near Detroit after she knocked on a white man's door for help, faded from the national news cycle, black feminists kept her story alive on social media with #RememberRenisha. The #FreeCeCe hashtag was used to bring attention to the case of black transgender woman CeCe McDonald who said she defended herself against a violent trans-phobic and racist attack that led to her manslaughter conviction. Months before hashtags supporting Jada emerged, black feminists used #FastTailedGirls to create a discussion about the hypersexualization of black girls and the dismissal of sexual attacks against them. That important conversation about black girls garnered seven million online impressions (Lemieux 2014).

Black Twitter's use of hashtags prompts the black social media community to recognize issues and respond to them. Moreover, hashtags reflect Black Twitter's opinion on social issues (André Brock 2012). Women and black Americans dominate social networks: 76 percent of women who are online use social media (Pew Research Center 2014) and blacks are

29 percent of online adults who use Twitter, more than any other racial group (Maeve Duggan and Aaron Smith 2013). Black women use Twitter more than any other demographic group (Aaron Smith 2014). Black feminists' use of hashtag activism is a unique fusion of social justice, technology and citizen journalism. It should serve as a fertile ground for emerging news for journalists, a point of connection for white feminists and a ripe area of study for academics. Twitter is often a site of resistance where black feminists challenge violence committed against women of color and they leverage the power of Black Twitter to bring attention and justice to women who rarely receive either.

## REFERENCES

Anderson, Monica. 2014. "As News Business Takes a Hit, the Number of Black Journalists Declines." Pew Research Center. Accessed August 1, 2014. http://www.pewresearch.org/fact-tank/2014/08/01/as-news-business-takes-a-hit-the-number-of-black-journalists-declines/.

Brock, André. 2012. "From the Blackhand Side: Twitter as a Cultural Conversation." *Journal of Broadcasting & Electronic Media* 56 (4): 529–549.

Byerly, Carolyn M., and Clint C. Wilson. 2009. "Journalism as Kerner Turns 40: Its Multicultural Problems and Possibilities." *Howard Journal of Communications* 20 (3): 209–221.

Crenshaw, Kimberlé W. 1991. "Mapping the Margins: Intersectionality, Identity Politics and Violence against Women of Color." *Stanford Law Review* 43 (6): 1241–1299.

Duggan, Maeve, and Aaron Smith. 2013. "Social Media Update 2013." December 30. Pew Research Center. Accessed December 30, 2013. http://pewinternet.org/Reports/2013/Social-Media-Update.aspx.

Lemieux, Jamilah. 2014. "Black Feminism Goes Viral." *Ebony Magazine* 69 (5): 126–131.

Pew Research Center. 2014. "Social Networking Fact Sheet." January. Accessed January 6, 2014. http://www.pewinternet.org/fact-sheets/social-networking-fact-sheet/.

Smith, Aaron. 2014. "African Americans and Technology Use." Pew Research Internet Project. Accessed January 6, 2014. http://www.pewinternet.org/2014/01/06/african-americans-and-technology-use/.

*Source:* Williams, Sherri. (2015). "Digital Defense: Black Feminists Resist Violence with Hashtag Activism." *Feminist Media Studies, 15*(2), 341–344.

# CHAPTER 58

## More Than a Poster Campaign: Redefining Colonial Violence

*Sarah Hunt*

Sarah Hunt is an assistant professor in the First Nations and Indigenous Studies Program and Department of Geography at the University of British Columbia. She is Kwagiulth (Kwakwaka'wakw) from Tsaxis, and has spent most of her life as a guest in Lkwungen territories. Hunt is a community-based researcher with a particular focus on issues facing women, girls, and two-spirit people. Her scholarship in Indigenous and legal geographies critically takes up questions of justice, gender, self-determination, and the spatiality of Indigenous law. Hunt's writing has been published in numerous books and scholarly journals, as well as in popular media outlets such as mediaINDIGENA. com, decolonization.org, and op-eds for the *Globe and Mail* and the CBC.

Nineteen years ago, when I started my undergraduate degree, I was introduced to Indigenous women's writing for the first time. Until then, the words in my own personal journal were the only reflections of Indigenous women's lives available to me. Reading the stories of Lee Maracle, Jeanette Armstrong, Beth Brant, Patricia Monture-Angus, and others, I was struck by both the prevalence of violence in their lives and the strength of resistance to this violence. Their stories of resilience sprung off the page, transforming moments of shame and silence into ones of strength and survival. After a family member took her own life, these stories inspired me to focus on issues of violence in our communities, and I've taken my direction from this calling ever since.

Over the years, much has changed in how violence against women is talked about. With the emergence of a discourse around 'the missing women', gendered violence is being recognized as a widespread reality in our homes, schools, cities, and streets. The conviction of a serial killer in Vancouver's downtown east side solidified the reality that our aunties have been preyed upon for far too long. But in talking with other Indigenous people across Turtle Island, I know the daily reality of interpersonal violence continues despite this increased awareness. After close to 20 years of talking about this issue, what unsettles me the most is the similarity of stories from girls in small towns and large cities, in urban centers and remote villages. Across this land, our daughters continue to be targeted for physical, mental, and emotional abuse on a daily basis, by people from both inside and outside our communities. Something needs to change in our strategies to stop this violence.

Colonialism relies on the widespread dehumanization of all Indigenous people—our children, two-spirits, men, and women—so colonial violence could be understood to impact all of us at the level of our denied humanity. Yet this dehumanization is felt most acutely in the bodies of Indigenous girls, women, two-spirit, and transgender people, as physical and sexual violence against us continues to be accepted as normal.

Our strategies to name gendered violence can themselves become part of the problem, as the language of 'the missing women' masks the brutal reality of how they become 'missing'. Girls and women don't simply disappear—they are beaten, murdered, kidnapped, violated, and raped. The language of 'bullying' in our schools also serves to mask the nature of this violence, which is not simply about online taunts or threats but about targeted assaults. It may be more palatable to use softer language to raise awareness, but, as the girls in our communities can tell us, the realities we're trying to change are anything but soft. We're fighting for our lives here, as our aunties and grandmas have been doing since colonialism began.

News stories of girls being killed or kidnapped continue to surface momentarily on the local newspaper and radio, without any follow up or outrage. Our 'disappearance' is still easily dismissed as mere blips on the radar of most Canadians. And, as those of us working with families and communities know, many more daily incidents of violence go untold, unheard, or unnoticed. Despite the national Stolen Sisters campaign, local marches, vigils, and other events to remember girls and women who've been killed, our efforts have yet to change the acceptance of daily violence enacted on the bodies of our loved ones.

Many of the strategies to address violence have further strengthened broad systems of colonial power, which are themselves inherently violent. We continue

to appeal to the Canadian legal system to address physical violence, calling for more policing or better laws, while knowing this system is set up to oppress, rather than help, us. The same colonial mentality that created the Indian Act to privilege the rights of men over women, and instituted residential schools to break down our family systems, serves as the foundation for the Canadian legal system. Surely we must engage with this powerful system, but appealing to law alone will not stop the violence.

So how do we begin to change norms around gendered violence without reinforcing its roots in colonial power? As we strategize, we must be careful not to reproduce the systems and ideologies that colonialism has introduced. Sexist, racist, and homophobic ideas have been internalized at many levels, but colonialism's stealthy ways make them hard to recognize.

As an example, one consequence of developing broad public awareness about the prevalence of violence against Indigenous women has been the privileging of some women's voices over others. Moving from Vancouver's downtown east side to offices in Ottawa and other urban centers across Turtle Island, efforts to name gendered violence have shifted from grassroots discussions to slick poster campaigns. In these moves, certain voices have been left behind, enacting a form of silencing that I believe is in crucial need of reparation. Rather than calling on our sisters in the sex trade to speak for themselves, others are asked to speak on their behalf. We must ask ourselves how colonial values continue to shape whose voices are seen as legitimate, while working to center the voices of the most marginalized women in our communities rather than only those of us with a colonial education.

So colonial violence can be understood as more than just interpersonal abuse—it is inherent in the systems that have shaped how we define ourselves and relate to one another as Indigenous people. It should go without saying that healing from violence requires rebuilding our individual and collective strength rather than reinforcing the power of the state. By centering local Indigenous knowledge in our understandings of leadership, honor, strength, and love, we can redefine 'power' as well as 'violence'. This requires relearning our stories and our cultural teaching in order to raise up the girls in our communities and respect them as leaders, mothers, warriors, and knowledge keepers.

Transforming our dehumanization must move beyond just poster campaigns and court cases, because their ability to enact change only goes so far. I believe it is only through building stronger relationships with one another, across the generations and across differences in education, ability, sexuality, and other social locations, that we can break down the stigma and shame resulting from generations of colonial violence. As we reinstate the roles of women and two-spirit people in systems of Indigenous governance and law, ending gendered violence can be understood as integral to self-determination. In the words of the late Patricia Monture-Angus, "Self-determination is principally, that is first and foremost, about our relationships. Communities cannot be self-governing until members of those communities are well and living in a responsible way. It is difficult for individuals to be self-determining until they are living as part of their community."[1]

## NOTE

1.  Monture-Angus, Patricia. *Journeying Forward: Dreaming First Nations' Independence.* Fernwood, 1999, p. 8.

*Source:* Hunt, Sarah. (2013). "More Than a Poster Campaign: Redefining Colonial Violence." *Decolonization: Indigeneity, Education & Society Blog.* Retrieved from: https://decolonization.wordpress.com/2013/02/14/more-than-a-poster-campaign-redefining-colonial-violence/.

## MURDERS AND DISAPPEARANCES OF ABORIGINAL WOMEN AND GIRLS

*Canadian Feminist Alliance for International Action (FAFIA)*

The Canadian Feminist Alliance for International Action (FAFIA) is an alliance of women's organizations at the national, provincial, territorial, and local levels. Its mandate is to advance women's equality in Canada by working for the full implementation of the international human rights treaties and agreements that Canada has ratified. FAFIA provides training and resources on women's human rights instruments and helps women to engage in using those instruments to address inequalities in their lives.

Aboriginal women and girls experience extremely high levels of violence in Canada. Aboriginal women in Canada report rates of violence including domestic violence and sexual assault 3.5 times higher than non-Aboriginal women. Young Aboriginal women are five times more likely than other Canadian women of the same age to die of violence. Aboriginal women and girls experience both high levels of sexual abuse and violence in their own families and communities, and high levels of stranger violence in the broader society.

> The RCMP documented 1,181 murders and disappearances of Aboriginal women and girls between 1980 and 2012.

Between 2005 and 2010, the Native Women's Association of Canada (NWAC), through its Sisters in Spirit project, documented the disappearances or murders of 582 Aboriginal women and girls over twenty years. But in 2010, the Government of Canada cut NWAC's funding for this ground breaking research project and NWAC was unable to continue this work.

NWAC has always believed that the scope of the violence is far greater than the cases it has been able to document through public sources. For many years, the inadequacy of data that identifies the victims and perpetrators of murders and disappearances of Aboriginal women and girls by race has been well known and acknowledged, including by Statistics Canada.

Late in 2013 the Royal Canadian Mounted Police (RCMP) commissioned a study on murders and disappearances of Aboriginal women and girls and released its findings in May 2014. The RCMP documented 1,181 murders and disappearances of Aboriginal women and girls between 1980 and 2012 with information from over 300 police forces. This confirmed the broad scope of the violence and the over representation of Aboriginal women and girls among murdered and missing women in Canada.

*Source:* Canadian Feminist Alliance for International Action (FAFIA). (n.d.). Excerpted from "Campaign of Solidarity with Aboriginal Women." Ottawa, ON: FAFIA. Retrieved from: http://fafia-afai.org/en/solidarity-campaign/.

# ACTIVIST ART 9

## WALKING WITH OUR SISTERS

Moccasin "Vamps"

*Source:* Photo courtesy of Walking With Our Sisters

Walking With Our Sisters is a commemorative art installation to honour the lives of missing and murdered Indigenous Women of Canada and the United States; to acknowledge the grief and torment families of these women continue to suffer; and to raise awareness of this issue and create opportunity for broad community-based dialogue on the issue.

Walking With Our Sisters is an entirely crowd-sourced project. From the artwork to the fundraising, even to the way the exhibit tour is being booked, it is all being fueled by hundreds and thousands of people who have chosen to become involved. Collectively we are creating one unified voice to honour these women and their families, and to call for attention to be paid to this issue. There is power in numbers, and there is power in art.

In June of 2012, a general call was issued on Facebook for people to create moccasin tops. The call was answered by women, men and children of all ages and races. By July 25, 2013, over 1,600 vamps had been received, almost tripling the initial goal of 600 and offering proof that the world is indeed filled with caring souls.

Each pair of moccasin tops are intentionally not sewn into moccasins to represent the unfinished lives of the women and girls.

This project is about these women, paying respect to their lives and existence on this earth. They are not forgotten. They are sisters, mothers, daughters, cousins, aunties, grandmothers, friends and wives. They have been cared for, they have been loved, and they are missing.

The Walking With Our Sisters Collective is made up of volunteers who form the national organizing committee.

Maria Campbell, Elder, Advisor on Traditional Protocol
Christi Belcourt, Helper, Community Support
Erin Konsmo, Helper, Two-Spirit, Communications & Youth Programming
Tracy Bear, Helper, Community Support
Tara Kappo, Helper, Finance & Community Support
Tony Belcourt, Helper, Advisor
Tracey Pawis, Helper, Community Support
Christine King, Helper, Tour Schedule

Laurie Odjick, Helper, Family Support
Shane Belcourt, Helper, Film & Web Adviser
Sherry Farrell Racette, Helper, Curatorial Team
Lisa Periard, Helper, Community Support
Ryan Rice, Helper, Curatorial Team
Maria Hupfield, Helper, Curatorial Team
Gregory A Scofield, Helper, Advisor
Lisa Shepherd, Helper, Community Support
Kim Anderson, Helper, Publication
Nathalie Bertin, Helper, Advisor
Kara Louttit, Helper, Community Support & Publication
Doreen Roman, Helper, Advisor & Publication
Rebecca Beaulne-Stuebing, Helper, Publication support
Tracie Louttit & Jodi Stonehouse, Helpers, WWOS Film Crew
Karon Shmon, Gabriel Dumont Institute Book Partner in Publishing

*Source:* Walking With Our Sisters. (2017). Excerpted from "About the Project" and "The WWOS Collective." Retrieved from: http://walkingwithoursisters.ca/.

# EVERY CLASS IN EVERY SCHOOL

*Catherine Taylor and Tracey Peter*

Catherine Taylor is the associate dean of arts and a professor in the Faculty of Education and the Department of Rhetoric, Writing, and Communications at the University of Winnipeg in Manitoba, Canada. She is highly acclaimed for her work on research ethics, LGBTQ well-being, and LGBTQ inclusive education. Taylor has led several large-scale national research projects that aim to build inclusive school environments for sexual and gender minority students and their parents.

Tracey Peter is the associate head of and a professor in the Department of Sociology at the University of Manitoba. She specializes in applied statistical research methods and survey design, and has published widely in the area of sexual and gender minority youth and other marginalized populations, particularly in the areas of inclusive education, mental health, and suicide prevention.

This report discusses the results of a national survey of Canadian high school students undertaken in order to investigate what life at school is like for students with sexual or gender minority status. The study sought to identify the forms and extent of students' experiences of homophobic and transphobic incidents at school, the impact of those experiences, and the efficacy of measures being taken by schools to combat these common forms of bullying. The study involved surveying over 3700 students from across Canada between December 2007 and June 2009.

Below are some of the findings:

- 70% of all participating students, LGBTQ and non-LGBTQ, reported hearing expressions such as "that's so gay" every day in school and almost half (48%) reported hearing remarks such as "faggot," "lezbo," and "dyke" every day in school.

- Almost 10% of LGBTQ students reported having heard homophobic comments from teachers daily or weekly (17% of trans students; 10% of female sexual minority students; and 8% of male sexual minority students). Even more LGBTQ students reported that they had heard teachers use negative gender-related or transphobic comments daily or weekly: 23% of trans students; 15% of male sexual minority students; and 12% of female sexual minority students.

- 74% of trans students, 55% of sexual minority students, and 26% of non-LGBTQ students reported having been verbally harassed about their gender expression.

- 37% of trans students, 32% of female sexual minority students, and 20% of male sexual minority students reported being verbally harassed daily or weekly about their sexual orientation.
- 68% of trans students, 55% of female sexual minority students, and 42% of male sexual minority students reported being verbally harassed about their perceived gender or sexual orientation. Trans youth may report experiencing particularly high levels of harassment on the basis of perceived sexual orientation because often trans individuals are perceived as lesbian, gay, or bisexual when they are not.
- More than one in five (21%) LGBTQ students reported being physically harassed or assaulted due to their sexual orientation.
- 20% of LGBTQ students and almost 10% of non-LGBTQ students reported being physically harassed or assaulted about their perceived sexual orientation or gender identity.
- Youth of colour, both LGBTQ and non-LGBTQ, are far less likely to know of any out LGBTQ students (67% compared to 81% of Caucasian and 87% of Aboriginal youth, LGBTQ and non-LGBTQ combined) or to know of any teachers or staff members who are supportive of LGBTQ students (48% knew of none, compared to 38% of Aboriginal and 31% of Caucasian youth, LGBTQ and non-LGBTQ combined).

- One of the most striking findings of the study is that 58% of non-LGBTQ youth find homophobic comments upsetting. This finding suggests that there is a great deal of potential solidarity for LGBTQ-inclusive education among heterosexual students.
- One in twelve heterosexual students reported being verbally harassed about their perceived sexual orientation and one in four about their gender expression.
- Almost 10% of non-LGBTQ youth reported being physically harassed or assaulted about their perceived sexual orientation or gender identity and more than 10% reported being physically harassed or assaulted because of their gender expression.
- Any given school is likely to have as many heterosexual students as LGBTQ students who are harassed about their sexual orientation or gender expression.

---

*Source:* Taylor, Catherine, & Peter, Tracey, with McMinn, T.L., Elliott, Tara, Beldom, Stacey, Ferry, Allison, Gross, Zoe, Paquin, Sarah, & Schachter, Kevin. (2011). Excerpted from *Every Class in Every School: The First National Climate Survey on Homophobia, Biphobia, and Transphobia in Canadian Schools. Final Report* (pp. 15, 16, 21, 26). Toronto, ON: Egale Canada Human Rights Trust.

# PART 5

## Gendering Globalization, Migration, and Activism

If women are to "clean up the mess," they have a right to challenge the people
and institutions which create the problems.
—*Peggy Antrobus, quoted in Joni Seager, "What's the Problem Here?"*
*in Earth Follies: Coming to Feminist Terms*
*with the Global Environmental Crisis (1993, p. 7)*

Part 5 examines the changing nature of gender relations in an increasingly globalized world shaped by the ideas and practices of neoliberalism, economic restructuring, and structural adjustment. We introduce students to gendered and racialized understandings of globalization and its unequal distribution of costs and benefits within and between countries in the economic North and South. We also look at movements organizing for gender and economic justice within and across communities, cultures, and borders.

## Part 5A: Gender and Global Restructuring

This section introduces students to feminist analyses of globalization, neo-liberalism, and structural adjustment policies, highlighting their differential impacts on privileged and marginalized social groups within and between the economic North and South. We examine in particular the effects of globalization on gendered experiences of migration, labour, economic security, violence, and health. We also begin to consider some of the ways in which activists are organizing for economic and social justice.

## Part 5B: Gender, Migration, and Citizenship

This section looks at the intersections between gender, citizenship, immigration status, and the state. We critically examine the social construction of categories like "immigrant women," "refugees," and "borders," and highlight how gendered and racialized laws and policies in the past and present regulate access to Canada and the United States. We explore how the status of non-citizen intersects with gender, race, class, ethnicity, religion, and so on to shape experiences of immigration and settlement, and we consider how immigrants have challenged discriminatory barriers.

## Part 5C: On (Not) Getting By in North America

Neo-liberalism and economic restructuring in a North American context have gendered impacts on economic security, paid and unpaid labour, and housing security. This section focuses on gendered experiences of poverty and homelessness in North America, including northern Canada, in the context of the neo-liberal dismantling of the welfare state and the criminalization of poor women in Canada, especially since the 1990s. We explore the regulation and stigmatization of one group of workers in neo-liberal and neo-colonial North America: sex workers. We also explore some analyses, proposals, and actions of contemporary anti-poverty activists.

## SNAPSHOTS & SOUNDWAVES 38

## WHAT IS NEO-LIBERAL GLOBALIZATION?

*Alison Jaggar*

Alison Jaggar is a professor of philosophy and women and gender studies at the University of Colorado–Boulder, and a distinguished research professor at the University of Birmingham in England. Her areas of interest include contemporary social, moral, and political philosophy from a feminist perspective and gendered aspects of global justice. She has published numerous works on these topics, including *Just Methods: An Interdisciplinary Feminist Reader, Abortion: Three Perspectives*, and *Gender and Global Justice*. Jaggar has been awarded numerous honours and fellowships throughout her career, including the Society for Women in Philosophy's Distinguished Philosopher of the Year in 1995, and the University of Colorado Gee Memorial Lectureship in 2011.

Interpreted broadly, the term *globalization* refers to any system of transcontinental travel and trade. However, contemporary globalization is distinguished by its integration of many local and national economies into a single global market, regulated by the World Trade Organization (WTO). This treaty organization was established in 1995 to determine the rules for global trade. WTO rules supersede the national law of any signatory nation and are rationalized by a distinctive version of liberal political theory, namely, neo-liberalism.

Although its name suggests that it is something novel, "neo-liberalism" in fact marks a retreat from the liberal social democracy of the years following World War II. It moves back toward the non-redistributive laissez faire liberalism of the seventeenth and eighteenth centuries, which held that the main function of government was to make the world safe and predictable for the participants in a market economy. Following are some main tenets of contemporary neo-liberalism.

### "Free" Trade

Neo-liberalism promotes the free flow of both traded goods and of capital. However, not only does it not require the free flow of labour, the third crucial factor of production, but it also seeks actively to control that flow. Although immigration from poorer to wealthier countries is currently at record levels, much of it is achieved in the teeth of draconian border controls that often cost would-be immigrants their lives.

## Opposition to Government Regulation

Neo-liberalism opposes government regulation of such aspects of production as wages, working conditions and environmental protections. Indeed, legislation intended to protect workers, consumers or the environment may be challenged as an unfair barrier to trade.

## Refusal of Responsibility for Social Welfare

Neo-liberalism presses governments to abandon the social welfare responsibilities that they have assumed over the twentieth century, such as providing allowances for housing, health care, education, disability and unemployment.

## Resource Privatization

The final feature of contemporary neo-liberalism is its push to bring all economically exploitable resources into private ownership. Public services are turned into profit-making enterprises, sometimes sold to foreign investors, and natural resources such as minerals, forests, water and land are opened up for commercial exploitation in the global market.

*Source:* Jaggar, Alison. (2002). Adapted from "Vulnerable Women and Neo-Liberal Globalization: Debt Burdens Undermine Women's Health in the Global South." *Theoretical Medicine and Bioethics, 23*(6), 425–426.

# THE IMF: VIOLATING WOMEN SINCE 1945

*Kavita Ramdas and Christine Ahn*

Kavita Ramdas is the strategy advisor at MADRE, an international women's human rights organization, and the senior advisor of global strategy to the Ford Foundation's president. Previously, she was president and CEO of the Global Fund for Women. Ramdas has broadly promoted women's human rights, social justice philanthropy, and international development through her membership and professional affiliations on the boards and advisory councils of a diverse array of organizations.

Christine Ahn is a writer, organizer, and policy analyst with expertise in Korea, globalization, militarism, women's rights, and philanthropy. She is the founder and International Coordinator of Women Cross DMZ, a global movement of women mobilizing to end the Korean War and reunify families. She is also the co-founder of the Korea Policy Institute, National Campaign to End the Korean War, and the Global Campaign to Save Jeju Island. Ahn is a columnist with *Foreign Policy in Focus*, and her writings have appeared in *The New York Times* and *The Nation*, among other publications.

As Dominique Strauss-Kahn, head of the world's most powerful financial institution, the International Monetary Fund (IMF), spends a few nights in Rikers Island prison awaiting a hearing, the world is learning a lot about his history of treating women as expendable sex objects. Strauss-Kahn has been charged with rape and forced imprisonment of a 32-year-old Guinean hotel worker at a $3,000-a-night luxury hotel in New York.

While the media dissects the attempted rape of a young African woman and begins to dig out more information about Strauss-Kahn's past indiscretions, we couldn't help but see this situation through the feminist lens of the "personal is political."

For many in the developing world, the IMF and its draconian policies of structural adjustment have systematically "raped" the earth and the poor and violated the human rights of women. It appears that the personal disregard and disrespect for women demonstrated by the man at the highest levels of leadership within the IMF is quite consistent with the gender bias inherent in the IMF's institutional policies and practice.

## Systematic Violation of Women's Human Rights

The IMF and the World Bank were established in the aftermath of World War II to promote international trade and monetary cooperation by giving governments loans in times of severe budget crises. Although 184 countries make up the IMF's membership, only five countries—France, Germany, Japan, Britain, and the United States—control 50 percent of the votes, which are allocated according to each country's contribution.

The IMF has earned its villainous reputation in the Global South because in exchange for loans, governments must accept a range of austerity measures known as structural adjustment programs (SAPs). A typical IMF package encourages export promotion over local production for local consumption. It also pushes for lower tariffs and cuts in government programs such as welfare and education. Instead of reducing poverty, the trillion dollars of loans issued by the IMF have deepened poverty, especially for women who make up 70 percent of the world's poor.

IMF-mandated government cutbacks in social welfare spending have often been achieved by cutting public sector jobs, which disproportionately impact women. Women hold most of the lower-skilled public sector jobs, and they are often the first to be cut. Also, as social programs like caregiving are slashed, women are expected to take on additional domestic responsibilities that further limit their access to education or other jobs.

In exchange for borrowing $5.8 billion from the IMF and World Bank, Tanzania agreed to impose fees for health services, which led to fewer women seeking hospital deliveries or post-natal care and, naturally, higher rates of maternal death. In Zambia, the imposition of SAPs led to a significant drop in girls' enrollment in schools and a spike in "survival or subsistence sex" as a way for young women to continue their educations.

But IMF's austerity measures don't just apply to poor African countries. In 1997, South Korea received $57 billion in loans in exchange for IMF conditionalities that forced the government to introduce "labor market flexibility," which outlined steps for the government to compress wages, fire "surplus workers," and cut government spending on programs and infrastructure. When the financial crisis hit, seven Korean women were laid off for every one Korean man. In a sick twist, the Korean

government launched a "get your husband energized" campaign encouraging women to support depressed male partners while they cooked, cleaned, and cared for everyone.

Nearly 15 years later, the scenario is grim for South Korean workers, especially women. Of all OECD countries, Koreans work the longest hours: 90 percent of men and 77 percent of women work over 40 hours a week. According to economist Martin Hart-Landsberg, in 2000, 40 percent of Korean workers were irregular workers; by 2008, 60 percent worked in the informal economy. The Korean Women Working Academy reports that today 70 percent of Korean women workers are temporary laborers.

## Selling Mother Earth

IMF policies have also raped the earth by dictating that governments privatize the natural resources most people depend on for their survival: water, land, forests, and fisheries. SAPs have also forced developing countries to stop growing staple foods for domestic consumption and instead focus on growing cash crops, like cut flowers and coffee for export to volatile global markets. These policies have destroyed the livelihoods of small-scale subsistence farmers, the majority of whom are women.

"IMF adjustment programs forced poor countries to abandon policies that protected their farmers and their agricultural production and markets," says Henk Hobbelink of GRAIN, an international organization that promotes sustainable agriculture and biodiversity. "As a result, many countries became dependent on food imports, as local farmers could not compete with the subsidized products from the North. This is one of the main factors in the current food crisis, for which the IMF is directly to blame."

In the Democratic Republic of Congo (DRC), IMF loans have paved the way for the privatization of the country's mines by transnational corporations and local elites, which has forcibly displaced thousands of Congolese people in a context where women and girls experience obscenely high levels of sexual slavery and rape in the eastern provinces. According to Gender Action, the World Bank and IMF have made loans to the DRC to restructure the mining sector, which translates into laying off tens of thousands of workers, including women and girls who depend on the mining operations for their livelihoods. Furthermore, as the land becomes mined and privatized, women and girls responsible for gathering water and firewood must walk even further, making them more susceptible to violent crimes.

## We Are Over It

Women's rights activists around the globe are consistently dumbfounded by how such violations of women's bodies are routinely dismissed as minor transgressions. Strauss-Kahn, one of the world's most powerful politicians whose decisions affected millions across the globe, was known for being a "womanizer" who often forced himself on younger, junior women in subordinate positions where they were vulnerable to his far greater power, influence, and clout. Yet none of his colleagues or fellow Socialist Party members took these reports seriously, colluding in a consensus shared even by his wife that the violation of women's bodily integrity is not in any sense a genuine violation of human rights.

Why else would the world tolerate the unearthly news that 48 Congolese women are raped every hour with deadening inaction? Eve Ensler speaks for us all when she writes, "I am over a world that could allow, has allowed, continues to allow 400,000 women, 2,300 women, or one woman to be raped anywhere, anytime of any day in the Congo. The women of Congo are over it too."

We live in a world where millions of women don't speak their truth, don't tell their dark stories, don't reveal their horror lived every day just because they were born women. They don't do it for the same reasons that the women in the Congo articulate—they are tired of not being heard. They are tired of men like Strauss-Kahn, powerful and in suits, believing that they can rape a black woman in a hotel room, just because they feel like it. They

are tired of the police not believing them or arresting them for being sex workers. They are tired of hospitals not having rape kits. They are tired of reporting rape and being charged for adultery in Iran, Pakistan, and Saudi Arabia.

## Fighting Back

For each one of them, and for those of us who have spent many years investing in the tenacity of women's movements across the globe, the courage and gumption of the young Guinean immigrant shines like the torch held by Lady Liberty herself. This young woman makes you believe we can change this reality. She refused to be intimidated. She stood up for herself. She fought to free herself—twice—from the violent grip of the man attacking her. She didn't care who he was—she knew she was violated and she reported it straight to the hotel staff, who went straight to the New York police, who went straight to JFK to pluck Strauss-Kahn from his first-class Air France seat.

In a world where it often feels as though wealth and power can buy anything, the courage of a young woman and the people who stood by her took our breath away. These stubborn, ethical acts of working-class people in New York City reminded us that women have the right to say "no." It reminded us that "no" does not mean "yes" as the Yale fraternities would have us believe, and, most importantly, that no one, regardless of their position or their gender, should be above the law. A wise woman judge further drove home the point about how critically important it is to value women's bodies when she denied Strauss-Kahn bail, citing his long history of abusing women.

Strauss-Kahn sits in his Rikers Island cell. It would be a great thing if his trial succeeds in ending the world's tolerance for those who discriminate and abuse women. We cannot tolerate it one second longer. We cannot tolerate it at the personal level, we must refuse to condone it at the professional level, and we must challenge it every time it we see it in the policies of global institutions like the International Monetary Fund.

*Editors' note:* The charges for attempted rape were dropped after this article was published, and Strauss-Kahn settled a civil lawsuit launched by the woman out of court. Other allegations of sexual assault followed, as did charges (for which he was later acquitted) of "aggravated pimping" for his alleged involvement in a prostitution ring. See "Profile: Dominique Strauss-Kahn," *BBC News*, June 12, 2015. http://www.bbc.com/news/world-europe-13405268.

*Source:* Ramdas, Kavita, & Ahn, Christine. (2011, May 19). "The IMF: Violating Women Since 1945." *Foreign Policy in Focus*. Washington, DC: Institute for Policy Studies. Retrieved from: http://www.fpif.org/articles/the_imf_violating_women_since_1945.

# CHAPTER 59

## The Gendered Politics and Violence of Structural Adjustment: A View from Jamaica

*Faye V. Harrison*

Faye V. Harrison is a professor of anthropology and African American studies at the University of Illinois at Urbana-Champaign. She is an award-winning sociocultural anthropologist specializing in the study of social inequalities, human rights, and intersections of race, gender, class, and (trans)national belonging (or not belonging). In 2013, she was elected to a five-year term as president of the International Union of Anthropological and Ethnological Sciences (IUAES). Harrison has published extensively on a diverse range of topics, including structural adjustment policies, poverty, the informal economy, political violence, and critical race feminist methodology as a tool for global research. She is the author of *Outsider Within: Reworking Anthropology in the Global Age*.

## AN ETHNOGRAPHIC WINDOW ON A CRISIS

"The ghetto not'ing but a sad shantytown now." This is what one of my friends and informants sadly remarked to me upon my 1992 visit to "Oceanview," a pseudonym for an impoverished slum neighborhood with a roughly 74 percent formal unemployment rate in the downtown district of the Kingston Metropolitan Area. Times were so hard that the tenements had deteriorated beyond repair. The conspicuous physical decline was a marker of the deepened socioeconomic austerity accompanying what some critics (e.g., *Race & Class* 1992) now consider to be the "recolonization" of Jamaica by "the new

conquistadors"—the policies and programs that the International Monetary Fund (IMF), the World Bank, and the Reagan and Bush administrations of the United States government designed to "adjust" and "stabilize" the country's revived export-oriented economy. These strategies for delivering third world societies from collapsing economies are informed by a development ideology that euphemizes the widening social disparities that have been the outcome of policies imposing an unbearable degree of austerity on living conditions. Hence, these policies have sacrificed ordinary people's—especially the poor's—basic needs in health care, housing, education, social services, and employment for those of free enterprise and free trade.

Since 1978, I have observed and conversed with Oceanview residents about the social, economic, and political conditions shaping their lived experiences and struggles for survival in this neighborhood (e.g., Harrison 1987a, b, 1988, 1991a, b). The late 1970s was a time of economic hardship and political turbulence, a time when the People's National Party's (PNP) democratic socialist path to economic development and social transformation was vehemently contested, blocked, and destabilized by political opponents both within and without the country and by the concerted economic force of an international recession, quadrupled oil prices, and a massive flight of both domestic and foreign capital. Life was certainly hard then, but, as one resident commented, "Cho, mahn; tings worse now." Despite the bright promises of political and economic "deliverance" made by the Jamaica Labour Party (JLP) and its major backer, the Reagan and later Bush administrations of the U.S. government, the 1980s and early 1990s—under the leadership of a much more conservative PNP—brought only a deepened poverty to the folk who people the streets and alleys of slum and shantytown neighborhoods like Oceanview. This deepening poverty is reflected, for example, in a serious decline in the conditions of public health. The implementation of structural adjustment policies has brought about alarming reductions in government health-care expenditures and promoted the privatization of more costly and less accessible medical care (Phillips 1994, 137). Those most heavily burdened by the impact of these deteriorating social conditions and capital-centered policies are women (Antrobus 1989) who serve as the major "social shock absorbers" (Sparr 1992, 31; 1994), mediating the crisis at the local level of households and neighborhoods. Nearly 50 percent of all Kingston's households are female-headed, giving women the major responsibilities for making ends meet out of virtually nothing (Deere et al. 1990, 52–53). Concentrated in the informal sector of the economy, these women, along with their children, are

most vulnerable to the consequences of malnutrition, hunger, and poor health: rising levels of morbidity and mortality (Phillips 1994, 142; Pan American Health Organization/World Health Organization 1992).

To appreciate and understand the effects, contradictions, and meanings that constitute the reality of a structurally adjusted pattern of production and trade, we must examine the everyday experiences, practices, discourses, and common sense of real people, particularly those encouraged to wait—and wait—for social and economic benefits to trickle down. In the interest of an ethnographically grounded view of Jamaica's current economic predicament, I present the case of Mrs. Beulah Brown, an admirable woman whose life story I collected over several years, to help elucidate the impact the ongoing crisis has on the everyday lives of ordinary Jamaicans, particularly poor urban women and those who depend most on them. A longtime household head and informal-sector worker like so many other Jamaican women, Mrs. Brown was once a community health aide with a government program that provided much-needed health services to a population to which such care would not have been available otherwise. Mrs. Brown would not have gotten or held that job for the years that she did without "the right political connections," something, unfortunately, that too few poor people ever obtain. Although visible benefits from membership in the local PNP group may have set her apart from most of her neighbors, the centrality of patronage-clientelism in local and national politics makes a former political client's experience an insightful window on the constraints and vulnerabilities built into Jamaica's political and economic policies.

Highlights from Mrs. Brown's life story lead us to the more encompassing story of postcolonial Jamaica's experience with debt, export-led development, and structural adjustment, and their combined impact on women workers as well as on neighborhood-level negotiations of crisis.

## A HARD-WORKING WOMAN'S STORY WITHIN A STORY

In the 1970s, Beulah Brown, then a middle-aged woman responsible for a two-generation household and extended family, worked as a community health aide under the combined aegis of a government public health program and a local urban redevelopment agency, two projects that owed their existence to the social-policy orientation of the reformist PNP administration. Mrs. Brown had begun her employment history as a worker in a factory manufacturing undergarments. However, she preferred household-based self-employment over the stringent regimentation of factory work. A woman with strong civic consciousness and organizing skills, she had worked her way into the leadership of the PNP group within the neighborhood and wider political division. By the late 1970s, she was no longer an officer; however, her membership in the party was still active.

Mrs. Brown was so effective at working with patients and exhibiting good citizenship that she was widely recognized and addressed as "Nurse Brown," the term *nurse* being a title of utmost respect. When Mrs. Brown made her daily rounds, she did more than expected of a health aide. She treated her patients as whole persons with a range of basic needs she felt obligated to help meet. To this end, she saw to it that they had nutritional food to eat, clean clothes to wear, and neat and orderly rooms in which to live. She was especially devoted to the elderly, but she also invested considerable energy in young mothers who were often merely children themselves. She shared her experiences and wisdom with them, admonishing them to eat healthy foods, read good books, and, given her religious worldview, "pray to the Lord Jesus Christ" so that their babies' characters and personalities would be positively influenced while still in the womb.

When I initially met her, Mrs. Brown was responsible for caring for her elderly father, her [disabled] sister, her sister's three daughters, and her own two daughters. At earlier times she had even minded a young niece who eventually joined her other siblings and mother, another of Mrs. Brown's sisters, in Canada. Despite many hardships, Beulah managed her household well enough to see to it that the children were fed, clothed, and schooled. Indeed, one of her nieces, Claudia, is now a nurse in New York City, and—"by the grace of God"—her eldest daughter, Cherry, is a graduate of the University of the West Indies. Unfortunately, Marie, the daughter who still remains at home, had difficulty getting and keeping wage work, whether in an office or factory, so she decided to make and sell children's clothes so she could work at home while minding her children. Despite the economic uncertainty of informal sector work, Marie appreciates its flexibility and the freedom from the "downpressive" (oppressive) industrial surveillance about which a number of former factory workers in Oceanview complain.

Because the community health aide job did not bring in enough income to support the household, Mrs. Brown found ways to augment her income. Mainly she made dresses, a skill and talent she had cultivated over most of her life. Years ago she had even had a small shop in Port Antonio that catered to locals as well as foreign tourists. That was before she gave up everything—her shop and her husband—to return home to Kingston to care for relatives who were going through some hard times. Besides her dressmaking enterprise, Mrs. Brown also baked and sold meat patties, bought and sold cheese, and sold ice from the deep freezer she had purchased with remittances from her twin sister in England and help from her church. Through political party connections gained through her earlier activism in the local PNP group, she also saw to it that her sister got a job cleaning streets in the government Crash Programme. Although her family managed better than most of their neighbors, survival was still an everyday struggle.

In the mid-1980s, Mrs. Brown lost her health aide job. The Community Health Aide Program suffered massive losses due to the retrenchment in public-sector employment stipulated by the structural-adjustment and stabilization measures imposed by the IMF and World Bank. Luckily, the layoff came around the time when the girls she had raised were coming of age and could work to support themselves and their families. By 1988, the household was made up of only Beulah, her second daughter, Marie, and Marie's three small children. Everyone else had moved on to independent residences in Kingston or emigrated to the U.S. and Canada to live with relatives, "a foreign," overseas. This dispersal relieved the household of considerable financial pressure, but to make ends meet, Beulah still had to intensify her informal means of generating income. She did more dressmaking and added baking wedding and birthday cakes to her list of money-making activities.

No matter how much work she did, she never seemed to be able to do more than barely make ends meet. With the devaluation of the Jamaican dollar and the removal of subsidies on basic consumer items like food, the costs of living had increased dramatically. What more could she do to keep pace with the inflationary trend designed to make Jamaican exports more competitive on the international market? She knew that she would never resort to the desperate illicit measures some of her neighbors had taken by "tiefing" ("thiefing") or dealing drugs. She simply refused to sell her soul to the devil for some of the "blood money" obtainable from the activities of local gangs—now called posses—that move from Kingston to the U.S. and back trafficking in substances like crack cocaine. Increasingly, especially with political patronage becoming more scarce, drug trafficking has become an important source of local subsistence and small-scale investment. However, the price paid for a life of crime is too high. She lamented that too many "youts" (youths) involved in the drug economy make the return trip home to Jamaica enclosed in deathly wooden crates.

Like most Caribbean people, Mrs. Brown has long belonged to and actively participated in an international family network extending from Jamaica to Great Britain, Canada, and the U.S. (Basch et al. 1994). Her sisters abroad had often invited her to visit

them, and they had also encouraged her to migrate so that she, too, could benefit from better opportunities. Before the mid-1980s, Mrs. Brown had been determined to remain at home caring for her family. Moreover, she loved her country, her church, and her party, and she wanted to help shape the direction of Jamaica's future. She strongly felt that someone had to remain in Jamaica to keep it going on the right course. Everyone couldn't migrate. "My home is here in Jamaica," she insisted adamantly.

These were her strong feelings *before* structural adjustment hit the heart of her home: her refrigerator, deep freezer, and kitchen table. In 1990 alone, the cost of chicken—a desirable entree to accompany rice and peas on Sunday—went up three times. The cost of even more basic staples also rose, making items such as fresh milk, cornmeal, and tomatoes (whose price increased 140 percent) more and more unaffordable for many people (Statistical Institute of Jamaica 1991).

Between 1987 and 1992, Mrs. Brown travelled abroad twice for extended visits with relatives in England, Canada, and the U.S. While away for nearly a year at a time, she "did a likkle babysitting and ting" to earn money that she was able to save for her own purposes. Her family treated her "like a queen," buying her gifts ("good camera, TV, radio, and ting"), not letting her spend her own money for living expenses, and paying for her air transportation from point to point along her international itinerary. The savings she managed to send and bring back home were key to her Oceanview household's survival. Her transnational family network, and the geographical mobility it offered, allowed her to increase her earnings by taking advantage of the marked wage differential between Jamaica and the countries where her relatives live (Ho 1993, 33). This particular financial advantage has led even middle-class Jamaican women to tolerate an otherwise embarrassing and humiliating decline in social status to work as nannies and domestic helpers in North American homes. International migration within the Caribbean region, as well as between it and major metropoles, has been a traditional survival strategy among Jamaicans since nineteenth-century post-emancipation society.

Harsh circumstances forced Mrs. Brown to join the larger wave of female emigrants from the Caribbean who, since the late 1960s, have outnumbered their male counterparts (Deere et al. 1990, 76; Ho 1993, 33). Thus far, Mrs. Brown has remained a "visitor," but she acknowledges the possibility and perhaps even the probability that someday soon she will join her sisters as a permanent resident abroad. Meanwhile, she continues to take care of business at home by informally generating and allocating resources within the kinship-mediated transnational social field within which her local life is embedded.

Mrs. Brown's story and many others similar to it are symptomatic of the current age of globalization, marked by a deepening crisis that policies such as structural adjustment and its complementary export-led development strategy attempt to manage in favor of the mobility and accumulation of transnational capital. Mrs. Brown's story, however, is only a story within a story about the dramatic plot-thickening details of Jamaica's nonlinear struggle for development and decolonization. Let us now place Beulah Brown's lived experience in a broader context, and in so doing, illuminate the forces and conditions that differentially affect Jamaica's hard-working women, particularly those who work in the informal sector and free trade zone. As we shall see, their dilemmas and struggles are closely interrelated.

## ONCE UPON A TIME: DILEMMAS OF DEVELOPMENT

### Deep into Debt

Postcolonial Jamaica, like many other third world and southern hemisphere countries, is beset by a serious case of debt bondage. Jamaica is embroiled in a crisis that can be traced back to the economic turmoil of the mid-1970s. By 1980, when the conservative JLP ousted the democratic socialist PNP from power, Jamaica's debt had doubled due to the extensive borrowing undertaken to absorb the impact the receding international economy was having on the country, to offset massive capital flight (a domestic and international panic response to the PNP's move to the left), and to underwrite state-initiated development projects. To stabilize and reinvigorate the collapsed economy, the JLP administration, with the support and guidance of the Reagan administration, relied on the IMF and the World Bank for massive loans to redress its critical balance of payments and fiscal deficits. Consequently, the country's indebtedness grew by leaps and bounds. As a result, Jamaica now owes more than U.S. $4 billion. Its debt servicing exceeds what it receives in loans and grants (Ferguson 1992, 62), and it devours 40 percent of the foreign exchange it earns from its exports, which are supposed to jump start the economy into a pattern of sustained development. The development strategy pursued since 1980—one that privileges private-sector export production—has been underwritten by these relations of indebtedness. The IMF, World Bank, and the U.S. government's Caribbean Basin Initiative (CBI) and USAID have delimited terms for Jamaica's economic restructuring that further integrate the island into a global hierarchy of free-trade relations. This global hierarchy is not only class- and racially biased (Köhler 1978); it is also fundamentally gendered (Antrobus 1989; Enloe 1989; Sparr 1994).

### The Path to Economic Growth and Social Crisis

The debt-constrained, export-led, and free trade–based development path that the Jamaican economy is following has failed to deliver the masses of Jamaican people from the dilemmas of persistent poverty and underdevelopment. Benefits from this development strategy have not trickled down the socioeconomic ladder. However, what have trickled down are the adverse effects of drastic austerity measures, which are the strings attached to aid from the IMF and World Bank. These strings stipulate that the government de-nationalize or privatize public sectors of the economy, cut back social services and public employment, devalue the Jamaican dollar, impose restraints on wages, liberalize imports, and remove subsidies and price controls on food and other consumer goods (Antrobus 1989, 20). These measures, along with the stipulated focus on export production, have resulted in increased unemployment, a decline in real wages for those fortunate enough to have regular incomes, a dramatic rise in the costs of living, and, with these, an increase in malnutrition and hunger, a general deterioration in public health, and an escalating incidence of drug abuse and violence—including violence against women (Antrobus 1989, 23). [...] Those bearing the heaviest burden in coping with today's social and economic austerity are women, a large proportion of whom have the responsibility—whether they are formally employed or not—to support households and family networks (Bolles 1991).

Although it has sacrificed ordinary people's basic needs, the debt bondage and free trade strategy has successfully restored "the military and economic foundations of U.S. superiority ... incorporating the Caribbean Basin countries into the U.S. military-industrial complex" (Deere et al. 1990, 157). A central aspect of the CBI has been the increased sale of U.S. exports to the Caribbean (McAfee 1991, 43). Exports from the Caribbean that receive duty-free entry into the U.S. market are produced in foreign and, to a considerable extent, U.S.-controlled free-trade zones where items (usually those of apparel and electronics) are assembled from raw materials and capital goods imported from the U.S. In other words, the Caribbean has become an offshore site for branch plants that are not generating the backward linkages and horizontal integration necessary for stimulating the domestic sectors of Jamaica's economy.

## Gender Inequality in Globalization

Transnational capital has appropriated the enterprising freedom to repatriate profits without any enforced obligations to invest in the host country's future; it has enjoyed the freedom to employ workers, to a great extent female, whose labor has been politically, legally, and culturally constructed to be cheap and expendable. As Enloe (1989, 160–163) argues, economic globalization depends upon laws and cultural presumptions about femininity, sexuality, and marriage that help to lower women's wages and benefits. For instance, transnational garment production has taken advantage of and reinforced the patriarchal assumptions that activities such as sewing are "natural" women's tasks requiring no special skill, training, or compensation; that jobs defined as skilled belong to men, who deserve to be remunerated for their special physical strength and training; that women are not the major breadwinners in their households and families and are really supported by their fathers or husbands (Safa 1994); and finally that women's needs should not direct the policies and practices of business management and development specialists.

The profitability, capital mobility, and structural power (Wolf 1990) constitutive of globalization are fundamentally gendered phenomena marked by a masculinist logic. Present-day strategies to adjust, stabilize, and facilitate capital accumulation implicate constructions of femininity and masculinity that, in effect, legitimate the superexploitation of the productive and reproductive labor of women, with women of color bearing the heaviest burdens (see Antrobus 1989; Deere et al. 1990; Enloe 1989) and being the most vulnerable targets of structural violence—the symbolic, psychological, and physical assaults against human subjectivities, physical bodies, and sociocultural integrity that emanate from situations and institutions structured in social, political, and economic dominance (Köhler 1978).

\*\*\*\*\*

## END OF STORY WITHIN A STORY—FOR NOW

Tired from feeling the weight of her 63 years, especially the past 10 of them, Mrs. Brown complained to me about the prohibitive costs of living and the unjust formula being used to devalue the Jamaican dollar so as to make the economy more penetrable for foreign investment. "And all at the people's expense!" As we waited at the airport for my departure time, she remarked that she didn't know how she could have made it through all her trials and tribulations if it weren't for the grace of God who gave her industry, creativity, and a loving family as gifts; her church, upon which she had always been able to depend for both spiritual guidance and material aid; and Blessed Sacrament School, its PTA, and the various other activities and community services based on the grounds of that strategic local sanctuary from political warfare and economic desperation. [...]

I am back home now, but I can't help but think—and worry—about Beulah and Oceanview in light of the global restructuring that affects life in the Caribbean as well as in the U.S., where the implementation of first world versions of structural adjustment are being felt and confronted. The economic restructuring occurring in the U.S. is only a variation on a wider structural adjustment theme reverberating across the globe. Policies implemented in the U.S. resemble the austerity measures the IMF and World Bank are imposing on "developing" nations: cutbacks in social spending and public investments in housing, education, and health care; deregulation of airline, trucking, banking, finance, and broadcasting industries; corporate union-busting; currency devaluation; divestment of public enterprises; the increasing privatization of public services; and dramatic alterations of the tax system, shifting the tax burden away from wealthy individuals and large corporations (Sparr 1992, 30–31).

Probing the political and moral economy of poverty in "the field" (cf. D'Amico-Samuels 1991) has led me to reconceptualize analytical units and boundaries in ways that discern and utilize points of articulation and conjuncture between, for instance, Beulah Brown and myself, and Jamaica and the U.S., for a deeper, more broadly situated, and more personally grounded understanding of structural adjustment's gendered assaults—its invidious structural violence.

## REFERENCES

Antrobus, Peggy. 1989. Crisis, Challenge, and the Experiences of Caribbean Women. *Caribbean Quarterly* 35(1&2):17–28.

Basch, Linda, Nina Glick Schiller, and Cristina Szanton Blanc. 1994. *Nations Unbound: Transnational Projects, Postcolonial Predicaments, and Deterritorialized Nation-States.* Langhorne: Gordon and Breach Science Publishers.

Bolles, A. Lynn. 1991. Surviving Manley and Seaga: Case Studies of Women's Responses to Structural Adjustment Policies. *Review of Radical Political Economy* 23(3&4):20–36.

D'Amico-Samuels, Deborah. 1991. Undoing Fieldwork: Personal, Political, Theoretical, and Methodological Implications. In *Decolonizing Anthropology: Moving Further toward an Anthropology for Liberation.* Ed. Faye V. Harrison. Washington: American Anthropological Association.

Deere, Carmen Diana, et al. 1990. *In the Shadows of the Sun: Caribbean Development Alternatives and U.S. Policy.* Boulder: Westview Press.

Enloe, Cynthia. 1989. *Bananas, Beaches and Bases: Making Feminist Sense of International Politics.* Berkeley: University of California Press.

Ferguson, James. 1992. Jamaica: Stories of Poverty. *Race & Class* 34(1):61–72.

Harrison, Faye V. 1987a. Crime, Class, and Politics in Jamaica. *TransAfrica Forum* 5(1):29–38.

Harrison, Faye V. 1987b. Gangs, Grassroots Politics, and the Crisis of Dependent Capitalism in Jamaica. In *Perspectives in U.S. Marxist Anthropology.* Ed. David Hakken and Hanna Lessinger. Boulder: Westview Press.

Harrison, Faye V. 1988. The Politics of Social Outlawry in Urban Jamaica. *Urban Anthropology and Studies in Cultural Systems and World Economic Development* 17(2&3):259–277.

Harrison, Faye V. 1991a. Ethnography as Politics. In *Decolonizing Anthropology: Moving Further toward an Anthropology for Liberation*. Ed. Faye V. Harrison. Washington: American Anthropological Association.

Harrison, Faye V. 1991b. Women in Jamaica's Urban Informal Economy: Insights from a Kingston Slum. In *Third World Women and the Politics of Feminism*. Ed. Chandra T. Mohanty et al. Bloomington: Indiana University Press.

Ho, Christine G.T. 1993. The Internationalization of Kinship and the Feminization of Caribbean Migration: The Case of Afro-Trinidadian Immigrants in Los Angeles. *Human Organization* 52(1):32–40.

Köhler, Gernot. 1978. Global Apartheid. *World Order Models Project*. Working Paper no. 7. New York: Institute for World Order.

McAfee, Kathy. 1991. *Storm Signals: Structural Adjustment and Development Alternatives in the Caribbean*. Boston: South End Press.

Pan American Health Organization/World Health Organization. 1992. *The Health of Women in the English-Speaking Caribbean*.

Phillips, Daphene. 1994. The IMF, Structural Adjustment, and Health in the Caribbean: Policy Change in Health Care in Trinidad and Tobago. *Twenty-First Century Policy Review* 2(1&2):129–149.

*Race & Class*. 1992. *The New Conquistadors* 34(1) (July–Sept.):1–114.

Safa, Helen. 1994. *The Myth of the Male Breadwinner: Women and Industrialization in the Caribbean*. Boulder: Westview Press.

Sparr, Pamela. 1992. How We Got into This Mess and Ways to Get Out. *Ms.* March/April:130.

Sparr, Pamela, ed. 1994. *Mortgaging Women's Lives: Feminist Critiques of Structural Adjustment*. London: Zed Books.

Statistical Institute of Jamaica. 1991. *Statistical Yearbook of Jamaica*. Kingston: Statistical Institute of Jamaica.

Wolf, Eric. 1990. Distinguished Lecture: Facing Power—Old Insights, New Questions. *American Anthropologist* 92(3):586–596.

*Source:* Harrison, Faye V. (1997). Excerpted from "The Gendered Politics and Violence of Structural Adjustment: A View from Jamaica." In Louise Lamphere, Helena Ragone, & Patricia Zavella (Eds.), *Situated Lives: Gender and Culture in Everyday Life* (pp. 451–457, 464–465). New York, NY: Routledge.

# CHAPTER 60

## Women's Labor Is Never *Cheap*: Gendering Global Blue Jeans and Bankers

*Cynthia Enloe*

Cynthia Enloe is a research professor in the Department of International Development, Community, and Environment at Clark University in Worcester, Massachusetts. Her teaching and research focus on the interplay of gendered politics in the national and international arenas. Enloe has published in *Ms.* magazine, and appeared on National Public Radio, Al Jazeera, C-Span, and the BBC. She is the author of numerous books, including *Maneuvers: The International Politics of Militarizing Women's Lives, The Curious Feminist, Nimo's War, Emma's War: Making Feminist Sense of the Iraq War,* and *Seriously! Investigating Crashes and Crises as if Women Mattered.* The following excerpt is taken from the second edition of her book *Bananas, Beaches and Bases: Making Feminist Sense of International Politics.*

On April 24, 2013, the collapse of the Rana Plaza building killed 1,129 Bangladeshis. Most of the dead were women, all of whom had been working in the five garment factories housed in the poorly constructed building. The collapse was the deadliest disaster in the history of the garment industry, a globalized industry long plagued by disasters. What made headlines around the world, however, was less the deaths of Bangladeshi women and more the discovery that the garments they had been sewing were for global brand-name companies. And even then, the collapse of the Rana Plaza building, on the sprawling fringe of Dhaka, the capital city, might not have attracted sustained international attention had this tragedy not come only five months after another Bangladeshi garment-factory tragedy. The workers who had died when that factory burned were mostly women, and they too had been sewing clothes for popularly known brand-name corporations, such as Walmart, Gap, and Tommy Hilfiger.

Would these headlined deaths significantly alter the deeply gendered politics of the international garment industry?

# THE DOOR OPENED INWARD

The factory door opened inward. That was a fire code violation. It would prove deadly.

It was November 24, 2012, when fire broke out in the Tazreen Fashions garment factory on the outskirts of Dhaka. The factory was nine stories high; the top three floors had been added illegally. The company had fifteen hundred employees and sales totaling $35 million per year. Women, who constituted 70 percent of the factory's workers, were at their sewing machines when they first smelled the smoke. Their supervisors told them not to worry, to stay at their machines.

In today's globally competitive garment industry, the men who own the factories producing jeans, bathing suits, lingerie, and basketball uniforms under contract for European and North American brand-name companies cannot risk falling behind in their production deadlines. Those deadlines are set by their global corporate clients, who want to put new fashions on store shelves more and more often, to match impatient consumers' expectations. The Bangladeshi factory owner's anxiety over meeting his global clients' tight production deadlines had trickled down to his assembly line supervisors. As the smoke seeped upward, they pushed the women to keep sewing.[1]

The fire spread. Women defied their supervisors and dashed for the exit doors. They and their male coworkers found most of the doors locked or blocked by piles of fabric. The owner later claimed that he had ordered the doors locked to prevent workers from stealing materials. Some women did find one unlocked door; it opened inward. In the smoke and confusion, scores of women were crushed against the door. Other women died when they jumped out of windows. Many met their deaths not far from where they had sewn the brand-name garments. A total of 112 workers, women and men, died in the Tazreen factory fire; hundreds more were injured.

One of the workers able to escape was Sumi Abedin. She has told of the fire, the locked doors, the blocked stairways, the confusion. A male coworker broke a window. As she jumped through it, she thought her life was ending, but that at least her parents would have her body to bury. She still wonders how she survived. When she was twenty-three, Sumi had migrated from a small rural village to the outskirts of sprawling Dhaka to seek paid work in one of the scores of garment factories sprouting all over Bangladesh. She took a job at Tazreen Fashions as a "senior" sewing machine operator, earning fifty-five dollars per month, almost twenty dollars more than the Bangladeshi garment worker's legally mandated average wage of just thirty-seven dollars per month. She tried to send part of her earnings home to her parents. For her fifty-five dollars per month, Sumi worked at Tazreen Fashions eleven hours per day, six days a week. She recalls seeing labels for Walmart, Disney, and Gap.[2]

The Tazreen Fashions fire made global headlines. It was not the first Bangladesh garment fire, however. Even before the deadly Tazreen fire, between 2006 and 2012, five hundred Bangladeshi workers had died—and many more had been injured—in other garment factory fires. Furthermore, the Tazreen tragedy would not be the last time that the deaths of Bangladeshi women garment workers would feature on the world's nightly news.

To many, it seemed as if the clock had spun backward. Women garment workers, locked in their flaming factories, jumping out of upper-story windows, meeting their deaths as a result of owners' abuses: was this March 21, 1911, all over again? That was the date of the infamous Triangle Shirtwaist Factory fire in lower Manhattan, in which so many Jewish, Irish, and Italian young women and men had perished: 129 women; 17 men. In March 2011, on the Triangle fire's hundredth anniversary, feminist labor historians reminded us that it had taken such a deadly fire to wake up the American public to the exploitive and unsafe working conditions on which the country's garment industry was built and to compel the all-male legislatures at the time to pass the country's first meaningful labor safety laws.[3] In the past century, had no lessons been learned? Why were we all still wearing clothes threaded with the exploitation of women workers?

The weeks following the 2012 Bangladesh garment factory fire produced exposés and calls for reform. We learned that in recent years Walmart, Tommy Hilfiger, Benetton, H&M, Zara, Sears, Mango, and Gap had put another layer of agents in between themselves and the women workers: suppliers. The global companies hired local suppliers, such as Success Apparel, to hire the local factory contractors. Those factory contractors, such as Tazreen Fashion's owner, were the men who, in turn, hired the sewers, pressers, and cutters. These men—the factory owners and the managers of the suppliers and contractors—had cultivated political ties to influential local Bangladeshi officials to ensure they would not be fined for safety violations and that they would be issued the questionable zoning permits. Some of the garment factory owners even held seats in the Bangladesh parliament. The profits of the global brand-name corporations depended on those local masculinized political relationships—whom they trusted, whom they bribed, whom they entertained.

As the fire's death toll mounted, some multinational company executives, worried about their global reputations, initially denied using Tazreen. They soon had to backtrack, however, when Bangladeshi labor advocates displayed their brands' labels and the documents that named them as Tazreen customers. In fact, one high-risk form of activism that Bangladesh labor advocates had resorted to was running into burning factory buildings to pull out company labels and garment orders in order to challenge what they predicted would be post-tragedy denials by global company executives.[4] [...]

The corporate strategy to assuage the concerns of rights-conscious consumers without jeopardizing profits has been to devise a system of workplace monitoring conducted under contract with "independent" accreditation monitors. Thus, as the ashes of the Tazreen fire still smoldered, some corporate executives

claimed that their companies had hired monitors to inspect their subcontractors' far-flung factories, and that Tazreen had met the monitors' safety and fairness standards. What the executives neglected to note, however, was that those reputedly independent monitoring organizations depended financially on their corporate clients for their own incomes. Furthermore, some monitors routinely subcontracted out their safety inspection work to local monitors, over whom they exerted only minimal quality control. [...]

Putting geographic and political distance between their own boardrooms and the factory floors where low-waged women sewed their products has been one of the core globalizing business strategies of current-era companies. Now, however, labor rights campaigners, such as those in Bangladesh, were not only running into burning buildings, but they were also forging international alliances (with groups such as the Amsterdam-based Clean Clothes Campaign and the Washington-based Workers Rights Coalition, which represented a coalition of anti-sweatshop colleges) in order to globalize corporate accountability.[5] It has not been easy.

By 2012, Bangladesh had become the world's second-largest garment exporter (China was first). When Bangladeshis had waged a war to gain their independence from Pakistan in 1971, there had been no garment factories in Bangladesh. But entrepreneurs and policy makers in the newly independent Bangladesh soon realized that the world's rapidly globalizing apparel industry provided their country with an opportunity to capitalize on a resource that the labor-intensive industry needed and that Bangladesh had in abundance: low-waged workers. By 2004, there were thirty-three hundred garment factories in Bangladesh. Together, they employed 1.7 million workers: 1,320,000 women and 380,000 men.[6] By 2012, the year of the Tazreen fire, the number of garment factories had grown to forty-five hundred, employing over 3 million Bangladeshi workers—that is, as many garment workers as the entire population of Albania. Many of the factory owners were Bangladeshi men, although overseas male entrepreneurs, too, were moving into Bangladesh's lucrative garment manufacturing sector. [...]

In Bangladesh, garment production was now more than Big Business; it was also Big Politics. Local businessmen sought to influence mayors, zoning boards, political parties, regulators, and parliament. Workers began to unionize. When the government, in support of the factory owners, suppressed their organizing efforts, workers called wildcat strikes. After an especially violent confrontation between striking workers and armed police, Bangladesh's prime minister, Sheikh Hasina (a woman, but head of a masculinized ruling party, the Awami League, closely allied with the male garment-industry owners), agreed to raise the country's minimum monthly wage from twenty-one dollars to thirty-seven dollars.[7] Still, at an average wage of thirty-seven dollars per month, Bangladesh remained the *cheapest* place for global apparel companies to produce their clothes. So the brand-name companies kept coming. The operations of the suppliers and the contractors kept expanding. The cost of the sewn products for the global brands and the retail prices of clothes for consumers were kept low not only by the low wages paid to Bangladeshi workers but also by both the factory owners' lack of investment in factory safety and health measures and by the global companies' lack of insistence on those safety and health measures.

The end of the quota-setting Multi-Fiber Agreement in 2005, an international agreement designed to protect garment workers' jobs in North America and Europe, made Bangladesh's garment factories all the more attractive to multinational brand companies in their constant search for low-cost contractors. When the Geneva-based World Trade Organization ruled that the MFA gave unfair advantage to developed countries, Los Angeles and New York garment workers lost thousands of jobs (many of them held by immigrant women), while the global garment companies became freer to roam the world in search of low-cost production.

Then in the early years of the twenty-first century, Chinese women garment workers, who had been calling wildcat strikes, succeeded in pressing for higher wages. This development added even more luster to Bangladesh's low-cost manufacturing. And at this gendered historical moment, Tazreen Fashions' factory burst into flames.

## GENDER MATTERS

It is all too easy to tell this tale of globalized garments, money, and death as if gender politics do not matter. It is all too comfortable for many commentators to narrate the story of the Tazreen factory fire—and the other factory disasters that followed soon after, not only in Bangladesh, but also in Pakistan, Cambodia, South Korea, and Mexico—as if it does not matter that the majority of the dead and injured were women. Women may be mentioned, they may be photographed and filmed, yet they are rarely interviewed by mainstream journalists about their complex experiences of being women factory workers. [...]

The majority of people trapped in the Tazreen fire—and in most garment factory disasters, which are so common today around the world—were not merely "workers." They were *women* workers. To stay incurious about these women's experiences as women leaves journalists, scholars, human rights activists, and citizens unable to reliably explain how and why women's labor is made *cheap*.

No one's labor is automatically cheap. It has to be *made* cheap. It is the deliberate manipulation of ideas about girls and women, and of notions of femininity, that empowers those who try to cheapen women's labor.

Chobi Mahmud grew up in Tangail, Bangladesh's northern district. She migrated from her family's rural village when she was a teenager. As her country's garment industry expanded, its workforce had become more feminized. Chobi entered the globalized garment workforce at a time when feminization of

Bangladesh's garment industry had progressed significantly. What had not been available to Chobi's mother had become available to her. In 1990, women had constituted only 28 percent of all of Bangladesh's garment workers. By contrast, in 2002, when Chobi was nineteen and speaking to a journalist, women's proportion of all Bangladesh's garment workers had grown to a remarkable 85 percent.[8]

That is, there was nothing "natural" about such a high proportion of women working in the twenty-first-century Bangladesh garment factories. It had been in part the result of male factory owners' coming to the realization that they could keep wages low—and thus keep the factories globally attractive to the executives of Nike, North Face, Walmart, Mango, H&M, and Tommy Hilfiger—if they began to feminize their workforces, to hire more young women from poor rural villages.

But it had taken a second change for this gendered formula to work: more and more young women in those villages had to change their own ideas about what they could do with their lives and to persuade their mothers and fathers to let them leave home. Without this effective redefinition of girlhood and feminine respectability, the global brand-name companies would not have migrated to Bangladesh.

Chobi, like most of these young factory women, was unmarried when she took a job in an urban factory. She and her fellow sewers started to earn wages for their work. They gained a sense of importance as they sent money back to their parents, who, in turn, soon realized that their daughters were more likely to send money home from their urban jobs than were their sons. With this realization, parents became less likely to define a daughter's goodness in terms of her marrying a young man of their choosing. Not only did the women factory workers put off marriage, but when they did marry they also often managed to negotiate a new division of household labor with their husbands. If they continued to work and bring home money after they married, many of Chobi's women factory friends were able to persuade their

husbands to start sharing in more of the housework. According to Mashuda Shefali Khatun, head of the Dhaka-based women's advocacy group Nari Uddug Kendra (Centre for Women's Initiatives), studies revealed that men married to women with paid jobs did more hours of housework than those men married to women without paid jobs.[9]

Many Bangladeshi women garment workers became acutely aware of the unfair, even dangerous, conditions under which they sewed seams, hems, and pockets—there were unclean toilets, long hours, poor ventilation, blocked stairways. When deciding whether to risk organizing and whether to risk taking part in protests, each woman garment worker had to weigh the gendered advantages of taking and keeping her paid factory job against her growing frustration at the exploitive collusion between an array of men: the global companies, their factory owners, and the local politicians who suppressed her wages, discouraged her organizing efforts, and endangered her health. That gendered calculus was fraught.

The Tazreen fire broke out at a particular moment in gendered local and international histories. Just as New York's Triangle Shirtwaist Factory fire of 1911 happened at a particular moment in the history of women's international migration and in the history of American women's suffrage organizing, so too the Tazreen fire of 2012 happened at a particular moment in transnational women's politics and in Bangladeshi women's own organizing. One popular racialized myth that has enabled the global companies and their local allies to cheapen women's labor holds that women on the social margins in affluent countries, and women living in poor countries, are less conscious of and less in need of their rights—or that they will pursue their rights only if tutored and led by more privileged women and men.

In reality, by 2012, Bangladeshi women's political thinking and organizing had become elaborate and sophisticated. Bangladesh's women activists had named, exposed, and campaigned against local men's acid-throwing intended to disfigure women and girls.

Other women activists not only had taken part in microfinance schemes but also had begun to expose how those schemes, intended to economically empower poor women, too often empowered men and left the women recipients burdened by debt. Some women also had begun to challenge Bangladesh's male-dominated political parties and religious clergy. Local feminists were supporting those Bangladeshi women who now, after decades of silence, were defying the powerful notions of nationalist pride and feminized sexualized shame to publicly tell their stories of having survived rape during the 1971 war for independence.

The politics of marriage, of parenting, of daughterhood, of women's friendships, of gendered divisions of paid and unpaid labor, of women's organizing, of feminized sexuality and silence—each of these politics is gendered. That is, each is shaped by acceptance of or resistance to certain ideas about femininity and masculinity. Those ideas are *political* insofar as they not only take power to legitimize and sustain but also take power to transform or debunk.

These ideas and the interlocking gendered politics they fuel are not timeless. They can be altered, sometimes only superficially, other times profoundly. Each one of these deeply gendered politics has been and continues to be a pillar of the international political economy of jeans, bikinis, dresses, sweatshirts, and tank tops. Making women visible is crucial to making reliable sense of the international politics of making women's labor *cheap*.

## HOW IS WOMEN'S LABOR MADE *CHEAP*?

It is commonplace to speak of "cheap women's labor." The phrase is used in public policy discussions as if cheapness were somehow inherent in women's work—especially in the work of those women pushed to the societal and international margins.

Reality is quite different: women's work is only as unrewarded or as low-paid as it is *made* to be.

Feminist investigators are always on the lookout for decisions—and the people who make and enforce those decisions. The international political economy works the way it does in part because of the decisions that have cheapened the value of women's work, making it either unpaid or low paid. These decisions are made invisible, however, when they are dismissed as being not decisions at all but merely the result of "natural" processes. Imagining anything as "natural" takes it out of the realm of politics. A lot of what goes on in international politics is left underinvestigated because it is mistakenly assumed to be natural. One of the hallmarks of unfeminist commentaries on international politics is their underestimation of power.

*\*\*\*\*\**

## THE BANKER AND THE SEAMSTRESS

Nike was a pioneer in shedding its factories. When Nike's Oregon-based male executives decided to rely on subcontractor factory-owners overseas, they chose South Korea. The government was friendly. In the 1970s, South Korea's government was deeply militarized; it was also tightly bound to the United States by a military alliance and was hosting fifty thousand American troops on scores of U.S. bases. To the Nike executives, this Cold War arrangement made South Korea seem a good bet for investment. But then came the South Koreans' successful popular prodemocracy movement of the mid-1980s, a movement in which women as university students and as factory workers played vital political roles. When South Korea's new civilian democratic political system replaced the military regime, and both the local women's movement and labor unions became more influential, Nike's executives ended their contracts with Korean factories and moved—with their Korean male subcontractors—to Indonesia and elsewhere.

Rural, migrant, young Indonesian women thereafter became a crucial part of the global profit formula for Nike—and Puma, Adidas, and Reebok.

By the start of the twenty-first century, garment factories had become part of the local landscape in countries that otherwise appeared politically dissimilar. Each pair of jeans, each blouse or bikini, was sewn, that is, with threads of particular gendered political hues. For instance, under apartheid, the white-dominated South African government officials had encouraged foreign companies to set up shop in Bantustans, a territorial scheme intended to bolster apartheid and the fiction of self-sustaining Black "homelands." Companies from Hong Kong, Taiwan, and Israel accepted Pretoria's invitation.[10] For their part, in 1986, Vietnamese Communist government officials adopted a new probusiness policy, called Doi Moi, to jump-start their country's postwar economy. Within several decades, the resultant government-promoted system would be described as the "generally opaque world of Vietnamese manufacturing with layers of contractors and subcontractors" that produced clothing and sneakers for the international market.[11] Meanwhile, in Fiji, the government compensated for a long-term slump in world sugar prices and a sharp fall in tourism revenues following a military coup by enticing Australian and New Zealand garment companies to set up factories with a special offer intended to undercut Fiji's Asian neighbors. Fijian officials hoped that Fijian women's sewing could paper over the problems caused by a weakened plantation economy, interethnic strife, and militarization.[12]

The international politics of garments stretched from the women at their sewing machines stitching the tricky pant-leg seam of a pair of blue jeans, to the men in boardrooms and ministerial offices drafting memos on loans and investments. Bankers, both in private banks and in international banking agencies such as the World Bank and the International Monetary Fund, have been prime movers in the globalization of the garment industry and its deliberate reliance on low-paid feminized workforces. Bankers,

however, do not talk with, much less bargain with, women sewing-machine operators. Bankers deal with corporate executives and with government officials, especially those men who dominate their countries' finance ministries.

These dealings take place behind closed doors and are often tense, and they also are usually masculinized. We know all too little about how the workings of diverse masculinities shape these important financial dealings. We do know that the outcomes not only determine women's lives but also depend on controlling women's lives. Bankers have tied their government and company loans to their borrowers' ability to promote internationally competitive garment exports. It has been a loan condition that has proved hard to meet without government officials and manufacturing executives taking deliberate steps to suppress the costs of manufacturing labor—that is, women's labor.

Lending and stitching—the two activities have become globally interdependent. Each has become a process reliant on bolstering gendered assumptions and gendered relationships: while the floors of the exporting garment factories remain feminized, the boardrooms of international lenders remain masculinized.

Risk-taking has been at the core of the masculinized conception of banking. Just as travel to "exotic" regions was once imagined to be a risky and therefore peculiarly masculine form of adventure, so today manly risk-taking is thought by many financiers to be integral to the globalized financial industry and to manly banking. The value assigned to risk-taking, furthermore, has become even greater since governments eagerly deregulated banking in the 1990s and the beginning of the twenty-first century. Widespread banking deregulation made a distinctly American, masculinized style of banking more popular in Britain, Ireland, Iceland, Spain, Greece, and Japan. This transnational masculinized banking style also helped sustain cooperative relations between otherwise fiercely competitive male bankers. It is a shared masculinized risk-taking style that makes their "world." It also has helped keep women, allegedly more risk averse than "manly men," on the margins of this "ceaselessly competitive" financial world.

Thousands of women today do work in global banking. They provide banking's crucial support services; but only occasionally do women gain promotions to the still-masculinized senior policy positions. In the United States, for instance, women constitute a mere 16 percent of all banking executives. Among those women trying to gain senior promotions into banks' higher echelons, where long hours and constant travel are unquestioned requisites for proving one's corporate commitment, the stubborn conventional politics of marriage and the politics of motherhood reinforce the masculinized character of the executive suites.

The banking industry's masculinized structure and culture would persist up to and even after the disastrous financial crash of 2008. By the later phases of the global financial crash, more women were making careers in the financial industry, some rising to middle management. Nonetheless, by 2013, no woman yet had served as head of one of the European Union's Central Banks, as president of the World Bank, as secretary of the U.S. Treasury, or as chancellor of the exchequer in Britain. Only in 2011 was the first woman—Christine Lagarde—chosen to head the International Monetary Fund. Only in 2014 was the first woman—Janet Yellen—appointed to the powerful post of chair of the U.S. Federal Reserve. And each of these breakthroughs was in large measure a response to concerted political pressure. By themselves, they are not proof that the patriarchal conventions of global banking have been radically subverted.[13]

The masculinization of international banking has been politically costly. It has destabilized governments, distorted public priorities, undermined inclusive democracy, and widened the gaps between rich and poor. Many European and developing countries carry huge international debts and are scarcely able to keep up with the astronomical interest payments owed to their foreign creditors, much less to repay the principal. But Japanese, British, German, American, and other large lenders and their governments fear that global default would topple the international political economy that has been so carefully constructed in the years since World War II. So lenders and their allies press debtor governments to make good on their mammoth debts. The most popular package of loan conditions—"structural adjustment"—combines cuts in a debtor government's expenditures on "nonproductive" public services (transport and food subsidies, health services, and education) with the expansion of exports: locally mined raw materials, locally grown plantation crops, or locally manufactured goods. Among the latter are garments. Unless they remain globally competitive in the export of garments, many of these indebted governments cannot pay off their international debts.

The centerpiece of the bankers' export strategy has been the export-processing zone. Indebted governments were encouraged by economists to set aside territory specifically for factories producing goods for the international market. Governments were to entice overseas companies to move their factories to these zones by offering to provide them with electricity, ports, and runways, as well as low-cost workers, and by offering tax holidays and police protection. Most attractive of all has been the governments' promise to provide "cheap labor." It should not be surprising that in most export-processing zones—in Sri Lanka, the Philippines, El Salvador, Nicaragua, and Panama—at least 70 percent of the workers are women.

The risk-taking globalized banker needs the conscientious seamstress to hold his world together. The local patriarchal politician and his financial advisors need the seamstress to keep the banker pacified. If the seamstress rebels, radically reimagining what it means to be a female citizen who sews for a living, her country may turn up on the bankers' list of "poor investments."

## PATRIARCHY IS NOT OLD-FASHIONED

Garment-company managers have continued to rely on four patriarchal assumptions to help them keep women's wages low in their factories. First, they have defined sewing as something that girls and women do "naturally" or "traditionally." An operation that a person does "naturally" is not a "skill," because a skill is something one has to be trained to do, for which one should then be rewarded. In reality, many a schoolgirl has struggled through her home economics class trying in vain to make the required skirt or apron. One garment-factory manager explained that he preferred to hire young Filipino women who did *not* know how to sew, so that "we don't have to undo the bad habits they've learned."[14] But the myth of women as "natural" sewers persists and is used by factory managers to deflate women garment workers' actual skills, thereby reducing their wages. Women sewing machinists have gone out on strike to force company executives to categorize their jobs as "skilled" jobs.[15]

Second, women's labor can be made and kept *cheap* by reserving allegedly skilled jobs for men. Women, the "natural" sewers, are assigned to the sewing machines; men are hired by managers to be the cutters and the pressers and to run specialized equipment, such as the zipper inserter. Workers who cut and press fabric and install zippers are paid more than those who sew. The managerial argument that running specialized machinery and pressing require the physical strength that only men have and skills that only men can learn ignores the technological options available and the physical demands made on women by housework and farming, while conveniently also overlooking the fact that some men are weaker and slower learners than some women.

Third, factory owners and managers justify paying women workers less than men, and less than a living wage, by imagining that women are merely secondary wage earners in their families. They prefer to ignore (most of the time) the reality that the rural parents of their young female employees have come to depend on the money that those young women, as "dutiful daughters," send home. Simultaneously, however, managers strategically manipulate the daughterly expectations when they try to persuade the women not to jeopardize their jobs by going out on strike. Executives of global apparel corporations take comfort in the outdated assumption that men—as fathers and husbands—are still the breadwinners. In the 1990s, feminists working inside, and lobbying from outside, powerful international agencies persuaded their economists and development experts to see that their "men-as-breadwinners" assumption was out of touch with economic reality. The assumption that men are breadwinners had been a boon to generations of garment-factory managers. Still today it is an erroneous assumption that allows managers to rationalize paying their women workers *as if* those women were being financially supported at home by a man.

In reality, divorce, abandonment, recession, AIDS, war, and separation have caused marked increases in the numbers of women who are the chief income earners—often the sole income earners—for their households. They support not only their own children but also the children of relatives, as well as elderly or impoverished parents. In 2006, outside of western Europe and North America, women were the heads of 25 percent or more of all households in Vietnam, Hong Kong, Lesotho, Namibia, Zimbabwe, Kenya, Burundi, Tanzania, Brazil, Peru, Venezuela, Colombia, El Salvador, Costa Rica, Nicaragua, Haiti, and Dominican Republic, to name only a few.[16]

Factory owners' and global clients' fourth self-serving claim is that the single woman at her machine, working eleven hours a day, six days a week, is not a "serious" member of the labor force because she intends to work only until she finds a husband and "settles down," thereafter to be supported by him. Consequently, so the modern managerial ideology of marriage goes, the single woman employee does not need to be paid as if she were a career worker: when she is sewing a collar for Gap or a back pocket for

Levi's, she is just going through "a phase." When male labor union leaders also share this same vision—that women's chief and lasting vocation is to be a good wife—the prospects for women's collective action grow even dimmer.

Thus keeping women's labor cheap requires patriarchal power. Cheapening women's labor requires alliances, vigilance, and daily effort. That effort is an integral part of what is called today's "international political economy." Factory managers alone cannot keep women's labor cheap: it takes a combination of willing allies—fathers and husbands, media producers, local and national officials, police forces, global executives, labor activists—holding and promoting patriarchal ideas. That is, the profits and tax revenues earned by businesses and governments rely on the perpetuation of certain ideas about skills, marriage, dutiful daughters, child care, feminine respectability, and fashion. The politics of the global garment industry are sustained by these patriarchal ideas, which maintain gendered relationships inside homes, within communities, and in and between governments, as well as on the factory floor.

To make feminist sense of the international politics of bankers and blue jeans—and dresses, sneakers, sweatshirts, and football uniforms—requires investigating a wide range of interlocking gendered mindsets and multiple political sites, as well as finding out who gains what from the perpetuation of those particular beliefs.

## NOTES

[Note that the endnotes were heavily edited down from the original due to space considerations.]

1.  This description of the Tazreen Fashions garment factory fire of November 24, 2012, in Bangladesh and its aftermath is based on the following reports: Vikas Bajaj, "Fire Ravages Bangladesh Factory, *International Herald Tribune*, November 26, 2012; Julfikar Ali Manik and Jim Yardley, "Garment Workers Stage Angry Protest after Bangladesh Fire," *New York Times*, November 27, 2012; Steven Greenhouse, "Documents Indicate Walmart Blocked Safety Push in Bangladesh," *New York Times*, December 6, 2012; Associated Press, "Factory in Bangladesh Lost Fire Clearance before Blaze," *New York Times*, December 8, 2012; "Fire Safety in Garment Factories," editorial, *New York Times*, December 10, 2012; Steven Greenhouse, "2nd Supplier for Walmart at Factory That Burned," *New York Times*, December 11, 2012; Julfikar Ali Manik and Jim Yardley, "Bangladesh Finds Gross Negligence in Factory Fire," *New York Times*, December 18, 2012; Amy Goodman, "Survivor of Bangladesh's Tazreen Factory Fire Urges U.S. Retailers to Stop Blocking Worker Safety," an interview with Sumi Abedin, *Democracy Now*, April 25, 2013, www.democracynow.org/2013/4/25/survivor_of_bangladeshs_tazreen_factory_fire.

2.  Goodman, "Survivor of Bangladesh's Tazreen Factory Fire ..."

3.  See, for instance, the Remember the Triangle Fire Coalition website created by feminist historians and devoted to the history—and lessons—of the 1911 Triangle Shirtwaist fire: www.rememberthetrianglefire.org; see also two documentary films describing the Triangle fire: Jamila Wignot, dir., *Triangle Fire*, American Experience, PBS, 2011; and Daphne Pinkerton, dir., *Triangle*, HBO, 2011.

4.  Greenhouse, "Documents Indicate Walmart Blocked Safety Push in Bangladesh"; Priyanka Borpujari, "Deadly Savings," *Boston Globe*, January 2, 2013.

5.  Clean Clothes Campaign, www.cleanclothes.org; Workers Rights Consortium, www.workersrights.org.

6.  National Garments Workers Federation, *Activity Reports, 1999–2004*, Dhaka, 2004, www.nadir.org/nadir/initiativ/agp/s26/banglad/index.htm#contence.

7.  Jim Yardley, "Fighting for Bangladesh Labor, and Ending Up in Pauper's Grave," *New York Times*, September 10, 2012.

8.  This interview was conducted by Swapna Majumdar, "Bangladesh Garment Workers Have Taste of Freedom," *Women's eNews*, July 15, 2002, http://womensenews.org/2002/07/bangladesh-garment-workers-have-taste-freedom/. The gender-disaggregated employment data cited here were collected by researchers at the Bangladesh Institute of Development Studies in Dhaka.

9.  Ibid.

10. I am indebted to Ann Seidman, an expert on foreign investment in South Africa, for this information. Interview with the author, Clark University, Worcester, MA, April 21, 1988.

11. Thomas Fuller, "Vietnam Accused of Abusing Drug Addicts," *New York Times*, September 8, 2011. See also Murray Hiebert, "Hanoi Courts Capitalist Investment," *Indochina Issues*, no. 67 (July 1986): 3–4. For a rather uncritical look at current government-approved labor organizing in Vietnam, see Kent Wong and An Le, *Organizing on Separate Shores: Vietnamese and Vietnamese Union Organizers* (Los Angeles: UCLA Center for Labor Research and Education, 2009).

12. Anthony B. Van Fossen, "Two Military Coups in Fiji," *Bulletin of Concerned Asian Scholars* 19 (November 4, 1988): 29; *Far Eastern Economic Review* (March 3, 1988): 49.

13. Lynn Ashburner, "Women Inside the Counting House: Women in Finance," in *Women and Work*, ed. Angela Coyle and Jane Skinner (London: Macmillan; New York: New York University Press, 1988), 130–51.

14. Interview by the author with a Levi's factory manager, Manila, March 1980. See also Noeleen Heyzer, *Daughters in Industry: Work, Skills, and Consciousness of Women Workers in Asia* (Kuala Lumpur: Women's Program, Asian and Pacific Development Centre, 1988).

15. Simon Godfrey, "Women Who Took on Ford in Equal Pay Fight," *The Guardian*, June 7, 2013.

16. Joni Seager, *The Penguin Atlas of Women in the World*, 4th ed. (New York: Penguin, 2009), 22–23.

*Source:* Enloe, Cynthia. (2014). Excerpted from "Chapter Seven: Women's Labor Is Never Cheap: Gendering Global Blue Jeans and Bankers." In *Bananas, Beaches and Bases: Making Feminist Sense of International Politics, 2nd Edition* (pp. 250–263, 274–282). Oakland, CA: University of California Press.

# CHAPTER 61

## Women behind the Labels: Worker Testimonies from Central America

*STITCH and the Maquila Solidarity Network*

STITCH is an independent, non-profit women's solidarity network that supports women workers in Central America and immigrant workers in the United States to plan and carry out labour organizing campaigns. By adopting a feminist perspective, STITCH seeks to sustain unions and women's and workers' rights through leadership development, training programs, and exchanges that increase women's organizing skills and build ties between workers and activists.

The Maquila Solidarity Network (MSN) is a labour and women's rights organization that supports the efforts of workers in global supply chains to win improved wages and working conditions, and therefore a better quality of life for themselves and their families. MSN works alongside women's and labour rights organizations, primarily in Mexico and Central America, on cases of workers' rights violations and on joint projects and initiatives focused on systemic issues in the garment industry.

## INTRODUCTION

The women whose stories appear in this booklet are [groundbreaking] union organizers. They are the women behind the clothing labels and food brands that have inspired campaigns against sweatshops across North America. They are emerging leaders of a growing movement of strong and committed women determined to improve conditions for themselves and their co-workers. They want jobs, yes, but dignified jobs, and wages that allow them to provide for themselves and their families.

## The Maquilas

Marie [and others] have worked in Central America's maquiladora garment factories, making brand-name apparel for the North American market. They organized workers in an industry with almost no unions and even fewer collective bargaining agreements.

Maquiladoras, also known as maquilas, are factories that assemble goods for export. In Central America, the majority of maquilas assemble clothing, almost all of which is exported to North America.

Guatemala and Honduras each have approximately 300 maquiladora factories. Yet, as of August 2000, there are only 10 maquilas with signed collective agreements in Honduras and none in Guatemala.

Countless studies of Central America's maquiladoras have documented inhumane working conditions: verbal, physical, and sexual abuse of women workers; and vehement union-busting tactics of employers. Reports of sweatshop abuses have generated citizen outcry in Central America and a growing anti-sweatshop movement in North America.

Companies have flocked to Central America not just for so-called cheap labour, but also because here they can operate with impunity. They face almost no regulation from local governments dependent on foreign investment to create employment, and little opposition from the local labor movement weakened by years of violent repression.

The workers' stories in this booklet reveal the human reality behind the statistics: how it feels to work a 16-hour shift in a crowded factory, the unrelenting pressure to produce more in less time, the continual harassment by supervisors, harassment that turns to repression when workers begin to organize to defend their rights. [...]

The interviews also reveal a less visible aspect of the maquila—how organizing experiences have changed women's lives.

For the first time, these women took on positions of leadership, and, in some cases, began to demand their rights at home as well as at work. Long after the initial campaigns were over, and in spite of the setbacks, the women who tell their stories in this booklet continue to organize for change, in other factories, in their personal lives, and in the broader union and social movement.

\*\*\*\*\*

## The Women behind the Labels

Too often, the media, and even the anti-sweatshop movement, present the women behind the labels and brands as helpless victims. We hope these stories of Central American women working for change will help challenge that notion.

The women who speak through the pages of *Women behind the Labels* share stories of organizing against all odds for better wages and working conditions, but also for justice, respect, and a better future for themselves and their children.

At some point, each of the women decides she can no longer accept the inhuman conditions forced upon her and her family and fellow workers. [...]

The interviews for this booklet were carried out by Marion Traub-Werner in October–December of 1998. [...]

> If you don't learn to defend yourself, you're in real trouble.
> —*Marie Mejia*

Marie Mejia is the lead organizer for the International Textile, Garment and Leather Workers Federation (ITGLWF)[1] maquila organizing project in Guatemala. For the past two years she has spent close to seven days a week going from house to house and maquila to maquila talking to workers about the benefits of organizing. Marie speaks from experience—as a former maquila worker, teenage domestic worker, and child laborer on coffee plantations.

The oldest of seven from a Mayan Indigenous family in the western province of San Marcos, Marie has lived several lifetimes in her 26 years. She started working at the age of 12. At 15, she left home to work in Mexico in order to help her family. That experience left her fiercely independent—a characteristic embodied in her determined step, her perfect posture, and her resolute voice.

Hearing about the interviews I was doing, Marie approached me one day and asked to participate. "You should really interview me," she said. "I have worked in just about every job there is." During the interview, I barely had to ask any questions. For two hours, Marie led me through an emotional journey, one she had not shared with many people. Later, she played the tapes for her siblings as a way of explaining to them what it was like for her to come of age away from them, her parents, and her country.

**Marion: What is your family like?**

**Marie:** I am the oldest of seven. I left school when I was 12. I went with my father to cut coffee outside of Tapachula in Mexico. When we arrived at the finca, the coffee harvest was over. The only work for women was collecting garbage, while the men worked clearing brush in the mountains. I helped my father clear brush even though they said it was "men's work." One day my father was bitten by a scorpion while working, and from then on he wouldn't let me do that work.

After a while there wasn't work for women or men. That's when I decided to go to Tapachula to get a job as a domestic worker. My father accompanied me to the house. I remember how he cried when the señora took me inside and closed the door. I could see him outside, just standing there. I only lasted two months in that first house. I was desperate to see my mother and father. I knew that if my father had reacted that way, my mother was sure to be feeling even worse. I went home for two months, and then had to return to Tapachula. That was in 1988.

I found work at another house, earning 80 pesos [U.S.$32] a month. But I didn't like it. I had problems with the grandfather who lived there. He was always watching me. Once, he pushed me into my room and locked me in. I found out later that he had raped all the maids that had come to work there. That's when I left. I worked at that house for five months.

At the next house I earned 150 pesos [U.S.$60] a month. It was only about three blocks from where I worked before. By that time, I was 16. I never went hungry in that house. Never. I had food and my own room, and nobody tried to come in. But I had to work very hard. The house was

huge, with something like five bathrooms and a big patio. I worked there for six years, until I ran into problems after the señor divorced and remarried. After living nine months with his new wife, I had to leave. She said I was paid too much for the amount of work that there was to do. Can you imagine? I did everything—washed and ironed their clothes, made their food, went to the market, mopped and scrubbed the floors. Everything. I would get up at 6:00 in the morning and be rushing all day until 10:00 or 10:30 at night when I finally could stop working.

**Marion: Are your parents ladino[2] or Indigenous?**

**Marie:** They are Indigenous. They speak Mam,[3] but my father never permitted us to learn to speak that dialect. When he was little, he didn't learn to speak Spanish, and had a lot of problems because of it. My mother still wears traditional dress. I did too when I was little, but I stopped when I was working in Tapachula.

**Marion: And in Tapachula, did you earn enough to help out your parents or just to support yourself?**

**Marie:** When I started I was earning 80 pesos a month. I kept 20 pesos for myself and gave the rest to my father, who used to come to Tapachula every month. Later, when I earned 150 pesos a month, I gave my father 120 and kept 30 for myself. And with those 30 pesos, I had to buy soap, shampoo, deodorant, towels, and all of that. It wasn't much, but I always tried to find a way to make the money last, because I was working there to help my family.

**Marion: How did you learn to sew?**

**Marie:** When I was having problems with the last señora, I started thinking about finding another kind of work. So I asked the señor if he would give me permission to study sewing for one hour a day.

My next job was working in a tailor shop. I earned very little, 10 pesos [U.S.$3.50] for each piece of clothing I finished. I made one piece a day, which meant I had only 10 pesos to pay for a room, food, and transportation. That was not enough, so I decided to look for work in a house again.

At the next house where I worked I earned good money, but I had to do the work of two. In the morning I made breakfast for the girls and took them to school. Then I made breakfast for the señora and her husband, the doctor. After that, I would go to the market, wash and iron the clothes, and clean the house. When the girls got back from school, I took them to ballet. I looked after those two girls as if they were my own; it was a huge responsibility. The girls had rooms of their own with separate bathrooms. Lots of clothes. Sheets for the bed. Everything had to be washed, and of course there was no washing machine.

The man who lived next door tried to warn me that the señora was bad, but I thought she was alright. I learned how wrong I was. I had just returned from going to visit my family when she accused me of stealing. She started going through my clothes. She even searched my underwear, which I think is what hurt me the most. The señora called the police and they came and took me to the station. The police commander said he would let me go if I would go out with him. I told him that he better arrest me, because I would never go out with him. He disgusted me.

I went to my old boss for help. He went the very next morning to a government official and got the charges dropped.

That was the last time I worked in a house. I decided to rent a small room and started working as a food vendor, making 30 pesos [U.S.$4.70] a day. There were a lot of problems with that job too, but the good thing about the job was that the vendors were organized and I started to learn

about unions. In 1996, I left Tapachula for good and came here to Guatemala.

**Marion: Is that when you started working in the maquila?**

Marie: Yes. My uncle suggested that since I liked sewing, I should try working in the maquila. So my brother and I went looking for work all along Avenida Petapa [the main industrial road]. At the Daimi factory we asked if there were any openings. I told them I was an operator, that I had experience. They hired both of us right away.

I had never worked in a factory and didn't know what to expect. But it didn't take long before I started to see how badly they treated people, how they yelled at them. A Korean supervisor named Señora Lee was the worst. You wouldn't believe how she mistreated people. She screamed at people in front of everyone. Her favorite phrases were: "Do you want to work? Yes or No?" Or, "Why don't you look for another job if you don't want to work?" And, "You are useless. You aren't worth a salary." When she yelled at the workers, most of the women would cry.

I was afraid that Señora Lee would yell at me, but the woman she scolded the most on our line was our line supervisor, Carmen. Who knows what she had against her? Señora Lee would throw pieces of clothing in her face. When she finally managed to get Carmen suspended, a few of us tried to stop the line. We couldn't do it because some of the workers refused to join us.

My pay for the first two weeks at Daimi was 90 quetzales [U.S.$15]. Oh, it made me want to cry. Every day I had to pay for four bus trips and food, and then to receive only 90 quetzales. It made me very angry, but I couldn't quit because my sister had just left her husband and we needed the money. The most I ever earned at Daimi was 365 quetzales [U.S.$60] for two weeks' work and that included all my overtime hours.

I didn't complain about the wages because I didn't know how much I was entitled to. At that point I didn't even know what the minimum wage was.

**Marion: What were the hours like?**

**Marie:** Long. We had to be at work at 7:00 in the morning, and then supposedly we'd be able to leave at 4:40 in the afternoon. But almost every day we had to work overtime until at least 7:40 p.m. The Koreans would stand in front of the door and not let anybody out. They would stand there and shout, "You, overtime." They'd even grab you and haul you inside. It didn't matter whether you wanted to work or not. They wouldn't let you out.

I worked all day sitting on a little stool, with only one short break for lunch. By the end of a 12-hour day, my body really hurt. And then there were the night shifts. Sometimes we would have to stay all night and maybe take a break to sleep three or four hours on the floor next to the machine. If I was doing pants, I would take a bunch down and cover myself so I wouldn't get too cold. In the morning, I would fold them back up like nothing had happened. They would give you breakfast in the morning and tell you to get to work. You have to learn to defend yourself during those all-nighters. It can be dangerous. Men and women stay together in a small area, and there have been cases of women being raped.

**Marion: How did you find out about the union?**

**Marie:** A young guy in the factory came and told me about Juan Jose, a student who was working as an organizer with the ITGLWF. I think he'd heard me complain about how little we got paid. He told me that there was a way to fix the situation. When I asked how, he told me that there were some students who wanted to help improve conditions in the maquilas, but that things would only improve

if we wanted them to change. He asked if he could give Juan Jose my address, and I said yes.

That next Sunday, Juan Jose came to my house. He explained how they worked, and that we needed to organize to improve conditions in all the factories. If we didn't, then the bosses would always treat our people this way. I told him I wanted to get involved; at that point my brother didn't want to. He didn't believe it could work.

I started going to meetings. We'd look over the lists of workers to identify people we might be able to recruit. Over time, I was able to recruit a number of people from my line.

Soon the owners started getting suspicious. They started watching us. About that time, there were several waves of firings. That was in 1997. I hardly knew anyone who was fired in the first round. I knew one person that was fired in the second. Then I was fired in the third round.

By then, I was one of the older workers. I was 24. Most of the workers were young people, 14, 15, and 18 years old. The bosses exploited them, yelled at them, hit them, made them work double shifts, and paid them less than the older workers. When workers are young, they don't complain when they are not paid properly. The owners hire young people because they often don't know their rights.

**Marion: How many workers were employed at Daimi?**

**Marie:** There were about 400 workers. We had five production lines, plus the people working in cutting, ironing, packing, buttons, and in the warehouse.

**Marion: What happened with the organizing effort in Daimi before and after you were fired?**

**Marie:** I was only able to talk with people on my line. You know more about people on your own line: what they're like, if they get along, if they stay when there is overtime, how they react if they are forced to stay extra hours, things like that.

Seven people on my line were with me. That's why the supervisors broke up the line. They moved some workers to other lines, and then fired the rest. The firings did the most damage.

We worked so hard to get the workers at Daimi to stand up for themselves. But despite all the problems in the factory, many workers wouldn't join with the union. Perhaps they were afraid. Some would even hide from us. Of course some did join, but many did not. I was very sad when they fired me. Still, the struggle continued inside the factory.

After I was fired, there were just a few union supporters left. Three of them, two girls and my brother—who had gotten active by then—placed an injunction on the factory. Then one of the girls quit, which left only my brother and the other girl.

The supervisors started really harassing my brother. When he showed up for work, they wouldn't give him anything to do. He just had to stay sitting in the office. They would try to scare him. Then they offered him money, but he didn't take it. They harassed him like that for about three days and then more or less left him in peace. They let him work on a line, but wouldn't give him any overtime. That meant he could only earn the minimum wage.

It was a difficult experience for my brother; it really affected him. He worked so hard to get people to support the struggle at Daimi. He'd get home at 10:00 at night after going with the organizers to visit the workers. But instead of supporting the union, people often made fun of it. Of course that made the owner feel good.

One night, the supervisors shut my brother inside the factory. When I called the factory to ask if my brother was there, they told me he wasn't. I called back later and they admitted he was there, but said I couldn't speak with him because they were "fixing a problem." I was desperate. I didn't

know what to do. I couldn't say anything to my uncle because he's with the military and wouldn't have supported the union. My brother was stuck there alone with management in the factory most of the night. He finally called at 1:00 in the morning and I went to the bus stop to wait for him. My sister came along. She was very angry with me. She blamed me for what had happened. A couple days later, my brother quit his job.

**Marion: Does the factory still exist?**

**Marie:** Yes, it exists. They changed the name and fired a supervisor, the Korean woman who was really bad. But the bad conditions and hiring of minors continues. And of course, some of the workers who were fired during the campaign still haven't gotten their severance pay.

That factory cost us a lot. The only thing we achieved was to scare the owner and maybe get a message to some of the workers. Some of them did begin to realize that organizing was a good thing.

**Marion: What did you do after you were fired?**

**Marie:** I looked for other work. I got a job in the same factory where my sister worked, Modas Montañas, also Korean-owned. They make pants from nylon. The wages were a bit better, but the conditions were really bad. We had to drink tap water, from dirty, greasy cups. The bathrooms didn't have doors, and the men made a hole in the wall that separated the bathrooms so they could look at us while we were using the bathroom.

There was tons of work. Eleven hundred pieces a day wasn't considered a lot. When we were forced to stay all night, they gave us food that made us sick. I got parasites while I was there.

The material we sewed was like little cat hairs. You'd have it all over your face and in your pores. Both my sister and I started to get throat infections.

The only good thing was that I managed to get permission to study on Saturdays. The director of personnel said I could work half-days on Saturdays and then go to class. He actually encouraged me to do it and said that I was very intelligent.

It was around that time that the coordinator of the ITGLWF's organizing project in Guatemala City asked me to come and work in the office. I wasn't sure about leaving because there are things about the maquila that I liked. You can learn a lot working in the maquila.

**Marion: What do you learn?**

**Marie:** You learn how to defend yourself. You learn to be strong. If not, everyone yells at you. The mechanic, the supervisor, the chief of production, the assistant, the operator behind you and the one in front of you, the inspectors…. The whole world yells at you. If you don't learn how to defend yourself, you're really in trouble. That kind of experience builds character. You learn how to stand up to people and tell them they don't have the right to yell at you.

What I like is that you can see the product of your work. You can see exactly what you've made. It's right up there on the board in front, that you're producing 100 pieces each hour. Then in the afternoon you can see that you've finished, say, 1,500 pieces and you can be proud of what you and your compañeros have accomplished. That's the good part of the maquila. Of course the bad part is the mistreatment, the low salaries, and the bad conditions.

Right from the beginning, I loved to sew. I make my own clothes, although less so now because I don't have a machine. But I decided to leave the maquila to work with the organizing project because I wanted to learn new things, for example, more about worker rights.

Here I'm learning about the conditions in other maquilas. We find that conditions are pretty much the same everywhere. Workers don't get paid well, they are treated badly, and their rights are violated.

Of course there are differences. In some maquilas workers are treated really badly, while in others conditions are slightly better. Another thing I've learned is that workers don't know what the minimum wage is or how much they are being paid for overtime. Some don't even know they are being robbed.

The most important thing I have learned is how to organize workers. It's funny, but if I hadn't been hired at Daimi, I probably would still be working in a maquila.

## NOTES

1. The International Textile, Garment and Leather Workers' Federation (ITGLWF) is an International Trade Secretariat bringing together 250 organizations associated with the apparel and textile industries in 130 countries, with a combined membership of 10 million workers.
2. Ladino or ladina refers to someone who is of mixed heritage. Indigenous people who wear western clothing are often referred to as ladino. The ladino ethnicity is considered one of the four broad ethnic categories in the country; the other ethnicities are Maya, Garifuna, and Xineo.
3. One of the Mayan dialects.

*Source:* STITCH and the Maquila Solidarity Network. (2000). Excerpted from "Introduction" and "If You Don't Learn to Defend Yourself, You're in Real Trouble." In *Behind the Labels: Worker Testimonies in Central America* (pp. ii–iii, 1–6). Toronto, ON: STITCH and the Maquila Solidarity Network.

# CHAPTER 62

## Trump and National Neoliberalism

*Sasha Breger Bush*

Sasha Breger Bush is an assistant professor in the Political Science Department at the University of Colorado–Denver. She teaches and researches about international political economy, global finance, and food and agriculture systems. She is the author of *Derivatives and Development: A Political Economy of Global Finance, Farming, and Poverty*.

The election of Donald Trump portends the completion of the U.S. Government's capture by wealthy corporate interests. Trump's election is widely seen in terms of a dispossessed and disenfranchised white, male working class, unsatisfied with neoliberal globalization and the insecurity and hardship it has unleashed, particularly across regions of the United States that were formerly manufacturing powerhouses (like the Rust Belt states of Pennsylvania, Michigan, Ohio, and Wisconsin, four states believed to have cost Hillary Clinton the election). While there is much truth to this perspective and substantial empirical evidence to support it, it would be a mistake to see Trump's victory wholly in these terms.

This election appears to be a key stage in the ongoing process of American democratic disintegration, though in my opinion Trump's election does not signal the beginning of a rapid descent into European-style fascism. Instead, the merger of state and corporate interests is proceeding along an already-established trajectory. American democracy has been under attack from large and wealthy corporate interests for a long time, with this process accelerating and gaining strength over the period of neoliberal globalization (roughly the early 1970s to the present). This time period is associated with the rise of powerful multinational corporations with economic and political might that rivals that of many national governments.

I am persuaded by the argument that the U.S. political system is not democratic at all, but rather an "inverted totalitarian" system. Political commentator Chris Hedges notes: "Inverted totalitarianism is different from classical forms of totalitarianism. It does not find its expression in a demagogue or charismatic leader but in the faceless anonymity of the corporate state." Citing the American political theorist Sheldon Wolin, Hedges argues that our inverted totalitarian system is one that retains the trappings of a democratic system—e.g. it retains the appearance of loyalty to "the Constitution, civil liberties, freedom of the press, [and] the independence of the judiciary"—all the while undermining the capacity of citizens to substantively participate and exert power over the system.

In my view, what Trump's election has accomplished is an unmasking of the corporate state. Trump gives inverted totalitarianism a persona and a face, and perhaps marks the beginning of a transformation from inverted totalitarianism to totalitarianism proper. By this I mean that I think we are entering a period in which our political system will come to look more obviously totalitarian, with ever fewer efforts made to conceal its true nature and with the demagoguery that we typically associate with this form of politics. In spite of this, it makes no sense to me to call the system toward which we are heading (that is, if we do not stand up and resist with all our might right this second) "fascism" or to make too close comparisons to the Nazis. The European fascists put their faith in the power of the state to remake society. I do not see this on the horizon for the liberal-capitalist US, where feelings of hatred and distrust towards an oversized federal government helped to elect Trump. Whatever totalitarian nightmare is on our horizon, it will be uniquely American: a kind of "corporate" or "market-based" totalitarianism that is unique in world history. With its orientation towards the needs of the marketplace and big business, it will resemble in many ways the system that we've been living under for decades. If the pre-Trump system of inverted totalitarianism solidified in the context of global neoliberalism, the period of corporate totalitarianism that we are entering now seems likely to be one characterized by what I call "national neoliberalism."

## TRUMP'S ELECTION DOESN'T MEAN THE END OF NEOLIBERALISM

Trump's election represents a triumph of neoliberal thinking and values. Perhaps most importantly, we should all keep in mind the fact that Americans just elected a businessman to the presidency. In spite of his Wall Street background and billionaire status,

Trump successfully cast himself as the "anti-establishment" candidate. This configuration—in which a top-one-percenter real estate tycoon is accepted as a political "outsider"—is a hallmark of neoliberal thinking. The fundamental opposition between market and government is a central dichotomy in the neoliberal narrative. In electing Trump, American voters are reproducing this narrative, creating an ideological cover for the closer connections between business and the state that are in store moving forward. (Indeed, Trump is already using the apparatus of the U.S. federal government to promote his own business interests). As states and markets further fuse in coming years, this representation of Trump and his administration—as being anti-government—will help immunize his administration from accusations of too-cozy relationships with big business. Trump's promises to "drain the swamp" by imposing Congressional term limits and constraints on lobbying activities by former political officials will also help to hide this relationship. (Has anyone else noticed that Trump only addresses half of the "revolving door," i.e., he plans to limit the lobbying of former politicians, but not the political roles of businessmen?)

Trump's Contract with the American Voter, his plan for the first 100 days in office, discusses policies and programs many of which are consistent with neoliberal thinking. (I interpret the term *neoliberalism* to emphasize at its core the importance of private property rights, market-based social organization, and the dangers of government intervention in the economy.) Trump's plan redirects the activities of the U.S. government along the lines touted by neoliberal "market fundamentalists" like Milton Friedman, who advocate limiting government's role to market-supportive functions like national defense and domestic law and order (Trump's proposals have a lot to do with altering immigration policy to "restore security"). Trump also plans to use government monies to revitalize physical infrastructure and create jobs. Other government functions, for example, health care provision and education as well as protecting the environment and public lands, are open for privatization and defunding in Trump's agenda. Under Trump, the scope of federal government activities will narrow, likely to infrastructure, national defense, and domestic policing and surveillance, even if overall government spending increases (as bond markets are predicting).

Trump also seems content to take neoliberal advice in regard to business regulation (less is best) and the role of the private sector in regulating itself (industry insiders understand regulatory needs better than public officials). Trump's plan for the first 100 days specifies "a requirement that for every new federal regulation, two existing regulations must be eliminated." As of the time of this writing, his selection of cabinet appointees illustrate a broad willingness to appoint businesspeople to government posts. As of mid-December 2016, a Goldman Sachs veteran, Steven Mnuchin, has been appointed Secretary of the Treasury; billionaire investor Wilbur Ross, Secretary of Commerce; fossil-fuel-industry supporter and Oklahoma Attorney General Scott Pruitt, EPA administrator; fast-food mogul Andrew Puzder, Secretary of Labor; Exxon-Mobil CEO Rex Tillerson, Secretary of State. Trump's business council is staffed by the CEOs of major U.S. corporations including JP Morgan Chase, IBM, and General Motors. To be fair, the "revolving door" between government and industry has been perpetuated by many of Trump's predecessors, with Trump poised to continue the tradition. But this is not to say that neoliberalism will continue going in a "business as usual" fashion. The world is about to get much more dangerous, and this has serious implications for patterns of global trade and investment.

## TRUMP'S ELECTION DOES MEAN THE END OF GLOBALISM

The nationalism, xenophobia, isolationism, and paranoia of Donald Trump are about to replace the significantly more cosmopolitan outlook of his post-WWII predecessors. While Trump is decidedly pro-business and pro-market, he most certainly does not see himself as a global citizen. Nor does he intend to maintain the United States' extensive global footprint or its relatively open trading network. In other words, while neoliberalism is not dead, it is being transformed into a geographically more fragmented and localized system (this is not only about the U.S. election, but also about rising levels of global protectionism and Brexit, among other anti-globalization trends around the world). I expect that the geographic extent of the U.S. economy in the coming years will coincide with the new landscape of U.S. allies and enemies, as defined by Donald Trump and his administration.

Trump's Contract with the American Voter outlines several policies that will make it more expensive and riskier to do business abroad. All of these need not occur; I think that even one or two of these changes will be sufficient to alter expectations in business communities about the benefits of certain cross-border economic relationships. Pulling the United States out of the TPP, along with threats to pull out of the Paris Climate Agreement and attempts to renegotiate NAFTA, is already signaling to other countries that the new administration will not be interested in international cooperation. A crackdown on foreign trading abuses will prompt retaliation. Labelling China a currency manipulator will sour relations between the two countries and prompt retaliation by China. As Trump goes forward with his anti-immigration and anti-Muslim rhetoric and policies, he will alienate the United States' traditional allies in Europe (at least until Europe elects its own nationalist and xenophobic leaders) and communities across the Global South. The U.S. election has already undermined performance in emerging markets, and bigoted rhetoric and policy will only increase anti-American sentiment in struggling economies populated largely by people of color. Add to this the risk of conflict posed by any number of the following: his antagonizing China, allying with Russia, deploying ground troops to stop ISIS, and pulling out of the Korean DMZ

[Demilitarized Zone], among other initiatives that seem likely to contribute to a more confrontational and violent international arena. All of this is to say that Trump will not have to intervene directly in the affairs of business in order to make it less international and more national. The new global landscape of conflict and risk, combined with elevated domestic spending on infrastructure and security, will bring U.S. business and investment back home nonetheless.

## NATIONAL NEOLIBERALISM AND STATE-MARKET RELATIONS

Fascist states are corporatist in nature, a state of affairs marked by a fusion of state and business functions and interests. In the fascist states on the European continent in the 1930s and 1940s—systems that fall under the umbrella of "national socialism"—the overwhelming power of the state characterized this relationship. Political theorist Sheldon Wolin writes in *Democracy, Inc.*, in regard to Nazi Germany and Fascist Italy (as well as Stalinist Russia), "The state was conceived as the main center of power, providing the leverage necessary for the mobilization and reconstruction of society."

By contrast, in Trump's America—where an emergent "national neoliberalism" may be gradually guiding us to a more overt and obvious corporate totalitarian politics—we can expect a similar fusion of state and market interests, but one in which the marketplace and big business have almost total power and freedom of movement. State and market in the U.S. will fuse further together in the coming years, leading some to make close parallels with European fascism. But it will do so not because of heavy handed government dictates and interventions, but rather because domestic privatization initiatives, appointments of businessmen to government posts, fiscal stimulus, and the business community's need for protection abroad will bring them closer. Corporate interests will merge with state interests not because corporations are commanded to, but rather because the landscape of risk and reward will shift and redirect investment patterns to a similar effect. This may be where a budding U.S. totalitarianism differs most starkly from its European cousins.

Of course, it helps that much of the fusion of state and market in the United States is already complete, what with decades of revolving doors and privatization initiatives spanning the military, police, prison, healthcare and educational sectors, among others. It will not take much to further cement the relationship.

***Source:*** Breger Bush, Sasha. (2014). "Trump and National Neoliberalism." *Dollars and Sense,* 328(January–February), 11–14. Retrieved from: http://dollarsandsense.org/archives/2016/1216bregerbush.html.

# SNAPSHOTS & SOUNDWAVES 40

## NO ONE IS ILLEGAL

### Vision, Demands, Organizing Pillars

**Our Vision**

No One Is Illegal is a migrant justice movement rooted in anti-colonial, anti-capitalist, ecological justice, Indigenous self-determination, anti-occupation, and anti-oppressive politics. We are part of a worldwide movement of resistance that strives and struggles for the freedom to stay, the freedom to move, and the freedom to return. We undertake to increase public awareness about the exploitation inherent in the immigration system and border controls, as well as interrelated systems of exploitation, capitalism, and race, gender, sexuality, and ability-based oppression. We mobilize tangible support for refugees, undocumented migrants, and (im)migrant workers, while also prioritizing solidarity with Indigenous land defenders. We struggle alongside allied anti-capitalist, anti-authoritarian, and anti-imperialist movements, and fight back through rallies and direct actions to affirm dignity and respect for our communities.

No One Is Illegal–Toronto (NOII–TO) strives to build a strong community organization of racialized migrants and allies [...] to create critical change for undocumented people in the country [Canada], while organizing against the forces of displacement.

Crucial to our vision is our commitment to promote the leadership of women and trans people of colour in our organization, and of individuals who have been directly impacted by unjust immigration policies.

**Our Organizing Pillars**

We organize around three pillars: status for all, access without fear, and support work for Indigenous sovereignty struggles. [...]

1.  Status for All. This work includes stopping deportations and ending detentions; stopping unjust immigration policies; ending exploitative and temporary migrant work; fighting back against the environmental, economic, and military forces that force people to move out of their homes in the first place; and creating a culture of resistance and building community power towards a global movement for justice, of which migrant justice is a part.

2. Access Without Fear. This is our campaign to push Immigration Enforcement out of our city and our province so that people can safely access the services and supports they need to live with dignity, and without fear of detention, deportation, or harassment.

3. Indigenous Sovereignty. For us, defending Indigenous sovereignty happens in two ways: responding to calls for solidarity as they emerge, and building an informed base of support for Indigenous sovereignty, particularly in migrant communities.

**Points of Unity Demands**

- An end to all deportations and detentions
- The implementation of a full and inclusive regularization program for all non-status people
- Access without fear to essential services for all undocumented people
- The recognition of Indigenous sovereignty
- An end to the exploitation of temporary workers
- An end to all imperialist wars and occupations
- An end to the use of Security Certificates and secret trials

*Source:* No One Is Illegal–Toronto. (n.d.). Adapted from "Vision, Demands, Organizing Pillars." Retrieved from: http://toronto.nooneisillegal.org/demands.

# CHAPTER 63

## Undoing Border Imperialism

*Harsha Walia and Jo-Anne Lee*

Harsha Walia is a South Asian activist, writer, and journalist, as well as the co-founder of the Vancouver chapter of No One Is Illegal. She has been involved in community-based grassroots migrant justice, feminist, anti-racist, Indigenous solidarity, anti-capitalist, Palestinian liberation, and anti-imperialist movements for over a decade. She is formally trained in law and works as an advocate with women in Vancouver's Downtown Eastside, one of the most impoverished neighbourhoods in Canada. Walia's writings have appeared in over fifty journals, anthologies, and magazines, including *Briarpatch*, *Feministing*, *FUSE Magazine*, *Rabble*, and *The Winter We Danced*. She is the author of the well-known book *Undoing Border Imperialism*.

Jo-Anne Lee is an associate professor in the Department of Gender Studies at the University of Victoria. She is a past president of the Canadian Research Institute for the Advancement of Women (CRIAW). Lee is trained as a sociologist, and her research focuses on anti-racist, decolonizing feminist theory and practice. She writes and researches in the areas of immigrant women, North American Asian and Asian Canadian feminisms, feminist participatory action research, and girlhood studies. Her path-breaking work in participatory action research uses popular theatre, video documentaries, digital media, and arts-based methods.

*M*igration, Mobility, and Displacement editor Jo-Ann Lee talks to activist and author Harsha Walia about her book *Undoing Border Imperialism*. Their conversation is transcribed below. You can also watch the interview in a series of three videos available on Vimeo: vimeo.com/album/3419590.

## DEFINING BORDER IMPERIALISM

Harsha describes the ways borders form a part of a broad system of power and empire that contribute to marginalization and racialization of vulnerable populations. She argues that it is not simply a matter of fixing a broken immigration system, but instead dismantling another tool of neoliberal oppression.

**Jo-Anne:** Let's talk a little bit about this concept of border imperialism, it's the topic of your new book, can you explain to the journal's readers what border imperialism is?

**Harsha:** The idea of borders is incomplete without a deeper analysis about how they actually function. Most conceptualizations of borders are just seen as markers of territory if you will, but in the ways that borders are experienced by people, they're a form of governmentality, they're a form of violence, and they operate not only on the site on which they exist but they operate internally as well as much more broadly. I was trying to find a way to talk about borders that really grasps their fluidity in some ways and at the same time their rigidity. And so for me the concept of border imperialism really is trying to encapsulate the ways in which borders function, the ways in which they govern our lives and particularly in which they are really a part of a broader system of power and empire.

There are four key concepts around imagining how borders work and conceptualizing how borders work. The first is that we can't talk about immigration as this kind of domestic issue, because that's how we've tended to look at immigration, as this domesticated framework of how immigrants come to the shores, come to the borders, how refugees come, and then how the state manages these migrant populations, but for me it's important to look at the starting point which is 'What creates a migrant?' 'What creates the displacement, what are the cycles of displacement and dispossession that create migrant populations?' Firstly looking at those systemic forces like war and empire and oppression and gender-persecution, etc., that are operating at a global level, that are asymmetrical, that are disproportionately impacting poor, brown and black bodies and particularly women. What are those forces of economic imperialism, free-trade agreements, militarization particularly in the Middle-East right now? You know the Middle-East is home to the largest stateless population, whether it's Palestine, Iraq or Afghanistan, what are these forces and how's the 'West', if you will, the global-North, complicit in these displacements and dispossessions? That's critical because one of the ways in which the state talks about migration is not only to domesticate it but to present itself as the benevolent manager of migration. We're supposed to be grateful that the Canadian Government is allowing and welcoming immigrants. And this is something that immigrants internalize, which is why for me, challenging borders is so important because it's also part of us, I'm a migrant myself, how do we shed that internalized racism, that sense of gratitude that we're supposed to have to the state and when we shift the lens back on the state as responsible and culpable for displacement and dispossession, and for managing migration and managing dispossession, then I think that it's part of our process to 'uninternalize' and shed those myths that we're told. That's a key part of conceptualizing border imperialism, to shift the focus from migrants and the process that migrants take and oftentimes the perilous journeys that migrants take and oftentimes the so-called 'illegal' irregular journeys that migrants take, and to place the responsibility onto the state for creating and managing and in many cases causing death and killings and violence on migrant bodies.

For me there are a few other pieces around border imperialism. One is the connection to racism and the ways in which immigration increasingly is not seen as racially coded, it's seen as more of a legal debate, whether you're legal or illegal, whether you're here, if you're following the proper channels. And this is particularly the debate in Europe as well and Australia and Canada and the United States right now, the difference—the discourse that differentiates between the so-called 'legal migrant' and the 'bogus migrant'. This is really coded, even though it's not explicitly so around race, because even though we don't explicitly talk about anti-Chinese, anti-Japanese, anti-South Asian migration in Canada when we're talking about migration we are talking about race, and one of the ways in which we see this is the fact that communities of colour are constantly seen as migrants despite their legal status. In the case of many communities of colour, even though those communities have resided on these lands for centuries, they're constantly depicted as 'the dual citizen', if you will; the Chinese-Canadian, the Indian-Canadian, the Muslim-Canadian, and that dual-status casts us as constant outsiders. Whereas white people are seen as belonging to Canada, no one really traces back where white people are from or which colonized ancestors white people come from. And that of course also displaces and continues to perpetrate settler-colonialism because whiteness is not indigenous to these lands. And so that's just one of the many ways in which racism continues to operate and to use immigration as a stand-in essentially to talk about people of colour, and the struggles that regardless of legal status that communities of colour continue to face, the precarity, impoverishment, the racism, the discrimination, etc. And those come out in different moments, right now in the context of the War on Terror it's impacting especially Muslim women in specific ways. The debates [around] the Niqāb, which are again couched as debates on secularism and religion, are essentially racial debates and are racial forms of violence inflicted on Muslim women's bodies.

And that's another piece around border imperialism, a connected third piece, the detention of migrants. We're seeing an explosion of migrant-detention particularly across Western countries, and the links to border-militarization. So the fact that migrants are increasingly being incarcerated, essentially for the crime

of trespassing a border, it's really important to unravel how migrant detention works because it is so normalized, people have taken for granted that migrants should be incarcerated because they are committing so-called illegal acts; migrants are passed as criminals. Media and politicians continue to regurgitate that notion of migrants as committing illegal acts. In Canada we have over 11,000 migrants who are detained every single year, it includes children. Canada is increasingly adopting the Australian model of mandatory detention, which means that, again, people are essentially being thrown into jail for the crime of migrating. And to me that's at the core of challenging borders, because if we look at what is the crime that has been committed, it's literally the crime of trespassing a border, which is a completely artificial construct. The state has imagined itself as an entity that can be harmed. That's what borders have created. It's given the state this personhood that is completely fake. Look at the ways in which migrant detention is part of the expansion of the prison industrial complex. How it is part and parcel of this ongoing war on brown and black bodies that operates through different logics. The war on black bodies and in particular Indigenous bodies, the over-incarceration of black communities, of Indigenous communities is happening simultaneously to the expansion of migrant detention. In Canada right now Indigenous women and migrant-detainees are the fastest growing prison populations. And of course racism underpins how that incarceration is justified. And also, particularly in the United States but increasingly in Canada, appropriations are making a killing from migrant detention and that's really important to name.

I just came from the United States and learned there were literally quotas in migrant holding-cells. Corporations like GEO are running migrant detention-centres and have quotas for how many migrant-detainees need to be in these detention-centres and when they're under quota they literally call up ICE, the Immigration and Customs Enforcement, and say, 'We're under-quota,' and ICE goes out and conducts a raid.

**Jo-Anne: It's like the policing technologies.**

**Harsha:** Yes. A very clear link between militarization and the profits that come from it. After 9/11 there were a number of CEOs of the prison industrial complex, who operate prison-companies, who came out in the business pages of financial papers across the United States, saying '9/11 will be good business for us.' So this self-perpetuating logic of needing to incarcerate people, that's another key component of border imperialism.

The final one is, and I think the critical one that's not often talked about when we talk about borders or at least is not linked in this way, is how capitalism is racialized and the key role that capitalism and labour plays in the context of managing migration. So while it's true that racism plays a huge role in underpinning the debate about migration, it's not the case that the state wants to get rid of all people of colour, because the state also needs cheap labour, and communities of colour have typically performed that role. At a global level as well, of course, the West relies on sweat-shop labour, on cheap labour, etc., but it also needs that source of labour in-house, it needs to in-source what it typically out-sources, for domestic work all the domesticated forms of labour the state needs internal to its borders. And so migrants have always been commodified as a source of cheap labour. And increasingly under the Temporary Foreign Worker Program, which Canada is drastically expanding, Canada now accepts more people under Temporary Foreign Worker programs than under Permanent Residence, which really is a challenge to this myth of Canada being so welcoming to immigrants and accepting Permanent Residents; it's not true.

Increasingly people are coming as indentured-labourers under a program that's 'Migrant Workers' in words, a form of modern-day slavery, where people live in egregious conditions, have no access to basic labour standards, live in worker compounds, have their travel documents confiscated and again are indentured labour. And this pool of labour is so vulnerable, again because people are cast as 'foreigners' and 'temporary' and so readily deportable, you know, at the whim of the employer, the employer can get rid of them. This program fills a really critical need within the Canadian State and Canadian Capital, which is to ensure a constant, cheap supply of labour while maintaining this racial hierarchy of whiteness. And so it resolves this core contradiction if you will of how to keep Canada white, how to keep Canada hegemonically white and to maintain white supremacy, but needing brown and black folks to be within the nation-state. So how to be in the nation-state but not of the nation-state and so the Temporary Foreign Worker program really is that model.

And it's important to note that the Temporary Foreign Worker program in Canada, is actually being replicated all across the world. The United States has looked at it as the model to follow. [...] In the context of Canada, when people, including liberal, migrant justice activists say, 'We need to fix this broken immigration system,' for me the response is actually, 'No.' because when we look at it through a lens of border imperialism, it's the perfect system, it's actually serving the purpose it's meant to, which is to serve neoliberalism and maintain racialized citizenship.

And I think that's the key part. We're not fixing a broken system, the system is functioning as it's intended to, which is why challenging border imperialism and understanding it as a framework means that we come to a different place which is not fixing or reforming the immigration system, it's completely dismantling it. Because one of the main things it does in addition to treating us as cheap labour and racializing us, it also pits us against each other. Migrants are divided between the good, desirable migrant, the model-minority, the one who will assimilate, integrate, etc., against those who aren't. And so for me the key to undoing border imperialism is understanding the way it works and to also have movements, not to act as border agents ourselves. How do we not perpetuate those divides within our communities and act as border agents about who has the right to migrate, and has the right to dignity. And so for me the challenge is also internal for our movements, to not reproduce systems of power where we decide who's worthy and who's not, and to undo border imperialism within our movements and our communities as well.

## INDIGENOUS SOLIDARITY

Here Harsha outlines the importance of respect for Indigenous knowledge and histories within the migrant justice movement. She explains how both Indigenous and migrant communities are forced into narratives of settler colonialism, and challenges us to imagine an alternative in life under Indigenous legal jurisdiction.

Jo-Anne: [...] You make an argument that the migrant justice movement, as a political movement, has to stand in solidarity with Indigenous sovereignty and self-determination. Could you expand on that because I think that's a very, very important point?

Harsha: I think for all movements, but particularly the migrant justice movement, it is so imperative to understand our responsibilities to Indigenous nations, to the lands on which we've come to reside, to not perpetuate settler-colonialism. And one of the ways in which settler-colonialism

operates of course is to tell immigrants this story, this false story that we're being accepted into and need to be grateful to the Canadian state and to whiteness, when again, in fact, whiteness is not indigenous to these lands. And so I think it is so important for us to know and to act in solidarity with the true stewards of these lands. And that's an important gesture not just symbolically but because it is also imperative to decolonize our own understanding of how we're migrating and where we're migrating to.

There's lots of communities that can draw links, particularly Palestinian refugees who are fleeing settler-colonialism and fleeing Israeli apartheid, are coming to a very similar reality when they're arriving on Turtle Island, which is this settler-colonial reality which is intent on annihilating and committing genocide against Indigenous people. Many communities can draw parallels about forces of dispossession and displacement, but at the same time I think it's important to not conflate our struggles as the same, in the sense that settler-colonialism is very different than informal, indirect colonialism that's impacted most of the global south, particularly countries that are former colonies. And also to realize that once we come to Canada, immigrants, because of the model-minority myth, because of a very selective immigration process, a lot of immigrants are actively pitted against Indigenous people. Anti-Native racism is immense within our communities, and we perpetuate it in many ways; this idea that we're immigrants, we toughed it out, we made it, how come Indigenous people who've lived here for so long can't make it within the system. And so I think it is so important for us to understand all of the struggles that Indigenous communities face, impoverishment, over-incarceration, all of those struggles flow directly from a legacy of settler-colonialism. And again to not perpetuate this myth of the so-called welfare bum lazy Indian etc., that we're indoctrinated into and to be really open in rejecting those stereotypes and not allowing ourselves to be used as a fulcrum against which Indigenous people are analyzed, essentially.

And so for me I think it's imperative, again it's not just an optional alliance. When we're talking about movement building, I think the migrant justice movement can decide to align with the labour movement or not, I think the migrant justice movement can decide to align with anti-poverty struggles or not. I think they should, but I do think that in the context of Indigenous struggles I don't think it's an optional alliance, I think that it's a responsibility. I think it's our responsibility to always centre Indigenous struggles within our movements because these are the lands on which we reside. And to prefigure relationships, so when we want to dismantle borders, and we want to dismantle colonial borders and capitalist white-supremacist borders, then when we come here what are our responsibilities to these lands? That's an important part of the migrant justice movement because for me the migrant justice movement is the freedom to move, the freedom to be mobile but it also doesn't mean that we can come onto these lands and do as we wish. It means that we have to honour and respect the lands and communities [that occupy the lands] that we're on, to understand the host laws. One of the ways, the very concrete ways, I think, in which the migrant justice movement can decolonize within our communities is in rejecting Canadian law and Canadian legal jurisdiction and educating ourselves on what are the host laws of these lands. What would it mean to live under and live alongside living, natural, Indigenous laws? What are our responsibilities under Indigenous laws? When we want to reject, when I want to reject Canadian laws and the Canadian notion of what a good citizen is, to me the corollary is, 'What is it to be a good human on this land according to Indigenous laws?' That is so critical.

**Jo-Anne:** [...] This principle of migrant justice standing in solidarity with Indigenous peoples' self-determination and reclaiming the land, it's [...] an ethical position that you're articulating here. Then moving along from that ethical position, you're outlining a political agenda too. Can you speak more to that political agenda? [...]

**Harsha:** Yes, I mean I think so much of it is in terms of the material, tangible ways in which we actually organize in solidarity with Indigenous communities, I think a big part of it is the unlearning, I think that is immense, particularly because we are so indoctrinated into learning a particular history. Most newcomers learn about Canada from the citizenship test. You know, as flawed as the education system is, most migrants don't even have access to that, particularly if they're coming at an older age, all we have access to is the deeply state-centred, white supremacist, complete erasure of Indigenous histories. And so I think as a first step it is so necessary for people doing migrant justice work to work within our communities to really build a strong understanding of settler-colonial history. And that is always a first step to understanding what the legacy has been, to understand how that legacy plays out today because it is ongoing.

And then using that history to really reject the leverage of us as the good, model-minority versus bad Indigenous people, because that history, it provides the context within which to reject those stereotypes. And to work within our communities through the various means that we have access to, so for me that means accessing and doing work through Punjabi media, radio stations and South-Asian print magazines for example. And really doing that work in our communities on our own terms. You know we obviously can't do that work through the mainstream media, we have to do it through our community networks, and to prioritize that. And that can be hard, especially in the migrant justice movement, our communities are in survival mode. You're literally fighting deportation and detention on a daily basis, so it seems like an impossible task to take on education work when people are trying to survive. Or to appear patronizing, if you will, to migrants, to be like 'How do you not know this?' The material is about the practice of being in relationship, being in community and seeing this as a long-term commitment to prioritizing that work as we're working alongside migrant communities to fight against the ways in which the state oppresses us.

I think that these systems are connected. It has been so important for different migrant justice organizers across this land to take on very seriously understanding and learning about Indigenous host laws. It's not a small thing, I think it's immense because a lot of communities are also going through this process of resurgence where people are uncovering their own understandings of what immigration law looks like, under Indigenous nationhood. And so for me that's meant working with a number of different Indigenous nations who have found and are articulating what they imagine an immigration policy would look like under Indigenous laws.

And again this is such a long term project, but for me it is so core because in rejecting the Canadian immigration system, to actually prefigure and centre as alternative Indigenous host laws is key. Because you know it is one thing to rail against the state, and we do it. We do it all the time! It is something else to say we need to be in solidarity with Indigenous nations, and we all do it in various ways. And I think the step beyond that is to actually imagine ourselves as actually living under Indigenous legal jurisdiction. And to understand our responsibilities under Indigenous legal jurisdiction, and to do the work to find out what that would mean first of all. And then to conduct and enact ourselves and to embody that is kind of the goal if you will. I mean it's a process

but it's also the goal, which is how do we understand ourselves as living under Indigenous host laws, under Indigenous legal jurisdiction, with the rules and responsibilities that come with that?

One very concrete example is, the *Unist'ot'en* camp, which is a resistance camp up in *Wet'suwet'en* territory. They've built a resistance camp in the pathway of over seven pipelines, including fracking pipelines, and they live on the land, on their traditional territory. They don't live on reserve and they're completely subsistent on traditional food systems: on hunting, on gathering. And revitalizing their clan system, and they're a governance system outside the band council essentially, right, so they're going through this process of revitalizing their governance systems. And one of the things that they do for anyone who wants to come to visit the camp, to show solidarity, is that you have to go through a process of questions; that before you enter the territory, the community can give free, prior and informed consent for you to enter into the territory. They ask a series of questions about whether you work for government or industry, what your intention is, how you will support the community. I've been through this checkpoint several times. For me when I say that I challenge borders, to me that is not a border, but it is a form of assertion of Indigenous autonomy that I completely respect. And I think that this is a key part of migrant justice movements is that we're rejecting artificial, arbitrary, violent borders but that we also understand and respect that we are entering into communities and into territories that have live ways of being and resurgent ways of being.

And so to me one really material way in which migrant justice movements can take on and embody what it means to understand ourselves as living on Indigenous lands and under Indigenous jurisdiction, is to go through these processes with Indigenous communities.

# DEFINING DECOLONIZATION

[Here] Harsha reflects on the concept of decolonization. Instead of prefiguring a radically new world as the goal of activism, she argues that we should look towards existing alternatives that are alive and well in Indigenous communities.

**Jo-Anne:** Now I want to segue into this question of the debate over decolonization, and [...] as you know there's a thing about how it's been taken up; on the one hand it seems to be conceptually slanted so that we want to decolonize everything, and then there's a reaction to that where we want to restrict it to retain its political power in Indigenous voices about decolonization, about decolonizing the land, reclaiming the territory. And as I read you, you're somewhere in between, I might be misreading you, but could you really articulate it for me, what your position is and why?

**Harsha:** [...] I actually think your reading is correct, if I were to give it thought. I think I do fall in the middle, for me definitely the primary struggle that one identifies decolonization with is undoubtedly Indigenous struggles, and particularly Indigenous struggles in a global context; you know against white settler colonialism in Canada and understanding decolonization, yeah, it's not just a metaphor to radicalize everything. It is a metaphor of reclamation of land, of culture, of nationhood, which has been resurgent on these lands for so long and that is alive. Again that there are alive laws on these lands, there are still laws and ceremonial protocols that govern how people are and how people need to be on these lands. So for me that is definitely the core of decolonization.

Again at a global level, which is how do we respect people's autonomy and how are borders actually violated across the global south; like military occupation and economic trade-agreements are constantly violating people's borders and autonomy. But I do also see the need to decolonize within our movements. You know and maybe I wouldn't use that term actually in the same ways, maybe I would find another word, but I don't know that another word exists.

---

*Source:* Walia, Harsha, & Lee, Jo-Anne. (2015). Excerpted from "Hasha Walia in Conversation with MM&D Editor Jo-Anne Lee." *Migration, Mobility, & Displacement,* *1*(1), 55–65. Retrieved from: http://mmduvic.ca/index.php/mmd/article/view/13643.

# CHAPTER 64

## Immigrant Women in Canada
## and the United States

*Leslie Nichols and Vappu Tyyskä*

Leslie Nichols earned a PhD in policy studies at Ryerson University and is currently an instructor in women and gender studies and social work at Wilfrid Laurier University. Her research explores the social conditions of diverse women in North America using intersectional feminist theory and methods, with a focus on work, immigration, and social well-being.

Vappu Tyyskä is a professor in the Department of Sociology at Ryerson University. Her research focuses on immigrant youth and intergenerational relations, immigrant women, and family violence in immigrant communities. She is currently working on projects that address intersections between social policy and immigration policy. Tyyskä is the author of *Youth and Society: The Long and Winding Road.*

## INTRODUCTION

Canada and the United States are nations with large numbers of immigrants. In Canada, according to 2011 census figures, 20.6% of the population is foreign-born, the largest proportion in the wealthy G8 countries. Most new immigrants are from Asia, with the three leading source countries in 2011 being the Philippines, China, and India (Canada Press 2013). In the total Canadian population, 19.1% are members of racialized groups and three-quarters of them are immigrants (Citizenship and Immigration Canada 2012). [...] European immigrants are a minority in recent years (Monger and Yankay 2013).

The gender balance is reflective of the general landscape of immigration. Over the past two decades women have outnumbered men as migrants (Labadie-Jackson 2008–2009). In fact, over half of the world's 214 million migrants are women (Deen 2013). As of 2011, one in five women in Canada was foreign born (Chui 2011), while in the US, immigrant women made up 12% of the female population in 2008 (Batalova 2009). South Asian and Hispanic women are the largest groups of immigrant women in Canada and the United States, respectively.

Against this backdrop, this chapter will show that "immigrant women" is a diverse category with respect to age, education, social class, family status, region, and membership in racialized groups. The chapter will outline the social construction of "immigrant women" as a category, based on the colonial history of Canada and the United States. It will address the issues faced by female migrants at different stages of their lives: as children and youth, adults, and older adults. For adult women, there will be a focus on employment outcomes and family lives including spousal relations, mothering, and interpersonal violence (IPV). The issues of identity and belonging faced by first- and second-generation young women will be taken up, along with the specific needs of senior immigrant women. While the focus will be on permanent residents, we will also provide examples from other migrant categories (refugees, temporary workers, undocumented migrants) where relevant.

## HISTORICAL CONSIDERATIONS: THE SOCIAL CONSTRUCTION OF "IMMIGRANT WOMEN"

Canada and the United States are clear examples of "settler" nations, in which colonizers came to a "new land" forging a new emphasis on a common destiny for all—an imagined community (Anderson 1983). Since the earliest days of the settlement of new world colonies, immigrant women have remained marginalized and disadvantaged in the establishment and perpetuation of the imagined communities of Canada and the United States. Gender and race are points of social identity that are often used to marginalize and categorize immigrants. The term *immigrant woman* is customarily used to label many women of colour, whether they are immigrants or not. "Immigrant woman" is a social category that names not only women who have come to live in Canada or the United States permanently, but specifically those women who do not fit the national idea of a woman, based on their characteristics or presumed social location (Folson 2004:30, 31).

When Canada and the United States were first colonized, British immigrant women were seen as co-creators of the imagined community, whose main role was to give birth to and raise British subjects. In the early years of settlement, women were only considered "immigrants" if they did not conform to a standard white British ideal (Arat-Koç 2006:200; Roberts 1979:201). Therefore, the creation of the nation-state involved the process of othering certain populations within and outside the Canadian and American state (Baines and Sharma 2002:85). [...]

In the case of Canada, the process of constructing an imagined Canadian woman was intimately tied to the larger colonialist and imperialist project of settling the nation and imagining its appropriate community and colour (Folson 2004; Carter 1996; Dua 2000; Arat-Koç 2006). White women settlers, rather than Indigenous women, were positioned as the "mothers of the nation" (Folson 2004; Arat-Koç 2006); they would reproduce the nation as appropriate marital partners and mothers who would give birth and raise its citizens. From the beginning of the colonization process, British immigrant women were not seen as outsiders, but rather co-settlers with their male counterparts. As Barbara Roberts (1979:201) notes, "the nation was the home and the home was the women; all were best British."

Along with Indigenous women, racialized Immigrant women did not fit into the imagined community. In 1908, the government declared that immigrants needed $200 to enter Canada and must travel to the country in one continuous journey (Dua 2000), effectively prohibiting South Asian women's entry. Conversely, a "bachelor society" of working male immigrants allowed the Canadian state and employers to keep the immigrant males' income artificially low on the grounds that they did not have families to support (Das Gupta 2000:229). At the same time, however, many advocated allowing South Asian women to enter the country out of fear that South Asian men would marry white women and "dilute" Canadian identity (Dua 2000:59, 68).

It was not until 1919 that South Asian married women were permitted to enter Canada (Das Gupta 2000: 221). This same logic was at work again in the government's decision to implement a head tax on Chinese immigrants in the late nineteenth and early twentieth century (Das Gupta 2000:220). In these two examples we can see how would-be immigrant women were constructed as a liability to the cultural and economic health of Canada's emerging imagined community and as a result were often simply refused entry to the country. And, when they were permitted entry, it was due to a fear that their absence would create a mixed race culture like the Métis (Carter 1996), who are offspring of the French Canadian population and First Nations. It is clear that racist and sexist sentiments have played a central role in guiding Canadian immigration policy. [...]

That race is a consideration in addition to gender in immigration policy is exemplified in the case of black Caribbean women, who came to Canada as domestic workers, after the first wave of British and Finnish domestic immigrants to Canada (1900–1930) (Das Gupta 2000:222). Unlike the group of white European women, Caribbean domestics were given temporary contracts and were not allowed to change their immigrant status once in Canada. When their contracts were done or not renewed, they were forced to go home, their job and status being entirely tied to their employer. It was not until 1981 that this group of immigrant women domestics (by now also including an increasing number of Filipinas) was finally allowed to apply for immigration to Canada after two years of employment (Das Gupta 2000). This immigrant community of female domestic workers has always been marginalized; originally, they were supposed to be single and only here temporarily and, even though this policy has changed throughout the years, the family reunification of this category of migrant women is still poor (Das Gupta 2000:224; Arat-Koç 2006). Ironically, the very women who are good enough to raise white Canadian children cannot raise their own children, who are not allowed entry with them (Das Gupta 2000:224).

Concerns over social reproduction, labour costs, and the welfare state also inform much recent immigration policy. Grace Chang outlines the panic in California over the presence of undocumented Mexican immigrant women who are seen to be a "burden to the state" and a drain on social welfare budgets (Chang 2000:2). The sexism in these assumptions ignores the ways in which immigrant women support working men in the home and therefore contribute to the economy through their unpaid domestic work, including childcare. Instead, the belief that these immigrant women absorb social welfare costs led to legislative changes (Chang 2000) that included a reduction of all kinds of social assistance, particularly to undocumented immigrants. Critics argue that as a result of this treatment, immigrant women are structurally disadvantaged as they are rendered "more receptive to scorned, low-paid service jobs once they arrive" (Chang 2000:16).

There are around 11 million undocumented immigrants in the United States, and the numbers of women among them are on the rise, from less than 20% 2 decades ago to around 34 to 45% currently. Women's share has risen simply because of rising poverty levels south of the border (see Case Example 1), and despite the hardships and dangers of crossing the border, these women share the sentiment "it's worth it" (Alvarez and Broder 2006).

## Case Example 1: More and More, Women Risk All to Enter US

TUCSON—It took years for Normaeli Gallardo, a single mother from Acapulco, to drum up the courage to join the growing stream of Mexican women illegally crossing the border on the promise of a job, in her case working in a Kansas meatpacking plant for $5.15 an hour.

First, she had to grapple with the idea of landing in an unfamiliar country, all alone, with no grasp of English and no place to live.

Then she had to imagine crossing the Arizona desert, where immigrants face heat exhaustion by

*continued*

day, frostbite by night, and the cunning of the "coyotes"—smugglers who charge as much as $1,500 to guide people into the United States and who make a habit of robbing and sexually assaulting them.

And finally, Ms. Gallardo, 38, who earned $50 a week at an Acapulco hotel, had to contemplate life without her two vivacious daughters, Isabel, 7, and Fernanda, 5. That once unimaginable trade-off—leaving her children behind so they could one day leave poverty behind—had suddenly become her only option.

She simply did not earn enough money, she said. If she paid the electric bill, she fell behind on rent; if she paid the water bill, she could forget about new clothes for the children. [...]

Undaunted by a backlash against illegal immigrants here, Ms. Gallardo is part of what some experts say is a largely unnoticed phenomenon: the increasing number of women, many without male companions, enduring danger and the risk of capture to come to the United States to work and to settle. [...]

**Source:** Excerpted from Alvarez and Broder 2006. Retrieved from www.nytimes.com/2006/01/10/national/10women.html?pagewanted=print&_r=0

# FEMINIST AND INTERSECTIONAL ANALYSIS

Feminism can help us better understand the ways in which women of various social positions and identities have differential access to rights and citizenship (Das Gupta 2000:222). [...] Analyzing the experiences of different groups of women brought in under different immigration schemes, through an intersectionality lens, can highlight the "complex and sometimes contradictory intersection of gender, class, race and nationality" (Arat-Koç 2006:199). These intersections are evident in immigrant women's experiences in the economy and the family, as will be detailed below.

# ADULT IMMIGRANT WOMEN

## Employment and Economic Experiences

Research on Canadian immigrants indicates that 1) economic difficulties are common for many years following migration to Canada; 2) more recent immigrants are not doing as well as those who immigrated to Canada prior to the 1990s; and 3) compared to Canadian-born degree holders, those immigrants who hold degrees do not fare as well, particularly if race is taken into account. To this we can add that 4) the reason for the poorer economic outcomes of more recent immigrants has to be linked to their racialized status. Further, 5) the difficult economic situation that newcomers face leads to difficulties in finding affordable housing and accessing healthcare, education, and training, along with low rates of home ownership (Tyyskä 2007).

Taking gender into account further complicates this picture. Immigrant men in both Canada and the United States are overrepresented as the principal applicant (the person making the immigration application) in the economic class, due to the tendency of men to be primary breadwinners. [...]

There is a clear gender division of labour between women and men in Canada and the US, whereby women tend to occupy service and caring work while men more commonly occupy manual labour positions in the primary and secondary sectors. This also holds for immigrants. Immigrant women in the US tend to work in office and administration support, nursing and domestic work, sales, and related industries while men work in construction, manufacturing, and extraction (Pearce 2006:1). Powers and Seltzer note that women tend to not advance in their careers as much as men, and end up holding fewer managerial and other powerful positions (1998:478). This is in keeping with the general distinction between men as primary breadwinners and women as primary caregivers in families. Meanwhile, there is evidence that many immigrant women in Canada tend to find full-time employment faster than immigrant men because they are willing to accept any survival job (Ali and Kilbride 2004).

This gender-based division of work is reflected in wages. In 2003 in America, 61.7% of immigrant women had a yearly income of less than US$25,000 compared to 54.4% of native-born women and 47.8% of immigrant men (Pearce 2006:2). Furthermore, in 2003 only 5.2% of immigrant women had an annual wage of US$75,000 or more, compared to 4.7% of native-born women and 10.8% of immigrant men (Pearce 2006:2). In Canada, the median income for immigrant women in 2010 was C$15,590 for very recent immigrants who arrived that same year (Statistics Canada 2013).

Immigrant women's economic and cultural integration is directly linked to the way women are positioned in immigration policy (Gabriel 2006; Arat-Koç 1999). Current Canadian immigration policies tend to favour those who have money, investments, or significant human capital (education, training, occupational skills, experience, and official language facility), as reflected in the points system introduced in 1967 (Gabriel 2006:162, 164, 171; Man 2004:135). The immigrant is positioned as a potential contributor to the labour market and the economy overall (Gabriel 2006:164). Because women often are not the primary applicant for immigration, they are marginalized in terms of their perceived lack of economic contributions (Gabriel 2006:172, 164; Arat-Koç 1999:36).

With the immigration regulations favouring men as principal applicants, there are benefits accruing to them. For example, Canadian language training programs were initially only available to men as the main breadwinners (Arat-Koç 1999:39). This is not in keeping with a reality in which immigrant women often end up working in the secondary labour market, supporting a male spouse as they complete their settlement programs, thereby contributing to the Canadian economy (Thobani 2000:39, 40). Despite changes in official language training programs, the current Language Instruction for Newcomers to Canada

(LINC) and Labour Market Language Training (LMLT) programs are not gender neutral. They limit eligibility to those who have been in Canada for less than a year and only some of the centres provide childcare for children from six months to six years old. Despite this childcare service, many women still miss language classes due to caring for children who are unable to attend their childcare facilities due to illness or other issues (Pothier 2012). [...]

# IMMIGRANT WOMEN AND FAMILIES

## Spousal Relations

It should be no surprise that transnational living can stress spousal relations; lengthy separations can result in extramarital affairs, couples growing apart, and negative emotions including "jealousy, hostility, depression and indifference" (Tyyskä 2008:60). Yet Guida Man (2003) found that while some Chinese immigrant women living in Vancouver, BC, Canada, dealt with spousal estrangement and extramarital affairs, others noted improvements in their spousal relationships while also reporting reduced domestic burdens because higher incomes allowed for the hiring of household help.

Some research indicates that immigrant women's employment may result in more egalitarian gender and family relations (Jain and Belsky 1997; Anisef, Kilbride, Ochocka, and Janzen 2001). However, research also indicates that women's employment may put pressure on men to perform domestic work, resulting in a loss of the traditional male breadwinner role and a negative impact on men's self-esteem (Ali and Kilbride 2004). Changes in traditional gender arrangements can at times result in tensions that can lead to either the onset or escalation of male violence against women and children (Tyyskä 2005, 2008).

Often within families, whether immigrant or nonmigrant, the husband/father holds more status than the wife/mother (Tyyskä 2002a, 2002b, 2003a). Intimate partner violence (IPV) is traditionally linked to patriarchy, which is present in all cultural groups. Studies of prevalence of IPV in immigrant families compared to nonmigrant families are mostly inconclusive. For example, a study by Janice Du Mont and associates (2012) found that immigrant women who have lived in Canada for more than 20 years and Canadian-born women reported no difference in risk of abuse. The accuracy of family violence rates is also in question, due to reluctance to report. Some American studies indicate that, when socioeconomic factors are taken into account, there is no difference from other social groups in rates of partner violence (Tjaden and Theonnes 2000; González-Guarda, Vasquez, and Mitrani 2009). Therefore, the higher rates in IPV among Hispanics over "whites" (Caetano, Field, Ramisetty-Mikler, and McGarth 2005) may reflect socioeconomic differences, in that the Hispanic population is one of the most economically marginalized in the US.

The issue of economic and other immigrant settlement stressors figures prominently in research on family violence. [...] Both Canadian and US research has shown that there is a connection between loss of employment status and an increase in the level of male/father aggression (Tyyskä 2005:127–128; González-Guarda, Vasquez, and Mitrani 2009). Rosa M. González-Guarda and associates (2009), also show violence as more likely within Hispanic couples where the woman makes more money than her male partner. This connection shows up in Canadian interviews with immigrant women who report that abuse either began (Tyyskä 2009) or intensified (Tyyskä 2005, 2008) upon immigration.

Changes in family composition may make it even more difficult for women to cope with violence. Many current immigrants arrive from countries where they had lived in extended families. As family members separate in migration, this possible source of deterrence to violence is removed (Morrison, Guruge, and Snarr 1999; Tyyskä 2008).

Lewis Okun notes that in the United States, women often take between 2.5 and 5 attempts to leave an unhealthy relationship before they are ultimately successful (1988:107, 113). Leaving a violent situation is made more complex by immigrant and racialized status. [...] Racialized women may view the family as a safe place from the harsh racist realities of the public world, despite the possible presence of violence in their lives. Rather than wanting to escape the traditional family, they will uphold it (Moghissi 1999). This attitude may contribute to keeping family violence a private matter, particularly in racialized immigrant families, in order to avoid the stigma. The cultural sensitivity in the community service–providing sector is not necessarily present to address this (Dinshaw 2005; Tyyskä, Dinshaw, Redmond, and Gomes 2012). The difficulties of addressing the issue are most starkly demonstrated in the case of "honour killings" of female members of the family. This topic is wrought with media sensationalism and misconceptions.

## Mothering

A key reason for migration is often the desire to improve children's lives. Canadian and American studies show that fear over children's potential economic hardships through their adulthood often leads to pressure exerted on children related to their education and career planning (Tyyskä 2005; Fuligni 1997).

Immigrant parents also worry about their children's relations and social behaviours with their peers (Wong 1999), spouse selection (Morrison, Guruge, and Snarr 1999; Zaidi and Shuraydi 2002), and maintenance of their culture (James 1999). There are often resultant tensions for immigrant youth, between their parents' expectations and their desire to fit into their social environment (Tyyskä 2003b). [...]

Thus, parenting roles may be strained due to role reversals between parents and their children, due to children learning the official or dominant language and culture at faster rates (Anisef et al. 2001) or acting as "cultural brokers" for the parents in their dealings with mainstream institutions such as schools, hospitals, or social services (Ali and Kilbride 2004; Creese, Dyck, and McLaren 1999; Tyyskä 2005, 2006).

An added complication is separation from extended family. Many immigrant families are not based on the typical North American nuclear family unit but count more relatives as their closest kin (Creese et al. 1999). While some families are able to arrive as multigenerational units (Noivo 1993), not every family is so lucky. Rather, it is common for one parent to arrive, followed by a spouse, children, and other family members. Therefore, one typical loss is that there are no longer extended family members to help with caring for and raising children, putting more pressure on parents and particularly mothers (Anisef et al. 2001; Tyyskä 2002b, 2003b). [...]

## YOUNG IMMIGRANT WOMEN

In most immigrant communities, parental expectations for sons and daughters differ (Tyyskä 2003b). Studies note that young men are subjected to less parental control, with more freedom and decision-making power in comparison to their sisters (Anisef et al. 2001; Handa 2003; Tyyskä 2001, 2006, 2007, 2008). Concerns about daughters were related to premarital dating and sexuality, while concerns about sons related to violence and drugs (Anisef et al. 2001; Tyyskä 2006, 2007, 2008).

Protectiveness of their children, particularly daughters, is heightened in Muslim and Asian families compared to Western cultures (Aapola, Gonick, and Harris 2005:93–94). Concerns about loss of cultural identity, in combination of fear of losing their children, have influenced many parents to push for conservative sexual norms. This most notably impacts girls, as they hold a significant location as "cultural vessels," who are expected to pass on to their children the culture's central norms, beliefs, and ideals (Handa 2003; Tyyskä 2006). However, this may lead

some young immigrant women to live in two worlds, manifested in hiding parts of their lives from their parents as a means of living up to the expectations of both their parents and peers. This often shows up in heightened mother-daughter conflict as mothers are deemed responsible for the socialization of their children, and particularly their daughters, into culturally approved behaviours (Dyck and McLaren 2002:9; Tyyskä 2006). However, there is a range of parenting practices from traditional (conservative or protective) to modern (liberal or permissive) in some communities (Tyyskä 2003b). [...]

## OLDER IMMIGRANT WOMEN

While the majority of current immigrants are younger arrivals, older adult immigration is increasing in both Canada and the United States. [...]

Older immigrant women have different needs and vulnerabilities. As Mark A. Leach (2008–2009:35, 36) notes in the American context, nonexistent or limited comprehension of English compounded with lack of familiarity with US society leads to greater reliance on familiar ties, which in turn can create isolation and lack of access to social services such as healthcare, transportation to healthcare, and other social services. Steven Ruggles and associates (2007) noted that 71% of recent older immigrants either spoke no English or did not speak it very well. Another issue that immigrant women tend to face more so than immigrant men is widowhood, as women tend to outlive men within both native-born and foreign-born couples. This results in the widow having to rely more on extended family members (Leach 2008–2009). Atsuko Matsuoka and associates (2012–2013) note a similar situation in the Canadian context: there are various factors leading to the abuse or vulnerability of older immigrant women, including social isolation, language difficulties, financial difficulties and dependency, and poor access to information and appropriate resources. These reflect the "intersection of systemic issues such as sexism, ageism, and racism in Canadian society" (Matsuoka, Guruge, Koehn, Beaulieu, and Ploeg 2012–2013:111). [...]

## CONCLUSION

Even though Canada and the United States are long past their "settler" periods of nation-building and are considered open, tolerant, and liberal societies, colonial, white, and patriarchal interests persist in the immigration policies of these nations. The processes of creating a "citizen" through structural mechanisms of inclusion and exclusion are well established. These processes show no signs of disappearing and, as we have demonstrated in this chapter, marginalize immigrant women. This is manifested in multiple ways. In the past, this could be seen in the denial of female immigrants' entry or admitting only married women. Current Canadian evidence of this includes the admission of women mostly within the family or domestic class immigration categories or as incoming spouses to male economic class immigrants, limiting their access to English language classes; and female immigrant youths' difficulties in integration into the new culture, combined with changes in parenting roles within the receiving society. As a result, immigrant women are denied full citizenship rights. Clearly, women have always occupied a marginal and dependent position in relation to the nation-state; they are reduced to their reproductive and nurturing capacities (Gabriel 2006:166) while their economic contributions are downplayed. This gendered role intersects with racial exclusion. As Enakshi Dua notes, the Canadian state (and this can be extended to the United States as well), remains, in the words of John A. Macdonald, a "white man's country" (2000:57).

## REFERENCES

Aapola, S., M. Gonick, and A. Harris (2005) *Young Femininity: Girlhood, Power and Social Change*. London: Palgrave Macmillan.

Ali, M. and K.M. Kilbride (2004) Forging New Ties: Improving Parenting and Family Support Services for New Canadians with Young Children. Ottawa: Human Resources and Skills Development Canada.

Alvarez, L. and J.M. Broder (2006) More and More, Women Risk All to Enter U.S. *New York Times*, 10 January. www.nytimes.com/2006/01/10/national/10women.html?pagewanted=all&_r=0

Anderson, B. (1983) *Imagined Communities: Reflections on the Origin and Spread of Nationalism*. London: Verso.

Anisef, P., K.M. Kilbride, J. Ochocka, and R. Janzen (2001) Parenting Issues of Newcomer Families in Ontario. Kitchener: Centre for Research and Education in Human Services and Centre of Excellence for Research on Immigration and Settlement.

Arat-Koç, S. (1999) Neo-Liberalism, State Restructuring and Immigration: Changes in Canadian Policies in the 1990s. *Journal of Canadian Studies* 34(2):31–56.

Arat-Koç, S. (2006) From "Mothers of the Nation" to Migrant Workers. In M. Gleason and A. Perry (eds.) *Rethinking Canada: The Promise of Women's History*, pp. 195–209. Don Mills: Oxford University Press.

Baines, D. and N. Sharma (2002) Migrant Workers as Non-Citizens: The Case against Citizenship as a Social Policy Concept. *Studies in Political Economy* 69:75–107.

Batalova, J. (2009) Immigrant Women in the United States. Washington: Migration Policy Institute. www.migrationinformation.org/USfocus/print.cfm?ID=763

Caetano, R., G.A. Field, S. Ramisetty-Mikler, and C. McGarth (2005) Intimate Partner Violence and Drinking Patterns among White, Black and Hispanic Couples in the U.S. *Journal of Substance Abuse* 11(2):123–138.

Canada Press (2013) Canada's Foreign-Born Population Soars to 6.8 Million. 8 May.

Carter, S. (1996) Categories and Terrains of Exclusion: Constructing the "Indian Woman" in the Early Settlement

Era in Western Canada. In J. Parr and M. Rosenfeld (eds.) *Gender and History in Canada*, pp. 30–49. Toronto: Copp Clark.

Chang, G. (2000) *Disposable Domestics: Immigrant Women Workers in the Global Economy*. Cambridge: South End Press.

Chui, T. (2011) Immigrant Women. Ottawa: Statistics Canada. www.statcan.gc.ca/pub/89-503-x/2010001/article/11528-eng.pdf

Citizenship and Immigration Canada (2012) Canada Facts and Figures: Immigration Overview Permanent and Temporary Residents. http://publications.gc.ca/collections/collection_2013/cic/Ci1-8-2012-eng.pdf

Creese, G., I. Dyck, and A. McLaren (1999) *Reconstituting the Family: Negotiating Immigration and Settlement*. Vancouver: RIIM Working Paper 99–10.

Das Gupta, T. (2000) Families of Native Peoples, Immigrants and People of Colour. In B. Crow and L. Gotell (eds.) *Open Boundaries: A Canadian Women's Studies Reader*, pp. 215–230. Toronto: Prentice Hall Canada.

Deen, T. (2013) Over 100 Million Women Lead Migrant Workers Worldwide. Inter Press Service News Agency. www.ipsnews.net/2013/04/over-100-million-women-lead-migrant-workers-worldwide

Dinshaw, F. (2005) Elder Abuse: South Asian Women Speak Up. Toronto: COSTI Immigrant Services.

Du Mont, J., I. Hyman, K. O'Brien, M. White, F. Odette, and V. Tyyskä (2012) Immigration Status and Abuse by a Former Partner [Research Summary]. Toronto: CERIS—The Ontario Metropolis Centre. www.ceris.metropolis.net/wp-content/uploads/2012/03/Exploring-intimate-partner-abuse.pdf (link no longer active)

Dua, E. (2000) "The Hindu Women's Question": Canadian Nation Building and the Social Construction of Gender for South Asian-Canadian Women. In A. Calliste and G.J. Sefa Dei (eds.) *Anti-Racist Feminism: Critical Race and Gender Studies*, pp. 55–72. Halifax: Fernwood Publishing.

Dyck, I. and A.T. McLaren (2002) Becoming Canadian? Girls, Home and School and Renegotiating Feminine Identity. Vancouver: RIIM.

Folson, R.B. (2004) Representation of the Immigrant. In R.B. Folson (ed.) *Calculated Kindness: Global Restructuring, Immigration and Settlement in Canada*, pp. 21–32. Halifax: Fernwood Publishing.

Fuligni, A.J. (1997) The Academic Achievement of Adolescents from Immigrant Families: The Roles of Family Background, Attitudes, and Behavior. *Child Development* 68(2):351–363.

Gabriel, C. (2006) A Question of Skills: Gender, Migration Policy and the Global Political Economy. In K. van der Pijl, L. Assassi, and D. Wigen (eds.) *Global Regulation: Managing Crises after the Imperial Turn*, pp. 163–176. New York: Palgrave Macmillan.

González-Guarda, R., E.P. Vasquez, and V.B. Mitrani (2009) Intimate Partner Violence, Depression and Resource Availability among a Community Sample of Hispanic Women. *Issues in Mental Health Nursing* 30:227–236.

Handa, A. (2003) *Of Silk Saris and Mini-Skirts: South Asian Girls Walk the Tightrope of Culture*. Toronto: Women's Press.

Jain, A. and J. Belsky (1997) Fathering and Acculturation: Immigrant Indian Families with Young Children. *Journal of Marriage and Family* 59:873–883.

James, C.E. (1999) *Seeing Ourselves: Exploring Race, Ethnicity and Culture*. 2nd ed. Toronto: Thompson Educational Publishing.

Labadie-Jackson, G. (2008–2009) Reflections on Domestic Work and the Feminization of Migration. *Campbell Review Law* 31:67–90.

Leach, M.A. (2008–2009) America's Older Immigrants: A Profile. *Generations* 32(4):34–39.

Man, G. (2003) The Experience of Middle Class Women in Recent Hong Kong Chinese Immigrant Families in Canada. In M. Lynn (ed.) *Voices: Essays on Canadian Families*. 2nd ed. Toronto: Thomson Nelson.

Man, G. (2004) Gender, Work and Migration: Deskilling Chinese Immigrant Women in Canada. *Women's Studies International Forum* 27:135–148.

Matsuoka, A., S. Guruge, S. Koehn, M. Beaulieu, and J. Ploeg (2012–2013) Prevention of Abuse of Older Women in the Post-Migration Context in Canada. *Canadian Review of Social Policy* 68/69:107–120.

Moghissi, H. (1999) Away from Home: Iranian Women, Displacement, Cultural Resistance and Change. *Journal of Comparative Family Studies* 30(2):207–218.

Monger, R. and J. Yankay (2013) U.S. Legal Permanent Residents: 2012. Office of Immigration Statistics, Policy Directorate. Washington: U.S. Department of Homeland Security.

Morrison, L., S. Guruge, and K.A. Snarr (1999) Sri Lankan Tamil Immigrants in Toronto: Gender, Marriage Patterns, and Sexuality. In G. Kelson and D. DeLaet (eds.) *Gender and Immigration*, pp. 144–162. New York: NYU Press.

Noivo, E. (1993) Ethnic Families and the Social Injuries of Class, Migration, Gender, Generation and Minority Status. *Canadian Ethnic Studies* 23(3):66–76.

Okun, L. (1988) Termination or Resumption of Cohabitation of Women in Battering Relationships: A Statistical Study. In G.T. Hotaling, D. Finkelhar, J.T. Kirkpatrick, and M.A. Straus (eds.) *Coping with Family Violence: Research and Policy Perspectives.* Thousand Oaks: Sage Press.

Pearce, S. (2006) *Immigrant Women in the United States: A Demographic Portrait.* Washington: American Immigration Law Foundation.

Pothier, M. (2012) *LINCing Literatices: Literacy Practices among Somali Refugee Women in the LINC Program.* University of Toronto: Unpublished Thesis.

Powers, M.G. and Q. Seltzer (1998) Occupational Status and Mobility among Undocumented Immigrants by Gender. *International Migration Review* 12:21–55.

Roberts, B. (1979) "A Work of Empire": Canadian Reformers and British Female Immigration. In L. Kealey (ed.) *A Not Unreasonable Claim: Women and Reform in Canada, 1880s–1920*s, pp. 185–201, 231–233. Toronto: Women's Press.

Ruggles, S., M. Sobek, C.A. Fitch, P.K. Hall, and C. Ronnander (2007) Integrated Public Use Microdata Series: Version 2.0. Historical Census Projects, Department of History, University of Minnesota.

Statistics Canada (2013) Table 054-0001—Immigrant Income, by Sex, Landing Age Group, Immigrant Admission Category, Years since Landing and Landing Year, 2010 Constant Dollars, Annual.

Thobani, S. (2000) Closing Ranks: Racism and Sexism in Canada's Immigration Policy. *Race and Class* 42(1):35–55.

Tjaden, P. and N. Theonnes (2000) Full Report of the Prevalence, Incidence, and Consequences of Violence against Women: Finding from the National Violence against Women Survey. Washington: National Institute of Justice.

Tyyskä, V. (2001) *Long and Winding Road: Adolescents and Youth in Canada Today.* Toronto: Canadian Scholars' Press.

Tyyskä, V. (2002a) Report of Key Informant Interviews—Toronto. Improving Parenting and Family Supports for New Canadians with Young Children: Focus on Resources for Service Providers (unpublished).

Tyyskä, V. (2002b) Report of Individual Interviews with Parents—Toronto. Improving Parenting and Family Supports for New Canadians with Young Children: Focus on Resources for Service Providers (unpublished).

Tyyskä, V. (2003a) Report of Focus Groups with Newcomer Parents. Improving Parenting and Family Supports for New Canadians with Young Children: Focus on Resources for Service Providers (unpublished).

Tyyskä, V. (2003b) Solidarity and Conflict: Teen-Parent Relationships in Iranian Immigrant Families in Toronto. In M. Lynn (ed.) *Voices: Essays on Canadian Families.* 2nd ed. pp. 312–331. Toronto: Nelson Canada.

Tyyskä, V. (2005) Immigrant Adjustment and Parenting of Teens: A Study of Newcomer Groups in Toronto, Canada. In V. Puuronen, J. Soilevuo-Grønnerød, and J. Herranen, *Youth-Similarities, Differences, Inequalities.* Joensuu: Joensuu University, Reports of the Karelian Institute, No. 1/2005.

Tyyskä, V. (2006) *Teen Perspectives on Family Relations in the Toronto Tamil Community.* CERIS Working Paper No. 45. March 2006. Toronto: CERIS.

Tyyskä, V. (2007) Immigrant Families in Sociology. In J.E. Lansford, K. Deater-Deckard, and M.H. Bornstein (eds.) *Immigrant Families in Contemporary Society*, pp. 83–99. New York: The Guilford Press.

Tyyskä, V. (2008) *Youth and Society: The Long and Winding Road.* 2nd ed. Toronto: Canadian Scholars' Press.

Tyyskä, V. (2009) *Families and Violence in Punjabi and Tamil Communities in Toronto.* CERIS Working Paper No. 74.

Toronto: CERIS. www.ceris.metropolis.net/Virtual%20
Library/WKPP%20List/WKPP2009/CWP74.pdf (link
no longer active)

Tyyskä, V., F. Dinshaw, C. Redmond, and F. Gomes (2012).
"Where We Have Come and Are Now Trapped": Views of
Victims and Service Providers on Abuse of Older Adults
in Tamil and Punjabi Families. *Canadian Ethnic Studies*
44(3):59–78.

Wong, S.K. (1999) Acculturation, Peer Relations, and
Delinquent Behaviour of Chinese-Canadian Youth.
*Adolescence* 34(133):107–119.

Zaidi, A. and M. Shuraydi (2002) Perceptions of Arranged
Marriages by Young Pakistani Muslim Women Living
in Western Society. *Journal of Comparative Family Studies*
33(4):37–57.

*Source:* Nichols, Leslie, & Tyyskä, Vappu. (2015).
Excerpted from "Immigrant Women in Canada and
the United States." In Harald Bauder & John Shields
(Eds.), *Immigrant Experiences in North America:
Understanding Settlement and Integration* (pp. 248–
272). Toronto, ON: Canadian Scholars' Press.

# CHAPTER 65

## The Door of No Return

*Leah Lakshmi Piepzna-Samarasinha*

Leah Lakshmi Piepzna-Samarasinha is a queer, chronically ill, and disabled nonbinary femme writer and cultural worker of Burger/Tamil Sri Lankan and Irish/Roma descent. She is the author of *Dirty River: A Queer Femme of Color Dreaming Her Way Home*, *Bodymap*, and *Consensual Genocide*. Her collection of poetry entitled *Love Cake* received a Lambda Literary Award in 2012. Piepzna-Samarasinha is currently a lead artist with the disability justice performance collective Sins Invalid.

Everyone in my family has run from something. Some of us run halfway across the world. Crossing a border's less like a family secret and more like a family tradition. Filling out paperwork, getting an immigration sponsorship, pretending we were 99 percent white, and flirting or saying "yes, ma'am" to the guard—all that stuff came to my family as natural as tears and sweat. Easy. It wasn't that far a leap from my grandparents sneaking into White Australia [to me deciding to] leave America, Guiliani, and $4.25 minimum wages for Canada in 1996.

*It's time, girl.*
Time for what?
*Time to be free.*

When you apply for Canadian immigration through marriage, your sponsor has to sign an undertaking that for the next ten years they're financially responsible for you. You can't go on welfare, you can't really go on disability. The government makes sure immigrants don't get to use any of the lovely Canadian social safety net that your taxes pay for. A lot of husbands tell their wives that that means they can't get divorced, telling them if they leave they will be deported. There's a law that makes that illegal, but the system doesn't always pay attention to it and the women don't always know. When my partner signs the undertaking, I know it is a problem but I also don't have an alternative.

Lining up in the snow. A line of migrants snaking out of the downtown immigration office when it was still on Dundas Street. Line out the door from before when it opened, but I was sick so I never got there before two or three. Long line of people afraid, clutching forms, talking softly in our own languages. Mean-ass barking lady telling us to speak up, telling us, "I DON'T UNDERSTAND YOUR ACCENT, DO YOU SPEAK ENGLISH?" Hour or two wait, me English speaking and American citizenship, but brown skinned, poor and queer and sick, and they still gave me the wrong form two or three times. That long line of pain and fear.

Soon they would move the office out to Etobicoke and strongly encourage everyone to shift to calling the 1-800 lines instead, so no one working or living downtown had to see the physical face of immigration, so we couldn't see each other, just alone waiting on the damn hold on the 1-800 number. I remember taking four buses out to Mississauga to the immigration consultant, who took a hundred bucks from us to explain the forms and tell us where to sign.

Sometime later, two winters and a spring and summer and two falls of poverty, off the books, shoveling snow, handing out flyers, landscaping paid in cash, packaging food for the Afri-Can food basket in exchange for tokens and a meal and a big food box, a huge amount of bulk food I bought via a credit card scam, and living off the rice and dhal and falafel mix that I had told the health food store was for a new chapter of Food Not Bombs, I get that narrow faded piss-yellow letter in the mail from immigration. The one that says I am landed in principle. Then the one that says I need to show up at the immigration center at 8:00 am on a certain day. When I talked about how hard it was and how broke we were, I remember my lover's mother saying, "But you know, it won't always be that way." I could see her remembering being just like us—twenty-two, broke, and immigrant. And here it was, that day. The day when things were no longer quite so hard. The day when I got a health insurance card, a social insurance number, the ability to rise out of the basement apartment to the world I'd been looking at through a smeared window.

When the postcard with the date and time showed up, I got up early. Dressed in my least patched-up best and took the subway all the way to Kipling to get there on time. The waiting room was that shit-diarrhea yellow of all institutional waiting rooms, filled with folks who looked just like some variation of me. The ones who had finally made it. When my name was called, I went to my Plexiglas cubicle. The lady there looked at my forms, and then looked at me. She handed me a long pale piss-yellow form through the slot. It said "FAMILY CLASS LANDED IMMIGRANT STATUS" on it.

I looked at her. "Um, this is the wrong one. I'm supposed to have a Humanitarian and Compassionate." I had gotten my free counselor in the partner abuse program to fill out all the forms and write a support letter so I wouldn't be bound to my partner and the undertaking for the next decade. I was still looking over my shoulder every time I left the house.

"Dear, I don't see anything about that. What do you mean?"

"Humanitarian and Compassionate. It's for when your sponsor was abusive."

"Well, dear, I'm not seeing anything about that here. And I have your landed. Do you want it or not?" She paused. "Dear. Don't break up a marriage over something like that."

What could I do? I had been waiting for this, this piece of paper. The one that would open the door to doctors and jobs, tax returns and bank accounts, ID and health insurance cards, a maybe easier time at the Greyhound border crossing. I nodded.

BAM. Stamp on the passport. Coveted, coveted document stapled into coveted, coveted passport. "Take the elevator downstairs, you can get your SIN number and OHIP application there."

I was silent. I'd passed through. But what now?

*Source:* Piepzna-Samarasinha, Leah Lakshmi. (2013). "The Door of No Return." In Harsha Walia (Ed.), *Undoing Border Imperialism* (pp. 81–84). Chico, CA: AK Press.

# CHAPTER 66

## Seeking Refuge from Homophobic and Transphobic Persecution

*Sharalyn Jordan and Christine Morrissey*

Sharalyn Jordan is an assistant professor in the Faculty of Education at Simon Fraser University in Burnaby, British Columbia. As a scholar-practitioner and educator in counselling psychology, she works at the nexus of mental health and social justice. Her recent and current projects explore the implications of homophobic and transphobic stigma, trauma, and intersectional oppressions for refugee protection, settlement, and mental health. Jordan's research uses critical, interpretive, and collaborative qualitative inquiry methods, and involves communities and participants in knowledge co-production. In 2015, she received a YMCA Power of the Peace Award for her work helping lesbian, gay, bisexual, transgender, and queer (LGBTQ) refugees to navigate the Canadian refugee system.

Christine Morrissey is the founder and member of the board of the Rainbow Refugee Committee. The Rainbow Refugee Committee is a Vancouver-based community group that supports people seeking refugee protection in Canada because of persecution based on sexual orientation, gender identity, gender expression, or HIV status.

Currently, no fewer than 76 countries criminalize same-sex sexual acts or gender variability. Many of these statutes can be traced to colonial imposition, specifically, the British penal code section 377. Direct criminalization and morality laws create the means for abuse of power by police and others in authority. Surveillance and threat is dispersed along networks of family, school, and community. Homophobic and transphobic violence often occurs out of the public eye, and unlike war or larger conflicts, people experience this violence in relative isolation. In some cases, religious teachings and psychiatric diagnosis are used to shame and pathologize people who live transgressive sexualities or genders. Stigmatization as evil or mentally ill further isolates people.

These brief accounts below were shared by QLGBT [Queer Lesbian Gay Bi and Trans] refugees now living in Canada, as part of our research project

"Un/Settling." These accounts highlight some of the complexities of persecution based on sexual orientation or gender identity.

A young woman from Nigeria was told to marry a man who was twenty years her elder. She confided in her sister that she was attracted to women and could not marry this man. The sister told her parents. The young woman was kept locked up and beaten regularly by her father for over a month. Rumours spread around her town. Her church publicly denounced her. When she was allowed out, she was assaulted by a gang of young men and neighbours threw rocks at her.

A trans woman from Mexico was picked up by police while walking home in the afternoon. They threatened to charge her with prostitution if she did not perform sexual acts and pay them a bribe. Officers were regularly waiting outside her apartment, following and harassing her.

Gay men who have fled Sri Lanka report being picked up from gay cruising areas by police. They were detained and assaulted by police, and forced to pay a bribe for their release. The police returned to their homes monthly to extort more money, threatening to out them or beat them if they did not pay.

Our research suggests the global terrain of protection and persecution for QLGBT people is in flux and often paradoxical. As Louis George Tin has described in the *Dictionary of Homophobia*,[1] Brazil hosts the largest Pride Parade in the world with over 3 million people celebrating. Yet Brazil also has the world's highest reported rate of homophobic and transphobic murders. While South Africa recognizes same-sex marriage, human rights organizations there report ten cases a week of 'corrective rape' targeting lesbians, most never investigated by police. QLGBT organizers in Poland have been targets of violence, with impunity or complicity from authorities, despite the human rights protections promised by European Union membership. We have heard Bogota described by one man as a great place to be gay but, by another person who spent ten years on the run within Colombia trying to escape death threats, as a terrifying city to be

gay. The first man was protected by his affluence, the second vulnerable because he was poor, and from an area controlled by drug cartels. Legal human rights protection does not translate into on-the-ground safety or access to state protection. Within the same country of origin, people's vulnerability or safety varies considerably based on social class, race, religion, ability to 'pass,' and social networks.

Queer Lesbian Gay Bi and Trans refugees that we know left their home countries because they were in danger, and many did not know that the risks they faced constituted persecution. Often it was only after they left their countries by any means possible that they learned that they could seek refugee protection. Asymmetrical im/mobilities—created by intersectional mobility exclusions based on racism, global north/south disparities, gender, and social class—enable and constrain who is able to leave, how people migrate, and options for permanent status.

In their migration, QLGBT asylum seekers encounter immigration and border systems that enable and restrict mobility based on the priorities of global capitalism, neocolonialism, and post-9/11 notions of security. Canada, along with other Western countries, is using increasingly stringent measures to screen out potential asylum seekers. According to Oxfam's report, *A Price Too High: The Cost of Australia's Approach to Asylum Seekers*,[2] Australia has spent over a billion dollars to detain and process asylum seekers offshore; a half-million dollars per refugee. Legislation before Canadian Parliament [at the time of writing] would result in detention of potential refugees, including children, for a full year. Canada Research Chair Catherine Dauvergne argues in *Making People Illegal: What Globalization Means for Migration and Law*[3] that the punitive impact of measures like these function to make asylum itself illegal.

Undertaking an asylum application entails accessing and working within a refugee system that was not designed with lesbian gay bi trans or queer refugees in mind. In the early 1990s, the Geneva Convention criteria for refugee protection stated that, "membership in a particular social group" was interpreted in Canada and by the United Nations High Commission on Refugees (UNHCR) to include those who face persecution based on their sexuality or gender identity. Yet, much work remains to be done to ensure that this protection is meaningful.

If a potential refugee makes it to a UNHCR office or one of the 21 countries that extend protection to QLGBT refugees, they must prove an often hidden and stigmatized identity, and their fear of persecution. QLGBT refugees have left countries where they have been under surveillance, arrested, extorted, and, for some, imprisoned or tortured, because of their sexuality or gender identity. Survival has required vigilance, secrecy, and conformity. The survival tactics do not necessarily disappear on departure. We know one man who spent 27 days in detention after making his way from Iran, through China, Indonesia, and Japan, before working up the nerve to tell his duty counsel he was gay. Shame, fear, and the impacts of trauma on memory interfere with people being able to make their case.

Refugee decision makers find sexual orientation and gender identity cases some of the hardest decisions to make. Law professor Nicole LaViolette argues that no other kind of claim requires people to provide such intimate testimony about such deeply stigmatized parts of their lives.

Without formal guidelines for adjudicators to follow, decision makers rely on their own background knowledge—often based in culturally encapsulated understandings of sexualities and genders—to assess the credibility of an applicant's identity claim. QLGBT refugees are evaluated against expected narratives of refugee flight and Western narratives of LGBT identity that do not necessarily apply. Fair decisions are hampered by the lack of reliable information about on-the-ground conditions for QLGBT people.

Refugee protection is not yet meaningfully accessible for queer or trans people facing persecution. Simultaneously, the right to asylum is in jeopardy, internationally and in Canada, for all asylum seekers.

QLGBT refugees are struggling to gain access to a protection system that is under-resourced and under erosion. Bringing about refugee protection for QLGBT people facing persecution, preventing further erosion of the refugee protection system that exists, and envisioning just approaches to asylum will require creative and committed political, policy, social service, community building, cultural, and scholarly work.

The social justice risks are as significant as the potentials—as are spelt out in the research of scholars such as Jasbir Puar, Sara Ahmed, Vivien Namaste, and Vancouver activist/scholar Fatima Jaffer. Raising the problem of sexuality or gender based persecution internationally risks othering cultures, faiths, or countries as monolithically and irredeemably homophobic. Moreover, we are mindful that presenting the need for QLGBT refugee settlement in Canada can entrench colonial narratives of rescue and binaries of developed vs. backwards or civilized vs. barbaric. Writing, speaking, and organizing around QLGBT refugee protection invites us into echoing homonationalist discourses that equate the West with progress and tolerance of QLGBT citizens with modernity. This homonationalism can ally dangerously with Islamophobia or xenophobia. As Fatima Jaffer explained at the July 2011 Salaam conference held in Vancouver, after 9/11 "I was being seen as not being queer and patriotic, not being Canadian in the way that it's being framed by the queer community."[4]

Post-Colonial Queer/Trans scholarship, antiracist organizing among QLGBT communities, QLGBT migrant organizing, and Queer and Trans intersectionality[5] all play critical roles in interrupting these problematic discourses and their repercussions. Bringing postcolonial, antiracist, Trans, and Queer perspectives into dialogue will enhance the community organizing, research, law, and policy efforts to create meaningful protection for QLGBT refugees. Collaborations among community organizations working with QLGBT refugees and researchers are contributing to this important dialogue—Rainbow

Refugee in Vancouver, AGIR [Action LGBTQ with Immigrants and Refugees] in Montreal, and a number of groups in Toronto are part of this effort. As well, bringing the knowledge constructed through these collaborations into dialogue with policymakers, lawyers, service providers, human rights organizations, and the wider public is a critical step in the social justice agenda for QLGBT refugees.

Recently the two of us met with officers of Citizenship and Immigration Canada (CIC), to iron out specifics of how Queer/LGBT community organizations can participate in sponsoring refugees facing homophobic or transphobic persecution. Among the many details we pointed out were the problems with application forms asking for *sex (male/female)* and *marital status*. We also raised the issue that, while waiting for resettlement, in often precarious conditions, QLGBT refugees continue to face homophobic or transphobic violence. In particular, we drew attention to the interminably long and dangerous waits faced by Ugandans, Nigerians, and other Africans who apply for refugee protection in Nairobi, Kenya. As the Canadian Council for Refugees documents,[6] the target for the Canadian processing centre in Nairobi remains 1000 people per year, despite a caseload[7] of over 7000 people who have willing sponsors in Canada.

Advocating for migration rights for same-sex partners (LEGIT.ca)[8] and refugee protection for QLGBT asylum seekers in Canada (rainbowrefugee.ca)[9] has taught us a few things about negotiating our way around boxes that confine and, through systems, exclude. Working towards human rights protection for those persecuted for their sexualities or gender identities raises complex intersectional social justice issues that call for alliance building, interdisciplinary scholarship, dialogue, and critical reflexivity in our advocacy and research.

## NOTES

1. Tin, L.G. (Ed.). (2008). *The Dictionary of Homophobia: A Global History of Gay & Lesbian Experience*. (Redburn, M., Trans.). British Columbia: Arsenal Pulp Press.

2. Bem, K., Field, N., Maclellan, N., Meyer, S. & Morris, T. (2007). A Price too High: The Cost of Australia's Approach to Asylum Seekers. Retrieved from http://resources.oxfam.org.au/filestore/originals/OAus-PriceTooHighAsylumSeekers-0807.pdf

3. Dauvergne, C. (2008). *Making People Illegal: What Globalization Means for Migration and Law*. Cambridge: Cambridge University Press.

4. Hainsworth, J. (2011, July 29). Homosexuality and Islam Not Opposing Forces. *Xtra!* Retrieved from https://www.dailyxtra.com/homosexuality-and-islam-not-opposing-forces-6673

5. Bilge, S. (2011, October 18). Developing Intersectional Solidarities: Plea for Queer Intersectionality. [Blog entry]. Retrieved from http://www.ideas-idees.ca/blog/developing-intersectional-solidarities-plea-queer-intersectionality

6. Canadian Council for Refugees. (n.d.). Nairobi: Long Delays-Sign the Statement, contact your MP and raise awareness. Retrieved from http://ccrweb.ca/en/nairobi-action

7. Canadian Council for Refugees. (n.d.). Nairobi: Long Delays-Sign the Statement, contact your MP and raise awareness. Retrieved from http://ccrweb.ca/en/nairobi-action

8. LEGIT. (2011). Home. Retrieved from http://www.legit.ca/

9. Rainbow Refuge Canada. (2011). About Rainbow Refugee. Retrieved from http://www.rainbowrefugee.ca/

*Source:* Jordan, Sharalyn, & Morrissey, Christine. (2012). "Seeking Refuge from Homophobic and Transphobic Persecution." In Malinda S. Smith & Fatima Jaffer (Eds.), *Beyond the Queer Alphabet: Conversations on Gender, Sexuality, & Intersectionality* (pp. 67–70). Ottawa, ON: Canadian Federation for the Humanities and Social Sciences.

# CHAPTER 67

## Nickel and Dimed: On (Not) Getting By in America

*Barbara Ehrenreich*

Barbara Ehrenreich is a highly influential American journalist, author, and activist, as well as the founder of the Economic Hardship Reporting Project. Beginning her professional life with a PhD in cell biology, she traded the sciences for social criticism, focusing especially on women's rights, economic justice, peace and war, and health and illness. She has written extensively for leading magazines and newspapers including the *New York Times*, *Time*, *Harper's Magazine*, *The Nation*, and *The Progressive*, and has also published over 20 books. Ehrenreich extended the article excerpted below into the full-length book *Nickel and Dimed: On (Not) Getting By in America*, which investigated the impacts of the 1996 welfare reforms on the working poor in the United States. The book, published in 2001, became a *New York Times* bestseller.

At the beginning of June 1998, I leave behind everything that normally soothes the ego and sustains the body—home, career, companion, reputation, ATM card—for a plunge into the low-wage workforce. There, I become another, occupationally much diminished "Barbara Ehrenreich"—depicted on job-application forms as a divorced homemaker whose sole work experience consists of housekeeping in a few private homes. I am terrified, at the beginning, of being unmasked for what I am: a middle-class journalist setting out to explore the world that welfare mothers are entering, at the rate of approximately 50,000 a month, as welfare reform kicks in. Happily, though, my fears turn out to be entirely unwarranted: during a month of poverty and toil, my name goes unnoticed and for the most part unuttered. In this parallel universe where my father never got out of the mines and I never got through college, I am "baby," "honey," "blondie," and, most commonly, "girl."

My first task is to find a place to live. I figure that if I can earn $7 an hour—which, from the want ads, seems doable—I can afford to spend $500 on rent, or maybe, with severe economies, $600. In the Key West area, where I live, this pretty much confines me to flophouses and trailer homes [....]

So I decide to make the common trade-off between affordability and convenience, and go for a $500-a-month efficiency thirty miles up a two-lane highway from the employment opportunities of Key West, meaning forty-five minutes if there's no road construction and I don't get caught behind some sun-dazed Canadian tourists. [...]

[...] My aim is nothing so mistily subjective as to "experience poverty" or find out how it "really feels" to be a long-term low-wage worker. I've had enough unchosen encounters with poverty and the world of low-wage work to know it's not a place you want to visit for touristic purposes; it just smells too much like fear. And with all my real-life assets—bank account, IRA, health insurance, multiroom home—waiting indulgently in the background, I am, of course, thoroughly insulated from the terrors that afflict the genuinely poor.

No, this is a purely objective, scientific sort of mission. The humanitarian rationale for welfare reform—as opposed to the more punitive and stingy impulses that may actually have motivated it—is that work will lift poor women out of poverty while simultaneously inflating their self-esteem and hence their future value in the labor market. Thus, whatever the hassles involved in finding child care, transportation, etc., the transition from welfare to work will end happily, in greater prosperity for all. Now there are many problems with this comforting prediction, such as the fact that the economy will inevitably undergo a downturn, eliminating many jobs. Even without a downturn, the influx of a million former welfare recipients into the low-wage labor market could depress wages by as much as 11.9 percent, according to the Economic Policy Institute (EPI) in Washington, D.C.

But is it really possible to make a living on the kinds of jobs currently available to unskilled people? Mathematically, the answer is no, as can be shown by taking $6 to $7 an hour, perhaps subtracting a dollar or two an hour for child care, multiplying by 160 hours a month, and comparing the result to the prevailing rents. According to the National Coalition for the Homeless, for example, in 1998 it took, on average nationwide, an hourly wage of $8.89 to afford

a one-bedroom apartment, and the Preamble Center for Public Policy estimates that the odds against a typical welfare recipient's landing a job at such a "living wage" are about 97 to 1. If these numbers are right, low-wage work is not a solution to poverty and possibly not even to homelessness.

\*\*\*\*\*

On the morning of my first full day of job searching, I take a red pen to the want ads, which are auspiciously numerous. Everyone in Key West's booming "hospitality industry" seems to be looking for someone like me—trainable, flexible, and with suitably humble expectations as to pay. I know I possess certain traits that might be advantageous—I'm white and, I like to think, well-spoken and poised—but I decide on two rules: One, I cannot use any skills derived from my education or usual work—not that there are a lot of want ads for satirical essayists anyway. Two, I have to take the best-paid job that is offered me and of course do my best to hold it; no Marxist rants or sneaking off to read novels in the ladies' room. [...]

So I put on what I take to be a respectful-looking outfit of ironed Bermuda shorts and scooped-neck T-shirt and set out for a tour of the local hotels and supermarkets. Best Western, Econo Lodge, and HoJo's all let me fill out application forms, and these are, to my relief, interested in little more than whether I am a legal resident of the United States and have committed any felonies. My next stop is Winn-Dixie, the supermarket, which turns out to have a particularly onerous application process, featuring a fifteen-minute "interview" by computer since, apparently, no human on the premises is deemed capable of representing the corporate point of view. I am conducted to a large room decorated with posters illustrating how to look "professional" (it helps to be white and, if female, permed) and warning of the slick promises that union organizers might try to tempt me with. The interview is multiple choice: Do I have anything, such as child-care problems, that might make it hard for me to get to work on time? Do I think safety on the job is the responsibility of management? Then, popping up cunningly out of the blue: How many dollars' worth of stolen goods have I purchased in the last year? Would I turn in a fellow employee if I caught him stealing? Finally, "Are you an honest person?"

Apparently, I ace the interview, because I am told that all I have to do is show up in some doctor's office tomorrow for a urine test. This seems to be a fairly general rule: if you want to stack Cheerio boxes or vacuum hotel rooms in chemically fascist America, you have to be willing to squat down and pee in front of some health worker (who has no doubt had to do the same thing herself). The wages Winn-Dixie is offering—$6 and a couple of dimes to start with—are not enough, I decide, to compensate for this indignity.

I lunch at Wendy's, where $4.99 gets you unlimited refills at the Mexican part of the Superbar, a comforting surfeit of refried beans and "cheese sauce." A teenage employee, seeing me studying the want ads, kindly offers me an application form, which I fill out, though here, too, the pay is just $6 and change an hour. Then it's off for a round of the locally owned inns and guesthouses. At "The Palms," let's call it, a bouncy manager actually takes me around to see the rooms and meet the existing housekeepers, who, I note with satisfaction, look pretty much like me—faded ex-hippie types in shorts with long hair pulled back in braids. Mostly, though, no one speaks to me or even looks at me except to proffer an application form. At my last stop, a palatial B&B, I wait twenty minutes to meet "Max," only to be told that there are no jobs now but there should be one soon, since "nobody lasts more than a couple weeks." (Because none of the people I talked to knew I was a reporter, I have changed their name to protect their privacy and, in some cases perhaps, their jobs.)

Three days go by like this, and, to my chagrin, no one out of the approximately twenty places I've applied calls me for an interview. I had been vain enough to worry about coming across as too educated for the jobs I sought, but no one even seems interested in finding out how overqualified I am. Only later will I realize that the want ads are not a reliable measure of the actual jobs available at any particular time. They are, as I should have guessed from Max's comment, the employers' insurance policy against the relentless turnover of the low-wage workforce. Most of the big hotels run ads almost continually, just to build a supply of applicants to replace the current workers as they drift away or are fired, so finding a job is just a matter of being at the right place at the right time and flexible enough to take whatever is being offered that day. This finally happens to me at one of the big discount hotel chains, where I go, as usual, for housekeeping and am sent, instead, to try out as a waitress at the attached "family restaurant," a dismal spot with a counter and about thirty tables that looks out on a parking garage and features such tempting fare as "Pollish [*sic*] sausage and BBQ sauce" on 95-degree days. [...]

So begins my career at the Hearthside, I shall call it, one small profit center within a global discount hotel chain, where for two weeks I work from 2:00 till 10:00 P.M. for $2.43 an hour plus tips. In some futile bid for gentility, the management has barred employees from using the front door, so my first day I enter through the kitchen, where a red-faced man with shoulder-length blond hair is throwing frozen steaks against the wall and yelling, "Fuck this shit!" "That's just Jack," explains Gail, the wiry middle-aged waitress who is assigned to train me. "He's on the rag again"—a condition occasioned, in this instance, by the fact that the cook on the morning shift had forgotten to thaw out the steaks. For the next eight hours, I run after the agile Gail, absorbing bits of instruction along with fragments of personal tragedy. All food must be trayed, and the reason she's so tired today is that she woke up in a cold sweat thinking of her boyfriend, who killed himself recently in an upstate prison. No refills on lemonade. And the reason he was in prison is that a few DUIs caught up with him, that's all, could have happened to anyone. Carry the creamers to the table in a monkey bowl, never in your hand. And after he was gone she spent several months living in her truck, peeing in a plastic pee bottle and reading by candlelight at night, but you can't live in a truck in the summer, since you need to have the windows down, which means anything can get in, from mosquitoes on up.

At least Gail puts to rest any fears I had of appearing overqualified. From the first day on, I find that of all the things I have left behind, such as home and identity, what I miss the most is competence. Not that I have ever felt utterly competent in the writing business, in which one day's success augers nothing at all for the next. But in my writing life, I at least have some notion of procedure: do the research, make the outline, rough out a draft, etc. As a server, though, I am beset by requests like bees: more iced tea here, ketchup over there, a to-go box for table fourteen, and where are the high chairs, anyway? Of the twenty-seven tables, up to six are usually mine at any time, though on slow afternoons or if Gail is off, I sometimes have the whole place to myself. There is the touch-screen computer-ordering system to master, which is, I suppose, meant to minimize server–cook contact, but in practice requires constant verbal fine-tuning: "That's gravy on the mashed, okay! None on the meatloaf," and so forth—while the cook scowls as if I were inventing these refinements just to torment him. Plus, something I had forgotten in the years since I was eighteen: about a third of a server's job is "side work" that's invisible to customers—sweeping, scrubbing, slicing, refilling, and restocking. If it isn't all done, every little bit of it, you're going to face the 6:00 P.M. dinner rush defenseless and probably go down in flames. I screw up dozens of times at the beginning, sustained in my shame entirely by Gail's support—"It's okay, baby, everyone does that sometime"—because, to my total surprise and despite the scientific detachment I am doing my best to maintain, I care. [...]

After a few days at the Hearthside, I feel the service ethic kick in like a shot of oxytocin, the nurturance hormone. The plurality of my customers are hard-working locals—truck drivers, construction workers, even housekeepers from the attached hotel—and I want them to have the closest to a "fine dining" experience that the grubby circumstances will allow. No "you guys" for me; everyone over twelve is "sir" or "ma'am." I ply them with iced tea and coffee refills; I return, mid-meal, to inquire how everything is; I doll up their salads with chopped raw mushrooms, summer squash slices, or whatever bits of produce I can find that have survived their sojourn in the cold-storage room mold-free.

\*\*\*\*\*

I could drift along like this, in some dreamy proletarian idyll, except for two things. One is management. If I have kept this subject on the margins thus far it is because I still flinch to think that I spent all those weeks under the surveillance of men (and later women) whose job it was to monitor my behavior for signs of sloth, theft, drug abuse, or worse. Not that managers and especially "assistant managers" in low-wage settings like this are exactly the class enemy. In the restaurant business, they are mostly former cooks or servers, still capable of pinch-hitting in the kitchen or on the floor, just as in hotels they are likely to be former clerks, and paid a salary of only about $400 a week. But everyone knows they have crossed over to the other side, which is, crudely put, corporate as opposed to human. Cooks want to prepare tasty meals; servers want to serve them graciously; but managers are there for only one reason—to make sure that money is made for some theoretical entity that exists far away in Chicago or New York, if a corporation can be said to have a physical existence at all. Reflecting on her career, Gail tells me ruefully that she had sworn, years ago, never to work for a corporation again. "They don't cut you no slack. You give and you give, and they take."

Managers can sit—for hours at a time if they want—but it's their job to see that no one else ever does, even when there's nothing to do, and this is why, for servers, slow times can be as exhausting as rushes. You start dragging out each little chore, because if the manager on duty catches you in an idle moment, he will give you something far nastier to do. So I wipe, I clean, I consolidate ketchup bottles and recheck the cheesecake supply, even tour the tables to make sure the customer evaluation forms are all standing perkily in their places—wondering all the time how many calories I burn in these strictly theatrical exercises. When, on a particularly dead afternoon, Stu [the assistant manager] finds me glancing at a *USA Today* a customer has left behind, he assigns me to vacuum the entire floor with the broken vacuum cleaner that has a handle only two feet long, and the only way to do that without incurring orthopedic damage is to proceed from spot to spot on your knees.

On my first Friday at the Hearthside there is a "mandatory meeting for all restaurant employees," which I attend, eager for insight into our overall marketing strategy and the niche (your basic Ohio cuisine with a tropical twist?) we aim to inhabit. But there is no "we" at this meeting. Phillip, our top manager except for an occasional "consultant" sent out by corporate headquarters, opens it with a sneer: "The break room—it's disgusting. Butts in the ashtrays, newspapers lying around, crumbs." This windowless little room, which also houses the time clock for the entire hotel, is where we stash our bags and civilian clothes and take our half-hour meal breaks. But a break room is not a right, he tells us. It can be taken away. We should also know that the lockers in the break room and whatever is in them can be searched at any time. Then comes gossip; there has been gossip; gossip (which seems to mean employees talking among themselves) must stop. Off-duty employees are henceforth barred from eating at the restaurant, because "other servers gather around them and gossip." When Phillip has exhausted his agenda of rebukes, Joan complains about the condition of the ladies' room and I throw in my two bits about the vacuum cleaner. But I don't see any backup coming from my fellow servers, each of whom has subsided into her own personal funk. [...]

The other problem, in addition to the less-than-nurturing management style, is that this job shows no sign of being financially viable. You might imagine, from a comfortable distance, that people who live, year in and year out, on $6 to $10 an hour have discovered some survival stratagems unknown to the middle class. But no. It's not hard to get my co-workers to talk about their living situations, because housing, in almost every case, is the principal source of disruption in their lives, the first thing they fill you in on when they arrive for their shifts. After a week, I have compiled the following survey:

- Gail is sharing a room in a well-known downtown flophouse for which she and a roommate pay about $250 a week. Her roommate, a male friend, has begun hitting on her, driving her nuts, but the rent would be impossible alone.
- Claude, the Haitian cook, is desperate to get out of the two-room apartment he shares with his girlfriend and two other, unrelated, people. As far as I can determine, the other Haitian men (most of whom only speak Creole) live in similarly crowded situations.
- Annette, a twenty-year-old server who is six months pregnant and has been abandoned by her boyfriend, lives with her mother, a postal clerk.
- Marianne and her boyfriend are paying $170 a week for a one-person trailer.
- Jack, who is, at $10 an hour, the wealthiest of us, lives in the trailer he owns, paying only the $400-a-month lot fee.
- The other white cook, Andy, lives on his dry-docked boat, which, as far as I can tell from his loving descriptions, can't be more than twenty feet long. He offers to take me out on it, once it's repaired, but the offer comes with inquiries as to my marital status, so I do not follow up on it.

- Tina and her husband are paying $60 a night for a double room in a Days Inn. This is because they have no car and the Days Inn is within walking distance of the Hearthside. When Marianne, one of the breakfast servers, is tossed out of her trailer for subletting (which is against the trailer-park rules), she leaves her boyfriend and moves in with Tina and her husband.
- Joan, who had fooled me with her numerous and tasteful outfits (hostesses wear their own clothes), lives in a van she parks behind a shopping center at night and showers in Tina's motel room. The clothes are from thrift shops.

It strikes me, in my middle-class solipsism, that there is gross improvidence in some of these arrangements. When Gail and I are wrapping silverware in napkins—the only task for which we are permitted to sit—she tells me she is thinking of escaping from her roommate by moving into the Days Inn herself. I am astounded: How can she even think of paying between $40 and $60 a day? But if I was afraid of sounding like a social worker, I come out just sounding like a fool. She squints at me in disbelief, "And where am I supposed to get a month's rent and a month's deposit for an apartment?" I'd been feeling pretty smug about my $500 efficiency, but of course it was made possible only by the $1,300 I had allotted myself for start-up costs when I began my low-wage life: $1,000 for the first month's rent and deposit, $100 for initial groceries and cash in my pocket, $200 stuffed away for emergencies. In poverty, as in certain propositions in physics, starting conditions are everything.

There are no secret economies that nourish the poor; on the contrary, there are a host of special costs. If you can't put up the two months' rent you need to secure an apartment, you end up paying through the nose for a room by the week. If you have only a room, with a hot plate at best, you can't save by cooking up huge lentil stews that can be frozen for the week ahead. You eat fast food, or the hot dogs and styrofoam cups of soup that can be microwaved in a convenience store.

If you have no money for health insurance [...] you go without routine care or prescription drugs and end up paying the price. Gail, for example, was fine until she ran out of money for estrogen pills. She is supposed to be on the company plan by now, but they claim to have lost her application form and need to begin the paperwork all over again. So she spends $9 per migraine pill to control the headaches she wouldn't have, she insists, if her estrogen supplements were covered. Similarly, Marianne's boyfriend lost his job as a roofer because he missed so much time after getting a cut on his foot for which he couldn't afford the prescribed antibiotic.

My own situation, when I sit down to assess it after two weeks of work, would not be much better if this were my actual life. The seductive thing about waitressing is that you don't have to wait for payday to feel a few bills in your pocket, and my tips usually cover meals and gas, plus something left over to stuff into the kitchen drawer I use as a bank. But as the tourist business slows in the summer heat, I sometimes leave work with only $20 in tips (the gross is higher, but servers share about 15 percent of their tips with the busboys and bartenders). With wages included, this amounts to about the minimum wage of $5.15 an hour. Although the sum in the drawer is piling up, at the present rate of accumulation it will be more than $100 short of my rent when the end of the month comes around. Nor can I see any expenses to cut. True, I haven't gone the lentil-stew route yet, but that's because I don't have a large cooking pot, pot holders, or a ladle to stir with (which cost about $30 at Kmart, less at thrift stores), not to mention onions, carrots, and the indispensable bay leaf. I do make my lunch almost every day—usually some slow-burning, high-protein combo like frozen chicken patties with melted cheese on top and canned pinto beans on the side. Dinner is at the Hearthside, which offers its employees a choice of BLT, fish sandwich, or hamburger for only $2. The burger lasts longest, especially if it's heaped with gut-puckering jalapenos, but by midnight my stomach is growling again.

So unless I want to start using my car as a residence, I have to find a second, or alternative, job. I call all the hotels where I filled out housekeeping applications weeks ago—the Hyatt, Holiday Inn, Econo Lodge, HoJo's, Best Western, plus a half dozen or so locally run guesthouses. Nothing. Then I start making the rounds again, wasting whole mornings waiting for some assistant manager to show up, even dipping into places so creepy that the front-desk clerk greets you from behind bulletproof glass and sells pints of liquor over the counter. But either someone has exposed my real-life housekeeping habits—which are, shall we say, mellow—or I am at the wrong end of some infallible ethnic equation: most, but by no means all, of the working housekeepers I see on my job searches are African Americans, Spanish-speaking, or immigrants from the Central European post-Communist world, whereas servers are almost invariably white and monolingually English-speaking. When I finally get a positive response, I have been identified once again as server material. Jerry's, which is part of a well-known national family restaurant chain and physically attached here to another budget hotel chain, is ready to use me at once. The prospect is both exciting and terrifying, because, with about the same number of tables and counter seats, Jerry's attracts three or four times the volume of customers as the gloomy old Hearthside.

*****

Management at Jerry's is generally calmer and more "professional" than at the Hearthside, with two exceptions. One is Joy, a plump, blowsy woman in her early thirties, who once kindly devoted several minutes to instructing me in the correct one-handed method of carrying trays but whose moods change disconcertingly from shift to shift and even within one. Then there's B.J., a.k.a. B.J.-the-bitch, whose contribution is to stand by the kitchen counter and yell, "Nita, your order's up, move it!" or, "Barbara, didn't you see you've got another table out there?

Come on, girl!" Among other things, she is hated for having replaced the whipped-cream squirt cans with big plastic whipped-cream-filled baggies that have to be squeezed with both hands—because, reportedly, she saw or thought she saw employees trying to inhale the propellant gas from the squirt cans, in the hope that it might be nitrous oxide. On my third night, she pulls me aside abruptly and brings her face so close that it looks as if she's planning to butt me with her forehead. But instead of saying, "You're fired," she says, "You're doing fine." The only trouble is I'm spending time chatting with customers: "That's how they're getting you." Furthermore I am letting them "run me," which means harassment by sequential demands: you bring the ketchup and they decide they want extra Thousand Island; you bring that and they announce they now need a side of fries; and so on into distraction. Finally she tells me not to take her wrong. She tries to say things in a nice way, but you get into a mode, you know, because everything has to move so fast.

I mumble thanks for the advice, feeling like I've just been stripped naked by the crazed enforcer of some ancient sumptuary law: No chatting for you, girl. No fancy service ethic allowed for the serfs. Chatting with customers is for the beautiful young college-educated servers in the downtown carpaccio joints, the kids who can make $70 to $100 a night. What had I been thinking? My job is to move orders from tables to kitchen and then trays from kitchen to tables. Customers are, in fact, the major obstacle to the smooth transformation of information into food and food into money—they are, in short, the enemy. And the painful thing is that I'm beginning to see it this way myself. […]

I make friends, over time, with the other "girls" who work my shift: Nita, the tattooed twenty-something who taunts us by going around saying brightly, "Have we started making money yet?" Ellen, whose teenage son cooks on the graveyard shift and who once managed a restaurant in Massachusetts but won't try out for management here because she prefers being a "common worker" and not "ordering people around." Easy-going fiftyish Lucy, with the raucous laugh, who limps toward the end of the shift because of something that has gone wrong with her leg, the exact nature of which cannot be determined without health insurance. We talk about the usual girl things—men, children, and the sinister allure of Jerry's chocolate peanut-butter cream pie—though no one, I notice, ever brings up anything potentially expensive, like shopping or movies. As at the Hearthside, the only recreation ever referred to is partying, which requires little more than some beer, a joint, and a few close friends. Still, no one here is homeless, or cops to it anyway, thanks usually to a working husband or boyfriend. All in all, we form a reliable mutual-support group: If one of us is feeling sick or overwhelmed, another one will "bev" a table or even carry trays for her. If one of us is off sneaking a cigarette or a pee, the others will do their best to conceal her absence from the enforcers of corporate rationality.

*****

I make the decision to move closer to Key West. First, because of the drive. Second and third, also because of the drive: gas is eating up $4 to $5 a day, and although Jerry's is as high-volume as you can get, the tips average only 10 percent, and not just for a newbie like me. Between the base pay of $2.15 an hour and the obligation to share tips with the busboys and dishwashers, we're averaging only about $7.50 an hour. Then there is the $30 I had to spend on the regulation tan slacks worn by Jerry's servers—a setback it could take weeks to absorb. (I had combed the town's two downscale department stores hoping for something cheaper but decided in the end that these marked-down Dockers, originally $49, were more likely to survive a daily washing.) Of my fellow servers, everyone who lacks a working husband or boyfriend seems to have a second job: Nita does something at a computer eight hours a day; another welds. Without the forty-five-minute commute, I can

picture myself working two jobs and having the time to shower between them.

So I take the $500 deposit I have coming from my landlord, the $400 I have earned toward the next month's rent, plus the $200 reserved for emergencies, and use the $1,100 to pay the rent and deposit on trailer number 46 in the Overseas Trailer Park, a mile from the cluster of budget hotels that constitute Key West's version of an industrial park. Number 46 is about eight feet in width and shaped like a barbell inside, with a narrow region—because of the sink and the stove—separating the bedroom from what might optimistically be called the "living" area, with its two-person table and half-sized couch. The bathroom is so small my knees rub against the shower stall when I sit on the toilet, and you can't just leap out of the bed, you have to climb down to the foot of it in order to find a patch of floor space to stand on. Outside, I am within a few yards of a liquor store, a bar that advertises "free beer tomorrow," a convenience store, and a Burger King—but no supermarket or, alas, laundromat. By reputation, the Overseas park is a nest of crime and crack, and I am hoping at least for some vibrant, multicultural street life. But desolation rules night and day, except for a thin stream of pedestrian traffic heading for their jobs at the Sheraton or 7-Eleven. There are not exactly people here but what amounts to canned labor, being preserved from the heat between shifts.

In line with my reduced living conditions, a new form of ugliness arises at Jerry's. First we are confronted—via an announcement on the computers through which we input orders—with the new rule that the hotel bar is henceforth off-limits to restaurant employees. The culprit, I learn through the grapevine, is the ultra-efficient gal who trained me—another trailer-home dweller and a mother of three. Something had set her off one morning, so she slipped out for a nip and returned to the floor impaired. This mostly hurts Ellen, whose habit it is to free her hair from its rubber band and drop by the bar for a couple of Zins before heading home at the end of the shift, but all of us feel the chill. Then the next day, when I go for straws, for the first time I find the dry-storage room locked. Ted, the portly assistant manager who opens it for me, explains that he caught one of the dishwashers attempting to steal something, and, unfortunately, the miscreant will be with us until a replacement can be found—hence the locked door. I neglect to ask what he had been trying to steal, but Ted tells me who he is—the kid with the buzz cut and the earring. You know, he's back there right now.

*****

When my month-long plunge into poverty is almost over, I finally land my dream job—housekeeping. I do this by walking into the personnel office of the only place I figure I might have some credibility, the hotel attached to Jerry's, and confiding urgently that I have to have a second job if I am to pay my rent and, no, it couldn't be front-desk clerk. "All right," the personnel lady fairly spits, "So it's house-keeping," and she marches me back to meet Maria, the housekeeping manager, a tiny, frenetic Hispanic woman who greets me as "babe" and hands me a pamphlet emphasizing the need for a positive attitude. The hours are nine in the morning till whenever, the pay is $6.10 an hour, and there's one week of vacation a year. I don't have to ask about health insurance once I meet Carlotta, the middle-aged African-American woman who will be training me. Carla, as she tells me to call her, is missing all of her top front teeth.

On that first day of housekeeping and last day of my entire project—although I don't yet know it's the last—Carla is in a foul mood. We have been given nineteen rooms to clean, most of them "checkouts," as opposed to "stayovers," that require the whole enchilada of bed-stripping, vacuuming, and bath-room-scrubbing. When one of the rooms that had been listed as a stay-over turns out to be a checkout, Carla calls Maria to complain, but of course to no

avail. "So make up the motherfucker," Carla orders me, and I do the beds while she sloshes around the bathroom. For four hours without a break, I strip and remake beds, taking about four and a half minutes per queen-sized bed, which I could get down to three if there were any reason to. We try to avoid vacuuming by picking up the larger specks by hand, but often there is nothing to do but drag the monstrous vacuum cleaner—it weighs about thirty pounds—off our cart and try to wrestle it around the floor. Sometimes Carla hands me the squirt bottle of "BAM" (an acronym for something that begins, ominously, with "butyric"; the rest has been worn off the label) and lets me do the bathrooms. No service ethic challenges me here to new heights of performance. I just concentrate on removing the pubic hairs from the bathtubs, or at least the dark ones that I can see. [...]

When I request permission to leave at about 3:30, another housekeeper warns me that no one has so far succeeded in combining housekeeping at the hotel with serving at Jerry's: "Some kid did it once for five days, and you're no kid." With that helpful informa-tion in mind, I rush back to number 46, down four Advils (the name brand this time), shower, stooping to fit into the stall, and attempt to compose myself for the oncoming shift. So much for what Marx termed the "reproduction of labor power," meaning the things a worker has to do just so she'll be ready to work again. The only unforeseen obstacle to that smooth transition from job to job is that my tan Jerry's slacks, which had looked reasonably clean by 40-watt bulb last night when I handwashed my Hawaiian shirt, prove by daylight to be mottled with ketchup and ranch-dressing stains. I spend most of my hour-long break between jobs attempting to remove the edible portions with a sponge and then drying the slacks over the hood of my car in the sun.

[...] At eight, Ellen and I grab a snack together standing at the mephitic end of the kitchen counter, but I can only manage two or three mozzarella sticks and lunch had been a mere handful of McNuggets. I am not tired at all, I assure myself, though it may be that there is simply no more "I" left to do the tiredness monitoring. What I would see, if I were more alert to the situation, is that the forces of destruction are already massing against me. There is only one cook on duty, a young man named Jesus ("Hay-Sue," that is) and he is new to the job. And there is Joy, who shows up to take over in the middle of the shift, wearing high heels and a long, clingy white dress and fuming as if she'd just been stood up in some cocktail bar.

Then it comes, the perfect storm. Four of my tables fill up at once. Four tables is nothing for me now, but only so long as they are obligingly staggered. As I bev table 27, tables 25, 28, and 24 are watching enviously. As I bev 25, 24 glowers because their bevs haven't even been ordered. Twenty-eight is four yuppyish types, meaning everything on the side and agonizing instructions as to the chicken Caesars. Twenty-five is a middle-aged black couple, who complain, with some justice, that the iced tea isn't fresh and the tabletop is sticky. But table 24 is the meteorological event of the century: ten British tourists who seem to have made the decision to absorb the American experience entirely by mouth. Here everyone has at least two drinks—iced tea and milk shake, Michelob and water (with lemon slice, please)—and a huge promiscuous orgy of breakfast specials, mozz sticks, chicken strips, quesadillas, burgers with cheese and without, sides of hash browns with cheddar, with onions, with gravy, seasoned fries, plain fries, banana splits. Poor Jesus! Poor me! Because when I arrive with their first tray of food—after three prior trips just to refill bevs—Princess Di refuses to eat her chicken strips with her pancake-and-sausage special, since, as she now reveals, the strips were meant to be an appetizer. Maybe the others would have accepted their meals, but Di, who is deep into her third Michelob, insists that everything else go back while they work on their "starters." [...]

Much of what happened next is lost in the fog of war. Jesus starts going under. The little printer on the counter in front of him is spewing out orders faster than he can rip them off, much less produce the meals. Even the invincible Ellen is ashen from stress.

I bring table 24 their reheated main courses, which they immediately reject as either too cold or fossilized by the microwave. When I return to the kitchen with their trays (three trays in three trips), Joy confronts me with arms akimbo: "What is this?" She means the food—the plates of rejected pancakes, hash browns in assorted flavors, toasts, burgers, sausages, eggs. "Uh, scrambled with cheddar," I try, "and that's ..." "NO," she screams in my face. "Is it a traditional, a super-scramble, an eye-opener?" I pretend to study my check for a clue, but entropy has been up to its tricks, not only on the plates but in my head, and I have to admit that the original order is beyond reconstruction. "You don't know an eye-opener from a traditional?" she demands in outrage. All I know, in fact, is that my legs have lost interest in the current venture and have announced their intention to fold. I am saved by a yuppie (mercifully not one of mine) who chooses this moment to charge into the kitchen to bellow that his food is twenty-five minutes late. Joy screams at him to get the hell out of her kitchen, please, and then turns on Jesus in a fury, hurling an empty tray across the room for emphasis.

I leave. I don't walk out, I just leave. I don't finish my side work or pick up my credit-card tips, if any, at the cash register or, of course, ask Joy's permission to go. And the surprising thing is that you *can* walk out without permission, that the door opens, that the thick tropical night air parts to let me pass, that my car is still parked where I left it. There is no vindication in this exit, no fuck-you surge of relief, just an overwhelming, dank sense of failure pressing down on me and the entire parking lot.

\*\*\*\*\*

In one month, I had earned approximately $1,040 and spent $517 on food, gas, toiletries, laundry, phone, and utilities. If I had remained in my $500 efficiency, I would have been able to pay the rent and have $22 left over (which is $78 less than the cash I had in my pocket at the start of the month). During this time, I bought no clothing except for the required slacks and no prescription drugs or medical care (I did finally buy some vitamin B to compensate for the lack of vegetables in my diet). Perhaps I could have saved a little on food if I had gotten to a supermarket more often, instead of convenience stores, but it should be noted that I lost almost four pounds in four weeks, on a diet weighted heavily toward burgers and fries.

How former welfare recipients and single mothers will (and do) survive in the low-wage workforce, I cannot imagine. Maybe they will figure out how to condense their lives—including child-raising, laundry, romance, and meals—into the couple of hours between full-time jobs. Maybe they will take up residence in their vehicles, if they have one. All I know is that I couldn't hold two jobs and I couldn't make enough money to live on with one. And I had advantages unthinkable to many of the long-term poor—health, stamina, a working car, and no children to care for and support. Certainly nothing in my experience contradicts the conclusion of Kathryn Edin and Laura Lein, in their recent book *Making Ends Meet: How Single Mothers Survive Welfare and Low-Wage Work*, that low-wage work actually involves more hardship and deprivation than life at the mercy of the welfare state. In the coming months and years, economic conditions for the working poor are bound to worsen, even without the almost inevitable recession. As mentioned earlier, the influx of former welfare recipients into the low-skilled workforce will have a depressing effect on both wages and the number of jobs available. A general economic downturn will only enhance these effects, and the working poor will of course be facing it without the slight, but nonetheless often saving, protection of welfare as a backup.

The thinking behind welfare reform was that even the humblest jobs are morally uplifting and psychologically buoying. In reality, they are likely to be fraught with insult and stress. But I did discover one redeeming feature of the most abject low-wage work—the camaraderie of people who are, in almost all cases, far too smart and funny and caring for the work they do and the wages they're paid. The hope, of course, is that someday these people will come to know what they're worth, and take appropriate action.

*Source:* Ehrenreich, Barbara. (1999). Excerpted from "Nickel-and-Dimed: On (Not) Getting By in America." *Harper's Magazine*, January, 37–52.

# CHAPTER 68

## When Sex Works: Labour Solidarity for Sex Workers Has Come a Long Way, but More Can Be Done

*Jenn Clamen and Kara Gillies*

Jenn Clamen is a faculty member in the Departments of History and Women's Studies at Concordia University in Montreal, Quebec. She is a coordinator at STELLA, a Montreal sex worker support organization.

Kara Gillies is a sex worker rights activist. In 2003, Clamen and Gillies founded the now-defunct Canadian Guild for Erotic Labour and are currently involved in sex worker-led movements for the total decriminalization of sex work. Clamen and Gillies have co-authored several pieces, including a chapter entitled "Working for Change: Sex Workers in the Union Struggle" (with Trish Salah) in *Selling Sex: Experience, Advocacy, and Research on Sex Work in Canada.*

In 2013, in *R. v. Bedford*, the Supreme Court of Canada declared three of Canada's prostitution laws unconstitutional, recognizing that criminal laws against prostitution contribute to the harms perpetrated against sex workers. The new sex work-related laws, introduced by the Conservative government (Bill C-36) in 2014 in response to the ruling, bear a striking resemblance to the ones that had been struck down a year prior, both in theory and application.

As the bill made its way through Parliament, many people and organizations allied with sex-worker rights groups spoke up against it, including LGBT rights groups, AIDS service organizations, women's groups, agencies working to end violence against women, and also, notably, unions. In Canada, sex workers have attempted for years to garner the support of the labour movement, and more recently unions like CUPE and OPSEU have made public their support for total decriminalization. But why is sex work a union issue in particular?

Sex work is rarely perceived as a form of work, but rather as a social problem that requires elimination or containment. Sometimes this entails viewing sex work as a morality issue, other times it involves constructing sex work as a negative manifestation of women's sexual exploitation or an individual pathology. While issues of economic insecurity and violence are at play in some sex workers' lives, they do not define who sex workers are or what sex work is about. Instead, we believe a more accurate definition is achieved by understanding sex work the way the workers themselves experience it—as a means of generating income and supporting themselves, their families, their needs, and their aspirations. In a word, sex work is work.

Understanding sex work in these terms is easier when we have a better sense of what the work is about. Whether working in massage parlours, in strip clubs, on the street or in other locales, sex workers are providing services of both a physical and emotional nature as well as interacting with clients, colleagues, management, other third parties, and the physical work environment. These interactions involve negotiating labour issues such as pay, work hours, services, professional responsibilities, and occupational health and safety. Like workers in other sectors, those in sex work worry about low wages, personal and workplace safety, the ability to take time off when they are sick, and access to state and employer benefits that enhance both their own and their families' wellbeing.

Unfortunately, the stigma surrounding most forms of sex work, and the accompanying resistance to treating it as "real" work, have hindered sex workers' ability to access basic labour rights, including those of minimum wage, reasonable hours, enforceable contracts, and secure working environments.

These obstacles are compounded by the continued criminalization of many aspects of sex work, especially prostitution. The purchase of, communication for, advertising of, and receiving a material benefit from sexual services are all illegal. Sex workers are directly criminalized if they communicate for work purposes in public places, as well as marginalized and subjected to violence and exploitation by criminal laws that make the actions of third parties and clients illegal. The absurdity of these prohibitions becomes clear

when one contemplates their hypothetical application to other work sectors.

Imagine working as a mechanic, but it being illegal for your customers to purchase your services, or for you to hire staff. Or envision being a hairstylist who is unable to advertise, or whose clients are unable to communicate what haircut they want and what price they are willing to pay. These are ludicrous scenarios, yet sex workers are currently legally required to work under such circumstances if they wish to avoid surveillance, arrest, and incarceration. Needless to say, most workers are unable to meet these requirements.

The criminalization of third parties creates further complications when it comes to realizing the labour rights of sex workers. Because the worker-third party relationship is often criminalized, many sex workers have difficulty addressing exploitation in their workplace, and seeking rights and protections under employment laws and before labour boards.

There are many supporters out there of sex workers' rights, but others see sex work as distinct from similar workers' struggles. We challenge this belief. While workers in every sector have their own specific sets of concerns, the commonalities override the differences. This is particularly true in the case of workers who have been cast to the margins of the labour market, and particularly for migrant sex workers, who have been the prime targets for arrest, detainment, and deportation, especially since the implementation of C-36.

Similar to sex workers, growing numbers of working people in multiple sectors have been relegated to the rank of independent contractor, denying them the various benefits associated with employee status. Women workers, including those in sex work, make up the majority of the part-time, contingent, temporary labour force and this precarious status undermines their economic security, ability to negotiate working conditions, and organizing efforts.

Migrant workers, including those in some erotic trades, are rendered vulnerable through the government's foreign worker programs, which create a market of temporary, expendable, underpaid labourers who lack the rights of either workers or citizens. Migrants who don't have formal status under these or other programs are further illegalized and left vulnerable to exploitation and abuse.

In an effort to overcome these barriers, sex worker rights groups have been visible for over 40 years in Canada, educating the public about sex work as an income-generating activity—as work. Part of this means promoting and upholding labour rights and labour protections for a diversity of workers in sex work, and recognizing informal labour that takes place on the street and other public spaces.

It also means fighting for recognition that all forms of sex work constitute legitimate labour and that sex workers are entitled to the same basic labour rights as other working people. These include the right to recognition and protection under labour, employment, and contract laws; the right to work independently, collectively, or for third parties; the right to enforceable work contracts (as independent contractors or employees); the right to labour organizing, whether in the form of professional associations or unionization; and, finally, the right to be free from criminal prosecution and other repressive state interference.

---

*Source:* Clamen, Jenn, & Gillies, Kara. (2016). "When Sex Works: Labour Solidarity for Sex Workers Has Come a Long Way, but More Can Be Done." *The Monitor, Canadian Centre for Policy Alternatives,* January/ February, 30–31.

# CHAPTER 69

## We Speak for Ourselves: Anti-Colonial and Self-Determined Responses to Young People Involved in the Sex Trade

*JJ and Ivo*

JJ is a youth activist, sister, and auntie who believes that to meet people where they are at requires more listening and supporting and less telling them what they should do. She has worked on the front lines doing youth and community organizing work for many years. JJ supports the direct resistance of youth and communities against violence from the state, and the self-determination of rights over body and space.

Ivo is a friend, colleague, and Indigenous community member who works in and with youth in the sex trade.

In discussion and debate over the sex trade and sex industries, the voices of young people are seldom heard. Young people involved in the sex trade, whether other options have run out or were not accessible in the first place, are rarely seen as possessing any form of agency and are often excluded from a rights-based approach that meets them where they are at. Further, the interconnections between the legacy of colonialism and approaches that try to "rescue" or "save" Indigenous youth involved in the sex trade, often through punitive measures of criminalization and detainment, aren't even discussed. Instead, it is common for policy makers, service providers, and others to speak on our behalf, as though they have the best knowledge of our experiences and our needs.

Below, I speak with a dear friend, colleague, and community member, Ivo, about our experiences working in, and working with, youth who are involved in the sex trade. And here we are speaking for ourselves.

## AN INTERVIEW WITH IVO

### Youth in the Sex Trade: Shame, Stigma, and Self-Determination

JJ: Can you tell me about your experiences working with young people who have been involved in the sex trade? Also, what has been your experience when other people bring up this issue of young people who are in the sex trade, particularly when other opportunities to get by may not be an option in their lives?

Ivo: To be honest, it's not something that we as young people disclose about ourselves or identify as—we don't always see ourselves as "sex workers." Even the phrase itself—*sex work*—is rarely talked about, but when people do bring up youth involved in the sex trade, it comes from the point of view that "we need to save these young people because they don't know what's good for them." The consensus that we as youth have the ability to make our own decisions, even if options are limited, is not there, and often our decisions are either not listened to, or they are second-guessed. In our society we are rarely consulted, when in fact we are the people most impacted by any decision really, and this goes for service providers as well. The interactions I've had with other youth in the sex trade is that on some level we're ashamed of what we've had to do and that on some level we feel fucked over. The sex industry is rarely talked about, even less so when we talk about the trade in North America or with youth. People often think that sex work is a "profession of desperation," and although I think that's sometimes true, a lot of people get jobs out of desperation. Whether it's working at McDonald's or whether it's working at some corporation, everyone needs a job to survive in this society—and so, any job could be considered a profession of desperation.

Add to that stigma, which prevents us from accessing so many things, and being younger, maybe we're not even eighteen yet, and you get a social context that isn't working. Younger people need jobs, but a lot of people don't hire younger folks, which means we need to find jobs under the table. I'm really fortunate that I've just turned eighteen and have a stable job at a health organization, but that doesn't happen for a lot of us. When we might be in bad situations and we need

money to survive, the sex trade becomes one of the few options available to us.

JJ: When you are young, say, sixteen, seventeen, eighteen, for example, and living on your own, you need to make more than minimum wage to survive. Given all those things you describe—living in a capitalist society, lack of employment opportunities, stigma and discrimination against both youth and people in the sex industry—what do you think are the important things that people need to know about young people who may be trading sex to get by and live, for money, shelter, or basic needs?

Ivo: I want people to know that like any job, we need support; we need some form of security. There are so many organizations that want to save us, and many of them rely on traumatizing stories of youth exploitation to get funding. However, they don't employ people who have real lived experiences to guide the work, and they don't talk to us to see what we actually need. When it comes down to it, if you don't have the lived experience or personal knowledge, how can you really understand something? How can you truly advocate for it? I want to be talked to by a peer, or someone who is Indigenous, or someone with life experience in the sex trade. I want to see more of those people talking to me! And talking about the trade in a way where the only option is *not* just about being a victim.

JJ: Why do you think people feel so uncomfortable talking about the reality of youth sex trade work?

Ivo: In our society, young people are viewed as sacred. And we are. We represent so many things, like light, hope, love. When we look at the sex industry, a lot of people think, "that could be my daughter." So it's this conflicting feeling where as a society we want to protect the younger generation, but at the same time we're constantly shaming them and telling them what they can and can't do; we're not providing ways for them to support themselves. I'm tired of being a young person and always having someone telling me what to do. As someone with life experience in the sex trade, I have the ability to identify when my body is able to accept someone else. I should have sovereignty over my own body.

**JJ: Why is it important to recognize youth self-determination in relation to the sex trade? Or to put it differently, what do you think self-determination for young people looks like? Like you said, there's a lot of speaking for, or speaking on behalf of, youth, particularly youth in the sex trade. For example, I hear older folks say things like "I'm doing this for the next generation," which is great, but I wonder why aren't we as young people speaking on behalf of ourselves? Why aren't we taking up that space? So, what does self-determination mean to you?**

Ivo: It means having a voice in decision-making processes—whether that be in our personal lives, in employment, in society, or in government. In terms of what self-determination means for youth in the sex trade, it's about having safe spaces for us to disclose what we're doing without fear of prosecution, or fear of being "saved." It's about healthy dialogues that are productive and supportive. We need spaces to talk honestly about the sex trade and what that means for people under eighteen, for example, without the fear of having someone call the cops, or family services, or priests, or whatever. For us as Indigenous peoples, we've faced those people before through the process of colonization, and we don't want to deal with them again.

**JJ: What you are offering is what I would call an anti-colonial critique or perspective on both the sex trade and the so-called saving people approach. [...]**

Ivo: Yes. It's about imposing one's ideals and lifestyle on others. People who do work from the savior mode are perpetuating a form of colonization. Society has given us few other options, but it's also important to recognize that some people might be ok with where they are at and there may be some of us who don't want to change. We should be respected for our decisions and supported for where we are at. [...]

We have specific needs and realities that should be supported. There are fundamental reasons why we do what we need to do to get by—for money, housing, food—but we have other needs as well, like security, safety, support, and autonomy. We survive on our own because we know that we might be in jeopardy if we access a social service outreach program; we might be shamed, stigmatized, or even prosecuted by being put into custody. [...]

I don't want to make the generalization that all sex work or social service agencies disregard youth voices—certainly many do not. Similarly, I don't want to make the generalization that all people in the sex trade even need access to support services! But I do know that when I've needed support as an Indigenous youth in the sex trade, it was rarely available. And when it was available, it wasn't the right kind of support; instead, it put me in further danger of criminalization.

I would like to see organizations stop turning people away because of their age and stop telling us what we can and can't do with our bodies. I'd also like to see people's views change about youth in the sex trade in general—we're not doing this because we are bored; we're doing it because we need to support ourselves, just like everyone else. And like anything else, we should have access to support services that actually support us without compromise. Meaning we should not be asked to compromise our trade or the protection we receive from law enforcement in order to do what we have to do. Yes, sex work needs to be decriminalized so we stop getting arrested and have more violence come from the police themselves, but we also need a lot more than that. People need to recognize that their way is not the only way; youth voices need to be listened to so people can understand that there are many ways that people survive—don't stigmatize us for what we do.

Instead, support us unconditionally. Youth with lived experience in the sex trade have valuable, legitimate, and expert knowledge—we deserve rights and we deserve to be recognized.

*Source:* JJ & Ivo. (2013). Excerpted from "We Speak for Ourselves: Anti-Colonial and Self-Determined Responses to Young People Involved in the Sex Trade." In Emily van der Meulen, Elya M. Durisin, & Victoria Love (Eds.), *Selling Sex: Experience, Advocacy, and Research on Sex Work in Canada* (pp. 74–77, 80–81). Vancouver, BC: UBC Press.

# CHAPTER 70

## Factsheet: Women and Restructuring in Canada

*Deborah Stienstra*

Deborah Stienstra is a professor and Jarislowsky Chair in Families and Work in the Department of Political Science, and director for the Centre for Families, Work and Well-being (CFWW) at the University of Guelph in Ontario. She has worked with various national organizations, including the Canadian Research Institute for the Advancement of Women, the Council of Canadians with Disabilities, the National Action Committee on the Status of Women, the Canadian Feminist Alliance for International Action, and the Canadian Voice of Women for Peace. Stienstra is the author of the book *About Canada: Disability Rights*.

Over the past three decades, Canada's economy has undergone significant restructuring by private companies and governments. This has caused tremendous changes for some communities, families, and individual lives. Women experience the effects of this restructuring in ways that directly increase their responsibilities and negatively affect their communities, families, and well-being. Restructuring affects particular groups of women more than others and in different ways. Think of seniors, recent immigrant women, single-parent mothers, and women with disabilities. They live with more serious effects of restructuring.

Lots of changes related to restructuring are happening right now or about to happen. Some signals are the significant downturn in the global economy in 2009, increased government involvement to address this, and the emerging public spending cuts to reduce deficits. Who is affected by these actions and how? This factsheet outlines some of the key issues for women in Canada as a result of restructuring and some actions women can take to address these issues. [...]

## WHAT IS RESTRUCTURING?

Restructuring is a process of change that has been happening in Canada and across the world for the past decades. It has its roots "in multiple sources, including globalized pressures on social spending, altered labor force realities, changing demographics and family relations, challenges over appropriate sites for government intervention, new reliance on public–private partnerships, and renewed roles for the voluntary or third sector."[1] The global economic downturn in 2009 intensified these changes and made a new wave of restructuring likely.

These changes are most often described in economic terms—companies downsize their workforce, governments try to reduce deficits and debts by eliminating or restricting public programs, and selling public or crown companies to private companies through privatization. Yet as feminist writers remind us, restructuring is changing the market, our governments as well as our communities, families, and social movements.[2] [...]

## WHAT ARE THE ISSUES FOR WOMEN?

Restructuring has impacts on both women and men, and the impacts are often more intensely experienced by those who have been marginalized in Canadian society as a result of gender, race, immigrant status, disability, or poverty. Using tools like intersectional feminist frameworks[3] and sex- and gender-based analysis,[4] we begin to see more precisely who is affected by which actions and what the longer-term impacts are of these changes.

In this factsheet we ask which women are affected most by the changes to the Canadian economy and society over the past decades, and which are most likely to be affected by the changes as a result of the recent economic downturn. Not surprisingly we find that single-parent mothers, women with disabilities, racialized women, recent immigrants, and poor women face increased intensified negative effects from both ongoing restructuring and the recent downturn.

We look [here at two] areas of restructuring and the effects on women:

- changing labour markets
- restructuring government programs [...]

We want to answer three questions:

- Where are the women?
- What are the effects of restructuring and the recession on women?
- Which women are most affected?

## 1. CHANGING LABOUR MARKETS

### Where Are the Women?

Today women make up almost half (47%) of Canada's labour force, much more than in the mid-1970s when they were just over one-third (37%) of the workforce. Most women (about three-quarters) work full-time and have historically. But women are much more likely than men to work part-time. Seven in 10 part-time employees are women and this has been consistent since the 1970s. As well, more women than men, and especially young women, are likely to hold more than one job at a time.[5]

Women continue to be concentrated in service-related occupations, administrative work, and teaching. Two-thirds of all employed women are found in these areas.[6] Racialized women are three times more likely than other women to be employed in manufacturing jobs.[7]

Women's hourly wage is 84% of men's, but the gap was significantly reduced among unionized women and men where women earn 94% of men's rate.[8] The gender gap is higher for full-time women between 25 and 54, with women earning 76 cents for each dollar men earned.[9]

Women without children systematically earn more than women with children. The gap is even greater for single-parent mothers.[10] In 2006, single-parent families headed by women had average earnings of $30,598 while father-led single-parent families had average earnings of $47,943 per year.[11]

Average earnings for immigrant workers are falling further behind that of Canadian-born workers, with average immigrant women's earnings plummeting from 85 cents for each dollar [earned by] Canadian-born women in 1980 to 56 cents in 2006.[12] Recent immigrant women who live in poverty are also likely to be racialized, have a university education, and live in the large urban areas of Toronto and Vancouver.[13]

One reason for lower earnings by racialized women, or those Statistics Canada calls "visible minority women," is that they are less likely to be employed even though they are better educated than other Canadian women. In 2000 their earnings were about 10% less than other Canadian women.[14] By 2005, this had grown to a 15% gap, as the average income of visible minority women was significantly below that of other women ($23,369 vs $27,673).[15]

Women with disabilities earn considerably less than women without disabilities and men with or without disabilities. Specifically, in 2006 women with disabilities earned approximately $11,000 per year less than men with disabilities. Women with disabilities who are unionized have better wages than women with disabilities who are not ($35,677 and $21,983), although they remain lower than men's.[16]

Aboriginal women are generally less likely than their non-Aboriginal counterparts to be part of the paid workforce and the unemployment rates are twice the rate for non-Aboriginal women.[17] Aboriginal women and men have lower than average incomes and less of an income gap between them. New findings show that with increasing education, Aboriginal women close the income gap with non-Aboriginal women.[18]

While these statistics illustrate the issues for different groups of women in the labour force, we do not have statistics to tell us about women who fit in more than one group, including Aboriginal women with disabilities or racialized women who are single parents. This is a significant gap in what we can know about women's situations.

## What Are the Effects of Restructuring and Recession on Women?

Four key issues emerge for women as a result of restructuring:

### (a) Impact on Women's Jobs and Income

There has been an increase in precarious or insecure work. Precarious work, including part-time, temporary, and multiple jobs, makes up approximately 40% of women's employment, compared to 30% of men's.[19] This type of work is normally low paid, with few or no benefits. When women lose these jobs, they may not be eligible for Employment Insurance (EI). "Only 39% of unemployed women are receiving employment insurance benefits (2008) replacing just 55% of their usual earnings when they are out of work."[20] Women in the provinces hardest hit by the 2009 recession have not benefited from Employment Insurance benefits. Only one in three women and men in Ontario and the Western provinces received EI benefits.[21]

### (b) Impact on Women's Well-Being

The negative impacts of restructuring on some women's jobs, income, and families is closely linked to women's well-being. When women face changes in their work life, it has ripple effects throughout their lives. Women with children who need to find childcare in order to spend more time in paid labour face challenges finding quality childcare. Plus, they have to juggle that expense. For single-parent mothers, the presence of young children shapes their employment and therefore their income.[22] During the recession of the 1990s, lone-parent mothers experienced a significant decline in their employment that was not the same for mothers of two-parent families.[23] Working-age women with disabilities noted that their life satisfaction is significantly affected by stress related to work, health, and finances.[24]

### (c) Impact on Families

During the most recent economic downturn, there has been a significant loss in men's jobs, especially in the manufacturing and natural resources industries like the boom-and-bust oil and gas industries and the forestry industry. Women have had to take on responsibility for more of the family income in heterosexual families, and more women over 55 are working, largely full-time, an increase of 5% since October 2008.[25]

### (d) Impact on Communities

During economic downturns, there is an increased demand for services, yet often fewer resources to deliver these. "Unlike most economic sectors, the non-profit sector typically sees an increase in the demand for services during an economic downturn, especially front-line organizations working in human and social services."[26] [...]

## 2. RESTRUCTURING GOVERNMENT PROGRAMS

### Where Are the Women?

Government programs are a significant source of income for women, especially for senior women, disabled women, and single-parent mothers. Government program transfers are a larger part of women's income than men's. This reliance on transfer programs is most significant for senior women. Government transfer programs account for over half (55%) the income of senior women. These programs provide only 15% of income for women between 55 and 64 and less than that for other age groups.[27]

Old Age Security (OAS) and Guaranteed Income Supplements (GIS) make up the single largest component of government transfer benefits received by women. The next largest were the Canada and Quebec Pension Plans, Child Tax benefits, social assistance benefits, and employment insurance payouts.[28]

Lone-parent families headed by women rely on government transfer payments for a relatively large share of their income. Government transfer programs accounted for over a quarter (27%) of all income for women-led lone-parent families in 2003. This compares with 11% of all income for male-headed lone-parent families and just 6% of that for two-parent families with children.[29] Many single-parent families led by women rely on social assistance as their main source of income.[30]

Employment Insurance is an increasingly important source of income for women, especially the special benefits. In 2008/9 twice as many women received the special EI benefits (maternity, parental, sickness, and compassionate care) than men (345,600 women vs 168,900 men). Yet during the same year, women made up only 38% of those receiving regular benefits (603,900 women and 1,038,600 men). In 2008/9, 36% of all female EI beneficiaries were receiving either maternity or parental benefits.[31] In 1997 the rules to qualify for EI benefits were significantly changed to the numbers of hours rather than weeks worked. Given that women work fewer hours than men, and are more likely to have precarious work without job security, the changes will have greater meaning for women.

It will mean fewer women will qualify to get EI during this economic downturn than during the 1980s recession. Under the old program of Unemployment Insurance, at the time of the last recession, in the late 1980s, almost 83% of unemployed women and 85% of unemployed men got benefits. Coverage dropped dramatically after the rules were changed. By 2008, only 39% of unemployed women and 45% of unemployed men were receiving employment insurance benefits, replacing just 55% of their usual earnings when they are out of work. In some parts of the country, coverage is much lower than that.[32]

Working-age people with disabilities were over three times as likely to receive government transfers in 2006 as adults without disabilities. Over 55% of women with disabilities had government transfers as a source of personal income while only 47% of men with disabilities did.[33] Many people with disabilities rely on provincial social assistance programs, or government disability benefit programs. The Canada Pension Plan Disability (CPP-D) is the major disability insurance program in Canada.[34] Several provinces have particular disability benefits programs, including Alberta (AISH), Ontario (ODSP), and BC, but none of the statistics available include a gender breakdown for the users. [...]

Women are also significant users of public services, including home care and disability supports programs and transportation. Although the statistics on home care usage are quite old, they illustrate that in 1996/97 at least 2.5% of Canadians over the age of 18 used homecare, most notably seniors and people with chronic illness.[35] As well, we know that the majority of long-term care home residents are women, both seniors and those under 65 who need continuing care.[36] Women with disabilities are more likely than men with disabilities to receive help from formal and informal providers for daily activities (67.4% versus 47.9%).[37]

Women are also in a majority of public service workers and thus are affected as workers by changes to government programs. They remain concentrated in the service sector workforce. In the health services, 80% of the workforce are women, although they remain clustered in the nursing professions; dental assistants, hygienists, and therapists; dietitians and nutritionists; and audiologists and speech-language pathologists.[38] Many other women work in the health services sector as personal care workers, cooks, cleaners, and laundry and clerical workers.[39]

## What Are the Effects of Restructuring and Recession on Women?

### (a) Eliminating and Reducing Public Services

As the number of claims to government programs increase and the funds become more limited, governments often choose to eliminate programs or reduce or restrict who can receive those programs.

The Employment Insurance program was radically changed for women in 1997 by linking eligibility to hours rather than weeks worked. Women in part-time and precarious work were affected most. Recent government changes intended to address the economic downturn in 2009 primarily targeted those who had been in relatively stable jobs before they were laid off. This has meant that many women have fallen through the cracks. "For women, the increase in the number of EI beneficiaries just matched the increase in the number of unemployed."[40]

More recently, at least two provincial governments have changed or restricted eligibility to some measures under social assistance programs that will especially affect people with disabilities. For example, the Ontario 2010 budget eliminated the special diet allowance for people on social assistance and replaced it with a health supplement, which is medically assessed and will only assist those with severe medical needs.[41] In the 2010 British Columbia budget, similar cuts were made to the range of medical equipment and supplies funded by the government. Eligibility for the monthly nutritional supplement was also tightened, including applicants now having to demonstrate they have at least two symptoms rather than one under the existing criteria.[42]

In 2002, the British Columbia government made dramatic cuts to legal aid services, primarily in the areas of family and poverty law. These cuts had the biggest effect on women who rely on legal aid to assist in divorce and custody disputes, as well as appeals related to welfare, Employment Insurance benefits, or housing.[43] [...]

### (b) Privatizing Government Services

Another way for governments to reduce expenditures on public programs has been to sell or transfer a service to a private, for-profit entity, without the same degree of public accountability or regulation.

The City of Vancouver privatized its bus services in 2008, which has significant and disproportionate impact on women, poor people, people with disabilities, and seniors who rely extensively on public transportation. The Bus Riders Union in Vancouver argues that "[w]omen are a majority of these bus riders. Many women, particularly women of colour, need public transit because they are concentrated in low-wage, night shift, temporary, part-time work, and have a lot of family responsibilities. They need reliable, affordable, and 24-hour public transit. As TransLink privatizes transit services, women have to deal with high fares, poor service, and barriers to [their] ability to get around."[44]

The parallel public transportation system for people with disabilities, HandyDart, was also privatized in October 2008. Before the first year under the new company was over, the drivers held a 10-week strike because of conflict with the employer about wages and benefits.[45] As a result of the contracting out of this service, the regional transportation has no authority to require binding arbitration or force a return to work.

British Columbia also undertook a massive privatization of public health services since 2003. At least 8,500 public sector jobs were eliminated in the health support services, and housekeeping services in 32 hospitals in the Lower Mainland and southern Vancouver Island were privatized.[46] The majority of the workers who lost their jobs and gained the privatized jobs were working-class women. In addition, many of these were women of colour from immigrant and non-immigrant backgrounds. A study of this shift illustrated that incomes for the privatized workers were very low, often below the poverty line, and working conditions were harsh. "Contracting out not only endangers the health of these workers, but the well-being of their families and the patients they serve."[47]

### (c) Downsizing Public Service Employment
Cuts to the British Columbia public service illustrate some of the significant impacts on women and their economic security. A 2005 report suggested three-quarters of the job cuts to health care, support services, education, and other areas of public service were jobs held by women.[48]

### (d) Impact on Women's Well-Being
All of these changes as a result of restructuring affect women's health and well-being. As public services are reduced, families are often left with the ongoing responsibility for care that remains. When services are provided in the home, such as home care, there is often an assumption that families, meaning primarily women, will provide support to fill any gaps. This increases stress, anxiety, and exhaustion for informal care providers.[49] Increased difficult conditions in a privatized service environment can also increase the negative impacts on women's health and well-being.[50]

## NOTES

1. Susan Prentice, "High Stakes: The 'Investable' Child and the Economic Reframing of Childcare," *Signs: Journal of Women in Culture and Society* (34) 2009: 701.
2. Isabella Bakker and Rachel Silvey, eds., *Beyond States and Markets: The Challenges of Social Reproduction* (London and New York: Routledge, 2008); Marianne H. Marchand and Anne S. Runyan, eds., *Gender and Global Restructuring: Sightings, Sights, and Resistances* (New York: Routledge, 2000); Isabella Bakker, ed., Introduction to *Rethinking Restructuring: Gender and Change in Canada* (Toronto: University of Toronto Press, 1996), pp. 3–25.
3. Marika Morris and Benita Bunjun, *Using Intersectional Feminist Frameworks in Research: A Resource for Embracing the Complexities of Women's Lives* (Ottawa: Canadian Research Institute for the Advancement of Women, 2007).
4. Barbara Clow, Ann Pederson, Margaret Haworth-Brockman, and Jennifer Bernier, *Rising to the Challenge: Sex and Gender-Based Analysis for Health Planning, Policy, and Research in Canada* (Halifax: Atlantic Centre of Excellence for Women's Health, 2009).
5. Statistics Canada, *Women in Canada: A Gender-Based Statistical Report* (5th ed.) (Ottawa: Minister of Industry, 2005).
6. Ibid.
7. Ibid.

8. Statistics Canada, *Economic Fact Sheet* (Ottawa: Minister of Industry, 2010).

9. Statistics Canada, "Census of Population, 2006," http://www12.statcan.ca/census-recensement/2006/as-sa/97-563/table/t7-eng.cfm.

10. Xuelin Zhang, Statistics Canada, *Earnings of Women with and without Children* (Ottawa: Minister of Industry, 2009).

11. Ibid.

12. Ibid.

13. Dominique Fleury, *A Study of Poverty and Working Poverty among Recent Immigrants to Canada* (Ottawa: Human Resources and Social Development Canada, 2007).

14. Statistics Canada, *Women in Canada: A Gender-Based Statistical Report* (5th ed.).

15. Canadian Association of Social Workers, *Comparing Women's Income in 2000 and 2005: Improvements and Disappointments* (Ottawa: CASW, 2009).

16. Human Resources and Skills Development Canada, *Federal Disability Report: Advancing the Inclusion of People with Disabilities* (Gatineau: HRSDC, 2009), p. 38.

17. Statistics Canada, *Women in Canada: A Gender-Based Statistical Report* (5th ed.).

18. Daniel Wilson and David MacDonald, *The Income Gap between Aboriginal Peoples and the Rest of Canada* (Ottawa: Canadian Centre for Policy Alternatives, 2010).

19. Monica Townson, *Women's Poverty and the Recession* (Ottawa: Canadian Centre for Policy Alternatives, 2009), p. 18.

20. Ibid., p. 7.

21. Ibid., p. 7.

22. Statistics Canada, *Women in Canada: Work Chapter Updates* (Ottawa: Minister of Industry, 2006).

23. Statistics Canada, *Women in Canada: A Gender-Based Statistical Report* (5th ed.).

24. Susan Crompton, *Living with Disability Series: Life Satisfaction of Working-Age Women with Disabilities* (Ottawa: Minister of Industry, 2010).

25. Yuquian Lu and Rene Morissette, "Women's Participation and Economic Downturns," *Perspectives*, Statistics Canada (May 2010): 18–22; Trish Hennessy and Armine Yalnizyan, *Canada's "He-cession"—Men Bearing Brunt of Rising Unemployment* (Ottawa: Canadian Centre for Policy Alternatives, Behind the Numbers (10)4, July 2009).

26. Lynne Toupin, *Managing People through Turbulent Times* (HR Council for the Voluntary & Nonprofit Sector, Trends & Issues, January 2009).

27. Statistics Canada, *Women in Canada: A Gender-Based Statistical Report* (5th ed.).

28. Ibid.

29. Ibid.

30. Townson, *Women's Poverty and the Recession*; Peter Dunn and Lea Caragata, *Preliminary SLID Findings* (Toronto: Lone Mothers: Building Social Inclusion, 2007).

31. Statistics Canada, *Women in Canada: A Gender-Based Statistical Report* (5th ed.).

32. Caledon Institute of Social Policy, *Canada's Shrunken Safety Net: Employment Insurance in the Great Recession* (Ottawa: Caledon Institute of Social Policy, Caledon Commentary, April 2009), p. 1.

33. Human Resources and Skills Development Canada (HRSDC).

34. Michael J. Prince, *Canadians Need a Medium-Term Sickness/Disability Income Benefit* (Ottawa: Caledon Institute of Social Policy, 2008).

35. Health Canada, "Health Care in Canada 1999: An Overview," http://www.hc-sc.gc.ca/hcs-sss/pubs/home-domicile/1999-home-domicile/situation-eng.php#a6.

36. Pat Armstrong, Madeline Boscoe, Barbara Clow, Karen R. Grant, Margaret Haworth-Brockman, Beth E. Jackson, Ann Pederson, Morgan Seeley, and Jane Springer, *A Place to Call Home: Long-Term Care in Canada* (Toronto: Fernwood, 2009), p. 34.

37. HRSDC.

38. Canadian Institute for Health Information, *Canada's Health Care Providers, 2007* (Ottawa: CIHI, 2007), p. 60.

39. Pat Armstrong, Hugh Armstrong, and Krista Scott-Dixon, *Critical to Care: The Invisible Women in Health Services* (Toronto: University of Toronto Press, 2008).

40. Andrew Jackson and Sylvain Schetagne, *Is EI Working for Canada's Unemployed? Analyzing the Great Recession* (Ottawa: Canadian Center for Policy Alternatives, Alternative Federal Budget 2010, Technical Paper, April 2010), p. 3.

41. Laurie Monsebraaten, "Anti-Poverty Advocates Decry Loss of Food Help," *The Star*, March 25, 2010.

42. B.C. Coalition of People with Disabilities, "March 2010 Medical Funding Cuts," http://www.bccpd.bc.ca/cutstomedical.htm.

43. Alison Brewin, *Women's Employment in B.C.: Effects of Government Downsizing and Policy Changes* (Vancouver: Canadian Centre for Policy Alternatives, B.C. Commentary (8)1, 2005); Sylvia Fuller and Lindsay Stephens, *Women's Employment in B.C.: Effects of Government Downsizing and Policy Changes* (Vancouver: Canadian Centre for Policy Alternatives, B.C. Commentary (8)1, 2005).

44. Bus Riders Union, "Women in Transit: Transit Is a Woman's Right," http://bru.vcn.bc.ca/women-in-transit.

45. Matthew Burrows, "HandyDart Strike Leaves Disabled Passengers Out in the Cold," *Straight.com, Vancouver's Online Source,* November 26, 2009, http://www.straight.com/article-272034/vancouver/disabled-left-out-cold.

46. Jane Stinson, Nancy Pollak, and Marcy Cohen, *The Pains of Privatization: How Contracting Out Hurts Health Support Workers, Their Families, and Health Care* (Vancouver: Canadian Centre for Policy Alternatives, 2005).

47. Ibid., p. 2.

48. Fuller and Stevens, *Women's Employment in B.C.*

49. Denyse Côté, Eric Gagnon, Claude Gilbert, Nancy Guberman, Francine Saillant, Nicole Thivierge, and Marielle Tremblay, *The Impact of the Shift to Ambulatory Care and of Social Economic Policies on Quebec Women* (Ottawa: Status of Women Canada, 1998).

50. Stinson et al., *The Pains of Privatization.*

_____

*Source:* Stienstra, Deborah. (2010). Excerpted from "Factsheet: Women and Restructuring in Canada" (pp. 1–16). Ottawa, ON: CRIAW. Retrieved from: http://www.criaw-icref.ca/sites/criaw/files/Women_and_Restructuring_Factsheet_June_2010.pdf.

# CHAPTER 71

## The Leaner, Meaner Welfare Machine: The Ontario Conservative Government's Ideological and Material Attack on Single Mothers

*Margaret Hillyard Little*

Margaret Hillyard Little is an anti-poverty activist and a professor in the Departments of Gender Studies and Political Studies at Queen's University. She holds the Sir Edward Peacock Chair in Gender and Politics. Her research focuses on the experiences of single mothers and abused women on welfare in Canada, neo-liberal welfare reform, and retraining initiatives for women on welfare. She has published many articles and two books, including *No Car, No Radio, No Liquor Permit: The Moral Regulation of Single Mothers in Ontario, 1920–1997*, which won the Floyd S. Chalmers Book Award. The following chapter presents some of her research about how single mothers fared in the aftermath of the mid-1990s welfare reforms in Ontario.

Marcey is recently divorced and trying to raise her 10-year-old son on welfare. She is anxious because the government has recently cut her welfare cheque by 22 percent. As a result, more than one-fifth of her income has disappeared overnight. She pleads with her landlord to lower the rent because she knows that she cannot feed her child *and* pay her rent. He agrees to lower the rent—provided she has sex with him occasionally. Because she refuses, she is forced to look for another place to rent, worrying about how she can pay first and last months' rent and move her belongings—all on a reduced welfare cheque (Interview 6, Kenora, February 25, 1999).

Katrina recently left her violent boyfriend when she was seven months pregnant. She applied for welfare and was told that she was eligible provided she went to three job sites per day looking for work. She traipsed up and down the streets of her small town with swollen ankles, inquiring about employment when she was obviously very pregnant and traumatized by the recent violence in her life. She suspects that her baby was born a month early because of this stress (Interview 4, Greater Toronto Area, May 1998). Belinda recently discovered that her welfare cheque was cancelled because they are investigating her for welfare fraud. Apparently someone has called the welfare fraud telephone line and reported that she is living with a spouse. She has no partner, but she is becoming friendly with a co-worker at her part-time job at the donut shop. They just talk while they're working—she hasn't even gone on a date. She suspects her ex-boyfriend of calling the welfare fraud line, but she does not know because all fraud complaints are anonymous (Interview 3, North Bay, January 28, 1999).

These are all true accounts of the lives of single mothers that reflect the impact of three major changes to welfare under the Conservative government in Ontario. While single mothers have always been harassed, forced to prove themselves deserving in order to receive welfare, this chapter will demonstrate how this level of scrutiny or moral regulation has greatly intensified under the Ontario Conservative government. This research is based on one-on-one interviews I have conducted with more than 30 workfare recipients across the province, interviews with anti-poverty activists, and 200 focus group interviews conducted by members of Ontario Workfare Watch, a non-profit organization established to monitor welfare changes across Ontario. I have conducted this type of research for more than a decade so I was surprised to find myself so overwhelmed by this recent trek across the province. Although I knew about the dismantling of our social programs, these interviews forced me to come face to face with the devastating results of these policy changes. You, too, will be shocked and alarmed when you read about the everyday struggles of single mothers who are simply trying to feed and care for their children as best they can.

## THE HISTORICAL AND NATIONAL CONTEXT

The poor have always been condemned in our society. Since the creation of the Elizabethan Poor Laws in the 1700s, our governments have divided between the worthy and unworthy poor. The Poor Laws required

the poor to complete a work test in order to be eligible for public charity. If you were strong enough to cut a cord of wood, you were generally considered ineligible for government help and expected to find your own work despite the massive unemployment and social upheaval that was occurring during the industrial revolution. If you were deemed worthy, you were given a few scanty provisions such as food and coal or you were eligible to live in a poorhouse, a disease-infested public home for the old, the sick, and single mothers.

With the creation of the modern welfare state in the early 20th century, we incorporated these same basic premises about poverty into our so-called modern welfare programs. Initially governments helped only poor widows and deserted mothers who proved to be both financially and morally deserving. These women would receive a penurious welfare cheque on which it was simply not enough to live. It was expected that these women would top up their welfare cheques with some part-time work that would not interfere with the time needed to care for their children. Eventually, governments expanded their welfare programs to include other types of single parents, such as divorced, unwed, and even single fathers. But every single parent had to prove continuously that they were both financially and morally deserving in order to receive government aid. Welfare administrators would scrutinize the cleanliness of the homes, the sleeping arrangements, the number and types of visitors to the homes, the dress and manner of the parent, the school records of the children, and many other aspects of daily life. All of this intense scrutiny was conducted in order to determine an applicant's worthiness. And once the welfare cheque was granted, home visits by welfare administrators continued in order to ensure that the recipient maintained a frugal and moral life.

But this is all in the past, you say. What does this have to do with today's poor single mothers? Although the moral regulation of poor single mothers has changed over time, it has persisted in new forms throughout the history of welfare. Today, single mothers still have to prove themselves both financially and morally deserving in order to receive welfare. And during the era of the Ontario Conservative government, there are more and more rules to determine just who is and who is not a worthy single mother.

The Ontario Conservative government is not the only guilty party when it comes to the moral regulation of poor single mothers. The federal government has made this possible when it dismantled the Canada Assistance Plan (CAP) and replaced it with the Canada Health and Social Transfer [CHST] in 1996. The CAP, established in 1966, provided unlimited cost-shared federal funding for welfare and promised to eradicate many of the punitive features of earlier welfare policies. In order to receive this federal grant, welfare programs had to meet three conditions: (1) benefits based solely on financial need; (2) all provincial residence requirements eradicated; and (3) an appeal board established in each province to protect recipients' rights.

While these CAP conditions had a number of limitations, they still helped to guarantee the poor a certain level of financial security (Little, 1999 Spring). The first condition is important to highlight for the purposes of this chapter. This stipulation prohibited workfare and other employment-tied welfare programs. Regardless of the reason for a citizen's impoverishment, regardless of the citizen's employment history, she or he was eligible for welfare simply because of poverty. Also, regardless of the moral character of an applicant, she or he was eligible for welfare provided she or he could prove economic need.

Despite the limitations of the CAP, it provided much more support to the poor than the CHST. With the CHST there is no federal funding specifically designated for welfare programs. Instead, each province receives a lump sum to spend on education, health, and welfare; each province can choose just how much to spend in each of these three areas. Given the popularity of health and education, provincial governments have begun to concentrate spending in these areas at the expense of welfare programs.

Under the CHST the federal government has erased almost all national standards for welfare. Poor Canadians no longer have a right to welfare based on economic need. Now the provinces can establish their own eligibility requirements. This change permits not only workfare but also any other eligibility criteria that the provincial and municipal governments wish to implement. It also allows provincial and municipal governments to refuse to grant a person welfare for any reason deemed appropriate. This has opened the door for a number of employment-tied welfare programs. We have now returned to the work test of the Elizabethan Poor Laws. It is not enough to be poor. You now must also prove that you are deserving. The implication is that you are responsible for the fact that you do not have a job during a time of high unemployment.

## THE IMPORTANCE OF MORAL REGULATION

To best understand how changes to Ontario welfare policy under the Ontario Conservative government have affected single mothers, I use the moral regulation approach (Corrigan & Sayer, 1985). [...]

There are five aspects of moral regulation, which makes it a useful concept for my own work on welfare. First, it highlights certain moral processes in society. The government and various social organizations are involved in processes to create and perpetuate certain power inequities, be they class, race, gender, sexual inequities, or others. But while these organizations are creating and maintaining these inequities, they are also creating and maintaining a certain moral order—a certain set of rules and regulations that establish what is moral and immoral. Second, this process of moral regulation is not static, but rather continuous. Once the rules and regulations are established, they need to be maintained. When these rules and regulations are challenged, the government and social organizations will reestablish or modify them.

Third, the public must accept this process of moral regulation. If the public does not agree with these moral codes, they can challenge these rules—they can vote for a different political party, run for political office, participate in a political protest, or even attempt to overthrow the government. Consequently the government needs legitimacy of the public to maintain its moral rules and regulations. Fourth, this process or moral regulation will meet resistance. These moral codes are usually not accepted by all. The government does not have absolute power to impose these moral codes. I want to highlight this aspect of moral regulation because it is sometimes confused with social control. Social control implies that those who make and administer the regulations are all-powerful and do not meet with resistance. Instead, moral regulation scholars insist that this set of moral rules and regulations can and will be challenged. Fifth, the relationship between the regulator and the regulated is beneficial to both. Even in the most unequal relationships created by moral codes, both parties have something to gain from this relationship. The regulated, or the weaker party, often needs the regulator, or the stronger party, for money, food, and shelter. But the regulator also needs the regulated to establish his or her status, to ensure his or her moral superiority. In the case of welfare, the poor need the welfare worker in order to receive their welfare cheques and survive. But at the same time, the welfare worker needs the poor in order to continue to have a job and status in society. Otherwise, the welfare worker will be without work and she or he will end up applying for welfare! (See Piven & Cloward, 1971.)

\*\*\*\*\*

# APPLICATION OF MORAL REGULATION TO ONTARIO WELFARE POLICY

The current welfare policy of Ontario is an excellent example of moral regulation at work. There are three policy changes under the Conservative government that have helped to perpetuate the notion that poor single mothers are morally undeserving. Both the welfare rate cuts and the implementation of workfare ensure that welfare is extremely stingy and punitive to its recipients. These two measures help to ensure that the current welfare policy meets the needs of capitalists. Today, capitalists in this increasingly globalized market economy are competing with companies all over the world. Local capitalists require workers who will work for lower wages and less benefits. When the local welfare policy is made more stingy and punitive, making it almost impossible to survive on welfare, it encourages the poor to compete with workers for any jobs available. This in turn allows local capitalists to reduce wages and benefits to workers because they know there is a desperate group of poor citizens who are willing to work for less. Whereas the first two policy changes meet the current needs of intensified capitalism, the third policy change reinforces certain moral codes of society. This third policy change, the heightened policing of welfare fraud, blatantly encourages the public to believe that all the poor are immoral cheaters who must be constantly investigated.

These welfare changes have had a dramatic impact on single mothers' lives. Not only is it increasingly difficult for single mothers to feed, clothe, and shelter their children, but it is almost impossible for them to insist that they are morally deserving of all the respect and dignity other citizens enjoy.

## Welfare Rate Cuts

One of the most dramatic changes to welfare policy in Ontario occurred in 1995 when all able-bodied welfare recipients had their cheques reduced by 21.6 percent. In the entire history of welfare, this was an unprecedented cut. While all welfare recipients have found this extremely difficult, single mothers have been particularly hurt by the cuts. With child-care responsibilities, these mothers have fewer opportunities to top up their scanty welfare cheques by finding employment. [...] The National Council of Welfare reported that single mothers have fallen further and further below the poverty line as a result of the Ontario welfare rate cuts. In 1995 single mothers in Ontario were $8,488 below the poverty line. After the welfare rate cuts they were $9,852 below the poverty line. In fact, the number of single mothers living on incomes less than *one half* of the poverty line jumped from 10.2 percent to 12.2 percent as a result of the welfare rate cuts (National Council of Welfare, 1995, 1996).

The everyday lives of single mothers have dramatically worsened. Single mothers whom I have interviewed told me that they have attempted suicide, reduced their food consumption to one meal a day, sold almost all their household furniture, moved in with abusive ex-partners—all in an attempt to survive the welfare rate cuts.

Given that food is one of the largest non-fixed items in many single mothers' budgets, this is where women are making huge sacrifices. Two-thirds of food bank recipients on welfare report going without food at least one day per month. Most of them report that they go without food one day a week or more. Twenty-one of the 30 single mothers whom I have recently interviewed across Ontario admit that they are eating less than three meals a day. One Aboriginal single mother said, "I always wondered how vegetarians survive—now I know. I never see meat anymore. Tonight's supper is popcorn and a stale muffin I got on sale" (Interview 1, Kenora, February 25, 1999). [...]

Many of the single mothers I interviewed were desperate to prove to me just how creative they were to provide food for their children. One mother opened up every kitchen cupboard at the beginning of the interview to show me that she had lots of food to feed her children, including food from the local food bank (Interview 12, Greater Toronto Area, May 1998).

Another single mother confided that she has a vegetable garden at a friend's house and she cans, freezes, and hides this food at her parent's home (Interview 6, Kenora, February 25, 1999).

Another woman went immediately to the grocery store after I handed her the honorarium at the end of the interview, stating that she had not gone grocery shopping in two months (Interview 10, Kenora, February 24, 1999).

In more than a decade of conducting interviews with single mothers, I have never seen them so desperate to prove to me that they are deserving and faithfully feeding their children. [...]

Even a telephone becomes a luxury for poor single mothers in the aftermath of the welfare rate cut. A recent survey of single mothers in Toronto found that as many as 27 percent of them had gone without telephone service some time during the last two years (Ontario Workfare Watch, 1999).

Telephones fulfill three very important functions for single mothers. First, they link a mother to emergency services, which are particularly important when you are raising children on your own. Second, they are essential for seeking employment opportunities, which is an obligation for many on welfare. Third, they link a single mother, who is often isolated in her own home, to family and friends.

Housing has become an enormous concern for single mothers since the welfare rate cuts. Without stable housing, life is thrown into a constant upheaval and is reduced to a desperate scramble to find shelter, temporary, permanent, good, or bad. Health suffers and damages the ability to make any long-term plans. Changes to welfare and tenant protection laws in Ontario have resulted in many people hanging on to their housing precariously, being forced into substandard accommodation or, worse, losing their housing altogether. Welfare benefits are paid in two parts: a shelter allowance plus a basic needs benefit that is supposed to cover all non-shelter costs. Maximum shelter allowances are far below the median rents actually paid by tenant households across Ontario.

While shelter allowances have been frozen, rents have continued to rise, shrinking the number of affordable units, putting thousands more people at risk of homelessness. These housing changes have dramatically affected single mothers. A number of single mothers interviewed had their electricity, gas, or telephones cut off. Others have been evicted and have moved themselves and their children into shelters. All of this has placed enormous stress upon poor single mothers, for once a single mother loses her housing, she is reported to the Children's Aid Society and she lives in fear that she will lose her child or children. [...]

Certainly my research supports the general belief that low-income women experience high degrees of violence and that this violence escalates when they become even more vulnerable. During my recent interviews, single mothers explained that they had experienced more difficulties with ex-partners, employers, and landlords. The Ontario shelter movement has reported that since the welfare rate cut, more women are returning to abusive partners in order to feed and clothe their children (Ontario Association of Interval and Transition Houses, 1997).

One Aboriginal woman told about her difficult decision to permit her abusive ex-partner to rejoin her and her son in their home. "With him here this month it's been such a change for me. I eat more often—I only ate once a day since the welfare rate cuts. I sleep better, I worry less. I have support" (Interview 12, Kenora, February 24, 1999). [...]

In more than one community, single mothers have complained that landlords have attempted to exchange sex for lower rents. "He [the landlord] told me that if I had sex with him he would take off $150 a month for rent," explained one single mother (Interview 6, Kenora, February 25, 1999). [...]

In one single mother's case, her ex-partner claimed that she had received $2,000 in child

support and immediately her welfare cheque was cut off. According to this mother, her ex-partner had threatened her with a knife and had previous charges, including assaulting two police officers. "I don't want to have to deal with him at all. Yet, here I was—being faced with welfare problems when I was in a shelter because he claimed he had given me money I'd never seen.... I was pretty stressed about that; they were even talking about charging me with fraud." She currently has $50 per month deducted from her cheque because of this support payment the welfare department claims she received. Once she charges her ex-partner with violence, the welfare department will stop deducting this money, but for several months she has been both financially and emotionally distressed because of this situation (Interview 4, Greater Toronto Area, May 1998).

Most welfare recipients are attempting to top up their miserable welfare cheques in whatever way they can. Because of childcare responsibilities, few single moms are able to find work to top up their welfare cheques. Only one single mother I interviewed reported any type of underground employment, which would have enhanced the welfare cheque. This woman, in a snowbound northern Ontario town, shared one pair of boots between herself and her son as they delivered newspapers.

Instead of doing underground employment, many women have increased the amount of caring work they do. Some women have moved in with their parent(s) and are caring for them in exchange for cheap rent. Others visit the home of their parent(s) or other family members and care for them in exchange for groceries or other necessities.

This welfare cut has severely reduced a single mother's economic independence. Where the welfare cheque in the past often meant a release from oppressive personal relationships, this is increasingly no longer the case. Instead, single mothers have had to once again rely upon abusive ex-partners, harassing landlords, or demanding family members—all in an effort to feed, clothe, and shelter their children.

## Workfare

From the introduction of welfare for single mothers in 1920 up until the arrival of the Ontario Conservative government, single mothers were considered a distinct category of welfare recipients whose primary responsibility was the care of their children. As a result, single mothers were not expected to look for full-time work. Instead, they were only encouraged to take work that did not interfere with their primary duty as mothers of the next generation. With the introduction of workfare, the Ontario Conservative government has dramatically altered the nature of welfare for single mothers. Now, all single mothers with school-aged children are expected to be participating in the workforce to the same degree as single men and women. In other words, single mothers are no longer fully recognized for their childcare responsibilities. Instead, they are treated very similarly to all other welfare recipients.

Treating single mothers with school-aged children as if they were *single* with no dependants creates enormous hardship for these mothers. [...]

Interviews with anti-poverty advocates revealed that "inadequate job searches" are the most common reasons given for cutting people off welfare. "I'm hearing about this all the time now. You can't appeal 'inadequate job searches' so it is an easy way to reduce the welfare case load," explains Lana Mitchell, a single mother and long-time coordinator of Low Income Peoples Involvement, an anti-poverty group in North Bay (Interview, North Bay, January 28, 1999). Consequently, welfare recipients feel enormous pressure to conduct these job searches despite how futile they know the search to be.

Retraining and educational upgrading has been severely restricted under workfare. Welfare support for post-secondary education was abolished in 1996: Now any education and training approved under Ontario Works must be short term and directed only at the fastest possible entry to the labour market. This has frustrated many of the single mothers interviewed.

Some of them have attempted to remain in university or college and scrape by on the Ontario Student Aid Program, but this requires them to carry huge debts that are much larger than the average student loan. Others have had to drop out of post-secondary education as a result of this policy change.

It is the Community Participation component that is the new aspect of this policy. This is what is publicly understood as workfare, unpaid work in return for welfare. Workfare recipients in this stream can be required to work up to 70 hours per month in a not-for-profit or public sector workplace.

A number of single mothers work part-time, but this only leads to further problems with the workfare administration. One mother's situation exemplified the difficulties of part-time employment: "I'll make too much money one month and they'll cut me off welfare and then the next month I'll make much less and I have to re-apply all over. I'm always running back and forth from the donut shop to the welfare office with these $90 pay stubs. They don't pay for the transportation to get down to the welfare office every two weeks." [...]

Community participants are not considered real workers. Although they are eligible for Workers' Compensation, the Employment Standards Act or Employment Insurance does not cover them. Also, it remains unclear whether workfare participants will be protected by the Ontario Human Rights Code, which protects workers against discrimination, including sexual and other harassment. [...]

Workfare participants cannot simply quit a placement. If you refuse an offer of employment, a community placement, or if you refuse to look for work, you are no longer eligible for welfare. If you are considered to not be making enough effort in this regard, you receive a warning and your case is refused within 30 days. If after the first warning you are still considered to not be making enough effort, your cheque is suspended for three months. Three months is a very long time when you have no other source of income or assets. After suspension you must re-apply and meet the requirements all over again in order to attempt to receive welfare benefits (Ministry of Community and Social Services, 2000).

The entire premise of workfare is that welfare recipients are lazy and require a "push" or incentive in order for them to find work. Nothing could be further from the truth. The reality is that most welfare recipients are on welfare for a very short time. The average amount of time a single employable person is on welfare is approximately one year. Single mothers average approximately three years even though they have small children. The largest study of welfare recipients in Ontario found that excluding those who were already working, going to school, were ill or had a disability, or reported that they had unavoidable childcare responsibilities, *three quarters* of single mothers were already looking for work (Ornstein, 1995). According to another study, 15 percent of single mothers were already doing volunteer work before workfare was implemented (Ontario Workfare Watch, 1999). […]

For the most part, these retraining and workfare schemes do not provide adequate childcare; it is up to the single mother to find her own childcare. One mother was granted childcare for only one of her three children. Another mother was told to find childcare for her three-month-old baby. Another mother had to pay $40 per week out of her welfare cheque to finance her own childcare while she participated in workfare (Ontario Workfare Watch, Interim Report, 1999).

All of these examples are against the stated regulations of workfare. They demonstrate that there is little recognition that parenting is the first concern of most single mothers. Instead, single mothers are blamed if they are not able to participate in retraining and workfare schemes. Money is deducted from their welfare cheques or they are told that they are ineligible for welfare at all—unless they participate in these programs. At the same time, single mothers are blamed if their children "act up at school" for lack of attention at home. This brings us back to a long history of contradictory expectations for single mothers on welfare. We have always expected single mothers on welfare to financially provide for their children. But at the same time we also expect these single mothers to adequately care for their children. Financial provision and mothering are contradictory expectations that are often impossible to meet. Workfare only exacerbates this contradiction, making women's unpaid caring work even more demanding and more invisible than it has been in the past.

## Welfare Fraud

The Ontario Conservative government has established a number of mechanisms to "stamp out" fraud. Several anti-fraud measures will be examined below to explore how single mothers, in particular, have been constructed as morally suspicious.

A number of new verification procedures have been created. Today, welfare workers can demand literally hundreds of different pieces of information, depending on the circumstances of the case, and they can refuse, delay, or cancel welfare payments if this information is not provided. People are often told to provide information that they cannot possibly obtain, or to provide it within impossibly short periods of time. This documentation includes their Social Insurance Number, OHIP number, proof of identity and birth date, complete information on income and assets, medical reports, information on budgetary requirements (lease, rent receipts, etc.), school attendance, employment activities, and status in Canada. Other documentation can, and is, demanded of people regularly. The information requirements frequently go well beyond what is required to establish a person's eligibility, suggesting that workers can use their discretion about what documentation must be provided.

Welfare recipients are often asked to provide such documentation within 10 working days or less. This is often difficult for single mothers who have to find childcare arrangements and additional transportation money to provide this information. And sometimes the documentation is very costly. For example, one single mother from North Bay said that her welfare worker had demanded that she provide monthly statements of her bankbook and those of her four children for the last three years. When she went to the bank to get these necessary documents, the bank official said it would cost $120 per hour to provide this documentation. Another single mother had to produce evidence that she had given up her car 15 years ago (Interview 1, Kingston, May 1999). Many women stated that they have been forced to locate violent ex-partners in order to obtain some of the necessary documentation (AWARE & the Single Mothers Support Network, 1999, p. 5). These are extremely intensive measures, which stigmatize those on welfare, encouraging the belief that welfare recipients are often thieves who must be caught. [...]

Immigrant and Aboriginal women have more difficulty obtaining the necessary documents for their welfare workers. Aboriginal women have to appeal to the Department of Indian [Affairs] and Northern Development to receive sworn documents. Birth certificates are not always available for Aboriginal or immigrant women, and the substitute documents require lengthy processing time. Also, people in smaller reserve communities tend not to have bank accounts; therefore, they are unable to provide the required bank statements. All of these exceptions require extra negotiation with the welfare caseworker (Interview 5, Kenora, February 26, 1999). [...]

In 1995 the Ontario Conservative government opened its provincial welfare fraud telephone [line]. Granting anonymity to the person who calls to report welfare fraud raises some interesting questions. If someone calls the police department to report noise or other bylaw violations, your name, address, and telephone number must be given. As a rule these identification details are given to the person you have complained about. In the case of welfare fraud, the caller does not have to take any responsibility for his or her actions due to the cloak of anonymity. The recipient will never be told who provoked an investigation into her case. It is also interesting to note who takes

advantage of and who is most often the scapegoat of these circumstances. According to welfare fraud evidence, single mothers are most often the targets of those who call the welfare office to report fraud. In the Ontario 1999 welfare fraud report, spouse-in-the-house issues were the second most common reason for people to call the welfare fraud telephone line. Also, according to interviews I conducted with anti-poverty advocates and community legal workers, it is generally believed that ex-partners are amongst the most likely people to call the welfare fraud line to report on single mothers' activities (Ontario Ministry of Community and Social Services, 1998).

The Ontario Conservative government has also dramatically changed its position on single mothers' spousal relationship. From 1987 until 1995, Ontario had the most progressive legislation in Canada regarding spousal relations. During this period, single mothers were permitted to live with a partner for up to three years before the government considered the couple common law and deducted the financial resources of the spouse from the welfare cheque. In August 1995, as part of an "anti-fraud" initiative, the Ontario Conservative government announced that single mothers [on welfare] would no longer be permitted to live with a spouse.

The impact of the Ontario Conservative government's anti-fraud campaign against single mothers in spousal relationships has been devastating. During the first eight months of this new amendment, more than 10,000 recipients were deemed ineligible under the new definition and cut off welfare, 89 percent of whom were women (*Falkiner et al. v. Her Majesty the Queen*). A number of women have been falsely accused of cohabiting with former spouses when these men have relocated to other countries, are dead, or are imprisoned. Some have been cut off assistance without a hearing, which would have demonstrated their innocence. In all cases, a single mother is considered guilty until she proves herself innocent—until she demonstrates that she is not in a spousal relationship. As many single mothers have realized, providing evidence that you are not in a spousal relationship is, indeed, a challenge (Little & Morrison, 1999).

Those single mothers who have remained on welfare have experienced more extensive and intrusive investigation into their lives. When a man moves into their home, they must fill out a questionnaire to determine whether the man is a boarder or a spouse. The 11-page questionnaire reveals that the definition of spouse is broad, encompassing an economic, social, and familial relationship. The questionnaire includes the following questions:

14) Do you and your co-resident have common friends?
15b) Do other people invite the two of you over together?
18) Do you and your co-resident spend spare time at home together?
24b) Does your co-resident ever do your laundry (or the children's)?
27) Who takes care of you and your co-resident when either of you are ill?
35a) Does your co-resident attend your children's birthday parties? (Ontario Ministry of Community and Social Services, 1995 October)

Such a questionnaire could hardly be more intrusive. And what makes it particularly insidious is that there is no rule regarding how many questions need to be answered in the affirmative in order to be declared in a spousal relationship. Even if the recipient succeeds in persuading the welfare worker that her co-resident is not a spouse, her status remains in question. According to the Ontario regulations, the same investigation will be carried out annually as long as the living arrangement continues. [...]

Community legal workers and welfare recipients spoke at length about how this change in spousal definition has deeply affected the lives of single mothers. In North Bay one mother was accused of being in a spousal relationship because her boarder drove her children to school. In another case, the mother

and father had never lived together, but the son was 18 years old and physically disabled. The father came over to help shower the child because the petite-framed mother could no longer do this on her own. This sharing of parental responsibility was considered evidence of a spousal relationship (Interview 3, North Bay, January 28, 1999). Another woman hides her engagement ring from her welfare worker because she is afraid this will be considered evidence that she is in a spousal relationship (Interview 5, North Bay, January 1999). The welfare department called one woman's house in Kenora and accused her of hanging men's clothes on her clothesline. "This was true, they were my son's and they were only out there for a couple hours," she explained (Interview 10, Kenora, February 1999). [...]

As well as implementing more mechanisms to "catch" welfare cheaters, the Ontario government has also dramatically increased the severity of the punishments. The Ontario Works Act permits recipients to be fined a maximum of $5,000 or six months' imprisonment if someone receives workfare payments that he or she is not entitled to. The new legislation punishes those who obstruct or knowingly give false information to a welfare worker. [...]

The impact of being accused of welfare fraud is incredibly damaging. One single mother in North Bay wept when she recounted her story of being wrongly charged with welfare fraud. She was charged for "undeclared income" and explained that she had received a welfare cheque when she had obtained full-time employment (ironically, her job was at the local welfare office). "I didn't even open up the cheque, I sent it right back, and I kept telling them to cancel my benefits," she explained. Then one day the police came to the welfare office where she was working and charged her with welfare fraud. The next day she woke up to find her name, address, and the fact that she had been charged with welfare fraud in the local newspaper and on the local radio station every half an hour for a whole day. "North Bay is a small community. My kids didn't want to go to school because they were bothered by other kids about it." Even though the charges were eventually dropped, this woman fears that she will never find employment again in North Bay. [...] (Interview 2, North Bay, January 1999).

The impact of welfare fraud charges is even more disturbing when one realizes that there is no evidence to support the government's obsession with welfare fraud. According to the most recent Ontario government welfare fraud report, there were 747 welfare fraud convictions of a 238,042 case load in 1998 to 1999, which means a welfare fraud rate of 0.3 percent. Of the more than 49,000 recipients suspected of fraud (as a result of complaints from [the] fraud line, information from welfare staff, information sharing with other governmental departments), more than two-thirds were found to have no fraud or error. So the vast majority of those suspected of fraud are not cheating the system (Ontario Ministry of Community and Social Services, January 2000).

It is important to remember that welfare recipients who violate technical rules, knowingly or otherwise, remain very poor as very few such cases involve significant amounts of money. Because the rules are many, complicated, and largely unknown to recipients, it is very possible for the most scrupulous person to break a regulation. Given that welfare payments are so inadequate, an important study from the U.S. suggests that most people on welfare supplement their welfare incomes in some manner (Edin & Lein, 1997). In my interviews all of the men admitted to receiving either gifts in kind or cash under the table to supplement their welfare cheques. The women interviewed did not have the same access to cash for work under the table, but they spoke instead of ways they hid additional food or resources from welfare workers. As one woman explained during my first interviews with single mothers more than a decade ago, "That's called abuse, but we call it survival" (Little, 1998).

*****

# CONCLUSION

These dramatic changes to the Ontario welfare policy have devastated the lives of poor single mothers. Because they are assumed to be undeserving, their benefits and other support services have been slashed. Because they are assumed to be lazy, there are coercive measures enforced to make sure that they are constantly looking for employment or participating in job-related activities. And because they are assumed to be cheaters, single mothers are constantly scrutinized by government workers, neighbours, landlords, teachers, and family. This is a highly intrusive, punitive welfare state that does not begin to treat its citizens with dignity or recognize their real needs. This results in a loss of both material and moral power for poor single mothers. Single mothers have lost material resources—now many of them are constantly anxious about their ability to provide food, shelter, and clothing for their children. But as well, single mothers have lost moral ground. The government has convinced the public that many single mothers are not deserving of public help. As a result, there is little public outcry about the many mean-spirited investigative procedures that the government now uses to determine who is and who is not deserving of welfare. These material and ideological changes not only affect single mothers; they affect all women. When welfare programs are miserly, punitive, and demeaning in nature, it affects the choices all women can make about their lives. It discourages women from leaving abusive partners and harassing employers in an attempt to create a new and brighter future. We must all open our eyes and take stock of what our welfare policies are doing to single mothers and their children for the results will have a lasting impact on the next generation.

# REFERENCES

AWARE & the Single Mothers Support Network. (November 1999). *Workfare or work fair: Perspectives on Ontario Works from single mothers*. Kingston.

Corrigan, P., & Sayer, D. (1985). *The great arch: English state formation as cultural revolution*. Oxford: Basil Blackwell.

Edin, K., & Lein, L. (1997). *Making ends meet: How single mothers survive welfare and low-wage work*. New York: Russell Sage Foundation.

*Falkiner et al. v. Her Majesty the Queen in right of Ontario as represented by the Ministry of Community and Social Services*, Court File no. 810/95 (Ontario Court [General Division] Divisional Court), Affidavit of Robert Fulton, October 25, 1995 as cited in Mosher, "Managing the disentitlement of women," in Sheila M. Neysmith (Ed.), *Restructuring caring labour: Discourse, state practice, and everyday life* (Toronto: Oxford University Press, 2000), p. 34.

Little, M. (1998). *No car, no radio, no liquor permit: The moral regulation of single mothers in Ontario, 1920–1997*. Toronto: Oxford University Press.

Little, M. (1999, Spring). The limits of Canadian democracy: The citizenship rights of poor women. *Canadian Review of Social Policy*, 43, 59, 76.

Little, M., & Morrison, L. (1999). The pecker detectors are back: Changes to the spousal definition in Ontario welfare policy. *Journal of Canadian Studies*, 34, 2, 110–136.

National Council of Welfare. (1995, 1996). *Poverty profile*. Ottawa: National Council of Welfare.

Ontario Association of Interval and Transition Houses. (1997). *Some impacts of the Ontario Works Act on survivors of violence against women*.

Ontario Ministry of Community and Social Services. (1995, October). *Residing with a spouse*. Family benefits policy guidelines 0203, 05.

Ontario Ministry of Community and Social Services. (1998, November 13). "Government anti-fraud initiatives save $100 million." News release, Toronto.

Ontario Ministry of Community and Social Services. (2000, January). "Welfare fraud control report, 1998–99." Toronto.

Ontario Ministry of Community and Social Services. (2000, May 5). "Nearly a half a million people move off welfare in Ontario." Press release.

Ontario Workfare Watch, Interim Report. (1999, April 30). *Broken promises: Welfare reform in Ontario*. Retrieved from: www.welfarewatch.toronto.on.ca/promises/report.htm.

Ornstein, M. (1995). *A profile of social assistance recipients in Ontario*. Toronto: Institute for Social Research, York University.

Piven, F.F., & Cloward, R.A. (1971). *Regulating the poor: The functions of public welfare*. New York: Pantheon Books.

## ONTARIO SOCIAL ASSISTANCE DOESN'T MEET BASIC HUMAN NEEDS

*Elaine Power*

Elaine Power is an associate professor in the School of Kinesiology and Health Studies and Department of Gender Studies at Queen's University in Kingston, Ontario. She is co-founder of the Kingston Action Group for Basic Income Guarantee. Her research is focused on issues relating to poverty, class, food, and health. She is the co-editor of *Neoliberal Governance and Health: Duties, Risks and Vulnerabilities.*

Six hundred and fifty-six dollars. $656.

That's the amount—per month—that the Ontario government provided in 2015 to social assistance recipients who were single and considered "able-bodied." Add in the GST credit and the Ontario Trillium Benefit for those living on low-incomes, and the total monthly income amounted to $740, whether you lived in Toronto, Thunder Bay, Ottawa, or anywhere else in the province.

Even if a single, able-bodied person on the social assistance program Ontario Works (OW) moved to Windsor, which has the lowest average rents in the province, and rented an "average" bachelor apartment, he or she would still have only $202 left over for the whole month after paying for housing. Two hundred and two dollars per month would have to pay for everything else, including food, transportation, clothing, and all other expenses of life, perhaps even utilities.

In my home community of Kingston, the average bachelor apartment costs 92 percent of the monthly income of a single person who was on OW in 2015. The monthly cost of a basic, nutritious diet, $297, takes another 40 percent. It doesn't add up.

Single individuals on the Ontario Disability Support Program (ODSP) fare a little bit better, with a total monthly income of $1,193. But disabilities usually come with extra costs. In some communities, the extra income disqualifies people from using their community food banks, even if they are hungry.

It is no wonder that two-thirds of households that rely on social assistance in Ontario are food insecure—in other words, they don't have enough money to buy the food they need for a healthy life. And food insecurity has a price. Researchers at the University of Toronto have found that health care costs among Ontario households increase dramatically as the severity of food insecurity increases. For those who are most food insecure, health care costs are 121 percent higher than they are for those who are food secure.

In other words, we all pay for poverty. This is no surprise. Research from all over the world, in dozens of countries, shows that those who are the poorest are sicker and die sooner than those who are wealthier, no matter the cause. Either we pay to allow people to meet their basic human needs for shelter and food, or we pay in other ways, through the health care system, the justice system, and the education system. Research also shows that every dollar we invest in reducing poverty will save us at least two dollars in the longer term.

And that is only the economic cost. The cost of poverty in human suffering is incalculable. The harsh reality is that people are sick and dying prematurely because of the terrible poverty they endure on our social assistance programs. If you attend a meeting of people who are trying to live on OW and ODSP, you will see the stress and ill effects of poverty written in their faces and on their bodies. If you ask them about their lives, you will hear stories that would make anyone weep for the indignities they face, and the sacrifices they make, every day.

The Ontario government promises reform. In the latest budget, it announced a basic income pilot project. It has also set up the Income Security Reform Working Group to undertake a comprehensive review of the income security system.

However, while we await the results of the basic income pilot project, which may be many years away, and the report of the Income Security Reform Working Group, social assistance rates remain unconscionably low. People living on Ontario Works and ODSP have waited through the 2009 *Ontario Poverty Reduction Act*, the 2010 Recommendations for an Ontario Income Security Review, and the 2012 *Brighter Prospects* report. They are tired of waiting, and they are understandably skeptical that yet another report will lead to change.

The need to increase social assistance rates is urgent. There is no reason to wait. Even if the income security review recommends a massive overhaul of our income security supports, the data are clear that social assistance recipients cannot meet basic human needs. It is time to increase social assistance rates, to improve the health and well-being of the poorest people in the province, and for the common good of all Ontarians.

*Source:* Power, Elaine. (2016, September 9). "Ontario Social Assistance Doesn't Meet Basic Human Needs." *Policy Options.* Retrieved from: http://policyoptions. irpp.org/magazines/september-2016/ontario-social-assistance-doesnt-meet-basic-human-needs/.

# SNAPSHOTS & SOUNDWAVES 42

## HOMELESSNESS IN CANADA

The Canadian Observatory on Homelessness (COH) is a non-partisan research and policy partnership between academics, policy and decision makers, service providers, and people with lived experience of homelessness. Housed at York University and led by Dr. Stephen Gaetz, the COH collaborates with partners to conduct and mobilize research that contributes to better, more effective solutions to homelessness.

### Canadian Definition of Homelessness

Homelessness describes the situation of an individual or family without stable, permanent, appropriate housing, or the immediate prospect, means and ability of acquiring it. It is the result of systemic or societal barriers, a lack of affordable and appropriate housing, the individual/household's financial, mental, cognitive, behavioural or physical challenges, and/or racism and discrimination. Most people do not choose to be homeless, and the experience is generally negative, unpleasant, stressful and distressing.

Homelessness describes a range of housing and shelter circumstances, with people being without any shelter at one end, and being insecurely housed at the other. That is, homelessness encompasses a range of physical living situations, organized here in a typology that includes 1) *Unsheltered*, or absolutely homeless and living on the streets or in places not intended for human habitation; 2) *Emergency Sheltered*, including those staying in overnight shelters for people who are homeless, as well as shelters for those impacted by family violence; 3) *Provisionally Accommodated*, referring to those whose accommodation is temporary or lacks security of tenure; and finally, 4) *At Risk of Homelessness*, referring to people who are not homeless, but whose current economic and/or housing situation is precarious or does not meet public health and safety standards. It should be noted that for many people homelessness is not a static state but rather a fluid experience, where one's shelter circumstances and options may shift and change quite dramatically and with frequency.

*Source:* Canadian Observatory on Homelessness. (2012). Excerpted from *Canadian Definition of Homelessness.* Toronto, ON: Canadian Observatory on Homelessness Press. Retrieved from: www.homelesshub.ca/homelessdefinition/.

# CHAPTER 72

## Fast Facts: Four Things to Know about Women and Homelessness in Canada

*Sadie McInnes*

Sadie McInnes is the special events and fundraising assistant at Head & Hands, a non-profit organization providing medical, social, and legal services for youth in Montreal, Quebec. Previously, she was a summer intern at the Canadian Centre for Policy Alternatives. McInnes recently completed her undergraduate degree in gender, sexuality, feminist, and social justice studies at McGill University.

Anywhere between 30,000 and 200,000 people are homeless in Canada, with another 1.7 million unable to afford adequate, suitable shelter. Winnipeg in particular has a history of housing shortages and inner-city poverty. In 2015 it was estimated that on a given night in the city there were at least 1,400 people experiencing homelessness. Winnipeg is also home to the largest urban Indigenous population in Canada and poverty rates among the highest in the country.

Unfortunately, much of the research on homelessness in Canada lacks a comprehensive gender-based analysis. It's time we pay attention to the unique experience of homeless women, and also take into account other identity-based barriers to housing and services that women face.

Here are four things you need to know about women's homelessness in Canada:

## 1. HOUSING AND SUPPORTS MUST BE ACCESSIBLE TO MOTHERS

As author Susan Scott writes in her 2007 book *All Our Sisters: Stories of Homeless Women in Canada*, "The presence of children can make it difficult for mothers to take any accommodation that happens to come up in the right price bracket. They have to think about safety, accessibility to schools, grocery stores, bus routes, and other amenities—if the landlord accepts children in the first place." That means mothers' concerns for their children may often trump their most affordable option for accommodation. Furthermore, mothers with children living in precarious housing who struggle with addictions may avoid entering drug treatment or emergency shelters for fear that their children will be removed from their care. These barriers are especially concerning in light of the fact that female lone-parent families are one of the demographics facing the highest rates of poverty in Canada.

## 2. WOMEN ARE MORE VULNERABLE TO HIDDEN HOMELESSNESS

For a number of reasons, women's homelessness is often hidden—sometimes as a result of experiences with violence. The Homelessness Hub's 2013 report on homelessness in Canada describes hidden homelessness as: "staying with a violent partner because she can't afford to leave; being bound to a pimp or a dealer; couch-surfing from one relative to another; or living in unhygienic and unsafe buildings and/or over-crowded conditions." This means women's struggle to gain and maintain housing is often not visible. However, in March 2013, of the individuals who used an inner city Winnipeg community-based Tenant Landlord Cooperation program that advocates on a tenant's behalf, 86% were female and 81% were Indigenous.

## 3. WOMEN ARE MOST OFTEN HOMELESS AS THE RESULT OF SOME FORM OF ABUSE

In 2010, 71% of women staying in shelters across Canada reported abuse as their reason for seeking refuge. In the Social Planning Council of Winnipeg's forthcoming gender analysis of the 2015 *Winnipeg Street Census,* nearly 60% of women cited family conflict, breakdown or violence as the reason for their first experience of homelessness, compared with 40% of men.

For many women, concerns for safety continue while homeless. It has been reported that as many as 91% of homeless women in Canada have experienced assault in their lifetime.

## 4. MULTIPLE IDENTITIES

Where women are marginalized along multiple identity axes, their likelihood of experiencing poverty and homelessness increases drastically, and their ability to access appropriate services declines. Women of Colour in general, and in particular Black and Indigenous women, face sexism which intersects with racism, classism, and colonialism, resulting in a high risk of homelessness. This can also be exacerbated by refugee or immigration status, as women often lack structural supports upon arrival in Canada.

Overwhelmingly, Indigenous women are the most impacted by poverty and homelessness, and are also the most likely to have their children apprehended by Child and Family Services. The overrepresentation of Indigenous children in the child welfare system is one of the many residual impacts of Canada's colonial history, and one facet of Canada's ongoing colonial project. According to Amnesty International, Indigenous women "have been pushed into dangerous situations of extreme poverty, homelessness, and prostitution that make it easy for men, both Aboriginal and non-Aboriginal, to be extremely violent towards them."

LGBTQ people are also overrepresented among the homeless, and are estimated to account for as much as 40% of the homeless population. Trans youth are particularly vulnerable. One in three trans youth will be rejected from a shelter while homeless, as a result of transphobic shelter policies that police gender presentation and expression.

The community organizations guiding CCPA-Manitoba's annual research collaboration, *The State of the Inner City Report,* have prioritized the need to better understand women's homelessness in Winnipeg, and how we can bring it to an end. This year's report will focus specifically on women's experiences of homelessness, and will map out—with the participation of women from the inner city—how public policy can make housing more accessible to women.

*Source:* McInnes, Sadie. (2016, August 26). "Four Things to Know about Women and Homelessness in Canada." Ottawa, ON: Canadian Centre for Policy Alternatives. Retrieved from: https://www.policyalternatives.ca/publications/commentary/fast-facts-4-things-know-about-women-and-homelessness-canada.

# CHAPTER 73

## The Little Voices of Nunavut: A Study of Women's Homelessness North of 60

*Qulliit Nunavut Status of Women Council*

The Qulliit Nunavut Status of Women Council works to advance women's equal participation in society by promoting changes in social, legal, and economic structures that hinder women. The Council is part of a pan-territorial steering committee of service providers and women's advocacy organizations that is currently conducting research on homelessness among northern women in Canada. The Qulliit Nunavut Status of Women Council took responsibility for the Nunavut component of this project. What follows is adapted from its 2007 report.

> They have a shelter here for men but nothing for women. It's because it was talked about, put in the news, put out there and they did it right away. Women have needed stuff for so long, but our voices are so little they can't hear them.
> —*Research Participant*

## DEFINING HOMELESSNESS

There is broad consensus in the literature that homelessness in general, and among women in particular, represents a continuum of circumstances. These include living on the street, seeking refuge in shelters, sleeping in the homes of friends or relatives, accepting shelter in return for sexual favours, remaining in households in which they and/or their children are subjected to various types of abuse, staying in accommodation that is unsafe and/or overcrowded, and paying for accommodation at the expense of other livelihood needs (such as food, clothing, and health care).

- *Visible* or *absolute homelessness* includes women who stay in emergency hostels and shelters and those who sleep rough in places considered unfit for human habitation, such as doorways, vehicles, and abandoned buildings

- *Relative homelessness* applies to those living in spaces that do not meet basic health and safety standards, including [spaces that lack] protection from elements, security of tenure, personal safety, and affordability

- *Hidden homelessness* includes women who are temporarily staying with friends or family or are staying with a man only in order to obtain shelter, and those living in households where they are subject to family conflict or violence
- *At risk of becoming homeless* can include those who are one step away from eviction, bankruptcy, or family separation

Although the number of women living on the street is increasing in many parts of Canada, street homelessness is not representative of most women's experiences. Definitions that focus on "absolute" or "visible" homelessness therefore leave most homeless women, especially those with children, out of homelessness counts and media portrayals of the issue. Women are more likely than men to be single parents, to work in low-paying and non-permanent employment, to take on caregiving roles when family members become incapacitated, [and] to suffer a dramatic decrease (averaging 33%) in household income in the case of separation or divorce. As well, domestic violence creates a need for housing that cannot be anticipated months in advance. In other words, women are dramatically impacted by "short-term changes and transitions which are often not captured by general affordability or adequacy measures" and are therefore "often overlooked in programmatic responses to homelessness" (Centre for Equality Rights in Accommodation, 2002).

Many women can often cycle through the various stages of homelessness described above. For example, 2.2 million adult women in Canada could be defined as at risk of homelessness because of poverty. All it takes is a small change in their circumstances (e.g., losing their employment, becoming ill) to throw them into hidden homelessness (i.e., staying with friends or family or anyone who will provide shelter). If this situation becomes untenable (e.g., they are no

longer welcome, [or] they are experiencing abuse), they can end up in a shelter if one is available or on the streets (absolute homelessness). If they return to an abusive situation simply in order to have shelter for themselves and their children, they are then back in a hidden homelessness situation. Or, if they are able to access appropriate and sufficient resources, they may be able to find accommodation again, but will remain at risk of homelessness. The stories in *A Study of Women's Homelessness North of 60* provide many different examples of how women move in and out of the various stages of homelessness.

## Theme Anthology no. 1: Every Woman Is Potentially at Risk

> There is not much distance from where you are to finding yourself on the other side of the fence.

This quote from one of the interviewees captures accurately how much of a reality homelessness has become for countless northern women. Homelessness in Nunavut has a very different reality than the circumstances generally found in southern Canada. The structure of small communities in this sparsely populated territory creates a sense of desperation when it comes to finding affordable housing, while other Nunavummiut are constantly at risk of losing their homes. The threat of homelessness exists for a broad range of women, from the unemployed, to members of the workforce who have no subsidized housing or don't earn enough to pay market rents, to Government of Nunavut employees who are in precarious possession of staff housing.

> I just can't afford the high cost of living and rent here. The housing situation is really desperate. That stress is what drives families apart and then other relatives are taking sides. Family is pitted against family all the time.

## Theme Anthology no. 2—Partners' Behaviour and Circumstances

> I put up with sexual abuse from my common law because leaving him leaves my children with no father. I didn't want them to suffer for mistakes they didn't even make.

A woman's intimate partner often plays a large role in the occurrence of homelessness in all areas of the country. The situation for northern women is unique, however.

The vast majority of the women interviewed have been victims of violence, or exposed to high levels of violence when moving from place to place. Several of the women became homeless when they made the decision to flee an abusive family member, most often their intimate partners. When asked what they believe is causing women's homelessness, the interviewees have been very forthcoming in noting violence as a serious problem requiring immediate intervention in the North.

> You go with this man even though you don't want to. You don't love him, you don't like him, but he has a bed to sleep on. You have no choice but to follow him because you need a place to sleep. It makes you sick inside, makes you lose your mind.

## Theme Anthology no. 3: Forced Eviction and Relocating to Another Community

> I fled from my violent husband from my home community. I couldn't stand the violence. Women are always running from their communities.

Forced eviction from social housing units was a reality for many of the women interviewed. A primary reason for eviction is that the male lists a unit under his name, exclusive of his female counterpart. If the relationship ends, becomes abusive, or if the woman becomes widowed, she is expected to evacuate her home. The vast majority of women who have shared stories of eviction have been forced out of their homes because of their partners' actions. Tenant damage is also another reason women become evicted from public housing.

> I got evicted on more than one occasion—three times actually. The first time it was because my first husband passed away and his name was on the lease. They made me leave. Another time my ex-boyfriend was vandalizing and his name was on the lease so we got kicked out. My family members are homeless too and have been for many years. I had a brother who was homeless. Bills ran up and he ended up moving to Yellowknife. He didn't want to come back because there is no housing over here. He would have waited for many years and he did not want that. His body was found in a cardboard box. My sister down in Ontario, she can't come back because she is ill, and the housing will be too long too and she don't want to come back because over here there is lots of drugs and alcohol. I also have another brother who is homeless in Calgary. I don't want Inuit to go through this. It's hard. It affects too many families of all cases.

## Theme Anthology no. 4—Lack of an Adequate Support System

> I haven't eaten a meal in over a week. I just feel so uncomfortable to do that at my brother's. If you are uncomfortable where you are staying, you feel like you're in the way of them. They want to help you but they are still pushing you away, making you feel uncomfortable.

Inuit women who are homeless in Nunavut survive because of the values that are placed on maintaining family ties and sharing. Fifty-four percent of Inuit currently live in overcrowded conditions, and 38.7% of them are considered in core need. This statistic is so high because the desperate lack of housing options forces these women to turn to friends and family. Women are often coming with more than just their own mouth to feed, and families can only provide so much. Three or four generations of families often huddle under one roof, which becomes a breeding ground for frustration. Women are forced to sleep in shifts, and if they are lucky enough to have a room, it is shared with several others. They have no privacy, and their tenure is based on the circumstances of others. If the home becomes violent and unbearable, the absence of alternative housing leaves the women feeling trapped. They often feel as though they are a burden to their families and end up moving from home to home, stripping them of stability. This also creates difficulty for women to maintain employment or access existing government programs if they do not have the security of a roof over their heads.

> I am going through that right now. My son and I are living with my brother and his family and it's a one-bedroom. It's really crowded, so then we start arguing and fighting. Everybody goes all over the place, so when it gets tense I have to find somewhere else to stay for the night. I won't go home for days. I just go from home to home, couch to couch, friends to friends. I'm so tired of that.

## Theme Anthology no. 5: Personal Wellness and Capacity

> I've thought about hiring someone to beat me up just so I can stay at the women's shelter.

> I know it sounds crazy, but that's what desperation does to your mind when you have no place to go.

Another determinant of homelessness in Nunavut women involves wellness and capacity.

A woman's potential for improving her position in life is often inhibited by her health and/or her perception of her own personal abilities.

> I don't think that it's because we're Inuk, but that most of us don't have the education to get good paying jobs to afford the high cost of rent up here. I know Inuit people don't have all these diplomas that people want, but we do have the skills to do it. We just need the opportunity, the chance.

Women often find themselves suffering from physical and emotional exhaustion, including feelings of disempowerment, which trap them in a cycle from which they can find no respite. Being incapable of sheltering/protecting themselves and their children results in feelings of worthlessness, eventually taxing every other area of their lives. They are stripped of all esteem, and poor health negatively infringes upon their capacity to better their situations. Many of the women interviewed stated that they have experienced a complete loss of identity, with no remaining sense of a culture that brought such a great sense of pride to their forebears.

## Theme Anthology no. 6: Community Institutions and Structures

> Students get housing right way, people coming in, government employees coming in. And they keep those houses open, even if they don't have staff to put in them. It's always the people that are from here that are homeless.

The structure of communities in Nunavut is what makes this homeless epidemic so unique. On the surface, many people fail to understand how things operate because it is so vastly dissimilar from southern Canadian communities. Iqaluit is currently the largest community in Nunavut, with a population of under 7,000, while the other 24 communities have significantly fewer people. The dynamics involved with the operation of our current institutions are often overlooked when examining our homeless situation.

Major issues include a lack of services and resources and the ineffectiveness of many existing services (partly because privacy and confidentiality are not respected). A harsh climate, the structure of family and intimate relationships in isolated conditions, issues of racism, and a vast northern terrain complicate communication and connectedness between Nunavut communities. Also critical is the high cost of living. Quite a large gap exists between the employed and unemployed, and if you are not benefiting from a Government of Nunavut salary, it is virtually impossible to get ahead. As of 2004, almost 50% of Nunavummiut were income-support clients (data supplied by the Department of Health and Social Services), which clearly illustrates the problematic economy currently in place.

> We owned our own home together; it was under both of our names and I don't think it was right to put his name under the home because it was a program for me and now we are separated because I have no job. But I'm very educated. I'm fighting so hard for my home. I was born and raised here. My ex just laughs at everybody, the whole community, he's got no respect for elders. I'm just all over, trying to find work and so on. It's so hard to put my life back together when I don't even have a place to call home.

## Theme Anthology no. 7 Cost of Living and Business Sector Practices

> The government is great at putting programs on. I can take all sorts of programs, but where's the jobs?

Cost of living is another unique circumstance of northern life. "It just doesn't make sense that the minimum wage is $8 an hour (or about $1,280 a month) when a one-bedroom apartment in Iqaluit can cost anywhere between $900–$1,600 per month" ("Most Nunavut Homeless," *Nunatsiaq News*, October 5, 2001). The cost of heating, electricity, and water is so high that many residents cannot afford to maintain accommodations without subsidy. According to Jackson, for example, (2006:15), the cost of supplying a gallon of water to a household is about the same as a gallon of gasoline.

> Can't afford to live here. The rent is too high and there's just not enough public housing. Affordable housing would solve a lot of problems here. I have been a house mother for the last 5 years and unemployed for 5 years, and I'm a surviving child of parents that went to residential school, and I have been healing on my own with the help of our wellness center and the programs they offer.

## Theme Anthology no. 8: Societal Indifference/Punitiveness toward the Homeless (Including Racism)

> There is no feeling worse than to be homeless, to be unloved, and to think that nobody in the community wants you....

Regardless of where you live in Canada, the homeless tend to be negatively stigmatized by other members of society. Homeless people are often judged and mistreated based on the stereotypes of what a homeless person is. The situation in Nunavut is no exception.

> A generation of Nunavummiut are growing up in desperate situations, where people value life less than they did in the past. Previously, Inuit had stable homes where traditions could be passed on. […] Now, the poor of Nunavut can't afford a permanent family home to provide stability. I see it as the absolute destruction of a culture. ("Homeless Shelter on the Rocks," *Nunatsiaq News*, March 11, 2005)

This sentiment is shared by many, as the Inuit way of life has become confused and eroded since they were forced into southern models of life.

The vast majority of women believe it would be more beneficial to go back to their traditional way of living. It was expressed in numerous interviews that "Qallunaat [non-Inuit people] are taking over our land." While most women maintain that they feel no prejudice toward White people, they feel the "White way of life" does not fit their traditional lifestyle and has further complicated their living situation. Women have also stated that "Qallunaat get houses faster," and "If I were a Qallunaaq, I'd probably have a house." Several of the women suggested [that] by simply looking at the homes owned by Inuit versus [those] of Qallunaat, … the message is clear as to who is valued the most. This gap continues to increase, suggesting a systematic failure. The government ought to implement strategies to help northern constituents help themselves, rather than displacing them in nontraditional "southern" models, which have proven unsuccessful.

> Qallunaats are running the show here. They get houses immediately. Nunavut used to be more community-oriented. Everyone helped each other out. We need to help everybody out like our ancestors did. Go back to Inuit culture. We need to go back to the traditional way of life.

## Theme Anthology no. 9: Climate/Weather

In the wintertime, it's cold right to the bone.

Although homelessness is a global issue, Inuit women face unique challenges that call for different solutions in the North. Homelessness tends to be invisible in Nunavut—people are not living on the street as you often see in southern cities because the harsh weather prevents them from doing so. On the most frigid days of the year, the climate can reach 60 below zero, forcing penniless women to pile into local establishments, hoping to make a cup of coffee span the day, or gathering at a friend or family member's already overcrowded home. The northern climate, combined with lack of available housing, is why homelessness in Nunavut shows itself in the average number of people per dwelling. With no homeless shelters for women anywhere in the territory, women are left relying on family to house them from the cold.

> Winter is so much harder. Existing buildings that aren't in use can be used to give women shelter from the cold at least. So many ladies are left out in the cold with no income when they separate from their partners. They have no income, no home, no hope of getting another house. I see so many situations like that and that's why everyone's house is so overcrowded.

# REFERENCES

Centre for Equality Rights in Accommodation. (2002). *Housing in Canada: Barriers to Equality*. Toronto: Centre for Equality Rights in Accommodation.

"Homeless shelter on the rocks." (March 11, 2005). *Nunatsiaq News*. Iqaluit, Nunavut.

Jackson, P. (2006). *Information Sharing on Homelessness in the North*. National Secretariat on Homelessness. Unpublished document.

"Most Nunavut homeless suffer in silence." (October 5, 2001). *Nunatsiaq News*. Iqaluit, Nunavut.

*Source:* Elliott, Shylah, van Bruggen, Rian, & Bopp, Judie. (2007). Adapted from *The Little Voices of Nunavut: A Study of Women's Homelessness North of 60* (pp. 3, 30–31, 50–71). Iqaluit, NU: Qulliit Nunavut Status of Women Council.

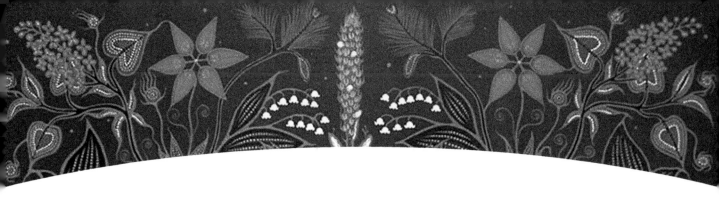

# PART 6

## Organizing for Change

More than ever, our societies need women with a vision of the future.
—*Rigoberta Menchú Tum, Nobel Peace Prize Laureate, quoted in "Appeal of the Nobel Peace Prize Laureates for the Children of the World: International Decade for a Culture of Peace and Non-Violence for the Children of the World (2001–2010)" (1999)*

The final section of the text explores contexts and examples of organizing for gender, racial, sexual, economic, environmental, and Indigenous justice within and across communities, cultures, and borders. The focus is primarily on contemporary neo-liberal and neo-colonial times.

### Part 6A: Feminist and Social Justice Movements in North America
This section offers an overview of diverse forms of contemporary feminist and social justice organizing in Canada and the United States. We explore specific sites of struggle and examples of activism, including Idle No More, Black Lives Matter, and trans activism. We also feature reflections and analyses on inclusive organizing and the future of feminist and social justice movements.

### Part 6B: Transnational Feminisms: Challenges and Possibilities
We conclude this text with a section that examines the promise and pitfalls of organizing across national borders in transnational or global feminist movements and networks. While problematizing historical notions of global "sisterhood," the chapters emphasize the importance of building transnational alliances that challenge the logic of neo-liberalism, global capitalism, and imperialism, and work to secure economic, social, environmental, and cultural rights.

# SNAPSHOTS & SOUNDWAVES 43

## ACTIVIST INSIGHT: THE IDLE NO MORE MANIFESTO

*Jessica Gordon and the Founders of Idle No More*

Jessica Gordon is one of the founding members of Idle No More, a movement that represents opposition to government and industries' disregard for Indigenous rights and environmental protection. She is a Cree/Saulteaux from Pasqua First Nation in Treaty Four territory and is a mother of five. She is most proud of the work she does empowering people to take control of the issues that affect them the most or those for which they feel most passionate. She is committed to working for the people relentlessly until the day she leaves this earth, and hopes to leave her children as well as future generations a legacy of tools to help them attain independence.

**We contend that:** The Treaties are nation-to-nation agreements between The Crown and First Nations who are sovereign nations. The Treaties are agreements that cannot be altered or broken by one side of the two Nations. The spirit and intent of the Treaty agreements meant that First Nations peoples would share the land, but retain their inherent rights to lands and resources. Instead, First Nations have experienced a history of colonization which has resulted in outstanding land claims, lack of resources, and unequal funding for services such as education and housing.

**We contend that:** The state of Canada has become one of the wealthiest countries in the world by using the land and resources. Canadian mining, logging, oil, and fishing companies are the most powerful in the world due to land and resources. Some of the poorest First Nations communities have mines or other developments on their land but do not get a share of the profit. The taking of resources has left many lands and waters poisoned—the animals and plants are dying in many areas in Canada. We cannot live without the land and water. We have laws older than this colonial government about how to live with the land.

**We contend that:** Currently, this government is trying to pass many laws so that reserve lands can also be bought and sold by big companies to get profit from resources. They are promising to share this time. Why would these promises be different from past promises? We will be left with nothing but poisoned water, land, and air. This is an attempt to take away sovereignty and the inherent right to land and resources from First Nations peoples.

**We contend that:** There are many examples of other countries moving towards sustainability, and we must demand sustainable development as well. We believe in healthy, just, equitable, and sustainable communities and have a vision and plan of how to build them.

Please join us in creating this vision.

---

*Source:* Gordon, Jessica, & the Founders of Idle No More. (2014). "The Idle No More Manifesto." In Kino-nda-niimi Collective (Ed.), *The Winter We Danced* (pp. 71–72). Winnipeg, MB: ARP Books.

**Sylvia McAdam, Parliament Hill in Ottawa, December 21, 2012**

*Source:* Photo by Nadya Kwandibens/Red Works Photography.

# CHAPTER 74

## Idle No More: Indigenous Activism and Feminism

*Sonja John*

Sonja John is an associate professor in political science and German as a foreign language at the University of Gondar in Ethiopia. She wrote her doctoral thesis in political science about the outcomes of the federal development program "Empowerment Zone" on the Pine Ridge Reservation. Previously, she graduated from two Master's programs, in Lakota leadership and management at Oglala Lakota College and in political science at Free University Berlin.

## INTRODUCTION

The grassroots movement Idle No More spread over the North American continent like a fire on the prairie. In October 2012, Sheelah McLean, Sylvia McAdam, Nina Wilson and Jessica Gordon, four women from the Canadian province of Saskatchewan, protested the federal omnibus budget bills C-45 and C-31 that would substantially diminish First Nations treaty, sovereignty and land rights. Idle No More locates itself within the framework of Indigenous renaissance, decoloniality and Indigenous activism. Although founded and led by Indigenous women, this group defines itself neither as a women's movement nor as an Indigenous movement. "We are a movement led by Indigenous women" (Sylvia McAdam, June 14, 2013).

Nonetheless, Idle No More members contemplate how feminist theory and praxis may have influenced the movement. Indeed, the movement applies strategies that have been theorized within Indigenous feminism for decades. Looking at Idle No More in particular, I will identify possible interleaving and commonalities as well as differences between feminist and Indigenous-decolonial concerns. Exemplified by the emancipative character of Idle No More, I will show under which circumstances struggles under the flags of resource conflicts and decoloniality can complement Indigenous feminism. Therefore, in the following, I will look at the activities and goals of the movement within the frameworks of Indigenous feminism as well as postcolonial feminism.

*****

# IDLE NO MORE: THE FORMATION OF A SOCIAL MOVEMENT

Idle No More formed to protest bill C-45 and bill C-31 at the end of the year 2012. This omnibus budget bill, introduced on October 18, 2012, would allow companies access to untapped resources by lifting regulations in these two areas hindering unlimited resource extraction: environmental protection and land and sovereignty rights of First Nations. A considerable amount of desired natural resources—predominantly oil—is located in Indigenous territories. Idle No More drew attention to the crucial points of the budget bill, especially to the proposed changes to the Indian Act and the Navigable Waters Protection Act; these would substantially impact sovereignty rights of First Nations as well as environmental protection policies. Three Indigenous women, Sylvia McAdam (Nehiyaw—in English Cree), Nina Wilson (Nakota and Nehiyaw) and Jessica Gordon (Pasqua), first discussed the bill in an internet chat room. When they decided to educate the public outside of the World Wide Web about this scheme, they drew in non-Indigenous political activist Sheelah McLean, well-known in Saskatoon for her anti-racist and anti-discrimination work. The women observed and indicated the violations of Indigenous land rights and the annulations of the principle of consent with First Nations. This principle prohibits the unilateral intervention of the settler state in Indigenous affairs "without the free, prior and informed consent of the indigenous peoples concerned" (UN 2007, 9). Anything but new, this key principle of the United Nations Declaration of the Rights of Indigenous Peoples of 2007 was also found in the Royal Proclamation from 1763, and was firmly established in Canadian law.

The twitter hashtag #IdleNoMore rapidly gained momentum and weight. In December 2012, the movement succeeded in carrying the protest from the internet into the streets of dozens of North American cities. At the second National Day of Action in January 2013, the protests gained global scope with rounddance flashmobs in North American cities, and supporting declarations of solidarity in front of numerous Canadian embassies on different continents. The goal of the movement is to "give the voices of our people a forum," to direct attention to the continuous constraints of fundamental rights and to pressure the Canadian government through collective actions to uphold existing rights and respect treaties as well as protect environmental laws (Idle No More 2012).

Idle No More defends treaties, Indigenous sovereignty and water; it's that simple (Sylvia McAdam, June 14, 2013). Of course, it is not that simple. On different levels, Idle No More faces unequal and unfavorable power relations. Although the law has been passed in the meantime, Idle No More continues to educate the public. The movement criticizes not only the amendments themselves but also the social and political contexts in which these changes occur.

I will look at the debates Idle No More intervenes in with the help of Anibal Quijano's (2000) concepts of coloniality. According to Quijano, the formation of the colonial power matrix depends on four dimensions: (1) control over authority; (2) appropriation of land; (3) control over gender and sexuality; and (4) control over subjectivity and knowledge. Further, Quijano stresses the effects of the interrelations of these spheres and how they limit access to education, knowledge and capital and how these, in turn, connect to racist discrimination. Along the four spheres defined by Quijano, I will introduce the goals of Idle No More.

# CONTROL OVER AUTHORITY

The Indian Act, passed in 1876, marks the end of the epoch of bilateral treaty agreements between the British Crown and First Nations. This Canadian act regulates who receives the official status *Indian*, how Indigenous societies are to be politically structured and governed, and how the Canadian government administers their land and resources. The traditional leaders and elder councils were replaced by nominated c*hiefs*. These *Indian Act chiefs* take up the role of administrator for the settler state. Canada established male-dominated administrative structures within (formerly mainly matrilineal and matriarchal) Indigenous societies. Until a few decades ago, women were excluded from governmental positions. Even in 2007, only five percent among the Assembly of First Nations (AFN), the umbrella organization of the *Indian Act Chiefs*, were women (Glenn/Green 2007, 230). Idle No More criticizes the representation of the chiefs and advocates for a more basic-democratic organization of First Nations. In its work, Idle No More stresses independence from and keeping a distance [from] the AFN; it does not intend to copy hierarchical structures within the grassroots movement. Idle No More also criticizes the Canadian state's failure to consult the AFN before introducing the law; this constitutes a violation of the principle of consent. However, Idle No More participants were even more appalled when they learned that some AFN chiefs met in consultations and gave their consent to Bill C-45—without communicating the issue to the Indigenous communities concerned, the very communities they represent (Sylvia McAdam, June 14, 2013). This may indicate that some chiefs are more committed to the Canadian state than to their own communities.

Most First Nations do not have accountability procedures in place to report to their members; they only report to the Canadian government (McAdam, June 15, 2013). The endeavors of Idle No More to pluralize the access to power and to expose the omnibus budget bill as a continuation of colonization did not remain unnoticed by the settler state. In August 2013, the Canadian Security Intelligence Service declared that Idle No More was under observation. The activities of the movement were characterized as a threat to national security. Reports of the observation were passed on to the AFN. Ironically, the chiefs learned from the Canadian Security Intelligence Service of the needs and demands of the very people they officially represent (CBC 2013).

However, the AFN cannot be confined in a black-and-white dichotomy. Several chiefs and major opposition parties in Ottawa have co-signed a joint declaration demanding "a fundamental change in the relationship of First Nations and the Crown" (Christoff 2013). In pre-Idle No More-times, this alliance and this outcome was unthinkable.

In the face of asymmetrical power relations, Idle No More also turned to the international arena. In addition to digital and analogous networking, the movement appealed to the United Nations (UN). Since Canada signed the UN Declaration of the Rights of Indigenous Peoples belatedly in 2010, First Nations in the country had the opportunity to call upon the UN Special Rapporteur on the Rights of Indigenous Peoples, at that time James Anaya. Representing Idle No More, Sylvia McAdam addressed the UN Permanent Forum on Indigenous Issues in May 2013. Thereupon, James Anaya announced he would observe the situation of First Nations in Canada. On October 14, 2013, an official hearing with James Anaya took place to which Idle No More sent delegates. […] In an immediate statement Anaya declared: "As a general rule, resource extraction should not occur on lands subject to Aboriginal claims without adequate consultations and a free, prior and informed consent of the Aboriginal peoples concerned" (Anaya 2013).

The consultation of the UN makes clear that Idle No More seeks to address and discuss Indigenous issues not only on the national but also on the international level. This is primarily because these issues are of international scope due to their treaty background, and secondly because the national government is not fulfilling its obligations. […]

## APPROPRIATION OF LAND

Idle No More argues that the settler state uses bill C-45 to continue its colonial conquering expedition. Through the Indian Act, the Canadian government claimed the position of proconsul of Indigenous resources having the authority to freely dispose of them—previously possible only under the condition of obtaining the explicit consent of the respective First Nations. With the changes to the Indian Act under bill C-45 (paragraphs 37, 39 and 40) the disposal of Indigenous land is considerably more easily achieved (Parliament of Canada 2012a). These amendments can be seen in a historic continuum; the founding and rise of settler states like the USA and Canada are based on Indigenous dispossession, dislocation and at times extinction. Bill C-45 follows elimination politics (from warfare to assimilation) that intend to separate the Indigenous population of the Americas from their land. Idle No More intervenes in these concrete resource wars with its rejection of the underlying capitalist exploitation logic as well as the white supremacist attitude of manifest destiny.

> We have never surrendered our land, our water or our resources; they were stolen from us.… Decolonization means restitution to First Nations what rightfully belongs to them. Justice means restitution. Justice means that my people not only survive but that they are able to flourish (McAdam, June 14, 2013).

[…] Another of Idle No More's major concerns constitutes the consequences of the amendments of the Navigable Waters Protection Act through bill C-45. Point 316 stipulates the renaming of the Navigable Waters Protection Act as the Navigation Protection Act. Water is no longer in the title, and water is no longer protected. Now this act no longer federally protects all water ways, but only those 3 oceans, 97 lakes and parts of 62 rivers listed (Parliament of Canada 2012b). The remaining water ways—99.7% of Canadian fresh water reserves—are no longer protected because development affecting these waters no longer requires environmental impact assessments (Ecojustice 2012). Environmental protection organizations, particularly the protest movement against Tar

Sands Oil, fracking and the Keystone XL Pipeline, were among the first to express support for and solidarity with Idle No More (Sheelah McLean, June 15, 2013). These bills were introduced to Parliament with the promise of economic development. Hence, the omnibus budget bill C-45 was renamed the "Jobs and Growth Act."

The concept of land is the most fundamental aspect of Indigeneity. Land is a barometer of intact communities, a marker of Native identity, the focal point of land-based creation stories and sacral practices, as well as a resource for cultural and socioeconomic stability. When Sylvia McAdam went into the woods to build a hunting cabin on treaty land and encouraged other Natives to do the same, she challenged the legitimacy of the Indian Act, the very foundation of the administration of First Nations' land, resources and self-government. Idle No More criticizes settler colonialism and resource extraction; it does not agitate against settlers but rather against continued colonialism and unleashed capitalism. The movement turns towards settlers because everybody depends on clean water and, as Idle No More stresses, only through combined efforts is change possible.

## CONTROL OVER GENDER AND SEXUALITY

In their analysis of contemporary internal political conflicts in First Nations communities, the Idle No More women point to the double form of discrimination based on race and gender. They argue that only through the exclusion of women from political roles was the introduction of the omnibus budget bill possible. The term *femicide* is used in the context of Indigenous women when referring to the *missing women* (Troian 2013) and also when referring to the systematic separation of Native women from their home communities and from leadership roles. Andrea Smith (2005) explains how colonization of First Nations became possible through gender-based violence and the forceful imposition of European gender roles on to Indigenous societies. Indigenous feminists stress that in the process of colonization, Indigenous cultures internalized gender-based discrimination that now continues to oppress women (St. Denis 2007, 45). Andrea Smith argues that decolonization and sovereignty are impossible to recuperate as long as Indigenous societies hold on to patriarchal gender systems introduced by agents of the settler state (Smith 2007, 100). [...]

When educating the public about contemporary Indigenous existence in Canada, Idle No More also draws upon the debates held by Indigenous feminists who highlight the harmful consequences of the colonial Indian Act to tribal (USA) respective band (Canada) membership and the status of Native women. Without formal Indian status, Natives lose the right of band membership and consequently the right to live on reserves. Before 1985, two-thirds of Indigenous people in Canada had lost their status and their land (Lawrence 2003, 6). In 1985, the Canadian government changed the membership criteria of the Indian Act and *permitted* First Nations to draft their own membership rules. Many of the First Nations voted to keep the externally introduced, yet in the meantime familiarized, discriminatory rules.[1]

The marginal subject position of Native women finds its equivalence in the movement. In the 1960s and 1970s, many women were active in the Red Power movement but subordinated themselves under men. The fish-in movement of 1964 in the US-state of Washington was initiated by Native women (Hightower Langston 2003, 117). Many women carried out the occupation of Alcatraz Island in 1969, as well as the occupation of the Bureau of Indian Affairs in Washington, DC in 1972, and the occupation of Wounded Knee in 1973 through the American Indian Movement (AIM). During that time women stayed in the background and did not articulate gender cleavage. [...]

As is true for many *women of color*, Indigenous women are confronted with the expectation that they should be loyal to their own people first, not to their gender. When they criticize oppression within their own communities, they tend to face accusations of betrayal and colonialism. Fay Blaney of the Aboriginal Women's Action Network of Canada states: "Patriarchy is so ingrained in our communities that it is now seen as a 'traditional trait'" (Blaney 2003, 158).

Hence, Blaney sees the main task of Indigenous feminism as addressing the internalized oppression of women within their home communities; otherwise this part of the colonial legacy would further politically weaken Indigenous societies. Bonita Lawrence and Kim Anderson (2005, 3) warn that band leaders should not reduce this debate to women's issues or misrepresent it as a threat to Native self-determination. Instead, they declare, attacks against Indigenous women—physical as well as political—constitute attacks against Indigenous sovereignty. Throughout Indian Country, women are referred to as the backbone of the nation. Marie Anna Jaimes Guerrero argues that any feminism that does not address the questions of land rights, sovereignty or government politics that systematically aim at destroying Native cultural practices, or that defines the participation of Native women as non-feminist, is "limited in vision and exclusionary in practice" (Guerrero 2012 [1997], 101). This brief insight into Indigenous feminism shows that "Native women's engagement with feminist politics is much more complex than generally depicted" (Smith 2007, 97).

Idle No More does not view women as an independent, separate group that has to fight against men. Instead, it views women as part of a collective that exists to achieve better conditions for everybody. Its members fight not only for women's rights but for group rights "together with all solidary people inside and outside of Canada" (McAdam, June 14, 2013). With this approach, Idle No More expresses its intersectional understanding of the conditions of oppression that are interlinked and can only be dealt with satisfactorily if reduced to individual issues.

There is an obvious strong presence of women in the movement. Sylvia McAdam reckons that the call to *defend the children* spoke more to women than to men. In a consultation with the elders' council—the traditional leadership that exists parallel with the Indian Act chiefs—about the consequences of the controversial bill C-45, the elders declared the traditional Nehiyaw law *Notawamissouin*, meaning protection of children in a broader sense:

> *Notawamissouin* means to defend for the children. And not just Indigenous children—all children. But it extends beyond that. You also have to defend for the animal children, the tree nation, the winged nation, the earth nation, all their children. And this law is sacred. It's peaceful, it's prayerful, and it's profound because it's not only that you are defending for this generation in our time but all the seven generations ahead (McAdam, June 14, 2013).

## CONTROL OVER SUBJECTIVITY AND KNOWLEDGE

The movement focuses on educating the public about the ecological consequences of bill C-45 and about the negative effects this law has on Indigenous self-determination, information that should have been spread by the federal government or the band leadership. It seems neither of these actants had the intention to inform the public:

> Even with our resounding 'No, you do not have our consent' they still put it through on December 14th. And it's unprecedented in the history of their Canadian Parliament that a bill that huge, a 450-page omnibus bill, to go through their Parliament in such a short time. It was introduced in the middle of October and became law on December 14th which is unheard of it. There was no proper debate, no proper consultation, no free prior and informed consent, nothing (McAdam June 14, 2013).

Idle No More educates the public on the local level through teach-ins and on the international level through digital networking, talks at conferences and presentations at the United Nations.

The movement also addresses interlinked issues of inequality in Canada. The workshop "Idle? Know More!", held in summer 2013, dealt with the construction of the *Other* in the dominant society over the markers of race, class, gender and sexuality. The workshop addressed the question how these practices of inequality and colonial oppression are being justified today (SAFE 2013). Idle No More sparked discussions on the issues raised that led to various conferences, talks and lectures, many of which were live streamed over the internet. Thus, an internet chat room discussion of four women has evolved into a global revolutionary education movement—a movement that is founded on the principles of non-hierarchy, broad participation and inclusion.

Idle No More does not only want to voice opposition; its members want to be part of a collective that is non-oppressive. Sheelah McLean expresses the openness of the movement when she invites people to become pro-active:

> You ask us: 'What can you do?' We ask you: 'What do you think needs to be done?' 'How can we help you to reach your goals?'
>
> (Sheelah McLean, June 15, 2013).

Keeping with the grassroots principle, McLean stresses that every voice has the same value. People should not wait until things get done for them, but should get together and find solutions. [...]

## EDUCATING, NOT ACCUSING

The movement Idle No More was formed to protest an omnibus budget bill. It drew attention to the consequences of bill C-45 and bill C-31—both the end of treaty relations between Canada and Indigenous nations and the harmful ecological consequences the bills held for the continent. Protest by Indigenous groups against laws detrimentally affecting their lives and group rights is not new. What is new is the quality and the approach of this mass movement. While the Red Power movement of past decades defined itself by conflict and used Native identity to keep the movement exclusive, Idle No More stresses commonalities and invites everybody to join.

Idle No More shows that Indigenous feminism—as political strategy and political project—can be strengthened through alliances built by engagement, participation and support by Native men and non-Natives working together. The emancipative character of Idle No More shows that feminist agendas and Indigenous struggles for decolonization do not have to contradict each other. Idle No More separates feminist rhetoric from the—in Indigenous contexts—frequently voiced allegation of acting colonial. Although they do share the Indigenous-feminist analysis of sexist and patriarchal power relations, the movement does not identify itself as feminist per se. Idle No More problematizes the shift in power structures in Native communities not by accusing but by educating. By applying this participative and inclusive approach, the emancipative character of Idle No More in the field of resource struggles and decoloniality can complement Indigenous feminism. By setting the anti-colonial struggle as central, Idle No More questions the legitimacy of (patriarchal) nation states. Such a political project imagines for colonized—and non-colonized—societies a more desirable, more just and more sustainably-oriented world beyond nation states.

## NOTE

1.  The Mi'kmaq lawyer Pamela D. Palmater (2011) argues for the introduction of more inclusive instead of exclusive membership rules; rather than measuring blood-quantum, cultural determinants should have more weight.

## REFERENCES

Anaya, James, 2013: Statement upon Conclusion of the Visit to Canada. Video. www.unsr.jamesanaya.org/videos/video-statement-upon-conclusion-of-the-visit-to-canada (November 8, 2013).

Blaney, Fay, 2003: Aboriginal Women's Action Network. In: Anderson, Kim/Lawrence, Bonita (ed.): Strong Women Stories. Native Vision and Community Survival. Toronto: Sumach Press, 156–171.

CBC, 2013: Thoughts on CSIS and Idle No More. Internet (audiofile; August 12, 2013): www.cbc.ca/bluesky/episodes/2013/08/12/thoughts-on-csis-and-idle-no-more (September 23, 2013).

Christoff, Stefan, 2013: Idle No More and Colonial Canada. In: Aljazeera, 30.1.2013. Internet: www.aljazeera.com/indepth/opinion/2013/01/20131289123344980.html (December 14, 2013).

Ecojustice, 2012: Bill C-45 and the Navigable Waters Protection Act (RSC 1985, C N-22). Internet: https://www.ecojustice.ca/wp-content/uploads/2015/03/NWPA_legal_backgrounder_November-20-2012.pdf (November 4, 2013).

Glenn, Colleen/Green, Joyce, 2007: Colleen Glenn. A Métis Feminist in Indian Rights for Indian Women, 1973–1979. In: Green, Joyce, (ed.): Making Space for Indigenous Feminism. Winnipeg: Fernwood Publishing, 233–240.

Guerrero, Marie Anna Jaimes, 2012 [1997]: Civil Rights versus Sovereignty. Native American Women in Life and Land Struggles. In: Alexander, M. Jacqui/Mohanty, Chandra Talpade (ed.): Feminist Genealogies, Colonial Legacies, Democratic Features. New York: Routledge, 101–124.

Hightower Langston, Donna, 2003: American Indian Women's Activism in the 1960s and 1970s. In: Hypatia, 18 (2), 114–132.

Idle No More, 2012: History of Idle No More Grassroots Movement. (December 10, 2013). Internet: www.idlenomore1.blogspot.ca/p/background-on-idle-no-more.html, link no longer active (April 15, 2013).

Lawrence, Bonita, 2003: Gender, Race, and the Regulation of Native Identity in Canada and the United States. An Overview. In: Hypatia, 18 (2), 3-31. http://dx.doi.org/10.1111/j.1527-2001.2003.tb00799.x.

Lawrence, Bonita/Anderson, Kim, 2005: Indigenous Women. The State of our Nations. In: Atlantis, 29 (2). Internet: http://forms.msvu.ca/atlantis/vol/292pdf/292intro.PDF (September 25, 2013).

McAdam, Sylvia, 2013: Personal Interview held on June 14, 2013.

McLean, Sheelah, 2013: Idle No More: The Movement. Session at the Native American and Indigenous Studies Annual Meeting, Saskatoon, SK, Canada (June 15, 2013).

Palmater, Pamela D., 2011: Beyond Blood. Rethinking Indigenous Identity. Saskatoon: Purich Publishing.

Parliament of Canada, 2012a: Jobs and Growth Act. (Changes of the Indian Act in Bill C-45). Internet: www.parl.gc.ca/HousePublications/Publication.aspx?Language=E&Mode=1&DocId=5942521&File=194#6 (November 4, 2013).

Parliament of Canada, 2012b: Jobs and Growth Act. (Änderungen des Navigable Waters Protection Act in der Bill C-45). Internet: www.parl.gc.ca/HousePublications/Publication.aspx?Language=E&Mode=1&DocId=5942521&File=344#25 (November 4, 2013).

Quijano, Anibal, 2000: Coloniality of Power, Eurocentrism, and Latin America. In: Views from the South, 1 (3), 533–580.

SAFE, 2013: Internet: www.safe-2011.blogspot.ca, link no longer active. [Website has been moved to: www.sites.google.com/site/sasksafe/.] (September 23, 2013).

Smith, Andrea, 2005: Conquest: Sexual Violence and American Indian Genocide. Cambridge: South End Press.

Smith, Andrea, 2007: Native Feminism, Sovereignty and Social Change. In: Green, Joyce, (ed.): Making Space for Indigenous Feminism. Winnipeg: Fernwood Publishing, 93–107.

St. Denis, Verna, 2007: Feminism Is for Everybody. Aboriginal Women, Feminism and Diversity. In: Green, Joyce, (ed.): Making Space for Indigenous Feminism. Winnipeg: Fernwood Publishing, 33–52.

Troian, Martha, 2013: Taking Control. Indigenous in Canada Compile Own Database on Missing and Murdered Women. (September 25, 2013). Internet: www.indiancountrytodaymedianetwork.com/2013/09/25/taking-control-canadas-aboriginals-compile-own-database-missing-and-murdered-women-151417 (November 18, 2013).

UN, 2007: United Nations Declaration of the Rights of Indigenous Peoples. UN document A/RES/61/295. Internet: http://www.un.org/esa/socdev/unpfii/documents/DRIPS_en.pdf (18.3.2014).

**Source:** John, Sonya. (2015). Excerpted from "Idle No More—Indigenous Activism and Feminism." *Theory in Action, 8*(4), 38-54.

# CHAPTER 75

## How a Black Lives Matter Toronto Co-Founder Sees Canada

*Zane Schwartz and Janaya Khan*

Zane Schwartz is a Michelle Lang Fellow at the *National Post* and *Calgary Herald* newspapers, covering politics and foreign affairs. He was previously a staff reporter at *Maclean's* and has also written for the *Globe and Mail* and the *Toronto Star*.

Janaya Khan is the co-founder of Black Lives Matter Toronto and the director of Gender Justice LA. Khan is an international advocate for social transformation, justice, and equality. Known as "future" within the BLM movement, Khan self-identifies as a Black, queer, gender non-conforming activist, Afrofuturist, boxer, and social justice educator. Their writings have been featured in publications including *The Feminist Wire*, *The Root*, and *Al Jazeera*.

Black Lives Matter Toronto claims that Canadian police, media, and society at large are inundated with anti-black racism. The organization, which started in the United States, is spreading across Canada, with protesters from Vancouver to Halifax chanting their slogans. Janaya Khan, one of the co-founders of the Toronto chapter, has been attending Pride for 10 years. On July 3, 2016, Khan helped lead the sit-in at the Toronto Pride parade that halted the march for half an hour. Khan sat down with *Maclean's* on Thursday afternoon.

**ZS: What was it like growing up as a black queer youth in Toronto?**

JK: Difficult. Difficult. There are very few resources for someone with an intersectional identity in general, let alone someone who is black, who identifies as queer and as gender non-conforming. Fast forward to my first Pride where I was really out for the first time. Having been there only about 20 minutes, I had my first interaction with the police at Pride. I have a history with interaction with the police that hasn't gone very well for me.

They've been very aggressive, often demanding ID and wanting information about where I'm going. I didn't have the language then. I didn't know I was being carded. It was so routine for people in my community that it just seemed like a natural occurrence that there would be that much police presence, that there would be that type of questioning. That was my first experience with a police officer at Pride, but that had been my experience my entire life in this city.

\*\*\*\*\*

ZS: **Between 2005 and 2015, the federal black inmate population in Canada grew by 69 per cent. That's the fastest growth rate for any group of people. For comparison, the number of Aboriginal people in prison grew by a little over 50 per cent during the same period. Right now the incarceration of black people in Canada is triple their representation in society. What would you like the federal government to do to address this?**

JK: I think there needs to be an intervention on several levels. We can easily say eliminate carding and that would suddenly be it. The reality is: so long as racism exists, prisons will exist. They work hand in hand together and so it's not a coincidence that the dramatic increase did go up in line with when carding practices became very normalized. On a federal level, look at Howard Sapers, who was the former prison watchdog who was fired by the Harper government [an election was called before Harper could replace Sapers and the new Prime Minister Justin Trudeau has kept him on]. On a federal level, the government is mandated to collect data on Indigenous populations. They're not mandated to collect data on black populations. So Sapers created a special report because of the dramatic way that black people's numbers were astronomical compared to their population. We make up 2.9 per cent of the population. We represent 10 per cent of the federal inmate population. As Black Lives Matter, we're an intersectional movement. We are not a movement that is only

fighting for black people. And so what happens in the Indigenous communities [is] often in line with what's happening in black communities. We are the two largest populations in the Canadian federal inmate population, so our struggles are intrinsically linked.

ZS: **Let's talk about Justin Trudeau. On May 17, he introduced legislation to protect the rights of transgender Canadians. Do you think he's doing enough to support black trans people and black LGBTQ+ people?**

JK: No. I think any time that we're changing legislation to make it more inclusive for people it's important, but I think we also need to ask the question, always at the end: "For whom does this serve?" "Who is this going to be transformative for?" And often times because legislation isn't considering anti-black racism, black people are lost in the holes, in the spaces, in the channels where racism exists, where disenfranchisement exists.

ZS: **In March, the United Nations commission on economic, social, and cultural rights harshly criticized Canada for the disproportionate number of black children in the foster care system and the high dropout rate amongst black youth. Are there things that Black Lives Matter is calling for in the way that federal or provincial policy deals with the foster care system, deals with the education system?**

JK: What we've been calling for recently and since our founding is the need for data and the need for research. When we are looking at these massive gaps where black youth are falling through, we need data to substantiate what we're seeing and what we're experiencing. I can say that especially because I was one of those black youth that grew up in the foster system. I grew up in group homes and spent time in women's shelters as a teenager.

When you have that type of experience it becomes very deeply personal to you. We shouldn't always have to use our personal experience to validate what we're saying when it's happening across the board. If we are making up 40 per cent of the youth that are in the foster care system [in Toronto], that is a state of emergency and it needs to be treated as such.

*****

ZS: **Do you see a difference in the way that anti-blackness manifests in Canada versus how it does in the United States?**

JK: We see two very different streams here than you find in the United States. A lot of how anti-black racism manifests here is in conjunction with anti-immigration sentiment because of the Somali community and also because of Islamophobia. The majority of black people in Canada actually don't identify as black Canadians. Our experience of being racialized in Canada is: "Where are you from?" "But where are you really from?" You know? You don't see that narrative in the States where it's like: "You don't belong here," "This isn't where you're from." *African Americans* and *black Americans* have been terms that people have used for decades, but the mainstream media doesn't refer to us as black Canadians. We don't refer to ourselves as that. So in a way you have the Canadian identity and you have the black identity and they've been separated.

ZS: **Do you think that's a reflection of how Canadian immigration policy for decades tried to foster a mosaic, as opposed to a melting pot in the United States? People are encouraged to sort of subsume themselves in the United States and consider themselves American whether they're Asian American, African American. Whereas, not only are black people in the**

Canadian media often referred to primarily as Somali or Guyanese, but you'd also see that with other communities where people are being referred to as say, Venezuelan not Latino. Is that part of it?

JK: Yeah, that's bigger than blackness. Racialized people are not often allowed to identify as Canadian, are not believed to be Canadian here. That type of nationality, I think that's reserved for white Canadians and I think white Canadians reserve that for themselves.

*****

ZS: **You've said that you've received death threats since the sit-in [at Toronto Gay Pride 2016], primarily from gay men.**

JK: Yes.

ZS: **Why do you think that is?**

JK: Gender and sexual diversity doesn't negate racism. I think that Pride has turned into something that is primarily for gay white men. In 1981, when the bathhouse raids took place, the population that was most deeply impacted, at least according to the media, was gay white men. Gay white men can assimilate into heteronormative culture, into straight culture in a way that someone like me never could. And because they're able to assimilate, they're able to create change and really inform what Pride Toronto is, what the Pride marches have looked like, who's a part of it and who isn't. So our action has challenged gay white men specifically and they've responded in white supremacist ways. That's really what we've seen.

ZS: **Have you informed the police? Have you asked for any kind of protection?**

**JK:** That would suggest that I believe that the police could protect me and that they were invested in my protection. I don't believe that.

**ZS: Are you afraid for your life?**

**JK:** The reality for black people now, in this moment in time in the world, is: whether you fight or not, you die anyway. So I'm going to fight. I think that fear is always a part of change, and I think fear is what makes people resist change, and I think we have to confront that fear head-on.

**ZS: You've called for an end to carding. Apart from carding, what would progress look like in terms of the relationship between police and black LGBTQ+ people?**

**JK:** You know, someone very smart said, "I'm an optimist by will and a pessimist by intellect." That is a very, very complicated thing to respond to, because at this particular moment I'm not sure what that would look like, because the entire institution and the entire practice of police officers are informed by racism and so …

**ZS: You're saying all police officers are racist?**

**JK:** No, I'm saying the institution.

**ZS: Can you explain the distinction as you see it?**

**JK:** There's police who are individuals. Those individuals are not the problem. The problem is the institution that houses them. The problem is the institutional practices that sort of perpetuate anti-black racism, and so long as those systems are in place the police are going to act out in ways that are racist, and they're going to act out in ways that are homophobic and transphobic, because that is the society that we live in. The police are a direct result of the society that we live in.

---

*Source:* Schwartz, Zane, & Khan, Janaya. (2016, July 8). Excerpted from "How a Black Lives Matter Toronto Co-Founder Sees Canada." *Maclean's*. Retrieved from: http://www.macleans.ca/news/canada/how-black-lives-matter-co-founder-janaya-khan-sees-canada/.

## 9 WAYS WE CAN MAKE SOCIAL JUSTICE MOVEMENTS LESS ELITIST AND MORE ACCESSIBLE

*Kai Cheng Thom*

Kai Cheng Thom is a writer, performer, and social worker based in Toronto and Montreal. Her writing has appeared in *Guts Magazine*, *Matrix Magazine*, and *Asian American Literary Review*, among other places. She is the author of the novel *Fierce Femmes and Notorious Liars: A Dangerous Trans Girl's Confabulous Memoir*, the poetry collection *A Place Called No Homeland*, and the children's book *From the Stars in the Sky to the Fish in the Sea*.

In my first year of college, I stopped calling myself an activist.

It took attending just a few meetings of the campus queer group for me to realize that I didn't fit in with everyone else. Despite the fact that I was definitely queer—*a pre-transition trans woman at the time*—I could tell immediately that I wasn't "queer enough" to fight for social justice alongside these university-educated revolutionaries who spoke with such confidence and rolled their eyes every time I opened my mouth.

I didn't know what "trigger warnings" or "intersectional systemic oppression" were. I didn't dress in ripped denim and black leather, or have a colorfully dyed, asymmetrical haircut. I wasn't white, like most of the people in the room. I didn't even know who this "Judith Butler" person that everyone seemed to love so much was.

Simply being racialized, a trans person, and survivor of abuse had apparently not prepared me to talk or think about racism, transphobia, or trauma in any valuable way. Neither had facilitating workshops on homophobia in my hometown.

And after a few weeks of feeling confused and invisible, I decided that I just wasn't smart enough to be an activist.

Six years, two degrees, one gender transition, and a bunch of published Internet rants later, I'm able to see that my feelings about those early forays into social justice weren't so much about my personal capacity or value as they were about exclusion and accessibility.

Social justice and feminist culture are incredible positive forces that transform the way we see ourselves and the world around us. Without social justice and the activist communities that form around it, I literally wouldn't be alive today.

But sometimes those same activist cultures can be unnecessarily exclusive—and worse, inaccessible and elitist. I even feel myself doing it sometimes:

I roll my eyes when someone at a community meeting

asks a "stupid question" about feminism. I snap unnecessarily when someone doesn't know the latest politically correct terminology. I make assumptions about people who I perceive (usually wrongly) as either too young to know anything or too old to be down.

Social justice is such a beautiful, powerful part of my life that I want—need—it to be open to those I care about, from my fifteen-year-old sister to my corporate lawyer friends to my racist grandparents.

So here, for your reading pleasure, are nine ways I'm trying to make my activism more accessible to everyone.

## 1. Welcome People Who Are Trying to Learn

Activist communities can be very loving, but they can also be cliquey and hostile to newcomers who don't speak the right language or even wear the right clothes.

At our worst, social justice culture is basically a rehash of high school, except that everyone is trying to one-up each other with how cool their politics are.

If we really want to create open, caring communities, then we have to create spaces (both online and IRL) where the learning process is welcome and valued. We have to celebrate the new possibilities that each new individual brings.

In practical terms, this means making sure that community meetings are open to newcomers, and that quieter and introverted folks are given opportunities to speak. It means that terminology is explained when necessary, and it means not using academic jargon to sound impressive.

Most of all, it means giving up the unrealistic—and frankly, oppressive—expectation that everyone should step into social justice conversations from an equal starting point—that everyone should or has to know exactly how to do everything perfectly, right away.

It means having the humility to know that all of us are, in fact, still amateurs at the work of making social justice ideas into reality.

## 2. Prioritize Physical and Economic Accessibility

If we, as activists and feminists, want to be accessible, then we need to—you know—actually *be accessible!*

As in, we need to make sure that disabled[1] folks can actually enter and comfortably get around in the spaces we use for work, meetings, conferences, workshops, parties, and every other event.

We also need to ensure that folks with children, people on welfare and fixed incomes, and basically anyone who might not have access to a lot of money and time can participate in community building.

Organizing childcare stations (this can be super fun), making events free or pay-what-you-can (it *can* be done!), and finding ways to compensate folks for "volunteer" work (which usually only middle class and wealthy folks can afford to do) are just a few examples of how this can be done.

These are some very basic practices that many community organizers tend to overlook, because society tends to [make] accessibility barriers invisible to those not affected by them.

Addressing even a few of these very simple things, however, completely changes who can participate in and benefit from activism.

## 3. Celebrate Age Diversity

What young intersectional feminist doesn't have a horror story about being trapped in a conversation with an older person who "just doesn't get it?"

And what older, veteran activist doesn't have a cringe-worthy anecdote about know-it-all youngsters who think that everything worth knowing can be found on a screen?

Ageism is a huge, unspoken problem in social justice culture.

Something I've noticed is that activist communities tend to be concentrated within an age range of 5–7 years, meaning that there is very little intergenerational overlap between them. This means there is little community memory to guide us. It also means that activism is not necessarily open to people creating and raising families.

An older feminist friend once said bitterly to me that "Activists all start out at 18 or 20, and then age out at 40. There [are] never any children or elders in social justice communities, which means they aren't really communities. They're just scenes."

These days, as I'm writing or organizing, I like to ask myself: Is my feminism one that I could see kids growing up with and participating in? Am I grounding myself in the wisdom of elders and mentors?

## 4. Make Room for Mistakes and Accountability

Sometimes I get really anxious about writing articles or organizing events about social justice. I've been part of one too many vicious Internet flame wars and public debates, and I know how intense and painful being publicly called out for making a mistake is.

I have friends who have sworn off feminism and community organizing for this very reason—because they said or did the wrong thing, and got burned for it.

We need to make room for people to make mistakes in their activism—and to grow from them.

I'm not saying that we should stop calling out oppressive language or behavior, or that we should tone police folks who are talking about the oppression they are directly experiencing. Definitely not—we have a right to speak up and to be angry about oppression.

I'm saying that doing the work of social justice is a skill that takes time, patience, and teaching to learn. I'm saying that we can't treat people as though they were disposable—try one out and throw them away if they don't work out.

We need to put our faith and our energy into showing each other how to do things right, rather than punishing each other for getting it wrong.

## 5. Value Intention and Action More than "Correct" Language

Obsession with "correct" language plays an enormous part in making social justice inaccessible to many people. Feminist terminology changes practically every day, it seems, and making a mistake with it can be cause for intense social backlash.

And no, I'm not one of those folks who is always moaning about how the "PC generation" is ruining the world. I know what it feels like to be constantly misgendered, to hear racist slurs about my people casually tossed out as a joke.

I believe that when people say things that reinforce oppression and cause pain, they should be made aware of it.

However, I'm also starting to realize that being considered a "good feminist" is an endeavor that can require an enormous amount of privilege: It takes time and a certain kind of education to read and keep up with social justice ideas. Not everyone's style of learning or thinking lends itself easily to learning new ways of thinking and talking.

Living in Quebec, where the majority language is French (in which it is virtually impossible to use gender-neutral pronouns) and having to exchange complex ideas when I can barely use certain French tenses, has given me a whole new appreciation for valuing folks' intentions and actions over their language use.

Instead of judging my relationships by whether or not my non-anglophone friends are using the correct terminology, I have to ask myself: Is this person genuinely trying to be respectful? How important is terminology or pronouns versus the way that someone treats me and acts on their values?

Some activists use the phrase "Intention doesn't matter—effect does" when it comes to using offensive language. I disagree. Intention and effect matter, because how we understand where someone is coming from can change the effect of what they are doing or saying.

## 6. Learning the Art of Calling In vs. Calling Out

When we do confront folks about talking or behaving oppressively, it can be super important to choose between "calling them in" (gently and lovingly explaining why they need to change what they are doing) and "calling them out" (responding with anger and social pressure).

Both are equally valuable and necessary tactics, but require judiciousness: Calling out is empowering because it allows oppressed individuals to respond and express valid emotions like rage and frustration. Calling in is useful because it allows folks who have done something oppressive to learn without feeling the need for defensiveness (well, that's how it works on a good day).

My personal guideline is that I only call folks out if I am directly affected by what they are doing or saying—that is, if their words or actions are harming me, and not someone that I'm trying to be an ally to. Calling someone out for doing something that impacts people with identities and experiences other than my own feels disingenuous and needlessly alienating.

## 7. Acknowledge and Break Down Activist Hierarchies

A dynamic we rarely acknowledge in activist communities is that there is a social hierarchy based on experience and popularity: Folks who are good at talking and writing usually have the most power, while those who have less experience and are less vocal have the least.

Often, we create miniature celebrities out of our favorite activists and social justice writers, vloggers, and artists: These are the people who get tons of "likes" on Facebook and shares on their blog posts.

When unacknowledged, these dynamics make social activism less accessible because they prevent new activists from being heard. Folks who don't have the time or ability to lead protests or write articles are excluded from taking the lead, even when the issue at hand affects them most.

Worst of all, activist social ladders can create a breeding ground for abuse, exploitation, and sexual harassment and assault. Too many of my acquaintances—particularly young women—have left social justice movements because of bad experiences with activist "celebrities."

The revolution starts at home: If our movements are going to undo the abuse of power in the world, we have to undo it in our own communities.

## 8. Value Everyone's Contributions

The best thing I ever got at a social justice conference was a dishtowel: Embroidered on it are the words "Everyone wants a revolution—no one wants to do the dishes."

It's easy to give someone glory and social cred for being an Internet personality or making a speech at a march. It's easy to get lost in judging other folks' value by how well they "speak feminist" or how many articles they've written.

It's harder to recognize and celebrate the invisible and unglamorous work like child raising and cooking and cleaning that has always traditionally been done by women, particularly migrants and women of color.

This, however, is the work that makes any "movement" possible, and is equally important as speaking on a panel or teaching at a university.

We need to start recognizing and centering this work, and the people who do it, in order to build truly accountable social justice communities.

## 9. Center Love

People always seem to forget about love in the movement.

We get caught up in righteous anger, in validating sadness, in the cold hard realities of violence and abuse. We talk about smashing the patriarchy, breaking the gender binary, shattering the glass ceiling.

This is all important, and very empowering, but I guess I'm tired of running on rage and despair alone.

So here's my access request to my social justice community: I want our activism to be fun. I want it to be fulfilling, and caring. I want it to be full of love.

And love—radical love, transformative love, the kind that brings people in and changes us over a million private revolutionary moments—doesn't leave people out of the movement.

## Note

1.   I am using disability-first and not person-first language here for [the] reasons [found here]: https://everydayfeminism.com/2012/12/im-not-a-person-with-a-disability/.

*Source:* Thom, Kai Cheng. (2015, September 27). "9 Ways We Can Make Social Justice Movements Less Elitist and More Accessible." Originally published on *Everyday Feminism*. Retrieved from: https://everydayfeminism.com/2015/09/social-justice-less-elitist/.

# A SENSE OF PLACE: EXPRESSIONS OF TRANS ACTIVISM NORTH OF LAKE NIPISSING

*Grey Kimber Piitaapan Muldoon, with Dan Irving*

Grey Kimber Piitaapan Muldoon is a performance artist and activist who explores vulnerabilities from all angles. In 2009, Muldoon, along with Dan Irving, conducted a series of interviews with eight two-spirit and trans activists living in Northern Ontario. These interviews were published in the article excerpted below.

Dan Irving is an associate professor teaching in the Human Rights and Sexuality Studies Program in the Institute of Interdisciplinary Studies at Carleton University. He is currently researching youth masculinities in times of socio-economic crisis, and trans and Two-Spirit individuals' experiences of unemployment and underemployment. Irving is the co-editor of *Trans Activism in Canada: A Reader*.

Most people, especially trans, two-spirit, and queer people, fear being confined by our past: many of us feel a need to deny our history daily to survive. I wonder about the possibility of continuity, bringing new meanings out of our past identities and circumstances.

Azilda is a hamlet on Whitewater Lake, near Sudbury, Ontario, where I grew up from 1982 to 2001. In the summer of 2009, I planned to return, queerly, after gender transition but before sex transition. My experience in Toronto's queer, social work, and activist spaces could not answer questions such as: "Are there (m)any other trans people in Sudbury?" "Will I get killed there?" "Can I be myself in First Nations spaces?" and "Does my desire to change my body relate to my spirit?" These questions were out of place. I yearned for my origins: for others like me.

I was not looking for those finding themselves out of place in a backwater. I wanted to question the idea of a backwater filled with ignorant "primitives," requiring enlightenment from the Silver City. So, I hitchhiked to Sudbury, North Bay, Thunder Bay, and Sault Ste. Marie, with analog tape and a recorder to interview people I did not yet know. These people had responded to a call out: "Looking for two-spirit, genderqueer, and trans people in the North to interview about their activism (gender identity-based or otherwise)." I went to every community where someone had responded. [...]

Everyone that I met was brave and inspiring. Everyone.

## Presenting Personal Narratives

*Starr Loon Danyals* is a trans woman in her early thirties who lives in downtown Sudbury. She has cats and offers me tea. She does presentations on trans experience and volunteers for the Women's Center and the Sudbury AIDS service organization. For her, activism is surviving and living your life as you are openly. She says that volunteering proves that she is a real person in the community because she contributes to it. When she was younger, she was going to be a Catholic priest. She still likes prayer and spirituality, but also thinks that what could be called God or a creator appreciates our using our freedom to be diverse. She never liked the hierarchy of the Church. It forced her out for being "gay" when she was 21. In her twenties she developed a drag queen persona named "Twilight Starr." Since 2007, she has been living as a woman. The harassment was worse for her when she was in her drag role and outside the clubs or bars than it has been for her as Starr Danyals, yet she stays inside sometimes for weeks because of the staring, threat of violence, and "flabbergasting" ignorance. She is a big-boned, tall woman and does not think she will ever pass, yet she does not see a man in her face: while tall like the women in her father's family, she sees her mom and the women from that side in her facial features. She has a blonde wig and black wig. The black one reminds her of her paternal relatives; the blonde one, of her mom's. Both sides are bilingual French-Canadian Catholics. Her mom is important to her, so she is working to make her relationship with her a good one.

* * * * *

*Ma-Nee Chacaby* is a two-spirit elder and lesbian woman who lives in Thunder Bay. Ma-Nee is wonderful to talk to. I highly recommend tea with her. She really likes being herself. She tells me so, over and over. Four years later, in response to her, I still think to myself: "How? How do I be myself, Ma-Nee?" Then I laugh at me. Her name, "Ma-Nee," was lost to her for a while, so she had to reclaim it. It refers to a hill covered in blueberries. Her apartment is covered in her artwork, mostly paintings. She likes to give these as gifts, creating a wealth of relationships through the presence of her work in other homes. She works in paint with the challenge of impaired eyes. She is in her sixties and has been working as an elder since she was 34. It was very hard for her to accept the need to do this work, as it means responsibility for others, and she has sometimes found it hard to be responsible even for only herself. She feels her two-spirit self in her work as a healer. It makes her able to empathize strongly with both men and women. She was raised speaking Cree and Ojibwe and learned English when she started school. She was raised to believe in a "higher power outside": "Like, trees. And, grass. And water. And rocks. Rocks are my stones—they're like my fathers and mothers, grandmothers. Rocks and stones are my grandparents."

Ma-Nee was a toddler when her grandmother (*kokum*) located her. She had been adopted into a French family. Her *kokum* raised her often miles away from anyone else, surviving by trapping, fishing, and eating moose near Ombabika, in the Lake Nipigon area. Her *kokum* told her about her own long life and about traditional roles for two-spirit persons before her death at age 104. Ma-Nee, then 15, wedded a man in a marriage arranged by her birth mother. The marriage was abusive and did not last long. Like my own family, there are many adoptions in Ma-Nee's. She has three children: two birth children and a daughter, Maya, whom Ma-Nee adopted when she was 15. Maya is now a language activist who lives in Toronto. Her daughter asks her to come to Toronto where it would be less lonely, but Ma-Nee likes being a 15-minute walk from the bush, and even Thunder Bay seems crowded to her. Her life has been full of activism and harsh retaliation. She was beaten up several times after coming out in 1988 on television during an interview about an equal rights protest action. Race was a factor in the attacks. Sometimes it was white people who attacked and sometimes it was Native people, who said they believed she was making it even worse for them, since they were already suffering racist attacks and did not need to be associated with gay people and suffer that violence (against gay people) too. Ma-Nee is an AA member and enjoys the (not queer) dances, but again feels lonely and rejected there. Most of Ma-Nee's chosen family are white gays and lesbians. (I meet some of them. They run the Women's Center, which welcomed trans people in 2009.) Yet she wishes there were more out Native gays and lesbians. They all leave, she knows, because life is too hard in Thunder Bay—but that is changing. She is trying to start a social group for cross-gender and two-spirit people with her friend Chris...

*Source:* Muldoon, Grey Kimber Piitaapan, with Irving, Dan. (2014). Excerpted from "A Sense of Place: Expressions of Trans Activism North of Lake Nipissing." In Dan Irving & Rupert Raj (Eds.), *Trans Activism in Canada: A Reader* (pp. 71–73, 76–77). Toronto, ON: Canadian Scholars' Press.

# CHAPTER 76

## The Future of Feminism

*Judy Rebick*

Judy Rebick is one of Canada's best-known feminists and political commentators. She is the former Sam Gindin Chair in Social Justice and Democracy at Ryerson University in Toronto, and former president of the National Action Committee on the Status of Women. She is the founding publisher of rabble.ca, a progressive, independent news and discussion site. Rebick makes regular appearances on television and radio, contributes frequently to newspapers and magazines, and has authored several books, including *Ten Thousand Roses: The Making of a Feminist Revolution, Occupy This!*, and *Transforming Power: From the Personal to the Political.*

In 1970, Canadian second-wave feminism emerged in its full glory in interaction with the state through the Royal Commission on the Status of Women and the Abortion Caravan; its subsequent development focused increasingly on the state. Thus, it is not surprising that the rise of neoliberalism, or corporate globalization, with its turn away from the social programs so essential to feminist organizing, resulted in a serious decline of the women's movement.

Second-wave feminism in Canada may not be dead, but it has lost its influence and visibility. [...] Many groups from second-wave feminism still remain and continue to do important work. For example, the recent push for a national child care campaign was led in large part by the same women who began the struggle in the 1960s and continued it through every broken promise. But like all social movements, the women's movement ebbs and flows, and today we are in more of an ebb than a flow.

Many women call themselves third-wave feminists. By "third wave" they mean a set of ideas that they see as quite different from those of the second wave. They are clearer from the outset on the intersection of various forms of domination, class, race, sex, and gender. They focus more on sexuality, although that is probably more a function of youth than of political difference. They have adopted the LGBT (Lesbian, Gay, Bisexual, Transgendered) approach to sexual orientation and see second wavers as transphobic. They are more focused on cultural interventions than on political and social interventions. In many ways, their development reflects the turn away from the state as a site of struggle. [...] I think third wavers do some interesting and important work, but they have not yet reached out to a wider layer of women in a way that is required to create a broad social movement.

My generation never called itself second wave. That was just a way for academics to distinguish between the two huge upsurges of women. The first wave won women the vote; the second gained them reproductive, economic, and legal rights. Feminist activism continued between the first and second waves, of course, and it perseveres today, but I don't yet see a mass movement dealing with gender issues. On the other hand, I think the division between generations exists in part because my generation has not made enough space for young women. The world is very different for young women today, and they should be in the lead of defining what a new feminism will look like.

Much conventional wisdom addresses the decline of the women's movement in Canada. Many blame it on identity politics. If feminists had only focused on what united women, they say, instead of on what divided them, the women's movement would have remained strong. It is true that the cross-class alliance of the women's movement was an important part of its power.

That there were a handful of women in positions of authority to promote the feminist agenda was critical to our success. But feminism would have betrayed its vision, and therefore lost its purpose, if it had continued to marginalize the poorest and most oppressed women to favour those more privileged.

In fact, the organizing of women of colour and their insistence that the women's movement belonged to them too breathed new life into a feminism that was co-opted by its own success at the end of the 1980s. As neoliberal globalization increased the gap between rich and poor, the challenge of maintaining a common vision among women became much greater. The global backlash against feminism and, in Canada, the federal state's funding cuts to women's groups made dealing with these difficulties even harder. The women's movement in Canada worked hard to find new ways to unite across differences. Today, the security state and the war on terror are further isolating already marginalized religious minorities and communities of colour.

[…] Gender itself is becoming a contested notion under neoliberalism. As Janine Brodie says so eloquently […]:

Since then, however, the issue of gender equality has been progressively erased from official policy discourses and practices. This disappearance of gender coincides with the implementation of neoliberal governing practices in Canada and most advanced liberal democracies. Although the scope and degree of neoliberal policy reform vary widely among these states, neoliberalism has greatly influenced the framing of citizenship claims as well as relationships between the state and both the private sector (the economy and civil society) and the private sphere (the individual and the family) (Brodie, 1997; Clarke, 2004). In the process, we have been submerged in a politics that seeks to reform and transform the irredeemably gendered subjects of the post-war welfare state into genderless and self-sufficient market actors. (Brodie, 2007: 165)

Carol Shields said it more poetically in her book *Unless* (2002: 99, emphasis in original): *"But we've come so far"*; that's the thinking. So far compared with fifty or a hundred years ago. Well, no, we've arrived at the new millennium and we haven't 'arrived' at all. We've been sent over to the side pocket of the snooker table and made to disappear."

As gender disappears, and class and race divisions among women grow, it is increasingly difficult for women to self-identify as a group. It was that identification, captured in the phrase "sisterhood is powerful," that was so central to second-wave feminism. Women are still hungry for that identification and gender solidarity, but the ground for it has shifted.

In English Canada, we spent many years struggling with the differences among women. The efforts of marginalized women to be heard in feminism have been central to its development. Young feminists begin with the understanding of difference that took us many years of blood, sweat, and mostly tears to develop. But somehow, in creating a new comprehension of feminism that, in the words of bell hooks (quoted in Lewis, n.d.), embraced the "recognition of difference without attaching privilege to difference," we have stopped seeing what women have in common, feeding into the neoliberal drive to eliminate gender as a category.

The Quebec women's movement evolved quite differently from that of English Canada. The later arrival of neoliberalism in Quebec meant that the women's movement continued to grow and make gains well into the late 1990s, most significantly a truly universal child care program. The social service cuts that so devastated the women's movement in most provinces were not as great in Quebec. On the other hand, the struggles around racism that so defined the women's movement in English Canada in the late '80s and the 1990s have not played out in the same way in Quebec, in part because of the influence of the national question. So the Quebec women's movement has not achieved the diversity of its English-Canadian counterpart. Nevertheless, the more general impact of neoliberalism is also manifest in Quebec.

Despite our differences, women today continue to face common problems. Feminists fought for universal child care and for men to assume their full share of child rearing, but neither battle has yet been won. The reality today is that most women are working longer hours outside the home than they used to but are still taking primary responsibility within it. Whether they are pressured to overwork so as to advance in their profession or whether they are obliged to hold two or three part-time jobs, most women struggle with the crushing burden of paid work combined with the still excessive demands of labour in the home.

Although I agree that we need to regender our understanding of the state, [...] I also believe that we must revisit the attention to the "private" sphere that was much more pronounced in the early years of the second wave. Women's equality will be possible only in a world that accepts nurturing and caring as important roles for both men and women. Gloria Steinem has said that her generation of feminists made it possible

for women to do what men traditionally did; now it is time for the opposite to occur. Men who wish to spend more time with their children and enjoy their lives will be our allies in challenging a society that values career and money alone. Yet such men are still few and far between. Even in countries where government policy encourages men to take parental leave, [...] the uptake is small.

We need a strategy that includes child care, a shorter work week, and improved parental leave for both men and women. But most of all, women must decide to stop carrying such an unfair share of the work of society. But as we learned in the second wave, the first step is to speak the name of the problem. In the 1960s, Betty Friedan (1963) spoke about the "problem with no name," thus sparking so much of the original second-wave activism. Today, that problem is too much work, too much pressure, too little time. It's a problem that women share with men but suffer from much more. This problem is not about the state but about women's continuing predominance in the private sphere. A different kind of struggle is required, one that focuses much more on education and new kinds of relationships than it does on engaging with the state.

Another continuing and related problem is the intractable hold of men on power. Second-wave feminists put on armour to enter the battlefields created by patriarchy. To challenge the way in which power is practiced, we need to challenge the men who hold it. In the 2005 Montreal roundtable to discuss my book about the Canadian women's movement, *Ten Thousand Roses*, journalist and filmmaker Francine Pelletier described the problem of the invisible glass ceiling. She said that although men initially welcome women into the workplace, they subsequently become uncomfortable with their presence and seek to marginalize them. It is difficult to name the problem because the men talk the talk of women's equality. Many young women in the audience nodded their heads in agreement. "It's so confusing," one young woman who works for an NGO told me. "We have strong feminists on our board, so how could our workplace be sexist? But it is. Women in leadership positions are always marginalized."

Both problems come from the fact that my generation of feminists failed to achieve its goal: to overturn the patriarchy. The system of male domination remains intact and is reinforced through male culture in the workplace, in politics, and in still too many families. This culture is not perpetrated solely by men. Many women in positions of power adopt the same methods of control as do their male colleagues. Our notions of leadership, for example, are still very masculinized. And certainly, the fact that so little value is placed on raising children or on caring for family, friends, and community is a sign that though, economically, we have moved radically from the family wage that allowed a male breadwinner to support a woman at home, in cultural terms, we have not moved very far at all.

At the beginning of the second wave, we were openly and actively challenging that male culture, but as our influence increased, we focused more and more on demands for reform and less and less on the deeper cultural and structural changes that would threaten patriarchy. Too many of us accepted a place within the patriarchal structures. In a 2004 interview I conducted with Frances Lankin, now the CEO of Toronto's United Way, she explained what happened to her feminist process once she became a minister in the Bob Rae government:

I came into government having worked in a consensus model, and we tried to work in government that way. But, I had to move quickly to match the style of that world—very top-down, directive, and not consensus oriented. People who knew me didn't understand how I could do it, but I did. I made it work and paid a price for that inside. I've found myself a lot in my life having to work in ways that I don't like. You get a strong training when you work in a male way of

doing things, and it sometimes takes over how you are as a person. I sometimes wish I could have worked more in a women's collective and had more balance. I think this is why I've been successful in a man's world.

I take pride in that but not in thinking that I've changed things to make it easier for women coming along. I think there's a lot of work for women to do to change the way in which institutions are run.

The pressure, as described by Lankin, to succeed as a woman in a traditionally male role almost always trumps the desire to change the way things are done to make room for other women. For one thing, all the hegemonic pressures push women in that direction; for another, we have no blueprint of any kind for making changes to deeply engrained hierarchical structures. The more power that resides in an organization, the harder it is to change.

How do we play the game but change the rules? As the poet Audre Lorde (1984: 110) so famously said, "The master's tools will never dismantle the master's house." But neither can we make change exclusively from the outside. The success of the second wave was in its ability to work both inside and outside the system: as some writers have put it, in and against the state. Once you are inside a system, however, the pressure to conform is tremendous. Feminists of my generation started as kick-ass radicals but were slowly co-opted. Italian philosopher Antonio Gramsci (1971: 389–90) called this hegemony, the way that capitalism maintains its ideological hold.

We need to explore new ways of decision making that entail cooperation rather than domination, inclusion rather than elitism, and new kinds of leadership that involve empowering others rather than aggrandizing ourselves. We tried to do this in the second wave but generally failed. In my view we internalized too many patriarchal ways of operating to successfully create non-hierarchical organizations.

Instead, as Jo Freeman states in her brilliant essay, "The Tyranny of Structurelessness" (1972–73), we created informal power that was even more inaccessible to marginalized women than the formal structures of power themselves. Today, we have the benefit of much more work, both academic and practical, in making decisions differently in realms ranging from popular education to participatory democracy. We know much more about creating egalitarian structures. Speaking truth to power, it turns out, is not enough. We must change the very nature of power.

A lot of young activists, seeing the dangers of co-option and the corruption of the existing political structures, choose to work completely outside of those structures. Young women ask me what I think of the impact of cyber feminism, for example. On the net you can communicate with large numbers of like-minded thinkers, developing ideas, debating issues, and even organizing protests. But unless we find ways to reach out to others who are not hooked into our networks, it is hard for me to see how we will effect change.

The World March of Women [2000] defined the priority of today's women's movement as fighting poverty and violence. Dealing with female poverty means dealing with neoliberalism. [...] With little or no discussion, welfare moms became part of the undeserving poor, and raising children was accorded even less economic and social value than it has had traditionally. When discussing why she should be a feminist, a young university professor recently asked me, "What's in it for me?" When you have access to privilege in a society that is so unequal, what's in it for you is the feeling that you are making a contribution to overcoming that inequity. Many people do see that need when it comes to solidarity with women and men in the developing countries but not so much within their own. The pressure, both financial and emotional, on poor women today is terrible. Racialized poor women or women in the sex trades face even greater marginalization and degradation. The horror that hundreds of Aboriginal women have disappeared,

not only from Vancouver's Downtown Eastside but also across the country, illustrates that authorities still consider some women's lives to be dispensable.

Feminist strategies for protecting and empowering women have saved thousands of lives, and attitudes that blamed women for the violence directed against them have changed radically. Yet male violence continues almost unabated, in Canada as elsewhere. Although improving laws and their application is critical, that won't eliminate male violence. A new feminism needs to debate strategies for ending violence against women. My own view is that these discussions must include men. Men have been active in combating male violence through the all-male White Ribbon Campaign. Anti-violence feminists have been quite critical of that campaign, maintaining that it often takes up the space and financing desperately needed by women's groups. It is certainly irritating that when you Google "violence against women," the White Ribbon Campaign comes up near the top. However, what I have in mind is not a male group that combats violence but a mixed discussion on the issue.

If we are to end violence against women, we must better understand how masculinization takes place and how it can be changed. From an early age, boys are still socialized to be aggressive, dominating, and competitive. There are few positive male role models in popular education. Boys still learn how to be men from patriarchal and often violent males, such as the heroes of team sports, action movies, and video games. And feminist men have to play a critical role in speaking out for a new masculinity that isn't based on the oppression of women.

Many young women identify as third-wave feminists. I see them as similar to the small group of women in the early and mid-1960s who identified as feminists. Years before the movement arose, women such as Simone de Beauvoir, Betty Friedan, and Doris Anderson were writing about the issues that would spawn it. Similarly, third-wave feminists are redefining feminism in new ways that focus on sexuality, the intersection of various forms of oppression, and the beauty myth. Not surprisingly, some of their ideas are a reaction to the excesses or absences of the generation before. They have also been heavily influenced by the postmodernism that has swept women's studies over the last number of years. To this old socialist feminist, the idea that intervening in strictly cultural arenas can change the world is highly idealistic and problematic. Without addressing the material reality of women, whether work time, child care, or violence, feminism will not find an echo among masses of women.

Nevertheless, sexuality and body image are central issues for feminism today. Several years ago, I had an e-mail conversation with Candice Steenburgen, a third-wave feminist academic, about sex. She told me, "We have no script about what equal sexual relationships look like." Second-wave feminists did challenge the male domination in relationships. However, though some individuals worked through their own relationships, we never really developed an understanding of what a new kind of equal relationship, whether heterosexual or lesbian, could be.

In her recent series about women and sex, Francine Pelletier (2005) reveals an incredibly broad diversity of women's sexual experience. She says that although women appear to have a lot of sexual agency today, you find something else when you dig deeper. She doesn't quite have the words to describe the lingering self-hatred that seems to remain from centuries of oppression and is fuelled by a massive industry designed to make us feel inadequate. We aren't thin enough, sexy enough, beautiful enough. We're too tall, too short, too loud, too quiet, too aggressive, too timid. What has changed is that no one now tells us we are too smart. Instead, the pressure today is to be smart, accomplished, *and* beautiful. And that pressure goes beyond youth with a terrifying explosion of cosmetic surgery.

As second-wave feminism began as a peace movement in Canada with the formation of the formidable Voice of Women (VOW), so peace must remain a central element of feminism. As VOW has always understood, women have the strongest interest in

ending war. This is not solely because, increasingly, women and children suffer most from war and because mass rapes have become a generalized instrument of war. It is also because war is a central prop to patriarchy. A world in which women hold equal power with men will be a world in which war is no longer either a method of domination or a method of dispute resolution. And ecofeminism, an important part of the second wave, has taken on even more significance in this day and age. As Sandra Delaronde put it during the 2005 Winnipeg roundtable on *Ten Thousand Roses*, "Second-wave feminism was focused on us as women and improving our status vis-à-vis men. Perhaps third wave feminism is about changing the world" (author's notes).

Indeed, most young feminists are more active in the global justice movement than in the women's movement. As a socialist feminist, I have always understood that women's equality can never be achieved in a capitalist system that is based on entrenched inequality. However, capitalism is not the only system of domination and inequality. The interlocking systems of capitalism, patriarchy, and colonialism produce the inequalities and injustice we seek to correct. Unless we challenge all those systems of domination, we will take two steps backward for every step forward. And the struggle to end this domination involves continuing engagement with the state but not in the almost exclusive focus that came to represent second-wave feminism. The personal is political too.

# REFERENCES

Brodie, Janine. 2007. "Putting Gender Back In: Women and Social Policy Reform in Canada." In Yasmin Abu-Laban, ed., *Gendering the Nation State: Canadian and Comparative Perspectives*. Vancouver: UBC Press, 2007. p. 165.

Freeman, Jo. 1972–73. "The Tyranny of Structurelessness." *Berkeley Journal of Sociology* 17: 151–65.

Friedan, Betty. 1963. *The Feminine Mystique*. New York: Random House.

Gramsci, Antonio. 1971. *Selections from the Prison Notebooks.* Edited by Q. Hoare and G.N. Smith. New York: International Publishers.

Lewis, Jone Johnson. n.d. "Women Voices: Quotations by Women—bell hooks." Available at http://womenshistory. about.com/library/qu/blquhook.htm.

Lorde, Audre. 1984. *Sister Outsider: Essays and Speeches.* Freedom: Crossing Press.

Pelletier, Francine. 2005. "Sex, Truth, and Videotape." CBC Broadcast, Virage Productions.

Shields, Carol. 2002. *Unless: A Novel.* London and New York: Random House Canada.

**Source:** Rebick, Judy. (2008). Excerpted from "The Future of Feminism." In Yasmin Abu-Laban (Ed.), *Gendering the Nation-State: Canadian and Comparative Perspectives* (pp. 252–259). Vancouver, BC: University of British Columbia Press.

## ACTIVIST INSIGHT: THIS COUNTRY'S HISTORY CANNOT BE DELETED

*Angela Y. Davis*

Angela Y. Davis is an American political activist, academic scholar, and author. She emerged as a prominent counterculture activist and radical in the 1960s as a leader of the Communist Party USA, and had close relations with the Black Panther Party through her involvement in the Civil Rights Movement. She co-founded Critical Resistance, an organization working to abolish the prison-industrial complex. She is a distinguished professor emerita at the University of California–Santa Cruz, in its History of Consciousness Department, and a former director of its Feminist Studies Department.

*In the immediate aftermath of the election of Donald Trump as President of the United States of America, hundreds of thousands of people took to the streets in protest. On January 21, 2017, prominent feminist and civil rights activist Angela Davis addressed a huge crowd at the historic "Women's March on Washington." The full text of her speech follows.*

At a challenging moment in our history, let us remind ourselves that we the hundreds of thousands, the millions of women, trans people, men and youth who are here at the Women's March, we represent the powerful forces of change that are determined to prevent the dying cultures of racism, hetero-patriarchy from rising again.

We recognize that we are collective agents of history and that history cannot be deleted like web pages. We know that we gather this afternoon on Indigenous land and we follow the lead of the first peoples who despite massive genocidal violence have never relinquished the struggle for land, water, culture, their people. We especially salute today the Standing Rock Sioux.

The freedom struggles of Black people that have shaped the very nature of this country's history cannot be deleted with the sweep of a hand. We cannot be made to forget that Black lives do matter. This is a country anchored in slavery and colonialism, which means for better or for worse the very history of the United States is a history of immigration and enslavement. Spreading xenophobia, hurling accusations of murder and rape and building walls will not erase history.

No human being is illegal.

The struggle to save the planet, to stop climate change, to guarantee the accessibility of water from the lands of the Standing Rock Sioux, to Flint, Michigan, to the West Bank and Gaza. The struggle to save our flora and fauna, to save the air—this is ground zero of the struggle for social justice.

This is a women's march and this women's march represents the promise of feminism as against the pernicious powers of state violence. An inclusive and intersectional feminism that calls upon all of us to join the resistance to racism, to Islamophobia, to antisemitism, to misogyny, to capitalist exploitation.

Yes, we salute the fight for 15. We dedicate ourselves to collective resistance.

Resistance to the billionaire mortgage profiteers and gentrifiers.

Resistance to the healthcare privateers.

Resistance to the attacks on Muslims and on immigrants. Resistance to attacks on disabled people.

Resistance to state violence perpetrated by the police and through the prison-industrial complex.

Resistance to institutional and intimate gender violence, especially against trans women of color.

Women's rights are human rights all over the planet and that is why we say freedom and justice for Palestine. We celebrate the impending release of Chelsea Manning. And Oscar López Rivera. But we also say free Leonard Peltier. Free Mumia Abu-Jamal. Free Assata Shakur.

Over the next months and years, we will be called upon to intensify our demands for social justice to become more militant in our defense of vulnerable populations. Those who still defend the supremacy of white male hetero-patriarchy had better watch out.

The next 1,459 days of the Trump administration will be 1,459 days of resistance: resistance on the ground, resistance in the classrooms, resistance on the job, resistance in our art and in our music.

This is just the beginning and in the words of the inimitable Ella Baker: "We who believe in freedom cannot rest until it comes." Thank you.

---

*Source:* Davis, Angela Y. (2017, January 22). "Angela Davis' Women's March Speech: 'This Country's History Cannot Be Deleted.'" *The Guardian*. Retrieved from: https://www.theguardian.com/commentisfree/2017/jan/22/angela-davis-womens-march-speech-countrys-history-cannot-be-deleted.

# CHAPTER 77

## Transnational Feminism

*Corinne L. Mason*

Corrine L. Mason is an associate professor of gender and women's studies and sociology at Brandon University in Manitoba. She conducts transnational critical race feminist analyses of development discourses and popular news media, focusing specifically on representations of LGBTIQ rights, violence against women, reproductive justice, and foreign aid. Her work has been published in *Feminist Formations*, *International Feminist Journal of Politics*, *Feminist Media*, and *Feminist Teacher*, among others. She is the author of *Manufacturing Urgency: Violence against Women and the Development Industry*.

## INTRODUCTION

The late 20th century saw a global explosion of attention to women's rights. In 1975, the United Nations announced the United Nation's Decade for Women to raise awareness of international women's rights. Four world conferences were held between 1975 and 1985 during which women from all over the world gathered to discuss such issues as gender discrimination, violence against women, poverty, health, armed conflict, the economy, the rights of girls, and the environment. Since these initial meetings, research on global gender inequality has increased immensely. Of women worldwide, 35% have experienced gendered violence in their lives (UN Women, 2014). Of all women who are employed, 50% work in vulnerable employment in the informal economy where there are no working regulations or protections for workers,

such as sexual harassment policies and the range of other workplace protections from injury and exploitation that some take for granted (UN Women, 2014). There is now growing consensus around the world that mobilizing for gender equality is a global project for the 21st century as well.

Transnational feminism constitutes a framework that can be used to address the challenges of working toward gender equality globally. Transnational feminism can be thought of as a two-pronged approach that analyzes shifts and changes in gender relations globally and builds feminist communities of resistance across and against borders. As a theoretical paradigm, transnational feminism examines how gender equality is manifested geographically (in various locations), and also traces historical structures of inequality.

Transnational feminism is specifically concerned with how colonialism and imperialism map onto current forms of global gender inequality. According to Ania Loomba (2005), colonialism can be defined as "conquest and control of other people's lands and goods" (p. 8). It may include the direct or indirect control of land and people by foreign occupiers, and in some cases, the settling of foreign populations and the displacement of those indigenous to the land (for example, Canada). Imperialism can be understood as the cultural and economic dependency and control over people and land that ensures that labour and markets are opened to imperial powers (p. 11). Transnational feminists work from the assumption that colonial and imperial projects have and continue to alter gender relations in significant ways that intersect with issues of health, poverty, the economy, and the environment. They also acknowledge that colonial and imperial projects have an impact on how these global issues are represented and discussed in feminist scholarship. Transnational feminists contend that current imperial projects, including dominant forms of economic globalization, affect women's lives and the ways in which feminists can align themselves in acts of global solidarity against systems of oppression.

This chapter offers an introduction to transnational feminist theories and activisms. First, this chapter will explain the concept of "transnational" by distinguishing transnational feminism from the terms *global* and *international* feminism. Second, this chapter will explore the differences between "global feminism" and transnational feminism. Third, the chapter will outline [two] issues of global significance where transnational feminists have made specific interventions: migration [...] and violence against women.[1] Fourth, feminist mobilizations across borders will be explored. By working through these key questions and issues, this chapter focuses on how power operates transnationally and how—with both successes and failures—transnational feminists are organizing and agitating for gender equality across borders.

## GLOBALIZATION, LOCAL/GLOBAL, AND THE TRANSNATIONAL

*Globalization* is a highly contested term and yet an essential one for transnational feminists. Globalization can be described as the increased movement and flows of peoples, information, and consumer culture across borders (Naples, 2002a, p. 8). For many, the term *globalization* might conjure images of the United States' companies such as McDonald's opening in Tanzania and Starbucks serving its coffee in Shanghai. The term might also evoke images of people crossing borders for holiday travel, of bananas from Latin America being imported into Canada, and of receiving cold calls from a United States' company that has outsourced its work to India. The term *globalization* appeals to people's optimistic visions of an interconnected world, where national identities and borders are becoming less important to the ways in which individuals move and interact, the services and goods people can access, and how companies do business. The largest corporations in the world, including Nestlé and Shell, are called multinational corporations (MNCs) or transnational corporations, meaning that these companies spread their work around the world, which is facilitated by processes of globalization.

Importantly, globalization has winners and losers. Critics of globalization say the costs outweigh the benefits since the benefits are not equally distributed. For Marchand and Runyan (2011), the term *globalization* is coded language that gives a positive spin on projects and processes that are actually imperialist in nature. They use the term *globalization-cum-imperialism* to denote the ways in which the term *globalization* masks the powerful forces behind changes in economies and cultures that create conditions in which some win and some lose. [...]

For feminists concerned with the negative impact of globalization on gender relations and on women in particular, globalization is neither inevitable nor unchanging, but rather a project shaped by social and political forces. In other words, globalization is a process, and therefore, it can be resisted. Marchand and Runyan (2011) find the term *global economic restructuring* a more accurate and effective one to describe the project of globalization-cum-imperialism. This process generally includes the dismantling of nationally funded social services and health care in favour of putting these services into an open market for private sector companies to own, deliver, and profit from. By seeing globalization through the lens of economic restructuring, the gendered impacts are more visible for study and can be challenged. For example, a major impact of globalization has been the increase in women's unpaid labour. Women do about 70% of the household work globally (Desai, 2002). Due to global economic restructuring, women are doing more unpaid care work than ever before. When countries liberalize their economies, many state supports for reproductive labour are effectively removed and women end up picking up the slack. Feminists have termed this the *double-burden* or *triple-burden* of labour where they perform not only paid work in the market and unpaid work for their families, but also the caregiving and domestic labour that might otherwise have been subsidized by the state. Among the impacts of global economic restructuring is also the increase in the price of goods, including food, that makes women more vulnerable to malnutrition as they often eat last after providing for family members (Desai, 2002, p. 20).

Transnational feminists conceptualize global economic restructuring as a useful way of understanding global power systems and cultural flows—and as a starting point for enacting change. This way of thinking about globalization is important for transnational feminist theories because scholars are interested in mapping changing politics, cultures, and economies and contributing to positive change.

Transnational feminist theory invites people to think differently about how culture is also subject to globalizing forces. Globalization has not meant that cultures have become homogeneous nor has it meant that the flow of Western products, services, and ideas proceed uniformly from the West to other countries

(Marchand & Runyan, 2011). Certainly, colonialism and imperialism shape the ways in which culture and capital flow, and it is important for transnational feminists to map how this happens as well as to note resistance to it. One way to think about how culture flows unpredictably under globalization is to take the example of the Mattel toy, the Barbie doll. In their canonical text *Scattered Hegemonies: Postmodernity and Transnational Feminist Practices*, Grewal and Kaplan (1994) use the example of the consumption of Barbie in India to describe the globalization of culture. Challenging the assumption that cultural flows are unidirectional (i.e., from the West to "the rest"), Grewal and Kaplan ask where, by whom, and for what reason some elements of culture are consumed and not others. Since Barbie is sold in India dressed in a sari while Ken is dressed in "American" clothes, some American culture is being consumed, but India's culture is also changing Barbie. Grewal and Kaplan ask that people think about what a Barbie dressed in a sari might communicate about the interplay between the global and the local, suggesting that although an American multinational corporation can impose culture, so can the recipient influence its production to a certain extent.

More than Barbie's dress, Grewal (2005) notes that most Barbie dolls sold in the United States in the 1990s were made in China, Malaysia, and Indonesia. The plastics of the doll were made in Taiwan from oil bought from Saudi Arabia. Her hair was made in Japan and the packaging was made in the United States. According to Grewal, the labour cost associated with Barbie was about 35 cents per Barbie and the labour was performed primarily by poorly paid Asian women in assembly line work. Most of the cost of Barbie is associated with shipping, marketing, and profit for Mattel. The example of Barbie demonstrates that the globalized production and consumption of Barbie is multidirectional and gendered in both labour and consumption. It also shows that the poor, Southern nations are positioned as sites of resources for the West where captive labour and markets are opened to Western powers through the project of globalization-cum-imperialism.

## Local/Global

Transnational feminists are particularly concerned with the terms *local* and *global*. Global is often used to denote the workings of globalization at a level that is supranational, or transgresses state borders. You may have heard the phrase "think global, act local," which promotes resistance to globalization. Resisting the harmful effects of globalization has involved taking local action, such as purchasing food at farmer's markets or checking the labels on clothing to ensure it has been traded fairly. These are complex consumer practices, and transnational feminists help us understand that the local and the global are not two distinct entities; instead, they are mutually constitutive spaces that cannot be separated (Grewal & Kaplan, 1994). In other words, the local and global are two interconnected aspects of the same phenomenon. [...]

## Transnational

According to Swarr and Nagar (2010), transnational feminist theory has grown out of two interconnected dialogues in the field of feminist studies: first, it has been employed by those seeking to question globalization and neo-liberalism, and to underscore social justice issues, including the creation of alliances across borders; and second, it has been used in feminist debates about Eurocentrism since the 1980s in feminist theory and writing, especially regarding issues of how stories of Other women's lives (including questions of voice, authority, identity, and representation) cross borders. But the very meaning of the term *transnational* is contested among scholars in the fields of postcolonial, Third World, and international feminisms. Laura Briggs, Gladys McCormick, and J. T. Way (2008) suggest that *transnationalism* is an overused term, taking on very different meanings in multiple disciplines (p. 625). For example, the term *transnational* can indicate migratory processes and capital circulations, or transnational flows of people and goods. The term is sometimes used to signal the

apparent powerlessness of the state to control trade and flows of people across its own borders. The term is also used to describe the world as borderless and interconnected. In fact, in the post-9/11 period especially, borders are very real and worthy of attention. Since passengers on commercial airlines attacked the New York World Trade Center on September 11, 2001, the way in which individuals cross some borders has changed dramatically. Some argue that in contrast to opening, borders are more entrenched and closed to some people than ever, and yet more open to capital. [...] Border crossings, and our varied experiences with crossing borders based on gender, race, class, sexuality, ability, and citizenship status, can tell us how borders continue to matter under globalization. [...] [Despite] its multiple and often conflicting usages, the term [*transnational*] allows its users to challenge the flattening of power relations between states.

The use of the term *transnational*, instead of *international* or *global*, marks some feminist theorists' refusal to valorize inequitable global systems. *International* usually refers to relations *between* nations. *Transnational* does a better job of getting at the social, economic, cultural, and political flows that *transcend* the boundaries of the nation-state (Mann, 2012, p. 356). Karen Booth (1998) suggests that the term *international* denotes Western power systems founded by global inequalities, including the United Nations. As Radika Mongia (2007) argues, the term *international* denotes equality between nations and does not take into account the power differentials between nations. Nor, I would add, can it adequately acknowledge cases where multiple nations (some acknowledged, some unacknowledged) may exist within a single state, as in the case of many Indigenous nations. [...]

For many transnational feminists, the term *transnational* is also a corrective term for the *global* in some feminist studies. According to Naples (2002a), the term *transnational* intertwines the global and the local and pays attention to the interplay between both sites, paying specific attention to how power operates within and between nations, and among and between women. *Global*, on the other hand, has come to represent theorizing and political organizing that assumes natural and inevitable solidarities among women globally. For transnational feminists Grewal and Kaplan, "global feminism has elided the diversity of women's agency in favor of a universalized Western model of women's liberation that celebrates individuality and modernity" (1994, p. 17). In other words, global feminism has come to represent a kind of theorizing and organizing among feminists that presents Western women as more advanced, modern, and liberated than their Third World sisters, and enables them to "save" their sisters from backward, patriarchal, and traditional men. Post-colonial theorist Gayatri Chakravorty Spivak (1988) coined the phrase, "White men saving brown women from brown men" to describe the ways in which Third World women are too often positioned in Western scholarship as agentless and waiting to be rescued. […]

### Terminology Note: *Third World*

The term *Third World* originated during the Cold War, a conflict that occurred between capitalist and communist states after the Second World War. Countries that had been previously colonized by European or North American countries were constructed as a third world in reference to the inequalities between them. Third World countries may have found formal independence from colonial powers during this period, but colonialization left profound disparities in wealth, the capacity to compete in a globalizing economy, the health and life expectancy of populations, and the political status of these nations. The comparable wealth and status of *First World* countries, such as Canada, Great Britain, and the United States, led these types of countries to exercise a great deal of power globally. The *Second World* referred to the Communist countries (Union of Soviet Socialist Republics, Cuba, China, and others), although this term was only meant by implication, as it was with

these countries that the United States and its allies were silently engaged in a major nuclear arms struggle. The term *Fourth World* has also emerged to refer to Indigenous societies that may be geographically and politically located in any of these countries. The term *Third World* has been problematized and also periodically reclaimed. Where *Third World* is used in this chapter, it appears as the language used by scholars under discussion.

To review, while a variety of scholars use the terms *global*, *international*, and *transnational* in many different ways, transnational feminists use the term *transnational* because they find it useful for feminist theorizing and organizing across and against borders, and for understanding globalization. Importantly, transnational feminist theorists continually reflect on the term *transnational* itself, especially its usage, and what it communicates.

## GLOBAL FEMINISM AND TRANSNATIONAL FEMINISM: KNOWING THE DIFFERENCE

Transnational feminism is often conceptualized as an alternative to global feminism, and has come to dominate Western feminist interventions into issues related to globalization. In 1984, Robin Morgan published *Sisterhood Is Global: The International Women's Movement Anthology*. Morgan envisioned a global sisterhood as a network of women from around the world, working together to address women's issues. While this text is not representative of all global feminist theorizing, and Morgan is not the only scholar I might cite here, this book demonstrates the most problematic aspects of global feminism that transnational feminists aim to address. In the text, Morgan suggests that because women from many countries around the world contributed to the anthology, it represents the state of women's issues globally. Significantly, each chapter is devoted to women's issues in different countries but there is little analysis of the connections and power differentials between women and countries. The anthology implies that if feminists know more about women's issues nation by nation, they can see that women around the world have connections to one another on the basis of their shared experiences under patriarchy. Learning about experiences of oppression other than your own is clearly a very desirable political goal, but Morgan, as the anthology editor, invited certain women to publish in the text and had control over the publishing of the anthology. A Western feminist, she collected and controlled women's stories for the anthology and provided the language of sisterhood to bring the chapters together, thus allowing it to be framed through a Western lens. This is significant because transnational feminists not only question what stories about Other women are being told, but who has the power to tell these stories.

Transnational feminists are concerned with how stories are told. According to Chandra T. Mohanty (2003), academic curricula—including the very text you are reading—"tell[s] a story—or tells many stories" (p. 238). [...] For example, global feminist scholarship on the body and sexuality, and specifically on what in the West is commonly described as "female genital mutilation," is routinely embedded in what Grewal and Kaplan (2001) call "the binary axis of tradition-modern" (p. 669). In other words, scholarship on this subject habitually produces "traditional" subjects that are agentless in a backward culture in order to establish more "modern" Western subjects. [...]

The difference between global and transnational feminism might be best understood by looking at scholarship and claims for women's rights during the so-called War on Terror. In the aftermath of the attack on the New York World Trade Center, global feminism has been particularly occupied with the "binary axis of traditional-modern" that Grewal and Kaplan (2001) identify. Some Western feminists have concerned themselves with the alleged subordination of women under Islamic laws and governance, focusing specifically on women's bodily autonomy and even more specifically on veiling practices. Using the hijab, burqa, and niqab as a stand-in for nuanced analyses of women's lives, and specifically their religious and cultural practices, some Western feminists claim that "Eastern" women are pawns in a grand patriarchal scheme. Muslim women, especially those who wear the hijab, burqa, and niqab, are used as symbols for the cultural backwardness, social conservatism, and extremism of Islamic fundamentalism of the "East."

Jennifer Fluri (2009) uses the term *corporal modernity* to describe the ways in which the visibility of the female body has become a yardstick to measure a nation's level of modernity or "progress" in the post-9/11 era. She critiques the association of visibility of the female body with power, suggesting instead that lack of cultural and historical context ignores the ways in which the War on Terror has provided a political context for using the body and its coverings or lack thereof as a measure of liberation. In other words, women living in cultures that glorify the uncovering of the body are considered progressive, while those that support the covering of the body are regressive. This is a problematic and oversimplified formula for understanding gendered relations of power and women's agency. Fluri's work can be read as a criticism of global feminism's inattention to geography and history, and the lack of attention paid to the interplay between "home" and "abroad." Fluri and other scholars including Mahmood (2005), Thobani (2007), and Moallem (2005) maintain that what some Western feminists ignore is that the burqa and other veiling practices provide corporeal privacy in public space, and have allowed women to resist public patriarchal structures in their lives. Isolating veiling practices as symbolic of oppression does not accurately trace the cultural and political changes that lead women to wear, or take off, burqas, niqabs, and hijabs. Ignoring contextual analyses and the voices of Muslim women, global feminists have overwhelmingly argued that Muslim women are forced to act against their own human agency, or the innate sense of individual autonomy and desire for freedom against the weight of custom and tradition. Muslim women in this strand of global feminist theorizing are thought of as living with false consciousness or internalized patriarchy, and in need of saving by their liberated Western sisters (Abu-Lughod, 2002; Razack, 2008).

What is also missing from this global feminist discourse is an acknowledgment of the United States' role in women's loss of freedom in Taliban-controlled Afghanistan—a regime they supported during the Soviet occupation of the 1980s. In feminist rescue narratives, no mention is made of the Revolutionary Association of Women of Afghanistan (RAWA) that was established in 1977 and remains active in promoting human rights, health care, education, and democratic and secular rule in Afghanistan (Naples, 2002b, p. 263). Instead, by employing the "traditional-modern binary axis," global feminist scholarship assumes that women are waiting to be saved (Grewal & Kaplan, 2001). [...]

Although the field is too broad to outline extensively here, this chapter turns now to sketch [two] focal issues of transnational feminism: migration [...] and violence against women.

## MIGRATION

The movements of culture, capital, and people under globalization are contradictory and complex. The tension between opening borders for the flows of global capital and culture and the desire of states to protect their borders from immigration is a major concern (Harvey, 2003; Walia, 2013). For transnational feminists, the increasing security measures at borders, especially in the post-9/11 period, is a concern. They argue that there are racist and imperialist dimensions to border security and control of individuals' movements, and a lack of justice-based responses to the effects of globalization (Magnet, 2011; Puar, 2007; Walia, 2013). While border crossings may be increasingly restricted by Western states, globalization simultaneously displaces people from poorer Southern regions due to instability, violence, and poverty. Migration has been and will likely continue to be a survival strategy for many.

"Care work" provides a good example of the ways in which migration is gendered and racialized. Care work is labour that is reproductive in nature, namely childrearing, elder care, and home care. One of the impacts of global economic restructuring has been the movement of women into the global workforce. These movements have resulted in a "crisis of care" that affects women around the world in different ways. In poorer Southern countries, global economic restructuring has pushed women into the workforce, and in the Western world, more women are working than ever before. While this represents increased economic independence for women, household duties have not been redistributed among members. In her foundational work, Arlie Hochschild (1989) found that women in the United States were working, on average, a full extra month above and beyond their productive duties. Calling this phenomenon the "second shift," Hochschild showed that unequal distribution of workload within households falls on women, or their community and family networks. When women are unable to work this "second shift," households seek employees to do this work for them. Families often hire low-paid child-care, home-care, and elder-care workers who are often un-unionized and have very few working rights and protections. Many women, in addition to taking care of their own children, provide child care for other families in their own homes because child care is un- or under-subsidized. Since most child care occurs within private homes, this issue remains a "private" issue and is considered a woman's personal responsibility. In Canada, this idea is reinforced by the fact that the Canada Revenue Agency (2015) provides a meagre universal child care benefit to individual families so they can choose their own child care options, rather than subsidize public child care across the country.

Global economic restructuring in the United States and Canada shapes the transnational migration patterns of women. Welfare state retrenchment in both countries means most families lack an adequate social safety net. In the United States, there is no guarantee of paid maternity or paternity leave, no public child care, and no universal health care system. In Canada, women working in the most precarious, piecemeal labour do not qualify for paid maternity leave, while paternity leave is often less valued, and women spend upwards of 30% of their annual income on publically available child care due to the lack of subsidized child care nationally (with the exception of the province of Quebec) (Macdonald & Friendly, 2014). Under increasing pressure from work and household-related needs, middle-class families have the option of hiring migrant workers to care for their children, especially relatively inexpensive live-in caregivers provided through the Canadian government's Live-in Caregiver Program (Citizenship and Immigration Canada, 2014).

Some families in economies like those of Canada and the United States find that public child care is too expensive, and they can only afford to hire private caregivers as long as they are inexpensive. Less privileged women from the poorer Southern nations are called on to fill this gap. Migration, according to Marchand and Runyan (2011), is "fashioned as the solution to child-care, eldercare, and healthcare crises in the North and un- and under- employment in the South" (p. 14). Ehrenreich and Hochschild (2003) use the phrase "global care chain" to denote the migration of women from poor, developing countries to developed ones as maids and nannies. Many countries, due to global economic restructuring and national debts, depend on remittances as a way to further develop their own economies (Rodriquez, 2008). Remittances are monetary transfers from foreign workers to their home country. For example, the Philippine state relies on the export of labour through national migration apparatuses. As Rodriquez (2008) suggests, "brokering workers" in this way ensures remittances; women who leave

poorer countries for richer ones, as caregivers, send money home to their families, especially to their own children and to bolster their nation's economy. However, this leaves a major care gap in their home nations and households.

As I alluded to, the global care chain is not an informal network of gendered and racialized labour. Rather, governments in the West are responding to the known crisis of care by investing in transnational recruitment of women as maids and nannies. Ehrenreich and Hochschild (2003) call this the "female underside of globalization," where women in poorer countries migrate to do what is considered women's work in richer countries. The state is involved in this aspect of migration as governments, such as in the Philippines, for example, train women for "women's work" outside of the country, which includes training to conform to norms of gender and sexuality (Rodriquez, 2008). While care work is available transnationally, poorer nations must promote and market their women as the best in the field, and often the cheapest, to compete on a global scale. For Ehrenreich and Hochschild (2003), the international division of labour is about more than reproductive labour such as caring for infants and children. In fact, they claim that *feelings* are "distributive resources" (p. 23). In other words, migrant domestic workers also engage in emotional labour. Similar to women workers in export processing zones who are expected to perform a "docile and dexterous" femininity along the global assembly line, nannies and maids are expected to perform femininity by nurturing and acting lovingly.

*****

## VIOLENCE AGAINST WOMEN

Another issue that is often covered by transnational feminist research is violence against women. [...]

In 2006, the UN Secretary-General launched an in-depth study on violence against women. According to the corresponding UN campaign entitled UNITE, violence against women is a universally unjustifiable crime that exists in every corner of the world. UNITE maintains that persistent discrimination against women lies at the root of the issue, and violence against women is unconfined to any culture, region, or country (UNITE, 2012). This in-depth study revealed that up to 70% of women globally experience violence in their lifetime. In Canada, a study of adolescents ages 15 to 19 found that 54% of girls had experienced "sexual coercion in a dating relationship" (UNITE, 2012). The United Nations includes forced marriages, human trafficking, dowry murders, and honour killings in its report on global violence against women. It also includes issues of violence against women in war and conflict situations. The United Nations reports that in the Democratic Republic of Congo, over 200,000 women have suffered from sexual violence during conflict. In Rwanda, between 250,000 and 500,000 women were raped during the 1994 genocide (UNITE, 2012).

## Globalization and Violence against Women

As noted at the outset of this chapter, globalization has meant an increase in women's paid employment in a range of sectors, including in the informal sector and in export manufacturing. Export processing zones (EPZ) are contradictory sites for women. While they may provide women with income, and perhaps more economic autonomy within the household, they are connected to violence against women in complicated ways. One of the most well-known EPZs is the *maquiladoras* of the borderlands between the United States and Mexico. The majority of maquiladora employees are young women. According to scholar Kathleen Staudt (2008), who studies EPZs near Ciudad Juarez, this city and women's work here are situated within a matrix of "femicide" (the killing of women).

The Mexican government's Programa industrial fronterizo (border industrialization program) was established in 1960 to facilitate foreign direct investment and global free trade regimes to be globally competitive and to develop. In 1994, Canada and

the United States solidified the North American Free Trade Agreement (NAFTA) with Mexico. One of many results of these two major trade programs is the growth of Ciudad Juarez, which has become home to hundreds of factories employing more than 200,000 workers, over half of them women (Staudt, 2008, p. 7). Although profitable for factory owners and investors, feminists have argued that the workers experience structural violence at the hands of "a global economy that has shrunk the real value of earnings in the export-processing economic development model that dominates in Juarez" (Staudt, 2008, pp. 7–8). Although there are more jobs in the city, they have come at a high price. On top of inadequate shelter, food, and wages, the fact that over 370 women have been murdered since 1993 within and around the EPZ has inflicted terror on the population (Staudt, 2008, p. x). While families of those missing, raped, and/or murdered in Juarez have rallied for justice, there has been little response nationally or internationally by governments, global institutions, or the development community. Serial killers and drug cartels are popular explanations among some scholars, and yet, violence within the home has simultaneously become commonplace. This suggests feminists should broaden their understanding of the systemic causes of violence in a community where gender conflicts have been sparked by changing patterns of labour for meager wages—all of which is couched in the heavily increased security of the United States and Mexican borders (Staudt, 2008, p. 143).

Since transnational feminists are interested in understanding the negative effects of global economic restructuring on women, they pay attention to the manifestations of violence. In particular, the example of violence in Ciudad Juarez connects the local and global since the violence experienced in the site is not one or the other, but rather connected to local manifestations of patriarchy, as well as transnational economic and political forces that are also deeply invested in maintaining these interlocking systems of oppression.

## Representing Violence against Women

Given the pervasiveness of gender violence globally, violence against women is a crucial issue for feminists. Still, feminist scholars commonly misrepresent violence against Other women in problematic ways (Narayan, 1997). Uma Narayan, a self-identified Third World feminist, has made foundational contributions to transnational feminism. Using the concept of "border crossing," Narayan suggests that information about dowry murders in India is shaped, distorted, and decontextualized when it crosses borders. The practice of dowry (transferring parental property to a daughter at the time of her marriage), and the violence associated with dowry (the abuse by husbands and in-laws related to this property exchange), is both complicated and changing, and yet, it is represented in Western contexts as a traditional and static practice that occurs regardless of class and caste. Narayan argues that only certain kinds of information about dowry and dowry-related violence is passed through a filter when it crosses borders, producing simple, quick facts and media-friendly sound bites. There is little coverage of violence against women in India in North American media, and dowry-related violence is rarely framed in terms of the general issue of domestic violence. This means that stories of dowry murder tend to cross borders with more frequency and currency than more complicated and nuanced reports of violence against women.

Narayan maintains that while dowry is a social, economic, political, religious, and cultural practice that varies over time and space, a "cultural explanation" is most often given when women experience violence related to this exchange (Narayan, 1997, p. 101). Western media's focus on widow/wife burning, and even on the dowry itself—a relatively lesser-known or misunderstood practice—as "alien," codes the practice as "Indian," and therefore Other. For Narayan, phenomena that seem "different," "alien," and "Other" cross borders with more regularity than do problems that seem to also affect so-called Western women. Unlike dating violence or domestic abuse, for example, dowry murders are misrepresented as foreign and unlike anything "at home" (Narayan, 1997, p. 102).

In Canada, popular discourse does not often represent violence against women as a cultural issue, even though the issue is systemic. According to Statistics Canada (1993), half of all women in Canada have experienced at least one incident of physical or sexual violence. In Canada, approximately 1200 Indigenous women have been murdered or gone missing since 1999, and over 200 of these cases remain unsolved (RCMP, 2014). With the exception of Indigenous communities and anti-violence advocates, popular discourse has not framed the violence as an issue of Canadian culture. While systemic in nature and related to gender and racial inequality, media reports of violence against women use individualized explanations related to mental health, stress, alcohol and drug abuse, or provocation. While these explanations are problematic in their own right and are complicated by feminist theorizing on the issue, it is important to contrast this framing of the issue in Canada with "cultural explanations" offered in regard to violence against Indian women. [...]

## ACTIVISM AND SOLIDARITY

Transnational feminists examine the negative effects of globalization on women's lives while also taking account of women's resistances. While recognizing the limitations of resistances, transnational feminists explore the possibilities of generating transformative change through solidarity activism. Transnational feminists, as they seek solidarity practices, are particularly critical of global feminism's assumption that women are natural or inevitable sisters in struggle. Much transnational feminist literature considers how to collaborate and resist structures of oppression globally, while also recognizing the differences among women. Feminist scholarship on globalization has too often focused on global economic, social, and political change without taking into account the way in which women's daily lives are shaped by globalization—outside of women's labour force participation and the feminization of poverty in the Third World. Through providing various case studies of women organizing against local, national, and transnational forces, transnational feminist scholars aim to demonstrate the power of women's activism and the potential of transnational feminist practices, without romanticizing grassroots resistance. Transnational feminist scholars, including Grewal and Kaplan (1994), use transnational feminism both as a theoretical and activist framework that aims to avoid "the old sisterhood model of intervention and salvation that is clearly tied to older models of center-periphery relations" (p. 19). Yet, "old sisterhood models" continue to shape mobilizations of feminists globally, especially in response to violence against women as I offer in the final discussion.

## SAVING OTHER WOMEN

In 2012, a 23-year-old female paramedic was gang raped by six men in a moving bus in South Delhi. She died in a Singapore hospital two weeks later (*Times of India*, 2014). The gang rape received widespread coverage by international media; so much, in fact, that the phrase "the Indian gang rape" became a shorthand descriptor for the event. Importantly, this violent crime provoked discussion among anti-violence advocates and feminist scholars about how to intervene in a so-called culture of rape in India.

As feminist author and activist Jaclyn Friedman argued on TVO's current affairs program *The Agenda with Steve Paikin* (TVO, 2013), while individuals talk about *rape culture* in North America, popular discourse does not often include the phrase *culture of rape*, and yet, this is the phrase circulated about India in light of the gang rape in 2012. These two terms are distinctive, and the difference is telling.

When feminists speak and write about rape culture, they often refer to the ways in which sexual violence against women is explicitly and tacitly accepted in Western culture. This may include representations of violence in movies, jokes, and even colloquial ways of speaking (e.g., "I just raped that exam"). When feminists and others speak and write about "cultures of rape," as they did in the case of India following the 2012 gang rape, anti-violence advocates drew on stereotypes of Indian culture as inherently hyper-violent, misogynist, backward, and traditional. As in the discussion of dowry murder from earlier in this chapter, the 2012 gang rape that happened on a bus in South Delhi was given a cultural explanation.

In practice, cultural explanations of sexual or domestic violence do not allow for women to build solidarities transnationally. In the case of "the Indian gang rape" as it is ubiquitously known, a cultural explanation disallowed for connections to be made between North American and Indian women, in particular, about the different manifestations of gendered violence at a local level. As Mohanty (2003) articulates, solidarities among and between women require the mapping of power and difference, and an exploration of common interests. When "the Indian gang rape" was described as a cultural issue, many feminists in North America positioned themselves as saviours.

One of the most explicit examples of Western feminist attempts to "save their global sisters" comes from the Harvard College Women's Center when it announced a policy task force entitled "Beyond Gender Equality" just following the highly publicized rape and murder in South Delhi. The Harvardites presumed a stance of superior knowledge and, implicitly, culture, as they offered "recommendations to India and other South Asian countries." Understandably angered by the assumption that Indian feminists needed North American expertise, the following letter was written to the Harvard task force and published online on the blog *Kafila* by Nivedita Menon (2013):

## Letter from Indian Feminists VRINDA GROVER, MARY E. JOHN, KAVITA PANJABI, SHILPA PHADKE, SHWETA VACHANI, URVASHI BUTALIA and others, to their siblings at Harvard

We're a group of Indian feminists and we are delighted to learn that the Harvard community—without doubt one of the most learned in the world—has seen fit to set up a Policy Task Force entitled 'Beyond Gender Equality' and that you are preparing to offer recommendations to India (and other South Asian countries) in the wake of the New Delhi gang rape and murder. Not since the days of Katherine Mayo have American women—and American feminists—felt such concern for their less privileged Third World sisters. Mayo's concern, at that time, was to ensure that the Indian State (then the colonial State) did not leave Indian women in the lurch, at the mercy of their men, and that it retained power and the rule of the just. Yours, we see, is to work towards ensuring that steps are put in place that can help the Indian State in its implementation of the recommendations of the Justice Verma Committee, a responsibility the Indian State must take up. This is clearly something that we, Indian feminists and activists who have been involved in the women's movement here for several decades, are incapable of doing, and it was with a sense of overwhelming relief that we read of your intention to step into this breach.

You might be pleased to know that one of us, a lawyer who led the initiative to put pressure on the Justice Verma Committee to have a public hearing with women's groups, even said in relief, when she heard of your plans, that she would now go on holiday and take a plane ride to see the Everest. Indeed, we are all relieved, for now we know that our efforts will not have been in vain: the oral evidence provided by 82 activists and organizations to the Justice Verma Committee—and which we believe substantially contributed to the framing of their report—will now be in safe American hands!

Perhaps you are aware that the Indian State has put in place an Ordinance on Sexual Assault that ignores many recommendations of the Justice Verma Committee? If not, we would be pleased to furnish you a copy of the Ordinance, as well as a chart prepared by us, which details which recommendations have been accepted and which not. This may be useful in your efforts to advise our government. One of the greatest things about sisterhood is that it is so global, feminism has built such strong international connections—such that whenever our first world sisters see that we are incapable of dealing with problems in our countries, they immediately step in to help us out and provide us with much needed guidance and support. We are truly grateful for this.

Perhaps you will allow us to repay the favour, and next time President Obama wants to put in place legislation to do with abortion, or the Equal Rights Amendment, we can step in and help and, from our small bit of experience in these fields, recommend what the United States can do.

Vrinda Grover (mere lawyer)
Mary E. John, Senior Fellow, Centre for Women's Development Studies, New Delhi
Kavita Panjabi, Professor of Comparative Literature, Jadavpur University, Kolkata
Shilpa Phadke, Assistant Professor, School of Media and Cultural Studies, Tata Institute of Social Sciences, Mubmai
Shweta Vachani, Senior Editor, Zubaan
Urvashi Butalia, Director, Zubaan
And many others.

**Source:** Menon, Nivedita. (2013). "Dear sisters (and brothers?) at Harvard." *Kafila*. Retrieved from https://kafila.online/2013/02/20/dear-sisters-and-brothers-at-harvard/.

[…] What this case demonstrates is how global solidarity cannot be assumed. Instead, global solidarity must be built through negotiations of power and difference across borders. It should go without saying that Third World women, to use Mohanty's (2003) term, are not waiting to be saved.

\*\*\*\*\*

## CONCLUSION

Transnational feminist theories aim to repair the failures and shortcomings of global feminism […]. Western feminism has too often homogenized all Third World women as an uncivilized Other, in need of empowerment and saving. For transnational feminists, representing women's issues within ongoing global economic restructuring, attending to the nuanced facets of women's lives, is necessary for cross-border coalitions. While global feminism tends to assume that women are natural and inevitable sisters in struggle against a universal form of patriarchy, transnational feminism uses a framework of analysis that emphasizes power and differences among women within the context of shifting global power relations, in addition to paying attention to gender inequalities within localities.

This chapter has outlined some of the major concerns for transnational feminists including the concept of globalization and flows of culture and capital; the mutually constitutive relationship, or the interplay, between the local and the global; […] collaborating across borders in research practices; migration and the international division of care labour; violence against women; and women's organizing. It is important to remember that transnational feminism is not a homogenous subfield of feminist theory with shared values, meaning, ideas, and languages (Swarr & Nagar, 2010, p. 3). Instead, transnational feminism is a diverse field of study in which theorists have intervened in a variety of questions pertaining to global women's issues. It is a field of inquiry into globalization and its effects, with no single, coherent position or strategy. As scholars remain reflexive and the flow of goods and cultures shift and transform, the field shifts and changes. As global economic restructuring continues to alter transnational systems of oppression, new opportunities for solidarity open up. Transnational feminists concerned with solidarity at the global level will continue to reframe their analyses of the world and women's place within it.

## NOTE

1.  A third example, the representation of global women's issues, was included in the original essay, but has been deleted here due to space considerations.

## REFERENCES

Abu-Lughod, L. (2002). Do Muslim women really need saving? Anthropological reflections on cultural relativism and its others. *American Anthropologist 104*(3), 783–790.

Booth, K. M. (1998). National mother, global whore, and transnational femocrats: The politics of AIDS and the construction of women at the World Health Organization. *Feminist Studies 24*(1), 115–139.

Briggs, L., McCormick, G., & Way, J. T. (2008). Transnationalism: A category of analysis. *American Quarterly 60*(3), 625–648.

Canada Revenue Agency. (2015). Universal child care benefit (UCCB). Retrieved from www.cra-arc.gc.ca/bnfts/uccb-puge/menu-eng.html (link no longer active)

Citizenship and Immigration Canada. (2014). Live-in Caregiver Program. Retrieved from www.cic.gc.ca/ENGLISH/work/caregiver/index.asp

Desai, M. (2002). Transnational solidarity: Women's agency, structural adjustment, and globalization. In N. Naples & M. Desai (Eds.), *Women's activism and globalization: Linking local struggles and transnational politics* (pp. 14–31). New York, NY: Routledge.

Ehrenreich, B., & Hochschild, A. R. (2003). *Global economy of care: Nannies, maids, and sex workers in the new economy.* London, UK: Sage Publications.

Fluri, J. (2009). The beautiful 'other': A critical examination of 'western' representations of Afghan feminine corporeal modernity. *Gender, Place and Culture 16*(3), 241–257.

Grewal, I. (2005). *Transnational America: Feminisms, diasporas, neoliberalisms.* Durham, NC: Duke University Press.

Grewal, I., & Kaplan, C. (Eds.). (1994). *Scattered hegemonies: Postmodernity and transnational feminist practices.* Minneapolis, MN: University of Minnesota Press.

Grewal, I., & Kaplan C. (2001). Global identities: Theorizing transnational studies of sexuality. *GLQ: A Journal of Lesbian and Gay Studies 7*(4), 663–679.

Harvey, D. (2003). *The new imperialism.* Oxford, UK: Oxford University Press.

Hochschild, A. R. (1989). *The second shift: Working parents and the revolution at home.* New York, NY: Viking Press.

Loomba, A. (2005). *Colonialism/postcolonialism* (2nd ed.). London, UK; New York, NY: Routledge.

Macdonald, D., & Friendly, M. (2014). The parent trap: Childcare fees in Canada's big cities. Centre for Policy Alternatives. Retrieved from www.policyalternatives.ca/sites/default/files/uploads/publications/National%20Office/2014/11/Parent_Trap.pdf

Magnet, S. A. (2011). *When biometrics fail: Gender, race and the technology of identity.* Durham, NC: Duke University Press.

Mahmood, S. (2005). *The politics of piety: Islamic revival and the feminist subject.* Princeton, NJ: Princeton University Press.

Mann, S. A. (2012). *Doing feminist theory: From modernity to postmodernity.* Oxford, UK: Oxford University Press.

Marchand, M., & Runyan, A. (Eds.). (2011). *Gender and global restructuring: Sightings, sites and resistances* (2nd ed.). New York, NY: Routledge.

Menon, N. (2013). Dear sisters (and brothers?) at Harvard. *Kafila.* Retrieved from https://kafila.online/2013/02/20/dear-sisters-and-brothers-at-harvard/

Moallem, M. (2005). *Between warrior brother and veiled sister: Islamic fundamentalism and the politics of patriarchy in Iran.* Berkley, CA: University of California Press.

Mohanty, C. T. (2003). *Feminism without borders: Decolonizing theory, practicing solidarity.* Durham, NC: Duke University Press.

Mongia, R. (2007). Historicizing state sovereignty: Inequality and the form of equivalence. *Comparative Studies in Society and History 49*(2), 384–411.

Morgan, R. (Ed.). (1984). *Sisterhood is global: The international women's movement anthology.* New York, NY: Anchor Press/Doubleday.

Naples, N. (2002a). Changing the terms: Community activism, globalization, and the dilemmas of transnational feminist praxis. In N. Naples & M. Desai (Eds.), *Women's activism and globalization: Linking local struggles and transnational politics* (pp. 3–14). New York, NY: Routledge.

Naples, N. (2002b). The challenges and possibilities of transnational feminist praxis. In N. Naples & M. Desai (Eds.), *Women's activism and globalization: Linking local struggles and transnational politics* (pp. 267–282). New York, NY: Routledge.

Narayan, U. (1997). *Dislocating cultures: Identities, traditions, and third world feminism.* New York, NY: Routledge.

Puar, J. (2007). *Terrorist assemblages: Homonationalism in queer times.* Durham, NC; London, UK: Duke University Press.

Razack, S. (2008). *Casting out: The eviction of Muslims from western law and politics.* Toronto, ON: University of Toronto Press.

Rodriquez, R. M. (2008). "The labor brokerage state and the globalization of Filipina care workers." *Signs: Journal of Women in Culture and Society 33*(4): 794–800.

Royal Canadian Mounted Police (RCMP). (2014). Missing and murdered aboriginal women: A national operational overview. Retrieved from http://www.rcmp-grc.gc.ca/pubs/mmaw-faapd-eng.pdf (link no longer active)

Spivak, G. C. (1988). Can the subaltern speak? In C. Nelson & L. Grossberg (Eds.), *Marxism and interpretation of culture* (pp. 271–313). Chicago, IL: University of Illinois Press.

Statistics Canada. (1993). The violence against women survey. Retrieved from www23.statcan.gc.ca/imdb/p2SV.pl?Function=getSurvey&SDDS=3896&lang=en&db=imdb&adm=8&dis=2

Staudt, K. (2008). *Violence and activism at the border: Gender, fear, and everyday life in Ciudad Jaurez.* Austin, TX: University of Texas Press.

Swarr, A. L., & Nagar, R. (2010). *Critical transnational feminist praxis.* New York, NY: SUNY Press.

Thobani, S. (2007). White wars: Western feminisms and the 'War on Terror.' *Feminist Theory 8*(2), 169–185.

Times of India. 2014. SC stays death penalty of 2 in Nirbhaya case. Retrieved from http://timesofindia.indiatimes.com/india/SC-stays-death-penalty-of-2-in-Nirbhaya-case/articleshow/38398073.cms

TVO. The Agenda with Steve Paikin. (2013, January 8). Jaclyn Friedman: A culture of rape? Retrieved from https://tvo.org/video/programs/the-agenda-with-steve-paikin/jaclyn-friedman-a-culture-of-rape

United Nations. (2012). UNITE to end violence against women. Retrieved from http://endviolence.un.org/

UN Women. (2014). Facts and figures: Ending violence against women. United Nations Entity for Gender Equality and the Empowerment of Women. Retrieved from www.unwomen.org/en/what-we-do/ending-violence-against-women/facts-and-figures

Walia, H. (2013). *Undoing border imperialism.* Oakland, CA: AK Press/Institute for Anarchist Studies.

*Source:* Mason, Corinne L. (2016). Excerpted from "Transnational Feminism." In Nancy Mandell & Jennifer Johnson (Eds.), *Feminist Issues: Race, Class, and Sexuality, 6th Edition* (pp. 62–73, 77–89). Toronto, ON: Pearson.

# CHAPTER 78

## Defying, Producing, and Overlooking Stereotypes? The Complexities of Mobilizing "Grandmotherhood" as Political Strategy

*May Chazan and Stephanie Kittmer*

May Chazan is an assistant professor in the Gender and Women's Studies Department and Canada Research Chair in Gender and Feminist Studies at Trent University in Peterborough, Ontario. With longstanding interests in gender, aging, and intergenerational solidarities, Chazan is working on a five-year study looking at why and how older women across North America are mobilizing and building alliances around crucial social issues, including climate justice, violence against Indigenous women, and global health inequalities. She is the author of *The Grandmothers' Movement: Solidarity and Survival in the Time of AIDS*.

Stephanie Kittmer holds a Master's degree in political economy from Carleton University in Ottawa, Ontario. Her research interests include social and local food movements, Indigenous studies and environmental conflict, and the political ecology of natural resources in Canada. She is currently working with the Ottawa Farmers' Market Association.

## INTRODUCTION

In March 2006, the Stephen Lewis Foundation (SLF), a Canadian organization dedicated to supporting community-based AIDS groups in sub-Saharan Africa, launched a new campaign with three central goals: (a) to raise awareness about the impacts of HIV/AIDS on African grandmothers who have lost their children and are left to raise their grandchildren; (b) to build solidarity among African and Canadian grandmothers; and (c) to support, through fundraising, groups of grandmothers in Africa (see www.grandmotherscampaign.org). In its first four years, from 2006 to 2010, this Grandmothers to Grandmothers Campaign (hereafter referred to as the Grandmothers' Campaign) exceeded all expectations. It mobilized some 10,000 Canadian women and an estimated three times as many women from across sub-Saharan Africa, linking them in a sophisticated transnational network. It raised over $9 million and organized a highly acclaimed national committee dedicated to advocacy. With hundreds of affiliated "grandmothers' groups" operating across Canada, this Campaign also made older women's mobilizations visible to the Canadian public.

This mobilization was not the first such phenomenon, however, to reveal the power of older women in Canada; rather, "granny activists" have been an integral part of Canadian (and North American) social justice and peace movements for the past quarter-century. Indeed, in 1987, a small group of older women gathered in Victoria, BC, Canada, to protest the arrival of ships that were carrying nuclear armaments through the Victoria Harbour. Calling themselves the "Raging Grannies," these women emerged as unexpected peace activists, using satire and outrageous "granny" outfits to draw attention to both their presence and their age (Acker & Brightwell, 2004; Roy, 2004). Since then, more than 70 Raging Grannies groups have formed across North America, most focusing on localized social and environmental justice issues.

As one of the most longstanding and well-known examples of older women's activism in North America, the Raging Grannies have received considerable attention from scholars seeking to move beyond research on the challenges associated with aging, to instead illuminate the potential contributions of older women in working for social change (see Grenier & Hanley 2007; Hutchinson & Wexler, 2007; Kutz-Flamenbaum, 2007; Narushima, 2004; Pedersen, 2010; Roy, 2004, 2007; Sawchuk, 2009 […]; among others). Collectively, these analyses shed light on the tactics and motivations of "granny" activists, the health benefits of political engagement in later life, and the specific ways in which older people deploy and resist stereotypes, particularly stereotypes of "frailty." Yet, studies on older women's mobilizations and activism remain limited; indeed, there is a distinct gap in scholarship on networks and initiatives beyond the Raging Grannies […]. Moreover, there remains little by way of critical feminist analysis within this

research. Scholars thus repeatedly call for more, more nuanced, and different kinds of investigations into older women's mobilizations.

This chapter heeds these calls. Drawing on insights from critical and feminist social mobilization studies, we examine the Grandmothers' Campaign as a powerful, new example of "granny" mobilization—one that has yet received only extremely limited scholarly attention (Chazan, 2015). Based on research undertaken with the Grandmothers' Campaign in its first 4 years of operation, our analysis pivots around three central questions: (a) what was being mobilized in this campaign between 2006 and 2010?; (b) how was this mobilization taking place and for what purposes?; and (c) what was being produced, consolidated, or challenged as a result?

Through this exploration, we suggest that, like the Raging Grannies, the Canadian Grandmothers' Campaign mobilized not only people and resources but also the discourse of "grandmotherhood": while not all members were biological grandmothers, by naming themselves as such, they deployed "grandmotherhood" as discourse, symbol, and identity. We also reveal the variety of ways members drew strategically—often in fractured, fluid, and contradictory ways—on this discourse on "grandmotherhood" in order to, among other reasons, position themselves with the moral legitimacy to work for a more-just future. Finally, we suggest that, through their collective actions and the discourses upon which they draw, these "grandmothers" were working to both challenge narratives of disengagement and marginality and, inadvertently, reinforce essentialist North American-centric assumptions about grandmotherhood.[1]

*****

The research upon which this chapter draws was carried out with members of the Grandmothers' Campaign and staff from the SLF; it also involved participating in and tracking the development of the Campaign's first 4 years. […] Conducted in three overlapping phases, the research was comprised collectively of a survey, interviews, archival research, and participant observation.

[...] When the Campaign was launched in March 2006, it was comprised of six disparate "grandmothers' groups." The watershed moment in its mobilization then came in August that year, when the SLF hosted a Grandmothers' Gathering in Toronto, bringing together 300 "grandmothers" from Canada and sub-Saharan Africa for three days, alongside an International AIDS Conference. Following this event, which was widely broadcast on Canadian and international media, the Campaign ballooned: over 100 Canadian groups formed in the two months following the Gathering, organizing into as a loose network coordinated by the SLF. Most Campaign members were in their mid-60s, retired or semi-retired, White, university-educated women; many had previous experience with social justice advocacy and some connection to the North American feminist and peace movements of the 1960s and 1970s. Many, though not all, were grandmothers, usually to very young grandchildren. [...]

## FINDINGS: UNDERSTANDING THE GRANDMOTHERS' CAMPAIGN

### What Was Being Mobilized in the Campaign's First Four Years?

Understanding what was being mobilized in the early years of the Grandmothers' Campaign requires a closer look at some of the Campaign's key events, pivotal texts, and central messages. What becomes evident is that, not only did this Campaign function to mobilize people and funds, but it did so by deploying (and redeploying) "grandmotherhood" as a powerful and emotive discourse (in line with analyses offered elsewhere by, for example, Hilhorst, 2003). Given its role as coordinator, the SLF has played a central role in shaping its discourses and goals. Two texts were particularly instrumental in this regard:

Stephen Lewis's 2005 Massey Lectures and the SLF's 2006 Toronto Statement.

In 2005, Lewis, the former United Nations Special Envoy for HIV/AIDS in Africa and well-known social democratic leader in Canada, delivered the prestigious Canadian Massey Lectures, which were aired nationally by the Canadian Broadcasting Corporation and published in the best-selling book, *Race against time*. In this popular lecture series, he evocatively described his encounters with "Africa's grandmothers" who were, in his view, carrying the heaviest burden of AIDS, as they buried their own children and were left, with little or no support, to care for their grandchildren. As Lewis (2005, pp. 50–51) stated:

> It leads me to want to say a word about grandmothers. They have emerged as the heroes of Africa. The physical ravaging of extended families ... means that grandmothers step in when there's no one else to tread. I wonder if such a situation has ever occurred before in the history of organized society?....
>
> The trauma of the grandmothers equals that of the orphans; in fact, every normal rhythm of life is violated as grandmothers bury their own children and then look after their orphan grandchildren. I remember, vividly, sitting under the trees, outside the Alex/Tara Children's Clinic in Alexandra Township in Johannesburg, with about twenty grandmothers as they told their heartbreaking stories of personal loss, one by one. I could barely imagine how they were functioning; every one of them had made that heart-wrenching trek to the graveyard, many more than once, and yet they spoke with a spunk and resilience that was positively supernatural.

His lectures (and his book) had an enormous impact in Canadian society and among international

HIV/AIDS organizations. In addition to bringing widespread visibility to what, for many, were the invisible impacts of the epidemic on older women, it was in these lectures that "grandmotherhood" was first mobilized within global AIDS response.

In other words, to an audience of many thousands, Lewis (2005) named older African women not as "elderly" or "caregivers," as they had previously been called in the advocacy materials of international organizations (e.g., see HAI, 2003; UNAIDS, 2004; WHO, 1999; World Bank, 2005), but as a group of "grandmothers." In so doing, he transformed them into people to whom international audiences could more easily relate; he produced them as women who were "enduring every conceivable hardship for the sake of their grandchildren," drawing on a universal love and altruism that "all grandmothers" presumably feel for their grandchildren. He also spoke not only of immeasurable tragedy, "wrenching" grief, and the "ravaging" of families, but also of heroism and resilience. By focusing unapologetically on women, he set the "grandmothers" squarely within a feminist agenda, noting the disproportionate caregiving burdens on women and viewing them as agents of change. Following this, the advocacy writings of several international initiatives began to include the language of "grandmothers and AIDS," including, for example, those of HelpAge International and the Global Action on Aging.

Framing the tragedies in southern Africa in emotive and politically charged terms, his intervention also primed the Canadian public for the then-pending Campaign launch. Indeed, when discussing what initially drew them to the Grandmothers' Campaign, almost every one of our participants said she had heard Lewis speak, most often in this lecture series, about the injustices borne by "Africa's grandmothers." Many explained that, when they heard him describe the conditions faced by "grandmothers" across the globe, they felt "no choice" but to do something. [...]

One year later, with the launch of its Campaign and the Toronto Gathering, the SLF remobilized

this same "grandmotherhood" discourse, imbuing it once again with very similar messaging. This was most evident in the Toronto Statement (see http://www.stephenlewisfoundation.org/assets/files/G2G/Toronto_statement.pdf), which was written by a team led by the SLF to reflect the mood and content of the Gathering. Read publicly at the Gathering by one Canadian and one African "grandmother," it mirrored the Massey Lectures and articulated what "grandmother to grandmother solidarity" would mean in the Campaign. An excerpt is as follows:

> As grandmothers from Africa and Canada, we were drawn together in Toronto for three days in August 2006 by our similarities: our deep love and undying devotion to our children and grandchildren; our profound concern about the havoc that HIV/AIDS has inflicted on the continent of Africa, and in particular on its women and its children; and our understanding that we have within us everything needed to surmount seemingly insurmountable obstacles. We are strong, we are determined, we are resourceful, we are creative, we are resilient, and we have the wisdom that comes with age and experience.

From the moment of its reading, this statement became the Campaign's central organizing text. Just as the Massey Lectures primed so many pending Campaign members to engage in this mobilization, the Toronto Statement became their call to action. [...]

## How Was "Grandmotherhood" Mobilized, and for What Purposes?

The Toronto Statement and the Massey Lectures were clearly important for naming older women as "grandmothers" and for mobilizing "grandmotherhood" in the first instance. In seeking to make sense of the shifting, strategic, and politically powerful meanings that have come to be attributed to "grandmother" in this context, the importance of these texts can certainly not be overemphasized. However, by looking at these texts alongside Campaign members' own perspectives, a more nuanced understanding emerges of how, and for what purposes, Canadian Campaign members remobilized these messages and thus redeployed "grandmotherhood."

In June 2010, one Campaign member clearly explained why she felt it was important to be viewed as a "grandmothers'" initiative. Her words reflect many of the findings captured in this research, pointing particularly to the personal and symbolic meanings she associated with "grandmotherhood" and to her strategic use of her "grandmother" position:

> Part of it is that we are "the grandmothers," if you know what I mean. You see, I think it helps that we call ourselves "grannies," regardless of whether we actually are. And it helps that we are speaking on behalf of the African "grannies" too. I mean, what politician is going to close the door on their grandmother? Also, we are never going to be treated harshly if we're demonstrating or heckling or anything. Because you don't mistreat a bunch of grandmothers. It's, I guess, it's the symbol of what a grandmother is: gentle but firm, someone who speaks with integrity and wisdom, someone you don't cross, someone who has the best interest of her children and grandchildren and the future generations of children at heart.

These words reveal a number of the ways in which being called "grandmothers" became a political strategy in this Campaign. First, she noted that being called "grandmothers," whether this is biologically the case or not, provides Campaign members with certain protections in activist circles; in line with Grenier and Hanley's (2007) analysis, they strategically used the stereotype of older women as innocent

and nonthreatening as a means of gaining access to certain political spaces that might otherwise not be available. Second, she described how "grandmotherhood" was deployed to increase their legitimacy as social justice actors, coupling "grandmotherhood" with wisdom and integrity. Third, she suggested that use of the word *grandmother* also invokes their good intentions—pointing to the ostensibly altruistic qualities of grandmothers in loving and caring for children—and positions them as having a rightful role to play in, and responsibility for, ensuring the well-being of future generations. Indeed many participants felt that their positions as older women, whether biological grandmothers or not, positioned them as "the grandmothers of the world"—a position of social grandmothering—holding them responsible for the future well-being of the world's children.

In addition to increasing their credibility, legitimacy, and power within global AIDS response, "grandmotherhood" has also served as an important basis for solidarity across the movement. [...]

Drawing on perceived universal notions of what it means to be mothers and grandmothers, and the knowledge that comes with the "passage" into grandmotherhood, Campaign members avowed common maternal connections with African "grandmothers." With the love for their grandchildren serving as a point of connection with African women, several Campaign members also reflected on the significance of the emotional and spiritual relations between Canadian and African women. Moreover, drawing on their feminist leanings, some regularly made reference to their "African sisters" as they discussed how their solidarity was based on what they saw as their shared positions as "grandmothers"—specifically by a sense of sameness among them because of their similar roles as grandmothers. They coupled this with their sense of injustice that, unlike themselves, their African counterparts were enduring the burdens of caregiving at a time when they should rightfully be released from such duties. This Campaign member's words are illustrative:

What creates our bond, or our solidarity, is that we are grandmothers, or we know what it means to be grandmothers. These are our sisters. We recognize our similarities—the love, the power, the responsibility vested in us. We simply have no choice but to work to support our sisters so that they might enjoy even a fraction of the less-pressured kind of life we have, and they deserve, at this stage. They should be free now, they should be cared for. They should not have to be caring for little children, especially with so much grief and in such poverty. (December, 2009)

Finally, while "grandmotherhood" has served as a powerfully mobilizing discourse within the Campaign, it is also particularly salient to consider how it has been drawn on not only strategically but also fluidly. As one Campaign member reflected:

In one instance, we are "grandmothers"— loving old ladies who are speaking from the perspective of wanting what is best for the world's children. We are above party politics. We speak with wisdom and truth. But we are not what you would expect entirely either because we aren't knitting, frail things, in our rockers. We're out making a difference in the world. We are movers and shakers. We are a force to be reckoned with. (May, 2010)

In what Bernstein (1997) describes as the "strategic deployment of identity," members of the Campaign maintained the label "grandmother's groups" even when no one in the group was a biological grandmother, making a strategic decision to draw on the instrumental symbolism associated with grandmotherhood. Importantly, women within the Campaign also tended to draw on different meanings associated with grandmotherhood at different times, a testament to the fluid and often inconsistent nature of the discourse. As demonstrated in the previous quote,

members of the Campaign considered themselves loving older women who could, by virtue of their roles as "grandmothers," relate to their African counterparts—in this way, they identified with stereotypes of grandmothers as necessarily loving and altruistic. Yet they refused to be seen as politically impotent or disengaged; they resisted the stereotype of "grannies" who are relegated to knitting needles and rocking chairs. Instead, they positioned themselves as "movers and shakers": professional, active women, making a difference in the world. Thus, they actively deployed "grandmotherhood" in fluid and fractured ways, drawing on it strategically to position themselves and mobilize others.

## What Was Produced or Challenged through These Mobilizations?

We turn now to our third and final question: What was produced as a result of these mobilizations? In asking this, we draw on Butler's (1999) idea that norms can be made or unmade through people's repeated actions. From this perspective, Campaign members' acts of organizing, and their repeated, strategic mobilizations of "grandmotherhood," could presumably function to challenge, destabilize, uphold, or consolidate certain norms. Examining our study findings through this theoretical lens, three central points emerge.

First, as articulated widely by our research participants, and as similarly expressed with respect to the Raging Grannies (Roy, 2004; Sawchuk, 2009), these "grandmothers'" mobilizations challenge certain stereotypes about older women as seemingly disengaged, inactive, and apolitical. As one Campaign member remarked in November 2008:

We are probably not what most people expect when they hear "grandmothers' movement." We're the early boomers; the women who fought for women's lib; the women who juggled raising families and having careers in a male-dominated world. We're educated, we're skilled, and we now have some time on our hands to reengage in a struggle that clearly isn't over yet. And many of us, myself included, have recently become grandmothers. We understand what this passage means and what responsibility it brings. We are continuing our feminist struggle, now resisting age discrimination too.

For many, the Campaign has been a site of continued resistance: a continuation of their longstanding involvement in feminist struggles, now with an expanded understanding of the intersecting oppressions of gender and age. By launching campaigns within their own communities, organizing rallies on Canada's Parliament Hill, presenting at meetings within the United Nations, attending international AIDS conferences, and packing the galleries of the Canadian House of Commons, these "grandmothers" are not only working to improve the lives of older women in sub-Saharan Africa, they are also resisting the continued and intertwined sexist and ageist stereotypes present both at home and abroad. In other words, through the acts of making themselves visible within national and international spaces that have often omitted older women, they are producing "grandmothers" as global social justice actors and as powerful advocates within global AIDS response. We concur with Roy (2004, p. 2), then, that "focusing on stories of women's resistance and agency dispels notions of passivity and quiet acceptance."

Second, through their mobilizations, these women are effectively defying stereotypes of later life as a time of isolation, marginalization, and frailty, and instead producing vibrant, well-networked "grandmother" communities in which members are actively engaged in lifelong learning. [...]

Across the Campaign, members expressed how learning has been integral to the movement, with already well-educated women expanding their knowledge on HIV/AIDS, Africa, and community organizing, among other areas. Many pointed to the sense of community that had developed; with "grandmother's groups" most often assembling as strangers with common interests, these have become important spaces of belonging at a time in life often associated with isolation and marginalization (Grenier & Hanley, 2007).

Third, while these mobilizations clearly dispel a number of dominant images associated with gender and aging, some of the ways in which "grandmotherhood" has been deployed in the Campaign also serve to consolidate certain unfounded narratives. Resonating strongly with Lewis's (2005) Massey Lectures and the SLF's Toronto Statement, many Campaign members described their solidarity with their African counterparts as rooted in a perception of some universal or shared experience, meaning, or passage of being "grandmothers," as discussed in the previous section of the chapter. [...]

These assumptions of sameness—often termed "strategic essentialism" (Spivak, 1995)—were clearly important for framing the Campaign's central concept of "grandmother to grandmother solidarity." At the same time, such assumptions also tend to homogenize experiences and meanings associated with grandmothering, potentially neglecting the multiple and distinct differences among "grandmothers" within this transnational Campaign. It is worth questioning, then, whether the meanings attributed to "grandmotherhood" within the Campaign were based predominantly on 21st-century, North American, middle-class norms (i.e., notions of the nuclear family structure and later life as a time of retirement), and whether the assumed "similarities among grandmothers" reflect the lives and perspectives of the African women involved. It is also worth asking whether this idea of a universal experience of grandmotherhood is necessary for maintaining solidarity or whether a more explicit understanding of social difference alongside well-developed shared goals could be equally potent, particularly when paired with continuing to deploy "grandmotherhood" strategically in order to gain political access and establish legitimacy.

Thus, in probing what was produced, challenged, or consolidated through these women's mobilizations, a complex picture emerges once again of the diverse ways this Campaign operated. Some of the ways in which "grandmotherhood" was deployed served to resist stereotypes about older women—producing "grandmothers" as global social justice actors, community builders, and lifelong learners. In other instances, however, these mobilizations functioned to homogenize what it means to be a "grandmother," depicting present-day, middle-class, North American ideals as a kind of global norm and thus minimizing the existence of, and reasons for, vast differences and inequalities.

## FINAL REFLECTIONS: RESISTING, PRODUCING, OVERLOOKING STEREOTYPES?

[...] Drawing on critical and feminist social mobilization scholarship (e.g., Cooper, 1995; Hilhorst, 2003; Tsing, 2005), what became evident was that the Grandmothers' Campaign effectively mobilized "grandmotherhood" as a discursive category, imbuing this with messages of intergenerational love, commonality among "grandmothers" around the world, power, injustice, and feminist struggle; in so doing, it appealed to Canada's large, politically engaged, aging population. Campaign members then further mobilized "grandmotherhood" as discourse and identity for the purposes of establishing legitimacy, gaining entrance into political spheres, and defining their solidarity. They drew on this language strategically, fluidly, and in fractured ways—at times using stereotypes of older women, at times resisting such grand narratives, and at times possibly even overlooking the implications of their discourses.

The SLF, along with many Campaign members, drew, for instance, on a universal notion of "grandmotherhood" as their basis for solidarity. This raises questions about whether such a strategy normalizes images of "grandmotherhood" according to certain White, middle-class, North American perspectives, thereby "Othering" those whose experiences or perspectives of what it means to be a "grandmother" differ. This analysis speaks to long-standing feminist debates around building solidarities across differences and the potentially deleterious effects of such strategic essentialisms (e.g., Mohanty, 2003; Spivak, 1995; among others). At the same time, adding to the sparse literature on how older women resist ageist and sexist stereotypes (Grenier & Hanley, 2007; Roy, 2004; Sawchuk, 2009; among others), members of the Grandmothers' Campaign also clearly challenged narratives of frailty, disengagement, and marginality. Their mobilizations thus provide new insights into how older women are producing themselves as political subjects at the global level and how they are effectively positioning themselves as community builders, lifelong learners, social justice advocates, and key actors in the global fight against HIV/AIDS.

## NOTE

1. Our analysis focuses explicitly on why, how, and to what effect the *Canadian* dimension of this mobilization was taking place; it is beyond the scope of this chapter to examine the southern African mobilizations or the transnational dynamics associated with this Campaign, although such analyses are available elsewhere (see Chazan 2013, 2015). Within the larger project, which sought to understand why and how older women were mobilizing and linking up in Canada and South Africa, the first author was responsible for designing and conducting the research, while the second author engaged in the Canadian component by transcribing interviews and assisting with a survey analysis.

# REFERENCES

Acker, A., & Brightwell, B. (2004). *Off our rockers and into trouble*. Victoria, BC: Touch Wood Editions.

Bernstein, M. (1997). Celebration and suppression: The strategic uses of identity by the lesbian and gay movement. *American Journal of Sociology, 103*(3), 531–565.

Butler, J. (1999). *Gender trouble: Feminism and the subversion of identity*. New York, NY: Routledge.

Chazan, M. (2013). Everyday mobilisations among grandmothers in South Africa: Survival, support and social change in the era of HIV/AIDS. *Ageing and Society*, November 2013, 1–25.

Chazan, M. (2015). *The grandmothers' movement: Solidarity and survival in the time of AIDS*. Montreal, QC: McGill-Queen's University Press.

Cooper, B. (1995). The politics of difference and women's associations in Niger: Of "prostitutes," the public, and politics. *Signs, 20*(4), 851–882.

Grenier, A., & Hanley, J. (2007). Older women and "frailty": Aged, gendered and embodied resistance. *Current Sociology, 55*(2), 211–228.

HelpAge International (HAI). (2003). *Forgotten families: Older people as carers of orphans and vulnerable children*. Retrieved from http://www.helpage.org/silo/files/forgotten-families-older-people-as-carers-of-orphans-and-vulnerable-children.pdf

Hilhorst, D. (2003). *The real world of NGOs: Discourses, diversity and development*. London, UK: Zed Books.

Hutchinson, S. L., & Wexler, B. (2007). Is "raging" good for health?: Older women's participation in the Raging Grannies. *Health Care for Women International, 28*, 88–118.

Kutz-Flamenbaum, R. (2007). Code Pink, Raging Grannies, and the Missile Dick Chicks: Feminist performance activism in the contemporary anti-war movement. *NWSA Journal, 19*(1), 89–105.

Lewis, S. (2005). *Race against time*. Toronto, ON: House of Anansi Press.

Mohanty, C. T. (2003). *Feminism without borders: Decolonizing theory, practicing solidarity*. Durham, NC: Duke University Press.

Narushima, M. (2004). A gaggle of Raging Grannies: The empowerment of older Canadian women through social activism. *International Journal of Lifelong Education, 25*, 28–42.

Pedersen, J. (2010). The Raging Grannies: Activist grandmothering for peace. *Journal of the Motherhood Initiative, 1*(1), 64–74.

Roy, C. (2004). *The Raging Grannies: Wild hats, cheeky songs, and witty actions for a better world*. Montreal, QC: Black Rose Books.

Roy, C. (2007). When wisdom speaks sparks fly: Raging Grannies perform humor as protest. *WSQ: Women's Studies Quarterly, 35*(3/4), 150–164.

Sawchuk, D. (2009). The Raging Grannies: Defying stereotypes and embracing aging through activism. *Journal of Women and Aging, 21*, 171–185.

Spivak, G. C. (1995). Subaltern studies: Deconstructing historiography. In D. Landry & G. MacLean (Eds.), *The Spivak reader: Selected works of Gayatri Spivak* (pp. 203–236). New York, NY: Routledge.

Tsing, A. (2005). *Friction: An ethnography of global connection*. Princeton, NJ: Princeton University Press.

UNAIDS. (2004). *Report on the global HIV/AIDS epidemic 2002*. Geneva, Switzerland: United Nations.

World Bank. (2005). Ageing and poverty in Africa and the role of social pensions. *Social Safety Nets Primer Notes, 19*. Retrieved from http://www.un.org/esa/socdev/ageing/documents/workshops/Tanzania/agpov0305.pdf

World Health Organization (WHO). (1999). *Impact of AIDS on older people in Africa: Zimbabwe case study*. Geneva, Switzerland: World Health Organization.

**Source:** Chazan, May, & Kittmer, Stephanie. (2016). Excerpted from "Defying, Producing, and Overlooking Stereotypes? The Complexities of Mobilizing 'Grandmotherhood' as Political Strategy?" *Journal of Women & Aging, 28*(4), 297–308.

# CHAPTER 79

## How Young Feminists Are Tackling Climate Justice in 2016

*Maria Alejandra Rodriguez Acha*

Maria Alejandra (Majandra) Rodriguez Acha is an anthropologist, educator, and climate justice activist from Peru. She is co-founder and co-coordinator of TierrActiva Perú, an activist collective and national network that works towards "system change, not climate change," thus seeking to highlight the linkages between all forms of oppression and the climate crisis.

*To the living memory of Berta Cáceres. Courageous woman, environmental defender, feminist, mother and inspiration to many.*

You might ask: feminism and climate change? *Young* feminism for climate *justice*?

Grassroots experiences are steadily shifting our awareness of climate change, from an abstract phenomenon of carbon levels and future impacts to an ever-more tangible, multi-layered issue that is bringing together all kinds of social, environmental and economic struggles.

We are increasingly recognizing and exposing that climate change is not about carbon emissions alone, but about an economic and political system that churns out emissions to keep its cogs turning and its growth unabated. The same system that, despite its capacity for generating financial wealth, has maintained and exacerbated poverty and inequality in its various forms.

## THE JUSTICE/FEMINISM NEXUS

As climate *justice* advocates, we recognize the root causes of the climate crisis: that as we take from the earth to produce and consume, we also take resources, lands and rights from others to enable this process. The changing climate resulting from this exploitative process further increases disparities, as its impacts hit vulnerable populations—who have done the least to contribute to this crisis—the hardest. And among those at the frontlines of climate impacts are the bodies, lives and livelihoods of women around the world—particularly rural and Indigenous women.

Women are half of the world's population, yet it does not surprise that our voices and perspectives continue to be undermined and silenced due to gender-based violence, stifling gender roles, persistently unbalanced political leadership, and continuing economic inequalities between men and women. In the face of climate change, this gendered inequality of rights, resources and power is expressed most glaringly in stark differences in death rates and vulnerability to natural disasters, particularly of women in rural areas and living under poverty thresholds.

As African eco-feminists describe:

> It is Africa's more than 500-million peasant and working-class women that carry the burden of immediate and long-term impacts of both fossil fuels extraction and energy production, and the false solutions to the climate crisis, including corporatized renewable energy. This is because of the patriarchal-capitalist division of labour, our greater responsibility for agricultural production and social reproduction of families and communities, and our structural exclusion from decision-making. (WoMin, 2015)

## THE PARIS AGREEMENT

As feminists for climate justice, we witnessed and denounced how the Paris climate talks (COP21) last December, hailed by media and world leaders as a historic summit and a diplomatic success, failed to adequately address both justice and gender concerns and solutions. Except for two brief mentions of gender regarding capacity-building and adaptation, gender equality, human rights and Indigenous rights are limited to the preamble of the agreement, with unclear binding or operational value—that is, largely decorative. Though gender was mentioned multiple times in earlier drafts thanks to delegate and constituency advocacy, and despite an increased recognition of gender linkages within the UNFCCC [United Nations Framework Convention on Climate Change] over recent years, the Paris agreement [by and large ignores gender]. Even by purely numerical criteria, gender inequality remains a trait of the climate talks, as about one in three delegates is a woman, as is one in ten heads of state.

The agreement further removes us from climate justice by allowing developed countries to shirk their fair shares: despite "efforts pursued" to limit the temperature increase to 1.5 degrees, voluntary pledges put us on a path to a 3 degree warmer world. As commitments are not forced to increase in ambition until 2023, by which time we will have likely met our 1.5 degrees emissions budget, the threat of relying on dangerous and so far non-existent techno-fixes and market schemes is all too real. Furthermore, tangible financial support for most vulnerable countries continues to be a question, as about one fourth of what is needed has been promised, and even less actually delivered—without which effective climate action cannot be taken on.

## FEMINIST ACTIVISM ON CLIMATE BEYOND PARIS

Despite its unjust outcome, COP21 was a space ripe for feminist climate activism, and climate justice movement-building moments. Civil-society organized events such as Feminist Trade Union Day, Indigenous Women's Day and Young Feminist Day, as well as activities held during the UNFCCC official Gender Day, helped bridge diverse constituencies and issues, and strengthen international alliances. Multiple actions, demonstrations and interventions calling for climate justice, fair shares, and gender-just solutions, and focusing on cross-cutting issues such as militarization—a top source of emissions not included in any national mitigation commitments—galvanized groups and caught media attention. The political moment also gave space for the creation of new activist groups, from LGBTI pour le Climat (LGBTI for the Climate) to the Young Feminists for Climate Justice, the latter acting primarily as a safe space for young women activists to share experiences and stories from their struggles and efforts for justice.

For many it is clear that the UNFCCC is an increasingly exhausted and limited arena for change.

Spaces for movement building are, however, multi-fold, and in diversity lies strength. In a post-COP21 context, further consolidating our movements implies the multiple feat of 1) not losing sight of the incremental progress we can still push for within UN-hosted platforms; 2) using what we can of the Paris agreement to hold governments accountable, as just days and weeks after COP21, governments ignored all lip-service done to climate ambition by giving out new oil permits and signing the TPP [Trans-Pacific Partnership]; and 3) at the same time, pushing our narrative and actions much beyond the UNFCCC. The latter implies a "soul-searching" task that we must collectively take on to release our movements from the constraints of diplomacy in an unequal, fossil-fuelled world.

From a climate justice perspective, addressing the root causes of the climate crisis also requires tackling social inequalities and eradicating forms of oppression that movements can also reproduce, including gender inequalities. This includes honoring the fact that the frontlines inhabited by women around the world are not just lines of crisis, but also *frontlines of change*. Local and national fights against fossil-fuel infrastructure, one of the most well-known of which is the successful campaign against the Keystone XL pipeline, are in many lesser-known cases around the world led by women whose bodies and territories are at the frontlines of extraction impacts, even when subject to sexual violence and repression.

As movements, we need to acknowledge these different contexts in which environmental and climate defense takes place, and fight for the protection of women human rights defenders everywhere. The recent murder of Berta Cáceres[1] should not be seen as an isolated incident, but as part of an increasing violence that seeks to suppress the voices of environmental defenders and women, particularly in the global south. Environmental and climate activists, volunteers, groups and movements everywhere must recognize these inequalities, stand up firmly against violence and demand justice for those at the frontlines.

To join and support these struggles, an important step is to transcend the narrative of woman as victim. In addition, we must be wary of essentialisms that place women and men in so-called "natural" categories and roles. This means, for example, rejecting attempts to solely task women with "taking care" of climate change, adding to women's "triple burden" of reproductive, productive and community caretaking. Ultimately, we must all take on and share roles and perspectives on care-taking, if we are to face the climate crisis and ensure the survival and wellbeing of our communities.

## A YOUTH MOVEMENT RISING

Young women and young feminists are in many regards leading the way and engaging in increasingly intersectional and gender-aware forms of advocacy. Though socially constructed age barriers both within and outside of movements for justice remain—at times leading to a marginalization of youth insights and concerns—youth groups globally are engaging in critical, transformative activism for climate and environmental justice.

In the coming months, we can strengthen and grow the Young Feminists for Climate Justice network, both through online exchange and collaboration, and in gatherings and forums for advocacy such as the 60th Commission on the Status of Women, the AWID Forum, the Women Deliver Conference, UNFCCC intersessionals, the Allied Media Conference, the IUCN World Conservation Congress and other local, national and international convergence spaces. Making spaces to get together as young women and young feminists to discuss our roles and experiences in climate advocacy, environmental activism and feminist movements is key, as is having platforms and tools to deepen our understandings on the linkages between social and environmental issues. Networks of exchange across borders enrich our local actions, struggles and initiatives.

Let's honor the endurance, commitment and courage of all peoples fighting for their health, livelihoods, environment and communities, and standing up against the climate crisis globally. Let's also acknowledge that there is much left to do, including facing the challenge of weaving increased solidarity and collaboration between environmentalists, feminists and justice advocates, to reconstruct our societies based on justice and respect for all people and our planet.

## NOTE

1. *Editors' Note*: Berta Cáceres, a Honduran Indigenous rights and environmental activist best known for her successful grassroots resistance to the Agua Zarca dam project, was murdered in 2016.

## REFERENCE

WoMin. (2015). "An African Ecofeminist Perspective on the Paris Climate Negotiations." Retrieved from: http://womin.org.za/an-african-ecofeminist-perspective.html.

*Source:* Rodriguez Acha, Maria Alejandra. (2017, March 8). "How Young Feminists Are Tackling Climate Justice in 2016." *HuffPost Blog* (originally published March 7, 2016). Retrieved from: https://www.huffingtonpost.com/maria-alejandra-rodriguez-acha/how-young-feminists-climate-justice_b_9369338.html.

## PUNA KUAKEA

*Joy Enomoto*

Joy Enomoto was born in Inglewood, California, to an African American, Caddo Indian, Punjabi mother from Dallas, Texas, and to a Hawaiian, Japanese, Scottish father from Makawao, Maui. Enomoto's work is concerned with decolonizing geography, plantation genealogies, and the salt water conversations that occur within the space of the diaspora. She explores the idea of creating and holding onto our own cartographies in a world of rising sea levels and the ongoing destruction of the seabed and ancestral homelands.

*Source:* Enomoto, Joy. (2013). "disappearing (Screenprints 30x22)." *Puna Kuakea.* Retrieved from: http://joyenomoto.weebly.com/puna-kuakea.html.

*Puna Kuakea* is a small screen print series reflecting on bleached corals. When corals are stressed by extreme conditions, they expel the algae living in their tissues. This shock to the system is often caused by warming temperatures and pollution. The health of the reef rests in its coral beds. If the corals do not reabsorb the algae in the near term they will die.

# CHAPTER 80

## Feminisms and the Social Media Sphere

*Mehreen Kasana*

Mehreen Kasana covers politics for *Bustle*. She writes on diverse topics including digital media, race, and religion, among others. Her work has been featured in international publications such as *The New York Times, Los Angeles Times, Al Jazeera America, Jadaliyya, BBC, Hazlitt*, and *Guernica* magazine. Previously, Kasana was the Front Page Editor for *The Huffington Post* and staff writer for *The Nation*, Pakistan.

I have maintained a coherent journal of my daily thoughts ever since I was eleven. Before that, there was the notorious "secret diary" that was never as much a secret as it was a source of entertainment for my elders. The diary dealt with what Anaïs Nin called the "immediate present." It involved gathering my immediate thoughts about lived experiences, which revealed the power of reaction that remained in a little girl's sensibilities instead of verbose critical perception. Writing had not been a conversation until I began blogging. There was little to no concern for visibility until, in my late teens, I used social media. After that, writing became hypervisible and often took the form of a clash of opinions between me and my readers. Depending on the context of the posts, it was a curse or a blessing, but more than that, it was a constant dialogue.

By the time I was in my late teens and had moved to the bustling heart of Lahore from a rather small city, I began blogging with no specific purpose in my mind; for me, it was simply to store my thoughts. After several posts, I gained popularity among the Pakistani blogging world for a post that humorously described the sociocultural meanings behind the certain ways Pakistani women don the *dupatta*. Several journalists found it hilarious and my blog was listed as one of the top blogs in *Guernica* magazine's "A Year in Digital Discoveries in 2010" (Khan 2010), in which the categories were "gender," "South Asia," and "Islam."

My history of slowly amassing thousands of readers and followers on social media is imperative for me to mention so that the chronology of my political blogging and the change of tone in my online presence becomes evident. After I established my voice as a Pakistani blogger, a political reality surfaced and became uncomfortably obvious: nonwhite voices, particularly Muslim and female, were treated and received as anthropological projects but rarely as sources of personal musings, in comparison to the kind of treatment white female bloggers received. There was always, and sadly perhaps always will be, a certain kind of Orientalist fascination that brown Muslim bloggers invoked in their global audiences. There was no escaping it.

In addition to the veils-and-harems image seeming to be evoked every single time a Muslim woman, such as myself, blogged, the deep hostility that many Western neoconservatives and even liberals held for Muslim women and their online presence was a source of constant harassment and undeserved animosity. Added to that bitter concoction was the presence of sexist bloggers—the majority of whom are male—who used all sorts of narratives to shut Muslim women bloggers down. In several unfortunate cases of harassment, Muslim women chose to give up their social media presence; but the support they received from their readers showed that they had garnered a network of solidarity and unity—regardless of the profiles of their readers.

For marginalized voices in social media spaces, solidarity becomes essential. With the increasingly dense and confusing landscape of communication spreading throughout the world, various political-activist groups are attempting to gain more access to information as well as more opportunities to engage in public speech. The power of social media, in this context, lies primarily in its support for civil society and social justice. It is through the tools of social media that a group of bloggers, including myself, coordinated our political voices and demands. The diversity of our network was undeniable and politically significant; Arab, South Asian, and African American bloggers and others coordinated their voices and highlighted political and social issues before their own audiences. Regardless of the outcome (or lack of it), these networks still exist and continue to raise voices for each other on a plethora of issues. One can describe this as transnational solidarity in online spaces.

Before further elaborating on the necessity of the counternarratives generated by solidarity in social media, I would like to share the work our group of bloggers and activists rendered online on several issues. The manner in which our network increased, followers sprung up, and voices consolidated our demands is unforgettable and further augmented our belief in transnational political unity in all sorts of media.

## TACKLING SEXISM, RACISM, AND OTHER "ISMS" IN E-SPACES

Just as offline spaces are rampant with sexist men, online venues have their own share of omnipresent sexist male bloggers who have taken it upon themselves to harangue and harass female bloggers on virtually every feminist issue. If the profile of the said female blogger also highlights that she is not white and, in fact, brown and Muslim, male Western sexist bloggers increase their virulent hatred by slinging a list of racist obscenities at those Muslim social media users. In many cases that I have observed and personally experienced, the kind of racism and sexism Muslim female bloggers face online is symptomatic of the post-9/11 discourse on Muslim womanhood; the Muslim woman needs to be either "saved" or "corrected" by Western liberalism. If, through her very own agency, she refuses to rejoice about Western savior liberalism yet also rejects Muslim male sexism, she is caught in a dichotomy of us versus them. This is an issue many female Muslim political bloggers face online. The discourse is uniquely narrow and provides very little space for Muslim women to navigate through and express themselves in.

Because of how depressing and even demoralizing the entire narrative is for Muslim women's agency and empowerment and for how mainstream Western media constructs an image of the perpetually distressed and suffering Muslim woman, young bloggers online from Bangladesh (Juthika Hassan), Pakistan (myself), Afghanistan (Sarah Rahimi), and beyond decided to tackle this racist and sexist imagery with actual photos, videos, and news of Muslim women doing wonderful things. In this attempt, humor was vital; expressing this, the blog that was created after this concept was called *Oppressed Brown Girls Doing Things*. Biting and sharp in its sarcastic tone, *OBGDT* went viral on social media and was featured on Racialicious's "Crush of the Week," where it was described as a blog with a "satiric take(down) of showing that Muslim/South Asian women may not need us Westerners, especially us Western feminists, the way we think we should be needed." Many Western feminists of varying ages and backgrounds joined the network to show support. During the time that I was one of the administrators of *OBGDT*, I had in-depth conversations with liberal feminists on different occasions and was told that the blog managed to create a necessary counternarrative and counterimagery to the conventionally described "oppressed" Muslim woman. Not only did that open their eyes but it also compelled them to take this objection raised by Muslim women bloggers to public spaces, including classrooms and conferences, so that the effect was not limited to blogging.

Another instance of using a brilliantly sardonic tone to counter racism and sexism online with relation to the Arab woman, specifically, and the Middle East and South Asia, in general, is the creation of the blog *Orientalism Is Alive* by Moroccan blogger Samia Errazzouki, joined by Libyan blogger Tasbeeh Herwees and myself, for the Pakistani category of the blog. As Ms. Errazzouki states, the blog is meant to serve "as an archive of the portrayal and coverage of the 'Orient' on mainstream media. The 'Orient' also includes the 'Other.' Let's point and laugh at the elementary analyses, sensationalist headlines, injection of exoticism, and reductionist coverage" (*Orientalism Is Alive*). The blog accrued followers as well as "haters," in Internet parlance, and revealed to those of us managing the posts not only that the image of the Orient elicits racist tropes and xenophobia in even the most self-proclaimed liberal Western circles but also that there is a perverse sexual fascination with the belly-dancing, harem-residing Middle Eastern woman. The blog used satire and sarcasm to tackle those tones and undertones of media of the Middle East and Central and South Asia.

Humor is an effective tool in attacking misguided views and we all used it generously because, in simple terms, there is nothing more energy draining than to constantly delve into a discourse that not only paints you as the Other but also demands that it speak over you and your politics. In this hypervisible yet invisible discourse on the Muslim woman, our voices on social media were perhaps the only discursive devices we had that did not undergo any kind of tailoring or censoring. The conventional narrative on gender and social justice concerning the Muslim woman is such that she is visible to us (her "oppression" and the subsequent need to "save" her) but she is frequently spoken over by her self-appointed saviors. Thus, solidarity with each other was not only natural but also essential in tackling polemical narratives against us.

Beyond the subjects of gender and Islam, social media and solidarity in the case of Palestine is an issue that deserves to be mentioned given how viciously Palestinian bloggers and social media users are attacked online. The unity that I have seen between Palestinian and Pakistani bloggers is something that I experienced most positively. This political support for each other is often described with the example of the friendship between Palestinian literary theorist and intellectual Edward Said and Pakistani antiwar activist and political scientist Eqbal Ahmad. Through this bond, many social media users—whether or not they belonged to the aforementioned nations—raised their voices for hunger strikers in Palestine. Given the absence of support for Palestinian freedom in mainstream media, bloggers from Palestine encouraged their global audience to take the issue on social media so that the plight of these Palestinians would not go unnoticed. [...]

But social media alone cannot carry and implement the entire political process of change. It requires the help of those offline and those with access to academia and other venues where individuals are informed and educated about these issues. As Clay Shirky (2011) notes, "Opinions are first transmitted by the media, and then they get echoed by friends, family members, and colleagues. It is in this second, social step that political opinions are formed. This is the step in which the Internet in general, and social media in particular, can make a difference.

As with the printing press, the Internet spreads not just media consumption but media production as well—it allows people to privately and publicly articulate and debate a welter of conflicting views" (6). The skepticism that arises in the face of social media activism is not entirely off point either; many issues have been manipulated, and even presented without any facts being backed up, for the sake of the elephantine egos of "slacktivists."

This, then, does not mean that activism on social media is all rosy pink. When it comes to liberal savior politics and the act of speaking over an identity, South America, Africa, and Asia are three regions that remain at the receiving ends of constant Western liberal speculation, misguided worry, and wobbly, faux activism. Whether it is Jason Russell's *Kony 2012*, which targeted young college students and other people for falling for a hoax under the pretense of saving Ugandan children from a warlord, or the "gay girl in Damascus," who was not gay or female or even in Damascus but was a white male blogger, Tom MacMaster, in Scotland, social media is rife with individuals capitalizing on social justice causes and faking "controversial" identities for their own selfish purposes. Because of the inevitability of being appropriated and even impersonated, social media provides a golden opportunity for insincere individuals to trivialize the danger and gravity of a political issue.

How does one fix this then? Only through more Indigenous voices on social media can we envisage and execute a network of activism and solidarity. [...]

## IMPERIALIST DISCOURSES ON SEXUAL IDENTITIES IN SOCIAL MEDIA

In 2013, an Avaaz petition was drafted by a young woman in the United Kingdom that stated that the European Union should intervene in Greece to "save the trans people from concentration camps." The petition received 29,449 votes; its target remains 30,000. As people went on to sign, endorsing the demand in good faith to "protect" trans individuals in Greece, Greek bloggers were enraged: they forgot that it was the constant historical interference coming from the European Union that, among other reasons, has brought Greece to where it is today. In *Human Rights and Empire: The Political Philosophy of Cosmopolitanism*, Costas Douzinas (2007) compellingly argues that the discourse on human rights is pervasively neoliberal. As nonprofit organizations, individual states, and multinational companies engage in propaganda-based sensationalism around human rights and the need to "save" minority-status citizens, they create a paradoxical situation in which acts of war are committed in the name of human rights. "Military humanism" is the running theme behind these expressions of misplaced worry and empathy.

Similarly, when a petition on social media went viral to "save the trans" in Pakistan, appealing to the American Congress to "do something," Pakistani social media users were surprised by the description in the petition made by a young American woman. It stated that Pakistani transgender citizens "have no political rights" and are "threatened with death every single day of their lives." The sensationalistic narrative of an imaginary Pakistan where the *khawaja sira* have no political rights and are hunted daily made little sense to Pakistanis living within the country, where Pakistani transgender citizens may not enjoy the best economic conditions, just like other Pakistanis under an increasingly neoliberal economy and capitalist state, but where their political rights remain unquestionable—the Supreme Court of Pakistan itself states that Pakistani transgender citizens deserve equal inheritance and job opportunity rights, among other rights, like any other person in the country. That petition, upon receiving dozens of corrections from Pakistanis, was eventually taken down. [...]

## RECLAIMING THE OTHER BODY

The female body undergoes multiple socializations from a young age. Whether it is socializing at the playground, where boys, from the very get-go, learn territorial ways of asserting their control over their surroundings, or trying to balance self-esteem in front of an aggressively sexualizing and objectifying male gaze-oriented world, the female body learns to adapt in such volatile conditions. While I was growing up as a Pakistani girl in the United States, my racial background was what made me stick out like a sore thumb in my classroom, in PE, and in other social situations. By the time I was in my teens and back in Pakistan, I had already internalized the Eurocentric standards of beauty I had witnessed since I was little. Returning to the motherland only reinforced it; Pakistan is one of the many South Asian countries where skin lightening and bleaching industries make profits on the very bodies of young women and even men who view brown skin as inferior and white skin as a social marker indicating beauty and also success.

How does social media play a role in reclaiming the Otherized body? It may not topple capitalist industries running on racist ideas of beauty yet, and it may not entirely uproot a society's tendency to delineate some bodies as superior to others, but it contains a richness of space and voice for those who wish to reclaim their identities and bodies. The majority expressing that aching desire are men and women from once colonized countries—brown and black bodies. *The Body Narratives* is one blog that curates the experiences of women of color. The three administrators of the blog introduce the reader to this e-symposium as a place where the dismantling of racist aesthetics takes place: "Aesthetics continues to be an essential basis by which we are judged, looked at, and ultimately defined as women. This space is an attempt to curate and document all the ways in which as Women of Colour we navigate, understand and own the embodiment of our narratives and

experiences. At the heart of this journey, we seek to uncover how our bodies belong to ourselves."

This act of reclaiming the female Otherized body is integral to feminism. Social media has provided many women of color the opportunity and space in which to vent their frustrations about how white-washed and suffocating beauty standards are for them. Usually unnoticed issues that still wound our self-perceptions are being taken up in these spaces, issues such as the racism present in fashion industries, the media preference shown for white bodies as opposed to nonwhite bodies in various instances, the alienation one feels as the demonized black or brown Other, how academia is still the ivory tower for brown and black girls, and more. Through our voicing our collective discontent and helplessness, these feminist spaces on social media provide women with the encouragement they definitely need in times of isolation and dejection. Sites like *The Body Narratives* run by brown and black women are not merely rant-ridden blogs but necessary archives of the personal and the political that can be and are used by individuals from similar backgrounds. There is nothing more reassuring than knowing that your experience of discomfiture is not a lone occurrence but is shared by someone else. A reaffirming expression like this one on social media helps in more than one way.

In 2011, I wrote a poem in January, as it was Body Positive Month and the theme for my poem stemmed from childhood experiences of racism I dealt with as a Pakistani girl (Kasana 2011). I dedicated the poem to a little girl, Zahra, in South Africa, who, as her father told me, was going through similar racist rounds in her own classroom. She felt that her brown skin marked her as inferior to other students in class. I had no idea that the poem would elicit such emotion that bloggers from other countries would message to thank me for my little poem. Not only did I receive supportive messages, but also my poem was read in several classrooms in Lahore as well as in Zahra's classroom in South Africa. For me and women like me, as well as young girls, these expressions of self-confidence, in a world that still thinks blue eyes and white skin confirm beauty, not only allay concerns about self-esteem but also are essential for pushing other women forward and out of the vicious cycle of self-hatred. My poem was only one of the million other expressions on social media of reclaiming the Other body.

## WHERE DO WE GO FROM HERE?

The power of social media in supporting social movements and organizing political change—or at least motivating it—is felt all over the globe by users online and observers offline. Digital technology ferments and catalyzes discourses on a range of issues on the political and social spectrum. Whether it is environmental issues, immigrant rights, antiwar protests, criticism against state policies, or support for activists around the world, social media has shown us the diversity, and sometimes maddening complexity, of political voices. But what makes social media so easy and effective is its decentralized nature; it is inexpensive, driven by networks, and entails few boundaries, if any. It is the democratic nature of social media that makes it accessible to users who wish to be heard. […]

Feminists around the globe have used social media to highlight an assortment of political issues. A development that became even more perceptible in online discourses was the decidedly divergent lines of thought between different kinds of feminisms. Social media also gives rise to the question, "What is female emancipation and empowerment?" This is not to promote a postmodernist take on feminist struggles that is ultimately destructive but to show how rich womanhood is, with its countless manifestations across thousands of cultures and communities, and to demonstrate how, as a result, a monolithic image of womanhood and a generalized approach to women's liberation does little for feminists who wish to alleviate female subjugation and misogyny. […]

Another form of solidarity with women in the virtual mass convergence of networked feminism is the mushrooming of blogs that name and shame sexual harassers online. After a cursory glance, the blogs may not seem so effective in nipping sexism in the bud, but once we venture further into the history of these blogs, we see that young women have successfully exposed their sexual harassers online and have, in one way or another, "ruined" their reputations and saved other women from further sexual harassment. One blog that works on the same theme, *How Many Women Find Street Harassment Flattering?*, bravely tells trolls off by stating, "If you have some kind of grudge against feminists, the admin of this site, or women in general, please turn around and leave." These feminist voices and their blogs are correct for being proud of their "feminist killjoy" credentials online; given how vast the Internet is and how incessant sexists can be, there is nothing better than a feminist who refuses to chew her words to make a chauvinistic bully step back.

However, feminists online must remain mindful of the digital gap between online feminists and offline feminists who for political, economic, and social reasons do not have access to the same sphere that we do. By solidifying our activism online with theirs offline, we can create a network of solidarity that encourages women from all spheres of life to relay their sentiments and aims to each other so that means can be achieved for empowerment of said objectives. Ronak Ghorbani of *Fem2.0* is correct when she says, "We tend to forget the women who aren't online—there is a digital divide—and I think that part of the feminist movement should be focused on reaching out to people face-to-face doing community work, doing international work. A lot of people are online but not everybody, not by a long shot." […]

By opening up more forums on topics that we usually hesitate to opine on—whether it is race, sex, religion, or any other subject—we can encourage women to reclaim these spaces and address intersecting problems within feminisms in addition to the problems we all face under patriarchy. This is one safe sphere ripe with golden chances and supporters that enable women to network with each other over varying issues, dreams, and even laments. Ultimately, the effectiveness of feminism in the blogosphere is inherently dependent on how active we feminists are in taking these issues to the offline world and spreading the same messages in those spheres as well.

## REFERENCES

*The Body Narratives* (blog). Tumblr. Last modified October 25, 2013. http://thebodynarratives.tumblr.com/.

Douzinas, Costas. 2007. *Human Rights and Empire: The Political Philosophy of Cosmopolitanism.* New York: Routledge-Cavendish.

Ghorbani, Ronak. 2010. "Tweeting Feminists Exploring Feminism and Social Media." *Fem 2.0*, April 15. http://www.fem2pt0.com/?p=1612.

*How Many Women Find Street Harassment Flattering?* (blog). Tumblr. Last modified October 25, 2013. http://howmanywomen.tumblr.com/.

Kasana, Mehreen. 2011. "Beautiful as You Are." *Mehreen Kasana* (blog). January 2. http://mehreenkasana.wordpress.com/2011/01/02/beautiful-as-you-are/.

Khan, Azmat. 2010. "Azmat Khan: A Year in Digital Discoveries." *Guernica*, December 30. http://www.guernicamag.com/daily/azmat_khan_a_year_in_digital_discoveries/.

*Oppressed Brown Girls Doing Things* (blog). Tumblr. Last modified October 24, 2013. http://oppressedbrowngirlsdoingthings.tumblr.com/ (link no longer active).

*Orientalism Is Alive* (blog). Tumblr. Last modified February 16, 2013. http://orientalismisalive.tumblr.com/.

Shirky, Clay. 2011. "The Political Power of Social Media: Technology, the Public Sphere, and Political Change." *Foreign Affairs* (Council on Foreign Relations), January/February. https://www.cc.gatech.edu/~beki/cs4001/Shirky.pdf.

**Source:** Kasana, Mehreen. (2014). Excerpted from "Feminisms and the Social Media Sphere." *WSQ: Women's Studies Quarterly, 42*(3–4), 236–249.

# FEMINISM WITHOUT BORDERS

*Building on the long history of feminist activism, in recent years women around the world have developed new transnational grassroots organizations to help them face the challenges of the 21st century. DAWN, AWID, and the Global Women's Strike are three examples.*

## Development Alternatives with Women for a New Era (DAWN)

Development Alternatives with Women for a New Era (DAWN) is a network of feminist scholars, researchers and activists from the economic South working for economic and gender justice and sustainable and democratic development. DAWN provides a forum for feminist research, analyses and advocacy on global issues (economic, social and political) affecting the livelihoods, living standards, rights and development prospects of women, especially poor and marginalized women, in regions of the South. Through research, analyses, advocacy and, more recently, training, DAWN seeks to support women's mobilization within civil society to challenge inequitable social, economic and political relations at global, regional and national levels, and to advance feminist alternatives.

Since the founding of DAWN in 1984, the network has been recognized as a significant agent in the development of south feminist analyses in gender and development and a key participant in the global feminist/women's movements. A political and ideological 'south' location-position remains vitally relevant in the era of globalization [...].

DAWN's feminism entails countering the material bases for social, economic and political inequalities, injustices and exclusions. DAWN envisions processes of economic and social development that are geared to enabling human rights and freedoms. DAWN draws strength from, and is committed to further empowering, the women's movement in the South. Its various activities include:

- developing and disseminating analyses of the economic, social, cultural and political processes which cause and perpetuate inequalities of gender, class, race and other forms of unfair social ordering and discrimination;
- engaging in global and regional inter-governmental and non-governmental forums and processes to challenge and change mainstream thinking, policy and practice which hurt poor women in the South;
- co-sponsoring global civil society initiatives aimed at achieving sustainable, equitable and gender-just social, economic and political development;
- contributing to selected reform initiatives instituted in response to feminist or civil society demands for global institutional or policy changes; and
- providing training in analysis and advocacy skills to young feminists from the South who are engaged (or interested) in working on global issues covered by the four DAWN themes: Political Economy of Globalization (PEG); Sexual and Reproductive Health and Rights (SRHR); Political Restructuring and Social Transformation (PRST); and Political Ecology and Sustainability (PEAS).

*Sources:* Development Alternatives with Women for a New Era (DAWN). (n.d.). Adapted from "About" and "Research and Analyses." Retrieved from: https://www.dawnnet.org/feminist-resources/about/main; https://www.dawnnet.org/feminist-resources/analyses/main.

## Association for Women's Rights in Development (AWID)

The Association for Women's Rights in Development (AWID) is an international feminist membership organization that works to achieve gender justice and women's human rights by strengthening the collective voice, impact and influence of global women's rights advocates, organizations and movements.

AWID began in 1982 and has grown and transformed since then into a truly global organization.

### Our Vision

A world where human rights and freedoms, environmental sustainability and gender justice are a lived reality for all people and the planet.

### Our Mission

We aim to be a driving force within the global community of feminist and women's rights activists, organizations and movements, strengthening our collective voice, influencing and transforming structures of power and decision-making, and advancing human rights, gender justice and environmental sustainability worldwide.

Working together is key for women's rights and gender justice to be a lived reality and we support feminist and women's rights organizations and movements to collaborate effectively across issues, regions and constituencies.

*Source:* Association for Women's Rights in Development (AWID). (2017). Excerpted from "Who We Are." Retrieved from: https://www.awid.org/who-we-are.

## Global Women's Strike/Huelga Mundial de Mujeres

**Invest in Caring, Not Killing**

Survival and caring are not prioritised; even caring for the survival of the planet is treated as 'unaffordable'. Yet +$1.67 trillion/year is spent on the military worldwide. 10% of this would provide the essentials of life for all: water, sanitation, basic health, nutrition, literacy, and a minimum income. Investing in carers redirects economic and social policies towards survival, health, and well-being—for every individual and for the planet which sustains us all.

The Global Women's Strike is a grassroots network with national co-ordinations in a number of countries. Invest in caring not killing is our strategy for change. Women, and men who support our goals, take action together on 8 March, International Women's Day, and throughout the year. We address power relations among us, and make sure that each of our campaigns is backed by our collective power. GWS works with and is supported by Payday, an international network of men.

Women from different sectors are involved: women of colour, Indigenous and rural women, mothers, women in waged work, LBGTQ, sex workers, religious activists, women with disabilities, older and younger women ...

**Global Women's Strike Demands**

*Petition to ALL Governments: A Living Wage for Mothers and Other Carers*
Caring for others is the foundation of every society, yet this work, done mostly by women, is devalued and underfunded.
We demand that:

1.  Every worker be paid a living wage, including mothers and other carers.
2.  National and international budgets redirect financial support and resources to mothers and other carers.

We demand a living wage for mothers and other carers because:

- Every worker is entitled to a living wage. Women do 2/3 of the world's work—in the home, on the land, and in the community—but most of this work is unwaged.
- Women are the primary carers everywhere in the world, fighting for the survival and well-being of children and sick, disabled, and elderly people, in the home and outside, in peace as in war. Women grow most of the world's food.
- Most carers, starting with mothers, get no wages and aren't considered workers.
- Many carers are themselves disabled; many are children caring for younger ones or for their disabled parents; many are grandparents leaving retirement to care for their children's children.
- Caring is demanding work but the skills it requires are undervalued even in the job market—domestic work, homecare, childcare, and even nursing are low paid.
- Valuing caring work would help to close the income gap between women and men. It would also draw more men into caring.
- Financial dependence when caring work is unwaged often traps women in violent relationships.

- Many mothers do several jobs and have to fit time with their children around their job—this is exhausting and stressful for all.
- When mothers are impoverished and overworked, children suffer: hunger, ill-health, violence, and exploitation.
- Mothers who have to return to other work soon after childbirth are less likely to breastfeed.
- Workers who take time off to care for children or other loved ones, lose pay, promotion, social security, and future pension.
- Devaluing caring work devalues people, relationships, and life itself.
- Investing in carers redirects economic and social policies towards survival, health, and well-being—for every individual and for the planet which sustains us all.

SIGN AT: https://www.facebook.com/livingwageformothersandothercarers/

---

*Source:* Global Women's Strike/Huelga Mundial de Mujeres. (2017). Retrieved from: https://www.facebook.com/GlobalWomensStrike/.

# COPYRIGHT ACKNOWLEDGEMENTS

Figure 13.1: "Women Olympic Stars Posing on Ship" by Bettmann. Copyright © Getty Images. Reprinted with permission of Getty Images.

Chapter 14: *Contesting Intersex: The Dubious Diagnosis* by Georgiann Davis (2015). Copyright © New York University Press. Reprinted with permission of NYU Press.

Chapter 15: "Dueling Dualisms" in *Sexing the Body: Gender Politics and the Construction of Sexuality* by Anne Fausto-Sterling (2000). New York: Basic Books. Reprinted with permission of Hachette Books Group.

---

## PART 2B

Chapter 16: "Women's Brains," from THE PANDA'S THUMB: More Reflections in Natural History by Stephen Jay Gould. Copyright © 1980 by Stephen Jay Gould. Used by permission of W. W. Norton & Company, Inc.

Chapter 17: "Freaks and Queers," in *Exile and Pride*, Eli Clare, pp. 85-109. Copyright, 2009, Eli Clare. All rights reserved. Republished by permission of the copyright holder, and the publisher, Duke University Press. www.dukeupress.edu.

Snapshots and Soundwaves 10: "Introduction: Imagined Futures" in *Feminist, Queer, Crip* by Alison Kafer. Copyright © 2013, Indiana University Press. Reprinted with permission of Indiana University Press.

Activist Art 2: "Alison Lapper Pregnant" by Marc Quinn (2005). Copyright © Marc Quinn.

http://marcquinn.com/artworks/alison-lapper. Reprinted with permission.

Snapshots and Soundwaves 11: "RACE—The Power of an Illusion: Ten Things Everyone Should Know about Race" by California Newsreel (2003). San Francisco, CA: California Newsreel. Retrieved from: http://newsreel.org/guides/race/10things.htm. Reprinted with permission of California Newsreel.

Chapter 18: Reproduced by permission of the American Anthropological Association from *American Anthropologist*, Volume 104, Issue 3, pages 783–790, September 2002. Not for sale or further reproduction.

Activist Art 3, Images: Technicolor Muslimah, *Portraits of American Muslim Women*, by Saba Taj (2011). Retrieved from: http://www.artbysaba.com/technicolor-muslimah-2011---2014. Reprinted with permission of Saba Taj.

---

## PART 2C

Chapter 19: "X: A Fabulous Child's Story" by Lois Gould © (1998), in Blyth McVicker Clinchy & Julie K. Norem (Eds.), *The Gender and Psychology Reader*. New York: NYU Press.

Snapshots and Soundwaves 12: Slightly modified from "Understanding Men: Gender Sociology and the New International Research on Masculinities" by Raewyn Connell (2002). *Social Thought and Research*, *24*(1–2): 13–31. Reprinted with permission of Social Thought and Research (STAR Journal).

Snapshots and Soundwaves 13: "It's the Masculinity, Stupid! An interview with Jackson Katz on the throwback allure of Donald Trump" by Jackson Katz & Jeremy Earp (2016, September 26). Copyright © Media Education Foundation. Reprinted from *Huffington*

## PART 2D

## PART 3C

## PART 4C

Chapter 45: Excerpted from "Through the Mirror of Beauty Culture" by Carla Rice, in Nancy Mandell & Jennifer Johnson (Eds.), *Feminist Issues: Race, Class, and Sexuality*, 6th Edition (2016). Toronto: Pearson. Originally published as "Chapter 7: In the Mirror of Beauty Culture" in *Becoming Women* (2014) by Carla Rice. Toronto: UTP Press. Reprinted with permission of publisher, University of Toronto Press, and Carla Rice.

Chapter 46: "Body Beautiful/Body Perfect: Challenging the Status Quo. Where do Women with Disabilities Fit In?" by Francine Odette (1994). *Canadian Women's Studies/les cahiers de la femme, 14*(3): 41–43. Reprinted with permission of author.

## PART 4D

Chapter 47: "The Women's Health Movement in Canada: Looking Back and Moving Forward" by Madeline Boscoe, Gwynne Basen, Ghislaine Alleyne, Barbara Bourrier-Lacroix, & Susan White, of the Canadian Women's Health Network (2005). *Canadian Woman Studies/les cahiers de la femme, 24*(1): 7–13. Reprinted with permission of Madeline Boscoe.

Snapshots and Soundwaves 31: Adapted from "About Us" and "History," Our Bodies Ourselves (2012). Retrieved from: www.ourbodiesourselves.org. Reprinted with permission of Our Bodies Ourselves.

Snapshots and Soundwaves 31, Image 1: *Our Bodies, Ourselves*, by Boston Women's Health Book Collective (1973). New York: Simon and Schuster. Reprinted with permission of Our Bodies Ourselves.

Snapshots and Soundwaves 31, Image 2: *Our Bodies, Ourselves*, by Boston Women's Health Book Collective, & Judy Norsigian (2011). New York: Simon and Schuster. Reprinted with permission of Our Bodies Ourselves.

Chapter 48: "Women, Disability, and the Right to Health" by Paula C. Pinto (2015), in Pat Armstrong and Ann Pederson (Eds.), *Women's Health: Intersections of Policy, Research, and Practice, Second Edition* (2015). Toronto: Women's Press. Copyright © Canadian Scholars' Press. Reprinted with permission.

Snapshots and Soundwaves 32, Image 1: Dahlgren G, Whitehead M. (1991). Policies and Strategies to Promote Social Equity in Health. Stockholm, Sweden: Institute for Futures Studies. Reprinted with permission of the Institute for Futures Studies.

Chapter 49: *First Peoples, Second Class Treatment: The Role of Racism in the Health and Well-being of Indigenous Peoples in Canada* by Billie Allan & Janet Smylie (2015). Toronto, ON: The Wellesley Institute. Reprinted with permission of Janet Smylie and the Well Living House (WLH).

Chapter 50: "HIV/AIDS, Globalisation, and the International Women's Movement" by Sisonke Msimang (2003), *Gender and Development, 11*(1): 109–113. Copyright © Oxfam GB, reprinted by permission of Taylor & Francis Ltd, www.tandfonline.com on behalf of Oxfam GB.

## PART 4E

Chapter 51: Excerpted from *Ten Thousand Roses* by Judy Rebick. Copyright © 2005 Judy Rebick. Reprinted in Canada by permission of Viking Canada/Penguin Canada, a division of Penguin Random House Canada Limited; reprinted in the United States by permission of Judy Rebick.

Chapter 52: Reprinted from the *American Indian Culture and Research Journal*, Volume 36, Number 3,

## PART 5A

## PART 5B

## PART 5C

## PART 6A

## PART 6B